# Philosophy of Law

edited, with introductions by

## Conrad Johnson
*University of Maryland*

MACMILLAN PUBLISHING COMPANY
*New York*
MAXWELL MACMILLAN CANADA
*Toronto*

Editor: *Maggie Barbieri*
Production Supervisor: *Karen Fortgang*, bookworks
Production Manager: *Linda Greenberg*
Cover Designer: Robert Freese

*This book was set in Palatino & Optima by V & M Graphics, Inc.
and was printed and bound by Book Press, Inc.*

Macmillan Publishing Company
866 Third Avenue, New York, New York 10022

Macmillan Publishing Company is part of
the Maxwell Communication Group of Companies.

Maxwell Macmillan Canada, Inc.
1200 Eglinton Avenue East
Suite 200
Don Mills, Ontario M3C 3N1

**Library of Congress Cataloging-in-Publication Data**

Philosophy of law / edited, with introductions by Conrad D. Johnson.
    p.    cm.
    ISBN 0–02–360935–4
    1. Law—Philosophy.    I. Johnson, Conrad D.
K231.P47 1993
340'.1—dc20                          92–2964
                                     CIP

Printing:  1  2  3  4  5  6  7      Year:  3  4  5  6  7  8  9

# Preface

The philosophy of law, for many centuries a preeminent topic of scholarly study, has in recent years taken on a new importance for the larger public. Critical scrutiny of law, particularly of major judicial decisions, has become a matter of intense public concern and participation. The most dramatic changes seem to have occurred in just the last two or three decades. Legal developments are now scrutinized in considerable detail in the media, and nominees to the Supreme Court are sometimes required to explain their judicial and legal philosophies to U.S. Senate committees and the public almost as if they were conducting an advanced seminar before the nation. Thus practical, applied, and public philosophizing now tends increasingly to have a legal focus. No doubt there are many reasons for these developments, but one may be the fact that in a diverse, pluralistic society that has no official religion and places a high value on individual liberty, this public philosophizing is, for those who seek participation in a public, collective process of principled reasoning and justification, "the only game in town." It is an important enterprise, arguably one of the best sources of moral community available in a democracy.

This text is designed for a philosophy of law course taken primarily by advanced undergraduates, but peopled also with a fair number of others, ranging from first-year college students to graduate students. The readings are moderately difficult. Although they require that the student have the ability to read carefully and analytically, they do not presuppose any courses in philosophy, logic, or government.

The aim of this text is to provide an introduction, not only to some of the recurrent legal debates but also to the background conceptual frameworks that constitute the setting for those debates. These are frameworks which one needs to know in order to understand how abstract political and legal philosophy applies to concrete issues. Introductions to each of the seven parts of the book are accordingly designed to provide conceptual organization for the readings that follow. Various court cases, ranging from two cases dealing with tort liability to a host of U.S. Supreme Court cases dealing with constitutional rights and liberties, help give concrete focus to large, often vague principles. The reprinted philosophical and legal essays represent but a sampling of an increasingly wide range of literature in the philosophy of law. To include anything more than a small sampling of this large body of excellent literature would make a text of manageable size impossible.

The questions placed at the end of the reading materials are designed to be used for any of several purposes. They may be used by the individual student as self-testing exercises after the reading has been completed. I have found in my own teaching of the philosophy of law that students often benefit most when they form small study groups for the purpose of testing one another on the reading, and for this too the questions may be useful. Teachers may wish to use some of the questions as starters for class discussion. In other cases, the questions may serve as topics for analytic papers. The questions are not written with any preconceived answer in mind, as if there were or could be somewhere an answer book containing all the "right" answers. Thus the hope is that the questions will elicit one kind of answer on superficial reflection, but another kind of answer upon deeper reflection. The aim is to place the emphasis on how well the question is analyzed and the answer argued for rather than on the actual answer itself. That is, after all, the nature of a genuinely interesting philosophical question. It must also be the primary concern where people with radically different beliefs about such matters as abortion and criminal punishment are learning to reason with one another on the basis of principle rather than simply reporting their conflicting opinions to one another.

Part 1, on concepts of law and legal system, deals with what is perhaps the most general part of legal philosophy's subject matter. This part of the book serves to tell some of the story of the grand debates in legal philosophy, particularly between natural law and legal positivism, and to provide examples of these debates in the form they currently take. Here, as elsewhere in the book, is material that could have been included in one or more other parts of the book and that can profitably be read in connection with them. Thus a substantial part of the reading in Part 1 is relevant to Part 3, on legal reasoning and its conceptual tools. Part 1 also includes material on the idea of the rule of law, an idea that has been central to the political philosophy of liberalism (Part 2) and a main target of criticism on the part of skeptics in the Critical Legal Studies movement (Part 5).

The organizing idea of Part 2 is individual liberty, its background theory, its boundaries, and its applications in contemporary constitutional law. The recent literature, to say nothing of court cases, in this area is truly massive, and even this large section gives only a small sampling. In addition to readings from J.S. Mill and Benjamin Constant, two important figures in the early days of classical liberalism, Part 2 contains John Rawls's "The Idea of an Overlapping Consensus," an especially important paper in the modern debate about the possibilities for society to find unity in diversity.

Part 2 also raises issues that overlap those in other parts of this book, most especially those in Part 3 on legal reasoning and its conceptual tools. During the last decade, decisions on the constitutional right of privacy have brought in their wake a philosophical debate about the kind of reasoning and justification that is appropriate to a court of law, especially to a court of final appeal. This debate, particularly as it applies to the *Griswold v. Connecticut, Roe v. Wade,* and *Bowers v. Hardwick* cases reprinted here, raises once again one of the oldest problems of legal philosophy: Whether moral reasoning and even moral philosophizing ought to be part of what judges do when they first reason to a conclusion and then attempt to provide a justification for it. The introduction and the rest of the readings in Part 3 are designed to introduce the student to some ideas that are important to an understanding of legal reasoning: the notions of deductive and inductive reasoning, analogy, and the concept of rights. While the concept of rights is ordinarily thought to belong primarily to moral and political philosophy and to the criticism of oppressive regimes, that concept also plays a central and special role in everyday legal reasoning. For this reason it seemed necessary to include some discussion of the logic of rights language along with the more usual topics of legal reasoning such as those of deductive inference and analogy.

Although this part of the book stands on its own and requires no background in logic, the introduction explains some of the connections between logic in the law and logic as it is more traditionally taught in college courses.

Part 4 provides a brief introduction to the topic of law and economics. Much recent writing in the area of law and economics consists of books or especially lengthy articles, often presupposing a good deal of knowledge of theoretical economics and therefore is inappropriate in an introductory text in the philosophy of law. The Posner and Dworkin debate, however, is an exception. Each piece contains much of general interest to political and legal philosophy. These two pieces, together with the account of some fundamental ideas of economic analysis of law in the editorial introduction, give a general overview of some of the philosophical problems raised by that new field of inquiry.

Part 5, on varieties of skepticism about legal reasoning, attempts to give some insight into what have been perhaps the two most important skeptical movements in legal thinking during this century, American Legal Realism and Critical Legal Studies. The two movements have important differences, though much in common. More important for our purposes, both are sources of skeptical questions about many of the most established and hallowed ideas of legal thinking: the rule of law, the predictability and uniformity offered by adherence to rules, liberalism as a coherent and adequate political philosophy, and so on.

Part 6, on theories of punishment, and Part 7, on responsibility, are closely related. The stage is set in Part 6 by representative readings from the retributive and utilitarian schools of thought, along with readings from writers taking what I call "mixed" views. The application of theory is discussed in the two cases: *Gregg v. Georgia,* which contains an extensive discussion of sentencing in capital cases, and *Payne v. Tennessee,* a case viewed by many as a triumph for the "victim's rights" movement and one that brings to the fore deep philosophical issues about the relationship between luck on the one hand and blameworthiness (punishability) on the other. Of course, criminal punishment as well as tort liability are typically made to depend on the judgment that the actor was in the appropriate sense "responsible," the topic of Part 7. That one acted in self-defense or that one was insane are legal defenses that both operate, though in different ways, to negate liability for otherwise law-breaking actions. Further, that there is a causal connection between one's negligent actions and harm to a plaintiff is a necessary component of a successful tort suit. These are all matters having to do with the actor's responsibility. It is part of the purpose of Part 7 to sort out different senses of the term "responsibility." The essays in this part all move in the direction of offering models or theories to organize our thinking about self-defense, insanity, and the foundations of tort liability.

Statute and case citations, in addition to footnotes, have in many instances been omitted without so specifying. In other instances the omission is indicated by means of asterisks or brackets. In the hope of minimizing confusion for those who wish to return to the original texts, footnotes retain their original numbering. Footnotes added by this editor are lettered rather than numbered.

I must here thank the reviewers who evaluated this project at various stages of its development: Claudia Card, University of Wisconsin at Madison; Gerald Dworkin, University of Illinois at Chicago; Alan R. Mabe, Florida State University; Michele M. Moody-Adams, University of Rochester; Kathleen Moore, Oregon State University; and George Schedler,

Southern Illinois University at Carbondale. I have benefited from the written comments of each and every one of these people. Their influence has been significant. Of course, I have not been able to incorporate all of their suggestions. Individually or collectively, they may well have preferred a quite different outcome.

I must thank the people at Macmillan, many of whose names I do not know, for their help and steady cooperation in bringing this text to the market. My editor, Maggie Barbieri, has been cheerfully helpful throughout. Her predecessor at Macmillan, Helen McInnis, encouraged the project's development at the beginning, and gave efficient guidance in the early stages. Laura Golden helped in the final stages of securing and collecting permissions.

Conrad Johnson

# Contents

# PART ONE

# What Law Is

One of the oldest questions in the philosophy of law concerns the very subject of the study: What *is* law? Initially, this question might seem to be of little importance. One might be tempted to say that it is a mere matter of definition, or that we already know well enough what law is. But the sheer volume of books and theories on the subject that has been developed over the centuries suggests the contrary: The concept of law is of great importance, and we cannot be certain that we already have a clear concept of what law is.

Why should this be so? Why should there be so much dispute, both theoretical and practical, about, say, whether the law is whatever the sovereign says it is, or whether it is what the highest court in the land has most recently pronounced it to be? Part of the explanation is that law is an ongoing enterprise in which many people participate and have a stake. Whether you are a legislator aiming to make law, a state's attorney charged with enforcing the law, a member of the police deciding whether to make an arrest, a judge charged with the duty of applying the law, or an ordinary citizen trying to understand your rights and duties and the ways in which your behavior might get you into trouble, the answer to the question will have important practical consequences. Whether there must be a commander for there to be law will have an important bearing on whether what we call "international law" really is law at all, that is, whether it is legally binding on courts and governments. If we conclude that law must be announced in advance before anyone is considered to be bound by it, that will have a bearing on how legislators ought to conceive of their task: on what they should be trying to do and on what will count as success and what as failure. And if we conceive of law's overriding function as the preservation of order, that will be relevant to whether laws and judicial decisions must respect individual rights.

Different answers to the question "What is law?" will no doubt seem appropriate to different people depending on one's individual perspective, whether that of ordinary citizen, judge, or legislator. An ordinary citizen who sees the law as an alien presence, a bare-knuckled expression of the overwhelming power of the state, will no doubt have a different concept of what law is from the citizen or official who acknowledges the moral authority of the state and sees law as a collective expression in which everyone can participate.

A concept of law is necessary, not only for participants in the ongoing enterprise of shaping and interpreting law, but for the nonparticipant observer as well. The clearest example is an anthropologist who is trying to understand a foreign culture, tribe, or nation. The anthropologist's job is to find out whether the culture contains anything that can correctly be called law. Imagine yourself in the anthropologist's position. If you have concluded that the culture does have law, you will want to know something about what it is: what it permits and requires, whether people have anything that you could call a legal right, and whether the law of the culture constitutes anything that you would call a system. You will need a concept of law in order to know what to look for. Do you look first to see if there is an all-powerful ruler who is generally obeyed? Do you look to see whether people are regularly made to suffer physical sanctions for doing certain things? Or do you examine primarily the explanations and justifications that people in that culture give one another when they deprive others of their liberty? If other observers strongly disagree with various claims that you have made about the law of the culture, your disagreement with them may force you to think more deeply and carefully about the concept that you have been using, whether or not you have really been aware of that concept and its implications.

Questions about what law is sometimes arise in highly general form. We might ask whether the arbitrary commands issued by an unpredictable tyrant constitute a system of law. Or we might question whether unlegislated custom in the community can ever count as law until it has been recognized in legislation. These are global questions, and they may seem not to have much connection to everyday concerns about the law. But particular legal disputes, the sort regularly handled by courts, can also touch on conceptual issues about the nature of law. For example, a recurrent problem in legal philosophy concerns the status of principles that have never been enacted by any legislature, but which are sometimes used by courts to fill out the meaning of enacted law. As some of the readings in Part 1 will illustrate, a principle such as, "No one will be allowed to profit from his own wrong," a principle never enacted by any legislature, is sometimes used in legal argument. If we conceive of such a principle as having legal force, that will favor those whose legal arguments rely on it. If the principle is thought to reflect only personal moral convictions and as having no particular legal status, that will undercut its usefulness in legal argument.

Philosophizing about law has usually been a reflection of debates taking place in the larger sphere of politics and philosophy. A current example of this, as we shall see, is the argument between natural law proponents and legal positivists. In its current form, the debate focuses on the proper role of the courts in interpreting and sometimes overturning legislation. On the one side are those who distrust courts, especially when they appeal to moral principles and unenacted moral rights as a reason for overturning enacted law; on the other side are those who distrust political majorities and have more confidence in the capacity of the courts to conduct moral reasoning. We need now to turn to the historical background of this debate.

## NATURAL LAW CONCEPTIONS

The terms "natural law" and "legal positivism" are only rough categories that enable us to start our thinking about the concept of law. We should pay attention to the differences among the many theories included under each category, as well as to the fact that there are views that do not clearly belong under either heading. Traditional natural law doctrines hold that there is an immutable order of justice, of right and wrong and of good and evil, that we are capable of knowing. Human efforts to make law are necessarily subordinate to this order. Though laws created by governments vary from one country to another and come into existence and change through the actions of human beings, natural law is everywhere the same and valid for all humanity. Its existence is prior to, and independent of, the existence of any human government. As such, the norms of natural law serve as a standard by which we can evaluate an existing legal order. Natural law conceptions have often been used to check the state's (or a king's) claim to virtually unlimited power. Thus the philosopher John Locke (1632–1704) used the notion of natural rights as the basis for a doctrine of justified revolution against tyranny.

When we think of evaluating the norms of an existing order, we should notice two different ways in which the norms of natural law might be used for this purpose. On one kind of view, we use the norms of natural law only to determine whether existing laws are just or unjust, good or bad. Our evaluation would not enable us to conclude that something which was claimed to be law was in reality not law at all. We could only conclude that such-and-such law was a bad law, or an unjust law, though its status *as law* would remain untouched. But there is another way of thinking of the evaluation of law, one that is more typical of natural law doctrines. It is the idea that the moral qualities of a law or a legal system are not really separable from the determination of *whether* it is law. In this view, one may not neatly separate the question, "Is this a just law?" from the question, "Is this law at all?" This thesis, characteristic of natural law conceptions, is sometimes called the *necessary connection thesis*. As we shall see, it is one of the main points of difference between natural law and legal positivism.

The natural law would be of little use to human beings if they could not know and apply its principles. One of the central and most controversial features of natural law conceptions is their claim that we can use human reason to come to know the natural law and then apply it to concrete problems. The broad outline of a typical natural law conception (an example is Aquinas's, contained in the readings) illustrates these controversial features. In such a view, the laws of human conduct can be understood by rational reflection on the human as rational animal. Like other animals, humans have certain natural inclinations, and from our understanding of these we can know the natural law. Thus human beings, with other things in nature, have an inclination to self-preservation, and from this we can grasp the natural law that human life is to preserved. In addition, humans have certain inclinations that are more specifically theirs among animals, such as the inclination to know the truth and to live in society. So ignorance is to be shunned, while cooperation and fellowship with others are to be promoted.

There have been many criticisms of the claim that inspection of "natural inclinations" will enable us to know the requirements of an objective law of nature. Human beings have many, often conflicting, inclinations. Among these are kindness and cooperation and self-control and discipline. But they also have inclinations to hatred and aggression, laxity and intemperance. How, by a mere examination of these varied tendencies, are we to tell which reflect natural law and which violate it? How do we know, apart from an examination of what human beings actually do, what is in accordance with their nature or essence? Critics have charged that the doctrine of natural law confuses two very different things. It confuses a descriptive law of nature (telling us how humans and animals behave) with a prescriptive law (telling us how they ought to behave), mistakenly attempting to derive the latter from the former. Even if natural law theories can avoid this objection, our ability to recognize the principles of natural law can at best only give us confusing, conflicting, and highly controversial guidance.

## LEGAL POSITIVISM

Criticism of natural law doctrines has come primarily from those belonging to the legal positivist school. Like the term "natural law," "legal positivism" is sufficiently broad that it serves as shelter for many different theories. In the readings that follow, John Austin, Hans Kelsen, and H.L.A. Hart are all legal positivists, though there are many differences among their theories of law. At the same time, though, legal positivists are largely united in the objections they raise against natural law doctrines. Understanding these criticisms is a key to understanding much of the motivation behind legal positivism. Perhaps the most important of the criticisms is the charge that, while claiming that there is a necessary connection between law and morality, natural law theories are unable to demonstrate that their moral judgments are validated by an objective moral order. Instead, they leave us with vague and often conflicting general precepts, such as, "Do good and avoid evil," and then base the validity of these precepts on nothing more than an appeal to our intuitions.

Jeremy Bentham (1748–1832), himself a legal positivist who had great influence on the thinking of later positivists, complained that appeals to intuition in moral thinking, particularly when they profess to be intuitions about a law of nature, served only to support despotism:

> Unnatural, when it means any thing, means unfrequent: and there it means something; although nothing to the present purpose. . . . All it can serve to express is, the disposition of the person who is talking of it: the disposition he is in to be angry at the thoughts of it. . . .
>
> The mischief common to all these ways of thinking and arguing (which, in truth, as we have seen, are but one and the same method, couched in different forms of words) is their serving as a cloke, and pretence, and aliment, to despotism: if not a despotism in practice, a despotism however in disposition: which is but too apt, when pretence and power offer, to show itself in practice.[1]

Bentham's main complaint about natural law thinking is that, if your opponent disagrees with your intuitions, there is no public, objective standard to which everyone can appeal as a way of settling the dispute without coercion. The matter then becomes a contest of wills rather than an appeal to reason. If reasoning and arguing from the norms of natural law are as unanchored and subjective as Bentham suggests they are, the necessary connection thesis

[1] Jeremy Bentham, *An Introduction to the Principles of Morals and Legislation* (1789), Chap. II, Para. XIV, n. 1.

would then imply that legal questions are infected with this same uncertainty and subjectivity. For if we can only know what human law is by knowing first what is permitted and required by natural law, and we have nothing but our conflicting intuitions about the natural law, then what human law permits or requires is also a matter of conflicting intuitions which cannot be authoritatively settled. And that seems especially intolerable, since one of the main functions of law is to provide a publicly demonstrable, objective basis for the settlement of disputes. So it is one of the main goals of legal positivism to provide a neutral analysis of important legal notions such as legal validity and what it is for a legal system to exist. The goal is to make it possible to determine what the law is without having to delve into questions about what is good, right, or just. This idea, that there is no necessary connection between law and morality, is sometimes called the *separation thesis*.

Taken by itself, the separation thesis does not deny the objectivity or demonstrability of moral judgments. Bentham is just one example of a philosopher who accepts the separation thesis without denying that moral judgments can be placed on a rational, objective foundation. While Bentham thought that natural law provided a shaky and dangerous basis for moral judgments, his proposal was to use the more objective basis provided by the utilitarian principle, that is, the principle of maximizing net pleasure in the world, so his proposal was not one of rejecting moral reasoning altogether. However, some who accept the separation thesis do take the further step of claiming that morality is irrational or has no objective basis.

## THE IDEA OF THE RULE OF LAW

Related to debates about the concept of law and the necessary connection thesis is the idea of the rule of law. Defenders of the idea of the rule of law often claim that the very concept of law itself involves adherence to certain precepts. Governing people by laws rather than commands or managerial direction involves the public promulgation of rules that are general, abstract, and stable—rules that are not targeted to particular individuals. Exercises of the power of government to interfere with individual liberty must be authorized under previously promulgated rules. It is not enough that power-wielding officials sincerely believe that depriving you of liberty would be a good thing. They must show that depriving you of liberty is authorized under preexisting rules. This constitutes a significant restriction on the application of power.

In recent years, one of the leading defenders of the rule of law idea has been F.A. Hayek.[2] Like many others, Hayek sees the importance of the rule of law primarily in the fact that it provides a secure framework for individual freedom, from which so many benefits flow. Only when individuals know in advance that there is some secure and clearly understood sphere of free action can they make and pursue plans. The rules provide the clear boundaries, without which there would be little real liberty. When the boundaries of liberty are unclear, the effect is the same as if liberty were severely restricted. Moreover, individual liberty is only protected when government resolutely adheres to its own promulgated rules and can be held accountable for arbitrary exercises of power outside of the rules.

[2] See, for example, F.A. Hayek, *The Road to Serfdom* (Chicago: The University of Chicago Press, 1944), and *The Constitution of Liberty* (Chicago: The University of Chicago Press, 1960).

The political philosophy that has most often been used to support the rule of law has been classical liberalism. This theory will be addressed more fully in Part 2. Here we need only a brief description of classical liberalism and its connection to the rule of law. The leading ideas are those of freedom and equality. In the classical version, individuals are to be left free to pursue their own ends so long as doing so does not encroach on the liberty of others, and all citizens stand as equals before laws which are general and public and make distinctions among citizens only on a basis that is in principle acceptable to all.

Some versions of liberalism claim that liberty is justified because it produces the greatest good (usually conceived as happiness) overall.[3] Other versions claim that individuals are to be respected as ends in themselves, as beings with goals and plans that are not to be usurped for the purpose of advancing anyone else's goals and plans.[4] Both versions provide reasons for taking the rule of law seriously. A clearly defined, protected sphere of individual liberty encourages people to do what they know best and want most to do well: to pursue their own good and their own plans. And a government that is limited to the enforcement of public, general, and abstract rules will find it difficult to usurp the individual's ends and replace them with its own.

## THE READINGS

**CONCEPTS OF LAW AND LEGAL SYSTEM.**  Still a prominent figure in Catholic theology and philosophy, St. Thomas Aquinas (1224–1274) also remains one of the best representatives of the natural law position. In working out his overall philosophical view, Aquinas sought to reconcile the Aristotelian and Christian world views. In his frequent citations of authorities ranging from the Bible to Aristotle ("the Philosopher"), we can see the way in which he draws both on ancient Greek and Christian sources. To support his view that the principles of natural law can be derived from an understanding of the nature of things, Aquinas adopted Aristotle's doctrine that all things—animals, plants, and even minerals—have their own inherent tendencies by virtue of their nature or essence. Just as iron has an inclination to combine with oxygen, human beings have an inclination to known the truth and to cooperate. In addition to reflecting on Aquinas's method of determining what the natural law is, readers should attend closely to Aquinas's conception of the differences and the relations between natural law, which is eternal and universally applicable, and human law, which is created by humans and varies from one society to another. The human law must be derived from the natural law, though "derivation" may include more than deductive derivation in the logician's sense.

Reading Aquinas for the first time can be daunting, especially for those unused to the order in which he presents arguments, objections, and answers to those objections. One can get Aquinas's own answer to the question that heads each section by going directly to the paragraph beginning, "On the contrary, . . . " and especially to that beginning "I answer

---

[3] John Stuart Mill's utilitarian account of liberty is the leading example. See the excerpt from his *On Liberty* (1859) in Part 2.

[4] Immanuel Kant is the clearest example. See his *Metaphysical Elements of Justice* (1797), a portion of which is reprinted in Part 6.

that. . . ." Then, by examining the separate objections and the separate replies to each, the reader can get a sense of the kinds of doubts and misconceptions Aquinas is trying to address and the kinds of arguments he uses against them.

John Austin (1790–1859) is preeminent by virtue of being the first legal positivist to work out an analytically detailed version of legal positivism. The basic ideas on which Austin draws are not new with him. His political and legal philosophy was strongly influenced by Jeremy Bentham's ideas and the writings of Thomas Hobbes (1588–1679).

Austin's account of law as command has a certain analytic elegance about it. The theory contains several key concepts that Austin first defines and then uses as building blocks. The most important notions are those of command, sanction, and duty. A command is the expression of a wish that another person do or not do something, where that wish is backed by a sanction. A sanction, in turn, is defined as an evil that will result if the command is not carried out. A duty is the correlative of a command, that is to say, where *A* commands *B* to do something, then *B* is under a duty, and *B* is only under a duty if there is someone who commands *B*. To this, Austin adds other concepts in order to explain what it is to be under a legal duty and what it is for an independent political society to exist. If there is a common, determinate, superior (i.e., a "sovereign") who enjoys a habit of obedience on the part of the bulk of a population, and if that sovereign is not in the habit of obeying anyone, then there is an independent political society, and the commands of that sovereign impose legal duties on members of that society. Notice that by this conception of legal duty, being under a legal duty is simply a matter of being under some sovereign's established power. Nothing is implied about the justice or the goodness of the sovereign's laws.

Few would dispute the claim that Oliver Wendell Holmes (1841–1935) was the first great American writer on law and jurisprudence. First as a writer on the law, then as chief justice of the Supreme Court of Massachusetts (1899–1902), and as associate justice of the U.S. Supreme Court (1902–1932), Holmes contributed much that was fresh, striking, and clear to legal thinking. His paper "The Path of the Law," reprinted here, may well be the most widely read paper by an American writing on jurisprudence.

Holmes is especially famous for his "bad man" conception of law: "If you want to know the law and nothing else," he advises his audience, "you must look at it as a bad man, who cares only for the material consequences which such knowledge enables him to predict, not as a good one, who finds his reasons for conduct, whether inside the law or outside of it, in the vaguer sanctions of conscience." Holmes thus takes a position about law and morality that in many respects is like that of legal positivism. Of course, Holmes is not saying that we should not care about being moral; he means, rather, that the law is an instrument of coercion, so that when one asks what the law is on some issue, one is interested in knowing what kind of behavior will lead to unpleasant consequences, whether they be fines or imprisonment, or merely the failure of one's contracts to hold up in court.

Holmes's ideas, with their focus on what legal officials can be expected actually to *do*, rather than on the abstract, general statements of law that one finds in textbooks, make him an early representative of the school of thought subsequently known as American Legal Realism. In this connection Holmes is famous for his claim that law is not merely a matter of logic, but of experience. By this he meant to reject the idea that a court's reaching a decision is simply a matter of finding some general proposition of law to serve as the major premise of a syllogism which, together with the facts of the case as the minor premise, would allow the judge more or less mechanically to deduce the proper decision for the case. (For more on this, see the introduction to Part 3 on legal reasoning.) Experience dictates that we must be prepared to make exceptions to general rules. Thus it is wrong to harm people, and this is usually the basis for legal action, but not when the harm is the result of a desirable free competition, such as two businesses competing for market share.

Hans Kelsen (1881–1973) may well be the most influential legal theorist of the twentieth century, though his influence has been somewhat greater outside the Anglo-American world than within it. His approach to legal theory is highly systematic and analytic.

Kelsen calls his theory the *pure theory* of law because it aims to be "pure" of, or uncontaminated by, two elements. First, the pure theory aims to avoid the mistake made by natural law theory, which mixes ideas of the just and the good with the concept of law. Legal theory must be separated from ideological considerations, which are extraneous to it. Second, the pure theory attempts to avoid the opposite mistake of turning legal theory into a kind of sociological or psychological study. To grasp the concept of law, Kelsen believes, one must employ the concept of a *norm*, or an *ought*, for only then do we have the conceptual tools that enable us, among other things, to distinguish between those whose commands are merely followed in fact and those whose commands ought to be followed. But how then do we determine whether there is a norm imposing an obligation, say, not to kill the innocent? We can only establish the validity of a norm by reference to another norm. To establish the validity of this norm, it would not be sufficient merely to establish the fact that *X* commanded that one not kill the innocent (even where *X* is God). That would only establish the validity of the norm when *combined* with some *further* norm such as, "One ought to do whatever *X* commands."

Kelsen's work draws our attention to the ways in which legal systems involve norms arranged in hierarchical order. If we ask why some particular person *P* is to be sent to jail, the answer might refer to the fact that *P* stole money and that there is a valid norm that makes stealing punishable. Why, we ask, is that a valid norm? Because it was enacted by the legislature, which is empowered to enact such laws. From what, then, does this legislature derive its authority? The answer may be that it comes from the constitution of the state, which was duly enacted in accordance with the U.S. Constitution.

Kelsen reminds us in this way that legal systems have a kind of pyramidal structure: The validity of norms at lower levels of the system traces back in every case to a single source at the top. Notice that the chain of reasoning about the validity of norms seems only to push the question further and further back: This norm is valid because of a second norm, which is in turn valid because of some further norm, and so on. But what is the ultimate source of their validity? Kelsen's answer to this question is that every legal system has a *basic norm* whose validity is not demonstrated by reference to any further norm, but is presupposed. Even though this presupposition is what ultimately enables us to distinguish between those who have genuine legal authority and those who do not, we can say nothing more about its validity than that it is presupposed. This aura of mystery that surrounds the concept of the basic norm has been one of the major causes of criticism of Kelsen's theory of law. The remedy for some of these defects is to be found in the concept of law developed by H.L.A. Hart.

H.L.A. Hart's *The Concept of Law* (1961) is a sustained attempt to apply the methods of contemporary analytic philosophy to developing a concept of law, especially in the setting of a modern legal system. Hart's efforts in that book are based on a thorough knowledge of earlier systematic writers like Austin and Kelsen. Hart is therefore able to build on their contributions while avoiding some of the defects of their theories.

In *The Concept of Law*, Hart begins with a criticism of Austin's notion of law as coercive command. One of the main difficulties with Austin's theory is its defective notion of legal obligation (or duty, as Austin usually calls it). To be under an obligation is not the same as being pressured or coerced to do something. If it were, we would have to say that when a gunman holds you up and demands your money or your life, the gunman has put you under an obligation. You might say afterwards, "I was *obliged* to turn over my money," but you would be incorrect in saying that you were under an *obligation* to turn over your money. In Austin's theory of legal obligation, being under a legal obligation *is* a lot like being threatened by a gunman, except that one is a member of a large group of people in the habit of obeying and the sovereign is the gunman. Austin's theory, it seems, tries to connect obligation and coercion far too closely. Our obligations do not cease to exist just when we stop being threatened; and being threatened, no matter how elaborate and well established the system issuing the threats, does not by itself add up to being under an obligation.

Hart, like Kelsen, wants us to notice that law enables us to distinguish between those who are *entitled* to command, or who have the authority to place us under a legal obligation, and those who do not. Law enables us to distinguish between a lawgiver and a powerful imposter, between a person's going through the motions of signing an official-looking piece of paper and the U.S. president's signing a bill into law. And law can serve to limit the range of commands that the sovereign can make binding on us. The president and Congress have no authority to make laws violating the First Amendment to the Constitution. Yet these ideas of entitlement, authority to govern, and limits on authority cannot be explained by Austin's simple model of a sovereign issuing commands backed by sanctions. Because limits could only come from having to obey someone's commands, and the sovereign is not in the habit of obeying anyone, the sovereign in Austin's model must be unlimited.

Something more is obviously needed if limits are to be accounted for. The concept needed to fill in this puzzle, according to Hart, is that of a social rule. Kelsen's account of a norm, particularly of a basic norm, is sketchy and somewhat mysterious. Hart gives a fuller account of the concept of a social rule, which he defines in terms of certain regularities of behavior combined with a shared attitude that he calls "the internal point of view." For example, if there is a social rule that men are to take their hats off to women in certain circumstances, then this means that there is a general pattern of behavior conforming to the rule, deviations from the rule meet with criticisms and pressures of various kinds, and deviations are regarded as a good reason for these pressures. In addition, the rule is viewed by some as a standard that applies to everyone. This latter feature is the "internal aspect" or point of view.

Notice that Hart's analysis of a rule takes us at least a step back toward the sociological analysis of law that Kelsen tries to avoid with his pure theory. But Hart's analysis has the great advantage of enabling us to explain what it is for a fundamental rule of a legal system to exist. This fundamental rule—Hart calls it "the rule of recognition"—is the counterpart to

Kelsen's basic norm. We do not have to think of this rule of recognition as somehow mysteriously presupposed to be valid. Instead, its existence is a matter of the behavior and attitudes of the appropriate group, in particular, of the various legal officials who regularly make and apply law.

Hart's theory retains one of the most characteristic features of legal positivism: the thesis of the separation of law and morality. The existence of a legal system and its rule of recognition is simply a matter of the appropriate group of people exhibiting certain attitudes and behavior with respect to recognizing and applying law. In this connection, Hart states two conditions that, in his view, are "minimum conditions necessary and sufficient for the existence of a legal system": (1) "those rules of behaviour which are valid according to the system's ultimate criteria of validity must be generally obeyed," and (2) "its rules of recognition specifying the criteria of legal validity and its rules of change and adjudication must be effectively accepted as common public standards of official behaviour by its officials."[5] Given these minimum conditions, a system of tyranny and oppression would count as a legal system so long as the governed obey, for whatever reasons, and those in power accept and apply certain rules. It would matter little what those rules are. Thus a legal system's existence does not entail that it, or its rule of recognition, is good or just.

Ronald Dworkin's "The Model of Rules" (1967) criticizes legal positivism, taking Hart's version of positivism as the primary object of attack. Dworkin's criticism of positivism rests on the distinction that Dworkin makes between rules and principles. Dworkin holds that Hart's concept of law, as a system that consists of rules only, fails to take into account the fact that lawyers and judges use principles as well as rules in their reasonings. The difference is that rules apply in an all-or-nothing fashion, while principles generate reasons that have the dimension of weight, the amount of which depends on the context. Reasoning about whether the plaintiff or the defendant should win a case in a difficult and new area of the law typically involves weighing many reasons against one another, and there is no simple recipe for determining the correct outcome, as the model of rules might seem to suggest.

Once we become aware of the existence and role of principles, we will see that they appear everywhere in the law, that they are deeply entrenched, and that they are every bit as important as rules. Legal rules using broad and elastic phrases such as "reasonable and just" or "due process" can only be properly understood and applied through the use of principles. In Dworkin's view, moreover, principles are binding on judges. This emerges clearly in the conceptual distinctions Dworkin makes among different senses of "discretion." Here his discussion touches on a favorite doctrine about legal reasoning held by many legal positivists: Any law, no matter how well formulated, contains "gaps" that judges are free to fill in at their discretion.

In Hart's version of the doctrine,[6] these gaps are due to what he calls *open texture*. Since laws are formulated and communicated using human language, and since human language uses general classifying terms (e.g., "rain," "vehicle," "harassment," or "drunkenness"),

---

[5] H.L.A. Hart, *The Concept of Law* (Oxford: The Clarendon Press, 1961), p. 113.

[6] See Hart, *The Concept of Law*, pp. 124–32. See also Hart's earlier "Positivism and the Separation of Law and Morals," *Harvard Law Review*, vol. 71, p. 593 (1958), and Lon Fuller's answer, "Positivism and Fidelity to Law—A Reply to Professor Hart," *Harvard Law Review*, vol. 71, p. 630 (1958).

there will always be some indeterminacy as to what counts as an instance falling under a term; for example, whether the misty wet day we experience is really rain, whether something is or is not a vehicle, whether certain behavior counts as harassment of a worker, or some other behavior counts as public drunkenness. When this point of indeterminacy is reached, the law can tell the judge no more, and the decision must be reached by using other values and standards. This marks the sphere of judicial discretion or freedom.

But in Dworkin's view, judges do not have discretion in this strong sense, for they are still bound by principles which are not merely there to be taken into account at the judge's pleasure. They require careful weighing and judgment if they are to be applied properly, but their relevance may not be ignored. And, while it may be extremely difficult to arrive at the correct decision after fully weighing all relevant considerations, there is, at least in a developed legal system, a uniquely correct answer for every legal question, no matter how difficult the question, and no matter how controversial the answer. As Dworkin summarizes his own view, "A proposition of law, like the proposition that Tom's contract is valid, is true if the best justification that can be provided for the body of propositions of law already shown to be true provides a better case for that proposition than for the contrary proposition that Tom's contract is not valid, but is false if that justification provides a better case for that contrary proposition than for it."[7] Rarely if ever are the justifications for contrary legal propositions equally strong, and so legal questions have a right answer, though not necessarily an easy one.

Dworkin's views about the role of principles in judicial decision have seemed to some to involve a return to natural law or, if not to natural law, then a return at least to the use of moral reasoning and even moral philosophy in judicial decision. To some, especially those who question the objectivity of moral reasoning, this seems to set the law adrift on a sea of uncertainty. This is one important way in which questions about the nature of law are linked to questions about the nature of legal reasoning. This issue is taken up again in Part 3 on legal reasoning.

Ronald Dworkin relies on the case of *Riggs v. Palmer* (1889) to illustrate the ways in which principles operate in legal reasoning to fill out, or even override, legal rules. In that case, a young man murdered his grandfather because he had suspected that his grandfather was about to change his will, cutting the grandson out of a rather substantial inheritance. The court had to decide whether the young man, in spite of his conviction for murder, could nevertheless inherit under the terms of his grandfather's will. The New York statute governing the formation and legal effects of wills was silent on cases in which a legatee (here the grandson) murders a testator (here the grandfather). Followed literally, the statute would allow the murderer to inherit. About one thing at least there is fairly wide agreement: The court deciding a case is supposed to apply the law. It is not the court's job to use opinion surveys to find out what people would prefer to have done, nor is it the job of the judges to implement their personal moral convictions. But is it correct to say that the law on this

---

[7] Ronald Dworkin, "No Right Answer?" in *Law, Morality, and Society: Essays in Honour of H.L.A. Hart*, ed. P.M.S. Hacker and J. Raz (Oxford: Clarendon Press, 1977), p. 82. Additional discussion of this thesis is in Stephen Munzer, "Right Answers, Preexisting Rights, and Fairness," *Georgia Law Review*, vol. 11, no. 5 (September 1977), p. 1055, and Dworkin's answer, pp. 1241–50.

matter is to be equated with the ordinary meaning of a statute? Or does law, properly conceived, include more than what is contained in a literal construal of the statutes? The court in *Riggs* thought that it does and concluded that the grandson was not entitled to inherit under the will because, in addition to statutes, the law includes principles, among them the principle that no one is to be allowed to profit from his own wrong.

**THE IDEA OF THE RULE OF LAW.**  In his article on the rule of law (1977), Joseph Raz claims that the importance and value of the rule of law tend to be exaggerated. Even if we do accept the idea that the rule of law implies adherence to certain precepts, this will not be enough to guarantee that a society that lives by the rule of law will be just, or even morally tolerable. For one thing, the expression "the rule of law" is often loosely used, with the result that different people pack into the concept their own particular conceptions of justice. But when the idea is applied in that way, it becomes virtually useless, for it implies that one must have developed, as Raz puts it, "a complete social philosophy" about individual rights, political freedoms, and distributive justice in order to know whether a system adheres to the rule of law. On the other hand, if we use a narrow concept of the rule of law, one that requires only that laws be public, general, and prospective rather than retroactive, then one can imagine a regime that adheres strictly to the rule of law, but has thoroughly odious laws. Part of Raz's claim is that, just as a person deserves no great moral credit for being incapable of doing certain evil things, a legal system deserves no high evaluation simply because its officials adhere to the rule of law and thus are not likely to treat people arbitrarily.

# Concepts of Law
## and Legal System

# St. Thomas Aquinas
# TREATISE ON LAW*

## OF THE ESSENCE OF LAW

### Whether Law Is Something Pertaining to Reason

*We proceed thus to the First Article:—*

*Objection* 1. It would seem that law is not something pertaining to reason. For the Apostle says (Rom. vii. 23): *I see another law in my members,* etc. But nothing pertaining to reason is in the members; since the reason does not make use of a bodily organ. Therefore law is not something pertaining to reason.

*Obj.* 2. Further, in the reason there is nothing else but power, habit, and act. But law is not the power itself of reason. In like manner, neither is it a habit of reason: because the habits of reason are the intellectual virtues of which we have spoken above.[a] Nor again is it an act of reason: because then law would cease, when the act of reason ceases, for instance, while we are asleep. Therefore law is nothing pertaining to reason.

*Obj.* 3. Further, the law moves those who are subject to it to act aright. But it belongs properly to the will to move to act, as is evident from what has been said above. Therefore law pertains, not to the reason, but to the will; according to the words of the Jurist (*Lib. i. ff., De Const. Prin.* leg. i.): *Whatsoever pleaseth the sovereign, has force of law.*

*On the contrary,* It belongs to the law to command and to forbid. But it belongs to reason to command, as stated above. Therefore law is something pertaining to reason.

*I answer that,* Law is a rule and measure of acts, whereby man is induced to act or is restrained from acting: for *lex* (law) is derived from *ligare* (to bind), because it binds one to act. Now the rule and measure of human acts is the reason, which is the first principle of human acts, as is evident from what has been stated above, since it belongs to the reason to direct to the end, which is the first principle in all matters of action, according to the Philosopher (*Phys.* ii.). Now that which is the principle in any genus, is the rule and measure of that genus: for instance, unity in the genus of numbers, and the first movement in the genus of movements. Consequently it follows that law is something pertaining to reason.

*Reply Obj.* 1. Since law is a kind of rule and measure, it may be in something in two ways. First, as in that which measures and rules: and since this is proper to reason, it follows that, in this way, law is in the reason alone.—Secondly, as in that which is measured and ruled. In this way, law is in all those things that are inclined to something by reason of some law: so that any inclination arising from a law, may be called a law, not essentially but by participation as it were. And thus the inclination of the members to concupiscence is called *the law of the members.*

*Reply Obj.* 2. Just as, in external action, we may consider the work and the work done, for instance the work of building and the house built; so in the acts of reason, we may consider the act itself of reason, i.e., to understand and to reason, and something produced by this act. With regard to the speculative reason, this is the first of all the definition; secondly, the proposition; thirdly, the syllogism or argument. And since also the practical reason makes use of a syllogism in respect of the work to be done, as stated above and as the Philosopher teaches

---

*Excerpts from *Treatise on Law*, Questions 90–91, 94–96 of *Summa Theologica*. Reprinted by permission of Benziger Publishers.

[a]Here and throughout various citations have been omitted.

(*Ethic.* vii. 3); hence we find in the practical reason something that holds the same position in regard to operations, as, in the speculative intellect, the proposition holds in regard to conclusions. Suchlike universal propositions of the practical intellect that are directed to actions have the nature of law. And these propositions are sometimes under our actual consideration, while sometimes they are retained in the reason by means of a habit.

*Reply Obj.* 3. Reason has its power of moving from the will, as stated above: for it is due to the fact that one wills the end, that the reason issues its commands as regards things ordained to the end. But in order that the volition of what is commanded may have the nature of law, it needs to be in accord with some rule of reason. And in this sense is to be understood the saying that the will of the sovereign has the force of law; otherwise the sovereign's will would savour of lawlessness rather than of law.

**Whether the Law Is Always Directed to the Common Good?**

*We proceed thus to the Second Article:*—

*Objection* 1. It would seem that the law is not always directed to the common good as to its end. For it belongs to law to command and to forbid. But commands are directed to certain individual goods. Therefore the end of the law is not always the common good.

*Obj.* 2. Further, the law directs man in his actions. But human actions are concerned with particular matters. Therefore the law is directed to some particular good.

*Obj.* 3. Further, Isidore says (*Etym.* v. 3): *If the law is based on reason, whatever is based on reason will be a law.* But reason is the foundation not only of what is ordained to the common good, but also of that which is directed to private good. Therefore the law is not only directed to the good of all, but also to the private good of an individual.

*On the contrary,* Isidore says (*Etym.* v. 21) that *laws are enacted for no private profit, but for the common benefit of the citizens.*

*I answer that* As stated above, the law belongs to that which is a principle of human acts, because it is their rule and measure. Now as reason is a principle of human acts, so in reason itself there is something which is the principle in respect of all the rest: wherefore to this principle chiefly and mainly law must needs be referred.—Now the first principle in practical matters, which are the object of the practical reason, is the last end: and the last end of human life is bliss or happiness, as stated above. Consequently the law must needs regard principally the relationship to happiness. Moreover, since every part is ordained to the whole, as imperfect to perfect; and since one man is a part of the perfect community, the law must needs regard properly the relationship to universal happiness. Wherefore the Philosopher, in the above definition of legal matters mentions both happiness and the body politic: for he says (*Ethic.* v. 1) that we call those legal matters *just, which are adapted to produce and preserve happiness and its parts for the body politic*: since the state is a perfect community, as he says in *Polit.* i. 1.

Now in every genus, that which belongs to it chiefly is the principle of the others, and the others belong to that genus in subordination to that thing: thus fire, which is chief among hot things, is the cause of heat in mixed bodies, and these are said to be hot in so far as they have a share of fire. Consequently, since the law is chiefly ordained to the common good, any other precept in regard to some individual work, must needs be devoid of the nature of a law, save in so far as it regards the common good. Therefore every law is ordained to the common good.

*Reply Obj.* 1. A command denotes an application of a law to matters regulated by the law. Now the order to the common good, at which the law aims, is applicable to particular ends. And in this way commands are given even concerning particular matters.

*Reply Obj.* 2. Actions are indeed concerned with particular matters: but those particular matters are referable to the common good, not as to a common genus or species, but as to a common final cause, according as the common good is said to be the common end.

*Reply Obj.* 3. Just as nothing stands firm with regard to the speculative reason except that which is traced back to the first indemonstrable principles, so nothing stands firm with regard to the practical reason, unless it be directed to the last end which is the common good: and whatever stands to reason in this sense, has the nature of a law.

### Whether the Reason of Any Man Is Competent to Make Laws?

*We proceed thus to the Third Article:—*

*Objection* 1. It would seem that the reason of any man is competent to make laws. For the Apostle says (Rom. ii. 14) that *when the Gentiles, who have not the law, do by nature those things that are of the law, . . .* they *are a law to themselves.* Now he says this of all in general. Therefore anyone can make a law for himself.

*Obj.* 2. Further, as the Philosopher says (*Ethic.* ii. 1), *the intention of the lawgiver is to lead men to virtue.* But every man can lead another to virtue. Therefore the reason of any man is competent to make laws.

*Obj.* 3. Further, just as the sovereign of a state governs the state, so every father of a family governs his household. But the sovereign of a state can make laws for the state. Therefore every father of a family can make laws for his household.

*On the contrary,* Isidore says (*Etym.* v. 10): *A law is an ordinance of the people whereby something is sanctioned by the Elders together with the Commonalty.*

*I answer that,* A law, properly speaking, regards first and foremost the order to the common good. Now to order anything to the common good, belongs either to the whole people, or to someone who is the vicegerent of the whole people. And therefore the making of a law belongs either to the whole people or to a public personage who has care of the whole people: since in all other matters the directing of anything to the end concerns him to whom the end belongs.

*Reply Obj.* 1. As stated above, a law is in a person not only as in one that rules, but also by participation as in one that is ruled. In the latter way each one is a law to himself, in so far as he shares the direction that he receives from one who rules him. Hence the same text goes on: *Who show the work of the law written in their hearts.*

*Reply Obj.* 2. A private person cannot lead another to virtue efficaciously: for he can only advise, and if his advice be not taken, it has no coercive power, such as the law should have, in order to prove an efficacious inducement to virtue, as the Philosopher says (*Ethic.* x. 9). But this coercive power is vested in the whole people or in some public personage, to whom it belongs to inflict penalties, as we shall state further on. Wherefore the framing of laws belongs to him alone.

*Reply Obj.* 3. As one man is a part of the household, so a household is a part of the state: and the state is a perfect community, according to *Polit.* i. 1. And therefore, as the good of one man is not the last end, but is ordained to the common good; so too the good of one household is ordained to the good of a single state, which is a perfect community. Consequently he that governs a family, can indeed make certain commands or ordinances, but not such as to have properly the force of law.

### Whether Promulgation Is Essential to a Law?

*We proceed thus to the Fourth Article:—*

*Objection* 1. It would seem that promulgation is not essential to a law. For the natural law above all has the character of law. But the natural law needs no promulgation.

Therefore it is not essential to a law that it be promulgated.

*Obj.* 2. Further, it belongs properly to a law to bind one to do or not to do something. But the obligation of fulfilling a law touches not only those in whose presence it is promulgated, but also others. Therefore promulgation is not essential to a law.

*Obj.* 3. Further, the binding force of a law extends even to the future, since *laws are binding in matters of the future*, as the jurists say (*Cod.* I., tit. *De lege et constit.* leg. vii.). But promulgation concerns those who are present. Therefore it is not essential to a law.

*On the contrary,* It is laid down in the *Decretals*, dist. 4, that *laws are established when they are promulgated*.

*I answer that,* As stated above, a law is imposed on others by way of a rule and measure. Now a rule or measure is imposed by being applied to those who are to be ruled and measured by it. Wherefore, in order that a law obtain the binding force which is proper to a law, it must needs be applied to the men who have to be ruled by it. Such application is made by its being notified to them by promulgation. Wherefore promulgation is necessary for the law to obtain its force.

Thus from the four preceding articles, the definition of law may be gathered; and it is nothing else than an ordinance of reason for the common good, made by him who has care of the community, and promulgated.

*Reply Obj.* 1. The natural law is promulgated by the very fact that God instilled it into man's mind so as to be known by him naturally.

*Reply Obj.* 2. Those who are not present when a law is promulgated, are bound to observe the law, in so far as it is notified or can be notified to them by others, after it has been promulgated.

*Reply Obj.* 3. The promulgation that takes place now, extends to future time by reason of the durability of written characters, by which means it is continually promulgated. Hence Isidore says (*Etym.* v. 3; ii. 10) that *lex* (law) *is derived from legere* (to read) *because it is written*.

## OF THE VARIOUS KINDS OF LAW

### Whether There Is a Natural Law?

*We proceed thus to the Second Article:—*

*Objection* 1. It would seem that there is no natural law in us. Because man is governed sufficiently by the eternal law: for Augustine says (*De Lib. Arb.* i) that *the eternal law is that by which it is right that all things should be most orderly*. But nature does not abound in superfluities as neither does she fail in necessaries. Therefore no law is natural to man.

*Obj.* 2. Further, by the law man is directed, in his acts, to the end, as stated above. But the directing of human acts to their end is not a function of nature, as is the case in irrational creatures, which act for an end solely by their natural appetite; whereas man acts for an end by his reason and will. Therefore no law is natural to man.

*Obj.* 3. Further, the more a man is free, the less is he under the law. But man is freer than all the animals, on account of his free-will, with which he is endowed above all other animals. Since therefore other animals are not subject to a natural law, neither is man subject to a natural law.

*On the contrary,* A gloss on Rom. ii. 14: *When the Gentiles, who have not the law, do by nature those things that are of the law,* comments as follows: *Although they have no written law, yet they have the natural law, whereby each one knows, and is conscious of, what is good and what is evil.*

*I answer that,* As stated above, being a rule and measure, can be in a person in two ways: in one way, as in him that rules and measures; in another way, as in that which is ruled and measured, since a thing is ruled and measured, in so far as it partakes of the rule or measure. Wherefore, since all things subject to Divine providence are ruled and measured by the eternal law, as was stated above; it is evident that all things partake somewhat of the eternal law, in so far as, namely, from its being imprinted on them, they derive their respective inclinations to their proper acts and ends. Now among all others, the rational creature is subject to Divine providence in the most excellent way, in so far as it partakes of a share of providence, by being provident both for itself and for others. Wherefore it has a share of the Eternal Reason, whereby it has a natural inclination to its proper act and end: and this participation of the eternal law in the rational creature is called the natural law. Hence the Psalmist after saying (Ps. iv. 6): *Offer up the sacrifice of justice,* as though someone asked what the works of justice are, adds: *Many say, Who showeth us good things?* in answer to which question he says: *The light of Thy countenance, O Lord, is signed upon us:* thus implying that the light of natural reason, whereby we discern what is good and what is evil, which is the function of the natural law, is nothing else than an imprint on us of the Divine light. It is therefore evident that the natural law is nothing else than the rational creature's participation of the eternal law.

*Reply Obj.* 1. This argument would hold, if the natural law were something different from the eternal law: whereas it is nothing but a participation thereof, as stated above.

*Reply Obj.* 2. Every act of reason and will in us is based on that which is according to nature, as stated above: for every act of reasoning is based on principles that are known naturally, and every act of appetite in respect of the means is derived from the natural appetite in respect of the last end. Accordingly the first direction of our acts to their end must needs be in virtue of the natural law.

*Reply Obj.* 3. Even irrational animals partake in their own way of the Eternal Reason, just as the rational creature does. But because the rational creature partakes thereof in an intellectual and rational manner, therefore the participation of the eternal law in the rational creature is properly called a law, since a law is something pertaining to reason, as stated above. Irrational creatures, however, do not partake thereof in a rational manner, wherefore there is no participation of the eternal law in them, except by way of similitude.

## Whether There Is a Human Law?

*We proceed thus to the Third Article:*—

*Objection* 1. It would seem that there is not a human law. For the natural law is a participation of the eternal law, as stated above. Now through the eternal law *all things are most orderly,* as Augustine states (*De Lib. Arb.* i. 6). Therefore the natural law suffices for the ordering of all human affairs. Consequently there is no need for a human law.

*Obj.* 2. Further, a law bears the character of a measure, as stated above. But human reason is not a measure of things, but vice versa, as stated in *Metaph* x., text 5. Therefore no law can emanate from human reason.

*Obj.* 3. Further a measure should be most certain, as stated in *Metaph.* x., text. 3. But the dictates of human reason in matters of conduct are uncertain, according to Wis. ix. 14: *The thoughts of mortal men are fearful, and our counsels uncertain.* Therefore no law can emanate from human reason.

*On the contrary,* Augustine (*De Lib. Arb.* i. 6) distinguishes two kinds of law, the one eternal, the other temporal, which he calls human.

*I answer that,* As stated above, a law is a dictate of the practical reason. Now it is to be observed that the same procedure takes place in the practical and in the speculative reason: for each proceeds from principles to conclusions, as stated above. Accordingly we conclude that just as, in the speculative reason, from naturally known indemonstrable principles, we draw the conclusions of the various sciences, the knowledge of which is not imparted to us by nature, but acquired by the efforts of reason, so too it is from the precepts of the natural law, as from general and indemonstrable principles, that the human reason needs to proceed to the more particular determination of certain matters. These particular determinations, devised by human reason, are called human laws, provided the other essential conditions of law be observed, as stated above. Wherefore Tully says in his *Rhetoric (De Invent. Rhet.* ii.) that *justice has its source in nature; thence certain things came into custom by reason of their utility; afterwards these things which emanated from nature and were approved by custom, were sanctioned by fear and reverence for the law.*

*Reply Obj.* 1. The human reason cannot have a full participation of the dictate of the Divine Reason, but according to its own mode, and imperfectly. Consequently, as on the part of the speculative reason, by a natural participation of Divine Wisdom, there is in us the knowledge of certain general principles, but not proper knowledge of each single truth, such as that contained in the Divine Wisdom; so too, on the part of the practical reason, man has a natural participation of the eternal law, according to certain general principles, but not as regards the particular determinations of individual cases, which are, however, contained in the eternal law. Hence the need for human reason to proceed further to sanction them by law.

*Reply Obj.* 2. Human reason is not, of itself, the rule of things: but the principles impressed on it by nature, are general rules and measures of all things relating to human conduct, whereof the natural reason is the rule and measure, although it is not the measure of things that are from nature.

*Reply Obj.* 3. The practical reason is concerned with practical matters, which are singular and contingent: but not with necessary things, with which the speculative reason is concerned. Wherefore human laws cannot have that inerrancy that belongs to the demonstrated conclusions of sciences. Nor is it necessary for every measure to be altogether unerring and certain, but according as it is possible in its own particular genus.

## OF THE NATURAL LAW

### Whether the Natural Law Is a Habit?

*We proceed thus to the First Article:—*

*Objection* 1. It would seem that the natural law is a habit. Because, as the Philosopher says (*Ethic.* ii. 5), *there are three things in the soul, power, habit, and passion.* But the natural law is not one of the soul's powers: nor is it one of the passions; as we may see by going through them one by one. Therefore the natural law is a habit.

*Obj.* 2. Further, Basil says that the conscience or *synderesis is the law of our mind;* which can only apply to the natural law. But the *synderesis* is a habit, as was shown in the First Part. Therefore the natural law is a habit.

*Obj.* 3. Further, the natural law abides in man always, as will be shown further on. But man's reason, which the law regards, does not always think about the natural law. Therefore the natural law is not an act, but a habit.

*On the contrary,* Augustine says (*De Bono Conjug.* xxi) that *a habit is that whereby something is done when necessary.* But such is not the natural law: since it is in infants and in the damned who cannot act by it. Therefore the natural law is not a habit.

*I answer that,* A thing may be called a habit in two ways. First, properly and essentially: and thus the natural law is not a habit. For it has been stated above that the natural law is something appointed by reason, just as a proposition is a work of reason. Now that which a man does is not the same as that whereby he does it: for he makes a becoming speech by the habit of grammar. Since then a habit is that by which we act, a law cannot be a habit properly and essentially.

Secondly, the term habit may be applied to that which we hold by a habit: thus faith may mean that which we hold by faith. And accordingly, since the precepts of the natural law are sometimes considered by reason actually, while sometimes they are in the reason only habitually, in this way the natural law may be called a habit. Thus, in speculative matters, the indemonstrable principles are not the habit itself whereby we hold those principles, but are the principles the habit of which we possess.

*Reply Obj.* 1. The Philosopher proposes there to discover the genus of virtue; and since it is evident that virtue is a principle of action, he mentions only those things which are principles of human acts, viz., powers, habits and passions. But there are other things in the soul besides these three: there are acts; thus *to will* is in the one that wills; again, things known are in the knower; moreover its own natural properties are in the soul, such as immortality and the like.

*Reply Obj.* 2. *Synderesis* is said to be the law of our mind, because it is a habit containing the precepts of the natural law, which are the first principles of human actions.

*Reply Obj.* 3. This argument proves that the natural law is held habitually: and this is granted.

*To the argument advanced in the contrary sense* we reply that sometimes a man is unable to make use of that which is in him habitually, on account of some impediment; thus, on account of sleep, a man is unable to use the habit of science. In like manner, through the deficiency of his age, a child cannot use the habit of understanding of principles, or the natural law, which is in him habitually.

## Whether the Natural Law Contains Several Precepts, or One Only?

*We proceed thus to the Second Article:*—

*Objection* 1. It would seem that the natural law contains, not several precepts, but one only. For law is a kind of precept, as stated above. If therefore there were many precepts of the natural law, it would follow that there are also many natural laws.

*Obj.* 2. Further, the natural law is consequent to human nature. But human nature, as a whole, is one; though, as to its parts, it is manifold. Therefore, either there is but one precept of the law of nature, on account of the unity of nature as a whole; or there are many, by reason of the number of parts of human nature. The result would be that even things relating to the inclination of the concupiscible faculty belong to the natural law.

*Obj.* 3. Further, law is something pertaining to reason, as stated above. Now reason is but one in man. Therefore there is only one precept of the natural law.

*On the contrary,* The precepts of the natural law in man stand in relation to practical matters, as the first principles to matters of demonstration. But there are several first indemonstrable principles. Therefore there are also several precepts of the natural law.

*I answer that,* As stated above, the precepts of the natural law are to the practical reason, what the first principles of demonstrations are to the speculative reason; because both are self-evident principles. Now a thing is said to be self-evident in two ways: first, in itself; secondly, in relation to us. Any proposition is said to be self-evident in itself, if its predicate is contained in the notion of the subject: although, to one who knows not the definition of the subject, it happens that such a proposition is not self-evident. For instance, this proposition, *Man is a rational being*, is, in its very nature, self-evident, since who says *man*, says *a rational being:* and yet to one who knows not what a man is, this proposition is not self-evident. Hence it is that, as Boethius says (*De Hebdom.*), certain axioms or propositions are universally self-evident to all; and such are those propositions whose terms are known to all, as, *Every whole is greater than its part*, and, *Things equal to one and the same are equal to one another.* But some propositions are self-evident only to the wise, who understand the meaning of the terms of such propositions: thus to one who understands that an angel is not a body, it is self-evident that an angel is not circumscriptively in a place: but this is not evident to the unlearned, for they cannot grasp it.

Now a certain order is to be found in those things that are apprehended universally. For that which, before aught else, falls under apprehension, is *being*, the notion of which is included in all things whatsoever a man apprehends. Wherefore the first indemonstrable principle is that *the same thing cannot be affirmed and denied at the same time*, which is based on the notion of *being* and *not-being*: and on this principle all others are based, as is stated in *Metaph.* iv., text. 9. Now as *being* is the first thing that falls under the apprehension simply, so *good* is the first thing that falls under the apprehension of the practical reason, which is directed to action: since every agent acts for an end under the aspect of good. Consequently the first principle in the practical reason is one founded on the notion of good, viz., that *good is that which all things seek after*. Hence this is the first precept of law, that *good is to be done and ensued, and evil is to be avoided*. All other precepts of the natural law are based upon this: so that whatever the practical reason naturally apprehends as man's good (or evil) belongs to the precepts of the natural law as something to be done or avoided.

Since, however, good has the nature of an end, and evil, the nature of a contrary, hence it is that all those things to which man has a natural inclination, are naturally apprehended by reason as being good, and consequently as objects of pursuit, and their contraries as evil, and objects of avoidance. Wherefore according to the order of natural inclinations, is the order of the precepts of the natural law. Because in man there is first of all an inclination to good in accordance with the nature which he has in common with all substances: inasmuch as every substance seeks the preservation of its own being, according to its nature: and by reason of this inclination, whatever is a means of preserving human life, and of warding off its obstacles, belongs to the natural law. Secondly, there is in man an inclination to

things that pertain to him more specially, according to that nature which he has in common with other animals: and in virtue of this inclination, those things are said to belong to the natural law, *which nature has taught to all animals\**, such as sexual intercourse, education of offspring and so forth. Thirdly, there is in man an inclination to good, according to the nature of his reason, which nature is proper to him: thus man has a natural inclination to know the truth about God, and to live in society: and in this respect, whatever pertains to this inclination belongs to the natural law; for instance, to shun ignorance, to avoid offending those among whom one has to live, and other such things regarding the above inclination.

*Reply Obj.* 1. All these precepts of the law of nature have the character of one natural law, inasmuch as they flow from one first precept.

*Reply Obj.* 2. All the inclinations of any parts whatsoever of human nature, *e.g.*, of the concupiscible and irascible parts, in so far as they are ruled by reason, belong to the natural law, and are reduced to one first precept, as stated above: so that the precepts of the natural law are many in themselves, but are based on one common foundation.

*Reply Obj.* 3. Although reason is one in itself, yet it directs all things regarding man; so that whatever can be ruled by reason, is contained under the law of reason.

## Whether All Acts of Virtue Are Prescribed by the Natural Law?

*We proceed thus to the Third Article:—*

*Objection* 1. It would seem that not all acts of virtue are prescribed by the natural law. Because, as stated above it is essential to a law that it be ordained to the common good. But some acts of virtue are ordained to the private good of the individual, as is evident especially in regard to acts of temperance. Therefore not all acts of virtue are the subject of natural law.

*\*Pandect. Just.* I., tit. i.

*Obj.* 2. Further, every sin is opposed to some virtuous act. If therefore all acts of virtue are prescribed by the natural law, it seems to follow that all sins are against nature: whereas this applies to certain special sins.

*Obj.* 3. Further, those things which are according to nature are common to all. But acts of virtue are not common to all: since a thing is virtuous in one, and vicious in another. Therefore not all acts of virtue are prescribed by the natural law.

*On the contrary,* Damascene says (*De Fide Orthod.* iii. 4) that *virtues are natural*. Therefore virtuous acts also are a subject of the natural law.

*I answer that,* We may speak of virtuous acts in two ways: first, under the aspect of virtuous; secondly as such and such acts considered in their proper species. If then we speak of acts of virtue, considered as virtuous, thus all virtuous acts belong to the natural law. For it has been stated that to the natural law belongs everything to which a man is inclined according to his nature. Now each thing is inclined naturally to an operation that is suitable to it according to its form: thus fire is inclined to give heat. Wherefore, since the rational soul is the proper form of man, there is in every man a natural inclination to act according to reason: and this is to act according to virtue. Consequently, considered thus, all acts of virtue are prescribed by the natural law: since each one's reason naturally dictates to him to act virtuously. But if we speak of virtuous acts, considered in themselves, i.e., in their proper species, thus not all virtuous acts are prescribed by the natural law: for many things are done virtuously, to which nature does not incline at first: but which, through the inquiry of reason, have been found by men to be conducive to well-living.

*Reply Obj.* 1. Temperance is about the natural concupiscenses of food, drink and sexual matters, which are indeed ordained to the natural common good, just as other matters of law are ordained to the moral common good.

*Reply Obj.* 2. By human nature we may mean either that which is proper to man—and in this sense all sins, as being against reason, are also against nature, as Damascene states (*De Fide Orthod.* ii. 30): or we may mean that nature which is common to man and other animals; and in this sense, certain special sins are said to be against nature; thus contrary to sexual intercourse, which is natural to all animals, is unisexual lust, which has received the special name of the unnatural crime.

*Reply Obj.* 3. This argument considers acts in themselves. For it is owing to the virtuous conditions of men, that certain acts are virtuous for some, as being proportionate and becoming to them, while they are vicious for others, as being out of proportion to them.

## Whether the Natural Law Is the Same in All Men?

*We proceed thus to the Fourth Article:*—

*Objection* 1. It would seem that the natural law is not the same in all. For it is stated in the Decretals (*Dist.* i.) that *the natural law is that which is contained in the Law and the Gospel*. But this is not common to all men; because, as it is written (Rom. x. 16). *all do not obey the gospel.* Therefore the natural law is not the same in all men.

*Obj.* 2. Further, *Things which are according to the law are said to be just,* as stated in *Ethic.* v. But it is stated in the same book that nothing is so universally just as not to be subject to change in regard to some men. Therefore even the natural law is not the same in all men.

*Obj.* 3. Further, as stated above, to the natural law belongs everything to which a man is inclined according to his nature. Now different men are naturally inclined to different things; some to the desire of pleasures, others to the desire of honours, and other men to other things. Therefore there is not one natural law for all.

*On the contrary,* Isidore says (*Etym.* v. 4): *The natural law is common to all nations.*

*I answer that,* As stated above, to the natural law belongs those things to which a man is inclined naturally: and among these it is proper to man to be inclined to act according to reason. Now the process of reason is from the common to the proper, as stated in *Phys.* i. The speculative reason, however, is differently situated in this matter, from the practical reason. For, since the speculative reason is busied chiefly with necessary things, which cannot be otherwise than they are, its proper conclusions, like the universal principles, contain the truth without fail. The practical reason, on the other hand, is busied with contingent matters, about which human actions are concerned: and consequently, although there is necessity in the general principles, the more we descend to matters of detail, the more frequently we encounter defects. Accordingly then in speculative matters truth is the same in all men, both as to principles and as to conclusions: although the truth is not known to all as regards the conclusions, but only as regards the principles which are called common notions. But in matters of action, truth or practical rectitude is not the same for all, as to matters of detail, but only as to the general principles: and where there is the same rectitude in matters of detail, it is not equally known to all.

It is therefore evident that, as regards the general principles whether of speculative or of practical reason, truth or rectitude is the same for all, and is equally known by all. As to the proper conclusions of the speculative reason, the truth is the same for all, but is not equally known to all: thus it is true for all that the three angles of a triangle are together equal to two right angles, although it is not known to all. But as to the proper conclusions of the practical reason, neither is the truth or rectitude the same for all, nor, where it is the same, is it equally known by all. Thus it is right and true for all to act according to reason: and from this principle it follows as a proper conclusion, that goods entrusted to another should be restored to their owner.

Now this is true for the majority of cases: but it may happen in a particular case that it would be injurious, and therefore unreasonable, to restore goods held in trust; for instance if they are claimed for the purpose of fighting against one's country. And this principle will be found to fail the more, according as we descend further into detail, *e.g.,* if one were to say that goods held in trust should be restored with such and such a guarantee, or in such and such a way; because the greater the number of conditions added, the greater the number of ways in which the principle may fail, so that it be not right to restore or not to restore.

Consequently we must say that the natural law, as to general principles, is the same for all, both as to rectitude and as to knowledge. But as to certain matters of detail, which are conclusions, as it were, of those general principles, it is the same for all in the majority of cases, both as to rectitude and as to knowledge; and yet in some few cases it may fail, both as to rectitude, by reason of certain obstacles (just as natures subject to generation and corruption fail in some few cases on account of some obstacle), and as to knowledge, since in some the reason is perverted by passion, or evil habit, or an evil disposition of nature; thus formerly, theft, although it is expressly contrary to the natural law, was not considered wrong among the Germans, as Julius Caesar relates (*De Bello Gall.* vi.).

*Reply Obj.* 1. The meaning of the sentence quoted is not that whatever is contained in the Law and the Gospel belongs to the natural law, since they contain many things that are above nature; but that whatever belongs to the natural law is fully contained in them. Wherefore Gratian, after saying that *the natural law is what is contained in the Law and the Gospel,* adds at once, by way of example, *by which everyone is commanded to do to others as he would be done by.*

*Reply Obj.* 2. The saying of the Philosopher is to be understood of things that are naturally just, not as general principles, but as conclusions drawn from them, having rectitude in the majority of cases, but failing in a few.

*Reply Obj.* 3. As, in man, reason rules and commands the other powers, so all the natural inclinations belonging to the other powers must needs be directed according to reason. Wherefore it is universally right for all men, that all their inclinations should be directed according to reason.

## Whether the Natural Law Can Be Changed?

*We proceed thus to the Fifth Article:—*

*Objection* 1. It would seem that the natural law can be changed. Because on Ecclus. xvii. 9, *He gave them instructions, and the law of life,* the gloss says: *He wished the law of the letter to be written, in order to correct the law of nature.* But that which is corrected is changed. Therefore the natural law can be changed.

*Obj.* 2. Further, the slaying of the innocent, adultery, and theft are against the natural law. But we find these things changed by God: as when God commanded Abraham to slay his innocent son (Gen. xxii. 2); and when He ordered the Jews to borrow and purloin the vessels of the Egyptians (Exod. xii. 35); and when He commanded Osee to take to himself *a wife of fornications* (Osee i. 2). Therefore the natural law can be changed.

*Obj.* 3. Further, Isidore says (*Etym.* v. 4) that *the possession of all things in common, and universal freedom, are matters of natural law.* But these things are seen to be changed by human laws. Therefore it seems that the natural law is subject to change.

*On the contrary,* It is said in the Decretals (*Dist.* v.): *The natural law dates from the creation of the rational creature. It does not vary according to time, but remains unchangeable.*

*I answer that,* A change in the natural law may be understood in two ways. First, by way of addition. In this sense nothing hinders the natural law from being changed: since many things for the benefit of human life have been added over and above the natural law, both by the Divine law and by human laws.

Secondly, a change in the natural law may be understood by way of subtraction, so that what previously was according to the natural law, ceases to be so. In this sense, the natural law is altogether unchangeable in its first principles: but in its secondary principles, which, as we have said, are certain detailed proximate conclusions drawn from the first principles, the natural law is not changed so that what it prescribes be not right in most cases. But it may be changed in some particular cases of rare occurrence, through some special causes hindering the observance of such precepts, as stated above.

*Reply Obj.* 1. The written law is said to be given for the correction of the natural law, either because it supplies what was wanting to the natural law; or because the natural law was perverted in the hearts of some men, as to certain matters, so that they esteemed those things good which are naturally evil; which perversion stood in need of correction.

*Reply Obj.* 2. All men alike, both guilty and innocent, die the death of nature: which death of nature is inflicted by the power of God on account of original sin, according to I Kings ii. 6: *The Lord killeth and maketh alive.* Consequently, by the command of God, death can be inflicted on any man, guilty or innocent, without any injustice whatever.— In like manner adultery is intercourse with another's wife; who is allotted to him by the law emanating from God. Consequently intercourse with any woman, by the command of God, is neither adultery nor fornication.—The same applies to theft, which is the taking of another's property. For whatever is taken by the command of God, to Whom all things belong, is not taken against the will of its owner, whereas it is in this that theft consists.—Nor is it only in human things, that whatever is commanded by God is right; but also in natural things, whatever is done by God, is, in some way, natural, as stated in the First Part.

*Reply Obj.* 3. A thing is said to belong to the natural law in two ways. First, because nature inclines thereto: *e.g.,* that one should not do harm to another. Secondly, because nature did not bring in the contrary: thus we might say that for man to be naked is of the natural law, because nature did not give him clothes, but art invented them. In this sense, *the possession of all things in common and universal freedom* are said to be of the natural law, because, to wit, the distinction of possessions and slavery were not brought in by nature, but devised by human reason for the benefit of human life. Accordingly the law of nature was not changed in this respect, except by addition.

## OF HUMAN LAW

### Whether It Was Useful for Laws to Be Framed by Men?

*We proceed thus to the First Article:—*

*Objection* 1. It would seem that it was not useful for laws to be framed by men. Because the purpose of every law is that man be made good thereby, as stated above. But men are more to be induced to be good willingly by means of admonitions, than against their will, by means of laws. Therefore there was no need to frame laws.

*Obj.* 2. Further, as the Philosopher says (*Ethic.* v. 4), *men have recourse to a judge as to animate justice.* But animate justice is better than inanimate justice, which is contained in laws. Therefore it would have been better for the execution of justice to be entrusted to the decision of judges, than to frame laws in addition.

*Obj.* 3. Further, every law is framed for the direction of human actions, as is evident from what has been stated above. But since human actions are about singulars, which are infinite in number, matters pertaining to the direction of human actions cannot be taken into sufficient consideration except by a wise man, who looks into each one of them.

Therefore it would have been better for human acts to be directed by the judgment of wise men, than by the framing of laws. Therefore there was no need of human laws.

*On the contrary,* Isidore says (*Etym.* v. 20): *Laws were made that in fear thereof human audacity might held in check, that innocence might be safeguarded in the midst of wickedness, and that the dread of punishment might prevent the wicked from doing harm.* But these things are most necessary to mankind. Therefore it was necessary that human laws should be made.

*I answer that,* As stated above, man has a natural aptitude for virtue; but the perfection of virtue must be acquired by man by means of some kind of training. Thus we observe that man is helped by industry in his necessities, for instance, in food and clothing. Certain beginnings of these he has from nature, viz., his reason and his hands; but he has not the full compliment, as other animals have, to whom nature has given sufficiency of clothing and food. Now it is difficult to see how man could suffice for himself in the matter of this training: since the perfection of virtue consists chiefly in withdrawing man from undue pleasures, to which above all man is inclined, and especially the young, who are more capable of being trained. Consequently a man needs to receive this training from another, whereby to arrive at the perfection of virtue. And as to those young people who are inclined to acts of virtue, by their good natural disposition, or by custom, or rather by the gift of God, paternal training suffices, which is by admonitions. But since some are found to be depraved, and prone to vice, and not easily amenable to words, it was necessary for such to be restrained from evil by force and fear, in order that, at least, they might desist from evildoing, and leave others in peace, and that they themselves, by being habituated in this way, might be brought to do willingly what hitherto they did from fear, and thus become virtuous. Now this kind of training, which compels through fear of punishment, is the discipline of laws. Therefore, in order that man might have peace and virtue, it was necessary for laws to be framed: for, as the Philosopher says (*Polit.* i. 2), *as man is the most noble of animals, if he be perfect in virtue, so is he the lowest of all, if he be severed from law and righteousness;* because man can use his reason to devise means of satisfying his lusts and evil passions, which other animals are unable to do.

*Reply Obj.* 1. Men who are well disposed are led willingly to virtue by being admonished better than by coercion: but men who are evilly disposed are not led to virtue unless they are compelled.

*Reply Obj.* 2. As the Philosopher says (*Rhet.* i. 1), *it is better that all things be regulated by law, than left to be decided by judges:* and this for three reasons. First, because it is easier to find a few wise men competent to frame right laws, than to find the many who would be necessary to judge aright of each single case.—Secondly, because those who make laws consider long beforehand what laws to make; whereas judgment on each single case has to be pronounced as soon as it arises: and it is easier for man to see what is right, by taking many instances into consideration, than by considering one solitary fact.— Thirdly, because lawgivers judge in the abstract and of future events; whereas those who sit in judgment judge of things present, towards which they are affected by love, hatred, or some kind of cupidity; wherefore their judgement is perverted.

Since then the animated justice of the judge is not found in every man, and since it can be deflected, it was necessary, whenever possible, for the law to determine how to judge, and for very few matters to be left to the decision of men.

*Reply Obj.* 3. Certain individual facts which cannot be covered by the law *have necessarily to be committed to the judges,* as the Philosopher says in the same passage: for instance, *concerning something that has happened or not happened,* and the like.

## Whether Every Human Law Is Derived from the Natural Law?

*We proceed thus to the Second Article:*—

*Objection* 1. It would seem that not every human law is derived from the natural law. For the Philosopher says (*Ethic.* v. 7) that *the legal just is that which originally was a matter of indifference.* But those things which arise from the natural law are not matters of indifference. Therefore the enactments of human laws are not all derived from the natural law.

*Obj.* 2. Further, positive law is contrasted with natural law, as stated by Isidore (*Etym.* v. 4) and the Philosopher (*Ethic.* v., *loc. cit.*). But those things which flow as conclusions from the general principles of the natural law belong to the natural law, as stated above. Therefore that which is established by human law does not belong to the natural law.

*Obj.* 3. Further, the law of nature is the same for all; since the Philosopher says (*Ethic.* v. 7) that *the natural just is that which is equally valid everywhere.* If therefore human laws were derived from the natural laws, it would follow that they too are the same for all: which is clearly false.

*Obj.* 4. Further, it is possible to give a reason for things which are derived from the natural law. But *it is not possible to give the reason for all the legal enactments of the lawgivers,* as the jurist says*. Therefore, not all human laws are derived from the natural law.

*On the contrary,* Tully says (*Rhetor.*ii): *Things which emanated from nature and were approved by custom, were sanctioned by fear and reverence for the laws.*

*I answer that,* As Augustine says (*De Lib. Arb.* i. 5), *that which is not just seems to be no law at all:* wherefore the force of a law depends on the extent of its justice. Now in human affairs a thing is said to be just, from being right, according to the rule of

*Pandect. Justin,* lib. i. ff., tit. iii., art. v., *De Leg. et Senat.*

reason. But the first rule of reason is the law of nature, as is clear from what has been stated above. Consequently every human law has just so much of the nature of law, as it is derived from the law of nature. But if in any point it deflects from the law of nature, it is no longer a law but a perversion of law.

But it must be noted that something may be derived from the natural law in two ways: first, as a conclusion from premises, secondly, by way of determination of certain generalities. The first way is like to that by which, in sciences, demonstrated conclusions are drawn from the principles: while the second mode is likened to that whereby, in the arts, general forms are particularized as to details: thus the craftsman needs to determine the general form of a house to some particular shape. Some things are therefore derived from the general principles of the natural law, by way of conclusions; *e.g.*, that *one must not kill* may be derived as a conclusion from the principle that *one should do harm to no man:* while some are derived therefrom by way of determination; *e.g.*, the law of nature has it that the evil-doer should be punished; but that he be punished in this or that way, is a determination of the law of nature.

Accordingly both modes of derivation are found in the human law. But those things which are derived in the first way, are contained in human law not as emanating therefrom exclusively, but have some force from the natural law also. But those things which are derived in the second way, have no other force than that of human law.

*Reply Obj.* 1. The Philosopher is speaking of those enactments which are by way of determination or specification of the precepts of the natural law.

*Reply Obj.* 2. This argument avails for those things that are derived from the natural law, by way of conclusions.

*Reply Obj.* 3. The general principles of the natural law cannot be applied to all men in the same way on account of the great variety of human affairs: and hence arises the diversity of positive laws among various people.

*Reply Obj.* 4. These words of the Jurist are to be understood as referring to decisions of rulers in determining particular points of the natural law: on which determinations the judgment of expert and prudent men is based as on its principles; in so far, to wit, as they see at once what is the best thing to decide.

Hence the Philosopher says (*Ethic.* vi. II) that in such matters, *we ought to pay as much attention to the undemonstrated sayings and opinions of persons who surpass us in experience, age and prudence, as to their demonstrations.*

## OF THE POWER OF HUMAN LAW

### Whether It Belongs to Human Law to Repress All Vices?

*We proceed thus to the Second Article:—*

*Objection* 1. It would seem that it belongs to human law to repress all vices. For Isidore says (*Etym.* v. 20) that *laws were made in order that, in fear thereof, man's audacity might be held in check.* But it would not be held in check sufficiently, unless all evils were repressed by law. Therefore human law should repress all evils.

*Obj.* 2. Further, the intention of the lawgiver is to make the citizens virtuous. But a man cannot be virtuous unless he forbear from all kinds of vice. Therefore it belongs to human law to repress all vices.

*Obj.* 3. Further, human law is derived from the natural law, as stated above. But all vices are contrary to the law of nature. Therefore human law should repress all vices.

*On the contrary,* We read in *De Lib. Arb.* i. 5: *It seems to me that the law which is written for the governing of the people rightly permits these things, and that Divine providence punishes them.* But Divine providence punishes nothing but vices. Therefore human law rightly allows some vices, by not repressing them.

*I answer that,* As stated above, law is framed as a rule or measure of human acts. Now a measure should be homogeneous with that which it measures, as stated in *Metaph.* x., text. 3, 4, since different things are measured by different measures. Wherefore laws imposed on men should also be in keeping with their condition, for, as Isidore says (*Etym.* v. 21), law should be *possible both according to nature, and according to the customs of the country.* Now possibility or faculty of action is due to an interior habit or disposition: since the same thing is not possible to one who has not a virtuous habit, as is possible to one who has. Thus the same is not possible to a child as to a full-grown man: for which reason the law for children is not the same as for adults, since many things are permitted to children, which in an adult are punished by law or at any rate are open to blame. In like manner many things are permissible to men not perfect in virtue, which would be intolerable in a virtuous man.

Now human law is framed for a number of human beings, the majority of whom are not perfect in virtue. Wherefore human laws do not forbid all vices, from which the virtuous abstain, but only the more grievous vices, from which it is possible for the majority to abstain; and chiefly those that are to the hurt of others, without the prohibition of which human society could not be maintained: thus human law prohibits murder, theft and suchlike.

*Reply Obj.* 1. Audacity seems to refer to the assailing of others. Consequently it belongs to those sins chiefly whereby one's neighbour is injured: and these sins are forbidden by human law, as stated.

*Reply Obj.* 2. The purpose of human law is to lead men to virtue, not suddenly, but gradually. Wherefore it does not lay upon the multitude of imperfect men the burdens of those who are already virtuous, viz., that they should abstain from all evil. Otherwise these imperfect ones, being unable to bear such precepts, would break out into yet greater evils: thus it is written (Prov. XXX. 33): *He that violently bloweth his nose, bringeth out blood;* and (Matth. ix. 17) that if *new wine,* i.e., precepts of a perfect life, is *put into old bottles,* i.e., into imperfect men, *the bottles break, and the wine runneth out,* i.e., the precepts are despised, and those men, from contempt, break out into evils worse still.

*Reply Obj.* 3. The natural law is a participation in us of the eternal law: while human law falls short of the eternal law. Now Augustine says (*De Lib. Arb.* i. 5): *The law which is framed for the government of states, allows and leaves unpunished many things that are punished by Divine providence. Nor, if this law does not attempt to do everything, is this a reason why it should be blamed for what it does.* Wherefore, too, human law does not prohibit everything that is forbidden by the natural law.

## Whether Human Law Prescribes Acts of All the Virtues?

*We proceed thus to the Third Article:—*

*Objection* 1. It would seem that human law does not prescribe acts of all the virtues. For vicious acts are contrary to acts of virtue. But human law does not prohibit all vices, as stated above. Therefore neither does it prescribe all acts of virtue.

*Obj.* 2. Further, a virtuous act proceeds from a virtue. But virtue is the end of law; so that whatever is from a virtue, cannot come under a precept of law. Therefore human law does not prescribe all acts of virtue.

*Obj.* 3. Further, law is ordained to the common good, as stated above. But some acts of virtue are ordained, not to the common good, but to private good. Therefore the law does not prescribe all acts of virtue.

*On the contrary,* The Philosopher says (*Ethic.* v. T) that the law *prescribes the performance of the acts of a brave man,* . . . *and the acts of the temperate man,* . . . *and the acts of the meek man: and in like manner as regards the other virtues and vices, prescribing the former, forbidding the latter.*

*I answer that,* The species of virtues are distinguished by their objects, as explained above. Now all the objects of virtues can be referred either to the private good of an individual, or to the common good of the multitude: thus matters of fortitude may be achieved either for the safety of the state, or for upholding the rights of a friend, and in like manner with the other virtues. But law, as stated above is ordained to the common good. Wherefore there is no virtue whose acts cannot be prescribed by the law. Nevertheless human law does not prescribe concerning all the acts of every virtue: but only in regard to those that are ordainable to the common good,—either immediately, as when certain things are done directly for the common good,—or mediately, as when a lawgiver prescribes certain things pertaining to good order, whereby the citizens are directed in the upholding of the common good of justice and peace.

*Reply Obj.* 1. Human law does not forbid all vicious acts, by the obligation of a precept, as neither does it prescribe all acts of virtue. But it forbids certain acts of each vice, just as it prescribes some acts of each virtue.

*Reply Obj.* 2. An act is said to be an act of virtue in two ways. First, from the fact that a man does something virtuous; thus the act of justice is to do what is right, and an act of fortitude is to do brave things: and in this way law prescribes certain acts of virtue.— Secondly an act of virtue is when a man does a virtuous thing in a way in which a virtuous man does it. Such an act always proceeds from virtue: and it does not come under a precept of law, but is the end at which every lawgiver aims.

*Reply Obj.* 3. There is no virtue whose act is not ordainable to the common good, as stated above, either mediately or immediately.

## Whether Human Law Binds a Man in Conscience?

*We proceed thus to the Fourth Article:—*

*Objection* 1. It would seem that human law does not bind a man in conscience. For an inferior power has no jurisdiction in a court of higher power. But the power of a man, which frames human law, is beneath the Divine power. Therefore human law cannot impose its precept in a Divine court, such as is the court of conscience.

*Obj.* 2. Further, the judgment of conscience depends chiefly on the commandments of God. But sometimes God's commandments are made void by human laws, according to Matth. xv. 6: *You have made void the commandment of God for your tradition.* Therefore human law does not bind a man in conscience.

*Obj.* 3. Further, human laws often bring loss of character and injury on man, according to Isa. x. 1 *et seq.*: *Woe to them that make wicked laws, and when they write, write injustice; to oppress the poor in judgment, and do violence to the cause of the humble of My people.* But it is lawful for anyone to avoid oppression and violence. Therefore human laws do not bind man in conscience.

*On the contrary*, It is written (1 Pet. ii. 19): *This is thankworthy, if for conscience . . . a man endure sorrows, suffering wrongfully.*

*I answer that*, Laws framed by man are either just or unjust. If they be just, they have the power of binding in conscience, from the eternal law whence they are derived, according to Prov. viii. 15: *By Me kings reign, and lawgivers decree just things.* Now laws are said to be just, both from the end, when, to wit, they are ordained to the common good,— and from their author, that is to say, when the law that is made does not exceed the power of the lawgiver,—and from their form, when, to wit, burdens are laid on the subjects, according to an equality of proportion and with a view to the common good. For, since one man is a part of the community, each man, in all that he is and has, belongs to the community; just as a part, in all that it is, belongs to the whole; wherefore nature inflicts a loss on the part, in order to save the whole: so that on this account, such laws as these, which impose proportionate burdens, are just and binding in conscience, and are legal laws.

On the other hand laws may be unjust in two ways: first, by being contrary to human good, through being opposed to the things mentioned above:—either in respect of the end, as when an authority imposes on his subjects burdensome laws, conducive, not to the common good, but rather to his own cupidity or vainglory;—or in respect of the author, as when a man makes a law that goes beyond the power committed to him;—or in respect of the form, as when burdens are imposed unequally on the community, although with a view to the common good. The like are acts of violence rather than laws; because as Augustine says (*De Lib. Arb.* i. 5), *a law that is not just, seems to be no law at all.* Wherefore such laws do not bind in conscience, except perhaps in order to avoid scandal or disturbance, for which cause a man should even yield his right, according to Matth. v. 40, 41: *If a man . . . take away thy coat, let go thy cloak also unto him; and whosoever will force thee one mile, go with him other two.*

Secondly, laws may be unjust through being opposed to the Divine good: such are the laws of tyrants inducing to idolatry, or to anything else contrary to the Divine law: and laws of this kind must nowise be observed, because, as stated in Acts v. 29, *we ought to obey God rather than men.*

*Reply Obj. 1.* As the Apostle says (Rom. xiii. 1, 2), all human power is from God . . . *therefore he that resisteth the power,* in matters that are within its scope, *resisteth the ordinance of God;* so that he becomes guilty according to his conscience.

*Reply Obj. 2.* This argument is true of laws that are contrary to the commandments of God, which is beyond the scope of (human) power. Wherefore in such matters human law should not be obeyed.

*Reply Obj. 3.* This argument is true of a law that inflicts unjust hurt on its subjects. The power that man holds from God does not extend to this: wherefore neither in such matters is man bound to obey the law, provided he avoid giving scandal or inflicting a more grievous hurt.

## QUESTIONS

1. Give an example of the way in which law, in commanding people to particular ends, can at the same time be directed to the common good.

2. Can human beings know everything there is to know about the eternal law?

3. Explain what Aquinas means by saying that "the rational creature is subject to Divine providence in the most excellent way."

4. Give concrete examples to illustrate why human law, in addition to natural law, is necessary for the governance of human affairs.

5. Would Aquinas accept legal moralism, that is, the view that the moral wrongness of certain behavior is in itself a reason for legally prohibiting it?

6. To determine what the natural law requires, we need to examine man's "natural inclinations." What are some of the problems in determining what man's natural inclinations are? How do we proceed in determining what the human being's natural inclinations are when we observe a conflict, say, between kindness and aggression?

7. Sketch as fully as you can Aquinas's view about whether we have a moral obligation to obey unjust laws.

8. Aquinas distinguishes between two ways in which something may be derived from the natural law: (i) "as a conclusion from premises," and (ii) "by way of determination of certain generalities." Give examples of your own, different from those Aquinas gives, to illustrate each kind of derivation. What if all human laws had to be derivable from the natural law using only method (i)?

# John Austin
# LAW AS THE SOVEREIGN'S COMMAND*

## LECTURE I

The matter of jurisprudence is positive law: law, simply and strictly so called: or law set by political superiors to political inferiors. But positive law (or law, simply and strictly so called) is often confounded with objects to which it is related by *resemblance*, and with objects to which it is related in the way of *analogy*: with objects which are *also* signified, *properly* and *improperly*, by the large and vague expression *law*. To obviate the difficulties springing from that confusion, I begin my projected Course with determining the province of jurisprudence, or with distinguishing the matter of jurisprudence from those various related objects: trying to define the subject of which I intend to treat, before I endeavour to analyse its numerous and complicated parts.

A law, in the most general and comprehensive acceptation in which the term, in its literal meaning, is employed, may be said to be a rule laid down for the guidance of an intelligent being by an intelligent being having power over him. Under this definition are concluded, and without impropriety, several species. It is necessary to define accurately the line of demarcation which separates these species from one another, as much mistiness and intricacy has been infused into the science of jurisprudence by their being confounded or not clearly distinguished. In the comprehensive sense above indicated, or in the largest meaning which it has, without extension by metaphor or analogy, the term *law* embraces the following objects:—Laws set by God to his human creatures, and laws set by men to men.

The whole or a portion of the laws set by God to men is frequently styled the law of nature, or natural law: being, in truth, the only natural law of which it is possible to speak without a metaphor, or without a blending of objects which ought to be distinguished broadly. But, rejecting the appellation Law of Nature as ambiguous and misleading, I name those laws or rules, as considered collectively or in a mass, the *Divine law*, or the *law of God*.

Laws set by men to men are of two leading or principal classes: classes which are often blended, although they differ extremely; and which, for that reason, should be severed precisely, and opposed distinctly and conspicuously.

Of the laws or rules set by men to men, some are established by *political* superiors, sovereign and subject: by persons exercising supreme and subordinate *government*, in independent nations, or independent political societies. The aggregate of the rules thus established, or some aggregate forming a portion of that aggregate, is the appropriate matter of jurisprudence, general or particular. To the aggregate of the rules thus established, or to some aggregate forming a portion of that aggregate, the term *law*, as used simply and strictly, is exclusively applied. But, as contradistinguished to *natural* law, or to the law of *nature* (meaning, by those expressions, the law of God), the aggregate of the rules, established by political superiors, is frequently styled *positive* law, or law existing *by position*. As contradistinguished to the rules which I style *positive morality*, and on which I shall touch immediately, the aggregate of the rules, established by political superiors, may also be marked commodiously with the name of *positive law*. For the sake, then, of getting a name brief and distinctive at once, and agreeably to frequent usage, I style that aggregate of rules, or any portion of that aggregate, *positive law*:

*From *The Province of Jurisprudence Determined, etc.*  All of Lecture I and part of Lecture VI.  First published in 1832. Margin annotations omitted by the editor.

though rules, which are *not* established by political superiors, are also *positive*, or exist by *position*, if they be rules or laws, in the proper signification of the term.

Though *some* of the laws or rules, which are set by men to men, are established by political superiors, *others* are *not* established by political superiors, or are not established by political superiors, in that capacity or character.

Closely analogous to human laws of this second class, are a set of objects frequently but *improperly* termed *laws*, being rules set and enforced by *mere opinion*, that is, by the opinions or sentiments held or felt by an indeterminate body of men in regard to human conduct. Instances of such a use of the term *law* are the expressions—'The law of honour;' 'The law set by fashion;' and rules of this species constitute much of what is usually termed 'International law.'

The aggregate of human laws properly so called belonging to the second of the classes above mentioned, with the aggregate of objects *improperly* but by *close analogy* termed laws, I place together in a common class, and denote them by the term *positive morality*. The name *morality* severs them from *positive law*, while the epithet *positive* disjoins them from the *law of God*. And to the end of obviating confusion, it is necessary or expedient that they *should* be disjoined from the latter by that distinguishing epithet. For the name *morality* (or *morals*), when standing unqualified or alone, denotes indifferently either of the following objects: namely, positive morality *as it is*, or without regard to its merits; and positive morality *as it would be*, if it conformed to the law of God, and were, therefore, deserving of *approbation*.

Besides the various sorts of rules which are included in the literal acceptation of the term law, and those which are by a close and striking analogy, though improperly, termed laws, there are numerous applications of the term law, which rest upon a slender analogy and are merely metaphorical or figurative. Such is the case when we talk of *laws* observed by the lower animals; of *laws* regulating the growth or decay of vegetables; of *laws* determining the movements of inanimate bodies or masses. For where *intelligence* is not, or where it is too bounded to take the name of *reason*, and, therefore, is too bounded to conceive the purpose of a law, there is not the *will* which law can work on, or which duty can incite or restrain. Yet through these misapplications of *a name*, flagrant as the metaphor is, has the field of jurisprudence and morals been deluged with muddy speculation.

Having suggested the *purpose* of my attempt to determine the province of jurisprudence: to distinguish positive law, the appropriate matter of jurisprudence, from the various objects to which it is related by resemblance, and to which it is related, nearly or remotely, by a strong or slender analogy: I shall now state the essentials of *a law* or *rule* (taken with the largest signification which can be given to the term *properly*).

Every *law* or *rule* (taken with the largest signification which can be given to the term *properly*) is a *command*. Or, rather, laws or rules, properly so called, are a *species* of commands.

Now, since the term *command* comprises the term *law*, the first is the simpler as well as the larger of the two. But, simple as it is, it admits of explanation. And, since it is the *key* to the sciences of jurisprudence and morals, its meaning should be analysed with precision.

Accordingly, I shall endeavour, in the first instance, to analyse the meaning of '*command*:' an analysis which I fear, will task the patience of my hearers, but which they will bear with cheerfulness, or, at least, with resignation, if they consider the difficulty of performing it. The elements of a science are precisely the parts of it which are explained least easily. Terms that are the largest, and, therefore, the simplest of a series, are without equivalent expressions into which we can resolve them *concisely*. And when we endeavour to *define* them, or to translate them into terms which we suppose are better understood, we are forced upon awkward and tedious circumlocutions.

If you express or intimate a wish that I shall do or forbear from some act, and if you will visit me with an evil in case I comply not with your wish, the *expression* or *intimation* of your wish is a *command*. A command is distinguished from other significations of desire, not by the style in which the desire is signified, but by the power and the purpose of the party commanding to inflict an evil or pain in case the desire be disregarded. If you cannot or will not harm me in case I comply not with your wish, the expression of your wish is not a command, although you utter your wish in imperative phrase. If you are able and willing to harm me in case I comply not with your wish, the expression of your wish amounts to a command, although you are prompted by a spirit of courtesy to utter it in the shape of a request. '*Preces* erant, sed *quibus contradici non posset.*' Such is the language of Tacitus, when speaking of a petition by the soldiery to a son and lieutenant of Vespasian.

A command, then, is a signification of desire. But a command is distinguished from other significations of desire by this peculiarity: that the party to whom it is directed is liable to evil from the other, in case he comply not with the desire.

Being liable to evil from you if I comply not with a wish which you signify, I am *bound* or *obliged* by your command, or I lie under a *duty* to obey it. If, in spite of that evil in prospect, I comply not with the wish which you signify, I am said to disobey your command, or to violate the duty which it imposes.

Command and duty are, therefore, correlative terms: the meaning denoted by each being implied or supposed by the other. Or (changing the expression) wherever a duty lies, a command has been signified; and whenever a command is signified, a duty is imposed.

Concisely expressed, the meaning of the correlative expressions is this. He who will inflict an evil in case his desire be disre-

garded, utters a command by expressing or intimating his desire: He who is liable to the evil in case he disregard the desire, is bound or obliged by the command.

The evil which will probably be incurred in case a command be disobeyed or (to use an equivalent expression) in case a duty be broken, is frequently called a *sanction*, or an *enforcement of obedience*. Or (varying the phrase) the command or the duty is said to be *sanctioned* or *enforced* by the chance of incurring the evil.

Considered as thus abstracted from the command and the duty which it enforces, the evil to be incurred by disobedience is frequently styled a *punishment*. But, as punishments, strictly so called, are only a *class* of sanctions, the term is too narrow to express the meaning adequately.

I observe that Dr. Paley, in his analysis of the term *obligation*, lays much stress upon the *violence* of the motive to compliance. In so far as I can gather a meaning from his loose and inconsistent statement, his meaning appears to be this: that unless the motive to compliance be *violent* or *intense*, the expression or intimation of a wish is not a *command*, nor does the party to whom it is directed lie under a *duty* to regard it.

If he means, *by a violent* motive, a motive operating with certainty, his proposition is manifestly false. The greater the evil to be incurred in case the wish be disregarded, and the greater the chance of incurring it on that same event, the greater, no doubt, is the *chance* that the wish will *not* be disregarded. But no conceivable motive will *certainly* determine to compliance, or no conceivable motive will render obedience inevitable. If Paley's proposition be true, in the sense which I have now ascribed to it, commands and duties are simply impossible. Or, reducing his proposition to absurdity by a consequence as manifestly false, commands and duties are possible, but are never disobeyed or broken.

If he means by a *violent* motive, an evil which inspires fear, his meaning is simply this: that the party bound by a command is bound by the prospect of an evil. For that which is not feared is not apprehended as an evil: or (changing the shape of the expression) is not an evil in prospect.

The truth is, that the magnitude of the eventual evil, and the magnitude of the chance of incurring it, are foreign to the matter in question. The greater the eventual evil, and the greater the chance of incurring it, the greater is the efficacy of the command, and the greater is the strength of the obligation: Or (substituting expressions exactly equivalent), the greater is the *chance* that the command will be obeyed, and that the duty will not be broken. But where there is the smallest chance of incurring the smallest evil, the expression of a wish amounts to a command, and, therefore, imposes a duty. The sanction, if you will, is feeble or insufficient; but still there *is* a sanction, and, therefore, a duty and a command.

By some celebrated writers (by Locke, Bentham, and, I think, Paley), the term *sanction*, or *enforcement of obedience*, is applied to conditional good as well as to conditional evil: to reward as well as to punishment. But, with all my habitual veneration for the names of Locke and Bentham, I think that this extension of the term is pregnant with confusion and perplexity.

Rewards are, indisputably, *motives* to comply with the wishes of others. But to talk of commands and duties as *sanctioned* or *enforced* by rewards, or to talk of rewards as *obliging* or *constraining t*o obedience, is surely a wide departure from the established meaning of the terms.

If *you* expressed a desire that *I* should render a service, and if you proffered a reward as the motive or inducement to render it, *you* would scarcely be said to *command* the service, nor should *I*, in ordinary language, be *obliged* to render it. In ordinary language, *you* would *promise* me a reward, on condition of my rendering the service, whilst *I* might be *incited* or *persuaded* to render it by the hope of obtaining the reward.

Again: If a law hold out a *reward* as an inducement to do some act, an eventual *right* is conferred, and not an *obligation* imposed, upon those who shall act accordingly: The *imperative* part of the law being addressed or directed to the party whom it requires to *render* the reward.

In short, I am determined or inclined to comply with the wish of another, by the fear of disadvantage or evil. I am also determined or inclined to comply with the wish of another, by the hope of advantage or good. But it is only by the chance of incurring *evil*, that I am *bound* or *obliged* to compliance. It is only by conditional *evil*, that duties are *sanctioned* or *enforced*. It is the power and the purpose of inflicting eventual *evil*, and *not* the power and the purpose of inflicting eventual *good*, which gives to the expression of a wish the name of a *command*.

If we put *reward* into the import of the term *sanction*, we must engage in a toilsome struggle with the current of ordinary speech; and shall often slide unconsciously, notwithstanding our efforts to the contrary, into the narrower and customary meaning.

It appears, then, from what has been premised, that the ideas or notions comprehended by the term *command* are the following. 1. A wish or desire conceived by a rational being, that another rational being shall do or forbear. 2. An evil to proceed from the former, and to be incurred by the latter, in case the latter comply not with the wish. 3. An expression or intimation of the wish by words or other signs.

It also appears from what has been premised, that *command*, *duty*, and *sanction* are inseparably connected terms: that each embraces the same ideas as the others, though each denotes those ideas in a peculiar order or series.

'A wish conceived by one, and expressed or intimated to another, with an evil to be inflicted and incurred in case the wish be disregarded,' are signified directly and indirectly by each of the three expressions. Each is the name of the same complex notion.

But when I am talking *directly* of the expression or intimation of the wish, I employ the term *command*: The expression or intimation of the wish being presented *prominently* to my hearer; whilst the evil to be incurred, with the chance of incurring it, are kept (if I may so express myself) in the background of my picture.

When I am talking *directly* of the chance of incurring the evil, or (changing the express) of the liability or obnoxiousness to the evil, I employ the term *duty*, or the term *obligation*: The liability or obnoxiousness to the evil being put foremost, and the rest of the complex notion being signified implicitly.

When I am talking *immediately* of the evil itself, I employ the term *sanction*, or a term of the like import: The evil to be incurred being signified directly; whilst the obnoxiousness to that evil, with the express or intimation of the wish, are indicated indirectly or obliquely.

To those who are familiar with the language of logicians (language unrivalled for brevity, distinctness, and precision), I can express my meaning accurately in a breath:— Each of the three terms *signifies* the same notion; but each *denotes* a different part of that notion, and *connotes* the residue.

Commands are of two species. Some are *laws* or *rules*. The other have not acquired an appropriate name, nor does language afford an expression which will mark them briefly and precisely. I must, therefore, note them as well as I can by the ambiguous and inexpressive name of 'occasional or *particular* commands.'

The term *laws* or *rules* being not infrequently applied to occasional or particular commands, it is hardly possible to describe a line of separation which shall consist in every respect with established forms of speech. But the distinction between laws and particular commands may, I think, be stated in the following manner.

By every command, the party to whom it is directed is obliged to do or to forbear.

Now where it obliges *generally* to acts or forbearances of a *class*, a command is a law or rule. But where it obliges to a *specific* act or forbearance, or to acts or forbearances which it determines *specifically* or *individually*, a command is occasional or particular. In other words, a class or description of acts is determined by a law or rule, and acts of that class or description are enjoined or forbidden generally. But where a command is occasional or particular, the act or acts, which the command enjoins or forbids, are assigned or determined by their specific or individual natures as well as by the class or description to which they belong.

The statement which I have given in abstract expressions I will now endeavour to illustrate by apt examples.

If you command your servant to go on a given errand, or *not* to leave your house on a given evening, or to rise at such an hour on such a morning, or to rise at that hour during the next week or month, the command is occasional or particular. For the act or acts enjoined or forbidden are specially determined or assigned.

But if you command him *simply* to rise at that hour, or to rise at that hour *always*, or to rise at that hour *till further orders*, it may be said, with propriety, that you lay down a *rule* for the guidance of your servant's conduct. For no specific act is assigned by the command, but the command obliges him generally to acts of a determined class.

If a regiment be ordered to attack or defend a post, or to quell a riot, or to march from their present quarters, the command is occasional or particular. But an order to exercise daily till further orders shall be given would be called a *general* order, and *might* be called a *rule*.

If Parliament prohibited simply the exportation of corn, either for a given period or indefinitely, it would establish a law or rule: a *kind* or *sort* of acts being determined by the command, and acts of that kind or sort being *generally* forbidden. But an order issued by Parliament to meet an impending scarcity, and stopping the exportation of corn *then shipped and in port*, would not be a law or rule, though issued by the sovereign legislature. The order regarding exclusively a specified quantity of corn, the negative acts or forbearances, enjoined by the command, would be determined specifically or individually by the determinate nature of their subject.

As issued by a sovereign legislature, and as wearing the form of a law, the order which I have now imagined would probably be *called* a law. And hence the difficulty of drawing a distinct boundary between laws and occasional commands.

Again: An act which is not an offence, according to the existing law, moves the sovereign to displeasure: and, though the authors of the act are legally innocent or unoffending, the sovereign commands that they shall be punished. As enjoining a specific punishment in that specific case, and as not enjoining generally acts or forbearances of a class, the order uttered by the sovereign is not a law or rule.

Whether such an order would be *called* a law, seems to depend upon circumstances which are purely immaterial: immaterial, that is, with reference to the present purpose, though material with reference to others. If made by a sovereign assembly deliberately, and with the forms of legislation, it would probably be called a law. If uttered by an absolute monarch, without deliberation or ceremony, it would scarcely be confounded with acts of legislation, and would be styled an arbitrary command. Yet, on either of these suppositions, its nature would be the same. It would not be a law or rule, but an occasional or particular command of the sovereign One or Number.

To conclude with an example which best illustrates the distinction, and which shows the importance of the distinction most conspicuously, *judicial commands* are commonly occasional or particular, although the commands which they are calculated to enforce are commonly laws or rules.

For instance, the lawgiver commands that thieves shall be hanged. A specific theft and a specified thief being given, the judge commands that the thief shall be hanged, agreeably to the command of the lawgiver.

Now the lawgiver determines a class or description of acts; prohibits acts of the class generally and indefinitely; and commands, with the like generality, that punishment shall follow transgression. The command of the lawgiver is, therefore, a law or rule. But the command of the judge is occasional or particular. For he orders a specific punishment, as the consequence of a specific offence.

According to the line of separation which I have now attempted to describe, a law and a particular command are distinguished thus:—Acts or forbearances of a *class* are enjoined *generally* by the former. Acts *determined specifically*, are enjoined or forbidden by the latter.

A different line of separation has been drawn by Blackstone and others. According to Blackstone and others, a law and a particular command are distinguished in the following manner:—A law obliges *generally* the members of the given community, or a law obliges *generally* persons of a given class. A particular command obliges a *single* person, or persons whom it determines *individually*.

That laws and particular commands are not to be distinguished thus, will appear on a moment's reflection.

For, *first*, commands which oblige generally the members of the given community, or commands which oblige generally persons of given classes, are not always laws or rules.

Thus, in the case already supposed; that in which the sovereign commands that all corn actually shipped for exportation be stopped and detained; the command is obligatory upon the whole community, but as it obliges them only to a set of acts individually assigned, it is not a law. Again, suppose the sovereign to issue an order, enforced by penalties, for a general mourning, on occasion of a public calamity. Now, though it is addressed to the community at large, the order is scarcely a rule, in the usual acceptation of the term. For, though it obliges generally the members of the entire community, it obliges to acts which it assigns specifically, instead of obliging generally to acts or forbearances of a class. If the sovereign commanded that *black* should be the dress of his subjects, his command would amount to a law. But if he commanded them to wear it on a specified occasion, his command would be merely particular.

And, *secondly*, a command which obliges exclusively persons individually determined, may amount, notwithstanding, to a law or a rule.

For example, A father may set a *rule* to his child or children: a guardian, to his ward: a master, to his slave or servant. And certain of God's *laws* were as binding on the first man, as they are binding at this hour on the millions who have sprung from his loins.

Most, indeed, of the laws which are established by political superiors, or most of the laws which are simply and strictly so called, oblige generally the members of the political community, or persons of a class. To frame a system of duties for every individual of the community, were simply impossible: and if it were possible, it were utterly useless. Most of the laws established by political superiors are, therefore, *general* in a twofold manner: as enjoining or forbidding generally acts of kinds or sorts; and as binding the whole community, or, at least, whole classes of its members.

But if we suppose that Parliament creates and grants an office, and Parliament binds the grantee to services of a given description, we suppose a law established by political superiors, and yet exclusively binding a specified or determinate person.

Laws established by political superiors, and exclusively binding specified or determinate persons, are styled, in the language of the Roman jurists, *privilegia*. Though that, indeed, is a name which will hardly denote them distinctly: for, like most of the leading terms in actual systems of law, it is not the name of a definite class of objects, but of a heap of heterogeneous objects.[1]

It appears, from what has been premised, that a law, properly so called, may be defined in the following manner.

A law is a command which obliges a person or persons.

But, as contradistinguished or opposed to an occasional or particular command, a law is a command which obliges a person or persons, and obliges *generally* to acts or forbearances of a *class*.

In language more popular but less distinct and precise, a law is a command which obliges a person or persons to a *course* of conduct.

Laws and other commands are said to proceed from *superiors,* and to bind or oblige *inferiors.* I will, therefore, analyse the meaning of those correlative expressions; and will try to strip them of a certain mystery, by which that simple meaning appears to be obscured.

*Superiority* is often synonymous with *precedence* or *excellence.* We talk of superiors in rank; of superiors in wealth; of superiors in virtue: comparing certain persons with certain other persons; and meaning that the former precede or excel the latter in rank, in wealth, or in virtue.

But, taken with the meaning wherein I here understand it, the term *superiority* signifies *might:* the power of affecting others with evil or pain, and of forcing them, through fear of that evil, to fashion their conduct to one's wishes.

---

[1]Where a *privilegium* merely imposes a duty, it exclusively obliges a determinate person or persons. But where a *privilegium* confers a right, and the right conferred *avails against the world at large,* the law is *privilegium* as viewed from a certain aspect, but it is also *a general law* as viewed from another aspect. In respect of the right conferred, the law exclusively regards a determinate person, and, therefore, is *privilegium.* In respect of the duty imposed, and corresponding to the right conferred, the law regards generally the members of the entire community.

For example, God is emphatically the superior of Man. For his power of affecting us with pain, and of forcing us to comply with his will, is unbounded and resistless.

To a limited extent, the sovereign One or Number is the superior of the subject or citizen: the master, of the slave or servant: the father, of the child.

In short, whoever can *oblige* another to comply with his wishes, is the *superior* of that other, so far as the ability reaches: The party who is obnoxious to the impending evil, being, to that same extent, the *inferior*.

The might or superiority of God, is simple or absolute. But in all or most cases of human superiority, the relation of superior and inferior, and the relation of inferior and superior, are reciprocal. Or (changing the expression) the party who is the superior as viewed from one aspect, is the inferior as viewed from another.

For example, To an indefinite, though limited extent, the monarch is the superior of the governed: his power being commonly sufficient to enforce compliance with his will. But the governed, collectively or in mass, are also the superior of the monarch: who is checked in the abuse of his might by his fear of exciting their anger; and of rousing to active resistance the might which slumbers in the multitude.

A member of a sovereign assembly is the superior of the judge: the judge being bound by the law which proceeds from that sovereign body. But, in his character of citizen or subject, he is the inferior of the judge: the judge being the minister of the law, and armed with the power of enforcing it.

It appears, then, that the term *superiority* (like the terms *duty* and *sanction*) is implied by the term *command*. For superiority is the power of enforcing compliance with a wish: and the expression or intimation of a wish, with the power and the purpose of enforcing it, are the constituent elements of a command.

'That *laws* emanate from *superiors*' is, therefore, an identical proposition. For the meaning which it affects to impart is contained in its subject.

If I mark the peculiar source of a given law, or if I mark the peculiar source of laws of a given class, it is possible that I am saying something which may instruct the hearer. But to affirm of laws universally 'that they flow from *superiors*,' or to affirm of laws universally 'that *inferiors* are bound to obey them,' is the merest tautology and trifling.

Like most of the leading terms in the sciences of jurisprudence and morals, the term *laws* is extremely ambiguous. Taken with the largest signification which can be given to the term properly, *laws* are a species of *commands*. But the term is improperly applied to various objects which have nothing of the imperative character: to objects which are *not* commands; and which, therefore, are *not* laws, properly so called.

Accordingly, the proposition 'that laws are commands' must be taken with limitations. Or, rather, we must distinguish the various meanings of the term *laws*; and must restrict the proposition to that class of objects which is embraced by the largest signification that can be given to the term properly.

I have already indicated, and shall hereafter more fully describe, the objects improperly termed laws, which are *not* within the province of jurisprudence (being either rules enforced by opinion and closely analogous to laws properly so called, or being laws so called by a metaphorical application of the term merely). There are other objects improperly termed laws (not being commands) which yet may properly be included within the province of jurisprudence. These I shall endeavour to particularise:—

1. Acts on the part of legislatures to *explain* positive law, can scarcely be called laws, in the proper signification of the term. Working no change in the actual duties of the governed, but simply declaring what those duties *are*, they properly are acts of *interpretation* by legislative authority. Or, to borrow an expression from the writers on the Roman Law, they are acts of *authentic* interpretation.

But, this notwithstanding, they are frequently styled laws; *declaratory* laws, or declaratory statutes. They must, therefore, be noted as forming an exception to the proposition 'that laws are a species of commands.'

It often, indeed, happens (as I shall show in the proper place), that laws declaratory in name are imperative in effect: Legislative, like judicial interpretation, being frequently deceptive; and establishing new law, under guise of expounding the old.

2. Laws to repeal laws, and to release from existing duties, must also be excepted from the proposition 'that laws are a species of commands.' In so far as they release from duties imposed by existing laws, they are not commands, but revocations of commands. They authorize or permit the parties, to whom the repeal extends, to do or to forbear from acts which they were commanded to forbear from or to do. And, considered with regard to *this,* their immediate or direct purpose, they are often named *permissive laws,* or, more briefly and more properly, *permissions.*

Remotely and indirectly, indeed, permissive laws are often or always imperative. For the parties released from duties are restored to liberties or rights: and duties answering those rights are, therefore, created or revived.

But this is a matter which I shall examine with exactness, when I analyse the expressions 'legal right,' 'permission by the sovereign or state,' and 'civil or political liberty.'

3. Imperfect laws, or laws of imperfect obligation, must also be excepted from the proposition 'that laws are a species of commands.'

An imperfect law (with the sense wherein the term is used by the Roman jurists) is a law which wants a sanction, and which, therefore, is not binding. A law declaring that certain acts are crimes, but annexing no punishment to the commission of acts of the class, is the simplest and most obvious example.

Though the author of an imperfect law signifies a desire, he manifests no purpose of enforcing compliance with the desire. But where there is not a purpose of enforcing compliance with the desire, the expression of a desire is not a command. Consequently, an imperfect law is not so properly a law, as counsel, or exhortation, addressed by a superior to inferiors.

Examples of imperfect laws are cited by the Roman jurists. But with us in England, laws professedly imperative are always (I believe) perfect or obligatory. Where the English legislature affects to command, the English tribunals not unreasonably presume that the legislature exacts obedience. And, if no specific sanction be annexed to a given law, a sanction is supplied by the courts of justice, agreeably to a general maxim which obtains in cases of the kind.

The imperfect laws, of which I am now speaking, are laws which are imperfect, in the sense of *the Roman jurists*: that is to say, laws which speak the desires of political superiors, but which their authors (by oversight or design) have not provided with sanctions. Many of the writers on *morals*, and on the so called *law of nature*, have annexed a different meaning to the term *imperfect*. Speaking of imperfect obligations, they commonly mean duties which are *not legal*: duties imposed by commands of God, or duties imposed by positive morality, as contradistinguished to duties imposed by positive law. An imperfect obligation, in the sense of the Roman jurists, is exactly equivalent to no obligation at all. For the term *imperfect* denotes simply, that the law wants the sanction appropriate to laws of the kind. An imperfect obligation, in the other meaning of the expression, is a religious or a moral obligation. The term *imperfect* does not denote that the law imposing the duty wants the appropriate sanction. It denotes that the law imposing the duty is *not* a law established by a political superior: that it wants that *perfect*, or that surer or more cogent sanction, which is imparted by the sovereign or state.

I believe that I have now reviewed all the classes of objects, to which the term *laws* is improperly applied. The laws (improperly so called) which I have here lastly enumerated, are (I think) the only laws which are not commands, and which yet may be properly included within the province of jurisprudence. But though these, with the so called laws set by opinion and the objects metaphorically termed laws, are the only laws which *really* are not commands, there are certain laws (properly so called) which may *seem* not imperative. Accordingly, I will subjoin a few remarks upon laws of this dubious character.

1. There are laws, it may be said, which *merely* create *rights*: And, seeing that every command imposes a *duty*, laws of this nature are not imperative.

But, as I have intimated already, and shall show completely hereafter, there are no laws *merely* creating *rights*. There are laws, it is true, which *merely* create *duties*: duties not correlating with correlating rights, and which, therefore may be styled *absolute*. But every law, really conferring a right, imposes expressly or tacitly a *relative* duty, or a duty correlating with the right. If it specify the remedy to be given, in case the right shall be infringed, it imposes the relative duty expressly. If the remedy to be given be not specified, it refers tacitly to pre-existing law, and clothes the right which it purports to create with a remedy provided by that law. Every law, really conferring a right, is, therefore, imperative: as imperative, as if its only purpose were the creation of a duty, or as if the relative duty, which it inevitably imposes, were merely absolute.

The meanings of the term *right*, are various and perplexed; taken with its proper meaning, it comprises ideas which are numerous and complicated; and the searching and extensive analysis, which the term, therefore, requires, would occupy more room than could be given to it in the present lecture. It is not, however, necessary, that the analysis should be performed here. I purpose, in my earlier lectures, to determine the province of jurisprudence; or to distinguish the laws established by political superiors, from the various laws, proper and improper, with which they are frequently confounded. And this I may accomplish exactly enough, without a nice inquiry into the import of the term *right*.

2. According to an opinion which I must notice *incidentally* here, though the subject to which it relates will be treated *directly* hereafter, *customary laws* must be excepted from the proposition 'that laws are a species of commands.'

By many of the admirers of customary laws (and, especially, of their German admirers), they are thought to oblige legally (independently of the sovereign or state), *because* the citizens or subjects have observed or kept them. Agreeably to this opinion, they are not the *creatures* of the sovereign or state, although the sovereign or state may abolish them at pleasure. Agreeably to this opinion, they are positive law (or law, strictly so called), inasmuch as they are enforced by the courts of justice: But, that notwithstanding, they exist *as positive law* by the spontaneous adoption of the governed, and not by position or establishment on the part of political superiors. Consequently, customary laws, considered as positive law, are not commands. And, consequently, customary laws, considered as positive law, are not laws or rules properly so called.

An opinion less mysterious, but somewhat allied to this, is not uncommonly held by the adverse party: by the party which is strongly opposed to customary law; and to all law made judicially, or in the way of judicial legislation. According to the latter opinion, all judge-made law, or all judge-made law established by *subject* judges is purely the creature of the judges by whom it is established immediately. To impute it to the sovereign legislature, or to suppose that it speaks the will of the sovereign legislature, is one of the foolish or knavish *fictions* with which lawyers, in every age and nation, have perplexed and darkened the simplest and clearest truths.

I think it will appear, on a moment's reflection, that each of these opinions is groundless: that customary law is *imperative*, in the proper signification of the term; and that all judge-made law is the creature of the sovereign or state.

At its origin, a custom is a rule of conduct which the governed observe spontaneously, or not in pursuance of a law set by a political superior. The custom is transmuted into positive law, when it is adopted as such by the courts of justice, and when the judicial decisions fashioned upon it are enforced by the power of the state. But before it is adopted by the courts, and clothed with the legal sanction, it is merely a rule of positive morality: a rule generally observed by the citizens or subjects; but deriving the only force, which it can be said to possess, from the general disapprobation falling on those who transgress it.

Now when judges transmute a custom into a legal rule (or make a legal rule not suggested by a custom), the legal rule which they establish is established by the sovereign legislature. A subordinate or subject judge is merely a minister. The portion of the sovereign power which lies at his disposition is merely delegated. The rules which he makes derive their legal force from authority given by the state: an authority which the state may confer expressly, but which it commonly imparts in the way of acquiescence. For, since the state may reverse the rules which he makes, and yet permits him to enforce them by the power of the political community, its sovereign will 'that his rules shall obtain as law' is clearly evinced by its conduct, though not by its express declaration.

The admirers of customary law love to trick out their idol with mysterious and imposing attributes. But to those who can see the difference between positive law and morality, there is nothing of mystery about it. Considered as rules of positive morality, customary laws arise from the consent of the governed, and not from the position or establishment of political superiors. But, considered as moral rules turned into positive laws, customary laws are established by the state: established by the state directly, when the customs are promulged in its statutes; established by the state circuitously, when the customs are adopted by its tribunals.

The opinion of the party which abhors judge-made laws, springs from their inadequate conception of the nature of commands.

Like other significations of desire, a command is express or tacit. If the desire be signified by *words* (written or spoken), the command is express. If the desire be signified by conduct (or by any signs of desire which are *not* words), the command is tacit.

Now when customs are turned into legal rules by decisions of subject judges, the legal rules which emerge from the customs are *tacit* commands of the sovereign legislature. The state, which is able to abolish, permits its ministers to enforce them: and it, therefore, signifies its pleasure, by that its voluntary acquiescence, 'that they shall serve as a law to the governed.'

My present purpose is merely this: to prove that the positive law styled *customary* (and all positive law made judicially) is established by the state directly or circuitously, and, therefore, is *imperative*. I am far from disputing, that law made judicially (or in the way of improper legislation) and law made by statute (or in the properly legislative manner) are distinguished by weighty differences. I shall inquire, in future lectures, what those differences are; and why subject judges, who are properly ministers of the law, have commonly shared with the sovereign in the business of making it.

I assume, then, that the only laws which are not imperative, and which belong to the subject-matter of jurisprudence, are the following:—1. Declaratory laws, or laws explaining the import of existing positive law. 2. Laws abrogating or repealing existing positive law. 3. Imperfect laws, or laws of imperfect obligation (with the sense wherein the expression is used by the Roman jurists).

But the space occupied in the science by these improper laws is comparatively narrow and insignificant. Accordingly, although I shall take them into account so often as I refer to them directly, I shall throw them out of account on other occasions. Or (changing the expression) I shall limit the term *law* to laws which are imperative, unless I extend it expressly to laws which are not. . . .

## LECTURE VI

. . . The superiority which is styled sovereignty, and the independent political society which sovereignty implies, is distinguished from other superiority, and from other society, by the following marks or characters:—
1. The *bulk* of the given society are in a *habit* of obedience or submission to a *determinate* and *common* superior: let that common superior be a certain individual person, or a certain body or aggregate of individual persons.
2. That certain individual, or that certain body of individuals, is *not* in a habit of obedience to a determinate human superior. Laws (improperly so called) which opinion sets or imposes, may permanently affect the conduct of that certain individual or body. To express or tacit commands of other determinate parties, that certain individual or body may yield occasional submission. But there is no determinate person, or determinate aggregate of persons, to whose commands, express or tacit, that certain individual or body renders habitual obedience.

Or the notions of sovereignty and independent political society may be expressed concisely thus. If a *determinate* human superior, *not* in a habit of obedience to a like superior, receive *habitual* obedience from the *bulk* of a given society, that determinate superior is sovereign in that society, and the society (including the superior) is a society political and independent.

To that determinate superior, the other members of the society are *subject*: or on that determinate superior, the other members of the society are *dependent*. The position of its other members towards that determinate superior, is *a state of subjection*, or *a state of dependence*. The mutual relation which subsists between that superior and them, may be styled *the relation of sovereign and subject*, or *the relation of sovereignty and subjection*.

Hence it follows, that it is only through an ellipsis, or an abridged form of expression, that the *society* is styled *independent*. The party truly independent (independent, that is to say, of a determinate human superior), is not the society, but the sovereign portion of the society: that certain member of the society, or that certain body of its members, to whose commands, expressed or intimated, the generality or bulk of its members render habitual obedience. Upon that certain person, or certain body of persons, the other members of the society are *dependent*: or to that certain person, or certain body of persons, the other members of the society are *subject*. By 'an independent political society,' or 'an independent and sovereign nation,' we mean a political society consisting of a sovereign and subjects, as opposed to a political society which is merely subordinate: that is to say, which is merely a limb or member of another political society, and which therefore consists entirely of persons in a state of subjection.

In order that a given society may form a society political and independent, the two distinguishing marks which I have mentioned above must unite. The *generality* of the given society must be in the *habit* of obedience to a *determinate* and *common* superior: whilst that determinate person, or determinate body of persons must *not* be habitually obedient to a determinate person or body. It is the union of that positive, with this negative mark, which renders that certain superior sovereign or supreme, and which renders that given society (including that certain superior) a society political and independent.

To show that the union of those marks renders a given society a society political and independent, I call your attention to the following positions and examples.

1. In order that a given society may form a society political, the generality or bulk of its members must be in a *habit* of obedience to a determinate and common superior.

In case the generality of its members obey a determinate superior, but the obedience be rare or transient and not habitual or permanent, the relation of sovereignty and subjection is not created thereby between that certain superior and the members of that given society. In other words, that determinate superior and the members of that given society do not become thereby an independent political society. Whether that given society be political and independent or not, it is not an independent political society whereof that certain superior is the sovereign portion.

For example: In 1815 the allied armies occupied France; and so long as the allied armies occupied France, the commands of the allied sovereigns were obeyed by the French government, and, through the French government, by the French people generally. But since the commands and the obedience were comparatively rare and transient, they were not sufficient to constitute the relation of sovereignty and subjection between the allied sovereigns and the members of the invaded nation. In spite of those commands, and in spite of that obedience, the French government was sovereign or independent. Or in spite of those commands, and in spite of that obedience, the French government and its subjects were an independent political society whereof the allied sovereigns were not the sovereign portion.

Now if the French nation, before the obedience to those sovereigns, had been an independent society in a state of nature or anarchy, it would not have been changed by the obedience into a society political. And it would not have been changed by the obedience into a society political, because the obedience was not habitual. For, inasmuch as the obedience was not habitual, it was not changed by the obedience from a society political and independent, into a society political but subordinate.—A given society, therefore, is not a society political, unless the generality of its members be in a *habit* of obedience to a determinate and common superior.

Again: A feeble state holds its independence precariously, or at the will of the powerful states to whose aggressions it is obnoxious. And since it is obnoxious to their aggressions, it and the bulk of its subjects render obedience to commands which they occasionally express or intimate. Such, for instance, is the position of the Saxon government and its subjects in respect of the conspiring sovereigns who form the Holy Alliance. But since the commands and the obedience are comparatively few and rare, they are not sufficient to constitute the relation of sovereignty and subjection between the powerful states and the feeble state with its subjects. In spite of those commands, and in spite of that obedience, the feeble state is sovereign or independent. Or in spite of those commands, and in spite of that obedience, the feeble state and its subjects are an independent political society whereof the powerful states are not the sovereign portion. Although the powerful states are permanently *superior*, and although the feeble state is permanently *inferior*, there is neither a *habit* of command on the part of the former, nor a *habit* of obedience on the part of the latter. Although the latter is unable to defend and maintain its independence, the latter is independent of the former in fact or practice.

From the example now adduced, as from the example adduced before, we may draw the following inference: that a given society is not a society political, unless the generality of its members be in a *habit* of obedience to a determinate and common superior.—By the obedience to the powerful states, the feeble state and its subjects are not changed from an independent, into a subordinate political society. And they are not changed by the obedience into a subordinate political society, because the obedience is not habitual. Consequently, if they were a natural society (setting that obedience aside), they would not be changed by that obedience into a society political.

2. In order that a given society may form a society political, habitual obedience must be rendered, by the *generality* or *bulk* of its members, to a determinate and *common* superior. In other words, habitual obedience must be rendered, by the *generality* or *bulk* of its members, to *one and the same* determinate person, or determinate body of persons.

Unless habitual obedience be rendered by the *bulk* of its members, and be rendered by the bulk of its members to *one and the same* superior, the given society is either in a state of nature, or is split into two or more independent political societies.

For example: In case a given society be torn by intestine war, and in case the conflicting parties be nearly balanced, the given society is in one of the two positions which I have now supposed.—As there is no common superior to which the bulk of its members render habitual obedience, it is not a political society single or undivided.—If the bulk of each of the parties be in a habit of obedience to its head, the given society is broken into two or more societies, which, perhaps, may be styled independent political societies.—If the bulk of each of the parties be not in that habit of obedience, the given society is simply or absolutely in a state of nature or anarchy. It is either resolved or broken into its individual elements, or into numerous societies of an extremely limited size: of a size so extremely limited, that they could hardly be styled societies independent and *political*. For, as I shall show hereafter, a given independent society would hardly be styled *political*, in case if fell short of a *number* which cannot be fixed with precision, but which may be called considerable, or not extremely minute.

3. In order that a given society may form a society political, the generality or bulk of its members must habitually obey a superior *determinate* as well as common.

On this position I shall not insist here. For I have shown sufficiently in my fifth lecture, that no indeterminate party can command expressly or tacitly, or can receive obedience or submission: that no indeterminate body is capable of corporate conduct, or is capable, as a body, of positive or negative deportment.

4. It appears from what has preceded, that, in order that a given society may form a society political, the bulk of its members must be in a habit of obedience to a certain and common superior. But, in order that the given society may form a society political and independent, that certain superior must *not* be habitually obedient to a determinate human superior.

The given society may form a society political and independent, although that certain superior be habitually affected by laws which opinion sets or imposes. The given society may form a society political and independent, although that certain superior render occasional submission to commands of determinate parties. But the society is not independent, although it may be political, in case that certain superior habitually obey the commands of a certain person or body.

Let us suppose, for example, that a viceroy obeys habitually the author of his delegated powers. And, to render the example complete, let us suppose that the viceroy receives habitual obedience from the generality or bulk of the persons who inhabit his province.—Now though he commands habitually within the limits of his province, and receives habitual obedience from the generality or bulk of its inhabitants, the viceroy is not sovereign within the limits of his province, nor are he and its inhabitants an independent political society. The viceroy, and (through the viceroy) the generality or bulk of its inhabitants, are habitually obedient or submissive to the sovereign of a larger society. He and the inhabitants of his province are therefore in a state of subjection to the sovereign of that larger society. He and the inhabitants of his province are a society political but subordinate, or form a political society which is merely a limb of another.

# QUESTIONS

1.  Using Austin's conception of sovereignty, analyze government and law in a democracy. Identify the sovereign. Using Austin's theory and nothing more, how would we determine whose "commands" are to be obeyed?

2.  What, in an Austinian theory, are courts doing when they create case law through their own interpretations of the sovereign's commands as issued through the legislature?

3.  How do I apply Austin's theory to determine whether a command imposes a certain legal obligation on me even though I personally am not in a habit of obeying the sovereign making that particular command? Could a sovereign in a foreign land place me under a legal obligation to pay tribute? Why or why not?

4.  Suppose that the sovereign consists of a group of three who rule together. Could one explain in Austinian fashion what it is for this *group* to issue commands, and for people to be in a habit of obeying *it* rather than this or that member of the group?

5.  Suppose that, in accordance with the constitution, a new sovereign $S_2$ succeeds the old sovereign $S_1$, and $S_2$ is sworn in officially at noon on July 1. Can you describe what is happening in Austinian terms? Who is in a habit of obeying whom? Is it possible for a people to be in the habit of obeying $S_1$ before noon, but then to be in a habit of obeying $S_2$ immediately after noon?

6.  We learn from history of various rulers who were privately in awe of some person—for example, an advisor, a family member, lover, mistress, and so forth—who powerfully influenced their decisions. Does the influence of such private persons make it unclear who the real (Austinian) sovereign is? Explain.

## *Oliver W. Holmes, Jr.*
## THE PATH OF THE LAW*

### THE PATH OF THE LAW[1]

When we study law we are not studying a mystery but a well known profession. We are studying what we shall want in order to appear before judges, or to advise people in such as way as to keep them out of court. The reason why it is a profession, why people will pay lawyers to argue for them or to advise them, is that in societies like ours the command of the public force is intrusted to the judges in certain cases, and the whole power of the state will be put forth, if necessary, to carry out their judgments and decrees. People want to know under what circumstances and how far they will run the risk of coming against what is so much stronger than themselves, and hence it becomes a business to find out when this danger is to be feared. The object of our study, then, is prediction, the prediction of the incidence of the public force through the instrumentality of the courts.

[1]An Address delivered by Mr. Justice Holmes, of the Supreme Judicial Court of Massachusetts, at the dedication of the new hall of the Boston University School of Law, on January 8, 1897. Copyrighted by O. W. Holmes, 1897.
*From *Harvard Law Review*, vol. 10 (1897), pp. 457-68.

The means of the study are a body of reports, of treatises, and of statutes, in this country and in England, extending back for six hundred years, and now increasing annually by hundreds. In these sibylline leaves are gathered the scattered prophecies of the past upon the cases in which the axe will fall. These are what properly have been called the oracles of the law. Far the most important and pretty nearly the whole meaning of every new effort of legal thought is to make these prophecies more precise, and to generalize them into a thoroughly connected system. The process is one, from a lawyer's statement of a case, eliminating as it does all the dramatic elements with which his client's story has clothed it, and retaining only the facts of legal import, up to the final analyses and abstract universals of theoretic jurisprudence. The reason why a lawyer does not mention that his client wore a white hat when he made a contract, while Mrs. Quickly would be sure to dwell upon it along with the parcel gilt goblet and the sea-coal fire, is that he foresees that the public force will act in the same way whatever his client had upon his head. It is to make the prophecies easier to be remembered and to be understood that the teaching of the decisions of the past are put into general propositions and gathered into text-books, or that statutes are passed in a general form. The primary rights and duties with which jurisprudence busies itself again are nothing but prophecies. One of the many evil effects of the confusion between legal and moral ideas, about which I shall have something to say in a moment, is that theory is apt to get the cart before the horse, and to consider the right or the duty as something existing apart from and independent of the consequences of its breach, to which certain sanctions are added afterward. But, as I shall try to show, a legal duty so called is nothing but a prediction that if a man does or omits certain things he will be made to suffer in this or that way by judgment of the court;—and so of a legal right.

The number of our predictions when generalized and reduced to a system is not unmanageably large. They present themselves as a finite body of dogma which may be mastered within a reasonable time. It is a great mistake to be frightened by the ever increasing number of reports. The reports of a given jurisdiction in the course of a generation take up pretty much the whole body of the law, and restate it from the present point of view. We could reconstruct the corpus from them if all that went before were burned. The use of the earlier reports is mainly historical, a use about which I shall have something to say before I have finished.

I wish, if I can, to lay down some first principles for the study of this body of dogma or systematized prediction which we call the law, for men who want to use it as the instrument of their business to enable them to prophesy in their turn, and, as bearing upon the study, I wish to point out an ideal which as yet our law has not attained.

The first thing for a business-like understanding of the matter is to understand its limits, and therefore I think it desirable at once to point out and dispel a confusion between morality and law, which sometimes rises to the height of conscious theory, and more often and indeed constantly is making trouble in detail without reaching the point of consciousness. You can see very plainly that a bad man has as much reason as a good one for wishing to avoid an encounter with the public force, and therefore you can see the practical importance of the distinction between morality and law. A man who cares nothing for an ethical rule which is believed and practised by his neighbors is likely nevertheless to care a good deal to avoid being made to pay money, and will want to keep out of jail if he can.

I take it for granted that no hearer of mine will misinterpret what I have to say as the language of cynicism. The law is the witness and external deposit of our moral life. Its history is the history of the moral development of the race. The practice of it, in spite of popular jests, tends to make good citizens and good men. When I emphasize the difference between law and morals I do so with reference to a single end, that of learning and understanding the law. For that purpose you must definitely master its specific marks, and it is for that that I ask you for the moment to imagine yourselves indifferent to other and greater things.

I do not say that there is not a wider point of view from which the distinction between law and morals becomes of secondary or no importance, as all mathematical distinctions vanish in presence of the infinite. But I do say that that distinction is of the first importance for the object which we are here to consider,— a right study and mastery of the law as a business with well understood limits, a body of dogma enclosed within definite lines. I have just shown the practical reason for saying so. If you want to know the law and nothing else, you must look at it as a bad man, who cares only for the material consequences which such knowledge enables him to predict, not as a good one, who finds his reasons for conduct, whether inside the law or outside of it, in the vaguer sanctions of conscience. The theoretical importance of the distinction is no less, if you would reason on your subject aright. The law is full of phraseology drawn from morals, and by the mere force of language continually invites us to pass from one domain to the other without perceiving it, as we are sure to do unless we have the boundary constantly before our minds. The law talks about rights, and duties, and malice, and intent, and negligence, and so forth, and nothing is easier, or, I may say, more common in legal reasoning, than to take these words in their moral sense, at some stage of the argument, and so to drop into fallacy. For instance, when we speak of the rights of man in a moral sense, we mean to mark the limits of interference with individual freedom which we think are prescribed by conscience, or by our ideal, however reached. Yet it is certain that many laws have been enforced in the past, and it is likely that some are enforced now, which are condemned by the

most enlightened opinion of the time, or which at all events pass the limit of interference as many consciences would draw it. Manifestly, therefore, nothing but confusion of thought can result from assuming that the rights of man in a moral sense are equally rights in the sense of the Constitution and the law. No doubt simple and extreme cases can be put of imaginable laws which the statute-making power would not dare to enact, even in the absence of written constitutional prohibitions, because the community would rise in rebellion and fight; and this gives some plausibility to the proposition that the law, if not a part of morality, is limited by it. But this limit of power is not coextensive with any system of morals. For the most part it falls far within the lines of any such system, and in some cases may extend beyond them, for reasons drawn from the habits of a particular people at a particular time. I once heard the late Professor Agassiz say that a German population would rise if you added two cents to the price of a glass of beer. A statute in such a case would be empty words, not because it was wrong, but because it could not be enforced. No one will deny that wrong statutes can be and are enforced, and we should not all agree as to which were the wrong ones.

The confusion with which I am dealing besets confessedly legal conceptions. Take the fundamental question, What constitutes the law? You will find some text writers telling you that it is something different from what is decided by the courts of Massachusetts or England, that it is a system of reason, that it is a deduction from principles of ethics or admitted axioms or what not, which may or may not coincide with the decisions. But if we take the view of our friend the bad man we shall find that he does not care two straws for the axioms or deductions, but that he does want to know what the Massachusetts or English courts are likely to do in fact. I am much of his mind. The prophecies of what the courts will do in fact, and nothing more pretentious, are what I mean by the law.

Take again a notion which as popularly understood is the widest conception which the law contains;—the notion of legal duty, to which already I have referred. We fill the word with all the content which we draw from morals. But what does it mean to a bad man? Mainly, and in the first place, a prophecy that if he does certain things he will be subjected to disagreeable consequences by way of imprisonment or compulsory payment of money. But from his point of view, what is the difference between being fined and being taxed a certain sum for doing a certain thing? That his point of view is the test of legal principles is shown by the many discussions which have arisen in the courts on the very question whether a given statutory liability is a penalty or a tax. On the answer to this question depends the decision whether conduct is legally wrong or right, and also whether a man is under compulsion or free. Leaving the criminal law on one side, what is the difference between the liability under the mill acts or statutes authorizing a taking by eminent domain and the liability for what we call a wrongful conversion of property where restoration is out of the question? In both cases the party taking another man's property has to pay its fair value as assessed by a jury, and no more. What significance is there in calling one taking right and another wrong from the point of view of the law? It does not matter, so far as the given consequence, the compulsory payment, is concerned, whether the act to which it is attached is described in terms of praise or in terms of blame, or whether the law purports to prohibit it or to allow it. If it matters at all, still speaking from the bad man's point of view, it must be because in one case and not in the other some further disadvantages, or at least some further consequences, are attached to the act by the law. The only other disadvantages thus attached to it which I ever have been able to think of are to be found in two somewhat insignificant legal doctrines, both of which might be abolished without much disturbance. One is, that a contract to do a prohibited act is unlawful, and the other, that, if one of two or more joint wrongdoers has to pay all the damages, he cannot recover contribution from his fellows. And that I believe is all. You see how the vague circumference of the notion of duty shrinks and at the same time grows more precise when we wash it with cynical acid and expel everything except the object of our study, the operations of the law.

Nowhere is the confusion between legal and moral ideas more manifest than in the law of contract. Among other things, here again the so called primary rights and duties are invested with a mystic significance beyond what can be assigned and explained. The duty to keep a contract at common law means a prediction that you must pay damages if you do not keep it,—and nothing else. If you commit a tort, you are liable to pay a compensatory sum. If you commit a contract, you are liable to pay a compensatory sum unless the promised event comes to pass, and that is all the difference. But such a mode of looking at the matter stinks in the nostrils of those who think it advantageous to get as much ethics into the law as they can. It was good enough for Lord Coke, however, and here, as in many other cases, I am content to abide with him. In Bromage *v.* Genning,[1] a prohibition was sought in the King's Bench against a suit in the marches of Wales for the specific performance of a covenant to grant a lease, and Coke said that it would subvert the intention of the covenantor, since he intends it to be at his election either to lose the damages or to make the lease. Sergeant Harris for the plaintiff confessed that he moved the matter against his conscience, and a prohibition was granted. This goes further than we should go now, but it shows what I venture to say has been the common law point of view from the beginning, although Mr. Harriman,

[1] 1 Roll. Rep. 368.

in his very able little book upon Contracts has been misled, as I humbly think, to a different conclusion.

I have spoken only of the common law, because there are some cases in which a logical justification can be found for speaking of civil liabilities as imposing duties in an intelligible sense. These are the relatively few in which equity will grant an injunction, and will enforce it by putting the defendant in prison or otherwise punishing him unless he complies with the order of the court. But I hardly think it advisable to shape general theory from the exception, and I think it would be better to cease troubling ourselves about primary rights and sanctions altogether, than to describe our prophecies concerning the liabilities commonly imposed by the law in those inappropriate terms.

I mentioned, as other examples of the use by the law of words drawn from morals, malice, intent, and negligence. It is enough to take malice as it is used in the law of civil liability for wrongs,—what we lawyers call the law of torts,—to show you that it means something different in law from what it means in morals, and also to show how the difference has been obscured by giving to principles which have little or nothing to do with each other the same name. Three hundred years ago a parson preached a sermon and told a story out of Fox's Book of Martyrs of a man who had assisted at the torture of one of the saints, and afterward died, suffering compensatory inward torment. It happened that Fox was wrong. The man was alive and chanced to hear the sermon, and thereupon he sued the parson. Chief Justice Wray instructed the jury that the defendant was not liable, because the story was told innocently, without malice. He took malice in the moral sense, as importing a malevolent motive. But nowadays no one doubts that a man may be liable, without any malevolent

motive at all, for false statements manifestly calculated to inflict temporal damage. In stating the case in pleading, we still should call the defendant's conduct malicious; but, in my opinion at least, the word means nothing about motives, or even about the defendant's attitude toward the future, but only signifies that the tendency of his conduct under the known circumstances was very plainly to cause the plaintiff temporal harm.[1]

In the law of contract the use of moral phraseology has led to equal confusion, as I have shown in part already, but only in part. Morals deal with the actual internal state of the individual's mind, what he actually intends. From the time of the Romans down to now, this mode of dealing has affected the language of the law as to contract, and the language used has reacted upon the thought. We talk about a contract as a meeting of the minds of the parties, and thence it is inferred in various cases that there is no contract because their minds have not met; that is, because they have intended different things or because one party has not known of the assent of the other. Yet nothing is more certain than that parties may be bound by a contract to things which neither of them intended, and when one does not know of the other's assent. Suppose a contract is executed in due form and in writing to deliver a lecture, mentioning no time. One of the parties thinks that the promise will be construed to mean at once, within a week. The other thinks that it means when he is ready. The court says that it means within a reasonable time. The parties are bound by the contract as it is interpreted by the court, yet neither of them meant what the court declares that they have said. In my opinion no one will understand the true theory of contract or be able even to discuss some fundamental questions intelligently until he has understood that all contracts are formal, that the making of a contract depends not on the agreement of two

---

[1]See Hanson *v.* Globe Newspaper Co., 159 Mass. 293, 302.

minds in one intention, but on the agreement of two sets of external signs,—not on the parties' having *meant* the same thing but on their having *said* the same thing. Furthermore, as the signs may be addressed to one sense or another,—to sight or to hearing,—on the nature of the sign will depend the moment when the contract is made. If the sign is tangible, for instance, a letter, the contract is made when the letter of acceptance is delivered. If it is necessary that the minds of the parties meet, there will be no contract until the acceptance can be read,—none, for example, if the acceptance be snatched from the hand of the offerer by a third person.

This is not the time to work out a theory in detail, or to answer many obvious doubts and questions which are suggested by these general views. I know of none which are not easy to answer, but what I am trying to do now is only by a series of hints to throw some light on the narrow path of legal doctrine, and upon two pitfalls which, as it seems to me, lie perilously near to it. Of the first of these I have said enough. I hope that my illustrations have shown the danger, both to speculation and to practice, of confounding morality with law, and the trap which legal language lays for us on that side of our way. For my own part, I often doubt whether it would not be a gain if every word of moral significance could be banished from the law altogether, and other words adopted which should convey legal ideas uncolored by anything outside the law. We should lose the fossil records of a good deal of history and the majesty got from ethical associations, but by ridding ourselves of an unnecessary confusion we should gain very much in the clearness of our thought.

So much for the limits of the law. The next thing which I wish to consider is what are the forces which determine its content and its growth. You may assume, with Hobbes and Bentham and Austin, that all law emanates from the sovereign, even when the first human beings to enunciate it are the judges, or you may think that law is the voice of the Zeitgeist, or what you like. It is all one to my present purpose. Even if every decision required the sanction of an emperor with despotic power and a whimsical turn of mind, we should be interested none the less, still with a view to prediction, in discovering some order, some rational explanation, and some principle of growth for the rules which he laid down. In every system there are such explanations and principles to be found. It is with regard to them that a second fallacy comes in, which I think it important to expose.

The fallacy to which I refer is the notion that the only force at work in the development of the law is logic. In the broadest sense, indeed, that notion would be true. The postulate on which we think about the universe is that there is a fixed quantitative relation between every phenomenon and its antecedents and consequents. If there is such a thing as a phenomenon without these fixed quantitative relations, it is a miracle. It is outside the law of cause and effect, and as such transcends our power of thought, or at least is something to or from which we cannot reason. The condition of our thinking about the universe is that it is capable of being thought about rationally, or, in other words, that every part of it is effect and cause in the same sense in which those parts are with which we are most familiar. So in the broadest sense it is true that the law is a logical development, like everything else. The danger of which I speak is not the admission that the principles governing other phenomena also govern the law, but the notion that a given system, ours, for instance, can be worked out like mathematics from some general axioms of conduct. This is the natural error of the schools, but it is not confined to them. I once heard a very eminent judge say that he never let a decision go until he was absolutely sure that it was right. So judicial dissent often is blamed, as if it meant simply that one side or the other were not doing their sums right, and, if they would take more trouble, agreement inevitably would come.

This mode of thinking is entirely natural. The training of lawyers is a training in logic. The processes of analogy, discrimination, and deduction are those in which they are most at home. The language of judicial decision is mainly the language of logic. And the logical method and form flatter that longing for certainty and for repose which is in every human mind. But certainty generally is illusion, and repose is not the destiny of man. Behind the logical form lies a judgment as to the relative worth and importance of competing legislative grounds, often an inarticulate and unconscious judgment, it is true, and yet the very root and nerve of the whole proceeding. You can give any conclusion a logical form. You always can imply a condition in a contract. But why do you imply it? It is because of some belief as to the practice of the community or of a class, or because of some opinion as to policy, or, in short, because of some attitude of yours upon a matter not capable of exact quantitative measurement, and therefore not capable of founding exact logical conclusions. Such matters really are battle grounds where the means do not exist for determinations that shall be good for all time, and where the decision can do no more than embody the preference of a given body in a given time and place. We do not realize how large a part of our law is open to reconsideration upon a slight change in the habit of the public mind. No concrete proposition is self-evident, no matter how ready we may be to accept it, not even Mr. Herbert Spencer's Every man has a right to do what he wills, provided he interferes not with a like right on the part of his neighbors.

Why is a false and injurious statement privileged, if it is made honestly in giving information about a servant? It is because it has been thought more important that information should be given freely, than that a man should be protected from what under other circumstances would be an actionable wrong. Why is a man at liberty to set up a business which he knows will ruin his neighbor? It is because the public good is supposed to be best subserved by free competition. Obviously such judgments of relative importance may vary in different times and places. Why does a judge instruct a jury that an employer is not liable to an employee for an injury received in the course of his employment unless he is negligent, and why do the jury generally find for the plaintiff if the case is allowed to go to them? It is because the traditional policy of our law is to confine liability to cases where a prudent man might have foreseen the injury, or at least the danger, while the inclination of a very large part of the community is to make certain classes of persons insure the safety of those with whom they deal. Since the last words were written, I have seen the requirement of such insurance put forth as part of the programme of one of the best known labor organizations. There is a concealed, half conscious battle on the question of legislative policy, and if any one thinks that it can be settled deductively, or once for all, I only can say that I think he is theoretically wrong, and that I am certain that his conclusion will not be accepted in practice *semper ubique et ab omnibus.*

Indeed, I think that even now our theory upon this matter is open to reconsideration, although I am not prepared to say how I should decide if a reconsideration were proposed. Our law of torts comes from the old days of isolated, ungeneralized wrongs, assaults, slanders, and the like, where the damages might be taken to lie where they fell by legal judgment. But the torts with which our courts are kept busy today are mainly the incidents of certain well known businesses. They are injuries to person or property by railroads, factories, and the like. The liability for them is estimated, and sooner or later goes into the price paid by the public. The public really pays the damages, and the question of liability, if pressed far enough, is really the question how far it is desirable that the public should insure the safety of those whose work it uses. It might be said that in such cases the chance of a jury finding for the defendant is merely a chance, once in a while rather arbitrarily interrupting the regular course of recovery, most likely in the case of an unusually conscientious plaintiff, and therefore better done away with. On the other hand, the economic value even of a life to the community can be estimated, and no recovery, it may be said, ought to go beyond that amount. It is conceivable that some day in certain cases we may find ourselves imitating, on a higher plane, the tariff for life and limb which we see in the Leges Barbarorum.

I think that the judges themselves have failed adequately to recognize their duty of weighing considerations of social advantage. The duty is inevitable, and the result of the often proclaimed judicial aversion to deal with such considerations is simply to leave the very ground and foundation of judgments inarticulate, and often unconscious, as I have said. When socialism first began to be talked about, the comfortable classes of the community were a good deal frightened. I suspect that this fear has influenced judicial action both here and in England, yet it is certain that it is not a conscious factor in the decisions to which I refer. I think that something similar has led people who no longer hope to control the legislatures to look to the courts as expounders of the Constitutions, and that in some courts new principles have been discovered outside the bodies of those instruments, which may be generalized into acceptance of the economic doctrines which prevailed about fifty years ago, and a wholesale prohibition of what a tribunal of lawyers does not think about right. I cannot but believe that if the training of lawyers led them habitually to consider more definitely

and explicitly the social advantage on which the rule they lay down must be justified, they sometimes would hesitate where now they are confident, and see that really they were taking sides upon debatable and often burning questions.

So much for the fallacy of logical form. Now let us consider the present condition of the law as a subject for study, and the ideal toward which it tends. We still are far from the point of view which I desire to see reached. No one has reached it or can reach it as yet. We are only at the beginning of a philosophical reaction, and of a reconsideration of the worth of doctrines which for the most part still are taken for granted without any deliberate, conscious, and systematic questioning of their grounds. The development of our law has gone on for nearly a thousand years, like the development of a plant, each generation taking the inevitable next step, mind, like matter, simply obeying a law of spontaneous growth. It is perfectly natural and right that it should have been so. Imitation is a necessity of human nature, as has been illustrated by a remarkable French writer, M. Tarde, in an admirable book, "Les Lois de l'Imitation." Most of the things we do, we do for no better reason that that our fathers have done them or that our neighbors do them, and the same is true of a larger part than we suspect of what we think. The reason is a good one, because our short life gives us no time for a better, but it is not the best. It does not follow, because we all are compelled to take on faith at second hand most of the rules on which we base our action and our thought, that each of us may not try to set some corner of his world in the order of reason, or that all of us collectively should not aspire to carry reason as far as it will go throughout the whole domain. In regard to the law, it is true, no doubt, that an evolutionist will hesitate to affirm universal validity for his social ideals, or for the principles which he thinks should be embodied in legislation. He is content if he can prove them best for here and now. He may be ready to admit that he knows nothing about an absolute best in the cosmos, and even that he knows next to nothing about a permanent best for men. Still it is true that a body of law is more rational and more civilized when every rule it contains is referred articulately and definitely to an end which it subserves, and when the grounds for desiring that end are stated or are ready to be stated in words.

At present, in very many cases, if we want to know why a rule of law has taken its particular shape, and more or less if we want to know why it exists at all, we go to tradition. We follow it into the Year Books, and perhaps beyond them to the customs of the Salian Franks, and somewhere in the past, in the German forests, in the needs of Norman kings, in the assumptions of a dominant class, in the absence of generalized ideas, we find out the practical motive for what now best is justified by the mere fact of its acceptance and that men are accustomed to it. The rational study of law is still to a large extent the study of history. History must be a part of the study, because without it we cannot know the precise scope of rules which it is our business to know. It is a part of the rational study, because it is the first step toward an enlightened skepticism, that is, toward a deliberate reconsideration of the worth of those rules. When you get the dragon out of his cave on to the plain and in the daylight, you can count his teeth and claws, and see just what is his strength. But to get him out is only the first step. The next is either to kill him, or to tame him and make him a useful animal. For the rational study of the law the black-letter man may be the man of the present, but the man of the future is the man of statistics and the master of economics. It is revolting to have no better reason for a rule of law than that so it was laid down in the time of Henry IV. It is still more revolting if the grounds upon which it was laid down have vanished long since, and the rule simply persists from blind imitation of the past. I am thinking of the technical rule as to trespass *ab initio*, as it is called, which I attempted to explain in a recent Massachusetts case.[1]

Let me take an illustration, which can be stated in a few words, to show how the social end which is aimed at by a rule of law is obscured and only partially attained in consequence of the fact that the rule owes its form to a gradual historical development, instead of being reshaped as a whole, with conscious articulate reference to the end in view. We think it desirable to prevent one man's property being misappropriated by another, and so we make larceny a crime. The evil is the same whether the misappropriation is made by a man into whose hands the owner has put the property, or by one who wrongfully takes it away. But primitive law in its weakness did not get much beyond an effort to prevent violence, and very naturally made a wrongful taking, a trespass, part of its definition of the crime. In modern times the judges enlarged the definition a little by holding that, if the wrongdoer gets possession by a trick or device, the crime is committed. This really was giving up the requirement of a trespass, and it would have been more logical, as well as truer to the present object of the law, to abandon the requirement altogether. That, however, would have seemed too bold, and was left to statute. Statutes were passed making embezzlement a crime. But the force of tradition caused the crime of embezzlement to be regarded as so far distinct from larceny that to this day, in some jurisdictions at least, a slip corner is kept open for thieves to contend, if indicted for larceny, that they should have been indicted for embezzlement, and if indicted for embezzlement, that they should have been indicted for larceny, and to escape on that ground.

Far more fundamental questions still await a better answer than that we do as our fathers have done. What have we bet-

[1]Commonwealth *v.* Rubin, 165 Mass. 453.

ter than a blind guess to show that the criminal law in its present form does more good than harm? I do not stop to refer to the effect which it has had in degrading prisoners and in plunging them further into crime, or to the question whether fine and imprisonment do not fall more heavily on a criminal's wife and children than on himself. I have in mind more far-reaching questions. Does punishment deter? Do we deal with criminals on proper principles? A modern school of Continental criminalists plumes itself on the formula, first suggested, it is said, by Gall, that we must consider the criminal rather than the crime. The formula does not carry us very far, but the inquiries which have been started look toward an answer of my questions based on science for the first time. If the typical criminal is a degenerate, bound to swindle or to murder by as deep seated an organic necessity as that which makes the rattlesnake bite, it is idle to talk of deterring him by the classical method of imprisonment. He must be got rid of; he cannot be improved, or frightened out of his structural reaction. If, on the other hand, crime, like normal human conduct, is mainly a matter of imitation, punishment fairly may be expected to help to keep it out of fashion. The study of criminals has been thought by some well known men of science to sustain the former hypothesis. The statistics of the relative increase of crime in crowded places like large cities, where example has the greatest chance to work, and in less populated parts, where the contagion spreads more slowly, have been used with great force in favor of the latter view. But there is weighty authority for the belief that, however this may be, "not the nature of the crime, but the dangerousness of the criminal, constitutes the only reasonable legal criterion to guide the inevitable social reaction against the criminal."[1]

The impediments to rational generalization, which I illustrated from the law of larceny, are shown in the other branches of the law, as well as in that of crime. Take the law of tort or civil liability for damages apart from contract and the like. Is there any general theory of such liability, or are the cases in which it exists simply to be enumerated, and to be explained each on its special ground, as is easy to believe from the fact that the right of action for certain well known classes of wrongs like trespass or slander has its special history for each class? I think that there is a general theory to be discovered, although resting in tendency rather than established and accepted. I think that the law regards the infliction of temporal damage by a responsible person as actionable, if under the circumstances known to him the danger of his act is manifest according to common experience, or according to his own experience if it is more than common, except in cases where upon special grounds of policy the law refuses to protect the plaintiff or grants a privilege to the defendant.[2] I think that commonly malice, intent, and negligence mean only that the danger was manifest to a greater or less degree, under the circumstances known to the actor, although in some cases of privilege malice may mean an actual malevolent motive, and such a motive may take away a permission knowingly to inflict harm, which otherwise would be granted

[1]Havelock Ellis, "The Criminal," 41, citing Garofalo. See also Ferri, "Sociologie Criminelle," *passim*. Compare Tarde, "La Philosophie Pénale."

[2]An example of the law's refusing to protect the plaintiff is when he is interrupted by a stranger in the use of a valuable way, which he has travelled adversely for a week less than the period of prescription. A week later he will have gained a right, but now he is only a trespasser. Examples of privilege I have given already. One of the best is competition in business.

on this or that ground of dominant public good. But when I stated my view to a very eminent English judge the other day, he said: "You are discussing what the law ought to be; as the law is, you must show a right. A man is not liable for negligence unless he is subject to a duty." If our difference was more than a difference in words, or with regard to the proportion between the exceptions and the rule, then, in his opinion, liability for an act cannot be referred to the manifest tendency of the act to cause temporal damage in general as a sufficient explanation, but must be referred to the special nature of the damage, or must be derived from some special circumstances outside of the tendency of the act, for which no generalized explanation exists. I think that such a view is wrong, but it is familiar, and I dare say generally is accepted in England.

Everywhere the basis of principle is tradition, to such an extent that we even are in danger of making the role of history more important that it is. The other day Professor Ames wrote a learned article to show, among other things, that the common law did not recognize the defence of fraud in actions upon specialties, and the moral might seem to be that the personal character of that defence is due to its equitable origin. But if, as I have said, all contracts are formal, the difference is not merely historical, but theoretic, between defects of form which prevent a contract from being made, and mistaken motives which manifestly could not be considered in any system that we should call rational except against one who was privy to those motives. It is not confined to specialties, but is of universal application. I ought to add that I do not suppose that Mr. Ames would disagree with what I suggest.

However, if we consider the law of contract, we find it full of history. The distinctions between debt, covenant, and assumpsit are merely historical. The classification of certain obligations to pay money, imposed by the law irrespective of any bargain as quasi contracts, is merely historical. The doctrine of consideration is merely historical. The effect given to a seal is to be explained by history alone.—Consideration is a mere form. Is it a useful form? If so, why should it not be required in all contracts? A seal is a mere form, and is vanishing in the scroll and in enactments that a consideration must be given, seal or no seal.—Why should any merely historical distinction be allowed to affect the rights and obligations of business men?

Since I wrote this discourse I have come on a very good example of the way in which tradition not only overrides rational policy, but overrides it after first having been misunderstood and having been given a new and broader scope than it had when it had a meaning. It is the settled law of England that a material alteration of a written contract by a party avoids it as against him. The doctrine is contrary to the general tendency of the law. We do not tell a jury that if a man ever has lied in one particular he is to be presumed to lie in all. Even if a man has tried to defraud, it seems no sufficient reason for preventing him from proving the truth. Objections of like nature in general go to the weight, not to the admissibility, of evidence. Moreover, this rule is irrespective of fraud, and is not confined to evidence. It is not merely that you cannot use the writing, but that the contract is at an end. What does this mean? The existence of a written contract depends on the fact that the offerer and offeree have interchanged their written expressions, not on the continued existence of those expressions. But in the case of a bond the primitive notion was different. The contract was inseparable from the parchment. If a stranger destroyed it, or tore off the seal, or altered it, the obligee could not recover, however free from fault, because the defendant's contract, that is, the actual tangible bond which he had sealed, could not be produced in the form in which it bound him. About a hundred years ago Lord Kenyon undertook to use his reason on this tradition, as he sometimes did to the detriment of the law, and, not understanding it, said he could see no reason why what was true of a bond should not be true of other contracts. His decision happened to be right, as it concerned a promissory note, where again the common law regarded the contract as inseparable from the paper on which it was written, but the reasoning was general, and soon was extended to other written contracts, and various absurd and unreal grounds of policy were invented to account for the enlarged rule.

I trust that no one will understand me to be speaking with disrespect of the law, because I criticise it so freely. I venerate the law, and especially our system of law, as one of the vastest products of the human mind. No one knows better than I do the countless number of great intellects that have spent themselves in making some addition or improvement, the greatest of which is trifling when compared with the mighty whole. It has the final title to respect that it exists, that it is not a Hegelian dream, but a part of the lives of men. But one may criticize even what one reveres. Law is the business to which my life is devoted, and I should show less than devotion if I did not do what in me lies to improve it, and, when I perceive what seems to me the ideal of its future, if I hesitated to point it out and to press toward it with all my heart.

Perhaps I have said enough to show the part which the study of history necessarily plays in the intelligent study of the law as it is today. In the teaching of this school and at Cambridge it is in no danger of being undervalued. Mr. Bigelow here and Mr. Ames and Mr. Thayer there have made important contributions which will not be forgotten, and in England the recent history of early English law by Sir Frederick Pollock and Mr. Maitland has lent the subject an almost deceptive charm. We must beware of the pitfall of antiquarianism, and must remember that for our purposes our only interest in the past is for the light it throws upon the present. I look forward to a time when the part played by history in the explanation of dogma shall be very small, and instead of ingenious research we shall spend our energy on a study of the ends sought to be attained and the reasons for desiring them. As a step toward that ideal it seems to me that every lawyer ought to seek an understanding of economics. The present divorce between the schools of political economy and law seems to me an evidence of how much progress in philosophical study still remains to be made. In the present state of political economy, indeed, we come again upon history on a larger scale, but there we are called on to consider and weigh the ends of legislation, the means of attaining them, and the cost. We learn that for everything we have to give up something else, and we are taught to set the advantage we gain against the other advantage we lose, and to know what we are doing when we elect.

There is another study which sometimes is undervalued by the practical minded, for which I wish to say a good word, although I think a good deal of pretty poor stuff goes under that name. I mean the study of what is called jurisprudence. Jurisprudence, as I look at it, is simply law in its most generalized part. Every effort to reduce a case to a rule is an effort of jurisprudence, although the name as used in English is confined to the broadest rules and most fundamental conceptions. One mark of a great lawyer is that he sees the application of the broadest rules. There is a story of a Vermont justice of the peace before whom a suit was brought by one farmer against another for breaking a churn. The justice took time to consider, and then said that he had looked through the statutes and could find nothing about churns, and gave judgment for the defendant. The same state of mind is shown in all our common digests and text-books. Applications of rudimentary rules of contract or tort are tucked away under the head of Railroads or Telegraphs or go to swell treatises on historical subdivisions, such as Shipping or Equity, or are gathered under an arbitrary title which is thought likely to appeal to the practical mind, such as Mercantile Law. If a man goes into law it pays to be a master of it, and to be a master of it means to look straight through all the dramatic incidents and to discern the true basis for prophecy. Therefore, it is well to have an accurate notion of what you mean by law, by a right, by a duty, by malice, intent, and negligence, by ownership, by possession, and so forth. I have in my mind cases in which the highest courts seem to me to have floundered because they had no clear ideas on some of these themes. I have illustrated their importance already. If a further illustration is wished, it may be found by reading the Appendix to Sir James Stephen's Criminal Law on the subject of possession, and then turning to Pollock and Wright's enlightened book. Sir James Stephen is not the only writer whose attempts to analyze legal ideas have been confused by striving for a useless quintessence of all systems, instead of an accurate anatomy of one. The trouble with Austin was that he did not know enough English law. But still it is a practical advantage to master Austin, and his predecessors, Hobbes and Bentham, and his worthy successors, Holland and Pollock. Sir Frederick Pollock's recent little book is touched with the felicity which marks all his works, and is wholly free from the perverting influence of Roman models.

The advice of the elders to young men is very apt to be as unreal as a list of the hundred best books. At least in my day I had my share of such counsels, and high among the unrealities I place the recommendation to study the Roman law. I assume that such advice means more than collecting a few Latin maxims with which to ornament the discourse,—the purpose for which Lord Coke recommended Bracton. If that is all that is wanted, the title "De Regulis Juris Antiqui" can be read in an hour. I assume that, if it is well to study the Roman law, it is well to study it as a working system. That means mastering a set of technicalities more difficult and less understood than our own, and studying another course of history by which even more than our own the Roman law must be explained. If any one doubts me, let him read Keller's "Der Römische Civil Process und die Actionen," a treatise on the praetor's edict, Muirhead's most interesting "Historical Introduction to the Private Law of Rome," and, to give him the best chance possible, Sohm's admirable Institutes. No. The way to gain a liberal view of your subject is not to read something else, but to get to the bottom of the subject itself. The means of doing that are, in the first place, to follow the existing body of dogma into its highest generalizations by the help of jurisprudence; next, to discover from history how it has come to be what it is; and, finally, so far as you can, to consider the ends which the several rules seek to accomplish, the reasons why those ends are desired, what is given up to gain them, and whether they are worth the price.

We have too little theory in the law rather than too much, especially on this final branch of study. When I was speaking of history, I mentioned larceny as an example to show how the law suffered from not having embodied in a clear form a rule which will accomplish its manifest purpose. In that case the trouble was due to the survival of forms coming from a time when a more limited purpose was entertained. Let me now give an example to show the practical importance, for the decision of actual cases, of understanding the reasons of the law, by taking an example from rules which, so far as I know, never have been explained or theorized about in any adequate way. I refer to statutes of limitation and the law of prescription. The end of such rules is obvious, but what is the justification for depriving a man of his rights, a pure evil as far as it goes, in consequence of the lapse of time? Sometimes the loss of evidence is referred to, but that is a secondary matter. Sometimes the desirability of peace, but why is peace more desirable after twenty years than before? It is increasingly likely to come without the aid of legislation. Sometimes it is said that, if a man neglects to enforce his rights, he cannot complain if, after a while, the law follows his example. Now if this is all that can be said about it, you probably will decide a case I am going to put, for the plaintiff; if you take the view which I shall suggest, you possibly will decide it for the defendant. A man is sued for trespass upon land, and justifies under a right of way. He proves that he has used the way openly and adversely for twenty years. but it turns out that the plaintiff had granted a license to a person whom he reasonably supposed to be the defendant's agent, although not so in fact, and therefore had assumed that the use of the way was permissive, in which case no right would be gained. Has the defendant gained a right or not? If his gaining it stands on the fault and neglect of the landowner in the ordinary sense, as seems commonly to be supposed, there has been no such neglect, and the right of way has not been acquired. But if I were the defendant's counsel, I should suggest that the foundation of the acquisition of rights by lapse of time is to be looked for in the position of the person who gains them, not in that of the loser. Sir Henry Maine has made it fashionable to connect the archaic notion of property with prescription. But the connection is further back than the first recorded history. It is in the nature of man's mind. A thing which you have enjoyed and used as your own for a long time, whether property or an opinion, takes root in your being and cannot be torn away without your resenting the act and trying to defend yourself, however you came by it. The law can ask no better justification than the deepest instincts of man. It is only by way of reply to the suggestion that you are disappointing the former owner, that you refer to his neglect having allowed the gradual dissociation between

himself and what he claims, and the gradual association of it with another. If he knows that another is doing acts which on their face show that he is on the way toward establishing such an association, I should argue that in justice to that other he was bound at his peril to find out whether the other was acting under his permission, to see that he was warned, and, if necessary, stopped.

I have been speaking about the study of the law, and I have said next to nothing of what commonly is talked about in that connection,—text-books and the case system, and all the machinery with which a student comes most immediately in contact. Nor shall I say anything about them. Theory is my subject, not practical details. The modes of teaching have been improved since my time, no doubt, but ability and industry will master the raw material with any mode. Theory is the most important part of the dogma of the law, as the architect is the most important man who takes part in the building of a house. The most important improvements of the last twenty-five years are improvements in theory. It is not to be feared as unpractical, for, to the competent, it simply means going to the bottom of the subject. For the incompetent, it sometimes is true, as has been said, that an interest in general ideas means an absence of particular knowledge. I remember in army days reading of a youth who, being examined for the lowest grade and being asked a question about squadron drill, answered that he never had considered the evolutions of less than ten thousand men. But the weak and foolish must be left to their folly. The danger is that the able and practical minded should look with indifference or distrust upon ideas the connection of which with their business is remote. I heard a story, the other day, of a man who had a valet to whom he paid high wages, subject to deduction for faults. One of his deductions was, "For lack of imagination, five dollars." The lack is not confined to valets. The object of ambition, power, generally presents itself nowadays in the form of money alone. Money is the most immediate form, and is a proper object of desire. "The fortune," said Rachel, "is the measure of the intelligence." That is a good text to waken people out of a fool's paradise. But, as Hegel says,[1] "It is in the end not the appetite, but the opinion, which has to be satisfied." To an imagination of any scope the most far-reaching form of power is not money, it is the command of ideas. If you want great examples read Mr. Leslie Stephen's "History of English Thought in the Eighteenth Century," and see how a hundred years after his death the abstract speculations of Descartes had become a practical force controlling the conduct of men. Read the works of the great German jurists, and see how much more the world is governed today by Kant than by Bonaparte. We cannot all be Descartes or Kant, but we all want happiness. And happiness, I am sure from having known many successful men, cannot be won simply by being counsel for great corporations and having an income of fifty thousand dollars. An intellect great enough to win the prize needs other food beside success. The remoter and more general aspects of the law are those which give it universal interest. It is through them that you not only become a great master in your calling, but connect your subject with the universe and catch an echo of the infinite, a glimpse of its unfathomable process, a hint of the universal law.

## QUESTIONS

1. Holmes says that "The rational study of law is still to a large extent the study of history." But he also says that "It is revolting to have no better reason for a rule of law than that so it was laid down in the time of Henry IV." Explain how these two claims can best be reconciled with one another.

2. What, judging from Holmes's discussion and examples, is the criterion that Holmes would use in deciding whether an exception ought to be made in a standing rule of law?

3. Holmes says that "The prophecies of what the courts will do in fact, and nothing more pretentious, are what I mean by the law." If we accept this line of thought, then what is the most defensible view about what the courts themselves—especially the highest court in the land, the Supreme Court—are trying to do when *they* try to determine what the law is on some question?

4. "If you want to know the law and nothing else, you must look at it as a bad man . . . ," says Holmes. Apply and compare the appropriateness of this as a recommendation to: (a) ordinary citizens; (b) legislators; (c) judges.

5. Holmes tells of "a Vermont justice of the peace before whom a suit was brought by one farmer against another for breaking a churn. The justice took time to consider, and then said that he had looked through the statutes and could find nothing about churns, and gave judgment for the defendant." What point is Holmes trying to make about the justice's reasoning? Think, if you can, of recent, actual examples of the kind of mistaken legal reasoning that Holmes is making fun of here. (Hint: Some of the judicial opinions reprinted in this textbook may be candidates.) Explain why they are good examples.

[1]Phil. des Rechts, § 190.

# Hans Kelsen
# LAW AS A NORMATIVE ORDER*

c) THE LAW AS A NORMATIVE COERCIVE ORDER; LEGAL COMMUNITY AND GANG OF ROBBERS The law as a coercive order is sometimes characterized by the statement that the law commands a certain behavior "under threat" of coercive acts, that is, of certain evils. But this formulation ignores the normative meaning with which coercive acts in general and sanctions in particular are stipulated by the legal order. The meaning of a threat is that an evil *will* be inflicted under certain conditions; the meaning of a legal order is that certain evils *ought to be* inflicted under certain conditions or—expressed more generally—that certain coercive acts ought to be executed under certain conditions. This is not only the subjective meaning of the acts by which the law is established but also their objective meaning. Only because this normative meaning is the objective meaning of these acts, do they have the character of law-stipulating, norm-creating, or norm- executing acts. The action of a highwayman who under threat commands somebody to surrender his money also has the subjective meaning of an "ought." If the situation created by such a command is described by saying that one individual expresses a will directed toward the behavior of another individual, then one merely describes the action of the first as an actually happening event. The behavior of the other individual, however, which is intended by the will of the first, cannot be described as something that actually takes place, because he does not yet behave and may not behave at all in the way that the first one had intended. It can only be described as something that according to the subjective meaning of the command ought to take place.

In this way every situation must be described in which one individual expresses a will directed toward the behavior of another individual. In this respect (namely, so far as only the subjective meaning of the acts are considered), there is no difference between describing the command of a robber and the command of a legal organ. The difference appears only when the objective meaning of the command is described, the command directed from one individual toward another. Then we attribute only to the command of the legal organ, not to that of the robber, the objective meaning of a norm binding the addressed individual. In other words, we interpret the one command, but not the other, as an objectively valid norm; and then we interpret in the one case the connection of the nonfulfillment of the command with a coercive act merely as a "threat" (i.e., a statement that an evil *will* be inflicted), whereas in the other case, we interpret this connection to mean that an evil *ought to be* inflicted. Therefore we interpret the actual infliction of the evil in the second situation as the application or execution of an objectively valid norm, stipulating a coercive act as a sanction, but in the first situation—if we offer a normative interpretation—as a crime.

But why do we interpret the subjective meaning of the one act also as its objective meaning, but not so of the other act? Why do we suppose that of the two acts, which both have the subjective meaning of an "ought," only one established a valid, that is, binding, norm? In other words: What is the reason for the validity of the norm that we consider to be the objective meaning of this act? This is the decisive question.

*From *The Pure Theory of Law*, translated by Max Knight (1967). Reprinted by permission of the Regents of the University of California and the University of California Press.

By analyzing the judgments that interpret the acts as legal (that is, as acts whose objective meaning is norms) we get the answer to the question. Such an analysis reveals the *presupposition* that makes such an interpretation possible.

Let us start from the earlier-mentioned interpretation of the killing of one individual by another as the execution of a death sentence and not as murder. Our interpretation is based on the recognition that the act of killing constitutes the execution of a court decision that has commanded the killing as a punishment. This means: We attribute to the act of the court the objective meaning of an individual norm and in this way interpret the individuals who perform the act, as a court. We do this, because we recognize the act of the court as the execution of a statute (that is, of general norms stipulating coercive acts) in which we see not only the subjective but also the objective meaning of an act that had been established by certain individuals whom we consider, for this reason, as legislators. For we regard the act of legislation as the execution of the constitution, that is, of general norms that, according to their subjective meaning, authorize these individuals to establish general norms prescribing coercive acts. In this way we interpret these individuals as legislative organs. By regarding the norms authorizing the legislative organ not only as the subjective but also as the objective meaning of an act performed by definite individuals, we interpret these norms as "constitution." For the historically first constitution such an interpretation is possible only, if we *presuppose* that one ought to behave according to the subjective meaning of the act, that one ought to perform coercive acts only under the conditions and in the manner the constitution stipulates; if, in other words, we presuppose a norm according to which (a) the act whose meaning is to be interpreted as "constitution" is to be regarded as establishing objectively valid norms, and (b) the individuals who establish this act as the constitutional authorities. As will be developed later, this norm is the basic norm, of the national legal order. It is not established by a positive legal act, but is presupposed, *if* the act mentioned under (a) is interpreted as establishing a constitution and the acts based on the constitutions are interpreted as legal acts. To make manifest this presupposition is an essential function of legal science. This presupposition is the ultimate (but in its character conditional and therefore hypothetical) reason for the validity of the legal order.

By making these statements we are considering, at this point, only a national legal order, that is, a legal order whose territorial sphere of validity is limited to the territory of a state. The reason for the validity of international law, whose territorial sphere of validity is not so limited, and the relationship of the international legal order to the national legal orders, are, for the present, outside our discussion.

It was observed earlier that the validity of a norm (which means that one ought to behave as the norm stipulates) should not be confounded with the effectiveness of the norm (which means that one, in fact, does so behave); but that an essential relation may exist between the two concepts, namely, that a coercive order, presenting itself as the law, is regarded as valid only if it is by and large effective. That means: The basic norm which is the reason for the validity of a legal order, refers only to a constitution which is the basis of an effective coercive order. Only if the actual behavior of the individuals conforms, by and large, with the subjective meaning of the acts directed toward this behavior—if, in other words, the subjective meaning is recognized as the objective meaning—only then are the acts interpreted as legal acts.

Now we are ready to answer the question why we do not attribute to the command of a robber, issued under threat of death, the objective meaning of a valid norm binding on the addressed victim; why we do not interpret this act as a legal act;

why we regard the realization of the threat as a crime, and not as the execution of a sanction.

An isolated act of one individual cannot be regarded as a legal act, its meaning cannot be regarded as a legal norm, because law, as mentioned, is not a single norm, but a system of norms; and a particular norm may be regarded as a legal norm only as a part of such a system. How about a situation, however, in which an organized gang systematically jeopardizes a certain territory by forcing the people living there, under threat, to surrender their money? In this situation we will have to distinguish between the order that regulates the mutual behavior of the members of this robber gang and the external order, that is, the commands that the members of the gang direct at outsiders under the threat of inflicting evils. For it is only in relation to outsiders that the group behaves as a *robber* gang. If robbery and murder were not forbidden in the relations between the robbers, no community, no robber *gang* would exist. Nevertheless, even the internal order of the gang may be in conflict with the coercive order, considered to be a legal order, valid for the territory in which the gang is active. Why is the coercive order that constitutes the community of the robber gang and comprises the internal and external order not interpreted as a legal order? Why is the subjective meaning of this coercive order (that one ought to behave in conformity with it) not interpreted as its objective meaning? Because no basic norm is presupposed according to which one ought to behave in conformity with this order. But why is no such basic norm presupposed? Because this order does not have the lasting effectiveness without which no basic norm is presupposed. The robbers' coercive order does not have this effectiveness, if the norms of the legal order in whose territorial sphere of validity the gang operates are actually applied to the robbers' activity as being illegal behavior; if the members of the gang are deprived of their liberty or their lives by coercive acts that are interpreted as imprisonment and death sentences; and if thus the activity of the gang is terminated—in short, if the coercive order regarded as the legal order is more effective than the coercive order constituting the gang.

If the validity of this coercive order is restricted to a certain territory and if it is effective within this territory in such a way that the validity of any other coercive order of this kind is excluded, then the coercive order may indeed be regarded as a legal order and the community constituted by it may be regarded as a "state"—even if its external activity is illegal according to positive international law. Thus, from the sixteenth to the beginning of the nineteenth century so-called pirate states existed along the northwest coast of Africa (Algiers, Tunis, Tripolis) whose ships preyed upon navigation in the Mediterranean. These communities were "pirates" only with respect to their exercise of force on ships of other states, in defiance of international law. Yet, their internal order presumably prohibited mutual employment of force, and this prohibition was by and large obeyed, so that the minimum of collective security existed which is the condition for the existence of a relatively lasting community constituted by a normative order.

Collective security or peace—as we have said—is a function that the coercive orders designated as "law" have in various degrees when they have reached a certain level of development. This function is an objectively determinable fact. The scientific statement that a legal order is pacifying the legal community, is not a value judgment. Specifically, this statement does not mean that the realization of justice is essential to the law; this value, therefore, cannot be made an element of the concept of law and can therefore not serve as a criterion for the distinction between a legal community and a robber gang. This, however, is the distinction made by St. Augustine who says in his Civitas Dei: "Set justice aside then, and what are kingdoms but thievish purchases? because what are thieves' purchases but little kingdoms?"[21] A state, which is according to Augustine a legal community, cannot exist without justice. "Where true justice is wanting, there can be no law. For what law does, justice does, and what is done unjustly, is done unlawfully." But what is justice? "Justice is a virtue distributing onto everyone his due. What justice is that then, that takes man from the true God and gives him unto the condemned fiends? Is this distribution according to due? Is not he that takes away thy possessions and gives them to one that has no claim to them, guilty of injustice, and is not he so likewise, that takes himself away from his Lord God, and gives himself to the service of the devil?"[22]

According to this reasoning, the law is a just coercive order and is distinguished from the coercive order of the robbers by the justice of its content.

That justice cannot be the criterion distinguishing law from other coercive orders follows from the relative character of the value judgment according to which a social order is just. Saint Augustine recognizes as "just" only that order which gives each his due, and applies this empty formula by saying that an order is just only when it gives the true God—who, to him, is the Judeo-Christian God, not the gods of the Romans—what is his due, namely the worship that is expressed in a certain cult; therefore, according to Augustine, an order that does not conform with this postulate, cannot be law, and the community based on this order cannot be a state, but only a robber gang. With this, Roman Law is denied the character of law. If justice is assumed to be the criterion for a normative order to be designated as "law," then the capitalistic coercive order of the West is not law from the point of view of the Communist ideal of justice, nor the Communist coercive order of

the Soviet Union from the point of view of the capitalist ideal of justice. A concept of law with such consequences is unacceptable by a positivist legal science. A legal order may be judged to be unjust from the point of view of a certain norm of justice. But the fact that the content of an effective coercive order may be judged unjust, is no reason to refuse to acknowledge this coercive order as a legal order. After the victory of the French Revolution in the eighteenth century and after the victory of the Russian Revolution in the twentieth, the other states showed the distinct inclination not to interpret the coercive orders established by the revolution as legal orders and the acts of the revolutionary governments as legal acts, because the one government had violated the monarchic principle of legitimacy and the other had abolished private property of the means of production. For the last-named reason, even American courts refused to acknowledge acts of the revolutionary Russian government as legal acts; the courts declared that these were not acts of a state, but of a robber gang. However, as soon as the revolution-born coercive orders turned out to be effective, they were recognized as legal orders, the governments as state governments, and their acts as state acts, that is, legal acts.

**D) LEGAL OBLIGATIONS WITHOUT SANCTIONS?** If the law is conceived of as a coercive order, then the formula by which the basic norm of a national legal order is expressed runs as follows: "Coercion of man against man ought to be exercised in the manner and under the conditions determined by the historically first constitution." The basic norm delegates the first constitution to prescribe the procedure by which the norms stipulating coercive acts are to be created. To be interpreted objectively as a legal norm, a norm must be the subjective meaning of an act

---

[21] Saint Augustine, *The City of God*, trans. by John Healy (Edinburgh: 1909). Vol. I, Book iv, chap. 4.
[22] *Ibid.*, Vol. II Book xix, chap. 21.

performed in this procedure, hence in accordance with the basic norm; besides, the norm must stipulate a coercive act or must be in essential relation to such a norm. Together with the basic norm the definition of law as a coercive order is presupposed.[23] From the definition of law as a coercive order follows that a behavior may be regarded as legally commanded (i.e., as the content of a legal obligation) only if the contrary behavior is made the condition of a coercive act directed against the individual thus behaving. It is to be noted, however, that the coercive act itself need not be commanded in this sense: its ordering and executing may be merely authorized.

Against the definition of law as a coercive order, that is, against the inclusion of the element of coercion into the concept of law, the objections have been raised (1) that legal orders actually contain norms that do not stipulate coercive acts: norms that permit or authorize a behavior, and also norms that command a behavior without attaching to the opposite behavior a coercive act; and (2) that the nonapplication of the norms that stipulate coercive acts are frequently not made the condition for coercive acts functioning as sanctions.

The second objection is not valid, because the definition of law as a coercive order can be maintained even if the norm that stipulates a coercive act is not itself essentially connected with a norm that attaches, in a concrete case, a sanction to the nonordering or nonexecuting of the coercive act—if, therefore, the coercive act stipulated in the general norm is to be interpreted objectively not as commanded but only as authorized or positively permitted (although the subjective meaning of the act by which the general norm stipulates the coercive act is a commanding). As for the first objection, the definition of law as a coercive order can be maintained even with respect to norms that authorize a behavior not having the charac-

ter of a coercive act; or norms that positively permit such a behavior insofar as they are *dependent* norms, because they are essentially connected with norms that stipulate the coercive acts. A typical example for norms cited as arguments against the inclusion of coercion into the definition of law are the norms of constitutional law. It is argued that the norms of the constitution that regulate the procedure of legislation do not stipulate sanctions as a reaction against nonobservance. Closer analysis shows, however, that these are dependent norms establishing only one of the conditions under which coercive acts stipulated by other norms are to be ordered and executed. Constitutional norms authorize the legislator to create norms—they do not command the creation of norms; and therefore the stipulation of sanctions do not come into question at all. If the provisions of the constitution are not observed, valid legal norms do not come into existence, the norms created in this way are void or voidable. This means: the subjective meaning of the acts established unconstitutionally and therefore not according to the basic norm, is not interpreted as their objective meaning or such a temporary interpretation is annulled.

The most important case of norms which according to traditional science of law constitute legal obligations without stipulating sanctions, is the so-called natural obligation. Natural obligations are obligations whose fulfillment cannot be asserted in a court, and whose nonfulfillment is not the condition of a civil execution. Still, one speaks of a legal obligation, because that which, in fulfillment of a so-called natural obligation, has been given by one individual to another cannot be recovered as an unjustified enrichment. If this is so, however, it merely means: A general norm is valid stipulating that: (1) if the beneficiary of a performance to which the performer was legally not obligated refuses restitution, civil execution ought to be

---

[23]But the basic norm is not identical with this definition. As a norm the basic norm is not a concept.

directed into the property of the beneficiary; and (2) the validity of this coercion-stipulating norm is restricted with respect to cases determined by the legal order. This situation, therefore, can be described as a restriction of the validity of a sanction-stipulating norm; it is not necessary to assume the existence of a sanctionless norm.

It is possible, of course, for a legislator to establish, in a procedure conforming with the basic norm, an act whose subjective meaning is a behavior-commanding norm, without (1) establishing an act whose subjective meaning is a norm prescribing a sanction as a reaction against the opposite behavior; and without (2) the possibility of describing the situation as "restriction of the validity of a sanction-stipulating norm." In this case the subjective meaning of the act in question cannot be interpreted as its objective meaning; the norm, which is the act's subjective meaning cannot be interpreted as a legal norm, but must be regarded as legally irrelevant.

And there are other reasons why the subjective meaning of an act established in conformity with the basic norm may be regarded as legally irrelevant: namely, if the subjective meaning of such an act is not a norm that commands, permits, or authorizes human behavior. A law, established strictly according to the constitution, may have a content that is not a norm, but the expression of a religious or political theory—for example, the statement that the law is given by God or that the law is just or that the law realizes the interest of the entire population. Or, to give another example, in the form of a constitutionally established statute the nation's congratulations may be conveyed to the head of the state on the occasion of an anniversary of his accession to power; this may be done in this form merely to invest the congratulations with special solemnity. After all, since constitutionally established acts are expressed by words, the acts may have any meaning whatever, not only the meaning of norms. If law is defined as norm

at all, legal science cannot dispense with the concept of legally irrelevant contents.

Since the law regulates the procedure by which it is itself created, one might distinguish this legally regulated procedure as *legal form* from the *legal content* established by the procedure, and speak of a legally irrelevant legal content. In traditional science of law this thought is expressed to some extent by the distinction between law in the formal sense and law in the material sense. This distinction acknowledges the fact that not only general behavior-regulating norms are issued in the form of laws, but also administrative decisions, such as the naturalization of a person, the approval of the state budget, or judicial decision (when, in certain cases, the legislator acts as a judge). But it would be more correct to speak of form of law and content of law rather than of law in the formal and in the material sense. However, the words "legal form" and "legal content" are unprecise and even misleading in this respect; in order to be interpreted as a legal act it is not only required that the act be established by a certain procedure, but also that the act have a certain subjective meaning. The meaning depends on the definition of law, presupposed together with the basic norm. If the law is not defined as a coercive order, but only as an order established according to the basic norm (and if, therefore, the basic norm is formulated as: one ought to behave as the historically first constitution prescribes), then sanctionless legal norms could exist, that is, legal norms that under certain conditions command a human behavior without another norm stipulating a sanction as a reaction against nonobservance. In this case the subjective meaning of an act, established in accordance with the basic norm—if this meaning is not a norm and in no relation to a norm—would be legally irrelevant. Then, a norm established by the constitutional legislator and commanding a certain behavior without attaching a coercive act to its nonobservance, could be distinguished from a moral norm only by its origin; and a legal norm established by custom could not be distinguished from a customarily established moral norm at all.

If the constitution has established custom as a law-creating fact, then all moral norms created by custom constitute a part of the legal order.

Therefore, then, a definition of law, which does not determine law as a coercive order, must be rejected (1) because only by including the element of coercion into the definition of law is the law clearly distinguished from any other social order; (2) because coercion is a factor of great importance for the cognition of social relationships and highly characteristic of the social orders called "law"; and, (3) particularly, because by defining law as a coercive order, a connection is accounted for that exists in the case most important for the cognition of the law, the law of the modern state: the connection between law and state. The modern state is, essentially a coercive order—a centralized coercive order, limited in its territorial validity.

Norms that are the subjective meaning of legislative acts and that command a certain behavior without the opposite behavior being made the condition of a sanction are very rare in modern legal orders. If the social orders designated as law *did* contain significant numbers of sanctionless norms, then the definition of law as a coercive order could be questioned; and if from the existing social orders designated as law the element of coercion were to disappear—as predicted by Marx's socialism—then these social orders would indeed fundamentally change their character. They would—from the point of view of the offered definition of law—lose their legal character, and the social orders constituted by them would lose their character as states. In Marxian terms the state—and along with the state, the law—would wither away.

E) DEPENDENT LEGAL NORMS  It was pointed out earlier that: if one norm commands a certain behavior and a second norm stipulates a sanction as reaction against nonobservance, the two norms are tied to each other. This is particularly true if a social order—as the legal order—commands a certain behavior specifically by attaching a coercive act as sanction to the opposite behavior. Therefore a behavior according to such an order may be regarded as commanded—and in case of a legal order as legally commanded—only so far as the opposite behavior is the condition of a sanction. If a legal order, such as a statute passed by parliament, contains one norm that prescribes a certain behavior and a second norm that attaches a sanction to the nonobservance of the first, then the first norm is not an independent norm, but fundamentally tied to the second; the first norm merely designates—negatively—the condition under which the second stipulates the sanction; and if the second one positively designates the condition under which it stipulates the sanction, then the first one is superfluous from the point of view of legislative technique. For example: If a civil code contains the norm that a debtor ought to pay back the received loan to the creditor; and the second norm that a civil execution ought to be directed into the property of the debtor if the debtor does not repay the loan; then everything prescribed by the first norm is contained conditionally in the second. Modern criminal codes usually do not contain norms that prohibit, like the Ten Commandments, murder, adultery, and other crimes; they limit themselves to attach penal sanctions to certain behavior. This shows clearly that a norm: "You shall not murder" is superfluous, if a norm is valid: "He who murders ought to be punished"; it shows, further, that the legal order indeed prohibits a certain behavior by attaching to it a sanction or that it commands a behavior by attaching a sanction to the opposite behavior.

Dependent are also those legal norms that positively permit a certain behavior. For—as shown before—they merely limit the sphere of validity of a legal norm that prohibits this behavior by attaching a sanction to the opposite. The example of self-defense has been cited earlier. Another example is found in the United Nations Charter. Article 2, paragraph 4, forbids all members to use force: the Charter attaches to the use of force the sanctions stipulated in Article 39. But the Charter permits in Article 51 the use of force as individual or collective self-defense by limiting the general prohibition of Article 2, paragraph 4. The named articles form a unit. The Charter could have combined them all in a single article forbidding all members to use force which does not have the character of individual or collective self-defense by making the thus restricted use of force the condition of a sanction. Yet another example: A norm prohibits the sale of alcoholic beverages, that is, makes it punishable; but this prohibition is restricted by another norm according to which the sale of these beverages, if a license is obtained, is not forbidden; that means that the sale is not punishable.

The second norm, restricting the sphere of validity of the first, is a dependent norm; it is meaningful only in connection with the first; both form a unit. Their contents may be expressed in the single norm: "If somebody sells alcoholic beverages without a state license, he ought to be punished." The function of the merely negative permission, consisting in the nonprohibition by the legal order of a certain behavior, need not be considered here because negative permission is not granted by a positive norm.

A legal norm may not only restrict the sphere of validity of another norm, but may entirely annul the validity. These derogating norms too are dependent norms, meaningful only in connection with other, sanction-stipulating norms. Further, legal norms authorizing a certain behavior are dependent norms likewise, if "authorizing" is understood to mean: confer upon an individual a legal power, that is, the power to create legal norms. These authorizing norms designate only one of the conditions under which—in

an independent norm—the coercive act is prescribed. These are the norms that authorize the creation of general norms: (1) the norms of the constitution which regulate legislation or institute custom as a law-creating fact; and (2) the norms that regulate judicial and administrative procedures in which the general norms created by statute or custom are applied by authorized courts and administrative officials through individual norms created by these organs.

To give an example: Suppose the legal order of a state prohibits theft by attaching to it in a statute the penalty of imprisonment. The condition of the punishment is not merely the fact that a man has stolen. The theft has to be ascertained by a court authorized by the legal order in a procedure determined by the norms of the legal order; the court has to pronounce a punishment, determined by statute or custom; and this punishment has to be executed by a different organ. The court is authorized to impose, in a certain procedure, a punishment upon the thief, only if in a constitutional procedure a general norm is created that attaches to theft a certain punishment. The norm of the constitution, which authorizes the creation of this general norm, determines a condition to which the sanction is attached. The rule of law that describes this situation says: "If the individuals authorized to legislate have issued a general norm according to which a thief is to be punished in a certain way; and if the court authorized by the Code of Criminal Proceedings in a procedure prescribed by this code has ascertained that an individual has committed theft; and if that court has ordered the legally determined punishment; then a certain organ ought to execute the punishment." By thus phrasing the rule of law that describes the law, it is revealed that the norms of the constitution which authorize the creation of general norms by regulating the organization and procedure of legislation; and the norms of a Code of Criminal Procedure which authorize the creation of the individual norms of the judicial court decisions by regulating the organization and procedure of the criminal courts, are dependent norms; for they determine only conditions under which the punitive sanctions are to be executed. The execution of all coercive acts stipulated by a legal order—including those that are ordered by an administrative procedure and those that do not have the character of sanctions—is conditioned in that manner. The constitutional creation of the general norms to be applied by courts and administrative agencies, and the creation of the individual norms by which these organs have to apply the general norms, are as much conditions of the execution of the coercive act as the ascertainment of the fact of the delict or as other circumstances which the legal norms have made the condition of coercive acts that are not sanctions. But the general norm that stipulates the coercive act under all these conditions is an independent legal norm—even if the coercive act is not commanded because its nonexecution is not made the condition of a further coercive act. If we say that in this case the coercive act is authorized, then the word "authorized" is used in a wider sense. It then does not merely mean conferring a legal power in the sense of a power to create legal norms, but also conferring the power to perform the coercive acts stipulated by the legal norms. In a wider sense, then, this power may also be designated as a legal power.

Dependent norms are, finally, also those that further determine the meaning of other norms, by defining a concept used in a second norm or by authentically interpreting a second norm otherwise. For example, a Criminal Code might contain an article saying: "By murder is to be understood the behavior of an individual which intentionally causes the death of another individual." This article defines murder; however, the article has normative character only in connection with another article that says: "If a man commits murder, the authorized court ought to

impose the death penalty." And this article, again, is inseparably connected with a third article that says: "The death penalty is to be carried out by hanging."

It follows, that a legal order may be characterized as a coercive order, even though not all its norms stipulate coercive acts: because norms that do not themselves stipulate coercive acts (and hence do not command, but authorize the creation of norms or positively permit a definite behavior) are dependent norms, valid only in connection with norms, that *do* stipulate coercive acts. Again, not all norms that stipulate a coercive act but only those that stipulate the coercive act as a reaction against a certain behavior (that is, as a sanction), command a specific, namely the opposite, behavior. This, therefore, is another reason why the law does not have exclusively a commanding or imperative character. Since a legal order, in the sense just described, is a coercive order, it may be described in sentences pronouncing that under specific conditions (that is, under conditions determined by the legal order) specific coercive acts ought to be performed. All legally relevant material contained in a legal order fits in this scheme of the rule of law formulated by legal science— the *rule of law* which is to be distinguished from the *legal norm* established by the legal authority.

## THE DYNAMIC ASPECT OF LAW

### 34. The Reason for the Validity of a Normative Order: The Basic Norm

A) THE MEANING OF THE SEARCH FOR THE REASON FOR VALIDITY If the law as a normative order is conceived as a system of norms that regulates the behavior of men, the question arises: What constitutes the unity of a multitude of norms—why does a certain norm belong to a certain order? And this question is closely tied to the question: Why is a norm valid, what is the reason for its validity?

A norm referring to the behavior of a human being is "valid" means that it is binding—that an individual ought to behave in the manner determined by the norm. It has been pointed out in an earlier context that the question why a norm is valid, why an individual ought to behave in a certain way, cannot be answered by ascertaining a fact, that is, by a statement that something *is*; that the reason for the validity of a norm cannot be a fact. From the circumstance that something *is* cannot follow that something *ought* to be; and that something *ought* to be, cannot be the reason that something *is*. The reason for the validity of a norm can only be the validity of another norm. A norm which represents the reason for the validity of another norm is figuratively spoken of as a higher norm in relation to a lower norm. It looks as if one could give as a reason for the validity of a norm the circumstance that it was established by an authority, human or divine; for example, the statement: "The reason for the validity of the Ten Commandments is that God Jehovah issued them on Mount Sinai"; or: "Men ought to love their enemies, because Jesus, Son of God, issued this command in his Sermon on the Mount." But in both cases the reason for the validity is not that God or his son issued a certain norm at a certain time in a certain place, but the tacitly presupposed norm that one ought to obey the commands of God or his son. To be true: In the syllogism whose major premise is the ought- statement asserting the validity of the higher norm: "One ought to obey God's commands," and whose conclusion is the ought-statement asserting the validity of the lower norm: "One ought to obey God's Ten Commandments," the assertion that God had issued the Ten Commandments, an "is-statement," as the minor premise, is an essential link. The Major premise and the minor premise are both conditions of the conclusion. But only the major premise, which is an *ought*-statement, is the *conditio per quam* in relation to the conclusion, which is also an *ought*-statement;

that is, the norm whose validity is stated in the major premise is the reason for the validity of the norm whose validity is stated in the conclusion. The *is*-statement functioning as minor premise is only the *conditio sine qua non* in relation to the conclusion; this means: the fact whose existence is asserted in the minor premise is not the reason for the validity of the norm whose validity is asserted in the conclusion.

The norm whose validity is stated in the major premise ("One ought to obey God's commands"), is included in the supposition that the norms, whose reason for validity is in question, originate from an authority, that is, from somebody competent to create valid norms; this norm bestows upon the norm-creating personality the "authority" to create norms. The mere fact that somebody commands something is no reason to regard the command as a "valid" norm, a norm binding the individual at whom it is directed. Only a competent authority can create valid norms; and such competence can only be based on a norm that authorizes the issuing of norms. The authority authorized to issue norms is subject to that norm in the same manner as the individuals are subject to the norms issued by the authority.

The norm which represents the reason for the validity of another norm is called, as we have said, the "higher" norm. But the search for the reason of a norm's validity cannot go on indefinitely like the search for the cause of an effect. It must end with a norm which, as the last and highest, is presupposed. It must be *presupposed*, because it cannot be "posited," that is to say: created, by an authority whose competence would have to rest on a still higher norm. This final norm's validity cannot be derived from a higher norm, the reason for its validity cannot be questioned. Such a presupposed highest norm is referred to in this book as basic norm. All norms whose validity can be traced back to one and the same basic norm constitute a system of norms, a normative order. The basic norm is the common source for the validity of all norms that belong to the same order—it is their common reason of validity. The fact that a certain norm belongs to a certain order is based on the circumstance that its last reason of validity is the basic norm of this order. It is the basic norm that constitutes the unity in the multitude of norms by representing the reason for the validity of all norms that belong to this order.

**B) THE STATIC AND THE DYNAMIC PRINCIPLE**
According to the nature of the reason for the validity two types of norm systems may be distinguished: a static and a dynamic type. The norms of the order of the first type are valid on the strength of the content: because their validity can be traced back to a norm under whose content the content of the norms in question can be subsumed as the particular under the general. Thus, for example, the validity of the norms "do not lie," "do not give false testimony," "do fulfill a promise," can be derived from a norm that prescribes to be truthful. From the norm to love one's neighbor one can derive the norm not to harm one's fellow man, not to damage him physically or morally, to help him in need, and—particularly—not to kill him. Perhaps one might reduce the norms of truthfulness and love for one's fellow man to a still higher norm, such as to be in harmony with the universe. On this norm a whole moral order may be founded. Since all norms of an order of this type are already contained in the content of the presupposed norm, they can be deduced from it by way of a logical operation, namely a conclusion from the general to the particular. This norm, presupposed as the basic norm, supplies both the reason for the validity and the content of the norms deduced from it in a logical operation. A system of norms, whose reason for validity and content is deduced from a norm presupposed as a basic norm, is a *static norm system*. The principle according to which the validity of the norms of this system is founded is a static principle.

However, the norm from whose content other norms are deduced in the described fashion can be regarded as basic norm only if its content is assumed to be directly evident. In fact, the reason for the validity and the content of norms of a moral system are frequently traced back to a norm considered to be directly evident. A norm is "directly evident" means that it is immanent in, or emanates from, reason. The concept of a directly evident norm presupposes the concept of a practical reason, that is, a norm-creating reason; but this concept is untenable, as will be shown, because the function of reason is knowing and not willing, whereas the creation of norms is an act of will. Therefore there can be no such things as norms which are valid only in virtue of their directly evident content. If a norm prescribing a definite human behavior is asserted to be directly evident, it is done because it is believed that it is created by the will of God or another superhuman authority or because it was created by custom and therefore—like everything customary—regarded as self-evident. It is, then, a norm created by an act of will. Its validity can, in the last analysis, be based only on a presupposed norm which prescribes that one ought to behave according to the commands of the norm-creating authority or according to the norms created by custom. This norm can supply only the reason for the validity, not the content of the norms based on it. These norms constitute a dynamic system of norms. The principle according to which the validity of the norms of this system is founded, is a dynamic principle.

The dynamic type is characterized by this: the presupposed basic norm contains nothing but the determination of a norm-creating fact, the authorization of a norm-creating authority or (which amounts to the same) a rule that stipulates how the general and individual norms of the order based on the basic norm ought to be created. For example: A father orders his child to go to school. The child answers: Why? The reply may be: Because the father so ordered and the child ought to obey the father. If the child continues to ask: Why ought I to obey the father, the answer may be: Because God has commanded "Obey Your Parents," and one ought to obey the commands of God. If the child now asks why one ought to obey the commands of God, that is, if the child questions the validity of this norm, then the answer is that this question cannot be asked, that the norm cannot be questioned—the reason for the validity of the norm must not be sought: the norm has to be presupposed. The content of the norm that started it—the child ought to go to school—cannot be derived from the basic norm. For the basic norm is limited to authorize a norm-creating authority, it is a rule according to which the norms of this system ought to be created. The validity of the norm that constituted the starting point of the question is not derived from its content; it cannot be deduced from the basic norm by a logical operation. It has to be created by an act of the father, and it is valid (if we formulate this according to tradition) because it was so created; or, formulated more correctly: because a basic norm is presupposed to be valid which authorizes this way of creating norms. A norm belongs to an order founded on such a basic norm, because it was created in a fashion determined by the basic norm—and not because it has a certain content. The basic norm supplies only the reason for the validity, but not at the same time the content of the norms constituting the system. Their content can only be determined by the acts by which the authority authorized by the basic norm, and the authorities in turn authorized by this authority, create the positive norms of this system. Another example: In a social community, a tribe, it is customary that a man who marries a girl pays a certain amount to her father or uncle. If the groom asks why he ought to do this, the answer is: because in this community such a payment has always been made, that is, because there is a custom to make this payment and because it is assumed to be self-evident that the individual

member of the tribe ought to behave as all other members customarily do. This is the basic norm of the normative order that constitutes the community. It establishes custom as norm-creating fact. The two examples illustrate the dynamic type of a norm system.

The static and dynamic principles may be combined in the same system if the presupposed basic norm, according to the dynamic principle, merely authorizes a norm-creating authority, and if this authority (or one authorized by it in turn) not only establishes norms by which other norm-creating authorities are delegated, but also norms in which the subjects are commanded to observe a certain behavior and from which further norms can be deduced, as from the general to the particular. The Ten Commandments not only establish parents as norm-creating authorities but also stipulate general norms from whose content special norms may be logically deduced without requiring a norm-creating act, such as, for example, Thou shalt not make unto thee any graven image, etc. A wealth of special moral norms may logically be deduced from the command to love one's enemy. In giving a reason for the validity of the norms deduced from such commands of God or Christ, the static principle is applied; in giving a reason for the validity of God's commands through the basic norm: "One ought to obey God's commands" and for the validity of Christ's commands through the basic norm: "One ought to obey Christ's commands," the dynamic principle is applied.

c) THE REASON FOR THE VALIDITY OF A LEGAL ORDER The norm system that presents itself as a legal order has essentially a dynamic character. A legal norm is not valid because it has a certain content, that is, because its content is logically deducible from a presupposed basic norm, but because it is created in a certain way—ultimately in a way determined by a presupposed basic norm. For this reason alone does the legal norm belong to the legal order whose norms are created according to this basic norm. Therefore any kind of content might be law. There is no human behavior which, as such, is excluded from being the content of a legal norm. The validity of a legal norm may not be denied for being (in its content) in conflict with that of another norm which does not belong to the legal order whose basic norm is the reason for the validity of the norm in question. The basic norm of a legal order is not a material norm which, because its content is regarded as immediately self-evident, is presupposed as the highest norm and from which norms for human behavior are logically deduced. The norms of a legal order must be created by a specific process. They are posited, that is, positive, norms, elements of a positive order. If by the constitution of a legal community is understood the norm or norms that determine how (that is, by what organs and by what procedure—through legislation or custom) the general norms of the legal order that constitute the community are to be created, then the basic norm is that norm which is presupposed when the custom through which the constitution has come into existence, or the constitution-creating act consciously performed by certain human beings, is objectively interpreted as a norm-creating fact; if, in the latter case, the individual or the assembly of individuals who created the constitution on which the legal order rests, are looked upon as norm-creating authorities. In this sense, the basic norm determines the basic fact of law creation and may in this respect be described as the constitution in a logical sense of the word (which will be explained later) in contradistinction to the constitution in the meaning of positive law. The basic norm is the presupposed starting point of a procedure: the procedure of positive law creation. It is itself not a norm created by custom or by the act of a legal organ; it is not a positive but a presupposed norm so far as the constitution-establishing authority is looked upon as the highest authority and can therefore not be regarded as authorized by the norm of a higher authority.

If the question as to the reason for the validity of a certain legal norm is raised, then the answer can only consist in the reduction to the basic norm of this legal order, that is, in the assertion that the norm was created—in the last instance—according to the basic norm. In the following pages we would like to consider only a national legal order, that is, a legal order limited in its validity to a specific space, the so-called territory of the state, and which is regarded as "sovereign," that is, as not subordinated to any higher legal order. We shall discuss the problem of the validity of the norms of a national legal order, at first without considering an international legal order superordinated to or included in it.

The question of the reason for the validity of a legal norm belonging to a specific national legal order may arise on the occasion of a coercive act; for example, when one individual deprives another of his life by hanging, and now the question is asked why this act is legal, namely the execution of a punishment , and not murder. This act can be interpreted as being legal only if it was prescribed by an individual legal norm, namely as an act that "ought" to be performed, by a norm that presents itself as a judicial decision. This raises the questions: Under what conditions is such an interpretation possible, why is a judicial decision present in this case, why is the individual norm created thereby a legal norm belonging to a valid legal order and therefore ought to be applied? The answer is: Because this individual norm was created in applying a criminal law that contains a general norm according to which (under conditions present in the case concerned) the death penalty ought to be inflicted. If we ask for the reason for the validity of this criminal law, then the answer is: the criminal law is valid because it was created by the legislature, and the legislature, in turn, is authorized by the constitution to create general norms. If we ask for the reason of the validity of the constitution, that is, for the reason of the validity of the norms regulating the creation of the general norms, we may, perhaps, discover an older constitution; that means the validity of the existing constitution is justified by the fact that it was created according to the rules of an earlier constitution by way of a constitutional amendment. In this way we eventually arrive at a historically first constitution that cannot have been created in this way and whose validity, therefore, cannot be traced back to a positive norm created by a legal authority; we arrive, instead, at a constitution that became valid in a revolutionary way, that is, either by breach of a former constitution or for a territory that formerly was not the sphere of validity of a constitution and of a national legal order based on it. If we consider merely the national legal order, not international law, and if we ask for the reason of the validity of the historically first constitution, then the answer can only be (if we leave aside God or "nature") that the validity of this constitution—the assumption that it is a binding norm—must be *presupposed* if we want to interpret (1) the acts performed according to it as the creation or application of valid general legal norms; and (2) the acts performed in application of these general norms as the creation or application of valid individual legal norms. Since the reason for the validity of a norm can only be another norm, the presupposition must be a norm: not one posited (i.e., created) by a legal authority, but a presupposed norm, that is, a norm presupposed if the subjective meaning of the constitution-creating facts and the subjective meaning of the norm-creating facts established according to the constitution are interpreted as their objective meaning. Since it is the basic norm of a legal order (that is, an order prescribing coercive acts), therefore this norm, namely the basic norm of the legal order concerned, must be formulated as follows: Coercive acts sought to be performed under the conditions and in the manner which the historically first constitution, and the norms created according to it, prescribe. (In short:

One ought to behave as the constitution prescribes.) The norms of a legal order, whose common reason for their validity is this basic norm are not a complex of valid norms standing coordinately side by side, but form a hierarchical structure of super- and subordinate norms. This structure of the legal order will be discussed later.

**d) The Basic Norm as Transcendental-logical Presupposition** To understand the nature of the basic norm it must be kept in mind that it refers directly to a specific constitution, actually established by custom or statutory creation, by and large effective, and indirectly to the coercive order created according to this constitution and by and large effective: the basic norm thereby furnishes the reason for the validity of this constitution and of the coercive order created in accordance with it. The basic norm, therefore, is not the product of free invention. It is not presupposed arbitrarily in the sense that there is a choice between different basic norms when the subjective meaning of a constitution-creating act and the acts created according to this constitution are interpreted as their objective meaning. Only if this basic norm, referring to a specific constitution, is presupposed, that is, only if it is presupposed that one ought to behave according to this specific constitution—only then can the subjective meaning of a constitution-creating act and of the acts created according to this constitution be interpreted as their objective meaning, that is, as objectively valid legal norms, and the relationships established by these norms as legal relations.

In presupposing the basic norm referring to a specific constitution, the contents of this constitution and of the national legal order created according to it is irrelevant—it may be a just or unjust order; it may or may not guarantee a relative condition of peace within the community established by it. The presupposition of the basic norm does not approve any value transcending positive law.

Insofar as only the presupposition of the basic norm makes it possible to interpret the subjective meaning of the constitution- creating act (and of the acts established according to the constitution) as their objective meaning, that is, as objectively valid legal norms, the basic norm as represented by the science of law may be characterized as the transcendental-logical condition of this interpretation, if it is permissible to use by analogy a concept of Kant's epistemology. Kant asks: "How is it possible to interpret without a metaphysical hypothesis, the facts perceived by our senses, in the laws of nature formulated by natural science?" In the same way, the Pure Theory of Law asks: "How is it possible to interpret without recourse to metalegal authorities, like God or nature, the subjective meaning of certain facts as a system of objectively valid legal norms describable in rules of law?" The epistemological answer of the Pure Theory of Law is: "By presupposing the basic norm that one ought to behave as the constitution prescribes, that is, one ought to behave in accordance with the subjective meaning of the constitution-creating act of will—according to the prescriptions of the authority creating the constitution." The function of this basic norm is to found the objective validity of a positive legal order, that is, to interpret the *subjective* meaning of the acts of human beings by which the norms of an effective coercive order are created, as their *objective* meaning. The foundation of the validity of a positive norm, that is, one established by an act of will and prescribing a certain behavior, is the result of a syllogistic procedure. In this syllogism, the major premise is the assertion about a norm regarded as objectively valid, according to which one ought to obey the commands of a certain person, that is, one ought to behave according to the subjective meaning of these commands; the minor premise is the assertion of the fact that this person has commanded to behave in a certain way; and the conclusion is the assertion of the validity of the norm: that one ought to

behave in this particular way. Thus the norm whose validity is stated in the major premise legitimizes the subjective meaning of the command, whose existence is asserted in the minor premise, as the command's objective meaning. For example: One ought to obey God's commands. God has commanded to obey the commands of the parents. Hence, one ought to obey the commands of the parents. Thus the subjective meaning of the act by which a father commands a certain behavior of his son is legitimized as its objective meaning, that is, as a binding norm.

The norm whose validity is asserted in the major premise is a basic norm if its objective validity is not questioned. It is not questioned if its validity cannot be based on a syllogistic procedure. And it cannot be so based, if the statement of the fact that this norm was established by an individual's act of will is not possible as the minor premise of a syllogism. This is the case when the person whose commands one ought to obey according to the norm now in question, is regarded as a highest authority, for example, God. Then the norm prescribing to obey the commands of this person has to be placed at the top of the syllogism as its major premise without  it being possible that the norm itself is stated in the form of a conclusion of a further syllogism. This means: the norm is *presupposed* as a basic norm.

For this reason, the norm: "One ought to obey the commands of God" is a basic norm on which the validity of the norm: "One ought to obey the commands of one's parents," is based. A theological ethics that regards God as the highest norm-creating authority cannot state that somebody else has ordered to obey the commands of God— because this would have to be an authority higher than God. And if the norm: "One ought to obey the commands of God" were presumed to be posited by God, it could not be the reason for the validity of God-created norms, because it would itself be a God-created norm. Nor can theological ethics in itself create such a norm (that is, command to obey the commands of God) because as cognition it cannot be a norm-creating authority. Therefore, the norm: "One ought to obey the commands of God," as the basic norm, cannot be the subjective meaning of an act of will; it can only be the meaning of an act of thinking. That means: Theological ethics can only state: "The command of the parents has the character of an objectively binding norm if we presuppose in our thinking the norm: 'One ought to obey the commands of God' (who has commanded to obey the commands of the parents)."[71]

Since a positivistic science of law regards the creator of the historically first constitution as the highest legal authority and therefore cannot maintain that the norm to obey the commands of the creator of the constitution is the subjective meaning of the act of will of an authority higher than the creator of the constitution—such as God's or nature's—so therefore, the science of law cannot base the validity of this norm on a syllogistic procedure. A positivistic science of law can only state that this norm is presupposed as a basic norm in the foundation of the objective validity of the legal norms, and therefore presupposed in the interpretation of an effective coercive order as a system of objectivity valid legal norms. Since this basic norm cannot be the meaning of an act of will; and since this norm (rather: the statement about it) is logically indispensable for the foundation of the objective validity of positive legal norms, it can only be the meaning of an act of thinking; the science of law can state no more than: the subjective

meaning of the acts by which legal norms are created can be interpreted as their objective meaning only if we presuppose in our juristic thinking the norm: "One ought to obey the prescriptions of the historically first constitution."

The science of law does not prescribe that one ought to obey the commands of the creator of the constitution. The science of law remains a merely cognitive discipline even in its epistemological statement that the basic norm is the condition under which the subjective meaning of the constitution-creating act, and the subjective meaning of the acts performed in accordance with the constitution, are interpreted as their objective meaning, as valid norms, even if the meaning of these acts is so interpreted by the legal science itself.[72]

By offering this theory of the basic norm, the Pure Theory of Law does not inaugurate a new method of legal cognition. It merely makes conscious what most legal scientists do, at least unconsciously, when they understand the mentioned facts not as causally determined, but instead interpret their subjective meaning as objectively valid norms, that is, as a normative legal order, without basing the validity of this order upon a higher, meta-legal norm, that is, upon a norm enacted by an authority superior to the legal authority; in other words, when they consider as law exclusively positive law. The theory of the basic norm is merely the result of an analysis of the procedure which a positivistic science of law has always applied.

[71]A norm which is the meaning of an act of thinking is not a norm whose content is directly evident. The Basic Norm of a positive legal order, as developed in that which follows is by no means directly evident.

[72]The question: "Who presupposes the basic norm? is answered by the Pure Theory as follows: The basic norm is presupposed by whoever interprets the subjective meaning of the constitution-creating act, and of the acts created according to the constitution, as the objective meaning of these acts, that is, as objectively valid norm. This interpretation is a cognitive function, not a function of the will. Since the science of law, as cognition, can only describe norms, and not prescribe anything, hence cannot create norms, I have occasionally expressed doubt against the view that the basic norm is also presupposed by the science of law ("Was ist ein Rechtsakt?" *Oesterreichische Zeitschrift für Oeffentliches Recht*, 1952). These doubts are eliminated by the distinction, presented in the text, between positing and presupposing a norm.

## QUESTIONS

1. Explain what Kelsen means by the *effectiveness* of a norm. Does the validity of a norm have any connection to its effectiveness? Does it have any connection to the effectiveness of anything? What role does the concept of law as a *system* of norms play in this?

2. What is meant by Kelsen's notion of creating norms by an act of will? Explain how the norm, "one ought never to kill the innocent" could be conceived as having been created by an act of will. If it were created in this way, what norm would be presupposed by that fact?

3. Give an example of a norm that can be deduced (in Kelsen's sense of deduction according to the static principle), from the norm, "one ought not to harm anyone."

4. Explain the difference, in Kelsen's view, between an act's having a "subjective" meaning, and its having an "objective" meaning.

5. State as fully as you can the criteria that Kelsen would have us use in determining whether a small band of international outlaws constituted a kind of legal system.

# *H. L. A. Hart*
## LAW AS THE UNION OF PRIMARY AND SECONDARY RULES*

### 1. A FRESH START

In [an earlier discussion] we have seen that, at various crucial points, the simple model of law as the sovereign's coercive orders failed to reproduce some of the salient features of a legal system. To demonstrate this, we did not find it necessary to invoke (as earlier critics have done) international law or primitive law which some may regard as disputable or borderline examples of law; instead we pointed to certain familiar features of municipal law in a modern state, and showed that these were either distorted or altogether unrepresented in this over-simple theory.

The main ways in which the theory failed are instructive enough to merit a second summary. First, it became clear that though of all the varieties of law, a criminal statute, forbidding or enjoining certain actions under penalty, most resembles orders backed by threats given by one person to others, such a statute nonetheless differs from such orders in the important respect that it commonly applies to those who enact it and not merely to others. Secondly, there are other varieties of law, notably those conferring legal powers to adjudicate or legislate (public powers) or to create or vary legal relations (private powers) which cannot, without absurdity, be construed as orders backed by threats. Thirdly, there are legal rules which differ from orders in their mode of origin, because they are not brought into being by anything analogous to explicit prescription. Finally, the analysis of law in terms of the sovereign, habitually obeyed and necessarily exempt from all legal limitation, failed to

*© Oxford University Press 1961. Reprinted from *The Concept of Law* by H. L. A. Hart (1961) by permission of Oxford University Press.

account for the continuity of legislative authority characteristic of a modern legal system, and the sovereign person or persons could not be identified with either the electorate or the legislature of a modern state.

It will be recalled that in thus criticizing the conception of law as the sovereign's coercive orders we considered also a number of ancillary devices which were brought in at the cost of corrupting the primitive simplicity of the theory to rescue it from its difficulties. But these too failed. One device, the notion of a tacit order, seemed to have no application to the complex actualities of a modern legal system, but only to very much simpler situations like that of a general who deliberately refrains from interfering with orders given by this subordinates. Other devices, such as that of treating power-conferring rules as mere fragments of rules imposing duties, or treating all rules as directed only to officials, distort the ways in which these are spoken of, thought of, and actually used in social life. This had no better claim to our assent than the theory that all the rules of a game are 'really' directions to the umpire and the scorer. The device, designed to reconcile the self-binding character of legislation with the theory that a statute is an order given to *others*, was to distinguish the legislators acting in their official capacity, as *one* person ordering *others* who include themselves in their private capacities. This device, impeccable in itself, involved supplementing the theory with something it does not contain: this is the notion of a rule defining what must be done to legislate; for it is only in conforming with such a rule that legislators have an official capacity and a separate personality to be contrasted with themselves as private individuals.

The last three chapters are therefore the record of a failure and there is plainly need for a fresh start. Yet the failure is an instructive one, worth the detailed consideration we have given it, because at each point where the theory failed to fit the facts it was possible to see at least in outline why it was

bound to fail and what is required for a better account. The root cause of failure is that the elements out of which the theory was constructed, viz. the ideas of orders, obedience, habits, and threats, do not include, and cannot by their combination yield, the idea of a rule, without which we cannot hope to elucidate even the most elementary forms of law. It is true that the idea of a rule is by no means a simple one: we have already seen in [an earlier discussion] the need, if we are to do justice to the complexity of a legal system, to discriminate between two different though related types. Under rules of the one type, which may well be considered the basic or primary type, human beings are required to do or abstain from certain actions, whether they wish to or not. Rules of the other type are in a sense parasitic upon or secondary to the first; for they provide that human beings may by doing or saying certain things introduce new rules of the primary type, extinguish or modify old ones, or in various ways determine their incidence or control their operations. Rules of the first type impose duties; rules of the second type confer powers, public or private. Rules of the first type concern actions involving physical movement or changes; rules of the second type provide for operations which lead not merely to physical movement or change, but to the creation or variation of duties or obligations.

We have already given some preliminary analysis of what is involved in the assertion that rules of these two types exist among a given social group, and in this chapter we shall not only carry this analysis a little farther but we shall make the general claim that in the combination of these two types of rule there lies what Austin wrongly claimed to have found in the notion of coercive orders, namely, 'the key to the science of jurisprudence'. We shall not indeed claim that wherever the word 'law' is 'properly' used this combination of primary and secondary rules is to be found; for it is clear that the diverse range of cases of which the word 'law' is used are not linked by any such simple uniformity, but by less direct relations—often of analogy of either form or content to a central case. What we shall attempt to show, in this and the succeeding chapters, is that most of the features of law which have proved most perplexing and have both provoked and eluded the search for definition can best be rendered clear, if these two types of rule and the interplay between them are understood. We accord this union of elements a central place because of their explanatory power in elucidating the concepts that constitute the framework of legal thought. The justification for the use of the word 'law' for a range of apparently heterogeneous cases is a secondary matter which can be undertaken when the central elements have been grasped.

## 2. THE IDEA OF OBLIGATION

It will be recalled that the theory of law as coercive orders, notwithstanding its errors, started from the perfectly correct appreciation of the fact that where there is law, there human conduct is made in some sense non-optional or obligatory. In choosing this starting point the theory was well inspired, and in building up a new account of law in terms of the interplay of primary and secondary rules we too shall start from the same idea. It is, however, here, at this crucial first step, that we have perhaps most to learn from the theory's errors.

Let us recall the gunman situation. A orders B to hand over his money and threatens to shoot him if he does not comply. According to the theory of coercive orders this situation illustrates the notion of obligation or duty in general. Legal obligation is to be found in this situation writ large; A must be the sovereign habitually obeyed and the orders must be general, prescribing courses of conduct not single actions. The plausibility of the claim that the gunman situation displays the meaning of obligation lies in the fact that it is certainly one in which we

would say that B, if he obeyed, was 'obliged' to hand over his money. It is, however, equally certain that we should misdescribe the situation if we said, on these facts, that B 'had an obligation' or a 'duty' to hand over the money. So from the start it is clear that we need something else for an understanding of the idea of obligation. There is a difference, yet to be explained, between the assertion that someone *was obliged* to do something and the assertion that he *had an obligation* to do it. The first is often a statement about the beliefs and motives with which an action is done: B was obliged to hand over his money may simply mean, as it does in the gunman case, that he believed that some harm or other unpleasant consequences would befall him if he did not hand it over and he handed it over to avoid those consequences. In such cases the prospect of what would happen to the agent if he disobeyed has rendered something he would otherwise have preferred to have done (keep the money) less eligible.

Two further elements slightly complicate the elucidation of the notion of being obliged to do something. It seems clear that we should not think of B as obliged to hand over the money if the threatened harm was, according to common judgments, trivial in comparison with the disadvantage or serious consequences, either for B or for others, of complying with the orders, as it would be, for example, if A merely threatened to pinch B. Nor perhaps should we say that B was obliged, if there were no reasonable grounds for thinking that A could or would probably implement his threat of relatively serious harm. Yet, though such references to common judgments of comparative harm and reasonable estimates of likelihood, are implicit in this notion, the statement that a person was obliged to obey someone is, in the main, a psychological one referring to the beliefs and motives with which an action was done. But the statement that someone *had an obligation* to do something is of a very different type and there are many signs of this difference. Thus not only is it the case that the facts about B's action and his beliefs and motives in the gunman case, though sufficient to warrant the statement that B was obliged to hand over his purse, are *not sufficient* to warrant the statement that he had an obligation to do this; it is also the case that facts of this sort, i.e. facts about beliefs and motives, are *not necessary* for the truth of a statement that a person had an obligation to do something. Thus the statement that a person had an obligation, e.g. to tell the truth or report for military service, remains true even if he believed (reasonably or unreasonably) that he would never be found out and had nothing to fear from disobedience. Moreover, whereas the statement that he had this obligation is quite independent of the question whether or not he in fact reported for service, the statement that someone was obliged to do something, normally carries the implication that he actually did it.

Some theorists, Austin among them, seeing perhaps the general irrelevance of the person's beliefs, fears, and motives to the question whether he had an obligation to do something, have defined this notion not in terms of these subjective facts, but in terms of the *chance* or *likelihood* that the person having the obligation will suffer a punishment or 'evil' at the hands of others in the event of disobedience. This, in effect, treats statements of obligation not as psychological statements but as predictions or assessments of chances of incurring punishment or 'evil'. To many later theorists this has appeared as a revelation, bringing down to earth an elusive notion and restating it in the same clear, hard, empirical terms as are used in science. It has, indeed, been accepted sometimes as the only alternative to metaphysical conceptions of obligation or duty as invisible objects mysteriously existing 'above' or 'behind' the world of ordinary, observable facts. But there are many reasons for rejecting this interpretation of statements of obligation as predictions, and it is not, in fact, the only alternative to obscure metaphysics.

The fundamental objection is that the predictive interpretation obscures the fact that, where rules exist, deviations from them are not merely grounds for a prediction that hostile reactions will follow or that a court will apply sanctions to those who break them, but are also a reason or justification for such reaction and for applying the sanctions. We have already drawn attention in Chapter IV to this neglect of the internal aspect of rules and we shall elaborate it later in this chapter.

There is, however, a second, simpler, objection to the predictive interpretation of obligation. If it were true that the statement that a person had an obligation meant that *he* was likely to suffer in the event of disobedience, it would be a contradiction to say that he had an obligation, e.g. to report for military service but that, owing to the fact that he had escaped from the jurisdiction, or had successfully bribed the police or the court, there was not the slightest chance of his being caught or made to suffer. In fact, there is no contradiction in saying this, and such statements are often made and understood.

It is, of course, true that in a normal legal system, where sanctions are exacted for a high proportion of offenses, an offender usually runs a risk of punishment; so, usually the statement that a person has an obligation and the statement that he is likely to suffer for disobedience will both be true together. Indeed, the connexion between these two statements is somewhat stronger than this: at least in a municipal system it may well be true that, unless *in general* sanctions were likely to be exacted from offenders, there would be little or no point in making particular statements about a person's obligations. In this sense, such statements may be said to presuppose belief in the continued normal operation of the system of sanctions much as the statement 'he is out' in cricket presupposes, though it does not assert, that players, umpire, and scorer will probably take the usual steps. Nonetheless, it is crucial for the understanding of the idea of obligation to see that in individual cases the statement that a person has an obligation under some rule and the prediction that he is likely to suffer for disobedience may diverge.

It is clear that obligation is not to be found in the gunman situation, though the simpler notion of being obliged to do something may well be defined in the elements present there. To understand the general idea of obligation as a necessary preliminary to understanding it in its legal form, we must turn to a different social situation which, unlike the gunman situation, includes the existence of social rules; for this situation contributes to the meaning of the statement that a person has an obligation in two ways. First, the existence of such rules, making certain types of behaviour a standard, is the normal, though unstated, background or proper context for such a statement; and, secondly, the distinctive function of such statement is to apply such a general rule to a particular person by calling attention to the fact that his case falls under it. We have already seen in Chapter IV that there is involved in the existence of any social rules a combination of regular conduct with a distinctive attitude to that conduct as a standard. We have also seen the main ways in which these differ from mere social habits, and how the varied normative vocabulary ('ought', 'must', 'should') is used to draw attention to the standard and to deviations from it, and to formulate the demands, criticisms, or acknowledgments which may be based on it. Of this class of normative words the words 'obligation' and 'duty' form an important sub-class, carrying with them certain implications not usually present in the others. Hence, though a grasp of the elements generally differentiating social rules from mere habits is certainly indispensable for understanding the notion of obligation or duty, it is not sufficient by itself.

The statement that someone has or is under an obligation does indeed imply the existence of a rule; yet it is not always the case that where rules exist the standard of behaviour required by them is conceived of in terms of obligation. 'He ought to have' and 'He had an obligation to' are not always interchangeable expressions, even though they are alike in carrying an implicit reference to existing standards of conduct or are used in drawing conclusions in particular cases from a general rule. Rules of etiquette or correct speech are certainly rules: they are more than convergent habits or regularities of behaviour; they are taught and efforts are made to maintain them; they are used in criticizing our own and other people's behaviour in the characteristic normative vocabulary. 'You ought to take your hat off', 'It is wrong to say "you was"'. But to use in connexion with rules of this kind the words 'obligation' or 'duty' would be misleading and not merely stylistically odd. It would misdescribe a social situation; for though the line separating rules of obligation from others is at points a vague one, yet the main rationale of the distinction is fairly clear.

Rules are conceived and spoken of as imposing obligations when the general demand for conformity is insistent and the social pressure brought to bear upon those who deviate or threaten to deviate is great. Such rules may be wholly customary in origin: there may be no centrally organized system of punishments for breach of the rules; the social pressure may take only the form of a general diffused hostile or critical reaction which may stop short of physical sanctions. It may be limited to verbal manifestations of disapproval or of appeals to the individuals' respect for the rule violated; it may depend heavily on the operation of feelings of shame, remorse, and guilt. When the pressure is of this last-mentioned kind we may be inclined to classify the rules as part of the morality of the social group and the obligation under the rules as moral obligation. Conversely, when physical sanctions are prominent or usual among the forms of pressure, even though these are neither closely defined nor administered by officials but are left to the community at large, we shall be inclined to classify the rules as a primitive or rudimentary form of law. We may, of course, find both these types of serious social pressure behind what is, in an obvious sense, the same rule of conduct; sometimes this may occur with no indication that one of them is peculiarly appropriate as primary and the other secondary, and then the question whether we are confronted with a rule of morality or rudimentary law may not be susceptible of an answer. But for the moment the possibility of drawing the line between law and morals need not detain us. What is important is that the insistence on importance or *seriousness* of social pressure behind the rules is the primary factor determining whether they are thought of as giving rise to obligations.

Two other characteristics of obligation go naturally together with this primary one. The rules supported by this serious pressure are thought important because they are believed to be necessary to the maintenance of social life or some highly prized feature of it. Characteristically, rules so obviously essential as those which restrict the free use of violence are thought of in terms of obligation. So too rules which require honesty or truth or require the keeping of promises, or specify what is to be done by one who performs a distinctive role or function in the social group are thought of in terms of either 'obligation' or perhaps more often 'duty'. Secondly, it is generally recognized that the conduct required by these rules may, while benefiting others, conflict with what the person who owes the duty may wish to do. Hence obligations and duties are thought of as characteristically involving sacrifice or renunciation, and the standing possibility of conflict between obligation or duty and interest is, in all societies, among the truisms of both the lawyer and the moralist.

The figure of a *bond* binding the person obligated, which is buried in the word 'obligation', and the similar notion of a debt latent in the world 'duty' are explicable in terms of these three factors, which distinguish rules of obligation or duty from other rules. In this figure, which haunts much legal thought, the social pressure appears as a chain binding those who have obligations so that they are not free to do what they want. The other end of the chain is sometimes held by the group or their official representatives, who insist on performance or exact the penalty: sometimes it is entrusted by the group to a private individual who may choose whether or not to insist on performance or its equivalent in value to him. The first situation typifies the duties or obligations of criminal law and the second those of civil law where we think of private individuals having rights correlative to the obligations.

Natural and perhaps illuminating though these figures or metaphors are, we must not allow them to trap us into a misleading conception of obligation as essentially consisting in some feeling of pressure or compulsion experienced by those who have obligations. The fact that rules of obligation are generally supported by serious social pressure does not entail that to have an obligation under the rules is to experience feelings of compulsion or pressure. Hence there is no contradiction in saying of some hardened swindler, and it may often be true, that he had an obligation to pay the rent but felt no pressure to pay when he made off without doing so. To *feel* obliged and to have an obligation are different though frequently concomitant things. To identify them would be one way of misinterpreting, in terms of psychological feelings, the important internal aspect of rules to which we drew attention in [an earlier discussion].

Indeed, the internal aspect of rules is something to which we must again refer before we can dispose finally of the claims of the predictive theory. For an advocate of that theory may well ask why, if social pressure is so important a feature of rules of obligation, we are yet so concerned to stress the inadequacies of the predictive theory; for it gives this very feature a central place by defining obligation in terms of the likelihood that threatened punishment or hostile re-action will follow deviation from certain lines of conduct. The difference may seem slight between the analysis of a statement of obligation as a prediction, or assessment of the chances, of hostile reaction to devia-tion, and our own contention that though this statement presupposes a background in which deviations from rules are generally met by hostile reactions, yet its characteristic use is not to predict this but to say that a person's case falls under such a rule. In fact, however, this difference is not a slight one. Indeed, until its importance is grasped, we cannot properly understand the whole dis-tinctive style of human thought, speech, and action which is involved in the existence of rules and which constitutes the normative structure of society.

The following contrast again in terms of the 'internal' and 'external' aspect of rules may serve to mark what gives this distinc-tion its great importance for the understand-ing not only of law but of the structure of any society. When a social group has certain rules of conduct, this fact affords an oppor-tunity for many closely related yet different kinds of assertion; for it is possible to be con-cerned with the rules, either merely as an observer who does not himself accept them, or as a member of the group which accepts and uses them as guides to conduct. We may call these respectively the 'external' and the 'internal points of view'. Statements made from the external point of view may them-selves be of different kinds. For the observer may, without accepting the rules himself as-sert that the group accepts the rules, and thus may from outside refer to the way in which *they* are concerned with them from the internal point of view. But whatever the rules are, whether they are those of games, like chess or cricket, or moral or legal rules, we can if we choose occupy the position of an observer who does not even refer in this way to the internal point of view of the group. Such an observer is content merely to record the regularities of observ-able behaviour in which conformity with the rules partly consists and those further regu-larities, in the form of the hostile reaction, reproofs, or punishments, with which devia-tions from the rules are met. After a time the external observer may, on the basis of the reg-ularities observed, correlate deviation with hostile reaction, and be able to predict with a fair measure of success, and to assess the chances that a deviation from the group's normal behaviour will meet with hostile re-action or punishment. Such knowledge may not only reveal much about the group, but might enable him to live among them with-out unpleasant consequences which would attend one who attempted to do so without such knowledge.

If, however, the observer really keeps austerely to this extreme external point of view and does not give any account of the manner in which members of the group who accept the rules view their own regular be-haviour, his description of their life cannot be in terms of rules at all, and so not in the terms of the rule-dependent notions of obli-gation or duty. Instead, it will be in terms of observable regularities of conduct, predic-tions, probabilities, and signs. For such an observer, deviations by a member of the group from normal conduct will be a sign that hostile reaction is likely to follow, and nothing more. His view will be like the view of one who, having observed the working of a traffic signal in a busy street for some time, limits himself to saying that when the light turns red there is a high probability that the traffic will stop. He treats the light merely as a natural *sign that* people will behave in cer-tain ways, as clouds are a *sign that* rain will come. In so doing he will miss out a whole dimension of the social life of those whom he is watching, since for them the red light is not merely a sign that others will stop: they look upon it as a *signal for* them to stop, and so a reason for stopping in conformity to rules which make stopping when the light is red a standard of behaviour and an obli-gation. To mention this is to bring into the account the way in which the group regards its own behaviour. It is to refer to the internal aspect of rules seen from their internal point of view.

The external point of view may very nearly reproduce the way in which the rules function in the lives of certain members of the group, namely those who reject its rules and are only concerned with them when and because they judge that unpleasant consequences are likely to follow violation. Their point of view will need for its expression, 'I was obliged to do it', 'I am likely to suffer for it if . . .', 'You will probably suffer for it if . . .', 'They will do that to you if . . .'. But they will not need forms of expression like 'I had an obligation' or 'You have an obligation' for these are required only by those who see their own and other persons' conduct from the internal point of view. What the external point of view, which limits itself to the observable regularities of behaviour, cannot reproduce is the way in which the rules function as rules in the lives of those who normally are the majority of society. These are the officials, lawyers, or private persons who use them, in one situation after another, as guides to the conduct of social life, as the basis for claims, demands, admissions, criticism, or punishment, viz., in all the familiar transactions of life according to rules. For them the violation of a rule is not merely a basis for the prediction that a hostile reaction will follow but a *reason* for hostility.

At any given moment the life of any society which lives by rules, legal or not, is likely to consist in a tension between those who, on the one hand, accept and voluntarily cooperate in maintaining the rules, and so see their own and other persons' behaviour in terms of the rules, and those who, on the other hand, reject the rules and attend to them only from the external point of view as a sign of possible punishment. One of the difficulties facing any legal theory anxious to do justice to the complexity of the facts is to remember the presence of both these points of view and not to define one of them

out of existence. Perhaps all our criticisms of the predictive theory of obligation may be best summarized as the accusation that this is what it does to the internal aspect of obligatory rules.

## 3. THE ELEMENTS OF LAW

It is, of course, possible to imagine a society without a legislature, courts or officials of any kind. Indeed, there are many studies of primitive communities which not only claim that this possibility is realized but depict in detail the life of a society where the only means of social control is that general attitude of the group towards its own standard modes of behaviour in terms of which we have characterized rules of obligation. A social structure of this kind is often referred to as one of 'custom'; but we shall not use this term, because it often implies that the customary rules are very old and supported with less social pressure than other rules. To avoid these implications we shall refer to such a social structure as one of primary rules of obligation. If a society is to live by such primary rules alone, there are certain conditions which, granted a few of the most obvious truisms about human nature and the world we live in, must clearly be satisfied. The first of these conditions is that the rules must contain in some form restrictions on the free use of violence, theft, and deception to which human beings are tempted but which they must, in general, repress, if they are to coexist in close proximity to each other. Such rules are in fact always found in the primitive societies of which we have knowledge, together with a variety of others imposing on individuals various positive duties to perform services or make contributions to the common life. Secondly, though such a society may exhibit the tension, already described, between those who accept the rules and those who reject the rules except where fear of social pressure induces them to conform, it is plain that the latter cannot be more than a minority, if so loosely organized a society of persons, approximately equal in physical strength, is to endure: for otherwise those who reject the rules would have too little social pressure to fear. This too is confirmed by what we know of primitive communities where, though there are dissidents and malefactors, the majority live by the rules seen from the internal point of view.

More important for our present purpose is the following consideration. It is plain that only a small community closely knit by ties of kinship, common sentiment, and belief, and placed in a stable environment, could live successfully by such a régime of unofficial rules. In any other conditions such a simple form of social control must prove defective and will require supplementation in different ways. In the first place, the rules by which the group lives will not form a system, but will simply be a set of separate standards, without any identifying or common mark, except of course that they are the rules which a particular group of human beings accepts. They will in this respect resemble our own rules of etiquette. Hence if doubts arise as to what the rules are or as to the precise scope of some given rule, there will be no procedure for settling this doubt, either by reference to an authoritative text or to an official whose declarations on this point are authoritative. For, plainly, such a procedure and the acknowledgment of either authoritative text or persons involve the existence of rules of a type different from the rules of obligation or duty which *ex hypothesi* are all that the group has. This defect in the simple social structure of primary rules we may call its *uncertainty*.

A second defect is the static character of the rules. The only mode of change in the rules known to such a society will be the slow process of growth, whereby courses of conduct once thought optional become first habitual or usual, and then obligatory, and the converse process of decay, when deviations, once severely dealt with, are first tolerated and then pass unnoticed. There will be no means, in such a society, of deliberately adapting the rules to changing circumstances, either by eliminating old rules or introducing new ones: for, again, the possibility of doing this presupposes the existence of rules of a different type from the primary rules of obligation by which alone the society lives. In an extreme case the rules may be static in a more drastic sense. This, though never perhaps fully realized in any actual community, is worth considering because the remedy for it is something very characteristic of law. In this extreme case, not only would there be no way of deliberately changing the general rules, but the obligations which arise under the rules in particular cases could not be varied or modified by the deliberate choice of any individual. Each individual would simply have fixed obligations or duties to do or abstain from doing certain things. It might indeed very often be the case that others would benefit from the performance of these obligations; yet if there are only primary rules of obligation they would have no power to release those bound from performance or to transfer to others the benefits which would accrue from performance. For such operations of release or transfer create changes in the initial positions of individuals under the primary rules of obligation, and for these operations to be possible there must be rules of a sort different from the primary rules.

The third defect of this simple form of social life is the *inefficiency* of the diffuse social pressure by which the rules are maintained. Disputes as to whether an admitted rule has or has not been violated will always occur and will, in any but the smallest societies, continue interminably, if there is no agency specially empowered to ascertain finally, and authoritatively, the fact of violation. Lack of such final and authoritative determinations is to be distinguished from another weakness associated with it. This is the fact that punishments for violations of the rules, and other forms of social pressure involving physical effort or the use of force, are not administered by a special agency but are left to the individuals affected or to the group at large. It is obvious that the waste of time involved in the group's unorganized efforts to catch and punish offenders, and the smouldering vendettas which may result from self help in the absence of an official monopoly of 'sanctions', may be serious. The history of law does, however, strongly suggest that the lack of official agencies to determine authoritatively the fact of violation of the rules is a much more serious defect; for many societies have remedies for this defect long before the other.

The remedy for each of these three main defects in this simplest form of social structure consists in supplementing the *primary* rules of obligation with *secondary* rules which are rules of a different kind. The introduction of the remedy for each defect might, in itself, be considered a step from the pre-legal into the legal world; since each remedy brings with it many elements that permeate law: certainly all three remedies together are enough to convert the régime of primary rules into what is indisputably a legal system. We shall consider in turn each of these remedies and show why law may most illuminatingly be characterized as a union of primary rules of obligation with such secondary rules. Before we do this, however, the following general points should be noted. Though the remedies consist in the introduction of rules which are certainly different from each other, as well as from the primary rules of obligation which they supplement, they have important features in common and are connected in various ways. Thus they may all be said to be on a different level from the primary rules, for they are all *about* such rules; in the sense that while primary rules are concerned with the actions that individuals must or must not do, these secondary rules are all concerned with the primary rules themselves. They specify the ways in which the primary rules may be conclusively ascertained, introduced, eliminated, varied, and the fact of their violation conclusively determined.

The simplest form of remedy for the *uncertainty* of the régime of primary rules is the introduction of what we shall call a 'rule of recognition'. This will specify some feature or features possession of which by a suggested rule is taken as a conclusive affirmative indication that it is a rule of the group to be supported by the social pressure it exerts. The existence of such a rule of recognition may take any of a huge variety of forms, simple or complex. It may, as in the early law of many societies, be no more than that an authoritative list or text of the rules is to be found in a written document or carved on some public monument. No doubt as a matter of history this step from the pre-legal to the legal may be accomplished in distinguishable stages, of which the first is the mere reduction to writing of hitherto unwritten rules. This is not itself the crucial step, though it is a very important one: what is crucial is the acknowledgment of reference to the writing or inscription as *authoritative*, i.e. as the *proper* way of disposing of doubts as to the existence of the rule. Where there is such an acknowledgment there is a very simple form of secondary rule: a rule for conclusive identification of the primary rules of obligation.

In a developed legal system the rules of recognition are of course more complex; instead of identifying rules exclusively by reference to a text or list they do so by reference to some general characteristic possessed by the primary rules. This may be the fact of their having been enacted by a specific body, or their long customary practice, or their relation to judicial decisions. Moreover, where more than one of such general characteristics are treated as identifying criteria, provision may be made for their possible conflict by their arrangement in an order of superiority, as by the common subordination of custom or precedent to statute, the latter being a 'superior source' of law. Such complexity may make the rules of recognition in a modern legal system seem very different from the simple acceptance of an authoritative text: yet even in this simplest form, such a rule brings with it many elements distinctive of law. By providing an authoritative mark it introduces, although in embryonic form, the idea of a legal system: for the rules are now not just a discrete unconnected set but are, in a simple way, unified. Further, in the simple operation of identifying a given rule as possessing the required feature of being an item on an authoritative list of rules we have the germ of the idea of legal validity.

The remedy for the *static* quality of the régime of primary rules consists in the introduction of what we shall call 'rules of change'. The simplest form of such a rule is that which empowers an individual or body of persons to introduce new primary rules for the conduct of the life of the group, or of some class within it, and to eliminate old rules. As we have already argued in [an earlier discussion] it is in terms of such a rule, and not in terms of orders backed by threats, that the ideas of legislative enactment and repeal are to be understood. Such rules of change may be very simple or very complex: the powers conferred may be unrestricted or limited in various ways: and the rules may, besides specifying the persons who are to legislate, define in more or less rigid terms the procedure to be followed in legislation. Plainly, there will be a very close connection between the rules of change and the rules of recognition: for where the former exists the latter will necessarily incorporate a reference to legislation as an identifying feature of the rules, though it need not refer to all the details of procedure involved in legislation. Usually some official certificate or official copy will, under the rules of recognition, be taken as a sufficient proof of due enactment. Of course if there is a social structure so simple that the only 'source of law' is legislation, the rule of recognition will simply specify enactment as the unique identifying mark or criterion of validity of the rules. This will be the case for example in the imaginary kingdom of Rex I depicted in [an earlier discussion]: there the rule of recognition would simply be that whatever Rex I enacts is law.

We have already described in some detail the rules which confer on individuals power to vary their initial positions under the primary rules. Without such private power-conferring rules society would lack some of the chief amenities which law confers upon it. For the operations which these rules make possible are the making of wills, contracts, transfers of property, and many other voluntarily created structures of rights and duties which typify life under law, though of course an elementary form of power-conferring rule also underlies the moral institution of a promise. The kinship of these rules with the rules of change involved in the notion of legislation is clear, and as recent theory such as Kelsen's has shown, many of the features which puzzle us in the institutions of contract or property are clarified by thinking of the operations of making a contract or transferring property as the exercise of limited legislative powers by individuals.

The third supplement to the simple régime of primary rules, intended to remedy the *inefficiency* of its diffused social pressure, consists of secondary rules empowering individuals to make authoritative determinations of the question whether, on a particular occasion, a primary rule has been broken. The minimal form of adjudication consists in such determinations, and we shall call the secondary rules which confer the power to make them 'rules of adjudication'. Besides identifying the individuals who are to adjudicate, such rules will also define the procedure to be followed. Like the other secondary rules these are on a different level from the primary rules: though they may be reinforced by further rules imposing duties on judges to adjudicate, they do not impose duties but confer judicial powers and a special status on judicial declarations about the breach of obligations. Again these rules, like the other secondary rules, define a group of important legal concepts: in this case the concepts of judge or court, jurisdiction and judgment. Besides these resemblances to the other secondary rules, rules of adjudication have intimate connexions with them. Indeed, a system which has rules of adjudication is necessarily also committed to a rule of recognition of an elementary and imperfect sort. This is so because, if courts are empowered to make authoritative determinations of the fact that a rule has been broken, these cannot avoid being taken as authoritative determinations of what the rules are. So the rule which confers jurisdiction will also be a rule of recognition, identifying the primary rules through the judgments of the courts and these judgments will become a 'source' of law. It is true that this form of rule of recognition, inseparable from the minimum form of jurisdiction, will be very imperfect. Unlike an authoritative text or a statute book, judgments may not be couched in general terms and their use as authoritative guides to the rules depends on a somewhat shaky inference from particular decisions, and the reliability of this must fluctuate both with the skill of the interpreter and the consistency of the judges.

It need hardly be said that in few legal systems are judicial powers confined to authoritative determinations of the fact of violation of the primary rules. Most systems have, after some delay, seen the advantages of further centralization of social pressure; and have partially prohibited the use of physical punishments or violent self help by private individuals. Instead they have supplemented the primary rules of obligation by further secondary rules, specifying or at least limiting the penalties for violation, and have conferred upon judges, where they have ascertained the fact of violation, the exclusive power to direct the application of penalties by other officials. These secondary rules provide the centralized official 'sanctions' of the system.

If we stand back and consider the structure which has resulted from the combination of primary rules of obligation with the secondary rules of recognition, change and adjudication, it is plain that we have here not only the heart of a legal system, but a most powerful tool for the analysis of much that has puzzled both the jurist and the political theorist.

Not only are the specifically legal concepts with which the lawyer is professionally concerned, such as those of obligation and rights, validity and source of law, legislation and jurisdiction, and sanction, best elucidated in terms of this combination of elements. The concepts (which bestride both law and political theory) of the state, of authority, and of an official require a similar analysis if the obscurity which still lingers about them is to be dissipated. The reason why an analysis in these terms of primary and secondary rules has this explanatory power is not far to seek. Most of the obscurities and distortions surrounding legal and political concepts arise from the fact that these essentially involve reference to what we have called the internal point of view: the view of those who do not merely record and predict behaviour conforming to rules, but *use* the rules as standards for the appraisal of their own and others' behaviour. This requires more detailed attention in the analysis of legal and political concepts than it has usually received. Under the simple régime of primary rules the internal point of view is manifested in its simplest form, in the use of those rules as the basis of criticism, and as the justification of demands for conformity, social pressure, and punishment. Reference to this most elementary manifestation of the internal point of view is required for the analysis of the basic concepts of obligation and duty. With the addition to the system of secondary rules, the range of what is said and done from the internal point of view is much extended and diversified. With this extension comes a whole set of new concepts and they demand a reference to the internal point of view for their analysis. These include the notions of legislation, jurisdiction, validity and, generally, of legal powers, private and public. There is a constant pull towards an analysis of these in the terms of ordinary or 'scientific', fact-stating or predictive discourse. But this can only reproduce their external aspect: to do justice to their distinctive, internal aspect we need to see the different ways in which the law-making operations of the legislator, the adjudication of a court, the exercise of private or official powers, and other 'acts-in-the-law' are related to secondary rules.

In the next chapter we shall show how the ideas of the validity of law and sources of law, and the truths latent among the errors of the doctrines of sovereignty may be rephased and clarified in terms of rules of recognition. But we shall conclude this chapter with a warning: though the combination of primary and secondary rules merits, because it explains many aspects of law, the central place assigned to it, this cannot by itself illuminate every problem. The union of primary and secondary rules is at the centre of a legal system; but it is not the whole, and as we move away from the centre we shall have to accommodate, in ways indicated in later chapters, elements of a different character.

## THE FOUNDATIONS OF A LEGAL SYSTEM

### I. Rule of Recognition and Legal Validity

According to the theory criticized in [an earlier discussion] the foundations of a legal system consist of the situation in which the majority of a social group habitually obey the orders backed by threats of the sovereign person or persons, who themselves habitually obey no one. This social situation is, for this theory, both a necessary and a sufficient condition of the existence of law. We have already exhibited in some detail the incapacity of this theory to account for some of the salient features of a modern municipal legal system: yet nonetheless, as its hold over the minds of many thinkers suggests, it does

contain, though in a blurred and misleading form, certain truths about certain important aspects of law. These truths can, however, only be clearly presented, and their importance rightly assessed, in terms of the more complex social situation where a secondary rule of recognition is accepted and used for the identification of primary rules of obligation. It is this situation which deserves, if anything does, to be called the foundations of a legal system. In this chapter we shall discuss various elements of this situation which have received only partial or misleading expression in the theory of sovereignty and elsewhere.

Wherever such a rule of recognition is accepted, both private persons and officials are provided with authoritative criteria for identifying primary rules of obligation. The criteria so provided may, as we have seen, take any one or more of a variety of forms: these include reference to an authoritative text; to legislative enactment; to customary practice; to general declarations of specified persons, or to past judicial decisions in particular cases. In a very simple system like the world of Rex I depicted in [an earlier discussion], where only what he enacts is law and no legal limitations upon his legislative power are imposed by customary rule or constitutional document, the sole criterion for identifying the law will be a simple reference to the fact of enactment by Rex I. The existence of this simple form of rule of recognition will be manifest in the general practice, on the part of officials or private persons, of identifying the rules by this criterion. In a modern legal system where there are a variety of 'sources' of law, the rule of recognition is correspondingly more complex: the criteria for identifying the law are multiple and commonly include a written constitution, enactment by a legislature, and judicial precedents. In most cases, provision is made for possible conflict by ranking these criteria in an order of relative subordination and primacy. It is in this way that in our system 'common law' is subordinate to 'statute'.

It is important to distinguish this relative *subordination* of one criterion to another from *derivation*, since some spurious support for the view that all law is essentially or 'really' (even if only 'tacitly') the product of legislation, has been gained from confusion of these two ideas. In our own system, custom and precedent are subordinate to legislation since customary and common law rules may be deprived of their status as law by statute. Yet they owe their status of law, precarious as this may be, not to a 'tacit' exercise of legislative power but to the acceptance of a rule of recognition which accords them this independent though subordinate place. Again, as in the simple case, the existence of such a complex rule of recognition with this hierarchical ordering of distinct criteria is manifested in the general practice of identifying the rules by such criteria.

In the day-to-day life of a legal system its rule of recognition is very seldom expressly formulated as a rule; though occasionally, courts in England may announce in general terms the relative place of one criterion of law in relation to another, as when they assert the supremacy of Acts of Parliament over other sources or suggested sources of law. For the most part the rule of recognition is not stated, but its existence is *shown* in the way in which particular rules are identified, either by courts or other officials or private persons or their advisors. There is, of course, a difference in the use made by courts of the criteria provided by the rule and the use of them by others: for when courts reach a particular conclusion on the footing that a particular rule has been correctly identified as law, what they say has a special authoritative status conferred on it by other rules. In this respect, as in many others, the rule of recognition of a legal system is like the scoring rule of a game. In the course of the game the general rule defining the activities which constitute scoring (runs, goals, &c.) is seldom formulated; instead it is *used* by officials and players in identifying the particular phases which count towards winning. Here too, the declarations of officials (umpire or scorer) have a special authoritative status attributed to them by other rules. Further, in both cases there is the possibility of a conflict between these authoritative applications of the rule and the general understanding of what the rule plainly requires according to its terms. This, as we shall see later, is a complication which must be catered for in any account of what it is for a system of rules of this sort to exist.

The use of unstated rules of recognition, by courts and others, in identifying particular rules of the system is characteristic of the internal point of view. Those who use them in this way thereby manifest their own acceptance of them as guiding rules and with this attitude there goes a characteristic vocabulary different from the natural expressions of the external point of view. Perhaps the simplest of these is the expression, 'It is the law that . . .', which we may find on the lips not only of judges, but of ordinary men living under a legal system, when they identify a given rule of the system. This, like the expression 'Out' or 'Goal', is the language of one assessing a situation by reference to rules which he in common with others acknowledges as appropriate for this purpose. This attitude of shared acceptance of rules is to be contrasted with that of an observer who records *ab extra* the fact that a social group accepts such rules but does not himself accept them. The natural expression of this external point of view is not 'It is the law that . . .' but 'In England they recognize as law . . . whatever the Queen in Parliament enacts . . . .' The first of these forms of expression we shall call an *internal statement* because it manifests the internal point of view and is naturally used by one who, accepting the rule of recognition and without stating the fact that it is accepted, applies the rule in recognizing some particular rule of the system as valid. The second form of expression we shall call an *external statement* because it is the natural language of an external observer of the system who, without himself accepting its rule of recognition, states the fact that others accept it.

If this use of an accepted rule of recognition in making internal statements is understood and carefully distinguished from an external statement of fact that the rule is accepted, many obscurities concerning the notion of legal 'validity' disappear. For the word 'valid' is most frequently, though not always, used, in just such internal statements, applying to a particular rule of a legal system, an unstated but accepted rule of recognition. To say that a given rule is valid is to recognize it as passing all the tests provided by the rule of recognition and so as a rule of the system. We can indeed simply say that the statement that a particular rule is valid means that it satisfies all the criteria provided by the rule of recognition. This is incorrect only to the extent that it might obscure the internal character of such statements; for, like the cricketers' 'Out', these statements of validity normally apply to a particular case a rule of recognition accepted by the speaker and others, rather than expressly state that the rule is satisfied.

Some of the puzzles connected with the idea of legal validity are said to concern the relation between the validity and the 'efficacy' of law. If by 'efficacy' is meant that the fact that a rule of law which requires certain behaviour is obeyed more often than not, it is plain that there is no necessary connexion between the validity of any particular rule and *its* efficacy, unless the rule of recognition of the system includes among its criteria, as some do, the provision (sometimes referred to as a rule of obsolescence) that no rule is to count as a rule of the system if it has long ceased to be efficacious.

From the inefficacy of a particular rule, which may or may not count against its validity, we must distinguish a general disregard of the rules of the system. This may be so complete in character and so protracted that we should say, in the case of a new system, that it had never established itself as the legal system of a given group, or, in the case of a once-established system, that it had ceased to be the legal system of the group. In either case, the normal context or background for making any internal statement in terms of the rules of the system is absent. In such cases it would be generally *pointless* either to assess the rights and duties of particular persons by reference to the primary rules of a system or to assess the validity of any of its rules by reference to its rules of recognition. To insist on applying a system of rules which had either never actually been effective or had been discarded would, except in special circumstances mentioned below, be as futile as to assess the progress of a game by reference to a scoring rule which had never been accepted or had been discarded.

One who makes an internal statement concerning the validity of a particular rule of a system may be said to *presuppose* the truth of the external statement of fact that the system is generally efficacious. For the normal use of internal statements is in such a context of general efficacy. It would however be wrong to say that statements of validity 'mean' that the system is generally efficacious. For though it is normally pointless or idle to talk of the validity of a rule of a system which has never established itself or has been discarded, none the less it is not meaningless nor is it always pointless. One vivid way of teaching Roman Law is to speak *as if* the system were efficacious still and to discuss the validity of particular rules and solve problems in their terms; and one way of nursing hopes for the restoration of an old social order destroyed by revolution, and rejecting the new, is to cling to the criteria of legal validity of the old régime. This is implicitly done by the White Russian who still claims property under some rule of descent which was a valid rule of Tsarist Russia.

A grasp of the normal contextual connection between the internal statement that a given rule of a system is valid and the external statement of fact that the system is generally efficacious, will help us see in its proper perspective the common theory that to assert the validity of a rule is to predict that it will be enforced by courts or some other official action taken. In many ways this theory is similar to the predictive analysis of obligation which we considered and rejected in the last chapter. In both cases alike the motive for advancing this predictive theory is the conviction that only thus can metaphysical interpretations be avoided: that either a statement that a rule is valid must ascribe some mysterious property which cannot be detected by empirical means or it must be a prediction of future behaviour of officials. In both cases also the plausibility of the theory is due to the same important fact: that the truth of the external statement of fact, which an observer might record, that the system is generally efficacious and likely to continue so, is normally presupposed by anyone who accepts the rules and makes an internal statement of obligation or validity. The two are certainly very closely associated. Finally, in both cases alike the mistake of the theory is the same: it consists in neglecting the special character of the internal statement and treating it as an external statement about official action.

This mistake becomes immediately apparent when we consider how the judge's own statement that a particular rule is valid functions in judicial decision; for, though here too, in making such a statement, the judge presupposes but does not state the general efficacy of the system, he plainly is not concerned to predict his own or others' official action. His statement that a rule is valid is an internal statement recognizing that the rule satisfies the tests for identifying what is to count as law in his court, and constitutes not a prophecy of but part of the *reason* for his decision. There is indeed a more plausible case for saying that a statement that a rule is valid is a prediction when such a statement is made by a private person; for in the case of conflict between unofficial statements of validity or invalidity and that

of a court in deciding a case, there is often good sense in saying that the former must then be withdrawn. Yet even here, as we shall see when we come . . . to investigate the significance of such conflicts between official declarations and the plain requirements of the rules, it may be dogmatic to assume that it is withdrawn as a statement now shown to be *wrong*, because it has falsely *predicted* what a court would say. For there are more reasons for withdrawing statements than the fact that they are wrong, and also more ways of being wrong than this allows.

The rule of recognition providing the criteria by which the validity of other rules of the system is assessed is in an important sense, which we shall try to clarify, an *ultimate* rule: and where, as is usual, there are several criteria ranked in order of relative subordination and primacy one of them is *supreme*. These ideas of the ultimacy of the rule of recognition and the supremacy of one of its criteria merit some attention. It is important to disentangle them from the theory, which we have rejected, that somewhere in every legal system, even though it lurks behind legal forms, there must be a sovereign legislative power which is legally unlimited.

Of these two ideas, supreme criterion and ultimate rule, the first is the easiest to define. We may say that a criterion of legal validity or source of law is supreme if rules identified by reference to it are still recognized as rules of the system, even if they conflict with rules identified by reference to the other criteria, whereas rules identified by reference to the latter are not so recognized if they conflict with the rules identified by reference to the supreme criterion. A similar explanation in comparative terms can be given of the notions of 'superior' and 'subordinate' criteria which we have already used. It is plain that the notions of a superior and a supreme criterion merely refer to a *relative* place on a scale and do not import any notion of legally *unlimited* legislative power. Yet 'supreme' and 'unlimited' are easy to confuse—at least in legal theory. One reason for this is that in the simpler forms of legal system the ideas of ultimate rule of recognition, supreme criterion, and legally unlimited legislature seem to converge. For where there is a legislature subject to no constitutional limitations and competent by its enactment to deprive all other rules of law emanating from other sources of their status as law, it is part of the rule of recognition in such a system that enactment by that legislature is the supreme criterion of validity. This is, according to constitutional theory, the position in the United Kingdom. But even systems like that of the United States in which there is no such legally unlimited legislature may perfectly well contain an ultimate rule of recognition which provides a set of criteria of validity, one of which is supreme. This will be so, where the legislative competence of the ordinary legislature is limited by a constitution which contains no amending power, or places some clauses outside the scope of that power. Here there is no legally unlimited legislature, even in the widest interpretation of 'legislature'; but the system of course contains an ultimate rule of recognition and, in the clauses of its constitution, a supreme criterion of validity.

The sense in which the rule of recognition is the *ultimate* rule of a system is best understood if we pursue a very familiar chain of legal reasoning. If the question is raised whether some suggested rule is legally valid, we must, in order to answer the question, use a criterion of validity provided by some other rule. Is this purported by-law of the Oxfordshire County Council valid? Yes: because it was made in exercise of the powers conferred, and in accordance with the procedure specified, by a statutory order made by the Minister of Health. At this first stage the statutory order provides the criteria in terms of which the validity of the by-law is assessed. There may be no practical need to go farther; but there is a standing possibility of doing so. We may query the validity of the statutory order and assess its validity in

terms of the statute empowering the minister to make such orders. Finally when the validity of the statute has been queried and assessed by reference to the rule that what the Queen in Parliament enacts is law, we are brought to a stop in inquiries concerning validity: for we have reached a rule which, like the intermediate statutory order and statute, provides criteria for the assessment of the validity of other rules; but it is also unlike them in that there is no rule providing criteria for the assessment of its own legal validity.

There are, indeed, many questions which we can raise about this ultimate rule. We can ask whether it is the practice of courts, legislatures, officials, or private citizens in England actually to use this rule as an ultimate rule of recognition. Or has our process of legal reasoning been an idle game with the criteria of validity of a system now discarded? We can ask whether it is a satisfactory form of legal system which has such a rule at its root. Does it produce more good than evil? Are there prudential reasons for supporting it? Is there a moral obligation to do so? These are plainly very important questions; but, equally plainly, when we ask them about the rule of recognition, we are no longer attempting to answer the same kind of question about it as those which we answered about other rules with its aid. When we move from saying that a particular enactment is valid, because it satisfies the rule that what the Queen in Parliament enacts is law, to saying that in England this last rule is used by courts, officials, and private persons as the ultimate rule of recognition, we have moved from an internal statement of law asserting the validity of a rule of the system to an external statement of fact which an observer of the system might make even if he did not accept it. So too when we move from the statement that a particular enactment is valid, to the statement that the rule of recognition of the system is an excellent one and the system based on it is one worthy of support, we have moved from a statement of legal validity to a statement of value.

Some writers, who have emphasized the legal ultimacy of the rule of recognition, have expressed this by saying that, whereas the legal validity of other rules of the system can be demonstrated by reference to it, its own validity cannot be demonstrated but is 'assumed' or 'postulated' or is a 'hypothesis'. This may, however, be seriously misleading. Statements of legal validity made about particular rules in the day-to-day life of a legal system whether by judges, lawyers, or ordinary citizens do indeed carry with them certain presuppositions. They are internal statements of law expressing the point of view of those who accept the rule of recognition of the system and, as such, leave unstated much that could be stated in external statements of fact about the system. What is thus left unstated forms the normal background or context of statements of legal validity and is thus said to be 'presupposed' by them. But it is important to see precisely what these presupposed matters are, and not to obscure their character. They consist of two things. First, a person who seriously asserts the validity of some given rule of law, say a particular statute, himself makes use of a rule of recognition which he accepts as appropriate for identifying the law. Secondly, it is the case that this rule of recognition, in terms of which he assesses the validity of a particular statute, is not only accepted by him but is the rule of recognition actually accepted and employed in the general operation of the system. If the truth of this presupposition were doubted, it could be established by reference to actual practice: to the way in which courts identify what is to count as law, and to the general acceptance of or acquiescence in these identifications.

Neither of these two presuppositions are well described as 'assumptions' of a 'validity', which cannot be demonstrated. We only need the word 'validity', and commonly only use it, to answer questions which arise *within* a system of rules where the status of a rule as a member of the system depends on its satisfying certain criteria provided by the rule of recognition. No such question can arise as to the validity of the very rule of recognition which provides the criteria; it can neither be valid nor invalid but is simply accepted as appropriate for use in this way. To express this simple fact by saying darkly that its validity is 'assumed but cannot be demonstrated', is like saying that we assume, but can never demonstrate, that the standard metre bar in Paris which is the ultimate test of the correctness of all measurement in metres, is itself correct.

A more serious objection is that talk of the 'assumption' that the ultimate rule of recognition is valid conceals the essentially factual character of the second presupposition which lies behind the lawyers' statements of validity. No doubt the practice of judges, officials, and others, in which the actual existence of a rule of recognition consists, is a complex matter. As we shall see later, there are certainly situations in which questions as to the precise content and scope of this kind of rule, and even as to its existence, may not admit of a clear or determinate answer. None the less it is important to distinguish 'assuming the validity' from 'presupposing the existence' of such a rule; if only because failure to do this obscures what is meant by the assertion that such a rule *exists*.

In the simple system of primary rules of obligation sketched in the last chapter, the assertion that a given rule existed could only be an external statement of fact such as an observer who did not accept the rules might make and verify by ascertaining whether or not, as a matter of fact, a given mode of behaviour was generally accepted as a standard and was accompanied by those features which, as we have seen, distinguish a social rule from mere convergent habits. It is in this way also that we should now interpret and verify the assertion that in England a rule—though not a legal one—exists that we must bare the head on entering a church. If such rules as these are found to exist in the actual practice of a social group, there is no separate question of their validity to be discussed, though of course their value or desirability is open to question. Once their existence has been established as a fact we should only confuse matters by affirming or denying that they were valid or by saying that 'we assumed' but could not show their validity. Where, on the other hand, as in a mature legal system, we have a system of rules which includes a rule of recognition so that the status of a rule as a member of the system now depends on whether it satisfies certain criteria provided by the rule of recognition, this brings with it a new application of the word 'exist'. The statement that a rule exists may now no longer be what it was in the simple case of customary rules—an external statement of the *fact* that a certain mode of behaviour was generally accepted as a standard in practice. It may now be an internal statement applying an accepted but unstated rule of recognition and meaning (roughly) no more than 'valid given the systems criteria of validity'. In this respect, however, as in others a rule of recognition is unlike other rules of the system. The assertion that it exists can only be an external statement of fact. For whereas a subordinate rule of a system may be valid and in that sense 'exist' even if it is generally disregarded, the rule of recognition exists only as a complex, but normally concordant, practice of the courts, officials, and private persons in identifying the law by reference to certain criteria. Its existence is a matter of fact.

## QUESTIONS

1. Hart criticizes Austin's theory on grounds that it takes law to be a "gunman situation writ large." Is Hart's conception of law so very different, after all, from such a system of coercion? Explain the differences, and comment on their importance.

2. Suppose that, in the nation of Roritaka, a small clique, using methods of terror and coercion, rules the country with an iron hand. Suppose also that, among the clique themselves, fairly clear and well-defined rules are used in determining how decisions are taken, who has what office within the government, and so forth. In Hart's analysis of law, does Roritaka have a genuine legal system that imposes genuine legal obligations on the subjects outside of the ruling clique?

3. Explain how an ordinary citizen has what are, in effect, legislative powers.

4. How would you go about finding out what the full, complex rule of recognition is in a legal system like that of the United States?

5. Explain how a rule of adjudication will also be a rule of recognition.

## Ronald Dworkin
# THE MODEL OF RULES I*

## I. EMBARRASSING QUESTIONS

Lawyers lean heavily on the connected concepts of legal right and legal obligation. We say that someone has a legal right or duty, and we take that statement as a sound basis for making claims and demands, and for criticizing the acts of public officials. But our understanding of these concepts is remarkably fragile, and we fall into trouble when we try to say what legal rights and obligations are. We say glibly that whether someone has a legal obligation is determined by applying 'the law' to the particular facts of his case, but this is not a helpful answer, because we have the same difficulties with the concept of law.

We are used to summing up our troubles in the classic questions of jurisprudence: What is 'the law'? When two sides disagree, as often happens, about a proposition 'of law', what are they disagreeing about, and how shall we decide which side is right? Why do we call what 'the law' says a matter of legal 'obligation'? Is 'obligation' here just a term of art, meaning only what the law says? Or does legal obligation have something to do with moral obligation? Can we say that we have, in principle at least, the same reasons for meeting our legal obligations that we have for meeting our moral obligations?

These are not puzzles for the cupboard, to be taken down on rainy days for fun. They are sources of continuing embarrassment, and they nag at our attention. They embarrass us in dealing with particular problems that we must solve, one way or another. Suppose a novel right-of-privacy case comes to court, and there is no statute or precedent claimed by the plaintiff. What role in the court's decision should be played by the fact that most people in the community think that private individuals are 'morally' entitled to that particular privacy? Supposing the Supreme Court orders some prisoner freed because the police used procedures that the Court now says are constitutionally forbidden, although the Court's earlier decisions upheld these procedures. Must the Court, to be consistent, free all other prisoners previously convicted through these same procedures?[1] Conceptual puzzles about 'the law' and 'legal obligation' become acute when a court is confronted with a problem like this.

These eruptions signal a chronic disease. Day in and day out we send people to jail, or take money away from them, or make them do things they do not want to do, under coercion of force, and we justify all of this by speaking of such persons as having broken the law or having failed to meet their legal obligations or having interfered with other people's legal rights. Even in clear cases (a bank robber or a wilful breach of contract), when we are confident that someone had a legal obligation and broke it, we are not able to give a satisfactory account of what that means, or why that entitles the state to punish or coerce him. We may feel confident that what we are doing is proper, but until we can identify the principles we are following we cannot be sure that they are sufficient, or whether we are applying them consistently. In less clear cases, when the issue of whether an obligation has been broken is for some reason controversial, the pitch of these nagging questions rises, and our responsibility to find answers deepens.

---

[1] See *Linkletter v. Walker*, 381 U. S. 618 (1965).

Certain lawyers (we may call them 'nominalists') urge that we solve these problems by ignoring them. In their view the concepts of 'legal obligation' and 'the law' are myths, invented and sustained by lawyers for a dismal mix of conscious and subconscious motives. The puzzles we find in these concepts are merely symptoms that they are myths. They are unsolvable because unreal, and our concern with them is just one feature of our enslavement. We would do better to flush away the puzzles and the concepts altogether, and pursue our important social objectives without this excess baggage.

This is a tempting suggestion, but it has fatal drawbacks. Before we can decide that our concepts of law and of legal obligation are myths, we must decide what they are. We must be able to state, at least roughly, what it is we all believe that is wrong. But the nerve of our problem is that we have great difficulty in doing just that. Indeed, when we ask what law is and what legal obligations are, we are asking for a theory of how we use those concepts and of the conceptual commitments our use entails. We cannot conclude, before we have such a general theory, that our practices are stupid or superstitious.

Of course, the nominalists think they know how the rest of us use these concepts. They think that when we speak of 'the law' we mean a set of timeless rules stocked in some conceptual warehouse awaiting discovery by judges, and that when we speak of legal obligation we mean the invisible chains these mysterious rules somehow drape around us. The theory that there are such rules and chains they call 'mechanical jurisprudence', and they are right in ridiculing its practitioners. Their difficulty, however, lies in finding practitioners to ridicule. So far they have had little luck in caging and exhibiting mechanical jurisprudents (all specimens captured—even Blackstone and Joseph Beale—have had to be released after careful reading of their texts).

In any event, it is clear that most lawyers have nothing like this in mind when they speak of the law and of legal obligation. A superficial examination of our practices is enough to show this for we speak of laws changing and evolving, and of legal obligation sometimes being problematical. In these and other ways we show that we are not addicted to mechanical jurisprudence.

Nevertheless, we do use the concepts of law and legal obligation, and we do suppose that society's warrant to punish and coerce is written in that currency. It may be that when the details of this practice are laid bare, the concepts we do use will be shown to be as silly and as thick with illusion as those the nominalists invented. If so, then we shall have to find other ways to describe what we do, and either provide other justifications or change our practices. But until we have discovered this and made these adjustments, we cannot accept the nominalists' premature invitation to turn our backs on the problems our present concepts provide.

Of course the suggestion that we stop talking about 'the law' and 'legal obligation' is mostly bluff. These concepts are too deeply cemented into the structure of our political practices—they cannot be given up like cigarettes or hats. Some of the nominalists have half-admitted this and said that the myths they condemn should be thought of as Platonic myths and retained to seduce the masses into order. This is perhaps not so cynical a suggestion as it seems; perhaps it is a covert hedging of a dubious bet.

If we boil away the bluff, the nominalist attack reduces to an attack on mechanical jurisprudence. Through the lines of the attack, and in spite of the heroic calls for the death of law, the nominalists themselves have offered an analysis of how the terms 'law' and 'legal obligation' should be used which is not very different from that of more classical philosophers. Nominalists present their analysis as a model of how legal institutions (particularly courts) 'really operate'. But their model differs mainly in emphasis from the theory first made popular by the nineteenth century philosopher John Austin, and now accepted in one form or another by most working and academic lawyers who hold views on jurisprudence. I shall call this theory, with some historical looseness, 'legal positivism'. I want to examine the soundness of legal positivism, particularly in the powerful form that Professor H. L. A. Hart has given to it. I choose to focus on his position, not only because of its clarity and elegance, but because here, as almost everywhere else in legal philosophy, constructive thought must start with a consideration of his views.

## 2. POSITIVISM

Positivism has a few central and organizing propositions as its skeleton, and though not every philosopher who is called a positivist would subscribe to these in the way I present them, they do define the general position I want to examine. These key tenets may be stated as follows:

(a) The law of a community is a set of special rules used by the community directly or indirectly for the purpose of determining which behavior will be punished or coerced by the public power. These special rules can be identified and distinguished by specific criteria, by tests having to do not with their content but with their *pedigree* or the manner in which they were adopted or developed. These tests of pedigree can be used to distinguish valid legal rules from spurious legal rules (rules which lawyers and litigants wrongly argue are rules of law) and also from other sorts of social rules (generally lumped together as 'moral rules') that the community follows but does not enforce through public power.

(b) The set of these valid legal rules is exhaustive of 'the law', so that if someone's case is not clearly covered by such a rule (because there is none that seems appropriate, or those that seem appropriate are vague, or for some other reason) then that case cannot be decided by 'applying the law.' It must be decided by some official, like a judge, 'exercising his discretion,' which means reaching beyond the law for some other sort of standard to guide him in manufacturing a fresh legal rule or supplementing an old one.

(c) To say that someone has a 'legal obligation' is to say that his case falls under a valid legal rule that requires him to do or to forbear from doing something. (To say he has a legal right, or has a legal power of some sort, or a legal privilege or immunity, is to assert, in a shorthand way, that others have actual or hypothetical legal obligations to act or not to act in certain ways touching him.) In the absence of such a valid legal rule there is no legal obligation; it follows that when the judge decides an issue by exercising his discretion, he is not enforcing a legal right as to that issue.

This is only the skeleton of positivism. The flesh is arranged differently by different positivists, and some even tinker with the bones. Different versions differ chiefly in their description of the fundamental test of pedigree a rule must meet to count as a rule of law.

Austin, for example, framed his version of the fundamental test as a series of interlocking definitions and distinctions.[1] He defined having an obligation as lying under a rule, a rule as a general command, and a command as an expression of desire that others behave in a particular way, backed by the power and will to enforce that expression in the event of disobedience. He distinguished classes of rules (legal, moral or

[1] J. Austin, *The Province of Jurisprudence Determined* (1832).

religious) according to which person or group is the author of the general command the rule represents. In each political community, he thought, one will find a sovereign—a person or a determinate group whom the rest obey habitually, but who is not in the habit of obeying anyone else. The legal rules of a community are the general commands its sovereign has deployed. Austin's definition of legal obligation followed from this definition of law. One has a legal obligation, he thought, if one is among the addressees of some general order of the sovereign, and is in danger of suffering a sanction unless he obeys that order.

Of course, the sovereign cannot provide for all contingencies through any scheme of orders, and some of his orders will inevitably be vague or have furry edges. Therefore (according to Austin) the sovereign grants those who enforce the law (judges) discretion to make fresh orders when novel or troublesome cases are presented. The judges then make new rules or adapt old rules, and the sovereign either overturns their creations or tacitly confirms them by failing to do so.

Austin's model is quite beautiful in its simplicity. It asserts the first tenet of positivism, that the law is a set of rules specially selected to govern public order, and offers a simple factual test—what has the sovereign commanded?—as the sole criterion for identifying those special rules. In time, however, those who studied and tried to apply Austin's model found it too simple. Many objections were raised, among which were two that seemed fundamental. First, Austin's key assumption that in each community a determinate group or institution can be found, which is in ultimate control of all other groups, seemed not to hold in a complex society. Political control in a modern nation is pluralistic and shifting, a matter of more or less, of compromise and cooperation and alliance, so that it is often impossible to say that any person or group has that

dramatic control necessary to qualify as an Austinian sovereign. One wants to say, in the United States for example, that the 'people' are sovereign. But this means almost nothing, and in itself provides no test for determining what the 'people' have commanded, or distinguishing their legal from their social or moral commands.

Second, critics began to realize that Austin's analysis fails entirely to account for, even to recognize, certain striking facts about the attitudes we take toward 'the law.' We make an important distinction between law and even the general orders of a gangster. We feel that the law's strictures—and its sanctions—are different in that they are obligatory in a way that the outlaw's commands are not. Austin's analysis has no place for any such distinction, because it defines an obligation as subjection to the threat of force, and so founds the authority of law entirely on the sovereign's ability and will to harm those who disobey. Perhaps the distinction we make is illusory—perhaps our feelings of some special authority attaching to the law is based on religious hangover or another sort of mass self-deception. But Austin does not demonstrate this, and we are entitled to insist that an analysis of our concept of law either acknowledge and explain our attitudes, or show why they are mistaken.

H. L. A. Hart's version of positivism is more complex than Austin's, in two ways. First, he recognizes, as Austin did not, that rules are of different logical kinds. (Hart distinguishes two kinds, which he calls 'primary' and 'secondary' rules). Second, he rejects Austin's theory that a rule is a kind of command, and substitutes a more elaborate general analysis of what rules are. We must pause over each of these points, and then note how they merge in Hart's concept of law.

Hart's distinction between primary and secondary rules is of great importance.[1] Primary rules are those that grant rights or impose obligations upon members of the

[1] See H. L. A. Hart, *The Concept of Law*, 89–96 (1961).

community. The rules of the criminal law that forbid us to rob, murder or drive too fast are good examples of primary rules. Secondary rules are those that stipulate how, and by whom, such primary rules may be formed, recognized, modified or extinguished. The rules that stipulate how Congress is composed, and how it enacts legislation, are examples of secondary rules. Rules about forming contracts and executing wills are also secondary rules because they stipulate how very particular rules governing particular legal obligations (*i.e.*, the terms of a contract or the provisions of a will) come into existence and are changed.

His general analysis of rules is also of great importance.[2] Austin had said that every rule is a general command, and that a person is obligated under a rule if he is liable to be hurt should he disobey it. Hart points out that this obliterates the distinction between being *obliged* to do something and being *obligated* to do it. If one is bound by a rule he is obligated, not merely obliged, to do what it provides, and therefore being bound by a rule must be different from being subject to an injury if one disobeys an order. A rule differs from an order, among other ways, by being *normative*, by setting a standard of behavior that has a call on its subject beyond the threat that may enforce it. A rule can never be binding just because some person with physical power wants it to be so. He must have *authority* to issue the rule or it is no rule, and such authority can only come from another rule which is already binding on those to whom he speaks. That is the difference between a valid law and the orders of a gunman.

So Hart offers a general theory of rules that does not make their authority depend upon the physical power of their authors. If we examine the way different rules come into being, he tells us, and attend to the

distinction between primary and secondary rules, we see that there are two possible sources of a rule's authority:[1]

(a) A rule may become binding upon a group of people because that group through its practices *accepts* the rule as a standard for its conduct. It is not enough that the group simply conforms to a pattern of behavior: even though most Englishmen may go to the movies on Saturday evening, they have not accepted a rule requiring that they do so. A practice constitutes the acceptance of a rule only when those who follow the practice regard the rule as binding, and recognize the rule as a reason or justification for their own behavior and as a reason for criticizing the behavior of others who do not obey it.

(b) A rule may also become binding in quite a different way, namely by being enacted in conformity with some *secondary* rule that stipulates that rules so enacted shall be binding. If the constitution of a club stipulates, for example, that by-laws may be adopted by a majority of the members, then particular by-laws so voted are binding upon all the members, not because of any practice of acceptance of these particular by-laws, but because the constitution says so. We use the concept of *validity* in this connection: rules binding because they have been created in a manner stipulated by some secondary rule are called 'valid' rules.

Thus we can record Hart's fundamental distinction this way: a rule may be binding (a) because it is accepted or (b) because it is valid.

Hart's concept of law is a construction of these various distinctions.[2] Primitive communities have only primary rules, and these are binding entirely because of practices of acceptance. Such communities cannot be

---

[2]*Id.* at 79–88.

[1]*Id.* at 97–107.

[2]*Id. passim*, particularly ch. 6.

said to have 'law,' because there is no way to distinguish a set of legal rules from amongst other social rules, as the first tenet of positivism requires. But when a particular community has developed a fundamental secondary rule that stipulates how legal rules are to be identified, the idea of a distinct set of legal rules, and thus of law, is born.

Hart calls such a fundamental secondary rule a 'rule of recognition'. The rule of recognition of a given community may be relatively simple ('What the king enacts is law') or it may be very complex (the United States Constitution, with all its difficulties of interpretation, may be considered a single rule of recognition). The demonstration that a particular rule is valid may therefore require tracing a complicated chain of validity back from that particular rule ultimately to the fundamental rule. Thus a parking ordinance of the city of New Haven is valid because it is adopted by a city council, pursuant to the procedures and within the competence specified by the municipal law adopted by the state of Connecticut, in conformity with the procedures and within the competence specified by the constitution of the state of Connecticut, which was in turn adopted consistently with the requirements of the United States Constitution.

Of course, a rule of recognition cannot itself be valid, because by hypothesis it is ultimate, and so cannot meet tests stipulated by a more fundamental rule. The rule of recognition is the sole rule in a legal system whose binding force depends upon its acceptance. If we wish to know what rule of recognition a particular community has adopted or follows, we must observe how its citizens, and particularly its officials, behave. We must observe what ultimate arguments they accept as showing the validity of a particular rule, and what ultimate arguments they use to criticize other officials or institutions. We can apply no mechanical test, but there is no danger of our confusing the rule of recognition of a community with its rules of morality. The rule of recognition is identified by the fact that its province is the operation of the governmental apparatus of legislatures, courts, agencies, policemen, and the rest.

In this way Hart rescues the fundamentals of positivism from Austin's mistakes. Hart agrees with Austin that valid rules of law may be created through the acts of officials and public institutions. But Austin thought that the authority of these institutions lay only in their monopoly of power. Hart finds their authority in the background of constitutional standards against which they act, constitutional standards that have been accepted, in the form of a fundamental rule of recognition, by the community which they govern. This background legitimates the decisions of government and gives them the cast and call of obligation that the naked commands of Austin's sovereign lacked. Hart's theory differs from Austin's also, in recognizing that different communities use different ultimate tests of law, and that some allow other means of creating law than the deliberate act of a legislative institution. Hart mentions 'long customary practice' and 'the relation [of a rule] to judicial decisions' as other criteria that are often used, though generally along with and subordinate to the test of legislation.

So Hart's version of positivism is more complex than Austin's, and his test for valid rules of law is more sophisticated. In one respect, however, the two models are very similar. Hart, like Austin, recognizes that legal rules have furry edges (he speaks of them as having 'open texture') and, again like Austin, he accounts for troublesome cases by saying that judges have and exercise discretion to decide these cases by fresh legislation.[1] (I shall later try to show why one who thinks of law as a special set of rules is almost inevitably drawn to account for difficult cases in terms of someone's exercise of discretion.)

[1]*Id.* ch. 7.

## 3. RULES, PRINCIPLES, AND POLICIES

I want to make a general attack on positivism, and I shall use H. L. A. Hart's version as a target, when a particular target is needed. My strategy will be organized around the fact that when lawyers reason or dispute about legal rights and obligations, particularly in those hard cases when our problems with these concepts seem most acute, they make use of standards that do not function as rules, but operate differently as principles, policies, and other sorts of standards. Positivism, I shall argue, is a model of and for a system of rules, and its central notion of a single fundamental test for law forces us to miss the important roles of these standards that are not rules.

I just spoke of 'principles, policies, and other sorts of standards'. Most often I shall use the term 'principle' generically, to refer to the whole set of these standards other than rules; occasionally, however, I shall be more precise, and distinguish between principles and policies. Although nothing in the present argument will turn on the distinction, I should state how I draw it. I call a 'policy' that kind of standard that sets out a goal to be reached, generally an improvement in some economic, political, or social feature of the community (though some goals are negative, in that they stipulate that some present feature is to be protected from adverse change.). I call a 'principle' a standard that is to be observed, not because it will advance or secure an economic, political, or social situation deemed desirable, but because it is a requirement of justice or fairness or some other dimension of morality. Thus the standard that automobile accidents are to be decreased is a policy, and the standard that no man may

profit by his own wrong a principle. The distinction can be collapsed by construing a principle as stating a social goal (*i.e.*, the goal of a society in which no man profits by his own wrong), or by construing a policy as stating a principle (*i.e.*, the principle that the goal the policy embraces is a worthy one), or by adopting the utilitarian thesis that principles of justice are disguised statements of goals (securing the greatest happiness of the greatest number). In some contexts the distinction has uses which are lost if it is thus collapsed.[1]

My immediate purpose, however, is to distinguish principles in the generic sense from rules, and I shall start by collecting some examples of the former. The examples I offer are chosen haphazardly; almost any case in a law school casebook would provide examples that would serve as well. In 1889 a New York court, in the famous case of *Riggs v. Palmer*,[2] had to decide whether an heir named in the will of his grandfather could inherit under that will, even though he had murdered his grandfather to do so. The court began its reasoning with this admission: 'It is quite true that statutes regulating the making, proof and effect of wills, and the devolution of property, if literally construed, and if their force and effect can in no way and under no circumstances be controlled or modified, give this property to the murderer.'[3] But the court continued to note that 'all laws as well as all contracts may be controlled in their operation and effect by general, fundamental maxims of the common law. No one shall be permitted to profit by his own fraud, or to take advantage of his own wrong, or to found any claim upon his own iniquity, or to acquire property by his own crime.'[4] The murderer did not receive his inheritance.

[1]See Chapter 4. See also Dworkin, 'Wasserstrom: The Judicial Decision', 75 *Ethics* 47 (1964), reprinted as 'Does Law Have a Function?', 74 *Yale Law Journal* 640 (1965).

[2]115 N. Y. 506, 22 N. E. 188 (1889).

[3]*Id.* at 509, 22 N. E. at 189.

[4]*Id.* at 511, 22 N. E. at 190.

In 1960, a New Jersey court was faced, in *Henningsen v. Bloomfield Motors, Inc.*[5] with the important question of whether (or how much) an automobile manufacturer may limit his liability in case the automobile is defective. Henningsen had bought a car, and signed a contract which said that the manufacturer's liability for defects was limited to 'making good' defective parts—'this warranty being expressly in lieu of all other warranties, obligations or liabilities.' Henningsen argued that, at least in the circumstances of his case, the manufacturer ought not to be protected by this limitation, and ought to be liable for the medical and other expenses of persons injured in a crash. He was not able to point to any statute, or to any established rule of law, that prevented the manufacturer from standing on the contract. The court nevertheless agreed with Henningsen. At various points in the court's argument the following appeals to standards are made: (a) '[W]e must keep in mind the general principle that, in the absence of fraud, one who does not choose to read a contract before signing it cannot later relieve himself of its burdens.'[1] (b) 'In applying that principle, the basic tenet of freedom of competent parties to contract is a factor of importance.'[2] (c) 'Freedom of contract is not such an immutable doctrine as to admit of no qualification in the area in which we are concerned.'[3] (d) 'In a society such as ours, where the automobile is a common and necessary adjunct of daily life, and where its use is so fraught with danger to the driver, passengers and the public, the manufacturer is under a special obligation in connection with the construction, promotion and sale of his cars. Consequently, the courts must examine purchase agreements closely to see if consumer and public interests are treated fairly.'[4] (e) '"[I]s there any principle which is more familiar or more firmly embedded in the history of Anglo-American law than the basic doctrine that the courts will not permit themselves to be used as instruments of inequity and injustice?"'[5] (f) '"More specifically the courts generally refuse to lend themselves to the enforcement of a 'bargain' in which one party has unjustly taken advantage of the economic necessities of other. . . ."'[6]

The standards set out in these quotations are not the sort we think of as legal rules. They seem very different from propositions like 'The maximum legal speed on the turnpike is sixty miles an hour' or 'A will is invalid unless signed by three witnesses'. They are different because they are legal principles rather than legal rules.

The difference between legal principles and legal rules is a logical distinction. Both sets of standards point to particular decisions about legal obligation in particular circumstances, but they differ in the character of the direction they give. Rules are applicable in an all-or-nothing fashion. If the facts a rule stipulates are given, then either the rule is valid, in which case the answer it supplies must be accepted, or it is not, in which case it contributes nothing to the decision.

This all-or-nothing is seen most plainly if we look at the way rules operate, not in law, but in some enterprise they dominate—a game, for example. In baseball a rule provides that if the batter has had three strikes, he is out. An official cannot consistently acknowledge that this is an accurate statement of a baseball rule, and decide that a batter who has had three strikes is not out.

---

[5] 32 N. J. 358, 161 A.2d 69 (1960).

[1] *Id.* at 386, 161 A.2d at 84.

[2] *Id.*

[3] *Id.* at 388, 161 A.2d at 86.

[4] *Id.* at 387, 161 A.2d at 85.

[5] *Id.* at 389, 161 A.2d at 86 (quoting Frankfurter, J., in *United States v. Bethlehem Steel*, 315 U. S. 289, 326 [1942]).

[6] *Id.*

Of course, a rule may have exceptions (the batter who has taken three strikes is not out if the catcher drops the third strike). However, an accurate statement of the rule would take this exception into account, and any that did not would be incomplete. If the list of exceptions is very large, it would be too clumsy to repeat them each time the rule is cited; there is, however, no reason in theory why they could not all be added on, and the more that are, the more accurate is the statement of the rule.

If we take baseball rules as a model, we find that rules of law, like the rule that a will is invalid unless signed by three witnesses, fit the model well. If the requirement of three witnesses is a valid rule, then it cannot be that a will has been signed by only two witnesses and is valid. The rule might have exceptions, but if it does then it is inaccurate and incomplete to state the rule so simply, without enumerating the exceptions. In theory, at least, the exceptions could all be listed, and the more of them that are, the more complete is the statement of the rule.

But this is not the way the sample principles in the quotations operate. Even those which look most like rules do not set out legal consequences that follow automatically when the conditions provided are met. We say that our law respects the principle that no man may profit from his own wrong, but we do not mean that the law never permits a man to profit from wrongs he commits. In fact, people often profit, perfectly legally, from their legal wrongs. The most notorious case is adverse possession—if I trespass on your land long enough, some day I will gain a right to cross your land whenever I please. There are many less dramatic examples. If a man leaves one job, breaking a contract, to take a much higher paying job, he may have to pay damages to his first employer, but he is usually entitled to keep his new salary. If a man jumps bail and crosses state lines to make a brilliant investment in another state, he may be sent back to jail, but he will keep his profits.

We do not treat these—and countless other counter-instances that can easily be imagined—as showing that the principle about profiting from one's wrongs is not a principle of our legal system, or that it is incomplete and needs qualifying exceptions. We do not treat counter-instances as exceptions (at least not exceptions in the way in which a catcher's dropping the third strike is an exception) because we could not hope to capture these counter-instances simply by a more extended statement of the principle. They are not, even in theory, subject to enumeration, because we would have to include not only these cases (like adverse possession) in which some institution has already provided that profit can be gained through a wrong, but also those numberless imaginary cases in which we know in advance that the principle would not hold. Listing some of these might sharpen our sense of the principle's weight (I shall mention that dimension in a moment), but it would not make for a more accurate or complete statement of the principle.

A principle like 'No man may profit from his own wrong' does not even purport to set out conditions that make its application necessary. Rather, it states a reason that argues in one direction, but does not necessitate a particular decision. If a man has or is about to receive something, as a direct result of something illegal he did to get it, then that is a reason which the law will take into account in deciding whether he should keep it. There may be other principles or policies arguing in the other direction—a policy of securing title, for example, or a principle limiting punishment to what the legislature has stipulated. If so, our principle may not prevail, but that does not mean that it is not a principle of our legal system, because in the next case, when these contravening considerations are absent or less weighty, the principle may be decisive. All that is meant, when we say that a particular principle is a principle of our law, is that the principle is one which officials must take into account, if it is relevant, as a consideration inclining in one direction or another.

The logical distinction between rules and principles appears more clearly when we consider principles that do not even look like rules. Consider the proposition, set out under '(d)' in the excerpts from the *Henningsen* opinion, that 'the manufacturer is under a special obligation in connection with the construction, promotion and sale of his cars'. This does not even purport to define the specific duties such a special obligation entails, or to tell us what rights automobile consumers acquire as a result. It merely states—and this is an essential link in the *Henningsen* argument—that automobile manufacturers must be held to higher standards than other manufacturers, and are less entitled to rely on the competing principle of freedom of contract. It does not mean that they may never rely on that principle, or that courts may rewrite automobile purchase contracts at will; it means only that if a particular clause seems unfair or burdensome, courts have less reason to enforce the clause than if it were for the purchase of neckties. The 'special obligation' counts in favor, but does not in itself necessitate, a decision refusing to enforce the terms of an automobile purchase contract.

This first difference between rules and principles entails another. Principles have a dimension that rules do not—the dimension of weight or importance. When principles intersect (the policy of protecting automobile consumers intersecting with principles of freedom of contract, for example), one who must resolve the conflict has to take into account the relative weight of each. This cannot be, of course, an exact measurement, and the judgment that a particular principle or policy is more important than another will often be a controversial one. Nevertheless, it is an integral part of the concept of a principle that it has this dimension, that it makes sense to ask how important or how weighty it is.

Rules do not have this dimension. We can speak of rules as being *functionally* important or unimportant (the baseball rule that three strikes are out is more important

than the rule that runners may advance on a balk, because the game would be much more changed with the first rule altered than the second). In this sense, one legal rule may be more important than another because it has a greater or more important role in regulating behavior. But we cannot say that one rule is more important than another within the system of rules, so that when two rules conflict one supersedes the other by virtue of its greater weight.

If two rules conflict, one of them cannot be a valid rule. The decision as to which is valid, and which must be abandoned or recast, must be made appealing to considerations beyond the rules themselves. A legal system might regulate such conflicts by other rules, which prefer the rule enacted by the higher authority, or the rule enacted later, or the more specific rule, or something of that sort. A legal system may also prefer the rule supported by the more important principles. (Our own legal system uses both of these techniques.)

It is not always clear from the form of a standard whether it is a rule or a principle. 'A will is invalid unless signed by three witnesses' is not very different in form from 'A man may not profit from his own wrong', but one who knows something of American law knows that he must take the first as stating a rule and the second as stating a principle. In many cases the distinction is difficult to make—it may not have been settled how the standard should operate, and this issue may itself be a focus of controversy. The first amendment to the United States Constitution contains the provision that Congress shall not abridge freedom of speech. Is this a rule, so that if a particular law does abridge freedom of speech, it follows that it is unconstitutional? Those who claim that the first amendment is 'an absolute' say that it must be taken in this way, that is, as a rule. Or does it merely state a principle, so that when an abridgement of speech is discovered, it is unconstitutional unless the context presents some other policy or principle which in the circumstances is weighty enough to permit the abridgement? That is the position of those who argue for what is called the 'clear and present danger' test or some other form of 'balancing'.

Sometimes a rule and a principle can play much the same role, and the difference between them is almost a matter of form alone. The first section of the Sherman Act states that every contract in restraint of trade shall be void. The Supreme Court had to make the decision whether this provision should be treated as a rule in its own terms (striking down every contract 'which restrains trade', which almost any contract does) or as a principle, providing a reason for striking down a contract in the absence of effective contrary policies. The Court construed the provision as a rule, but treated that rule as containing the word 'unreasonable', and as prohibiting only 'unreasonable' restraints of trade.[1] This allowed the provision to function logically as a rule (whenever a court finds that the restraint is 'unreasonable' it is bound to hold the contract invalid) and substantially as a principle (a court must take into account a variety of other principles and policies in determining whether a particular restraint in particular economic circumstances is 'unreasonable').

Words like 'reasonable', 'negligent', 'unjust', and 'significant' often perform just this function. Each of these terms makes the application of the rule which contains it depend to some extent upon principles or policies lying beyond the rule, and in this way makes that rule itself more like a principle. But they do not quite turn the rule into a principle, because even the least confining of these terms restricts the kind of other principles and policies on which the rule depends. If we are bound by a rule that says that 'unreasonable' contracts are void, or that grossly 'unfair' contracts will not be enforced, much more judgment is required than if the quoted terms were omitted. But suppose a case in which some consideration of policy

or principle suggests that a contract should be enforced even though its restraint is not reasonable, or even though it is grossly unfair. Enforcing these contracts would be forbidden by our rules, and thus permitted only if these rules were abandoned or modified. If we were dealing, however, not with a rule but with a policy against enforcing unreasonable contracts, or a principle that unfair contracts ought not to be enforced, the contracts could be enforced without alteration of the law.

## 4. PRINCIPLES AND THE CONCEPT OF LAW

Once we identify legal principles as separate sorts of standards, different from legal rules, we are suddenly aware of them all round us. Law teachers teach them, lawbooks cite them, legal historians celebrate them. But they seem most energetically at work, carrying most weight, in difficult lawsuits like *Riggs* and *Henningsen*. In cases like these, principles play an essential part in arguments supporting judgments about particular legal rights and obligations. After the case is decided, we may say that the case stands for a particular rule (e.g., the rule that one who murders is not eligible to take under the will of his victim). But the rule does not exist before the case is decided; the court cites principles as its justification for adopting and applying a new rule. In *Riggs*, the court cited the principle that no man may profit from his own wrong as a background standard against which to read the statute of wills and in this way justified a new interpretation of that statute. In *Henningsen*, the court cited a variety of intersecting principles and policies as authority for a new rule respecting manufacturers' liability for automobile defects.

An analysis of the concept of legal obligation must therefore account for the important role of principles in reaching particular

[1] *Standard Oil v. United States*, 221 U.S. 1, 60 (1911); *United States v. American Tobacco Co.*, 221 U.S. 106, 180 (1911).

decisions of law. There are two very different tacks we might take:

(a) We might treat legal principles the way we treat legal rules and say that some principles are binding as law and must be taken into account by judges and lawyers who make decisions of legal obligation. If we took this tack, we should say that in the United States, at least, the 'law' includes principles as well as rules.

(b) We might, on the other hand, deny that principles can be binding the way some rules are. We would say, instead, that in cases like *Riggs* or *Henningsen* the judge reaches beyond the rules that he is bound to apply (reaches, that is, beyond the 'law') for extra-legal principles he is free to follow if he wishes.

One might think that there is not much difference between these two lines of attack, that it is only a verbal question of how one wants to use the word 'law'. But that is a mistake, because the choice between these two accounts has the greatest consequences for an analysis of legal obligation. It is a choice between two *concepts* of a legal principle, a choice we can clarify by comparing it to a choice we might make between two concepts of a legal rule. We sometimes say of someone that he 'makes it a rule' to do something, when we mean that he has chosen to follow a certain practice. We might say that someone has made it a rule, for example, to run a mile before breakfast because he wants to be healthy and believes in a regimen. We do not mean, when we say this, that he is *bound* by the rule that he must run a mile before breakfast, or even that he regards it as binding upon him. Accepting a rule as binding is something different from making it a rule to do something. If we use Hart's example again, there is a difference between saying that Englishmen make it a

rule to see a movie once a week, and saying that the English have a rule that one must see a movie once a week. The second implies that if an Englishman does not follow the rule, he is subject to criticism or censure, but the first does not. The first does not exclude the possibility of a *sort* of criticism—we can say that one who does not see movies is neglecting his education—but we do not suggest that he is doing something wrong *just* in not following the rule.[1]

If we think of the judges of a community as a group, we could describe the rules of law they follow in these two different ways. We could say, for instance, that in a certain state the judges make it a rule not to enforce wills unless there are three witnesses. This would not imply that the rare judge who enforces such a will is doing anything wrong just for that reason. On the other hand we can say that in that state a rule of law requires judges not to enforce such wills; this does imply that a judge who enforces them is doing something wrong. Hart, Austin and other positivists, of course, would insist on this latter account of legal rules; they would not at all be satisfied with the 'make it a rule' account. It is not a verbal question of which account is right. It is a question of which describes the social situation more accurately. Other important issues turn on which description we accept. If judges simply 'make it a rule' not to enforce certain contracts, for example, then we cannot say, before the decision, that anyone is 'entitled' to that result, and that proposition cannot enter into any justification we might offer for the decision.

The two lines of attack on principles parallel these two accounts of rules. The first tack treats principles as binding upon judges, so that they are wrong not to apply the principles when they are pertinent. The second tack treats principles as summaries of what most judges 'make it a principle' to do when forced to go beyond the standards that bind them. The choice between these approaches

---

[1] The distinction is in substance the same as that made by Rawls, 'Two Concepts of Rules', 64 *Philosophical Review* 3 (1955).

will affect, perhaps even determine, the answer we can give to the question whether the judge in a hard case like *Riggs* or *Henningsen* is attempting to enforce pre-existing legal rights and obligations. If we take the first tack, we are still free to argue that because such judges are applying binding legal standards they are enforcing legal rights and obligations. But if we take the second, we are out of court on that issue, and we must acknowledge that the murderer's family in *Riggs* and the manufacturer in *Henningsen* were deprived of their property by an act of judicial discretion applied *ex post facto*. This may not shock many readers—the notion of judicial discretion has percolated through the legal community—but it does illustrate one of the most nettlesome of the puzzles that drive philosophers to worry about legal obligation. If taking property away in cases like these cannot be justified by appealing to an established obligation, another justification must be found, and nothing satisfactory has yet been supplied.

In my skeleton diagram of positivism, previously set out, I listed the doctrine of judicial discretion as the second tenet. Positivists hold that when a case is not covered by a clear rule, a judge must exercise his discretion to decide that case by what amounts to a fresh piece of legislation. There may be an important connection between this doctrine and the question of which of the two approaches to legal principles we must take. We shall therefore want to ask whether the doctrine is correct, and whether it implies the second approach, as it seems on its face to do. En route to these issues, however, we shall have to polish our understanding of the concept of discretion. I shall try to show how certain confusions about that concept and in particular a failure to discriminate different senses in which it is used, account for the popularity of the doctrine of discretion. I shall argue that in the sense in which the doctrine does have a bearing on our treatment of principles, it is entirely unsupported by the arguments the positivists use to defend it.

## 5. DISCRETION

The concept of discretion was lifted by the positivists from ordinary language, and to understand it we must put it back in *habitat* for a moment. What does it mean, in ordinary life, to say that someone 'has discretion?' The first thing to notice is that the concept is out of place in all but very special contexts. For example, you would not say that I either do or do not have discretion to choose a house for my family. It is not true that I have 'no discretion' in making that choice, and yet it could be almost equally misleading to say that I do have discretion. The concept of discretion is at home in only one sort of context: when someone is in general charged with making decisions subject to standards set by a particular authority. It makes sense to speak of the discretion of a sergeant who is subject to orders of superiors, or the discretion of a sports official or contest judge who is governed by a rule book or the terms of the contest. Discretion, like the hole in a doughnut, does not exist except as an area left open by a surrounding belt of restriction. It is therefore a relative concept. It always makes sense to ask, 'Discretion under which standards?' or 'Discretion as to which authority?' Generally the context will make the answer to this plain, but in some cases the official may have discretion from one stand-point though not from another.

Like almost all terms, the precise meaning of 'discretion' is affected by features of the context. The term is always colored by the background of understood information against which it is used. Although the shadings are many, it will be helpful for us to recognize some gross distinctions.

Sometimes we use 'discretion' in a weak sense, simply to say that for some reason the standards an official must apply cannot be applied mechanically but demand the use of judgment. We use this weak sense when the context does not already make that clear, when the background our audience assumes does not contain that piece of information. Thus we might say, 'The sergeant's orders left him a great deal of discretion', to those who do not know what the sergeant's orders were or who do not know something that made those orders vague or hard to carry out. It would make perfect sense to add, by way of amplification, that the lieutenant had ordered the sergeant to take his five most experienced men on patrol but that it was hard to determine which were the most experienced.

Sometimes we use the term in a different weak sense, to say only that some official has final authority to make a decision and cannot be reviewed and reversed by any other official. We speak this way when the official is part of a hierarchy of officials structured so that some have higher authority but in which the patterns of authority are different for different classes of decision. Thus we might say that in baseball certain decisions, like the decision whether the ball or the runner reached second base first, are left to the discretion of the second base umpire, if we mean that on this issue the head umpire has no power to substitute his own judgment if he disagrees.

I call both of these senses weak to distinguish them from a stronger sense. We use 'discretion' sometimes not merely to say that an official must use judgment in applying the standards set him by authority, or that no one will review that exercise of judgment, but to say that on some issue he is simply not bound by standards set by the authority in question. In this sense we say that a sergeant has discretion who has been told to pick any five men for patrol he chooses or that a judge in a dog show has discretion to judge airedales before boxers if the rules do not stipulate an order of events. We use this sense not to comment on the vagueness or difficulty of the standards, or on who has the final word in applying them, but on their range and the

decisions they purport to control. If the sergeant is told to take the five most experienced men, he does not have discretion in this strong sense because that order purports to govern his decision. The boxing referee who must decide which fighter has been the more aggressive does not have discretion, in the strong sense, for the same reason.[1]

If anyone said that the sergeant or the referee had discretion in these cases, we should have to understand him, if the context permitted, as using the term in one of the weak senses. Suppose, for example, the lieutenant ordered the sergeant to select the five men he deemed most experienced, and then added that the sergeant had discretion to choose them. Or the rules provided that the referee should award the round to the more aggressive fighter, with discretion in selecting him. We should have to understand these statements in the second weak sense, as speaking to the question of review of the decision. The first weak sense—that the decisions take judgment—would be otiose, and the third, strong sense is excluded by the statements themselves.

We must avoid one tempting confusion. The strong sense of discretion is not tantamount to license, and does not exclude criticism. Almost any situation in which a person acts (including those in which there is no question of decision under special authority, and so no question of discretion) makes relevant certain standards of rationality, fairness, and effectiveness. We criticize each other's acts in terms of these standards, and there is no reason not to do so when the acts are within the center rather than beyond the perimeter of the doughnut of special authority. So we can say that the sergeant who was given discretion (in the strong sense) to pick a patrol did so stupidly or maliciously or carelessly, or that

[1] I have not spoken of that jurisprudential favorite, 'limited' discretion, because that concept presents no special difficulties if we remember the relativity of discretion. Suppose the sergeant is told to choose from 'amongst' experienced men, or to 'take experience into account'. We might say either that he has (limited) discretion in picking his patrol, or (full) discretion to either pick amongst experienced men or decide what else to take into account.

the judge who had discretion in the order of viewing dogs made a mistake because he took boxers first although there were only three airedales and many more boxers. An official's discretion means not that he is free to decide without recourse to standards of sense and fairness, but only that his decision is not controlled by a standard furnished by the particular authority we have in mind when we raise the question of discretion. Of course this latter sort of freedom is important; that is why we have the strong sense of discretion. Someone who has discretion in this third sense can be criticized, but not for being disobedient, as in the case of the soldier. He can be said to have made a mistake, but not to have deprived a participant of a decision to which he was entitled, as in the case of a sports official or contest judge.

We may now return, with these observations in hand, to the positivists' doctrine of judicial discretion. That doctrine argues that if a case is not controlled by an established rule, the judge must decide it by exercising discretion. We want to examine this doctrine and to test its bearing on our treatment of principles; but first we must ask in which sense of discretion we are to understand it.

Some nominalists argue that judges always have discretion, even when a clear rule is in point, because judges are ultimately the final arbiters of the law. This doctrine of discretion uses the second weak sense of that term, because it makes the point that no higher authority reviews the decisions of the highest court. It therefore has no bearing on the issue of how we account for principles, any more than it bears on how we account for rules.

The positivists do not mean their doctrine this way, because they say that a judge has no discretion when a clear and established rule is available. If we attend to the positivists' arguments for the doctrine we may suspect that they use discretion in the first weak sense to mean only that judges must sometimes exercise judgment in applying legal standards. Their arguments call attention to the fact that some rules of law are vague (Professor Hart, for example, says that all rules of law have 'open texture'), and that some cases arise (like *Henningsen*) in which no established rule seems to be suitable. They emphasize that judges must sometimes agonize over points of law, and that two equally trained and intelligent judges will often disagree.

These points are easily made; they are commonplace to anyone who has any familiarity with law. Indeed, that is the difficulty with assuming that positivists mean to use 'discretion' in this weak sense. The proposition that when no clear rule is available discretion in the sense of judgment must be used is a tautology. It has no bearing, moreover, on the problem of how to account for legal principles. It is perfectly consistent to say that the judge in *Riggs*, for example, had to use judgment, and that he was bound to follow the principle that no man may profit from his own wrong. The positivists speak as if their doctrine of judicial discretion is an insight rather than a tautology, and as if it does have a bearing on the treatment of principles. Hart, for example, says that when the judge's discretion is in play, we can no longer speak of his being bound by standards, but must speak rather of what standards he 'characteristically uses'.[1] Hart thinks that when judges have discretion, the principles they cite must be treated on our second approach, as what courts 'make it a principle' to do.

It therefore seems that positivists, at least sometimes, take their doctrine in the third, strong sense of discretion. In that sense it does bear on the treatment of principles; indeed, in that sense it is nothing less than a restatement of our second approach. It is the same thing to say that when a judge runs out of rules he has discretion, in the sense that he is not bound by any standards from the

[1] H. L. A. Hart, *The Concept of Law*, 144 (1961).

authority of law, as to say that the legal standards judges cite other than rules are not binding on them.

So we must examine the doctrine of judicial discretion in the strong sense. (I shall henceforth use the term 'discretion' in that sense.) Do the principles judges cited in cases like *Riggs* or *Henningsen* control their decisions, as the sergeant's orders to take the most experienced men or the referee's duty to choose the more aggressive fighter control the decisions of these officials? What arguments could a positivist supply to show that they do not?

(1) A positivist might argue that principles cannot be binding or obligatory. That would be a mistake. It is always a question, of course, whether any particular principle is *in fact* binding upon some legal official. But there is nothing in the logical character of a principle that renders it incapable of binding him. Suppose that the judge in *Henningsen* had failed to take any account of the principle that automobile manufacturers have a special obligation to their consumers, or the principle that the courts seek to protect those whose bargaining position is weak, but had simply decided for the defendant by citing the principle of freedom of contract without more. His critics would not have been content to point out that he had not taken account of considerations that other judges have been attending to for some time. Most would have said that it was his duty to take the measure of these principles and that the plaintiff was entitled to have him do so. We mean no more, when we say that a *rule* is binding upon a judge, than that he must follow it if it applies, and that if he does not he will on that account have made a mistake.

It will not do to say that in a case like *Henningsen* the court is only 'morally' obligated to take particular principles into account, or that it is 'institutionally' obligated, or obligated as a matter of judicial 'craft', or something of that sort. The question will still remain why this type of obligation (whatever we call it) is different from the obligation that rules impose upon judges, and why it entitles us to say that principles and policies are not part of the law but are merely extra-legal standards 'courts characteristically use'.

(2) A positivist might argue that even though some principles are binding, in the sense that the judge must take them into account, they cannot determine a particular result. This is a harder argument to assess because it is not clear what it means for a standard to 'determine' a result. Perhaps it means that the standard *dictates* the result whenever it applies so that nothing else counts. If so, then it is certainly true that the individual principles do not determine results, but that is only another way of saying that principles are not rules. Only rules dictate results, come what may. When a contrary result has been reached, the rule has been abandoned or changed. Principles do not work that way; they incline a decision one way, though not conclusively, and they survive intact when they do not prevail. This seems no reason for concluding that judges who must reckon with principles have discretion because a set of principles *can* dictate a result. If a judge believes that principles he is bound to recognize point in one direction and that principles pointing in the other direction, if any, are not of equal weight, then he must decide accordingly, just as he must follow what he believes to be a binding rule. He may, of course, be wrong in his assessment of the principles, but he may also be wrong in his judgment that the rule is binding. The sergeant and the referee, we might add, are often in the same boat. No one factor dictates which soldiers are the most experienced or which fighter the more aggressive. These officials must make judgments of the relative weights of these various factors; they do not on that account have discretion.

(3) A positivist might argue that principles cannot count as law because their authority, and even more so their weight, are

congenitally *controversial*. It is true that generally we cannot *demonstrate* the authority or weight of a particular principle as we can sometimes demonstrate the validity of a rule by locating it in an act of Congress or in the opinion of an authoritative court. Instead, we make a case for a principle, and for its weight, by appealing to an amalgam of practice and other principles in which the implications of legislative and judicial history figure along with appeals to community practices and understandings. There is no litmus paper for testing the soundness of such a case—it is a matter of judgment, and reasonable men may disagree. But again this does not distinguish the judge from other officials who do not have discretion. The sergeant has no litmus paper for experience, the referee none for aggressiveness. Neither of these has discretion, because he is bound to reach an understanding, controversial or not, of what his orders or the rules require, and to act on that understanding. That is the judge's duty as well.

Of course, if the positivists are right in another of their doctrines—the theory that in each legal system there is an ultimate *test* for binding law like Professor Hart's rule of recognition—it follows that principles are not binding law. But the incompatibility of principles with the positivists' theory can hardly be taken as an argument that principles must be treated any particular way. That begs the question; we are interested in the status of principles because we want to evaluate the positivists' model. The positivist cannot defend his theory of a rule of recognition by fiat; if principles are not amenable to a test he must show some other reason why they cannot count as law. Since principles seem to play a role in arguments about legal obligation (witness, again, *Riggs* and *Henningsen*), a model that provides for that role has some initial advantage over one

that excludes it, and the latter cannot properly be inveighed in its own support.

These are the most obvious of the arguments a positivist might use for the doctrine of discretion in the strong sense, and for the second approach to principles. I shall mention one strong counter-argument against that doctrine and in favor of the first approach. Unless at least some principles are acknowledged to be binding upon judges, requiring them as a set to reach particular decisions, then no rules, or very few rules, can be said to be binding upon them either.

In most American jurisdictions, and now in England also, the higher courts not infrequently reject established rules. Common law rules—those developed by earlier court decisions—are sometimes overruled directly, and sometimes radically altered by further development. Statutory rules are subjected to interpretation and reinterpretation, sometimes even when the result is not to carry out what is called the 'legislative intent.'[1] If courts had discretion to change established rules, then these rules would of course not be binding upon them, and so would not be law on the positivists' model. The positivist must therefore argue that there are standards, themselves binding upon judges, that determine when a judge may overrule or alter an established rule, and when he may not.

When, then, is a judge permitted to change an existing rule of law? Principles figure in the answer in two ways. First, it is necessary, though not sufficient, that the judge find that the change would advance some principle, which principle thus justifies the change. In *Riggs* the change (a new interpretation of the statute of wills) was justified by the principle that no man should profit from his own wrong; in *Henningsen* the previously recognized rules about automobile manufacturers' liability were altered on the basis of the principles I quoted from the opinion of the court.

---

[1]See Wellington and Albert, 'Statutory Interpretation and the Political Process: A Comment on Sinclair v. Atkinson', 72 *Yale L. J.* 1547 (1963).

But not any principle will do to justify a change, or no rule would ever be safe. There must be some principles that count and others that do not, and there must be some principles that count for more than others. It could not depend on the judge's own preferences amongst a sea of respectable extra-legal standards, any one in principle eligible, because if that were the case we could not say that any rules were binding. We could always imagine a judge whose preferences amongst extra-legal standards were such as would justify a shift or radical reinterpretation of even the most entrenched rule.

Second, any judge who proposes to change existing doctrine must take account of some important standards that argue against departures from established doctrine, and these standards are also for the most part principles. They include the doctrine of 'legislative supremacy', a set of principles that require the courts to pay a qualified deference to the acts of the legislature. They also include the doctrine of precedent, another set of principles reflecting the equities and efficiencies of consistency. The doctrines of legislative supremacy and precedent incline toward the *status quo*, each within its sphere, but they do not command it. Judges are not free, however, to pick and choose amongst the principles and policies that make up these doctrines—if they were, again, no rule could be said to be binding.

Consider, therefore, what someone implies who says that a particular rule is binding. He may imply that the rule is affirmatively supported by principles the court is not free to disregard, and which are collectively more weighty than other principles that argue for a change. If not, he implies that any change would be condemned by a combination of conservative principles of legislative supremacy and precedent that the court is not free to ignore. Very often, he will imply both, for the conservative principles, being principles and not rules, are usually not powerful enough to save a common law rule or an aging statute that is entirely unsupported by substantive principles the court is bound to respect. Either of these implications, of course, treats a body of principles and policies as law in the sense that rules are; it treats them as standards binding upon the officials of a community, controlling their decisions of legal right and obligation.

We are left with this issue. If the positivists' theory of judicial discretion is either trivial because it uses 'discretion' in a weak sense, or unsupported because the various arguments we can supply in its defense fall short, why have so many careful and intelligent lawyers embraced it? We can have no confidence in our treatment of that theory unless we can deal with that question. It is not enough to note (although perhaps it contributes to the explanation) that 'discretion' has different senses that may be confused. We do not confuse these senses when we are not thinking about law.

Part of the explanation, at least, lies in a lawyer's natural tendency to associate laws and rules, and to think of 'the law' as a collection or system of rules. Roscoe Pound, who diagnosed this tendency long ago, thought that English speaking lawyers were tricked into it by the fact that English uses the same word, changing only the article, for 'a law' and 'the law'.[1] (Other languages, on the contrary, use two words: 'loi' and 'droit', for example, and 'Gesetz' and 'Recht'.) This may have had its effect, with the English speaking positivists, because the expression 'a law' certainly does suggest a rule. But the principal reason for associating law with rules runs deeper, and lies, I think, in the fact that legal education has for a long time consisted of teaching and examining those established rules that form the cutting edge of law.

In any event, if a lawyer thinks of law as a system of rules, and yet recognizes, as he must, that judges change old rules and introduce new ones, he will come naturally to the theory of judicial discretion in the strong sense.

---

[1]R. Pound, *An Introduction to the Philosophy of Law* 56 (rev. ed. 1954).

In those other systems of rules with which he has experience (like games), the rules are the only special authority that govern official decisions, so that if an umpire could change a rule, he would have discretion as to the subject matter of that rule. Any principles umpires might mention when changing the rules would represent only their 'characteristic' preferences. Positivists treat law like baseball revised in this way.

There is another, more subtle consequence of this initial assumption that law is a system of rules. When the positivists do attend to principles and policies, they treat them as rules *manquées*. They assume that *if* they are standards of law they must be rules, and so they read them as standards that are trying to be rules. When a positivist hears someone argue that legal principles are part of the law, he understands this to be an argument for what he calls the 'higher law' theory, that these principles are the rules of a law about the law.[1] He refutes this theory by pointing out that these 'rules' are sometimes followed and sometimes not, that for every 'rule' like 'no man shall profit from his own wrong' there is another competing 'rule' like 'the law favors security of title', and that there is no way to test the validity of 'rules' like these. He concludes that these principles and policies are not valid rules of a law above the law, which is true, because they are not rules at all. He also concludes that they are extra-legal standards which each judge selects according to his own lights in the exercise of his discretion, which is false. It is as if a zoologist had proved that fish are not mammals, and then concluded that they are really only plants.

## 6. THE RULE OF RECOGNITION

This discussion was provoked by our two competing accounts of legal principles. We have been exploring the second account, which the positivists seem to adopt through their doctrine of judicial discretion, and we

have discovered grave difficulties. It is time to return to the fork in the road. What if we adopt the first approach? What would the consequences of this be for the skeletal structure of positivism? Of course we should have to drop the second tenet, the doctrine of judicial discretion (or, in the alternative, to make plain that the doctrine is to be read merely to say that judges must often exercise judgment). Would we also have to abandon or modify the first tenet, the proposition that law is distinguished by tests of the sort that can be set out in a master rule like Professor Hart's rule of recognition? If principles of the *Riggs* and *Henningsen* sort are to count as law, and we are nevertheless to preserve the notion of a master rule for law, then we must be able to deploy some test that all (and only) the principles that do count as law meet. Let us begin with the test Hart suggests for identifying valid *rules* of law, to see whether these can be made to work for principles as well.

Most rules of law, according to Hart, are valid because some competent institution enacted them. Some were created by a legislature, in the form of statutory enactments. Others were created by judges who formulated them to decide particular cases, and thus established them as precedents for the future. But this test of pedigree will not work for the *Riggs* and *Henningsen* principles. The origin of these as legal principles lies not in a particular decision of some legislature or court, but in a sense of appropriateness developed in the profession and the public over time. Their continued power depends upon this sense of appropriateness being sustained. If it no longer seemed unfair to allow people to profit by their wrongs, or fair to place special burdens upon oligopolies that manufacture potentially dangerous machines, these principles would no longer play much of a role in new cases, even if they had never been overruled or repealed. (Indeed, it hardly makes sense to speak of principles like these as being

[1] See, e.g., Dickinson. 'The Law Behind Law (pts. 1 & 2)', 29, *Columbia Law Review* 112, 254 (1929).

'overruled' or 'repealed'. When they decline they are eroded, not torpedoed.)

True, if we were challenged to back up our claim that some principle is a principle of law, we would mention any prior cases in which that principle was cited, or figured in the argument. We would also mention any statute that seemed to exemplify that principle (even better if the principle was cited in the preamble of the statute, or in the committee reports or other legislative documents that accompanied it). Unless we could find some such institutional support, we would probably fail to make out our case, and the more support we found, the more weight we could claim for the principle.

Yet we could not devise any formula for testing how much and what kind of institutional support is necessary to make a principle a legal principle, still less to fix its weight at a particular order of magnitude. We argue for a particular principle by grappling with a whole set of shifting, developing and interacting standards (themselves principles rather than rules) about institutional responsibility, statutory interpretation, the persuasive force of various sorts of precedent, the relation of all these to contemporary moral practices, and hosts of other such standards. We could not bolt all of these together into a single 'rule', even a complex one, and if we could the result would bear little relation to Hart's picture of a rule of recognition, which is the picture of a fairly stable master rule specifying 'some feature or features possession of which by a suggested rule is taken as a conclusive affirmative indication that it is a rule. . .'[1]

Moreover, the techniques we apply in arguing for another principle do not stand (as Hart's rule of recognition is designed to) on an entirely different level from the principles they support. Hart's sharp distinction between acceptance and validity does not hold. If we are arguing for the principle that a man should not profit from his own wrong, we could cite the acts of courts and legislatures that exemplify it, but this speaks as much to the principle's acceptance as its validity. (It seems odd to speak of a principle as being valid at all, perhaps because validity is an all-or-nothing concept, appropriate for rules, but inconsistent with a principle's dimension of weight.) If we are asked (as we might well be) to defend the particular doctrine of precedent, or the particular technique of statutory interpretation, that we used in this argument, we should certainly cite the practice of others in using that doctrine or technique. But we should also cite other general principles that we believe support that practice, and this introduces a note of validity into the chord of acceptance. We might argue, for example, that the use we make of earlier cases and statutes is supported by a particular analysis of the point of the practice of legislation or the doctrine of precedent, or by the principles of democratic theory, or by a particular position on the proper division of authority between national and local institutions, or something else of that sort. Nor is this path of support a one-way street leading to some ultimate principle resting on acceptance alone. Our principles of legislation, precedent, democracy, or federalism might be challenged too; and if they were we should argue for them, not only in terms of practice, but in terms of each other and in terms of the implications of trends of judicial and legislative decisions, even though this last would involve appealing to those same doctrines of interpretation we justified through the principles we are now trying to support. At this level of abstraction, in other words, principles rather hang together than link together.

So even though principles draw support from the official acts of legal institutions, they do not have a simple or direct enough connection with these acts to frame that

[1]H. L. A. Hart, *The Concept of Law* 92 (1961).

connection in terms of criteria specified by some ultimate master rule of recognition. Is there any other route by which principles might be brought under such a rule?

Hart does say that a master rule might designate as law not only rules enacted by particular legal institutions, but rules established by *custom* as well. He has in mind a problem that bothered other positivists, including Austin. Many of our most ancient legal rules were never explicitly created by a legislature or a court. When they made their first appearance in legal opinions and texts, they were treated as already being part of the law because they represented the customary practice of the community, or some specialized part of it, like the business community. (The examples ordinarily given are rules of mercantile practice, like the rules governing what rights arise under a standard form of commercial paper.)[1] Since Austin thought that all law was the command of a determinate sovereign, he held that these customary practices were not law until the courts (as agents of the sovereign) recognized them, and that the courts were indulging in a fiction in pretending otherwise. But that seemed arbitrary. If everyone thought custom might in itself be law, the fact that Austin's theory said otherwise was not persuasive.

Hart reversed Austin on this point. The master rule, he says, might stipulate that some custom counts as law even before the courts recognize it. But he does not face the difficulty this raises for his general theory because he does not attempt to set out the criteria a master rule might use for the purpose. It cannot use, as its only criterion, the provision that the community regard the practice as *morally* binding, for this would not distinguish legal customary rules from moral customary rules, and of course not all of the community's long-standing customary moral obligations are enforced at law. If, on the other hand, the test is whether the community regards the customary practice as *legally* binding, the whole point of the master rule is undercut, at least for this class of legal rules. The master rule, says Hart, marks the transformation from a primitive society to one with law, because it provides a test for determining social rules of law other than by measuring their acceptance. But if the master rule says merely that whatever other rules the community accepts as legally binding are legally binding, then it provides no such test at all, beyond the test we should use were there no master rule. The master rule becomes (for these cases) a non-rule of recognition; we might as well say that every primitive society has a secondary rule of recognition, namely the rule that whatever is accepted as binding is binding. Hart himself, in discussing international law, ridicules the idea that such a rule could be a rule of recognition, by describing the proposed rule as 'an empty repetition of the mere fact that the society concerned . . . observes certain standards of conduct as obligatory rules'.[2]

Hart's treatment of custom amounts, indeed, to a confession that there are at least some rules of law that are not binding because they are valid under standards laid

---

[1] See Note, 'Custom and Trade Usage: Its Application to Commercial Dealings and the Common Law', 55 *Columbia Law Review* 1192 (1955), and materials cited therein at 1193 n. 1. As that note makes plain, the actual practices of courts in recognizing trade customs follow the pattern of applying a set of general principles and policies rather than a test that could be captured as part of a rule of recognition.

[2] H. L. Hart, *The Concept of Law* 230 (1961). A master rule might specify some particular feature of a custom that is independent of jthe community's attitude; it might provide, for example, that all customs of very great age, or all customs having to do with negotiable instruments count as law. I can think of no such features that in fact distinguish the customs that have been recognized as law in England or America, however. Some customs that are not legally enforceable are older than some that are, some practices relating to commercial paper are enforced and others not, and so forth. In any event, even if a distinguishing feature were found tht identified all rules of law established by custom, it would remain unlikely that such a feature could be found for principles which vary widely in their subject matter and pedigree and some of which are of very recent origin.

down by a master rule but are binding—like the master rule—because they are accepted as binding by the community. This chips at the neat pyramidal architecture we admired in Hart's theory: we can no longer say that only the master rule is binding because of its acceptance, all other rules being valid under its terms.

This is perhaps only a chip, because the customary rules Hart has in mind are no longer a very significant part of the law. But it does suggest that Hart would be reluctant to widen the damage by bringing under the head of 'custom' all those crucial principles and policies we have been discussing. If he were to call these part of the law and yet admit that the only test of their force lies in the degree to which they are accepted as law by the community or some part thereof, he would very sharply reduce that area of the law over which his master rule held any dominion. It is not just that all the principles and policies would escape its sway, though that would be bad enough. Once these principles and policies are accepted as law, and thus as standards judges must follow in determining legal obligations, it would follow that *rules* like those announced for the first time in *Riggs* and *Henningsen* owe their force at least in part to the authority of principles and policies, and so not entirely to the master rule of recognition.

So we cannot adapt Hart's version of positivism by modifying his rule of recognition to embrace principles. No tests of pedigree, relating principles to acts of legislation, can be formulated, nor can his concept of customary law, itself an exception to the first tenet of positivism, be made to serve without abandoning that tenet altogether. One more possibility must be considered, however. If no rule of recognition can provide a test for identifying principles, why not say that principles are ultimate, and *form* the rule of recognition of our law? The answer to the general question 'What is valid law in an American jurisdiction?' would then require us to state all the principles (as well

as ultimate constitutional rules) in force in that jurisdiction at the time, together with appropriate assignments of weight. A positivist might then regard the complete set of these standards as the rule of recognition of the jurisdiction. This solution has the attraction of paradox, but of course it is an unconditional surrender. If we simply designate our rule of recognition by the phrase 'the complete set of principles in force', we achieve only the tautology that law is law. If, instead, we tried actually to list all the principles in force we would fail. They are controversial, their weight is all important, they are numberless, and they shift and change so fast that the start of our list would be obsolete before we reached the middle. Even if we succeeded we would not have a key for law because there would be nothing left for our key to unlock.

I conclude that if we treat principles as law we must reject the positivists' first tenet, that the law of a community is distinguished from other social standards by some test in the form of a master rule. We have already decided that we must then abandon the second tenet—the doctrine of judicial discretion—or clarify it into triviality. What of the third tenet, the positivists' theory of legal obligation?

This theory holds that a legal obligation exists when (and only when) an established rule of law imposes such an obligation. It follows from this that in a hard case—when no such established rule can be found—there is no legal obligation until the judge creates a new rule for the future. The judge may apply that new rule to the parties in the case, but this is *ex post facto* legislation, not the enforcement of an existing obligation.

The positivists' doctrine of discretion (in the strong sense) required this view of legal obligation, because if a judge has discretion there can be no legal right or obligation—no entitlement—that he must enforce. Once we abandon that doctrine, however, and treat principles as law, we raise the possibility that a legal obligation might be imposed by a constellation of principles as well as by an established rule. We might want to say that a legal obligation exists whenever the case supporting such an obligation, in terms of binding legal principles of different sorts, is stronger than the case against it.

Of course, many questions would have to be answered before we could accept that view of legal obligation. If there is no rule of recognition, no test for law in that sense, how do we decide which principles are to count, and how much, in making such a case? How do we decide whether one case is better than another? If legal obligation rests on an undemonstrable judgment of that sort, how can it provide a justification for a judicial decision that one party had a legal obligation? Does this view of obligation square with the way lawyers, judges and laymen speak, and is it consistent with our attitudes about moral obligation? Does this analysis help us to deal with the classical jurisprudential puzzles about the nature of law?

These questions must be faced, but even the questions promise more than positivism provides. Positivism, on its own thesis, stops short of just those puzzling, hard cases that send us to look for theories of law. When we read these cases, the positivist remits us to a doctrine of discretion that leads nowhere and tells nothing. His picture of law as a system of rules has exercised a tenacious hold on our imagination, perhaps through its very simplicity. If we shake ourselves loose from this model of rules, we may be able to build a model truer to the complexity and sophistication of our own practices.

## QUESTIONS

1. Providing an example of each, explain carefully Dworkin's distinctions (a) between principles in the specific sense and policies, and (b) between principles in the generic sense and rules.

2. Reflect on the ways in which a theory of law—Hart's, say—properly earns the title, "legal positivist." Could you defend the view that Dworkin's account in "The Model of Rules," despite his protests to the contrary, is itself really just a new version of legal positivism?

3. What would Dworkin say about Holmes's claim that "judicial dissent often is blamed, as if it meant simply that one side or the other were not doing their sums right, and, if they would take more trouble, agreement inevitably would come"?

4. Recall Hart's discussion of the secondary rules of a legal system. Is there room in Hart's concept of a rule to include what Dworkin calls "principles"?

5. Suppose that a court, say, the Supreme Court, makes a mistake in deciding a first-instance, hard case. Does the fact that that mistake was made then have a bearing on what the law is? If so, why, and under what circumstances?

# Court of Appeals of New York
## RIGGS v. PALMER*

EARL, J.   On the 13th day of August, 1880, Francis B. Palmer made his last will and testament, in which he gave small legacies to his two daughters, Mrs. Riggs and Mrs. Preston, the plaintiffs in this action, and the remainder of his estate to his grandson, the defendant Elmer E. Palmer, subject to the support of Susan Palmer, his mother, with a gift over to the two daughters, subject to the support of Mrs. Palmer in case Elmer should survive him and die under age, unmarried, and without any issue. The testator, at the date of his will, owned a farm, and considerable personal property. He was a widower, and thereafter, in March, 1882, he was married to Mrs. Bresee, with whom, before his marriage, he entered into an antenuptial contract, in which it was agreed that in lieu of dower and all other claims upon his estate in case she survived him she should have her support upon his farm during her life, and such support was expressly charged upon the farm. At the date of the will, and subsequently to the death of the testator, Elmer lived with him as a member of his family, and at his death was 16 years old. He knew of the provisions made in his favor in the will, and, that he might prevent his grandfather from revoking such provisions, which he had manifested some intention to do, and to obtain the speedy enjoyment and immediate possession of his property, he willfully murdered him by poisoning him. He now claims the property, and the sole question for our determination is, can he have it?

The defendants say that the testator is dead; that his will was made in due form, and has been admitted to probate; and that therefore it must have effect according to the letter of the law. It is quite true that statutes regulating the making, proof, and effect of wills and the devolution of property, if literally construed, and if their force and effect can in no way and under no circumstances be controlled or modified, give this property to the murderer. The purpose of those statutes was to enable testators to dispose of their estates to the objects of their bounty at death, and to carry into effect their final wishes legally expressed; and in considering and giving effect to them this purpose must be kept in view. It was the intention of the law-makers that the donees in a will should have the property given to them. But it never could have been their intention that a donee who murdered the testator to make the will operative should have any benefit under it. If such a case had been present to their minds, and it had been supposed necessary to make some provision of law to meet it, it cannot be doubted that they would have provided for it. It is a familiar canon of construction that a thing which is within the intention of the makers of a statute is as much within the statute as if it were within the letter; and a thing which is within the letter of the statute is not within the statute unless it be within the intention of the makers. The writers of laws do not always express their intentions perfectly, but either exceed it or fall short of it, so that judges are to collect it from probable or rational conjectures only, and this is called "rational interpretation;" and Rutherford, in his Institutes, (page 420,) says: "Where we make use of rational interpretation, sometimes we restrain the meaning of the writer so as to take in less, and sometimes we extend or enlarge his meaning so as to take in more than his words express." Such a construction ought to be put upon a statute as will best answer the intention which the makers had in view, for *qui hæret litera, hæret in cortice.* In Bac. Abr. "Statutes," 1, 5; Puff.

*22 N.E. 188 (1889).

Law Nat. bk. 5, c. 12; Ruth. Inst. 422, 427, and in Smith's Commentaries 814, many cases are mentioned where it was held that matters embraced in the general words of statutes nevertheless were not within the statutes, because it could not have been the intention of the law-makers that they should be included. They were taken out of the statutes by an equitable construction; and it is said in Bacon: "By an equitable construction a case not within the letter of a statute is sometimes holden to be within the meaning, because it is within the mischief for which a remedy is provided. The reason for such construction is that the law-makers could not set down every case in express terms. In order to form a right judgment whether a case be within the equity of a statute, it is a good way to suppose the law-maker present, and that you have asked him this question: Did you intend to comprehend this case? Then you must give yourself such answer as you imagine he, being an upright and reasonable man, would have given. If this be that he did mean to comprehend it, you may safely hold the case to be within the equity of the statute; for while you do no more than he would have done, you do not act contrary to the statute, but in conformity thereto." 9 Bac. Abr. 248. In some cases the letter of a legislative act is restrained by an equitable construction; in others, it is enlarged; in others, the construction is contrary to the letter. The equitable construction which restrains the letter of a statute is defined by Aristotle as frequently quoted in this manner: *Æquitas est correctio legis generaliter latæ qua parte deficit*. If the lawmakers could, as to this case, be consulted, would they say that they intended by their general language that the property of a testator or of an ancestor should pass to one who had taken his life for the express purpose of getting his property? In 1 B. Comm. 91, the learned author, speaking of the construction of statutes says: "If there arise out of them collaterally any absurd consequences manifestly contradictory to common reason, they are with regard to those collateral consequences void. * * * Where some collateral matter arises out of the general words, and happens to be unreasonable, there the judges are in decency to conclude that this consequence was not foreseen by the parliament, and therefore they are at liberty to expound the statute by equity, and only *quoad hoe* disregard it;" and he gives as an illustration, if an act of parliament gives a man power to try all causes that arise within his manor of Dale, yet, if a cause should arise in which he himself is party, the act is construed not to extend to that, because it is unreasonable that any man should determine his own quarrel. There was a statute in Bologna that whoever drew blood in the streets should be severely punished, and yet it was held not to apply to the case of a barber who opened a vein in the street. It is commanded in the decalogue that no work shall be done upon the Sabbath, and yet giving the command a rational interpretation founded upon its design the Infallible Judge held that it did not prohibit works of necessity, charity, or benevolence on that day.

What could be more unreasonable than to suppose that it was the legislative intention in the general laws passed for the orderly, peaceable, and just devolution of property that they should have operation in favor of one who murdered his ancestor that he might speedily come into the possession of his estate? Such an intention is inconceivable. We need not, therefore, be much troubled by the general language contained in the laws. Besides, all laws, as well as all contracts, may be controlled in their operation and effect by general, fundamental maxims of the common law. No one shall be permitted to profit by his own fraud, or to take advantage of his own wrong, or to found any claim upon his own iniquity, or to acquire property by his own crime. These maxims are dictated by public policy, have their foundation in universal law administered in all civilized countries, and have nowhere been superseded by statutes. They were applied in the decision of the case of Insurance Co. v. Armstrong, 117 U.S. 599, 6 Sup. Ct. Rep. 877. There it was held that the person who procured a policy upon the life of another, payable at his death, and then murdered the assured to make the policy payable, could not recover thereon. Mr. Justice FIELD, writing the opinion, said: "Independently of any proof of the motives of Hunter in obtaining the policy, and even assuming that they were just and proper, he forfeited all rights under it when, to secure its immediate payment, he murdered the assured. It would be a reproach to the jurisprudence of the country if one could recover insurance money payable on the death of a party whose life he had feloniously taken. As well might he recover insurance money upon a building that he had willfully fired." These maxims, without any statute giving them force or operation, frequently control the effect and nullify the language of wills. A will procured by fraud and deception, like any other instrument, may be decreed void, and set aside; and so a particular portion of a will may be excluded from probate, or held inoperative, if induced by the fraud or undue influence of the person in whose favor it is. Allen v. McPherson, 1 H. L. Cas. 191; Harrison's Appeal, 48 Conn. 202. So a will may contain provisions which are immoral, irreligious, or against public policy, and they will be held void.

Here there was no certainty that this murderer would survive the testator, or that the testator would not change his will, and there was no certainty that he would get this property if nature was allowed to take its course. He therefore murdered the testator expressly to vest himself with an estate. Under such circumstances, what law, human or divine, will allow him to take the estate and enjoy the fruits of his crime? The will spoke and became operative at the death of the testator. He caused that death, and thus by his crime made it speak and have operation. Shall it speak and operate in his favor? If he had met the testator, and taken his property by force, he would have had no title to it. Shall he acquire title by murdering him? If he had gone to the testator's house, and by force compelled him, or by fraud or undue influence had induced him, to will him his property, the law would not allow him to hold it. But can he give effect and operation to a will by murder, and yet take the property? To answer these questions in the affirmative it seems to me would be a reproach to the jurisprudence of our state, and an offense against public policy. Under the civil law, evolved from the general principles of natural law and justice by many generations of jurisconsults, philosophers, and statesmen, one cannot take property by inheritance or will from an ancestor or benefactor whom he has murdered. Dom. Civil Law, pt. 2, bk. 1, tit. 1, § 3; Code Nap. § 727; Mack. Rom. Law, 530, 550. In the Civil code of Lower Canada the provisions on the subject in the Code Napoleon have been substantially copied. But, so far as I can find, in no country where the common law prevails has it been deemed important to enact a law to provide for such a case. Our revisers and law-makers were familiar with the civil law, and they did not deem it important to incorporate into our statutes its provisions upon this subject. This is not a *casus omissus*. It was evidently supposed that the maxims of the common law were sufficient to regulate such a case, and that a specific enactment for that purpose was not needed. For the same reasons the defendant Palmer cannot take any of this property as heir. Just before the murder he was not an heir, and it was not certain that he ever would be. He might have died before his grandfather, or might have been disinherited by him. He made himself an heir by the murder, and he seeks to take property as the fruit of his crime. What has before been said as to him as legatee applies to him with equal force as an heir. He cannot vest himself with title by crime. My view of this case does not inflict upon Elmer any greater or other punishment for his crime than the law specifies. It takes from him no property, but simply holds that he shall not acquire property by his crime, and thus be rewarded for its commission.

Our attention is called to Owens v. Owens, 100 N. C. 240, 6 S. E. Rep. 794, as a case quite like this. There a wife had been convicted of being an accessory before the fact to the murder of her husband, and it was held that she was nevertheless entitled to dower. I am unwilling to assent to the doctrine of that case. The statutes provide dower for a wife who has the misfortune to survive her husband, and thus lose his support and protection. It is clear beyond their purpose to make provision for a wife who by her own crime makes herself a widow, and willfully and intentionally deprives herself of the support and protection of her husband. As she might have died before him, and thus never have been his widow, she cannot by her crime vest herself with an estate. The principle which lies at the bottom of the maxim *volenti non fit injuria* should be applied to such a case, and a widow should not, for the purpose of acquiring, as such, property rights, be permitted to allege a widowhood which she has wickedly and intentionally created.

The facts found entitled the plaintiffs to the relief they seek. The error of the referee was in his conclusion of law. Instead of granting a new trial, therefore, I think the proper judgment upon the facts found should be ordered here. The facts have been passed upon twice with the same result,— first upon the trial of Palmer for murder, and then by the referee in this action. We are therefore of opinion that the ends of justice do not require that they should again come in question. The judgment of the general term and that entered upon the report of the referee should therefore be reversed, and judgment should be entered as follows: That Elmer E. Palmer and the administrator be enjoined from using any of the personalty or real estate left by the testator for Elmer's benefit; that the devise and bequest in the will to Elmer be declared ineffective to pass the title to him; that by reason of the crime of murder committed upon the grandfather he

is deprived of any interest in the estate left by him; that the plaintiffs are the true owners of the real and personal estate left by the testator, subject to the charge in favor of Elmer's mother and the widow of the testator, under the antenuptial agreement, and that the plaintiffs have costs in all the courts against Elmer. All concur, except GRAY, J., who reads dissenting opinion, and DANFORTH, J., concurs.

GRAY, J., (*dissenting.*) This appeal presents an extraordinary state of facts, and the case, in respect of them, I believe, is without precedent in this state. The respondent, a lad of 16 years of age, being aware of the provisions in his grandfather's will, which constituted him the residuary legatee of the testator's estate, caused his death by poison, in 1882. For this crime he was tried, and was convicted of murder in the second degree, and at the time of the commencement of this action he was serving out his sentence in the state reformatory. This action was brought by two of the children of the testator for the purpose of having those provisions of the will in the respondent's favor canceled and annulled. The appellants' argument for a reversal of the judgment, which dismissed their complaint, is that the respondent unlawfully prevented a revocation of the existing will, or a new will from being made, by his crime; and that he terminated the enjoyment by the testator of his property, and effected his own succession to it, by the same crime. They say that to permit the respondent to take the property willed to him would be to permit him to take advantage of his own wrong. To sustain their position the appellants' counsel has submitted an able and elaborate brief, and, if I believed that the decision of the question could be effected by considerations of an equitable nature, I should not hesitate to assent to views which commend themselves to the conscience. But the matter does not lie within the domain of conscience. We are bound by the rigid rules of law, which have been established by the legislature, and within the limits of which the determination of this question is confined. The question we are dealing with is whether a testamentary disposition can be altered, or a will revoked, after the testator's death, through an appeal to the courts, when the legislature has by its enactments prescribed exactly when and how wills may be made, altered, and revoked, and apparently, as it seems to me, when they have been fully complied with, has left no room for the exercise of an equitable jurisdiction by courts over such matters. Modern jurisprudence, in recognizing the right of the individual, under more or less restrictions, to dispose of his property after his death, subjects it to legislative control, both as to extent and as to mode of exercise. Complete freedom of testamentary disposition of one's property has not been and is not the universal rule, as we see from the provisions of the Napoleonic Code, from the systems of jurisprudence in countries which are modeled upon the Roman law, and from the statutes of many of our states. To the statutory restraints which are imposed upon the disposition of one's property by will are added strict and systematic statutory rules for the execution, alteration, and revocation of the will, which must be, at least substantially, if not exactly, followed to insure validity and performance. The reason for the establishment of such rules, we may naturally assume, consists in the purpose to create those safeguards about these grave and important acts which experience has demonstrated to be the wisest and surest. That freedom which is permitted to be exercised in the testamentary disposition of one's estate by the laws of the state is subject to its being exercised in conformity with the regulations of the statutes. The capacity and the power of the individual to dispose of his property after death, and the mode by which that power can be exercised, are matters of which the legislature has assumed the entire control, and has undertaken to regulate with comprehensive particularity.

The appellants' argument is not helped by reference to those rules of the civil law, or to those laws of other governments, by which the heir, or legatee, is excluded from benefit under the testament if he has been convicted of killing, or attempting to kill, the testator. In the absence of such legislation here, the courts are not empowered to institute such a system of remedial justice. The deprivation of the heir of his testamentary succession by the Roman law, when guilty of such a crime, plainly was intended to be in the nature of a punishment imposed upon him. The succession, in such a case of guilt, escheated to the exchequer. See Dom. Civil Law, pt. 2, bk. 1, tit. 1. § 3. I concede that rules of law which annul testamentary provisions made for the benefit of those who have become unworthy of them may be based on principles of equity and of natural justice. It is quite reasonable to suppose that a testator would revoke or alter his will, where his mind has been so angered and changed as to make him unwilling to have his will executed as it stood. But these principles only suggest sufficient reasons for the enactment of laws to meet such cases.

The statutes of this state have prescribed various ways in which a will may be altered or revoked; but the very provision defining the modes of alteration and revocation implies a prohibition of alteration or revocation in any other way. The words of the section of the statute are: "No will in writing, except in the cases hereinafter mentioned, nor any part thereof, shall be revoked or altered otherwise," etc. Where, therefore, none of the cases mentioned are met by the facts, and the revocation is not in the way described in the section, the will of the testator is unalterable. I think that a valid will must continue as a will always, unless revoked in the manner provided by the statutes. Mere intention to revoke a will does not have the effect of revocation. The intention to revoke is necessary to constitute the effective revocation of a will, but it must be demonstrated by one of the acts contemplated by the statute. As WOODWORTH, J., said in Dan v. Brown, 4 Cow. 490: "Revocation is an act of the mind, which must be demonstrated by some outward and visible sign of revocation." The same learned judge said in that case: "The rule is that if the testator lets the will stand until he dies, it is his will; if he does not suffer it to do so, it is not his will." And see Goodright v. Glazier, 4 Burrows, 2512, 2514; Pemberton v. Pemberton, 13 Ves. 290. The finding of fact of the referee that presumably the testator would have altered his will had he known of his grandson's murderous intent cannot affect the question. We may concede it to the fullest extent; but still the cardinal objection is undisposed of,—that the making and the revocation of a will are purely matters of statutory regulation, by which the court is bound in the determination of questions relating to these acts.

Two cases,—in this state and in Kentucky,— at an early day, seem to me to be much in point. Gains v. Gains, 2 A. K. Marsh. 190, was decided by the Kentucky court of appeals in 1820. It was there urged that the testator intended to have destroyed his will, and that he was forcibly prevented from doing so by the defendant in error or devisee; and it was insisted that the will, though not expressly, was thereby virtually, revoked. The court held, as the act concerning wills prescribed the manner in which a will might be revoked, that, as none of the acts evidencing revocation were done, the intention could not be substituted for the act. In that case the will was snatched away, and forcibly retained. In 1854, Surrogate BRADFORD, whose opinions are entitled to the highest consideration, decided the case of Leaycraft v. Simmons, 3 Bradf. Sur. 35. In that case the testator, a man of 89 years of age, desired to make a codicil to his will, in order to enlarge the provisions for his daughter. His son, having the custody of the instrument, and the one to be prejudiced by the change, refused to produce the will at testator's request, for the purpose of alteration. The learned surrogate refers to the provisions of the civil law for such and other cases of unworthy conduct in the heir or

legatee, and says: "Our statute has undertaken to prescribe the mode in which wills can be revoked [citing the statutory provision.] This is the law by which I am governed in passing upon questions touching the revocation of wills. The whole of this subject is now regulated by statute; and a mere intention to revoke, however well authenticated, or however defeated, is not sufficient." And he held that the will must be admitted to probate. I may refer also to a case in the Pennsylvania courts. In that state the statute prescribed the mode for repealing or altering a will, and in Clingan v. Micheltree, 31 Pa. St. 25, the supreme court of the state held, where a will was kept from destruction by the fraud and misrepresentation of the devisee, that to declare it canceled as against the fraudulent party would be to enlarge the statute.

I cannot find any support for the argument that the respondent's succession to the property should be avoided because of his criminal act, when the laws are silent. Public policy does not demand it; for the demands of public policy are satisfied by the proper execution of the laws and the punishment of the crime. There has been no convention between the testator and his legatee; nor is there any such contractual element, in such a disposition of property by a testator, as to impose or imply conditions in the legatee. The appellants' argument practically amounts to this: that, as the legatee has been guilty of a crime, by the commission of which he is placed in a position to sooner receive the benefits of the testamentary provision, his rights to the property should be forfeited, and he should be divested of his estate. To allow their argument to prevail would involve the diversion by the court of the testator's estate into the hands of persons whom, possibly enough, for all we know, the testator might not have chosen or desired as its recipients. Practically the court is asked to make another will for the testator. The laws do not warrant this judicial action, and mere presumption would not be strong enough to sustain it. But, more than this, to concede the appellants' views would involve the imposition of an additional punishment or penalty upon the respondent. What power or warrant have the courts to add to the respondent's penalties by depriving him of property? The law has punished him for his crime, and we may not say that it was an insufficient punishment. In the trial and punishment of the respondent the law has vindicated itself for the outrage which he committed, and further judicial utterance upon the subject of punishment or deprivation of rights is barred. We may not, in the language of the court in People v. Thornton, 25 Hun, 456, "enhance the pains, penalties, and forfeitures provided by law for the punishment of crime." The judgment should be affirmed, with costs.

# QUESTIONS

1. Does the court in *Riggs* depart from the original meaning of the written statutes, or not?

2. Suppose that evidence from legislative hearings shows that the possibility of someone committing murder in order to inherit had been mentioned, and it was then briefly dismissed with the comment, "Then there will be someone profiting from murder. But we can't make the legislation overly complex by trying to deal with every hypothetical possibility that is suggested." Would that make a difference to the outcome of this case? Should it?

3. Is Judge Gray right in saying that, in deciding against Elmer, the court is, in effect, both remaking the will and remaking the legislation of the legislature?

4. What arguments can be given to support the claim that the principle, "No one shall be permitted to profit by his own fraud, or to take advantage of his own wrong. . . ." is a legal principle, valid and binding as such, and not merely a moral principle, i.e., a widely shared moral opinion with no particular legal force?

5. Dissenting, Judge Gray says that there is no support for the argument that the "respondent's succession to the property should be avoided because of his criminal act, when the laws are silent. Public policy does not demand it. . . ." Can you think of any reasons of public policy against allowing the inheritance? Can you think of any reasons *in favor?*

# The Idea of the Rule of Law

## *Joseph Raz*[*]
# THE RULE OF LAW AND ITS VIRTUE[*]

F.A. Hayek has provided one of the clearest and most powerful formulations of the ideal of the rule of law: 'stripped of all technicalities this means that government in all its actions is bound by rules fixed and announced beforehand—rules which make it possible to foresee with fair certainty how the authority will use its coercive powers in given circumstances, and to plan one's individual affairs on the basis of this knowledge'.[1] At the same time the way he draws certain conclusions from this ideal illustrates one of the two main fallacies in the contemporary treatment of the doctrine of the rule of law: the assumption of its overriding importance. My purpose is to analyse the ideal of the rule of law in the spirit of Hayek's quoted statement of it and to show why some of the conclusions which he drew from it cannot be thus supported. But first we must be put on our guard against the other common fallacy concerning the rule of law.

Not uncommonly when a political ideal captures the imagination of large numbers of people its name becomes a slogan used by supporters of ideals which bear little or no relation to the one it originally designated. The fate of 'democracy' not long ago and of 'privacy' today are just two examples of this familiar process. In 1959 the International Congress of Jurists meeting in New Delhi gave official blessing to a similar perversion of the doctrine of the rule of law.

The function of the legislature in a free society under the Rule of Law is to create and maintain the conditions which will uphold the dignity of man as an individual. This dignity requires not only the recognition of his civil and political rights but also the establishment of the social, economic, educational and cultural conditions which are essential to the full development of his personality.[2]

The report goes on to mention or refer to just about every political ideal which has found support in any part of the globe during the post-war years.

If the rule of law is the rule of the good law then to explain its nature is to propound a complete social philosophy. But if so the term lacks any useful function. We have no need to be converted to the rule of law just in order to discover that to believe in it is to believe that good should triumph. The rule of law is a political ideal which a legal system may lack or may possess to a greater or lesser degree. That much is common ground. It is also to be insisted that the rule of law is just one of the virtues which a legal system may possess and by which it is to be judged. It is not to be confused with democracy, justice, equality (before the law or otherwise), human rights of any kind or respect for persons or for the dignity of man. A non-democratic legal system, based on the denial of human rights, on extensive poverty, on racial segregation, sexual inequalities, and religious persecution may, in principle, conform to the requirements of the rule of law better than any of the legal

[*]© Joseph Raz 1979. Reprinted from *The Authority of Law: Essays on Law and Morality* by Joseph Raz (1979) by permission of Oxford University Press.

[*]First published in *The Law Quarterly Review* (1977). A draft of this paper was presented to a conference sponsored by the Liberty Fund and the University of San Francisco. I am grateful to Rolf Sartorius, Douglas Hutchinson, and David Libling for useful suggestions on ways to improve an early draft of the paper.

[1] *The Road to Serfdom* (London, 1944)π, p. 54.

[2] Clause 1 of the report of Committee I of the International Congress of Jurists at New Delhi, 1959.

systems of the more enlightened Western democracies. This does not mean that it will be better than those Western democracies. It will be an immeasurably worse legal system, but it will excel in one respect: in its conformity to the rule of law.

Given the promiscuous use made in recent years of the expression 'the rule of law' it is hardly surprising that my claim will alarm many. We have reached the stage in which no purist can claim that truth is on his side and blame the others for distorting the notion of the rule of law. All that I can claim for my account is, first, that it presents a coherent view of one important virtue which legal systems should possess and, secondly, that it is not original, that I am following in the footsteps of Hayek and of many others who understood 'the rule of law' in similar ways.

## 1. THE BASIC IDEA

'The rule of law' means literally what it says: the rule of the law. Taken in its broadest sense this means that people should obey the law and be ruled by it.[3] But in political and legal theory it has come to be read in a narrower sense, that the government shall be ruled by the law and subject to it. The ideal of the rule of law in this sense is often expressed by the phrase 'government by law and not by men'. No sooner does one use these formulas than their obscurity becomes evident. Surely government must be both by law and by men. It is said that the rule of law means that all government action must have foundation in law, must be authorized by law. But is not that a tautology? Actions not authorized by law cannot be the actions of the government as a government. They would be without legal effect and often unlawful.

It is true that we can elaborate a political notion of government which is different from the legal one: government as the loca-

tion of real power in the society. It is in this sense that one can say that Britain is governed by The City or by the trade unions. In this sense of 'government' it is not a tautology to say that government should be based on law. If the trade union ruling a country breaks an industrial relations law in order to impose its will on the Parliament or if the President or the F.B.I. authorize burglaries and conspire to pervert justice they can be said to violate the rule of law. But here 'the rule of law' is used in its original sense of obedience to law. Powerful people and people in government, just like anybody else, should obey the law. This is no doubt correct, and yet does it exhaust the meaning of the rule of law? There is more to the rule of law than the law and order interpretation allows. It means more even than law and order applied to the government. I shall proceed on the assumption that we are concerned with government in the legal sense and with the conception of the rule of law which applies to government and to law and is no mere application of the law and order conception.

The problem is that now we are back with our initial puzzle. If government is, by definition, government authorized by law the rule of law seems to amount to an empty tautology, not a political ideal.

The solution to this riddle is in the difference between the professional and the lay sense of 'law'. For the lawyer anything is the law if it meets the conditions of validity laid down in the system's rules of recognition or in other rules of the system.[4] This includes the constitution, parliamentary legislation, ministerial regulations, policemen's orders, the regulations of limited companies, conditions imposed in trading licenses, etc. To the layman the law consists only of a subclass of these. To him the law is essentially a set of open, general, and relatively stable laws. Government by law and not by men is not

---

[3]C.f., on this sense of the phrase. Jennings, *The Law and the Constitution* (London. 1933). pp. 42–5.

[4]I am here following Hart, *The Concept of Law* (Oxford, 1961), pp. 97–107.

a tautology if 'law' means general, open, and relatively stable law. In fact, the danger of this interpretation is that the rule of law might set too strict a requirement, one which no legal system can meet and which embodies very little virtue. It is humanly inconceivable that law can consist only of general rules and it is very undesirable that it should. Just as we need government both by laws and by men, so we need both general and particular laws to carry out the jobs for which we need the law.

The doctrine of the rule of law does not deny that every legal system should consist of both general, open, and stable rules (the popular conception of law) and particular laws (legal orders), an essential tool in the hands of the executive and the judiciary alike. As we shall see, what the doctrine requires is the subjection of particular laws to general, open, and stable ones. It is one of the important principles of the doctrine that *the making of particular laws should be guided by open and relatively stable general rules*.

This principle shows how the slogan of the rule of law and not of men can be read as a meaningful political ideal. The principle does not, however, exhaust the meaning of 'the rule of law' and does not by itself illuminate the reasons for its alleged importance. Let us, therefore, return to the literal sense of 'the rule of law'. It has two aspects: (1) that people should be ruled by the law and obey it, and (2) that the law should be such that people will be able to be guided by it. As was noted above, it is with the second aspect that we are concerned: the law must be capable of being obeyed. A person conforms with the law to the extent that he does not break the law. But he obeys the law only if part of his reason for conforming is his knowledge of the law. Therefore, if the law is to be obeyed *it must be capable of guiding the behaviour of its subjects*. It must be such that they can find out what it is and act on it.

This is the basic intuition from which the doctrine of the rule of law derives: the law must be capable of guiding the behavior of its subjects. It is evident that this conception of the rule of law is a formal one. It says nothing about how the law is to be made: by tyrants, democratic majorities, or any other way. It says nothing about fundamental rights, about equality, or justice. It may even be thought that this version of the doctrine is formal to the extent that it is almost devoid of content. This is far from the truth. Most of the requirements which were associated with the rule of law before it came to signify all the virtues of the state can be derived from this one basic idea.

## 2. SOME PRINCIPLES

Many of the principles which can be derived from the basic idea of the rule of law depend for their validity or importance on the particular circumstances of different societies. There is little point in trying to enumerate them all, but some of the more important ones might be mentioned:

(1) *All laws should be prospective, open, and clear*. One cannot be guided by a retroactive law. It does not exist at the time of action. Sometimes it is then known for certain that a retroactive law will be enacted. When this happens retroactivity does not conflict with the rule of law (though it may be objected to on other grounds). The law must be open and adequately publicized. If it is to guide people they must be able to find out what it is. For the same reason its meaning must be clear. An ambiguous, vague, obscure, or imprecise law is likely to mislead or confuse at least some of those who desire to be guided by it.

(2) *Laws should be relatively stable*. They should not be changed too often. If they are frequently changed people will find it difficult to find out what the law is at any given moment and will be constantly in fear that the law has been changed since they last learnt what it was. But more important still is the fact that people need to know the law not only for short-term decisions (where to

park one's car, how much alcohol is allowed duty free, etc.) but also for long-term planning. Knowledge of at least the general outlines and sometimes even of details of tax law and company law are often important for business plans which will bear fruit only years later. Stability is essential if people are to be guided by law in their long-term decisions.[5]

Three important points are illustrated by this principle. First, conformity to the rule of law is often a matter of degree, not only when the conformity of the legal system as a whole is at stake, but also with respect to single laws. A law is either retroactive or not, but it can be more or less clear, more or less stable, etc. It should be remembered, however, that by asserting that conformity to the principles is a matter of degree, it is not meant that the degree of conformity can be quantitatively measured by counting the number of infringements, or some such method. Some infringements are worse than others. Some violate the principles in a formal way only, which does not offend against the spirit of the doctrine. Secondly, the principles of the rule of law affect primarily the content and form of the law (it should be prospective, clear, etc.) but not only them. They also affect the manner of government beyond what is or can usefully be prescribed by law. The requirement of stability cannot be usefully subject to complete legal regulation. It is largely a matter for wise governmental policy. Thirdly, though the rule of law concerns primarily private citizens as subject to duties and governmental agencies in the exercise of their powers (on which more below), it is also concerned with the exercise of private powers. Power-conferring rules are designed to guide behaviour and should conform to the doctrine of rule of law if they are to be capable of doing so effectively.

(3) *The making of particular laws (particular legal orders) should be guided by open, stable, clear, and general rules*. It is sometimes assumed that the requirement of generality is of the essence of the rule of law. This notion derives (as noted above) from the literal interpretation of 'the rule of law' when 'law' is read in its lay connotations as being restricted to general, stable, and open law. It is also reinforced by a belief that the rule of law is particularly relevant to the protection of equality and that equality is related to the generality of law. The last belief is, as has often been noted before, mistaken. Racial, religious, and all manner of discrimination are not only compatible but often institutionalized by general rules.

The formal conception of the rule of law which I am defending does not object to particular legal orders as long as they are stable, clear, etc. But of course particular legal orders are mostly used by government agencies to introduce flexibility into the law. A police constable regulating traffic, a licensing authority granting a licence under certain conditions, all these and their like are among the more ephemeral parts of the law. As such they run counter to the basic idea of the rule of law. They make it difficult for people to plan ahead on the basis of their knowledge of the law. This difficulty is overcome to a large extent if particular laws of an ephemeral status are enacted only within a framework set by general laws which are more durable and which impose limits on the unpredictability introduced by the particular orders.

Two kinds of general rules create the framework for the enactment of particular laws: those which confer the necessary powers for making valid orders and those which impose duties instructing the power-holders how to exercise their powers. Both have equal importance in creating a stable framework for the creation of particular legal orders.

---

[5]Of course, uncertainty generated by instability of law also affects people's planning of action. If it did not, stability would not have any impact either. The point is that only if the law is stable are people guided by *their knowledge of the content of the law*.

Clearly, similar considerations apply to general legal regulations which do not meet the requirement of stability. They too should be circumscribed to conform to a stable framework. Hence the requirement that much of the subordinate administrative law-making should be made to conform to detailed ground rules laid down in framework laws. It is essential, however, not to confuse this argument with democratic arguments for the close supervision of popularly elected bodies over law-making by non-elected ones. These further arguments may be valid but have nothing to do with the rule of law, and though sometimes they reinforce rule of law type arguments, on other occasions they support different and even conflicting conclusions.

(4) *The independence of the judiciary must be guaranteed.* It is of the essence of municipal legal systems that they institute judicial bodies charged, among other things, with the duty of applying the law to cases brought before them and whose judgments and conclusions as to the legal merits of those cases are final. Since just about any matter arising under any law can be subject to a conclusive court judgment, it is obvious that it is futile to guide one's action on the basis of the law if when the matter comes to adjudication the courts will not apply the law and will act for some other reasons. The point can be put even more strongly. Since the court's judgment establishes conclusively what is the law in the case before it, the litigants can be guided by law only if the judges apply the law correctly.[6] Otherwise people will only be able to be guided by their guesses as to what the courts are likely to do—but these guesses will not be based on the law but on other considerations.

The rules concerning the independence of the judiciary—the method of appointing judges, their security of tenure, the way of fixing their salaries, and other conditions of service—are designed to guarantee that they will be free from extraneous pressures and independent of all authority save that of the law. They are, therefore, essential for the preservation of the rule of law.

(5) *The principles of natural justice must be observed.* Open and fair hearing, absence of bias, and the like are obviously essential for the correct application of the law and thus, through the very same considerations mentioned above, to its ability to guide action.

(6) *The courts should have review powers over the implementation of the other principles.* This includes review of both subordinate and parliamentary legislation and of administrative action, but in itself it is a very limited review—merely to ensure conformity to the rule of law.

(7) *The courts should be easily accessible.* Given the central position of the courts in ensuring the rule of law (see principles 4 and 6) it is obvious that their accessibility is of paramount importance. Long delays, excessive costs, etc., may effectively turn the most enlightened law into a dead letter and frustrate one's ability effectively to guide oneself by the law.

(8) *The discretion of the crime-preventing agencies should not be allowed to pervert the law.* Not only the courts but also the actions of the police and the prosecuting authorities can subvert the law. The prosecution should not be allowed, for example, to decide not to prosecute for commission of certain crimes, or for crimes committed by certain classes of offenders. The police should not be allowed to allocate its resources so as to avoid all effort to prevent and detect certain crimes or prosecute certain classes of criminals.

This list is very incomplete. Other principles could be mentioned and those which have been mentioned need further elaboration and further justification (why—as required by the sixth principle—should the courts and not some other body be in charge of reviewing conformity to the rule of law?

---

[6] I am not denying that courts also make law. This principle of the rule of law applies to them primarily in their duty to apply the law. As law-makers they are subject to the same principles as all law-makers.

etc.).[7] My purpose in listing them was merely to illustrate the power and fruitfulness of the formal conception of the rule of law. It should, however, be remembered that in the final analysis the doctrine rests on its basic idea that the law should be capable of providing effective guidance. The principles do not stand on their own. They must be constantly interpreted in the light of the basic idea.

The eight principles listed fall into two groups. Principles 1 to 3 require that the law should conform to standards designed to enable it effectively to guide action. Principles 4 to 8 are designed to ensure that the legal machinery of enforcing the law should not deprive it of its ability to guide through distorted enforcement and that it shall be capable of supervising conformity to the rule of law and provide effective remedies in cases of deviation from it. All the principles directly concern the system and method of government in matters directly relevant to the rule of law. Needless to say, many other aspects in the life of a community may, in more indirect ways, either strengthen or weaken the rule of law. A free press run by people anxious to defend the rule of law is of great assistance in preserving it, just as a gagged press or one run by people wishing to undermine the rule of law is a threat to it. But we need not be concerned here with these more indirect influences.

## 3. THE VALUE OF THE RULE OF LAW

One of the merits of the doctrine of the rule of law I am defending is that there are so many values it does not serve. Conformity to the rule of law is a virtue, but only one of the many virtues a legal system should possess. This makes it all the more important to be clear on the values which the rule of law does serve.

The rule of law is often rightly contrasted with arbitrary power. Arbitrary power is broader than the rule of law. Many forms of arbitrary rule are compatible with the rule of law. A ruler can promote general rules based on whim or self-interest, etc., without offending against the rule of law. But certainly many of the more common manifestations of arbitrary power run foul of the rule of law. A government subjected to the rule of law is prevented from changing the law retroactively or abruptly or secretly whenever this suits its purposes. The one area where the rule of law excludes all forms of arbitrary power is in the law-applying function of the judiciary where the courts are required to be subject only to the law and to conform to fairly strict procedures.[8] No less important is the restraint imposed by the rule of law on the making of particular laws and thus on the powers of the executive. The arbitrary use of power for personal gain, out of vengeance or favouritism, is most commonly manifested in the making of particular legal orders. These possibilities are drastically restricted by close adherence to the rule of law.

'Arbitrary power' is a difficult notion. We have no cause to analyse it here. It seems, however, that an act which is the exercise of power is arbitrary only if it was done either with indifference as to whether it will serve the purposes which alone can justify use of that power or with belief that it will not serve them. The nature of the purposes alluded to varies with the nature of the power. This condition represents 'arbitrary power' as a subjective concept. It all depends on the state of mind of the men in power. As such the rule of law does not bear directly on the extent of arbitrary power. But around its subjective core the notion of arbitrary power

---

[7] Similar lists of principles have been discussed by various authors. English writers have been mesmerized by Dicey's unfortunate doctrine for too long. For a list similar to mine see Lon Fuller's *The Morality of Law*, 2nd ed., ch. 2. His discussion of many of the principles is full of good sense. My main reason for abandoning some of his principles is a difference of views on conflicts between the laws of one system.

[8] The rule of law itself does not exclude all the possibilities of arbitrary law-making by the courts.

has grown a hard objective edge. Since it is universally believed that it is wrong to use public powers for private ends any such use is in itself an instance of arbitrary use of power. As we have seen the rule of law does help to curb such forms of arbitrary power.

But there are more reasons for valuing the rule of law. We value the ability to choose styles and forms of life, to fix long-term goals and effectively direct one's life towards them. One's ability to do so depends on the existence of stable, secure frameworks for one's life and actions. The law can help to secure such fixed points of reference in two ways: (1) by stabilizing social relationships which but for the law may disintegrate or develop in erratic and unpredictable ways; (2) by a policy of self-restraint designed to make the law itself a stable and safe basis for individual planning. This last aspect is the concern of the rule of law.

This second virtue of the rule of law is often, notably by Hayek, identified as the protection of individual freedom. This is right in the sense of freedom in which it is identified with an effective ability to choose between as many options as possible. Predictability in one's environment does increase one's power of action.[9] If this is freedom, well and good. The important thing is to remember that this sense of freedom differs from what is commonly meant by political freedom. Political freedom consists of: (1) the prohibition of certain forms of behaviour which interfere with personal freedom and (2) the limits imposed on the powers of public authorities in order to minimize interference with personal freedom. The criminal offences against the person are an example of the first mode of protecting personal freedom, the disability of the government to restrict freedom of movement—an example of the second. It is in connection with political freedom in this sense that con-

stitutionally guaranteed rights are of great importance. The rule of law may be yet another mode of protecting personal freedom. But it has no bearing on the existence of spheres of activity free from governmental interference and is compatible with gross violations of human rights.

More important than both these considerations is the fact that observance of the rule of law is necessary if the law is to respect human dignity. Respecting human dignity entails treating humans as persons capable of planning and plotting their future. Thus, respecting people's dignity includes respecting their autonomy, their right to control their future. A person's control over his life is never complete. It can be incomplete in any one of several respects. The person may be ignorant of his options, unable to decide what to do, incapable of realizing his choices or frustrated in his attempts to do so, or he may have no choice at all (or at least none which is worth having). All these failures can occur through natural causes or through the limitations of the person's own character and abilities.

Naturally, there are many ways in which one person's action may affect the life of another. Only some such interferences will amount to an offence to the dignity or a violation of the autonomy of the person thus affected. Such offences can be divided into three classes: insults, enslavement, and manipulation. (I am using the last two terms in a somewhat special sense.) An insult offends a person's dignity if it consists of or implies a denial that he is an autonomous person or that he deserves to be treated as one. An action enslaves another if it practically denies him all options through the manipulation of the environment. (Though it may be for a length of time—as in real slavery—I mean to include here also coercing another to act in a certain way on a

---

[9]But then welfare law and governmental manipulation of the economy also increase freedom by increasing--if successful--people's welfare. If the rule of law is defended as the bulwark of freedom in this sense, it can hardly be used to oppose in principle governmental management of the economy.

single occasion.) One manipulates a person by intentionally changing his tastes, his beliefs or his ability to act or decide. Manipulation—in other words—is manipulation of the person, of those factors relevant to his autonomy which are internal to him. Enslavement is the elimination of control by changing factors external to the person.

The law can violate people's dignity in many ways. Observing the rule of law by no means guarantees that such violations do not occur. But it is clear that deliberate disregard for the rule of law violates human dignity. It is the business of law to guide human action by affecting people's options. The law may, for example, institute slavery without violating the rule of law. But deliberate violation of the rule of law violates human dignity. The violation of the rule of law can take two forms. It may lead to uncertainty or it may lead to frustrated and disappointed expectations. It leads to the first when the law does not enable people to foresee future developments or to form definite expectations (as in cases of vagueness and most cases of wide discretion). It leads to frustrated expectations when the appearance of stability and certainty which encourages people to rely and plan on the basis of the existing law is shattered by retroactive law-making or by preventing proper law-enforcement, etc. The evils of uncertainty are in providing opportunities for arbitrary power and restricting people's ability to plan for their future. The evils of frustrated expectations are greater. Quite apart from the concrete harm they cause they also offend dignity in expressing disrespect for people's autonomy. The law in such cases encourages autonomous action only in order to frustrate its purpose. When such frustration is the result of human action or the result of the activities of social institu-

tions then it expresses disrespect. Often it is analogous to entrapment: one is encouraged innocently to rely on the law and then that assurance is withdrawn and one's very reliance is turned into a cause of harm to one. A legal system which does in general observe the rule of law treats people as persons at least in the sense that it attempts to guide their behaviour through affecting the circumstances of their action. It thus presupposes that they are rational autonomous creatures and attempts to affect their actions and habits by affecting their deliberations.

Conformity to the rule of law is a matter of degree. Complete conformity is impossible (some vagueness is inescapable) and maximal possible conformity is on the whole undesirable (some controlled administrative discretion is better than none). It is generally agreed that general conformity to the rule of law is to be highly cherished. But one should not take the value of the rule of law on trust nor assert it blindly. Disentangling the various values served by the rule of law helps to assess intelligently what is at stake in various possible or actual violations. Some cases insult human dignity, give free rein to arbitrary power, frustrate one's expectations, and undermine one's ability to plan. Others involve only some of these evils. The evil of different violations of the rule of law is not always the same despite the fact that the doctrine rests on the solid core of its basic idea.

## 4. THE RULE OF LAW AND ITS ESSENCE

Lon Fuller[10] has claimed that the principles of the rule of law which he enumerated are essential for the existence of law. This claim if true is crucial to our understanding not only of the rule of law but also of the relation

---

[10] In *The Morality of Law*, 2nd ed. (Yale, 1969), Fuller's argument is complex and his claims are numerous and hard to disentangle. Many of his claims are weak and unsupportable. Others are suggestive and useful. It is not my purpose to analyse or evaluate them. For a sympathetic discussion see R. E. Sartorius, *Individual Conduct and Social Norms* (Encino, California, 1975), ch. 9.

of law and morality. I have been treating the rule of law as an ideal, as a standard to which the law ought to conform but which it can and sometimes does violate most radically and systematically. Fuller, while allowing that deviations from the ideal of the rule of law can occur, denies that they can be radical or total. A legal system must of necessity conform to the rule of law to a certain degree, he claims. From this claim he concludes that there is an essential link between law and morality. Law is necessarily moral, at least in some respects.

It is, of course, true that most of the principles enumerated in section 2 above cannot be violated altogether by any legal system.[11] Legal systems are based on judicial institutions. There cannot be institutions of any kind unless there are general rules setting them up. A particular norm can authorize adjudication in a particular dispute, but no number of particular norms can set up an institution. Similarly retroactive laws can exist only because there are institutions enforcing them. This entails that there must be prospective laws instructing those institutions to apply the retroactive laws if the retroactive laws are to be valid. In the terminology of H.L.A. Hart's theory one can say that at least some of the rules of recognition and of adjudication of every system must be general and prospective. Naturally they must also be relatively clear if they are to make any sense at all, etc.

Clearly, the extent to which generality, clarity, prospectivity, etc., are essential to the law is minimal and is consistent with gross violations of the rule of law. But are not considerations of the kind mentioned sufficient to establish that there is necessarily at least some moral value in every legal system? I think not. The rule of law is essentially a negative value. The law inevitably creates a great danger of arbitrary power—the rule of law is designed to minimize the danger created by the law itself. Similarly, the law may be unstable, obscure, retrospective, etc., and thus infringe people's freedom and dignity. The rule of law is designed to prevent this danger as well. Thus the rule of law is a negative virtue in two senses: conformity to it does not cause good except through avoiding evil and the evil which is avoided is evil which could only have been caused by the law itself. It is thus somewhat analogous to honesty when this virtue is narrowly interpreted as the avoidance of deceit. (I do not deny that honesty is normally conceived more broadly to incorporate other virtuous acts and inclinations.) The good of honesty does not include the good of communication between people, for honesty is consistent with a refusal to communicate. Its good is exclusively in the avoidance of the harm of deceit—and not deceit by others but by the honest person himself. Therefore, only a person who can deceive can be honest. A person who cannot communicate cannot claim any moral merit for being honest. A person who through ignorance or inability cannot kill another by poison deserves no credit for it. Similarly, that the law cannot sanction arbitrary force or violations of freedom and dignity through total absence of generality, prospectivity, or clarity is no moral credit to the law. It only means that there are some kinds of evil which cannot be brought about by the law. But this is no virtue in the law just as it is no virtue in the law that it cannot rape or murder (all it can do is sanction such actions).

Fuller's attempt to establish a necessary connection between law and morality fails. In so far as conformity to the rule of law is a moral virtue it is an ideal which should but may fail to become a reality. There is another argument, however, which establishes an essential connection between the law and

---

[11]I am not adopting here Fuller's conception of the law, but rather I am following my own adaptation of Hart's conception. Cf. Hart's *The Concept of Law* and my *Practical Reason and Norms* (1975), pp. 132–54. Therefore, the discussion which follows is not a direct assessment of Fuller's own claims.

the rule of law, though it does not guarantee any virtue to the law. Conformity to the rule of law is essential for securing whatever purposes the law is designed to achieve. This statement should be qualified. We could divide the purposes a law is intended to serve into two kinds: those which are secured by conformity with the law in itself and those further consequences of conformity with the law or of knowledge of its existence which the law is intended to secure. Thus a law prohibiting racial discrimination in government employment has as its direct purpose the establishment of racial equality in the hiring, promotion, and conditions of service of government employees (since discriminatory action is a breach of law). Its indirect purposes may well be to improve race relations in the country in general, prevent a threat of a strike by some trade unions, or halt the decline in popularity of the government.

Conformity to the rule of law does not always facilitate realization of the indirect purposes of the law, but it is essential to the realization of its direct purposes. These are achieved by conformity with the law which is secured (unless accidentally) by people taking note of the law and guiding themselves accordingly. Therefore, if the direct purposes of the law are not to be frustrated it must be capable of guiding human behaviour, and the more it conforms to the principles of the rule of law the better it can do so.

In section 2 we saw that conformity to the rule of law is one among many moral virtues which the law should possess. The present consideration shows that the rule of law is not merely a moral virtue—it is a necessary condition for the law to be serving directly any good purpose at all. Of course, conformity to the rule of law also enables the law to serve bad purposes. That does not show that it is not a virtue, just as the fact that a sharp knife can be used to harm does not show that being sharp is not a good-making characteristic for knives. At most it shows that from the point of view of the present consideration it is not a moral good. Being sharp is an inherent good-making characteristic of knives. A good knife is, among other things, a sharp knife. Similarly, conformity to the rule of law is an inherent value of laws, indeed it is their most important inherent value. It is of the essence of law to guide behaviour through rules and courts in charge of their application. Therefore, the rule of law is the specific excellence of the law. Since conformity to the rule of law is the virtue of law in itself, law as law regardless of the purposes it serves, it is understandable and right that the rule of law is thought of as among the few virtues of law which are the special responsibility of the courts and the legal profession.

Regarding the rule of law as the inherent or specific virtue of law is a result of an instrumental conception of law. The law is not just a fact of life. It is a form of social organization which should be used properly and for the proper ends. It is a tool in the hands of men differing from many others in being versatile and capable of being used for a large variety of proper purposes. As with some other tools, machines, and instruments a thing is not of the kind unless it has at least some ability to perform its function. A knife is not a knife unless it has some ability to cut. The law to be law must be capable of guiding behaviour, however inefficiently. Like other instruments, the law has a specific virtue which is morally neutral in being neutral as to the end to which the instrument is put. It is the virtue of efficiency; the virtue of the instrument as an instrument. For the law this virtue is the rule of law. Thus the rule of law is an inherent virtue of the law, but not a moral virtue as such.

The special status of the rule of law does not mean that conformity with it is of no moral importance. Quite apart from the fact that conformity to the rule of law is also a moral virtue, it is a moral requirement when necessary to enable the law to perform useful social functions; just as it may be of moral importance to produce a sharp knife when it is required for a moral purpose. In the case of the rule of law this means that it is virtually always of great moral value.

## 5. SOME PITFALLS

The undoubted value of conformity to the rule of law should not lead one to exaggerate its importance. We saw how Hayek noted correctly its relevance for the protection of freedom. We also saw that the rule of law itself does not provide sufficient protection of freedom. Consider, however, Hayek's position. He begins with a grand statement which inevitably leads to exaggerated expectations:

> The conception of freedom under the law that is the chief concern of this book rests on the contention that when we obey laws, in the sense of general abstract rules laid down irrespective of their application to us we are not subject to another man's will and are therefore free. It is because the lawgiver does not know the particular cases to which his rule will apply, and it is because the judge who applies them has no choice in drawing the conclusions that follow from the existing body of rules and the particular facts of the case, that it can be said that laws and not men rule. . . . As a true law should not name any particulars, so it should especially not single out any specific persons or group of persons.[13]

Then, aware of the absurdity to which this passage leads, he modifies his line, still trying to present the rule of law as the supreme guarantor of freedom:

> The requirement that the rules of true law be general does not mean that sometimes special rules may not apply to different classes of people if they refer to properties that only some people possess. There may

be rules that can apply to women or to the blind or to persons above a certain age. (In most instances it would not even be necessary to name the class of people to whom the rule applies: only a woman, for example, can be raped or got with child.) Such distinctions will not be arbitrary, will not subject one group to the will of others, if they are equally recognized as justified by those inside and those outside the group. This does not mean that there must be unanimity as to the desirability of the distinction, but merely that individual views will not depend on whether the individual is in the group or not.[14]

But here the rule of law is transformed to encompass a form of government by consent and it is this which is alleged to guarantee freedom. This is the slippery slope leading to the identification of the rule of law with the rule of the good law.

Hayek's main objection is to governmental interference with the economy:

> We must now turn to the kinds of governmental measures which the rule of law excludes in principle because they cannot be achieved by merely enforcing general rules but, of necessity, involve arbitrary discrimination between persons. The most important among them are decisions as to who is to be allowed to provide different services or commodities, at what prices or in what quantities—in other words, measures designed to control the access to different trades and occupations, the terms of sale, and the amounts to be produced or sold.
>
> There are several reasons why all direct control of prices by government is irreconcilable with a functioning free system, whether the government actually fixes prices or merely lays down rules by which the permissible prices are to be determined. In

---

[13]F. A. Hayek, *The Constitution of Liberty* (Chicago, 1960), pp. 153–4.
[14]Ibid., p. 154.

the first place it is impossible to fix prices according to long-term rules which will effectively guide production. Appropriate prices depend on circumstances which are constantly changing and must be continually adjusted to them. On the other hand, prices which are not fixed outright but determined by some rule (such as that they must be in a certain relation to cost) will not be the same for all sellers and, for this reason, will prevent the market from functioning. A still more important consideration is that, with prices different from those that would form on a free market, demand and supply will not be equal, and if the price control is to be effective, some method must be found for deciding who is to be allowed to buy or sell. This would necessarily be discretionary and must consist of *ad hoc* decisions that discriminate between persons on essentially arbitrary grounds.[15]

Here again it is clear that arguments which at best show that certain policies are wrong for economic reasons are claimed to show that they infringe the rule of law and the making of supposedly misguided but perfectly principled particular orders is condemned as an arbitrary exercise of power.

Since the rule of law is just one of the virtues the law should possess, it is to be expected that it possesses no more than prima facie force. It has always to be balanced against competing claims of other values. Hence Hayek's arguments, to the extent that they show no more than that some other goals inevitably conflict with the rule of law, are not the sort of arguments which could, in

principle, show that pursuit of such goals by means of law is inappropriate. Conflict between the rule of law and other values is just what is to be expected. Conformity to the rule of law is a matter of degree, and though, other things being equal, the greater the conformity the better—other things are rarely equal. A lesser degree of conformity is often to be preferred precisely because it helps realization of other goals.

In considering the relation between the rule of law and other values the law should serve, it is of particular importance to remember that the rule of law is essentially a negative value. It is merely designed to minimize the harm to freedom and dignity which the law may cause in its pursuit of its goals however laudable these may be. Finally, regarding the rule of law as the inherent excellence of the law means that it fulfils essentially a subservient role. Conformity to it makes the law a good instrument for achieving certain goals, but conformity to the rule of law is not itself an ultimate goal. This subservient role of the doctrine shows both its power and its limitations. On the one hand, if the pursuit of certain goals is entirely incompatible with the rule of law, then these goals should not be pursued by legal means. But on the other hand one should be wary of disqualifying the legal pursuit of major social goals in the name of the rule of law. After all, the rule of law is meant to enable the law to promote social good, and should not be lightly used to show that it should not do so. Sacrificing too many social goals on the altar of the rule of law may make the law barren and empty.

[15]F. A. Hayek, *The Constitution of Liberty* (Chicago, 1960), pp. 227–8.

## QUESTIONS

1. In the passage Raz quotes, Hayek says, "As a true law should not name any particulars, so it should especially not single out any specific persons or group of persons." Explain what the issue is here. What, if anything, is bad about laws that single out persons or groups of persons? Is it possible for laws to apply differently to different classes of people without "singling them out" in the bad sense?

2. Does it help to make legislatures in a democracy more responsive to the people if government acts strictly according to laws that it has announced well in advance? Explain why or why not.

3. Raz says, "Like other instruments, the law has a specific virtue which is morally neutral in being neutral as to the end to which the instrument is put. It is the virtue of efficiency; the virtue of the instrument as an instrument." Suppose that a defender of the rule of law answers, "The rule of law is not simply a virtue of efficiency, because it can make it more difficult for would-be tyrants to achieve their ends. It can be quite an annoying obstacle for the would-be tyrant to be required to stick to laws he has already enacted rather than simply to do what he wants when he wants it. Moreover, adherence to the rule of law qualifies as a moral virtue, because it involves respect for people, their plans, and their reasonable expectations." Who has the better case, Raz or the defender of the moral quality of the rule of law?

4. Raz argues that "[p]redictability in one's environment does increase one's power of action." But then Raz goes on to argue that this is not what is meant by *political* freedom, which involves limits imposed on public authorities "in order to minimize interference with personal freedom." Does it increase your personal freedom if you can know very clearly what behavior of yours will lead to punishments, and what behavior will not? If authorities are required to adhere to public rules that make the behavior of authorities generally predictable, would that yield greater political freedom (on Raz's definition of political freedom)?

# PART TWO

# The Limits of the Authority of Society Over the Individual

Law shapes and controls our behavior. It does this by establishing disincentives as well as incentives of various kinds, ranging from outright coercion to taxes and the enforcement, under certain conditions, of contracts, wills, and trusts. Coercion, of course, is the most familiar method of control. But to coerce people is a serious matter and in need of justification. Unless there is some special and powerful justification, we think that it is wrong for one individual to coerce another by making demands backed by threats. The situation is not very different when individuals are being coerced by the state. Given the importance and value of liberty and the necessity of criminal laws, government and citizens alike must have clear guidance about the kinds of behavior that are regulated by the criminal law. Without this guidance, the individual's and society's great interest in individual liberty is all too likely to get lost in the political demands of the moment. To demand that there be a law against behavior one does not like is a natural and often dangerous temptation.

## LIBERTY AND LIBERALISM

There would be no reason to concern ourselves with the problems of demarcating a sphere of individual liberty if liberty itself were of no great importance. Our contemporary preoccupation with legal issues about individual privacy, victimless crimes, paternalistic interferences with liberty, and preventing people from being deeply offended derives from our commitment to individual liberty.

This commitment to individual liberty has long presented a fundamental conflict which today is again giving rise to a major public debate. On the one hand, we are committed to the liberty of the individual against the power of the majority, acting through the law, to control the individual's behavior. On the other hand, it is part of the democratic ideal that the enactment of laws for social control belongs to the people acting through the principle of majority rule.

The most interesting and controversial cases that the legal system is likely to confront are precisely those in which some have reason to fear that the majoritarian political process has encroached, or will encroach, on their liberties. The first task of philosophy is to examine the justification for respecting individual liberty. With this in mind, we will be in a better position to deal with cases in which individual liberty conflicts with the will of the majority.

Notice that there is an argument, at least superficially appealing, that can be made in favor of the will of the majority whenever it conflicts with the liberties valued by a smaller group. Between the liberty of the majority to enact the legal restrictions it wants and the liberty of a minority to be free of those restrictions, the argument goes, is a question of weighing one liberty against the other. And this favors the liberty of the majority, since there are more people in the majority.

There is something wrong with this argument. It is the job of philosophy not only to recognize that it is wrong but also to explain why. And if we can explain why individual liberty is important enough to take precedence over the will of the majority, we will be in a better position to explain when it should have priority.

Utilitarianism, using the principle that government and laws are to be designed to promote the greatest overall happiness, has long been prominent in attempts to defend a sphere of individual liberty from the law's encroachment. But unless the utilitarian defense of liberty is carefully stated, it is likely to run into the same kind of snag. For if the object is to promote the greatest overall balance of happiness over discontent, it would again seem that the majority ought to get its way. Weighing the majority's desire to impose restrictions on behavior against the minority's desire to be free of those restrictions, the majority, especially if large enough, is almost sure to win the utilitarian weighing. The choice becomes a matter of satisfying the wants of a larger, or of a smaller, group of people.

Sophisticated utilitarian defenses of liberty, such as John Stuart Mill's (an excerpt from which is reprinted here), avoid objections such as these by stressing that it is the long-term interests of human beings, not their immediate good feelings, that law and government should facilitate. In the pursuit of happiness, individuals are in a far better position to make wise and informed choices than is the state. And, since the unrestricted operation of the majority rule principle so easily leads to self-indulgent excesses on the part of the majority, it is important to recognize the right of the individual to be free in all matters that do not, as Mill puts it, "prejudicially affect the interests of others."

Other thinkers, like F. A. Hayek,[1] put special stress on an idea already present in Mill's thinking: No government or legislature could possibly possess anywhere near the total amount of information that individuals have about their own lives, behavior, and happiness. So long as individuals are not permitted to injure or coerce one another, the order

---

[1]See, for example, Hayek's *The Constitution of Liberty* (Chicago: University of Chicago Press, 1960), and several of the essays in Hayek's *Studies in Philosophy, Politics and Economics* (London: Routledge & Kegan Paul, 1967).

that they spontaneously achieve for themselves will be superior to any order that government could attempt to impose on them.

As a public justification of liberty in a pluralistic democracy, utilitarianism gives rise to some further problems. In a pluralistic democracy, there are many religious views, lifestyles, and ethnic groups. Within the separate subgroups, no doubt, solidarity and social unity can be readily achieved. United by their particular beliefs about God, sin, and salvation, members of a homogeneous religious community will have little difficulty in developing a sense of unity and belonging. So too for many nonreligious groups. And, in a society in which individual liberty is viewed as a right, these groups will be able to live with one another as well. But what will be the public basis, the publicly recognized justification, of that liberty? Even if a theoretically sound utilitarian justification can be given for individual liberty, utilitarianism itself is based on a conception of the good that members of some of these groups do not, indeed could not, accept. That happiness should be the main aim of government and law is likely to be controversial in a pluralistic society.

Whether, and if so how, to find a public and unifying basis of justifying liberty has caused much debate recently. One line of approach is to abandon hope for a public basis and the social unity it can provide. If we take this path, we assume that there is no independent, objective basis on which to compare claims and resolve disputes between groups and viewpoints. Social peace, if it exists at all, will have to be based on a kind of unstable mutual accommodation of interests, a *modus vivendi*,[2] among groups whose power relations could change at any time.

Another approach is to defend liberty on some basis other than a controversial concept of the good. An approach of this sort might then proceed either by attempting to defend liberty without any reliance at all on the idea that liberty will do good in the world, or by attempting to find a noncontroversial good that liberty is supposed to promote.

John Rawls, in an article reprinted here, provides still another approach, what he calls an "overlapping consensus." According to this line of thought, social unity within a diverse society does not require agreement of entire world-views, religious and metaphysical beliefs, or moral visions. It requires agreement only on certain core values and conceptions of political justice.

## THE PROPER SPHERE OF INDIVIDUAL LIBERTY

Everyone, except the most deeply committed, thoroughgoing anarchists, believes that the state has some legitimate authority to limit individual liberty, and ought, as a matter of policy, to do so. The problem is to draw the line between that which is, and that which is not, the proper business of the state to control by coercion. What is sought is not just any line, but one that is both defensible in theory and applicable in practice.

When we attempt to delineate a sphere of individual liberty, it is natural to begin with Mill's distinctions in *On Liberty*. In his introduction to that essay, Mill says that "the only purpose for which power can be rightfully exercised over any member of a civilized

---

[2]This problem, along with the idea of a modus vivendi, is set out in Charles E. Larmore, *Patterns of Moral Complexity* (New York: Cambridge University Press, 1987), especially Chap. 4.

community, against his will, is to prevent harm to others." Later, he gives some additional clues, drawing a contrast between those actions which, though "hurtful to others or wanting in due consideration for their welfare," do not violate any "constituted rights." It is only that behavior which "affects prejudicially the interests of others" that properly comes within the jurisdiction of society.

These are admittedly vague phrases, but they do give us some rough but useful guidelines. For example, public behavior may be coarse, crude, and disgusting, and may hurt the feelings of other people. Does that mean that it prejudicially affects people's interests? Not necessarily. A person's *interests* include those things that have fairly extensive connections with his or her various goals and wants. Thus one has an interest in good health and in the security of having health-care insurance for oneself and one's family. One has an interest in succeeding at one's chosen profession and in getting a promotion and a raise. These are interests partly because of their deep connections to so many other things: Health is important to virtually any achievement or enjoyment, as is security against the financial burdens of ill health. Similarly, success in one's profession is typically an interest because so many other aspects of oneself are invested in it. But one generally does not have an interest in getting a vanilla ice cream cone within the next hour, no matter how nice it would be to have one. Joel Feinberg, who has attempted one of the most extensive analyses of the concept of interests, characterizes them as "all those things in which one has a stake."[3] Our interests are connected to our wants and preferences, but are not to be identified with them. We may not get what we like, want, or prefer, but it does not automatically follow that our interests have been set back.

Mill thinks that conduct violating "constituted rights" automatically comes within society's coercive authority. What does Mill mean by this? In particular, does it mean anything different from the earlier formula about conduct that causes "harm to others"?

The answer to this begins to emerge when we remember that there are certain kinds of behavior that do great damage when widely engaged in, though particular instances may cause no appreciable harm to anyone. Pollution of the atmosphere is one example of such behavior. Embezzlement of a small amount of money from a large institution is another. Thus it is unlikely that any one person's driving a polluting automobile in the Los Angeles area causes harm to anyone. Nor does one relatively small instance of embezzlement threaten the integrity of financial institutions or the profitability of a single bank, much less the value of an individual shareholder's stock. But both the polluter and the embezzler do wrong, and the behavior of each is an appropriate target for coercion. Indeed, even if there were no law against pollution or embezzlement, we would have good reason to conclude that there ought to be laws prohibiting them, because each is the sort of behavior that many people would engage in if permitted to, with serious harm as the result. The law, then, imposes the specific duties not to pollute or embezzle. This provides the basis for saying that polluting or embezzling would violate constituted rights.

But many line-drawing problems remain. Beginning with some of Mill's own remarks about the authority of society over the individual, philosophers have attempted to make distinctions among types of reasons commonly offered as justification for applying legal coercion. Introducing the "one very simple principle" that guides his essay, Mill recognizes

---

[3]Joel Feinberg, *Harm to Others* (New York: Oxford University Press, 1984), p. 34.

the prevention of harm to others as *the one* fully sufficient reason for applying coercion, while the good of the person coerced is not sufficient. Each of these kinds of reasons corresponds to a principle about the legitimacy of coercion.

Feinberg has provided an extensive list of such principles,[4] and one's philosophical position about the legitimate and desirable use of the state's coercive power can roughly be defined by the subset of these principles that one accepts. Thus the *harm principle* states that a good reason for penal legislation is that it will probably be effective in preventing harm to persons other than the actor. The *offense principle* states that the probable prevention of serious offense to persons other than the actor constitutes a good reason for such legislation.

Although there are many other principles on Feinberg's list, two more are of special interest here: *legal paternalism*, which states that preventing harm to the actor is always a good reason for a legal prohibition, and *legal moralism*, which states that the inherent wrongness, apart from offense or any kind of harm, of behavior is by itself a good reason for a legal prohibition against it. The kinds of considerations allowed by the last three principles—preventing offense to others, preventing harm to the actor, and incorporating morality for its own sake in the law—form the basis of three subsections in this part of the book.

## CONSTITUTIONAL PRIVACY AND OTHER PRIVACY INTERESTS

Many of the most controversial cases in constitutional law today have to do with what is usually called the constitutional "right of privacy." We should be careful not to confuse the "privacy" at issue in these cases with what is often meant by that term in other contexts. Indeed, there are a number of quite different interests that people have, all of which have been designated as privacy interests. Thus we frequently think of violations of privacy as having to do with spying, listening in on people's conversations, going through files to get information about individuals, publishing embarrassing facts about them, and so on. The interest that people have in not having these things happen to them is one kind of privacy interest. And it is necessary to explain why this interest in controlling information and impressions about oneself is as important as it is. It is a different kind of interest, however, from the interests which have been the focus of many controversial constitutional cases having to do with a right of privacy. Whether people have the right to buy and use contraceptives or pornography, or whether women have a right to have an abortion, focus on interests in making certain autonomous choices without interference from the state. The focus is primarily on privacy as individual sovereignty, and thus the constitutional privacy cases recall philosophical questions about the extent of society's legitimate control over the individual.

Since the U.S. Constitution explicitly recognizes various individual rights in such matters as freedom of speech and religion (First Amendment), security against unreasonable searches and seizures (Fourth Amendment), and being compelled to be a witness against oneself (Fifth Amendment), the debates about the individual's sovereignty over self are no idle philosophical exercise. Indeed, they would seem to draw, out of necessity, on philosophical theory.

[4]Ibid., pp. 26–27.

Initially, though, we must recognize a complicating factor: When courts decide issues about constitutional rights, they are constrained both by the written document and by the precedents set by many constitutional decisions over the years. Many will be quick to point out that the contours of liberty set forth in a philosophical theory do not automatically apply to constitutional law. As Justice Holmes remarked in his much quoted dissent in *Lochner v. New York*,[5] "The 14th Amendment does not enact Mr. Herbert Spencer's *Social Statics*." Some would be prepared to apply this comment to just about every other book in addition to Herbert Spencer's *Social Statics*. Indeed, the extent to which constitutional theory can be or ought to be independent of moral theory is itself a hotly debated topic, one that will arise again in Part 3. For that reason, the privacy cases included here could well be used to apply and illustrate questions about legal reasoning that we shall encounter later.

## THE READINGS

**LIBERTY AND LIBERALISM.**  The author and politician Benjamin Constant (1767–1830) counts today as one of the fathers of Western liberal thought. His famous distinction between the liberty of the ancients and the liberty of the moderns was part of his analysis of what went wrong in the aftermath of the French Revolution. The liberty of the ancients consisted in the collective exercise of sovereignty, or control, over the affairs of the community. Liberty in this sense is neither empty nor unimportant; indeed, it can be highly invigorating to a people who find in it a sense of belonging to a strong community rather than to a collection of isolated individuals.

But this kind of liberty also implies, as Constant puts it, that the individual "could himself be deprived of his status, stripped of his privileges, banished, put to death, by the discretionary will of the whole to which he belonged." For the moderns, the more important liberty is that of individual independence—of freedom *from* social control, of the liberty that involves the knowledge that one has a right, in certain matters at least, to decide and act on one's own, without social supervision and control. To this day, liberalism continues to struggle with the problem of reconciling the claims of collective control with the claims of individual sovereignty over one's own life. And, in any case, as Constant recognizes, we no longer have the option of going back to an earlier age in which the liberty of the ancients reigns.

John Stuart Mill (1806–1873), philosopher, economist, and social reformer, was also one of the leading intellectual figures of his century. John Stuart was a genius from childhood, and his father, the utilitarian philosopher James Mill, gave him a rigorous education beginning with Greek at the age of 3 and political economy at 13. The younger Mill became a leading exponent of utilitarianism, though he abandoned Bentham's conception of good as equivalent to pleasure, and developed in its place a broader definition of good as "the permanent interests of man as a progressive being."

Mill's classic *On Liberty* (1859) is an attempt to use this broader definition of good to provide a utilitarian justification for an individual's right to liberty, at least in all matters where harm to others is not involved. Several factors, Mill believes, work together to make individual choice the best strategy for producing happiness. The most important of these are the twin

[5]198 U. S. 45, 25 S. Ct. 539 (1905).

facts that (1) individuals know far more about their particular circumstances and what will lead to their happiness than the wisest legislators could possibly know, and (2) individuals have a greater immediate interest in making correct decisions regarding their own happiness.

Mill's broader conception of good comes into play in his claim that the very exercise of autonomous choice not only gives satisfaction to the individual but also, more importantly, is good in itself. Human behavior is evaluated not merely by its external results, but by its internal motivation. Professions of faith, saying prayers, and doing good deeds are all much diminished in value when they are done without the right conviction and internal motivation. And coercion is an ineffective instrument for producing behavior that is done with conviction and feeling.

John Rawls's "The Idea of an Overlapping Consensus" (1987) addresses a characteristically modern problem for liberalism's defense of individual liberty: finding some basis for social unity, for a common public justification of individual liberty, within a diverse, pluralistic society. A society that values individual liberty will have to carry on a continuing public debate about the proper balance between the majority's freedom to enact the restrictions it wants and the individual's right to be free of social control. Neither a theological nor a utilitarian theory will do as a basis for public justification, if only because such views presuppose beliefs and values which are not widely shared. And it would not be consistent with democratic ideas of freedom and equality for one group to impose its vision of the good and the just on the rest of society. Rawls also rejects as inadequate what he calls a "modus vivendi," or a mutual accommodation of interests that happens to have been achieved among groups, but is not based on any shared principle. That would be no moral foundation for social unity.

Rawls believes that under these constraints we must rely on an overlapping consensus which derives from our particular political tradition. When there is an overlapping consensus, people agree on certain political and constitutional principles, but do not need to agree on everything, not even on what supports their political and constitutional convictions. In a diverse society, for example, there must be at least some virtues that are widely shared. As Rawls puts it, these are the virtues of political cooperation like "tolerance and being ready to meet others halfway, and the virtue of reasonableness and the sense of fairness." But people do not need to share comprehensive moral views about such things as the nature of the good, or the nature of virtue and vice. Nor do they need to debate, in a public forum, whether there really is a natural law ordained by God, or whether producing the greatest overall happiness is really the ultimate end of human action.

Rawls's discussion leaves us with some important questions. If the overlapping consensus derives from a particular political tradition, which tradition are we to use when evaluating a society very different from our own? Would someone in the tradition of Western liberalism even have a basis for criticizing a non-Western, non-liberal regime? The applicability of Rawls's account may be too limited.[6]

**OFFENSE TO OTHERS.** "No man is an island," the saying goes, and it is indeed hard to find instances of behavior that affect only the agent. This is particularly so because of the human

---

[6]See Joseph Raz, "Facing Diversity: The Case of Epistemic Abstinence," *Philosophy & Public Affairs*, vol. 19, no. 1 (Winter 1990), pp. 3–46.

tendency to take an interest in what others are doing and then to be either delighted or of-fended. If one's behavior is offensive to others, how can it be regarded as conduct that af-fects only oneself? Indeed, one's behavior can deeply affect others, causing annoyance, distraction, disgust, and even horror. But one thing is immediately clear: We do not want to accept the idea that the mere dislike of others for what we are doing should operate as a kind of veto on our behavior. The liberty to do only those things to which no one seriously ob-jects is, as Hart points out, "plainly quite nugatory."[7] At the same time, we should not have to conclude that any offensive behavior, no matter how deeply, intentionally, uselessly, and avoidably offensive, should be legally protected so long as it does not cause harm.

The first case raising issues about offensive behavior is that of *Hustler Magazine v. Falwell* (1988). That case arose from a jury's finding that the publication of a parody of the nationally known minister Jerry Falwell caused him emotional distress for which he could recover compensatory and punitive damages. In *Hustler Magazine*, the U.S. Supreme Court held that a public figure can recover such damages only if, in addition to being patently offensive and intended to inflict emotional injury, the speech could not reasonably have been interpreted as stating actual facts about the public figure. The reason for this height-ened protection of speech made against public figures is the First Amendment, the rationale of which is to maintain vigorous debate in a democracy. And, perhaps most important here, however outrageous the *Hustler* parody of Falwell may have been, it is not possible to lay down a "principled standard" as Chief Justice Rehnquist puts it, distinguishing truly out-rageous expression from that which is not.

The case of *United States v. Eichman* (1990) again illustrates this central conflict be-tween society's interest in protecting free expression of opinion and society's interest in pro-tecting people from behavior that many regard as offensive. This case concerned a statute designed to protect the flag; it did not concern a jury judgment for damages based on actual emotional injury. In the *Eichman* case, the Supreme Court held that the prosecution, under the Flag Protection Act of 1989, of Shawn Eichman and others for burning the flag during a political protest was unconstitutional because it was inconsistent with the First Amendment's guarantee of free expression. Society's interest in protecting free expression is so clear and so deep that the offensiveness of an idea or its expression does not justify a prohibition. The language of Justice Brennan's opinion would seem to exclude any weigh-ing of other factors, such as whether there was an alternative, less offensive way of express-ing the idea in question. Justice Stevens's opinion, on the other hand, does entertain the possibility of weighing such factors as whether the prohibition is supported by a valid soci-etal interest and whether the prohibition leaves the speaker free to express the same ideas by some other means.

Kent Greenawalt's lecture on insults and epithets begins with a fundamental insight that must guide our application of virtually any rule, whether it be a personal rule or the First Amendment to the United States Constitution: In order to know precisely *what* is for-bidden or permitted by a rule, we need to know *why* the rule exists in the first place. Insults are obviously speech in some sense, but do they fall under the rationale of the First Amendment's prohibition on "abridging freedom of speech"? One thing we should notice is

---

[7]H. L. A. Hart, *Law, Liberty, and Morality* (Stanford, Calif.: Stanford University Press, 1963), p. 47.

that we use language for all sorts of purposes, some of which appropriately come under the protection of the Constitution, others of which do not. Thus language is used to make particular and general statements of fact or value, and such uses should be protected because of the importance of such freedom in the effective operation of a stable democracy where debate and public understanding are essential. But language is also used primarily to alter the situation in some way, such as to command, to demean, and to enter into a conspiracy, among other things, and there is no similar reason for protecting such uses of language from legal penalty, particularly when they are abusive uses.

Greenawalt discusses four bases for legal suppression of abusive language: the likelihood of physical violence, psychological hurt to the object of abuse, general offensiveness, and destructive long-term effects from reinforcement of negative attitudes. The first of these is unfortunately limited: The small and the weak and those disinclined to fight are often vulnerable to insults, but insulting them may not raise the probability of violence. So Greenawalt's suggestion is that we should not ask whether the particular victim of insult is likely to fight, but whether many people, so insulted, would be likely to respond with force. In addition, protection of people from psychological hurt as well as prevention of the reinforcement of negative attitudes are equally important reasons for the legal suppression of abusive language.

Rosemarie Tong's discussion raises an issue not yet covered in this part of the book, namely, the effects of certain kinds of pornography on women. Her discussion of pornography begins with an important distinction: between *erotica* and *thanatica*. Her definition of thanatica as representations of "sexual exchanges devoid or nearly devoid of mutual or self respect," such that the representation is degrading to at least one of the participants, is intended to distinguish it from erotica, which involves depictions of sex, but as typically involving mutual pleasure and never in a way that degrades one of the participants. The distinction between erotica and thanatica then bears directly on the larger question of whether pornography causes harm. Tong's view is that thanatica are *harmful* to all women, though not *hurtful* to all women, and that erotica, by contrast, are not harmful to women, though some women regard erotica as offensive. Although harm is caused by thanatica, and this would constitute a theoretical basis for establishing a legal remedy of some kind, the fact that not all women are hurt by thanatica means that the time is not yet ripe for such a remedy.

**PATERNALISM.** Generally, paternalism is the view that protecting a person from harm is always a good reason for limiting that person's freedom. Applied to the authority of the state, paternalism is the view that protecting people from harming themselves is always a good reason for applying legal coercion. John Stuart Mill's opposition to paternalism was so clear and emphatic that he used the example of a person's own good as his main illustration of what social coercion may *not* be used to bring about. We may prohibit someone, such as a sentry or pilot, from being drunk on duty, but we may not use the power of the state to prevent him from being drunk at home alone, even though we might thus be allowing him to harm himself. Mill's reasons, as we have seen, have to do both with the far greater likelihood of the individual knowing the best path to her or his own good, and with the value of autonomy, even if one's decision turns out to be mistaken.

It is not always easy to find examples of legal prohibitions that are based solely on paternalistic considerations. Where paternalistic reasons for limits on liberty are given, closer inspection will often show that there are nonpaternalistic reasons for those same limits. For example, laws requiring motorcyclists to wear helmets might seem to be based on purely paternalistic considerations. But if the burden of medical expenses resulting from motorcycle injuries is carried by society, the state may be justified in imposing certain restrictions on helmetless motorcycle riders in order to protect the interests of people other than the rider.

In addition to the general framework it provides, Gerald Dworkin's (1972) essay on paternalism provides us with some clues about how the antipaternalist would deal with someone who was about to sell him- or herself into slavery, or with someone about to do a rash, self-endangering thing. Selling oneself into slavery would seem to belong to a special category because it involves exercising one's liberty in order to give up one's liberty. If the value of individual liberty is the main reason for being opposed to paternalism in the first place, we should also refuse to enforce contracts for slavery, contracts which would severely limit future choices of the would-be slave. Dworkin suggests that when we are dealing with people who are about to do a rash thing based on a serious misconception about what will happen, such as jumping out a fifth-story window believing that one will float upwards, we are well justified in interfering, because the person would undoubtedly not do that if he or she really understood the consequences. It is different, though, in the case of people who know well what the consequences and their probabilities are, but who love risk taking much more than the average person.

The right to die case of *Cruzan v. Director, Missouri Department of Health* (1990) poses a slightly different issue about paternalism. Our claim to act for another person would seem to have better justification in cases in which the person for whom we are acting is somehow not competent. Our concern to respect what a person would want if rational and not mistaken, or what a person would choose if she were capable of making an informed choice or any choice at all, often leads to the next best thing, what has been called a "substituted judgment." In cases where a brain-damaged person lives in a persistent vegetative state requiring active medical intervention to go on living, much can depend on judgments about whether that person would have wanted to be allowed to die. Because of greatly increased possibilities for prolonging life through technologically advanced medical intervention, respect for the individual patient's autonomy requires that the patient give informed consent to life-sustaining intervention. In *Cruzan*, Chief Justice Rehnquist notes that a corollary of this doctrine of informed consent is the right to refuse treatment. But the incompetence of the patient, Nancy Cruzan, made such actual consent impossible. Prior to the case, the Missouri Supreme Court had refused Nancy Cruzan's family the right to have her water and feeding tube disconnected on grounds that they had not presented "clear and convincing evidence" that this is what she would have wanted.

*Cruzan* was the first right to die case considered by the Supreme Court and led to the decision excerpted here. Surveying some of the history and difficulties involved in attempting to make a judgment in place of an incompetent person and recognizing that patients in a vegetative state like Cruzan's have both a right to privacy and a right to give informed consent, the Supreme Court upheld the constitutionality of the Missouri law setting the standard of "clear and convincing evidence." The Cruzan family eventually returned to the

Missouri court. On this occasion, some of Nancy Cruzan's co-workers testified that she had told them she would never want to live like a "vegetable." This testimony persuaded the state court to rule that there was clear and convincing evidence of her wishes. Nancy Cruzan died on December 26, 1990, 12 days after having been disconnected from the tube that supplied her with food and water.

LEGAL MORALISM. When the criminalization of behavior is debated, an additional kind of reason, one not falling under any of the above categories, is sometimes offered. Legal moralists claim that the moral wrongness of behavior—even where there is no harm to anyone and the private location of the behavior eliminates any direct offense to others—is by itself a good reason to impose a legal prohibition on it. Legal moralism should not be confused with the view that the law ought to coincide, in large part, with morality. Of course it is true that laws against theft and murder, among many other examples, coincide with morality. But they are not, or need not be, enacted *simply* because theft and murder are morally wrong; they are enacted for the different reason that theft and murder involve harming others.

It is not always easy to find clear examples of legal moralist beliefs. When someone claims that a certain kind of behavior ought to be illegal simply because it is wrong or a sin, that claim may still be based on the idea of harm, even though it makes no reference to harm. It may turn out that the one making that claim also believes that all wrongs somehow involve harms, or that there is a God who punishes all sins. It may also turn out that many convictions only appear to us to be legal moralist because we do not appreciate the ways in which they are based on false beliefs—even outright superstitions—about the harm that will result from transgressions of the moral code. Even some who are quite clearly legal moral-ists often defend their position by using a mixture of arguments from other sources, for ex-ample, arguments that the failure to enforce a society's deeply held moral convictions will lead to the disintegration of society, since moral convictions are the social "glue" holding a people together, and without legal reinforcement of these convictions, the very identity of the society will be threatened.[8]

James Fitzjames Stephen (1829–1894), an English legal scholar, judge, and onetime disciple of Mill's utilitarian philosophy, published *Liberty, Equality, Fraternity* (1873) as an attack on liberalism in general and John Stuart Mill's *On Liberty* in particular. Taking a legal moralist position, Stephen directs several related challenges at Mill's liberalism. The most general is that the various parts of the law, including most criminal law and the law of contracts, cannot be explained by Mill's simple rationale of preventing harm. Were we to stick consistently to Mill's principles, very much of what we know and want in the law would have to be discarded. Moreover, Stephen thinks Mill is forced to engage in some in-tellectual contortions in his attempt to prove that laws which he himself would approve fit his principles.

Stephen's conception of the role of law begins with the idea that the object of "morally intolerant legislation. . . . is to establish, to maintain, and to give power to that which the legis-lator regards as a good moral system or standard." This is clear legal moralism. The legislator is

---

[8]Patrick Devlin, "Morals and the Criminal Law," in *The Enforcement of Morals* (New York: Oxford University Press, 1965).

to begin with a conception of moral good and moral right. The object of legislation is to implant these standards and to give as much effect to them as possible.

But Stephen, like many other legal moralists, takes pains to acknowledge that the criminal law has significant limitations as a device for making people moral. The criminal law is the "roughest engine" for many purposes including this one, and it obviously would not succeed, say, in forcing people to be charitable or kind. Stephen also recognizes the importance of individual privacy, so he rejects the sweeping proposal of "treating vice in general as a crime." In addition, Stephen thinks that the law will only bring upon itself condemnation and disrepute if anything is punished which is not also strenuously condemned by public opinion. All of this highlights a feature of typical legal moralism which it is important to understand: The legal moralist holds that the moral wrongness of certain behavior is always *a* reason for legislation against it, not that it is always a *sufficient* reason. But with such limitations having been acknowledged, Stephen's legal moralism still emerges intact and robust. Legal condemnation serves to give vent to feelings of anger and resentment and hatred. These feelings, when directed toward what Stephen calls "the grosser forms of vice," are entirely natural and healthy, and giving vent to them "in a regular public and legal manner" is often reason enough for the legal prohibition.

INDIVIDUAL SOVEREIGNTY AND CONSTITUTIONAL PRIVACY. Few cases in constitutional law have been more controversial or of greater philosophical interest than *Griswold v. Connecticut* (1965). As the first in a series of "right to privacy" cases, *Griswold* struck down as unconstitutional a Connecticut statute that made illegal the use, sale, or counseling in the use or sale, of articles or instruments "for the purpose of preventing conception." From the time it was announced right up to the present day, opponents of this decision have usually begun their criticism with the observation that the United States Constitution makes no mention anywhere of a "right of privacy." Stating the opinion of the Court, Justice Douglas spoke of "penumbras" and "emanations" from the Bill of Rights, particularly from the First, Third, Fourth, Fifth, and Ninth Amendments. Indeed, the right of privacy existed prior to the Constitution itself: "We deal with a right of privacy older than the Bill of Rights," Justice Douglas writes.

On the one side of this controversy, there are those who believe that the Bill of Rights can only be understood as articulating a conception of individual rights, as presupposing a theory of the limits of the law's authority over the individual. In this view, those who interpret the Constitution must work toward the most coherent, theoretically defensible application of it they can, whether or not the framers of the Constitution anticipated all the eventualities the courts would one day have to deal with.

On the other side of the controversy is a view already contained in Justice Black's dissenting opinion in *Griswold*. It is that the courts must stick as much as possible to the specific, formulated terms of the Constitution and attempt to understand them as a reasonable person at the time of the framers would have understood them. In this view, if there is grand theorizing to do about the desirability of a right not specifically mentioned in the Constitution, that is the job of those who enact law; it is not up to the courts whose job is only to apply law. "I like my privacy as well as the next one," says Justice Black, "but I am nevertheless compelled to admit that government has a right to invade it unless prohibited by some specific constitutional provision."

Both sides in this controversy recognize that the concept of a right of privacy that derives from "emanations" and "penumbras" calls upon courts to make many important judgments about the precise contours of such a right. Since *Griswold*, the Court has, among other things, had to consider whether this right includes the possession at home of an obscene film,[9] a woman's decision to have an abortion (*Roe v. Wade*), the presentation of obscene materials in a commercial movie theater,[10] and homosexual sodomy (*Bowers v. Hardwick*).

*Roe v. Wade* (1973) illustrates the reasons for the political and philosophical controversies arising from the right of privacy cases perhaps better than any other. The most obvious of these is that the political conflict over abortion has evoked some of the most emotionally heated discussions of public issues that have occurred in the history of the nation. The Court's holding in *Roe* put it squarely on one side of this conflict, with the result that views about the correctness of *Roe* have been one of the main criteria used by both sides to determine the acceptability of nominees to serve on the Court.

But this particular political conflict should not be allowed to obscure other disagreements of deeper philosophical interest that arise out of *Roe*. These disagreements can be seen more clearly when we recognize that the decision in that case, and especially the opinion given in justification of that decision, have been criticized by many who nevertheless strongly believe that abortion ought to be recognized as a woman's right. The main criticisms of *Roe* include the following: (a) The claim that a fetus is a person under the Constitution—a crucial claim of abortion opponents—was dismissed with hardly any argument. (b) In doing so, the Court failed to base its decision on a neutral principle which all who are committed to the Constitution can accept. (c) The Court, in effect, arrogated to itself the power to define personhood, and this kind of self-arrogation threatens the whole idea of constitutional rights. Since rights belong to persons and not things, one's rights can be taken away if one's personhood can be defined away. (d) The boundaries of personhood actually drawn by the Court—six to seven months into pregnancy, the approximate point of viability of the fetus outside the mother's womb—are arbitrary and shifting and thus should be made by a legislature, not a court.

It is in the spirit of sidestepping these objections that Donald Regan's "Rewriting *Roe v. Wade*" (1979) was written. His argument does not challenge the claim that the fetus is a person from the point of conception, nor does it attempt to draw new boundaries defining personhood. Instead, his argument is guided by the analogy of samaritan laws. A stranger (the fetus) does not have an unlimited claim on the samaritan (the pregnant woman) for whatever is necessary to the continuation of life. By using the analogy of samaritan law, Regan's attempt can be seen as making use of a classic device for basing a decision on what is sometimes called "neutral principle": Samaritan law can be seen as a neutral principle on which to base the permissibility of abortion because Samaritan law has long existed, and its applicability to the fetus-as-person can be grasped once the details of the

---

[9]*Stanley v. Georgia*, 394 U. S. 557, 89 S. Ct. 1243 (1969).
[10]*Paris Adult Theatre I v. Slaton*, 413 U. S. 49, 93 S. Ct. 2628 (1973).

analogy are understood. If the analogy is a sound one, it can be argued that the permissibility of abortion has long been implicit in the law and is no arbitrary creation of a court.

*Bowers v. Hardwick* (1986), another right of privacy decision, also touches upon a number of the issues covered in this book. Hardwick had been arrested for homosexual sodomy in his home by a police officer who was already there legally. The latter fact is important because of the great difficulty, to say nothing of reluctance, that there usually is in prosecuting people for such things as sodomy or the use of contraceptives, when these activities take place in private homes. At issue was the constitutionality of the Georgia statute, which prohibited both homosexual and heterosexual sodomy. A bitterly divided Court held, by a slim majority, that the constitutional right of privacy does not extend to homosexual sodomy. As might be expected in discussions of the proper boundaries of a right of privacy that is already recognized, the main issue was the underlying rationale of the general right. Justice White's majority opinion held that there is no connection between the earlier cases on privacy and the present one, there being no connection between marriage, family relationships, and so on, and homosexual sodomy. Justice Brennan's minority opinion, on the other hand, claimed that the rationale for protecting privacy in marital and familial situations applies as well to homosexual relationships.

When we look to the deeper rationale of a recognized right in order to determine its more precise boundaries, we need some conception of what will count as an adequate rationale. The Court's majority stressed the long standing illegality and perceived immorality of homosexual sodomy, while Justice Brennan emphasized the importance of privacy in the exercise of individual autonomy. If the rationale is that the rights recognized in the Constitution are to reflect traditional moral views, then what exactly are these traditional moral views, and how do we go about determining what they are? To be considered moral in the first place, must those views be consistent and based on true beliefs, or does virtually any kind of reaction, if sufficiently widespread, count as a moral view? And if it is the value of individual liberty and autonomy that underlies the right of privacy, then what is the proper sphere of that liberty?

Robert Bork's "Judicial Moral Philosophy and the Right of Privacy" (1990) criticizes the judicial recognition of a constitutional right of privacy. Approving of the decision in *Bowers* but disagreeing with the constitutional right to an abortion announced in *Roe*, Bork argues that judges ought to follow the original meaning of the Constitution as a written document. They should not attempt to decide constitutional questions in accordance with the reasoning and principles of a coherent political philosophy since doing so is not provided for within the original meaning of the document. Bork has defended the originalist conception partly because of his view that appeals to moral and political philosophy are too subjective and uncertain to be used as a basis for law. This objection recalls the debate between natural law and legal positivism in Part 1 and anticipates the debate about legal reasoning taken up in Part 3.

**OTHER PRIVACY INTERESTS.** The chapter from Stanley I. Benn's *A Theory of Freedom* (1988) serves to remind us that there is another important privacy interest, one that centers on our concern about controlling the information and perceptions that others get of us. We think it violates another person's privacy to secretly photograph him or her at home alone, not so much because it violates that person's autonomy, but because it involves gaining impressions (images and the impressions to which they give rise) of that person in circumstances where one should be able to be confident that other people will observe constraints. Why should this be the case? On what principle(s) do we base our objection to invasions of this privacy interest? Stanley Benn's discussion of privacy attempts to analyze this more familiar idea of privacy. His analysis, while recognizing the importance of privacy in protecting people from harms that others may do to them, is nevertheless based on a principle of respect for persons. Finding oneself as the object of scrutiny, one is no longer able to think of oneself as "pure freedom, as originator and chooser," and this brings one to think of oneself as limited, as a fixed entity, a thing in the world. Benn's analysis implies that at some deeper level there is a connection between privacy and autonomy.

# Liberty and Liberalism

## *Benjamin Constant*

# THE LIBERTY OF THE ANCIENTS COMPARED WITH THAT OF THE MODERNS*

Gentlemen,

I wish to submit for your attention a few distinctions, still rather new, between two kinds of liberty: these differences have thus far remained unnoticed, or at least insufficiently remarked. The first is the liberty the exercise of which was so dear to the ancient peoples; the second the one the enjoyment of which is especially precious to the modern nations. If I am right, this investigation will prove interesting from two different angles.

Firstly, the confusion of these two kinds of liberty has been amongst us, in the all too famous days of our revolution, the cause of many an evil. France was exhausted by useless experiments, the authors of which, irritated by their poor success, sought to force her to enjoy the good she did not want, and denied her the good which she did want.

Secondly, called as we are by our happy revolution (I call it happy, despite its excesses, because I concentrate my attention on its results) to enjoy the benefits of representative government, it is curious and interesting to discover why this form of government, the only one in the shelter of which we could find some freedom and peace today, was totally unknown to the free nations of antiquity.

I know that there are writers who have claimed to distinguish traces of it among some ancient peoples, in the Lacedaemonian republic for example, or amongst our ancestors the Gauls; but they are mistaken.

The Lacedaemonian government was a monastic aristocracy, and in no way a representative government. The power of the kings was limited, but it was limited by the ephors, and not by men invested with a mission similar to that which election confers today on the defenders of our liberties. The ephors, no doubt, though originally created by the kings, were elected by the people. But there were only five of them. Their authority was as much religious as political; they even shared in the administration of government, that is, in the executive power. Thus their prerogative, like that of almost all popular magistrates in the ancient republics, far from being simply a barrier against tyranny, became sometimes itself an insufferable tyranny.

The regime of the Gauls, which quite resembled the one that a certain party would like to restore to us,[a] was at the same time theocratic and warlike. The priests enjoyed unlimited power. The military class or nobility had markedly insolent and oppressive privileges; the people had no rights and no safeguards.

In Rome the tribunes had, up to a point, a representative mission. They were the organs of those plebeians whom the oligarchy—which is the same in all ages—had submitted, in overthrowing the kings, to so harsh a slavery. The people, however, exercised a

*From *Benjamin Constant: Political Writings* (1988), translated and edited by Biancamaria Fontana. Pages 309–12, 316–19. Reprinted by permission of Cambridge University Press and Dr. Biancamaria Fontana. [All subsequent footnotes in this selection are those of Dr. Fontana.]

[a]If the model of the ancient republics had dominated the politics of the Jacobins, during the Restoration the return to feudal liberty became the ideal of the monarchical 'reformers'. The most influential contemporary source is: Robert de Montlosier, *De la monarchie française*. For a survey of the political interpretations of France's feudal past, see: Stanley Mellon, *The Political Uses of History, a Study of Historians in the French Restoration* (Stanford, California, 1958); Shirley M. Gruner, 'Political Historiography in Restoration France,' *History and Theory*, 8 (1969), 346–65.

large part of the political rights directly. They met to vote on the laws and to judge the patricians against whom charges had been levelled: thus there were, in Rome, only feeble traces of a representative system.

This system is a discovery of the moderns, and you will see, Gentlemen, that the condition of the human race in antiquity did not allow for the introduction or establishment of an institution of this nature. The ancient peoples could neither feel the need for it, nor appreciate its advantages. Their social organization led them to desire an entirely different freedom from the one which this system grants to us.

Tonight's lecture will be devoted to demonstrating this truth to you.

First ask yourselves, Gentlemen, what an Englishman, a Frenchman, and a citizen of the United States of America understand today by the word 'liberty'.

For each of them it is the right to be subjected only to the laws, and to be neither arrested, detained, put to death or maltreated in any way by the arbitrary will of one or more individuals. It is the right of everyone to express their opinion, choose a profession and practise it, to dispose of property, and even to abuse it; to come and go without permission, and without having to account for their motives or undertakings. It is everyone's right to associate with other individuals, either to discuss their interests, or to profess the religion which they and their associates prefer, even simply to occupy their days or hours in a way which is most compatible with their inclinations or whims. Finally it is everyone's right to exercise some influence on the administration of the government, either by electing all or particular officials, or through representations, petitions, demands to which the authorities are more or less compelled to pay heed. Now compare this liberty with that of the ancients.

The latter consisted in exercising collectively, but directly, several parts of the complete sovereignty; in deliberating, in the public square, over war and peace; in form-

ing alliances with foreign governments; in voting laws, in pronouncing judgements; in examining the accounts, the acts, the stewardship of the magistrates; in calling them to appear in front of the assembled people, in accusing, condemning or absolving them. But if this was what the ancients called liberty, they admitted as compatible with this collective freedom the complete subjection of the individual to the authority of the community. You find among them almost none of the enjoyments which we have just seen form part of the liberty of the moderns. All private actions were submitted to a severe surveillance. No importance was given to individual independence, neither in relation to opinions, nor to labour, nor, above all, to religion. The right to choose one's own religious affiliation, a right which we regard as one of the most precious, would have seemed to the ancients a crime and a sacrilege. In the domains which seem to us the most useful, the authority of the social body interposed itself and obstructed the will of individuals. Among the Spartans, Therpandrus could not add a string to his lyre without causing offence to the ephors. In the most domestic of relations the public authority again intervened. The young Lacedaemonian could not visit his new bride freely. In Rome, the censors cast a searching eye over family life. The laws regulated customs, and as customs touch on everything, there was hardly anything that the laws did not regulate.

Thus among the ancients the individual, almost always sovereign in public affairs, was a slave in all his private relations. As a citizen, he decided on peace and war; as a private individual, he was constrained, watched and repressed in all his movements; as a member of the collective body, he interrogated, dismissed, condemned, beggared, exiled, or sentenced to death his magistrates and superiors; as a subject of the collective body he could himself be deprived of his status, stripped of his privileges, banished, put to death, by the discretionary will of the whole to which he belonged. Among the moderns, on the contrary, the individual, independent in his private life, is, even in the freest of states, sovereign only in appearance. His sovereignty is restricted and almost always suspended. If, at fixed and rare intervals, in which he is again surrounded by precautions and obstacles, he exercises this sovereignty, it is always only to renounce it. . . .

The share which in antiquity everyone held in national sovereignty was by no means an abstract presumption as it is in our own day. The will of each individual had real influence: the exercise of this will was a vivid and repeated pleasure. Consequently the ancients were ready to make many a sacrifice to preserve their political rights and their share in the administration of the state. Everybody, feeling with pride all that his suffrage was worth, found in this awareness of his personal importance a great compensation.

This compensation no longer exists for us today. Lost in the multitude, the individual can almost never perceive the influence he exercises. Never does his will impress itself upon the whole; nothing confirms in his eyes his own cooperation.

The exercise of political rights, therefore, offers us but a part of the pleasures that the ancients found in it, while at the same time the progress of civilization, the commercial tendency of the age, the communication amongst peoples, have infinitely multiplied and varied the means of personal happiness.

It follows that we must be far more attached than the ancients to our individual independence. For the ancients when they sacrificed that independence to their political rights, sacrificed less to obtain more; while in making the same sacrifice, we would give more to obtain less.

The aim of the ancients was the sharing of social power among the citizens of the same fatherland: this is what they called liberty. The aim of the moderns is the enjoyment of security in private pleasures; and they call liberty the guarantees accorded by institutions to these pleasures.

I said at the beginning that, through their failure to perceive these differences, otherwise well–intentioned men caused infinite evils during our long and stormy revolution. God forbid that I should reproach them too harshly. Their error itself was excusable. One could not read the beautiful pages of antiquity, one could not recall the actions of its great men, without feeling an indefinable and special emotion, which nothing modern can possibly arouse. The old elements of a nature, one could almost say, earlier than our own, seem to awaken in us in the face of these memories. It is difficult not to regret the time when the faculties of man developed along an already trodden path, but in so wide a career, so strong in their own powers, with such a feeling of energy and dignity. Once we abandon ourselves to this regret, it is impossible not to wish to imitate what we regret. This impression was very deep, especially when we lived under vicious governments, which, without being strong, were repressive in their effects; absurd in their principles; wretched in action; governments which had as their strength arbitrary power; for their purpose the belittling of mankind; and which some individuals still dare to praise to us today, as if we could ever forget that we have been the witnesses and the victims of their obstinacy, of their impotence and of their overthrow. The aim of our reformers was noble and generous. Who among us did not feel his heart beat with hope at the outset of the course which they seemed to open up? And shame, even today, on whoever does not feel the need to declare that acknowledging a few errors committed by our first guides does not mean blighting their memory or disowning the opinions which the friends of mankind have professed throughout the ages.

But those men had derived several of their theories from the works of two philosophers who had themselves failed to recognize the changes brought by two thousand years in the dispositions of mankind. I shall perhaps at some point examine the system of the most illustrious of these philosophers, of Jean–Jacques Rousseau, and I shall show that, by transposing into our modern age an extent of social power, of collective sovereignty, which belonged to other centuries, this sublime genius, animated by the purest love of liberty, has nevertheless furnished deadly pretexts for more than one kind of tyranny. No doubt, in pointing out what I regard as a misunderstanding which it is important to uncover, I shall be careful in my refutation, and respectful in my criticism. I shall certainly refrain from joining myself to the detractors of a great man. When chance has it that I find myself apparently in agreement with them on some one particular point, I suspect myself; and to console myself for appearing for a moment in agreement with them on a single partial question, I need to disown and denounce with all my energies these pretended allies.

Nevertheless, the interests of truth must prevail over considerations which make the glory of a prodigious talent and the authority of an immense reputation so powerful. Moreover, as we shall see, it is not to Rousseau that we must chiefly attribute the error against which I am going to argue; this is to be imputed much more to one of his successors, less eloquent but no less austere and a hundred times more exaggerated. The latter, the abbé de Mably, can be regarded as the representative of the system which, according to the maxims of ancient liberty, demands that the citizens should be entirely subjected in order for the nation to be sovereign, and that the individual should be enslaved for the people to be free.

The abbé de Mably,[a] like Rousseau and many others, had mistaken, just as the ancients did, the authority of the social body for liberty; and to him any means seemed good if it extended his area of authority over that recalcitrant part of human existence whose independence he deplored. The regret he expresses everywhere in his works is that the law can only cover actions. He would have liked it to cover the most fleeting thoughts and impressions; to pursue man relentlessly, leaving him no refuge in which he might escape from its power. No sooner did he learn, among no matter what people, of some oppressive measure, then he thought he had made a discovery and proposed it as a model. He detested individual liberty like a personal enemy; and whenever in history he came across a nation totally deprived of it, even if it had no political liberty, he could not help admiring it. He went into ecstasies over the Egyptians, because, as he said, among them everything was prescribed by the law, down to relaxations and needs: everything was subjected to the empire of the legislator. Every moment of the day was filled by some duty; love itself was the object of this respected intervention, and it was the law that in turn opened and closed the curtains of the nuptial bed. . . .

## QUESTIONS

1. Why would anyone have been content, as many of the French Revolutionaries seem to have been, to establish a political system that fails to provide for Constant's "liberty of the moderns"? (Compare J.S. Mill's comment in Chapter 1 of *On Liberty*: "The notion that the people have no need to limit their power over themselves might seem axiomatic, when popular government was a thing only dreamed about, or read of as having existed at some distant period of the past.")

[a]Gabriel Bonnot de Mably, *De la législation ou principes des lois.*

2. Explain whether you agree or disagree with the following comment: "The concepts of freedom and equality are broad, elastic concepts. Consequently, each scheme, that providing for the liberty of the ancients, and that providing for the liberty of the moderns, can provide in its separate way both for freedom, and for equality."

3. Constant defends the importance of what we would call the rule of law. The rule of law requires, among other things, clear and certain definitions of what counts as a crime—definitions that remain unchanged over long periods of time. Is the rule of law likely to be as important under a system in which liberty of the ancients prevails?

4. Imagine and compare: (a) a world in which the constitutions and governments of all nations are organized to promote their citizens' liberty, but in the sense of Constant's "liberty of the ancients," and (b) a world in which all constitutions and governments are organized to promote their citizens' liberty in the sense of the "liberty of the moderns." Other things being equal, would (a) or (b) be the world likely to have more wars between nations?

## *John Stuart Mill*
# ON LIBERTY*

. . . The object of this Essay is to assert one very simple principle, as entitled to govern absolutely the dealings of society with the individual in the way of compulsion and control, whether the means used be physical force in the form of legal penalties, or the moral coercion of public opinion. That principle is, that the sole end for which mankind are warranted, individually or collectively, in interfering with the liberty of action of any of their number, is self–protection. That the only purpose for which power can be rightfully exercised over any member of a civilised community, against his will, is to prevent harm to others. His own good, either physical or moral, is not a sufficient warrant. He cannot rightfully be compelled to do or forbear because it will be better for him to do so, because it will make him happier, because, in the opinions of others, to do so would be wise, or even right. These are good reasons for remonstrating with him, or reasoning with him, or persuading him, or entreating him, but not for compelling him, or visiting him with any evil in case he do otherwise. To justify that, the conduct from which it is desired to deter him, must be calculated to produce evil to some one else. The only part of the conduct of any one, for which he is amenable to society, is that which concerns others. In the part which merely concerns himself, his independence is, of right, absolute. Over himself, over his own body and mind, the individual is sovereign.

It is, perhaps, hardly necessary to say that this doctrine is meant to apply only to human beings in the maturity of their faculties. We are not speaking of children, or of young persons below the age which the law may fix as that of manhood or womanhood. Those who are still in a state to require being taken care of by others, must be protected against their own actions as well as against external injury. For the same reason, we may leave out of consideration those backward states of society in which the race itself may

*From *On Liberty*, parts of Chaps. 1 and 2; all of Chap. 4. First published in 1859.

be considered as in its nonage. The early difficulties in the way of spontaneous progress are so great, that there is seldom any choice of means for overcoming them; and a ruler full of the spirit of improvement is warranted in the use of any expedients that will attain an end, perhaps otherwise unattainable. Despotism is a legitimate mode of government in dealing with barbarians, provided the end be their improvement, and the means justified by actually effecting that end. Liberty, as a principle, has no application to any state of things anterior to the time when mankind have become capable of being improved by free and equal discussion. Until then, there is nothing for them but implicit obedience to an Akbar or a Charlemagne, if they are so fortunate as to find one. But as soon as mankind have attained the capacity of being guided to their own improvement by conviction or persuasion (a period long since reached in all nations with whom we need here concern ourselves), compulsion, either in the direct form or in that of pains and penalties for non–compliance, is no longer admissible as a means to their own good, and justifiable only for the security of others.

It is proper to state that I forego any advantage which could be derived to my argument from the idea of abstract right, as a thing independent of utility. I regard utility as the ultimate appeal on all ethical questions; but it must be utility in the largest sense, grounded on the permanent interests of man as a progressive being. Those interests, I contend, authorise the subjection of individual spontaneity to external control, only in respect to those actions of each, which concern the interest of other people. If any one does an act hurtful to others, there is a *prima facie* case for punishing him, by law, or, where legal penalties are not safely applicable, by general disapprobation. There are also many positive acts for the benefit of others which he may rightfully be compelled to perform; such as, to give evidence in a court of justice; to bear his fair share in the common defence, or in any other joint work necessary to the interest of the society of which he enjoys the protection; and to perform certain acts of individual beneficence, such as saving a fellow–creature's life, or interposing to protect the defenceless against ill–usage, things which whenever it is obviously a man's duty to do, he may rightfully be made responsible to society for not doing. A person may cause evil to others not only by his actions but by his inaction, and in either case he is justly accountable to them for the injury. The latter case, it is true, requires a much more cautious exercise of compulsion than the former. To make anyone answerable for doing evil to others, is the rule; to make him answerable for not preventing evil, is, comparatively speaking, the exception. Yet there are many cases clear enough and grave enough to justify that exception. In all things which regard the external relations of the individual, he is *de jure* amenable to those whose interests are concerned, and if need be, to society as their protector. There are often good reasons for not holding him to the responsibility; but these reasons must arise from the special expediencies of the case: either because it is a kind of case in which he is on the whole likely to act better, when left to his own discretion, than when controlled in any way in which society have it in their power to control him; or because the attempt to exercise control would produce other evils, greater than those which it would prevent. When such reasons as these preclude the enforcement of responsibility, the conscience of the agent himself should step into the vacant judgment seat, and protect those interests of others which have no external protection; judging himself all the more rigidly, because the case does not admit of his being made accountable to the judgment of his fellow-creatures.

But there is a sphere of action in which society, as distinguished from the individual, has, if any, only an indirect interest; comprehending all that portion of a person's life and conduct which affects only himself, or if it also affects others, only with their free, voluntary, and undeceived consent and participation. When I say only himself, I mean directly, and in the first instance: for whatever affects himself, may affect others through himself; and the objection which may be grounded on this contingency, will receive consideration in the sequel. This, then, is the appropriate region of human liberty. It comprises, first, the inward domain of consciousness; demanding liberty of conscience, in the most comprehensive sense; liberty of thought and feeling; absolute freedom of opinion and sentiment on all subjects, practical or speculative, scientific, moral, or theological. The liberty of expressing and publishing opinions may seem to fall under a different principle, since it belongs to that part of the conduct of an individual which concerns other people; but, being almost of as much importance as the liberty of thought itself, and resting in great part on the same reasons, is practically inseparable from it. Secondly, the principle requires liberty of tastes and pursuits; of framing the plan of our life to suit our own character; of doing as we like, subject to such consequences as may follow: without impediment from our fellow–creatures, so long as what we do does not harm them, even though they should think our conduct foolish, perverse, or wrong. Thirdly, from this liberty of each individual, follows the liberty, within the same limits, of combination among individuals; freedom to unite, for any purpose not involving harm to others: the persons combining being supposed to be of full age, and not forced or deceived.

No society in which these liberties are not, on the whole, respected, is free, whatever may be its form of government; and none is completely free in which they do not exist absolute and unqualified. The only freedom which deserves the name, is that of pursuing our own good in our own way, so long as we do not attempt to deprive others of theirs, or impede their efforts to obtain it. Each is the proper guardian of his own health, whether bodily, or mental and spiritual. Mankind are greater gainers by suffering each other to live as seems good to themselves, than by compelling each to live as seems good to the rest. . . .

It still remains to speak of one of the principal causes which make diversity of opinion advantageous, and will continue to do so until mankind shall have entered a stage of intellectual advancement which at present seems at an incalculable distance. We have hitherto considered only two possibilities: that the received opinion may be false, and some other opinion, consequently, true; or that, the received opinion being true, a conflict with the opposite error is essential to a clear apprehension and deep feeling of its truth. But there is a commoner case than either of these; when the conflicting doctrines, instead of being one true and the other false, share the truth between them; and the nonconforming opinion is needed to supply the remainder of the truth, of which the received doctrine embodies only a part. Popular opinions, on subjects not palpable to sense, are often true, but seldom or never the whole truth. They are a part of the truth; sometimes a greater, sometimes a smaller part, but exaggerated, distorted, and disjoined from the truths by which they ought to be accompanied and limited. Heretical opinions, on the other hand, are generally some of these suppressed and neglected truths, bursting the bonds which kept them down, and either seeking reconciliation with the truth contained in the common opinion, or fronting it as enemies, and setting themselves up, with similar exclusiveness, as the whole truth. The latter case is hitherto the most frequent, as, in the human mind, one-sidedness has always been the rule, and many-sidedness the exception. Hence, even in revolutions of opinion, one part of the truth usually sets while another rises. Even progress, which ought to superadd, for the most part only substitutes, one partial and incomplete truth for another; improvement consisting chiefly in this, that the new fragment of truth is more wanted, more adapted to the needs of the time, than that which it displaces. Such being the partial character of prevailing opinions, even when resting on a true foundation, every opinion which embodies somewhat of the portion of truth which the common opinion omits, ought to be considered precious, with whatever amount of error and confusion that truth may be blended. No sober judge of human affairs will feel bound to be indignant because those who force on our notice truths which we should otherwise have overlooked, overlook some of those which we see. Rather, he will think that so long as popular truth is one-sided, it is more desirable than otherwise that unpopular truth should have one-sided asserters too; such being usually the most energetic, and the most likely to compel reluctant attention to the fragment of wisdom which they proclaim as if it were the whole.

Thus, in the eighteenth century, when nearly all the instructed, and all those of the uninstructed who were led by them, were lost in admiration of what is called civilization, and of the marvels of modern science, literature, and philosophy, and while greatly overrating the amount of unlikeness between the men of modern and those of ancient times, indulged the belief that the whole of the difference was in their own favour; with what a salutary shock did the paradoxes of Rousseau explode like bombshells in the midst, dislocating the compact mass of one-sided opinion, and forcing its elements to recombine in a better form and with additional ingredients. Not that the current opinions were on the whole farther from the truth than Rousseau's were; on the contrary, they were nearer to it; they contained more of positive truth, and very much less of error. Nevertheless, there lay in Rousseau's doctrine, and has floated down the stream of opinion along with it, a considerable amount of exactly those truths which the popular opinion wanted; and these are the deposit which was left behind when the flood subsided. The superior worth of sim-

plicity of life, the enervating and demoralising effect of the trammels and hypocrisies of artificial society, are ideas which have never been entirely absent from cultivated minds since Rousseau wrote; and they will in time produce their due effect, though at present needing to be asserted as much as ever, and to be asserted by deeds, for words, on this subject, have nearly exhausted their power.

In politics, again, it is almost a commonplace, that a party of order or stability, and a party of progress or reform, are both necessary elements of a healthy state of political life; until the one or the other shall have so enlarged its mental grasp as to be a party equally of order and of progress, knowing and distinguishing what is fit to be preserved from what ought to be swept away. Each of these modes of thinking derives its utility from the deficiencies of the other; but it is in a great measure the opposition of the other that keeps each within the limits of reason and sanity. Unless opinions favourable to democracy and to aristocracy, to property and to equality, to co-operation and to competition, to luxury and to abstinence, to sociality and individuality, to liberty and discipline, and all the other standing antagonisms of practical life, are expressed with equal freedom, and enforced and defended with equal talent and energy, there is no chance of both elements obtaining their due; one scale is sure to go up, and the other down. Truth, in the great practical concerns of life, is so much a question of the reconciling and combining of opposites, that very few have minds sufficiently capacious and impartial to make the adjustment with an approach to correctness, and it has to be made by the rough process of a struggle between combatants fighting under hostile banners. On any of the great open questions just enumerated, if either of the two opinions has a better claim than the other, not merely to be tolerated, but to be encouraged and countenanced, it is the one which happens at the particular time and place to be in a minority. That is the opinion which, for the time being, represents the neglected interests, the side of human well-being which is in danger of obtaining less than its share. I am aware that there is not, in this country, any intolerance of differences of opinion on most of these topics. They are adduced to show, by admitted and multiplied examples, the universality of the fact, that only through diversity of opinion is there, in the existing state of human intellect, a chance of fair play to all sides of the truth. When there are persons to be found, who form an exception to the apparent unanimity of the world on any subject, even if the world is in the right, it is always probable that dissentients have something worth hearing to say for themselves, and that truth would lose something by their silence.

It may be objected, 'But *some* received principles, especially on the highest and most vital subjects, are more than half-truths. The Christian morality, for instance, is the whole truth on that subject, and if any one teaches a morality which varies from it, he is wholly in error.' As this is of all cases the most important in practice, none can be fitter to test the general maxim. But before pronouncing what Christian morality is or is not, it would be desirable to decide what is meant by Christian morality. If it means the morality of the New Testament, I wonder that any one who derives his knowledge of this from the book itself, can suppose that it was announced, or intended, as a complete doctrine of morals. The Gospel always refers to a pre-existing morality, and confines its precepts to the particulars in which that morality was to be corrected, or superseded by a wider and higher; expressing itself, moreover, in terms most general, often impossible to be interpreted literally, and possessing rather the impressiveness of poetry or eloquence than the precision of legislation. To extract from it a body of ethical doctrine, has never been possible without eking it out from the Old Testament, that is, from a system elaborate indeed, but in many respects barbarous, and intended only for a

barbarous people. St. Paul, a declared enemy to this Judaical mode of interpreting the doctrine and filling up the scheme of his Master, equally assumes a pre-existing morality, namely that of the Greeks and Romans; and his advice to Christians is in a great measure a system of accommodation to that; even to the extent of giving an apparent sanction to slavery. What is called Christian, but should rather be termed theological, morality, was not the work of Christ or the Apostles, but is of much later origin, having been gradually built up by the Catholic church of the first five centuries, and though not implicitly adopted by moderns and Protestants, has been much less modified by them than might have been expected. For the most part, indeed, they have contented themselves with cutting off the additions which had been made to it in the middle ages, each sect supplying the place by fresh additions, adapted to its own character and tendencies. That mankind owe a great debt to this morality, and to its early teachers, I should be the last person to deny; but I do not scruple to say of it, that it is, in many important points, incomplete and one-sided, and that unless ideas and feelings, not sanctioned by it, had contributed to the formation of European life and character, human affairs would have been in a worse condition than they now are. Christian morality (so called) has all the characters of a reaction; it is, in great part, a protest against Paganism. Its ideal is negative rather than positive; passive rather than active; Innocence rather than Nobleness; Abstinence from Evil, rather than energetic Pursuit of Good: in its precepts (as has been well said) 'thou shalt not' predominates unduly over 'thou shalt'. In its horror of sensuality, it made an idol of asceticism, which has been gradually compromised away into one of legality. It holds out the hope of heaven and the threat of hell, as the appointed and appropriate motives to a virtuous life: in this falling far below the best of the ancients, and doing what lies in it to give to human morality an essentially selfish character, by disconnecting each man's feelings of duty from the interests of his fellow-creatures, except so far as a self-interested inducement is offered to him for consulting them. It is essentially a doctrine of passive obedience; it inculcates submission to all authorities found established; who indeed are not to be actively obeyed when they command what religion forbids, but who are not to be resisted, far less rebelled against, for any amount of wrong to ourselves. And while, in the morality of the best Pagan nations, duty to the State holds even a disproportionate place, infringing on the just liberty of the individual; in purely Christian ethics, that grand department of duty is scarcely noticed or acknowledged. It is in the *Koran*, not the New Testament, that we read the maxim—'A ruler who appoints any man to an office, when there is in his dominions another man better qualified for it, sins against God and against the State.' What little recognition the idea of obligation to the public obtains in modern morality, is derived from Greek and Roman sources, not from Christian; as, even in the morality of private life, whatever exists of magnanimity, highmindedness, personal dignity, even the sense of honour, is derived from the purely human, not the religious part of our education, and never could have grown out of a standard of ethics in which the only worth, professedly recognised, is that of obedience.

I am as far as any one from pretending that these defects are necessarily inherent in the Christian ethics, in every manner in which it can be conceived, or that the many requisites of a complete moral doctrine which it does not contain, do not admit of being reconciled with it. Far less would I insinuate this of the doctrines and precepts of Christ himself. I believe that the sayings of Christ are all, that I can see any evidence of their having been intended to be; that they are irreconcilable with nothing which a comprehensive morality requires; that everything which is excellent in ethics may be brought within them, with no greater vio-

lence to their language than has been done to it by all who have attempted to deduce from them any practical system of conduct whatever. But it is quite consistent with this, to believe that they contain, and were meant to contain, only a part of the truth; that many essential elements of the highest morality are among the things which are not provided for, nor intended to be provided for, in the recorded deliverances of the Founder of Christianity, and which have been entirely thrown aside in the system of ethics erected on the basis of those deliverances by the Christian Church. And this being so, I think it a great error to persist in attempting to find in the Christian doctrine that complete rule for our guidance, which its author intended it to sanction and enforce, but only partially to provide. I believe, too, that this narrow theory is becoming a grave practical evil, detracting greatly from the value of the moral training and instruction, which so many well-meaning persons are now at length exerting themselves to promote. I much fear that by attempting to form the mind and feelings on an exclusively religious type, and discarding those secular standards (as for want of a better name they may be called) which heretofore co-existed with and supplemented the Christian ethics, receiving some of its spirit, and infusing into it some of theirs, there will result, and is even now resulting, a low, abject, servile type of character, which, submit itself as it may to what it deems the Supreme Will, is incapable of rising to or sympathising in the conception of Supreme Goodness. I believe that other ethics than any which can be evolved from exclusively Christian sources, must exist side by side with Christian ethics to produce the moral regeneration of mankind; and that the Christian system is no exception to the rule, that in an imperfect state of the human mind, the interests of truth require a diversity of opinions. It is not necessary that in ceasing to ignore the moral truths not contained in Christianity, men should ignore any of those which it does contain. Such prejudice, or oversight, when it occurs, is altogether an evil; but it is one from which we cannot hope to be always exempt, and must be regarded as the price paid for an inestimable good. The exclusive pretension made by a part of the truth to be the whole, must and ought to be protested against; and if a reactionary impulse should make the protestors unjust in their turn, this one-sidedness, like the other, may be lamented, but must be tolerated. If Christians would teach infidels to be just to Christianity, they should themselves be just to infidelity. It can do truth no service to blink the fact, known to all who have the most ordinary acquaintance with literary history, that a large portion of the noblest and most valuable moral teaching has been the work, not only of men who did not know, but of men who knew and rejected the Christian faith.

I do not pretend that the most unlimited use of the freedom of enunciating all possible opinions would put an end to the evils of religious or philosophical sectarianism. Every truth which men of narrow capacity are in earnest about, is sure to be asserted, inculcated, and in many ways even acted on, as if no other truth existed in the world, or at all events none that could limit or qualify the first. I acknowledge that the tendency of all opinions to become sectarian is not cured by the freest discussion, but is often heightened and exacerbated thereby; the truth which ought to have been, but was not, seen, being rejected all the more violently because proclaimed by persons regarded as opponents. But it is not on the impassioned partisan, it is on the calmer and more disinterested bystander, that this collision of opinions works its salutary effect. Not the violent conflict between parts of the truth, but the quiet suppression of half of it, is the formidable evil; there is always hope when people are forced to listen to both sides; it is when they attend only to one that errors harden into prejudices, and truth itself ceases to have the effect of truth, by being exaggerated into falsehood. And since there are few mental attributes more rare than that judicial faculty which can sit in intelligent judgment between two sides of a question, of which only one is represented by an advocate before it, truth has no chance but in proportion as every side of it, every opinion which embodies any fraction of the truth, not only finds advocates, but is so advocated as to be listened to.

We have now recognised the necessity of the mental well-being of mankind (on which all their other well-being depends) of freedom of opinion, and freedom of the expression of opinion, on four distinct grounds; which we will now briefly recapitulate.

First, if any opinion is compelled to silence, that opinion may, for aught we can certainly know, be true. To deny this is to assume our own infallibility.

Secondly, though the silenced opinion be an error, it may, and very commonly does, contain a portion of truth; and since the general or prevailing opinion on any subject is rarely or never the whole truth, it is only by the collision of adverse opinions that the remainder of the truth has any chance of being supplied.

Thirdly, even if the received opinion be not only true, but the whole truth; unless it is suffered to be, and actually is, vigorously and earnestly contested, it will, by most of those who receive it, be held in the manner of a prejudice, with little comprehension or feeling of its rational grounds. And not only this, but, fourthly, the meaning of the doctrine itself will be in danger of being lost, or enfeebled, and deprived of its vital effect on the character and conduct: the dogma becoming a mere formal profession, inefficacious for good, but cumbering the ground, and preventing the growth of any real and heartfelt conviction, from reason or personal experience.

Before quitting the subject of freedom of opinion, it is fit to take some notice to those who say, that the free expression of all opinions should be permitted, on condition that the manner be temperate, and do not pass the bounds of fair discussion. Much might be said on the impossibility of fixing where these supposed bounds are to be placed; for if the test be offence to those whose opinion is attacked, I think experience testifies that this offence is given whenever the attack is telling and powerful, and that every opponent who pushes them hard, and whom they find it difficult to answer, appears to them, if he shows any strong feeling on the subject, an intemperate opponent. But this, though an important consideration in a practical point of view, merges in a more fundamental objection. Undoubtedly the manner of asserting an opinion, even though it be a true one, may be very objectionable, and may justly incur severe censure. But the principal offences of the kind are such as it is mostly impossible, unless by accidental self-betrayal, to bring home to conviction. The gravest of them is, to argue sophistically, to suppress facts or arguments, to misstate the elements of the case, or misrepresent the opposite opinion. But all this, even to the most aggravated degree, is so continually done in perfect good faith, by persons who are not considered, and in many other respects may not deserve to be considered, ignorant or incompetent, that it is rarely possible on adequate grounds conscientiously to stamp the misrepresentation as morally culpable; and still less could law presume to interfere with this kind of controversial misconduct. With regard to what is commonly meant by intemperate discussion, namely invective, sarcasm, personality, and the like, the denunciation of these weapons would deserve more sympathy if it were ever proposed to interdict them equally to both sides; but it is only desired to restrain the employment of them against the prevailing opinion: against the unprevailing they may not only be used without general disapproval, but will be likely to obtain for him who uses them the praise of honest zeal and righteous indignation. Yet whatever mischief arises from their use, is greatest when they are employed against the comparatively defenceless; and whatever unfair advantage can be derived by any opinion from this mode of asserting it, accrues almost exclusively to

received opinions. The worst offence of this kind which can be committed by a polemic, is to stigmatise those who hold the contrary opinion as bad and immoral men. To calumny of this sort, those who hold any unpopular opinion are peculiarly exposed, because they are in general few and uninfluential, and nobody but themselves feels much interested in seeing justice done them; but this weapon is, from the nature of the case, denied to those who attack a prevailing opinion: they can neither use it with safety to themselves, nor, if they could, would it do anything but recoil on their own cause. In general, opinions contrary to those commonly received can only obtain a hearing by studied moderation of language, and the most cautious avoidance of unnecessary offence, from which they hardly ever deviate even in a slight degree without losing ground: while unmeasured vituperation employed on the side of the prevailing opinion, really does deter people from professing contrary opinions, and from listening to those who profess them. For the interest, therefore, of truth and justice, it is far more important to restrain this employment of vituperative language than the other; and, for example, if it were necessary to choose, there would be much more need to discourage offensive attacks on infidelity, than on religion. It is, however, obvious that law and authority have no business with restraining either, while opinion ought, in every instance, to determine its verdict by the circumstances of the individual case; condemning every one, on whichever side of the argument he places himself, in whose mode of advocacy either want of candour, or malignity, bigotry, or intolerance of feeling manifest themselves; but not inferring these vices from the side which a person takes, though it be the contrary side of the question to our own: and giving merited honour to every one, whatever opinion he may hold, who has calmness to see and honesty to state what his opponents and their opinions really are, exaggerating nothing to their discredit, keeping nothing back which tells, or can be supposed to tell, in their favour. This is the real morality of public discussion: and if often violated, I am happy to think that there are many controversialists who to a great extent observe it, and a still greater number who conscientiously strive towards it.

## OF THE LIMITS TO THE AUTHORITY OF SOCIETY OVER THE INDIVIDUAL

What, then, is the rightful limit to the sovereignty of the individual over himself? Where does the authority of society begin? How much of human life should be assigned to individuality, and how much to society?

Each will receive its proper share, if each has that which more particularly concerns it. To individuality should belong the part of life in which it is chiefly the individual that is interested; to society, the part which chiefly interests society.

Though society is not founded on a contract, and though no good purpose is answered by inventing a contract in order to deduce social obligations from it, every one who receives the protection of society owes a return for the benefit, and the fact of living in society renders it indispensable that each should be bound to observe a certain line of conduct towards the rest. This conduct consists first, in not injuring the interests of one another; or rather certain interests, which, either by express legal provision or by tacit understanding, ought to be considered as rights; and secondly, in each person's bearing his share (to be fixed on some equitable principle) of the labours and sacrifices incurred for defending the society or its members from injury and molestation. These conditions society is justified in enforcing at all costs to those who endeavour to withhold fulfilment. Nor is this all that society may do. The acts of an individual may be hurtful to others, or wanting in due consideration for their welfare, without going the length of violating any of their constituted rights. The offender may then be justly punished by opinion, though not by law. As soon as any part of a person's conduct affects prejudicially the interests of others, society has jurisdiction over it, and the question whether the general welfare will or will not be promoted by interfering with it, becomes open to discussion. But there is no room for entertaining any such question when a person's conduct affects the interests of no persons besides himself, or needs not affect them unless they like (all the persons concerned being of full age, and the ordinary amount of understanding). In all such cases there should be perfect freedom, legal and social, to do the action and stand the consequences.

It would be a great misunderstanding of this doctrine to suppose that it is one of selfish indifference, which pretends that human beings have no business with each other's conduct in life, and that they should not concern themselves about the well-doing or well-being of one another, unless their own interest is involved. Instead of any diminution, there is need of a great increase of disinterested exertion to promote the good of others. But disinterested benevolence can find other instruments to persuade people to their good, than whips and scourges, either of the literal or the metaphorical sort. I am the last person to undervalue the self-regarding virtues; they are only second in importance, if even second, to the social. It is equally the business of education to cultivate both. But even education works by conviction and persuasion as well as by compulsion, and it is by the former only that, when the period of education is past, the self-regarding virtues should be inculcated. Human beings owe to each other help to distinguish the better from the worse, and encouragement to choose the former and avoid the latter. They should be for ever stimulating each other to increased exercise of their higher faculties, and increased direction of their feelings and aims towards wise instead of foolish, elevating instead of degrading, objects and contemplations. But neither one person, nor any number of persons is warranted in saying to another human creature of ripe years, that he shall not do with his life for his own benefit what he chooses to do with it. He is the person most interested in his own well-being: the interest which any other person, except in cases of strong personal attachment, can have in it, is trifling, compared with that which he himself has; the interest which society has in him individually (except as to his conduct to others) is fractional, and altogether indirect: while, with respect to his own feelings and circumstances, the most ordinary man or woman has means of knowledge immeasurably surpassing those that can be possessed by any one else. The interference of society to overrule his judgment and purposes in what only regards himself, must be grounded on general presumptions: which may be altogether wrong, and even if right, are as likely as not to be misapplied to individual cases, by persons no better acquainted with the circumstances of such cases than those are who look at them merely from without. In this department, therefore, of human affairs, Individuality has its proper field of action. In the conduct of human beings towards one another, it is necessary that general rules should for the most part be observed, in order that people may know what they have to expect; but in each person's own concerns, his individual spontaneity is entitled to free exercise. Considerations to aid his judgment, exhortations to strengthen his will, may be offered to him, even obtruded on him, by others; but he himself is the final judge. All errors which he is likely to commit against advice and warning, are far outweighed by the evil of allowing others to constrain him to what they deem his good.

I do not mean that the feelings with which a person is regarded by others, ought not to be in any way affected by his self-regarding qualities or deficiencies. This is neither possible nor desirable. If he is eminent in any of the qualities which conduce to his own good, he is, so far, a proper object of admiration. He is so much the nearer to the ideal perfection of human nature. If he is grossly deficient in those qualities, a sentiment the opposite of admiration will follow.

There is a degree of folly, and a degree of what may be called (though the phrase is not unobjectionable) lowness or depravation of taste, which, though it cannot justify doing harm to the person who manifests it, renders him necessarily and properly a subject of distaste, or, in extreme cases, even of contempt: a person could not have the opposite qualities in due strength without entertaining these feelings. Though doing no wrong to any one, a person may so act as to compel us to judge him, and feel to him, as a fool, or as a being of an inferior order: and since this judgment and feeling are a fact which he would prefer to avoid, it is doing him a service to warn him of it beforehand, as of any other disagreeable consequence to which he exposes himself. It would be well, indeed, if this good office were much more freely rendered than the common notions of politeness at present permit, and if one person could honestly point out to another that he thinks him in fault, without being considered unmannerly or presuming. We have a right, also, in various ways, to act upon our unfavourable opinion of any one, not to the oppression of his individuality, but in the exercise of ours. We are not bound, for example, to seek his society; we have a right to avoid it (though not to parade the avoidance), for we have a right to choose the society most acceptable to us. We have a right, and it may be our duty, to caution others against him, if we think his example or conversation likely to have a pernicious effect on those with whom he associates. We may give others a preference over him in optional good offices, except those which tend to his improvement. In these various modes a person may suffer very severe penalties at the hand of others, for faults which directly concern only himself; but he suffers these penalties only in so far as they are the natural, and, as it were, the spontaneous consequences of the faults themselves, not because they are purposely inflicted on him for the sake of punishment. A person who shows rashness, obstinacy, self-conceit—who cannot live within moderate means—who cannot restrain himself from hurtful indulgences—who pursues animal pleasures at the expense of those of feeling and intellect—must expect to be lowered in the opinion of others, and to have a less share of their favourable sentiments; but of this he has no right to complain, unless he has merited their favour by special excellence in his social relations, and has thus established a title to their good offices, which is not affected by his demerits towards himself.

What I contend for is, that the inconveniences which are strictly inseparable from the unfavourable judgment of others, are the only ones to which a person should ever be subjected for the portion of his conduct and character which concerns his own good, but which does not affect the interests of others in their relations with him. Acts injurious to others require a totally different treatment. Encroachment on their rights; infliction on them of any loss or damage not justified by his own rights; falsehood or duplicity in dealing with them; unfair or ungenerous use of advantages over them; even selfish abstinence from defending them against injury—these are fit objects of moral reprobation, and, in grave cases, of moral retribution and punishment. And not only these acts, but the dispositions which lead to them, are properly immoral, and fit subjects of disapprobation which may rise to abhorrence. Cruelty of disposition; malice and ill-nature; that most anti-social and odious of all passions, envy; dissimulation and insincerity; irascibility on insufficient cause, and resentment disproportioned to the provocation; the love of domineering over others; the desire to engross more than one's share of advantages (the πλεονεξια of the Greeks); the pride which derives gratification from the abasement of others; the egotism which thinks self and its concerns more important than everything else, and decides all doubtful questions in its own favour;—these are moral vices, and constitute a bad and odious moral character: unlike the self-regarding faults previously mentioned, which are not properly immoralities, and to whatever pitch they may be carried, do not constitute wickedness. They may be proofs of any amount of folly, or want of personal dignity and self-respect; but they are only a subject of moral reprobation when they involve a breach of duty to others, for whose sake the individual is bound to have care for himself. What are called duties to ourselves are not socially obligatory, unless circumstances render them at the same time duties to others. The term duty to oneself, when it means anything more than prudence, means self-respect or self-development; and for none of these is any one accountable to his fellow creatures, because for none of them is it for the good of mankind that he be held accountable to them.

The distinction between the loss of consideration which a person may rightly incur by defect of prudence or of personal dignity, and the reprobation which is due to him for an offence against the right of others, is not a merely nominal distinction. It makes a vast difference both in our feelings and in our conduct towards him, whether he displeases us in things in which we think we have a right to control him, or in things in which we know that we have not. If he displeases us, we may express our distaste, and we may stand aloof from a person as well as from a thing that displeases us; but we shall not therefore feel called on to make his life uncomfortable. We shall reflect that he already bears, or will bear, the whole penalty of his error; if he spoils his life by mismanagement, we shall not, for that reason, desire to spoil it still further: instead of wishing to punish him, we shall rather endeavour to alleviate his punishment, by showing him how he may avoid or cure the evils his conduct tends to bring upon him. He may be to us an object of pity, perhaps of dislike, but not of anger or resentment; we shall not treat him like an enemy of society: the worst we shall think ourselves justified in doing is leaving him to himself, if we do not interfere benevolently by showing interest or concern for him. It is far otherwise if he has infringed the rules necessary for the protection of his fellow-creatures, individually or collectively. The evil consequences of his acts do not then fall on himself, but on others; and society, as the protector of all its members, must retaliate on him; must inflict pain on him for the express purpose of punishment, and must take care that it be sufficiently severe. In the one case, he is an offender at our bar, and we are called on not only to sit in judgment on him, but, in one shape or another, to execute our own sentence: in the other case, it is not our part to inflict any suffering on him, except what may incidentally follow from our using the same liberty in the regulation of our own affairs, which we allow to him in his.

The distinction here pointed out between the part of a person's life which concerns only himself, and that which concerns others, many persons will refuse to admit. How (it may be asked) can any part of the conduct of a member of society be a matter of indifference to the other members? No person is an entirely isolated being; it is impossible for a person to do anything seriously or permanently hurtful to himself, without mischief reaching at least to his near connections, and often far beyond them. If he injures his property, he does harm to those who directly or indirectly derived support from it, and usually diminishes, by a greater or less amount, the general resources of the community. If he deteriorates his bodily or mental faculties, he not only brings evil upon all who depended on him for any portion of their happiness, but disqualifies himself for rendering the services which he owes to his fellow-creatures generally; perhaps becomes a burthen on their affection or benevolence; and if such conduct were very frequent, hardly any offence that is committed would detract more from the general sum of good. Finally, if by his vices or follies a person does no direct harm to others, he is nevertheless (it may be said) injurious by his example; and ought to be compelled to control himself, for the sake of those whom the sight or knowledge of his conduct might corrupt or mislead.

And even (it will be added) if the consequences of misconduct could be confined to the vicious or thoughtless individual, ought society to abandon to their own guidance those who are manifestly unfit for it? If protection against themselves is confessedly due to children and persons under age, is not society equally bound to afford it to persons of mature years who are equally incapable of self-government? If gambling, or drunkenness, or incontinence, or idleness, or uncleanliness, are as injurious to happiness, and as great a hindrance to improvement, as many or most of the acts prohibited by law, why (it may be asked) should not law, so far as is consistent with practicability and social convenience, endeavour to repress these also? And as a supplement to the unavoidable imperfections of law, ought not opinion at least to organise a powerful police against these vices, and visit rigidly with social penalties those who are known to practise them? There is no question here (it may be said) about restricting individuality, or impeding the trial of new and original experiments in living. The only things it is sought to prevent are things which have been tried and condemned from the beginning of the world until now; things which experience has shown not to be useful or suitable to any person's individuality. There must be some length of time and amount of experience, after which a moral or prudential truth may be regarded as established: and it is merely desired to prevent generation after generation from falling over the same precipice which has been fatal to their predecessors.

I fully admit that the mischief which a person does to himself may seriously affect, both through their sympathies and their interests, those nearly connected with him, and in a minor degree, society at large. When, by conduct of this sort, a person is led to violate a distinct and assignable obligation to any other person or persons, the case is taken out of the self-regarding class, and becomes amenable to moral disapprobation in the proper sense of the term. If, for example, a man, through intemperance or extravagance, becomes unable to pay his debts, or, having undertaken the moral responsibility of a family, becomes from the same cause incapable of supporting or educating them, he is deservedly reprobated, and might be justly punished; but it is for the breach of duty to his family or creditors, not for the extravagance. If the resources which ought to have been devoted to them, had been diverted from them for the most prudent investment, the moral culpability would have been the same. George Barnwell murdered his uncle to get money for his mistress, but if he had done it to set himself up in business, he would equally have been hanged. Again, in the frequent case of a man who causes grief to his family by addiction to bad habits, he deserves reproach for his unkindness or ingratitude; but so he may for cultivating habits not in themselves vicious, if they are painful to those with whom he passes his life, or who from personal ties are dependent on him for their comfort. Whoever fails in the consideration generally due to the interests and feelings of others, not being compelled by some more imperative duty, or justified by allowable self-preference, is a subject of moral disapprobation for that failure, but not for the cause of it, nor for the errors, merely personal to himself, which may have remotely led to it. In like manner, when a person disables himself, by conduct purely self-regarding, from the performance of some definite duty incumbent on him to the public, he is guilty of a social offence. No person ought to be punished simply for being drunk; but a soldier or a policeman should be punished for being drunk on duty. Whenever, in short, there is a definite damage, or a definite risk of damage, either to an individual or to the public, the case is taken out of the province of liberty, and placed in that of morality or law.

But with regard to the merely contingent, or, as it may be called, constructive injury which a person causes to society, by conduct which neither violates any specific duty to the public, nor occasions perceptible hurt to any assignable individual except himself; the inconvenience is one which society can afford to bear, for the sake of the greater good of human freedom. If grown persons are to be punished for not taking proper care of themselves, I would rather it were for their own sake, than under pretence of preventing them from impairing their capacity of rendering to society benefits which society does not pretend it has a right to exact. But I cannot consent to argue the point as if society had no means of bringing its weaker members up to its ordinary standard of rational conduct, except waiting till they do something irrational, and then punishing them, legally or morally, for it. Society has had absolute power over them during all the early portion of their existence: it has had the whole period of childhood and nonage in which to try whether it could make them capable of rational conduct in life. The existing generation is master both of the training and the entire circumstances of the generation to come; it cannot indeed make them perfectly wise and good, because it is itself so lamentably deficient in goodness and wisdom; and its best efforts are not always, in individual cases, its most successful ones; but it is perfectly well able to make the rising generation, as a whole, as good as, and a little better than, itself. If society lets any considerable number of its members grow up mere children, incapable of being acted on by rational consideration of distant motives, society has itself to blame for the consequences. Armed not only with all the powers of education, but with the ascendancy which the authority of a received opinion always exercises over the minds who are least fitted to judge for themselves; and aided by the *natural* penalties which cannot be prevented from falling on those who incur the distaste or the contempt of those who know them; let not society pretend that it needs, besides all this, the power to issue commands and enforce obedience in the personal concerns of individuals, in which, on all principles of justice and policy, the decision ought to rest with those who are able to abide the consequences. Nor is there anything which tends more to discredit and frustrate the better means of influencing conduct, than a resort to the worse. If there be among those whom it is attempted to coerce into prudence or temperance, any of the material of which vigorous and independent characters are made, they will infallibly rebel against the yoke. No such person will ever feel that others have a right to control him in his concerns, such as they have to prevent him from injuring them in theirs; and it easily comes to be considered a mark of spirit and courage to fly in the face of such usurped authority, and do with ostentation the exact opposite of what it enjoins; as in the fashion of grossness which succeeded, in the time of Charles II, to the fanatical moral intolerence of the Puritans. With respect to what is said of the necessity of protecting society from the bad example set to others by the vicious or the self–indulgent; it is true that bad example may have a pernicious effect, especially the example of doing wrong to others with impunity to the wrong-doer. But we are now speaking of conduct which, while it does no wrong to others, is supposed to do great harm to the agent himself: and I do not see how those who believe this, can think otherwise than that the example, on the whole, must be more salutary than hurtful, since, if it displays the misconduct, it displays also the painful or degrading consequences which, if the conduct is justly censured, must be supposed to be in all or most cases attendant on it.

But the strongest of all the arguments against the interference of the public with purely personal conduct, is that when it does interfere, the odds are that it interferes wrongly, and in the wrong place. On questions of social morality, of duty to others, the opinion of the public, that is, of an over-ruling majority, though often wrong, is likely to be still oftener right; because on such questions they are only required to judge of their own interests; of the manner in which some mode of conduct, if allowed to be practised, would affect themselves. But the opinion of a similar majority, imposed as a law on the minority, on questions of self-regarding conduct, is quite as likely to be wrong as right; for in these cases public opinion means, at the best, some people's opinion of what is good or bad for other people; while very often it does not even mean that; the public, with the most perfect indifference, passing over the pleasure or convenience of those whose conduct they censure, and considering only their own preference. There are many who consider as an injury to themselves any conduct which they have a distaste for, and resent it as on outrage to their feelings; as a religious bigot, when charged with disregarding the religious feelings of others, has been known to retort that they disregard his feelings, by persisting in their abominable worship or creed. But there is no parity between the feeling of a person for his own opinion, and the feeling of another who is offended at his holding it; no more than between the desire of a thief to take a purse, and the desire of the right owner to keep it. And a person's taste is as much his own peculiar concern as his opinion or his purse. It is easy for any one to imagine an ideal public, which leaves the freedom and choice of individuals in all uncertain matters undisturbed, and only requires them to abstain from modes of conduct which universal experience has condemned. But where has there been seen a public which set any such limit to its censorship? or when does the public trouble itself about universal experience? In its interferences with personal conduct it is seldom thinking of anything but the enormity of acting or feeling differently from itself; and this standard of judgment, thinly disguised, is held up to mankind as the dictate of religion and philosophy, by nine-tenths of all moralists and speculative writers. These teach that things are right because they are right; because we feel them to be so. They tell us to search in our own minds and hearts for laws of conduct binding on ourselves and on all others. What can the poor public do but apply these instructions, and make their own personal feelings of good and evil, if they are tolerably unanimous in them, obligatory on all the world?

The evil here pointed out is not one which exists only in theory; and it may perhaps be expected that I should specify the instances in which the public of this age and country improperly invests its own preferences with the character of moral laws. I am not writing an essay on the aberrations of existing moral feeling. That is too weighty a subject to be discussed parenthetically, and by way of illustration. Yet examples are necessary, to show that the principle I maintain is of serious and practical moment, and that I am not endeavouring to erect a barrier against imaginary evils. And it is not difficult to show, by abundant instances, that to extend the bounds of what may be called moral police, until it encroaches on the most unquestionably legitimate liberty of the individual, is one of the most universal of all human propensities.

As a first instance, consider the antipathies which men cherish on no better grounds than that persons whose religious opinions are different from theirs, do not practise their religious observances, especially their religious abstinences. To cite a rather trivial example, nothing in the creed or practice of Christians does more to envenom the hatred of Mahomedans against them, than the fact of their eating pork. There are few acts which Christians and Europeans regard with more unaffected disgust, than Mussulmans regard this particular mode of satisfying hunger. It is, in the first place, an offence against their religion; but this circumstance by no means explains either the degree or the kind of their repugnance; for wine also is forbidden by their religion, and to partake of it is by all Mussulmans accounted wrong, but not disgusting. Their aversion to the flesh of the 'unclean beast' is, on the contrary, of that peculiar character, resembling an instinctive antipathy, which the idea of uncleanness, when once it thoroughly sinks into the feelings, seems always to excite even in those whose personal habits are anything but scrupulously cleanly, and of which the sentiment of religious impurity, so intense in the Hindoos, is a remarkable example. Suppose now that in a people, of whom the majority were Mussulmans, the majority should insist upon not permitting pork to be eaten within the limits of the country. This would be nothing new in Mahomedan countries.[1] Would it be a legitimate exercise of the moral authority of public opinion? and if not, why not? The practice is really revolting to such a public. They also sincerely think that it is forbidden and abhorred by the Deity. Neither could the prohibition be censured as religious persecution. It might be religious in its origin, but it would not be persecution for religion, since nobody's religion makes it a duty to eat pork. The only tenable ground of condemnation would be, that with the personal tastes and self-regarding concerns of individuals the public has no business to interfere.

To come somewhat nearer home: the majority of Spaniards consider it a gross impiety, offensive in the highest degree to the Supreme Being, to worship him in any other manner than the Roman Catholic; and no other public worship is lawful on Spanish soil. The people of all Southern Europe look upon a married clergy as not only irreligious, but unchaste, indecent, gross, disgust-

---

[1]The case of the Bombay Parsees is a curious instance in point. When this industrious and enterprising tribe, the descendants of the Persian fire-worshippers, flying from their native country before the Caliphs, arrived in Western India, they were admitted to toleration by the Hindoo sovereigns, on condition of not eating beef. When those regions afterwards fell under the dominion of Mahomedan conquerors, the Parsees obtained from them a continuance of indulgence, on condition of refraining from pork. What was at first obedience to authority became second nature, and the Parsees to this day abstain both from beef and pork. Though not required by their religion, the double abstinence has had time to grow into a custom of their tribe; and custom, in the East, is a religion.

ing. What do Protestants think of these perfectly sincere feelings, and of the attempt to enforce them against non-Catholics? Yet, if mankind are justified in interfering with each other's liberty in things which do not concern the interests of others, on what principle is it possible consistently to exclude these cases? or who can blame people for desiring to suppress what they regard as a scandal in the sight of God and man? No stronger case can be shown for prohibiting anything which is regarded as a personal immorality, than is made out for suppressing these practices in the eyes of those who regard them as impieties; and unless we are willing to adopt the logic of persecutors, and to say that we may persecute others because we are right, and that they must not persecute us because they are wrong, we must beware of admitting a principle of which we should resent as a gross injustice the application to ourselves.

The preceding instances may be objected to, although unreasonably, as drawn from contingencies impossible among us: opinion, in this country, not being likely to enforce abstinence from meats, or to interfere with people for worshipping, and for either marrying or not marrying, according to their creed or inclination. The next example, however, shall be taken from an interference with liberty which we have by no means passed all danger of. Wherever the Puritans have been sufficiently powerful, as in New England, and in Great Britain at the time of the Commonwealth, they have endeavoured, with considerable success, to put down all public, and nearly all private, amusements: especially music, dancing, public games, or other assemblages for purposes of diversion, and the theatre. There are still in this country large bodies of persons by whose notions of morality and religion these recreations are condemned; and those persons belonging chiefly to the middle class, who are the ascendant power in the present social and political condition of the kingdom, it is by no means impossible that persons of these sentiments may at some time or other command a majority in Parliament. How will the remaining portion of the community like to have the amusements that shall be permitted to them regulated by the religious and moral sentiments of the stricter Calvinists and Methodists? Would they not, with considerable peremptoriness, desire these intrusively pious members of society to mind their own business? This is precisely what should be said to every government and every public, who have the pretension that no person shall enjoy any pleasure which they think wrong. But if the principle of the pretension be admitted, no one can reasonably object to its being acted on in the sense of the majority, or other preponderating power in the country; and all persons must be ready to conform to the idea of a Christian commonwealth, as understood by the early settlers in New England, if a religious profession similar to theirs should ever succeed in regaining its lost ground, as religions supposed to be declining have so often been known to do.

To imagine another contingency, perhaps more likely to be realised than the one last mentioned. There is confessedly a strong tendency in the modern world towards a democratic constitution of society, accompanied or not by popular political institutions. It is affirmed that in the country where this tendency is most completely realised—where both society and the government are most democratic—the United States—the feeling of the majority, to whom any appearance of a more showy or costly style of living than they can hope to rival is disagreeable, operates as a tolerably effectual sumptuary law, and that in many parts of the Union it is really difficult for a person possessing a very large income, to find any mode of spending it, which will not incur popular disapprobation. Though such statements as these are doubtless much exaggerated as a representation of existing facts, the state of things they describe is not only a conceivable and possible, but a probable result of democratic feeling, combined with the notion that the public has a right to a veto on the manner in which individuals shall spend their incomes. We have only further to suppose a considerable diffusion of Socialist opinions, and it may become infamous in the eyes of the majority to possess more property than some very small amount, or any income not earned by manual labour. Opinions similar in principle to these, already prevail widely among the artisan class, and weigh oppressively on those who are amenable to the opinion chiefly of that class, namely, its own members. It is known that the bad workmen who form the majority of the operatives in many branches of industry, are decidedly of opinion that bad workmen ought to receive the same wages as good, and that no one ought to be allowed, through piecework or otherwise to earn by superior skill or industry more than others can without it. And they employ a moral police, which occasionally becomes a physical one, to deter skilful workmen from receiving, and employers from giving, a larger remuneration for a more useful service. If the public have any jurisdiction over private concerns, I cannot see that these people are in fault, or that any individual's particular public can be blamed for asserting the same authority over his individual conduct, which the general public asserts over people in general.

But, without dwelling on supposititious cases, there are, in our own day, gross usurpations upon the liberty of private life actually practised, and still greater ones threatened with some expectation of success, and opinions propounded which assert an unlimited right in the public not only to prohibit by law everything which it thinks wrong, but in order to get at what it thinks wrong, to prohibit any number of things which it admits to be innocent.

Under the name of preventing intemperance, the people of one English colony, and of nearly half the United States, have been interdicted by law from making any use whatever of fermented drinks, except for medical purposes: for prohibition of their sale is in fact, as it is intended to be, prohibition of their use. And though the impracticability of executing the law has caused its repeal in several of the States which had adopted it, including the one from which it derives its name, an attempt has notwithstanding been commenced, and is prosecuted with considerable zeal by many of the professed philanthropists, to agitate for a similar law in this country. The association, or 'Alliance' as it terms itself, which has been formed for this purpose, has acquired some notoriety through the publicity given to a correspondence between its Secretary and one of the very few English public men who hold that a politician's opinions ought to be founded on principles. Lord Stanley's share in this correspondence is calculated to strengthen the hopes already built on him, by those who know how rare such qualities as are manifested in some of his public appearances, unhappily are among those who figure in political life. The organ of the Alliance, who would 'deeply deplore the recognition of any principle which could be wrested to justify bigotry and persecution', undertakes to point out the 'broad and impassable barrier' which divides such principles from those of the association. 'All matters relating to thought, opinion, conscience, appear to me', he says, 'to be without the sphere of legislation; all pertaining to social act, habit, relation, subject only to a discretionary power vested in the State itself, and not in the individual, to be within it.' No mention is made of a third class, different from either of these, viz. acts and habits which are not social, but individual; although it is to this class, surely, that the act of drinking fermented liquors belongs. Selling fermented liquors, however, is trading, and trading is a social act. But the infringement complained of is not the liberty of the seller, but on that of the buyer and consumers; since the State might just as well forbid him to drink wine, as purposely make it impossible for him to obtain it. The Secretary, however, says, 'I claim, as a citizen, a right to legislate whenever my social rights are invaded by the social act of another.' And now for the definition of these 'social rights'. 'If anything invades my social rights, certainly the traffic in strong drink does. It destroys my primary right of security, by constantly creating and stimulating social disorder. It invades my right of equality, by deriving a profit from the creation of a misery I am taxed to support. It impedes my right to free moral and intellectual development, by surrounding my path with dangers, and by weakening and demoralising society, from which I have a right to claim mutual aid and intercourse.' A theory of 'social rights', the like of which probably never before found its way into distinct language: being nothing short of this—that it is the absolute social right of every individual, that every other individual shall act in every respect exactly as he ought; that whosoever fails thereof in the smallest particular, violates my social right, and entitles me to demand from the legislature the removal of the grievance. So monstrous a principle is far more dangerous than any single interference with liberty; there is no violation of liberty which it would not justify; it acknowledges no right to any freedom whatever, except perhaps to that of holding opinions in secret, without ever disclosing them: for, the moment an opinion which I consider noxious passes any one's lips, it invades all the 'social rights' attributed to me by the Alliance. The doctrine ascribes to all mankind a vested interest in each other's moral, intellectual, and even physical perfection, to be defined by each claimant according to his own standard.

Another important example of illegitimate interference with the rightful liberty of the individual, not simply threatened, but long since carried into triumphant effect, is Sabbatarian legislation. Without doubt, abstinence on one day in the week, so far as the exigencies of life permit, from the usual daily occupation, though in no respect religiously binding on any except Jews, is a highly beneficial custom. And inasmuch as this custom cannot be observed without a general consent to that effect among the industrious classes, therefore, in so far as some persons by working may impose the same necessity on others, it may be allowable and right that the law should guarantee to each the observance by others of the custom, by suspending the greater operations of industry on a particular day. But this justification, grounded on the direct interest which others have in each individual's observance of the practice, does not apply to the self-chosen occupations in which a person may think fit to employ his leisure; nor does it hold good, in the smallest degree, for legal restrictions of amusements. It is true that the amusement of some is the day's work of others; but the pleasure, not to say the useful recreation, of many, is worth the labour of a few, provided the occupation is freely chosen, and can be freely resigned. The operatives are perfectly right in thinking that if all worked on Saturday, seven days' work would have to be given for six days' wages: but so long as the great mass of employments are suspended, the small number who for the enjoyment of others must still work, obtain a proportional increase of earnings; and they are not obliged to follow those occupations, if they prefer leisure to emolument. If a further remedy is sought, it might be found in the establishment by custom of a holiday on some other day of the week for those particular classes of persons. The only ground, therefore, on which restrictions on Sunday amusements can be defended, must be that they are religiously wrong; a motive of legislation which never can be too earnestly protested against. 'Deorum injuriæ Diis curæ'. It remains to be proved that society or any of its officers holds a commission from on high to avenge any supposed offence to Omnipotence, which is not also a wrong to our fellow creatures. The notion that it is one man's duty that another should be religious, was the foundation of all the religious persecutions ever perpetrated, and if admitted, would fully justify them. Though the feeling which breaks out in the repeated attempts to stop railway travelling on Sunday, in the resistance to the opening of Museums, and the like, has not the cruelty of the old persecutors, the state of mind indicated by it is fundamentally the same. It is a determination not to tolerate others in doing what is permitted by their religion, because it is not permitted by the persecutor's religion. It is a belief that God not only abominates the act of the misbeliever, but will not hold us guiltless if we leave him unmolested.

I cannot refrain from adding to these examples of the little account commonly made of human liberty, the language of downright persecution which breaks out from the press of this country, whenever it feels called on to notice the remarkable phenomenon of Mormonism. Much might be said on the unexpected and instructive fact, that an alleged new revelation, and a religion founded on it, the product of palpable imposture, not even supported by the *prestige* of extraordinary qualities in its founder, is believed by hundreds of thousands, and has been made the foundation of a society, in the age of newspapers, railways, and the electric telegraph. What here concerns us is, that this religion, like other and better religions, has its martyrs; that its prophet and founder was, for his teaching, put to death by a mob; that others of its adherents lost their lives by the same lawless violence; that they were forcibly expelled, in a body, from the country in which they first grew up; while, now that they have been chased into a solitary recess in the midst of a desert, many in this country openly declare that it would be right (only that it is not convenient) to send an expedition against them, and compel them by force to conform to the opinions of other people. The article of the Mormonite doctrine which is the chief provocative to the antipathy which thus breaks through the ordinary restraints of religious tolerance, is its sanction of polygamy; which, though permitted to Mahomedans, and Hindoos, and Chinese, seems to excite unquenchable animosity when practised by persons who speak English, and profess to be a kind of Christians. No one has a deeper disapprobation that I have of this Mormon institution; both for other reasons, and because, far from being in any way countenanced by the principle of liberty, it is a direct infraction of that principle, being a mere rivetting of the chains of one-half of the community, and an emancipation of the other from reciprocity of obligation towards them. Still, it must be remembered that this religion is as much voluntary on the part of the women concerned in it, and who may be deemed the sufferers by it, as is the case with any form of the marriage institution; and however surprising this fact may appear, it has its explanation in the common ideas and customs of the world, which teaching women to think marriage the one thing needful, make it intelligible that many a woman should prefer being one of several wives, to not being a wife at all. Other countries are not asked to recognise such unions, or release any portion of their inhabitants from their own laws on the score of Mormonite opinions. But when the dissentients have conceded to the hostile sentiments of others, far more than could justly be demanded; when they have left the countries to which their doctrines were unacceptable, and established themselves in a remote corner of the earth, which they have been the first to render habitable to human beings; it is difficult to see on what principles but those of tyranny they can be prevented from living there under what laws they please, provided they commit no aggression on other nations, and allow perfect freedom of departure to those who are dissatisfied with their ways. A recent writer, in some respects of considerable merit, proposes (to use his own words) not a crusade, but a *civilizade*, against this polygamous community, to put an end to what seems to him a retrograde step in civilisation. It also appears so to me, but I am not aware that any community has a right to force another to be civilised. So long as the sufferers by the bad law do not invoke assistance from other communities, I cannot admit that persons entirely unconnected with them ought to step in and require that a condition of things with which all who are directly interested appear to be satisfied, should be put an end to because it is a scandal to persons some thousands of miles distant, who have no part or concern in it. Let them send missionaries, if they please, to preach against it; and let them, by any fair means (of which silencing the teachers is not one), oppose the progress of similar doctrines among their own people. If civilisation has got the better of barbarism when barbarism had the world to itself, it is too much to profess to be afraid lest barbarism, after having been fairly got under, should revive and conquer civilisation. A civilisation that can thus succumb to its vanquished enemy, must first have become so degenerate, that neither its appointed priests and teachers, nor anybody else, has the capacity, or will take the trouble, to stand up for it. If this be so, the sooner such a civilisation receives notice to quit, the better. It can only go on from bad to worse, until destroyed and regenerated (like the Western Empire) by energetic barbarians.

## QUESTIONS

1. How would Mill answer the charge that, while insisting that government leave a sphere of liberty for the individual, we as individuals may, in effect, take away that individual's freedom by making our own hostile judgments about him or her?

2. Mill says that "When, by conduct of this sort, a person is led to violate a distinct and assignable obligation to any other person or persons, the case is taken out of the self-regarding class and becomes amenable to moral disapprobation in the proper sense of the term." What criterion should we use in determining whether an action violates such an obligation? Consider the advantages and disadvantages of each of the following answers: (a) existing law; (b) whether that particular action would harm another person; (c) whether harm would be caused by that kind of action if everyone did it; (d) whether harm would be caused by that kind of action if it were generally permitted; (e) whether most people believe that harm would be caused by that kind of action if it were generally permitted; (f) whether that kind of action injures interests which ought to be considered as rights.

3. Mill says that "The interference of society to overrule his judgment and purposes in what only regards himself must be grounded on general presumptions." What does this mean? Is it true? Explain.

4. Mill says that "when a person disables himself, by conduct purely self-regarding, from the performance of some definite duty incumbent on him to the public, he is guilty of a social offense. No person ought to be punished simply for being drunk; but a soldier or a policeman should be punished for being drunk on duty." Given that even a parent's drunkenness at home can make him or her less fit to be a parent, how much difficulty does Mill's concession here create for his own thesis about individual liberty?

5. Mill sometimes speaks of behavior that "affects others" and sometimes of that which "affects the interests of others." How would you explain the difference between the two?

6. Some kinds of action, such as embezzlement, perjury, espionage, and contempt of court, are prohibited and punishable even though they do not always cause harm. Should such laws make only *harm-causing* actions of embezzlement, perjury, and so on, punishable? What would Mill say, and why?

## *John Rawls*
# THE IDEA OF AN OVERLAPPING CONSENSUS*

The aims of political philosophy depend on the society it addresses. In a constitutional democracy one of its most important aims is presenting a political conception of justice that can not only provide a shared public basis for the justification of political and social institutions but also helps ensure stability from one generation to the next. Now, a basis of justification that rests on self- or group-interests alone cannot be stable; such a basis must be, I think, even when moderated by skilful constitutional design, a mere *modus vivendi*, dependent on a fortuitous conjunction of contingencies. What is needed is a regulative political conception of justice that can articulate and order in a principled way the political ideals and values of a democratic regime, thereby specifying the aims the constitution is to achieve and the limits it must respect. In addition, this political conception needs to be such that there is some hope of its gaining the support of an overlapping consensus, that is, a consensus in which it is affirmed by the opposing religious, philosophical and moral doctrines likely to thrive over generations in a more or less just constitutional democracy, where the criterion of justice is that political conception itself.

In the first part of my discussion (Secs I-II) I review three features of a political conception of justice and note why a conception with these features is appropriate given the historical and social conditions of a modern democratic society, and in particular, the condition I shall refer to as the fact of pluralism. The second part (Secs III-VII) takes up four illustrative—but I think misplaced—objections we are likely to have to the idea of an overlapping consensus, and to its corollary that social unity in a democracy cannot rest on a shared conception of the meaning, value and

purpose of human life. This corollary does not imply, as one might think, that therefore social unity must rest solely on a convergence of self- and group-interests, or on the fortunate outcome of political bargaining. It allows for the possibility of stable social unity secured by an overlapping consensus on a reasonable political conception of justice. It is this conception of social unity for a democratic society I want to explain and defend.

By way of background, several comments. When Hobbes addressed the contentious divisions of his day between religious sects, and between the Crown, aristocracy and middle-classes, the basis of his appeal was self-interest: men's fear of death and their desire for the means of a commodious life. On this basis he sought to justify obedience to an existing effective (even if need be absolute) sovereign. Hobbes did not think this form of psychological egoism was true; but he thought it was accurate enough for his purposes. The assumption was a political one, adopted to give his views practical effect. In a society fragmented by sectarian divisions and warring interests, he saw no other common foothold for political argument.

How far Hobbes's perception of the situation was accurate we need not consider, for in our case matters are different. We are the beneficiaries of three centuries of democratic thought and developing constitutional practice; and we can presume not only some public understanding of, but also some allegiance to, democratic ideals and values as realized in existing political institutions. This opens the way to elaborate the idea of an overlapping consensus on a political conception of justice: such a consensus, as we shall see, is moral both in its object and grounds, and so is distinct from a consensus, inevitably fragile, founded solely on self- and group-interest, even

*© Oxford University Press 1987. Reprinted from the *Oxford Journal of Legal Studies*, vol. 7, no. 1 (1987), pp. 1–25.

when ordered by a well-framed constitution.[1] The idea of an overlapping consensus enables us to understand how a constitutional regime characterized by the fact of pluralism might, despite its deep divisions, achieve stability and social unity by the public recognition of a reasonable political conception of justice.

# I

The thesis of the first part of my discussion is that the historical and social conditions of a modern democratic society require us to regard a conception of justice for its political institutions in a certain way. Or rather, they require us to do so, if such a conception is to be both practicable and consistent with the limits of democratic politics. What these conditions are, and how they affect the features of a practicable conception, I note in connection with three features of a political conception of justice, two of which I now describe, leaving the third for the next section.

The first feature of a political conception of justice is that, while such a conception is, of course, a moral conception, it is a moral conception worked out for a specific kind of subject, namely, for political, social and economic institutions.[2] In particular, it is worked out to apply to what we may call the 'basic structure' of a modern constitutional democracy. (I shall use 'constitutional democracy', and 'democratic regime', and similar phrases interchangeably.) By this structure I mean a society's main political, social and economic institutions, and how they fit together into one unified scheme of social cooperation. The focus of a political conception of justice is the framework of basic institutions and the principles, standards and precepts that apply to them, as well as how those norms are expressed in the character and attitudes of the members of society who realize its ideals. One might suppose that this first feature is already implied by the meaning of a political conception of justice: for if a conception does not apply to the basic structure of society, it would not be a political conception at all. But I mean more than this, for I think of a political conception of justice as a conception framed in the first instance[3] solely for the special case of the basic structure.

The second feature complements the first: a political conception is not to be understood as a general and comprehensive moral conception that applies to the political order, as if this order was only another subject, another kind of case, falling under that conception.[4] Thus, a political conception of justice is

---

[1]Occasionally I refer to the Hobbesian strand in liberalism, by which I mean the idea that ordered liberty is best achieved by skilful constitutional design framed to guide self- (family-) and group-interests to work for social purposes by the use of various devices such as balance of powers and the like; it can be found in Montesquieu's *Spirit of Laws*(1748), Hume's essay 'That Politics may be reduced to a Science' (1741), in Madison's *Federalist*, Number 10 (1788), and in Kant's 'Perpetual Peace" (1796). This strand becomes purely Hobbesian to the extent that it sees self- (family-) and group-interests as the only available, or the only politically relevant, kind of motivation; of course, Montesquieu, Hume, Madison and Kant did not hold this view.

[2]In saying that a conception is moral I mean, among other things, that this content is given by certain ideals, principles and standards; and that these norms articulate certain values, in this case political values.

[3]The phrase 'in the first instance' indicates that we are to focus first on the basic structure. Should we find a reasonably satisfactory conception of justice for this case, we can then try to extend it to further cases, of which one of the most important is the relations between states and the system of cooperation between them. I accept Kant's view in 'Perpetual Peace' that a world state would be either an oppressive autocracy, or continually disturbed by open or latent civil wars between regions and peoples. Hence we would look for principles to regulate a confederation of states and to specify the powers of its several members. We also need to clarify how the principles of justice apply to associations within the state. On this, see the remarks in 'The Basic Structure as Subject', Secs II and IX, in *Values and Morals*, eds A. I. Goldman and Jaegwon Kim (Reidel, 1978).

[4]I think of a moral conception as general when it applies to a wide range of subjects of appraisal (in the limit of all subjects universally), and as comprehensive when it includes conceptions of what is of value in human life, ideals of personal virtue and character, and the like, that are to inform much of our conduct (in the limit of our

different from many familiar moral doctrines, for these are widely understood as general and comprehensive views. Perfectionism and utilitarianism are clear examples, since the principles of perfection and utility are thought to apply to all kinds of subjects ranging from the conduct of individuals and personal relations to the organization of society as a whole, and even to the law of nations. Their content as political doctrines is specified by their application to political institutions and questions of social policy. Idealism and Marxism in their various forms are also general and comprehensive. By contrast, a political conception of justice involves, so far as possible, no prior commitment to any wider doctrine. It looks initially to the basic structure and tries to elaborate a reasonable conception for that structure alone.

Now one reason for focusing directly on a political conception for the basic structure is that, as a practical political matter, no general and comprehensive view can provide a publicly acceptable basis for a political conception of justice.[5] The social and historical conditions of modern democratic regimes have their origins in the Wars of Religion following the Reformation and the subsequent development of the principle of toleration, and in the growth of constitutional government and of large industrial market economies. These conditions profoundly affect the requirements of a workable conception of justice: among other things, such a conception must allow for a diversity of general and comprehensive doctrines, and for the plurality of conflicting, and indeed incommensurable, conceptions of the meaning, value and purpose of human life (or what I shall call for short 'conceptions of the good') affirmed by the citizens of democratic societies.[6]

This diversity of doctrines—the fact of pluralism—is not a mere historical condition that will soon pass away; it is, I believe, a permanent feature of the public culture of modern democracies. Under the political and social conditions secured by the basic rights and liberties historically associated with these regimes, the diversity of views will persist and may increase. A public and workable agreement on a single general and comprehensive conception could be maintained only by the oppressive use of state power.[7] Since

life as a whole). Many religious and philosophical doctrines tend to be general and fully comprehensive. See also footnote 23.

[5] By a publicly acceptable basis I mean a basis that includes ideals, principles and standards that all members of society can not only affirm but also mutually recognize before one another. A public basis involves, then, the public recognition of certain principles as regulative of political institutions, and as expressing political values that the constitution is to be framed to realize.

[6] It is a disputed question whether and in what sense conceptions of the good are incommensurable. For our purposes, here, incommensurability is to be understood as a political fact, an aspect of the fact of pluralism: namely, the fact that there is no available political understanding as to how to commensurate these conceptions for settling questions of political justice.

[7] For convenience, I give a fuller list of these social and historical conditions, beginning with the three already mentioned above: (1) the fact of pluralism; (2) the fact of the permanence of pluralism, given democratic institutions; (3) the fact that agreement on a single comprehensive doctrine presupposes the oppressive use of state power. Four additional ones are: (4) the fact that an enduring and stable democratic regime, one not divided into contending factions and hostile classes, must be willingly and freely supported by a substantial majority of at least its politically active citizens; (5) the fact that a comprehensive doctrine, whenever widely, if not universally, shared in society, tends to become oppressive and stifling; (6) the fact that reasonably favourable conditions (administrative, economic, technological and the like), which make democracy possible, exist; and finally, (7) the fact that the political culture of a society with a democratic tradition implicitly contains certain fundamental intuitive ideas from which it is possible to work up a political conception of justice suitable for a constitutional regime. (This last is important when we characterize a political conception of justice in the next section.) We may think of the first six of these seven conditions as known by common sense, that is, as known from our shared history and the evident features and aspects of our political culture and present circumstances. They belong to what we might refer to as the common sense political sociology of democratic societies. When

we are concerned with securing the stability of a constitutional regime, and wish to achieve free and willing agreement on a political conception of justice that establishes at least the constitutional essentials, we must find another basis of agreement than that of a general and comprehensive doctrine.[8] And so, as this alternative basis, we look for a political conception of justice that might be supported by an overlapping consensus.

We do not, of course, assume that an overlapping consensus is always possible, given the doctrines currently existing in any democratic society. It is often obvious that it is not, not at least until firmly held beliefs change in fundamental ways.[9] But the point of the idea of an overlapping consensus on a political conception is to show how, despite a diversity of doctrines, convergence on a political conception of justice may be achieved and social unity sustained in long-run equilibrium, that is, over time from one generation to the next.

## II

So far I have noted two features of a political conception of justice: first, that it is expressly framed to apply to the basic structure of society: and second, that it is not to be seen as derived from any general and comprehensive doctrine.

Perhaps the consequences of these features are clear. Yet it may be useful to survey them. For while no one any longer supposes that a practicable political conception for a constitutional regime can rest on a shared devotion to the Catholic or the Protestant Faith, or to any other religious view, it may still be thought that general and comprehensive philosophical and moral doctrines might serve in this role. The second feature denies this not only for Hegel's idealism and Marxism, and for teleological moral views, as I have said, but also for many forms of liberalism as well. While I believe that in fact any workable conception of political justice for a democratic regime must indeed be in an appropriate sense liberal—I come back to this question later—its liberalism will not be the liberalism of Kant or of J.S. Mill, to take two prominent examples.

Consider why: the public role of a mutually recognized political conception of justice is to specify a point of view from which all citizens can examine before one another whether or not their political institutions are just. It enables them to do this by citing what are recognized among them as valid and sufficient reasons singled out by that conception itself.[10] Questions of political justice can be discussed on the same basis by all citizens, whatever their social position, or more particular aims and interests, or their religious, philosophical or moral views. Justification in matters of political justice is addressed to others who disagree with us, and therefore it proceeds from some consensus: from premises that we and others recognize as true, or as reasonable for the purpose of reaching a working agreement on the fundamentals of political justice. Given the fact of pluralism, and given that justification begins from some consensus, no general and comprehensive doctrine can assume the role of a publicly acceptable basis or political justice.

---

elaborating a political conception of justice, we must bear in mind that it must be workable and practicable in a society in which the first six conditions obtain.

[8] Here I assume that free and willing agreement endorsed by our considered convictions on due reflection, or in what I have elsewhere called 'reflective equilibrium'. See *A Theory of Justice*, pp 19ff, 48ff.

[9] How these beliefs might change is discussed later in Secs VI–VII.

[10] I suppose these reasons to be specified by the ideals, principles and standards of the mutually acknowledged political conception, which is, as noted earlier, a moral conception. Thus political institutions are not thought of as justified to all citizens simply in terms of a happy convergence of self- or group-interest, and the like. This conception of justification is in contrast with the Hobbesian strand in the tradition of liberal thought; it is found in Rousseau's *Social Contract* (1762) and plays a central role in Hegel's *Philosophy of Right* (1821).

From this conclusion it is clear what is problematic with the liberalisms of Kant and Mill. They are both general and comprehensive moral doctrines: general in that they apply to a wide range of subjects, and comprehensive in that they include conceptions of what is of value in human life, ideals of personal virtue and character that are to inform our thought and conduct as a whole. Here I have in mind Kant's ideal of autonomy and his connecting it with the values of the Enlightenment, and Mill's ideal of individuality and his connecting it with the values of modernity. These two liberalisms both comprehend far more than the political.[11] Their doctrines of free institutions rest in large part on ideals and values that are not generally, or perhaps even widely, shared in a democratic society. They are not a practicable public basis of a political conception of justice and I suspect the same is true of many liberalisms besides those of Kant and Mill.

Thus we come to a third feature of a political conception of justice, namely, it is not formulated in terms of a general and comprehensive religious, philosophical or moral doctrine but rather in terms of certain fundamental intuitive ideas viewed as latent in the public political culture of a democratic society. These ideas are used to articulate and order in a principled way its basic political values. We assume that in any such society there exists a tradition of democratic thought, the contents of which is at least intuitively familiar to citizens generally. Society's main institutions, together with the accepted forms of their interpretation, are seen as a fund of implicitly shared fundamental ideas and principles. We suppose that these ideas and principles can be elaborated into a political conception of justice, which we hope can gain the support of an overlapping consensus. Of course, that this can be done can be verified only by actually elaborating a political conception of justice and exhibiting the way in which it could be thus supported. It's also likely that more than one political conception may be worked up from the fund of shared political ideas; indeed, this is desirable, as these rival conceptions will then compete for citizens' allegiance and be gradually modified and deepened by the contest between them.

Here I cannot, of course, even sketch the development of a political conception. But in order to convey what is meant, I might say that the conception I have elsewhere called 'justice as fairness' is a political conception of this kind.[12] It can be seen as starting with the fundamental intuitive idea of political society as a fair system of social cooperation between citizens regarded as free and equal persons, and as born into the society in which they are assumed to lead a complete life. Citizens are further described as having certain moral powers that would enable them to take part in social cooperation. The problem of justice is then understood as that of specifying the fair terms of social cooperation between citizens so conceived. The conjecture is that by working out such ideas, which I view as implicit in the public political culture, we can in due course arrive at widely acceptable principles of political justice.[13]

---

[11]For Kant again see 'What is Enlightenment?' and for Mill see especially 'On Liberty' (1859), Ch III, pars 1-9.

[12]For the fullest discussion, see *A Theory of Justice* (1971). I have discussed justice as fairness as a political conception in 'Justice as Fairness: Political not Metaphysical', *Philosophy and Public Affairs*, Summer 1985. Ronald Dworkin's liberal conception of equality is, I think, another example of a political conception of justice. See his *A Matter of Principle* (Cambridge, Harvard University Press, 1986), the essays in part Three on liberalism and justice.

[13]These principles will express and give certain weights to familiar political values such as liberty and equality, fair equality of opportunity, and the efficient design of institutions to serve the common good, and the like. But we can arrive at a political conception of justice in a very different way, namely, by balancing these competing values directly against one another and eventually adjusting them to one another in the light of the overall balance, or pattern, of values that seems best to us. A procedure of this kind is suggested by Sir Isaiah Berlin; see for example his essay 'Equality', in *Concepts and Categories* (Oxford, 1980), p 100. The advantage of starting with the fundamental intuitive idea of society as a fair system of social cooperation may be that we do not simply

The details are not important here. What is important is that, so far as possible, these fundamental intuitive ideas are not taken for religious, philosophical or metaphysical ideas. For example, when it is said that citizens are regarded as free and equal persons, their freedom and equality are to be understood in ways congenial to the public political culture and explicable in terms of the design and requirements of its basic institutions. The conception of citizens as free and equal is, therefore, a political conception, the content of which is specified in connection with such things as the basic rights and liberties of democratic citizens.[14] The hope is that the conception of justice to which this conception of citizens belongs will be acceptable to a wide range of comprehensive doctrines and hence supported by an overlapping consensus.

But, as I have indicated and should emphasize, success in achieving consensus requires that political philosophy try to be, so far as possible, independent and autonomous from other parts of philosophy, especially from philosophy's long-standing problems and controversies. For given the aim of consensus, to proceed otherwise would be self-defeating. But as we shall see (in Sec IV) we may not be able to do this entirely when we attempt to answer the objection that claims that aiming for consensus implies scepticism or indifference to religious, philosophical or moral truth. Nevertheless, the reason for avoiding deeper questions remains. For as I have said above, we can present a political view either by starting explicitly from within a general and comprehensive doctrine, or we can start from fundamental intuitive ideas regarded as latent in the public political culture. These two ways of proceeding are very dif-

ferent, and this difference is significant even though we may sometimes be forced to assert certain aspects of our own comprehensive doctrine. So while we may not be able to avoid comprehensive doctrines entirely, we do what we can to reduce relying on their more specific details, or their more disputed features. The question is: what is the least that must be asserted; and if it must be asserted, what is its least controversial form?

Finally, connected with a political conception of justice is an essential companion conception of free public reason. This conception involves various elements. A crucial one is this: just as a political conception of justice needs certain principles of justice for the basic structure to specify its content, it also needs certain guidelines of enquiry and publicly recognized rules of assessing evidence to govern its application. Otherwise, there is no agreed way for determining whether those principles are satisfied, and for settling what they require of particular institutions, or in particular situations. Agreement on a conception of justice is worthless—not an effective agreement at all—without agreement on these further matters. And given the fact of pluralism, there is, I think, no better practicable alternative than to limit ourselves to the shared methods of, and the public knowledge available to, common sense, and the procedures and conclusions of science when these are not controversial. It is these shared methods and this common knowledge that allows us to speak of *public reason.*[15] As I shall stress later on, the acceptance of this limit is not motivated by scepticism or indifference to the claims of comprehensive doctrines; rather, it springs from the fact of pluralism, for this fact

---

balance values directly in the light of an overall pattern, but see how the values and their weights are arrived at in the way they are specified by the deliberations of the parties in the original position. Here I refer to the details of how justice as fairness is worked out. The thought here is that these details provide a clearer conception of how weights may be determined than the idea of balancing in the light of an overall pattern. But perhaps the idea of society as a fair system of social cooperation might itself be regarded as such a pattern, in which case the two procedures could coincide.

[14]On this, see 'Political not Metaphysical', Sec V.

[15]For a fuller discussion, see *A Theory of Justice*, Sec 34, and 'Kantian Constructivism', Lect II, pp 535–543.

means that in a pluralist society free public reason can be effectively established in no other way.[16]

## III

I now turn to the second part of my discussion (Secs III–VII) and take up four objections likely to be raised against the idea of social unity founded on an overlapping consensus on a political conception of justice. These objections I want to rebut, for they can prevent our accepting what I believe is the most reasonable basis of social unity available to us. I begin with perhaps the most obvious objection, namely, that an overlapping consensus is a mere *modus vivendi*. But first several explanatory comments.

Earlier I noted what it means to say that a conception of justice is supported by an overlapping consensus. It means that it is supported by a consensus including the opposing religious, philosophical and moral doctrines likely to thrive over generations in the society effectively regulated by that conception of justice. These opposing doctrines we assume to involve conflicting and indeed incommensurable comprehensive conceptions of the meaning, value and purpose of human life (or conceptions of the good), and there are no resources within the political view to judge those conflicting conceptions. They are equally permissible provided they respect the limits imposed by the principles of political justice. Yet despite the fact that there are opposing comprehensive conceptions affirmed in society, there is no difficulty as to how an overlapping consensus may exist. Since different premises may lead to the same conclusions, we simply suppose that the

essential elements of the political conception, its principles, standards and ideals, are theorems, as it were, at which the comprehensive doctrines in the consensus intersect or converge.

To fix ideas I shall use a model case of an overlapping consensus to indicate what is meant; and I shall return to this example from time to time. It contains three views: one view affirms the political conception because its religious doctrine and account of faith lead to a principle of toleration and underwrite the fundamental liberties of a constitutional regime; the second view affirms the political conception on the basis of a comprehensive liberal moral doctrine such as those of Kant and Mill; while the third supports the political conception not as founded on any wider doctrine but rather as in itself sufficient to express political values that, under the reasonably favourable conditions that make a more or less just constitutional democracy possible, normally outweigh whatever other values may oppose them. Observe about this example that only the first two views—the religious doctrine and the liberalism of Kant or Mill—are general and comprehensive. The political conception of justice itself is not; although it does hold that under reasonably favourable conditions, it is normally adequate for questions of political justice. Observe also that the example assumes that the two comprehensive views agree with the judgments of the political conception in this respect.

To begin with the objection: some will think that even if an overlapping consensus should be sufficiently stable, the idea of political unity founded on an overlapping consensus must still be rejected, since it abandons the hope of political community and settles

---

[16]Two other elements of the idea of free public reason in justice as fairness are these: the first is a publicly recognized conception of everyone's (rational) advantage, or good, to be used as an agreed basis of interpersonal comparisons in matters of political justice. This leads to an account of primary goods. See 'Social Unity and Primary Goods', in A. K. Sen and B. Williams, eds. *Utilitarianism and Beyond* (Cambridge University Press, 1982), Secs I–V. The second further element is the idea of publicity, which requires that the principles of political justice and their justification (in their own terms) be publicly available to all citizens, along with the knowledge of whether their political institutions are just or unjust. See 'Kantian Constructivism', Lect II, pp 535–543.

instead for a public understanding that is at bottom a mere *modus vivendi*. To this objection, we say that the hope of political community must indeed be abandoned, if by such a community we mean a political society united in affirming a general and comprehensive doctrine. This possibility is excluded by the fact of pluralism together with the rejection of the oppressive use of state power to overcome it. I believe there is no practicable alternative superior to the stable political unity secured by an overlapping consensus on a reasonable political conception of justice. Hence the substantive question concerns the significant features of such a consensus and how these features affect social concord and the moral quality of public life. I turn to why an overlapping consensus is not a mere *modus vivendi*.[17]

A typical use of the phrase '*modus vivendi*' is to characterize a treaty between two states whose national aims and interests put them at odds. In negotiating a treaty each state would be wise and prudent to make sure that the agreement proposed represents an equilibrium point: that is, that the terms and conditions of the treaty are drawn up in such a way that it is public knowledge that it is not advantageous for either state to violate it. The treaty will then be adhered to because doing so is regarded by each as in its national interest, including its interest in its reputation as a state that honours treaties. But in general both states are ready to pursue their goals at the expense of the other, and should conditions change they may do so. This background highlights the way in which a treaty is a mere *modus vivendi*. A similar background is present when we think of social consensus founded on self- or group-interests, or on the outcome of political bargaining: social unity is only apparent as its stability is contingent on circumstances remaining such as not to upset the fortunate convergence of interests.

Now, that an overlapping consensus is quite different from a *modus vivendi* is clear from our model case. In that example, note two aspects: first, the object of consensus, the political conception of justice, is itself a moral conception. And second, it is affirmed on moral grounds, that is, it includes conceptions of society and of citizens as persons, as well as principles of justice, and an account of the cooperative virtues through which those principles are embodied in human character and expressed in public life. An overlapping consensus, therefore, is not merely a consensus on accepting certain authorities, or on complying with certain institutional arrangements, founded on a convergence of self- or group-interests. All three views in the example affirm the political conception: as I have said, each recognizes its concepts, principles and virtues as the shared content at which their several views coincide. The fact that those who affirm the political conception start from within their

[17]Note that what is impracticable is not *all* values of community (recall that a community is understood as an association or society whose unity rests on a comprehensive conception of the good) but only *political* community and its values. Justice as fairness assumes, as other liberal political views do also, that the values of community are not only essential but realizable, first in the various associations that carry on their life within the framework of the basic structure, and second in those associations that extend across the boundaries of nation-states, such as churches and scientific societies. Liberalism rejects the state as a community because, among other things, it leads to the systematic denial of basic liberties and to the oppressive use of the state's monopoly of (legal) force. I should add that in the well-ordered society of justice as fairness citizens share a common aim, and one that has high priority: namely, the aim of political justice, that is, the aim of ensuring that political and social institutions are just, and of giving justice to persons generally, as what citizens need for themselves and want for one another. It is not true, then, that on a liberal view citizens have no fundamental common aims. Nor is it true that the aim of political justice is not an important part of their identity (using the terms 'identity', as is now often done, to include the basic aims and projects by reference to which we characterize the kind of person we very much want to be). But this common aim of political justice must not be mistaken for (what I have called) a conception of the good. For a discussion of this last point see Amy Gutmann, 'Communitarian Critics of Liberalism', *Philosophy and Public Affairs*. Summer 1985, p 311, footnote 14.

own comprehensive view, and hence begin from different premises and grounds, does not make their affirmation any less religious, philosophical or moral, as the case may be.

The preceding two aspects (moral object and moral grounds) of an overlapping consensus connect with a third aspect, that of stability: that is, those who affirm the various views supporting the political conception will not withdraw their support of it should the relative strength of their view in society increase and eventually become dominant. So long as the three views are affirmed and not revised, the political conception will still be supported regardless of shifts in the distribution of political power. We might say: each view supports the political conception for its own sake, or on its own merits; and the test for this is whether the consensus is stable with respect to changes in the distribution of power among views. This feature of stability highlights a basic contrast between an overlapping consensus and a *modus vivendi*, the stability of which does depend on happenstance and a balance of relative forces.

This becomes clear once we change our example and include the views of Catholics and Protestants in the sixteenth century. We no longer have an overlapping consensus on the principle of toleration. At that time both faiths held that it was the duty of the ruler to uphold the true religion and to repress the spread of heresy and false doctrine. In this case the acceptance of the principle of toleration would indeed be a mere *modus vivendi*, because if either faith becomes dominant, the principle of toleration will no longer be followed. Stability with respect to the distribu-

tion of power no longer holds. So long as views held by Catholics and Protestants in the sixteenth century are very much in the minority, and are likely to remain so, they do not significantly affect the moral quality of public life and the basis of social concord. For the vast majority in society are confident that the distribution of power will range over and be widely shared by views in the consensus that affirm the political conception of justice for its own sake. But should this situation change, the moral quality of political life will also change in ways I assume to be obvious and to require no comment.

The preceding remarks prompt us to ask which familiar conceptions of justice can belong to a consensus stable with respect to the distribution of power. It seems that while some teleological conceptions can so belong, others quite possibly cannot, for example, utilitarianism.[18] Or at least this seems to be the case unless certain assumptions are made limiting the content of citizens' desires, preferences, or interests.[19] Otherwise there appears to be no assurance that restricting or suppressing the basic liberties of some may not be the best way to maximize the total (or average) social welfare. Since utilitarianism in its various forms is a historically prominent and continuing part of the tradition of democratic thought, we may hope there are ways of construing or revising utilitarian doctrine so that it can support a conception of justice appropriate for a constitutional regime, even if it can do so only indirectly[20] as a means to the greatest welfare. Insofar as utilitarianism is likely to persist in a well-ordered society, the overlapping consensus is in that case all the more stable and secure.

[18]Here I mean the view of Bentham, Edgeworth and Sidgwick, and of such contemporary writers as R. B. Brandt in *A Theory of the Good and the Right* (Oxford, 1979), R. M. Hare in *Moral Thinking* (Oxford, 1981), and J. J. C. Smart in *Utilitarianism: For and Against* (Cambridge, 1973).

[19]Desires, preferences and interests are not the same but have distinct features: and these differences play an important part in different versions of utilitarianism espoused by the writers mentioned in the previous footnote. I believe, however, that the general point in the text holds against all these versions.

[20]The adverb 'indirectly' here refers to indirect utilitarianism so-called. For a clear account of J. S. Mill's view as exemplifying this doctrine, see John Gray, *Mill on Liberty: A Defence* (London, 1983).

## IV

I turn to the second objection to the idea of an overlapping consensus on a political conception of justice: namely, that the avoidance of general and comprehensive doctrines implies indifference or scepticism as to whether a political conception of justice is true. This avoidance may appear to suggest that such a conception might be the most reasonable one for us even when it is known not to be true, as if truth were simply beside the point. In reply, it would be fatal to the point of a political conception to see it as sceptical about, or indifferent to, truth, much less as in conflict with it. Such scepticism or indifference would put political philosophy in conflict with numerous comprehensive doctrines, and thus defeat from the outset its aim of achieving an overlapping consensus. In following the method of avoidance, as we may call it, we try, so far as we can, neither to assert nor to deny any religious, philosophical or moral views, or their associated philosophical accounts of truth and the status of values. Since we assume each citizen to affirm some such view or other, we hope to make it possible for all to accept the political conception as true, or as reasonable, from the standpoint of their own comprehensive view, whatever it may be.[21]

Properly understood, then, a political conception of justice need be no more indifferent, say, to truth in morals than the principle of toleration, suitably understood, need be indifferent to truth in religion. We simply apply the principle of toleration to philosophy itself. In this way we hope to avoid philosophy's long-standing controversies, among them controversies about the nature of truth and the status of values as expressed by realism and subjectivism. Since we seek an agreed basis of public justification in matters of justice, and since no political agreement on those disputed questions can reasonably be expected, we turn instead to the fundamental intuitive ideas we seem to share through the public political culture. We try to develop from these ideas a political conception of justice congruent with our considered convictions on due reflection. Just as with religion, citizens situated in thought and belief within their comprehensive doctrines, regard the political conception of justice as true, or as reasonable, whatever the case may be.

Some may not be satisfied with this: they may reply that, despite these protests, a political conception of justice must express indifference or scepticism. Otherwise it could not lay aside fundamental religious, philosophical and moral questions because they are politically difficult to settle, or may prove intractable. Certain truths, it may be said, concern things so important that differences about them have to be fought out, even should this mean civil war. To this we say first, that questions are not removed from the political agenda, so to speak, solely because they are a source of conflict. Rather, we appeal to a political conception of justice to distinguish between those questions that can be reasonably removed from the political agenda and those that cannot, all the

---

[21]It is important to see that the view that philosophy in the classical sense as the search for truth about a prior and independent moral order cannot provide the shared basis for a political conception of justice (asserted in 'Political not Metaphysical', p 230) does not presuppose the controversial metaphysical claim that there is no such order. The above paragraph makes clear why it does not. The reasons I give for that view are historical and sociological, and have nothing to do with metaphysical doctrines about the status of values. What I hold is that we must draw the obvious lessons of our political history since the Reformation and the Wars of Religion, and the development of modern constitutional democracies. As I say in Sec I above, it is no longer reasonable to expect us to reach *political* agreement on a general and comprehensive doctrine as a way of reaching political agreement on constitutional essentials, unless, of course, we are prepared to use the apparatus of the state as an instrument of oppression. If we are not prepared to do that, we must, as a practical matter, look for what I have called a political conception of justice.

while aiming for an overlapping consensus. Some questions still on the agenda will be controversial, at least to some degree; this is normal with political issues.

To illustrate: from within a political conception of justice let's suppose we can account both for equal liberty of conscience, which takes the truths of religion off the political agenda, and the equal political and civil liberties, which by ruling out serfdom and slavery takes the possibility of those institutions off the agenda.[22] But controversial issues inevitably remain: for example, how more exactly to draw the boundaries of the basic liberties when they conflict (where to set 'the wall between church and state'); how to interpret the requirements of distributive justice even when there is considerable agreement on general principles for the basic structure; and finally, questions of policy such as the use of nuclear weapons. These cannot be removed from politics. But by avoiding comprehensive doctrines we try to bypass religion and philosophy's profoundest controversies so as to have some hope of uncovering a basis of a stable overlapping consensus.

Nevertheless in affirming a political conception of justice we may eventually have to assert at least certain aspects of our own comprehensive (by no means necessarily fully comprehensive)[23] religious or philosophical doctrine. This happens whenever someone insists, for example, that certain questions are so fundamental that to ensure their being rightly settled justifies civil strife. The religious salvation of those holding a particular religion, or indeed the salvation of a whole people, may be said to depend on it. At this point we may have no alternative but to deny this, and to assert the kind of thing we had hoped to avoid. But the aspects of our view that we assert should not go beyond what is necessary for the political aim of consensus. Thus, for example, we may assert in some form the doctrine of free religious faith that supports equal liberty of conscience; and given the existence of a just constitutional regime, we deny that the concern for salvation requires anything incompatible with that liberty. We do not state more of our comprehensive view than we think would advance the quest for consensus.

The reason for this restraint is to respect, as best we can, the limits of free public reason (mentioned earlier at the end of Sec II). Let's suppose that by respecting these limits we succeed in reaching an overlapping consensus on a conception of political justice. Some might say that reaching this reflective agreement is itself sufficient grounds for regarding that conception as true, or at any rate highly probable. But we refrain from this further step: it is unnecessary and may interfere with the practical aim of finding an agreed public basis of justification. The idea of an overlapping consensus leaves this step to be taken by citizens individually in accordance with their own general and comprehensive views.

---

[22] To explain: when certain matters are taken off the political agenda, they are no longer regarded as proper subjects for political decision by majority or other plurality voting. In regard to equal liberty of conscience and rejection of slavery and serfdom, this means that the equal basic liberties in the constitution that cover these matters are taken as fixed, settled once and for all. They are part of the public charter of a constitutional regime and not a suitable topic for on-going public debate and legislation, as if they can be changed at any time, one way or the other. Moreover, the more established political parties likewise acknowledge these matters as settled. Of course, that certain matters are taken off the political agenda does not mean that a political conception of justice should not explain why this is done. Indeed, as I note above, political conception should do precisely this. For thinking of basic rights and liberties as taking certain questions off the political agenda I am indebted to Stephen Holmes.

[23] I think of a doctrine as fully comprehensive if it covers all recognized values and virtues within one rather precisely articulated system; whereas a doctrine is only partially comprehensive when it comprises a number of non-political values and virtues and is rather loosely articulated. This limited scope and looseness turns out to be important with regard to stability in Sec VI–VII below.

In doing this a political conception of justice completes and extends the movement of thought that began three centuries ago with the gradual acceptance of the principle of toleration and led to the non-confessional state and equal liberty of conscience. This extension is required for an agreement on a political conception of justice given the historical and social circumstances of a democratic society. In this way the full autonomy of democratic citizens connects with a conception of political philosophy as itself autonomous and independent of general and comprehensive doctrines. In applying the principles of toleration to philosophy itself it is left to citizens individually to resolve for themselves the questions of religion, philosophy and morals in accordance with the views they freely affirm.

## V

A third objection is the following: even if we grant that an overlapping consensus is not a *modus vivendi*, it may be said that a workable political conception must be general and comprehensive. Without such a doctrine on hand, there is no way to order the many conflicts of justice that arise in public life. The idea is that the deeper the conceptual and philosophical bases of those conflicts, the more general and comprehensive the level of philosophical reflection must be if their roots are to be laid bare and an appropriate ordering found. It is useless, the objection concludes, to try to work out a political conception of justice expressly for the basic structure apart from any comprehensive doctrine. And as we have just seen, we may be forced to refer, at least in some way, to such a view.[24]

This objection is perfectly natural: we are indeed tempted to ask how else could these conflicting claims be adjudicated. Yet part of the answer is found in the third view in our model case: namely, a political conception of justice regarded not as a consequence of a comprehensive doctrine but as in itself sufficient to express values that normally outweigh whatever other values oppose them, at least under the reasonably favourable conditions that make a constitutional democracy possible. Here the criterion of a just regime is specified by that political conception; and the values in question are seen from its principles and standards, and from its account of the co-operative virtues of political justice, and the like. Those who hold this conception have, of course, other views as well, views that specify values and virtues belonging to other parts of life; they differ from citizens holding the two other views in our example of an overlapping consensus in having no fully (as opposed to partially)[25] comprehensive doctrine within which they see all values and virtues as being ordered. They don't say such a doctrine is impossible, but rather practically speaking unnecessary. Their conviction is that within the scope allowed by the basic liberties and the other provisions of a just constitution, all citizens can pursue their way of life on fair terms and properly respect its (non-public) values. So long as those constitutional guarantees are secure, they think no conflict of values is likely to arise that would justify their opposing the political conception as a

---

[24]It is essential to distinguish between general and comprehensive views we think of as abstract. Thus, when justice as fairness begins from the fundamental intuitive idea of society as a fair system of cooperation and proceeds to elaborate that idea, the resulting conception of political justice may be said to be abstract. It is abstract in the same way that the conception of a perfectly competitive market, or of general economic equilibrium, is abstract: that is, it singles out, or focuses on, certain aspects of society as especially significant from the standpoint of political justice and leaves others aside. But whether the conception that results itself is general and comprehensive, as I have used those terms, is a separate question. I believe the conflicts implicit in the fact of pluralism force political philosophy to present conceptions of justice that are abstract, if it is to achieve its aims; but the same conflicts prevent those conceptions from being general and comprehensive.

[25]For the distinction between a doctrine's being fully vs partially comprehensive, see footnote 23 Sec IV.

whole, or on such fundamental matters as liberty of conscience, or equal political liberties, or basic civil rights, and the like.

Those holding this partially comprehensive view might explain it as follows. We should not assume that there exist reasonable and generally acceptable answers for all or even for many questions of political justice that might be asked. Rather we must be prepared to accept the fact that only a few such questions can be satisfactorily resolved. Political wisdom consists in identifying those few, and among them the most urgent. That done, we must frame the institutions of the basic structure so that intractable conflicts are unlikely to arise; we must also accept the need for clear and simple principles, the general form and content of which we hope can be publicly understood. A political conception is at best but a guiding framework of deliberation and reflection which helps us reach political agreement on at least the constitutional essentials. If it seems to have cleared our view and made our considered convictions more coherent; if it has narrowed the gap between the conscientious convictions of those who accept the basic ideas of a constitutional regime, then it has served its practical political purpose. And this remains true even though we can't fully explain our agreement: we know only that citizens who affirm the political conception, and who have been raised in and are familiar with the fundamental ideas of the public political culture, find that, when they adopt its framework of deliberation, their judgments converge sufficiently so that political cooperation on the basis of mutual respect can be maintained. They view the political conception as itself normally sufficient and may not expect, or think they need, greater political understanding than that.

But here we are bound to ask: how can a political conception of justice express values

that, under the reasonably favourable conditions that make democracy possible, normally outweigh whatever other values conflict with them? One way is this. As I have said, the most reasonable political conception of justice for a democratic regime will be, broadly speaking, liberal. But this means, as I will explain in the next section, that it protects the familiar basic rights and assigns them a special priority; it also includes measures to ensure that all persons in society have sufficient material means to make effective use of those basic rights. Faced with the fact of pluralism, a liberal view removes from the political agenda the most divisive issues, pervasive uncertainty and serious contention about which must undermine the bases of social cooperation.

The virtues of political cooperation that make a constitutional regime possible are, then, *very great virtues*. I mean, for example, the virtues of tolerance and being ready to meet others halfway, and the virtue of reasonableness and the sense of fairness. When these virtues (together with the modes of thought and sentiments they involve) are widespread in society and sustain its political conception of justice, they constitute a very great public good, part of society's political capital.[26] Thus, the values that conflict with the political conception of justice and its sustaining virtues may be normally outweighed because they come into conflict with the very conditions that make fair social cooperation possible on a footing of mutual respect.

Moreover, conflicts with political values are much reduced when the political conception is supported by an overlapping consensus, the more so the more inclusive the consensus. For in this case the political conception is not viewed as incompatible with basic religious, philosophical and moral values. We avoid having to consider the claims

---

[26] The term 'capital' is appropriate and familiar in this connection because these virtues are built up slowly over time and depend not only on existing political and social institutions (themselves slowly built up), but also on citizens' experience as a whole and their knowledge of the past. Again, like capital, these virtues depreciate, as it were, and must be constantly renewed by being reaffirmed and acted from in the present.

of the political conception of justice against those of this or that comprehensive view; nor need we say that political values are intrinsically more important than other values and that's why the latter are overridden. Indeed, saying that is the kind of thing we hope to avoid, and achieving an overlapping consensus enables us to avoid it.

To conclude: given the fact of pluralism, what does the work of reconciliation by free public reason, and thus enables us to avoid reliance on general and comprehensive doctrines, is two things: first, identifying the fundamental role of political values in expressing the terms of fair social cooperation consistent with mutual respect between citizens regarded as free and equal; and second, uncovering a sufficiently inclusive concordant fit among political and other values as displayed in an overlapping consensus.

## VI

The last difficulty I shall consider is that the idea of an overlapping consensus is utopian; that is, there are not sufficient political, social, or psychological forces either to bring about an overlapping consensus (when one does not exist), or to render one stable (should one exist). Here I can only touch on this intricate question and I merely outline one way in which such a consensus might come about and its stability made secure. For this purpose I use the idea of a liberal conception of political justice, the content of which I stipulate to have three main elements (noted previously): first, a specification of certain basic rights, liberties and opportunities (of the kind familiar from constitutional democratic regimes); second, an assignment of a special priority to those rights, liberties and opportunities, especially with respect to the claims of the general good and of perfectionist values; and third, measures assuring to all citizens adequate all-purpose means to make effective use of their basic liberties and opportunities.[27]

Now let's suppose that at a certain time, as a result of various historical events and contingencies, the principles of a liberal conception have come to be accepted as a mere *modus vivendi*, and that existing political institutions meet their requirements. This acceptance has come about, we may assume, in much the same way as the acceptance of the principle of toleration as a *modus vivendi* came about following the Reformation: at first reluctantly, but nevertheless as providing the only alternative to endless and destructive civil strife. Our question, then, is this: how might it happen that over generations the initial acquiescence in a liberal conception of justice as a *modus vivendi* develops into a stable and enduring overlapping consensus? In this connection I think a certain looseness in our comprehensive views, as well as their not being fully comprehensive, may be particularly significant. To see this, let's return to our model case.

One way in which that example is atypical is that two of the three doctrines were described as fully general and comprehensive, a religious doctrine of free faith and the comprehensive liberalism of Kant or Mill. In these cases the acceptance of the political conception was said to be derived from and to depend solely on the comprehensive doctrine. But how far in practice does the allegiance to a political conception actually

---

[27] A fuller idea of the content of a liberal conception of justice is this: (1) political authority must respect the rule of law and a conception of the common good that includes the good of every citizen; (2) liberty of conscience and freedom of thought is to be guaranteed; and this extends to the liberty to follow one's conception of the good, provided it does not violate the principles of justice; (3) equal political rights are to be assured, and in addition freedom of the press and assembly, the right to form political parties, including the idea of a loyal opposition; (4) fair equality of opportunity and free choice of occupation are to be maintained against a background of diverse opportunities; and (5) all citizens are to be assured a fair share of material means so that they are suitably independent and can take advantage of their equal basic rights, liberties and fair opportunities. Plainly each of these elements can be understood in different ways, and so there are many liberalisms. However, I think of them all as sharing at least the three mentioned in the text.

depend on its derivation from a comprehensive view? There are several possibilities. For simplicity distinguish three cases: the political conception is derived from the comprehensive doctrine; it is not derived from but is compatible with that doctrine; and last, the political conception is incompatible with it. In everyday life we have not usually decided, or even thought much about, which of these cases hold. To decide among them would raise highly complicated issues; and it is not clear that we need to decide among them. Most people's religious, philosophical and moral doctrines are not seen by them as fully general and comprehensive, and these aspects admit of variations of degree. There is lots of slippage, so to speak, many ways for the political conception to cohere loosely with those (partially) comprehensive views, and many ways within the limits of a political conception of justice to allow for the pursuit of different (partially) comprehensive doctrines. This suggests that many if not most citizens come to affirm their common political conception without seeing any particular connection, one way or the other, between it and their other views. Hence it is possible for them first to affirm the political conception and to appreciate the public good it accomplishes in a democratic society. Should an incompatibility later be recognized between the political conception and their wider doctrines, then they might very well adjust or revise these doctrines rather than reject the political conception.[28]

At this point we ask: in virtue of what political values might a liberal conception of justice gain an allegiance to itself? An allegiance to institutions and to the conception that regulates them may, of course, be based in part on long-term self- and group-interests, custom and traditional attitudes, or simply on the desire to conform to what is expected and normally done. Widespread allegiance may also be encouraged by institutions securing for all citizens the political values included under what Hart calls the minimum content of natural law. But here we are concerned with the further bases of allegiance generated by a liberal conception of justice.[29]

Now when a liberal conception effectively regulates basic political institutions, it meets three essential requirements of a stable constitutional regime. First, given the fact of pluralism—the fact that necessitates a liberal regime as a *modus vivendi* in the first place—a liberal conception meets the urgent political requirement to fix, once and for all, the content of basic rights and liberties, and to assign them special priority. Doing this takes those guarantees off the political agenda and puts them beyond the calculus of social interests, thereby establishing clearly and firmly the terms of social cooperation on a footing of mutual respect. To regard that calculus as relevant in these matters leaves the status and content of those rights and liberties still unsettled; it subjects them to the shifting circumstances of time and place, and by greatly raising the stakes of political controversy, dangerously increases the insecurity and hostility of public life. Thus, the unwillingness to take these matters off the agenda perpetuates the deep divisions latent in society; it betrays a readiness to revive those antagonisms in the hope of gaining a more favourable position should later

[28]Note that here we distinguish between the initial allegiance to, or appreciation of, the political conception and the later adjustment or revision of comprehensive doctrines to which that allegiance or appreciation leads when inconsistencies arise. These adjustments or revisions we may suppose to take place slowly over time as the political conception shapes comprehensive views to cohere with it. For much of this approach I am indebted to Samuel Scheffler.

[29]See the *The Concept of Law*, (Oxford, 1961), pp 189–195, for what Hart calls the minimum content of natural law. I assume that a liberal conception (as do many other familiar conceptions) includes this minimum content; and so in the text I focus on the basis of the allegiance such a conception generates in virtue of the distinctive content of its principles.

circumstances prove propitious. So, by contrast, securing the basic liberties and recognizing their priority achieves the work of reconciliation and seals mutual acceptance on a footing of equality.

The second requirement is connected with a liberal conception's idea of free public reason. It is highly desirable that the form of reasoning a conception specifies should be, and can publicly be seen to be, correct and reasonably reliable in its own terms.[30] A liberal conception tries to meet these desiderata in several ways. As we have seen, in working out a political conception of justice it starts from fundamental intuitive ideas latent in the shared public culture; it detaches political values from any particular comprehensive and sectarian (non-public) doctrine; and it tries to limit that conception's scope to matters of political justice (the basic structure and its social policies). Further, (as we saw in Sec II) it recognizes that an agreement on a political conception of justice is to no effect without a companion agreement on guidelines of public enquiry and rules for assessing evidence. Given the fact of pluralism, these guidelines and rules must be specified by reference to the forms of reasoning available to common sense, and by the procedures and conclusions of science when not controversial. The role of these shared methods and this common knowledge in applying the political conception makes reason *public*; the protection given to freedom of speech and thought makes it *free*. The claims of religion and philosophy (as previously emphasized) are not excluded out of scepticism or indifference, but as a condition of establishing a shared basis for free public reason.

A liberal conception's idea of public reason also has a certain simplicity. To illustrate: even if general and comprehensive teleological conceptions were acceptable as political conceptions of justice, the form of

public reasoning they specify would be politically unworkable. For if the elaborate theoretical calculations involved in applying their principles are publicly admitted in questions of political justice (consider, for example, what is involved in applying the principle of utility to the basic structure), the highly speculative nature and enormous complexity of these calculations are bound to make citizens with conflicting interests highly suspicious of one another's arguments. The information they presuppose is very hard if not impossible to obtain, and often there are insuperable problems in reaching an objective and agreed assessment. Moreover, even though we think our arguments sincere and not self-serving when we present them, we must consider what it is reasonable to expect others to think who stand to lose when our reasoning prevails. Arguments supporting political judgments should, if possible, not only be sound but such that they can be publicly seen to be sound. The maxim that justice must not only be done, but be seen to be done, holds good not only in law but in free public reason.

The third requirement met by a liberal conception is related to the preceding ones. The basic institutions enjoined by such a conception, and its conception of free public reason—when effectively working over time—encourage the cooperative virtues of political life: the virtue of reasonableness and a sense of fairness, a spirit of compromise and a readiness to meet others halfway, all of which are connected with the willingness if not the desire to cooperate with others on political terms that everyone can publicly accept consistent with mutual respect. Political liberalism tests principles and orders institutions with an eye to their influence on the moral quality of public life, on the civic virtues and habits of mind their public recognition tends to foster, and which are

[30] Here the phrase 'in its own terms' means that we are not at present concerned with whether the conception in question is true, or reasonable (as the case may be), but with how easily its principles and standards can be correctly understood and reliably applied in public discussion.

needed to sustain a stable constitutional regime. This requirement is related to the preceding two in this way. When the terms of social cooperation are settled on a footing of mutual respect by fixing once and for all the basic liberties and opportunities with their priority, and when this fact itself is publicly recognized, there is a tendency for the essential cooperative virtues to develop. And this tendency is further strengthened by successful conduct of free public reason in arriving at what are regarded as just policies and fair understandings.

The three requirements met by a liberal conception are evident in the fundamental structural features of the public world it realizes, and in its effects on citizens' political character, a character that takes the basic rights and liberties for granted and disciplines its deliberations in accordance with the guidelines of free public reason. A political conception of justice (liberal or otherwise) specifies the form of a social world—a background framework within which the life of associations, groups and individual citizens proceeds. Inside that framework a working consensus may often be secured by a convergence of self- or group-interests; but to secure stability that framework must be honoured and seen as fixed by the political conception, itself affirmed on moral grounds.

The conjecture, then, is that as citizens come to appreciate what a liberal conception does, they acquire an allegiance to it, an allegiance that becomes stronger over time. They come to think it both reasonable and wise for them to confirm their allegiance to its principles of justice as expressing values that, under the reasonably favourable conditions that make democracy possible, normally counterbalance whatever values may oppose them. With this an overlapping consensus is achieved.

## VII

I have just outlined how it may happen that an initial acquiescence in a liberal conception of justice as a mere *modus vivendi* changes over time into a stable overlapping consensus. Thus the conclusion just reached is all we need to say in reply to the objection that the idea of such a consensus is utopian. Yet to make this conclusion more plausible, I shall indicate, necessarily only briefly, some of the main assumptions underlying the preceding account of how political allegiance is generated.

First, there are the assumptions contained in what I shall call a reasonable moral psychology, that is, a psychology of human beings as capable of being reasonable and engaging in fair social cooperation. Here I include the following: (I) besides a capacity for a conception of the good, people have a capacity to acquire conceptions of justice and fairness (which specify fair terms of cooperation) and to act as these conceptions require; (2) when they believe that institutions or social practices are just, or fair (as these conceptions specify), they are ready and willing to do their part in those arrangements provided they have reasonable assurance that others will also do their part; (3) if other persons with evident intention strive to do their part in just or fair arrangements, people tend to develop trust and confidence in them; (4) this trust and confidence becomes stronger and more complete as the success of shared cooperative arrangements is sustained over a longer time; and also (5) as the basic institutions framed to secure our fundamental interests (the basic rights and liberties) are more firmly and willingly recognized.

We may also suppose that everyone recognizes what I have called the historical and social conditions of modern democratic societies: (i) the fact of pluralism and (ii) the fact of its permanence, as well as (iii) the fact that this pluralism can be overcome only by the oppressive use of state power (which presupposes a control of the state no group possesses). These conditions constitute a common predicament. But also seen as part of this common predicament is (iv) the fact of moderate scarcity and (v) the fact of there being numerous possibilities of gains from well-organized social cooperation, if only co-operation can be established on fair terms. All these conditions and assumptions characterize the circumstances of political justice.

Now we are ready to draw on the preceding assumptions to answer once again the question: how might an overlapping consensus on a liberal conception of justice develop from its acceptance as a mere *modus vivendi*? Recall our assumption that the comprehensive doctrines of most people are not fully comprehensive, and how this allows scope for the development of an independent allegiance to a liberal conception once how it works is appreciated. This independent allegiance in turn leads people to act with evident intention in accordance with liberal arrangements, since they have reasonable assurance (founded on past experience) that others will also comply with them. So gradually over time, as the success of political cooperation continues, citizens come to have increasing trust and confidence in one another.

Note also that the success of liberal institutions may come as a discovery of a new social possibility: the possibility of a reasonably harmonious and stable pluralist society. Before the successful and peaceful practice of toleration in societies with liberal political institutions there was no way of knowing of that possibility. It can easily seem more natural to believe, as the centuries' long practice of intolerance appeared to confirm, that social unity and concord requires agreement on a general and comprehensive religious, philosophical or moral doctrine. Intolerance was accepted as a condition of social order and stability.[31] The weakening of that belief helps to clear the way for liberal institutions. And if we ask how the doctrine of free faith might develop, perhaps it is connected with the fact that it is difficult, if not impossible, to believe in the damnation of those with whom we have long cooperated on fair terms with trust and confidence.

To conclude: the third view of our model case, seen as a liberal conception of justice, may encourage a mere *modus vivendi* to develop eventually into an overlapping consensus precisely because it is not general and comprehensive. The conception's limited scope together with the looseness of our comprehensive doctrines allows leeway for it to gain an initial allegiance to itself and thereby to shape those doctrines accordingly as conflicts arise, a process that takes place gradually over generations (assuming a reasonable moral psychology). Religions that once rejected toleration may come to accept it and to affirm a doctrine of free faith; the comprehensive liberalisms of Kant and Mill, while viewed as suitable for non-public life and as possible bases for affirming a constitutional regime, are no longer proposed as political conceptions of justice. On this account an overlapping consensus is not a happy coincidence, even if aided as it no doubt must be by historical good fortune, but is rather in part the work of society's public tradition of political thought.

## VIII

I conclude by commenting briefly on what I have called political liberalism. We have seen that this view steers a course between the Hobbesian strand in liberalism—liberalism as a *modus vivendi* secured by a convergence of self- and group-interests as coordinated and balanced by well-designed constitutional arrangements—and a liberalism founded on a comprehensive moral doctrine such as that of Kant or Mill. By itself, the former cannot secure an enduring social unity, the latter cannot gain sufficient agreement. Political liberalism is represented in our model case of an overlapping consensus by the third view once we take the political conception in question as liberal. So understood political liberalism is the view that under the rea-

---

[31]Hume remarks on this in par 6 of 'Liberty of the Press' (1741).

sonably favourable conditions that make constitutional democracy possible, political institutions satisfying the principles of a liberal conception of justice realize political values and ideals that normally outweigh whatever other values oppose them.

Political liberalism must deal with two basic objections: one is the charge of scepticism and indifference, the other that it cannot gain sufficient support to assure compliance with its principles of justice. Both of these objections are answered by finding a reasonable liberal conception of justice that can be supported by an overlapping consensus. For such a consensus achieves compliance by a concordant fit between the political conception and general and comprehensive doctrines together with the public recognition of the very great value of the political virtues. But as we saw, success in finding an overlapping consensus forces political philosophy to be, so far as possible, independent of and autonomous from other parts of philosophy, especially from philosophy's long-standing problems and controversies. And this in turn gives rise to the objection that political liberalism is sceptical of religious and philosophical truth, or indifferent to their values. But if we relate the nature of a political conception to the fact of pluralism and with what is essential for a shared basis of free public reason, this objection is seen to be mistaken. We can also note (see the end of Sec IV) how political philosophy's independence and autonomy from other parts of philosophy connects with the freedom and autonomy of democratic citizenship.

Some may think that to secure stable social unity in a constitutional regime by looking for an overlapping consensus detaches political philosophy from philosophy and makes it into politics. Yes and no: the politician, we say, looks to the next election, the statesman to the next generation, and philosophy to the indefinite future. Philosophy sees the political world as an on-going system of cooperation over time, in perpetuity practically speaking. Political philosophy is related to politics because it must be concerned, as moral philosophy need not be, with practical political possibilities.[32] This has led us to outline, for example, how it is possible for the deep divisions present in a pluralistic society to be reconciled through a political conception of justice that gradually over generations becomes the focus of an overlapping consensus. Moreover, this concern with practical possibility compels political philosophy to consider fundamental institutional questions and the assumptions of a reasonable moral psychology.

Thus political philosophy is not mere politics: in addressing the public culture it takes the longest view, looks to society's permanent historical and social conditions, and tries to mediate society's deepest conflicts. It hopes to uncover and to help to articulate, a shared basis of consensus on a political conception of justice drawing upon citizens' fundamental intuitive ideas about their society and their place in it. In exhibiting the possibility of an overlapping consensus in a society with a democratic tradition confronted by the fact of pluralism, political philosophy assumes the role Kant gave to philosophy generally: the defence of reasonable faith. In our case this becomes the defence of reasonable faith in the real possibility of a just constitutional regime.

---

[32]On this point, see the instructive remarks by Joshua Cohen, 'Reflections on Rousseau: Autonomy and Democracy', *Philosophy and Public Affairs* Summer 1986, pp 296f.

# QUESTIONS

1. Rawls's idea of an overlapping consensus is meant to apply to political societies. Describe what an overlapping consensus among a private group of three friends would be like. Then change your description enough to turn it into what Rawls calls a modus vivendi.

2. Rawls says, "success in achieving consensus requires that political philosophy try to be, so far as possible, independent and autonomous from other parts of philosophy, especially from philosophy's long-standing problems and controversies." Explain concretely what he means by this, using the example of abortion. Think of two people with directly conflicting views about the permissibility of abortion, one believing that abortion is forbidden by God and contrary to the natural order of the universe, while the other believes that to prohibit abortion is to impose a kind of slavery on women. If they were taking Rawls's advice in an effort to conduct public discussion on the basis of an "overlapping consensus," how would they proceed?

3. Rawls claims that a mere modus vivendi, whether among nations or among individuals in society, is not affirmed on moral grounds. Why does he say this? Explain what is different about an overlapping consensus that justifies saying that it is affirmed on moral grounds.

4. Give an example of a philosophical view that would count as a comprehensive moral conception. Explain carefully why it is a comprehensive conception.

5. Rawls has been criticized for holding that our political consensus must arise out of political ideas and understandings already in our culture. One author says, "When Americans say that all human beings are created equal and endowed with certain inalienable rights, we intend this not as a description of our local convictions but, rather, as universal truths, valid everywhere and binding on all." [William A. Galston, "Pluralism and Social Unity," Ethics 99 (July 1989), p. 725.] Is there any objective, widely shared basis that a Rawlsian can use to argue that Hitlerism, Stalinism, and apartheid are unjust, bad, or undesirable?

6. Sketch as completely as you can the standards of inquiry and evidence (what Rawls calls the "basis for free public reason") that would prevail in a liberal society.

# Offense to Others

## *United States Supreme Court**
# HUSTLER MAGAZINE v. FALWELL

CHIEF JUSTICE REHNQUIST delivered the opinion of the Court.

Petitioner Hustler Magazine, Inc., is a magazine of nation-wide circulation. Respondent Jerry Falwell, a nationally known minister who has been active as a commentator on politics and public affairs, sued petitioner and its publisher, petitioner Larry Flynt, to recover damages for invasion of privacy, libel, and intentional infliction of emotional distress. The District Court directed a verdict against respondent on the privacy claim, and submitted the other two claims to a jury. The jury found for petitioners on the defamation claim, but found for respondent on the claim for intentional infliction of emotional distress and awarded damages. We now consider whether this award is consistent with the First and Fourteenth Amendments of the United States Constitution.

The inside front cover of the November 1983 issue of Hustler Magazine featured a "parody" of an advertisement for Campari Liqueur that contained the name and picture of respondent and was entitled "Jerry Falwell talks about his first time." This parody was modeled after actual Campari ads that included interviews with various celebrities about their "first times." Although it was apparent by the end of each interview that this meant the first time they sampled Campari, the ads clearly played on the sexual double entendre of the general subject of "first times." Copying the form and layout of these Campari ads, Hustler's editors chose respondent as the featured celebrity and drafted an alleged "interview" with him in which he states that his "first time" was during a drunken incestuous rendezvous with his mother in an outhouse. The Hustler parody portrays respondent and his mother as drunk and immoral, and suggests that respondent is a hypocrite who preaches only when he is drunk. In small print at the bottom of the page, the ad contains the disclaimer, "ad parody—not to be taken seriously." The magazine's table of contents also lists the ad as "Fiction; Ad and Personality Parody."

Soon after the November issue of Hustler became available to the public, respondent brought this diversity action in the United States District Court for the Western District of Virginia against Hustler Magazine, Inc., Larry C. Flynt, and Flynt Distributing Co., Inc. Respondent stated in his complaint that publication of the ad parody in Hustler entitled him to recover damages for libel, invasion of privacy, and intentional infliction of emotional distress. The case proceeded to trial.[1] At the close of the evidence, the District Court granted a directed verdict for petitioners on the invasion of privacy claim. The jury then found against respondent on the libel claim, specifically finding that the ad parody could not "reasonably be understood as describing actual facts about [respondent] or actual events in which [he] participated." The jury ruled for respondent on the intentional infliction of emotional distress claim, however, and stated that he should be awarded $100,000 in compensatory damages, as well as $50,000 each in punitive damages from petitioners.[2] Petitioners' motion for judgment notwithstanding the verdict was denied.

On appeal, the United States Court of Appeals for the Fourth Circuit affirmed the judgment against petitioners. The court rejected petitioners' argument that the "actual malice" standard of *New York Times Co. v. Sullivan*, 376 U. S. 254 (1964), must be met before respondent can recover for emotional

---

*485 U. S. 46 (1988). Numerous citations omitted without so specifying.

[1]While the case was pending, the ad parody was published in Hustler Magazine a second time.

[2]The jury found no liability on the part of Flynt Distributing Co., Inc. It is consequently not a party to this appeal.

distress. The court agreed that because respondent is concededly a public figure, petitioners are "entitled to the same level of first amendment protection in the claim for intentional infliction of emotional distress that they received in [respondent's] claim for libel." But this does not mean that a literal application of the actual malice rule is appropriate in the context of an emotional distress claim. In the court's view, the *New York Times* decision emphasized the constitutional importance not of the falsity of the statement or the defendant's disregard for the truth, but of the heightened level of culpability embodied in the requirement of "knowing . . . or reckless" conduct. Here, the *New York Times* standard is satisfied by the state-law requirement, and the jury's finding, that the defendants have acted intentionally or recklessly.[3] The Court of Appeals then went on to reject the contention that because the jury found that the ad parody did not describe actual facts about respondent, the ad was an opinion that is protected by the First Amendment. As the court put it, this was "irrelevant," as the issue is "whether [the ad's] publication was sufficiently outrageous to constitute intentional infliction of emotional distress."[4] Petitioners then filed a petition for rehearing en banc, but this was denied by a divided court. Given the importance of the constitutional issues involved, we granted certiorari.

This case presents us with a novel question involving First Amendment limitations upon a State's authority to protect its citizens from the intentional infliction of emotional distress. We must decide whether a public figure may recover damages for emotional harm caused by the publication of an ad parody offensive to him, and doubtless gross and repugnant in the eyes of most. Respondent would have us find that a

State's interest in protecting public figures from emotional distress is sufficient to deny First Amendment protection to speech that is patently offensive and is intended to inflict emotional injury, even when that speech could not reasonably have been interpreted as stating actual facts about the public figure involved. This we decline to do.

At the heart of the First Amendment is the recognition of the fundamental importance of the free flow of ideas and opinions on matters of public interest and concern. "[T]he freedom to speak one's mind is not only an aspect of individual liberty—and thus a good unto itself—but also is essential to the common quest for truth and the vitality of society as a whole." We have therefore been particularly vigilant to ensure that individual expressions of ideas remain free from governmentally imposed sanctions. The First Amendment recognizes no such thing as a "false" idea. As Justice Holmes wrote, "when men have realized that time has upset many fighting faiths, they may come to believe even more than they believe the very foundations of their own conduct that the ultimate good desired is better reached by free trade in ideas—that the best test of truth is the power of the thought to get itself accepted in the competition of the market . . . ." *Abrams* v. *United States,* 250 U. S. 616, 630 (1919) (dissenting opinion).

The sort of robust political debate encouraged by the First Amendment is bound to produce speech that is critical of those who hold public office or those public figures who are "intimately involved in the resolution of important public questions or, by reason of their fame, shape events in areas of concern to society at large." Justice Frankfurter put it succinctly in *Baumgartner* v. *United States,* 322 U. S. 665, 673-674 (1944),

---

[3]Under Virginia law, in an action for intentional infliction of emotional distress a plaintiff must show that the defendant's conduct (1) is intentional or reckless; (2) offends generally accepted standards of decency or morality; (3) is causally connected with the plaintiff's emotional distress; and (4) caused emotional distress that was severe. 797 F. 2d, at 1275, n. 4 (citing *Womack* v. *Eldridge,* 215 Va. 388, 210 S. E. 2d 145 (1974).

[4]The court below also rejected several other contentions that petitioners do not raise in this appeal.

when he said that "[o]ne of the prerogatives of American citizenship is the right to criticize public men and measures." Such criticism, inevitably, will not always be reasoned or moderate; public figures as well as public officials will be subject to "vehement, caustic, and sometimes unpleasantly sharp attacks." "[T]he candidate who vaunts his spotless record and sterling integrity cannot convincingly cry 'Foul!' when an opponent or an industrious reporter attempts to demonstrate the contrary."

Of course, this does not mean that *any* speech about a public figure is immune from sanction in the form of damages. Since *New York Times Co.* v. *Sullivan, supra,* we have consistently ruled that a public figure may hold a speaker liable for the damage to reputation caused by publication of a defamatory falsehood, but only if the statement was made "with knowledge that it was false or with reckless disregard of whether it was false or not." False statements of fact are particularly valueless; they interfere with the truth-seeking function of the marketplace of ideas, and they cause damage to an individual's reputation that cannot easily be repaired by counterspeech, however persuasive or effective. But even though falsehoods have little value in and of themselves, they are "nevertheless inevitable in free debate," and a rule that would impose strict liability on a publisher for false factual assertions would have an undoubted "chilling" effect on speech relating to public figures that does have constitutional value. "Freedoms of expression require 'breathing space.'" This breathing space is provided by a constitutional rule that allows public figures to recover for libel or defamation only when they can prove both that the statement was false and that the statement was made with the requisite level of culpability.

Respondent argues, however, that a different standard should apply in this case because here the State seeks to prevent not reputational damage, but the severe emotional distress suffered by the person who is the subject of an offensive publication. In respondent's view, and in the view of the Court of Appeals, so long as the utterance was intended to inflict emotional distress, was outrageous, and did in fact inflict serious emotional distress, it is of no constitutional import whether the statement was a fact or an opinion, or whether it was true or false. It is the intent to cause injury that is the gravamen of the tort, and the State's interest in preventing emotional harm simply outweighs whatever interest a speaker may have in speech of this type.

Generally speaking the law does not regard the intent to inflict emotional distress as one which should receive much solicitude, and it is quite understandable that most if not all jurisdictions have chosen to make it civilly culpable where the conduct in question is sufficiently "outrageous." But in the world of debate about public affairs, many things done with motives that are less than admirable are protected by the First Amendment. In *Garrison* v. *Louisiana,* 379 U. S. 64 (1964), we held that even when a speaker or writer is motivated by hatred or ill-will his expression was protected by the First Amendment:

> "Debate on public issues will not be uninhibited if the speaker must run the risk that it will be proved in court that he spoke out of hatred; even if he did speak out of hatred, utterances honestly believed contribute to the free interchange of ideas and the ascertainment of truth."

Thus while such a bad motive may be deemed controlling for the purposes of tort liability in other areas of the law, we think the First Amendment prohibits such a result in the area of public debate about public figures.

Were we to hold otherwise, there can be little doubt that political cartoonists and satirists would be subjected to damages awards without any showing that their work falsely defamed its subject. Webster's defines a caricature as "the deliberately distorted picturing or imitating of a person, literary style, etc. by exaggerating features or mannerisms for satirical effect." Webster's New Unabridged Twentieth Century Dictionary of the English Language 275 (2d ed. 1979). The appeal of the political cartoon or caricature is often based on exploitation of unfortunate physical traits or politically embarrassing events—an exploitation often calculated to injure the feelings of the subject of the portrayal. The art of the cartoonist is often not reasoned or evenhanded, but slashing and one-sided. One cartoonist expressed the nature of the art in these words:

"The political cartoon is a weapon of attack, of scorn and ridicule and satire; it is least effective when it tries to pat some politician on the back. It is usually as welcome as a bee sting and is always controversial in some quarters." Long, The Political Cartoon: Journalism's Strongest Weapon, The Quill, 56, 57 (Nov. 1962).

Several famous examples of this type of intentionally injurious speech were drawn by Thomas Nast, probably the greatest American cartoonist to date, who was associated for many years during the post-Civil War era with Harper's Weekly. In the pages of that publication Nast conducted a graphic vendetta against William M. "Boss" Tweed and this corrupt associates in New York City's "Tweed Ring." It has been described by one historian of the subject as "a sustained attack which in its passion and effectiveness stands alone in the history of American graphic art." M. Keller, The Art and Politics of Thomas Nast 177 (1968). Another writer explains that the success of the Nast cartoon was achieved "because of the emotional impact of its presentation. It continuously goes beyond the bounds of good taste and conventional manners." C. Press, The Political Cartoon 251 (1981).

Despite their sometimes caustic nature, from the early cartoon portraying George Washington as an ass down to the present day, graphic depictions and satirical cartoons have played a prominent role in public and political debate. Nast's castigation of the Tweed Ring, Walt McDougall's characterization of Presidential candidate James G. Blaine's banquet with the millionaires at Delmonico's as "The Royal Feast of Belshazzar," and numerous other efforts have undoubtedly had an effect on the course and outcome of contemporaneous debate. Lincoln's tall, gangling posture, Teddy Roosevelt's glasses and teeth, and Franklin D. Roosevelt's jutting jaw and cigarette holder have been memorialized by political cartoons with an effect that could not have been obtained by the photographer or the portrait artist. From the viewpoint of history it is clear that our political discourse would have been considerably poorer without them.

Respondent contends, however, that the caricature in question here was so "outrageous" as to distinguish it from more traditional political cartoons. There is no doubt that the caricature of respondent and his mother published in Hustler is at best a distant cousin of the political cartoons described above, and a rather poor relation at that. If it were possible by laying down a principled standard to separate the one from the other, public discourse would probably suffer little or no harm. But we doubt that there is any such standard, and we are quite sure that the pejorative description "outrageous" does not supply one. "Outrageousness" in the area of political and social discourse has an inherent subjectiveness about it which would allow a jury to impose liability on the basis of the jurors' tastes or views, or perhaps on the basis of their dislike of a particular expression. An "outrageousness" standard thus runs afoul of our longstanding refusal to allow damages to be awarded because the speech in question may have an adverse emotional impact on the audience. See *NAACP v. Claiborne Hardware Co.*, 458 U. S. 886, 910 (1982) ("Speech does not lose its protected character . . . simply because it may embarrass others or coerce them into action").

And, as we stated in *FCC* v. *Pacifica Foundation*, 438 U. S. 726 (1978):

"[T]he fact that society may find speech offensive is not a sufficient reason for suppressing it. Indeed, if it is the speaker's opinion that gives offense, that consequence is a reason for according it constitutional protection. For it is a central tenet of the First Amendment that the government must remain neutral in the marketplace of ideas."

See also *Street* v. *New York* ("It is firmly settled that . . . the public expression of ideas may not be prohibited merely because the ideas are themselves offensive to some of their hearers").

Admittedly, these oft-repeated First Amendment principles, like other principles, are subject to limitation. We recognized in *Pacifica Foundation*, that speech that is "'vulgar,' 'offensive,' and 'shocking'" is "not entitled to absolute constitutional protection under all circumstances." In *Chaplinsky* v. *New Hampshire*, 315 U. S. 568 (1942), we held that a State could lawfully punish an individual for the use of insulting "'fighting' words—those which by their very utterance inflict injury or tend to incite an immediate breach of the peace." These limitations are but recognition of the observation in *Dun & Bradstreet, Inc.* v. *Greenmoss Builders, Inc.* that this Court has "long recognized that not all speech is of equal First Amendment importance." But the sort of expression involved in this case does not seem to us to be governed by any exception to the general First Amendment principles stated above.

We conclude that public figures and public officials may not recover for the tort of intentional infliction of emotional distress by reason of publications such as the one here at issue without showing in addition that the publication contains a false statement of fact which was made with "actual malice," *i.e.,* with knowledge that the statement was false or with reckless disregard as to whether or not it was true. This is not merely a "blind application" of the *New York Times* standard, it reflects our considered judgment that such a standard is necessary to give adequate "breathing space" to the freedoms protected by the First Amendment.

Here it is clear that respondent Falwell is a "public figure" for purposes of First Amendment law.[5] The jury found against respondent on his libel claim when it decided that the Hustler ad parody could not "reasonably be understood as describing actual facts about [respondent] or actual events in which [he] participated." The Court of Appeals interpreted the jury's finding to be that the ad parody "was not reasonably believable," and in accordance with our custom we accept this finding. Respondent is thus relegated to this claim for damages awarded by the jury for the intentional infliction of emotional distress by "outrageous" conduct. But for reasons heretofore stated this claim cannot, consistently with the First Amendment, form a basis for the award of damages when the conduct in question is the publication of a caricature such as the ad parody involved here. The judgment of the Court of Appeals is accordingly

*Reversed.*

---

[5]Neither party disputes this conclusion. Respondent is the host of a nationally syndicated television show and was the founder and president of a political organization formerly known as the Moral Majority. He is also the founder of Liberty University in Lynchburg, Virginia, and is the author of several books and publications. Who's Who in America 849 (44th ed. 1986–1987).

# QUESTIONS

1. Crucial to the outcome in *Hustler Magazine* was the fact that Jerry Falwell, as a "public figure," was not entitled to the same degree of protection from emotional distress as people who are not public figures. What rationale is there for making this distinction between public figures and others? Would there also be a rationale for protecting speech—even scurrilous parodies—directed at whole groups of people, for example, ethnic, religious, or minority groups? Explain why or why not.

2. The Court's opinion held that "'Outrageous' in the area of political and social discourse has an inherent subjectiveness about it. . . ." Could one also claim that the concept of a "public figure" has an inherent subjectiveness about it? Are professors public figures? Are student columnists in student newspapers public figures? Officers of campus student groups? (Notice what is mentioned in footnote 5 of the Court's opinion to support the contention that Falwell is a public figure.)

3. The Court's opinion quotes Justice Holmes, who said "[T]he best test of truth is the power of the thought itself to get itself accepted." In your opinion, how relevant are Holmes's words, given that the parody of Falwell explicitly disavowed being a statement of fact?

4. The Court makes clear that, where criticism of public figures is involved, there is an especially strong social interest in allowing full and free criticism, even where scurrilous parodies are involved. Some claim that there is also an especially strong social interest in allowing the robust debate on college and university campuses. Is there a reason for giving an especially wide latitude to freedom of expression on campuses, even permitting personal attacks and parodies, or should the same standards apply on campuses as apply anywhere else? Or is there some reason for enforcing stricter codes of politeness and civility on campuses than are appropriate elsewhere in society?

## *United States Supreme Court**
## UNITED STATES v. EICHMAN

JUSTICE BRENNAN delivered the opinion of the court.

In these consolidated appeals, we consider whether appellees' prosecution for burning a United States flag in violation of the Flag Protection Act of 1989 is consistent with the First Amendment. Applying our recent decision in *Texas* v. *Johnson*[a], the District Courts held that the Act cannot constitutionally be applied to appellees. We affirm. . . .

II

Last term in *Johnson*, we held that a Texas statute criminalizing the desecration of venerated objects, including the United States flag, was unconstitutional as applied to an individual who had set such a flag on fire during a political demonstration. The Texas statute provided that "[a] person commits an offense if he intentionally or knowingly desecrates

*110 S. Ct. 2404 (1990). Numerous citations omitted without so specifying.
[a]109 S. Ct. 2533 (1989).

. . . [a] national flag," where "desecrate" meant to "deface, damage, or otherwise physically mistreat in a way that the actor knows will seriously offend one or more persons likely to observe or discover his action." Tex. Penal Code Ann. § 42.09 (1989). We first held that Johnson's flag-burning was "conduct 'sufficiently imbued with elements of communication' to implicate the First Amendment." We next considered and rejected the State's contention that, under *United States* v. *O'Brien*, 391 U. S. 367 (1968), we ought to apply the deferential standard with which we have reviewed Government regulations of conduct containing both speech and non-speech elements where "the governmental interest is unrelated to the suppression of free expression." *Id.*, at 377. We reasoned that the State's asserted interest in "preserving the flag as a symbol of nationhood and national unity," was an interest "related 'to the suppression of free expression' within the meaning of *O'Brien*" because the State's concern with protecting the flag's symbolic meaning is implicated "only when a person's treatment of the flag communicates some message." We therefore subjected the statute to "'the most exacting scrutiny,'" quoting *Boos* v. *Barry*, 485 U. S. 312, 321 (1988), and we concluded that the States's asserted interests could not justify the infringement on the demonstrator's First Amendment rights.

After our decision in *Johnson*, Congress passed the Flag Protection Act of 1989.[3] The Act provides in relevant part:

"(a)(1) Whoever knowingly mutilates, defaces, physically defiles, burns, maintains on the floor or ground, or tramples upon any flag of the United States shall be fined under this title or imprisoned for not more than one year, or both.

"(2) This subsection does not prohibit any conduct consisting of the disposal of a flag when it has become worn or soiled.

"(b) As used in this section, the term 'flag of the United States' means any flag of the United States, or any part thereof, made of any substance, of any size, in a form that is commonly displayed." 18 U. S. C. A. § 700 (Supp. 1990).

The Government concedes in this case, as it must, that appellees' flag-burning constituted expressive conduct, Brief for United States 28; but invites us to reconsider our rejection in *Johnson* of the claim that flag-burning as a mode of expression, like obscenity or "fighting words," does not enjoy the full protection of the First Amendment. Cf. *Chaplinsky* v. *New Hampshire*, 315 U. S. 568, 572 (1942). This we decline to do.[4] The only remaining question is whether the Flag Protection Act is sufficiently distinct from the Texas statute that it may constitutionally be applied to proscribe appellees' expressive conduct.

The Government contends that the Flag Protection Act is constitutional because, unlike the statute addressed in *Johnson*, the Act does not target expressive conduct on the basis of the content of its message. The Government asserts an interest in "protect[ing] the physical integrity of the flag under all circumstances" in order to safeguard the flag's identity "'as the unique and unalloyed symbol of the Nation.'" Brief for United States 28, 29. The Act proscribes conduct (other than disposal) that damages or mistreats a flag, without regard to the actor's motive, his intended message, or the likely effects of his conduct on onlookers. By contrast, the Texas statute expressly prohibited only those acts of physical flag desecration "that the actor knows will seriously offend" onlookers, and

---

[3]The Act replaced the then-existing federal flag-burning statute, which Congress perceived might be unconstitutional in light of *Johnson*. Former 18 U. S. C. § 700(a) prohibited "knowingly cast[ing] contempt upon any flag of the United States by publicly mutilating, defacing, defiling, burning, or trampling upon it."

[4]We deal here with concededly political speech and have no occasion to pass on the validity of laws regulating commercial exploitation of the image of the United States flag. See *Texas* v. *Johnson*, 491 U. S. ——, ——, n. 10 (1989); cf. *Halter* v. *Nebraska*, 205 U. S. 34 (1907).

the former federal statute prohibited only those acts of desecration that "cas[t] contempt upon" the flag.

Although the Flag Protection Act contains no explicit content-based limitation on the scope of prohibited conduct, it is nevertheless clear that the Government's asserted *interest* is "related 'to the suppression of free expression,'" and concerned with the content of such expression. The Government's interest in protecting the "physical integrity" of a privately owned flag[5] rests upon a perceived need to preserve the flag's status as a symbol of our Nation and certain national ideals. But the mere destruction or disfigurement of a particular physical manifestation of the symbol, without more, does not diminish or otherwise affect the symbol itself in any way. For example, the secret destruction of a flag in one's own basement would not threaten the flag's recognized meaning. Rather, the Government's desire to preserve the flag as a symbol for certain national ideals is implicated "only when a person's treatment of the flag communicates [a] message" to others that is inconsistent with those ideals.[6] *Id.*, at —.

Moreover, the precise language of the Act's prohibitions confirms Congress' interest in the communicative impact of flag destruction. The Act criminalizes the conduct of anyone who "knowingly mutilates, defaces, physically defiles, burns, maintains on the floor or ground, or tramples upon any flag." 18 U. S. C. A. § 700(a)(1) (Supp. 1990). Each of the specified terms—with the possible exception of "burns"—unmistakably connotes disrespectful treatment of the flag and suggests a focus on those acts likely to damage the flag's symbolic value.[7] And the explicit exemption in § 700 (a)(2) for disposal of "worn or soiled" flags protects certain acts traditionally associated with patriotic respect for the flag.[8]

As we explained in *Johnson, supra*, "[I]f we were to hold that a State may forbid flag-burning wherever it is likely to endanger the flag's symbolic role, but allow it wherever burning a flag promotes that role—as where, for example, a person ceremoniously burns a

[5]Today's decision does not affect the extent to which the Government's interest in protecting publicly owned flags might justify special measures on their behalf. See *Spence* v. *Washington*, 418 U. S. 405, 408–409 (1974); cf. *Johnson, supra*, at ——, n. 8.

[6]Aside from the flag's association with particular ideals, at some irreducible level the flag is emblematic of the Nation as a sovereign entity. Appellant's *amicus* asserts that the Government has a legitimate non-speech-related interest in safeguarding this "eminently practical legal aspect of the flag, as an incident of sovereignty." Brief for the Speaker and the Leadership Group of the United States House of Representatives [as] *Amicus Curiae* 25. This interest has firm historical roots: "While the symbolic role of the flag is now well-established, the flag was an important incident of sovereignty before it was used for symbolic purposes by patriots and others. When the nation's founders first determined to adopt a national flag, they intended to serve specific functions relating to our status as a sovereign nation." *Id.*, at 9; see *id.*, at 5 (noting "flag's `historic function' for such sovereign purposes as marking `our national presence in schools, public buildings, battleships and airplanes'") (citation omitted).

We concede that the Government has a legitimate interest in preserving the flag's function as an "incident of sovereignty," though we need not address today the extent to which this interest may justify any laws regulating conduct that would thwart this core function, as might a commercial or like appropriation of the image of the United States flag. *Amicus* does not, and cannot, explain how a statute that penalizes anyone who knowingly burns, mutilates, or defiles any American flag is designed to advance this asserted interest in maintaining the association between the flag and the Nation. Burning a flag does not threaten to interfere with this association in any way; indeed, the flag-burner's message depends in part on the viewer's ability to make this very association.

[7]For example, "defile" is defined as "to make filthy; to corrupt the purity or perfection of; to rob of chastity; to make ceremonially unclean; tarnish; dishonor." Webster's Third New International Dictionary 592 (1976). "Trample" is defined as "to tread heavily so as to bruise, crush, or injure; to inflict injury or destruction: have a contemptuous or ruthless attitude." *Id.*, at 2425.

[8]The Act also does not prohibit flying a flag in a storm or other conduct that threatens the physical integrity of the flag, albeit in an indirect manner unlikely to communicate disrespect.

dirty flag—we would be . . . permitting a State to 'prescribe what shall be orthodox' by saying that one may burn the flag to convey one's attitude toward it and its referents only if one does not endanger the flag's representation of nationhood and national unity." Although Congress cast the Flag Protection Act in somewhat broader terms than the Texas statute at issue in *Johnson*, the Act still suffers from the same fundamental flaw: it suppresses expression out of concern for its likely communicative impact. Despite the Act's wider scope, its restriction on expression cannot be "'justified without reference to the content of the regulated speech.'" . . . We decline the Government's invitation to reassess this conclusion in light of Congress' recent recognition of a purported "national consensus" favoring a prohibition on flag-burning. Brief for United States 27. Even assuming such a consensus exists, any suggestion that the Government's interest in suppressing speech becomes more weighty as popular opposition to that speech grows is foreign to the First Amendment.

## III

"'National unity as an end which officials may foster by persuasion and example is not in question.'" Government may create national symbols, promote them, and encourage their respectful treatment.[9] But the Flag Protection Act goes well beyond this by criminally proscribing expressive conduct because of its likely communicative impact.

We are aware that desecration of the flag is deeply offensive to many. But the same might be said, for example, of virulent ethnic and religious epithets, see *Terminiello* v. *Chicago*, 337 U. S. 1 (1949), vulgar repudiations of the draft, see *Cohen* v. *California*, 403 U. S. 15 (1971), and scurrilous caricatures, see *Hustler Magazine, Inc.* v. *Falwell*, 485 U. S. 46 (1988). "If there is a bedrock principle underlying the First Amendment, it is that the Government may not prohibit the expression of an idea simply because society finds the idea itself offensive or disagreeable." *Johnson, supra*, at ——. Punishing desecration of the flag dilutes the very freedom that makes this emblem so revered, and worth revering. The judgments are

*Affirmed.*

Justice Stevens with whom The Chief Justice, Justice White and Justice O'Connor join, dissenting.

The Court's opinion ends where proper analysis of the issue should begin. Of course "the Government may not prohibit the expression of an idea simply because society finds the idea itself offensive or disagreeable." None of us disagrees with that proposition. But it is equally well settled that certain methods of expression may be prohibited if (a) the prohibition is supported by a legitimate societal interest that is unrelated to suppression of the ideas the speaker desires to express; (b) the prohibition does not entail any interference with the speaker's freedom to express those ideas by other means; and (c) the interest in allowing the speaker complete freedom of choice among alternative methods of expression is less important than the societal interest supporting the prohibition.

Contrary to the position taken by counsel for the flag burners in *Texas* v. *Johnson*, it is now conceded that the Federal Government has a legitimate interest in protecting the symbolic value of the American flag. Obviously that value cannot be measured, or even described, with any precision. It has at least these two components: in times of national crisis, it inspires and motivates the average citizen to make personal sacrifices in order to achieve societal goals of overriding importance; at all times, it serves as a reminder of the paramount importance of pursuing the ideals that characterize our society.

---

[9]See, *e.g*, 36 U. S. C. §§ 173–177 (suggesting manner in which flag ought to be displayed).

The first question the Court should consider is whether the interest in preserving the value of that symbol is unrelated to suppression of the ideas that flag burners are trying to express. In my judgment the answer depends, at least in part, on what those ideas are. A flag burner might intend various messages. The flag burner may wish simply to convey hatred, contempt, or sheer opposition directed at the United States. This might be the case if the flag were burned by an enemy during time of war. A flag burner may also, or instead, seek to convey the depth of his personal conviction about some issue, by willingly provoking the use of force against himself. In so doing, he says that "my disagreement with certain policies is so strong that I am prepared to risk physical harm (and perhaps imprisonment) in order to call attention to my views." This second possibility apparently describes the expressive conduct of the flag burners in these cases. Like the protesters who dramatized their opposition to our engagement in Vietnam by publicly burning their draft cards—and who were punished for doing so—their expressive conduct is consistent with affection for this country and respect for the ideals that the flag symbolizes. There is at least one further possibility: a flag burner may intend to make an accusation against the integrity of the American people who disagree with him. By burning the embodiment of America's collective commitment to freedom and equality, the flag burner charges that the majority has forsaken that commitment—that continued respect for the flag is nothing more than hypocrisy. Such a charge may be made even if the flag burner loves the country and zealously pursues the ideals that the country claims to honor.

The idea expressed by a particular act of flag burning is necessarily dependent on the temporal and political context in which it occurs. In the 1960's it may have expressed opposition to the country's Vietnam policies, or at least to the compulsory draft. In *Texas* v. *Johnson*, it apparently expressed opposition to the platform of the Republican Party. In these cases, the respondents have explained that it expressed their opposition to racial discrimination, to the failure to care for the homeless, and of course to statutory prohibitions of flag burning. In any of these examples, the protestors may wish both to say that their own position is the only one faithful to liberty and equality, and to accuse their fellow citizens of hypocritical indifference to—or even of a selfish departure from—the ideals which the flag is supposed to symbolize. The ideas expressed by flag burners are thus various and often ambiguous.

The Government's legitimate interest in preserving the symbolic value of the flag is, however, essentially the same regardless of which of many different ideas may have motivated a particular act of flag burning. As I explained in my dissent in *Johnson*, the flag uniquely symbolizes the ideas of liberty, equality, and tolerance—ideas that Americans have passionately defended and debated throughout our history. The flag embodies the spirit of our national commitment to those ideals. The message thereby transmitted does not take a stand upon our disagreements, except to say that those disagreements are best regarded as competing interpretations of shared ideals. It does not judge particular policies, except to say that they command respect when they are enlightened by the spirit of liberty and equality. To the world, the flag is our promise that we will continue to strive for these ideals. To us, the flag is a reminder both that the struggle for liberty and equality is unceasing, and that our obligation of tolerance and respect for all of our fellow citizens encompasses those who disagree with us—indeed, even those whose ideas are disagreeable or offensive.

Thus, the Government may—indeed, it should—protect the symbolic value of the flag without regard to the specific content of the flag burners' speech. The prosecution in this case does not depend upon the object of the defendants' protest. It is, moreover, equally clear that the prohibition does not entail any interference with the speaker's freedom to express his or her ideas by other means. It may well be true that other means of expression may be less effective in drawing attention to those ideas, but that is not itself a sufficient reason for immunizing flag burning. Presumably a gigantic fireworks display or a parade of nude models in a public park might draw even more attention to a controversial message, but such methods of expression are nevertheless subject to regulation.

This case therefore comes down to a question of judgment. Does the admittedly important interest in allowing every speaker to choose the method of expressing his or her ideas that he or she deems most effective and appropriate outweigh the societal interest in preserving the symbolic value of the flag? This question, in turn, involves three different judgments: (1) The importance of the individual interest in selecting the preferred means of communication; (2) the importance of the national symbol; and (3) the question whether tolerance of flag burning will enhance or tarnish that value. The opinions in *Texas* v. *Johnson* demonstrate that reasonable judges may differ with respect to each of these judgments.

The individual interest is unquestionably a matter of great importance. Indeed, it is one of the critical components of the idea of liberty that the flag itself is intended to symbolize. Moreover, it is buttressed by the societal interest in being alerted to the need for thoughtful response to voices that might otherwise go unheard. The freedom of expression protected by the First Amendment embraces not only the freedom to communicate particular ideas, but also the right to communicate them effectively. That right, however, is not absolute—the communicative value of a well-placed bomb in the Capitol does not entitle it to the protection of the First Amendment.

Burning a flag is not, of course, equivalent to burning a public building. Assuming that the protester is burning his own flag, it causes no physical harm to other persons or to their property. The impact is purely symbolic, and it is apparent that some thoughtful persons believe that impact, far from depreciating the value of the symbol, will actually enhance its meaning. I most respectfully disagree. Indeed, what makes this case particularly difficult for me is what I regard as the damage to the symbol that has already occurred as a result of this Court's decision to place its stamp of approval on the act of flag burning. A formerly dramatic expression of protest is now rather commonplace. In today's marketplace of ideas, the public burning of a Vietnam draft card is probably less provocative than lighting a cigarette. Tomorrow flag burning may produce a similar reaction. There is surely a direct relationship between the communicative value of the act of flag burning and the symbolic value of the object being burned.

The symbolic value of the American flag is not the same today as it was yesterday. Events during the last three decades have altered the country's image in the eyes of numerous Americans, and some now have difficulty understanding the message that the flag conveyed to their parents and grandparents—whether born abroad and naturalized or native born. Moreover, the integrity of the symbol has been compromised by those leaders who seem to advocate compulsory worship of the flag even by individuals whom it offends, or who seem to manipulate the symbol of national purpose into a pretext for partisan disputes about meaner ends. And, as I have suggested, the residual value of the symbol after this Court's decision in *Texas* v. *Johnson* is surely not the same as it was a year ago.

Given all these considerations, plus the fact that the Court today is really doing nothing more than reconfirming what it has already decided, it might be appropriate to defer to the judgment of the majority and merely apply the doctrine of *stare decisis* to the case at hand. That action, however, would not honestly reflect my considered judgment concerning the relative importance of the conflicting interests that are at stake. I remain persuaded that the consider-ations identified in my opinion in *Texas* v. *Johnson* are of controlling importance in this case as well.

Accordingly, I respectfully dissent.

## QUESTIONS

1. Is it possible to (quoting Justice Stevens) "protect the symbolic value of the flag without regard to the specific content of the flag burners' speech"?

2. Among the factors Justice Stevens cites in determining whether expression may be prohibited is whether the prohibition entails "interference with the speaker's freedom to express those ideas by other means." Could Shawn Eichman have expressed his ideas about the government's domestic and foreign policy without burning the flag?

3. See the quotation from the *Chaplinsky* case in the Greenawalt article (the next reading). Could burning the flag of the United States on the U.S. Capitol steps be regarded as "fighting" words? Explain why or why not, and what difference this conclusion would make.

4. The Court makes a distinction between limitations on expression that are "content-based" and those that are not. Explain the concept of a content-based limitation, giving some examples of limitations on expression that you believe would *not* be content-based.

5. Justice Stevens, in his dissenting opinion, says that "The flag embodies the spirit of our national commitment to those ideals [of liberty, equality, and tolerance]. The message transmitted does not take a stand upon our disagreements, except to say that those disagreements are best regarded as competing interpretations of shared ideals." Is this message favoring liberty, equality, and tolerance neutral with respect to *all* disagreements? Ought we to tolerate only those disagreements that are about "competing interpretations of shared ideals"?

6. Read the excerpt from J.S. Mill's *On Liberty* that is reprinted earlier in Part 2. Mill argues that freedom of opinion is a fundamental means of promoting knowledge and truth. Would this rationale of the right of free expression tend to support the freedom to burn the flag or not? Do you agree with the Court in *Chaplinsky v. New Hampshire* (315 U.S. 568), that "such utterances [as Chaplinsky's] are no essential part of any exposition of ideas, and are of such slight social value as a step to truth that any benefit that may be derived from them is clearly outweighed by the social interest in order and morality"? Is there perhaps an additional rationale for freedom of expression that goes beyond Mill's concern for advancing truth and knowledge?

## Kent Greenawalt
# INSULTS AND EPITHETS: ARE THEY PROTECTED SPEECH?*

## I. INTRODUCTION

. . . Extremely harsh personal insults and epithets directed against one's race, religion, ethnic origin, gender, or sexual preference pose a problem for democratic theory and practice. Should such comments be forbidden because they lead to violence, because they hurt, or because they contribute to domination and hostility? Or should they be part of a person's freedom to speak his or her mind? Any country with a liberal democracy faces this dilemma. In the United States, one forum for resolution is the judiciary, which applies the first amendment and analogous state constitutional provisions.

I shall look at insults and epithets in light of the different uses of language. This perspective hardly provides the last word about what insults and epithets should be allowed, but it helps illuminate what is at stake. I begin with some brief general comments about reasons for free speech and about uses of language.[4] I then address the force of insults and epithets in various contexts. I consider four claims about the damage they may do, as measured against their value as expression. I then tie the analysis to existing and possible first amendment doctrine.[5]

## II. REASONS FOR FREE SPEECH AND USES OF LANGUAGE

The reasons for free speech are central for proper principles of free speech. This is plainly true about legislative choice. Which communications a legislature should leave free will depend on why many communications should be free. Given language that is as open-ended as that of our free speech and free press clauses, the reasons for free speech also bear closely on the scope of constitutional principles that guide courts.

We can divide the reasons to give speech more protection than most other kinds of actions into consequential and nonconsequential reasons. Consequential reasons concern the good effects of a practice. Despite some modern challenges to this traditional idea, liberty of speech contributes to discovery of truth. Worries about inequality among communicators and about people's tendency to believe what is conventional and what serves irrational desires are well founded. But the government's suppression of what it deems to be false is hardly more conducive to growth in understanding than wide liberty of expression. Such liberty also promotes accommodation of interests. Despite causing occasional divisiveness, it can enhance social stability by reducing resentment. Freedom of thought and expression promote individual autonomy and the development of personality. Talk about one's ideas and feelings is a vital emotional outlet. Conventions of free speech may help teach a healthy tolerance of differences. In a liberal democracy, citizens can perform a responsible political role only if they have available a wide range of information and opinions. Free criticism of government officials and policy is a strong check on the abuse of political authority.

---

*From *Rutgers Law Review*, vol. 42, no. 2 (Winter 1990), pp. 288–307. Reprinted by permission of *Rutgers Law Review*.

[4]These comments outline major themes of a book entitled K. GREENAWALT, SPEECH CRIME, AND THE USES OF LANGUAGE (1989). A discussion of reasons for free speech appears in Greenawalt, *Free Speech Justifications*, 89 COLUM L. REV. 119 (1989).

[5]My discussion of insults and epithets draws heavily on the chapters in *Speech, Crime, and the Uses of Language*, *supra* note 4. On many subjects, they contain a more detailed analysis and fuller citations.

Nonconsequential reasons for liberties do not depend on what happens after a person is restricted. The simple denial of liberty is itself a wrong, and typically takes the form of an injustice or denial of right. It is argued that, under our dominant social contract theory, most speech is within a private domain, not subject to control by a government of limited powers. It is also claimed that restricting speech neither treats citizens as autonomous and rational nor accords them the dignity and equal status they warrant under a democratic government. I shall not today try to develop these claims and their reach. My judgment is that these arguments do not set clear standards for which communications should be left free. Together with the consequential reasons, they do help indicate what interferences with expression are most troublesome, and they operate as counters in favor of freedom.

What communications do the reasons for free speech cover? In a liberal democracy, the need is great for freedom of discourse about public affairs, but the reasons for liberty of speech are much broader, reaching all subjects of human concern. They clearly cover general statements of fact, such as "rapid inflation causes social instability," and particular statements of fact, such as "the Soviet Union exploded a nuclear device yesterday." They also cover general and particular assertions of value: "love is the greatest good" and "you should not lie to your friend about your grades." The reasons have much less force for assertions that the speaker knows or believes to be false.

The reasons for free speech hardly apply at all to some sorts of communications. Consider two people agreeing to commit a crime. Their words of agreement represent commitments to action, not assertions of fact or value. Their words change the normative environment they inhabit, creating new obligations and claims. The communications are situation-altering; they are much more "action" than "expression." It should come as no surprise that the punishment of ordinary conspiracies has rarely been thought to raise problems of free speech. Orders, offers of agreement, and invitations, such as "just try to hit me," are similar to agreements in their situation-altering character. I claim that these communicative activities may be regulated essentially without reference to principles of free speech. I make the same claim about what I call manipulative threats and offers. Suppose Gertrude tells Claude that she will give him two thousand dollars if he hires her or that she will disclose his criminal past if he does not hire her. Her comment to Claude sets in play consequences that would not otherwise occur; it is situation-altering.[6]

Hovering between situation-altering utterances and ordinary assertions of fact and value are what I call weak imperatives. These "weak imperatives" are requests and encouragements that do not sharply alter the listener's normative environment. If Gertrude says, "please hire Joseph" or "kill him, Claude," her immediate aim is to produce action, but she has not created new rights or new obligations or new consequences of Claude's behavior. Weak imperatives often indicate beliefs about values and facts and cannot always be disentangled from them. They are covered to a degree by a principle of free speech, but they may often be prohibited when assertions of fact and value must be free.

Forgive this speedy, superficial sketch of some general views about the uses of language and the reasons for free speech. It sets the discussion of insults and epithets in a broader context.

---

[6]On the other hand, if Gertrude merely warns Claude about what she would do in any event, "I am going to divorce you if you don't spend more time at home," her words reveal her natural response to circumstances and are like ordinary predictions about what will happen in the future. Such warning threats are covered by a principle of free speech.

## III. STRONG INSULTS AND GROUP EPITHETS

One feature of strong insults and epithets is that they tend to shock those at whom they are directed *and* others who hear. They are not expressions that are used in civil conversation or academic discourse. A setting like this lecture presents a problem: how much to risk offending by speaking the upsetting words and phrases; how much to risk failure to come to terms with the real issues by avoiding the words that shock. I shall indicate briefly the sorts of remarks we are considering, and then use them sparingly. Many strong insults use coarse language in a highly derogatory way: "You are a stupid bastard," "cheating prick," "conniving bitch," "fucking whore." Others may be strong without any single shocking word: "You are as yellow as the sun;" "your mother must have discovered your father in a pigpen." Broadly, epithets are words and phrases that attribute good, bad, or neutral qualities; but usually epithets are thought of as negative. Some epithets denigrate on the basis of race, religion, ethnic origin, gender, or sexual preference. Among these are "wop," "kike," "spick," "Polack," "nigger," "pansy," "cunt," "honkey," "slant-eyes," and perhaps "WASP."

This summary account allows me to make some obvious points. Group epithets frequently strengthen other insulting words. Group epithets and other words of insult often are spoken against someone in a face-to-face encounter, but they are also used before friendly audiences to put down outsiders. The strength of insults and group epithets varies; much depends on tone of voice, context, and prior relationships. Saying just when words and phrases pass beyond the bounds of civil discourse at any moment in history is daunting. If the law is to restrict insults and group epithets, the task of categorizing which insults and group epithets should be restricted is formidable.

## IV. INSULTS AND GROUP EPITHETS AS USES OF LANGUAGE

I turn now to how insults and epithets function as uses of language. The *meaning* of most insults and epithets amounts to mixed assertions of facts and values. Words like "stupid" and "cheating" have fairly definite content. The significance of group epithets is much vaguer, but they call to mind whatever "negative" qualities are associated with a group, qualities such as laziness, greed, dishonesty, stupidity, vulgarity. They also indicate a harsh unfavorable judgment about members of the group. If insults and group epithets involve assertions of fact and value, then does it follow that they are covered by a principle of freedom of speech? Even if they are covered, their restriction *might* still be warranted because these comments are too dangerous or too misleading; but should we recognize candidly that restriction is an exception to the privilege speakers usually have to choose their own terms to express their views? When insults and group epithets are spoken about people who are not present, they are indeed an extremely crude way to attribute characteristics and render judgments.[7]

In contrast, when insults and epithets are employed face-to-face, the analysis of their use becomes more complicated. Indeed, in such encounters, abusive remarks often approach closer to action and may even amount to situation-altering utterances. At the extreme, social convention might establish that certain insults invite or even "demand" set responses: calling a man "chicken" to his face might be understood as a challenge to fight. In that event, uttering the insult would be a situation-altering utterance. The phrase, "you are chicken," seems to have some fact and value content, but if this just happens to be how one invites a fight, the insult could be little more than a challenge. In any event, the situation-altering aspect matters more than any message about the qualities of the person

---

[7] This is true at least if the speaker's aim does not include having the comments relayed to those insulted.

challenged. Probably no insults function generally with this kind of precision in modern western societies, but conventions among various subgroups may approximate this kind of clarity. In settings where a person utters abusive words that are understood by him and his listener to invite a fight, the communication is dominantly situation-altering.

The circumstance is subtly different when a speaker, without overtly inviting a fight, hopes to provoke such anger in the listener that a fight will ensue.[8] If the speaker tries to manipulate the listener into fighting, his own expressive interests remain slim; but for the listener the import of the insult differs now. He is angered by the very bad things that have been said. *His* reaction is partly to the intense message of facts and values.[9]

Often a speaker consciously sets out to wound and humiliate a listener. He aims to make the other feel degraded and hated, and chooses words to achieve that effect.[10] In what they accomplish, insults of this sort are a form of psychic assault; they do not differ much from physical assaults, like slaps or pinches, that cause no real physical hurt. Usually, the speaker believes the listener possesses the characteristics that are indicated by his humiliating and wounding remarks,[11] but the speaker selects the most abusive form of expression to impose the maximum hurt.

His aim diminishes the expressive importance of the words. He does not use words to inform, nor is he really attempting to indicate his feelings. His aim is to wound, and the congruence of what he says with his actual feelings is almost coincidental.[12]

Many speakers who want to humiliate and wound would also welcome a fight. But in many of the cruelest instances in which abusive words are used, no fight is contemplated: white adults shout epithets at black children walking to an integrated school; strong men insult much smaller women.[13]

For many persons, serious use of group epithets is regarded as reprehensible and is quite rare; and serious use of strongly insulting words face-to-face occurs only during moments of high emotion. Out of frustration and anger a person hurls words of intense feeling that are also meant to wound; he does not expect responsive physical force but is not careful to avoid it. Abusive words in these situations are a true barometer of feelings, and, as such, have substantial importance as expression.

I have suggested that the circumstances in which people insult each other vary a good deal. For some, the reasons for free speech are more relevant than for others.

The remainder of my discussion is organized around the harms that insults and

---

[8]For purposes of clarity, I am describing a sharp distinction that is clearly drawn and perceptively analyzed in J. FEINBERG, OFFENSE TO OTHERS 226–32 (1985). Often the two aspects, conventional challenge and anger provocation, will be mixed in such a way that even a thoughtful speaker aware of his own state of mind might have a hard time saying which he is doing.

[9]It has been suggested that "fighting words" trigger an automatic reaction. See J. NOWAK, R. ROTUNDA & J. YOUNG, CONSTITUTIONAL LAW § 16.37, at 942 43 (3d ed. 1986); Rutzick, *Offensive Language and the Evolution of First Amendment Protection*, 9 HARV. C.R.-C.L. L. REV. 1, 8 (1974). No doubt these words can trigger intense responses that reduce control, but many listeners must still be able to use some judgment about their chances in a physical conflict, and are not likely to attack an abuser who is also pointing a gun at them.

[10]*See generally* Delgado, *Words That Wound: A Tort Action for Racial Insults, Epithets, and Name-Calling*, 17 HARV. C.R.-C.L. L. REV. 133 (1982); Downs, *Skokie Revisited: Hate Group Speech and the First Amendment*, 60 NOTRE DAME L. REV. 629 (1985). *See also* J. FEINBERG, *supra* note 8, at 30, 89–91.

[11]A speaker might not carry the attitudes the words imply. For example, a woman with no prejudice against Italian-Americans who wished to hurt a particular Italian-American man who annoyed her might say "You wop," hoping that expression would be wounding to him.

[12]On this point, Donald Downs writes, *supra* note 10, at 651, "[W]hen the *primary* purpose of speech is not communication, but rather the infliction of harm, the law can no longer construe any resulting harm as a secondary result."

[13]*See generally* A. MONTAGU, THE ANATOMY OF SWEARING (1967).

group epithets can do. I review four main bases for suppressing abusive language: (1) the danger of immediate violence; (2) psychological hurt that one is the object of abuse; (3) general offense that such language is used; and (4) destructive long term effects from the attitudes reinforced by abusive remarks. I comment about existing law and sensible legislative and constitutional approaches.

## V. THE DANGER OF VIOLENT RESPONSE

Insults and group epithets can cause listeners to react with violence. I concentrate on the situation in which violence is used against the speaker, and the person provoked to violence, or a friend, is the immediate object of abuse.[14] Words highly likely to provoke violence are ordinarily made criminal by breach of the peace or disorderly conduct provisions. Under the *Model Penal Code's* section on disorderly conduct, adopted in substance by some jurisdictions, one must purposely or recklessly create a risk of "public inconvenience, annoyance or alarm" by making "offensively coarse utterance, gesture or display" or by addressing "abusive language to any person present."[15] The Code also forbids harassment; one commits a violation if, with a purpose to harass, he "insults, taunts or challenges another in a manner likely to provoke violent or disorderly response."[16]

Much is unclear about how the first amendment applies to abusive remarks, but courts have steadily assumed that restriction is permissible if the danger of responsive violence is great. The leading case was decided almost half a century ago.[17] Chaplinsky, a Jehovah's Witness, was annoying some people with his proselytizing. A city marshall warned him to "go slow."[18] Chaplinsky replied that the marshall was a "God damned racketeer" and "a damned Fascist," and that the whole government of Rochester was comprised of Fascists.[19] He was convicted under a statute that forbade addressing "any offensive, derisive or annoying word to any other person . . . [or] call[ing] him by any offensive or derisive name. . . ."[20] Despite the political nature of Chaplinsky's remarks and their being addressed to an official, who presumably was trained to restrain himself, the Supreme Court upheld the conviction. It said:

> There are certain well-defined and narrowly limited classes of speech, the prevention and punishment of which have never been thought to raise any Constitutional problem. These include the lewd and obscene, the profane, the libelous, and the insulting or "fighting" words—those which by their very utterance inflict injury or tend to incite an immediate breach of the peace. . . . [S]uch utterances are no essential part of any exposition of ideas, and are of such slight social value as a step to truth that any benefit that may be derived from them is clearly outweighed by the social interest in order and morality.[21]

Reasoning that the state court had construed the statute only to cover words that "men of common intelligence would understand [to be] likely to cause an average addressee to fight," the Supreme Court decided

---

[14]Thus, I am putting aside circumstances in which abusive remarks lead others to act violently against the victim of abuse.

[15]MODEL PENAL CODE § 250.2(1)(b) (1962).

[16]*Id*. § 250.4(2).

[17]Chaplinsky v. New Hampshire, 315 U.S. 568 (1942).

[18]State v. Chaplinsky, 91 N.H. 310, 313 (1941).

[19]*Chaplinsky*, 315 U.S. at 569.

[20]*Id*.

[21]*Id*. at 571–72.

that the statute was neither too vague nor an undue impairment of liberty.

Two major developments have occurred since *Chaplinsky*. In *Cohen v. California*,[22] the Supreme Court overturned the conviction of a young man who wore a jacket saying "Fuck the Draft." It stressed the emotive elements of communication and their constitutional protection. Given *Cohen*,[23] not all remarks that amount to fighting words can be simply dismissed as lacking any expressive value. The second development was a series of per curiam opinions in which the Court invalidated statutes directed at offensive language as overbroad and vague.[24] The Court emphasized the lack of danger of immediate violence.

The prospect of immediate responsive violence is a proper basis for restricting abusive words, but when is such restriction warranted? I shall focus on three aspects: the speaker's aims and understanding, the probability of violence, and the breadth of circumstances against which that probability is assessed.

I have suggested that when a speaker tries to provoke a fight, his expressive interest is slight; his remarks represent a course of action and may be punished. What if the speaker is not aiming to start a fight, but understands, or should understand, that his words may have that effect? The lowest appropriate standard of culpability would require some understanding of danger by the speaker. A speaker who was actually *unaware* that the sorts of words he used might provoke violence should be protected. If persons are punished for speaking words they do not realize can cause harm, open

communication is threatened. As far as the Constitution is concerned, it should be enough that the speaker know the propensity of his words, even if, in his rage, he did not consider their likely effect. Ignorance about the effect of words should provide a constitutional defense, but a failure to bring one's understanding to bear should not.

How likely should responsive violence have to be for remarks to be punished on that basis? The *Chaplinsky* court wrote of "words likely to cause an average addressee to fight."[25] This phrase has ambiguities and is probably not to be taken literally. The first ambiguity concerns the persons to be counted among potential addressees: everyone, only people to whom a phrase really "applies," or all those likely to be angered by having the label applied to them? Someone of French origin reacts differently to being called a "Polack" than someone of Polish origin. Unless an epithet is one to which most people react with great anger,[26] "average addressee" should include only those to whom the epithet might apply. Another ambiguity is how an "average addressee" is to be conceived. The *Chaplinsky* language reflects the propensity of courts to imagine male actors for most legal problems. Women, as well as children and older people, are potential addressees for most abusive phrases; but outside of quarrels among intimates, abusive words are very often spoken by and to younger men, frequently after alcohol has been drunk. The average person to whom insulting words *are actually* addressed may be more ready to fight than the average *potential* addressee. Even if we focus on those actually addressed,[27] probably no words

---

[22]403 U.S. 15 (1971).

[23]Of course, the Supreme Court might at some future time decide to abandon the reasoning of *Cohen*.

[24]*See, e.g.*, Gooding v. Wilson, 405 U.S. 518 (1972); Lewis v. City of New Orleans, 415 U.S. 130 (1974). *See also* Rosenfeld v. New Jersey, 408 U.S. 901 (1972).

[25]State v. Chaplinsky, 91 N.H. 310, 320 (1941).

[26]Sometimes it can be an insult to place a person in a category which both speaker and listener know is literally inappropriate. Calling a boy or man "a little girl" may be a way to impute cowardice or other "weakness."

[27]To quantify crudely why it matters which group counts: if 80 percent of young men respond by fighting and only 20 percent of the much larger remaining pool of potential addressees respond in that way, and if the

now cause the average listener to respond with violence. In any event, that is too stringent as a minimum constitutional test. Suppose a study showed that twenty percent of listeners respond violently to certain words spoken in certain contexts. That should be enough to restrict. The standard should be whether provoking violence is a substantial probability.

Against what situations is the likelihood of violence to be gauged? If this danger is the overriding reason for restraint, the simplest approach is exemplified by the *Model Penal Code*: make the likelihood of violence an inquiry into particular circumstances. This approach, however, is deeply troubling. Imagine that in an area where few blacks live,[28] a twenty-five year old white man of average size and strength waits for a bus with a single black person, and the white directs a torrent of insults and racial epithets at his black companion. Does it matter if the black listener is (1) a strong twenty-year old man, (2) a seventy-year-old man on crutches, (3) a very small woman of fifty, or (4) a child of nine? Only in the first setting is violence likely. Can the same remark be punishable if directed at the one person able to respond and constitutionally protected if directed at people not able to match the speaker physically? Even asking this question suggests two propositions. The first, to which I shall return, is that proper reasons for restraint go beyond preventing immediate violence. The second is that even if preventing such violence is the main reason for restraint, some principle of "equalization of victims" is called for. Inquiry should not concentrate on the perceived capacity of a particular victim to respond physically.[29] The test should be whether remarks of that sort in that context

would cause many listeners to respond forcibly. Neither statutory nor constitutional standards should require that a particular addressee be, or appear, likely to react violently.

## VI. WOUNDING THE LISTENER WHO IS ABUSED

Abusive words can be deeply wounding to their victims, but is that a proper basis for criminal penalties or civil liability? Much harsh language is a natural part of heated personal exchanges and strong disagreements about ideas. Since few of us are able and inclined to modulate our discourse to the magnitude of a subject, the law must tolerate many words that hurt. The Supreme Court has been right to invalidate criminal provisions that reach broadly to offensive or opprobrious language.

If the use of any words can be punished because they wound, it is only a small subcategory of all those that hurt, a category narrowed in terms of the speaker's aims, damage to the listener, the way language is used, or some combination of these criteria. Suppose that four men think humiliating a Hispanic woman who is standing alone would be "fun." They use their harshest words to insult her gender and ethnic origin, and call her a "whore." Their words wound deeply. Remarks whose dominant object is to hurt and humiliate, not to assert facts or values, have very limited expressive value. Their harm can be serious. Viewed alone, behavior like this should not be constitutionally protected against punishment.[30] This conclusion fits the actual language of *Chaplinsky*, which speaks of words "which by their very utterance inflict injury *or* tend to incite an immediate breach of the peace."[31]

---

abusive words are addressed to young men more than the remaining pool together, then the average potential addressee (the whole pool) would not fight, but the average actual addressee would fight.

[28]I add this fact to reduce the possibility that a defenseless black might call on others who are on, or waiting for, the next bus for retaliation.

[29]Subsequently, I consider the relevance of bystanders and their attitudes.

[30]*See, e.g.*, Downs, *supra* note 10; Delgado, supra note 10 (on civil liability).

[31]Chaplinsky v. New Hampshire, 315 U.S. 568, 572 (1942) (emphasis added).

But line-drawing problems are severe. The speaker's motives may be mixed, and separating an intent to humiliate from an honest but crude statement of views is often difficult. A general criminal prohibition of abusive words designed to hurt and humiliate probably should be judged unconstitutional.[32] However, penalties are proper when, as in my example, someone has initiated contact with a person just to harass him or her;[33] they are also proper when abusive language accompanies a clear intent to intimidate someone from exercising legally protected rights.

My conclusions about remarks that tend to provoke violence have a crucial bearing here. I have recommended a principle of equalization of victims. That principle, which would protect some victims not likely to respond with physical force, implicitly recognizes the legitimacy of protecting against deep hurt. The test whether words would cause many listeners to fight is a good test for whether remarks have passed the boundaries of what innocent citizens should be expected to tolerate. The hurt in a particular instance may not correlate with a willingness to fight; indeed, words may hurt the defenseless more than those who are able to strike back. However, the sorts of comments about which *some* listeners do fight are the ones that hurt the most. The propensity to generate a violent response is partly a measure of the intensity of hurt; this is a powerful reason why a listener's apparent capacity to fight back should not be an element of the speaker's crime.

If the particular victim's fighting capacity should be disregarded, so also should some other features of confrontational situations. The number of people supporting the abusive speaker and the presence of bystanders who might help the victim should be irrelevant, though these affect the likelihood of a physical clash. A more subtle point concerns groups whose members are generally less likely to fight. Suppose women, or members of a particular ethnic group, are much less likely to fight than are men, or members of other ethnic groups. That does not mean the listeners are less hurt when insulted. I have proposed that the difference in likely physical response is irrelevant for words that apply generally, but what of abusive words that apply peculiarly to the group in question? Is equivalent abuse more protected if the broad class of addressees is less likely to fight? The answer should be "no." An ethnic slur should be treated like other ethnic slurs of similar viciousness.[34] Calling a woman a "cunt" should be treated like calling a man a "prick." When the question is asked if words "of this sort" would lead many addressees to fight, the inquiry about the words should abstract from the inclinations to fight of the particular class abused.

Words that wound may lead to civil recovery in place of, or in addition to, criminal penalties. A standard for civil damages can be vaguer than is acceptable for criminal liability. Presently, the main vehicle for recovery in tort is infliction of emotional distress.[35] That tort requires extremely outrageous conduct and severe emotional distress. When these conditions are met, liability for abusive words is appropriate. However, an absolute privilege is needed for some communications with general public significance, as the Supreme Court has held for parodies of important public figures.[36]

---

[32] *See* State v. Harrington, 67 Or. App. 608, 680 P.2d 666 (1984).

[33] This behavior bears some resemblance to making a telephone call in order to harass. It has been assumed that this behavior is punishable, even though the prospect of immediate violence is absent.

[34] I do not underestimate how difficult it may be to decide what slurs are similarly vicious.

[35] *See generally* Note, *First Amendment Limits on Tort Liability for Words Intended to Inflict Severe Emotional Distress*, 85 COLUM. L. REV. 1749 (1985).

[36] *See* Hustler Magazine v. Falwell, 108 S. Ct. 876 (1988).

Do some abusive expressions hurt so generally in face-to-face conversations that they should be singled out as actionable? The most obvious candidates are racial and ethnic epithets and slurs. Similar remarks directed at religion, sexual preference, and gender might also be reached. Even for race and ethnicity, determining which expressions should be treated as wrongful is worrisome. One problem is that those secure in a favored status can accept denigrating terms that apply to their privileged position with less distress than can those who know the terms reflect a wide dislike of their group. "Honkey" hurts a lot less than "nigger," and "WASP" hurts a lot less than "kike."[37] Despite these line-drawing difficulties, a substantial argument exists for a special rule allowing recovery when speakers seriously try to injure and demean with racial and ethnic insults.[38]

## VII. OFFENSIVENESS

The third possible basis for restricting strong insults and group epithets is "general offensiveness." When the words and phrases I have mentioned are seriously used, they shock. They disturb people who are not the subject of abuse and they do so regardless of their message. However, determining what words are acceptable depends heavily on social context; and conventional restraints on language have loosened considerably in the last few decades. In the United States, no words or expressions should be illegal simply because they offend those who hear them.[39]

Someone's disquiet at listening to objectionable language is not nearly as great as his distress that he or his loved ones are the direct object of humiliating language. People who strongly wish not to be exposed to coarse language should avoid settings where use of that language is likely. In certain more formal settings, constraints on use of language are appropriate. Lawyers in court may not curse opposing counsel or judges, because curses are destructive of civility in court proceedings. A more debatable situation is a public meeting at which citizens are free to speak. If other citizens need to attend the meeting, flagrantly abusive language is directed toward a kind of captive audience and it may undermine the attempt to maintain reasoned discourse. However, it is arguable that citizens participating in open meetings should probably have the freedom of more informal settings.

*Cohen v. California*[40] and other cases indicate that the Constitution does not permit prohibition based on the offensiveness of language alone. However, the Supreme Court supposes that offense can be the basis for restriction in limited settings. It has upheld discipline of a high school student for offensive remarks at a school assembly[41] and federal restrictions on the broadcast of coarse words on daytime radio.[42] Both decisions are highly questionable. People are free to switch their dials and few children listen to daytime radio; the school remarks were part of a campaign speech that exceeded good taste but was neither shockingly abusive nor extremely coarse.[43]

---

[37] See Delgado, *supra* note 10, at 180.

[38] See id.

[39] See, e.g., M. NIMMER, NIMMER ON FREEDOM OF SPEECH 2–30 (1984); Rutzick, *supra* note 9, at 27. For an elaborate and sophisticated account of varieties of offensiveness and the circumstances in which offensive behavior may properly be punished in a liberal society, see J. FEINBERG, *supra* note 8, at 1–96.

[40] 403 U.S. 15 (1971).

[41] Bethel School Dist. v. Fraser, 478 U.S. 675, (1986).

[42] FCC v. Pacifica Found., 438 U.S. 726 (1978).

[43] The student gave the following speech at a high school assembly in support of a candidate for student government office:

Nevertheless, the Court's general position that there should be regulation in some narrow settings is sound.

## VIII. LONG-TERM HARMS

The fourth reason for suppressing strong insults and group epithets is the avoidance of long-term harms. I shall say a brief word about the quality of public discourse before concentrating on harms that relate to social resentment and inequality. Some have argued that *Cohen v. California* gave insufficient weight to maintaining a civil quality to public discourse.[44] Coarseness and abuse may negatively affect reasoned discourse, but the government should not be in the business generally of setting standards for acceptable speech.[45] It is no coincidence that the less privileged and more radical are those who often use words and phrases that might be judged to impair civil discourse. Drawing distinctions between what is civil and what is not is difficult, and government control of the terms of discussion should not sanitize expressions of outrage.

The more troubling question involves the long-term effects of insults and epithets that reinforce feelings of prejudice and inferiority and contribute to social patterns of domination. Although repetition of some personal insults, such as "you fat slob," can undermine self-esteem, the effect of most such insults is contained and dissipates fairly quickly. Epithets and more elaborate slurs that reflect stereotypes about race, ethnic group, religion, sexual preference, and gender may cause continuing hostility and psychological damage. The harms need not depend on whether listeners are the objects of the epithets or slurs. All-male conversations in which women are denigrated can support male prejudices, and women's feelings of resentment and inferiority may derive from knowing how they are talked about as well as reacting to how they are talked to. If one focuses on these long-term harms, the particular audience is not of primary importance; laws in other countries that are specifically directed against racial, ethnic, and religious epithets and slurs[46] do not make the audience critical.

---

I know a man who is firm—he's firm in his pants, he's firm in his shirt, his character is firm—but most . . . of all, his belief in you, the students of Bethel, is firm.

Jeff Kuhlman is a man who takes his point and pounds it in. If necessary, he'll take an issue and nail it to the wall. He doesn't attack things in spurts—he drives hard, pushing and pushing until finally—he succeeds.

Jeff is a man who will go to the very end—even the climax—, for each and every one of you.

So vote for Jeff for A.S.B. vice-president—he'll never come between you and the best our high school can be. *Bethel School Dist.*, 478 U.S. at 687, (Brennan, J., concurring).

[44]*See e.g.*, A. BICKEL, MORALITY OF CONSENT 72–73 (1975).

[45]*See e.g.*, Farber, *Civilizing Public Discourse: An Essay on Professor Bickel, Justice Harlan, and the Enduring Significance of* Cohen v. California, 1980 DUKE L.J. 283.

[46]*See generally* E. BARENDT, FREEDOM OF SPEECH 163–65 (1985); L. BOLLINGER, THE TOLERANT SOCIETY 38–39 (1986); Arkes, *Civility and the Restriction of Speech: Rediscovering the Defamation of Groups*, 1974 SUP. CT. REV. 281, 283–84; Note, *A Communitarian Defense of Group Libel Laws*, 101 HARV. L. REV. 682, 689–94 (1988). In a Public Order Act of 1986, the British Parliament amended previous enactments to provide that "[a] person who uses threatening, abusive or insulting words or behaviour, or displays any written material which is threatening, abusive or insulting is guilty . . . if (a) he intends thereby to stir up racial hatred, or (b) having regard to all the circumstances racial hatred is likely to be stirred up thereby." Public Order Act, 1986, ch. 64, §18. A similar standard governs publication or distribution of material, public performance or recording of plays, and radio and television broadcasts. Id. §§19–22. For the Federal Republic of Germany, relevant statutes and interpretations, as well as recent legislative reform, are carefully described in Stein, *History Against Free Speech: The New German Law Against the "Auschwitz"—and Other—"Lies,"* 85 MICH. L. REV. 277 (1986). Although some foreign legislation seems very broad to American eyes, Lee Bollinger has observed that other countries are able to distinguish racist rhetoric from other speech: "It seems a significant piece of corroborating evidence that virtually every

Whether a law of this type would be held unconstitutional in the United States is very dubious. In *Beauharnais v. Illinois*,[47] in 1952, the Supreme Court did uphold a conviction under a law that forbade publications portraying "depravity, criminality, unchastity, or lack of virtue of a class of citizens, of any race, color, creed or religion [in a way that exposes those citizens] to contempt, derision, or obloquy or which is productive of breach of the peace or riots."[48] Beauharnais had organized distribution of a leaflet asking city officials to resist the invasion of the Negro and warning that if "the need to prevent the white race from becoming mongrelized by the negro will not unite us, then the aggressions, . . . rapes, robberies, knives, guns and marijuana of the negro, surely will."[49] The Court assimilated this speech to group libel, instances in which something defamatory is said about a small group in such a way that the damaging remark falls on members of the group: for example, "the [fifteen member] firm of Mix and Nix is a bunch of crooks."[50] The Court mentioned the danger of racial riots which a legislature might reasonably think is made more likely by racist speech.[51] In subsequent years, the Court's protection of civil libel, the *Cohen* case, and invalidations of breach of the peace and disorderly conduct statutes that lacked reference to immediate danger of violence, have largely undermined the authority of

*Beauharnais.* The case has occasionally been cited in peripheral contexts, but the prevailing assumption has been that a statute as broad as that one from Illinois would not stand, and that a publication like the one in that case would be protected. In cases that arose out of the intense controversy over whether Nazis might march in uniform in Skokie, a city inhabited by many Jewish survivors of the Holocaust, appellate judges acted on these premises, striking down ordinances designed to keep the Nazis out and indicating that a Nazi march could not be altogether foreclosed.[52]

During the last two decades the Supreme Court has emphasized that discrimination among communications on the basis of content is constitutionally suspect. When a law is directed at group epithets and slurs, words are made illegal because they place people in certain categories and are critical of members of those categories. This is certainly content discrimination. It may be said in response that much of the harm of these abusive words derives from nonconscious response to their force, not from conscious consideration of the overall message.[53] Nevertheless, if a law forbids comments made generally or to third persons about members of groups, and it covers the "ordinary" language of the publication in *Beauharnais* as well as harsh epithets, what is being suppressed really is a message whose content

---

other western democracy does draw such a distinction in their [sic] law; the United States stands virtually alone in the degree to which it has decided legally to tolerate racist rhetoric." See L. BOLLINGER, *supra*, at 8.

[47]343 U.S. 250 (1952).

[48]*Id.* at 251.

[49]*Id.* at 252.

[50]*See generally* Note, *Group Defamation: Five Guiding Factors*, 64 TEX. L. REV. 591 (1985).

[51]*Beauharnais*, 343 U.S. at 259. The Court sustained the refusal of the Illinois courts to entertain truth as a defense, on the ground that a state might, and did, require "good motives" and "justifiable ends" as well as truth, and if these requisites could not be satisfied the court did not need to consider evidence of truth. *Id.*

This aspect of the Court's opinion is unsatisfying, because the trial court did not indicate that it would consider truth if Beauharnais also made a showing of "good motives" and "justifiable ends." I assume that courts cannot reject motives and ends as unjustifiable because they disapprove of the political program that is urged.

[52]*See* Collin v. Smith, 578 F.2d 1197 (7th Circ. 1978), *cert. denied*, 439 U.S. 916 (1978); *see also* D. RICHARDS, TOLERATION AND THE CONSTITUTION 191–92 (1986).

[53]Also, people are left free to express any facts or values about members of the group in less obnoxious words.

and intensity is judged hurtful and obnoxious. This language cannot be characterized as "low value" speech, except by virtue of a judgment about its substantive message.

Some proponents of laws of this type have argued that if such speech is tolerated, the government implicitly endorses a message that is contrary to our fundamental values.[54] That is not so. The government permits all kinds of speech contrary to our constitutional values; that is an aspect of freedom of speech. The government can promote equality by its own actions, by education and advocacy, by regulating actions other than speech. Allowing racist rhetoric does not show support of racism. It is true that in a society where less privileged members of minorities may identify the majority with the government, government passivity may be perceived as support. But more emphasis on the government's direct commitment to positive values of equality is a better way to show support than silencing speakers.

Many countries have reasonably concluded that suppression of messages of race and ethnic hate is warranted, at some cost to free speech, because values of equality and dignity are so central and so vulnerable.[55] The issue is close, but my own judgment coincides with the prevailing academic assumption that a law like that in *Beauharnais* should be held unconstitutional. Part of the reason is the difficulty in seeing how the line of permissible restriction would be drawn

once the harm of messages was treated as a proper basis for suppression.

One conceivable way to meet this objection to restricting messages of fact and value would be to forbid only "false" speech about members of groups.[56] Such speech would lack "full value" because of falsity, and prohibiting it would not open the door for broad prohibitions of speech. Unfortunately, aiming at false speech of this kind would either be ineffectual or dangerous. Suppose that the "false" remarks to be criminalized were those that asserted definite facts about members of groups that were demonstrably false and were known to be false by those making the assertions, for example, "Every single black person in this country scores lower on standard intelligence tests than the worst scoring white person." Punishing those who make such false assertions would have a very slight effect on hate literature. To have any bite, the law's coverage of punishable false statements would have to include matters of opinion or much vaguer and ambiguous factual assertions. As far as free speech is concerned, opinions may not be labeled true or false. With respect to vague factual assertions, trials would afford merchants of hate an opportunity to indicate their meanings in full detail, using that public forum to present damaging facts about the group they despise as unsympathetically as possible.[57] Two conclusions emerge. If falsity is an aspect of criminal liability, people

---

[54] See, e.g., Note, *supra* note 46, at 690–91.

[55] See *supra* note 46.

[56] See, e.g., Note, *supra* note 46.

[57] *Beauharnais* is instructive as to these difficulties. The leaflet in question asserted, among other things, that "if the need to prevent being mongrelized by the Negro did not unite white people, the rapes, robberies, knives, guns and marijuana of the Negro, surely will." 343 U.S. 250, 252 (1952). The *desirability* of white people uniting is a matter of opinion; the likelihood that that will happen is a prediction of vague and uncertain future facts that cannot be punished. Exactly what Negroes are said to be doing to bring about "mongrelization" is much too unclear to amount to a punishable assertion of facts. That leaves the statement about the "rapes, robberies," et cetera. What exactly is being claimed here: that all Negroes engage in these bad acts, that most do, that a higher proportion of Negroes than whites do? The first proposition is absurd and the second is probably demonstrably false, but Beauharnais might say at his trial: "Well, all I meant factually is that the percentages are a lot higher among Negroes and that for this reason, the safety of neighborhoods will deteriorate if Negroes move in." I do not know what was true in Chicago around 1950, but we do know that Beauharnais offered to

should be punishable only for clear assertions of fact, and much vague scurrilous comment about groups would remain unpunishable. Trials about truth could easily do much more damage than the original communications. Whatever the constitutional status of a law precisely limited to false assertions of fact, adopting such a law would be senseless.

If racial and ethnic epithets and slurs are to be made illegal by separate legal standards, the focus should be on face-to-face encounters, targeted vilification aimed at members of the audience.[58] As to these, expressive value is slight, because the aim is to wound and humiliate, or to start a fight. Since fighting words are already punishable and the tort of extreme emotional distress is available, what would be the significance of separate provisions for the language of group vilification? They could stand as symbolic statements that such language is peculiarly at odds with our constitutional values; and they could relieve prosecutors, or plaintiffs, from having to establish all the requisites of a more general offense or tort.[59]

Some lesser showing of immediate injury is appropriate for words that historically have inflicted grave humiliations and damage to ideals of equality and continue to do so. Of course, special treatment for class-based insults in face-to-face settings would be a modest exception to "content neutrality," but one that is warranted in light of the values involved.

In closing, I want briefly to consider the import of an ideal of civic courage, an ideal eloquently propounded by Justice Brandeis, for strong insults and group epithets.[60] If a principle of free speech *assumes* that people are hardy or *aims* to help them become so, perhaps coarse and even hurtful comments should be protected in the rough and tumble of vigorous dialogue. But group epithets and slurs designed to wound listeners are another matter. Being impervious to epithets when one is a member of a privileged majority is much easier than when one belongs to a reviled minority, and a general encouragement of civic courage may be more likely if targeted racial and religious abuse is not allowed. Even "courageous citizens" should not be expected to swallow such abuse without deep hurt, and being the victim of such abuse may not contribute to hardiness in ways that count positively for a democratic society.

---

prove truth, and that around 1989, at least judged by convictions, the percentage of blacks who commit many serious crimes is higher than the percentage of whites who do so.

[58]*See* Delgado, *supra* note 10; Downs, *supra* note 10.

[59]*See* Delgado, *supra* note 10, at 151–57. For criminal liability, I am inclined to think that either a purpose to initiate contact in order to humiliate or an attempt to intimidate should be constitutionally required. That is, punishment should not be allowed if during a heated conversation a person decides to wound another with such remarks, unless the remarks also are of a sort that often lead to violence.

[60]*See* Whitney v. California, 274 U.S. 357, 372 (1927) (Brandeis, J., concurring).

## QUESTIONS

1. Apply Greenawalt's views to the case of *United States v. Eichman*. Do they tend to support the holding in that case, or not?

2. How satisfactory is Greenawalt's distinction between words that are assertions and words that are "situation-altering"?

3. Suppose that, precisely *because* certain words are deeply insulting and upsetting, only those words can adequately express certain attitudes or convictions. What would follow from this as to whether such insults and epithets should be legally suppressed?

4. Greenawalt says: "The test whether words would cause many listeners to fight is a good test of whether remarks have passed the boundaries of what innocent persons should tolerate." Suppose J says, "I knew that what I said to M would really be offensive to a lot of people, but I also knew M to be more thick-skinned than the average person, and would be able to take it." Should J be held liable for making the insulting remark because most people in M's position would have been deeply hurt by it? Or should the proper criterion be whether the average *thick-skinned* person would tolerate the remark without fighting?

5. What rules governing speech and other expressive behavior would, on Greenawalt's view of insults and epithets, be appropriate for college campuses? Be as specific as you can. Do you think such rules would go too far, or not far enough?

6. Should there be a prohibition on speech that is *both* denigrating toward minority groups *and* false? Do you share Greenawalt's suspicion that court trials arising from such a law would only give a wider airing to the false claims in question?

## Rosemarie Tong
# FEMINISM, PORNOGRAPHY AND CENSORSHIP*

In 1976 a group called Women Against Violence in Pornography and Media was formed. Its first action was a 600-woman march down Broadway, the major pornography strip in San Francisco, to protest pornography as "anti-woman propaganda."[1] Since that march, feminists have been concerned lest their activities be used as an excuse to usher in an era of censorship. In recent months they have re-examined their position, noting that they are opposed *primarily* to public displays of pornographic material in which women are represented in a degrading manner. Despite such qualifications, however, feminist "anti-porn" campaigns continue to draw heavy criticism. Some opponents insist that pornography is a seamless web, that it is impossible to distinguish between its benign and malign modalities. Others claim that even if such distinctions

*© From *Social Theory and Practice*, vol. 8, no. 1 (Winter 1982), pp. 1–17. Reprinted by permission of *Social Theory and Practice* and the author.
[1]D. E. H. Russell and Laura Lederer, "Questions We Get Asked Most Often," in *Take Back the Night: Women on Pornography*, ed. Laura Lederer (New York: Morrow & Co., 1980), p. 23.

could be made, it would matter little insofar as the feminist cause is concerned since the Constitution protects "stereotypes degrading to women."[2]

What this paper argues is that a certain kind of pornography is degrading, that it is possible to distinguish this type of pornography from other types, and that Constitutional principles, somewhat different than those stressed in the Supreme Court's leading obscenity decisions,[3] warrant the imposition of legal constraints on publicly-disseminated, degrading pornographic material. Nonetheless, though such legal constraints are justified in principle, in practice they should not be imposed if other less coercive, extra-legal means of control are available.

## What Makes Some but Not All Pornography Degrading?

**A. Erotica and thanatica generally defined:** The term "pornography" is derived from the Greek *pornographos*, meaning "writing (sketching) of harlots."[4] Thus, the depictions of various forms of sexual intercourse on the walls of a house of prostitution in Pompeii were literally *pornographos*.[5] Such explicit sketches, intended as aphrodisiacs, left far less to the imagination than their oral or written counterparts—they frequently "told" more than a thousand words. Still such murals pale when set beside the photographs and motion pictures spawned by contemporary pornographers. Since audiences probably have more difficulty distancing themselves from what they have seen than what they have heard or

read, and since they are more prone to believe what they see rather than what they hear or read, pornography may indeed make a deeper, more lasting impression on the viewer's consciousness than, say, a sexually-explicit monologue or novel.

Because of such considerations, many feminists are concerned that pornography will have a negative effect on sexual attitudes and sexual behavior. Now if by pornography is understood "a view of sensual delight in the erotic celebration of the body,"[6] or the depiction of a "mutually pleasurable, sexual expression between people who have enough power to be there by positive choice,"[7] then most feminists have no objection to it whatsoever although they would prefer that it be termed "erotica." In contrast, if by pornography is meant "verbal or pictorial material which represents or describes sexual behavior that is degrading or abusive to one or more of the participants *in such a way as to endorse the degradation*,"[8] then most feminists are opposed to it. Feminists generally term such pornography "hardcore." Insofar as it involves the affirmation of self or mutual destruction (depersonalization), I term it "thanatic" (from the Greek *thanatos*, having to do with death). Since I claim only that *publicly-disseminated, degrading thanatica* are Constitutionally unprotected, it seems advisable to distinguish more precisely between erotica and thanatica.

**B. Erotica and thanatica precisely differentiated:** The essential difference between erotica and thanatica cannot be that the one but not the other portrays sex within marriage,

[2] Alan Dershowitz as cited by A. Berger in "Pornography: Is Censorship the Answer?" *Boston Real Paper*, September 14, 1979.

[3] See Roth v. United States, 354 U.S. 476, 487 (1975); Miller v. California, 413 U.S. 15, 24 (1973); Paris Adult Theater I v. Slaton, 413 U.S. 49 (1973).

[4] See, for example, *Webster's Third New International Dictionary*.

[5] See David A. J. Richards, *The Moral Criticism of Law* (Encino, Cal.: Dickenson Co., 1977), p. 63.

[6] Ibid., p. 71.

[7] Gloria Steinem, "Erotica and Pornography: A Clear and Present Difference," in Lederer, *Take Back the Night*, p. 37.

[8] Helen E. Longino, "Pornography, Oppression, and Freedom: A Closer Look," in *Take Back the Night*, p. 43.

teaching that the only proper "genital commotion"[9] is one with the voluntary aim of reproducing the species; and this because neither erotica nor thanatica are Augustinian in inspiration or motivation.[10] Both of these pornographic modes depict sexual relations between fornicators, adulterers, sodomists, and so forth who use, whenever necessary, the appropriate contraceptive devices. Feminists have no objections to depictions of extra-marital sexual liaisons *per se*. On the contrary, given certain conditions they endorse them. Indeed to engage in sexual activity solely for the purposes of procreation may count as dangerous sex for those feminists who have led the battle for reproductive freedom and population control. Similarly, it may count as perverted for those feminists who maintain that the *raison d'être* of "genital commotion" is pleasure or the expression of love, and not the conception of children.

But if the difference between erotica and thanatica is not some debate about the relationship between sex and procreation, is it some controversy about the relationship between sex and love? Certainly, love is not the *leit-motif* of thanatica. If anything, hate is. And admittedly, when love is divorced from sex the results can be quite devastating, especially for the inexperienced woman. One of the most haunting scenes in a recent movie, *Diary of a Mad Housewife*, occurs when the frazzled, rooster-pecked housewife is given a seductive nightgown as unanticipated severance pay from her callous "lover." The woman nearly breaks down on the spot. Yet even if love frequently enhances sexual exchanges and even if sexual intimacies often add a dimension to love relation

ships, love is neither a necessary nor a sufficient condition for sexual pleasure, and vice versa.[11] If this is so, the distinction between erotica and thanatica cannot be that whereas the latter does not depict sex as linked with love the former does. The message of erotica may not be hate, but neither is it love in the sense of a relatively durable, inter-personal commitment. Rather it is enjoyment. And on occasion, if not frequently, the most enjoyable sexual experience may be one that is encumbered neither with the responsibilities of love nor with some of its more romanticized illusions.

But to say that erotica depict sexual exchanges as enjoyable is not to suggest that thanatica fail to do this. Nonetheless, it is initially plausible to make this claim. Whereas erotica frequently show people kissing, fondling or hugging each other, thanatica often show people—especially men—kicking, hitting or whipping other people—usually women. Ordinarily most people enjoy kisses more than kicks. Still it is quite possible to enjoy a kick more than a kiss; and this not only because the enjoyment of pleasure and pain is largely a matter of personal preference, but because pleasure and pain sensations frequently combine to create very enjoyable sexual exchanges:

> Pain is normally a part of the erotic frenzy; bodies that delight to be bodies for the joy they give each other, seek to find each other, to unite, to confront each other in every possible manner. There is in erotic love a tearing away from the self, transport, ecstasy; suffering also tears through the limits of the ego, it is transcendence, a paroxysm; pain has always played a great part in orgies; it

[9] For an explanation of this phrase see H. Gardiner, "Moral Principles Toward a Definition of the Obscene," *Law and Contemporary Problems* 20 (1955): 567.

[10] See Augustine, *The City of God*. St. Thomas Aquinas is in accord with Augustine's view. Of the emission of semen apart from generation in marriage, he wrote, "after the sin of homicide whereby a human nature already in existence is destroyed, this type of sin appears to take new place, for by it the generation of human nature is precluded." Thomas Aquinas, *On the Truth of the Catholic Faith: Summa Contra Gentiles*, (Garden City, New York: Image Books, 1955) trans. V. Bourke, p. 146.

[11] See Fred Berger, "Pornography, Sex, and Censorship," *Social Theory and Practice* 4 (1977): 192–204.

is well known that the exquisite and the painful intermesh: a caress can become torture, torment can give pleasure.[12]

Given these considerations, erotica, no less than thanatica, can depict persons enjoying pain-sensations as well as pleasure-sensations.[13]

If this is the case, then, what does distinguish between erotica and thanatica? Seemingly, it is that unlike erotica, thanatica depict people not only enjoying pain but inflicting it as proof of their superiority or accepting it as proof of their inferiority. In other words, thanatica represent sexual exchanges devoid or nearly devoid of mutual or self respect; they display sexual exchanges which are degrading in the sense and to the degree that the desires and experiences of at least one participant are not regarded by the other participant(s) as having a validity and a subjective importance *equal* to his/her/their own. I regard your desires and experiences as *less* valid and important than mine. And so I force myself upon you despite your protestations; or I hurt you to amuse myself or indulge my sexual fantasies or needs. Or I regard your desires and experiences as *more* valid and important than mine, in which case I lose my self respect, make myself an object, and not only let you do with me as you will but come to think it is your right to so abuse me.[14] In either event the representation of such degrading behavior is thanatic to the extent that it not only depicts but celebrates (condones) and encourages either the callous frustration of one's own or someone else's preferences as a sexual being or, worse, the intentional violation of one's own or someone else's rights as a sexual being. It is this type of

pornography—degrading thanatica—to which most feminists take particular objection. As they and others see it, if any type of sexually explicit material warrants censorship, it is this.

## The Constitution and Degrading Thanatica

At this point the predictable objection is made that although there may be constitutional grounds for restricting degrading thanatic behavior, these grounds cannot be invoked to restrict *representations* of such harmful behavior and this because such depictions are not harmful *per se*. To this objection there are three replies: (1) Although such thanatic material may not be harmful per se, it causes persons to engage in harmful behavior; (2) Thanatic material does not have to be harmful in order to be Constitutionally censorable; and (3) Thanatic material is harmful. Although feminists have made use of all these arguments, they have tended to favor the first. This is unfortunate because of these arguments, the third is, as I shall suggest, the strongest.

*Argument One*: The first argument—that there is an intimate connection between viewing degrading thanatica and engaging in corresponding forms of behavior—is based on a common sense belief that there is an intimate relationship between thought and action. This belief is expressed, for example, by parents who fear that their children's conduct will be deleteriously affected as a result of viewing too much explicit sex or violence on television. This belief is so strong among some that a defense of "prolonged, intense, involuntary, subliminal television intoxication"[15] was offered on behalf of 15-year-old Ronald Zamora. Supposedly Ronnie would not have murdered an aged, neighborhood

---

[12]Simone de Beauvoir, *The Second Sex*, trans. H. M. Parshley (New York: Random House, Vintage Books, 1952, 1974), pp. 444–5.

[13]For a further explanation of the difference between sensation-pleasure and enjoyment-pleasure, see Gilbert Ryle, "Pleasure," in *Moral Concepts*, ed. Joel Feinberg (New York: Oxford University Press, 1969).

[14]See Thomas E. Hill, Jr., "Servility and Self-Respect," *The Monist* 57 (1973): 87–104.

[15]Quoted by Hugo A. Bedau, "Rough Justice: The Limits of Novel Defenses," *Hastings Center Report* 8 (1978): 8.

woman had he not been under the influence of Kojak, that rough-and-tumble police
detective. Interestingly, the jury rejected Zamora's defense. As they saw it, the thought-
action relation, though strong, is not one of
cause and necessary effect. Thousands of
children who watched *Kojak* remained utterly benign in action even if their thoughts
were malign. Like them, Zamora had it in
his power to control his actions in a way that
he could not have been expected to control
his thoughts.

But if there be reason to doubt that children usually, or even frequently, do what
they see or think, then it becomes hard to
argue, with any surety, that adults who routinely view thanatica are very likely to perpetrate thanatic acts. In other words, it becomes
difficult to conclude with Susan Brownmiller
that "the anti-female propaganda that perme-
ates our nation's cultural output promotes a
climate in which acts of sexual hostility directed against women are not only tolerated
but ideologically encouraged."[16] In fact if the
1979 Commission on Obscenity and Pornography was correct, then there is "no evidence
. . . that exposure to explicit sexual materials
plays a significant role in the causation of
delinquent or criminal behavior among youth
or adults."[17] Indeed, exposure to such material may be therapeutic, a convenient cathartic
device for relieving sexual repressions and
tensions non-violently.[18] Nonetheless, such
empirical evidence needs to be weighed
against more recent studies which show a cor-
relation between exposure to violent pornographic materials and committing sexually
abusive or violent acts against women.[19]
Should such studies be confirmed, then the
causal link between viewing thanatica and

perpetrating sexually-abusive acts may be
more firmly established.

But even if empirical evidence of the latter sort should increase, it would have to increase tremendously to support the claim
that some feminists may be tempted to
make, namely that degrading thanatica constitute a "clear and present danger" to
women. As Wendy Kaminer has pointed
out, the clear and present danger standard
would actually afford greater legal protection to pornography than current obscenity
laws.[20] It is easier to prove that a given instance of "unprotected nonspeech" is "obscene" than to prove that a given instance of
protected speech constitutes a real danger.
In a "clear and present" danger case the government must demonstrate, with direct factual evidence, that speech is occurring in a
context in which it poses a serious, substantive, and immediate danger that Congress or
the states have a right to protect against.
Thus, to use the standard example, falsely
shouting "Fire!" in a crowded theater might
be punished because it is so closely linked to
subsequent harmful actions. So in order to
win its case in a pornography proceeding
the State would have to show that as an immediate result of viewing *Snuff*, a movie in
which a woman was supposed to have *actually* been tortured, mutilated and murdered,
most male viewers would, as soon as the opportunity presented itself, sexually assault
and brutally murder a woman. But the fact
of the matter is that it is not at all certain
whether viewing *Snuff* has the same sort of
behavioral effect on an audience as yelling
"Fire!" does. This coupled with the fact that
the clear and present danger test has been
manipulated in such ways as to restrict in-

---

[16]Susan Brownmiller, *Against Our Will: Men, Women and Rape* (New York: Simon & Schuster, Inc., 1975).

[17]United States Commission on Obscenity and Pornography, *Report of the Commission on Obscenity and Pornography* (D.C.: G.P.O., 1979), p. 27.

[18]See G. Gorer, *The Danger of Equality* (New York: Weybright and Talley, 1966).

[19]See Section IV, "Research on the Effects on Pornography," in Lederer, *Take Back the Night*, pp. 185–238.

[20]Wendy Kaminer, "Pornography and the First Amendment: Prior Restraints and Private Action," in *Take Back the Night*, p. 245.

nocuous expression and political dissent[21] as well as truly dangerous expression makes it less than the instrument of choice for combatting degrading thanatica.

*Argument Two*: Realizing this, many feminists have attempted to rest their case for the censorship of degrading thanatica on the second argument listed above—namely, that material does not have to be harmful *per se* in order to be Constitutionally censorable. The success of this argument depends on whether or not the so-called "offense-principle" is a legitimate liberty-limiting principle. Many students of John Stuart Mill claim that it is, and this despite the fact that Mill often wrote as if the prevention of private or public harm were the only valid ground for state coercion.[22]

> ". . . there are many acts which, being directly injurious only to the agents themselves, ought not to be legally interdicted, but which, if done publicly, are a violation of good manners, and coming thus within the category of offences against others, may rightfully be prohibited. Of this kind are offences against public decency. . . ."[23]

But why may such "harmless" offenses as public nudity, indecency, public displays of "dirty" pictures and the like be validly restricted? Are they not "symbolic speech," expressions of opinion entitled to the same protection which safeguards historical, scientific, theological, philosophical, political and moral questions? Perhaps not. As Mill sees it, such offenses are not really speech, because they do not have the same "redeeming social value" peculiar to assertion, criticism, advocacy, and debate. Consequently, they may be restricted without much ado.[24]

In the nineteenth century this line of reasoning could probably have been accepted without grave consequences. The case for free love and sex, when it was made, was generally made on the soap box or in the pamphlet. Depictions of unorthodox sexual exchanges were relatively few and this simply because pictorial modes of communication were underdeveloped. Today, however, the *seen* word is more dominant than the spoken or written word. Television and film convey just as much information as oral tradition or the "Gutenberg" media (newspapers, journals, pamphlets, books). It seems, then, that forms of communication which show rather than state or print a message are entitled to just as much, if not more, protection as other more traditional forms of expression. If this is so, then some other reason, other than lack of social value, must be found to restrict "harmless" offenses such as the depiction of degrading thanatic behavior.

That reason may well be that a pluralistic democracy can withstand only so much in the way of ethnic, racial and sexist slurs, and only so many denigrating expressions, before its viability is threatened. "There are," as D. A. J. Richards observes "certain demonstrable moral virtues or character traits—public spiritedness, civic responsibility, democratic tolerance, mutual respect—which citizens of a stable constitutional democracy must have."[25] This may be the intuition behind Joel Feinberg's attempt to add credence to the offense principle as a liberty-limiting principle. He argues that offensive expression may be restricted provided that it is universally offensive and publicly flaunted. An

---

[21]See, for example, Schenck v. United States, 249 U.S. 47 (1919); Dennis v. United States, 341 U.S. 494 (1951); N.Y. Times Co. v. United States, 403 U.S. 713 (1971).

[22]See John Stuart Mill, *On Liberty*, ed. David Spitz (New York: W. W. Norton & Co., 1975).

[23]Ibid., Chapter 5, paragraph 7.

[24]See Joel Feinberg, "'Harmless Immoralities' and Offensive Nuisances," in *Rights, Justice and the Bounds of Liberty*, (Princeton: Princeton University Press, 1980), p. 71.

[25]Richards, *Moral Criticism*, p. 75.

offense is of the universal sort when it can be expected to evoke reactions such as shame, embarrassment, repugnance, repulsion or disgust "from almost any person chosen at random, taking the nation as a whole, and not because the individual selected belongs to some faction, clique or party."[26] It is publicly flaunted when non-consenting individuals can avoid it only by unreasonably inconveniencing themselves,[27] by foregoing, limiting or altering their forays into the public marketplace.

If Feinberg is correct, the implications are these: On almost any account degrading thanatica are universally offensive; not only women but most men (hopefully) are offended by depictions of men treating women as pieces of meat ready to be branded or butchered on the altar of male sexual entertainment. And even if most men and a few women are not offended by such depictions, Feinberg's standard of universality can be supplemented to discount such obtuseness. Feinberg asserts that even if the population as a whole is not offended by "[p]ublic cross-burnings, displays of swastikas, 'jokes' that ridicule Americans of Polish descent told on public media, public displays of banners with large and abusive caricatures of the Pope,"[28] such expressions should be curtailed nonetheless because it is insulting behavior of a type "bound to upset, alarm, anger, or irritate those it insults:"

> Those who are taunted by such conduct will understandably suffer intense and complicated emotions. They might be frightened or wounded; and their blood might boil in wrath. Yet the law cannot permit them to accept the challenge and vent their anger in retaliatory aggression.[29]

And since the law cannot expect them to cope with their rage either, it might, as it has in the past, silence or sanction those who would abuse, mock, or otherwise offend their fellow citizens. In 1939, for example, in a standard prosecution for "disorderly, threatening, insulting language or behavior in public places, and acts which annoy, obstruct, or are offensive to others," Ninfo, a Christian Front street orator, was convicted for shouting "If I had my way, I would hang all the Jews in this country. I wish I had $100,000 from Hitler. I would show those damn Jews what I would do, you mockies, you damn Jews, you scum."[30] Therefore, whether degrading thanatica offend the entire population or not, provided that they are profoundly upsetting to most women, there may be cause for legal intervention. Still, if those who take offense at degrading thanatica can "easily and effectively" avoid them, then such depictions may not be legitimately restricted. In other words, no matter how universally offensive a given thanatic film of the degrading variety is, provided that it is not flaunted or foisted upon unwilling spectators, it may be viewed no matter how many non-viewers are repulsed, embarrassed or shamed at the mere thought that others are viewing it.[31]

This seems to have been behind the Court's thinking in *Stanley v. Georgia*,[32] the decision which held that Georgia could not constitutionally convict Stanley merely for possessing in his home an obscene film for his own viewing. After citing the First Amendment right of

---

[26]Ibid., p. 88.

[27]Ibid., p. 89.

[28]Ibid., p. 88.

[29]Ibid., p. 89.

[30]See David Reisman, "Democracy and Defamation: Control of Group Libel," *Columbia Law Review* 42 (1942): 751.

[31]See H. L. A. Hart, *Law, Liberty, and Morality*, The Harry Camp Lectures (Stanford, Cal.: Stanford University Press, 1963).

[32]405 U.S. 113 (1973).

Stanley to receive information and ideas, the Court appealed to the constitutional right of privacy: "for also fundamental is the right to be free, except in very limited circumstances, from unwanted governmental intrusions into one's privacy."[33] Significantly, this decision did not protect what Feinberg's "reasonable avoidability" criterion might protect, namely, the viewing of degrading thanatica in discreetly-operated but publicly-accessible adult theaters. Some Justices seem to have been persuaded by Alexander Bickel's argument that to grant the right not only to read and see obscene material in the privacy of one's home but also "to obtain obscene books and pictures in the market, or to foregather in public places—discreet, but accessible to all—with others who share a taste for the obscene" is "to affect the world about the rest of us, and to impinge on other privacies and other interests, as those concerned with the theater in New York have found, apparently to their surprise."[34]

Bickel's obvious, and relatively non-controversial, point seems to be that in this society it is very difficult to circumvent obscene material, including degrading thanatica. His stronger claim is that it is not only difficult but virtually impossible to avoid such contact: "Perhaps each of us can, if he wishes, effectively avert the eye and stop the ear. Still, what is commonly read and seen and heard and done intrudes upon us all, wanted or not, for it constitutes our environment."[35]

Admittedly, the fact that everyone reads *Hustler* (the *Times*), listens to "punk" rock (Debussy), and plays pushpin (chess) does affect the quality of life in these United States.

But the fact that such habits affect the quality of life for all is not in itself a strong enough reason to censor, say, "punk." Assuming that it is not harmful and that it is reasonably avoidable, it still has to be demonstrated that "punk" is universally offensive. And even if it is, it also has to be shown that *restricting* such "noise" does not erode basic democratic virtues such as tolerance.

*Argument Three:* Realizing how difficult it is to apply the offense principle sagaciously,[36] some feminists have instead rested their case for censorship on the third argument above: namely, that degrading thanatica are *per se* harmful. Supposedly the harm constituted by publicly-disseminated degrading thanatica is akin to the type of harm constituted by defamation. Therefore, ". . . [t]he manufacture and distribution of material which defames and threatens all members of a class by its recommendation of abusive and degrading behavior toward some members of that class simply in virtue of their membership in it"[37] is a likely candidate for censorship provided that "group libel" is a viable legal concept.

"Group libel" is an underdeveloped concept in American law. Defamatory attacks upon social groups fall pretty much outside the scope of existing law, because the traditions of individualism are very powerful in the United States. American legal thought is phrased in terms of the "individual" and the "state," and the law of defamation, such as it is,[38] is conceived of as a protection against *individual* injury, just as the law of assault and battery is a protection for *indi-*

---

[33] Ibid., p. 564.

[34] Alexander M. Bickel, *The Morality of Consent* (New Haven: Yale University Press, 1975), p. 74.

[35] Ibid.

[36] Joel Feinberg claims that the best example of perverse judicial zeal to avenge mere offense is cited by Zechariah Chafee: "The white slave traffic was first exposed by W. T. Stead in a magazine article, 'The Maiden Tribute.' The English law did absolutely nothing to the profiteers in vice, but put Stead in prison for a year for writing about an indecent subject." Chafee, *Free Speech in the United States* (Cambridge, Mass.: Harvard University Press, 1941), p. 151.

[37] Longino, "Pornography, Oppression, and Freedom," in *Take Back the Night*, p. 50.

[38] Given that First Amendment doctrine is the result of little more than fifty years of Court discussion, it is not surprising that the law of defamation needs sharpening.

*vidual* life and limb. Thus the discovery of an adequate defense for groups against defamation must cope not only with many technical impediments but with the customary refusal of American law to appreciate the role of groups in the social process.[39]

One thing seems clear: legal theorists are not likely to turn to the criminal law to forge a group-libel doctrine. Those who tried this tack embarrassed themselves by modeling group-libel statutes on seditious libel statutes. This was a strategic error, because the First Amendment was drafted and adopted by men who were reacting against the English common law of seditious libel. They were deeply disturbed that persons could be punished, as they were in England, for

> the intention of (1) exciting disaffection, hatred, or contempt against the sovereign, or the government and constitution of the kingdom, or either house of parliament, or the administration of justice, *or* (2) exciting his majesty's subjects to attempt, otherwise than by lawful means, the alteration of any matter in church or state by law established, *or* (3) to promote feelings of ill will and hostility between different classes.[40]

And even if the word "intention" is deleted above, it still seems excessive to *punish* people for casting public aspersions on groups, especially powerful groups.

Consequently, the only salvation for the notion of group libel would seem to be the civil law. But two sources of difficulty have discouraged the courts from permitting let alone encouraging group libel suits: One is the feeling that no particular plaintiff can be hurt, or, if hurt, can show anything but the most speculative claim for damages. The other is the variety of procedural obstacles which are involved in actions by amorphous groups. And where liberalism has made its impact, the courts frequently express the fear that suits for group attacks would curb unduly the guarantees or needs for freedom of speech and of the press.[41]

The first difficulty is overcome by observing that in individual libel suits, the fact that the defendant did not know the plaintiff, or meant someone else, or a fictitious character, does not exculpate him; nor does the fact that he did not intend to injure the plaintiff.[42] Moreover, in such cases a showing of actual pecuniary damage is not a necessary ingredient of the action. The umbrella of a few *presumed* pecuniary items in lieu of some *actual* items is permitted by the courts to cover a large amount of mental anguish, embarrassment, and suffering of the defendant. So there is no reason why either proof of intent or proof of actual pecuniary damages would have to be a necessary ingredient in *group* libel suits.

The second difficulty is also dispelled but only by first articulating the mistaken assumptions upon which it rests. Where a group is large the courts guess that the plaintiff cannot possibly be hurt, simply as a member of the group. Salmond thought it obvious that "no action would lie at the suit of anyone for saying that all mankind is vicious and depraved, or even for alleging that all clergymen are hypocrites or all lawyers dishonest."[43] In part, his assumption is that as the number of the libelled group expands, the extravagance of the defendant's assertions will discredit him. But this is not necessarily so. To the extent they are believed, statements such as "all lawyers are dishonest" or "all cops are pigs" can cause harm to lawyers or policemen as a group, and derivatively to every individual lawyer or policeman. And the harm

---

[39]Reisman, "Democracy and Defamation," p. 734.

[40]Chafee, *Free Speech*, p. 506.

[41]Reisman, "Democracy and Defamation," pp. 767–8.

[42]See Prosser, *Handbook of the Law of Torts* (1941), p. 316 and following.

[43]John Salmond, *Torts; 7th Edition* (1928), p. 529.

caused to racial or ethnic minorities—to Blacks, to Jews, to Poles, to American Indians—as a result of systematic defamation is even more real; no member of these groups escapes some psychic or material hurt as a consequence of the attacks upon the groups with which he is voluntarily or involuntarily identified. "But," as David Riesman points out, "even if no reliable estimate could be obtained of the damages suffered by the plaintiff or his group as the result of what the defendant said, the courts could avoid the issue of compensation by awarding nominal damages, and, where warranted, punitive ones estimated not according to the plaintiff's hurt but with an eye to deterring the defendant and other potential offenders." Riesman goes on to suggest that "there is the possibility of injunction against substantial repetition of a suable wrong," and that such an injunction may be preferable to orchestrating and then proliferating complicated group suits.[44]

If Riesman is correct, then women may well have a case for civil suit or even injunctive relief against the public-dissemination of degrading thanatica. To be sure, the perils of "previous restraint" loom in the background. Following Blackstone, American courts have understood freedom of speech as meaning the absence of restraints on publication in advance as distinguished from civil or criminal liability for libelous matter when published.[45] But if what is to be said is known in advance and has been said many times before, the decision to apply a sanction before public dissemination does not seem so ominous. And since the plot and message of hard-core "porn" films (degrading thanatica) is all too predictable, by barring them from the marketplace no new truth will be lost, and women will be spared the psychic hurt and loss of esteem they suf-

fer as the result of the same sadistic message about sex, violence, and women being reiterated *ad nauseam*.

At this point it might be objected that in an analogous case, the proposed Nazi march in Skokie, the National Socialist Party ultimately won judicial permission to not only march in the predominantly Jewish community of Skokie but to wear their swastikas,[46] and this despite the fact that their message of anti-Semitism was all too familiar, their action "universally offensive," and their mode of presentation deliberately nonavoidable. Although the court did not deny "that the proposed demonstration would seriously disturb, emotionally and mentally, at least some, and probably many, of the village's residents,"[47] it nonetheless proclaimed that

> it is better to allow those who preach racial hate to expend their venom in rhetoric rather than [for us to] be panicked into embarking on the dangerous course of permitting the government to decide what its citizens may see and hear. . . . The ability of American Society to tolerate the advocacy even of the hateful doctrines espoused by the plaintiffs without abandoning its commitment to freedom of speech and assembly is perhaps the best protection we have against the establishment of any Nazi-type regime in this country.[48]

But what if the Nazis wanted to march every week in Skokie, or what if they systematically scheduled a march in a different Jewish community every weekend, or what if, as Susan Brownmiller speculates, "the bookstores and movie theaters lining Forty-second Street in New York City were devoted not to the humiliation of women by rape and torture, as they currently are, but

---

[44]Reisman, "Democracy and Defamation," p. 771.

[45]Blackstone, *Commentaries* 4 (1862), pp. 151–3.

[46]Cited in Nat Hentoff, *The First Freedom* (New York: Dell, 1980).

[47]Ibid., p. 322.

[48]Ibid.

to a systematized, commercially successful propaganda machine depicting the sadistic pleasures of gassing Jews or lynching blacks?"[49] Would not the courts reconsider their stance on democratic tolerance and the need to develop a position on mutual respect? After all, it is not as if the National Socialist Party could not get its anti-Semitic message across in ways that do not entail the intentional insult of Jews in what amounts to their own backyards. Democratic tolerance is, as D. A. J. Richards observed, an important civic virtue; but so too is mutual respect. If a constitutional democracy is to remain stable, both of these virtues have to be practiced. The one cannot be sacrificed for the other.

## CONCLUSION

If this paper makes any claim, it is that the Courts have not only failed to make the necessary distinction between erotica and thanatica, but to understand the precise harm that pornography presents. In its leading obscenity decisions the Supreme Court implied that erotica as well as thanatica are harmful, and that their harmful effects were likely to be felt in either the near or distant future. The Court determined that a state legislature could restrict publicly-disseminated pornographic material because it is reasonable to assume a probable connection between exposure to obscene material and subsequent anti-social behavior (rape, child-molestation, incest, and so on).[50] But as I have argued only one sort of pornography is harmful— namely thanatica—and it is harmful to women *now*. Unlike erotica, which may be offensive to some women, thanatica are harmful to all women to the degree that they are meant to degrade and defame females.

Admittedly, some women insist that they are not personally distressed, bothered, or otherwise hurt by thanatica. But the fact that some women are not *hurt* by thanatica does not mean that they are not *harmed* thereby. To be harmed is to have one's legitimate interests violated. To be hurt by such violations is to be painfully aware that one's legitimate interests have indeed been violated. There are times, however, when persons fail to realize that they have been harmed. In such instances, what they don't know literally can't hurt them. Joel Feinberg gives the example of a husband who is unaware of his wife's infidelity. What the cuckolded husband doesn't know isn't hurting him, but it certainly is harming him:

> An undetected adultery damages one of the victim's "interests in domestic relations," just as an unknown libelous publication can damage his interest in a good reputation, or an undetected trespass on his land can damage his interest in "the exclusive enjoyment and control" of that land.[51]

Similarly, even though some women are not hurt by thanatica, they are harmed since their interest in being perceived as persons worthy of respect is violated.

Nonetheless, because not all women are hurt by thanatica, it is probably best not to seek a legal remedy at this time. For now education through consciousness-raising may be the most acceptable way to curb publicly-disseminated thanatica. But if education proves ineffective and if *most* women begin to appreciate how thanatica harm them, then the solution may be to expand slander and libel doctrine to encompass pictorial as well as verbal and written modes of defamation.

Contrary to the opinion of some, the Constitution does not obdurately protect degrading stereotypes. If it did, defamation would be sanctioned by neither the criminal nor the civil law. As it stands, it is penalized

---

[49] Brownmiller, *Against Our Will*, p. 395.
[50] Roth v. United States, 354 U.S. at 485, citing Chaplinsky v. New Hampshire, 315 U.S. 568, 572 (1942).
[51] Joel Feinberg, *Social Philosophy* (Englewood Cliffs, N.J.: Prentice Hall Inc., 1973), p. 27.

by both; and there is nothing inherently unconstitutional about group-libel doctrine or civil suits aimed at impeding the flow of publicly-disseminated thanatica. Admittedly, the crucial gains in respect cannot be secured by legal remedies alone. Stopping or slowing down thanatica will not automatically make women the equals of men, but when all other meaningful alternatives have been exhausted, a legal remedy seems preferable to none.

## QUESTIONS

1. Tong claims that "thanatica are harmful to all women to the degree that they are meant to degrade and defame females." Does this mean that the intention with which pornography (or thanatica) is produced and sold is itself what makes the material harmful? If not, then give an alternative explanation of what Tong means by this. If you think that this is its meaning, explain how the very intention itself can make harmful that which would otherwise be harmless.

2. Tong says that "only one sort of pornography is harmful—namely thanatica." How does one support this claim? How does Tong support it? Though Tong characterizes (or *defines*) erotica as having the "message" of "enjoyment," is this sufficient to guarantee that erotica are not, as a matter of fact, harmful?

3. What are Tong's reasons for holding that there should not yet be legal penalties for producing and selling thanatica, even though thanatica harm all women? Do you agree with this reasoning?

4. Explain as best you can how, in a view like Tong's, thanatica harm women, remembering that, according to Tong: (1) all women are harmed by thanatica; (2) some women are neither hurt nor offended by such materials; (3) their harmfulness depends on the degree to which they were meant to be degrading.

# Paternalism

## *Gerald Dworkin*
# PATERNALISM*

Neither one person, nor any number of persons, is warranted in saying to another human creature of ripe years, that he shall not do with his life for his own benefit what he chooses to do with it. *Mill*

I do not want to go along with a volunteer basis. I think a fellow should be compelled to become better and not let him use his discretion whether he wants to get smarter, more healthy or more honest. *General Hershey*

I take as my starting point the "one very simple principle" proclaimed by Mill in *On Liberty* . . . "That principle is, that the sole end for which mankind are warranted, individually or collectively, in interfering with the liberty of action of any of their number, is self-protection. That the only purpose for which power can be rightfully exercised over any member of a civilized community, against his will, is to prevent harm to others. He cannot rightfully be compelled to do or forbear because it will be better for him to do so, because it will make him happier, because, in the opinion of others, to do so would be wise, or even right."[1]

This principle is neither "one" nor "very simple." It is at least two principles; one asserting that self-protection or the prevention of harm to others is sometimes a sufficient warrant and the other claiming that the individual's own good is *never* a sufficient warrant for the exercise of compulsion either by the society as a whole or by its individual members. I assume that no one with the possible exception of extreme pacifists or anarchists questions the correctness of the first half of the principle. This essay is an examination of the negative claim embodied in Mill's principle—the objection to paternalistic interferences with a man's liberty.

## I

By paternalism I shall understand roughly the interference with a person's liberty of action justified by reasons referring exclusively to the welfare, good, happiness, needs, interests or values of the person being coerced. One is always well-advised to illustrate one's definitions by examples but it is not easy to find "pure" examples of paternalistic interferences. For almost any piece of legislation is justified by several different kinds of reasons and even if historically a piece of legislation can be shown to have been introduced for, purely paternalistic motives, it may be that advocates of the legislation with an anti-paternalistic outlook can find sufficient reasons justifying the legislation without appealing to the reasons which were originally adduced to support it. Thus, for example, it may be that the original legislation requiring motorcyclists to wear safety helmets was introduced for purely paternalistic reasons. But the Rhode Island Supreme Court recently upheld such legislation on the grounds that it was "not persuaded that the legislature is powerless to prohibit individuals from pursuing a course of conduct which could conceivably result in their becoming public charges," thus clearly introducing reasons of a quite different kind. Now I regard this decision as being based on reasoning of a very dubious nature but it illustrates the kind of problem one has in finding examples. The following is a list of the kinds of interferences I have in mind as being paternalistic.

*Copyright © 1972, *The Monist*, La Salle, Illinois 61301. Reprinted by permission.
[1]J. S. Mill, *Utilitarianism* and *On Liberty* (Fonatana Library Edition, ed. by Mary Warnock, London, 1962), p. 135. All further quotes from Mill are from this edition unless otherwise noted.

## II

1. Laws requiring motorcyclists to wear safety helmets when operating their machines.
2. Laws forbidding persons from swimming at a public beach when lifeguards are not on duty.
3. Laws making suicide a criminal offense.
4. Laws making it illegal for women and children to work at certain types of jobs.
5. Laws regulating certain kinds of sexual conduct, e.g. homosexuality among consenting adults in private.
6. Laws regulating the use of certain drugs which may have harmful consequences to the user but do not lead to anti-social conduct.
7. Laws requiring a license to engage in certain professions with those not receiving a license subject to fine or jail sentence if they do engage in the practice.
8. Laws compelling people to spend a specified fraction of their income on the purchase of retirement annuities. (Social Security)
9. Laws forbidding various forms of gambling (often justified on the grounds that the poor are more likely to throw away their money on such activities than the rich who can afford to).
10. Laws regulating the maximum rates of interest for loans.
11. Laws against duelling.

In addition to laws which attach criminal or civil penalties to certain kinds of action there are laws, rules, regulations, decrees, which make it either difficult or impossible for people to carry out their plans and which are also justified on paternalistic grounds. Examples of this are:

1. Laws regulating the types of contracts which will be upheld as valid by the courts, e.g. (an example of Mill's to which I shall return) no man may make a valid contract for perpetual involuntary servitude.
2. Not allowing as a defense to a charge of murder or assault the consent of the victim.
3. Requiring members of certain religious sects to have compulsory blood transfusions. This is made possible by not allowing the patient to have recourse to civil suits for assault and battery and by means of injunctions.
4. Civil commitment procedures when these are specifically justified on the basis of preventing the person being committed from harming himself. (The D.C. Hospitalization of the Mentally Ill Act provides for involuntary hospitalization of a person who "is mentally ill, and because of that illness, is likely to injure *himself* or others if allowed to remain at liberty." The term injure in this context applies to unintentional as well as intentional injuries.)
5. Putting fluorides in the community water supply.

All of my examples are of existing restrictions on the liberty of individuals. Obviously one can think of interferences which have not yet been imposed. Thus one might ban the sale of cigarettes, or require that people wear safety-belts in automobiles (as opposed to merely having them installed) enforcing this by not allowing motorists to sue for injuries even when caused by other drivers if the motorist was not wearing a seat-belt at the time of the accident.

I shall not be concerned with activities which though defended on paternalistic grounds are not interferences with the liberty of persons, e.g. the giving of subsidies in kind rather than in cash on the grounds that the recipients would not spend the money on the goods which they really need, or not including a $1000 deductible provision in a basic protection automobile insurance plan on the ground that the people who would elect it could least afford it. Nor shall I be concerned with measures such as "truth-in-advertising" acts and the Pure Food and Drug legislation which are often attacked as paternalistic but which should not be considered so. In these cases all that is provided—it is true by the use of compulsion—is information which it is presumed that rational persons are interested in having in order to make wise decisions. There is no interference with the liberty of the consumer unless one wants to stretch a point beyond good sense and say that his liberty to apply for a loan without knowing the true rate of interest is diminished. It is true that sometimes there is sentiment for going further than providing information, for example when laws against usurious interest are passed preventing those who might wish to contract loans at high rates of interest from doing so, and these measures may correctly be considered paternalistic.

## III

Bearing these examples in mind let me return to a characterization of paternalism. I said earlier that I meant by the term, roughly, interference with a person's liberty for his own good. But as some of the examples show the class of persons whose good is involved is not always identical with the class of person's whose freedom is restricted. Thus in the case of professional licensing it is the practitioner who is directly interfered with and it is the would-be patient whose interests are presumably being served. Not allowing the consent of the victim to be a defense to certain types of crime primarily affects the would-be aggressor but it is the interests of the willing victim that we are trying to protect. Sometimes a person may fall into both classes as would be the case if we banned the manufacture and sale of cigarettes and a given manufacturer happened to be a smoker as well.

Thus we may first divide paternalistic interferences into "pure" and "impure" cases. In "pure" paternalism the class of persons whose freedom is restricted is identical with the class of persons whose benefit is intended to be promoted by such restrictions. Examples: the making of suicide a crime, requiring passengers in automobiles to wear seat-belts, requiring a Christian Scientist to receive a blood transfusion. In the case of "impure" paternalism in trying to protect the welfare of a class of persons we find that the only way to do so will involve restricting the freedom of other persons besides those who are benefited. Now it might be thought that there are no cases of "impure" paternalism since any such case could always be justified on non-paternalistic grounds, i.e. in terms of preventing harms to others. Thus we might ban cigarette manufacturers from continuing to manufacture their product on the grounds that we are preventing them from causing illness to others in the same way that we prevent other manufacturers from releasing pollutants into the atmosphere, thereby causing danger to the members of the community. The difference is, however, that in the former but not the latter case the harm is of such a nature that it could be avoided by those individuals affected if they so chose. The incurring of the harm requires, so to speak, the active co-operation of the victim. It would be mistaken theoretically and hypocritical in practice to assert that our interference in such cases is just like our interference in standard cases of protecting others from harm. At the very least someone interfered with in this way can reply that no one is complaining about his activities. It may be that impure paternalism requires arguments or reasons of a stronger kind in order to be justified since there are persons who are losing a portion of their liberty and they do not even have the solace of having it be done "in their own interest." Of course in some sense, if paternalistic justifications are ever correct then we are protecting others, we are preventing some from injuring others, but it is important to see the differences between this and the standard case.

Paternalism then will always involve limitations on the liberty of some individuals in their own interest but it may also extend to interferences with the liberty of parties whose interests are not in question.

## IV

Finally, by way of some more preliminary analysis, I want to distinguish paternalistic interferences with liberty from a related type with which it is often confused. Consider, for example, legislation which forbids employees to work more than, say, 40 hours per week. It is sometimes argued that such legislation is paternalistic for if employees desired such a restriction on their hours of work they could agree among themselves to impose it voluntarily. But because they do not the society imposes its own conception of their best interests upon them by the use of coercion. Hence this is paternalism.

Now it may be that some legislation of this nature is, in fact, paternalistically motivated. I am not denying that. All I want to point out is that there is another possible way of justifying such measures which is not paternalistic in nature. It is not paternalistic because as Mill puts it in a similar context such measures are "required not to overrule the judgment of individuals respecting their own interest, but to give effect to that judgment: they being unable to give effect to it except by concert, which concert again cannot be effectual unless it receives validity and sanction from the law."[2]

The line of reasoning here is a familiar one first found in Hobbes and developed with great sophistication by contemporary economists in the last decade or so. There are restrictions which are in the interests of a class of persons taken collectively but are such that the immediate interest of each individual is furthered by his violating the rule when others adhere to it. In such cases the individuals involved may need the use of compulsion to give effect to their collective judgment of their own interest by guaranteeing each individual compliance by the others. In these cases compulsion is not used to achieve some benefit which is not recognized to be a benefit by those concerned, but rather because it is the only feasible means of achieving some benefit which *is* recognized as such by all concerned. This way of viewing matters provides us with another characterization of paternalism in general. Paternalism might be thought of as the use of coercion to achieve a good which is not recognized as such by those persons for whom the good is intended. Again while this formulation captures the heart of the matter—it is surely what Mill is objecting to in *On Liberty*—the matter is not always quite like that. For example when we force motorcyclists to wear helmets we are trying to promote a good—the protection of the person from injury—which is surely recognized by most of the individuals concerned. It is not that a cyclist doesn't value his bodily integrity; rather, as a supporter of such legislation would put it, he either places, perhaps irrationally, another value or good (freedom from wearing a helmet) above that of physical well-being or, perhaps, while recognizing the danger in the abstract, he either does not fully appreciate it or he under-estimates the likelihood of its occurring. But now we are approaching the question of possible justifications of paternalistic measures and the rest of this essay will be devoted to that question.

## V

I shall begin for dialectical purposes by discussing Mill's objections to paternalism and then go on to discuss more positive proposals.

---

[2] J. S. Mill, *Principles of Political Economy* (New York: P.F. Collier and Sons, 1900), p. 442.

An initial feature that strikes one is the absolute nature of Mill's prohibitions against paternalism. It is so unlike the carefully qualified admonitions of Mill and his fellow Utilitarians on other moral issues. He speaks of self-protection as the *sole* end warranting coercion, of the individuals own goals as *never* being a sufficient warrant. Contrast this with his discussion of the prohibition against lying in *Util*.

> Yet that even this, rule, sacred as it is, admits of possible exception, is acknowledged by all moralists, the chief of which is where the with-holding of some fact . . . would save an individual . . . from great and unmerited evil.[3]

The same tentativeness is present when he deals with justice.

> It is confessedly unjust to break faith with any one: to violate an engagement, either express or implied, or disappoint expectations raised by our own conduct, at least if we have raised these expectations knowingly and voluntarily. Like all the other obligations of justice already spoken of, this one is not regarded as absolute, but as capable of being overruled by a stronger obligation of justice on the other side.[4]

This anomaly calls for some explanation. The structure of Mill's argument is as follows:

1. Since restraint is an evil the burden of proof is on those who propose such restraint.
2. Since the conduct which is being considered is purely self-regarding, the normal appeal to the protection of the interests of others is not available.

3. Therefore we have to consider whether reasons involving reference to the individuals own good, happiness, welfare, or interests are sufficient to overcome the burden of justification.
4. We either cannot advance the interests of the individual by compulsion, or the attempt to do so involves evil which outweigh the good done.
5. Hence the promotion of the individual's own interests does not provide a sufficient warrant for the use of compulsion.

Clearly the operative premise here is (4) and it is bolstered by claims about the status of the individual as judge and appraiser of his welfare, interests, needs, etc.

> With respect to his own feelings and circumstances, the most ordinary man or woman has means of knowledge immeasurably surpassing those that can be possessed by any one else.[5]
> He is the man most interested in his own well-being: the interest which any other person, except in cases of strong personal attachment, can have in it, is trifling, compared to that which he himself has.[6]

These claims are used to support the following generalizations concerning the utility of compulsion for paternalistic purposes.

> The interferences of society to overrule his judgment and purposes in what only regards himself must be grounded on general presumptions; which may be altogether wrong, and even if right, are as likely as not to be misapplied to individual cases.[7]
> But the strongest of all the arguments against the interference of the public with

---

[3] Mill, *Utilitarianism* and *On Liberty*, p. 174.
[4] *Ibid.*, p. 299.
[5] *Ibid.*, p. 207.
[6] *Ibid.*, p. 206.
[7] *Ibid.*, p. 207.

purely personal conduct is that when it does interfere, the odds are that it interferes wrongly and in the wrong place.[8]

All errors which the individual is likely to commit against advice and warning are far outweighed by the evil of allowing others to constrain him to what they deem his good.[9]

Performing the utilitarian calculation by balancing the advantages and disadvantages we find that:

> Mankind are greater gainers by suffering each other to live as seems good to themselves, than by compelling each other to live as seems good to the rest.[10]

From which follows the operative premise (4).

This classical case of a utilitarian argument with all the premises spelled out is not the only line of reasoning present in Mill's discussion. There are asides, and more than asides, which look quite different and I shall deal with them later. But this is clearly the main channel of Mill's thought and it is one which has been subjected to vigorous attack from the moment it appeared—most often by fellow Utilitarians. The link that they have usually seized on is, as Fitzjames Stephen put it, the absence of proof that the "mass of adults are so well acquainted with their own interests and so much disposed to pursue them that no compulsion or restraint put upon them by any others for the purpose of promoting their interest can really promote them."[11] Even so sympathetic a critic as Hart is forced to the conclusion that:

In Chapter 5 of his essay Mill carried his protests against paternalism to lengths that may now appear to us as fantastic. . . . No doubt if we no longer sympathise with this criticism this is due, in part, to a general decline in the belief that individuals know their own interest best.[12]

Mill endows the average individual with "too much of the psychology of a middle-aged man whose desires are relatively fixed, not liable to be artificially stimulated by external influences; who knows what he wants and what gives him satisfaction of happiness; and who pursues these things when he can."[13]

Now it is interesting to note that Mill himself was aware of some of the limitations on the doctrine that the individual is the best judge of his own interests. In his discussion of government intervention in general (even where the intervention does not interfere with liberty but provides alternative institutions to those of the market) after making claims which are parallel to those just discussed, e.g.

> People understand their own business and their own interests better, and care for them more, than the government does, or can be expected to do.[14]

He goes on to an intelligent discussion of the "very large and conspicuous exceptions" to the maxim that:

> Most persons take a juster and more intelligent view of their own interest, and of the

[8] Ibid., p. 214.

[9] Ibid., p. 207.

[10] Ibid., p. 138.

[11] J. F. Stephen, *Liberty, Equality, Fraternity* (New York: Henry Holt & Co., n.d.), p. 24.

[12] H. L. A. Hart, *Law, Liberty and Morality* (Stanford: Stanford University Press, 1963), p. 32.

[13] Ibid., p. 33.

[14] Mill, *Principles*, II, 448.

means of promoting it than can either be prescribed to them by a general enactment of the legislature, or pointed out in the particular case by a public functionary.[15]

Thus there are things

of which the utility does not consist in ministering to inclinations, nor in serving the daily uses of life, and the want of which is least felt where the need is greatest. This is peculiarly true of those things which are chiefly useful as tending to raise the character of human beings. The uncultivated cannot be competent judges of cultivation. Those who most need to be made wiser and better, usually desire it least, and, if they desired it, would be incapable of finding the way to it by their own lights.
. . . A second exception to the doctrine that individuals are the best judges of their own interest, is when an individual attempts to decide irrevocably now what will be best for his interest at some future and distant time. The presumption in favor of individual judgment is only legitimate, where the judgment is grounded on actual, and especially on present, personal experience; not where it is formed antecedently to experience, and not suffered to be reversed even after experience has condemned it.[16]

The upshot of these exceptions is that Mill does not declare that there should never be government interference with the economy but rather that

. . . in every instance, the burden of making out a strong case should be thrown not on those who resist but on those who recommend government interference. Letting alone, in short, should be the general practice:

every departure from it, unless required by some great good, is a certain evil.[17]

In short, we get a presumption not an absolute prohibition. The question is why doesn't the argument against paternalism go the same way?

I suggest that the answer lies in seeing that in addition to a purely utilitarian argument Mill uses another as well. As a Utilitarian Mill has to show, in Fitzjames Stephen's words, that:

Self-protection apart, no good object can be attained by any compulsion which is not in itself a greater evil than the absence of the object which the compulsion obtains.[18]

To show this is impossible; one reason being that it isn't true. Preventing a man from selling himself into slavery (a paternalistic measure which Mill himself accepts as legitimate), or from taking heroin, or from driving a car without wearing seat-belts may constitute a lesser evil than allowing him to do any of these things. A consistent Utilitarian can only argue against paternalism on the grounds that it (as a matter of fact) does not maximize the good. It is always a contingent question that may be refuted by the evidence. But there is also a non-contingent argument which runs through *On Liberty*. When Mill states that "there is a part of the life of every person who has come to years of discretion, within which the individuality of that person ought to reign uncontrolled either by any other person or by the public collectively" he is saying something about what it means to be a person, an autonomous agent. It is because coercing a person for his own good denies this status as an independent entity that Mill objects to it so strongly and in such absolute terms. To

[15] *Ibid.*, II, 458.
[16] *Ibid.*, II, 459.
[17] *Ibid.*, II, 451.
[18] Stephen, p. 49.

be able to choose is a good that is independent of the wisdom of what is chosen. A man's "mode of laying out his existence is the best, not because it is the best in itself, but because it is his own mode."[19]

> It is the privilege and proper condition of a human being, arrived at the maturity of his faculties, to use and interpret experience in his own way.[20]

As further evidence of this line of reasoning in Mill consider the one exception to his prohibition against paternalism.

> In this and most civilised countries, for example, an engagement by which a person should sell himself, or allow himself to be sold, as a slave, would be null and void; neither enforced by law nor by opinion. The ground for thus limiting his power of voluntarily disposing of his own lot in life, is apparent, and is very clearly seen in this extreme case. The reason for not interfering, unless for the sake of others, with a person's voluntary acts, is consideration for his liberty. His voluntary choice is evidence that what he so chooses is desirable, or at least endurable, to him, and his good is on the whole best provided for by allowing him to take his own means of pursuing it. But by selling himself for a slave, he abdicates his liberty; he foregoes any future use of it beyond that single act.
>
> He therefore defeats, in his own case, the very purpose which is the justification of allowing him to dispose of himself. He is no longer free; but is thenceforth in a position which has no longer the presumption in its favour, that would be afforded by his voluntarily remaining in it. The principle of freedom cannot require that he should be free not to be free. It is not freedom to be allowed to alienate his freedom.[21]

Now leaving aside the fudging on the meaning of freedom in the last line it is clear that part of this argument is incorrect. While it is true that *future* choices of the slave are not reasons for thinking that what he chooses then is desirable for him, what is at issue is limiting his immediate choice; and since this choice is made freely, the individual may be correct in thinking that his interests are best provided for by entering such a contract. But the main consideration for not allowing such a contract is the need to preserve the liberty of the person to make future choices. This gives us a principle—a very narrow one—by which to justify some paternalistic interferences. Paternalism is justified only to preserve a wider range of freedom for the individual in question. How far this principle could be extended, whether it can justify all the cases in which we are inclined upon reflection to think paternalistic measures justified remains to be discussed. What I have tried to show so far is that there are two strains of argument in Mill—one a straightforward Utilitarian mode of reasoning and one which relies not on the goods which free choice leads to but on the absolute value of the choice itself. The first cannot establish any absolute prohibition but at most a presumption and indeed a fairly weak one given some fairly plausible assumptions about human psychology; the second while a stronger line of argument seems to me to allow on its own grounds a wider range of paternalism than might be suspected. I turn now to a consideration of these matters.

## VI

We might begin looking for principles governing the acceptable use of paternalistic power in cases where it is generally agreed that it is legitimate. Even Mill intends his principles to be applicable only to mature individuals, not

[19] Mill, *Utilitarianism* and *On Liberty*, p. 197.
[20] *Ibid.*, p. 186.
[21] *Ibid.*, pp. 235–236.

those in what he calls "non-age". What is it that justifies us in interfering with children? The fact that they lack some of the emotional and cognitive capacities required in order to make fully rational decisions. It is an empirical question to just what extent children have an adequate conception of their own present and future interests but there is not much doubt that there are many deficiencies. For example it is very difficult for a child to defer gratification for any considerable period of time. Given these deficiencies and given the very real and permanent dangers that may befall the child it becomes not only permissible but even a duty of the parent to restrict the child's freedom in various ways. There is however an important moral limitation on the exercise of such parental power which is provided by the notion of the child eventually coming to see the correctness of his parent's interventions. Parental paternalism may be thought of as a wager by the parent on the child's subsequent recognition of the wisdom of the restrictions. There is an emphasis on what could be called future-oriented consent—on what the child will come to welcome, rather than on what he does welcome.

The essence of this idea has been incorporated by idealist philosophers into various types of "real-will" theory as applied to fully adult persons. Extensions of paternalism are argued for by claiming that in various respects, chronologically mature individuals share the same deficiencies in knowledge, capacity to think rationally, and the ability to carry out decisions that children possess. Hence in interfering with such people we are in effect doing what they would do if they were fully rational. Hence we are not really opposing their will, hence we are not really interfering with their freedom. The dangers of this move have been sufficiently exposed by Berlin in his Two Concepts of Liberty. I see no gain in theoretical clarity nor in practical advantage in trying to pass over the real nature of the interferences with liberty that we impose on others. Still the basic notion of consent is important and seems to me the

only acceptable way of trying to delimit an area of justified paternalism.

Let me start by considering a case where the consent is not hypothetical in nature. Under certain conditions it is rational for an individual to agree that others should force him to act in ways in which, at the time of action, the individual may not see as desirable. If, for example, a man knows that he is subject to breaking his resolves when temptation is present, he may ask a friend to refuse to entertain his requests at some later stage.

A classical example is given in the Odyssey when Odysseus commands his men to tie him to the mast and refuse all future orders to be set free, because he knows the power of the Sirens to enchant men with their songs. Here we are on relatively sound ground in later refusing Odysseus' request to be set free. He may even claim to have changed his mind but since it is just such changes that he wished to guard against we are entitled to ignore them.

A process analogous to this may take place on a social rather than individual basis. An electorate may mandate its representatives to pass legislation which when it comes time to "pay the price" may be unpalatable. I may believe that a tax increase is necessary to halt inflation though I may resent the lower pay check each month. However in both this case and that of Odysseus the measure to be enforced is specifically requested by the party involved and at some point in time there is genuine consent and agreement on the part of those persons whose liberty is infringed. Such is not the case for the paternalistic measures we have been speaking about. What must be involved here is not consent to specific measures but rather consent to a system of government, run by elected representatives, with an understanding that they may act to safeguard our interests in certain limited ways.

I suggest that since we are all aware of our irrational propensities, deficiencies in cognitive and emotional capacities and avoidable and unavoidable ignorance it is rational and prudent for us to in effect take out "social insurance policies". We may argue for and against proposed paternalistic measures in terms of what fully rational individuals would accept as forms of protection. Now, clearly since the initial agreement is not about specific measures we are dealing with a more-or-less blank check and therefore there have to be carefully defined limits. What I am looking for are certain kinds of conditions which make it plausible to suppose that rational men could reach agreement to limit their liberty even when other men's interests are not affected.

Of course as in any kind of agreement schema there are great difficulties in deciding what rational individuals would or would not accept. Particularly in sensitive areas of personal liberty, there is always a danger of the dispute over agreement and rationality being a disguised version of evaluative and normative disagreement.

Let me suggest types of situations in which it seems plausible to suppose that fully rational individuals would agree to having paternalistic restrictions imposed upon them. It is reasonable to suppose that there are "goods" such as health which any person would want to have in order to pursue his own good—no matter how that good is conceived. This is an argument that is used in connection with compulsory education for children but it seems to me that it can be extended to other goods which have this character. Then one could agree that the attainment of such goods should be promoted even when not recognized to be such, at the moment, by the individuals concerned.

An immediate difficulty that arises stems from the fact that men are always faced with competing goods and that there may be reasons why even a value such as health—or indeed life—may be overridden by competing values. Thus the problem with the Christian Scientist and blood transfusions. It may be more important for him to reject "impure substances" than to go on living. The difficult problem that must be faced is whether one can give sense to the notion of a person irrationally attaching weights to competing values.

Consider a person who knows the statistical data on the probability of being injured when not wearing seat belts in an automobile and knows the types and gravity of the various injuries. He also insists that the inconvenience attached to fastening the belt every time he gets in and out of the car outweighs for him the possible risks to himself. I am inclined in this case to think that such a weighing is irrational. Given his life-plans which we are assuming are those of the average person, his interests and commitments already undertaken, I think it is safe to predict that we can find inconsistencies in his calculations at some point. I am assuming that this is not a man who for some conscious or unconscious reasons is trying to injure himself nor is he a man who just likes to "live dangerously". I am assuming that he is like us in all the relevant respects but just puts an enormously high negative value on inconvenience—one which does not seem comprehensible or reasonable.

It is always possible, of course to assimilate this person to creatures like myself. I, also, neglect to fasten my seat belt and I concede such behavior is not rational but not because I weigh the inconvenience differently from those who fasten the belts. It is just that having made (roughly) the same calculation as everybody else I ignore it in my actions. [Note: a much better case of weakness of the will than those usually given in ethics texts.] A plausible explanation for this deplorable habit is that although I know in some intellectual sense what the probabilities and risks are I do not fully appreciate them in an emotionally genuine manner.

We have two distinct types of situation in which a man acts in a non-rational fashion. In one case he attaches incorrect weights to some of his values; in the other he neglects to act in accordance with his actual preferences and desires. Clearly there is a stronger and more persuasive argument for paternalism in the latter situation. Here we are really not—by assumption—imposing a good on another person. But why may we not extend our interference to what we might call evaluative delusions? After all in the case of cognitive delusions we are prepared, often, to act against the expressed will of the person involved. If a man believes that when he jumps out the window he will float upwards—Robert Nozick's example—would not we detain him, forcibly if necessary? The reply will be that this man doesn't wish to be injured and if we could convince him that he is mistaken as to the consequences of his action he would not wish to perform the action. But part of what is involved in claiming that a man who doesn't fasten his seat-belts is attaching an irrational weight to the inconvenience of fastening them is that if he were to be involved in an accident and severely injured he would look back and admit that the inconvenience wasn't as bad as all that. So there is a sense in which if I could convince him of the consequences of his action he also would not wish to continue his present course of action. Now the notion of consequences being used here is covering a lot of ground. In one case it's being used to indicate what will or can happen as a result of a course of action and in the other it's making a prediction about the future evaluation of the consequences—in the first sense—of a course of action. And whatever the difference between facts and values—whether it be hard and fast or soft and slow—we are genuinely more reluctant to consent to interferences where evaluative differences are the issue. Let me now consider another factor which comes into play in some of these situations which may make an important difference in our willingness to consent to paternalistic restrictions.

Some of the decisions we make are of such a character that they produce changes which are in one or another way irreversible. Situations are created in which it is difficult or impossible to return to anything like the initial stage at which the decision was made. In particular some of these changes will make it impossible to continue to make reasoned choices in the future. I am thinking specifically of decisions which involve taking drugs that are physically or psychologically addictive and those which are destructive of one's mental and physical capacities.

I suggest we think of the imposition of paternalistic interferences in situations of this kind as being a kind of insurance policy which we take out against making decisions which are far-reaching, potentially dangerous and irreversible. Each of these factors is important. Clearly there are many decisions we make that are relatively irreversible. In deciding to learn to play chess I could predict in view of my general interest in games that some portion of my free-time was going to be pre-empted and that it would not be easy to give up the game once I acquired a certain competence. But my whole life-style was not going to be jeopardized in an extreme manner. Further it might be argued that even with addictive drugs such as heroin one's normal life plans would not be seriously interfered with if an inexpensive and adequate supply were readily available. So this type of argument might have a much narrower scope than appears to be the case at first.

A second class of cases concerns decisions which are made under extreme psychological and sociological pressures. I am not thinking here of the making of the decision as being something one is pressured into— e.g. a good reason for making duelling illegal is that unless this is done many people might have to manifest their courage and integrity in ways in which they would rather not do so—but rather of decisions such as that to commit suicide which are usually made at a point where the individual is not thinking clearly and calmly about the nature of his decision. In addition, of course, this comes under the previous heading of all-too-irrevocable decision. Now there are practical steps which a society could take if it wanted to decrease the possibility of suicide—for example, not paying social security benefits to the survivors or as religious institutions do, not allowing such persons to be buried with the same status as natural deaths. I think we may count these as interferences with the liberty of persons to attempt suicide and the question is whether they are justifiable.

Using my argument schema the question is whether rational individuals would consent to such limitations. I see no reason for them to consent to an absolute prohibition- but I do think it is reasonable for them to agree to some kind of enforced waiting period. Since we are all aware of the possibility of temporary states, such as great fear or depression, that are inimical to the making of well-informed and rational decsions, it wouldbe prudent for all of us if there were some kind of institutional arrangement whereby we were restrained from making a decision which is (all too) irreversible. What this would be like in practice is difficult to envisage and it may be that if no practical arrangements were feasible then we would have to conclude that there should be no restriction at all on this kind of action. But we might have a "cooling off" period, in much the same way that we now require couples who file for divorce to go through a waiting period. Or, more far-fetched, we might imagine a Suicide Board composed of a psychologist and another member picked by the applicant. The Board would be required to meet and talk with the person proposing to take his life, though its approval would not be required.

A third class of decisions—these classes are not supposed to be disjoint—involves dangers which are either not sufficiently understood or appreciated correctly by the persons involved. Let me illustrate, using the example of cigarette smoking, a number of possible cases.

1. A man may not know the facts—e.g. smoking between 1 and 2 packs a day shortens life expectancy 6.2 years, the costs and pain of the illness caused by smoking, etc.

2. A man may know the facts, wish to stop smoking, but not have the requisite will-power.

3. A man may know the facts but not have them play the correct role in his calculation because, say, he discounts the danger psychologically because it is remote in time and/or inflates the attractiveness of other consequences of his decision which he regards as beneficial.

In case 1 what is called for is education, the posting of warnings, etc. In case 2 there is no theoretical problem. We are not imposing a good on someone who rejects it. We are simply using coercion to enable people to carry out their own goals. (Note: There obviously is a difficulty in that only a subclass of the individuals affected wish to be prevented from doing what they are doing.) In case 3 there is a sense in which we are imposing a good on someone since given his current appraisal of the facts he doesn't wish to be restricted. But in another sense we are not imposing a good since what is being claimed—and what must be shown or at least argued for—is that an accurate accounting on his part would lead him to reject his current course of action. Now we all know that such cases exist, that we are prone to disregard dangers that are only possibilities, that immediate pleasures are often magnified and distorted.

If in addition the dangers are severe and far-reaching we could agree to allowing the state a certain degree of power to intervene in such situations. The difficulty is in specifying in advance, even vaguely, the class of cases in which intervention will be legitimate.

A related difficulty is that of drawing a line so that it is not the case that all ultra-hazardous activities are ruled out, e.g. mountain-climbing, bull-fighting, sports-car racing, etc. There are some risks—even very great ones— which a person is entitled to take with his life.

A good deal depends on the nature of the deprivation—e.g. does it prevent the person from engaging in the activity completely or merely limit his participation—and how important to the nature of the activity is the absence of restriction when this is weighed against the role that the activity plays in the life of the person. In the case of automobile seat belts, for example, the restriction is trivial in nature, interferes not at all with the use or enjoyment of the activity, and does, I am assuming, considerably reduce a high risk of serious injury. Whereas, for example, making mountain climbing illegal prevents completely a person engaging in an activity which may play an important role in his life and his conception of the person he is.

In general the easiest cases to handle are those which can be argued about in the terms which Mill thought to be so important—a concern not just for the happiness or welfare, in some broad sense, of the individual but rather a concern for the autonomy and freedom of the person. I suggest that we would be most likely to consent to paternalism in those instances in which it preserves and enhances for the individual his ability to rationally consider and carry out his own decisions.

I have suggested in this essay a number of types of situations in which it seems plausible that rational men would agree to granting the legislative powers of a society the right to impose restrictions on what Mill calls "self-regarding" conduct. However, rational men knowing something about the resources of ignorance, ill-will and stupidity available to the law-makers of a society—a

good case in point is the history of drug legislation in the United States—will be concerned to limit such intervention to a minimum. I suggest in closing two principles designed to achieve this end.

In all cases of paternalistic legislation there must be a heavy and clear burden of proof placed on the authorities to demonstrate the exact nature of the harmful effects (or beneficial consequences) to be avoided (or achieved) and the probability of their occurrence. The burden of proof here is twofold—what lawyers distinguish as the burden of going forward and the burden of persuasion. That the authorities have the burden of going forward means that it is up to them to raise the question and bring forward evidence of the evils to be avoided. Unlike the case of new drugs where the manufacturer must produce some evidence that the drug has been tested and found not harmful, no citizen has to show with respect to self-regarding conduct that it is not harmful or promotes his best interests. In addition the nature and cogency of the evidence for the harmfulness of the course of action must be set at a high level. To paraphrase a formulation of the burden of proof for criminal proceedings—better 10 men ruin themselves than one man be unjustly deprived of liberty.

Finally I suggest a principle of the least restrictive alternative. If there is an alternative way of accomplishing the desired end without restricting liberty then although it may involve great expense, inconvenience, etc. the society must adopt it.

## QUESTIONS

1. Dworkin says that "part of what is involved in claiming that the man who doesn't fasten his seat-belts is attaching an incorrect weight to the inconvenience of fastening them is that if he were involved in an accident and severely injured he would look back and admit that the inconvenience wasn't as bad as all that." Do you agree with this statement as it stands? In particular, if he does have an accident, and he wishes he now had the chance to do it differently, does that show that he was attaching an incorrect weight to the inconvenience?

2. We have rules forbidding athletes from using steroids in preparation for athletic competitions. Yet if there were no such rules, many, if not most, athletes in certain high-level competitions would undoubtedly use them. Is this prohibition paternalism in Dworkin's sense?

3. Consider again the contract to sell oneself into slavery. If, in order to protect the ability to make free choices in the future, we decide to make such contracts unenforceable, does that involve taking away anyone's liberty? Compare that to a criminal prohibition forbidding one from doing something one is otherwise free to do.

4. A roulette wheel or other game of chance, even if fair, is openly designed to make the gambling house a net winner in the long run, with individual gamblers the net losers. Could one defend the claim that those who gamble are necessarily making a mistake about their own interests?

5. Could one plausibly argue that those who engage in dangerous sports like skydiving and hang gliding necessarily make mistakes in calculating their own good, and thus that their decisions to do these things are irrational?

6. Give your ranking of the desirability of the following three possibilities: (a) making legally compulsory the wearing of helmets while motorcycle riding, (b) compelling motorcycle riders to pay for insurance to cover the costs of injuries due to not wearing helmets, or (c) neither (a) nor (b), allowing the costs of injuries to fall on the injured.

7. Do you lose any of your autonomy when you (a) sell yourself into slavery? (b) join the military? (c) get married? (d) promise to take care of the neighbor's dog while your neighbor is out of town? Are there any differences in kind among (a) to (d), or are there only differences in degree?

## United States Supreme Court*
# CRUZAN v. DIRECTOR, MISSOURI DEPT. OF HEALTH

Chief Justice REHNQUIST delivered the opinion of the Court.

Petitioner Nancy Beth Cruzan was rendered incompetent as a result of severe injuries sustained during an automobile accident. Co-petitioners Lester and Joyce Cruzan, Nancy's parents and co-guardians, sought a court order directing the withdrawal of their daughter's artificial feeding and hydration equipment after it became apparent that she had virtually no chance of recovering her cognitive faculties. The Supreme Court of Missouri held that because there was no clear and convincing evidence of Nancy's desire to have life-sustaining treatment withdrawn under such circumstances, her parents lacked authority to effectuate such a request.

On the night of January 11, 1983, Nancy Cruzan lost control of her car as she traveled down Elm Road in Jasper County, Missouri. The vehicle overturned, and Cruzan was discovered lying face down in a ditch without detectable respiratory or cardiac function. Paramedics were able to restore her breathing and heartbeat at the accident site, and she was transported to a hospital in an unconscious state. An attending

*110 S. Ct. 2841 (1990). Numerous citations omitted without so specifying.

neurosurgeon diagnosed her as having sustained probable cerebral contusions compounded by significant anoxia (lack of oxygen). The Missouri trial court in this case found that permanent brain damage generally results after 6 minutes in an anoxic state; it was estimated that Cruzan was deprived of oxygen from 12 to 14 minutes. She remained in a coma for approximately three weeks and then progressed to an unconscious state in which she was able to orally ingest some nutrition. In order to ease feeding and further the recovery, surgeons implanted a gastrostomy feeding and hydration tube in Cruzan with the consent of her then husband. Subsequent rehabilitative efforts proved unavailing. She now lies in a Missouri state hospital in what is commonly referred to as a persistent vegetative state: generally, a condition in which a person exhibits motor reflexes but evinces no indications of significant cognitive function.

The State of Missouri is bearing the cost of her care.

After it had become apparent that Nancy Cruzan had virtually no chance of regaining her mental faculties her parents asked hospital employees to terminate the artificial nutrition and hydration procedures. All agree that such a removal would cause her death. The employees refused to honor the request without court approval. The parents then sought and received authorization from the state trial court for termination. The court found that a person in Nancy's condition had a fundamental right under the State and Federal Constitutions to refuse or direct the withdrawal of "death prolonging procedures." The court also found that Nancy's "expressed thoughts at age twenty-five in somewhat serious conversation with a housemate friend that if sick or injured she would not wish to continue her life unless she could live at least halfway normally suggests that given her present condition she would not wish to continue on with her nutrition and hydration."

The Supreme Court of Missouri reversed by a divided vote. The court recognized a right to refuse treatment embodied in the common-law doctrine of informed consent, but expressed skepticism about the application of that doctrine in the circumstances of this case. The court also declined to read a broad right of privacy into the State Constitution which would "support the right of a person to refuse medical treatment in every circumstance," and expressed doubt as to whether such a right existed under the United States Constitution. It then decided that the Missouri Living Will statute, Mo.Rev.Stat. § 459.010 *et seq.* (1986), embodied a state policy strongly favoring the preservation of life. The court found Cruzan's statements to her roommate regarding her desire to live or die under certain conditions were "unreliable for the purpose of determining her intent," "and thus insufficient to support the co-guardians claim to exercise substituted judgment on Nancy's behalf." It rejected the argument that Cruzan's parents were entitled to order the termination of her medical treatment, concluding that "no person can assume that choice for an incompetent in the absence of the formalities required under Missouri's Living Will statutes or the clear and convincing, inherently reliable evidence absent here." The court also expressed its view that "[b]road policy questions bearing on life and death are more properly addressed by representative assemblies" than judicial bodies.

We granted certiorari to consider the question of whether Cruzan has a right under the United States Constitution which would require the hospital to withdraw life-sustaining treatment from her under these circumstances.

At common law, even the touching of one person by another without consent and without legal justification was a battery. Before the turn of the century, this Court observed that "[n]o right is held more sacred, or is more carefully guarded, by the common law, than the right of every individual to the possession and control of his own person, free from all restraint or interference of others, unless by clear and unquestionable authority of law." *Union Pacific R. Co. v. Botsford*, 141 U.S. 250, 251. This notion of bodily integrity has been embodied in the requirement that informed consent is generally required for medical treatment. Justice Cardozo, while on the Court of Appeals of New York, aptly described this doctrine. "Every human being of adult years and sound mind has a right to determine what shall be done with his own body; and a surgeon who performs an operation without his patient's consent commits an assault, for which he is liable in damages." *Schloendorff v. Society of New York Hospital*, 211 N.Y. 125, 129–30, 105 N.E. 92, 93 (1914). The informed consent doctrine has become firmly entrenched in American tort law.

The logical corollary of the doctrine of informed consent is that the patient generally possesses the right not to consent, that is, to refuse treatment. Until about 15 years ago and the seminal decision in *In re Quinlan*, 70 N.J. 10, 355 A.2d 647, the number of right-to-refuse-treatment decisions were relatively few. Most of the earlier cases involved patients who refused medical treatment forbidden by their religious beliefs, thus implicating First Amendment rights as well as common law rights of self-determination. More recently, however, with the advance of medical technology capable of sustaining life well past the point where natural forces would have brought certain death in earlier times, cases involving the right to refuse life-sustaining treatment have burgeoned.

In the *Quinlan* case, young Karen Quinlan suffered severe brain damage as the result of anoxia, and entered a persistent vegetative state. Karen's father sought judicial approval to disconnect his daughter's respirator. The New Jersey Supreme Court granted the relief, holding that Karen had a right of privacy grounded in the Federal Constitution to terminate treatment. Recognizing this right was not absolute, however, the court balanced it against asserted state interests. Noting that the State's interest "weakens and the individual's right to privacy grows as the degree of bodily invasion increases and the prognosis dims," the court concluded that the state interests had to give way in that case. The court also concluded that the "only practical way" to prevent the loss of Karen's privacy right due to her incompetence was to allow her guardian and family to decide "whether she would exercise it in these circumstances."

After *Quinlan*, however, most courts have based a right to refuse treatment either solely on the common law right to informed consent or on both the common law right and a constitutional privacy right. See L. Tribe, *American Constitutional Law* § 15–11, p. 1365 (2d ed. 1988). In *Superintendent of Belchertown State School v. Saikewicz*, 373 Mass. 728, 370 N.E. 2d 417, the Supreme Judicial Court of Massachusetts relied on both the rights of privacy and the right of informed consent to permit the withholding of chemotherapy from a profoundly-retarded 67-year-old man suffering from leukemia. Reasoning that an incompetent person retains the same rights as a competent individual "because the value of human dignity extends to both," the court adopted a "substituted judgment" standard whereby courts were to determine what an incompetent individual's decision would have been under the circumstances. Distilling certain state interests from prior case law—the preservation of life, the protection of the interests of innocent third parties, the prevention of suicide, and the maintenance of the ethical integrity of the medical profession—the court recognized the first interest as paramount and noted it was greatest when an affliction was curable, "as opposed to the State interest where, as here, the issue is not whether, but when, for how long, and at what cost to the individual [a] life may be briefly extended."

In *In re Storar*, the New York Court of Appeals declined to base a right to refuse treatment on a constitutional privacy right. Instead, it found such a right "adequately supported" by the informed consent doctrine. In *In re Eichner* (decided with *In re Storar, supra*) an 83-year-old man who had suffered brain damage from anoxia entered a vegetative state and was thus incompetent to consent to the removal of his respirator. The court, however, found it unnecessary to reach the question of whether his rights could be exercised by others since it found the evidence clear and convincing from statements made by the patient when competent that he "did not want to be maintained in a vegetative coma by use of a respirator." In the companion *Storar* case, a 52-year-old man suffering from bladder cancer had been profoundly retarded during most of his life. Implicitly rejecting the approach taken in *Saikewicz, supra*, the court reasoned that due to such life-long incompetency, "it is unrealistic to attempt to determine whether he would want to continue potentially life prolonging treatment if he were competent." As the evidence showed that the patient's required blood transfusions did not involve excessive pain and without them his mental and physical abilities would deteriorate, the court concluded that it should not "allow an incompetent patient to bleed to death because someone, even someone as close as a parent or sibling, feels that this is best for one with an incurable disease."

Many of the later cases build on the principles established in *Quinlan, Saikewicz* and *Storar/Eichner*. For instance, in *In re Conroy*, the same court that decided *Quinlan* considered whether a nasogastric feeding tube could be removed from an 84-year-old incompetent nursing-home resident suffering irreversible mental and physical ailments. While recognizing that a federal right of privacy might apply in the case, the court, contrary to its approach in *Quinlan*, decided to base its decision on the common-law right to self-determination and informed consent. "On balance, the right to self-determination ordinarily outweighs any countervailing state interests, and competent persons generally are permitted to refuse medical treatment, even at the risk of death. Most of the cases that have held otherwise, unless they involved the interest in protecting innocent third parties, have concerned the patient's competency to make a rational and considered choice."

Reasoning that the right of self-determination should not be lost merely because an individual is unable to sense a violation of it, the court held that incompetent individuals retain a right to refuse treatment. It also held that such a right could be exercised by a surrogate decisionmaker using a "subjective" standard when there was clear evidence that the incompetent person would have exercised it. Where such evidence was lacking, the court held that an individual's right could still be invoked in certain circumstances under objective "best interest" standards. Thus, if some trustworthy evidence existed that the individual would have wanted to terminate treatment, but not enough to clearly establish a person's wishes for purposes of the subjective standard, and the burden of a prolonged life from the experience of pain and suffering markedly outweighed its satisfactions, treatment could be terminated under a "limited-objective" standard. Where no trustworthy evidence existed, and a person's suffering would make the administration of life-sustaining treatment inhumane, a "pure-objective" standard could be used to terminate treatment. If none of these conditions obtained, the court held it was best to err in favor of preserving life.

The court also rejected certain categorical distinctions that had been drawn in prior refusal-of-treatment cases as lacking substance for decision purposes: the distinction between actively hastening death by terminating treatment and passively allowing a person to die of a disease; between treating individuals as an initial matter versus withdrawing treatment afterwards; between ordinary versus extraordinary treatment; and between treatment by artificial feeding versus other forms of life-sustaining medical procedures. As to the last item, the court acknowledged the "emotional significance" of food, but noted that feeding by implanted tubes is a "medical procedur[e] with inherent risks and possible side effects, instituted by skilled healthcare providers to compensate for impaired physical functioning" which analytically was equivalent to artificial breathing using a respirator.

In contrast to *Conroy*, the Court of Appeals of New York recently refused to accept less than the clearly expressed wishes of a patient before permitting the exercise of her right to refuse treatment by a surrogate decision maker. There, the court, over the objection of the patient's family members, granted an order to insert a feeding tube into a 77-year-old woman rendered incompetent as a result of several strokes. While continuing to recognize a common-law right to refuse treatment, the court rejected the substituted judgment approach for asserting it "because it is inconsistent with our fundamental commitment to the notion that no person or court should substitute its judgment as to what would be an acceptable quality of life for another. Consequently, we adhere to the view that, despite its pitfalls and inevitable uncertainties, the inquiry must always be narrowed to the patient's expressed intent, with every effort made to minimize the opportunity for error." The court held that the record lacked the requisite clear and convincing evidence of the patient's expressed intent to withhold life-sustaining treatment.

Other courts have found state statutory law relevant to the resolution of these issues. In *Conservatorship of Drabick*, the California Court of Appeal authorized the removal of a nasogastric feeding tube from a 44-year-old man who was in a persistent vegetative state as a result of an auto accident. Noting

that the right to refuse treatment was grounded in both the common law and a constitutional right of privacy, the court held that a state probate statute authorized the patient's conservator to order the withdrawal of life-sustaining treatment when such a decision was made in good faith based on medical advice and the conservatee's best interests. While acknowledging that "to claim that [a patient's] 'right to choose' survives incompetence is a legal fiction at best," the court reasoned that the respect society accords to persons as individuals is not lost upon incompetence and is best preserved by allowing others "to make a decision that reflects [a patient's] interests more closely than would a purely technological decision to do whatever is possible." See also *In re Conservatorship of Torres*, 357 N. W. 2d 332 (Minn. 1984) (Minnesota court had constitutional and statutory authority to authorize a conservator to order the removal of an incompetent individual's respirator since in patient's best interests).

In *In re Estate of Longeway*, the Supreme Court of Illinois considered whether a 76-year-old woman rendered incompetent from a series of strokes had a right to the discontinuance of artificial nutrition and hydration. Noting that the boundaries of a federal right of privacy were uncertain, the court found a right to refuse treatment in the doctrine of informed consent. The court further held that the State Probate Act impliedly authorized a guardian to exercise a ward's right to refuse artificial sustenance in the event that the ward was terminally ill and irreversibly comatose. Declining to adopt a best interests standard for deciding when it would be appropriate to exercise a ward's right because it "lets another make a determination of a patient's quality of life," the court opted instead for a substituted judgment standard. Finding the "expressed intent" standard utilized in *O'Connor, supra,* too rigid, the court noted that other clear and convincing evidence of the patient's intent could be considered. The court also adopted the "consensus opinion [that] treats artificial nutrition and hydration as medical treatment.". . .

As these cases demonstrate, the common-law doctrine of informed consent is viewed as generally encompassing the right of a competent individual to refuse medical treatment. Beyond that, these decisions demonstrate both similarity and diversity in their approach to decision of what all agree is a perplexing question with unusually strong moral and ethical overtones. State courts have available to them for decision a number of sources—state constitutions, statutes, and common law—which are not available to us. In this Court, the question is simply and starkly whether the United States Constitution prohibits Missouri from choosing the rule of decision which it did. This is the first case in which we have been squarely presented with the issue of whether the United States Constitution grants what is in common parlance referred to as a "right to die." We follow the judicious counsel of our decision in *Twin City Bank v. Nebeker*, where we said that in deciding "a question of such magnitude and importance . . . it is the [better] part of wisdom not to attempt, by any general statement, to cover every possible phase of the subject."

[1] The Fourteenth Amendment provides that no State shall "deprive any person of life, liberty, or property, without due process of law." The principle that a competent person has a constitutionally protected liberty interest in refusing unwanted medical treatment may be inferred from our prior decisions. In *Jacobson v. Massachusetts*, for instance, the Court balanced an individual's liberty interest in declining an unwanted smallpox vaccine against the State's interest in preventing disease. Decisions prior to the incorporation of the Fourth Amendment into the Fourteenth

Amendment analyzed searches and seizures involving the body under the Due Process Clause and were thought to implicate substantial liberty interests.

Just this Term, in the course of holding that a State's procedures for administering antipsychotic medication to prisoners were sufficient to satisfy due process concerns, we recognized that prisoners possess "a significant liberty interest in avoiding the unwanted administration of antipsychotic drugs under the Due Process Clause of the Fourteenth Amendment." *Washington v. Harper*, ("The forcible injection of medication into a nonconsenting person's body represents a substantial interference with that person's liberty"). Still other cases support the recognition of a general liberty interest in refusing medical treatment.

But determining that a person has a "liberty interest" under the Due Process Clause does not end the inquiry;[7] "whether respondent's constitutional rights have been violated must be determined by balancing his liberty interests against the relevant state interests." *Youngberg v. Romeo*.

Petitioners insist that under the general holdings of our cases, the forced administration of life-sustaining medical treatment, and even of artificially-derived food and water essential to life, would implicate a competent person's liberty interest. Although we think the logic of the cases discussed above would embrace such a liberty interest, the dramatic consequences involved in refusal of such treatment would inform the inquiry as to whether the deprivation of that interest is constitutionally permissible. But for purposes of this case, we assume that the United States Constitution would grant a competent person a constitutionally protected right to refuse lifesaving hydration and nutrition.

---

[7]Although many state courts have held that a right to refuse treatment is encompassed by a generalized constitutional right of privacy, we have never so held. We believe this issue is more properly analyzed in terms of a Fourteenth Amendment liberty interest. *See Bowers v. Hardwick,* 478 U.S. 186, 194-195, 106 S. Ct. 2841, 2846,92 L.Ed.2d 140(1986).

Petitioners go on to assert that an incompetent person should possess the same right in this respect as is possessed by a competent person. . . .

[2] The difficulty with petitioners' claim is that in a sense it begs the question: an incompetent person is not able to make an informed and voluntary choice to exercise a hypothetical right to refuse treatment or any other right. Such a "right" must be exercised for her, if at all, by some sort of surrogate. Here, Missouri has in effect recognized that under certain circumstances a surrogate may act for the patient in electing to have hydration and nutrition withdrawn in such a way as to cause death, but it has established a procedural safeguard to assure that the action of the surrogate conforms as best it may to the wishes expressed by the patient while competent. Missouri requires that evidence of the incompetent's wishes as to the withdrawal of treatment be proved by clear and convincing evidence. The question, then, is whether the United States Constitution forbids the establishment of this procedural requirement by the State. We hold that it does not.

[3] Whether or not Missouri's clear and convincing evidence requirement comports with the United States Constitution depends in part on what interests the State may properly seek to protect in this situation. Missouri relies on its interest in the protection and preservation of human life, and there can be no gainsaying this interest. As a general matter, the States—indeed, all civilized nations—demonstrate their commitment to life by treating homicide as serious crime. Moreover, the majority of States in this country have laws imposing criminal penalties on one who assists another to commit suicide. We do not think a State is required to remain neutral in the face of an informed and voluntary decision by a physically-able adult to starve to death.

[4] But in the context presented here, a State has more particular interests at stake. The choice between life and death is a deeply personal decision of obvious and overwhelming finality. We believe Missouri may legitimately seek to safeguard the personal element of this choice through the imposition of heightened evidentiary requirements. It cannot be disputed that the Due Process Clause protects an interest in life as well as an interest in refusing life-sustaining medical treatment. Not all incompetent patients will have loved ones available to serve as surrogate decisionmakers. And even where family members are present, "[t]here will, of course, be some unfortunate situations in which family members will not act to protect a patient." *In re Jobes*, 108 N.J. 394, 419, 529 A.2d 434, 477 (1987). A State is entitled to guard against potential abuses in such situations. Similarly, a State is entitled to consider that a judicial proceeding to make a determination regarding an incompetent's wishes may very well not be an adversarial one, with the added guarantee of accurate factfinding that the adversary process brings with it. Finally, we think a State may properly decline to make judgments about the "quality" of life that a particular individual may enjoy, and simply assert an unqualified interest in the preservation of human life to be weighed against the constitutionally protected interests of the individual.

[5] In our view, Missouri has permissibly sought to advance these interests through the adoption of a "clear and convincing" standard of proof to govern such proceedings. "The function of a standard of proof, as that concept is embodied in the Due Process Clause and in the realm of factfinding, is to 'instruct the factfinder concerning the degree of confidence our society thinks he should have in the correctness of factual conclusions for a particular type of adjudication.'" "This Court has mandated an intermediate standard of proof—'clear and convincing evidence'—when the individual interests at stake in a state proceeding are both 'particularly important' and 'more substantial than mere loss of money.'" Thus, such a standard has been required in deportation proceedings, in denaturalization

proceedings, in civil commitment proceedings, and in proceedings for the termination of parental rights. Further, this level of proof, "or an even higher one, has traditionally been imposed in cases involving allegations of civil fraud, and in a variety of other kinds of civil cases involving such issues as . . . lost wills, oral contracts to make bequests, and the like."

We think it self-evident that the interests at stake in the instant proceedings are more substantial, both on an individual and societal level, than those involved in a run-of-the-mine civil dispute. But not only does the standard of proof reflect the importance of a particular adjudication, it also serves as "a societal judgment about how the risk of error should be distributed between the litigants." The more stringent the burden of proof a party must bear, the more that party bears the risk of an erroneous decision. We believe that Missouri may permissibly place an increased risk of an erroneous decision on those seeking to terminate an incompetent individual's life-sustaining treatment. An erroneous decision not to terminate results in a maintenance of the status quo; the possibility of subsequent developments such as advancements in medical science, the discovery of new evidence regarding the patient's intent, changes in the law, or simply the unexpected death of the patient despite the administration of life-sustaining treatment, at least create the potential that a wrong decision will eventually be corrected or its impact mitigated. An erroneous decision to withdraw life-sustaining treatment, however, is not susceptible of correction. In *Santosky*, one of the factors which led the Court to require proof by clear and convincing evidence in a proceeding to terminate parental rights was that a decision in such a case was final and irrevocable. The same must surely be said of the decision to discontinue hydration and nutrition of a patient such as Nancy Cruzan, which all agree will result in her death.

It is also worth noting that most, if not all, States simply forbid oral testimony entirely in determining the wishes of parties in transactions which, while important, simply do not have the consequences that a decision to terminate a person's life does. At common law and by statute in most States, the parole evidence rule prevents the variations of the terms of a written contract by oral testimony. The statute of frauds makes unenforceable oral contracts to leave property by will, and statutes regulating the making of wills universally require that those instruments be in writing. There is no doubt that statutes requiring wills to be in writing, and statutes of frauds which require that a contract to make a will be in writing, on occasion frustrate the effectuation of the intent of a particular decedent, just as Missouri's requirement of proof in this case may have frustrated the effectuation of the not-fully-expressed desires of Nancy Cruzan. But the Constitution does not require general rules to work faultlessly; no general rule can.

[6] In sum, we conclude that a State may apply a clear and convincing evidence standard in proceedings where a guardian seeks to discontinue nutrition and hydration of a person diagnosed to be in a persistent vegetative state. We note that many courts which have adopted some sort of substituted judgment procedure in situations like this, whether they limit consideration of evidence to the prior expressed wishes of the incompetent individual, or whether they allow more general proof of what the individual's decision would have been, require a clear and convincing standard of proof for such evidence.

[7] The Supreme Court of Missouri held that in this case the testimony adduced at trial did not amount to clear and convincing proof of the patient's desire to have hydration and nutrition withdrawn. In so doing, it reversed a decision of the Missouri trial court which had found that the evidence "suggest[ed]" Nancy Cruzan would not have

desired to continue such measures, App. to Pet. for Cert. A98, but which had not adopted the standard of "clear and convincing evidence" enunciated by the Supreme Court. The testimony adduced at trial consisted primarily of Nancy Cruzan's statements made to a housemate about a year before her accident that she would not want to live should she face life as a "vegetable," and other observations to the same effect. The observations did not deal in terms with withdrawal of medical treatment or of hydration and nutrition. We cannot say that the Supreme Court of Missouri committed constitutional error in reaching the conclusion that it did.

[8] Petitioners, alternatively contend that Missouri must accept the "substituted judgment" of close family members even in the absence of substantial proof that their views reflect the views of the patient. They rely primarily upon our decisions in *Michael H. v. Gerald D.*, 491 U.S. ——, 109 S.Ct. 2333, 105 L.Ed.2d 91 (1989), and *Parham v. J.R.*, 442 U.S. 584, 99 S.Ct. 2493, 61 L.Ed.2d 101 (1979). But we do not think these cases support their claim. In *Michael H.*, we *upheld* the constitutionality of California's favored treatment of traditional family relationships; such a holding may not be turned around into a constitutional requirement that a State *must* recognize the primacy of those relationships in a situation like this. And in *Parham*, where the patient was a minor, we also *upheld* the constitutionality of a state scheme in which parents made certain decisions for mentally ill minors. Here again petitioners would seek to turn a decision which allowed a State to rely on family decision making into a constitutional requirement that the State recognize such decision making. But constitutional law does not work that way.

No doubt is engendered by anything in this record but that Nancy Cruzan's mother and father are loving and caring parents. If the State were required by the United States Constitution to repose a right of "substituted judgement" with anyone, the Cruzans would surely qualify. But we do not think the Due Process Clause requires the State to repose judgment on these matters with anyone but the patient herself. Close family members may have a strong feeling—a feeling not at all ignoble or unworthy, but not entirely disinterested, either—that they do not wish to witness the continuation of the life of a loved one which they regard as hopeless, meaningless, and even degrading. But there is no automatic assurance that the view of close family members will necessarily be the same as the patient's would have been had she been confronted with the prospect of her situation while competent. All of the reasons previously discussed for allowing Missouri to require clear and convincing evidence of the patient's wishes lead us to conclude that the State may choose to defer only to those wishes, rather than confide the decision to close family members.

The judgment of the Supreme Court of Missouri is

*Affirmed* . . . .

Justice SCALIA, concurring.

The various opinions in this case portray quite clearly the difficult, indeed agonizing, questions that are presented by the constantly increasing power of science to keep the human body alive for longer than any reasonable person would want to inhabit it. The States have begun to grapple with these problems through legislation. I am concerned, from the tenor of today's opinions, that we are poised to confuse that enterprise as successfully as we have confused the enterprise of legislating concerning abortion—requiring it to be conducted against a background of federal constitutional imperatives that are unknown because they are being newly crafted from Term to Term. That would be a great misfortune.

While I agree with the Court's analysis today, and therefore join in its opinion, I would have preferred that we announce, clearly and promptly, that the federal courts have no business in this field; that American law has always accorded the State the power to prevent, by force if necessary, suicide—including suicide by refusing to take appropriate measures necessary to preserve one's life; that the point at which life becomes "worthless," and the point at which the means necessary to preserve it become "extraordinary" or "inappropriate," are neither set forth in the Constitution nor known to the nine Justices of this Court any better than they are known to nine people picked at random from the Kansas City telephone directory; and hence, that even when it *is* demonstrated by clear and convincing evidence that a patient no longer wishes certain measures to be taken to preserve her life, it is up to the citizens of Missouri to decide, through their elected representatives, whether that wish will be honored. It is quite impossible (because the Constitution says nothing about the matter) that those citizens will decide upon a line less lawful than the one we would choose; and it is unlikely (because we know no more about "life-and-death" than they do) that they will decide upon a line less reasonable.

The text of the Due Process Clause does not protect individuals against deprivations of liberty *simpliciter*. It protects them against deprivations of liberty "without due process of law." To determine that such a deprivation would not occur if Nancy Cruzan were forced to take nourishment against her will, it is unnecessary to reopen the historically recurrent debate over whether "due process" includes substantive restrictions. . . . It is at least true that no "substantive due process" claim can be maintained unless the claimant demonstrates that the State has deprived him of a right historically and traditionally protected against State interference.

At common law in England, a suicide—defined as one who "deliberately puts an end to his own existence, or commits any unlawful malicious act, the consequences of which is his own death," 4 W. Blackstone, Commentaries *189—was criminally liable. *Ibid.* Although the States abolished the penal-

ties imposed by the common law (*i.e.* forfeiture and ignominious burial), they did so to spare the innocent family, and not to legitimize the act. Case law at the time of the Fourteenth Amendment generally held that assisting suicide was a criminal offense.

Petitioners rely on three distinctions to separate Nancy Cruzan's case from ordinary suicide: (1) that she is permanently incapacited and in pain; (2) that she would bring on her death not by any affirmative act but by merely declining treatment that provides nourishment; and (3) that preventing her from effectuating her presumed wish to die requires violation of her bodily integrity. None of these suffices. Suicide was not excused even when committed "to avoid those ills which [persons] had not the fortitude to endure." "The life of those to whom life has become a burden—of those who are hopelessly diseased or fatally wounded—nay, even the lives of criminals condemned to death, are under the protection of the law, equally as the lives of those who are in the full tide of life's enjoyment, and anxious to continue to live." Thus a man who prepared a poison, and placed it within reach of his wife, "to put an end to her suffering" from a terminal illness was convicted of murder; the "incurable suffering of the suicide, as a legal question, could hardly affect the degree of criminality. . . ." Nor would the imminence of the patient's death have affected liability. "The lives of all are equally under the protection of the law, and under that protection to their last moment. . . . [Assisted suicide] is declared by the law to be murder, irrespective of the wishes or the condition of the party to whom the poison is administered. . . ."

The second asserted distinction—suggested by the recent cases canvassed by the Court concerning the right to refuse treatment, *ante*, at 2846–2850—relies on the dichotomy between action and inaction. Suicide, it is said, consists of an affirmative act to end one's life; refusing treatment is not an affirmative act "causing" death, but merely a passive acceptance of the natural process of dying. I readily acknowledge that the distinction between action and inaction has some bearing upon the legislative judgment of what ought to be prevented as suicide—though even there it would seem to me unreasonable to draw the line precisely between action and inaction, rather than between various forms of inaction. It would not make much sense to say that one may not kill oneself by walking into the sea, but may sit on the beach until submerged by the incoming tide; or that one may not intentionally lock oneself into a cold storage locker, but may refrain from coming indoors when the temperature drops below freezing. Even as a legislative matter, in other words, the intelligent line does not fall between action and inaction but between those forms of inaction that consist of abstaining from "ordinary" care and those that consist of abstaining from "excessive" or "heroic" measures. Unlike action *vs.* inaction, that is not a line to be discerned by logic or legal analysis, and we should not pretend that it is.

But to return to the principal point for present purposes: the irrelevance of the action-inaction distinction. Starving oneself to death is no different from putting a gun to one's temple as far as the common-law definition of suicide is concerned; the cause of death in both cases is the suicide's conscious decision to "pu[t] an end to his own existence." Of course the common law rejected the action-inaction distinction in other contexts involving the taking of human life as well. In the prosecution of a parent for the starvation death of her infant, it was no defense that the infant's death was "caused" by no action of the parent but by the natural process of starvation, or by the infant's natural inability to provide for itself. . . .

It is not surprising, therefore, that the early cases considering the claimed right to refuse medical treatment dismissed as specious the nice distinction between "passively submitting to death and actively seeking it. The distinction may be merely verbal, as it would be if an adult sought death by starvation instead of a drug. If the State may interrupt one mode of self-destruction, it may with equal authority interfere with the other."

The third asserted basis of distinction—that frustrating Nancy Cruzan's wish to die in the present case requires interference with her bodily integrity—is likewise inadequate, because such interference is impermissible only if one begs the question whether her refusal to undergo the treatment on her own is suicide. It has always been lawful not only for the State, but even for private citizens, to interfere with bodily integrity to prevent a felony. That general rule has of course been applied to suicide. At common law, even a private person's use of force to prevent suicide was privileged. It is not even reasonable, much less required by the Constitution, to maintain that although the State has the right to prevent a person from slashing his wrists it does not have the power to apply physical force to prevent him from doing so, nor the power, should he succeed, to apply, coercively if necessary, medical measures to stop the flow of blood. The state-run hospital, I am certain, is not liable under 42 U.S.C. § 1983 for violation of constitutional rights, nor the private hospital liable under general tort law, if, in a State where suicide is unlawful, it pumps out the stomach of a person who has intentionally taken an overdose of barbiturates, despite that person's wishes to the contrary.

Justice BRENNAN, with whom Justice MARSHALL and Justice BLACKMUN join, dissenting.

"Medical technology has effectively created a twilight zone of suspended animation where death commences while life, in some form, continues. Some patients, however, want no part of a life sustained only by medical technology. Instead, they prefer a plan of medical treatment that allows nature to take its course and permits them to die with dignity."

Nancy Cruzan has dwelt in that twilight zone for six years. She is oblivious to her surroundings and will remain so. Her body twitches only reflexively, without consciousness. The areas of her brain that once thought, felt, and experienced sensations have degenerated badly and are continuing to do so. The cavities remaining are filing with cerebro-spinal fluid. The " 'cerebral cortical atrophy is irreversible, permanent, progressive and ongoing.' " "Nancy will never interact meaningfully with her environment again. She will remain in a persistent vegetative state until her death." Because she cannot swallow, her nutrition and hydration are delivered through a tube surgically implanted in her stomach.

A grown woman at the time of the accident, Nancy had previously expressed her wish to forgo continuing medical care under circumstances such as these. Her family and her friends are convinced that this is what she would want. A guardian ad litem appointed by the trial court is also convinced that this is what Nancy would want. Yet the Missouri Supreme Court, alone among state courts deciding such a question, has determined that an irreversibly vegetative patient will remain a passive prisoner of medical technology—for Nancy, perhaps for the next 30 years.

Today the Court, while tentatively accepting that there is some degree of constitutionally protected liberty interest in avoiding unwanted medical treatment, including life-sustaining medical treatment such as artificial nutrition and hydration, affirms the decision of the Missouri Supreme Court. The majority opinion, as I read it, would affirm that decision on the ground that a State may require "clear and convincing" evidence of Nancy Cruzan's prior decision to forgo life-sustaining treatment under circumstances such as hers in order to ensure that her actual wishes are honored. Because I believe that Nancy Cruzan has a fundamental right to be free of unwanted artificial nutrition and hydration, which right is not outweighed by any interests of the State, and because I find that the improperly biased procedural obstacles imposed by the Missouri Supreme Court impermissibly burden that right, I respectfully dissent. Nancy Cruzan is entitled to choose to die with dignity.

# I

## A

"[T]he timing of death—once a matter of fate—is now a matter of human choice." Office of Technology Assessment Task Force, Life Sustaining Technologies and the Elderly 41 (1988). Of the approximately two million people who die each year, 80% die in hospitals and long-term care institutions,[3] and perhaps 70% of those after a decision to forgo life-sustaining treatment has been made. Nearly every death involves a decision whether to undertake some medical procedure that could prolong the process of dying. Such decisions are difficult and personal. They must be made on the basis of individual values, informed by medical realities, yet within a framework governed by law. The role of the courts is confined to defining that framework, delineating the ways in which government may and may not participate in such decisions.

The question before this Court is a relatively narrow one: whether the Due Process Clause allows Missouri to require a now incompetent patient in an irreversible persistent vegetative state to remain on life support absent rigorously clear and convincing evidence that avoiding the treatment represents the patient's prior, express choice.

[3]See President's Commission for the Study of Ethical Problems in Medicine and Biomedical and Behavioral Research, Deciding to Forego Life Sustaining Treatment 15, n. 1, and 17–18 (1983) (hereafter President's Commission).

If a fundamental right is at issue, Missouri's rule of decision must be scrutinized under the standards this Court has always applied in such circumstances. As we said in *Zablocki v. Redhail*, if a requirement imposed by a State "significantly interferes with the exercise of a fundamental right, it cannot be upheld unless it is supported by sufficiently important state interests and is closely tailored to effectuate only those interests." . . .

**B**

The starting point for our legal analysis must be whether a competent person has a constitutional right to avoid unwanted medical care. Earlier this Term, this Court held that the Due Process Clause of the Fourteenth Amendment confers a significant liberty interest in avoiding unwanted medical treatment. Today, the Court concedes that our prior decisions "support the recognition of a general liberty interest in refusing medical treatment." The Court, however, avoids discussing either the measure of that liberty interest or its application by assuming, for purposes of this case only, that a competent person has a constitutionally protected liberty interest in being free of unwanted artificial nutrition and hydration. Justice O'CONNOR's opinion is less parsimonious. She openly affirms that "the Court has often deemed state incursions into the body repugnant to the interests protected by the Due Process Clause," that there is a liberty interest in avoiding unwanted medical treatment and that it encompasses the right to be free of "artificially delivered food and water."

But if a competent person has a liberty interest to be free of unwanted medical treatment, as both the majority and Justice O'CONNOR concede, it must be fundamental. "We are dealing here with [a decision] which involves one of the basic civil rights of man." Whatever other liberties protected by the Due Process Clause are fundamental,

"those liberties that are 'deeply rooted in this Nation's history and tradition'" are among them. . . .

The right to be free from medical attention without consent, to determine what shall be done with one's own body, *is* deeply rooted in this Nation's traditions, as the majority acknowledges. This right has long been "firmly entrenched in American tort law" and is securely grounded in the earliest common law. "'Anglo-American law starts with the premise of thoroughgoing self determination. It follows that each man is considered to be master of his own body, and he may, if he be of sound mind, expressly prohibit the performance of lifesaving surgery, or other medical treatment.'" "The inviolability of the person" has been held as "sacred" and "carefully guarded" as any common law right. Thus, freedom from unwanted medical attention is unquestionably among those principles "so rooted in the traditions and conscience of our people as to be ranked as fundamental."

That there may be serious consequences involved in refusal of the medical treatment at issue here does not vitiate the right under our common law tradition of medical self-determination. It is "a well-established rule of general law . . . that it is the patient, not the physician, who ultimately decides if treatment—any treatment—is to be given at all. . . . The rule has never been qualified in its application by either the nature or purpose of the treatment, or the gravity of the consequences of acceding to or foregoing it." . . .

No material distinction can be drawn between the treatment to which Nancy Cruzan continues to be subject—artificial nutrition and hydration—and any other medical treatment. The artificial delivery of nutrition and hydration is undoubtedly medical treatment. The technique to which Nancy Cruzan is subject—artificial feeding through a gastrostomy tube—involves a tube implanted surgically into her stomach through incisions in her abdominal wall. It may obstruct the intestinal tract, erode and pierce the stomach wall or cause leakage of the stomach's contents into the abdominal cavity. The tube can cause pneumonia from reflux of the stomach's contents into the lung. See Bernard & Forlaw, Complications and Their Prevention, in Enteral and Tube Feeding 553 (J. Rombeau & M. Caldwell eds. 1984). Typically, and in this case (see Tr. 377) commercially prepared formulas are used, rather than fresh food. See Matarese, Enteral Alimentation, in Surgical Nutrition 726 (J. Fischer ed. 1983). The type of formula and method of administration must be experimented with to avoid gastrointestinal problems. The patient must be monitored daily by medical personnel as to weight, fluid intake and fluid output; blood tests must be done weekly.

Artificial delivery of food and water is regarded as medical treatment by the medical profession and the Federal Government. According to the American Academy of Neurology, "[t]he artificial provision of nutrition and hydration is a form of medical treatment . . . analogous to other forms of life-sustaining treatment, such as the use of the respirator. When a patient is unconscious, both a respirator and an artificial feeding device serve to support or replace normal bodily functions that are compromised as a result of the patient's illness." Position of the American Academy of Neurology on Certain Aspects of the Care and Management of the Persistent Vegetative State Patient, 39 Neurology 125 (Jan. 1989). See also Council on Ethical and Judicial Affairs of the American Medical Association, Current Opinions, Opinion 2.20 (1989) ("Life-prolonging medical treatment includes medication and artificially or technologically supplied respiration, nutrition or hydration"); President's Commission 88 (life-sustaining treatment includes respirators, kidney dialysis machines, special feeding procedures). The Federal Government permits the cost of the medical devices and formulas used in enteral feeding to be reimbursed under Medicare. . . .

Nor does that fact that Nancy Cruzan is now incompetent deprive her of her fundamental rights. . . . As the majority recognizes, the question is not whether an incompetent has constitutional rights, but how such rights may be exercised. As we explained in *Thompson v. Oklahoma*, "[t]he law must often adjust the manner in which it affords rights to those whose status renders them unable to exercise choice freely and rationally. Children, the insane, and *those who are irreversibly ill with loss of brain function, for instance, all retain 'rights,'* to be sure, but often such rights are only meaningful as they are exercised by agents acting with the best interests of their principals in mind." "To deny [its] exercise because the patient is unconscious or incompetent would be to deny the right."

## III

This is not to say that the State has no legitimate interests to assert here. As the majority recognizes, Missouri has a *parens patriae* interest in providing Nancy Cruzan, now incompetent, with as accurate as possible a determination of how she would exercise her rights under these circumstances. Second, if and when it is determined that Nancy Cruzan would want to continue treatment, the State may legitimately assert an interest in providing that treatment. But *until* Nancy's wishes have been determined, the only state interest that may be asserted is an interest in safe-guarding the accuracy of that determination.

Accuracy, therefore, must be our touchstone. Missouri may constitutionally impose only those procedural requirements that serve to enhance the accuracy of a determination of Nancy Cruzan's wishes or are at least consistent with an accurate determination. The Missouri "safeguard" that the Court upholds today does not meet that standard. The determination needed in this context is whether the incompetent person would choose to live in a persistent vegetative state on life-support or to avoid this medical treatment. Missouri's rule of decision imposes a markedly asymmetrical evidentiary burden. Only evidence of specific statements of treatment choice made by the patient when competent is admissible to support a finding that the patient, now in a persistent vegetative state, would wish to avoid further medical treatment. Moreover, this evidence must be clear and convincing. No proof is required to support a finding that the incompetent person would wish to continue treatment.

## A

The majority offers several justifications for Missouri's heightened evidentiary standard. First, the majority explains that the State may constitutionally adopt this rule to govern determinations of an incompetent's wishes in order to advance the State's substantive interests, including its unqualified interest in the preservation of human life. Missouri's evidentiary standard, however, cannot rest on the State's own interest in a particular substantive result. To be sure, courts have long erected clear and convincing evidence standards to place the greater risk of erroneous decisions on those bringing disfavored claims. In such cases, however, the choice to discourage certain claims was a legitimate, constitutional policy choice. In contrast, Missouri has no such power to disfavor a choice by Nancy Cruzan to avoid medical treatment, because Missouri has no legitimate interest in providing Nancy with treatment until it is established that this represents her choice. See *supra*, at 2869–2870. Just as a State may not override Nancy's choice directly, it may not do so indirectly through the imposition of a procedural rule.

The majority claims that the allocation of the risk of error is justified because it is more important not to terminate life-support for someone who would wish it continued than to honor the wishes of someone who would not. An erroneous decision to terminate life-support is irrevocable, says

the majority, while an erroneous decision not to terminate "results in a maintenance of the status quo." See *ante*, at 2854. But, from the point of view of the patient, an erroneous decision in either direction is irrevocable. An erroneous decision to terminate artificial nutrition and hydration, to be sure, will lead to failure of that last remnant of physiological life, the brain stem, and result in complete brain death. An erroneous decision not to terminate life-support, however, robs a patient of the very qualities protected by the right to avoid unwanted medical treatment. His own degraded existence is perpetuated; his family's suffering is protracted; the memory he leaves behind becomes more and more distorted.

Even a later decision to grant him his wish cannot undo the intervening harm. But a later decision is unlikely in any event. "[T]he discovery of new evidence," to which the majority refers, *ibid.*, is more hypothetical than plausible. The majority also misconceives the relevance of the possibility of "advancements in medical science," *ibid.*, by treating it as a reason to force someone to continue medical treatment against his will. The possibility of a medical miracle is indeed part of the calculus, but it is a part of the *patient's* calculus. If current research suggests that some hope for cure or even moderate improvement is possible within the life-span projected, this is a factor that should be and would be accorded significant weight in assessing what the patient himself would choose.

## C

I do not suggest that States must sit by helplessly if the choices of incompetent patients are in danger of being ignored. See *ante*, at 2853. Even if the Court had ruled that Missouri's rule of decision is unconstitutional, as I believe it should have, States would nevertheless remain free to fashion procedural protections to safeguard the interests of incompetents under these circumstances. The

Constitution provides merely a framework here: protections must be genuinely aimed at ensuring decisions commensurate with the will of the patient, and must be reliable as instruments to that end. Of the many States which have instituted such protections, Missouri is virtually the only one to have fashioned a rule that lessens the likelihood of accurate determinations. In contrast, nothing in the Constitution prevents States from reviewing the advisability of a family decision, by requiring a court proceeding or by appointing an impartial guardian ad litem.

### D

Finally, I cannot agree with the majority that where it is not possible to determine what choice an incompetent patient would make, a State's role as *parens patriae* permits the State automatically to make that choice itself. See *ante*, at 2855 (explaining that the Due Process Clause does not require a State to confide the decision to "anyone but the patient herself"). Under fair rules of evidence, it is improbable that a court could not determine what the patient's choice would be. Under the rule of decision adopted by Missouri and upheld today by this Court, such occasions might be numerous. But in neither case does it follow that it is constitutionally acceptable for the State invariably to assume the role of deciding for the patient. A State's legitimate interest in safeguarding a patient's choice cannot be furthered by simply appropriating it.

The majority justifies its position by arguing that, while close family members may have a strong feeling about the question, "there is no automatic assurance that the view of close family members will necessarily be the same as the patient's would have been had she been confronted with the prospect of her situation while competent." *Ibid*. I cannot quarrel with this observation. But it leads only to another question: Is there any reason to suppose that a State is

more likely to make the choice that the patient would have made than someone who knew the patient intimately? To ask this is to answer it. As the New Jersey Supreme Court observed: "Family members are best qualified to make substituted judgments for incompetent patients not only because of their peculiar grasp of the patient's approach to life, but also because of their special bonds with him or her. . . . It is . . . they who treat the patient as a person, rather than a symbol of a cause." The State, in contrast, is a stranger to the patient.

A State's inability to discern an incompetent patient's choice still need not mean that a State is rendered powerless to protect that choice. But I would find that the Due Process Clause prohibits a State from doing more than that. A State may ensure that the person who makes the decision on the patient's behalf is the one whom the patient himself would have selected to make that choice for him. And a State may exclude from consideration anyone having improper motives. But a State generally must either repose the choice with the person whom the patient himself would most likely have chosen as proxy or leave the decision to the patient's family.

### IV

As many as 10,000 patients are being maintained in persistent vegetative states in the United States, and the number is expected to increase, significantly, in the near future. See Cranford, *supra* n. 2 at 27, 31. Medical technology, developed over the past 20 or so years, is often capable of resuscitating people after they have stopped breathing, or their hearts have stopped beating. Some of those people are brought fully back to life. Two decades ago, those who were not and could not swallow and digest food, died. Intravenous solutions could not provide sufficient calories to maintain people for more than a short time. Today, various forms of artificial feeding have been developed that are able to keep people metabolically alive for years, even decades. In addition, in this century, chronic or degenerative ailments have replaced communicable diseases as the primary causes of death. The 80% of Americans who die in hospitals are "likely to meet their end . . . 'in a sedated or comatose state; betubed nasally, abdominally and intravenously; and far more like manipulated objects than like moral subjects.'" A fifth of all adults surviving to age 80 will suffer a progressive dementing disorder prior to death.

"[L]law, equity and justice must not themselves quail and be helpless in the face of modern technological marvels presenting questions hitherto unthought of." *In re Quinlan*, 70 N.J. 10, 44, 355 A.2d 647, 665, cert. denied, 429 U.S. 922, 97 S.Ct. 319, 50 L.Ed.2d 289 (1976). The new medical technology can reclaim those who would have been irretrievably lost a few decades ago and restore them to active lives. For Nancy Cruzan, it failed, and for others with wasting incurable disease it may be doomed to failure. In these unfortunate situations, the bodies and preferences and memories of the victims do not escheat to the State; nor does our Constitution permit the State or any other government to commandeer them. No singularity of feeling exists upon which such a government might confidently rely as *parens patriae*. The President's Commission, after years of research, concluded:

"In few areas of health care are people's evaluations of their experiences so varied and uniquely personal as in their assessments of the nature and value of the processes associated with dying. For some, every moment of life is of inestimable value; for others, life without some desired level of mental or physical ability is worthless or burdensome. A moderate degree of suffering may be an important means of personal growth and religious experience to one person, but only frightening or despicable to another." President's Commission 276.

Yet Missouri and this Court have displaced Nancy's own assessment of the processes associated with dying. They have discarded evidence of her will, ignored her values and deprived her of the right to a decision as closely approximating her own choice as humanly possible. They have done so disingenuously in her name, and openly in Missouri's own. That Missouri and this Court may truly be motivated only by concern for incompetent patients makes no matter. As one of our most prominent jurists warned us decades ago: "Experience should teach us to be most on our guard to protect liberty when the government's purposes are beneficent. . . . The greatest dangers to liberty lurk in insidious encroachment by men of zeal, well meaning but without understanding."

I respectfully dissent.

## QUESTIONS

1. Nancy Cruzan, though incompetent at the time her family argued that she be disconnected from life-sustaining treatment, was nevertheless competent at an earlier time in her life. In the case of *Superintendent of Belchertown State School v. Saikewicz*, mentioned in Justice Rehnquist's opinion, the patient, Joseph Saikewicz, was severely retarded and had never been competent. How should one determine what such a patient *would* want if competent?

2. When the case involves the hypothetical choices of an incompetent person, it is natural to use the legal device of a presumption, which serves to place the burden of proof on one side or the other. Should there be a presumption in favor of continuing life support,

so that clear and convincing evidence must be produced to show that such is *not* what the patient would want? Or should there be a presumption against, or no presumption one way or the other?

3. In such cases where a surrogate decision maker must be found, should there be a presumption in favor of a family member? What factors in a relationship between family member and patient would tend to qualify or disqualify him or her for that position?

4. Would it be more appropriate to put the *Cruzan* case under the heading of legal moralism rather than paternalism? Explain.

# Legal Moralism

## *James Fitzjames Stephen*
# THE DOCTRINE OF LIBERTY IN ITS APPLICATION TO MORALS*

. . . These explanations enable me to restate without fear of misapprehension the object of morally intolerant legislation. It is to establish, to maintain, and to give power to that which the legislator regards as a good moral system or standard. For the reasons already assigned I think that this object is good if and in so far as the system so established and maintained is good. How far any particular system is good or not is a question which probably does not admit of any peremptory final decision; but I may observe that there are a considerable number of things which appear good and bad, though no doubt in different degrees, to all mankind. For the practical purpose of legislation refinements are of little importance. In any given age and nation virtue and vice have meanings which for that purpose are quite definite enough. In England at the present day many theories about morality are current, and speculative men differ about them widely, but they relate not so much to the question whether particular acts are right or wrong, as to the question of the precise meaning of the distinction, the manner in which the moral character of particular actions is to be decided, and the reasons for preferring right to wrong conduct. The result is that the object of promoting virtue and preventing vice must be admitted to be both a good one and one sufficiently intelligible for legislative purposes.

If this is so, the only remaining questions will be as to the efficiency of the means at the disposal of society for this purpose, and the cost of their application. Society has at its disposal two great instruments by which vice may be prevented and virtue promoted—namely, law and public opinion; and law is either criminal or civil. The use of each of these instruments is subject to certain limits and conditions, and the wisdom of attempting to make men good either by Act of Parliament or by the action of public opinion depends entirely upon the degree in which those limits and conditions are recognized and acted upon.

First, I will take the case of criminal law. What are the conditions under which and the limitations within which it can be applied with success to the object of making men better? In considering this question it must be borne in mind that criminal law is at once by far the most powerful and by far the roughest engine which society can use for any purpose. Its power is shown by the fact that it can and does render crime exceedingly difficult and dangerous. Indeed, in civilized society it absolutely prevents avowed open crime committed with the strong hand, except in cases where crime rises to the magnitude of civil war. Its roughness hardly needs illustration. It strikes so hard that it can be enforced only on the gravest occasions, and with every sort of precaution against abuse or mistake. Before an act can be treated as a crime, it ought to be capable of distinct definition and of specific proof, and it

---

*From *Liberty, Equality, Fraternity*, Chap. 4. First published in 1873.

ought also to be of such a nature that it is worth while to prevent it at the risk of inflicting great damage, direct and indirect, upon those who commit it. These conditions are seldom, if ever, fulfilled by mere vices. It would obviously be impossible to indict a man for ingratitude or perfidy. Such charges are too vague for specific discussion and distinct proof on the one side, and disproof on the other. Moreover, the expense of the investigations necessary for the legal punishment of such conduct would be enormous. It would be necessary to go into an infinite number of delicate and subtle inquiries which would tear off all privacy from the lives of a large number of persons. These considerations are, I think, conclusive reasons against treating vice in general as a crime.

The excessive harshness of criminal law is also a circumstance which very greatly narrows the range of its application. It is the *ratio ultima* of the majority against persons whom its application assumes to have renounced the common bonds which connect men together. When a man is subjected to legal punishment, society appeals directly and exclusively to his fears. It renounces the attempt to work upon his affections or feelings. In other words, it puts itself into distinct, harsh, and undisguised opposition to his wishes; and the effect of this will be to make him rebel against the law. The violence of the rebellion will be measured partly by the violence of the passion the indulgence of which is forbidden, and partly by the degree to which the law can count upon an ally in the man's own conscience. A law which enters into a direct contest with a fierce imperious passion, which the person who feels it does not admit to be bad, and which is not directly injurious to others, will generally do more harm than good; and this is perhaps

the principal reason why it is impossible to legislate directly against unchastity, unless it takes forms which every one regards as monstrous and horrible. The subject is not one for detailed discussion, but any one who will follow out the reflections which this hint suggests will find that they supply a striking illustration of the limits which the harshness of criminal law imposes upon its range.

If we now look at the different acts which satisfy the conditions specified, it will, I think, be found that criminal law in this country actually is applied to the suppression of vice and so to the promotion of virtue to a very considerable extent; and this I say is right.

The punishment of common crimes, the gross forms of force and fraud, is no doubt ambiguous. It may be justified on the principle of self-protection, and apart from any question as to their moral character. It is not, however, difficult to show that these acts have in fact been forbidden and subjected to punishment not only because they are dangerous to society, and so ought to be prevented, but also for the sake of gratifying the feeling of hatred—call it revenge, resentment, or what you will—which the contemplation of such conduct excites in healthily constituted minds. If this can be shown, it will follow that criminal law is in the nature of a persecution of the grosser forms of vice, and an emphatic assertion of the principle that the feeling of hatred and the desire of vengeance above-mentioned are important elements of human nature which ought in such cases to be satisfied in a regular public and legal manner.

The strongest of all proofs of this is to be found in the principles universally admitted and acted upon as regulating the amount of punishment. If vengeance affects, and ought to affect, the amount of punishment, every circumstance which aggravates or extenuates the wickedness of an act will operate in aggravation or diminution of punishment. If the object of legal punishment is simply the prevention of specific acts, this will not be the case. Circumstances which extenuate the wickedness of the crime will often operate in aggravation of punishment. If, as I maintain, both objects must be kept in view, such circumstances will operate in different ways according to the nature of the case.

A judge has before him two criminals, one of whom appears, from the circumstances of the case, to be ignorant and depraved, and to have given way to very strong temptation, under the influence of the other, who is a man of rank and education, and who committed the offence of which both are convicted under comparatively slight temptation. I will venture to say that if he made any difference between them at all every judge on the English bench would give the first man a lighter sentence than the second.

What should we think of such an address to the prisoners as this? You, A, are a most dangerous man. You are ignorant, you are depraved, and you are accordingly peculiarly liable to be led into crime by the solicitations or influence of people like your accomplice B. Such influences constitute to men like you a temptation practically all but irresistible. The class to which you belong is a large one, and is accessible only to the coarsest possible motives. For these reasons I must put into the opposite scale as heavy a weight as I can, and the sentence of the court upon you is that you be taken to the place from whence you came and from thence to a place of execution, and that there you be hanged by the neck till you are dead. As to you, B, you are undoubtedly an infamous wretch. Between you and your tool A there can, morally speaking, be no comparison at all. But I have nothing to do with that. You belong to a small and not a dangerous class. The temptation to which you gave way was slight, and the impression made upon me by your conduct is that you really did not care very much whether you committed this crime or not. From a moral point of view, this may perhaps increase your guilt; but it shows that the motive to be overcome is less powerful in your case than in A's. You belong, moreover, to a class, and occupy a position in society, in which exposure and loss of character are much dreaded. This you will have to undergo. Your case is a very odd one, and it is not likely that you will wish to commit such a crime again, or that others will follow your example. Upon the whole, I think that what has passed will deter others from such conduct as much as actual punishment. It is, however, necessary to keep a hold over you. You will therefore be discharged on your own recognizance to come up and receive judgment when called upon, and unless you conduct yourself better for the future, you will assuredly be so called upon, and if you do not appear, your recognizance will be inexorably forfeited.

Caricature apart, the logic of such a view is surely unimpeachable. If all that you want of criminal law is the prevention of crime by the direct fear of punishment, the fact that a temptation is strong is a reason why punishment should be severe. In some instances this actually is the case. It shows the reason why political crimes and offences against military discipline are punished so severely. But in most cases the strength of the temptation operates in mitigation of punishment, and the reason of this is that criminal law operates not merely by producing fear, but also indirectly, but very powerfully, by giving distinct shape to the feeling of anger, and a distinct satisfaction to the desire of vengeance which crime excites in a healthy mind.

Other illustrations of the fact that English criminal law does recognize morality are to be found in the fact that a considerable number of acts which need not be specified are treated as crimes merely because they are regarded as grossly immoral.

I have already shown in what manner Mr Mill deals with these topics. It is, I venture to think, utterly unsatisfactory. The impression it makes upon me is that he feels that such acts ought to be punished, and that he is able to reconcile this with his fundamental principles only by subtleties quite unworthy of him. Admit the relation for which I am contending between law and morals, and all becomes perfectly clear. All the acts referred to are unquestionably wicked. Those who do them are ashamed of them. They are all capable of being clearly defined and specifically proved or disproved, and there can be no question at all that legal punishment reduces them to small dimensions, and forces the criminals to carry on their practices with secrecy and precaution. In other words, the object of their suppression is good, and the means adequate. In practice this is subject to highly important qualifications, of which I will only say here that those who

have due regard to the incurable weaknesses of human nature will be very careful how they inflict penalties upon mere vice, or even upon those who make a trade of promoting it, unless special circumstances call for their infliction. It is one thing however to tolerate vice so long as it is inoffensive, and quite another to give it a legal right not only to exist, but to assert itself in the face of the world as an 'experiment in living' as good as another, and entitled to the same protection from law.

I now pass to the manner in which civil law may and does, and as I say properly, promote virtue and prevent vice. This is a subject so wide that I prefer indicating its nature by a few illustrations to attempting to deal with it systematically. It would, however, be easy to show that nearly every branch of civil law assumes the existence of a standard of moral good and evil which the public at large have an interest in maintaining, and in many cases enforcing—a proceeding which is diametrically opposed to Mr Mill's fundamental principles.*

The main subject with which law is conversant is that of rights and duties, and all the commoner and more important rights and duties presuppose some theory of morals. Contracts are one great source of rights and duties. Is there any country in the world the courts of which would enforce a contract which the Legislature regarded as immoral? and is there any country in which there would be much

---

*Mr Morley says on this: 'A good deal of rather bustling ponderosity is devoted to proving that the actual laws do in many points assume the existence of a standard of moral good and evil, and that this proceeding is diametrically opposed to Mr Mill's fundamental principles. To this one would say first that the actual existence of laws of any given kind is wholly irrelevant to Mr Mill's contention, which is that it would be better if laws of such a kind did not exist. Secondly, Mr Mill never says, nor is it at all essential to his doctrine to hold, that a government ought not to have "a standard of moral good and evil which the public at large have an interest in maintaining, and in many instances enforcing." He only set apart a certain class of cases to which the right or duty of enforcement of the criminal standard does not extend—self-regarding cases.'

As to the first point, surely it is not irrelevant to show that Mr Mill is at issue with the practical conclusions to which most nations have been led by experience. Those to whom I address myself may be disposed to doubt whether a principle which condemns so many of the institutions under which they live can be right.

difficulty in specific cases in saying whether the object or the consideration of a contract was or was not immoral? Other rights are of a more general nature, and are liable to be violated by wrongs. Take the case of a man's right to his reputation, which is violated by defamation. How, without the aid of some sort of theory of morals, can it be determined whether the publication of defamatory matter is justifiable or not?

Perhaps the most pointed of all illustrations of the moral character of civil law is to be found in the laws relating to marriage and inheritance. They all proceed upon an essentially moral theory as to the relation of the sexes. Take the case of illegitimate children. A bastard is *filius nullius*—he inherits nothing, he has no claim on his putative father. What is all this except the expression of the strongest possible determination on the part of the Legislature to recognize, maintain, and favour marriage in every possible manner as the foundation of civilized society? It has been plausibly maintained that these laws bear hardly upon bastards, punishing them for the sins of their parents. It is not necessary to my purpose to go into this, though it appears to me that the law is right. I make the remark merely for the sake of showing to what lengths the law does habitually go for the purpose of maintaining the most important of all moral principles, the principle upon which one great department of it is entirely founded. It is a case in which

a good object is promoted by efficient and adequate means.

These illustrations are so strong that I will add nothing more to them from this branch of the law, but I may refer to a few miscellaneous topics which bear on the same subject. Let us take first the case of sumptuary laws. Mr Mill's principles would no doubt condemn them, and, as they have gone out of fashion, it may be said, that unless my principle does so too, it is the worse for my principle. I certainly should not condemn sumptuary laws on the principle that the object in view is either bad or improper for legislation. I can hardly imagine a greater blessing to the whole community than a reduction in the lavish extravagance which makes life so difficult and laborious. It is difficult for me to look at a lace machine with patience. The ingenuity which went to devise it might have made human life materially happier in a thousand ways, and its actual effect has been to enable a great number of people to wear an imitation of an ornament which derives what little merit it has principally from its being made by hand. If any one could practically solve the problem of securing the devotion of the higher forms of human ingenuity to objects worthy of them, he would be an immense benefactor to his species. Life, however, has become so complicated, vested interests are so powerful and so worthy of respect, it is so clear that the enforcement

---

As to the second point, Mr Mill says in express words: 'Society, as society, has no right to decide anything to be wrong which concerns only the individual.' This I think is equivalent to denying that society ought to have a moral standard, for by a moral standard I understand a judgment that certain acts are wrong, whoever they concern. Whether they concern the agent only or others as well, is and must be an accident. Mr Morley, however, thinks that Mr Mill's opinion was that society may and ought to have a moral standard, but ought not to enforce it in the case of self-regarding acts. I say, and attempt throughout the whole of this chapter to prove, that as regards the 'moral coercion of public opinion,' this is neither possible nor desirable, and that as regards legal coercion, the question whether it is possible and desirable depends upon considerations drawn from the nature of law, civil and criminal. Whether I am right or wrong I cannot see that I have not understood Mr Mill, or that I have not contradicted him.

of any conceivable law upon such a subject would be impossible, that I do not think anyone in these days would be found to propose one. In a simpler age of the world and in a smaller community such laws may have been very useful. The same remarks apply to laws as to the distribution of property and to the regulation of trade.

Laws relating to education and to military service and the discipline of the army have a moral side of the utmost importance. Mr Mill would be the first to admit this; indeed, in several passages of his book he insists on the fact that society has complete control over the rising generation as a reason why it should not coerce adults into morality. This surely is the very opposite of the true conclusion. How is it possible for society to accept the position of an educator unless it has moral principles on which to educate? How, having accepted that position and having educated people up to a certain point, can it draw a line at which education ends and perfect moral indifference begins? When a private man educates his family, his superiority over them is founded principally on his superior age and experience; and as this personal superiority ceases, the power which is founded upon it gradually ceases also. Between society at large and individuals the difference is of another kind. The fixed principles and institutions of society express not merely the present opinions of the ruling part of the community, but the accumulated results of centuries of experience, and these constitute a standard by which the conduct of individuals may be tried, and to which they are in a variety of ways, direct and indirect, compelled to conform. This, I think, is one of the meanings which may be attached to the assertion that education never ceases. As a child grows into a man, and as a young man grows into an old man, he is brought under the influence of successive sets of educators, each of whom sets its mark upon him. It is no uncommon thing to see aged parents taught by their grown-up children lessons learned by the children in their intercourse with their own generation. All of us are continually educating each other, and in every instance this is and must be a process at once moral and more or less coercive.*

As to Mr Mill's doctrine that the coercive influence of public opinion ought to be exercised only for self-protective purposes, it seems to me a paradox so startling that it is almost impossible to argue against it. A single consideration on the subject is sufficient to prove this. The principle is one which it is impossible to carry out. It is like telling a rose that it ought to smell sweet only for the purpose of affording pleasure to the owner of the ground in which it grows. People form and express their opinions on each other, which, collectively, form public opinion, for a thousand reasons; to amuse themselves; for the sake of something to talk about; to gratify this or that momentary feeling; but the effect of such opinions, when formed, is quite

*Mr Morley says in reference to this passage and the preceding passages from pp. 153–4: 'Mr. Stephen . . . proves the contradictory of assertions which his adversary never made, as when he cites judicial instances which imply the recognition of morality by the law.' I think Mr Morley misunderstands my argument, which nevertheless appears to me very plain. It is simply this: I say laws can and do promote virtue and diminish vice by coercion in the cases and in the ways specified, and their interference does more good than harm. The contradictory of this proposition would be that in the cases specified legal interference does more harm than good. Surely, if Mr Mill's general principle is true, this must follow from it. Therefore in denying it I deny a necessary inference from the principle which I attack.

independent of the grounds of their formation. A man is tried for murder, and just escapes conviction. People read the trial from curiosity; they discuss it for the sake of the discussion; but if, by whatever means, they are brought to think that the man was in all probability guilty, they shun his society as they would shun any other hateful thing. The opinion produces its effect in precisely the same way whatever was its origin.

The result of these observations is that both law and public opinion do in many cases exercise a powerful coercive influence on morals, for objects which are good in the sense explained above, and by means well calculated to attain those objects, to a greater or less extent at a not inadequate expense. If this is so, I say law and public opinion do well, and I do not see how either the premises or the conclusion are to be disproved.

Of course there are limits to the possibility of useful interference with morals, either by law or by public opinion; and it is of the highest practical importance that these limits should be carefully observed. The great leading principles on the subject are few and simple, though they cannot be stated with any great precision. It will be enough to mention the following:

(1) Neither legislation nor public opinion ought to be meddlesome. A very large proportion of the matters upon which people wish to interfere with their neighbours are trumpery little things which are of no real importance at all. The busybody and world-betterer who will never let things alone, or trust people to take care of themselves, is a common and a contemptible character. The commonplaces directed against these small creatures are perfectly just, but to try to put them down by denying the connection between law and morals is like shutting all light and air out of a house in order to keep out gnats and blue-bottle flies.

(2) Both legislation and public opinion, but especially the latter, are apt to be most mischievous and cruelly unjust if they proceed upon imperfect evidence. To form and express strong opinions about the wickedness of a man whom you do not know, the immorality or impiety of a book you have not read, the merits of a question on which you are uninformed, is to run a great risk of inflicting a great wrong. It is hanging first and trying afterwards, or more frequently not trying at all. This, however, is no argument against hanging after a fair trial.

(3) Legislation ought in all cases to be graduated to the existing level of morals in the time and country in which it is employed. You cannot punish anything which public opinion, as expressed in the common practice of society, does not strenuously and unequivocally condemn. To try to do so is a sure way to produce gross hypocrisy and furious reaction. To be able to punish, a moral majority must be overwhelming. Law cannot be better than the nation in which it exists, though it may and can protect an acknowledged moral standard, and may gradually be increased in strictness as the standard rises. We punish, with the utmost severity, practices which in Greece and Rome went almost uncensured. It is possible that a time may come when it may appear natural and right to punish adultery, seduction, or possibly even fornication, but the prospect is, at present, indefinitely remote, and it may be doubted whether we are moving in that direction.

(4) Legislation and public opinion ought in all cases whatever scrupulously to respect privacy. To define the province of

privacy distinctly is impossible, but it can be described in general terms. All the more intimate and delicate relations of life are of such a nature that to submit them to unsympathetic observation, or to observation which is sympathetic in the wrong way, inflicts great pain, and may inflict lasting moral injury. Privacy may be violated not only by the intrusion of a stranger, but by compelling or persuading a person to direct too much attention to his own feelings and to attach too much importance to their analysis. The common usage of language affords a practical test which is almost perfect upon this subject. Conduct which can be described as indecent is always in one way or another a violation of privacy.

There is one perfect illustration of this, of which I may say a few words. It is the case of the confessional and casuistry generally. So far as I have been able to look into the writings of casuists, their works appear to contain a spiritual penal code, in which all the sins of act and thought, of intention and imagination, which it is possible for men to commit, are described with legal minuteness and with specific illustrations, and are ranged under the two heads of mortal and venial, according as they subject the sinner to eternal damnation or only to purgatory. Nothing can exceed the interest and curiosity of some of the discussions conducted in these strange works, though some of them (by no means so large a proportion as popular rumour would suggest) are revolting. So far as my observation has gone, I should say that nothing can be more unjust than the popular notion that the casuists explained away moral obligations. Escobar in particular (Pascal's *bete noire*) gives me rather the impression of a sort of half-humorous simplicity.*

The true objection to the whole system, and the true justification of the aversion with which it has been regarded, is that it is perhaps the greatest intrusion upon privacy, the most audacious and successful invasion by law of matters which lie altogether out of the reach of law, recorded in history. Of course if the postulate on which it is founded is true—if, in fact, there is a celestial penal code which classifies as felonies or misdemeanours punishable respectively with hell or purgatory all human sins—and if priests have the power of getting the felonies commuted into misdemeanours by confession and absolution—there is no more to be said; but this supposition need not be seriously considered. It is, I think, impossible to read the books in question without feeling convinced that a trial in a court which administers such laws upon evidence supplied exclusively by the criminal must be either a mere form, a delusion of a very mischievous kind, or a process which would destroy all the self respect of the person submitted to it and utterly confuse all his notions of right and wrong, good and evil. That justice should be done without the

---

*His habit of putting all his illustrations in the first person has a very strange effect. Here for instance is a catalogue of the mortal sins which an advocate may commit. 'Defendi litem injustam, seu minus probabilem, quando minimè poteram, et debebam de minori probabilitate consulentem admonere. Ob studii defectum falso de probabilitate causae judicavi, quam improbabilem omnino post studium rejicerem. Induxi partem ad pactum, cum nulla justitia inniti cognoscerem, et nihil ab altero posset exigi nisi parum aliquid quod fortasse daretur in vexationis redemptionem.' (I got my client too good terms in a compromise.) 'Plures causaes quam discutere poteram suscepi' (I held briefs in too many committee-rooms at once.) 'Leges, statuta et ordinationes ignoravi' (I did not know all the local government acts), &c., &c.—Escobar, Theol. Mor. 286. The last appears to me to be a very hard law. It is difficult to imagine the state of mind of a man who really thought that he was authorized to declare as a part of the law of God, that a lawyer who did not know all 'laws, statutes, and ordinances' would be eternally damned unless he repented.

fullest possible knowledge of every fact connected with every transgression is impossible. That every such fact should be recalled, analyzed, dwelt upon, weighed and measured, without in a great measure renewing the evil of the act itself, and blunting the conscience as to similar acts in future, seems equally impossible. That any one human creature should ever really strip his soul stark naked for the inspection of any other, and be able to hold up his head afterwards, is not, I suppose, impossible, because so many people profess to do it; but to lookers-on from the outside it is inconceivable.

The inference which I draw from this illustration is that there is a sphere, none the less real because it is impossible to define its limits, within which law and public opinion are intruders likely to do more harm than good. To try to regulate the internal affairs of a family, the relations of love or friendship, or many other things of the same sort, by law or by the coercion of public opinion, is like trying to pull an eyelash out of a man's eye with a pair of tongs. They may put out the eye, but they will never get hold of the eyelash.

These, I think, are the principal forms in which society can and actually does promote virtue and restrain vice. It is impossible to form any estimate of the degree in which it succeeds in doing so, but it may perhaps be said that the principal importance of what is done in this direction by criminal law is that in extreme cases it brands gross acts of vice with the deepest mark of infamy which can be impressed upon them, and that in this manner it protects the public and accepted standard of morals from being grossly and openly violated. In short, it affirms in a singularly emphatic manner a principle which is absolutely inconsistent with and contradictory to Mr Mill's—the principle, namely, that there are acts of wickedness so gross and outrageous that, self-protection apart, they must be prevented as far as possible at any cost to the offender, and punished, if they occur, with exemplary severity.

As for the influence of public opinion upon virtue and vice, it is incalculably great, but it is difficult to say much as to its extent, because its influence is indefinite, and is shown in an infinite variety of ways. It must also be observed that, though far more powerful and minute than the influence of law, it is infinitely less well instructed. It is also exceedingly liable to abuse, for public opinion is multiform, and may mean the gossip of a village or the spite of a coterie, as well as the deliberate judgment of a section of the rational part of mankind. On the other hand, its power depends on its nature and on the nature of the person on whom it acts. A calm, strong, and rational man will know when to despise and when to respect it, though no rules can be laid down on the subject. It is, however, clear that this much may be said of it in general. If people neither formed nor expressed any opinions on their neighbours' conduct except in so far as that conduct affected them personally, one of the principal motives to do well and one of the principal restraints from doing ill would be withdrawn from the world. . . .

# QUESTIONS

1. Stephen says that "Legislation ought in all cases to be graduated to the existing level of morals. . . ." Does this imply that the moral standards which the law ought to reflect simply *are* nothing more or less than the prevailing moral opinions of society?

2. Read the opinions in the *Bowers v. Hardwick* case, and then consider the following: Using the criteria Stephen sets forth for determining when it is appropriate to criminalize behavior, would he favor laws like the Georgia statute prohibiting sodomy?

3. In his attempt to illustrate his claim that the law is already deeply committed to punishing vice as such, Stephen says that "every circumstance which aggravates or extenuates the wickedness of an act will operate in aggravation or diminution of punishment." In his comment on Stephen in *Law, Liberty, and Morality*, H.L.A. Hart says that "this argument is a *non sequitur* generated by Stephen's failure to see that the questions 'What sort of conduct may justifiably be punished?' and 'How severely should we punish different offenses?' are distinct and independent questions." Is Hart's criticism correct?

4. Mill acknowledges that his principles of liberty do not apply to the very young, but only to adults. Stephen then says: "How is it possible for society to accept the position of an educator unless it has moral principles on which to educate? How, having accepted that position and having educated people up to a certain point, can it draw a line at which education ends and perfect moral indifference begins?" Are these valid criticisms of Mill's position?

5. Stephen says that "criminal law is in the nature of a persecution of the grosser forms of vice, and an emphatic assertion of the principle that the feeling of hatred and the desire of vengeance . . . are important elements of human nature which ought in such cases to be satisfied in a regular public and legal manner." Here there is both a descriptive claim about the criminal law and a normative claim that a certain desire for vengeance ought to be satisfied using the law. Evaluate each separately.

6. Could a respectable argument be made that failure to criminalize inherently immoral behavior will sometimes lead to harm to society and its members, and thus that a justification for legal moralism indirectly falls under Mill's principles of criminal legislation?

7. Stephen says that "the object of morally intolerant legislation . . . . is to establish . . . that which the legislator regards as a good moral system or standard." What moral standards should legislators regard as good when they are legislating for a pluralistic society in which there is much about which people disagree and about which they think that disagreement is possible for reasonable persons?

# Individual Sovereignty
# and Constitutional Privacy

## *United States Supreme Court*[*]
# GRISWOLD v. CONNETICUT

MR. JUSTICE DOUGLAS delivered the opinion of the Court.

Appellant Griswold is Executive Director of the Planned Parenthood League of Connecticut. Appellant Buxton is a licensed physician and a professor at the Yale Medical School who served as Medical Director for the League at its Center in New Haven—a center open and operating from November 1 to November 10, 1961, when appellants were arrested.

They gave information, instruction, and medical advice to *married persons* as to the means of preventing conception. They examined the wife and prescribed the best contraceptive device or material for her use. Fees were usually charged, although some couples were serviced free.

The statutes whose constitutionality is involved in this appeal are §§53-32 and 54-196 of the General Statutes of Connecticut (1958 rev.). The former provides:

"Any person who uses any drug, medicinal article or instrument for the purpose of preventing conception shall be fined not less than fifty dollars or imprisoned not less than sixty days nor more than one year or be both fined and imprisoned."

Section 54-196 provides:

"Any person who assists, abets, counsels, causes, hires or commands another to commit any offense may be prosecuted and punished as if he were the principal offender."

The appellants were found guilty as accessories and fined $100 each, against the claim that the accessory statute as so applied violated the Fourteenth Amendment. The Appellate Division of the Circuit Court affirmed.

We think that appellants have standing to raise the constitutional rights of the married people with whom they had a professional relationship. . . . Certainly the accessory should have standing to assert that the offense which he is charged with assisting is not, or cannot constitutionally be, a crime. . . .

Coming to the merits, we are met with a wide range of questions that implicate the Due Process Clause of the Fourteenth Amendment. Overtones of some arguments suggest that *Lochner* v. *New York,* 198 U. S. 45, should be our guide. But we decline that invitation. We do not sit as a super-legislature to determine the wisdom, need, and propriety of laws that touch economic problems, business affairs, or social conditions. This law, however, operates directly on an intimate relation of husband and wife and their physician's role in one aspect of that relation.

The association of people is not mentioned in the Constitution nor in the Bill of Rights. The right to educate a child in a school of the parents' choice—whether public or private or parochial—is also not mentioned. Nor is the right to study any particular subject or any foreign language. Yet the First Amendment has been construed to include certain of those rights.

By *Pierce* v. *Society of Sisters*, the right to educate one's children as one chooses is made applicable to the States by the force of the First and Fourteenth Amendments. By *Meyer* v. *Nebraska*, the same dignity is given the right to study the German

[*]381 U. S. 479 (1965). Numerous citations omitted without so specifying.

language in a private school. In other words, the State may not, consistently with the spirit of the First Amendment, contract the spectrum of available knowledge. The right of freedom of speech and press includes not only the right to utter or to print, but the right to distribute, the right to receive, the right to read and freedom of inquiry, freedom of thought, and freedom to teach—indeed the freedom of the entire university community. Without those peripheral rights the specific rights would be less secure. And so we reaffirm the principle of the *Pierce* and the *Meyer* cases.

In *NAACP* v. *Alabama*, we protected the "freedom to associate and privacy in one's associations," noting that freedom of association was a peripheral First Amendment right. Disclosure of membership lists of a constitutionally valid association, we held, was invalid "as entailing the likelihood of a substantial restraint upon the exercise by petitioner's members of their right to freedom of association." In other words, the First Amendment has a penumbra where privacy is protected from governmental intrusion. In like context, we have protected forms of "association" that are not political in the customary sense but pertain to the social, legal, and economic benefit of the members. In *Schware* v. *Board of Bar Examiners*, 353 U. S. 232, we held it not permissible to bar a lawyer from practice, because he had once been a member of the Communist Party. The man's "association with that Party" was not shown to be "anything more than a political

faith in a political party" and was not action of a kind proving bad moral character. . . .

The foregoing cases suggest that specific guarantees in the Bill of Rights have penumbras, formed by emanations from those guarantees that help give them life and substance. Various guarantees create zones of privacy. The right of association contained in the penumbra of the First Amendment is one, as we have seen. The Third Amendment in its prohibition against the quartering of soldiers "in any house" in time of peace without the consent of the owner is another facet of that privacy. The Fourth Amendment explicitly affirms the "right of the people to be secure in their persons, houses, papers, and effects, against unreasonable searches and seizures." The Fifth Amendment in its Self-Incrimination Clause enables the citizen to create a zone of privacy which government may not force him to surrender to his detriment. The Ninth Amendment provides: "The enumeration in the Constitution, of certain rights, shall not be construed to deny or disparage others retained by the people."

The Fourth and Fifth Amendments were described in *Boyd* v. *United States*, as protection against all governmental invasions "of the sanctity of a man's home and the privacies of life."\* We recently referred in *Mapp* v. *Ohio*, 367 U. S. 643, 656, to the Fourth Amendment as creating a "right to privacy, no less important than any other right carefully and particularly reserved to the people."

---

\*The Court said in full about this right of privacy:

"The principles laid down in this opinion [by Lord Camden in *Entick* v. *Carrington*, 19 How. St. Tr. 1029] affect the very essence of constitutional liberty and security. They reach farther than the concrete form of the case then before the court, with its adventitious circumstances; they apply to all invasions on the part of the government and its employes of the sanctity of a man's home and the privacies of life. It is not the breaking of his doors, and the rummaging of his drawers, that constitutes the essence of the offence; but it is the invasion of his indefeasible right of personal security, personal liberty and private property, where that right has never been forfeited by his conviction of some public offence—it is the invasion of this sacred right which underlies and constitutes the essence of Lord Camden's judgment. Breaking into a house and opening boxes and drawers are circum-

We have had many controversies over these penumbral rights of "privacy and repose." These cases bear witness that the right of privacy which presses for recognition here is a legitimate one.

The present case, then, concerns a relationship lying within the zone of privacy created by several fundamental constitutional guarantees. And it concerns a law which, in forbidding the *use* of contraceptives rather than regulating their manufacture or sale, seeks to achieve its goals by means having a maximum destructive impact upon that relationship. Such a law cannot stand in light of the familiar principle, so often applied by this Court, that a "governmental purpose to control or prevent activities constitutionally subject to state regulation may not be achieved by means which sweep unnecessarily broadly and thereby invade the area of protected freedoms." *NAACP* v. *Alabama*, 377 U. S. 288, 307. Would we allow the police to search the sacred precincts of marital bedrooms for telltale signs of the use of contraceptives? The very idea is repulsive to the notions of privacy surrounding the marriage relationship.

We deal with a right of privacy older than the Bill of Rights—older than our political parties, older than our school system. Marriage is a coming together for better or for worse, hopefully enduring, and intimate to the degree of being sacred. It is an association that promotes a way of life, not causes; a harmony in living, not political faiths; a bilateral loyalty, not commercial or social projects. Yet it is an association for as noble a purpose as any involved in our prior decisions.

*Reversed.*

MR. JUSTICE GOLDBERG, whom THE CHIEF JUSTICE and MR. JUSTICE BRENNAN join, concurring.

I agree with the Court that Connecticut's birth-control law unconstitutionally intrudes upon the right of marital privacy, and I join in its opinion and judgment. Although I have not accepted the view that "due process" as used in the Fourteenth Amendment incorporates all of the first eight Amendments, I do agree that the concept of liberty protects those personal rights that are fundamental, and is not confined to the specific terms of the Bill of Rights. My conclusion that the concept of liberty is not so restricted and that it embraces the right of marital privacy though that right is not mentioned explicitly in the Constitution is supported both by numerous decisions of this Court, referred to in the Court's opinion, and by the language and history of the Ninth Amendment. In reaching the conclusion that the right of marital privacy is protected, as being within the protected penumbra of specific guarantees of the Bill of Rights, the Court refers to the Ninth Amendment. I add these words to emphasize the relevance of that Amendment to the Court's holding. . . .

This Court, in a series of decisions, has held that the Fourteenth Amendment absorbs and applies to the States those specifics of the first eight amendments which express fundamental personal rights. The language and history of the Ninth Amendment reveal that the Framers of the Constitution believed that there are additional fundamental rights, protected from governmental infringement, which exist alongside those fundamental rights specifically mentioned in the first eight constitutional amendments.

---

stances of aggravation; but any forcible and compulsory extortion of a man's own testimony or of his private papers to be used as evidence to convict him of crime or to forfeit his goods, is within the condemnation of that judgment. In this regard the Fourth and Fifth Amendments run almost into each other." 116 U. S., at 630.

The Ninth Amendment reads, "The enumeration in the Constitution, of certain rights, shall not be construed to deny or disparage others retained by the people." The Amendment is almost entirely the work of James Madison. It was introduced in Congress by him and passed the House and Senate with little or no debate and virtually no change in language. It was proffered to quiet expressed fears that a bill of specifically enumerated rights could not be sufficiently broad to cover all essential rights and that the specific mention of certain rights would be interpreted as a denial that others were protected.

In presenting the proposed Amendment, Madison said:

"It has been objected also against a bill of rights, that, by enumerating particular exceptions to the grant of power, it would disparage those rights which were not placed in that enumeration; and it might follow by implication, that those rights which were not singled out, were intended to be assigned into the hands of the General Government, and were consequently insecure. This is one of the most plausible arguments I have ever heard urged against the admission of a bill of rights into this system; but, I conceive, that it may be guarded against. I have attempted it, as gentlemen may see by turning to the last clause of the fourth resolution [the Ninth Amendment]." I Annals of Congress 439 (Gales and Seaton ed. 1834).

Mr. Justice Story wrote of this argument against a bill of rights and the meaning of the Ninth Amendment:

"In regard to . . . [a] suggestion, that the affirmance of certain rights might disparage others, or might lead to argumentative implications in favor of other powers, it might be sufficient to say that such a course of reasoning could never be sustained upon any solid basis. . . . But a conclusive answer is, that such an attempt may be interdicted (as it has been) by a positive declaration in such a bill of rights that the enumeration of certain rights shall not be construed to deny or disparage others retained by the people." II Story, Commentaries on the Constitution of the United States 626-627 (5th ed. 1891).

He further stated, referring to the Ninth Amendment:

"This clause was manifestly introduced to prevent any perverse or ingenious misapplication of the well-known maxim, that an affirmation in particular cases implies a negation in all others; and, *e converso*, that a negation in particular cases implies an affirmation in all others."

These statements of Madison and Story make clear that the Framers did not intend that the first eight amendments be construed to exhaust the basic and fundamental rights which the Constitution guaranteed to the people.

While this Court has had little occasion to interpret the Ninth Amendment, "[i]t cannot be presumed that any clause in the constitution is intended to be without effect." In interpreting the Constitution, "real effect should be given to all the words it uses." The Ninth Amendment to the Constitution may be regarded by some as a recent discovery and may be forgotten by others, but since 1791 it has been a basic part of the Constitution which we are sworn to uphold. To hold that a right so basic and fundamental and so deep-rooted in our society as the right of privacy in marriage may be infringed because that right is not guaranteed in so many words by the first eight amendments to the Constitution is to ignore the Ninth Amendment and to give it no effect whatsoever.

Moreover, a judicial construction that this fundamental right is not protected by the Constitution because it is not mentioned in explicit terms by one of the first eight amendments or elsewhere in the Constitution would violate the Ninth Amendment, which specifically states that "[t]he enumeration in the Constitution, of certain rights, shall not be *construed* to deny or disparage others retained by the people." . . . (Emphasis added.)

MR. JUSTICE BLACK, with whom MR. JUSTICE STEWART joins, dissenting.

I agree with my Brother STEWART's dissenting opinion. And like him I do not to any extent whatever base my view that this Connecticut law is constitutional on a belief that the law is wise or that its policy is a good one. In order that there may be no room at all to doubt why I vote as I do, I feel constrained to add that the law is every bit as offensive to me as it is to my Brethren of the majority and my Brothers HARLAN, WHITE and GOLDBERG who, reciting reasons why it is offensive to them, hold it unconstitutional. There is no single one of the graphic and eloquent strictures and criticisms fired at the policy of this Connecticut law either by the Court's opinion or by those of my concurring Brethren to which I cannot subscribe—except their conclusion that the evil qualities they see in the law make it unconstitutional. . . .

The Court talks about a constitutional "right of privacy" as though there is some constitutional provision or provisions forbidding any law ever to be passed which might abridge the "privacy" of individuals. But there is not. There are, of course, guarantees in certain specific constitutional provisions which are designed in part to protect privacy at certain times and places with respect to certain activities.

Such, for example, is the Fourth Amendment's guarantee against "unreasonable searches and seizures." But I think it belittles that Amendment to talk about it as though it protects nothing but "privacy." To treat it that way is to give it a niggardly interpretation, not the kind of liberal reading I think any Bill of Rights provision should be given. The average man would very likely not have his feelings soothed any more by having his property seized openly than by having it seized privately and by stealth. He simply wants his property left alone. And a person can be just as much, if not more, irritated, annoyed and injured by an unceremonious public arrest by a policeman as he is by a seizure in the privacy of his office or home.

One of the most effective ways of diluting or expanding a constitutionally guaranteed right is to substitute for the crucial word or words of a constitutional guarantee another word or words, more or less flexible and more or less restricted in meaning. This fact is well illustrated by the use of the term "right of privacy" as a comprehensive substitute for the Fourth Amendment's guarantee against "unreasonable searches and seizures." "Privacy" is a broad, abstract and ambiguous concept which can easily be shrunken in meaning but which can also, on the other hand, easily be interpreted as a constitutional ban against many things other than searches and seizures. I have expressed the view many times that First Amendment freedoms, for example, have suffered from a failure of the courts to stick to the simple language of the First Amendment in construing it, instead of invoking multitudes of words substituted for those the Framers used. For these reasons I get nowhere in this case by talk about a constitutional "right of privacy" as an emanation from one or more constitutional provisions.[1] I like my privacy as well as the next one, but I am nevertheless compelled to admit that government has a right to invade it unless prohibited by some specific constitutional provision. For these reasons I cannot agree with the Court's judgment and the reasons it gives for holding this Connecticut law unconstitutional.

This brings me to the arguments made by my Brothers HARLAN, WHITE and GOLDBERG for invalidating the Connecticut law. Brothers HARLAN[2] and WHITE would invalidate it by reliance on the Due Proces Clause of the Fourteenth Amendment, but Brother GOLDBERG, while agreeing with Brother HARLAN, relies also on the Ninth Amendment. I have no doubt that the Connecticut law could be applied in such a way as to abridge freedom of speech and press and therefore violate the First and Fourteenth Amendments. My disagreement with the Court's opinion holding that there is such a violation here is a narrow one, relating to the application of the First Amendment to the facts and circumstances of this particular case. But my disagreement with Brothers HARLAN, WHITE and GOLDBERG is more basic. I think that if properly construed neither the Due Process Clause nor the Ninth Amendment, nor both together, could under any circumstances be a proper basis for invalidating the Connecticut law. I discuss the due process and Ninth Amendment arguments together because on analysis they turn out to be the same thing—merely using different words to claim for this Court and the federal judiciary power to invalidate any legislative act which the judges find irrational, unreasonable or offensive.

The due process argument which my Brothers HARLAN and WHITE adopt here is based, as their opinions indicate, on the premise that this Court is vested with power to invalidate all state laws that it considers to be arbitrary, capricious, unreasonable, or oppressive, or on this Court's belief that a particular state law under scrutiny has no "rational or justifying" purpose, or is offensive to a "sense of fairness and justice." If these formulas based on "natural justice," or others which mean the same thing, are to prevail, they require judges to determine what is or is not constitutional on the basis of their own appraisal of what laws are unwise or unnecessary. The power to make such decisions is of course that of a legislative body. Surely it has to be admitted that no provision of the Constitution specifically gives such blanket power to courts to exercise such a supervisory veto over the wisdom

[1] The phrase "right to privacy" appears first to have gained currency from an article written by Messrs. Warren and (later Mr. Justice) Brandeis in 1890 which urged that States should give some form of tort relief to persons whose private affairs were exploited by others. The Right to Privacy, 4 Harv. L. Rev. 193. Largely as a result of this article, some States have passed statutes creating such a cause of action, and in others state courts have done the same thing by exercising their powers as courts of common law. See generally 41 Am. Jur. 926–927. Thus the Supreme Court of Georgia, in granting a cause of action for damages to a man whose picture had been used in a newspaper advertisement without his consent, said that "A right of privacy in matters purely private is . . . derived from natural law" and that "The conclusion reached by us seems to be . . . thoroughly in accord with natural justice, with the principles of the law of every civilized nation, and especially with the elastic principles of the common law . . . ." *Pavesich* v. *New England Life Ins. Co.,* 122 Ga. 190, 194, 218, 50 S. E. 68, 70, 80. Observing that "the right of privacy . . . presses for recognition here," today this Court, which I did not understand to have power to sit as a court of common law, now appears to be exalting a phrase which Warren and Brandeis used in discussing grounds for tort relief, to the level of a constitutional rule which prevents state legislatures from passing any law deemed by this court to interfere with "privacy."

[2] Brother Harlan's views are spelled out at greater length in his dissenting opinion in *Poe* v. *Ullman,* 367 U.S. 497, 539–555.

and value of legislative policies and to hold unconstitutional those laws which they believe unwise or dangerous. I readily admit that no legislative body, state or national, should pass laws that can justly be given any of the invidious labels invoked as constitutional excuses to strike down state laws. But perhaps it is not too much to say that no legislative body ever does pass laws without believing that they will accomplish a sane, rational, wise and justifiable purpose. While I completely subscribe to the holding of *Marbury* v. *Madison*, 1 Cranch 137, and subsequent cases, that our Court has constitutional power to strike down statutes, state or federal, that violate commands of the Federal Constitution, I do not believe that we are granted power by the Due Process Clause or any other constitutional provision or provisions to measure constitutionality by our belief that legislation is arbitrary, capricious or unreasonable, or accomplishes no justifiable purpose, or is offensive to our own notions of "civilized standards of conduct." Such an appraisal of the wisdom of legislation is an attribute of the power to make laws, not of the power to interpret them. The use by federal courts of such a formula or doctrine or whatnot to veto federal or state laws simply takes away from Congress and States the power to make laws based on their own judgment of fairness and wisdom and transfers that power to this Court for ultimate determination—a power which was specifically denied to federal courts by the convention that framed the Constitution. . . .

My Brother GOLDBERG has adopted the recent discovery that the Ninth Amendment as well as the Due Process Clause can be used by this Court as authority to strike down all state legislation which this Court thinks violates "fundamental principles of liberty and justice," or is contrary to the "traditions and [collective] conscience of our people." He also states, without proof satisfactory to me, that in making decisions on this basis judges will not consider "their personal and private notions." One may ask how they can avoid considering them. Our Court certainly has no machinery with which to take a Gallup Poll.[13] And the scientific miracles of this age have not yet produced a gadget which the Court can use to determine what traditions are rooted in the "[collective] conscience of our people." Moreover, one would certainly have to look far beyond the language of the Ninth Amendment[14] to find that the Framers vested in this Court any such awesome veto powers over law-making, either by the States or by the Congress. Nor does anything in the history of the Amendment offer any support for such a shocking doctrine. The whole history of the adoption of the Constitution and Bill of Rights points the other way, and the very material quoted by my Brother GOLDBERG shows that the Ninth Amendment was intended to protect against the idea that "by enumerating

[13]Of course one cannot be oblivious to the fact that Mr. Gallup has already published the results of a poll which he says show that 46% of the people in this country believe schools should teach about birth control. Washington Post, May 21, 1965, p. 2, col. 1. I can hardly believe, however, that Brother GOLDBERG would view 46% of the persons polled as so overwhelming a proportion that this Court may now rely on it to delcare that the Connecticut law infringes "fundamental" rights, and overrule the long-standing view of the people of Connecticut expressed through their elected representatives.

[14]U.S. Const., Amend. IX, provides:
"The enumeration in the Constitution, of certain rights, shall not be construed to deny or disparage others retained by the people."

particular exceptions to the grant of power" to the Federal Government, "those rights which were not singled out, were intended to be assigned into the hands of the General Government [the United States], and were consequently insecure."[15] That Amendment was passed, not to broaden the powers of this Court or any other department of "the General Government," but, as every student of history knows, to assure the people that the Constitution in all its provisions was intended to limit the Federal Government to the powers granted expressly or by necessary implication. If any broad, unlimited power to hold laws unconstitutional because they offend what this Court conceives to be the "[collective] conscience of our people" is vested in this Court by the Ninth Amendment, the Fourteenth Amendment, or any other provision of the Constitution, it was not given by the Framers, but rather has been bestowed on the Court by the Court. This fact is perhaps responsible for the peculiar phenomenon that for a period of a century and a half no serious suggestion was ever made that the Ninth Amendment, enacted to protect state powers against federal invasion, could be used as a weapon of federal power to prevent state legislatures from passing laws they consider appropriate to govern local affairs. Use of any such broad, unbounded judicial authority would make of this Court's members a day-to-day constitutional convention.

I repeat so as not be misunderstood that this Court does have power, which it should exercise, to hold laws unconstitutional where they are forbidden by the Federal Constitution. My point is that there is no provision of the Constitution which either expressly or impliedly vests power in this Court to sit as a supervisory agency over acts of duly constituted legislative bodies and set aside their laws because of the Court's belief that the legislative policies adopted are unreasonable, unwise, arbitrary, capricious or irrational. The adoption of such a loose, flexible, uncontrolled standard for holding laws unconstitutional, if ever it is finally achieved, will amount to a great unconstitutional shift of power to the courts which I believe and am constrained to say will be bad for the courts and worse for the country. Subjecting federal and state laws to such an unrestrained and unrestrainable judicial control as to the wisdom of legislative enactments would, I fear, jeopardize the separation of governmental powers that the Framers set up and at the same time threaten to take away much of the power of States to govern themselves which the Constitution plainly intended them to have.

I realize that many good and able men have eloquently spoken and written, sometimes in rhapsodical strains, about the duty of this Court to keep the Constitution in tune with the times. The idea is that the Constitution must be changed from time to time and that this Court is charged with a duty to make those changes. For myself, I must with all deference reject that philosophy. The Constitution makers knew the need for change and provided for it. Amendments suggested by the people's

---

[15] 1 Annals of Congress 439. See also II Story, Commentaries on the Constitution of the United States (5th ed. 1891): "This clause was manifestly introduced to prevent any perverse or ingenious misapplication of the well-known maxim, that an affirmation in particular cases implies a negation in all others; and, *e converso*, that a negation in particular cases implies an affirmation in all others. The maxim, rightly understood, is perfectly sound and safe; but it has often been strangely forced from its natural meaning into the support of the most dangerous political heresies." *Id.*, at 651 (footnote omitted).

elected representatives can be submitted to the people or their selected agents for ratification. That method of change was good for our Fathers, and being somewhat old-fashioned I must add it is good enough for me. And so, I cannot rely on the Due Process Clause or the Ninth Amendment or any mysterious and uncertain natural law concept as a reason for striking down this state law. The Due Process Clause with an "arbitrary and capricious" or "shocking to the conscience" formula was liberally used by this Court to strike down economic legislation in the early decades of this century, threatening, many people thought, the tranquility and stability of the Nation. See, *e.g., Lochner* v. *New York,* 198 U. S. 45. That formula, based on subjective considerations of "natural justice," is no less dangerous when used to enforce this Court's views about personal rights than those about economic rights. . . .

## QUESTIONS

1. How might the "zones of privacy" type of argument used by Justice Douglas be used to strike down *economic* legislation limiting, say, the sorts of contracts that one can enter into?

2. Some would claim that the sheer number of amendments referred to as having "penumbras" and "emanations" and supposedly adding up to a right of privacy makes the whole argument implausible, and that, to be convincing, such an argument would need to show that some specifically guaranteed right involved some specific right of privacy. Do you agree?

3. Read what Justice Black says about the origin of the phrase "right to privacy" in footnote 1 of his dissenting opinion. Do you agree with those who claim that some of the opinions in the *Griswold* case play fast and loose with the distinction between privacy and autonomy? Does *Griswold* still have something to do with privacy, even if privacy is understood in the narrow sense as having to do with the security of information and impressions about oneself?

4. In his dissent, Justice Black says that "One of the most effective ways of diluting or expanding a constitutionally guaranteed right is to substitute for the crucial word or words of a constitutional guarantee another word or words, more or less flexible and more or less restricted in meaning." To what extent is this a fair criticism? Is anyone proposing that the *word* "privacy" replace some other word or words in the Constitution? Does any argument in the majority opinion rest on such a replacement?

5. The Ninth Amendment to the U.S. Constitution reads: "The enumeration in the Constitution, of certain rights, shall not be construed to deny or disparage others retained by the people." Read this as literally as you can, paying close attention to the exact words being used. What does it mean? What, in your view, is the most plausible interpretation of the intent of those who wrote and adopted this form of words?

## *United States Supreme Court**

## ROE v. WADE

Mr. Justice Blackmun delivered the opinion of the Court. The Texas statutes that concern us here are Arts. 1191–1194 and 1196 of the State's Penal Code.[1] These make it a crime to "procure an abortion," as therein defined, or to attempt one, except with respect to "an abortion procured or attempted by medical advice for the purpose of saving the life of the mother." Similar statutes are in existence in a majority of the States. . . .

Jane Roe,[4] a single woman who was residing in Dallas County, Texas, instituted this federal action in March 1970 against the District Attorney of the county. She sought a declaratory judgment that the Texas criminal abortion statutes were unconstitutional on their face, and an injunction restraining the defendant from enforcing the statutes.

Roe alleged that she was unmarried and pregnant; that she wished to terminate her pregnancy by an abortion "performed by a competent, licensed physician, under safe, clinical conditions"; that she was unable to get a "legal" abortion in Texas because her life did not appear to be threatened by the continuation of her pregnancy; and that she could not afford to travel to another jurisdiction in order to secure a legal abortion under safe conditions. She claimed that the Texas statutes were unconstitutionally vague and that they abridged her right of personal privacy, protected by the First, Fourth, Fifth, Ninth, and Fourteenth Amendments. By an amendment to her complaint Roe purported to sue "on behalf of herself and all other women" similarly situated. . . .

Three reasons have been advanced to explain historically the enactment of criminal abortion laws in the 19th century and to justify their continued existence.

It has been argued occasionally that these laws were the product of a Victorian social concern to discourage illicit sexual conduct. Texas, however, does not advance this justification in the present case, and it appears that no court or commentator has taken the argument seriously. . . .

A second reason is concerned with abortion as a medical procedure. When most criminal abortion laws were first enacted, the procedure was a hazardous one for the woman. This was particularly true prior to the development of antisepsis. Antiseptic techniques, of course, were based on discoveries by Lister, Pasteur, and others first announced in 1867, but were not generally accepted and employed until about the turn of the century. Abortion mortality was high. Even after 1900, and perhaps until as late the development of antibiotics in the 1940's,

---

*410 U. S. 113 (1973). Numerous citations omitted without so specifying.

[1]"Article 1191.  Abortion

"If any person shall designedly administer to a pregnant woman or knowingly procure to be administered with her consent any drug or medicine, or shall use towards her any violence or means whatever externally or internally applied, and thereby procure an abortion, he shall be confined in the penitentiary not less than two nor more than five years; if it be done without her consent, the punishment shall be doubled. By 'abortion' is meant that the life of the fetus or embryo shall be destroyed in the woman's womb or that a premature birth thereof be caused.

"Art. 1192.  Furnishing the means

"Whoever furnishes the means for procuring an abortion knowing the purpose intended is guilty as an accomplice.

"Art. 1193.  Attempt at abortion

standard modern techniques such as dilation and curettage were not nearly so safe as they are today. Thus, it has been argued that a State's real concern in enacting a criminal abortion law was to protect the pregnant woman, that is, to restrain her from submitting to a procedure that placed her life in serious jeopardy.

Modern medical techniques have altered this situation. Appellants and various *amici* refer to medical data indicating that abortion in early pregnancy, that is, prior to the end of the first trimester, although not without its risk, is now relatively safe. . . .

The third reason is the State's interest—some phrase it in terms of duty—in protecting prenatal life. Some of the argument for this justification rests on the theory that a new human life is present from the moment of conception. The State's interest and general obligation to protect life then extends, it is argued, to prenatal life. Only when the life of the pregnant mother herself is at stake, balanced against the life she carries within her, should the interest of the embryo or fetus not prevail. Logically, of course, a legitimate state interest in this area need not stand or fall on acceptance of the belief that life begins at conception or at some other point prior to live birth. In assessing the State's interest, recognition may be given to the less rigid claim that as long as at least *potential life* is involved, the State may assert

interests beyond the protection of the pregnant woman alone.

It is with these interests, and the weight to be attached to them, that this case is concerned.

. . . [T]he Court has recognized that a right of personal privacy, or a guarantee of certain areas or zones of privacy, does exist under the Constitution. In varying contexts, the Court or individual Justices have, indeed, found at least the roots of that right in the First Amendment, *Stanley* v. *Georgia*, in the Fourth and Fifth Amendments, in the penumbras of the Bill of Rights, *Griswold* v. *Connecticut*; in the Ninth Amendment; or in the concept of liberty guaranteed by the first section of the Fourteenth Amendment. These decisions make it clear that only personal rights that can be deemed "fundamental" or "implicit in the concept of ordered liberty," *Palko* v. *Connecticut*, are included in this guarantee of personal privacy. They also make it clear that the right has some extension to activities relating to marriage, *Loving* v. *Virginia*, U. S. 1, 12 (1967); procreation, *Skinner* v. *Oklahoma*, contraception, *Eisenstadt* v. *Baird*; family relationships, *Prince* v. *Massachusetts*; and child rearing and education, *Pierce* v. *Society of Sisters*.

This right of privacy, whether it be founded in the Fourteenth Amendment's concept of personal liberty and restrictions upon state action, as we feel it is, or, as the District Court

---

"If the means used shall fail to produce an abortion, the offender is nevertheless guilty of an attempt to produce abortion, provided it be shown that such means were calculated to produce that result, and shall be fined not less than one hundred nor more than one thousand dollars.

"Art. 1194. Murder in producing abortion

"If the death of the mother is occasioned by an abortion so produced or by an attempt to effect the same it is murder."

"Art. 1196. By medical advice

"Nothing in this chapter applies to an abortion procured or attempted by medical advice for the purpose of saving the life of the mother."

The foregoing Articles, together with Art. 1195, compose Chapter 9 of Title 15 of the Penal Code. Article 1195, not attacked here, reads:

"Art. 1195. Destroying unborn child.

"Whoever shall during parturition of the mother destroy the vitality or life in a child in a state of being born and before actual birth, which child would otherwise have been born alive, shall be confined in the penitentiary for life or for not less than five years."

[4]The name is a pseudonym.

determined, in the Ninth Amendment's reservation of rights to the people, is broad enough to encompass a woman's decision whether or not to terminate her pregnancy. The detriment that the State would impose upon the pregnant woman by denying this choice altogether is apparent. Specific and direct harm medically diagnosable even in early pregnancy may be involved. Maternity, or additional offspring, may force upon the woman a distressful life and future. Psychological harm may be imminent. Mental and physical health may be taxed by child care. There is also the distress, for all concerned, associated with the unwanted child, and there is the problem of bringing a child into a family already unable, psychologically and otherwise, to care for it. In other cases, as in this one, the additional difficulties and continuing stigma of unwed motherhood may be involved. All these are factors the woman and her responsible physician necessarily will consider in consultation.

On the basis of elements such as these, appellant and some *amici* argue that the woman's right is absolute and that she is entitled to terminate her pregnancy at whatever time, in whatever way, and for whatever reason she alone chooses. With this we do not agree. Appellant's arguments that Texas either has no valid interest at all in regulating the abortion decision, or no interest strong enough to support any limitation upon the woman's sole determination, are unpersuasive. The Court's decisions recognizing a right of privacy also acknowledge that some state regulation in areas protected by that right is appropriate. As noted above, a State may properly assert important interests in safeguarding health, in maintaining medical standards, and in protecting potential life. At some point in pregnancy, these respective interests become sufficiently compelling to sustain regulation of the factors that govern the abortion decision. The privacy right involved, therefore, cannot be said to be absolute. In fact, it is not clear to us that the claim asserted by some *amici* that one has an unlimited right to do with one's body as one pleases bears a close relationship to the right of privacy previously articulated in the Court's decisions. . . .

The appellee and certain *amici* argue that the fetus is a "person" within the language and meaning of the Fourteenth Amendment. In support of this, they outline at length and in detail the well-known facts of fetal development. If this suggestion of personhood is established, the appellant's case, of course, collapses, for the fetus' right to life would then be guaranteed specifically by the Amendment. The appellant conceded as much on reargument. On the other hand, the appellee conceded on reargument that no case could be cited that holds that a fetus is a person within the meaning of the Fourteenth Amendment.

The Constitution does not define "person" in so many words. Section 1 of the Fourteenth Amendment contains three references to "person." . . . But in nearly all these instances, the use of the word is such that it has application only postnatally. None indicates, with any assurance, that it has any possible pre-natal application.

All this, together with our observation, *supra*, that throughout the major portion of the 19th century prevailing legal abortion practices were far freer than they are today, persuades us that the word "person," as used in the Fourteenth Amendment, does not include the unborn. . . .

This conclusion, however, does not of itself fully answer the contentions raised by Texas, and we pass on to other considerations.

The pregnant woman cannot be isolated in her privacy. She carries an embryo and, later, a fetus, if one accepts the medical definitions of the developing young in the human uterus. The situation therefore is inherently different from marital intimacy, or bedroom possession of obscene material, or marriage, or procreation, or education, with which *Eisenstadt* and *Griswold, Stanley, Loving, Skinner*, and *Pierce* and *Meyer* were respectively concerned. . . .

Texas urges that, apart from the Fourteenth Amendment, life begins at conception and is present throughout pregnancy, and that, therefore, the State has a compelling interest in protecting that life from and after conception. We need not resolve the difficult question of when life begins. When those trained in the respective disciplines of medicine, philosophy, and theology are unable to arrive at any consensus, the judiciary, at this point in the development of man's knowledge, is not in a position to speculate as to the answer.

. . . [W]e do not agree that, by adopting one theory of life, Texas may override the rights of the pregnant woman that are at stake. We repeat, however, that the State does have an important and legitimate interest in preserving and protecting the health of the pregnant woman, whether she be a resident of the State or a nonresident who seeks medical consultation and treatment there, and that it has still *another* important and legitimate interest in protecting the potentiality of human life. These interests are separate and distinct. Each grows in substantiality as the woman approaches term and, at a point during pregnancy, each becomes "compelling."

With respect to the State's important and legitimate interest in the health of the mother, the "compelling" point, in the light of present medical knowledge, is at approximately the end of the first trimester. This is so because of the now-established medical fact, referred to above at 149, that until the end of the first trimester mortality in abortion may be less than mortality in normal childbirth. It follows that, from and after this point, a State may regulate the abortion procedure to the extent that the regulation reasonably relates to the preservation and protection of maternal health. Examples of permissible state regulation in this area are requirements as to the qualifications of the person who is to perform the abortion; as to the licensure of that person; as to the facility in which the procedure is to be performed,

that is, whether it must be a hospital or may be a clinic or some other place of less-than-hospital status; as to the licensing of the facility; and the like.

This means, on the other hand, that, for the period of pregnancy prior to this "compelling" point, the attending physician, in consultation with his patient, is free to determine, without regulation by the State, that, in his medical judgment, the patient's pregnancy should be terminated. If that decision is reached, the judgment may be effectuated by an abortion free of interference by the State.

With respect to the State's important and legitimate interest in potential life, the "compelling" point is at viability. This is so because the fetus then presumably has the capability of meaningful life outside the mother's womb. State regulation protective of fetal life after viability thus has both logical and biological justifications. If the State is interested in protecting fetal life after viability, it may go so far as to proscribe abortion during that period, except when it is necessary to preserve the life or health of the mother.

Measured against these standards, Art. 1196 of the Texas Penal Code, in restricting legal abortions to those "procured or attempted by medical advice for the purpose of saving the life of the mother," sweeps too broadly. The statute makes no distinction between abortions performed early in pregnancy and those performed later, and it limits to a single reason, "saving" the mother's life, the legal justification for the procedure. The statute, therefore, cannot survive the constitutional attack made upon it here. . . .

To summarize and to repeat:

1. A state criminal abortion statute of the current Texas type, that excepts from criminality only a *life-saving* procedure on behalf of the mother, without regard to pregnancy stage and without recognition of the other interests involved, is violative of the Due Process Clause of the Fourteenth Amendment.

(a) For the stage prior to approximately the end of the first trimester, the abortion decision and its effectuation must be left to the medical judgment of the pregnant woman's attending physician.

(b) For the stage subsequent to approximately the end of the first trimester, the State, in promoting its interest in the health of the mother, may, if it chooses, regulate the abortion procedure in ways that are reasonably related to maternal health.

(c) For the stage subsequent to viability, the State in promoting its interest in the potentiality of human life may, if it chooses, regulate, and even proscribe, abortion except where it is necessary, in appropriate medical judgment, for the preservation of the life or health of the mother.

2. The State may define the term "physician," as it has been employed in the preceding paragraphs of this Part XI of this opinion, to mean only a physician currently licensed by the State, and may proscribe any abortion by a person who is not a physician as so defined. . . .

This holding, we feel, is consistent with the relative weights of the respective interests involved, with the lessons and examples of medical and legal history, with the lenity of the common law, and with the demands of the profound problems of the present day. The decision leaves the State free to place increasing restrictions on abortion as the period of pregnancy lengthens, so long as those restrictions are tailored to the recognized state interests. The decision vindicates the right of the physician to administer medical treatment according to his professional judgment up to the points where important state interests provide compelling justifications for intervention. Up to those points, the abortion decision in all its aspects is inherently, and primarily, a medical decision, and basic responsibility for it must rest with the physician. If an individual practitioner abuses the privilege of exercising proper medical judgment, the usual remedies, judicial and intra-professional, are available. . . .

MR. JUSTICE REHNQUIST, dissenting . . . I have difficulty in concluding, as the Court does, that the right of "privacy" is involved in this case. Texas, by the statute here challenged, bars the performance of a medical abortion by a licensed physician on a plaintiff such as Roe. A transaction resulting in an operation such as this is not "private" in the ordinary usage of that word. Nor is the "privacy" that the Court finds here even a distant relative of the freedom from searches and seizures protected by the Fourth Amendment to the Constitution, which the Court has referred to as embodying a right to privacy.

If the Court means by the term "privacy" no more than that the claim of a person to be free from unwanted state regulation of consensual transactions may be a form of "liberty protected by the Fourteenth Amendment, there is no doubt that similar claims have been upheld in our earlier decisions on the basis of that liberty. I agree with the statement of MR. JUSTICE STEWART in his concurring opinion that the "liberty," against deprivation of which without due process the Fourteenth Amendment protects, embraces more than the rights found in the Bill of Rights. But that liberty is not guaranteed absolutely against deprivation, only against deprivation without due process of law. The test traditionally applied in the area of social and economic legislation is whether or not a law such as that challenged has a rational relation to a valid state objective. The Due Process Clause of the Fourteenth Amendment undoubtedly does place a limit, albeit a broad one, on legislative power to enact laws such as this. If the Texas statute were to prohibit an abortion even where the mother's life is in jeopardy, I have little doubt that such a statute would lack a rational relation to a valid state objective. But the Court's sweeping invalidation of any restrictions on abortion during the first trimester is impossible to justify under that standard, and the conscious weighing of competing factors that the Court's opinion apparently substitutes for the established test is far more appropriate to legislative judgment than to a judicial one. . . .

As in *Lochner* and similar cases applying substantive due process standards to economic and social welfare legislation, the adoption of the compelling state interest standard will inevitably require this Court to examine the legislative policies and pass on the wisdom of these policies in the very process of deciding whether a particular state interest put forward may or may not be "compelling." The decision here to break pregnancy into three distinct terms and to outline the permissible restrictions the State may impose in each one, for example, partakes more of judicial legislation than it does of a determination of the intent of the drafters of the Fourteenth Amendment.

The fact that a majority of the States reflecting, after all, the majority sentiment in those States, have had restrictions on abortions for at least a century is a strong indication, it seems to me, that the asserted right to an abortion is not "so rooted in the traditions and conscience of our people as to be ranked as fundamental." Even today, when society's views on abortion are changing, the very existence of the debate is evidence that the "right" to an abortion is not so universally accepted as the appellant would have us believe. . . .

## QUESTIONS

1. If the fetus is considered to be a person from the point of conception, does that by itself have implications for the permissibility of abortions in cases of rape or incest?

2. Some argue that it is misleading or outright mistaken to say that a woman's right to have an abortion really has anything to do with *privacy.* Do you agree, or not?

3. What are the advantages and/or disadvantages of each of the following as the point at which full personhood (i.e., having moral rights and rights under the Constitution) is thought to begin: (a) conception; (b) viability; (c) birth? Are there advantages and/or disadvantages in thinking of personhood as being a matter of degree?

4. Why should viability be considered the "compelling" point at which the interest in protecting potential life becomes especially weighty?

5. The Court says that "the word 'person,' as used in the Fourteenth Amendment, does not include the unborn." Suppose that it could indeed be shown that the word "person," as used by those who wrote and adopted the Constitution, was not understood either by them or their audience to include the unborn. Would that mean that the rights of the unborn have no "textual" basis in the Constitution? If, in spite of this, it could be established that, from a *moral* point of view, the unborn are truly persons, would that make a difference for the way in which *Roe* ought to have been decided? Explain and defend your answers.

6. Consider the following argument: "In the process in which an egg becomes fertilized, then develops into a fetus, and then eventually becomes a child, no sharp line demarcating personhood from nonpersonhood can be drawn. A fertilized egg is no more a child or human person than a poppy seed is a flowering poppy. And the fact that both the fertilized egg and the seed can develop into something different from what they are, and by a process that proceeds smoothly and by degrees no more shows this to be false than the fact that day gradually develops out of night shows that there is no fundamental difference between night and day. Therefore, the Court in *Roe* did the right thing in rejecting the contention that human personhood begins at conception, and instead concluding that

the legitimate interest in protecting potential human life "grows in substantiality as the woman approaches term. . . . " Do you agree with this? What reasons are there for and against thinking of human personhood as developing by degrees rather than coming on the scene all at once? Does your answer to this question depend on whether we are asking about personhood for constitutional purposes, or for ordinary purposes of everyday moral judgment? Explain and defend your answers.

## Donald H. Regan
# REWRITING ROE v. WADE*

## I. THE PREGNANT WOMAN AS SAMARITAN

In this Section of the essay, I shall attempt to locate the abortion problem in the doctrinal landscape of samaritan law. Some readers will object that the abortion problem does not belong in that landscape at all, that I am looking at the wrong map. We usually think of samaritan problems as problems involving *omissions*. The established general principle that one does not have to volunteer aid (which I shall refer to as the "bad-samaritan principle") is normally thought of as equivalent to the notion that there is no liability for a failure to act. But the behavior of a woman who secures an abortion does not look like an omission. It looks like an act. So does the behavior of anyone who helps her. Perhaps the bad-samaritan principle is irrelevant. The first project for this part of the essay, then, is to explain why the abortion problem should be regarded as a problem in samaritan law.

Once we have established that we are looking at the right map, we shall attempt to orient ourselves with regard to some important landmarks, such as the established exceptions and apparent exceptions to the bad-samaritan principle. Two important propositions will appear. First, the abortion case is distinguishable in some significant re-

spects from every other case in which a duty to aid is imposed. A respectable argument can therefore be made that if the pregnant woman is to be treated consistently with other potential samaritans, it is impermissible to impose on her even a trivially burdensome duty to aid. Many readers will not be persuaded by such an argument, however. They will believe that even if the pregnant woman is distinguishable from every other potential samaritan on whom duties to aid are imposed, still the cumulative force of the *similarities* of the abortion case to various other cases where duties are imposed makes it clear that the pregnant woman may be subjected to some burdens. That brings us to the second proposition: There is *no* other potential samaritan on whom burdens are imposed which are as extensive and as physically invasive as the burdens of pregnancy and childbirth. Even if the pregnant woman should be regarded as "eligible for compulsion to samaritanism" to some extent, she is by no means the most eligible member of the family of potential samaritans. It is not acceptable to subject her to specially extensive and specially invasive burdens, as laws forbidding abortion do.

By now every reader who has given any rein at all to his imagination will have thought up at least two or three objections to

*From *Michigan Law Review*, vol. 77 (1979). Excerpts only. Reprinted by permission of *Michigan Law Review* and the author.

the claim that laws forbidding abortion are inconsistent with the general tenor of samaritan law. There are many possible objections to be dealt with, and I cannot deal with them all at once. In order that the reader shall not be distracted by impatience to know when I will deal with his particular objections, let me indicate the order of treatment of the major topics in what follows. First, I shall explain why abortion is a samaritanism problem. Second, I shall examine the extent and nature of the burdens imposed on women by anti-abortion statutes. I shall concentrate on the physical and psychological burdens of pregnancy and childbirth, and I shall explain why I think these burdens are more important to the *constitutional* argument concerning abortion than the burdens of child-rearing or the psychological cost of giving up a child for adoption. (It is worth mentioning now that one of the reasons laws forbidding abortion are not validated by analogy to the "parenthood exception" to the bad-samaritan principle is that the burdens of pregnancy and childbirth are physically invasive in a way the burdens imposed on parents are not. As I shall show, physical invasions are specially disfavored by our common and constitutional law. I think this is not the only distinction between the pregnant woman and the parent, but it may well be the most important distinction for my purposes.) Third, I shall explain why the pregnant woman is different from every other potential samaritan on whom common-law duties to aid are imposed, including the parent, the social host, the innocent or negligent creator of a dangerous situation, the samaritan who voluntarily begins to give aid an may be forbidden to terminate the aid, and so on. In the process I shall explain why it is not an adequate defense of laws against abortion that pregnancy is "voluntary". Fourth, I shall distinguish the abortion case from certain exceptions and apparent exceptions to the bad-samaritan principle created by statute, notably the military draft. (The draft involves burdens closely compa-rable to the burdens of pregnancy, but the draft, I shall argue, is *not* a problem in samaritan law, however much it may seem so at first.) Finally, a few summary remarks will conclude this part of the essay.

## A. Is Samaritan Law Relevant?

The bad-samaritan principle depends on a distinction between acts and omissions. It would exempt from all liability a physically healthy adult who watched an unrelated child drown in a foot of water, maliciously refusing to pull the child out. It would not, however, permit the adult to hold the child under that water. One might argue that the pregnant woman does not even come within the general scope of the bad-samaritan principle because aborting a fetus, or securing an abortion, is not an omission but a positive act, like holding the child under.

It is clear that from one perspective securing an abortion looks like a positive act. It should also be clear that from another perspective it does not. Carrying a fetus and giving birth are burdensome, disruptive, uncomfortable, and usually to some extent painful activities. In effect, the fetus makes continuing demands for aid on the woman who carries it. The fetus is not like a child being held under water, whose prospects would be satisfactory if the adult holding it under would merely go away. The fetus is much more like the child drowning on its own, who needs the adult bystander to rescue it. The principal difference between the demands of the fetus and the "demand" the child drowning on its own makes of an adult bystander is that the fetus's demands are much greater. If the adult bystander may refuse aid to the drowning child, then surely the same general principle (leaving aside the possibility of relevant exceptions to the principle, which will be discussed later) allows the pregnant woman to refuse aid to the fetus.

The point of the bad-samaritan principle is to establish that, as a general proposition, one does not have to give aid whenever another requires it. One can turn one's back on another's need, declining to subordinate one's own interests. One can choose not to be involved. When a woman secures an abortion in order to avoid the burdens imposed by an unwanted fetus, she is doing just what the bad-samaritan principle, in its standard applications, is designed to allow. It may seem odd to suggest that securing an abortion is really an "omission", but if we want the "act/omission"[3] distinction to reflect the values underlying the bad-samaritan principle, then that is how abortion ought to be viewed.

Suppose that a fetus and the pregnant woman carrying it were attached in such a way that the fetus could be removed without damaging it physically. The removed fetus would eventually die unless it was placed in some other womb, but it would come out of the original carrier's womb in just the same condition it was inside. If this were the way pregnancy worked, it would be much easier to see that the general right of non-subordination or non-involvement embodied in the bad-samaritan principle would entitle the woman to remove the fetus at any time, unless she had waived or forfeited the right. It would be easier to see the woman who did *not* remove an unwanted fetus was engaged in a continuing course of charitable conduct, which general samaritan law would permit her to terminate at any time. There are certain situations, to be discussed below, in which one who has started to give aid may not stop. But the general principle is that merely giving aid does not commit one to continuing it.

Now, pregnancy does not work the way I have suggested. It is not possible (at least at the stages of pregnancy where abortions are commonly done, and where they are safest and most desirable for the woman) to remove the fetus without making it inviable. This should make no difference to the conclusion that the woman is permitted by the bad-samaritan principle to remove the fetus. One reason it might be thought to make a difference is that the fetus which was removed without being damaged would have a chance of survival, if another willing carrier could be found in time, whereas the aborted fetus will certainly die. But the bad-samaritan principle protects even omissions that are certain to result in the death of the person denied aid. Unless the pregnant woman falls within some exception to the principle, the principle would permit her to remove the fetus without damaging it, assuming that were possible, even if it were known that the fetus would die because no other carrier could be found. Therefore the fact the fetus is certain to die does not remove the woman from the scope of the principle.

It might be suggested that removing the fetus in a way which renders it inviable is more clearly an "act" than simply removing the fetus without damaging it. But this does not seem right. It may be that removing the fetus in a way which renders it inviable is likely to be a more complicated act, or a more difficult act. But it is no more an act. Like the mere removing, it is an act in one sense, but it ought to be viewed as an omission, or as part of a course of conduct amounting in overall effect to an omission, under the bad-samaritan principle. It is the only way, in the real world, for a pregnant woman to discontinue the burdensome course of aid to the fetus.[4]

I have argued that abortion must be allowed if we are to respect the pregnant woman's

---

[3]The principle is discussed by Prosser in a section entitled "Acts and Omissions". W. Prosser, THE LAW OF TORTS §56 (4th ed. 1971).

[4]Another possible objection to the argument in the text runs as follows: Removing-the-fetus-without-damaging-it and removing-the-fetus-and-rendering-it-inviable differ with respect to the actor's intention. In the latter case, but not the former, the death of the fetus is a *means* to the protection of the mother. Therefore, in the latter case but not the former the removal of the fetus is impermissible. This is the Doctrine of Double Effect. A great deal has been written about the Doctrine, and I shall not discuss it here. I do not think it has a place in moral

interest in being free to refuse aid, an interest we protect for other potential samaritans. There are two possible counter-arguments, designed to show that we do not really value the potential samaritan's freedom to refuse aid as much as the existence of the bad-samaritan principle might suggest.

The first counter-argument involves the notion that we do not value the potential samaritan's freedom to be uninvolved—rather, we believe only that involvement should not be *legally compelled*. This suggestion strikes me as somewhat odd, but it is not incoherent. A full discussion of the suggestion would be interesting. For the present, however, it suffices to observe that this suggestion does not constitute a reason for thinking that abortion should be treated differently from other samaritan problems. The pregnant woman's involvement with the fetus she carries is not originally created by law, but if she does not desire the involvement, then, in the absence of laws forbidding abortion, she will have no difficulty terminating it. Laws forbidding abortion *compel* her continuing involvement just as much as a general law requiring one to be a Good Samaritan would compel the reluctant adult bystander to be involved with the drowning child.

The second counter-argument suggests that we do not really value either the potential samaritan's freedom to be uninvolved in every case *or* freedom from legally compelled involvement. Instead, it is suggested, the bad-samaritan principle is a response to various difficulties in formulating legal rules requiring aid. In many situations where a person is in need of aid, there will be more than one potential samaritan. Each potential samaritan will be in a position to ask, "Why should I be the one to give aid?" Similarly, in many situations involving potential samaritans, it will be unclear just how much the samaritan ought to be required to do in the way of attempting a rescue, or whatever. Frequently, also, it will be difficult to establish a clear causal connection between the failure to give aid and the harm to the person who needed aid. It may seem that the bad-samaritan principle is a sort of *per se* rule designed to avoid all these difficulties by establishing a general, easily understood, and easily applied rule of non-liability. If so, it may also seem that the abortion case should be an exception to the *per se* rule. When a woman is pregnant and the fetus is in need of her continuing aid, there is no doubt who must provide the aid; there is no doubt what aid is required; and there will be no difficulty in identifying the woman's refusal of aid, if she has an abortion, as the cause of the harm to the fetus.

One answer to this argument is that even if the bad-samaritan principle were a *per se*

---

reasoning, but that is beside the point. I also do not think it is part of American law, and that is very much to the point. In many situations, appeal to the act/omission distinction may resemble argument based on the Doctrine of Double Effect, but the two sorts of argument are not the same, *see* Foot, *The Problem of Abortion and the Doctrine of the Double Effect*, in P. Foot, VIRTUES AND VICES (1978), and the latter is not important in our law.

Anyone familiar with the literature on abortion will have assumed, correctly, that I owe the idea of the pregnant woman as samaritan to Judith Thomson's revelatory article, *A Defense of Abortion*, 1 PHILOSOPHY & PUB. AFF. 47 (1971). It is worth noting that Thomson does not unequivocally claim that securing an abortion should be viewed as an omission rather than as an act. Much of her essay seems to be based on this implicit premise, but when she addresses the issue directly, she apparently prefers to view abortion as an act of killing justified by principles regarding self-defense. I think a highly plausible argument can be made along these lines, and I shall devote a brief Section II to the self-defense argument. But I prefer to rely primarily on the bad-samaritan principle. I find it very plausible to view securing an abortion as a refusal-to-aid, and it is clear that our law allows refusals-to-aid for less weighty resons than it requires for killing, even in self-defense. (In saying this, I do not mean to suggest that the reasons which may support an abortion are not weighty. They are.) One reason Thomson may have had for preferring the self-defense line does not concern me. For purposes of *moral* argument, which she was engaged in, it is much less clear that we accept the bad-samaritan principle than that we recognize a right of self-defense. But there is no doubt that the bad-samaritan principle is a principle of American law.

rule of the sort described, it would not be clear that abortion cases should constitute an exception. There is no question about whose aid is required in the abortion case, and there is no question that a refusal of aid will be the cause of harm to the fetus. Nor is there doubt about what aid is required if the fetus is to survive. But the difficulty about the magnitude of aid which inclines us to a *per se* rule is not primarily the difficulty of deciding how much aid is required. It is the difficulty of deciding how much may justly be required of the potential samaritan. If we did not think there were limits to the aid that could justly be required, we could solve the "how much aid" difficulty by requiring the potential samaritan to do everything in his power that might conceivably be useful. As I shall show in the next Section, the burdens of pregnancy and childbirth are considerable, and they are burdens of a sort disfavored by our legal tradition. They are also far greater than the burdens imposed under exceptions to the bad-samaritan principle on any other potential samaritans, except (possibly) parents. The case for making an exception of the abortion situation would be problematic even if the *per se* analysis were correct and our commitment to the bad-samaritan principle were much weaker than the present scope of the principle suggests.

In any event, I do not think the bad-samaritan principle is adequately explained as a *per se* rule. I do not deny that some legal rules are of this type. Nor do I deny that for someone out of sympathy with the idea that an individual should be free to refuse aid, this sort of *per se* analysis may be the most appealing justification of the bad-samaritan principle available. But it is clear to me that if the difficulties we have mentioned were the only support for the bad-samaritan principle, the principle in its present broad form would not be part of the common law. There are many individual cases not involving abortion in which none of the difficulties

mentioned is serious. If these difficulties were the only basis for the bad-samaritan principle, then instead of a flat rule we would consider the issue of samaritans' duties case by case and develop more specific rules. The uncertainty created would be no greater than that created by many hard-to-apply common law rules, and the gain in clarity about what we were doing would be considerable. The common law recognizes the bad-samaritan principle because it does value the freedom to refuse aid, to resist subordination even in trivial ways, to remain uninvolved. If this freedom is important, it is as important for the pregnant woman as for anyone else.

One final point should be mentioned in this Section. It will seem to some readers that even if the *woman's* act of securing an abortion can be viewed as an omission, the same cannot be said of the act of any doctor who assists her by performing the abortion. I agree that the doctor looks more "active" than the woman. That is not primarily because he performs the abortion while the woman suffers it. Rather it is because the doctor is not freeing *himself* from the fetus's demands for future aid, as the woman is freeing herself. The question, then, is whether the doctor is shielded from liability by arguments establishing the woman's freedom to refuse aid.

I do not know of any authority on whether a third party may assist a potential samaritan who needs help in refusing aid. The reason for the lack of authority is clear. It is only in the unusual case, like the abortion situation, that anything resembling a positive act is necessary for the samaritan to refuse aid. There is some law on third-party intervention in the context of the right of self-defense (or, from the point of view of the third party, the context of defense of others). In that context, the currently dominant view, and the view which is still gaining ground, is that third parties are entitled to intervene.

For myself, I find it easy to conclude that if the woman is free to secure an abortion, the doctor should be able to help her. Although I find it easy to conclude this, I do not have much to say in support of my conclusion. I do have one observation. When abortion is forbidden by law, many women suffer severe injury or even death from illegal or self-induced abortions. If we assume that women should not be seeking abortions in the first place, it is possible to ignore this large cost, saying that the women have only themselves to blame. But it seems perverse to say that given the general tenor of samaritan law a woman ought to be permitted to refuse aid to the fetus, and yet to say that she may not receive assistance in this course when the assistance would avoid much suffering and when it is voluntarily offered and privately arranged. . . .

## C. Exceptions to the Bad-Samaritan Principle

I turn now to the matter of comparing the pregnant woman to other potential samaritans who are required to give aid under standard exceptions to the bad-samaritan principle. It is worth repeating something I have said before: My object is not to show that by traditional standards the pregnant woman is indistinguishable from the totally uninvolved bystander who may refuse even the most trivial aid. The pregnant woman is not totally uninvolved. She is sufficiently involved that we could appropriately impose slight burdens of aid on her, if imposing slight burdens would do the fetus any good. Unfortunately, imposing slight burdens on her will not do the fetus any good. It is very large burdens or nothing. What I propose to show in this Section is that even if the pregnant woman is sufficiently involved to justify imposing some small duty of aid, she is still *less* "eligible for compulsion" than any of the other potential samaritans who figure in the standard exceptions to the bad-samaritan principle. Her situation is distinguishable, in ways that make her a less appropriate subject for compulsion, from the situation of

every other potential samaritan on whom duties are imposed. If we consider in addition that the duties imposed on those other samaritans are ordinarily trivial, both absolutely and in comparison with the burdens of pregnancy and childbirth, it should become clear why I suggest that laws forbidding abortion are out of line with the general framework of samaritan law.

Two of the standard exceptions to the bad-samaritan principle can be disposed of quickly. One is the "statutory duty" exception. Any discussion of the bad-samaritan principle can be expected to include the observation that there *is* a duty to aid if some statute imposes such a duty. Now, statutes forbidding abortion are (on my analysis) statutes imposing a duty to aid. So it might seem that the pregnant woman falls squarely within the first standard exception we look at. But the statutory duty exception, considered as a *general* exception, is not relevant to our purposes. The claim that there is a duty if some statute creates such a duty assumes that the statute in question is constitutional, whereas I am arguing precisely that anti-abortion statutes are unconstitutional because they make an exception to the bad-samaritan principle that is unacceptable given the general state of samaritan law. It is relevant, of course, to compare anti-abortion statutes, and the duty they impose, with other *specific* duty-creating statutes and the duties they impose. Those other statutes are part of the "general state of samaritan law". I shall discuss some other statutory duties, including the draftee's duty of military service, in Section D below.

The other standard exception to the bad-samaritan principle that we can deal with summarily is the "contract" exception. Duties to aid may be undertaken by contract. It might be suggested that when a woman marries, or perhaps when a woman has sexual intercourse, she enters into an implied contract with her husband or with the man involved to carry and deliver any conceptus that results. If there is such an implied contract, the fetus can be regarded as a third-party beneficiary. We do not ordinarily enforce contractual duties by criminal sanctions, but contractual duties to aid the helpless can appropriately be so enforced in some circumstances. The trouble with this argument, of course, is that it is absurd to suggest that sex or marriage always carries with it an implied promise to bear a child. Even among people who are married, there are just too many who do not want children.[28] In arguing against the existence of an implied contract on the basis of what people want, I assume that we are talking about a contract implied "in fact". We sometimes imply contracts "in law" without caring what the parties want. If that possibility is relevant at all in the present context, it is under the heading of "status" exceptions to the bad-samaritan principle, to which I now turn.[29]

**1. EXCEPTIONS BASED ON STATUS OR RELATIONSHIP** There are a number of cases in which a duty to render aid is based on the status of the potential samaritan, or on the relationship between the potential samaritan and the person in need of aid.[30] A common carrier has a duty to aid a passenger; the master of a ship has a duty to aid a member of his crew; a jailer must aid his prisoner. Others on whom duties to aid are imposed are innkeepers (*vis-à-vis* their guests), storeowners (*vis-à-vis* their customers), employers of all kinds (*vis-à-vis* their employees), schools (*vis-à-vis* their pupils), social hosts, spouses, and parents.

The situation of the pregnant woman can be distinguished from the situations of all these other potential samaritans on whom duties are imposed. In fact, in almost every case there is more than one significant ground of distinction. A ground of distinction which is common to all of the cases, however, is the degree of voluntariness of the assumption of the status or relationship on which the duty to aid is based. Every one of the statuses or relationships I have just named is entered into voluntarily. The condition (or status, or relationship with the fetus) of pregnancy is *not* chosen voluntarily by those women who, once pregnant, want abortions. Some readers may think the distinction just suggested is more apparent than real. I do propose to discuss it further. First, let us consider the extent to which pregnancy is voluntary.

I think it may safely be assumed that most pregnancies *of women who want abortions* are not intentional.[31] Unintended pregnancies may occur for a variety of reasons. Many result from contraceptive failure. (If contraceptive methods of very high effectiveness, say 98%, were used carefully and

---

[28]To be sure, we may say that mariage involves an implied promise to have children, *meaning* that unwillingness to beget or bear children is or ought to be a ground for divorce. That is obviously quite a different matter.

[29]The text ignores the possibility of an express contract to carry the fetus. Given problems of proof (unless we require such a contract to be in writing), and given the reluctance of the common law to grant specific performance of contracts for personal services, it is not clear that even an express contract ought to be enforceable. Certainly, however, a woman who has made an express contract to carry a fetus is a much more appropriate subject for compulsion than one who has not. Fortunately, we need not decide whether a woman should be allowed to bind herself by an express contract not to have an abortion. I am prepared to restrict the argument of this essay, and my conclusions, to women who have not made the attempt.

[30]*See generally* RESTATMENT(SECOND) OF TORTS §§314, 314A, 314B (1965); W. PROSSER, *supra* note 3, at 340–43; W. LaFAYE & A. SCOTT, *supra* note 5, at 184.

[31]To be sure, there will be cases where the woman becomes pregnant intentionally and then changes her mind about having the child; but these cases will be comparatively rare. (If the practice of amniocentesis to determine the fetus's sex, followed by abortion of a fetus of the undesired sex, becomes more common, the case in question may not be so rare. That does not affect what I say in the remainder of this note.) In any case which is identifiably of this type, the case for denying the woman an abortion is very much stronger than in the usual case of a pregnancy which is unwanted from the beginning. Whether the case for denying an abortion is strong enough is a harder question. Some of the relevant considerations are canvassed later on, in the discussion of duties

consistently, there would be hundreds of thousands of pregnancies a year caused by contraceptive failure in a large population such as that of the United States.) Many more, probably, result from inept or inattentive use of contraceptives, or from occasional non-use. And many result from persistent non-use, caused by ignorance, laziness, the expense or disruptiveness of many contraceptive methods, pressure from male partners not to use contraception, and a variety of other possible psychological causes. In none of these cases has the woman who becomes pregnant chosen to be pregnant.

It might be argued, of course, that in every case where a woman becomes pregnant (except the case of rape), she has voluntarily done *something*. She has given in to pressure not to use contraception; or she has given in to her own laziness. If she has done neither of these things—if she is a victim of contraceptive failure despite responsible contraceptive use, or even if she is totally and excusably ignorant about methods of contraception—she has at least had sex. Assuming she is not so ignorant as to be unaware of the connection between intercourse and pregnancy, can she not be said to have assumed the risk of conception?

It is true that in every case in which a woman becomes pregnant (still excepting the case of rape), she has voluntarily had sex. Voluntariness, however, is something that admits of degrees. As Harry Wellington has pointed out, having sex may be more a matter of choice than eating, but it is an act to which most of us feel a strong compulsion.[32] It is clear to me that the choice to have sex is ordinarily not as "voluntary" as the choice to be an innkeeper, or a storeowner, or whatever.

It might be suggested that even if an innkeeper (for example) voluntarily chooses (in a strong sense of "voluntary") to be an innkeeper, he does not choose to be a good samaritan to his guests. He does not even choose that any of his guests shall ever need his aid (beyond room and board). All he *chooses* is to run the *risk* that some guest will have an accident or other misfortune which requires special aid. In other words, the innkeeper does just what the woman does when she has sex. He takes a risk. If the innkeeper may be compelled to be a samaritan when the event he does not want occurs, why not the woman as well?

This suggestion overlooks important differences between the innkeeper and the woman. The innkeeper may not want to be a good samaritan. But he actively invites the formation of the relationship on which his duty of aid is based. The innkeeper wants guests. The woman does not want the fetus. What is true of the innkeeper is true of every other potential samaritan mentioned at the beginning of this Subsection (with the possible exception of the parent, to be discussed shortly). In some cases, the relationship which is the basis for the duty of aid is a relationship of some intimacy in which the potential samaritan chooses the *particular* individual with whom the relationship is to be formed. (I have in mind the relationship of spouse to spouse and of host to social guest.) This obviously makes it easier to accept the imposition of a duty to aid. Innkeepers, storekeepers, and so on, do not choose their guests or customers with such particularity. Even so, unlike the unwillingly pregnant woman, they actively seek the formation of the relationship. That is the point of their calling.

The reference to the innkeeper's "calling" suggests another observation. The innkeeper, the storekeeper, and so on, are all engaged in providing a service for pay. They are engaged in economic enterprise. That clearly contributes to the feeling that it is acceptable

---

created by the voluntary commencement of aid, [section titled "Voluntarily Beginning Aid"]. I think we can leave this unusual case unresolved without impairing the general argument.

[32]Wellington, *Common Law Rules and Constitutional Double Standards: Some Notes on Adjudication*, 83 YALE L.J. 221, 308 (1973).

to impose duties of aid, to treat them as having "assumed the risk".[33] In fact, every potential samaritan on the list at the beginning of this Subsection (still excepting the parent) not only invites the formation of the relationship but *either* chooses the other party to the relationship with particularity *or* is engaged in an economic activity.[34]

There is another respect in which all the potential samaritans discussed in this Subsection differ from the pregnant woman. All the relationships under discussion—of innkeeper to guest, shopkeeper to customer, parent to child, and so on—are relationships in which the second-named party would *expect* aid from the first. The potential samaritan in any of these categories who refuses aid will disappoint expectations which are likely to exist in fact and which we regard as reasonable. It might be suggested that the expectations exist only because of the legal duties to aid, but I think that suggestion is simply false. Even in the absence of legal duties, most innkeepers would aid guests who fell ill (both for humanitarian reasons and because it would be bad for business to refuse), most social hosts would aid their guests, and so on. Substantial expectations of aid would exist regardless of the legal rule, and one justification for the legal rule is that it protects these expectations. The fetus, in contrast, has no expectations to be protected. (Lest there be any doubt, I have been talking in this paragraph about psychological expectations, not "legal" expectations. The claim that the fetus has no expectations is not a *petitio principii*. It is, I believe, an empirical fact.)

Before we move on to compare the pregnant woman to the parent, let us summarize what we have established so far. There is undeniably *some* reason to regard the pregnant woman as "eligible for compulsion" for the benefit of the fetus. She has (except in the case of rape) voluntarily done an act which created the risk that her aid would be required. On the other hand, the pregnant woman seems a notably less apt candidate for compulsion than the other potential samaritans we have considered. Surely she should not be compelled to undertake greater burdens then they. And yet, so long as there are laws forbidding abortion, she is compelled to undertake much greater burdens than they. The aid required of innkeepers and the others is trivial. It is usually something on the order of calling a doctor or sending for medicine. As one of my colleagues put it, we speak easily of the innkeeper's duty to aid his guests, but we would hardly require an innkeeper to give up a kidney for transplanting into a guest whose kidneys had failed. That would be a duty comparable to the duty anti-abortion laws impose on the pregnant woman.

Probably the most troublesome comparison, for my argument, is the comparison between the pregnant woman and the parent. I have explicitly excepted the parent from some of the claims made in this Subsection about other potential samaritans whose duties are based on status or relationship. It is not true of all parents, as it is true of all innkeepers, that they have invited the relationship with their child. It is not true of any parents that they have chosen the particular individual with whom to establish the parent-child relationship; and it is true of very few parents, if any, that they have children primarily for economic reasons. In addition, the burdens of being a parent are considerably greater than the burdens of aid imposed on innkeepers and the like. All in all, it may seem that the parallel between the parent and the pregnant woman is very close.

---

[33]W. Prosser, *supra* note 3, at 339.

[34]The claim in the text might be denied with respect to jails and *public* schools. These cases are special for a different reason: the duties to aid, to the extent they are not imposed on individuals who are providing services for pay, are imposed on the *state*. Whatever value we attach to an individual's being free to refuse aid, we do not attach the same value to the state's having a similar freedom, especially where the relevant relationship, with the prisoner or the public school pupil, is not only "invited" but coerced.

There are, however, significant differences between the parent and the pregnant woman who wants an abortion, differences which make parenthood look much more "voluntary" than unwanted pregnancy. The woman who does not want to be a parent, or the couple who do not want to be parents, can give their child up for adoption. There are costs associated with giving the child up, as I have already noted. But if, as I have argued, these costs are not enough so that the burdens of parenthood count for purposes of samaritan analysis as being imposed on women by laws forbidding abortion, then neither are they great enough so that the burdens of parenthood cannot be avoided by parents.[35] It is much more plausible to view keeping the child as a voluntary assumption of the burdens of raising the child than to view having sex as a voluntary assumption of the burdens of pregnancy and childbirth.

We can make the same point in a slightly different way. It is true that the law imposes burdens of care on parents. It is also true that what we normally think of as "the burdens of parenthood" are very great. But it is not really true that the law imposes on parents all the "burdens of parenthood". Most parents assume most of the burdens voluntarily. They keep their child. They feed it, and care for it, generally speaking. What the law is likely to punish the parent for is some particular refusal of aid fairly localized in time. (Even where the parent's failure is a long-term course of general neglect, the parent is arguably being punished as much for failure to enlist other assistance on the child's behalf as for anything else.) The parent, much more than the pregnant woman,

creates the relationship with the child. The parent who refuses aid, much more than the pregnant woman who has an abortion, is like the samaritan who harms the object of his "assistance" by voluntarily embarking on a course of aid and then terminating it after other potential samaritans have turned their attention elsewhere, satisfied that the need is being met. (An extended comparison of the pregnant woman with the samaritan who volunteers aid and then terminates it is reserved for the next Subsection.)

Finally, it is worth emphasizing again that the burdens of parenthood, however great they are, are not physically invasive as the burdens of pregnancy and childbirth. For better or worse, our tradition assigns special disvalue to the imposition of pain or extreme physical discomfort and to actual invasion of the body. I have suggested earlier, with my compulsory-organ-donation and burning-building hypotheticals, that we would stop far short of imposing on parents the sort of physical burdens anti-abortion laws impose on women.[36]

**2. VOLUNTARILY BEGINNING AID** There is substantial authority for the proposition that one who voluntarily begins to aid another assumes certain duties.[37] The aid must be provided in a non-negligent manner, and in some circumstances the aid may not be terminated. It might be argued that a pregnant woman has embarked on a course of aid to the fetus which she may not terminate by an abortion.

The principal objection to this argument is that the pregnant woman has not "voluntarily" begun to aid the fetus. I have already

---

[35]In years past, when giving the child up for adoption may have been harder to arrange than it is today, it was probably easier to arrange some informal "farming-out" of the child.

[36]As a last word on parenthood, it is worth noting that one sort of burden is arguably imposed on parents who are no more eligible for compulsion than unintentionally pregnant women. I have in mind support obligations imposed of fathers who did not want a child. I think the argument of this essay casts some doubt on the constitutionality of such support obligations. But for the reader who thinks such obligations are obviously constitutional (and I assume most readers will fall into this category), it should suffice to note that financial impositions of this sort are much less disfavored than the physical imposition involved in forbidding abortion.

[37]RESTATEMENT (SECOND) OF TORTS §§323, 324 (1965); W. PROSSER, *supra* note 3, at 343–48.

discussed the degree of voluntariness of the woman's choice. I have conceded that, except in the case of rape, her connection with the fetus is not totally involuntary. But in most cases the pregnant woman has not knowingly and intentionally offered the fetus any assistance at all. At most she has taken a small risk, and lost. All of the cases about "voluntarily beginning aid" involve potential samaritans who, unlike the pregnant woman, have knowingly and intentionally embarked on a course of assistance to someone in need.[38]

In addition, the cases where voluntarily beginning aid has been found to create a duty are ordinarily cases where the "aid" in question has left the recipient worse off, as where a landlord causes injury by performing negligently a repair he was not obligated to perform, or where a half-hearted samaritan terminates a rescue-in-progress short of completion after other potential rescuers have disappeared, thinking that matters were under control. When a pregnancy is terminated, however, the fetus is no worse off than it was before the only action of the woman that could possibly be construed as the beginning of aid, namely the sexual act as a result of which the fetus was conceived.

This "no worse off" argument may seem fanciful. I admit it is an argument many people are likely to be uncomfortable with. It nonetheless deserves to be taken seriously. The point is *not* just that the fetus is no worse off dead than alive.[39] The point is that the fetus which is conceived and then aborted is not made worse off *by the entire course of the woman's conduct.*[40] This is a significant distinction between the abortion case and most cases where a duty is founded upon a voluntary undertaking to aid.

At this point, it might be suggested that there are certain cases where a samaritan who begins a rescue may not terminate it, despite the fact that his whole course of conduct leaves the person in need of rescue no worse off. The *Restatement (Second) of Torts* suggests in a comment that one who has pulled a drowning man halfway to shore with a rope might not be permitted simply to drop the rope and walk away, even if no other potential rescuer has been discouraged.[41] Similarly, the *Restatement* says that one who has pulled another out of a trench filled with poisonous gas may not then throw him back in even though he is left no worse off than before the rescue was begun.[42]

These cases both differ significantly from the abortion situation. As to the drowning

---

[38]The discussion in the text may remind the reader of another traditional exception to the bad-samaritan principle, involving people who negligently or innocently create dangerous situations. That exception is the subject of the next Subsection.

[39]Since the fetus does not have and has never had any conscious desire to live, I think it can be argued plausibly that it is not worse off dead than alive. But that is not the present point.

[40]The reader who does take the argument in the text seriously may object that if the abortion causes pain to the fetus, then the fetus is made worse off by the woman's entire course of conduct. However, if we take account of the pain caused the fetus, we ought to take account also of the pleasures of its earlier life in the womb (a life for which many inhabitants of the harsher world outside reportedly pine). How we are to estimate the balance of pain and pleasure here I do not know. Conceivably the balance would weigh against a late saline abortion. In any event, early abortions, by whatever technique, can hardly cause the fetus much pain.

It might also be objected that in saying the fetus is no worse off having been conceived and aborted than if it had never been conceived at all, I am overlooking the possibility that the fetus has a soul. I do not claim much knowledge about the fortunes of fetal souls, but it seems to me that if the fetus has a soul, then it is betr off (and therefore no worse off) for being conceived and aborted and spending eternity in Limbo, than if it had not been conceived at all.

[41]RESTATEMENT (SECOND) OF TORTS § 323, comment e (1965).

[42]RESTATEMENT (SECOND) OF TORTS § 324, comment g (1965).

man, the *Restatement* only surmises that the half-hearted samaritan may not abandon the rescue. It may seem obvious to many readers that the rescue may not be abandoned, but if so, I suspect it is because the picture that springs to mind is of a relatively effortless pulling-to-shore. If we imagine instead a rescue that requires a long-sustained and painful effort, it should seem much less clear that the samaritan who has done no harm and displaced no other rescuer may not quit. For the benefit of any reader who thinks even the highly burdensome rescue may not be terminated, it is worth noting that there is *still* a significant difference between the drowning man and the fetus. One of the reasons we would be appalled (in the case of the easy rescue, perhaps only troubled in the case of the difficult rescue) by the samaritan who abandoned the drowning man halfway to shore is that the samaritan would have raised expectations in the drowning man and then disappointed them. The fetus, as I have observed before, has no expectations.

As to the samaritan who has pulled someone from a gas-filled trench and may not throw him back, the point here is that once the unfortunate is pulled from the trench, the rescue (or that part of it) is complete. Throwing the person rescued back into the trench is not in any sense a refusal to aid. Securing an abortion, while it is in some respects a positive act like throwing the person back into the trench, is the only way the pregnant woman can deny future aid to the fetus. Indeed, it is the only way she can deny very *burdensome* aid which, we should note once more, she never really volunteered in the first place.[43]

**3. HARM OR DANGER CAUSED BY THE POTENTIAL SAMARITAN** There is authority for the proposition that one who injures another, or one who creates a situation which is dangerous to another, has a duty to take steps to minimize the injury or danger, even if it was innocently caused.[44] For example, it has been held that when a vehicle becomes disabled in a position where it blocks a highway, the driver of the vehicle, even though utterly free of fault, has a duty to set out flares or otherwise warn oncoming traffic.[45]

This exception to the bad-samaritan principle is distinctive. It contemplates a duty to aid where the potential samaritan has neither chosen to become involved with the person in need of aid nor invited the formation of a relationship. It might be suggested that the pregnant woman is analogous to the samaritan who innocently creates a dangerous situation. It might be suggested that the pregnant woman has put the fetus in a dangerous situation. Even if she is free of fault, may she not, like the driver of the disabled vehicle, be required to give aid?

There is a significant difference between the pregnant woman and the driver of the disabled vehicle, a difference we have already discussed in another context. If we allow a potential samaritan to refuse aid to someone he has harmed or endangered, he will have made the other worse off by his entire course of conduct. The pregnant woman who has an abortion, however, does not make the fetus worse off by her entire course of conduct. For all practical purposes, the abortion leaves the fetus in just the state it was in before it was conceived. Allowing a woman to have an abortion is therefore quite different

[43]It may seem that the "no worse off" aspect of my argument would tend to justify neonate infanticide. That claim can be rejected for either of two reasons. First, once the infant is born, the woman can refuse further aid with less cost to the infant simply by giving it up for adoption. Second, we can argue that the woman has waived her right to refuse aid sometime before the infant is born. I think a waiver argument is probably adequate to justify the Court's holding in *Roe v. Wade* that third-trimester abortions may be prohibited in most circumstances.

[44]RESTATEMENT (SECOND) OF TORTS §§ 321, 322 (1965); W. PROSSER, *supra* note 3. at 342–43.

[45]*E.g.*, Scatena v. Pittsburgh & New England Trucking, 2 Mass. App. Ct. 638, 319 N.E.2d 730 (1974).

from allowing a driver simply to walk away from a disabled vehicle blocking a highway on a foggy night.

The reader may wonder whether the "no worse off" idea is really as important as I suggest. It is a difference between the abortion case and the disabled vehicle case, but is it a difference that matters? We sometimes allow a person to escape liability even though he clearly makes another worse off, as where, through no fault of the driver, a vehicle goes out of control and kills someone instantly. If the driver in such a case escapes liability even though he makes his victim worse off, can the duty to aid in the disabled-vehicle case really be explained as simply a duty not to make the victim worse off?

I think the "no worse off" idea *is* important. Where an out-of-control vehicle kills someone instantly, the question of aid to the victim does not arise, because the harm happens all at once. Where the harm does not happen all at once, courts have apparently decided that the right to refuse involvement does not extend to a right to refuse aid to those one has made worse off, even innocently. To make someone worse off, or to put someone is a position where he is likely to be made worse off, is to become involved. The right to non-involvement can be regained only by undoing the damage one has done.

A corollary is that the right to non-involvement ought to be regained once the damage has been undone. Nothing in the cases involving danger innocently caused suggests that the potential samaritan must do more than undo the damage. If the pregnant woman who has an abortion leaves the fetus no worse off than before it was conceived, nothing in those cases suggests that a pregnant woman must instead carry the fetus and thereby confer on it a substantial net benefit.

I have discussed the duty to aid of a potential samaritan who has innocently caused harm or danger. There is a similar, and more firmly established, duty to aid when one has *negligently* caused harm or danger. Now, I have conceded the existence of a duty to aid even when the potential samaritan is innocent, and it might seem that I have therefore answered the strongest possible case against my position. I have eschewed reliance on the fact that many women who become pregnant are entirely innocent and would clearly be excused from any duty to aid that fell only on potential samaritans who *negligently* caused harm or danger. On the other hand, it could be argued that I have made things too easy for myself. It would not be surprising if potential samaritans who negligently caused harm or danger were subjected to more extensive duties of aid than potential samaritans who cause harm or danger innocently. If this were the case, and if it could be argued that most women who become pregnant unwillingly are at least negligent, then I would have made things easier than they should be. In fact, there is no evidence that greater duties are imposed on negligent than on innocent potential samaritans. Even if duties are imposed more consistently on the negligent, the burdens imposed are no greater. Accordingly (returning to my perennial final point), it is as true of the negligent potential samaritan as of the innocent potential samaritan that the duties of aid imposed on him are completely trivial compared to the burdens of pregnancy and childbirth.

## 4. EROSION OF THE BAD-SAMARITAN PRINCIPLE

Scholars do not like the bad-samaritan principle, and they are eager to claim that the principle is being eroded away. Perhaps it is, but if so, then the erosion is very slow indeed.

Two recent cases that might be cited as evidence of erosion are *Tarasoff v. Board of Regents*[46] and *Farwell v. Keaton*.[47] In *Tarasoff*, the California Supreme Court held that a

[46]17 Cal. 3d 425, 551 P. 2d 334, 131 Cal Rptr. 14 (1976).
[47]396 Mich. 281, 240 N.W.2d 217 (1976).

psychotherapist had a duty to warn a person against whom the therapist's patient made a death threat. In *Farwell*, the Michigan Supreme Court said a teenage boy had a duty not to abandon in a parked car a friend who was unconscious from a beating by other boys, suffered during a night of drinking and "cruising" in search of female companionship.

*Farwell* may represent a slight extension of traditional duties to aid, but the relationship of participants in a social "joint venture" is closely analogous to the relationship of host and guest. Most importantly, the relationship is undertaken knowingly and voluntarily. In addition, there is an element of reciprocity in the relationship that is absent in most samaritan cases. This is a case where the court might plausibly find that a bilateral contract to give minor aid is implied "in fact".

*Tarasoff* appears unusual at first because the duty found by the court runs to a party not directly involved in the relationship that gives rise to the duty. But the case is not really very striking. There is clear precedent for duties to third parties in cases where the potential samaritan has a more extensive duty to control the behavior of another—for example the duty of a jailer to prevent the escape of his prisoners, or of an employer to control his employees.[48] The fact that a psychotherapist does not have a full-fledged duty to control his patient should not prevent us from recognizing, in the duty to warn, a weaker analogue. It is relevant that the role of psychotherapist, like the role of jailer or employer, is undertaken voluntarily and, ordinarily, for pay.

I cannot discuss every case which might be cited as evidence that the bad-samaritan principle is disappearing. I think there is little persuasive evidence for this proposition. In any event, even scholars who see the rule weakening are thinking of its application to cases where the burdens on the potential samaritan are trivial. Thus Prosser suggests that the bad-samaritan principle may erode to the point where "the mere knowledge of serious peril, threatening death or great bodily harm to another, which an identified defendant might avoid *with little inconvenience*, creates a sufficient relation . . . to impose a duty of action."[49] Or more recently, Marshall Shapo: "I have evolved as a working principle that one has a duty to aid others in situations in which hazardous conditions necessitate assistance for the preservation of life and of physical integrity, and in which one possesses the power to expend energy in that task without serious inconvenience or possibility of harm to herself."[50]

Whatever else may be said of the supposed duty of a woman to carry a fetus, it is not a duty that can be discharged "with little inconvenience" or even "without serious inconvenience or possibility of harm".

## D. Statutory Duties

A variety of statutes create duties to act for the benefit of others and therefore create either exceptions or apparent exceptions to the bad-samaritan principle. As I have noted previously, the truth of the general proposition that statutes may create duties to aid does not undermine my argument against laws forbidding abortion, because the general proposition presupposes that the statutes in question are constitutional. However, since my argument is an equal protection argument, based in part on the claim that pregnant women are treated worse than other potential samaritans, it is important to compare laws forbidding abortion with other specific statutes or statutory schemes imposing duties to act.

The most arresting statutorily created exception (or, as I think, apparent exception) to the bad-samaritan principle is the military

[48]W. Prosser, *supra* note 3, at 349–50.
[49]*Id.* at 343 (emphasis added).
[50]M. Shapo, The Duty To Act: Tort Law, Power, and Public Policy 69 (1977).

draft. (Though the draft is not currently in force, there is talk of reinstituting it, and its *constitutionality* is not currently doubted, which is the key fact for our purposes.) One of my principal themes has been that the burdens imposed on pregnant women by laws forbidding abortion are significantly greater than, and different in kind from, the burdens imposed on other potential samaritans. The only potential samaritans who are subjected to burdens at all comparable to the burdens of pregnancy and childbirth are parents (whom I have already discussed) and military draftees.

Now, we could attempt to distinguish laws forbidding abortion from the military draft by reference to the nature of the burdens imposed in the two cases. We could suggest that the burdens of pregnancy and childbirth, even if not greater than the burdens imposed on draftees, are more constitutionally objectionable. They involve invasions of the body, and they more directly touch on the specially sensitive area of sexual intimacy.[51] This does not seem to me a sufficient ground of distinction between anti-abortion laws and the draft.

Draftees are likely to be subjected to a good deal of forced exercise under unpleasant and demanding conditions. For many, this will result in considerable discomfort and even pain. To be sure, the draftee is not compelled to allow another person to grow inside his body, and it might be argued that the pains of military training make the body a more versatile and useful instrument for varied physical activities, while pregnancy makes the woman's body less adapted to physical activities other than carrying a fetus. But these differences do not alter the fact that compulsory military service involves a considerable *physical* invasion.

As to the suggestion that forbidding abortion touches on a zone of special intimacy, that is true, but I am not certain the draft is so different. The draftee is presented with a new group of associates he has no hand in picking. He will eat with them, sleep in close proximity to them, share bathroom facilities with them, and spend most of his leisure time with them. Intimate associational interests of the draftee are strongly affected. Even as to sex, the draftee is taken away from whatever sexual relationships or patterns of sexual behavior he has established for himself in his civilian life and he is thrown into a new society that is likely to have and to enforce by considerable social pressure expectations regarding both what he shall say about sex and what he shall do about it. Remembering that the draftee's tour of duty normally lasts two years while the pregnant woman's lasts nine months, I am not persuaded that the burdens of pregnancy and childbirth are clearly greater than, or importantly different in kind from the burdens of military conscription.[52]

To my mind, the crucial difference between the pregnant woman denied an abortion and the military draftee is this: The woman is being required to aid a specific other individual (the fetus); the draftee is not. Rightly or wrongly, our tradition distinguishes between obligations to aid particular individuals and obligations to promote a more broadly based public interest. (This, incidentally, is why the draft is only an *apparent* exception to the bad-samaritan principle. The bad-samaritan principle applies only when aid to specific individuals is in issue.)

In the opinion that established the constitutionality of the draft, the unanimous Court gave most of its attention to a federalism question—whether the power to conscript belonged to Congress or to the states.[53] The Court gave the thirteenth amendment issue,

---

[51]For a suggestion along these lines, see Gerety, *Redefining Privacy*, 12 HARV. C.R.-C.L.L. REV. 233, 275 n. 153 (1977).

[52]The text notwithstanding, a *possible* argument to the effect that the burdens imposed by laws forbidding abortion are greater than the burdens imposed by the draft was suggested in note 27 *supra*.

[53]Selective Draft Law Cases, 245 U.S. 366 (1918).

which is the relevant issue for our purposes, short shrift. That issue is discussed explicitly only in the final paragraph of the opinion:

> Finally, as we are unable to conceive upon what theory the exaction by government from the citizen of the performance of his supreme and noble duty of contributing to the defense of the rights and honor of the nation, as the result of a war declared by the great representative body of the people, can be said to be the imposition of involuntary servitude in violation of the prohibitions of the Thirteenth Amendment, we are constrained to the conclusion that the contention to that effect is refuted by its mere statement.[54]

If the Justices were genuinely unable to conceive how the draft could be said to impose involuntary servitude, they were deficient in imagination. But the point of their rebuttal is clear. It does not offend the traditions of a free people to require citizens to perform their "supreme and noble duty of contributing to the defense of the rights and honor of the nation". When the nation calls and the public welfare is at stake, the citizen must respond.

In answer to the suggestion that the draftee serves a public interest while the pregnant woman denied an abortion serves only the interest of the fetus, it might be argued that every interest protected by state power becomes *ipso facto* a public interest. There is something to this. I am protected by law against gratuitous physical assault, and that suggests that in some sense there must be a public interest in so protecting me. Still, the public interest involved is ultimately based on my private interest in physical integrity. Similarly, if the prohibition on abortion is justified on the ground that the fetus has a right to life (as it commonly is these days), then the ultimate public interest is in protecting the private interest of the fetus. This public interest is not enough to justify compelling the pregnant woman to carry the fetus. The reason is that in *every* potential samaritan case there is a public interest in protecting the person in need of aid which is precisely analogous to the public interest in saving the fetus. We cannot rely on this public interest in the abortion situation and ignore it elsewhere.

The draft appeals to a more public, or more general, public interest—in national security. It simply does not present the same issue as abortion. There is a difference between the idea that an individual is not his brother's keeper, which underlies the bad-samaritan principle, and the idea that a citizen owes nothing to society at large.[55]

If the difference between the draft and laws forbidding abortion is what I have suggested, then laws forbidding abortion might well be constitutional if they were justified on grounds other than the right to life of the fetus. In particular, it seems that if there were a genuine national commitment to population growth, abortion could be prohibited in furtherance of that commitment. This will strike some readers as a curious and unacceptable conclusion, but it is a conclusion I am prepared to accept. We do sometimes require great sacrifices in the public interest. The draft is the most extreme example. If it

---

[54]245 U.S. at 390.

[55]It may seem that the distinction between public interest and private interest, which I rely on in the text, is a weak reed on which to base a constitutional argument. The idea that private property can be taken only for "public use" has arguably not been a significant limitation on the power of eminent domain. The idea that government can regulate only businesses "affected with a public interest" is as dead as any constitutional doctrine can hope to be. A full-scale discussion of the public/private distinction, while interesting, would take us far beyond a reasonable scope for this essay. Whatever the difficulty of drawing the line in other contexts, it seems to me there is an intuitively arresting difference between making someone serve in the military, in defense of interests which are plainly public if any are, and making someone carry a fetus, for the benefit of the fetus or the child it might become.

were necessary to require women to bear children in the pursuit of a goal similar to national security, I see no reason why that sacrifice could not be required.

In addition to the duty of military service, there are many other statutorily created duties to act for the benefit of others. There are duties to fight forest fires, to work on public roads, to submit to quarantine for infectious disease, to be a witness or a juror. There is the lawyer's duty to serve some indigent clients without compensation, the duty of the master of a ship to rescue at sea,[56] the duty of children to contribute to the support or medical expenses of impoverished parents. Although this list is not exhaustive, I believe a discussion of these representative duties will suffice.

The first thing to say about all of these statutory duties is that they impose burdens very much lighter than the burdens of pregnancy and childbirth. Just as the parenthood exception to the bad-samaritan principle is the only common law exception which resembles laws forbidding abortion in the magnitude of the burdens imposed, so the draft, which I have already discussed, is the only statutory exception or apparent exception which is comparable in this respect.

Every one of these statutory duties differs from the duty to carry a fetus (imposed by laws forbidding abortion) in other ways as well. The duties to fight forest fires, to work on public roads, and to submit to quarantine are, I believe, no longer of great practical importance. Also, like the duty to be a witness or a juror, they all involve *public* service—they are not duties to aid specific other individuals, but rather duties to benefit the community at large. The duty of the lawyer to serve indigent clients might also be regarded as a duty of public service, promoting the public interest in seeing justice done.

If this "public" interest seems too closely tied to the private interest of the lawyer's client (since the lawyer does work *for* his client in a way the witness and the juror do not), we can also observe of both the lawyer's duty and the duty of the master of a ship to rescue at sea that these duties are attached to activities ordinarily undertaken for pay. Furthermore, the lawyer and the ship's master are required to render services of *kinds* that they have shown a general willingness to render by their choice of occupation. The same cannot be said of the unwillingly pregnant woman. With regard to the last statutory duty, the duty of children to support impoverished parents, I have always had doubts about the constitutionality of statutes imposing such a duty. People do not choose their parents; they do not even choose to *have* parents. Many states have statutes imposing duties of filial support, but the constitutionality of such statutes has never been passed on by the Supreme Court.[57] Even if such statutes are constitutional, they are distinguishable from laws forbidding abortion. The burdens imposed by filial support statutes, while significant, are monetary. Also, I assume that anyone inclined to defend filial support statutes would rely on the claim that the child was merely repaying the parent for benefits received, a claim which cannot be made in the abortion case.

## E. Final Comments

I have argued that abortion is a problem in samaritan law, and I have compared the situation of the pregnant woman with the situations of other potential samaritans and others (such as draftees) who are not strictly speaking potential samaritans (because it is not other *individuals* who require their aid) but who are compelled to act for the benefit of

[56]46 U.S.C. § 728 (1976).

[57]The closest the Court has come was to vacate, with a request for clarification on whether there was an adequate state ground, a California Supreme Court decision that such a statute was unconstitutional under the federal Constitution, or under the California constitution, or both. Department of Mental Hygiene v. Kirchner, 380 U.S. 194 (1965).

persons besides themselves. As I have noted, the situation of the pregnant woman has no perfect analogue. There is no other case in which noninvolvement on the part of the potential samaritan requires something that looks so much like a positive act; and there is no other case in which the potential samaritan has contributed to the existence of a relationship with the person in need of aid with just the same degree of voluntariness. Expanding on the last point, I have conceded that by having sex the pregnant woman has (except in the case of rape) done *something* that gives us *some* reason to compel her to aid the fetus. On the other hand, the pregnant woman has not done as much to establish a relationship with the fetus as has the parent to establish a relationship with her child, the voluntary rescuer to establish a relationship with the object of the rescue, or even the innkeeper to establish a relationship with his guest. If we bear in mind that no other potential samaritan is required to bear burdens as physically invasive as the burdens of pregnancy and childbirth, and if we bear in mind also that no other potential samaritan (with the possible,

but doubtful,[58] exception of the parent) is subjected to burdens remotely comparable in magnitude to the burdens imposed on the pregnant woman, we conclude that laws forbidding abortion are at odds with the general spirit of samaritan law.[59]

One final point. When I suggest that the woman should not be compelled to subordinate her interests to those of the fetus, I sometimes meet with the response: "But if she is allowed to have an abortion, the fetus is subordinated. It is just a question of who shall be subordinated to whom." In a sense, of course, this is correct. There is a conflict of interest between the woman and the fetus, and someone is going to lose. But that is true in every samaritan situation. There is a conflict between the distressed party's need for aid and the potential rescuer's desire not to give it. The point is that our law generally resolves this conflict in favor of the potential samaritan. When a woman is pregnant, it is the fetus that needs aid and the woman who is in a position to give it. If the conflict between the woman and the fetus is to be resolved consistently with the resolutions of the most closely analogous cases, the woman must prevail.

[58]*See* discussion [above at the end of the section entitled "Exceptions Based on a Status or Relationship"].

[59]An issue I have not mentioned is whether, in view of the greater responsibility for the fetus of the woman who has sex without taking measures against conception, a state could make access to abortion conditional on responsible contraceptive use. In theory, this suggestion has considerable appeal. But there are difficulties. Many women are excusably ignorant concerning contraceptive methods. Perhaps before the state makes contraceptive use a prerequisite to abortion it must do a better job of contraceptive education. Also, there are significant side effects from many contraceptive methods. If, as I have argued, the woman who conceives and then has an abortion does not make the fetus worse off by her entire course of conduct, it is not clear that the woman should be required to run any risk to herself in order to avoid these consequences to the fetus. Most significantly, the invasions and uncertainty involved in *enforcing* a rule that conditioned abortion on responsible contraceptive use would be extreme. More could be said on this topic, but since no state has attempted to condition abortion on contraceptive use, no more need be said in this essay.

## QUESTIONS

1. What does Regan mean by a *"per se* rule of liability" in the law? Are determinations of *moral blameworthiness* ever governed by something like a *per se* rule?

2. In addition to the bad samaritan law Regan refers to, there is also much legal tradition supporting the claim that a parent owes a special duty of care to his or her child. Is the situation of the pregnant woman sufficiently analogous to the parent's situation to undercut the bad samaritan analogy of Regan's? Explain why or why not.

3. Think of reasons for, and reasons against, the view that there is a duty to continue helping someone whom one has already begun to help.

4. Regan says, "The pregnant woman who has an abortion . . . does not make the fetus worse off by her entire course of conduct." Analyze Regan's reasons for saying this. Suppose that the father of the fetus performs the abortion. Is he making the fetus worse off by his entire course of conduct? Suppose that an unrelated physician (not the father) performs the abortion. What answer then?

5. Analyze Regan's reasons for saying that "if there were a genuine national commitment to population growth, abortion could be prohibited in furtherance of that commitment." Whether or not you ultimately agree with this conclusion, do you agree with this conclusion *given his analysis*? Do you accept the analysis itself? Why or why not?

6. Ronald Dworkin (in "The Great Abortion Case," *The New York Review of Books*, June 29, 1989, pp. 49–54) says, of views like Regan's: "[A]bortion normally requires a physical attack on the fetus, not just a failure to come to its aid. And in any case parents are invariably made an exception to the general doctrine under which people are not required to save others." Either develop this kind of argument against Regan's view, or defend Regan's view against the objection.

## *United States Supreme Court**
### BOWERS v. HARDWICK

JUSTICE WHITE delivered the opinion of the Court.

In August 1982, respondent was charged with violating the Georgia statute criminalizing sodomy[1] by committing that act with another adult male in the bedroom of respondent's home. After a preliminary hearing, the District Attorney decided not to present the matter to the grand jury unless further evidence developed.

*478 U. S. 186 (1986). Numerous footnotes have been omitted without so specifying.
[1]Ga. Code Ann. §16–6–2 (1984) provides, in pertinent part, as follows:
"(a) a person commits the offense of sodomy when he performs or submits to any sexual act involving the sex organs of one person and the mouth or anus of another. . . .
"(b) A person convicted of the offense of sodomy shall be punished by imprisonment for not less than one nor more than 20 years. . . ."

Respondent then brought suit in the Federal District Court, challenging the constitutionality of the statute insofar as it criminalized consensual sodomy.[2] He asserted that he was a practicing homosexual, that the Georgia sodomy statute, as administered by the defendants, placed him in imminent danger of arrest, and that the statute for several reasons violates the Federal Constitution. The District Court granted the defendants' motion to dismiss for failure to state a claim, relying on *Doe* v. *Commonwealth's Attorney for the City of Richmond*, 403 F. Supp. 1199 (ED Va. 1975), which this Court summarily affirmed, 425 U. S. 901 (1976). . . .

Because other Courts of Appeals have arrived at judgments contrary to that of the Eleventh Circuit in this case,[3] we granted the State's petition for certiorari questioning the holding that its sodomy statute violates the fundamental rights of homosexuals. We agree with the State that the Court of Appeals erred, and hence reverse its judgment.

This case does not require a judgment on whether laws against sodomy between consenting adults in general, or between homosexuals in particular, are wise or desirable. It raises no question about the right or propriety of state legislative decisions to repeal their laws that criminalize homosexual sodomy, or of state court decisions invalidating those laws on state constitutional grounds. The issue presented is whether the Federal Constitution confers a fundamental right upon homosexuals to engage in sodomy and hence invalidates the laws of the many States that still make

such conduct illegal and have done so for a very long time. The case also calls for some judgment about the limits of the Court's role in carrying out its constitutional mandate.

We first register our disagreement with the Court of Appeals and with respondent that the Court's prior cases have construed the Constitution to confer a right of privacy that extends to homosexual sodomy and for all intents and purposes have decided this case. The reach of this line of cases was sketched in *Carey* v. *Population Services International*, 431 U. S. 678, 685 (1977). *Pierce* v. *Society of Sisters*, 268 U. S. 510 (1925), and *Meyer* v. *Nebraska*, 262 U. S. 390 (1923), were described as dealing with child rearing and education; *Prince* v. *Massachusetts*, 321 U. S. 158 (1944), with family relationships; *Skinner* v. *Oklahoma ex rel. Williamson*, 316 U. S. 535 (1942), with procreation; *Loving* v. *Virginia*, 388 U. S. 1 (1967), with marriage; *Griswold* v. *Connecticut, supra*, and *Eisenstadt* v. *Baird, supra*, with contraception; and *Roe* v. *Wade*, 410 U. S. 113 (1973), with abortion. The latter three cases were interpreted as construing the Due Process Clause of the Fourteenth Amendment to confer a fundamental individual right to decide whether or not to beget or bear a child.

Accepting the decisions in these cases and the above description of them, we think it evident that none of the rights announced in those cases bears any resemblance to the claimed constitutional right of homosexuals to engage in acts of sodomy that is asserted in this case. No connection between family, marriage, or procreation on the one hand and

---

[2]John and Mary Doe were also plaintiffs in the action. They alleged that they wished to engage in sexual activity proscribed by §16–6–2 in the privacy of their home, App. 3, and that they had been "chilled and deterred" from engaging in such activity by both existence of the statute and Hardwick's arrest. *Id.*, at 5. The District Court held, however, that because they had neither sustained, nor were in immediate danger of sustaining, any direct injury from the enforcement of the statute, they did not have proper standing to maintain the action. *Id.*, at 18. The Court of Appeals affirmed the District Court's judgment dismissing the Does' claim for lack of standing, 760 F. 2d 1202, 1206–1207 (1985), and the Does do not challenge that holding in this Court.

The only claim properly before the Court, therefore, is Hardwick's challenge to the Georgia statute as applied to consensual homosexual sodomy. We express no opinion on the constitutionality of the Georgia statute as applied to other acts of sodomy.

[3]See *Baker* v. *Wade*, 769 F. 2d 289, reh'g denied, 774 F. 2d 1285 (CA5 1985)(en banc). *Dronenburg* v. *Zech*, 239 U. S. App. D.C. 229, 741 F. 2d 1388, reh'g denied, 241 U. S. App. D. C. 262, 746 F. 2d 1579 (1984).

homosexual activity on the other has been demonstrated, either by the Court of Appeals or by respondent. Moreover, any claim that these cases nevertheless stand for the proposition that any kind of private sexual conduct between consenting adults is constitutionally insulated from state proscription is unsupportable. Indeed, the Court's opinion in *Carey* twice asserted that the privacy right, which the *Griswold* line of cases found to be one of the protections provided by the Due Process Clause, did not reach so far.

Precedent aside, however, respondent would have us announce, as the Court of Appeals did, a fundamental right to engage in homosexual sodomy. This we are quite unwilling to do. It is true that despite the language of the Due Process Clauses of the Fifth and Fourteenth Amendments, which appears to focus only on the processes by which life, liberty, or property is taken, the cases are legion in which those Clauses have been interpreted to have substantive content, subsuming rights that to a great extent are immune from federal or state regulation or proscription. Among such cases are those recognizing rights that have little or no textual support in the constitutional language. *Myers, Prince,* and *Pierce* fall in this category, as do the privacy cases from *Griswold* to *Carey*.

Striving to assure itself and the public that announcing rights not readily identifiable in the Constitution's text involves much more than the imposition of the Justices' own choice of values on the States and the Federal Government, the Court has sought to identify the nature of the rights qualifying for heightened judicial protection. In *Palko* v. *Connecticut*, it was said that this category includes those fundamental liberties that are "implicit in the concept of ordered liberty," such that "neither liberty nor justice would exist if [they] were sacrificed." A different description of fundamental liberties appeared in *Moore* v. *East Cleveland*, where they are characterized as those liberties that are "deeply rooted in this Nation's history and tradition." See also *Griswold* v. *Connecticut*.

It is obvious to us that neither of these formulations would extend a fundamental right to homosexuals to engage in acts of consensual sodomy. Proscriptions against that conduct have ancient roots. See generally, Survey on the Constitutional Right to Privacy in the Context of Homosexual Activity, 40 Miami U. L. Rev. 521, 525 (1986). Sodomy was a criminal offense at common law and was forbidden by the laws of the original thirteen States when they ratified the Bill of Rights. In 1868, when the Fourteenth Amendment was ratified, all but 5 of the 37 States in the Union had criminal sodomy laws. In fact, until 1961, all 50 States outlawed sodomy, and today, 24 States and the District of Columbia continue to provide criminal penalties for sodomy performed in private and between consenting adults. Against this background, to claim that a right to engage in such conduct is "deeply rooted in this Nation's history and tradition" or "implicit in the concept of ordered liberty" is, at best, facetious.

Nor are we inclined to take a more expansive view of our authority to discover new fundamental rights imbedded in the Due Process Clause. The Court is most vulnerable and comes nearest to illegitimacy when it deals with judge-made constitutional law having little or no cognizable roots in the language or design of the Constitution. That this is so was painfully demonstrated by the face-off between the Executive and the Court in the 1930's, which resulted in the repudiation of much of the substantive gloss that the Court had placed on the Due Process Clause of the Fifth and Fourteenth Amendments. There should be, therefore, great resistance to expand the substantive reach of those Clauses, particularly if it requires redefining the category of rights deemed to be fundamental. Otherwise, the Judiciary necessarily takes to itself further authority to govern the country without express constitutional authority. The claimed right pressed on us today falls far short of overcoming this resistance.

Respondent, however, asserts that the result should be different where the homosexual conduct occurs in the privacy of the home. He relies on *Stanley* v. *Georgia*, 394 U. S. 557 (1969), where the Court held that the First Amendment prevents conviction for possessing and reading obscene material in the privacy of his home: "If the First Amendment means anything, it means that a State has no business telling a man, sitting alone in his house, what books he may read or what films he may watch."

*Stanley* did protect conduct that would not have been protected outside the home, and it partially prevented the enforcement of state obscenity laws; but the decision was firmly grounded in the First Amendment. The right pressed upon us here has no similar support in the text of the Constitution, and it does not qualify for recognition under the prevailing principles for construing the Fourteenth Amendment. Its limits are also difficult to discern. Plainly enough, otherwise illegal conduct is not always immunized whenever it occurs in the home. Victimless crimes, such as the possession and use of illegal drugs do not escape the law where they are committed at home. *Stanley* itself recognized that its holding offered no protection for the possession in the home of drugs, firearms, or stolen goods. And if respondent's submission is limited to the voluntary sexual conduct between consenting adults, it would be difficult, except by fiat, to limit the claimed right to homosexual conduct while leaving exposed to prosecution adultery, incest, and other sexual crimes even though they are committed in the home. We are unwilling to start down that road.

Even if the conduct at issue here is not a fundamental right, respondent asserts that there must be a rational basis for the law and that there is none in this case other than the presumed belief of a majority of the electorate in Georgia that homosexual sodomy is immoral and unacceptable. This is said to be an inadequate rationale to support the law. The law, however, is constantly based on notions of morality, and if all laws representing essentially moral choices are to be invalidated under the Due Process Clause, the courts will be very busy indeed. Even respondent makes no such claim, but insists that majority sentiments about the morality of homosexuality should be declared inadequate. We do not agree, and are unpersuaded that the sodomy laws of some 25 States should be invalidated on this basis.

Accordingly, the judgment of the Court of Appeals is

*Reversed.*

CHIEF JUSTICE BURGER, concurring.

I join the Court's opinion but I write separately to underscore my view that in constitutional terms there is no such thing as a fundamental right to commit homosexual sodomy.

As the Court notes, the proscriptions against sodomy have very "ancient roots." Decisions of individuals relating to homosexual conduct have been subject to state intervention throughout the history of Western Civilization. Condemnation of those practices is firmly rooted in Judeao-Christian moral and ethical standards. Homosexual sodomy was a capital crime under Roman law. See Code Theod. 9.7.6; Code Just. 9.9.31. See also D. Bailey, Homosexuality in the Western Christian Tradition 70–81 (1975). During the English Reformation when powers of the ecclesiastical courts were transferred to the King's Courts, the first English statute criminalizing sodomy was passed. 25 Hen. VIII, c. 6. Blackstone described "the infamous crime against nature" as an offense of "deeper malignity" than rape, an heinous act "the very mention of which is a disgrace to human nature," and "a crime not fit to be named." Blackstone's Commentaries *215. The common law of England, including its prohibition of sodomy, became the received law of Georgia and the other Colonies. In 1816 the Georgia Legislature passed the statute at issue here, and that statute has been continuously in force in one form or another since that time. To hold that the act of homosexual sodomy is somehow protected as a fundamental right would be to cast aside millennia of moral teaching.

This is essentially not a question of personal "preferences" but rather that of the legislative authority of the State. I find nothing in the Constitution depriving a State of the power to enact the statute challenged here.

JUSTICE POWELL, concurring.

I join the opinion of the Court. I agree with the Court that there is no fundamental right—*i.e.*, no substantive right under the Due Process Clause—such as that claimed by respondent, and found to exist by the Court of Appeals. This is not to suggest, however, that respondent may not be protected by the Eighth Amendment of the Constitution. The Georgia statute at issue in this case, Ga. Code Ann. §16–6–2, authorizes a court to imprison a person for up to 20 years for a single private, consensual act of sodomy. In my view, a prison sentence for such conduct—certainly a sentence of long duration—would create a serious Eighth Amendment issue. Under the Georgia statute a single act of sodomy, even in the private setting of a home, is a felony comparable in terms of the possible sentence imposed to serious felonies such as aggravated battery, §16–5–24, first degree arson, §16–7–60 and robbery, §16–8–40.

In this case, however, respondent has not been tried, much less convicted and sentenced. Moreover, respondent has not raised the Eighth Amendment issue below. For these reasons this constitutional argument is not before us.

JUSTICE BLACKMUN, with whom JUSTICE BRENNAN, JUSTICE MARSHALL, and JUSTICE STEVENS join, dissenting.

This case is no more about "a fundamental right to engage in homosexual sodomy," as the Court purports to declare, than *Stanley* v. *Georgia* was about a fundamental right to watch obscene movies, or *Katz* v. *United States* was about a fundamental right to place interstate bets from a telephone booth. Rather, this case is about " the most comprehensive of rights and the right most valued by civilized men," namely, "the right to be let alone." *Olmstead* v. *United States.*

The statute at issue, Ga. Code Ann. §16–6–2, denies individuals the right to decide for themselves whether to engage in particular forms of private, consensual sexual activity. The Court concludes that §16–6–2 is valid essentially because "the laws of . . . many States . . . still make such conduct illegal and have done so for a very long time." But the fact that the moral judgments expressed by statutes like §16–6–2 may be "natural and familiar . . . ought not to conclude our judgment upon the question whether statutes embodying them conflict with the Constitution of the United States." *Roe* v. *Wade.* Like Justice Holmes, I believe that "[i]t is revolting to have no better reason for a rule of law than that so it was laid down in the time of Henry IV. It is still more revolting if the grounds upon which it was laid down have vanished long since, and the rule simply persists from blind imitation of the past." Holmes, The Path of the Law, 10 Harv. L. Rev. 457, 469 (1897). I believe we must analyze respondent's claim in the light of the values that underlie the constitutional right to privacy. If that right means anything, it means that, before Georgia can prosecute its citizens for making choices about the most intimate aspects of their lives, it must do more than assert that the choice they have made is an "'abominable crime not fit to be named among Christians.'" *Herring* v. *State.*

I

In its haste to reverse the Court of Appeals and hold that the Constitution does not "confe[r] a fundamental right upon homosexuals to engage in sodomy," the Court relegates the actual statute being challenged to a footnote and ignores the procedural posture of the case before it. A fair reading of the statute and of the complaint clearly reveals that the majority has distorted the question this case presents.

First, the Court's almost obsessive focus on homosexual activity is particularly hard to justify in light of the broad language Georgia has used. Unlike the Court, the Georgia Legislature has not proceeded on the assumption that homosexuals are so different from other citizens that their lives may be controlled in a way that would not be tolerated if it limited the choices of those other citizens. Rather, Georgia has provided that "[a] person commits the offense of sodomy when he performs or submits to any sexual act involving the sex organs of one person and the mouth or anus of another." The sex or status of the persons who engage in the act is irrelevant as a matter of state law. In fact, to the extent I can discern a legislative purpose for Georgia's 1968 enactment of §16–6–2, that purpose seems to have been to broaden the coverage of the law to reach heterosexual as well as homosexual activity.[1] I therefore see no basis for the Court's decision to treat this case as an "as applied" challenge to §16–6–2, or for Georgia's attempt, both in its brief and at oral argument, to defend §16–6–2 solely on the grounds that it prohibits homosexual activity. Michael Hardwick's standing may rest in significant part on Georgia's apparent willingness to enforce against homosexuals a law it seems not to have any desire to enforce against heterosexuals. But his claim that §16–6–2 involves an unconstitutional intrusion into his privacy and his right of intimate association does not depend in any way on his sexual orientation.

Second, I disagree with the Court's refusal to consider whether §16–6–2 runs afoul of the Eighth or Ninth Amendments or the Equal Protection Clause of the Fourteenth Amendment. Respondent's complaint expressly invoked the Ninth Amendment, see App. 6, and he relied heavily before this Court on *Griswold* v. *Connecticut*, which identifies that Amendment as one of the specific constitutional provisions giving "life and substance" to our understanding of privacy. More importantly, the procedural posture of the case requires that we affirm the Court of Appeals' judgment if there is *any* ground on which respondent may be entitled to relief. This case is before us on petitioner's motion to dismiss for failure to state a claim, Fed. Rule Civ. Proc. 12(b)(6). It is a well settled principle of law that "a complaint should not be dismissed merely because a plaintiff's allegations do not support the particular legal theory he advances, for the court is under a duty to examine the complaint to determine if the allegations provide for relief on any possible theory." Thus, even if respondent did not advance claims based on the Eighth or Ninth Amendments, or on the Equal Protection Clause, his complaint should not be dismissed if any of those provisions could entitle him to relief. I need not reach either the Eighth Amendment or the Equal Protection Clause issues because I believe that Hardwick has stated a cognizable claim that §16–6–2 interferes with constitutionally protected interests in privacy and freedom of intimate association. But neither the Eighth Amendment nor the Equal Protection Clause is so clearly irrelevant that a claim resting on either provision should be peremptorily dismissed. The Court's cramped reading of the issue before it makes for a short opinion, but it does little to make for a persuasive one.

---

[1] Until 1968, Georgia defined sodomy as "the carnal knowledge and connection against the order of nature, by man with man, or in the same unnatural manner with woman." Ga. Crim. Code §26–5901 (1933). In *Thompson* v. *Aldredge*, 187 Ga. 467, 200 S. E. 799 (1939), the Georgia Supreme Court held that §26–5901 did not prohibit lesbian activity. And in *Riley* v. *Garrett*, 219 Ga. 345, 133 S.E. 2d 367 (1963), the Georgia Supreme Court held that §26–5901 did not prohibit heterosexual cunnilingus. Georgia passed the act-specific statute currently in force "perhaps in response to the restrictive court decisions such as *Riley*," Note, The Crimes Against Nature, 16 J. Pub. L. 159, 167, n. 47 (1967).

## II

"Our cases long have recognized that the Constitution embodies a promise that a certain private sphere of individual liberty will be kept largely beyond the reach of government." In construing the right to privacy, the Court has proceeded along two somewhat distinct, albeit complementary, lines. First, it has recognized a privacy interest with reference to certain *decisions* that are properly for the individual to make. Second, it has recognized a privacy interest with reference to certain *places* without regard for the particular activities in which the individuals who occupy them are engaged. The case before us implicates both the decisional and the spatial aspects of the right to privacy.

## A

The Court concludes today that none of our prior cases dealing with various decisions that individuals are entitled to make free of governmental interference "bears any resemblance to the claimed constitutional right of homosexuals to engage in acts of sodomy that is asserted in this case." While it is true that these cases may be characterized by their connection to protection of the family, the Court's conclusion that they extend no further than this boundary ignores the warning in *Moore* v. *East Cleveland*, against "clos[ing] our eyes to the basic reasons why certain rights associated with the family have been accorded shelter under the Fourteenth Amendment's Due Process Clause." We protect those rights not because they contribute, in some direct and material way, to the general public welfare, but because they form so central a part of an individual's life. "[T]he concept of privacy embodies the 'moral fact that a person belongs to himself and not others nor to society as a whole.'" And so we protect the decision whether to marry precisely because marriage "is an association that promotes a way of life, not causes; a harmony in living, not political faiths; a bilateral loyalty, not commercial or social projects." *Griswold* v. *Connecticut*. We protect the decision whether to have a child because parenthood alters so dramatically an individual's self-definition, not because of demographic considerations or the Bible's command to be fruitful and multiply. And we protect the family because it contributes so powerfully to the happiness of individuals, not because of a preference for stereotypical households. The Court recognized in *Roberts* that the "ability independently to define one's identity that is central to any concept of liberty" cannot truly be exercised in a vacuum; we all depend on the "emotional enrichment of close ties with others."

Only the most willful blindness could obscure the fact that sexual intimacy is "a sensitive, key relationship of human existence, central to family life, community welfare, and the development of human personality," *Paris Adult Theatre I* v. *Slayton*. The fact that individuals define themselves in a significant way through their intimate sexual relationships with others suggests, in a Nation as diverse as ours, that there may be many "right" ways of conducting those relationships, and that much of the richness of a relationship will come from the freedom an individual has to *choose* the form and nature of these intensely personal bonds.

In a variety of circumstances we have recognized that a necessary corollary of giving individuals freedom to choose how to conduct their lives is acceptance of the fact that different individuals will make different choices. For example, in holding that the clearly important state interest in public education should give way to a competing claim by the Amish to the effect that extended formal schooling threatened their way of life, the Court declared: "There can be no assumption that today's majority is 'right' and the Amish and others like them are 'wrong.' A way of life that is odd or even erratic but interferes with no rights or interests of others is not to be condemned because it is different." *Wisconsin* v. *Yoder*. The Court claims that its decision today merely refuses to recognize a fundamental right to engage in homosexual sodomy; what the Court really has refused to recognize is the fundamental interest all individuals have in controlling the nature of their intimate associations with others.

## B

The behavior for which Hardwick faces prosecution occurred in his own home, a place to which the Fourth Amendment attaches special significance. The Court's treatment of this aspect of the case is symptomatic of its overall refusal to consider the broad principles that have informed our treatment of privacy in specific cases. Just as the right to privacy is more than the mere aggregation of a number of entitlements to engage in specific behavior, so too, protecting the physical integrity of the home is more than merely a means of protecting specific activities that often take place there. Even when our understanding of the contours of the right to privacy depends on "reference to a 'place,'" *Katz* v. *United States*, "the essence of a Fourth Amendment violation is 'not the breaking of [a person's] doors, and the rummaging of his drawers,' but rather is 'the invasion of his indefeasible right of personal security, personal liberty and private property.'" *California* v. *Ciraolo*.

The Court's interpretation of the pivotal case of *Stanley* v. *Georgia* is entirely unconvincing. *Stanley* held that Georgia's undoubted power to punish the public distribution of constitutionally unprotected, obscene material did not permit the State to punish the private possession of such material. According to the majority here, *Stanley* relied entirely on the First Amendment, and thus, it is claimed, sheds no light on cases not involving printed materials. But that is not what *Stanley* said. Rather, the *Stanley* Court anchored its holding in the Fourth Amendment's special protection for the individual in his home:

"'The makers of our Constitution undertook to secure conditions favorable to the pursuit of happiness. They recognized the significance of man's spiritual nature, of his feelings and of his intellect. They knew that only a part of the pain, pleasure and satisfactions of life are to be found in material things. They sought to protect Americans in their beliefs, their thoughts, their emotions and their sensations.'

"These are the rights that appellant is asserting in the case before us. He is asserting the right to read or observe what he pleases—the right to satisfy his intellectual and emotional needs in the privacy of his own home."

The central place that *Stanley* gives Justice Brandeis' dissent in *Olmstead*, a case raising *no* First Amendment claim, shows that *Stanley* rested as much on the Court's understanding of the Fourth Amendment as it did on the First. Indeed, in *Paris Adult Theatre I* v. *Slaton*, the Court suggested that reliance on the Fourth Amendment not only supported the Court's outcome in *Stanley* but actually was *necessary* to it: "If obscene material unprotected by the First Amendment in itself carried with it a 'penumbra' of constitutionally protected privacy, this Court would not have found it necessary to decide *Stanley* on the narrow basis of the 'privacy of the home,' which was hardly more than a reaffirmation that 'a man's home is his castle.'" "The right of the people to be secure in their . . . houses," expressly guaranteed by the Fourth Amendment, is perhaps the most "textual" of the various constitutional provisions that inform our understanding of the right to privacy, and thus I cannot agree with the Court's statement that "[t]he right pressed upon us here has no . . . support in the text of the Constitution." Indeed, the right of an individual to conduct intimate relationships in the intimacy of his or her own home seems to me to be the heart of the Constitution's protection of privacy.

## III

The Court's failure to comprehend the magnitude of the liberty interests at stake in this case leads it to slight the question whether petitioner, on behalf of the State, has justified Georgia's infringement on these interests. I believe that neither of the two general justifications for §16–6–2 that petitioner has advanced warrants dismissing respondent's challenge for failure to state a claim.

First, petitioner asserts that the acts made criminal by the statute may have serious adverse consequences for "the general public health and welfare," such as spreading communicable diseases or fostering other criminal activity. Inasmuch as this case was dismissed by the District Court on the pleadings, it is not surprising that the record before us is barren of any evidence to support petitioner's claim.[3] In light of the state of the record, I see no justification for the Court's attempt to equate the private, consensual sexual activity at issue here with the "possession in the home of drugs, firearms, or stolen goods," to which *Stanley* refused to extend its protection. None of the behavior so mentioned in *Stanley* can properly be viewed as "[v]ictimless": drugs and weapons are inherently dangerous, and for property to be "stolen," someone must have been wrongfully deprived of it. Nothing in the record before the Court provides any justification for finding the activity forbidden by §16–6–2 to be physically dangerous, either to the persons engaged in it or to others.[4]

The core of petitioner's defense of §16-6-2, however, is that respondent and others who engage in the conduct prohibited by §16–6–2 interfere with Georgia's exercise of the "'right of the Nation and of the States to maintain a decent society,'" *Paris Adult Theater I* v. *Slaton*. Essentially, petitioner argues, and the Court agrees, that the fact that the acts described in §16–6–2 "for hundreds of years, if not thousands, have been uniformly condemned as immoral" is a sufficient reason to permit a State to ban them today.

I cannot agree that either the length of time a majority has held its convictions or the passions with which it defends them can withdraw legislation from this Court's scrutiny. . . .[5] As Justice Jackson wrote so eloquently for the Court in *West Virginia*

---

[3] Even if a court faced with a challenge to §16–6–2 were to apply simple rational-basis scrutiny to the statute, Georgia would be required to show an actual connection between the forbidden acts and the ill effects it seeks to prevent. The connection between the acts prohibited by §16–6–2 and the harms identified by petitioner in his brief before this Court is a subject of hot dispute, hardly amenable to dismissal under Federal Rule of Civil Procedure 12(b)(6). Compare, *e.g.,* Brief for Petitioner 36–37 and Brief for David Robinson, Jr., as *Amicus Curiae* 23–28, on the one hand, with *People* v. *Onofre*, 51 N.Y. 2d 476, 489, 415 N. E. 2d 936, 941 (1980); Brief for the Attorney General of the State of New York, joined by the Attorney General of the State of California, as *Amici Curiae* 11–14; and Brief for the American Psychological Association and American Public Health Association as *Amici Curiae* 19–27, on the other.

[4] Although I do not think it necessary to decide today issues that are not even remotely before us, it does seem to me that a court could find simple, analytically sound distinctions between certain private, consensual sexual conduct, on the one hand, and adultery and incest (the only two vaguely specific "sexual crimes" to which the majority points, *ante,* at 9) on the other. For example, marriage, in addition to its spiritual aspects, is a civil contract that entitles the contracting parties to a variety of governmentally provided benefits. A State might define the contractual commitment necessary to become eligible for these benefits to include a commitment of fidelity and then punish individuals for breaching that contract. Moreover, a State might conclude that adultery is likely to injure third persons, in particular, spouses and children of persons who engage in extramarital affairs. With respect to incest, a court might well agree with respondent that the nature of familial relationships renders true consent to incestuous activity sufficiently problematical that a blanket prohibition of such activity is warranted. See Tr. of Oral Arg. 21–22. Notably, the Court makes no effort to explain why it has chosen to group private, consensual homosexual activity with adultery and incest rather than with private, consensual heterosexual activity by unmarried persons or, indeed, with oral or anal sex within marriage.

[5] The parallel between *Loving* and this case is almost uncanny. There, too, the State relied on a religious justification for its law. Compare 388 U. S., at 3 (quoting trial court's statement that "Almighty God created the races

*Board of Education* v. *Barnette*, "we apply the limitations of the Constitution with no fear that freedom to be intellectually and spiritually diverse or even contrary will disintegrate the social organization . . . . [F]reedom to differ is not limited to things that do not matter much. That would be a mere shadow of freedom. The test of its substance is the right to differ as to things that touch the heart of the existing order." It is precisely because the issue raised by this case touches the heart of what makes individuals what they are that we should be especially sensitive to the rights of those whose choices upset the majority.

The assertion that "traditional Judeo-Christian values proscribe" the conduct involved cannot provide an adequate justification for §16–6–2. That certain, but by no means all, religious groups condemn the behavior at issue gives the State no license to impose their judgments on the entire citizenry. The legitimacy of secular legislation depends instead on whether the State can advance some justification for its law beyond its conformity to religious doctrine. Thus, far from buttressing his case, petitioner's invocation of Leviticus, Romans, St. Thomas Aquinas, and sodomy's heretical status during the Middle Ages undermines his suggestion that §16–6–2 repre-

sents a legitimate use of secular coercive power.[6] A State can no more punish private behavior because of religious intolerance than it can punish such behavior because of racial animus. "The Constitution cannot control such prejudices, but neither can it tolerate them. Private biases may be outside the reach of the law, but the law cannot, directly or indirectly give them effect." No matter how uncomfortable a certain group may make the majority of this Court, we have held that "[m]ere public intolerance or animosity cannot constitutionally justify the deprivation of a person's physical liberty." *O'Connor* v. *Donaldson*.

Nor can §16–6–2 be justified as a "morally neutral" exercise of Georgia's power to "protect the public environment," *Paris Adult Theatre I*. Certainly, some private behavior can affect the fabric of society as a whole. Reasonable people may differ about whether particular sexual acts are moral or immoral, but "we have ample evidence for believing that people will not abandon morality, will not think any better of murder, cruelty and dishonesty, merely because some private sexual practice which they abominate is not punished by law." H. L. A. Hart, Immorality and Treason, reprinted in The Law as Literature 220, 225 (L. Blom-Cooper ed. 1961). Petitioner and the Court

---

white, black, yellow, malay and red, and he placed them on separate continents . . . . The fact that he separated the races shows that he did not intend for the races to mix"), with Brief for Petitioner 20–21 (relying on the Old and New Testaments and the writings of St. Thomas Aquinas to show that "traditional Judeo-Christian values proscribe such conduct"). There, too, defenders of the challenged statute relied heavily on the fact that when the Fourteenth Amendment was ratified, most of the States had similar prohibitions. There, too, at the time the case came before the Court, many of the States still had criminal statutes concerning the conduct at issue. Compare 388 U. S., at 6, n. 5 (noting that 16 States still outlawed interracial marriage), with *ante*, 6–7 (noting that 24 States and the District of Columbia have sodomy statutes). Yet the Court held, not only that the individious racism of Virginia's law violated the Equal Protection Clause, but also that the law deprived the Lovings of due process by denying them the "freedom of choice to marry" that had "long been recognized as one of the vital personal rights essential to the orderly pursuit of happiness by free men."

[6] The theological nature of the origin of Anglo-American antisodomy statutes is patent. It was not until 1533 that sodomy was made a secular offense in England. 25 Hen. VIII, cap. 6. Until that time, the offense was, in Sir James Stephen's words, "merely ecclesiastical." 2 J. Stephen, A History of the Criminal Law of England 430 (1883). Pollock and Maitland similarly observed that "[t]he crime against nature . . . . was so closely connected with heresy that the vulgar had but one name for both." 2 F. Pollock & F. Maitland, The History of English Law 554 (1895). The transfer of jurisdiction over prosecutions for sodomy to the secular courts seems primarily due to the alteration of ecclesiastical jurisdiction attendant on England's break with the Roman Catholic Church, rather than to any new understanding of the sovereign's interest in preventing or punishing the behavior involved. Cf. E. Coke, The Third Part of the Institutes of the Laws of England, ch. 10 (4th ed. 1797).

fail to see the difference between laws that protect public sensibilities and those that enforce private morality. Statutes banning public sexual activity are entirely consistent with protecting the individual's liberty interest in decisions concerning sexual relations: the same recognition that those decisions are intensely private which justifies protecting them from governmental interference can justify protecting individuals from unwilling exposure to the sexual activities of others. But the mere fact that intimate behavior may be punished when it takes place in public cannot dictate how States can regulate intimate behavior that occurs in intimate places. See *Paris Adult Theatre I* ("marital intercourse on a street corner or a theater stage" can be forbidden despite the constitutional protection identified in *Griswold* v. *Connecticut*).

This case involves no real interference with the rights of others, for the mere knowledge that other individuals do not adhere to one's value system cannot be a legally cognizable interest, let alone an interest that can justify invading the houses, hearts, and minds of citizens who choose to live their lives differently.

## IV

It took but three years for the Court to see the error in its analysis in *Minersville School District* v. *Gobitis* and to recognize that the threat to national cohesion posed by a refusal to salute the flag was vastly outweighed by the threat to those same values posed by compelling such a salute. See *West Virginia Board of Education* v. *Barnette*, 319 U. S. 624 (1943). I can only hope that here, too, the Court soon will reconsider its analysis and conclude that depriving individuals of the right to choose for themselves how to conduct their intimate relationships poses a far greater threat to the values most deeply rooted in our Nation's history than tolerance of nonconformity could ever do. Because I think the Court today betrays those values, I dissent.

JUSTICE STEVENS, with whom JUSTICE BRENNAN and JUSTICE MARSHALL join, dissenting.

Like the Statute that is challenged in this case, the rationale of the Court's opinion applies equally to the prohibited conduct regardless of whether the parties who engage in it are married or unmarried, or are of the same or different sexes. Sodomy was condemned as an odious and sinful type of behavior during the formative period of the common law. That condemnation was equally damning for heterosexual and homosexual sodomy. Moreover, it provided no special exemption for married couples. The license to cohabit and to produce legitimate offspring simply did not include any permission to engage in sexual conduct that was considered a "crime against nature."

The history of the Georgia statute before us clearly reveals this traditional prohibition of heterosexual, as well as homosexual, sodomy. Indeed, at one point in the 20th century, Georgia's law was construed to permit certain sexual conduct between homosexual women even though such conduct was prohibited between heterosexuals. The history of the statutes cited by the majority as proof for the proposition that sodomy is not constitutionally protected similarly reveals a prohibition on heterosexual, as well as homosexual, sodomy.[8]

Because the Georgia statute expresses the traditional view that sodomy is an immoral kind of conduct regardless of the identity of the persons who engage in it, I believe that a proper analysis of its constitutionality requires consideration of two questions: First, may a State totally prohibit the described conduct by means of a neutral law applying without exception to all persons subject to its jurisdiction? If not, may the State save the

---

[8]A review of the statutes cited by the majority discloses that, in 1791, in 1868, and today, the vast majority of sodomy statutes do not differentiate between homosexual and heterosexual sodomy.

statute by announcing that it will only enforce the law against homosexuals? The two questions merit separate discussion.

# I

Our prior cases make two propositions abundantly clear. First, the fact that the governing majority in a State has traditionally viewed a particular practice as immoral is not a sufficient reason for upholding a law prohibiting the practice: neither history nor tradition could save a law prohibiting miscegenation from constitutional attack.[9] Second, individual decisions by married persons, concerning the intimacies of their physical relationship, even when not intended to produce offspring, are a form of "liberty" protected by the Due Process Clause of the Fourteenth Amendment. *Griswold* v. *Connecticut*. Moreover, this protection extends to intimate choices by unmarried as well as married persons.

In consideration of claims of this kind, the Court has emphasized the individual interest in privacy, but its decisions have actually been animated by an even more fundamental concern. As I wrote some years ago:

> "These cases do not deal with the individual's interest in protection from unwarranted public attention, comment, or exploitation. They deal, rather, with the individual's right to make certain unusually important decisions that will affect his own, or his family's, destiny. The Court has referred to such decisions as implicating 'basic values,' as being 'fundamental,' and as being dignified by history and tradition. The character of the Court's language in

these cases brings to mind the origins of the American heritage of freedom—the abiding interest in individual liberty that makes certain state intrusions on the citizen's right to decide how he will live his own life intolerable. Guided by history, our tradition of respect for the dignity of individual choice in matters of conscience and the restraints implicit in the federal system, federal judges have accepted the responsibility for recognition and protection of these rights in appropriate cases."

Society has every right to encourage its individual members to follow particular traditions in expressing affection for one another and in gratifying their personal desires. It, of course, may prohibit an individual from imposing his will on another to satisfy his own selfish interests. It also may prevent an individual from interfering with, or violating, a legally sanctioned and protected relationship, such as marriage. And it may explain the relative advantages and disadvantages of different forms of intimate expression. But when individual married couples are isolated from observation by others, the way in which they voluntarily choose to conduct their intimate relations is a matter for them—not the State—to decide.[10] The essential "liberty" that animated the development of the law in cases like *Griswold*, *Eisenstadt*, and *Carey* surely embraces the right to engage in nonreproductive, sexual conduct that others may consider offensive or immoral.

Paradoxical as it may seem, our prior cases thus establish that a State may not prohibit sodomy within "the sacred precincts of marital bedrooms," *Griswold*, 381 U. S., at 485, or, indeed, between unmarried heterosexual adults. *Eisenstadt*, 405 U. S., at 453. In

[9]See *Loving* v. *Virginia*, 388 U. S. 1 (1967). Interestingly, miscegenation was once treated as a crime similar to sodomy. See Hawley & McGregor, The Criminal Law, at 287 (discussing crime of sodomy); *id.*, at 288 (discussing crime of miscegenation).

[10]Indeed, the Georgia Attorney General concedes that Georgia's statute would be unconstitutional if applied to a married couple. Significantly, Georgia passed the current statute three years after the Court's decision in *Griswold*.

all events, it is perfectly clear that the State of Georgia may not totally prohibit the conduct proscribed by §16–6–2 of the Georgia Criminal Code.

## II

If the Georgia statute cannot be enforced as it is written—if the conduct it seeks to prohibit is a protected form of liberty for the vast majority of Georgia's citizens—the State must assume the burden of justifying a selective application of its law. Either the persons to whom Georgia seeks to apply its statute do not have the same interest in "liberty" that others have, or there must be a reason why the State may be permitted to apply a generally applicable law to certain persons that it does not apply to others.

The first possibility is plainly unacceptable. Although the meaning of the principle that "all men are created equal" is not always clear, it surely must mean that every free citizen has the same interest in "liberty" that the members of the majority share. From the standpoint of the individual, the homosexual and the heterosexual have the same interest in deciding how he will live his own life, and, more narrowly, how he will conduct himself in his personal and voluntary associations with his companions. State intrusion into the private conduct of either is equally burdensome.

The second possibility is similarly unacceptable. A policy of selective application must be supported by a neutral and legitimate interest—something more substantial than a habitual dislike for, or ignorance about, the disfavored group. Neither the State nor the Court has identified any such interest in this case. The Court has posited as a justification for the Georgia statute "the presumed belief of a majority of the electorate in Georgia that homosexual sodomy is immoral and unacceptable." But the Georgia electorate has expressed no such belief—instead, its representatives enacted a law that presumably reflects the belief that *all sodomy* is immoral and unacceptable. Unless the Court is prepared to conclude that such a law is constitutional, it may not rely on the work product of the Georgia Legislature to support its holding. For the Georgia statute does not single out homosexuals as a separate class meriting special disfavored treatment.

Nor, indeed, does the Georgia prosecutor even believe that all homosexuals who violate this statute should be punished. This conclusion is evident from the fact that the respondent in this very case has formally acknowledged in his complaint and in court that he has engaged, and intends to continue to engage, in the prohibited conduct, yet the State has elected not to process criminal charges against him. As JUSTICE POWELL points out, moreover, Georgia's prohibition on private, consensual sodomy has not been enforced for decades. The record of nonenforcement, in this case and in the last several decades, belies the Attorney General's representations about the importance of the State's selective application of its generally applicable law.[12]

Both the Georgia statute and the Georgia prosecutor thus completely fail to provide the Court with any support for the conclusion that homosexual sodomy, *simpliciter*, is considered unacceptable conduct in that State, and that the burden of justifying a selective application of the generally applicable law has been met.

[12]It is, of course, possible to argue that a statute has a purely symbolic role. Cf. *Carey* v. *Population Services International*, 431 U. S. 678, 715, n. 3 (1977) (STEVENS, J., concurring in part and concurring in judgment) ("The fact that the State admittedly has never brought a prosecution under the statute . . . is consistent with appellants' position that the purpose of the statute is merely symbolic"). Since the Georgia Attorney General does not even defend the statute as written, however, the State cannot possibly rest on the notion that the statute may be defended for its symbolic message.

## III

The Court orders the dismissal of respondent's complaint even though the State's statute prohibits all sodomy; even though that prohibition is concededly unconstitutional with respect to heterosexuals; and even though the State's *post hoc* explanations for selective application are belied by the State's own actions. At the very least, I think it clear at this early stage of the litigation that respondent has alleged a constitutional claim sufficient to withstand a motion to dismiss.[13]

I respectfully dissent.

## QUESTIONS

1. Justice Stevens's opinion focuses on the fact that the Georgia statute applies both to homosexual and heterosexual sodomy, and that this brings with it dangers of selective application of the law. Answer the following hypothetical argument designed to reply to this objection: "Such laws are not selectively enforced. In fact, they are quite uniformly *un*enforced, and typically enacted with the expectation that they will not be enforced. They serve an entirely different function—an educative, moral tutelary function. When a case under such a statute does come before the courts, it is very rare, and, as in *Bowers*, usually the result of a deliberate plan to test the law's constitutionality in court."

2. Justice Blackmun, in discussing whether homosexual sodomy in the privacy of one's home is like the possession of drugs or firearms, says that "Nothing in the record before the Court provides any justification for finding the activity forbidden by [the statute] to be physically dangerous, either to the persons engaged in it or to others." In 1986 (though more than at the present time), an especially large percentage of AIDS cases were attributable to homosexual sodomy. Would this fact have any legal or moral bearing on this issue, or not?

3. In his concurring opinion, Chief Justice Burger says that "To hold that the act of homosexual sodomy is somehow protected as a fundamental right would be to cast aside millennia of moral teaching." Similarly, Justice White's opinion mentions the "ancient roots" of the proscription against homosexual sodomy. What is the relevance here of "millenia of moral teaching"? In answering this, evaluate each of the following possibilities as an interpretation of this argument: Long-standing moral teaching (a) informs as to what the framers of the Constitution must have had in mind when they adopted its provisions; (b) establishes the true extent of the State's moral authority to legislate; (c) is the best indicator of the extent of individual liberty that we can successfully live with today; (d) tells us what is "implicit in the concept of ordered liberty."

4. Justice Powell might well have voted with the minority (thus changing the outcome of this case) if Hardwick had in fact been tried and convicted. If such a conviction *would*

---

[13]Indeed, at this stage, it appears that the statute indiscriminately authorizes a policy of selective prosecution that is neither limited to the class of homosexual persons nor embraces all persons in that class, but rather applies to those who may be arbitrarily selected by the prosecutor for reasons that are not revealed either in the record of this case or in the text of the statute. If that is true, although the text of the statute is clear enough, its true meaning may be "so intolerably vague that evenhanded enforcement of the law is a virtual impossibility." *Marks* v. *United States*, 430 U. S. 188, 198 (1977)(STEVENS, J., concurring in part and dissenting in part).

have raised an Eighth Amendment issue, should Powell have voted with the minority anyway, even though Hardwick was never actually tried? If such a statute as this one is routinely *not* enforced, is there any issue about "cruel and unusual" punishment to worry about?

5. Ronald Dworkin (in "The Great Abortion Case," *The New York Review of Books*, June 29, 1989, pp. 49-54) says that "if we must reject the right to an abortion because abortion is not mentioned in the Constitution, then we must also reject a great number of other, unquestioned constitutional rights that lawyers frequently describe in language not to be found there either." [Dworkin mentions as examples such unquestioned rights as the right to use contraceptives, the right to vote, to travel between states, and so on.] Does Dworkin's comment have an application to the majority opinion in *Bowers*? Explain.

## *Robert Bork*
# JUDICIAL MORAL PHILOSOPHY AND THE <u>RIGHT OF PRIVACY</u>*

The years of the Burger and Rehnquist Courts also saw the "right of privacy" invented by the Warren Court mature into a judicial power to dictate moral codes of sexual conduct and procreation for the entire nation. The Court majority adopted an extreme individualistic philosophy in these cases, seeming to assert that society, acting through government, had very little legitimate interest in such matters.

*Griswold* v. *Connecticut*[17] invalidated a law prohibiting the use of contraceptives on the ground that government must not enter the marital bedroom. That focus, spurious as it was, at least seemed to confine the "right of privacy" to areas of life that all Americans would agree should remain private. But almost at once a Court majority began to alter the new right's rationale and hence to expand its coverage in unpredictable ways.

Massachusetts enacted a law regulating the distribution rather than the use of contraceptives. The law provided the married persons could obtain contraceptives to prevent pregnancy on prescription only, and single persons could not obtain contraceptives for the purpose of preventing pregnancy but only to prevent the spread of disease. It was not apparent that the law made much sense, but that is not the same as being unconstitutional. In 1972, in *Eisenstadt* v. *Baird*,[18] the Supreme Court invalidated the statute under the equal protection clause of the fourteenth amendment and began the transformation of the right of privacy:

> If under *Griswold* the distribution of contraceptives to married persons cannot be prohibited, a ban on distribution to unmarried persons would be equally impermissible. It is true that in *Griswold* the right of privacy in question inhered in the marital relationship. Yet the marital couple is not an independent entity with a mind and heart of its own,

[17]381 U.S. 479 (1965).
[18]405 U.S.438, 453 (1972).

but an association of two individuals each with a separate intellectual and emotional makeup. If the right of privacy means anything, it is the right of the *individual,* married or single, to be free from unwarranted governmental intrusion into matters so fundamentally affecting a person as the decision whether to bear or beget a child.

*Griswold* did not, of course, deal with distribution of contraceptives but with a prohibition of use. That case, moreover, rested upon a rhetorical appreciation of marriage and the marital bedroom. Now that rhetorical line was dropped because the Massachusetts statute treated married couples and single persons differently, and the Court wanted to strike down the law as to unmarried people. Significantly the argument of the Court shifted from the sanctity of a basic institution, marriage, to the sanctity of individual desires. The unmarried individual has, as a matter of fact, the freedom to decide whether to bear or beget a child, of course, because he or she has the right to choose whether or not to copulate. But that did not seem enough to the Court, perhaps because copulation should not be burdened either by marital status or by abstinence from its pleasures. There may or may not be something to be said for this as a matter of morality, but there is nothing to be said for it as constitutional law. The Constitution simply does not address the subject.

Nor after *Eisenstadt* were we much further along in knowing what it is that the right of privacy does cover. In order to apply the precedent to the next litigant's claim to be free of a law on the grounds of privacy, one would have to know whether the challenged governmental regulation was "unwarranted," which is in no way defined by the opinion, and whether the regulation concerned a matter "so fundamentally affecting a person as the decision whether to bear

or beget a child." The opinion gives no guidance for deciding that issue either. It was impossible to tell from *Eisenstadt* where the right of privacy might strike next. We soon learned.

The subject of abortion had been fiercely debated in state legislatures for many years. It raises profound moral issues upon which people of good will can and do disagree, depending upon whether they view a fetus as fully human, and therefore not to be killed for anyone's convenience, or whether they think the fetus less than human so that the desires of the pregnant woman should be paramount. Whatever the proper resolution of the moral debate, a subject which there is no need to address here, few people imagined that the Constitution resolved it. In 1973 a majority of the Supreme Court did imagine just that in *Roe* v. *Wade.*[19]

In an opinion of just over fifty-one pages, Justice Blackmun writing for a majority of seven Justices, employed the right of privacy to strike down the abortion laws of most states and to set severe limitations upon the states' power to regulate the subject at all. From the beginning of the Republic until that day, January 22, 1973, the moral question of what abortions should be lawful had been left entirely to state legislatures. The discovery this late in our history that the question was not one for democratic decision but one of constitutional law was so implausible that it certainly deserved a fifty-one-page explanation. Unfortunately, in the entire opinion there is not one line of explanation, not one sentence that qualifies as legal argument. Nor has the Court in the sixteen years since ever provided the explanation lacking in 1973. It is unlikely that it ever will, because the right to abort, whatever one thinks of it, is not to be found in the Constitution.

The *Roe* opinion began with a brief recitation of the statute challenged, the appealability of the orders below, and the power of the Court to

---

[19]410 U.S. 113 (1973).

decide the issue, and then turned to the history of abortion and the interests of the state in regulating the topic through its criminal code. Justice Blackmun canvassed ancient attitudes, including those of the Persian Empire, the Greeks, the Romans, and the "Ephesian, Soranos, often described as the greatest of the ancient gynecologists. . . ."[20] He placed the Hippocratic Oath, which forbids aiding an abortion, in historical context, suggesting that the oath was not at first highly regarded and that its later popularity was due in large measure to the rise of Christianity. The opinion then traced the English common and statutory law as well as the American law on the subject before devoting sections to the positions of the American Medical Association, the American Public Health Association, and the American Bar Association. None of this, it will be noted, is of obvious relevance to the Constitution. Nor was any of this material employed as history that might illuminate the meaning of any provision of the Constitution.

The *Roe* opinion next discussed three reasons said to explain the enactment of laws limiting the right to abort: "a Victorian social concern to discourage illicit sexual conduct";[21] concern for the hazards abortion posed for women; and concern for prenatal life. Note that the very concept of sexual conduct that is "illicit" is dismissed with the pejorative "Victorian." This accurately reflects the Court majority's allegiance to untrammeled individualism and its position in our cultural wars. And the Court did not decide that the statutes were invalid because obsolete—that, for example, state legislatures had been moved by concern for women's health that modern medicine had rendered irrelevant. A statute may be enacted for one reason, retained for another, and be none the less constitutional for that. Had that rationale for invalidity been advanced, moreover, states could have responded by reenacting their laws out of an

expressed desire to protect the unborn. That was not what the Court had in mind.

The explanation of the true basis for the unconstitutionality of so many statutes begins with the sentence, "The Constitution does not explicitly mention any right of privacy."[22] The existence of such a right is nonetheless defended by citing a series of cases to demonstrate that "the Court has recognized that a right of personal privacy, or a guarantee of certain areas or zones of privacy, does exist under the Constitution." Nobody has ever quarrelled with the proposition that certain zones or aspects of privacy or freedom are protected by the Constitution. Justice Blackmun cited cases decided under the first, fourth, and fifth amendments. But those differed entirely from the right he was creating in that they had specific textual support. He got closer to his solution when he moved to concepts previously employed by Courts that lacked support in the actual Constitution for what they wanted to do. The opinion cited the "penumbras of the Bill of Rights," relied upon by Justice Douglas in *Griswold* v. *Connecticut*, Justice Goldberg's reliance upon the ninth amendment in the same case, and the concept of liberty in the due process clause of the fourteenth amendment. *Roe* continued:

> These decisions make it clear that only personal rights that can be deemed "fundamental" or "implicit in the concept of ordered liberty [*Palko v. Connecticut*]," are included in this guarantee of personal privacy. They also make it clear that the right has some extension to activities relating to marriage [*Loving v. Virginia*]; procreation [*Skinner v. Oklahoma*]; contraception [*Eisenstadt v. Baird*]; family relationships [*Prince v. Massachusetts*]; and child rearing and education [*Pierce v. Society of Sisters: Meyer v. Nebraska*].

[20]*Id.* at 130.
[21]*Id.* at 148.
[22]*Id.* 152–53.

*Skinner*[23] and *Eisenstadt,*[24] as we have seen in this chapter and the one preceding, involved the Court's creation of new rights without support in constitutional text or history. *Pierce*[25] and *Meyer,*[26] as we saw two chapters back, used the same methodology of creating rights but at least reflected the first amendment. *Prince*[27] denied claims by a Jehovah's Witness to be free of the state's child labor laws on grounds of religious freedom and the equal protection of the laws. The case related to marriage, *Loving,*[28] struck down an antimiscegenation law on the grounds that the racial classification violated the equal protection clause and also the right of liberty under the due process clause, though the latter holding also seemed to depend upon the invidious racial classification. This is not a very impressive list of cases to support the claimed right of abortion. They do not bear upon the subject at all. Some of the cases were clearly instances of judicial rewriting of the Constitution, others at least enforced values found in actual provisions of the Constitution, and still others denied the rights claimed. None of them remotely addresses the issue of abortion, and none of them even mentions a right of privacy. It is difficult, therefore, to understand why the *Roe* opinion supposes that these cases show the extension or reach of the right of privacy. They do nothing of the sort. Marshaling these decisions as if they were precedents merely emphasized the absence of support for the right. The invented right of privacy had not been applied in any Supreme Court case other than ones involving contraception.

Nonetheless, without any analysis, the Roe opinion then immediately decided the issue before the Court by simple assertion:

This right of privacy, whether it be founded in the Fourteenth Amendment's concept of personal liberty and restrictions upon state action, as we feel it is, or, as the District Court determined, in the Ninth Amendment's reservations of rights to the people is broad enough to encompass a woman's decision whether or not to terminate her pregnancy.[29]

That is it. That is the crux of the opinion. The Court did not even feel obliged to settle the question of where the right of privacy or the subsidiary right to abort is to be attached to the Constitution's text. The opinion seems to regard that as a technicality that really does not matter, and indeed it does not, since the right does not come out of the Constitution but is forced into it. The opinion does not once say what principle defines the new right so that we might know both why it covers a liberty to abort and what else it might cover in the future. We are told only that wherever the right may be located and whatever it may cover, it is "broad enough" for present purposes. This is not legal reasoning but fiat.

The *Roe* opinion then legislated the rules the Court considered appropriate for abortions by balancing the interests of the woman and those of the state. To do that, of course, the Court had implicitly to decide which interests were legitimate and how much weight should be ascribed to each one. That, being unguided by the Constitution, was an exercise in moral and political philosophy, or would have been if some reasoning had been articulated. The upshot, in any event, was that in the first trimester of pregnancy the abortion decision must be left to

[23]316 U.S. 535 (1942).
[24]405 U.S. 438 (1972).
[25]268 U.S. 510 (1925).
[26]262 U.S. 390 (1923).
[27]321 U.S. 158 (1944).
[28]388 U.S. 1 (1967).
[29]410 U.S. at 153. 164–65.

the woman and the medical judgment of her physician. After that and up to the point where the fetus can live outside the womb, the point of viability, the state may regulate the abortion procedure but only in ways related to the health of the mother. Subsequent to viability "the State in promoting its interest in the potentiality of human life may, if it chooses, regulate, and even proscribe, abortion" except where it is necessary to preserve the mother's life or health.

Justice Rehnquist's dissent pointed out that it was very curious to decide the case under the rubric of privacy since a transaction resulting in an operation by a physician is not "private."[30] Justice White's dissent, which Justice Rehnquist joined, summed up the trouble with *Roe:*

> I find nothing in the language or history of the Constitution to support the Court's judgment. The Court simply fashions and announces a new constitutional right for pregnant mothers and, with scarcely any reason or authority for its action, invests that right with sufficient substance to override most existing state abortion statutes. The upshot is that the people and the legislatures of the 50 States are constitutionally disentitled to weigh the relative importance of the continued existence and development of the fetus, on the one hand, against a spectrum of possible impacts on the mother, on the other hand. As an exercise of raw judicial power, the Court perhaps has authority to do what it does today; but it in my view its judgment is an improvident and extravagant exercise of the power of judicial review that the Constitution extends to this Court.[31]

In the years since 1973, no one, however pro-abortion, has ever thought of an argument that even remotely begins to justify *Roe* v. *Wade* as a constitutional decision. Justice Blackmun frequently discusses the case in public, but the only justification he offers is not legal but moral: the case, he says, is a milestone on women's march to equality. There is certainly room for argument about that. There is no room for argument about the conclusion that the decision was the assumption of illegitimate judicial power and a usurpation of the democratic authority of the American people.

On the last day it sat in 1989, a bitterly divided Court decided *Webster* v. *Reproductive Health Services*,[32] a challenge to statutory restrictions Missouri has placed upon the abortion procedure. The crucial restriction was the law's requirement that before performing an abortion on a woman twenty or more weeks pregnant, the physician first determine whether the unborn child is viable. Five Justices upheld that regulation, which seemed to narrow the scope of *Roe.* Three Justices, Rehnquist, White, and Kennedy, employed a standard of review which necessarily, though not explicitly, completely undermines *Roe,*[33] while one Justice, Scalia,[34] stated that *Roe* should expressly be overruled. Justice O'Connor upheld the statute but stated that that could be done without bringing *Roe* into question.[35] Both sides in the abortion controversy at once announced that the Court had made a momentous decision. It is true enough that states now appear to have some unknown degree of additional power to control the incidents of abortion but *Webster* was neither the calamity that the pro-abortion groups bewailed ("the court is

---

[30] 410 U.S. at 171, 172 (Rehnquist, J., dissenting).

[31] 410 U.S. at 221–22 (White, J., dissenting).

[32] 57 U.S.L.W. 5023 (U.S. July 3, 1989).

[33] *Id.* at 5025. (plurality op. of Rehnquist. (J.).

[34] *Id.* at 5034 (Scalia, J., concurring).

[35] *Id.* at 5031 (O'Connor, J., concurring).

waging war on women") nor the great victory that the anti-abortionists proclaimed ("we will produce an avalanche of legislation"). Though *Webster* altered little that was fundamental, it does signal the potential for such change. In *Roe*, the Justices split seven to two in favor of a right to abort. Now there are four Justices who favor that right, four who think it does not exist, and one who does not reach the issue.

Attempts to overturn *Roe* will continue as long as the Court adheres to it. And, just so long as the decision remains, the Court will be perceived, correctly, as political and will continue to be the target of demonstrations, marches, television advertisements, mass mailings, and the like. *Roe*, as the greatest example and symbol of the judicial usurpation of democratic prerogatives in this century, should be overturned. The Court's integrity requires that. But even if the case is relegated to the dustbin of history where *Dred Scott* and *Lochner* lie, the right of privacy and the judicial techniques and attitudes it represents are likely to remain. A more fundamental rethinking of legitimate judicial power than the mere demise of *Roe* would signify is required.

The privacy right had come to another crucial point three years earlier in *Bowers* v. *Hardwick*.[36] A narrow majority of the Court there upheld, at least as to homosexual sodomy, a Georgia statute making all sodomy criminal. This was significant, and may even have presaged *Webster*, for there seems little doubt that the impulse, it was no more than that, underlying *Roe* would have struck down the sodomy statute in *Hardwick*.

A police officer, who entered Hardwick's home lawfully, observed Hardwick engaged in homosexual sodomy and made an arrest. The district attorney, however, decided not to prosecute—there had been no criminal prosecutions under the statute for decades—and so Hardwick brought suit to have the

law declared unconstitutional. Though he alleged that he was in imminent danger of arrest as a practicing homosexual, that was obviously not so, and the suit was surely brought to seek a declaration that would equate the constitutionality, and hence the presumed morality, of homosexual and heterosexual conduct. Hardwick's suit, in a word, rested upon nothing in the Constitution and so was one more sortie in our cultural war.

The Supreme Court upheld the law by a five-to-four vote. Justice White, writing for the majority, stated: "The issue presented is whether the Federal Constitution confers a fundamental right upon homosexuals to engage in sodomy and hence invalidates the laws of the many States that still make such conduct illegal and have done so for a very long time."[37] This statement of the issue was somewhat problematical, because the statute on its face applied to all forms of sodomy, heterosexual as well as homosexual, and, given the history of its enforcement, Hardwick was in no greater danger of prosecution than any heterosexual.

The court of appeals had found the statute unconstitutional by relying on Supreme Court precedent that we have already canvassed in this and previous chapters. Justice White found those precedents inapplicable, however, by categorizing them as dealing with child rearing and education, family relationships, procreation, marriage, contraception, and abortion. There was, he said, no connection between those subjects and homosexual sodomy. That was true enough, though, since those cases never did offer a rationale, it is hard to put them into categories except retroactively and as a matter of description rather than analysis.

But Hardwick, quite aside from the precedent, asked the Court to announce a fundamental right to engage in homosexual sodomy. Justice White's response showed

---

[36]478 U.S. 186 (1986).
[37]*Id.* at 190.

that he knew the Court had long been performing a questionable function in this area. "It is true that despite the language of the Due Process Clauses of the Fifth and Fourteenth Amendments, which appears to focus only on the process by which life, liberty, or property is taken, the cases are legion in which those Clauses have been interpreted to have substantive content. . . . Among such cases are those recognizing rights that have little or no textual support in the constitutional language."[38] Then:

> Striving to assure itself and the public that announcing rights not readily identifiable in the Constitution's text involves much more than the imposition of the Justices' own values on the States and the Federal Government, the Court has sought to identify the nature of the rights qualifying for heightened judicial protection.

That passage contains no suggestion that the Court had succeeded in its striving. Justice White noted two formulations of the Justices' attempts to assure themselves, and us, that they were not merely imposing their own values. In *Palko* v. *Connecticut*, a 1937 decision, it was said that the fundamental liberties to be protected, though not found in the text of the Constitution, included those "implicit in the concept of ordered liberty," so that "neither liberty nor justice would exist if [they] were sacrificed."[39] Forty years later, in *Moore* v. *East Cleveland*, the formulation of protected freedoms was those that are "deeply rooted in this Nation's history and tradition."[40]

This is pretty vaporous stuff. Compare the phrases used by *Palko* and *Moore* with the provisions of the Bill of Rights. The latter at least specify what liberty is to be protected. Whatever line-drawing must be done starts from a solid base, the guarantee of freedom of speech, of freedom from unreasonable searches and seizures, and the like. By contrast, the judge-created phrases specify no particular freedom, but merely assure us, in sonorous phrases, that they, the judges, will know what freedoms are required when the time comes. One would think something more is required as the starting place for a line of reasoning that leads to the negation of statutes duly enacted by elected representatives. "Ordered liberty" is a splendid phrase but not a major premise. It might be thought that ordered liberty is just what the Constitution was intended to establish for the nation and that it is therefore more than a little surprising, and perhaps presumptuous, that Justices should describe their task in a way that suggests they are completing a design the Founders left unfinished. Both the amendment process, specified in the Constitution, and the processes of legislation are means by which the design of order and liberty can be elaborated and improved. The phrase *Palko* used rather too clearly indicates that the Justices may rewrite the Constitution. Nor is it terribly reassuring to be told they will rewrite it only to save liberties the Founders overlooked but which are nevertheless so essential that neither liberty nor justice can exist without them. The suggestion that such rights were overlooked in the Constitution and then systematically overlooked through two centuries of amendments is , to be candid, preposterous.

The *Moore* formulation is less grandiose but hardly offers more guidance. Liberties that are deeply rooted in our history and tradition and that now need protection must be matters the Founders left to the legislature, either because they assumed no legislature would be mad enough to do away with them or because they wished to allow the legislature discretion to regulate the area as

---

[38]*Id.* at 191.
[39]302 U.S. 319, 325, 326 (1937).
[40]431 U.S. 494, 503 (1977).

they saw fit. In any event, history is not binding, and tradition is useful to remind us of the wisdom and folly of the past, not to chain us to either. No constitutional doctrine holds that history and tradition may not be departed from when the people think there is good reason to do so. Our history and tradition, like those of any nation, display not only adherence to great moral principles but also instances of profound immorality. Opinions about which is which will differ at any one time and change over time. The judge who states that tradition and morality are his guides, therefore, leaves himself free to pick through them for those particular freedoms that he prefers. History and tradition are very capacious suitcases, and a judge may find a good deal pleasing to himself packed into them, if only because he has packed the bags himself.

Because homosexual sodomy has been proscribed for centuries, Justice White said the claim that such conduct was "deeply rooted in this nation's history and tradition" was "at best, facetious."[41] He expressed the *Bowers* majority's unwillingness to make a more expansive view of its authority to discover new fundamental rights in the due process clause. "The Court is most vulnerable and comes nearest to illegitimacy when it deals with judge-made constitutional law having little or no cognizable roots in the language or design of the Constitution." That is quite right, or almost so. Perhaps he had to put the matter as one of coming "nearest to illegitimacy" in order not to of-

fend members of the majority who had joined decisions that had no roots in the "language or design of the Constitution," but on this topic there is no question of near or far. When constitutional law is judge-made and not rooted in the text or structure of the Constitution, it does not approach illegitimacy, it *is* illegitimate, root and branch.*

Justice Blackmun wrote for the four dissenters.[42] His opinion has been widely praised by the commentators of the popular press with such terms as "eloquent" and "passionate." Those things it may be. But eloquence and passion are poor substitutes for judicial reasoning, and the *Bowers* dissent, the natural outcome of *Griswold* v. *Connecticut* and *Roe* v. *Wade,* is a constitutional debacle. The opinion will repay close examination nonetheless, for here, for the first time, a Justice embarks upon the enterprise law school theorists have been urging upon the Court as its proper function—the enterprise of articulated moral philosophy. Blackmun began with the observation that the case was not about a fundamental right to engage in homosexual sodomy but about "the most comprehensive of rights and the right most valued by civilized men,' namely, 'the right to be let alone.'" There is, of course, no general constitutional right to be let alone, or there would be no law. This was merely the general, undefined right of privacy again. Though it is difficult to be sure, Justice Blackmun seems to have located this free-floating right, or rather free-floating judicial power, alternatively in the due process clause

[41]478 U.S. at 194.

*As a judge, I had earlier reached the same result by a somewhat different route. The Navy had discharged a petty officer for engaging in such conduct in the barracks with a young recruit. The former petty officer challenged his discharge and contended before our court that the right of privacy cases created a general rule that government may not interfere with an individual's intimate decisions regarding his or her own body. My opinion examined those cases, found in them "no explanatory principle that informs a lower court how to reason about what is and what is not encompassed by the right of privacy," and refused to invent a right to homosexual conduct, saying that "If the revolution in sexual mores that appellant proclaims is in fact ever to arrive, we think it must arrive through the moral choices of the people and their elected representatives, not through the ukase of this court." *Dronenburg* v. *Zech* 741 F.2d 1388, 1395, 1397 (1984). Since the right of privacy cases rest upon no constitutional principle, but are themselves mere judicial ukases, that position still seems to me correct.

[42]478 U.S. at 199 (Blackmun, J., dissenting)

of the fourteenth amendment or in the ninth amendment. We have discussed the due process clause's lack of substance, and the ninth amendment, as will be shown [in a chapter not reprinted here], simply does not create any rights a court may enforce against any government. In *Roe,* Justice Blackmun had attached privacy to the due process clause of the fourteenth amendment. But, as in *Roe,* where in the Constitution a Justice chooses to insert a right he had made up is of small significance, more a matter of aesthetic preference than of legal significance.

Justice Blackmun went on to explain that the Court construed the right to privacy by proceeding along two lines. "First, [the Court] has recognized a privacy interest with reference to certain decisions that are properly for the individual to make. [He cited *Roe* v. *Wade* and *Pierce* v. *Society of Sisters*]. Second, [the Court] has recognized a privacy interest with reference to certain *places* without regard for the particular activities in which the individuals who occupy them are engaged."[43] Neither of these withstands even cursory examination.

The first line of argument gives itself away at once with the qualification that the Court protects the right to make those decisions that are *"properly"* the individual's to make. What is proper is not an objective fact but a moral choice to be made by someone, and the *Bowers* dissent says the moral choice is for judges. That is bad enough, but the next question is whether the judges can at least frame criteria that guide them to their choice and explain to us why the choice is correct and what is likely to be the judges' next choice on behalf of the individual against society. From the evidence of Blackmun's *Roe* opinion there are no such criteria, or at least none that the Justices care to share with us. *Bowers,* on the other hand, confirms the conclusion that there are no such criteria by trying to explain them to us. The dissent chastises the majority for stating that prior cases had related to the protection of the family. That may be so, Blackmun

said in a truly startling argument, but the rights to be protected extended beyond that, because "We protect those rights [associated with the family] not because they contribute, in some direct and material way, to the general public welfare, but because they form so central a part of an individual's life. '[T]he concept of privacy embodies the "moral fact that a person belongs to himself and not others nor to society as a whole."'" It is doubtful that there are any moral "facts," as opposed to moral convictions, but if there are, this is not one of them and cannot be so long as we live in a society. If the opinion meant what it said, four members of the Court viewed the state of nature, in which every individual is free to be for himself and no one else, as the moral condition contemplated by the Constitution. That view of the individual and his obligations can hardly be taken seriously. In our view of morality and responsibility, no husband or wife, no father or mother, should act on the principle that a "person belongs to himself and not others." No citizen should take the view that no part of him belongs to "society as a whole." Under that notion, there would be no moral obligation to obey the law and it would certainly be impossible to draft an army to defend the nation. Here and elsewhere some Justices have enunciated a position of extreme individualism, which amounts necessarily to an attitude of moral relativism. If all that counts is the gratification of the individual, then morality is completely privatized and society may make no moral judgments that are translated into law.

The dissent cannot really mean what it said and, indeed, no Justice takes any such position consistently. None could since all law is based upon moral judgments. There is, for example, no basis for worker safety laws other than the moral judgment that it is wrong to endanger workers' lives and limbs in order to produce goods at lower cost. There is no objection to segregation or even to slavery other than moral disapproval. No

---

[43]*Id.* at 204.

one suggests that the fourteenth amendment, which ended the one, and the thirteenth amendment, which ended the other, are based on anything other than morality. Justice White rejected Justice Blackmun's point as phrased by Hardwick. Hardwick made the argument that has become common in these cases. White said he asserted that "there must be a rational basis for the law and that there is none in this case other than the presumed belief of a majority of the electorate in Georgia that homosexual sodomy is immoral and unacceptable. This is said to be an inadequate rationale to support the law. The law, however, is constantly based on notions of morality, and if all laws representing essentially moral choices are to be invalidated under the Due Process Clause, the courts will be very busy indeed."[44]

Justice Blackmun attempted to repair his position somewhat by claiming that "what the Court really has refused to recognize is the fundamental interest all individuals have in controlling the nature of their intimate associations with others."[45] "Intimate associations," of course, means sex. It has never been thought, until the rampant individualism of the modern era, that all individuals are entitled, as a matter of constitutional right, to engage in any form of sexual activity that appealed to them. The dissent had no real reply to the majority's observation that if the constitutional argument is "limited to the voluntary sexual conduct between consenting adults, it would be difficult, except by fiat, to limit the claimed right to homosexual conduct while leaving exposed to prosecution adultery, incest, and other sexual crimes even though they are committed in the home." Indeed it would. When the community decides that certain sexual conduct is permissible and other conduct is not, courts have no way of disagreeing about the line drawn except by saying that judges'

morality is superior to that of the majority of the citizenry and is, for that reason, to be transformed into a constitutional standard.

The dissent's second line of argument, that a right to privacy attached because Hardwick's behavior occurred in his own home, "a place to which the Fourth Amendment attaches special significance,"[46] fares no better. The fourth amendment states that citizens are to be secure in their homes from unreasonable searches and seizures; it does not even remotely suggest that anything done in the home has additional constitutional protection. Moreover, that amendment specifically recognizes the government's right to enter a home under a proper warrant, or if the search is reasonable. That certainly suggests that the privacy of the home is less than absolute. Many actions taken entirely in one's home can nonetheless be punished by law. Of course the Constitution and much legislation protect the privacy of the home in many respects, but they also leave much that is done in the home unprotected. When Justice Blackmun extrapolates from protections that exist to create a new protection not to be found in existing law, he performs precisely the same logical leap that enabled Justice Douglas to invent a right of privacy in the first place. Thus, it is appropriate that Justice Blackmun should end this section of his opinion with the observation that the "right of an individual to conduct intimate relationships in the intimacy of his or her own home seems to me to be the heart of the Constitution's protection of privacy."

The dissent makes a point of the fact that Hardwick's behavior was not physically dangerous to those engaged in it or to others and refers to "victimless" activity. That, as we have reason to know, is not true. But, in any event, physical danger does not exhaust the categories of harms society may seek to prevent by legislation, and no activity that

[44]478 U.S. at 196.
[45]478. U.S. at 206 (Blackmun, J., dissenting): 195–96 (opinion of the Court).
[46]478 U.S. at 206, 208 (Blackmun, J., dissenting).

society thinks immoral is victimless. Knowledge that an activity is taking place is a harm to those who find it profoundly immoral. That statement will be taken as repressive by many, but only because they really do not disapprove of the conduct involved in *Bowers*. If the sexual conduct involved was bestiality, they might agree that it could be prohibited by law, although the only objection to it is moral.

There is vast confusion upon this point. In the seminar on constitutional theory I taught with Alex Bickel, I took the position at one time that it was no business of society what conduct that did not harm another person took place out of sight. Indeed, my position then, though not my reasons, was almost identical to that of the *Bowers* dissent. Bickel posed a hypothetical. Suppose, he said, that on an offshore island there lived a man who raised puppies entirely for the pleasure of torturing them to death. The rest of us are not required to witness the torture, nor can we hear the screams of the animals. We just know what is taking place and we are appalled. Can it be that we have no right, constitutionally or morally, to enact legislation against such conduct and to enforce it against the sadist? I cannot now remember what, if any, answer I gave; certainly, whatever it was it was not a very good one. Bickel was right. Moral outrage is a sufficient ground for prohibitory legislation.

Many people will argue that Bickel's hypothetical does not at all resemble a law against consensual homosexual sodomy since cruelty to animals is involved in the former. We have already dealt with that argument. There is no objection to the torturing of puppies for pleasure except that it outrages our morality. There is, indeed, no objection to forcible rape in the home or to the sexual abuse of a child there, except a moral objection. But, it will be said, those cases do not involve consent or do not involve a consent the person is mature enough to give intelligently. Those are not objections to the comparison. They are merely statements that the

speaker perceives a moral distinction in consent. But the perception of a moral distinction does not affect the point being made that morality, standing alone, is a sufficient rationale to support legislation. In fact, for most people, consent does not solve everything: they would favor laws punishing the torture of a consenting masochist or the provision of cocaine to a willing purchaser. I am sure to be attacked on the ground that I see no moral distinction between forcible rape and consenting sexual activity between adults. That is not true. I do see a clear moral difference. But the subject for discussion is not my morality. Nor is it the case that the moral difference between consent and non-consent means that only behavior involving the latter may be punished by law. If a majority of my fellow citizens decide that the cases, while not alike, are nevertheless similar enough so that both actions should be made criminal, while I may disagree with them morally, the fact that I am a judge does not mean that I am entitled to displace their moral judgment with my own. A robe is entirely irrelevant to the worth or power of one's moral views. A judge is also a voter, and it is in the polling booth that his moral views count.

The dissenting opinion also made the elementary error of confusing its power to override legislated morality when that morality conflicts with the Constitution and its power to override legislated morality when that morality conflicts with nothing in the Constitution but only with the judge's preferences. I have heard this argument when I sat on the bench: why, if you allow people to legislate their morality, it is said, they can decide that morality requires racial segregation. The argument is that if courts allow people to legislate on the basis of morality, the people will legislate immoral laws. There could hardly be a clearer statement that what those who want activist courts actually fear is rule by the people. The people cannot, of course, reflect any racist morality in law, because that notion of morality is placed out of bounds by the fourteenth amendment.

But the dissent went beyond denying that morality could be a basis for law and contended that if the morality was based in religion, that fact made the law worse. The Georgia Attorney General had argued that traditional Judeo-Christian values proscribed homosexual sodomy. The dissent correctly noted that conformity to religious doctrine is not enough to sustain secular legislation, but the opinion went further:

> [F]ar from buttressing his case, [the Attorney General's] invocation of Leviticus, Romans, St. Thomas Aquinas, and sodomy's heretical status during the Middle Ages undermines his suggestion that [the statute] represents a legitimate use of secular coercive power. A *State can no more punish private behavior because of religious intolerance than it can punish such behavior because of racial animus.*[47]

The fact that a moral view is embodied in religious doctrine does not convert either the view or the doctrine into religious intolerance. The Constitution prohibits punishing a person because of his religious beliefs; to do that would be religious intolerance. All religions of which I am aware condemn murder. One supposes that the dissenters would not find a homicide statute undermined by that fact. Indeed, if a religious parallel or basis for a law makes the law suspect, the Court should reexamine statutes punishing perjury since Jews and Christians believe that God has commanded, "Thou shalt not bear false witness."

There is a further paradox in the judicial objection to morality as the basis for legislation. Judges who vigorously deny elected representatives the right to base law on morality simultaneously claim for themselves the right to create constitutional law on the basis of morality, their morality. There being nothing in the Constitution prohibiting legislated morality, the only opposition to it rests upon a moral view. The *Bowers* dissent said as much when it stated as a "moral fact" that a person belongs to himself and not to others or to society. Moral relativism is, after all, one moral position. But the imposition of moral relativism upon legislatures by judges is not, strictly speaking, moral relativism in itself. It is more accurately described as the belief that the only valid and trustworthy morality is the judges'. That being the case, even should *Roe* be overruled, we have no idea what the "right of privacy"—or some other judge-made moral principle—may accomplish next.

## QUESTIONS

1. Of the hypothetical man who, we discover, raises puppies on an island in order to torture them, Bork says: "There is no objection to the torturing of puppies for pleasure except that it outrages our morality." Is this true? Indeed, is moral outrage even the best justification available for having a law against puppy torture? What if the puppy torture took place without anyone finding out?

2. Bork says that "no activity that society thinks immoral is victimless." What if "society" thinks that interracial dating or marriage is immoral? Would the knowledge that interracial dating is taking place constitute a genuine harm to those who think it immoral?

3. Bork says: "I am sure to be attacked on the ground that I see no moral distinction between forcible rape and consenting sexual activity between adults. That is not true. I do see a clear moral difference. But the subject for discussion is not my morality." Suppose

[47]*Id.* at 211–12 (emphasis added).

for a moment that this moral difference *is* one that can be demonstrated to every reasonable person's satisfaction, and that it is not merely a matter of *Bork's* morality, *my* morality, or *yours.* Would it then be appropriate for a judge to make distinctions on that same basis among legal cases? Would it then be so terribly important to leave the matter to be decided in the polling booth?

4.  Hardwick's arrest in his home for homosexual sodomy was unusual and, in any ordinary course of events, highly improbable. Can you think of some reason, or function, for such laws to remain on the books even if they are almost never enforced? Is this reason or function a legitimate one?

5.  Criticizing Justice Blackmun's opinion in *Bowers,* Bork says: "If the opinion meant what it said, four members of the Court viewed the state of nature, in which every individual is free to be for himself and no one else, as the moral condition contemplated by the Constitution." Is this a fair criticism?

# Other Privacy Interests

## Stanley Benn
# THE PRINCIPLE OF PRIVACY*

## 1. THE SEMANTICS OF PRIVACY

### A . The Categories of Privacy

I remarked [in an earlier discussion] that the rights of privacy were relative newcomers to the human rights scene and for that reason were still in need of precise definition and needed to make a place for themselves by elbowing out of the way some applications of other, well-established rights, such as the freedom to observe, to report, and to inquire. I hope to show in this chapter and in the one following how, by considering their *telé*, one can go quite a long way in delineating the bounds of particular human rights where they appear to conflict with others. But it will greatly assist the inquiry if we can first clarify some confusions in the use of *privacy*.

Though many of the scholars and official committees who have ventured into this perplexing area have thought that deciding on a definition of 'privacy' was indispensable as a preliminary to reviewing the principles which should govern attempts to protect it, others have despaired of constructing such a definition. Though paradigm cases of invasions of privacy are recognized readily enough, they are so disparate that there seems little chance of framing a comprehensive but determinate definition on which an enforceable legal right might be grounded. Paradigm instances are already covered indirectly by principles of equity, laws of defamation, and so on; beyond other piecemeal legislation, the courts might be relied upon, they say, to assimilate other related problems to these established paradigms as they arise.

Others, reluctant to leave to the courts a margin of discretion so wide as to be legislative rather than judicial, have offered a variety of definitions, some stressing the exclusion of publicity, others the protection of areas of personal activity from interference and intrusion, still others the psychological isolation of the subject in his privacy, and more besides. More remarkable than this, however, is the failure of such writers to agree on the category to which privacy belongs. Some, Warren and Brandeis, appear to *define* it as a right.[1] This tends to load, if not entirely to beg, the question whether anyone ought to have the power to deny access to any information, places, or activity called "private"; alternatively, the very definition of privacy would have to include or take into account the reasons why some matters but not others should enjoy the protection of such a power. Definition and justification then become inextricably confused.

A.F. Westin, the author of a major work on privacy, is not helpful. He says in one sentence that privacy is "a claim" and in the next that it is a "voluntary . . . withdrawal of a person from the general society . . . either in a state of solitude . . . or in a condition of anonymity or reserve"; that is, privacy is a state or even an act of withdrawal.[2] Lusky calls it "a condition enjoyed by one who can control the communication of information about himself,"[3] and W. L. Morison follows him in part, though the "condition" that he favors is that "of an individual when he is free from interference with his intimate personal affairs by others."[4]

---

*From *A Theory of Freedom* (1988), Chap. 14. Reprinted by permission of Cambridge University Press.

[1] S.D. Warren and L.D. Brandeis, "The Right to Privacy," *Harvard Law Review*, (1890): 1934.

[2] A.F. Westin, *Privacy and Freedom* (New York, 1967), 7.

[3] L. Lusky, "Invasion of Privacy: A Clarification of Concepts," *Columbia Law Review* 72 (1972): 709.

[4] New South Wales Parliamentary Papers, No. 170. (1972–73); W.L. Morison, *Report on the Law of Privacy* (Sydney, 1973), 3.

On the very same page that Lusky defines "privacy" as a controlling condition, however, he also declares that we "ought to avoid welding together the descriptive and legal aspects of the concept. . . . Our basic term should refer to the interest whose protection is under consideration."[5] Yet to refer to privacy as "an interest" itself presupposes that it is something people would be better (or believe they would be better) for having, and that already amounts to an evaluative presupposition in favor of privacy. Nor is there any reason for thinking that there is anything logically primitive about privacy considered as an interest; there could be opportunities for privacy which would benefit no one, in which no one could conceivably have an interest. Indeed, some lonely people might find the notion of an interest in privacy almost unintelligible. Nor is there anything pleonastic in attributing to someone an interest in privacy, as there would be if privacy were necessarily an interest. I shall suggest later that the interests people do have in privacy and its protection are very diverse, deriving in many cases from other interests, some personal, some commercial, some political. We need to understand then how the different privacy categories—claims, states, interests, and rights—are related. That will clear the way to the more substantive question, whether there are reasons for saying that persons, natural and corporate, have a right to it.

**A. PRIVACY AS A STATE.** I take the logically most primitive notion of privacy to be that of the simple state of being private, that is, of not sharing an experience, a place, or knowledge with anyone else. A more complex variant notion is of a state in which either there is no sharing or there is sharing only because the subjects want to share; so a group of persons are conversing privately if all are there by agreement and are not observed or overheard by anyone not of their party.

**B. PRIVACY AS A POWER.** Privacy as a state shared by agreement leads naturally enough to the conception of privacy as an ability or power to control access by others to a private object (to a private place, to information, or to an activity). This is the ability to maintain the state of being private or to relax it as, and to the degree that, and to whom, one chooses.

**C. PRIVACY AS AN INTEREST.** Someone has an interest in privacy in the sense that it would be *in his interest* to have it, if he would be better off for being in a private state or for having the power to control access to it. Whether he would really be better off for it might be more contentious than either whether he is actually in the state or whether he has the power, since whether he is better off on account of his being private is an evaluative matter, even when it is what he desires; we certainly cannot take it for granted that giving a person what he wants is necessarily in his interest. Adults as well as children can be made worse off by giving them what they want. (They may not be a sufficient reason, of course, for refusing them, if they have a right to it. Respect for persons requires that ordinarily one does not substitute one's own judgment for that of the person whose well-being is in question. He has a right to make his own mistakes.)

**D. PRIVACY OF A RIGHT.** A person enjoys privacy as of right if he possesses the normative capacity to decide whether to maintain or relax the state of being private. A normative order provides Alan with a normative capacity if Betty's status within the order will be changed or will remain unchanged, according to whether Alan decides to give or to relieve her from some reason for acting or for forbearing. So by inviting her into his house, where she would otherwise have a reason not to be, he relieves her of that reason for forbearance. Once invited in, she no

[5]Lusky, "Invasion of Privacy," 709.

longer has a reason not to be there, unless Alan, as the right-holder, subsequently asks her to leave; that would create for her a new reason for action. So if someone has a legal right to privacy, he also has a way of controlling others' access to and participation in his private states; for when the courts put their authority, and ultimately the police power, behind a person's claims, they supply other people with a motive for respecting them, whether they already had one or not.

Moral rights do not motivate in the same way. Nevertheless, anyone who, in exercising a moral right, sustains or creates a reason for action for other people may in fact motivate them, if they are rational. For to have a reason is to have an action commitment and not to act on it in the absence of any contrary commitment is to be irrational. Though our conversation in a secluded spot in a public park may not be protected by law, someone overhearing it may acknowledge that in asking him to move away we invoke a moral right to privacy, supplying him thereby with a reason for going. Of course, someone who does not acknowledge the right, at least under these conditions, recognizes no reason for going. Or he may acknowledge the reason but still refuse to go. But not to be motivated by a reason that one acknowledges to be a reason is one of the ways of being irrational.

E. PRIVATE OBJECTS. "Private rooms," "private affairs," and "private correspondence" belong to the category of privacy rights. There are legal, moral, or conventional norms that constitute reasons not to try to share or participate in such objects without the permission of the specified holder of the privacy right.

The use of *private* in such a context invokes a norm; it only indirectly describes a state of affairs. Rather, it signals the sort of behavior which is appropriate to the object. So it is not misapplied in a given instance just because some people pry or gatecrash. If, however, it became the practice to enter some particular room marked "Private" without waiting for permission, one would be inclined to say that the room was no longer private. But that would be not simply a description of a new situation in which the occupant's *ability* to control access had broken down, but rather a recognition that the signal was now misapplied, that the occupant's right to exclude having lapsed, it was now *appropriate* to enter uninvited.

## B. Privacy, Secrecy, and Confidentiality

Both individuals and corporate persons, including governments, may be able to control access to information and to places like military establishments which are described as "secret" rather than "private." Secrecy overlaps with privacy; for instance, a person confiding private information to a friend may ask him to "keep his secret." But for a matter to be private it is not sufficient that it be kept secret and consequently not publicized. It must not be public in the further sense that the person in question is not liable, in principle, to answer for it in terms of principles, procedures, or standards held to promote a wider "public interest."[6] No one, not even a politician, has to justify painting his dining room table yellow before a court of law, nor to answer for it to his electorate; it is not something for which he has a public responsibility. He acts, we say, not in his official role, but as a private citizen. A private citizen, unlike a public official, has no special duties for which he is publicly answerable. Again, the directors of a private business, while subject to the ground rules of private-business games, can do as they like within those rules, without having to answer to anyone outside the business, but only to their

---

[6]Cp. Lusky's reference to privacy as "the area of individual non-accountability, in which one can think and speak and act without having to *justify* to Big Brother or anyone else." Ibid., 707.

shareholders, who are participants in the corporate person to which the relevant privacy attaches.

This conception of privacy is closely bound to the liberal ideal. The totalitarian claims that everything a person is and does has significance for society at large. He sees the state as the self-conscious organization of civil society, existing for society's well-being. The public or political universe is all-inclusive: *all* roles are public, and every function, whether political, economic, scholarly, or artistic, can be interpreted as creating a public responsibility for and in its performance.

The liberal cannot give absolute specifications, however, for what is private and what is not, because privacy is context relative. I do not mean that standards differ between cultures. That is also true, but it is a different kind of relativity. *Within the one culture* the same matter may count as private or not, relative to the social nexus in which it is embedded. The rest of the politician's family may call him to account for painting the dining room table, just as the firm's shareholders may call its directors to account. He may do what he chooses with his bedroom, but others besides himself (his family may say) have a legitimate interest which he is not entitled to disregard in the furnishings in the dining room. What is private in this sense is not a matter of what I am *able* to control, but what I am at liberty to deal with simply according to my own taste or discretion, without regard to anyone's interests but my own, and that will depend on rules of law, morals, or conventions according to context. That is not to say that the private area is confined to what does not *affect* others' interests—to what J.S. Mill called "self-regarding" actions. I may be at liberty to disregard the way some act of mine affects the interests of others as when I cut my prices in a free market. What I charge may well be my own private affair, even though it affects other sellers. Conversely, if one believed that in deciding whether to Φ Alan ought to have regard to the public interest, then, even though no procedure existed in practice for calling him publicly to account for his decision whether to Φ, one would resist his claim that whether he should Φ was his private affair.

*Private* and *secret* are alike Janus-headed: they can be used either purely descriptively or in a way that invokes norms, standards, or principles. A secret code is one that is not understood, and is intended not to be understood except by a group of initiates. When the enemy secretly breaks it, it is no longer secret. But the official key to the code marked "Secret" is like letters marked "private": The mark invokes a rule that objects so marked should not be "shared in" except by those who are appropriately authorized according to the rule. Invoking the rule is itself, of course, a way of implementing de facto control if there are sanctions that operate against those who disregard it.

Nevertheless, though the extensions of *private* and *secret* overlap, they are not interchangeable concepts. Much that is properly called "secret" (military plans, details of security organizations and so on) is not also private just because these are matters of public interest, even though they are not, and ought not to be, publicized. Equally, information considered private, in the sense that it is of a kind that ought to be within the control of the person it concerns, may nevertheless be made public de facto by, for instance, a press report, without its normative status being affected.

A further complication arises from the association of privacy with confidentiality, which is to be found on both sides of the public/private divide. A confidential relationship is one in which it is understood that communications are *not to be shared* with non-authorized outsiders. The phrase points to an unambiguously normative relationship. One could not define confidentiality except with reference to the complex of obligations laid on a recipient of information within a particular norm-governed role relationship, such as that between solicitor or bank manager and client. Confidentiality operates as norm-based protection both of what is private and what is public but secret.

## C. Corporate Privacy

The sense in which a corporation's affairs can be private requires a somewhat more complex analysis, for the range of persons having free access to private places, information, and so forth will depend on formal rules defining membership of the corporation, and specifying which of its role bearers are to have free access to what. A shop foreman, though a member of the organization, might still be refused access to the books, on the ground that they were private, and this would be quite different from refusing him a peep at the letters the manager received from his wife. Any person can count both as insider and as outsider. As insider, he does not require permission or invitation respecting matters to which his role entitles him to free access; however, as an outsider—one whose role does not entitle him to access—he will require it.

Any part of the corporation's operations for which it was answerable as an official agency would not be among its private affairs. A public corporation like British Rail or the Australian Broadcasting Corporation does not have private affairs, though some of its business may be secret or confidential. And within the total frame of reference of the corporation, some matters, rooms, cupboards, even correspondence, may be called private because the role bearer entitled to control them has very wide discretion in what he does with them, even though the corporation might ultimately be held externally accountable for it.

Secret government defense contracts of a private firm would hardly count among its private affairs. For a start, it would have obligations, not rights, of secrecy, obligations owed to the public at large, or to the public's authorized representatives, the government. It is not a player with a free hand in the ordinary game of competitive business.

## 2. THE ETHICS OF PRIVACY

There is an important distinction to be made between privacy claims grounded on intimate and personal interests, and those necessary for the success of social practices valued on other grounds. Privacy claims inevitably compete with other interests, such as freedom of scientific inquiry, news reporting, business and administrative data collection, and so on. In trying to strike a proper balance between them, we need to take careful account of the different kinds of interest that privacy control serves to protect. Intimate and personal affairs are one kind to which our culture in particular attaches importance; but there is no reason to think that when we come to assign priorities, especially for legislation, privacy will always stand in the same relation to competing interests no matter what types of interest a privacy right would defend. The best way, then, to set about deciding how much importance to give to privacy will be to prepare a typology of privacy interests, of the different ways in which people might be better off for being able to control access. We may then be in a better position, instead of confusing practical issues with appeals to omnibus rights of privacy, to decide, with reasons, what weight to give to each, or rather , to decide their priorities (I shall say something later about attaching "weights" to arguments). All this, however, must wait until the next chapter. In this one, I shall provide a justification for a widespread concern for privacy that is not necessarily related to any interest at all.

### A. Respect for Persons, Noninterference, and the Principle of Privacy

"Why," asks little (or not-so-little) Johnny, "mustn't I peep at people through cracks in their curtains? Why do they get cross with me when they catch me at it? What harm does it do?" The last question is a trap: Many (but not all) people resent being spied on, stared at, gossiped about, or clinically exhibited as interesting specimens, even when no harm is either done or intended. Their reason for resentment may on occasion be overridden by legitimate, not to say important, interests in free inquiry; we may then be content to treat peeping as just a breach of good taste or good manners, better not regulated by law. Nevertheless, claims to privacy rights will be seen in sharper perspective if we grasp what underlies the resentment.

There is nothing intrinsically objectionable in observing the world, including its inhabitants, and in sharing one's discoveries with anyone who finds them interesting, and this is not on account of any special claims on behalf of, for instance, scientific inquiry or a public interest in the discovery of truth. For I take as a fundamental principle in morals a general liberty to do whatever one chooses unless someone else has good grounds to interfere to prevent it, grounds that would appeal to any rational person. The onus of justification, in brief, lies with the advocate of restraint, not on the person restrained. In Chapter 5 I derived this principle of noninterference from the principle of respect for persons. Is there any principle that can reverse this onus in favor of a prima facie claim that Alan should not observe a report on Betty unless Betty agrees to it, *whatever* Betty is about? Is there a principle of privacy extending prima facie immunity to inquiry to all human activities, or is it rather that there is general freedom to inquire, observe, and report on human affairs, as on other things, unless a special case can be made out for denying it with respect to certain activities that are specifically private?

The first possibility may appear at first sight extravagant, even as a prima facie claim. Anyone, it may be said, who wants to remain unobserved and unidentified should stay at home or go out only in disguise. Yet there is a difference between happening to be seen and having someone closely observe and perhaps record and report on what one is doing, even in a public place. Nor is the resentment that some people feel at being watched necessarily connected with fears of damaging disclosures in the Sunday papers or in graduate theses in social science. How reasonable is it, then, for a person to resent being treated as a redstart might be treated by a birdwatcher?[7]

I have postulated a kind if intrusion which does no obvious damage. It is not like publishing details of someone's sex life and ruining his career. That would affect his interests, and I am trying to isolate for the moment reasons for immunity to observation, reporting , and so on that do not depend on interests but on the principle of privacy deriving from respect for persons.

What is resented is not simply being watched, but being watched without leave. If observation were intrinsically or consequentially damaging, it might be objectionable even if done with consent. In the present instance, consent would remove all grounds for objection. Observation of this sort is not evidently a breach of the principle of noninterference, or if it is, the interference is of a very indirect kind. Threatening a man with penalties or taking away his stick are

---

[7]John Buxton relates how, in a prisoner-of-war camp in Germany, he organized a dawn-to-dusk vigil to observe the nesting and mating behavior of redstarts. A fellow prisoner, A.N.L. Munby, put the redstarts's point of view:

> When your mind is set on mating
> It is highly irritating
> To see an ornithologist below:
> Though it may be nature-study,
> To a bird it's merely bloody
> Awful manners. Can't he see that he's de trop!

From *Lyra Catenata* (printed privately, 1948), quoted in John Buxton, The Redstart (London, 1950).

both direct interferences that would prevent a man from beating his donkey. But if he stops simply because he is being watched, the interference is of a quite different kind. He could continue if he chose; being observed affects his action only by changing his own perception of it. The observer makes the action impossible only in the sense that the agent now sees it in a different light, through the eyes, as it were, of the observer. The intrusion is not therefore obviously objectionable as an interference with the agent's freedom. There are, it is true, kinds of action, such as ones that depend on surprise, that could be made objectively impossible merely by someone's watching and reporting on them. But my present purpose is to inquire whether a general case, not depending on special conditions of that sort, can be made out against such intrusions.

Of course, there is always a danger that information may be used to harm someone. Tyrannical governments or unscrupulous individuals may misuse information amassed about people to their disadvantage. The more one knows about an individual, the greater one's power to damage him. A utilitarian might say that fears of this kind are the only reasonable ground for objecting in general to being watched. Eliza Doolittle resents Professor Higgins's recording her speech in Covent Garden because she believes that a girl of her class subject to so close a scrutiny must be in danger of police persecution: "You dunno what it means to me. They'll take away my character and drive me on the streets for speaking to gentlemen." But the resentment of the bystanders is excited, not by some possible disadvantageous consequence of the phonetician's ability to spot their origins by their accents, but by something else which is intrinsic to Higgins's performance. "See here," one says, "what call have you to know about people what never offered to meddle with

you? . . . You take us for dirt under your feet, dont you? Catch you taking liberties with a gentleman!"[8] What this man resents is surely that Higgins is failing in respect for persons; he is treating people like objects or specimens—like "dirt"—and not like subjects with sensibilities and aspirations of their own, capable, as mere specimens are not, of reciprocal relations with the observer. This failure is, of course, precisely what Eliza, in her later incarnation—the ladylike creation of Pygmalion-Higgins's artistry—complains of too.

Finding oneself an object of scrutiny, as the focus of someone else's attention, brings one to a new consciousness of oneself, as something seen through another's eyes. Indeed, according to Sartre, it is a necessary condition for knowing oneself *as* anything at all that one should conceive oneself as an object of scrutiny.[9] It is only through the regard of another that the observed becomes aware of himself as an object, knowable, having a determinate character, in principle predictable. His consciousness as subject of pure freedom, as originator and chooser, is at once assailed by it: He is fixed as *something* , with limited probabilities rather than infinite, indeterminate possibilities. Sartre's account of human relations is of an obsessional need to master an unbearable alien freedom that undermines one's belief in one's own freedom; for Ego is aware of Alter not only as a fact, an object in his world, but also as the subject of a quite independent world of Alter's own, wherein Ego himself figures as a mere object. The relationship between them is therefore essentially hostile. Each, doubting his own freedom, is driven to assert the primacy of his own subjectivity and to demand its acknowledgment by the other. But the struggle is self-frustrating: Alter's reassurance would be worthless to Ego unless it were freely given, for if it were not it would be just another fact of Ego's own subjective world, yet

---

[8]G.B. Shaw, *Pygmalion,* Act 1 (Shaw's idiosyncratic punctuation).
[9]J.P. Sartre, *L'être et le néant* (Paris, 1953), Part 3, "Le pour-autrui."

the freedom to give the reassurance would at once refute it, for Alter's freedom entails the *objective* appearance of Ego, as something determined, in Alter's world.

What Sartre conceived as a phenomenologically necessary dilemma reappears in R.D. Laing's *The Divided Self*[10] as a characteristically schizoid perception of the world, the response of a personality denied free development, trying to preserve itself from domination by hiding away a "real self" where it cannot be absorbed or overwhelmed. The schizoid cannot believe fully in his own existence as a person. He may need to be observed in order to be convinced that he exists, if only in someone else's world. Yet, resenting the necessity to be what the other perceives him to be, he may try at the same time to hide, often in irrationality. His predicament, like Sartre's, may seem to him not to arise from the *manner* of his being observed, but to be implicit in the very relation of observer to observed.

Sartre, however, does not show why the awareness of others as subjects must evoke so hostile a response. Even if it were true that my consciousness of my own infinite freedom is shaken by my being made aware that in the eyes of another I have only limited possibilities, still if I am not free, it is not his regard that confines me; his regard only draws my attention to the truth I was able formerly to disregard. And if I am free after all, then his regard makes no difference. And if there is really a dilemma here, may I not infer from it that the other sees me too, not only as object, but as possessing the same subjectivity as he does himself, and therefore has the same problem as I? Could this not be as much a bond between us as a source of resentment, each according the other the same dignity as at least a subject from his own point of view?

It is because the schizoid cannot believe in himself as a person that he cannot form such a bond, or accept the respectful regard of another. So every glance is a threat or an insult. Still, even for the nonschizoid, there are ways of looking at a person that do diminish him, that provide cause for offense as real as any physical assault. Women complain of such looks as forms of sexual harassment. But that cannot be a sufficient reason, of course, either for the victim to go into hiding or for others to go around with their eyes shut. It does suggest, however, that if, as a doctor, one has occasion to make someone an object of scrutiny and study or, as a clinician, the topic for a lecture, the patient will have grounds for resentment if the doctor appears insensible to the fact that he is examining a person, to whom being observed makes a difference, and who will also have an independent view and evaluation of what is discovered or demonstrated by the examination.

It is a mistake to think that the only objection to such an examination is that an incautious examiner could cause damage to a sensitive patient's mental state, for that might sometimes be avoided by watching the patient secretly. To treat someone without respect is not to harm him—it is more like insulting him. Nor is it scrutiny as such that is offensive, but only the fact that the scrutiny is unlicensed.

The principle of privacy provides reasons, then, which restrict Alan's freedom of action in certain respects on account of the need for Betty's agreement. It is not the case, of course, that Betty's having a certain attitude toward *anything* that Alan proposes to do would alone be sufficient for her wishes to be a relevant consideration. She will certainly have attitudes and wishes about some actions of Alan's that do not affect her own enterprise at all; if she dislikes cruelty to animals and would be pleased if Alan stopped beating his donkey, that would not itself be a reason for Alan to stop. It is the conception of Betty as chooser, as engaged in a creative enterprise, that grounds reasons

---

[10] R.D. Laing, *The Divided Self* (Harmondsworth, 1965).

for others. So her preferences are considerations for Alan only if what Alan does makes a difference to the conditions under which she makes her choices, denying an option or changing the significance for her of acts which remain open, Betty may disapprove of Alan's watching Caroline or overhearing her conversation with Desmond, but Betty's own conditions for action remain unaffected. On the other hand, if Caroline knows that Alan is listening, his intrusion alters Caroline's consciousness of herself and of her experiences in relation to her world. Formerly self-forgetful, she may now be conscious of her opinions as candidates for Alan's approval or contempt. But even without self-consciousness of this kind, her immediate enterprise—her conversation with Desmond—may be changed for her merely by Alan's presence. I am not supposing a private conversation about Caroline's personal affairs. What is at issue is the change in the way Caroline apprehends her own performance, whatever the topic. Alan's uninvited intrusion is an impertinence because he treats it as of no consequence that he may have effected a change in Caroline's perception of herself. Of course, no damage may have been done; Caroline may actually enjoy performing before an enlarged audience. But her wishes in the matter are always a relevant consideration, as Betty's are not, and in the absence of some overriding reason, if Caroline is inclined to object, she has legitimate grounds. True, there are situations, as in university common rooms, where there is a kind of conventional license to join ongoing conversations. A railway compartment offers a similar license in Italy but not in England. In such situations, if one does not wish to be overheard, one must either whisper or stay silent. Equally, there are conditions in which it would be rude to engage in a private conversation; polite guests do not whisper to each other at a dinner party. Conventions create public occasions where rights of privacy are overridden.

The underpinning of a claim not to be watched or listened to without leave will be more general if it can be grounded in this way on the principle of respect for persons, rather than on a utilitarian duty to avoid inflicting damage. Respect for persons will sustain an objection to secret watching that may do no actual harm to anyone. Covert observation—spying—is objectionable because it deliberately deceives a person about his world: It thwarts, on the basis of reasons that are not his own, the agent's attempts to make rational choices. The objection, then, is not that observing Alan would hurt his feelings. To protect his feelings by keeping him in ignorance of what was happening, so far from eliminating the injury to Alan, would exacerbate it by the further insult of deliberately falsifying his self-perception: Thinking himself master of his private world, he would behave the more intriguingly for his manipulator's ends. One cannot respect someone as engaged on an enterprise worthy of consideration if one knowingly and deliberately alters his conditions of action while concealing the fact from him.

The offense is different in this case from Alan's open intrusion on Caroline's conversation. There, Alan's attentions were liable to frustrate Caroline's attempt to communicate privately with Desmond, or, even if she had no such intention, it would be liable to affect her conversational enterprise by changing her perception of it, altering it by virtue only of her knowing that Alan was listening. In the case of covert observation, Caroline is unaware of Alan, yet she is wronged because Alan is deliberately "making a fool of her," by falsifying her beliefs about what she is about. Suppose her to be in a situation in which she might be observed but in which she chooses to act privately; for anyone to watch without her knowledge is to show disrespect not only for the privacy she has chosen, but for her as a chooser, since it implies a disregard for the way she chooses to present herself to the world. A policeman may treat suspected wrongdoers like this only if there are good grounds for believing in a need to frustrate what they are about, overriding their rights as persons to privacy. Psychiatrists may be justified in treating the insane in the same way, but only to the extent that the insane are incapable of rational choice and in need of tutelage, and that the goal of secret surveillance is the subject's own welfare. Insanity does not legitimize turning people into exhibits for public entertainment, however, as was the practice in former times.

The close connection between the general principle of privacy and the principle of respect for persons may account for much of the resentment evoked by the idea of a central data bank collating all that is known about an individual from his past contacts with government agencies or his past use of credit-granting facilities. Much has been made, of course, of the dangers of computerized data banks. The information supplied to and by them may be false or, if true, may still put a person in a false light by drawing attention, for instance, to delinquencies of a distant past now lived down. A good deal of legislative ingenuity has been exercised, accordingly, to devise appropriate safeguards against the use of information power. Yet for some objectors it altogether misses the point: It is resented that anyone, even a most trustworthy official, should be able at will to satisfy any curiosity, to possess himself of a composite picture which, even though accurate in detail, still permits him to interpret it in a way the subject finds humiliating, and is powerless to influence, because it is done without his knowledge, let alone his consent. One may feel humiliated when one regards the image of oneself that another sees as despicable, and whether or not one believes it to be just, or may be unable not to identify with it. Since what others know about him can radically affect a person's view of himself, to treat the collation of personal information about him as a purely technical problem of safeguards is to disregard his claim to consideration as a person to whom respect is due.

I have argued as if the principle of respect clearly defined the boundaries of the person. But this is not altogether clear. If someone stares at my face, I cannot help seeing his gaze as focused on me. I am no less self-conscious if I catch him scrutinizing the clothes I am wearing. But should I resent scrutiny of the clothes I am not wearing—a suit, perhaps, that I have given to a charity? Or of my car, in the street outside my home or in the service station? What counts for this purpose as *me?* It is not enough that I do not *want* something to be observed; for the principle of respect to be relevant, it must be something about my own person that is in question, otherwise any mere wish of mine would be a prima facie reason for everyone to refrain from observing and reporting on anything at all. And though prima facie reasons are not conclusive, this one seems no reason at all. For I do not make something a part of my person by having feelings about it. The principle of privacy proposed is that a person who desires that he himself should not be an object of scrutiny has a reasonable prima facie claim to immunity. But the ground is not in his desiring but in the relation between himself as an object of scrutiny and as a conscious, experiencing subject and agent. And it clearly not enough for someone simply to say that something pertains to him as a person and therefore shares his immunity; he needs a reason for saying so.

The intimate connection between the concept of the self and one's body would seem to put that beyond question (though a schizoid perception of the world suggests that dissociation even of these closely linked concepts is not beyond the bounds of possibility). Beyond that point, cultural norms cannot be disregarded. In a possessive individualist culture in which a person's property is seen as a extension of his personality, an index to his social standing, a measure of his achievement, or an expression of his taste, to look critically at his clothes or his car is to look critically at him. In other cultures the standards might well be different. The notion each person has of his own extension, of the boundaries of his personality—what can count for him as an occasion for personal pride or shame—is unquestionably culture-variant. Consequently, the application even of a quite general principle of privacy will be affected by culturally variant norms, regarding, for instance, family or property.

## B. The Force of the General Principle of Privacy

The principle amounts only to a prima facie ground for limiting the freedom of others to observe and report, placing upon them a burden of justification but not overriding any special reasons for observing and reporting. Unsupported by special reasons, it may be quite insufficient to sustain a case for legal restraints; the protection of privacy in general may be less important, perhaps, than the danger to political freedom from legal restrictions on reporting. An obligation to show a reasonable public interest in every instance of reporting would result in an overtimorous press. The courts have been properly wary of recognizing rights that might discourage if not disable the press from publicizing what *ought* to be exposed.

General principles are reasons, but not conclusive reasons. They point to what needs to be justified, where the onus lies, and what can count as justification. Consider the difficult case of the privacy of celebrities. According to a learned American judge, the law "recognizes a legitimate public curiosity about the personality of celebrities, and about a great deal of otherwise private and personal information about them."[11] But is all curiosity equally legitimate or might there be something about the kind of celebrity that legitimizes curiosity about some aspects of the person but not about others? Is there no difference, say, between a serious historian's curiosity about what (and who) prompted President Johnson's decision not to run for office a second time and the curiosity to which the Sunday gossip columnists appeal? If the person is in the public eye for some performance he intends to be public or which is in its nature public, such as conducting an orchestra, this may make "human interest" stories about him more entertaining and exciting than stories about an unknown. But the fact that many people enjoy that kind of entertainment is not a reason for overriding the principle of privacy; for though there is a presumptive liberty to do whatever there is not a reason not to do, the claim to have whatever one enjoys is rationally restricted. To treat even an entertainer's life simply as material for entertainment is to pay no more regard to him as a person than to an animal in a menagerie. Of course, anyone who courts publicity, as many entertainers do, can hardly complain if he is understood to be offering a general license. But merely to be a celebrity—even a willing celebrity—does not disable someone from claiming the consideration due to a person. Admittedly, it opens up a range of special claims to information about him, to override his general claim to privacy. Candidates for appointment to the United States Supreme Court must expect to be quizzed about their business integrity. Or to take a rather different case, because an eminent conductor participates in a public activity with a public tradition, anyone choosing conducting as a profession must expect his musical experience—where he was trained, who has influenced his interpretations—to be matters of legitimate interest to others concerned as he is with music. But this is not a warrant for prying into other facts about him that have nothing at all to do with his music: his taste in wines, perhaps, or in women. The principle of privacy will properly give way in one area, but would stand in any other to which the special overriding grounds were irrelevant. For the principle is not limited in its application; it is a prima facie reason for immunity from publication in respect of *anything* a person does.

[11]See W.L. Prosser, "Privacy," *California Law Review,* vol. 48 (1960) 416–17.

# QUESTIONS

1. Benn says, of spying on another: "Thinking himself master of his private world, he would behave the more intriguingly for his manipulator's ends." What is the manipulation Benn is talking about here? Does such spying necessarily involve manipulation?

2. Benn says: "Since what others know about him can radically affect a person's view of himself, to treat the collation of personal information about him as a purely technical problem of safeguards is to disregard his claim to consideration as a person to whom respect is due." Suppose that A finds out about B's embarrassing past, but neither B nor anyone else finds out that A has found out. Does A's knowledge of B then affect B's view of himself? Defend Benn's view against the claim that it is only the *effect* on B of finding out, not the finding out itself, that is what is wrong in violating privacy.

3. If we were not the kind of creatures who tend to look at ourselves through the eyes of observers, would we still have reasons to want privacy?

4. Comment on Benn's view that "for a matter to be private . . . . It must not be public in the further sense that the person in question is not liable, in principle, to answer for it in terms of principles, procedures, or standards held to promote a wider 'public interest.'"

5. Explain the differences, as Benn would put it, between the ways in which moral and legal rights "motivate."

6. To what extent does Benn's analysis of privacy make it a subcategory of autonomy?

7. Explain how the boundaries of one's right of privacy can depend on culturally variant customs and conventions.

# PART THREE

# Legal Reasoning and Its Conceptual Tools

Reasoning about the law is an important part of what lawyers and judges do. In constitutional democracies, it is also a process in which ordinary citizens participate. This is so because legal reasoning is involved in two closely related tasks: *predicting* the behavior of others, especially of officials, and *justifying* decisions and actions, of both officials and ordinary citizens. Whether or not I can have any influence on what an official will do, I may still be deeply interested in predicting that official's decisions: What that person does may determine the fine I have to pay, if any; whether I will be sent to jail; or whether doing what I had planned to do will get me into trouble or will yield special benefits for me. In predicting what will happen, it will help to be able to replicate in my thinking the reasoning about the law that these power-wielding people will engage in. If I know that they are serious about the law, then I must also be serious about what it requires and allows, if only to enable my predictions to be more reliable.

Fortunately, our involvement in the legal process can go way beyond prediction. Lawyers provide arguments in court supporting their client's claim of innocence, claim for damages, or defense against civil suit or criminal charges. In providing these arguments, lawyers appeal to the law and to the judge's commitment to uphold the law. Judges provide arguments in their opinions supporting their decision in a particular case, and in this they attempt to show the parties to the dispute, the legal community, and the public in general that their decision was justified by the law, that the decision was not an exercise of bare, arbitrary power.

This process of justifying a lawyer's claim or a court's decision involves an interaction among people. One justifies the claim or decision publicly, *to* others, in terms they publicly acknowledge and are committed to uphold. Whether it is the substantive general principles of law or the process of adjudication that is acknowledged by the parties, the claim or decision is justified in impersonal terms. If this interaction is to be successful, the participants must be reasonable and must be able to presume that they are in turn dealing with reasonable people—people who recognize the requirements of logic and the importance of consistency.

The proper study of legal reasoning includes the study of logic. The reason for this is that logic, especially formal logic, sharpens the concepts we use: concepts such as the deductive validity of an argument, what it is for two statements to be logically inconsistent, and whether an added premise will turn an invalid argument into a valid one. But logic, in the strict sense of that term as used by logicians and studied in college courses, constitutes only the bare bones of what philosophers of law refer to as "legal reasoning." We may all agree that judicial decisions set precedents, but logic alone will not tell us what precedent they establish. Nor will logic alone tell us when two parties who come before a court are similarly situated and deserve the same treatment. However, judges and lawyers often must reach conclusions on matters like these, and the philosophy of law has traditionally concerned itself with problems about the reasoning they use and ought to use in deciding what the law is. This is legal reasoning in a broader sense—reasoning that includes, but is not exhausted by, formal logic.

When we consider the problems of legal reasoning, it is important to bear in mind that a theory of legal reasoning may be meant primarily as a descriptive account or as a prescriptive (normative) account. Thus a theory of the behavior of judges on appeals courts might be descriptive only. If such an account laid great stress on the ways in which judges in certain kinds of cases always cite the rules laid down by other judges rather than the rules as enacted by the legislature, that would not imply that judges ought to reason in that way; only that they do. And a prescriptive theory of legal reasoning is not necessarily proposed as an accurate description of the way judges or lawyers reason, only of how they ought to reason.

Though this distinction between descriptive and prescriptive is important to keep in mind when reading and thinking about theories of legal reasoning, there seems to be an easy explanation for the fact that legal philosophers often blur the difference between descriptive and prescriptive in their writings, sometimes referring to "what judges do" as if it were automatically what judges *ought* to do. The explanation is that law and legal reasoning are complex and subtle phenomena, the patterns and forms of which have been developed over many hundreds of years by many people confronted with the necessity of dealing with real practical problems. Those who philosophize on these topics should take very seriously the way existing case-law embodies the actual reasonings of judges and lawyers. Only then is one in a position to make recommendations about how they ought to reason.

Finally, our interest here focuses on reasoning as it figures in the justification of legal conclusions, not as it concerns their discovery. Methods of discovering the law are many and often private, but the justification of legal conclusions is a public process in which everyone has a stake. One judge may find that the most reliable way of finding the right legal precedents to follow and cite is to use the research of a certain young law clerk whose grasp of legal materials is especially quick and accurate. Another may rely on the method of looking first at the legal opinions of another particularly influential judge. Still another may simply follow first intuitions about a case, at least after a good night's sleep and a cup or two of coffee. These methods are all methods of discovery, and they may even support reasons such as, "This is probably right, because it's my first clear intuition on how this case should be decided," or "This is probably right because it's my clerk's view of the matter, and she is very sharp and has been very reliable in the past." But these reasons would not count in the public arena as good reasons in support of legal conclusions. In fact, whether these methods are even reliable in the first place depends on whether they lead to conclusions that are independently justifiable according to publicly acknowledged standards of legal reasoning. If citing your law clerk's sound intuitions is to count as a reason supporting a legal conclusion, it must first be demonstrated that those intuitions are sound, and that requires an independent investigation of what the law is. So one might as well just go directly to the primary question: What is the law on this, and how do I publicly show that this the law?

## USES OF LEGAL REASONING

So far we have only a broad, general picture of the subject matter of legal reasoning: It concerns the kinds of reasons that are appropriate in legal argument, that is, argument designed to reach legally justified conclusions and to establish publicly that they are legally justified. Before considering some of the main problems about legal reasoning, let us consider some of its typical uses. We shall begin with simple and instructive logical models of legal reasoning, although we shall ultimately have to recognize the many ways in which legal reasoning is far more complex than these models suggest.

LEGISLATION AND PRECEDENT. When courts decide cases, they are not supposed to decide arbitrarily, but according to some rule, principle, or standard. Without prejudging any questions about what kind of a standard this is, let us here simply call it a rule. What are the sources of these rules? There are mainly two: legislation and precedent. Legislated rules have several distinguishing features. They are explicitly formulated by a person or collective body claiming to have the authority to create legal duties and rights by their actions, and in so enacting the rule, it is their intention to alter in some way the structure of legal duties and rights. As such, the particular formulation of a legislated rule carries a special authority that other formulations do not. If you or I say, using our own paraphrase, "What this statute means is such-and-such . . . ," *our* statement of what it means does not carry the authority of the actual, literal formulation found in the statute book. It is one of the distinguishing marks of legislation that its formulation is not intended to capture any legal truths that were somehow already there, but to create legal distinctions. So its actual formulation in the statute book has a special status.

Rules of precedent, on the other hand, do not really have any of these characteristics. The core idea is that of *stare decisis,* or the notion of abiding by decided cases. Starting from there, the problem is to determine what was decided and how far that earlier decision applies to cases coming after it. What is needed is a rule. While rules of precedent are often enough formulated, they are not formulated by persons claiming the authority to alter legal rights and duties *by* any "enactment" of the rule. Legal experts attempt to give accurate formulations of these rules in their textbooks; judges formulate these rules when they survey the state of the law in their opinions; and law students and teachers do the same when discussing the law. But none of these formulations creates law, and none of the people doing the formulating claims to be making law or to have the authority to make law by dint of stating such a formulation. Unlike legislated rules, then, rules of precedent have no specially authoritative formulation. This is as one would expect given the rules of precedent are formulated in the spirit of accurately stating law that is already there, rather than of making new law.

The legislated rules that figure in legal argument, then, have a fairly clear identifiable source: the enactments of legislatures. But, while rules of precedent have a clear enough source (the holdings in already decided cases), the problem is to determine what rule of precedent is generated by those earlier decisions. In practice, of course, judges and lawyers manage somehow to work through this problem, sometimes brilliantly, but more often by muddling through. Describing what is and what ought to be going on from a logical and philosophical point of view, however, can be quite a challenge. To understand this challenge, it helps to understand the concepts of deduction and induction, two concepts that have come up again and again in traditional accounts of legal reasoning.

**DEDUCTION AND INDUCTION.** In the logician's strict sense, an argument is deductively valid if it is impossible for the premises all to be true while the conclusion is false. Deductive validity is therefore a relation between premises and conclusion. By itself, it assures us neither of the truth of the premises nor of the truth of the conclusion, but only that *if* the premises are all true, the conclusion must also be true. The following is a deductively valid argument.

$P_1$: Anyone who litters the park is subject to a fine of $100.
$P_2$: Mary litters the park.
_____
C: Therefore, Mary is subject to a fine of $100.

We do not need to know whether premise $P_1$, or premise $P_2$, or the conclusion is true in order to know that the argument is valid. Given this notion of a deductively valid argument, the process of logical deduction is then the step-by-step process of reasoning which, by assuming truth for the premises and seeing to it that truth is preserved at each step, aims at producing a deductively valid argument.

Many arguments have premises that support the argument's conclusion, but do not necessitate it, as do the premises of a deductively valid argument. Logicians usually call such arguments inductive arguments, and their strength, or the amount of support the premises give to the conclusion, is a matter of degree. This broad concept of an inductive argument contrasts with the all-or-nothing concept of deductive validity. Sometimes, however, when it is said that an argument is an inductive argument, especially in legal and scientific contexts, what is meant is that the argument moves from premises about particulars to a general conclusion. The following is an example of an inductive argument in this narrower sense.

P: Apples A, B, and C, taken at random from this sack, are red.
_____
C: All of the apples in this sack are red.

Though clearly not deductively valid, this argument is inductive in both the broad and narrow senses: The premise supports the conclusion, and the argument moves from particular to general.

Induction in this narrower sense has a natural and obvious place in legal reasoning. Inferring a general legal rule from a particular case or set of cases constitutes a kind of inductive argument. One observes that, of the two cases involving such-and-such fact situation, the court's decision was in favor of the plaintiff; therefore, whenever in the future the fact situation is such-and-such, the law calls for a decision in favor of the plaintiff. A rule like this one, lawyers sometimes say, *fits* the decided cases. What they mean is that this rule, combined with a statement of the fact situations in previously decided cases, allows us to deduce the decisions in those cases.

A rule's fit with earlier cases is a weighty factor. And it is nearly a necessary condition for concluding that the rule is the precedent set by those cases. Thus if the decision in previous cases were all in favor of the defendant, any rule that would have required decision in favor of the plaintiff most of the time would not be a correct statement of precedent. But we cannot say that fit is a strictly necessary condition for the correctness of a rule of precedent. Some earlier decisions may have little precedential value; others may have to be rejected as outright mistaken. A laboratory analogy may be useful here. When plotting a curve representing the general relation between two variables, one might recognize that some pieces of data are to be rejected as wholly unreliable. It is likewise so when legal rules are being extracted from the data of earlier cases. (A good illustration of a conflict between the need to make a decision fit with earlier cases and the idea that some of those decisions carry little weight because they were mistaken in the first place can be found in the majority and dissenting opinions in *Payne v. Tennessee,* reprinted in Part 6.)

Even if a fit with earlier decisions is a near necessary condition for singling out a rule as the precedent established by those cases, it is far from being a sufficient condition, since there are many other rules that fit earlier decisions. And yet these various rules of equally good fit would call for opposite decisions in cases still to be decided. It is clear that those who reason about what the law is must reach far beyond mere fit with past decisions if they are to find a reasonable basis for singling out some particular rule as *the* established rule. Looking for such a reasonable basis in the opinions that judges usually provide with the court's decision, some have been attracted to what seems to be an easy solution. If one can find a suggested formulation of a rule in the opinion accompanying the decision, then that is to be taken as the law. Coming from a court and written by a judge, it would seem to have special authority. But this solution has the major disadvantage of supposing that courts, in effect, are mini-legislatures. If judges can make law by singling out a particular rule, then they are doing more than deciding an individual case; they are in effect making law for many future cases. All the familiar objections against allowing courts to act as legislatures can be raised against any strong version of this proposal: Judges are not elected, sometimes serving for life; they do not have the time or political position to make law wisely; it is part of the genius of case-law that general rules emerge incrementally from the piecemeal contribution made by many cases responding to many concrete fact situations, rather than in some one court's formulation of a rule, and so on.

**ANALOGY.** The use of analogical argument is common both in legal and in moral contexts. It is sufficiently different from deductive and inductive arguments to be considered separately from them. Analogical argument draws on similarities. Suppose that there is a rule against keeping livestock in one's own home. Does the rule then apply to pigs kept as pets? To answer this, it is natural to seek analogies. Is keeping a pet pig more like keeping livestock, or more like keeping a housecat? Among the similarities are the fact that (we may suppose) neither the pig nor the cat is being kept in order eventually to be marketed or eaten, and each of the owners of these animals has the kind of affection for the animal that would be unlikely were it nothing more than livestock. Dissimilarities include the fact that pigs are generally regarded as livestock while cats are not. Unlike the inductive argument which proceeds from particulars to general rules, some analogical arguments do not involve inferences to rules. In this case, the argument might have the following form:

$P_1$: A pet cat is not livestock and is therefore not prohibited.

$P_2$: This pet pig has more similarity to a pet cat than to livestock.

C: This pet pig is not prohibited.

This argument gives no hint about any rule for dealing with future cases. It yields only the judgment that this pet pig is not prohibited, providing no rule for deciding whether a pet snake, cow, horse, or anything else for that matter, even a different pet pig, is prohibited. These matters are left open for later decision. Of course, analogical arguments can be general, as this one would be if the conclusion were about pet pigs in general, and not just about this one. We would then have a conclusion that extends beyond this particular pet pig to future pet pigs. If this pet pig does not fall under the prohibition, neither do they, unless there is some relevant difference that distinguishes their case from this one.

This last conclusion raises what is undoubtedly the main problem about analogy and similarity and their use in analogical arguments. The conclusion follows from one of the most fundamental, yet abstract, principles of justice: the formal principle that *like cases are to be treated alike.*[1] This principle is formal because by itself it tells us nothing about what counts as making things similar and what is simply irrelevant. Any *two* things, whether they are sunsets, people, or fact situations, are different in some ways; otherwise they would not be different sunsets, people, or fact situations. And it takes little ingenuity to find *some* similarities in two things, no matter how different they may otherwise be. How, then, do we get a handle on the problem of whether a pet pig is more similar to a pet cat than it is to livestock? And what, if anything, could make the next domestic pig be considered sufficiently different that it would count as livestock rather than a pet?

In some cases, the search for analogies is guided mainly by the need to find some basis or other upon which consensus can be established, such that a decision which seems right to everyone can be reached and can command wide agreement. One of the primary functions of law, after all, is to provide a stable resolution of disputes without leaving people with the sense that an arbitrary decision is being imposed on them. The philosopher and historian David Hume (1711–1776) once said:

[1] Chaim Perelman, *The Idea of Justice and the Problem of Argument,* trans. John Petrie (New York: The Humanities Press, 1963), Chap. 1; Aristotle, *Nichomachean Ethics,* bk. V.

Sometimes the interests of society may require a rule of justice in a particular case; but may not determine any particular rule, among several, which are all equally beneficial. In that case, the slightest *analogies* are laid hold of, in order to prevent that indifference and ambiguity, which would be the source of perpetual dissension.[2]

If eliminating ambiguity and consequent dissension is the main goal, Hume thought, then we need search only for analogies that, as a matter of psychological fact, simply strike most people as right. We follow their natural associations of ideas.

Hume's suggestion seems to be correct for some cases, but we must remember that people's automatic responses can sometimes be destructive, biased, and without rational foundation—mere prejudices. And would Hume's suggestion help in settling whether a pet pig is to be prohibited as livestock or allowed as a pet? It seems not. He is speaking of the possibility that several rules are equally beneficial and one must somehow be singled out. In this case, we would also need to examine the *purpose* and *rationale* of the rule that forbids the keeping of livestock at home. If we discover that the rule was enacted to implement the policy of keeping barnyard filth out of residential areas, then it would be relevant to demonstrate that a domestic pig can be as clean as a housecat. If the policy behind the rule is to protect religious or other sensibilities from being offended in a country where pigs, though not housecats, are regarded as disgusting, that would put the matter in a different light.

## RECURRING ISSUES ABOUT LEGAL REASONING

Certain issues about legal reasoning have been recurrent and important partly because the way judges and lawyers reason about the law has a great practical impact on people's lives. Questions about what the law is and the kind of reasoning that is appropriate to it ultimately bear on how power is distributed in society, on whether law's function is to constrain the exercise of power, and if so, how. Even such arguments as whether judicial reasoning is best described as deductive or inductive are not mere issues about correct description, for behind them is often a political philosophy about how judicial reasoning ought to proceed. And behind a political philosophy about how judicial reasoning ought to proceed is some conception of how it can proceed. What ought to be is limited by what can be. The following are some of the main recurring issues about the actual practice of legal reasoning.

LEGAL CERTAINTY.  Since legal reasoning leads to conclusions that deeply affect people's behavior and lives, certainty and predictability are an important standard by which methods of legal reasoning are judged. Without some real measure of legal certainty, law and the rule of law degenerate into a pretense, serving not to establish public limits on governmental power that everyone can understand and point to in defense of their liberties, but as a cover giving the look of respectability to arbitrary exercises of power. If one plaintiff is granted a benefit today and another who appears to be in a similar situation is denied the same benefit tomorrow, it is understandable that the second plaintiff is going to feel unfairly

[2]David Hume, *An Enquiry Concerning the Principles of Morals,* ed. P.H. Nidditch (Oxford: Clarendon Press, 1975), sec. III, part II, 157 (first published in 1748).

treated unless a plausible difference between the two cases can be demonstrated. So to some, methods of reasoning that undercut legal certainty are unacceptable because they are inconsistent with the primary functions of law, predictability and fairness.

Recall from the discussion above that both the method of induction and the method of analogy seem to bring considerable indeterminacy with them. If one is generally worried about the effects of indeterminacy on legal certainty, the development and interpretation of precedent are likely to be special sources of concern, for both rely heavily on induction and analogy. There seem to be no clear, fixed criteria that we can use in checking a rule of precedent to see if it is the correct rule deriving from a line of cases; nor are there clear criteria for demonstrating the correctness of an analogical argument.

Some philosophers, while admitting that there are no such clear criteria, claim that judges must rely on "intuition," "feel," or "hunch" and that judges will recognize the rightness of a right answer to a hard case when confronted with its full set of facts. In this view, the reasons why the answer is right may not be capable of articulation, but the fact *that* it is right can be grasped. No doubt judges must rely to some extent on intuition, just as anyone in most any department of life must sometimes rely on intuition. But extensive reliance on intuition is not likely to provide for legal certainty in a pluralistic society in which moral convictions are diverse and potentially conflicting. Such a society makes especially great demands on the public justification of exercises of power.

**THE ROLE OF MORAL REASONING.** In the history of legal philosophy, concerns about legal certainty have often occasioned debates about the proper relationship between moral reasoning and legal reasoning. One of the main subthemes of the longstanding debate between legal positivists and proponents of natural law is whether the requirements of natural law are knowable by reason, publicly demonstrable, and sufficiently clear to provide concrete guidance. People with different moral convictions have widely differing views about such things as justice in the distribution of wealth, the proper domain of individual liberty, whether abortion is wrong, and what constitutes due process of law. At a minimum, legal positivists have doubted the possibility of publicly demonstrating the validity of moral judgments on topics like these. Thus, as we saw in Part 1 of this book, one of the guiding ideas behind legal positivism is to separate questions abut law from questions about morality, in this way securing the separation of legal reasoning from moral reasoning. In this view, moral reasoning is too subjective, mystifying, and irresolvable to rely on in legal contexts. Were moral reasoning necessarily embedded in legal argument, it would only infect the law with the endless controversies characteristic of morality. This would be especially intolerable in the law, since the main function of law is to settle disputes, put an end to argument, and get on with deploying the state's power in an orderly way.

From this it is clear that the degree to which one will be impressed with this line of argument will depend on the degree to which one thinks of moral reasoning as hopelessly subjective or irrational and as tending to incite controversy rather than to quell it. If one believes that the moral opinion that slavery is wrong is ultimately nothing more than a personal preference having a status like one's preference for strawberry ice cream over vanilla, then one will probably have doubts about relying on moral judgments in situations where objective validation is especially important. In moral philosophy, various forms of subjectivism have gone in and out of fashion, alternating with more objectivist moods. Since our attention here must focus primarily on problems in the philosophy of law, we cannot get sidetracked too far into moral philosophy. But certain points about moral reasoning should be kept in mind. One is that we should not allow the superficial disagreements and heated rhetoric of moralizing to deceive us into thinking that there is no underlying foundation which would support agreement, at least in a cooler hour. Neither in science and mathematics nor in ethics does the existence of heated controversy show that there is no right answer. Second, the belief that ethical questions are subjective frequently rests on a shallow understanding of the subtleties and complexities of ethical reasoning, and here both experience and study are needed to remedy the deficiency. Those who believe that moral judgment and argument are primarily matters of trading one opaque, unreasoned opinion for another are almost inevitably headed for skepticism and despair about morality.

Finally, moral argument and justification may have a different kind of claim to be embedded in legal argument, one that is independent of the goal of legal certainty. It is important in a democracy in which the governed are conceived to be free persons that the actions of officials, ranging from judicial decisions to enactments of the legislature, be based on a foundation of moral defensibility. It is not enough to say, "This is our decision; it needs no justification other than our power." The giving of orders backed by nothing more than threats and cutting off all requests for moral justification might promote legal certainty, but is not the giving of law to a *free* people. As one writer puts it, "The public morality of law creates a certain kind of moral community, one in which political officials answer to the public not only for following the rules but also for their conscientious adherence to shared political principles."[3]

LEGISLATIVE INTENT AND LEGISLATIVE INTERPRETATION. Those who see reliance on analogical and moral reasoning as threatening to legal certainty have often recommended reliance on legislation instead. The basic model of drawing legal inferences from existing legislation is deductive. A legislated rule functions as the major premise in a syllogistic argument in which the minor premise states the relevant facts of a case and a legal conclusion is drawn as a deductive inference. If, as in the U.S. Constitution's statement of qualifications for being president (Art. II, Sec. 1), a legislated rule states that no "Person be eligible to that Office who shall not have attained to the Age of thirty five Years" (major premise), and Smith has not attained thirty-five years of age (minor premise), then it follows deductively that Smith is not now eligible to be president (conclusion). Restricting courts to the role of deductively drawing inferences from legislated rules is thought to be the best way to provide for legal certainty, as well as democratic accountability. The existence of a legislated rule, which is to say a rule whose written, specially authoritative formulation is to be found in the statute books, is supposed to provide for certainty: It means what it says, and what it says is there for all to see. The fact that judges, who are not chosen by popular vote and often serve for life, are restricted to deducing conclusions from rules given by the legislature is supposed to provide for democratic accountability: The people or their elected representative enact the law, and the law is applied as written.

[3]Stephen Macedo, *Liberal Virtues: Citizenship, Virtue, and Community in Liberal Constitutionalism* (Oxford: Clarendon Press, 1990), p. 86.

This is the simple legislative-deductive model, drawn in stark outline in order to show its basic appeal. One immediate problem is interpreting the meaning of legislation itself. We know the First Amendment to the Constitution says that "Congress shall make no law respecting an establishment of religion, or prohibiting the free exercise thereof," but we still need to know what counts as a "religion." There are clear cases, of course, but there are beliefs that may be hard or controversial to classify, like vegetarianism. How are we supposed to determine what, for purposes of the First Amendment, counts as a religion? In recent years, some legal scholars and government lawyers, including the former Attorney General  Edwin Meese III, have tried to advance a "jurisprudence of original meaning." Proponents claim that judges are to interpret the Constitution according to its original meaning, which is "the meaning of the constitutional language at issue to the society that adopted it." This meaning, they point out, is not some draftsman's or legislator's subjective meaning, but the objective meaning of the language itself, that is (quoting Justice O.W. Holmes), "what those words would mean in the mouth of a normal speaker of English, using them in the circumstances in which they were used. . . ."[4] What about words and phrases in legislation (taking the Constitution again as an example) whose meaning is vague or ambiguous? We begin with dictionaries and other contemporaneous sources of usage, like the debates that took place over enactment of the legislation. Where these sources fail to give a determinate answer, we try to find that meaning "which, without departing from the literal import of the words, best harmonizes with the nature and objects, the scope and design of the instrument."[5]

The focus on an original meaning that is supposed to be tightly tied to an authoritative, legislated formulation of law is an attempt to remove legal reasoning as much as possible from the vagaries of moral reasoning and, ultimately, of moral philosophy, placing it at the service of the majority acting through the legislative process. Critics of original meaning jurisprudence claim that the idea of a statute's, and especially of the U.S. Constitution's, original meaning as something that can be divorced from moral reasoning and moral philosophy, cannot survive close scrutiny. Critics say that, when the proponent of original meaning jurisprudence admits that interpretation requires harmonizing "with the nature and objects, the scope and design of the instrument," moral philosophy is virtually inescapable, particularly in view of the fact that the constitution was deeply inspired by the ideas of moral and political philosophers.


## SOME CONCEPTUAL TOOLS OF LEGAL REASONING: RIGHTS AND DUTIES

Though the language of rights is frequently the currency of heated political debate and revolutionary talk, the concept of a right plays an important role in legal reasoning, even in its most routine forms. The concept of rights may be best known as a rhetorical tool, but it is also a fundamental conceptual tool of lawyers and judges, and the kind of structure the concept of a right imposes on legal arguments therefore belongs to the study of legal reasoning, not just to legal rhetoric. In their everyday reasonings, lawyers concern themselves with whether one of the

[4]From *Report to the Attorney General: Original Meaning Jurisprudence: A Sourcebook* (Office of Legal Policy, U.S. Department of Justice, March 12, 1987), p. 9.
[5]See ibid., p. 11 (quoting Justice Joseph Story).

parties to a contract has a right to damages arising out of the other party's breach of the contract; whether a trustee has a right to sell certain properties belonging to the trust; and whether some public official has the right to issue the orders she issued. In political argument, one hears such claims as the claim that all humans have a right to a decent life, including food, shelter, and medical care; that everyone has the right to the use and enjoyment of their property; or that animals have the right not to be killed or experimented upon to serve human purposes. It will be clear just from these few examples that talk of rights in political argument has both reflected and occasioned controversy. Thus some would deny that everyone has a right to a decent life, if that means anything more than that no one may interfere with one's attempts to earn a decent living. Some would deny that there is an unrestricted right to enjoy one's own abundant property as long as there are people who do not have a decent life. And others, while perhaps admitting that humans have a duty not to mistreat animals, would insist that animals are not the kind of creature that is even capable of having a right in the first place. The controversies attendant on rights claims have thus driven thinkers to provide an analysis of rights and the different things that can be meant by claiming that someone has right.

An initial distinction is that between legally recognized rights and moral rights which are not necessarily recognized in the law. Claims about the existence of moral rights can in turn be claims made from a point of view of critical morality, or from a point of view of prevailing morality. Usually, when people claim that there are human rights like, say, a right to a decent life, the point of view is that of critical morality: All persons have a moral right to a decent life simply by virtue of being human. As a moral right, its existence does not depend on its being recognized by the institutions of society. Indeed, people usually make claims about moral rights precisely in order to criticize existing institutions and to bring about the institutional recognition of those rights. On other occasions, statements about moral rights are meant rather as descriptions of the prevailing moral views in a given society or circle. Since prevailing morality can be defective or actually evil, what prevailing morality recognizes as a moral right may have no ultimate validity.

No doubt this century's most influential contribution to the analysis of rights has been that of Wesley N. Hohfeld, who sought to distinguish among the different meanings of rights assertions.[6] Hohfeld believed that when ordinary people and even lawyers talk about rights, they often confuse different concepts. The phrase, "*P* has a right to_____," is, in ordinary usage, multiply ambiguous and can have any of the following meanings (or combination of them).

LIBERTY. Hohfeld somewhat misleadingly called this a privilege, and some prefer to call it a permission. To have a liberty to do *X* is equivalent to not having a duty not to do *X*. For example, you ordinarily have the right to play with balloons in your own living room. By this is meant only that you are not under a duty to play with balloons in your living room. Hohfeld would have been very strict insisting that we not call this a right, though he recognized that the term is commonly enough used to mean the same as "liberty."

POWER. If you own an automobile, it might be said that you have the right to transfer ownership of it to someone else. Having a right in this context means something different: You have the power to alter the structure of legal relations. By transferring the title to the car, the various

[6]Wesley N. Hohfeld, *Fundamental Legal Conceptions* (New Haven: Yale University Press, 1919).

rights, powers, liberties, and so forth, that you once enjoyed with respect to the automobile are shifted to another person. Powers exist all over the legal landscape. A legislature has the power, subject to certain conditions, to enact laws; the U.S. president has the power to command the armed forces and "militia of the several States"; and individuals have the power to make wills and enter into contracts. Those who enjoy such legal powers typically also need legal liberties to make use of them. But in Hohfeld's view that does not alter the fact that a power is fundamentally different from a liberty.

IMMUNITY. Something else that in loose parlance is occasionally called a right is really an immunity. To have a legal immunity is to have a kind of freedom from someone else's legal power. Thus the Fifth Amendment to the U.S. Constitution says that no person shall "be subject for the same offence to be twice put in jeopardy of life or limb." This deprives government of a legal power that governments sometimes have. The same amendment also says that no one "shall be compelled in any criminal case to be a witness against himself," and this is sometimes spoken of as one's Fifth Amendment "right," thought it is an immunity in the Hohfeldian analysis.

CLAIM-RIGHTS. If A and B have agreed that A will mow B's lawn for $20, and A now mows B's lawn, then A has a claim-right to $20 from B, and B has a duty to pay A the $20. The existence of one person's claim and another person's correlative duty is the sure mark of what Hohfeld himself calls a right. Thus one does not simply have a claim-right in isolation. Someone else must have a correlative duty. (It follows that if there were only one being in the universe, that being could not have a claim-right.) The importance of not confusing claim-rights with liberties can be illustrated with the example of entering into a competition. You may have the liberty to enter and win a game, but that does not involve the claim-right to win, for that would entail someone's duty to let you win, or even to provide you with a win. In fact, others too have the liberty to compete and, if they win, to prevent you from winning. Similarly, you have the liberty to acquire a certain piece of land, but that does not include a right to acquire it unless some special circumstances obtain, for example, the owner is under a contract to sell it to you for a given price and you have now exercised your option. Without having a right to acquire possession, someone else may do so first.

LOGICAL RELATIONS AMONG HOHFELDIAN CONCEPTS. Each of these concepts—liberty, power, immunity, and claim-right—really involves a relation among persons or other entities, like corporations. Each of these concepts, then, can only be fully understood by understanding both its *correlative,* and its *opposite.* To find the correlative of A's right, power, immunity, and so forth, we must reflect on what must be true about some *other* entity B. Thus if A has a claim-right to such-and-such, it is only because some other person or entity has a duty to provide A with such-and-such. So if all human beings have a right to adequate health care, there must be some person, persons, or entity (like government or society as a whole) that has the duty to provide adequate health care. If A has a liberty to do such-and-such, it is only because some other person does not have a right (Hohfeld calls this a *no-right*) that A not do such-and-such. If A has a power to change some aspect of legal relations in the world, it is only because some other person is under a *liability* to such change. If A has an immunity to certain kinds of changes of legal relations, that implies that some other person has a *disability* to bring about such changes.

The *opposite* of a concept is simply its logical negation. Thus the negation of A's having a liberty to do so-and-so is A's duty not to do so-and-so. A's not having a power to alter some legal relation amounts to A's disability to alter that legal relation. A's lack of an immunity from someone's power amounts to A's liability to that power, and the negation of A's right is A's no-right.

Sometimes several of these concepts will apply at once to the same person and with respect to the same object. As an example, take the case of an individual's right of free speech in a constitutional democracy. Clearly, part of what is involved is a liberty: One is under no legal duty not to express one's opinions. But a constitution also protects individuals against what governments might try to do in the future. If there is a constitutional provision restricting the powers of government to pass laws forbidding speech, that constitutional provision imposes a disability on government, conferring thereby an immunity on individuals. All of this may occur without imposing on the legislature any outright duty not to enact restrictive laws. It may be both sufficient and desirable to have only a constitutional provision disempowering the legislature.

Hohfeld's concepts refer to legal relations. Indeed, some philosophers have thought that rights assertions are especially at home in the law, but not in morality where we cannot be sure that they are institutionally underwritten. Nevertheless, people do make rights assertions that are moral rather than legal in character. When they do, their assertion is not necessarily accompanied by any belief that the right in question ought to be enforced by law, even in principle. We can easily think of analogues in morality and moral thinking to the legal concepts of claim-right, liberty, power, and immunity. Thus a promise can give rise to a moral right of the promisor against the promisee, even where legal enforcement of the promise would be out of the question. Moral liberties exist wherever one has no moral duty to refrain from an action, like the moral liberty to eat less lunch today than yesterday, or to eat no lunch at all. Moral powers include the power to make a morally binding promise, or the power of a parent of a small child to entrust the child's care to another adult. And the many limitations on our moral powers over others confer correlative moral immunities on them. We have moral immunities from becoming anyone's duty-bound slave and from having moral duties imposed upon us by the whims of total strangers.

## THE READINGS

**INTERPRETATION, ANALOGY, AND PRECEDENT.** One of the severest critics of English Common Law, which is to say, the English law that developed incrementally and mostly out of the decisions of cases, was Jeremy Bentham (1748–1832). Bentham's criticisms were varied and stinging.[7] A principal criticism of Bentham's was that traditional Common Law was so confused, incoherent, and uncertain that judges and lawyers were able to interpret it any way they wanted to with essentially no check on their power. Such a state of affairs is destructive of individual liberty, because no one can be sure of the limits of law or its

---

[7] Gerald J. Postema, *Bentham and the Common Law Tradition* (Oxford: Clarendon Press, 1986).

enforcement. The excerpt reprinted here illustrates how uncertain the derivation of rules from earlier decisions can be, both as a matter of logic and practice, and how that uncertainty can have the same practical effect for the governed as the enactment of an ex post facto law.

The excerpt from Ronald Dworkin's 1986 book *Law's Empire,* along with the accompanying *McLoughlin v. O'Brian* (1983) case discussed in that excerpt, illustrate how an idealized judge ("Hercules") might approach the difficult problem of extrapolating the law from a series of judicial decisions in order to apply that law to a new case of a kind that judges have not encountered before. One of Dworkin's main ideas is that judges are to interpret and apply the law so as to give it as much coherence and unity—which he calls "integrity"—as possible. In doing this, they attempt to make the law speak with a single, consistent voice, so that citizens are treated with equality and fairness. The process can be likened, he thinks, to the writing of a chain novel in which a number of earlier chapters have already been written by many different authors, and it now falls to the present author to write the latest chapter in a way that will best cohere with what has gone before, making the best novel that one can make. Those who are preoccupied with maximizing certainty and minimizing controversial judicial interpretation may have doubts about the extent to which these objectives can be achieved if judicial interpretation is modeled after literary interpretation, and judges are assigned the job of working toward overall coherence and integrity. But Dworkin's careful explanation, of how Hercules could sort through various interpretations of case-law, rejecting some as lacking fit with the decisions while rejecting others as stating no genuine principle at all, illustrates some of the many sources to which legal reasoning can appeal.

Robert Bork's view, at least of the judicial interpretation of constitutional law, is strikingly different from Dworkin's. The excerpt from Bork's 1990 book illustrates some of the main concerns of proponents of the jurisprudence of original meaning. Bork is worried that if judges do not rigidly fasten their interpretations of the Constitution to the actual formulations found there, they will entangle themselves, improperly, in the political process of making laws, a process that ought, in Bork's view, to be guided by the procedures of majority rule and of constitutional amendment. Like others who defend the jurisprudence of original meaning, Bork makes a distinction between subjective and objective intentions of those who ratified the Constitution. We are to search for the objective intention, which "must be taken to be what the public of that time would have understood the words to mean." What we might know about the private, subjective intentions of the ratifiers is simply irrelevant.

Most of Bork's arguments had been advanced in one form or other before his book appeared. Stephen Macedo's book *The New Right v. The Constitution* (1987) is addressed to Bork's arguments that favor interpreting the Constitution in accordance with original meaning. Macedo's claim is that the search for original meaning rests on an unjustifiably skeptical view of morality and an excessive willingness to acquiesce in what the majority wants, no matter whether the majority is motivated by reason or by prejudice and passion. Both the ratifiers of the Constitution and the document itself invite the use of moral philosophy in its interpretation, Macedo argues. Moreover, the jurisprudence of original meaning turns against itself, both in that the Constitution itself contains much that can reasonably be understood as an invitation to interpret its broad phrases by using moral principle and in that regarding majority rule as the only objective foundation of rights itself presupposes a moral philosophy, albeit a defective one, of "might makes right."

**RIGHTS.**  The next subsection, on the concept of rights and its conceptual near relations, begins with an excerpt from a classic work in moral and political theory, John Stuart Mill's *Utilitarianism* (1863). Mill's discussion is valuable for several reasons. One is that it provides us with a kind of conceptual map, allowing us to trace the interrelations among the concepts of justice, obligation, rights, and social sanctions. Another is that Mill does this partly by exploring the etymology of the concept of justice in order to come up with a unifying account of the various things that people regard as required by justice. Examples of these include allowing each to have what is a matter of legal entitlement; giving to each what is deserved; not breaking faith; being impartial, and so on. In giving his unifying account, Mill tries to show that our contemporary concept of justice is in fact the result of several historical layers of influence, among them Hebrew, Greek, and Roman. His overall purpose in exploring the concept of justice and rights is to demonstrate that the peculiar stringency and force of the idea of justice, of the strongly felt notion that doing an injustice is wrong in itself, derives from an impulse of self-defense combined with the feeling of sympathy, and that justice is consistent with the utilitarian program of promoting happiness in the world.

Duty, or obligation, Mill says, "is a thing which may be *exacted* from a person." When we call something wrong, we imply that the one who does it ought to be punished. But, even though the legal concept of punishment helps us to define duty, we must remember that punishment can take different forms, including outright legal punishment, the informal pressures of opinion and criticism, and the internal reproaches of one's own conscience. The particular combination of these sanctions that happens to be appropriate will presumably define the nature of the duty in question. The concept of duty and of wrong thus enables us to distinguish what is characteristic of morality from that which is a matter of general good-doing or expediency.

But this distinction does not reach all the way to a definition of the concept of justice, for justice is a subdepartment of morality. To delineate this section of morality, Mill relies on an old distinction of jurisprudence and moral theory: the distinction between duties of imperfect obligation, which do not have corresponding rights, and those of perfect obligation, which do. A good example of the former would be the duty of charity, as ordinarily understood. A duty of charity is a duty to help the needy, and you have obviously failed in this duty if you have never helped the needy. At the same time, though, no particular needy person can claim to have a right to your aid, for you have considerable discretion in choosing the beneficiaries of your help. A duty to pay a merchant for delivered goods, however, is a duty of perfect obligation, because that particular worker has a right to your payment. Justice, then, is that branch of morality which concerns duties to which corresponding rights attach. The right to equal treatment, the right to get what one deserves, the right to one's due under a contract, and the right to retain one's property all correspond to duties, the violation of which would be not merely a bad thing, but an injustice.

Gerald Postema's (1989) discussion, while acknowledging the contributions of Mill and Hohfeld, reflects more recent thinking on the subject. His discussion throws some new light on what rights are and on how talk of rights is to be placed on the conceptual map along with normative ideas of goals, duties, and liabilities. Unlike Hohfeld, who attempted to categorize rights assertions and then show what each assertion logically entails, Postema maintains that the particular package of protections, what he calls the *exercise-respect (E-R) structure,* depends on the moral and political theory that is taken to justify that right in the first place. This E-R structure can be likened to a combination of Hohfeldian duties, liberties, powers, immunities, and so forth, that goes with a right. So when someone asserts that P has a right to X, we must know a good deal about the interest of P that grounds this assertion if we are to argue intelligently about any particular E-R structure appropriate to that right. What is common to all rights assertions is their claim that the bearer of the right has an interest that ought in some way to be respected by others and protected by society. Beyond that, normative theory is necessary to spell out the nature of the appropriate protections. As Postema summarizes this more recent understanding of the concept of rights, "It has always been recognised that what rights *there are* . . . is a morally/politically substantive matter. It is now clear that *what it is to have or enjoy* any given right is also in large part a morally/politically substantive matter."

# Interpretation, Analogy, and Precedent

## Jeremy Bentham
# NO CUSTOMARY LAW COMPLETE*

**1.** If it be thus with the statute law, how is it, let any one imagine with the customary? A customary law is not expressed in words: now in what words should it present itself? It has no parts: how should it exhibit any? It is one single indivisible act, capable of all manner of constructions. Under the customary law there can scarcely be said to be a right or a wrong in any case. How should there? Right is the conformity to a rule, wrong the deviation from it: but here there is no rule established, no measure to discern by, no standard to appeal to: all is uncertainty, darkness, and confusion.

**2.** It is evident enough that the mute sign, the act of punishment, which is all there is properly speaking of a customary law, can express nothing of itself to any who have not some other means of informing themselves of the occasion on which it was given: that the act of hanging for example, is no definition of the act of stealing, and that a blow which is given to a dog (for here dogs and men are put upon the same footing) is no lesson to the dog who is in the next yard, or to the whelp that will have been begotten by one of them a year hence. If then it can serve as a rule to any distance or for any length of time, some account of the case must be taken and handed down by somebody: which somebody stands then in the place of a legislator. But of the boundless group of circumstances with which the act punished must necessarily have been attended, how many and which of them were considered as material? what were received as inculpative? what were not suffered to operate in the way of exculpation? to what circumstances was it owing that the punishment was so great? to what others that it was no greater? These and a multitude of other circumstances which it would be needless to repeat must all be taken into the account in the description of the case. But let the case be delineated ever so exactly, it is still but that individual case that is delineated: to make a rule that can serve for cases yet to come, a new process must be carried on: the historian must give place to the metaphysician; and a general rule must be created by abstraction out of this particular proceeding. And by whom then shall the abstraction be performed? by every man for himself, or by some one for all the rest? In the latter case that one man, be he whoever he will, if his rule comes to be adopted and adhered to, that one man becomes in effect the legislator. . . .

**9.** But the general rule extracted no matter how, from these particular *data*, and which if there were a law in the case, would be the law, is after all absurd and mischievous: perhaps it was so from the very first, that is the decisions on which it is grounded were so at the first moment of their being made. But at any rate it would be so if applied now to the matter at present in dispute. To decide then according to *this* rule would be mischievous in one way: but to depart from *any* rule which is to be deemed to have been established would be mischievous in another way. It is only in as far as subsequent decisions are rendered conformable to the rules that are fairly to be drawn from prior decisions that such prior decisions can answer, in any even the most imperfect degree, the purpose of a law. Whenever the chain of conformity, such as it is, is broken, the anomalous decision whatever it is, does all

---

*From *Of Laws in General*, ed. H.L.A. Hart, Chap. 15, sections 1–2 and 9–12. Reprinted by permission of The Athlone Press, London. Bentham's footnotes are indicated by letters, and footnotes to these notes are indicated by asterisks. Editorial footnotes (Hart's) are indicated by numerals. Margin annotations omitted.

the mischief that can be done by an *ex post facto* law. If the question be of a penal nature in the one way it absolves without reason, or the other way it punishes without warning: in a matter of purely civil competition, it subjects the unsuccessful party to a privation or to a burthen which as far as they go have the effect of a punishment without cause. This it does by its own single efficacy: add to which that in the way of example it gives a shock which from hand to hand is felt by the whole fabric of customary law. Nor is the mischief cured till a strong body of connected decisions either in confirmation of the first anomalous one or in opposition to it have repaired the broken thread of analogy and brought back the current of reputation to its old channel. I speak in metaphors: since in metaphors only on a subject like the present can one speak. This being the case, whenever any past decision, in itself apparently absurd, is brought in the character of a law to govern the proposed decision in the case of litigation, there are two maxims that point different ways and press for opposite determinations. As this dilemma is occurring at every turn, lawyers are of course continually called upon to embrace the one side of it or the other. Accordingly then as the inconveniences on the one side or those or the other have been accustomed to press upon their imaginations with the greatest force they insensibly contract a general propensity to lean on the one side or the other. They form themselves like the Proculians and the Sabinians of old,[1] though on a ground of much greater extent and importance into different parties: *Stare decisis* is the maxim of the one; *salus reipublicae* or something like it, the motto of the other: both perhaps partisans of utility, though of utility viewed through a different medium: the one of the general utility which results from the adherence to established precedents: the other, of the particular utility which results from the bringing back the current of decision at any rate into the channel of original utility from which the force of precedent they suppose had drawn it aside: the one enamoured of uniformity, the mother of security and peace: the other, of Natural Justice or Equity or Right Reason or by whatever other name the phantom is best known.

10. Given the documents from whence the law that is to govern in a given case is to be abstracted, it is required to find that law. A question arises concerning the title to an article of property. A deed copied from one drawn by a conveyancer of great name and since copied from by a thousand others, but now impeached for the first time; a decision badly reported upon the face of it but taken from a printed book of high authority; a decision well reported upon the face of it but taken from a printed book of low authority; a decision indifferently reported and taken from a book without a name; a corresponding string of unprinted cases; an ancient treatise, and the decisions which it quotes and which when examined make against it; these together with the dictates of utility in the abstract, are all candidates at the same time for the prerogative of legislation:— which of all these outstanding authorities ought to carry it?[e] When the circle has been squared, this problem will be solved.[f]

---

[1] The Proculians were a school of lawyers founded in the reign of Augustus by Antistius Labeo, but named after his pupil Sempronius Proculus. The Sabinians, who were founded by Ateius Capito, a jurist in the reigns of Augustus and Tiberius, were named after his pupil Masurius Sabinus, and formed a rival school.

[e] There are various other species of authorities, which it would be to no purpose to insist upon: for example
1. Maxims: which are unconnected scraps of general treatises.
2. Opinions of counsel: which are treatises on the particular cases laid before them.
3. Pleadings: (that is formularies of procedure settled by counsel) which carry with them their opinion concerning the validity of these pleadings.
    There are also various circumstances which may give different degrees of weight to authorities of the same species.
1. The reputation of the counsel who advised; or of the judge who decided.

**11.** From a set of *data* like these a law is to be extracted by every man who can fancy that he is able: by each man, perhaps a different law: and these then are the *monades* which meeting together constitute the rules which taken together constitute that inimitable and unimprovable production of enlightened reason, that fruit of concord, pledge of liberty in every country in which it is found, the common or customary law.

Caligula published his laws in small characters: but still he published them: he hung them up high, but still he hung them up. English judges neither hang up their laws, nor publish them. They go further; they will not suffer it to be done by others: and if there be any dependence to be placed in any rule of common law, whosoever takes upon him to do it, well or ill, he may be punished. The rule is indeed falling into desuetude: but it has lately been recognized; it has never been disclaimed; and it may be enforced at any time. Whosoever takes upon him to do any such service to his country does it, like the Grecian lawgiver, with a halter about his neck.[2]

It appears then, that the customary law is a fiction from beginning to end: and it is in the way of fiction if at all that we must speak of it.

The customary law, you say, punishes theft with hanging: be it so. But by what law is this done? who made it? when was it made? where is it to be found? what are the parts that it contains? by what words is it expressed? Theft, you say, is taking under certain circumstances: but taking by whom? taking of what? under what circumstances? taking by a person of such a sort, taking a thing of such a sort, taking under such and such circumstances. But how know you this?—because so it has been adjudged. What then? Not if it be a taking by any other person, nor if of any other thing, nor if under any other circumstances? O yes, in many other cases: if by whom then? and if of what? and if under what circumstances? if *by* a person of such another sort, if *of* a thing of such another sort, if *under* such and such circumstances? But how do you know this is the case? because I think it ought to be so, because I believe it would be so: because such and such persons believe it ought to be so or would be so. But how *came* you to think so? and how came *they* to think so? and what if I think different and as many people with me, *quorum ego judicium* (as saith the courtly Cicero, to his friend)[g] *longe antepono tuo*, happen to, tell me, I say, where is your law then?

---

2. The rank and fullness of the court; was it before the Master of the Rolls, or before the Chancellor: at a judge's chambers, at Nisi prius, *in Banco*, or at the House of Lords?

3. The solemnity of argumentation—how many times argued? by how many counsel on a side?

4. The solemnity of decision—did the Chief Justice deliver the opinion of the court: or did the judges give their opinion *seriatim*?

5. The number of stages in the cause—was it a decision acquiesced in, or a decision confirmed upon an appeal?

These are a part of the topics which may occasionally be thrown into the scale, all adding to the perplexity of the inquiry, and to the uncertainty of the result.

[f]Mathematicians, when a question presents itself they are not acquainted with, call it *x*: if there comes another, they call it *y*: and so they go on investigating the nature of it by means of its relation to other quantities which they are acquainted with. It remains in this state of obscurity for a certain time, but at last out it comes in the intelligible and familiar shape of one, two, three, four, and so forth. Thus it is in mathematics: but in jurisprudence under the customary law, the object is as much unknown at the end as at the first: it is *x, y* for ever more.

[2]Demosthenes in his speech against Theocrates (139–141) contrasts the incessant legislative changes at Athens with the permanence achieved at Locri in Italy, where anyone proposing a change in the laws of Zeleucus must do so with a halter round his neck, which was removed or tightened till he died according to the approval or disapproval with which the proposal was received.

[g]Tuscul. Disput. in principio.[3]

[3]Cicero, *Tusculan Disputations*, v.4.12 : 'A. Non mihi videtur ad beate vivendum satis posse virtutem. M. At hercule Bruto meo videtur, cuius ego iudicium, pace tua dixerim, longe antepone tuo.'

But for peace sake let your notion be the right one: no matter why nor wherefore. I am content to abide by it, and to acknowledge that all others ought and are bound to do so, too. Be pleased then to give it words for us to know it by.—And are these then the words? is this paper the standard we are to measure an act by in order to see whether it be an act of theft or no?—Then is this a law and you the legislator.

**12.** In short, if there be still a man who will stand up for the existence and certainty of a rule of customary law, give him everything he asks, he must still have recourse to fiction to produce any such rule: if it appears in any shape it must clothe itself in the similitude of some particular provision of the nature of statute law: it must purport to be, it must pretend to be a provision of statute law, although it be no such thing. To enable ourselves to conceive and express the influence which a rule of this sort may have over the whole system of law and at the same time to distinguish it from the real entity whose semblance it usurps, it may be called after the name of that which it would be if it were anything, with the particle *quasi* prefixed to it; according to the usage of the Roman Law.[h] Upon this plan a rule of customary law describing for example, what is to be looked upon as theft, may be styled a quasi-law against theft: which quasi-law will accordingly have its quasi-imperative, quasi-limitative, quasi-exceptive provisions, and so on.[i]

[h]Fragm. on Govt.[1]

[i]This is not the place to enter into a complete detail of the imperfections of the customary law: for such a description the proper place seems to be the title of *Digestion:* since in proportion to the imperfections of such part of the law as is in this form will be the benefits of the salutary operation which consists in reducing it to the form of statutory law. The imperfections which are here brought to view are no others than what transpired, as it were of themselves, in the course of the discussion which seemed necessary in order to give a view of the characteristic nature of this modification of the law. One other capital imperfection may just be hinted in a few words. I mean that which consists in the *unaccommodatingness* of the rules. Every decision that is given is spun out of some vague maxim, conceived in general terms without exceptions, and without any regard to times and circumstances: a maxim conceived in words which whenever put together, were put together, a thousand to one else, by persons who have no such case as the particular one in question present to their view. It admits of no temperaments, no compromises, no compositions: none of these qualifications which a legislator would see the necessity of applying. Even when it aims at utility, which perhaps is now and then, it either falls short of the mark or overshoots it. A sort of testimony in recognition of this truth is contained in the magnificent and well known adage, *fiat justitia ruat coelum.* Though heaven were wrecked, let justice be adhered to. Heaven may always be preserved when the law that governs is the work of the legislator. Hence the hardness of heart which is a sort of endemical disease of lawyers where that part of the law which is in the customary form is predominant in the system. Mischief being almost their incessant occupation, and the greatest merits they can attain being the firmness with which they persevere in the task of doing partial evil for the sake of that universal good which consists in a steady adherence to established rules, a judge thus circumstanced is obliged to divest himself of that anxious sensibility, which is one of the most useful as well as amiable qualities of the legislator. An empire shall run to ruin and the lawyer drive on in the same track as if nothing were the matter.

Familiarized with the prospect of all those miseries which are attendant on poverty, disappointment, and disgrace, accustomed even to heap those miseries on the heads of those by whom he knows them to be unmerited, he eases himself by habit of the concern which the prospect of them would produce in an unexperienced mind: the unconcerned spectator of the agonies, just as a man whose trade is in blood becomes insensible to the sufferings which accompany the stroke of death. It must be no common share of humanity that can induce him, nor any common share of wisdom that can enable him to keep this rigour within the bounds presented by utility, and the necessary regard to uniformity of decisions. By men of ordinary mould the dictates of utility in these circumstances may easily be lost sight of altogether: and a precedent the most absurd and mischievous conformed to with as much tranquility as an equally apposite precedent of a complexion the most reasonable and salutary.

[1]*A Fragment on Government*, Ch. 1, para. 12 n., §§10 and 11 (Bowring, i, 263. n.).

## QUESTIONS

1. Bentham says that "customary law is not expressed in words." Would Bentham's argument against customary law be undercut by pointing out that people who live in a society typically understand the customs of their society quite well, whether or not they have been expressed in words, and that customary *law* need be no different? Why or why not?

2. It is sometimes said that customary law, and custom generally, are in many ways superior to legislation, for customary law embodies the great collective wisdom of the decisions and adjustments that have been made by many people over a long time, while legislation does not. Give your reasons for agreeing or disagreeing with this view.

3. One of Bentham's main objections to customary law is that it cannot be known with certainty, and that "whenever the chain of conformity . . . is broken, the anomalous decision whatever it is, does all the mischief that can be done by an *ex post facto* law." For what parts of the law is this objection likely to be the most serious, and for what parts the least serious?

4. Bentham gives a long list of questions about the customary law, and what it does or does not punish. How and to what extent are these questions answered under law that is not customary, but legislated?

## *Ronald Dworkin*
## INTEGRITY IN LAW*

. . . A judge deciding *McLoughlin* or *Brown* adds to the tradition he interprets; future judges confront a new tradition that includes what he has done. Of course literary criticism contributes to the traditions of art in which authors work; the character and importance of that contribution are themselves issues in critical theory. But the contribution of judges is more direct, and the distinction between author and interpreter more a matter of different aspect of the same process. We can find an even more fruitful comparison between literature and law, therefore, by constructing an artificial genre of literature that we might call the chain novel.

In this enterprise a group of novelists writes a novel *seriatim*; each novelist in the chain interprets the chapters he has been given in order to write a new chapter, which is then added to what the next novelist receives, and so on. Each has the job of writing his chapter so as to make the novel being constructed the best it can be, and the complexity of this task models the complexity of deciding a hard case under law as integrity. The imaginary literary enterprise is fantastic but not unrecognizable. Some novels have actually been written in this way, though mainly for a debunking purpose, and certain parlor games for rainy weekends in English country houses have something of the same structure. Television soap operas span decades with the same characters and some minimal continuity of personality and plot, though they are written by different teams of authors even in different weeks. In our example, however, the novelists are expected to take their responsibilities of continuity more

*Reprinted by permission of the publishers from *Law's Empire* by Ronald Dworkin, Cambridge, Mass.: Harvard University Press, Copyright © 1986 by Ronald Dworkin. Pp. 229–66.

seriously; they aim jointly to create, so far as they can, a single unified novel that is the best it can be.[1]

Each novelist aims to make a single novel of the material he has been given, what he adds to it, and (so far as he can control this) what his successors will want or be able to add. He must try to make this the best novel it can be construed as the work of a single author rather than, as is the fact, the product of many different hands. That calls for an overall judgment on his part, or a series of overall judgments as he writes and rewrites. He must take up some view about the novel in progress, some working theory about its characters, plot, genre, theme, and point, in order to decide what counts as continuing it and not as beginning anew. If he is a good critic, his view of these matters will be complicated and multifaceted, because the value of a decent novel cannot be captured from a single perspective. He will aim to find layers and currents of meaning rather than a single, exhaustive theme. We can, however, in our now familiar way give some structure to any interpretation he adopts, by distinguishing two dimensions on which it must be tested. The first is what we have been calling the dimension of fit. He cannot adopt any interpretation, however complex, if he believes that no single author who set out to write a novel with the various readings of character, plot, theme, and point that interpretation describes could have written substantially the text he has been given. That does not mean his interpretation must fit every bit of the text. It is not disqualified simply because he claims that some lines or tropes are accidental, or even that some events of plot are mistakes because they work against the literary ambitions the interpretation states. But the interpretation he takes up must nevertheless flow throughout the text; it must have general explanatory power, and it is flawed if it leaves unexplained some major structural aspect of the text, a subplot treated as having great dramatic importance or a dominant and repeated metaphor. If no interpretation can be found that is not flawed in that way, then the chain novelist will not be able fully to meet his assignment; he will have to settle for an interpretation that captures most of the text, conceding that it is not wholly successful. Perhaps even that partial success is unavailable; perhaps every interpretation he considers is inconsistent with the bulk of the material supplied to him. In that case he must abandon the enterprise, for the consequence of taking the interpretive attitude toward the text in question is then a piece of internal skepticism: that nothing can count as continuing the novel rather than beginning anew.

He may find, not that no single interpretation fits the bulk of the text, but that more than one does. The second dimension of interpretation then requires him to judge which of these eligible readings makes the work in progress best, all things considered. At this point his more substantive aesthetic judgments, about the importance or insight or realism or beauty of different ideas the novel might be taken to express, come into play. But the formal and structural considerations that dominate on the first dimension figure on the second as well, for even when neither of two interpretations is disqualified out of hand as explaining too little, one may show the text in a better light because it fits more of the text or provides a more interesting integration of style and content. So the distinction between the two dimensions is less crucial or profound than it might seem. It is a useful analytical device that helps us

---

[1]Perhaps this is an impossible assignment; perhaps the project is doomed to produce not just an impossibly bad novel but no novel at all, because the best theory of art requires a single creator or, if more than one, that each must have some control over the whole. (But what about legends and jokes? What about the Old Testament, or in some theories, the *Iliad?*) I need not push that question further, because I am interested only in the fact that the assignment makes sense, that each of the novelists in the chain can have some grasp of what he is asked to do, whatever misgivings he might have about the value or character of what will then be produced.

give structure to any interpreter's working theory or style. He will form a sense of when an interpretation fits so poorly that it is unnecessary to consider its substantive appeal, because he knows that this cannot outweigh its embarrassments of fit in deciding whether it makes the novel better, everything taken into account, than its rivals. This sense will define the first dimension for him. But he need not reduce his intuitive sense to any precise formula; he would rarely need to decide whether some interpretation barely survives or barely fails, because a bare survivor, no matter how ambitious or interesting it claimed the text to be, would almost certainly fail in the overall comparison with other interpretations whose fit was evident.

We can now appreciate the range of different kinds of judgments that are blended in this overall comparison. Judgments about textual coherence and integrity, reflecting different formal literary values, are interwoven with more substantive aesthetic judgments that themselves assume different literary aims. Yet these various kinds of judgments, of each general kind, remain distinct enough to check one another in an overall assessment, and it is that possibility of contest, particularly between textual and substantive judgments, that distinguishes a chain novelist's assignment from more independent creative writing. Nor can we draw any flat distinction between the stage at which a chain novelist interprets the text he has been given and the stage at which he adds his own chapter, guided by the interpretation he has settled on. When he begins to write he might discover in what he has written a different, perhaps radically different, interpretation. Or he might find it impossible to write in the tone or theme he first took up, and that will lead him to reconsider other interpretations he first rejected. In either case he returns to the text to reconsider the lines it makes eligible.

## Scrooge

We can expand this abstract description of the chain novelist's judgment through an example. Suppose you are a novelist well down the chain. Suppose Dickens never wrote *A Christmas Carol,* and the text you are furnished, though written by several people, happens to be the first part of that short novel. You consider these two interpretations of the central character: Scrooge is inherently and irredeemably evil, an embodiment of the untarnished wickedness of human nature freed from the disguises of convention he rejects; or Scrooge is inherently good but progressively corrupted by the false values and perverse demands of high capitalist society. Obviously it will make an enormous difference to the way you continue the story which of these interpretations you adopt. If you have been given almost all of *A Christmas Carol* with only the very end to be written—Scrooge has already had his dreams, repented, and sent his turkey—it is too late for you to make him irredeemably wicked, assuming you think, as most interpreters would, that the text will not bear that interpretation without too much strain. I do not mean that no interpreter could possibly think Scrooge inherently evil after his supposed redemption. Someone might take that putative redemption to be a final act of hypocrisy, though only at the cost of taking much else in the text not at face value. This would be a poor interpretation, not because no one could think it a good one, but because it is in fact, on all the criteria so far described, a poor one.[2]

But now suppose you have been given only the first few sections of *A Christmas Carol.* You find that neither of the two interpretations you are considering is decisively ruled out by anything in the text so far; perhaps one would better explain some minor incidents of plot that must be left unconnected on the other, but each interpretation can be seen generally to flow through the abbreviated text as a whole. A competent

[2]See the debate cited in Chapter 2. n. 16.

novelist who set out to write a novel along either of the lines suggested could well have written what you find on the pages. In that case you have a further decision to make. Your assignment is to make of the text the best it can be, and you will therefore choose the interpretation you believe makes the work more significant or otherwise better. That decision will probably (though not inevitably) depend on whether you think that real people somewhat like Scrooge are born bad or are corrupted by capitalism. But it will depend on much else as well, because your aesthetic convictions are not so simple as to make only this aspect of a novel relevant to its overall success. Suppose you think that one interpretation integrates not only plot but image and setting as well; the social interpretation accounts, for example, for the sharp contrast between the individualistic fittings and partitions of Scrooge's countinghouse and the communitarian formlessness of Bob Cratchit's household. Now your aesthetic judgment—about which reading makes the continuing novel better as a novel—is itself more complex because it must identify and trade off different dimensions of value in a novel. Suppose you believe that the original sin reading is much the more accurate depiction of human nature, but that the sociorealist reading provides a deeper and more interesting formal structure for the novel. You must then ask yourself which interpretation makes the work of art better on the whole. You may never have reflected on that sort of question before—perhaps the tradition of criticism in which you have been trained takes it for granted that one or the other of these dimensions is the more important—but that is no reason why you may not do so now. Once you make up your mind you will believe that the correct interpretation of Scrooge's character is the interpretation that makes the novel better on the whole, so judged.

This contrived example is complex enough to provoke the following apparently important question. Is your judgment about the best way to interpret and continue the sections you have been given of *A Christmas Carol* a free or a constrained judgment? Are you free to give effect to your own assumptions and attitudes about what novels should be like? Or are you bound to ignore these because you are enslaved by a text you cannot alter? The answer is plain enough: neither of these two crude descriptions—of total creative freedom or mechanical textual constraint—captures your situation, because each must in some way be qualified by the other. You will sense creative freedom when you compare your task with some relatively more mechanical one, like direct translation of a text into a foreign language. But you will sense constraint when you compare it with some relatively less guided one, like beginning a new novel of your own.

It is important not only to notice this contrast between elements of artistic freedom and textual constraint but also not to misunderstand its character. It is *not* a contrast between those aspects of interpretation that are dependent on and those that are independent of the interpreter's aesthetic convictions. And it is not a contrast between those aspects that may be and those that cannot be controversial. For the constraints that you sense as limits to your freedom to read *A Christmas Carol* so as to make Scrooge irredeemably evil are as much matters of judgment and conviction, about which different chain novelists might disagree, as the convictions and attitudes you call on in deciding whether the novel would have been better if he had been irredeemably evil. If the latter convictions are "subjective" (I use the language of external skepticism, reluctantly, because some readers will find it helpful here) then so are the former. Both major types of convictions any interpreter has—about which readings fit the text better or worse and about which of two readings makes the novel substantively better—are internal to his overall scheme of beliefs and attitudes; neither type is independent of that scheme in some way that the other is not.

That observation invites the following objection. "If an interpreter must in the end rely on what seems right to him, as much in deciding whether some interpretation fits as in deciding whether it makes the novel more attractive, then he is actually subject to no genuine constraint at all, because no one's judgment can be constrained except by external, hard facts that everyone must agree about." The objection is misconceived because it rests on a piece of dogmatism. It is a familiar part of our cognitive experience that some of our beliefs and convictions operate as checks in deciding how far we can or should accept or give effect to others, and the check is effective even when the constraining beliefs and attitudes are controversial. If one scientist accepts stricter standards for research procedure than another, he will believe less of what he would like to believe. If one politician has scruples that another politician in good faith rejects, the first will be constrained when the second is not. There is no harm, once again, in using the language of subjectivity the external skeptic favors. We might say that in these examples the constraint is "internal" or "subjective." It is nevertheless phenomenologically genuine, and that is what is important here. We are trying to see what interpretation is like from the point of view of the interpreter, and from that point of view the constraint he feels is as genuine as if it were uncontroversial, as if everyone else felt it as powerfully as he does. Suppose someone then insists that from an "objective" point of view there is no real constraint at all, that the constraint is *merely* subjective. If we treat this further charge as the external skeptic's regular complaint, then it is pointless and misleading in the way we noticed in Chapter 2. It gives a chain novelist no reason to doubt or abandon the conclusions he reaches, about which interpretations fit the text well enough to count, for example, or so poorly that they must be rejected if other interpretations, otherwise less attractive, are available.

The skeptical objection can be made more interesting, however, if we weaken it in the following way. It now insists that a felt constraint may sometimes be illusory not for the external skeptic's dogmatic reason, that a genuine constraint must be uncontroversial and independent of other beliefs and attitudes, but because it may not be sufficiently disjoint, within the system of the interpreter's more substantive artistic convictions, ever actually to check or impede these, even from his point of view.[3] That is a lively possibility, and we must be on guard against it when we criticize our own or other people's interpretive arguments. I made certain assumptions about the structure of your aesthetic opinions when I imagined your likely overall judgment about *A Christmas Carol*. I assumed that the different types of discrete judgments you combine in your overall opinion are sufficiently independent of one another, within the system of your ideas, to allow some to constrain others. You reject reading Scrooge's supposed redemption as hypocritical for "formal" reasons about coherence and integration of plot and diction and figure. A decent novel (you think) would not make a hypocritical redemption the upshot of so dramatic and shattering an event as Scrooge's horrifying night. These formal convictions are independent of your more substantive opinions about the competing value of different literary aims: even if you think a novel of original sin would be more exciting, that does not transform your formal conviction into one more amenable to the original sin interpretation. But suppose I am wrong in these assumptions about your mental life. Suppose we discover in the process of argument that your formal convictions are actually soldered to and driven by more substantive ones. Whenever you prefer a reading of some text on substantive grounds, your formal convictions automatically adjust to endorse it as a decent reading of that text.

[3]See *A Matter of Principle* chap. 7.

You might, of course, only be pretending that this is so, in which case you are acting in bad faith. But the adjustment may be unconscious, in which case you think you are constrained but, in the sense that matters, you actually are not. Whether any interpreter's convictions actually check one another, as they must if he is genuinely interpreting at all, depends on the complexity and structure of his pertinent opinions as a whole.

Our chain-novel example has so far been distorted by the unrealistic assumption that the text you were furnished miraculously had the unity of something written by a single author. Even if each of the previous novelists in the chain took his responsibilities very seriously indeed, the text you were given would show the marks of its history, and you would have to tailor your style of interpretation to that circumstance. You might not find any interpretation that flows through the text, that fits everything the material you have been given treats as important. You must lower your sights (as conscientious writers who join the team of an interminable soap opera might do) by trying to construct an interpretation that fits the bulk of what you take to be artistically more fundamental in the text. More than one interpretation may survive this more relaxed test. To choose among these, you must turn to your background aesthetic convictions, including those you will regard as formal. Possibly no interpretation will survive even the relaxed test. That is the skeptical possibility I mentioned earlier: you will then end by abandoning the project, rejecting your assignment as impossible. But you cannot know in advance that you will reach that skeptical result. You must try first. The chain-novel fantasy will be useful in the later argument in various ways, but that is the most important lesson it teaches. The wise-sounding judgment that no one interpretation could be best must be earned and defended like any other interpretive claim.

## A Misleading Objection

A chain novelist, then, has many difficult decisions to make, and different chain novelists can be expected to make these differently. But his decisions do not include, nor are they properly summarized as, the decision whether and how far he should depart from the novel-in-progress he has been furnished. For he has nothing he *can* depart from or cleave to until he has constructed a novel-in-process from the text, and the various decisions we have canvassed are all decisions he must make just to do this. Suppose you have decided that a socorealist interpretation of the opening sections of *A Christmas Carol* makes that text, on balance, the best novel-so-far it can be, and so you continue the novel as an exploration of the uniformly degrading master-servant relation under capitalism rather than as a study of original sin. Now suppose someone accuses you of rewriting the "real" novel to produce a different one that you like better. If he means that the "real" novel can be discovered in some way other than by a process of interpretation of the sort you conducted, then he has misunderstood not only the chain-novel enterprise but the nature of literature and criticism. Of course, he may mean only that he disagrees with the particular interpretive and aesthetic convictions on which you relied. In that case your disagreement is not that he thinks you should respect the text, while you think you are free to ignore it. Your disagreement is more interesting: you disagree about what respecting this text means.

## LAW: THE QUESTION OF EMOTIONAL DAMAGES

Law as integrity asks a judge deciding a common-law case like *McLoughlin* to think of himself as an author in the chain of common law. He knows that other judges have decided cases that, although not exactly like his case, deal with related problems; he must think of their decisions as part of a long story he must interpret and then continue, according to his own judgment of how to make the developing story as good as it can be. (Of course the best story for him means best from the standpoint of political morality, not aesthetics.) We can make a rough distinction once again between two main dimensions of this interpretive judgment. The judge's decision—his postinterpretive conclusions—must be drawn from an interpretation that both fits and justifies what has gone before, so far as that is possible. But in law as in literature the interplay between fit and justification is complex. Just as interpretation within a chain novel is for each interpreter a delicate balance among different types of literary and artistic attitudes so in law it is a delicate balance among political convictions of different sorts; in law as in literature these must be sufficiently related yet disjoint to allow an overall judgment that trades off an interpretation's success on one type of standard against its failure on another. I must try to exhibit that complex structure of legal interpretation, and I shall use for that purpose an imaginary judge of superhuman intellectual power and patience who accepts law as integrity.

Call him Hercules.[4] In this and the next several chapters we follow his career by noticing the types of judgments he must make and tensions he must resolve in deciding a variety of cases. But I offer this caution in advance. We must not suppose that his answers to the various questions he encounters *define* law as integrity as a general conception of law. They are the answers I now think best. But law as integrity consists in an approach, in questions rather than answers, and other lawyers and judges who accept it would give different answers from his to the questions it asks. You might think other answers would be better. (So might I, after further thought.) You might, for example, reject

Hercules' views about how far people's legal rights depend on the reasons past judges offered for their decisions enforcing these rights, or you might not share his respect for what I shall call "local priority" in common-law decisions. If you reject these discrete views because you think them poor constructive interpretations of legal practice, however, you have not rejected law as integrity but rather have joined its enterprise.

## Six Interpretations

Hercules must decide *McLoughlin*. Both sides in that case cited precedents; each argued that a decision in its favor would count as going on as before, as continuing the story begun by the judges who decided those precedent cases. Hercules must form his own view about that issue. Just as a chain novelist must find, if he can, some coherent view of character and theme such that a hypothetical single author with that view could have written at least the bulk of the novel so far, Hercules must find, if he can, some coherent theory about legal rights to compensation for emotional injury such that a single political official with that theory could have reached most of the results the precedents report.

He is a careful judge, a judge of method. He begins by setting out various candidates for the best interpretation of the precedent cases even before he reads them. Suppose he makes the following short list: (1) No one has a moral right to compensation except for physical injury. (2) People have a moral right to compensation for emotional injury suffered at the scene of an accident against anyone whose carelessness caused the accident but have no right to compensation for emotional injury suffered later. (3) People should recover compensation for emotional injury when a practice of requiring compensation in their circumstances would diminish the overall costs of accidents or otherwise

---

[4]Hercules played an important part in *Taking Rights Seriously* chap. 4.

make the community richer in the long run. (4) People have a moral right to compensation for any injury, emotional or physical, that is the direct consequence of careless conduct, no matter how unlikely or unforeseeable it is that that conduct would result in the injury. (5) People have a moral right to compensation for emotional or physical injury that is the consequence of careless conduct, but only if that injury was reasonably foreseeable by the person who acted carelessly. (6) People have a moral right to compensation for reasonably foreseeable injury but not in circumstances when recognizing such a right would impose massive and destructive financial burdens on people who have been careless out of proportion to their moral fault.

These are all relatively concrete statements about rights and, allowing for a complexity in (3) we explore just below, they contradict one another. No more than one can figure in a single interpretation of the emotional injury cases. (I postpone the more complex case in which Hercules constructs an interpretation from competitive rather than contradictory principles, that is, from principles that can live together in an overall moral or political theory though they sometimes pull in different directions.)[5] Even so, this is only a partial list of the contradictory interpretations someone might wish to consider; Hercules chooses it as his initial short list because he knows that the principles captured in these interpretations have actually been discussed in the legal literature. It will obviously make a great difference which of these principles he believes provides the best interpretation of the precedents and so the nerve of his postinterpretive judgment. If he settles on (1) or (2), he must decide for Mr. O'Brian; if on (4), for Mrs. McLoughlin. Each of the others requires further thought, but the line of reasoning each suggests is different. (3) invites an economic calculation. Would it reduce the cost of accidents to ex-

tend liability to emotional injury away from the scene? Or is there some reason to think that the most efficient line is drawn just between emotional injuries at and those away from the scene? (5) requires a judgment about foreseeability of injury, which seems to be very different, and (6) a judgment both about foreseeability and the cumulative risk of financial responsibility if certain injuries away from the scene are included.

Hercules begins testing each interpretation on his short list by asking whether a single political official could have given the verdicts of the precedent cases if that official were consciously and coherently enforcing the principles that form the interpretation. He will therefore dismiss interpretation (1) at once. No one who believed that people never have rights to compensation for emotional injury could have reached the results of those past decisions cited in *McLoughlin* that allowed compensation. Hercules will also dismiss interpretation (2), though for a different reason. Unlike (1), (2) fits the past decisions; someone who accepted (2) as a standard would have reached these decisions, because they are all allowed recovery for emotional injury at the scene and none allowed recovery for injury away from it. But (2) fails as an interpretation of the required kind because it does not state a principle of justice at all. It draws a line that it leaves arbitrary and unconnected to any more general moral or political consideration.

What about (3)? It might fit the past decisions, but only in the following way. Hercules might discover through economic analysis that someone who accepted the economic theory expressed by (3) and who wished to reduce the community's accident costs would have made just those decisions. But it is far from obvious that (3) states any principle of justice or fairness. Remember the distinction between principles and policies we discussed toward the end of the last chapter. (3) supposes that it is desirable to reduce accident

---

[5]See the discussion of critical legal studies later in this chapter.

costs overall. Why? Two explanations are possible. The first insists that people have a right to compensation whenever a rule awarding compensation would produce more wealth for the community overall than a rule denying it. This has the form, at least, of a principle because it describes a general right everyone is supposed to have. I shall not ask Hercules to consider (3) understood in that way now, because he will study it very carefully.[a] The second, quite different, explanation suggests that it is sometimes or even always in the community's general interest to promote overall wealth in this way, but it does not suppose that anyone has any right that social wealth always be increased. It therefore sets out a policy that government might or might not decide to pursue in particular circumstances. It does not state a principle of justice, and so it cannot figure in an interpretation of the sort Hercules now seeks.[6]

Law as integrity asks judges to assume, so far as this is possible, that the law is structured by a coherent set of principles about justice and fairness and procedural due process, and it asks them to enforce these in the fresh cases that come before them, so that each person's situation is fair and just according to the same standards. That style of adjudication respects the ambition integrity assumes, the ambition to be a community of principle. But as we saw,[b] integrity does not recommend what would be perverse, that we should all be governed by the same goals and strategies of policy on every occasion. It does not insist that a legislature that enacts one set of rules about compensation today, in order to make the community richer on the whole, is in any way committed to serve that same goal of policy tomor-

row. For it might then have other goals to seek, not necessarily in place of wealth but beside it, and integrity does not frown on this diversity. Our account of interpretation, and our consequent elimination of interpretation (3) read as a naked appeal to policy, reflects a discrimination already latent in the ideal of integrity itself.

We reach the same conclusion in the context of *McLoughlin* through a different route, by further reflection on what we have learned about interpretation. An interpretation aims to show what is interpreted in the best light possible, and an interpretation of any part of our law must therefore attend not only to the substance of the decisions made by earlier officials but also to how—by which officials in which circumstances—these decisions were made. A legislature does not need reasons of principle to justify the rules it enacts about driving, including rules about compensation for accidents, even though these rules will create rights and duties for the future that will then be enforced by coercive threat. A legislature may justify its decision to create new rights for the future by showing how these will contribute, as a matter of sound policy, to the overall good of the community as a whole. There are limits to this kind of justification, as we noticed[c]. The general good may not be used to justify the death penalty for careless driving. But the legislature need not show that citizens already have a moral right to compensation for injury under particular circumstances in order to justify a statute awarding damages in those circumstances.

Law as integrity assumes, however, that judges are in a very different position from legislators. It does not fit the character of a

---

[a]In a chapter not reprinted here.

[6]The disagreement between Lords Edmund Davies and Scarman in *McLoughlin,* described in Chapter 1, was perhaps over just this claim. Edmund Davies's suggestions, about the arguments that might justify a distinction between compensable and non-compensable emotional injury, seemed to appeal to arguments of policy Scarman refused to acknowledge as appropriate.

[b]In a chapter not reprinted here.

[c]In a chapter not reprinted here.

community of principle that a judge should have authority to hold people liable in damages for acting in a way he concedes they had no legal duty not to act. So when judges construct rules of liability not recognized before, they are not free in the way I just said legislators are. Judges must make their common-law decision on grounds of principle, not policy: they must deploy arguments why the parties actually had the "novel" legal rights and duties they enforce at the time the parties acted or at some other pertinent time in the past.[7] A legal pragmatist would reject that claim. But Hercules rejects pragmatism. He follows law as integrity and therefore wants an interpretation of what judges did in the earlier emotional damage cases that shows them acting in the way he approves, not in the way he thinks judges must decline to act. It does not follow that he must dismiss interpretation (3) read in the first way I described, as supposing that past judges acted to protect a general legal right to compensation when this would make the community richer. For if people actually have such a right, others have a corresponding duty, and judges do not act unjustly in ordering the police to enforce it. The argument disqualifies interpretation (3) only when this is read to deny any such general duty and to rest on grounds of policy alone.

## Expanding the Range

Interpretations (4), (5), and (6) do, however, seem to pass these initial tests. The principles of each fit the past emotional injury decisions, at least on first glance, if only because none of these precedents presented facts that would discriminate among them. Hercules must now ask, as the next stage of his investigation, whether any one of the three must be ruled out because it is incompatible with the bulk of legal practice more generally. He must test each interpretation against other past judicial decisions, beyond those involving emotional injury, that might be thought to engage them. Suppose he discovers, for example, that past decisions provide compensation for physical injury caused by careless driving only if the injury was reasonably foreseeable. That would rule out interpretation (4) unless he can find some principled distinction between physical and emotional injury that explains why the conditions for compensation should be more restrictive for the former than the latter, which seems extremely unlikely.

Law as integrity, then, requires a judge to test his interpretation of any part of the great network of political structures and decisions of his community by asking whether it could form part of a coherent theory justifying the network as a whole. No actual judge could compose anything approaching a full interpretation of all his community's law at once. That is why we are imagining a Herculean judge of superhuman talents and endless time. But an actual judge can imitate Hercules in a limited way. He can allow the scope of his interpretation to fan out from the cases immediately in point to cases in the same general area or department of law, and then still farther, so far as this seems promising. In practice even this limited process will be largely unconscious: an experienced judge will have a sufficient sense of the terrain surrounding his immediate problem to know instinctively which interpretation of a small set of cases would survive if the range it must fit were expanded. But sometimes the expansion will be deliberate and controversial. Lawyers celebrate dozens of decisions of that character, including several on which the modern law of negligence was built.[8] Scholarship offers other important examples.[9]

[7] See *Taking Rights Seriously*, chap. 4.

[8] See *Thomas v. Winchester*, 6 N.Y. 397, and *MacPherson v. Buick Motor Co.*, 217 N.Y. 382, 111 N.E., 1050.

[9] C. Haar and D. Fessler, *The Wrong Side of the Tracks* (New York, 1986), is a recent example of integrity working on a large canvas.

Suppose a modest expansion of Hercules' range of inquiry does show that plaintiffs are denied compensation if their physical injury was not reasonably foreseeable at the time the careless defendant acted, thus ruling out interpretation (4). But this does not eliminate either (5) or (6). He must expand his survey further. He must look also to cases involving economic rather than physical or emotional injury, where damages are potentially very great: for example, he must look to cases in which professional advisers like surveyors or accountants are sued for losses others suffer through their negligence. Interpretation (5) suggests that such liability might be unlimited in amount, no matter how ruinous in total, provided that the damage is foreseeable, and (6) suggests, on the contrary, that liability is limited just because of the frightening sums it might otherwise reach. It one interpretation is uniformly contradicted by cases of that sort and finds no support in any other area of doctrine Hercules might later inspect, and the other is confirmed by the expansion, he will regard the former as ineligible, and the latter alone will have survived. But suppose he finds, when he expands his study in this way, a mixed pattern. Past decisions permit extended liability for members of some professions but not for those of others, and this mixed pattern holds for other areas of doctrine that Hercules, in the exercise of his imaginative skill, finds pertinent.

The contradiction he has discovered, though genuine, is not in itself so deep or pervasive as to justify a skeptical interpretation of legal practice as a whole, for the problem of unlimited damages, while important, is not so fundamental that contradiction within it destroys the integrity of the larger system. So Hercules turns to the second main dimension, but here, as in the chain-novel example, questions of fit surface again, because an interpretation is *pro tanto* more satisfactory if it shows less damage to integrity than its rival. He will therefore consider whether interpretation (5) fits the expanded legal record better than (6). But this cannot be a merely mechanical decision; he cannot simply count the number of past decisions that must be conceded to be "mistakes" on each interpretation. For these numbers may reflect only accidents like the number of cases that happen to have come to court and not been settled before verdict. He must take into account not only the numbers of decisions counting for each interpretation, but whether the decisions expressing one principle seem more important or fundamental or wide-ranging than the decisions expressing the other. Suppose interpretation (6) fits only those past judicial decisions involving charges of negligence against one particular profession—say, lawyers—and interpretation (5) justifies all other cases, involving all other professions, and also fits other kinds of economic damage cases as well. Interpretation (5) then fits the legal record better on the whole, even if the number of cases involving lawyers is for some reason numerically greater, unless the argument shifts again, as it well might, when the field of study expands even more.

Now suppose a different possibility: that though liability has in many and varied cases actually been limited to an amount less than interpretation (5) would allow, the opinions attached to these cases made no mention of the principle of interpretation (6), which has in fact never before been recognized in official judicial rhetoric. Does that show that interpretation (5) fits the legal record much better, or that interpretation (6) is ineligible after all? Judges in fact divide about this issue of fit. Some would not seriously consider interpretation (6) if no past judicial opinion or legislative statement had ever explicitly mentioned its principle. Others reject this constraint and accept that the best interpretation of some line of cases may lie in a principle that has never been recognized explicitly but that nevertheless offers a brilliant account of the actual decision, showing them in a better light than ever before.[10] Hercules will confront this issue as a special question of political morality. The political history of the community is *pro tanto* a better history, he thinks, if it shows judges making plain to their public, through their opinions, the path that later judges guided by integrity will follow and if it shows judges making decisions that give voice as well as effect to convictions about morality that are widespread throughout the community. Judicial opinions formally announced in law reports, moreover, are themselves acts of the community personified that, particularly if recent, must be taken into the embrace of integrity.[11] These are among his reasons for somewhat preferring an interpretation that is not too novel, not too far divorced from what past judges and other officials said as well as did. But he must set these reasons against his more substantive political convictions about the relative moral value of the two interpretations, and if he believes that interpretation (6) is much superior from that perspective, he will think he makes the legal record better overall by selecting it even at the cost of the more procedural values. Fitting what judges did is more important than fitting what they said.

Now suppose an even more unpatterned record. Hercules finds that unlimited liability has been enforced against a number of professions but has not been enforced against a roughly equal number of others, that no principle can explain the distinction, that judicial rhetoric is as split as the actual decisions, and that this split extends into other kinds of actions for economic damage. He might expand his field of survey still further, and the picture might change if he does. But let us suppose he is satisfied that it will not. He will then decide that the question of fit can play no more useful role in his deliberations even on the second dimension. He must now emphasize the more plainly substantive aspects of that dimension: he must decide which interpretation shows the legal record to be the best it can be from the standpoint of substantive political morality. He will comprise and compare two stories. The first supposes that the community personified has adopted and is enforcing the principle of foreseeability as its test of moral responsibility for damage caused by negligence, that the various decisions it has reached are intended to give effect to that principle, though it has often lapsed and reached decisions that foreseeability would condemn. The second supposes, instead, that the community has adopted and is enforcing the principle of foreseeability limited by some overall ceiling on liability, though it has often lapsed from that principle. Which story shows the community in a better light, all things considered, from the standpoint of political morality?

Hercules' answer will depend on his convictions about the two constituent virtues of political morality we have considered: justice and fairness.[12] It will depend, that is, not only on his beliefs about which of these principles is superior as a matter of abstract justice but also about which should be followed, as a matter of political fairness, in a community whose members have the moral convictions his fellow citizens have. In some cases the two kinds of judgment—the judgment of justice and that of fairness—will come together. If Hercules and the public at large share the view that people are entitled to be compensated fully whenever they are injured by others' carelessness, without regard to

[10] See, for example, Benjamin Cardozo's decision in *Hynes v. New York Central R.R. Co.,* 231 N.Y. 229.

[11] These various arguments why a successful interpretation must achieve some fit with past judicial opinions as well as with the decisions themselves are discussed in Chapter 9 in the context of past legislative statements.

[12] I have in mind the distinction and the special sense of fairness described in Chapter 6.

how harsh this requirement might turn out to be, then he will think that interpretation (5) is plainly the better of the two in play. But the two judgments will sometimes pull in different directions. He may think that interpretation (6) is better on grounds of abstract justice, but know that this is a radical view not shared by any substantial portion of the public and unknown in the political and moral rhetoric of the times. He might then decide that the story in which the state insists on the view he thinks right, but against the wishes of the people as a whole, is a poorer story, on balance. He would be preferring fairness to justice in these circumstances, and that preference would reflect a higher-order level of his own political convictions, namely his convictions about how a decent government committed to both fairness and justice should adjudicate between the two in this sort of case.

Judges will have different ideas of fairness, about the role each citizen's opinion should ideally play in the state's decision about which principles of justice to enforce through its central police power. They will have different higher-level opinions about the best resolution of conflicts between these two political ideals. No judge is likely to hold the simplistic theory that fairness is automatically to be preferred to justice or vice versa. Most judges will think that the balance between the opinions of the community and the demands of abstract justice must be struck differently in different kinds of cases. Perhaps in ordinary commercial or private law cases, like *McLoughlin*, an interpretation supported in popular morality will be deemed superior to one that is not, provided it is not thought very much inferior as a matter of abstract justice. But many judges will think the interpretive force of popular morality very much weaker in constitutional cases like *Brown*, because they will think the point of the Constitution is in part to protect individuals from what the majority thinks right.[13]

## Local Priority

I must call special attention to a feature of Hercules' practice that has not yet clearly emerged. His judgments of fit expand out from the immediate case before him in a series of concentric circles. He asks which interpretations on his initial list fit past emotional injury cases, then which ones fit cases of accidental damage to the person more generally, then which fit damage to economic interests, and so on into areas each further and further from the original *McLoughlin* issue. This procedure gives a kind of local priority to what we might call "departments" of law. If Hercules finds that neither of two principles is flatly contradicted by the accidental damage cases of his jurisdiction, he expands his study into, say, contract cases to see which of these principles, if either, fits contract decisions better. But in Hercules' view, if one principle does *not* fit accident law at all—if it is contradicted by almost every decision in the area that might have confirmed it—this counts dramatically against it as an eligible interpretation of that body of law, even if it fits other areas of the law superbly. He will not treat this doctrine of local priority as absolute, however; he will be ready to override it, as we shall soon see, in some circumstances.

The compartmentalization of law into separate departments is a prominent feature of legal practice. Law schools divide courses and their libraries divide treatises to distinguish emotional from economic or physical injury, intentional from unintentional torts, tort from crime, contract from other parts of common law, private from public law, and constitutional law from other parts of public law. Legal and judicial arguments respect these traditional divisions. Judicial opinions normally begin by assigning the case in hand to some department of law, and the precedents and statutes considered are usually

---

[13]But see the discussion of "passivism" as a theory of constitutional adjudication in Chapter 10.

drawn exclusively from that department. Often the initial classification is both controversial and crucial.

Compartmentalization suits both conventionalism and pragmatism, though for different reasons. Departments of law are based on tradition, which seems to support conventionalism, and they provide a strategy a pragmatist can manipulate in telling his noble lies: he can explain that his new doctrine need not be consistent in principle with past decisions because the latter, properly understood, belong to a different department. Law as integrity has a more complex attitude toward departments of law. Its general spirit condemns them, because the adjudicative principle of integrity asks judges to make the law coherent as a whole, so far as they can, and this might be better done by ignoring academic boundaries and reforming some departments of law radically to make them more consistent in principle with others.[14] But law as integrity is interpretive, and compartmentalization is a feature of legal practice no competent interpretation can ignore.

Hercules responds to these competing impulses by seeking a constructive interpretation of compartmentalization. He tries to find an explanation of the practice of dividing law into departments that shows that practice in its best light. The boundaries between departments usually match popular opinion; many people think that intentional harm is more blameworthy than careless harm, that the state needs a very different kind of justification to declare someone guilty of a crime than it needs to require him to pay compensation for damage he has caused, that promises and other forms of explicit agreement or consent are a special kind of reason for state coercion, and so forth.

Dividing departments of law to match that sort of opinion promotes predictability and guards against sudden official reinterpretations that uproot large areas of law, and it does this in a way that promotes a deeper aim of law as integrity. If legal compartments make sense to people at large, they encourage the protestant attitude integrity favors, because they allow ordinary people as well as hard-pressed judges to interpret law within practical boundaries that seem natural and intuitive.

Hercules accepts that account of the point of compartmentalization, and he shapes his doctrine of local priority accordingly. He allows the doctrine most force when the boundaries between traditional departments of law track widely held moral principles distinguishing types of fault or responsibility, and the substance of each department reflects those moral principles. The distinction between criminal and civil law meets that test. Suppose Hercules thinks, contrary to most people's opinion, that being made to pay compensation is just as bad as being made to pay a fine, and therefore that the distinction between criminal and civil law is unsound in principle. He will nevertheless defer to local priority. He will not claim that criminal and civil law should be treated as one department; he will not argue that a criminal defendant's guilt need only be established as probable rather than beyond a reasonable doubt because the probable standard fits the combined department as well as any other.

But Hercules will not be so ready to defer to local priority when his test is not met, when traditional boundaries between departments have become mechanical and arbitrary, either because popular morality has shifted or because the substance of the departments no longer reflects popular opinion.[15]

---

[14]See the discussion of different levels of integrity in Chapter 11.

[15]The disagreement between Lords Diplock and Edmund Davies, on the one hand, and Viscount Dilhorne on the other, in the notorious blasphemy case *R. v. Lemon* [1979] 1 All ER 898, illustrates the importance of not ignoring this connection between changes in popular morality and the boundaries of local priority. The former insisted that the law of blasphemy be interpreted to reflect developments in other parts of criminal law; the latter that blasphemy, for some unexplained reason, be counted an isolated domain of its own.

Compartments of law do sometimes grow arbitrary and isolated from popular conviction in that way, particularly when the central rules of the departments were developed in different periods. Suppose the legal tradition of a community has for many decades separated nuisance law, which concerns the discomfort of interference that activities on one person's land cause to neighbors, from negligence law, which concerns the physical or economic or emotional injuries someone's carelessness inflicts on others. Suppose that the judges who decided the crucial nuisance cases disdained any economic test for nuisance; they said that an activity counts as a nuisance, and must therefore be stopped, when it is not a "natural" or traditional use of the land, so that someone who starts a factory on land traditionally used for farming is guilty of nuisance even though the factory is an economically more efficient use. But suppose that in recent years judges have begun to make economic cost crucial for negligence. They say that someone's failure to take precautions against injuring others is negligent, so that he is liable for the resulting injury if the precaution was "reasonable" in the circumstances, and that the economic cost of the precaution counts in deciding whether it was in fact reasonable.

The distinction between negligence and nuisance law no longer meets Hercules' test, if it ever did. It makes some sense to distinguish nuisance from negligence if we assume that nuisance is intentional while negligence is unintentional; then the distinction tracks the popular principle that it is worse to injure someone knowingly than unknowingly. But the developments in negligence law I just described are not consistent with that view of the distinction, because failing to guard against an accident is not necessarily unintentional in the required sense. So Hercules would be ready to ignore the traditional boundary between these two departments of law. If he thought that the

"natural use" test was silly, and the economic cost test much more just, he would argue that the negligence and nuisance precedents should be seen as one body of law, and that the economic cost test is a superior interpretation of that unified body. His argument would probably be made easier by other legal events that already had occurred. The intellectual climate that produced the later negligence decisions would have begun to erode the assumption of the earlier nuisance cases, that novel enterprises that annoy people are necessarily legal wrongs. Perhaps the legislature would have adopted special statutes rearranging liability for some new forms of inconvenience, like airport noise, that the "natural" theory has decided or would decide in what seems the wrong way, for example. Or perhaps judges would have decided airport cases by straining the historical meaning of "natural" to reach decisions that seemed sensible given developing technology. Hercules would cite these changes as supporting his interpretive argument consolidating nuisance and negligence. If he persuades the profession of his view, nuisance and negligence will no longer be distinct departments of law but joint tenants of a new province which will shortly attract a new name attached to new law school courses and new treatises. This process is in fact under way in Anglo-American law, as is, though less securely, a new unification of private law that blurs even the long-established and once much firmer boundary between contract and tort.

## A PROVISIONAL SUMMARY

In [a later discussion[d]] we continue constructing Hercules' working theory of law as integrity by exploring in more detail issues raised in three departments of adjudication: common-law cases, cases turning on statutes, and cases of constitutional dimension.

---

[d]Not reprinted here.

But first we will take stock, though this means some repetition, and then consider certain objections to the argument so far. Judges who accept the interpretive ideal of integrity decide hard cases by trying to find, in some coherent set of principles about people's rights and duties, the best constructive interpretation of the political structure and legal doctrine of their community. They try to make that complex structure and record the best these can be. It is analytically useful to distinguish different dimensions or aspects of any working theory. It will include convictions about both fit and justification. Convictions about fit will provide a rough threshold requirement that an interpretation of some part of the law must meet if it is to be eligible at all. Any plausible working theory would disqualify an interpretation of our own law that denied legislative competence or supremacy outright or that claimed a general principle of private law requiring the rich to share their wealth with the poor. That threshold will eliminate interpretations that some judges would otherwise prefer, so the brute facts of legal history will in this way limit the role any judge's personal convictions of justice can play in his decisions. Different judges will set this threshold differently. But anyone who accepts law as integrity must accept that the actual political history of his community will sometimes check his other political convictions in his overall interpretive judgment. If he does not—if his threshold of fit is wholly derivative from and adjustable to his convictions of justice, so that the latter automatically provide an eligible interpretation—then he cannot claim in good faith to be interpreting his legal practice at all. Like the chain novelist whose judgments of fit automatically adjusted to his substantive literary opinions, he is acting from bad faith or self-deception.

Hard cases arise, for any judge, when his threshold test does not discriminate between two or more interpretations of some statute or line of cases. Then he must choose between eligible interpretations by asking which shows the community's structure of institutions and decisions—its public standards as a whole—in a better light from the standpoint of political morality. His own moral and political convictions are now directly engaged. But the political judgment he must make is itself complex and will sometimes set one department of his political morality against another: his decision will reflect not only his opinions about justice and fairness but his higher-order convictions about how these ideals should be compromised when they compete. Questions of fit arise at this stage of interpretation as well, because even when an interpretation survives the threshold requirement, any infelicities of fit will count against it, in the ways we noticed, in the general balance of political virtues. Different judges will disagree about each of these issues and will accordingly take different views of what the law of their community, properly understood, really is.

Any judge will develop, in the course of his training and experience, a fairly individualized working conception of law on which he will rely, perhaps unthinkingly, in making these various judgments and decisions, and the judgments will then be, for him, a matter of feel or instinct rather than analysis. Even so, we as critics can impose structure on his working theory by teasing out its rules of thumb about fit—about the relative importance of consistency with past rhetoric and popular opinion, for example—and its more substantive opinions or leanings about justice and fairness. Most judges will be like other people in their community, and fairness and justice will therefore not often compete for them. But judges whose political opinions are more eccentric or radical will find that the two ideals conflict in particular cases, and they will have to decide which resolution of that conflict would show the community's record in the best light. Their working conceptions will accordingly include higher-order principles that have proved necessary to that further decision. A particular judge may think or assume, for example, that political decisions should mainly respect majority opinion, and yet believe that this requirement relaxes and even disappears when serious constitutional rights are in question.

We should now recall two general observations we made in constructing the chain-novel model, because they apply here as well. First, the different aspects or dimensions of a judge's working approach—the dimensions of fit and substance, and of different aspects of substance—are in the last analysis all responsive to his political judgment. His convictions about fit, as these appear either in his working threshold requirement or analytically later in competition with substance, are political not mechanical. They express his commitment to integrity: he believes that an interpretation that falls below his threshold of fit shows the record of the community in an irredeemably bad light, because proposing that interpretation suggests that the community has characteristically dishonored its own principles. When an interpretation meets the threshold, remaining defects of fit may be compensated, in his overall judgment, if the principles of that interpretation are particularly attractive, because then he sets off the community's infrequent lapses in respecting these principles against its virtue in generally observing them. The constraint fit imposes on substance, in any working theory, is therefore the constraint of one type of political conviction on another in the overall judgment which interpretation makes a political record the best it can be overall, everything taken into account. Second, the mode of this constraint is the mode we identified in the chain novel. It is not the constraint of external hard fact or of interpersonal consensus. But rather the structural constraint of different kinds of principle within a system of principle, and it is none the less genuine for that.

No mortal judge can or should try to articulate his instinctive working theory so far, or make that theory so concrete and detailed, that no further thought will be necessary case by case. He must treat any general principles or rules of thumb he has followed in the past as provisional and stand ready to abandon these in favor of more sophisticated and searching analysis when the occasion demands. These will be moments of special difficulty for any judge, calling for fresh political judgments that may be hard to make. It would be absurd to suppose that he will always have at hand the necessary background convictions of political morality for such occasions. Very hard cases will force him to develop his conception of law and his political morality together in a mutually supporting way. But it is nevertheless possible for any judge to confront fresh and challenging issues as a matter of principle, and this is what law as integrity demands of him. He must accept that in finally choosing one interpretation over another of a much contested line of precedents, perhaps after demanding thought and shifting conviction, he is developing his working conception of law in one rather than another direction. This must seem to him the right direction as a matter of political principle, not just appealing for the moment because it recommends an attractive decision in the immediate case. There is, in this counsel, much room for deception, including self-deception. But on most occasions it will be possible for judges to recognize when they have submitted an issue to the discipline it describes. And also to recognize when some other judge has not.

## SOME FAMILIAR OBJECTIONS

### Hercules Is Playing Politics

Hercules has completed his labors in *McLoughlin*. He declares that the best interpretation of the emotional damage cases, all things considered, is (5): the law allows compensation for all emotional injury directly caused by careless driving and foreseeable by a reasonably thoughtful motorist. But he concedes that in reaching that conclusion he has relied on his own opinion that this principle is better—fairer and more just—than any other that is eligible on what he takes to be the right criteria of fit. He also concedes that this opinion is controversial: it is not shared by all of his fellow judges, some of whom therefore think that some other interpretation, for example (6), is superior. What complaints are his arguments likely to attract? The first in the list I propose to consider accuses Hercules of ignoring the actual law of emotional injury and substituting his own views about what the law should be.

How shall we understand this objection? We might take it in two very different ways. It might mean that Hercules was wrong to seek to justify his interpretation by appealing to justice and fairness because it does not even survive the proper threshold test of fit. We cannot assume, without reviewing the cases Hercules consulted, that this argument is mistaken. Perhaps this time Hercules nodded; perhaps if he had expanded the range of his study of precedents further he would have discovered that only one interpretation did survive, and this discovery would then have settled the law, for him, without engaging his opinions about the justice of requiring compensation for accidents. But it is hardly plausible that even the strictest threshold test of fit will always permit only one interpretation, so the objection, understood this way, would not be a general objection to Hercules' methods of adjudication but only a complaint that he had misapplied his own methods in the particular case at hand.

We should therefore consider the second, more interesting reading of the objection: this claims that a judge must never rely on his personal convictions about fairness or justice the way Hercules did in this instance. Suppose the critic says, "The correct interpretation of a line of past decisions can always be discovered by morally neutral means, because the correct interpretation is just a matter of discovering what principles the judges who made these decision intended to lay down, and that is just a matter of historical fact." Hercules will point out that this critic needs a political reason for his dictum that interpretations must match the intentions of past judges. That is an extreme form of the position we have already considered, that an interpretation is better if it fits what past judges said as well as did, and even that weaker claim depends on the special arguments of political morality I described. The critic supposes that these special reasons are not only strong but commanding; that they are so powerful that a judge always does wrong even to consider an interpretation that does not meet the standard they set, no matter how well that interpretation ties together, explains, and justifies past decisions.

So Hercules' critic, if his argument is to have any power, is not relying on politically neutral interpretive convictions after all. He, too, has engaged his own background convictions of political morality. He thinks the political values that support his interpretive style are of such fundamental importance as to eliminate any competing commands of justice altogether. That may be a plausible position, but it is hardly uncontroversial and is in no sense neutral. His difference with Hercules is not, as he first suggested, about whether political morality is relevant in deciding what the law is, but about which principles of morality are sound and therefore decisive of that issue. So the first, crude objection, that Hercules has substituted his own political convictions for the politically neutral correct interpretation of the past law, is an album of confusions.

## Hercules Is a Fraud

The second objection is more sophisticated. Now the critic says, "It is absurd to suppose that there is any single correct interpretation of the emotional injury cases. Since we have discovered two interpretations of these cases, neither of which can be preferred to the other on 'neutral' grounds of fit, no judge would be forced by the adjudicative principle of integrity to accept either. Hercules has chosen one on frankly political grounds; his choice reflects only his own political morality. He has no choice in the circumstances but to legislate in that way. Nevertheless it is fraudulent for him to claim that he has discovered, through his political choice, what the *law* is. He is only offering his own opinion about what it should be."

This objection will seem powerful to many readers, and we must take care not to weaken it by making it seem to claim more than it does. It does not try to reinstate the idea of conventionalism, that when convention runs out a judge is free to improve the law according to the right legislative standards; still less the idea of pragmatism that he is always free to do this, checked only by considerations of strategy. It acknowledges that judges must choose between interpretations that survive the test of fit. It insists only that there can be no best interpretation when more than one survives that test. It is an objection, as I have framed it, from within the general idea of law as integrity; it tries to protect that idea from corruption by fraud.

Is the objection sound? Why is it fraudulent, or even confusing, for Hercules to offer his judgment as a judgment of law? Once again, two somewhat different answers—two ways of elaborating the objection—are available, and we cannot do credit to the objection unless we distinguish them and consider each. The first elaboration is this: "Hercules' claim is fraudulent because it suggests that there can be a right answer to the question whether interpretation (5) or (6) is fairer or more just; since political morality is subjective there cannot be a single right answer to that question, but only answers." This is the challenge of moral skepticism I discussed at length. . . .[e] I cannot escape saying something more about it now, but I will use a new critic, with a section of his own, to do so. The second elaboration does not rely on skepticism: "Hercules is a fraud

even if morality is objective and even if he is right that the principle of foreseeability he settled on is objectively fairer and more just. He is a fraud because he pretends he has discovered what the law is, but he has only discovered what is should be." That is the form of the objection I shall consider here.

We ask of a conception of law that it provide an account of the grounds of law—the circumstances under which claims about what the law is should be accepted as true or sound—that shows why law licenses coercion. Law as integrity replies that the grounds of law lie in integrity, in the best constructive interpretation of past legal decisions, and that law is therefore sensitive to justice in the way Hercules recognizes. So there is no way Hercules *can* report his conclusion about Mrs. McLoughlin's case except to say that the law, as he understands it, is in her favor. If he said what the critic recommends, that she has no legal right to win but has a moral right that he proposes to honor, he would be *misstating* his view of the matter. He would think that a true account of some situations—if he found the law too immoral to enforce, for example—but not of this one. A critic might disagree with Hercules at many levels. He might reject law as integrity in favor of conventionalism or pragmatism or some other conception of law. Or he might accept it but reach different conclusions from Hercules because he holds different ideas about the necessary requirements of fit, or different convictions about fairness or justice or the relation between them. But he can regard Hercules' use of "law" as fraudulent (or grammatically wrong) only if he suffers from the semantic sting, only if he assumes that claims of law are somehow out of order when they are not drawn directly from some set of factual criteria for law every competent lawyer accepts.

One aspect of the present objection, however, might be thought immune from my arguments against the rest. Even if we

[e]Not reprinted here.

agree that Hercules' conclusions about Mrs. McLoughlin are properly presented as conclusions of law, it might seem extravagant to claim that these conclusions in any way follow from integrity understood as a distinct political ideal. Would it not be more accurate to say that integrity is at work in Hercules' calculations just up to the point at which he has rejected all interpretations that fail the threshold test of fit, but that integrity play no part in selecting among those that survive that test? Should we not say that his conception of law is really two conceptions: law as integrity supplemented, when integrity gives out, by some version of natural law theory? This is not a very important objection; it only suggests a different way of reporting the conclusions it no longer challenges. Nevertheless the observation that prompts it is too crude. For it is a mistake to think that the idea of integrity is irrelevant to Hercules' decision once that decision is no longer a matter of his convictions about fit but draws on his sense of fairness or justice as well.

The spirit of integrity, which we located in fraternity, would be outraged if Hercules were to make his decision in any way other than by choosing the interpretation that he believes best from the standpoint of political morality as a whole. We accept integrity as a political ideal because we want to treat our political community as one of principle, and the citizens of a community of principle aim not simply at common principles, as if uniformity were all they wanted, but the best common principles politics can find. Integrity is distinct from justice and fairness, but it is bound to them in that way: integrity makes no sense except among people who want fairness and justice as well. So Hercules' final choice of the interpretation he believes sounder on the whole—fairer and more just in the right relation—flows from his initial commitment to integrity. He makes that choice at the moment and in the way integrity both permits and requires, and it is therefore deeply misleading to say that he has abandoned the ideal at just that point.

## Hercules Is Arrogant and Anyway a Myth

I shall deal much more briefly with two less important critics who nevertheless must be heard. I have been describing Hercules' methods in what some will call a subjective way, by describing the questions he must answer and judgments he must make for himself. Other judges would answer these differently, and you might agree with one of them rather than Hercules. We shall consider in a moment whether any of this means that neither Hercules nor any other judge or critic can be "really" right about what the law is. But Hercules' opinion will be controversial no matter how we answer that philosophical question, and his new critic seizes just on the fact of controversiality, untainted by any appeal to either external or internal skepticism. "Whether or not there are right answers to the interpretive questions on which Hercules' judgment depends, it is unfair that the answer of one judge (or a bare majority of judges on a panel) be accepted as final when he has no way to *prove*, against those who disagree, that his opinion is better."

We must return, for an answer, to our more general case for law as integrity. We want our officials to treat us as tied together in an association of principle, and we want this for reasons that do not depend on any identity of conviction among these officials, either about fit or about the more substantive principles an interpretation engages. Our reasons endure when judges disagree, at least in detail, about the best interpretation of the community's political order, because each judge still confirms and reinforces the principled character of our association by striving, in spite of the disagreement, to reach his own opinion instead of turning to the usually simpler task of fresh legislation. But even if this were not so, the present objection could not count as an objection to law as integrity distinctly, for it would apply in its full force to pragmatism or to conventionalism, which becomes pragmatism in any case hard enough to come before an appellate court. How can it be fairer for judges to enforce their own views about the best future, unconstrained by any requirement of coherence with the past, than the more complex but no less controversial judgments that law as integrity requires?

Another minor critic appears. His complaint is from a different quarter. "Hercules," he says "is a myth. No real judge has his powers, and it is absurd to hold him out as a model for others to follow. Real judges decide hard cases much more instinctively. They do not construct and test various rival interpretations against a complex matrix of intersecting political and moral principles. Their craft trains them to see structure in facts and doctrine at once; that is what thinking as a lawyer really is. If they decided to imitate Hercules, trying in each case to secure some general theory of law as a whole, they would be paralyzed while their docket choked." This critic misunderstands our exercise. Hercules is useful to us just because he is more reflective and self-conscious than any real judge need be or, given the press of work, could be. No doubt real judges decide most cases in a much less methodical way. But Hercules shows us the hidden structure of their judgments and so lays these open to study and criticism. We must be careful to distinguish, moreover, two senses in which he might be said to have more powers than any actual judge could. He works so much more quickly (and has so much more time available) that he can explore avenues and ideas they cannot; he can pursue, not just one or two evident lines in expanding the range of cases he studies but all the lines there are. That is the sense in which he can aim at more than they: he can aim at a comprehensive theory, while theirs must be partial. But he has no vision into transcendental mysteries opaque to them. His judgments of fit and political morality are made on the same material and have the same character as theirs. He does what they would do if they had a career to devote to a single decision; they need, not a different conception of law from his, but skills of craft husbandry and efficiency he has never had to cultivate.

Now this critic trims his sails. "In any case Hercules has too much theory for easy cases. Good judges just know that the plain meaning of a plain statute, or a crisp rule always applied and never doubted in precedent, is law, and that is all there is to it. It would be preposterous, not just time-consuming, to subject these undoubted truths to interpretive tests on each occasion. So law as integrity, with its elaborate and top-heavy structure, is at best a conception for hard cases alone. Something much more like conventionalism is a better interpretation of what judges do in the easy ones." The distinction between easy and hard cases at law is neither so clear nor so important as this critic assumes, as we shall see[f], but Hercules does not need that point now. Law as integrity explains and justifies easy cases as well as hard ones; it also shows why they are easy. It is obvious that the speed limit in California is 55 because it is obvious that any competent interpretation of California traffic law must yield that conclusion. So easy cases are, for law as integrity, only special cases of hard ones, and the critic's complaint is then only what Hercules himself would be happy to concede: that we need not ask questions when we already know the answer.

[f]In a chapter not reprinted here.

## QUESTIONS

1. Dworkin says that an interpretation [like (2)] that "draws a line that it leaves arbitrary and unconnected to any more general moral or political consideration" is not even a principle in the required sense and must be ruled out by Hercules. Suppose that a legislature draws a legal drinking age line at 18, or at 21. Is this similarly arbitrary and therefore unacceptable? Why or why not?

2. Elsewhere in his book, Dworkin explains the notion of law as integrity by giving examples of "checkerboard" laws that result from that very familiar political and legislative phenomenon, compromise. For example, suppose that the nation is bitterly and evenly divided over the morality of abortion, approximately half believing that it is morally permissible and a woman's right, the other half believing that it amounts to murder of the unborn. It would seem clearly unacceptable to compromise by passing a law prohibiting abortions for women born in even-numbered years, and permitting abortions for women born in odd-numbered years. Explain why.

3. Some critics claim that moral judgments and opinions, like the opinions that slavery is unjust and that murder is wrong, are not *objective,* and that this vitiates Dworkin's whole conception of what Hercules is supposed to be doing. Think carefully about the various things that could plausibly be meant by the claim that moral judgments are, or are not, objective. For each of these meanings that you specify, answer the questions: *Are* moral judgments objective in this sense? Does it matter whether they are?

4. Read the excerpt from Bentham ("No Customary Law Complete"). How would Dworkin address Bentham's various doubts about customary law and the mischief of ex post facto law arising from breaking "the chain of conformity"?

## *Appeals Courts**
## McLOUGHLIN v. O'BRIAN

. . . May 6. LORD WILBERFORCE. My Lords, this appeal arises from a very serious and tragic road accident which occurred on October 19, 1973, near Withersfield, Suffolk. The appellant's husband, Thomas McLoughlin, and three of her children, George, aged 17, Kathleen, aged 7, and Gillian, nearly 3, were in a Ford motor car: George was driving. A fourth child, Michael, then aged 11, was a passenger in a following motor car driven by Mr. Pilgrim: this car did not become involved in the accident. The Ford car was in collision with a lorry driven by the first respondent and owned by the second respondent. That lorry had been in collision with another lorry driven by the third respondent and owned by the fourth respondent. It is admitted that the accident to the Ford car was caused by the respondents' negligence. It is necessary to state what followed in full detail.

As a result of the accident, the appellant's husband suffered bruising and shock; George suffered injuries to his head and face, cerebral concussion, fractures of both scapullae and bruising and abrasions; Kathleen suffered concussion, fracture of the right clavicle, bruising, abrasions and shock; Gillian was so seriously injured that she died almost immediately.

*1 A.C. 410 (1983)

At the time, the appellant was at her home about two miles away; an hour or so afterwards the accident was reported to her by Mr. Pilgrim, who told her that he thought George was dying, and that he did not know the whereabouts of her husband or the condition of her daughter. He then drove her to Addenbrooke's Hospital, Cambridge. There she saw Michael, who told her that Gillian was dead. She was taken down a corridor and through a window she saw Kathleen, crying, with her face cut and begrimed with dirt and oil. She could hear George shouting and screaming. She was taken to her husband who was sitting with his head in his hands. His shirt was hanging off him and he was covered in mud and oil. He saw the appellant and started sobbing. The appellant was then taken to see George. The whole of his left face and left side was covered. He appeared to recognise the appellant and then lapsed into unconsciousness. Finally, the appellant was taken to Kathleen who by now had been cleaned up. The child was too upset to speak and simply clung to her mother. There can be no doubt that these circumstances, witnessed by the appellant, were distressing in the extreme and were capable of producing an effect going well beyond that of grief and sorrow.

The appellant subsequently brought proceedings against the respondents. At the trial, the judge assumed, for the purpose of enabling him to decide the issue of legal liability, that the appellant subsequently suffered the condition of which she complained. This was described as severe shock, organic depression and a change of personality. Numerous symptoms of a physiological character are said to have been manifested. The details were not investigated at the trial, the court being asked to assume that the appellant's condition had been caused or contributed to by shock, as distinct from grief or sorrow, and that the appellant was a person of reasonable fortitude.

On these facts, or assumed facts, the trial judge (Boreham J.) gave judgment for the re-

spondents holding, in a most careful judgment reviewing the authorities, that the respondents owed no duty of care to the appellant because the possibility of her suffering injury by nervous shock, in the circumstances, was not reasonably foreseeable.

On appeal by the appellant the judgment of Boreham J. was upheld, but not on the same ground. Stephenson L.J. took the view that the possibility of injury to the appellant by nervous shock *was* reasonably foreseeable and that the respondents owed the appellant a duty of care. However, he held that considerations of policy prevented the appellant from recovering. Griffiths L.J. held that injury by nervous shock to the appellant was "readily foreseeable" but that the respondents owed no duty of care to the appellant. The duty was limited to those on the road nearby. Cumming-Bruce L.J. agreed with both judgments. The appellant now appeals to this House. The critical question to be decided is whether a person in the position of the appellant, i.e. one who was not present at the scene of grievous injuries to her family but who comes upon those injuries at an interval of time and space, can recover damages for nervous shock.

Although we continue to use the hallowed expression "nervous shock," English law, and common understanding, have moved some distance since recognition was given to this symptom as a basis for liability. Whatever is unknown about the mind-body relationship (and the area of ignorance seems to expand with that of knowledge), it is now accepted by medical science that recognisable and severe physical damage to the human body and system may be caused by the impact, through the senses, of external events on the mind. There may thus be produced what is as identifiable an illness as any that may be caused by direct physical impact. It is safe to say that this, in general terms, is understood by the ordinary man or woman who is hypothesised by the courts in situations where claims for negligence are made. Although in the only case which has reached this House (*Bourhill* v. *Young* [1943] A.C. 92) a claim for damages in respect of "nervous shock" was rejected on its facts, the House gave clear recognition to the legitimacy, in principle, of claims of that character: As the result of that and other cases, assuming that they are accepted as correct, the following position has been reached:

1. While damages cannot, at common law, be awarded for grief and sorrow, a claim for damages for "nervous shock" caused by negligence can be made without the necessity of showing direct impact or fear of immediate personal injuries for oneself. The reservation made by Kennedy J. in *Dulieu* v. *White & Sons* [1901] 2 K.B. 669, though taken up by Sargant L.J. in *Hambrook* v. *Stokes Brothers* [1925] 1 K.B. 141, has not gained acceptance, and although the respondents, in the courts below, reserved their right to revive it, they did not do so in argument. I think that it is now too late to do so. The arguments on this issue were fully and admirably stated by the Supreme Court of California in *Dillon* v. *Legg* (1968) 29 A.L.R. 3d 1316.

2. A plaintiff may recover damages for "nervous shock" brought on by injury caused not to him- or herself but to a near relative, or by the fear of such injury. So far (subject to 5 below), the cases do not extend beyond the spouse or children of the plaintiff (*Hambrook* v. *Stokes Brothers* [1925] 1 K.B. 141, *Boardman* v. *Sanderson* [1964] 1 W.L.R. 1317, *Hinz* v. *Berry* [1970] 2 Q.B. 40—including foster children—(where liability was assumed) and see *King* v. *Phillips* [1953] 1 Q.B. 429).

3. Subject to the next paragraph, there is no English case in which a plaintiff has been able to recover nervous shock damages where the injury to the near relative occurred out of sight and earshot of the plaintiff. In *Hambrook* v. *Stokes Brothers* an express distinction was made between shock caused by what the mother saw with her own eyes and what she might have been told by bystanders, liability being excluded in the latter case.

4. An exception from, or I would prefer to call it an extension of, the latter case, has been made where the plaintiff does not see or hear the incident but comes upon its immediate aftermath. In *Boardman* v. *Sanderson* the father was within earshot of the accident to his child and likely to come upon the scene: he did so and suffered damage from what he then saw. In *Marshall* v. *Lionel Enterprises Inc.* [1972] 2 O.R. 177, the wife came immediately upon the badly injured body of her husband. And in *Benson* v. *Lee* [1972] V.R. 879, a situation existed with some similarity to the present case. The mother was in her home 100 yards away, and, on communication by a third party, ran out to the scene of the accident and there suffered shock. Your Lordships have to decide whether or not to validate these extensions.

5. A remedy on account of nervous shock has been given to a man who came upon a serious accident involving numerous people immediately thereafter and acted as a rescuer of those involved (*Chadwick* v. *British Railways Board* [1967] 1 W.L.R. 912). "Shock" was caused neither by fear for himself nor by fear or horror on account of a near relative. The principle of "rescuer" cases was not challenged by the respondents and ought, in my opinion, to be accepted. But we have to consider whether, and how far, it can be applied to such cases as the present.

Throughout these developments, as can be seen, the courts have proceeded in the traditional manner of the common law from case to case, upon a basis of logical necessity. If a mother, with or without accompanying children, could recover on account of fear for herself, how can she be denied recovery on account of fear for her accompanying children? If a father could recover had he seen his child run over by a backing car, how can he be denied recovery if he is in the immediate vicinity and runs to the child's assistance? If a wife and mother could recover if she had witnessed a serious accident to her husband and children, does she fail because she was a short distance away and immediately rushes to the scene (cf. *Benson v. Lee*)? I think that unless the law is to draw an arbitrary line at the point of direct sight and sound, these arguments require acceptance of the extension mentioned above under 4 in the interests of justice.

If one continues to follow the process of logical progression, it is hard to see why the present plaintiff also should not succeed. She was not present at the accident, but she came very soon after upon its aftermath. If, from a distance of some 100 yards (cf. *Benson v. Lee*), she had found her family by the roadside, she would have come within principle 4 above. Can it make any difference that she comes upon them in an ambulance, or, as here, in a nearby hospital, when, as the evidence shows, they were in the same condition, covered with oil and mud, and distraught with pain? If Mr. Chadwick can recover when, acting in accordance with normal and irresistible human instinct, and indeed moral compulsion, he goes to the scene of an accident, may not a mother recover if, acting under the same motives, she goes to where her family can be found?

I could agree that a line can be drawn above her case with less hardship than would have been apparent in *Boardman* v. *Sanderson* [1964] 1 W.L.R. 1317 and *Hinz* v. *Berry* [1970] 2 Q.B. 40, but so to draw it would not appeal to most people's sense of justice. To allow her claim may be, I think it is, upon the margin of what the process of logical progression would allow. But where the facts are strong and exceptional, and, as I think, fairly analogous, her case ought, prima facie, to be assimilated to those which have passed the test.

To argue from one factual situation to another and to decide by analogy is a natural tendency of the human and the legal mind. But the lawyer still has to inquire whether, in so doing, he has crossed some critical line behind which he ought to stop. That is said to be the present case. The reasoning by which the Lords Justices decided not to grant relief to the plaintiff is instructive.

Both Stephenson L.J. and Griffiths L.J. accepted that the "shock" to the plaintiff was foreseeable; but from this, at least in presentation, they diverge. Stephenson L.J. considered that the defendants owed a duty of care to the plaintiff, but that for reasons of policy the law should stop short of giving her damages: it should limit relief to those on or near the highway at or near the time of the accident caused by the defendants' negligence. He was influenced by the fact that the courts of this country, and of other common law jurisdictions, had stopped at this point: it was indicated by the barrier of commercial sense and practical convenience. Griffiths L.J. took the view that although the injury to the plaintiff was foreseeable, there was no duty of care. The duty of care of drivers of motor vehicles was, according to decided cases, limited to persons and owners of property on the road or near to it who might be directly affected. The line should be drawn at this point. It was not even in the interest of those suffering from shock as a class to extend the scope of the defendants' liability: to do so would quite likely delay their recovery by immersing them in the anxiety of litigation.

I am impressed by both of these arguments, which I have only briefly summarised. Though differing in expression, in the end, in my opinion, the two presentations rest upon a common principle, namely that, at the margin, the boundaries of a man's responsibility for acts of negligence have to be fixed as a matter of policy. Whatever is the correct jurisprudential analysis, it does not make any essential difference whether one says, with Stephenson L.J., that there is a duty but, as a matter of policy, the consequences of breach of it ought to be limited at a certain point, or whether, with Griffiths L.J., one says that the fact that consequences may be foreseeable does not automatically impose a duty of care, does not do so in fact where policy indicates the contrary. This is an approach which one can see very clearly from the way in which Lord Atkin stated the neighbour principle in

*Donoghue* v. *Stevenson* [1932] A.C. 562, 580: "persons who are so closely and directly affected by my act that I ought reasonably to have them in contemplation as being so affected. . . ." This is saying that foreseeability must be accompanied and limited by the law's judgment as to persons who ought, according to its standards of value or justice, to have been in contemplation. Foreseeability, which involves a hypothetical person, looking with hindsight at an event which has occurred, is a formula adopted by English law, not merely for defining, but also for limiting, the persons to whom duty may be owed, and the consequences for which an actor may be held responsible. It is not merely an issue of fact to be left to be found as such. When it is said to result in a duty of care being owed to a person or a class, the statement that there is a "duty of care" denotes a conclusion into the forming of which considerations of policy have entered. That foreseeability does not of itself, and automatically, lead to a duty of care is, I think, clear. I gave some examples in *Anns* v. *Merton London Borough Council* [1978] A.C. 728, 752, *Anns* itself being one. I may add what Lord Reid said in *McKew* v. *Holland & Hannen & Cubitts (Scotland) Ltd.* [1969] 3 All E.R. 1621, 1623:

> "A defender is not liable for a consequence of a kind which is not foreseeable. But it does not follow that he is liable for every consequence which a reasonable man could foresee."

We must then consider the policy arguments. In doing so we must bear in mind that cases of "nervous shock," and the possibility of claiming damages for it, are not necessarily confined to those arising out of accidents on public roads. To state, therefore, a rule that recoverable damages must be confined to persons on or near the highway is to state not a principle in itself, but only an example of a more general rule that recoverable damages must be confined to those within sight and sound of an event caused by negligence or, at least, to those in close, or very close, proximity to such a situation.

The policy arguments against a wider extension can be stated under four heads.

First, it may be said that such extension may lead to a proliferation of claims, and possibly fraudulent claims, to the establishment of an industry of lawyers and psychiatrists who will formulate a claim for nervous shock damages, including what in America is called the customary miscarriage, for all, or many, road accidents and industrial accidents.

Secondly, it may be claimed that an extension of liability would be unfair to defendants, as imposing damages out of proportion to the negligent conduct complained of. In so far as such defendants are insured, a large additional burden will be placed on insurers, and ultimately upon the class of persons insured—road users or employers.

Thirdly, to extend liability beyond the most direct and plain cases would greatly increase evidentiary difficulties and tend to lengthen litigation.

Fourthly, it may be said—and the Court of Appeal agreed with this—that an extension of the scope of liability ought only to be made by the legislature, after careful research. This is the course which has been taken in New South Wales and the Australian Capital Territory.

The whole argument has been well summed up by Dean Prosser (*Prosser, Torts*, 4th ed. (1971), p. 256):

> "The reluctance of the courts to enter this field even where the mental injury is clearly foreseeable, and the frequent mention of the difficulties of proof, the facility of fraud, and the problem of finding a place to stop and draw the line, suggest that here it is the nature of the interest invaded and the type of damage which is the real obstacle."

Since he wrote, the type of damage has, in this country at least, become more familiar and less deterrent to recovery. And some of the arguments are susceptible of answer.

Fraudulent claims can be contained by the courts, who, also, can cope with evidentiary difficulties. The scarcity of cases which have occurred in the past, and the modest sums recovered, give some indication that fears of a flood of litigation may be exaggerated—experience in other fields suggests that such fears usually are. If some increase does occur, that may only reveal the existence of a genuine social need: that legislation has been found necessary in Australia may indicate the same thing.

But, these discounts accepted, there remains, in my opinion, just because "shock" in its nature is capable of affecting so wide a range of people, a real need for the law to place some limitation upon the extent of admissible claims. It is necessary to consider three elements inherent in any claim: the class of persons whose claims should be recognised; the proximity of such persons to the accident; and the means by which the shock is caused. As regards the class of persons, the possible range is between the closest of family ties—of parent and child, or husband and wife—and the ordinary bystander. Existing law recognizes the claims of the first: it denies that of the second, either on the basis that such persons must be assumed to be possessed of fortitude sufficient to enable them to endure the calamities of modern life, or that defendants cannot be expected to compensate the world at large. In my opinion, these positions are justifiable, and since the present case falls within the first class, it is strictly unnecessary to say more. I think, however, that it should follow that other cases involving less close relationships must be very carefully scrutinised. I cannot say that they should never be admitted. The closer the tie (not merely in relationship, but in care) the greater the claim for consideration. The claim, in any case, has to be judged in the light of the other factors, such as proximity to the scene in time and place, and the nature of the accident.

As regards proximity to the accident, it is obvious that this must be close in both time and space. It is, after all, the fact and consequence of the defendant's negligence that must be proved to have caused the "nervous shock." Experience has shown that to insist on direct and immediate sight or hearing would be impractical and unjust and that under what may be called the "aftermath" doctrine one who, from close proximity, comes very soon upon the scene should not be excluded. In my opinion, the result in *Benson* v. *Lee* [1972] V.R. 879 was correct and indeed inescapable. It was based, soundly, upon

"direct perception of some of the events which go to make up the accident as an entire event, and this includes . . . the immediate aftermath . . ." (p.880.)

The High Court's majority decision in *Chester* v. *Waverley Corporation* (1939) 62 C.L.R. 1, where a child's body was found floating in a trench after a prolonged search, may perhaps be placed on the other side of a recognisable line (Evatt J. in a powerful dissent placed it on the same side), but in addition, I find the conclusion of Lush J. to reflect developments in the law.

Finally, and by way of reinforcement of "aftermath" cases, I would accept, by analogy with "rescue" situations, that a person of whom it could be said that one could expect nothing else than that he or she would come immediately to the scene—normally a parent or a spouse—could be regarded as being within the scope of foresight and duty. Where there is not immediate presence, account must be taken of the possibility of alterations in the circumstances, for which the defendant should not be responsible.

Subject only to these qualifications, I think that a strict test of proximity by sight or hearing should be applied by the courts.

Lastly, as regards communication, there is no case in which the law has compensated shock brought about by communication by a third party. In *Hambrook* v. *Stokes Brothers* [1925] 1 K.B. 141, indeed, it was said that liability would not arise in such a case and this is surely right. It was so decided in *Abramzik v. Brenner* (1967) 65 D.L.R. (2d) 651. The shock must come through sight or hearing of the event or of its immediate aftermath. Whether some equivalent of sight or hearing, e.g. through simultaneous television, would suffice may have to be considered.

My Lords, I believe that these indications, imperfectly sketched, and certainly to be applied with common sense to individual situations in their entirety, represent either the existing law, or the existing law with only such circumstantial extension as the common law process may legitimately make. They do not introduce a new principle. Nor do I see any reason why the law should retreat behind the lines already drawn. I find on this appeal that the appellant's case falls within the boundaries of the law so drawn. I would allow her appeal. . . .

LORD BRIDGE OF HARWICH. My Lords, looking back I think it is possible to discern that there only ever were two clear lines of limitation of a defendant's liability for "nervous shock" for which any rational justification could be advanced in the light both of the state of the law of negligence and the state of medical science as judicially understood at the time when those limitations were propounded. In 1888 it was, no doubt, perfectly sensible to say: "Damages arising from mere sudden terror unaccompanied by any actual physical injury, but occasioning a nervous or mental shock, cannot . . . be considered a consequence which, in the ordinary course of things, would flow from . . . negligence" (*Victorian Railway Commissioners v. Coultas*, 13 App.Cas. 222, 225). Here the test, whether of duty or of remoteness, can be recognised as a relatively distant ancestor of the modern criterion of reasonable foreseeability. Again, in 1901 it was, I would suppose, equally sensible to limit a defendant's liability for "nervous shock" which could "reasonably or actually be expected" to be such as was suffered by a plaintiff who was himself physically endangered by the defendant's negligence (*Dulieu* v. *White &*

*Sons* [1901] 2 K.B. 669, 675). But once that line of limitation has been crossed, as it was by the majority in *Hambrook* v. *Stokes Brothers* [1925] 1 K.B. 141, there can be no logical reason whatever for limiting the defendant's duty to persons in physical proximity to the place where the accident, caused by the defendant's negligence, occurred. Much of the confusion in the authorities since *Bourhill* v. *Young* [1943] A.C. 92, including, if I may say so, the judgments of the courts below in the instant case, has arisen, as it seems to me, from the deference still accorded, notwithstanding the acceptance of the *Hambrook* principle, to dicta of their Lordships in *Bourhill* v. *Young* which only make sense if understood as based on the limited principle of liability propounded by Kennedy J. in *Dulieu* v. *White & Sons* [1901] 2 K.B. 669, and adopted in the dissenting judgment of Sargant L.J. in *Hambrook* v. *Stokes Brothers*.

My Lords, before returning to the policy question, it is, I think, highly instructive to consider the decision of the Supreme Court of California in *Dillon* v. *Legg*, 29 A.L.R. 3d 1316. Before this decision the law of California, and evidently of other states of the Union, had adhered to the English position before *Hambrook* v. *Stokes Brothers*, that damages for nervous shock could only be recovered if resulting from the plaintiff's apprehension of danger to himself and, indeed, this view had been affirmed by the Californian Supreme Court only five years earlier. The majority in *Dillon* v. *Legg* adopted a contrary view in refusing a motion to dismiss a mother's claim for damages for emotional trauma caused by seeing her infant daughter killed by a car as she crossed the road.

In delivering the majority judgment of the court, Tobriner J. said, at pp. 1326–1327:

"Since the chief element in determining whether defendant owes a duty or an obligation to plaintiff is the foreseeability of the risk, that factor will be of prime concern in every case. Because it is inherently intertwined with foreseeability such duty or obligation must necessarily be adjudicated only upon a case-by-case basis. We cannot now predetermine defendant's obligation in every situation by a fixed category; no immutable rule can establish the extent of that obligation for every circumstance of the future. We can, however, define guidelines which will aid in the resolution of such an issue as the instant one. We note, first, that we deal here with a case in which plaintiff suffered a shock which resulted in physical injury and we confine our ruling to that case. In determining, in such a case, whether defendant should reasonably foresee the injury to plaintiff, or, in other terminology, whether defendant owes plaintiff a duty of due care, the courts will take into account such factors as the following: (1) Whether plaintiff was located near the scene of the accident as contrasted with one who was a distance away from it. (2) Whether the shock resulted from a direct emotional impact upon plaintiff from the sensory and contemporaneous observance of the accident, as contrasted with learning of the accident from others after its occurrence. (3) Whether plaintiff and the victim were closely related, as contrasted with an absence of any relationship or the presence of only a distant relationship. The evaluation of these factors will indicate the *degree* of the defendant's foreseeability: obviously defendant is more likely to foresee that a mother who observes an accident affecting her child will suffer harm than to foretell that a stranger witness will do so. Similarly, the degree of foreseeability of the third person's injury is far greater in the case of his contemporaneous observance of the accident than that in which he subsequently learns of it. The defendant is more likely to foresee that shock to the nearby, witnessing mother will cause physical harm than to anticipate that someone distant from the accident will suffer more than a temporary emotional reaction. All these elements, of course, shade into each other; the fixing of obligation, inti-

mately tied into the facts, depends upon each case. In light of these factors the court will determine whether the accident and harm was *reasonably* foreseeable. Such reasonable foreseeability does not turn on whether the particular plaintiff as an individual would have in actuality foreseen the exact accident and loss; it contemplates that courts, on a case-to-case basis, analysing all the circumstances, will decide what the ordinary man under such circumstances should reasonably have foreseen. The courts thus mark out the areas of liability, excluding the remote and unexpected. In the instant case, the presence of all the above factors indicates that plaintiff has alleged a sufficient prima facie case. Surely the negligent driver who causes the death of a young child may reasonably expect that the mother will not be far distant and will upon witnessing the accident suffer emotional trauma. As Dean Prosser has stated: 'when a child is endangered, it is not beyond contemplation that its mother will be somewhere in the vicinity, and will suffer serious shock.' (*Prosser, Torts,* p. 353. See also 2 *Harper & James, The Law of Torts,* p. 1039) We are not now called upon to decide whether, in the absence or reduced weight of some of the above factors, we would conclude that the accident and injury were not reasonably foreseeable and that therefore defendant owed no duty of due care to plaintiff. In future cases the court will draw lines of demarcation upon facts more subtle than the compelling one alleged in the complaint before us."

The leading minority judgment [Burke J., at p. 1333] castigated the majority for embarking on a first excursion into the "fantastic realm of infinite liability," a colourful variant of the familiar "floodgates" argument.

In approaching the question whether the law should, as a matter of policy, define the criterion of liability in negligence for causing psychiatric illness by reference to some test other than that of reasonable foreseeability it is well to remember that we are concerned only with the question of liability of a defendant who is, ex hypothesi, guilty of fault in causing the death, injury or danger which has in turn triggered the psychiatric illness. A policy which is to be relied on to narrow the scope of the negligent tortfeasor's duty must be justified by cogent and readily intelligible considerations, and must be capable of defining the appropriate limits of liability by reference to factors which are not purely arbitrary. A number of policy considerations which have been suggested as satisfying these requirements appear to me, with respect, to be wholly insufficient. I can see no grounds whatever for suggesting that to make the defendant liable for reasonably foreseeable psychiatric illness caused by his negligence would be to impose a crushing burden on him out of proportion to his moral responsibility. However liberally the criterion of reasonable foreseeability is interpreted, both the number of successful claims in this field and the quantum of damages they will attract are likely to be moderate. I cannot accept as relevant the well-known phenomenon that litigation may delay recovery from a psychiatric illness. If this were a valid policy consideration, it would lead to the conclusion that psychiatric illness should be excluded altogether from the heads of damage which the law will recognise. It cannot justify limiting the cases in which damages will be awarded for psychiatric illness by reference to the circumstances of its causation. To attempt to draw a line at the furthest point which any of the decided cases happen to have reached, and to say that it is for the legislature, not the courts, to extend the limits of liability any further, would be, to my mind, an unwarranted abdication of the court's function of developing and adapting principles of the common law to changing conditions, in a particular corner of the common law which exemplifies, par excellence, the important and indeed necessary part which that function has to play." In the end I believe that the policy question depends on weighing against each other two conflicting considerations. On the one hand, if the criterion of liability is to be reasonable foreseeability simpliciter, this must, precisely because questions of causation in psychiatric medicine give rise to difficulty and uncertainty, introduce an element of uncertainty into the law and open the way to a number of arguable claims which a more precisely fixed criterion of liability would exclude. I accept that the elements of uncertainty is an important factor. I believe that the "floodgates" argument, however, is, as it always has been, greatly exaggerated. On the other hand, it seems to me inescapable that any attempt to define the limit of liability by requiring, in addition to reasonable foreseeability, that the plaintiff claiming damages for psychiatric illness should have witnessed the relevant accident, should have been present at or near the place where it happened, should have come upon its aftermath and thus have had some direct perception of it, as opposed to merely learning of it after the event, should be related in some particular degree to the accident victim—to draw a line by reference to any of these criteria must impose a largely arbitrary limit of liability. I accept, of course, the importance of the factors indicated in the guidelines suggested by Tobriner J. in *Dillon* v. *Legg*, 29 A.L.R. 3d 1316 as bearing upon the *degree* of foreseeability of the plaintiff's psychiatric illness. But let me give two examples to illustrate what injustice would be wrought by any such hard and fast lines of policy as have been suggested. First, consider the plaintiff who learned after the event of the relevant accident. Take the case of a mother who knows that her husband and children are staying in a certain hotel. She reads in her morning newspaper that it has been the scene of a disastrous fire. She sees in the paper a photograph of unidentifiable victims trapped on the top floor waving for help from the windows. She learns shortly afterwards that all her family have perished. She suffers an acute psychiatric illness. That her illness in these circumstances was a reasonably foreseeable consequence of the events resulting from the fire is undeniable. Yet, is the law to deny her damages as against a defendant whose negligence was responsible for the fire simply on the ground that an important link in the chain of causation of her psychiatric illness was supplied by her imagination of the agonies of mind and body in which her family died, rather than by direct perception of the event? Secondly, consider the plaintiff who is unrelated to the victims of the relevant accident. If rigidly applied, an exclusion of liability to him would have defeated the plaintiff's claim in *Chadwick* v. *British Railways Board* [1967] 1 W.L.R. 912. The Court of Appeal treated that case as in a special category because Mr. Chadwick was a rescuer. Now, the special duty owed to a rescuer who voluntarily places himself in physical danger to save others is well understood, and is illustrated by *Haynes* v. *Harwood* [1935] 1 K.B. 146, the case of the constable injured in stopping a runaway horse in a crowded street. But in relation to the psychiatric consequences of witnessing such terrible carnage as must have resulted from the Lewisham train disaster, I would find it difficult to distinguish in principle the position of a rescuer, like Mr. Chadwick, from a mere spectator as, for example, an uninjured or only slightly injured passenger in the train, who took no part in the rescue operations but was present at the scene after the accident for some time, perforce observing the rescue operations while he waited for transport to take him home.

My Lords, I have no doubt that this is an area of the law of negligence where we should resist the temptation to try yet once more to freeze the law in a rigid posture which would deny justice to some who, in

the application of the classic principles of negligence derived from *Donoghue* v. *Stevenson* [1932] A.C. 562, ought to succeed, in the interests of certainty, where the very subject matter is uncertain and continuously developing, or in the interests of saving defendants and their insurers from the burden of having sometimes to resist doubtful claims. I find myself in complete agreement with Tobriner J. in *Dillon* v. *Legg*, 29 A.L.R. 3d 1316, 1326 that the defendant's duty must depend on reasonable foreseeability and

"must necessarily be adjudicated only upon a case-by-case basis. We cannot now predetermine defendant's obligation in every situation by a fixed category; no immutable rule can establish the extent of that obligation for every circumstance of the future."

To put the matter in another way, if asked where the thing is to stop, I should answer, in an adaptation of the language of Lord Wright (in *Bourhill* v. *Young* [1943] A.C. 92, 110) and Stephenson L.J. [1981] Q.B. 599, 612, "where in the particular case the good sense of the judge, enlightened by progressive awareness of mental illness, decides."

I regret that my noble and learned friend, Lord Edmund-Davies, who criticises my conclusion that in this area of the law there are no policy considerations sufficient to justify limiting the liability of negligent tortfeasors by reference to some narrower criterion than that of reasonable foreseeability, stops short of indicating his view as to where the limit of liability should be drawn or as to the nature of the policy considerations (other than the "floodgates" argument, which I understand he rejects) which he would invoke to justify such a limit.

My Lords, I would accordingly allow the appeal. . . .

# QUESTIONS

1. In several places there is mention of the danger of opening the "floodgates" to litigation unless some arbitrary decision of policy, rather than of principle, is made. Explain (a) why the concern about opening the floodgates is thought to call for a policy decision, (b) how, as a policy decision, it would be arbitrary, and (c) why a decision of principle would be different from a policy decision, and presumably nonarbitrary.

2. As one of the policy arguments against extending liability, Lord Wilberforce mentions that it "would be unfair to defendants, as imposing damages out of proportion to the negligent conduct complained of." Do you agree with this? If you agree, explain the standard you would use in deciding whether damages are "out of proportion to the negligent conduct." If you disagree, explain why.

3. Lord Wilberforce says, "Whatever is unknown about the mind-body relationship . . . , it is now accepted by medical science that recognisable and severe physical damage to the human body . . . may be caused by the impact, through the senses, of external events on the mind." How might the development of knowledge of this sort extend the range of liability under the already existing principle that one is responsible for the reasonably foreseeable consequences of one's negligent behavior?

## Robert Bork
## THE ORIGINAL UNDERSTANDING*

What was once the dominant view of constitutional law—that a judge is to apply the Constitution according to the principles intended by those who ratified the document—is now very much out of favor among the theorists of the field. In the legal academies in particular, the philosophy of original understanding is usually viewed as thoroughly passé, probably reactionary, and certainly—the most dreaded indictment of all—"outside the mainstream." That fact says more about the lamentable state of the intellectual life of the law, however, than it does about the merits of the theory.

In truth, only the approach of original understanding meets the criteria that any theory of constitutional adjudication must meet in order to possess democratic legitimacy.

Only that approach is consonant with the design of the American Republic.

### THE CONSTITUTION AS LAW: NEUTRAL PRINCIPLES

When we speak of "law," we ordinarily refer to a rule that we have no right to change except through prescribed procedures. That statement assumes that the rule has a meaning independent of our own desires. Otherwise there would be no need to agree on procedures for changing the rule. Statutes, we agree, may be changed by amendment or repeal. The Constitution may be changed by amendment pursuant to the procedures set out in article V. It is a necessary implication

*Reprinted with permission of The Free Press, a Division of Macmillan, Inc. from *The Tempting of America: The Political Seduction of the Law* by Robert H. Bork. Copyright © 1990 by Robert H. Bork.

of the prescribed procedures that neither statute nor Constitution should be changed by judges. Though that has been done often enough, it is in no sense proper.

What is the meaning of a rule that judges should not change? It is the meaning understood at the time of the law's enactment. Though I have written of the understanding of the ratifiers of the Constitution, since they enacted it and made it law, that is actually a shorthand formulation, because what the ratifiers understood themselves to be enacting must be taken to be what the public of that time would have understood the words to mean. It is important to be clear about this. The search is not for a subjective intention. If someone found a letter from George Washington to Martha telling her that what he meant by the power to lay taxes was not what other people meant, that would not change our reading of the Constitution in the slightest. Nor would the subjective intentions of all the members of a ratifying convention alter anything. When lawmakers use words, the law that results is what those words ordinarily mean. If Congress enacted a statute outlawing the sale of automatic rifles and did so in the Senate by a vote of 51 to 49, no court would overturn a conviction because two senators in the majority testified that they really had intended only to prohibit the *use* of such rifles. They said "sale" and "sale" it is. Thus, the common objection to the philosophy of original understanding—that Madison kept his notes of the convention at Philadelphia secret for many years—is off the mark. He knew that what mattered was public understanding, not subjective intentions. Madison himself said that what mattered was the intention of the ratifying conventions. His notes of the discussions at Philadelphia are merely evidence of what informed public men of the time thought the words of the Constitution meant. Since many of them were also delegates to the various state ratifying conventions, their understanding informed the debates in those conventions. As Professor Henry Monaghan of Columbia has said, what counts is what the public understood.[1] Law is a public act. Secret reservations or intentions count for nothing. All that counts is how the words used in the Constitution would have been understood at the time. The original understanding is thus manifested in the words used and in secondary materials, such as debates at the conventions, public discussions, newspaper articles, dictionaries in use at the time, and the like. Almost no one would deny this; in fact almost everyone would find it obvious to the point of thinking it fatuous to state the matter—except in the case of the Constitution. Why our legal theorists make an exception for the Constitution is worth exploring.

The search for the intent of the lawmaker is the everyday procedure of lawyers and judges when they must apply a statute, a contract, a will, or the opinion of a court. To be sure, there are differences in the way we deal with different legal materials, which was the point of John Marshall's observation in *McCulloch* v. *Maryland* that "we must never forget, that it is *a constitution* we are expounding."[2] By that he meant that narrow, legalistic reasoning was not to be applied to the document's broad provisions, a document that could not, by its nature and uses, "partake of the prolixity of a legal code." But he also wrote there that it was intended that a provision receive a "fair and just interpretation," which means that the

---

[1] Monaghan, *Stare Decisis and Constitutional Adjudication*, 88 Colum. L. Rev. 723, 725–27 (1988) ("The relevant inquiry must focus on the *public* understanding of the language when the Constitution was developed. Hamilton put it well: 'whatever may have been the intention of the framers of a constitution, or of a law, that intention is to be sought for in the instrument itself, according to the usual & established rules of construction.' " [emphasis in original: footnotes omitted]).

[2] 17 U.S. (4 Wheat.) 316, 407 (1819).

judge is to interpret what is in the text and not something else. And, it will be recalled, in *Marbury* v. *Madison* Marshall placed the judge's power to invalidate a legislative act upon the fact that the judge was applying the words of a written document.[3] Thus, questions of breadth of approach or of room for play in the joints aside, lawyers and judges should seek in the Constitution what they seek in other legal texts: the original meaning of the words.[4]

We would at once criticize a judge who undertook to rewrite a statute or the opinion of a superior court, and yet such judicial rewriting is often correctable by the legislature or the superior court, as the Supreme Court's rewriting of the Constitution is not. At first glance, it seems distinctly peculiar that there should be a great many academic theorists who explicitly defend departures from the understanding of those who ratified the Constitution while agreeing, at least in principle, that there should be no departure from the understanding of those who enacted a statute or joined a majority opinion. A moment's reflection suggests, however, that Supreme Court departures from the original meaning of the Constitution are advocated *precisely because* those departures are not correctable democratically. The point of the academic exercise is to be free of democracy in order to impose the values of an elite upon the rest of us.

If the Constitution is law, then presumably its meaning, like that of all other law, is the meaning the lawmakers were under-stood to have intended. If the Constitution is law, then presumably, like all other law, the meaning the lawmakers intended is as binding upon judges as it is upon legislatures and executives. There is no other sense in which the Constitution can be what article VI proclaims it to be: "Law."[5] It is here that the concept of neutral principles, which Wechsler said were essential if the Supreme Court was not to be a naked power organ, comes into play. Wechsler, it will be recalled, in expressing his difficulties with the decision in *Brown* v. *Board of Education*,[6] said that courts must choose principles which they are willing to apply neutrally, apply, that is, to all cases that may fairly be said to fall within them.[7] This is a safeguard against political judging. No judge will say openly that any particular group or political position is always entitled to win. He will announce a principle that decides the case at hand, and Wechsler had no difficulty with that if the judge is willing to apply the same principle in the next case, even if it means that a group favored by the first decision is disfavored by the second. That was precisely what Arthur M. Schlesinger, Jr., said that the Black–Douglas wing of the Court was unwilling to do. Instead, it pretended to enunciate principles but in fact warped them to vote for interest groups.[8]

The Court cannot, however, avoid being a naked power organ merely by practicing the neutral application of legal principle. The Court can act as a legal rather than a political institution only if it is neutral as well in

---

[3] 5 U.S. (1 Cranch) 137, 177–79 (1803).

[4] *See also* Scalia. *Originalism: The Lesser Evil*, 57 U. Cin. L. Rev. 849, 853 (1989) (It is a canard to interpret Marshall's observation in *McCulloch* as implying that our interpretation of the Constitution must change from age to age. "The real implication was quite the opposite: Marshall was saying that the Constitution had to be interpreted generously because the powers conferred upon Congress under it had to be broad enough to serve not only the needs of the federal government originally discerned but also the needs that might arise in the future. If constitutional interpretation could be adjusted as changing circumstances required, a broad initial interpretation would have been unnecessary.").

[5] U.S. CONST. art. VI.

[6] 347 U.S. 483 (1954).

[7] *See* Chapter 3 [not reprinted here].

[8] Schlesinger, *The Supreme Court: 1947*, FORTUNE, vol. 35, Jan. 1947, at 73, 201–02.

the way it derives and defines the principles it applies. If the Court is free to choose any principle that it will subsequently apply neutrally, it is free to legislate just as a political body would. Its purported resolution of the Madisonian dilemma is spurious, because there is no way of saying that the correct spheres of freedom have been assigned to the majority and the minority. Similarly, if the Court is free to define the scope of the principle as it sees fit, it may, by manipulating the principle's breadth, make things come out the way it wishes on grounds that are not contained in the principle it purports to apply. Once again, the Madisonian dilemma is not resolved correctly but only according to the personal preferences of the Justices. The philosophy of original understanding is capable of supplying neutrality in all three respects—in deriving, defining, and applying principle.

## NEUTRALITY IN THE DERIVATION OF PRINCIPLE

When a judge finds his principle in the Constitution as originally understood, the problem of the neutral derivation of principle is solved. The judge accepts the ratifiers' definition of the appropriate ranges of majority and minority freedom. The Madisonian dilemma is resolved in the way that the founders resolved it, and the judge accepts the fact that he is bound by that resolution as law. He need not, and must not, make unguided value judgments of his own.

This means, of course, that a judge, no matter on what court he sits, may never create new constitutional rights or destroy old ones. Any time he does so, he violates not only the limits to his own authority but, and for that reason, also violates the rights of the legislature and the people. To put the matter another way, suppose that the United States, like the United Kingdom, had no written constitution and, therefore, no law to apply to strike down acts of the legislature. The

⁹U.S. CONST. amend. 1.

U.S. judge, like the U.K. judge, could never properly invalidate a statute or an official action as unconstitutional. The very concept of unconstitutionality would be meaningless. The absence of a constitutional provision means the absence of a power of judicial review. But when a U.S. judge is given a set of constitutional provisions, then, as to anything not covered by those provisions, he is in the same position as the U.K. judge. He has no law to apply and is, quite properly, powerless. In the absence of law, a judge is a functionary without a function.

This is not to say, of course, that majorities may not add to minority freedoms by statute, and indeed a great deal of the legislation that comes out of Congress and the state legislatures does just that. The only thing majorities may not do is invade the liberties the Constitution specifies. In this sense, the concept of original understanding builds in a bias toward individual freedom. Thus, the Supreme Court properly decided in *Brown* that the equal protection clause of the fourteenth amendment forbids racial segregation or discrimination by any arm of government, but, because the Constitution addresses only governmental action, the Court could not address the question of private discrimination. Congress did address it in the Civil Rights Acts of 1964 and in subsequent legislation, enlarging minority freedoms beyond those mandated by the Constitution.

## NEUTRALITY IN THE DEFINITION OF PRINCIPLE

The neutral definition of the principle derived from the historic Constitution is also crucial. The Constitution states its principles in majestic generalities that we know cannot be taken as sweepingly as the words alone might suggest. The first amendment states that "Congress shall make no law . . . abridging the freedom of speech,"⁹ but no one has ever supposed that Congress could not make some speech unlawful or that it could not make all speech illegal in certain places, at certain times, and under certain circumstances. Justices Hugo Black and William O. Douglas often claimed to be first amendment absolutists, but even they would permit the punishment of speech if they thought it too closely "brigaded" with illegal action. From the beginning of the Republic to this day, no one has ever thought Congress could not forbid the preaching of mutiny on a ship of the Navy or disruptive proclamations in a courtroom.

But the question of neutral definition remains and is obviously closely related to neutral application. Neutral application can be gained by defining a principle so narrowly that it will fit only a few cases. Thus, to return to *Griswold*,[10] we can make neutral application possible by stating the principle to be that government may not prohibit the use of contraceptives by married couples. But that tactic raises doubts as to the definition of the principle. Why does it extend only to married couples? Why, out of all forms of sexual behavior, only to the use of contraceptives? Why, out of all forms of behavior in the home, only to sex? There may be answers, but if there are, they must be given.

Thus, once a principle is derived from the Constitution, its breadth or the level of generality at which it is stated becomes of crucial importance. The judge must not state the principle with so much generality that he transforms it. The difficulty in finding the proper level of generality has led some critics to claim that the application of the original understanding is actually impossible. That sounds fairly abstract, but an example will make clear both the point and the answer to it.

In speaking of my view that the fourteenth amendment's equal protection clause requires black equality, Dean Paul Brest said:

The very adoption of such a principle, however, demands an arbitrary choice among levels of abstraction. Just what *is* "the general principle of equality that applies to all cases"? Is it the "core idea of *black* equality" that Bork finds in the original understanding (in which case Alan Bakke [a white who sued because a state medical school gave preference in admissions to other races] did not state a constitutionally cognizable claim), or a broader principle of "*racial* equality" (so that, depending on the precise content of the principle, Bakke might have a case after all), or is it a still broader principle of equality that encompasses discrimination on the basis of gender (or sexual orientation) as well? . . .

. . . The fact is that all adjudication requires making choices among the levels of generality on which to articulate principles, and all such choices are inherently non-neutral. No form of constitutional decisionmaking can be salvaged if its legitimacy depends on satisfying Bork's requirements that principles be "neutrally derived, defined and applied."[11]

If Brest's point about the impossibility of choosing the level of generality upon neutral criteria is correct, we must either resign ourselves to a Court that is a "naked power organ" or require the Court to stop making "constitutional" decisions. But Brest's argument seems to me wrong, and I think a judge committed to original understanding can do what Brest says he cannot. We may use Brest's example to demonstrate the point.

The role of a judge committed to the philosophy of original understanding is not to "*choose*" a level of abstraction." Rather, it is to find the meaning of a text—a process which includes finding its degree of generality, which is part of its meaning—and to apply

---

[10]*Griswold* v. *Connecticut*, 381 U.S. 479 (1965).

[11]Brest, *The Fundamental Rights Controversy: The Essential Contradictions of Normative Constitutional Scholarship*, 90 Yale L.J. 1063, 1091–92 (1981) (footnotes omitted).

that text to a particular situation, which may be difficult if its meaning is unclear. With many if not most textual provisions, the level of generality which is part of their meaning is readily apparent. The problem is most difficult when dealing with the broadly stated provisions of the Bill of Rights. It is to the latter that we confine discussion here. In dealing with such provisions, a judge should state the principle at the level of generality that the text and historical evidence warrant. The equal protection clause was adopted in order to protect the freed slaves, but its language, being general, applies to all persons. As we might expect, and as Justice Miller found in the *Slaughter-House Cases*,[12] the evidence of what the drafters, the Congress that proposed the clause, and the ratifiers understood themselves to be requiring is clearest in the case of race relations. It is there that we may begin in looking for evidence of the level of generality intended. Without meaning to suggest what the historical evidence in fact shows, let us assume we find that the ratifiers intended to guarantee that blacks should be treated by law no worse than whites, but that it is unclear whether whites were intended to be protected from discrimination in favor of blacks. On such evidence, the judge should protect only blacks from discrimination, and Alan Bakke would not have had a case. The reason is that the next higher level of generality above black equality, which is racial equality, is not shown to be a constitutional principle, and therefore there is nothing to be set against a current legislative majority's decision to favor blacks. Democratic choice must be accepted by the judge where the Constitution is silent. The test is the reasonableness of the distinction, and the level of generality chosen by the ratifiers determines that. If the evidence shows the ratifiers understood racial equality to have been the principle they were enacting, Bakke would have a case. In cases concerning gender and sexual orientation, however,

interpretation is not additionally assisted by the presence of known intentions. The general language of the clause, however, continues to subject such cases to the test of whether statutory distinctions are reasonable. Sexual differences obviously make some distinctions reasonable while others have no apparent basis. That has, in fact, been the rationale on which the law has developed. Society's treatment of sexual orientation is based upon moral perceptions, so that it would be difficult to say that the various moral balances struck are unreasonable.

Original understanding avoids the problem of the level of generality in equal protection analysis by finding the level of generality that interpretation of the words, structure, and history of the Constitution fairly supports. This is a solution generally applicable to all constitutional provisions as to which historical evidence exists. There is, therefore, a form of constitutional decision-making that satisfies the requirement that principles be neutrally defined.

To define a legal proposition or principle involves simultaneously stating its contents and its limits. When you state what *is* contained within the clause of the first amendment guarantee of the free exercise of religion, you necessarily state what is *not* contained within that clause. Because the first amendment guarantees freedom of speech, judges are required reasonably to define what is speech and what is its freedom. In doing these things, the judge necessarily decides that some things are not speech or are not abridgments of its freedom. As to things outside the proposition, the speech clause gives the judge no power to do anything. Because it is only the content of a clause that gives the judge any authority, where that content does not apply, he is without authority and is, for that reason, forbidden to act. The elected legislator or executive may act where not forbidden; his delegation of power from the people

---

[12]*Slaughter-House Cases*, 83 U.S. (16 Wall.) 36 (1873).

through an election is his authority. But the judge may act only where authorized and must do so in those cases; his commission is to apply the law. If a judge should say that the freedom of speech clause authorizes him to abolish the death penalty, we would unanimously say that he had exceeded the bounds of his lawful authority. The judge's performance is not improved if, following *Griswold* v. *Connecticut*, he adds four more inapplicable provisions to his list of claimed authorizations and claims that five inapplicable provisions give him the authority one alone did not. Where the law stops, the legislator may move on to create more; but where the law stops, the judge must stop.

## NEUTRALITY IN THE APPLICATION OF PRINCIPLE

The neutral or nonpolitical application of principle has been discussed in connection with Wechsler's discussion of the *Brown* decision.[13] It is a requirement, like the others, addressed to the judge's integrity. Having derived and defined the principle to be applied, he must apply it consistently and without regard to his sympathy or lack of sympathy with the parties before him. This does not mean that the judge will never change the principle he has derived and defined. Anybody who has dealt extensively with law knows that a new case may seem to fall within a principle as stated and yet not fall within the rationale underlying it. As new cases present new patterns, the principle will often be restated and redefined. There is nothing wrong with that; it is, in fact, highly desirable. But the judge must be clarifying his own reasoning and verbal formulations and not trimming to arrive at results desired on grounds extraneous to the Constitution. This requires a fair degree of sophistication and self-consciousness on the part of the judge. The only external discipline to which the judge is subject is the scrutiny of professional observers who will be able to tell over a period of time whether he is displaying intellectual integrity.

An example of the nonneutral application of principle in the service of a good cause is provided by *Shelley* v. *Kraemer*,[14] a 1948 decision of the Supreme Court striking down racially restrictive covenants. Property owners had signed agreements limiting occupancy to white persons. Despite the covenants, some whites sold to blacks, owners of other properties sued to enforce the covenants, and the state courts, applying common law rules, enjoined the blacks from taking possession.

The problem for the Supreme Court was that the Constitution restricts only action by the state, not actions by private individuals. There was no doubt that the racial restrictions would have violated the equal protection clause of the fourteenth amendment had they been enacted by the state legislature. But here state courts were not the source of the racial discrimination, they merely enforced private agreements according to the terms of those agreements. The Supreme Court nonetheless held that "there has been state action in these cases in the full and complete sense of the phrase."[15]

In a 1971 article in the Indiana Law Journal,[16] I pointed out the difficulty with *Shelley*, for which I was severely taken to task in my Senate hearings and elsewhere. That criticism consisted entirely of the observation that I had disapproved of a case that favored blacks and was therefore hostile to civil rights. Both the fact that many commentators had criticised *Shelley* and my

[13] *See* Chapter 3 [not reprinted here].
[14] 334 U.S. 1 (1948).
[15] *Id.* at 19.
[16] Bork, *Neutral Principles and Some First Amendment Problems*, 47 Ind. L.J. 1 (1971).

approval of other cases that favored blacks were ignored. The implicit position taken by some senators and activist groups was that a judge must always rule for racial minorities. That is a position I reject, because it requires political judging. Members of racial minorities should win when the law, honestly applied, supports their claim and not when it does not. *Shelley* v. *Kraemer* rested upon a theory that cannot be honestly applied, and, in the event, has not been applied at all.

The Supreme Court in *Shelley* said that the decision of a state court under common law rules constitutes the action of the state and therefore is to be tested by the requirements of the Constitution. The racial discrimination involved was not the policy of the state courts but the desire of private individuals, which the courts enforced pursuant to normal, and neutral, rules of enforcing private agreements. The impossibility of applying the state action ruling of *Shelley* in a neutral fashion may easily be seen. Suppose that a guest in a house becomes abusive about political matters and is ejected by his host. The guest sues the host and the state courts hold that the property owner has a right to remove people from his home. The guest then appeals to the Supreme Court, pointing out that the state, through its courts, has upheld an abridgment of his right of free speech guaranteed by the first amendment and made applicable to the states by the fourteenth. The guest cites *Shelley* to show that this is state action and therefore the case is constitutional. There is no way of escaping that conclusion except by importing into the rule of *Shelley* qualifications and limits that themselves have no foundation in the Constitution or the case. Whichever way it decided, the Supreme Court would have to treat the case as one under the first amendment and displace state law with constitutional law.

It is necessary to remember that absolutely anything, from the significant to the frivolous, can be made the subject of a complaint filed in a state court. Whether the state court dismisses the suit out of hand or proceeds to the merits of the issue does not matter; any decision is, according to *Shelley*, state action and hence subject to constitutional scrutiny. That means that all private conduct may be made state conduct with the result that the Supreme Court will make the rules for all allowable or forbidden behavior by private individuals. That is not only a complete perversion of the Constitution of the United States, it makes the Supreme Court the supreme legislature. The result of the neutral application of the principle of *Shelley* v. *Kraemer* would be both revolutionary and preposterous. Clearly, it would not be applied neutrally, and it has not been, which means that it fails Wechsler's test.

*Shelley* was a political decision. As such, it should have been made by a legislature. It is clear that Congress had the power to outlaw racially restrictive covenants. Subsequently, in fact, in a case in which as Solicitor General I filed a brief supporting the result reached, the Supreme Court held that one of the post–Civil War civil rights acts did outlaw racial discrimination in private contracts.[17] That fact does not, however, make *Shelley* a proper constitutional decision, however much its result may be admired on moral grounds.

Judicial adherence to neutral principles, in the three senses just described, is a crucial element of the American doctrine of the separation of powers. Since the Court's invocation of the Constitution is final, the judiciary is the only branch of the government not subject to the ordinary checks and balances that pit the powers of the other branches against each other. If it is to be faithful to the constitutional design, therefore, the Court must check itself.

---

[17] *Runyon* v. *McCrary*, 427 U.S. 160 (1976).

## THE ORIGINAL UNDERSTANDING
## OF ORIGINAL UNDERSTANDING

The judicial role just described corresponds to the original understanding of the place of courts in our republican form of government. The political arrangements of that form of government are complex, its balances of power continually shifting, but one thing our constitutional orthodoxy does not countenance is a judiciary that decides for itself when and how it will make national policy, when and to what extent it will displace executives and legislators as our governors. The orthodoxy of our civil religion, which the Constitution has aptly been called, holds that we govern ourselves democratically, except on those occasions, few in number though crucially important, when the Constitution places a topic beyond the reach of majorities.

The structure of government the Founders of this nation intended most certainly did not give courts a political role. The debates surrounding the Constitution focused much more upon theories of representation than upon the judiciary, which was thought to be a comparatively insignificant branch. There were, however, repeated attempts at the Constitutional Convention in Philadelphia to give judges a policymaking role. The plan of the Virginia delegation, which, amended and expanded, ultimately became the Constitution of the United States, included a proposal that the new national legislature be controlled by placing a veto power in a Council of Revision consisting of the executive and "a convenient number of the National Judiciary."[18] That proposal was raised four times and defeated each time. Among the reasons, as reported in James Madison's notes, was the objection raised by

Elbridge Gerry of Massachusetts that it "was quite foreign from the nature of ye. office to make them judges of policy of public measures."[19] Rufus King, also of Massachusetts, added that judges should "expound the law as it should come before them, free from the bias of having participated in its formation."[20] Judges who create new constitutional rights are judges of the policy of public measures and are biased by having participated in the policy's formation.

The intention of the Convention was accurately described by Alexander Hamilton in *The Federalist* No. 78: "[T]he judiciary, from the nature of its functions, will always be the least dangerous to the political rights of the Constitution; because it will be least in a capacity to annoy or injure them."[21] The political rights of the Constitution are, of course, the rights that make up democratic self-government. Hamilton obviously did not anticipate a judiciary that would injure those rights by adding to the list of subjects that were removed from democratic control. Thus, he could say that the courts were "beyond comparison the weakest of the three departments of power," and he appended a quotation from the "celebrated Montesquieu": "Of the three powers above mentioned [the others being the legislative and the executive], the JUDICIARY is next to nothing." This is true because judges were, as King said, merely to "expound" law made by others.

Even if evidence of what the founders thought about the judicial role were unavailable, we would have to adopt the rule that judges must stick to the original meaning of the Constitution's words. If that method of interpretation were not common in the law, if James Madison and Justice Joseph Story had never endorsed it, if Chief Justice John

---

[18]P. Bator, P. Mishkin, D. Meltzer & D. Shapiro, *Hart and Wechsler's The Federal Courts and the Federal System* 7 (3d ed. 1988) quoting 1 Farrand, *The Records of the Federal Convention* 21 (May 29) (1911).

[19]*Ibid., quoting* 1 Farrand. *The Records of the Federal Convention* 97–98, 109 (June 4) (1911).

[20]*Ibid.*

[21]*The Federalist* No. 78, at 465–66 (A. Hamilton) (C. Rossiter ed. 1961).

Marshall had rejected it, we would have to invent the approach of original understanding in order to save the constitutional design. No other method of constitutional adjudication can confine courts to a defined sphere of authority and thus prevent them from assuming powers whose exercise alters, perhaps radically, the design of the American Republic. The philosophy of original understanding is thus a necessary inference from the structure of government apparent on the face of the Constitution.

## THE CLAIMS OF PRECEDENT AND THE ORIGINAL UNDERSTANDING

The question of precedent is particularly important because, as Professor Henry Monaghan of Columbia University law school notes, "much of the existing constitutional order is at variance with what we know of the original understanding."[22] Some commentators have argued from this obvious truth that the approach of original understanding is impossible or fatally compromised, since they suppose it would require the Court to declare paper money unconstitutional and overturn the centralization accomplished by abandoning restrictions on congressional powers during the New Deal.[23] There is in these instances a great gap between the original understanding of the constitutional structure and where the nation stands now. But the conclusion does not follow. To suppose that it does is to confuse the descriptive with the normative. To say that prior courts have allowed, or initiated, deformations of the Constitution is not enough

to create a warrant for present and future courts to do the same thing.

All serious constitutional theory centers upon the duties of judges, and that comes down to the question: What should the judge decide in the case now before him? Obviously, an originalist judge should not deform the Constitution further. Just as obviously, he should not attempt to undo all mistakes made in the past. Whatever might have been the proper ruling shortly after the Civil War, if a judge today were to decide that paper money is unconstitutional, we would think he ought to be accompanied not by a law clerk but by a guardian. At the center of the philosophy of original understanding, therefore, must stand some idea of when the judge is bound by prior decisions and when he is not.[24]

Many people have the notion that following precedent (sometimes called the doctrine of *stare decisis*) is an ironclad rule. It is not, and never has been.[25] As Justice Felix Frankfurter once explained, "*stare decisis* is a principle of policy and not a mechanical formula of adherence to the latest decision, however recent and questionable, when such adherence involves collision with a prior doctrine more embracing in its scope, intrinsically sounder, and verified by experience."[26] Thus, in Justice Powell's words, "[i]t is . . . not only [the Court's] prerogative but also [its] duty to re-examine a precedent where its reasoning or understanding of the Constitution is fairly called into question."[27] The Supreme Court frequently overrules its own precedent. In 1870, *Hepburn* v. *Griswold*[28] held it unconstitutional to make paper money legal tender for antecedent debts, but

---

[22]Monaghan, *supra* note 1, at 727.

[23]*Id.; see also* Bittker, *The Bicentennial of the Jurisprudence of Original Intent: The Recent Past*, 77 Calif. L. Rev. 235 (1989).

[24]*See* Scalia, *supra* note 4, at 861–65.

[25]Monaghan, *supra* note 1, at 741–43; Maltz, *Some Thoughts on the Death of Stare Decisis in Constitutional Law*, 1980 Wis. L. Rev. 467, 494–96 ("it seems fair to say that if a majority of the Warren or Burger Court has considered a case wrongly decided, no constitutional precedent—new or old—has been safe.").

[26]*Helvering* v. *Hallock*, 309 U.S. 106, 119 (1940).

[27]*Mitchell* v. *W. T. Grant Co.*, 416 U.S. 600, 627–28 (1974) (Powell, J., concurring).

[28]75 U.S. (8 Wall.) 603 (1870).

in 1871 *Hepburn* was overruled in the *Legal Tender Cases*.[29] The New Deal Court swiftly began overruling or ignoring precedent, some of it of fifty years' standing, and often did so by five-to-four votes. Indeed, the Court has overruled important precedent in cases where nobody asked it to do so. *Swift* v. *Tyson* held in 1842 that federal courts could apply a "general law" independent of the state law that would apply had the suit been brought in a state court sitting nearby.[30] The rule lasted for ninety-six years until *Erie Railroad Co.* v. *Tompkins* did away with it in 1938.[31] *Plessy* v. *Ferguson*,[32] and the rule of separate-but-equal in racial matters, lasted fifty-eight years before it was dispatched in *Brown* v. *Board of Education*.[33] In a period of sixteen years the Court took three different positions with respect to the constitutionality of federal power to impose wage and price regulations on states and localities as employers.[34] Indeed, Justice Blackmun explained recently in the last of these decisions that prior cases, even of fairly recent vintage, should be reconsidered if they "disserve[] principles of democratic self-governance."[35] Every year the Court overrules a number of its own precedents. As the example given show, both recent and ancient precedents are vulnerable.

The practice of overruling precedent is particularly common in constitutional law, the rationale being that it is extremely difficult for an incorrect constitutional ruling to be corrected through the amendment process. Almost all Justices have agreed with

Felix Frankfurter's observation that "the ultimate touchstone of constitutionality is the Constitution itself and not what we have said about it."[36] But that, of course, is only a partial truth. It is clear, in the first place, that Frankfurter was talking about the Supreme Court's obligations with respect to its own prior decisions. Lower courts are not free to ignore what the Supreme Court has said about the Constitution, for that would introduce chaos into the legal system as courts of appeal refused to follow Supreme Court rulings and district courts disobeyed their appellate courts' orders. Secondly, what "the Constitution itself" says may, as in the case of paper money, be irretrievable, not simply because of "what [the Justices] have said about it," but because of what the nation has done or become on the strength of what the Court said.

It is arguable that the text of the Constitution counsels some ambivalence about precedent. Article VI states: "This Constitution, and the Laws of the United States which shall be made in Pursuance thereof" are to be "the supreme Law of the Land."[37] That could be taken to mean that recourse is continually to be had to the text of the Constitution and statutes without regard to prior judicial decisions since the latter are not given the status of supreme law. But article III vests the "judicial Power" in the Supreme Court and lower federal courts.[38] At the time of the ratification, judicial power was known to be to some degree confined by an obligation to respect precedent. Whatever may be made of

[29]79 U.S. (12 Wall.) 457 (1871).

[30]41 U.S. (16 Pet.) 1 (1842).

[31]304 U.S. 64 (1938).

[32]163 U.S. 537 (1896).

[33]347 U.S. 483 (1954).

[34]Compare *Maryland* v. *Wirtz*, 392 U.S. 183 (1968); *National League of Cities* v. *Usery*, 426 U.S. 833 (1976); *Garcia* v. *San Antonio Metropolitan Transit Authority*, 469 U.S. 528 (1985).

[35]469 U.S. 528, 547 (1985).

[36]*Graves* v. *New York*, 306 U.S. 466, 491–92 (1939) (Frankfurter, J., concurring).

[37]U.S. CONST. art. VI, cl. 2.

[38]U.S. CONST. art. III, § 1.

that, it has been commonly understood that a judge looking at an issue for the second time is, or should be, less free than one who looks at it for the first time. In constitutional law, as in all law, there is great virtue in stability. Governments need to know their powers, and citizens need to know their rights; expectations about either should not lightly be upset.

The law currently has no very firm theory of when precedent should be followed and when it may be ignored or overruled. It is an important subject nonetheless, and it is particularly so to a judge who abides by the original understanding, because, as Monaghan said, so much of our constitutional order today does not conform to the original design of the Constitution. If we do not possess anything worthy of being called a theory of precedent, it is possible at least to suggest some of the factors that should be considered when facing a question of following or overruling a prior decision.

No question arises, of course, unless the judge concludes that the prior constitutional decision, which is urged as controlling his present decision, was wrong. In making that determination, particular respect is due to precedents set by courts within a few decades of a provision's ratification since the judges of that time presumably had a superior knowledge of the original meaning of the Constitution. Similarly, precedents that reflect a good-faith attempt to discern the original understanding deserve far more respect than those that do not. Here, there are not only the claims of stability and continuity in the law, but respect for the knowledge and intelligence of those who have gone before. Today's judge should reflect that if the prior court has been wrong, he too may fall into error.

But if the judge concludes that a prior decision was wrong, he faces additional considerations. The previous decision on the subject may be clearly incorrect but nevertheless have become so embedded in the life of the nation, so accepted by the society, so

fundamental to the private and public expectations of individuals and institutions, that the result should not be changed now. This is a judgment addressed to the prudence of a court, but it is not the less valid for that. Judging is not mechanical. Many rules are framed according to predictions of their likely effects, and it is entirely proper for a decision to overrule or not to overrule to be affected by a prediction of the effects likely to flow from that. Thus, it is too late to overrule not only the decision legalizing paper money but also those decisions validating certain New Deal and Great Society programs pursuant to the congressional powers over commerce, taxation, and spending. To overturn these would be to overturn most of modern government and plunge us into chaos. No judge would dream of doing it. It was never too late to overrule the line of cases represented by *Lochner*, because they were unjustifiable restrictions on governmental power, and allowing additional regulation of economic matters did not produce any great disruption of institutional arrangements. Similarly, it will probably never be too late to overrule the right of privacy cases, including *Roe* v. *Wade*, because they remain unaccepted and unacceptable to large segments of the body politic, and judicial regulation could at once be replaced by restored legislative regulation of the subject.

To say that a decision is so thoroughly embedded in our national life that it should not be overruled, even though clearly wrong, is not necessarily to say that its principle should be followed in the future. Thus, the expansion of Congress's commerce, taxing, and spending powers has reached a point where it is not possible to state that, as a matter of articulated doctrine, there are any limits left. That does not mean, however, that the Court must necessarily repeat its mistake as congressional legislation attempts to reach new subject areas. Cases now on the books would seem to mean that Congress could, for example, displace state law on such subjects as marriage and divorce, thus ending such federalism as remains. But the Court could refuse to extend the commerce power so far without overruling its prior decisions, thus leaving existing legislation in place but not giving generative power to the faulty principle by which that legislation was originally upheld. It will be said that this is a lawless approach, but that is not at all clear. The past decisions are beyond reach, but there remains a constitutional principle of federalism that should be regarded as law more profound than the implications of the past decisions. They cannot be overruled, but they can be confined to the subject areas they concern. Similarly, there may be no real point in overturning the decision in *Griswold* v. *Connecticut*. It was important in its immediate consequences since no jurisdiction wants to enforce a law against the use of contraceptives by married couples. But that does not mean that *Roe* v. *Wade* should not be overruled or that the spurious right of privacy that *Griswold* created should ever be used to invalidate a statute again. *Griswold* has had generative power, spawning a series of wrong decisions, and will certainly bring a series of new and unjustifiable claims before the federal courts. But should it become apparent that the Court will not apply it again, the stream of claims will dwindle and ultimately dry up. A case like *Shelley* v. *Kraemer* has generated no subsequent decisions and is most unlikely to. The Supreme Court has refused to follow its rationale, and there would be no point in overruling the decision. There are times when we cannot recover the transgressions of the past, when the best we can do is say to the Court, "Go and sin no more."[39]

Finally, it should be said that those who adhere to a philosophy of original understanding are more likely to respect precedent than those who do not. As Justice Scalia has said, if revisionists can ignore "the most solemnly and democratically adopted text of the Constitution and its Amendments . . . on the basis of current values, what possible basis could there be for enforced adherence to a legal decision of the Supreme Court?"[40] Indeed, it is apparent from our recent history that the Justices most inclined to rewrite the Constitution have the least patience with precedent that stands in their way. If you do not care about stability, if today's result is all-important, there is no occasion to respect either the constitutional text or the decisions of your predecessors.

The interpretation of the Constitution according to the original understanding, then, is the only method that can preserve the Constitution, the separation of powers, and the liberties of the people. Only that approach can lead to what Felix Frankfurter called the "fulfillment of one of the greatest duties of a judge, the duty not to enlarge his authority. That the Court is not the maker of policy but is concerned solely with questions of ultimate power, is a tenet to which all Justices have subscribed. But the extent to which they have translated faith into works probably marks the deepest cleavage among the men who have sat on the Supreme Bench. . . . The conception of significant achievement on the Supreme Court has been too much identified with largeness of utterance, and too little governed by inquiry into the extent to which judges have fulfilled their professed role in the American constitutional system."[41]

[39]*See* R. Berger, *Death Penalties* 82–83 n. 29 (1982) (Berger makes this statement while referring to a Supreme Court decision that in my judgment is unquestionably correct. His misapplication of the biblical command in this context, however, does not detract from his general point about *stare decisis*—that past errors in particular cases should not be expanded and elaborated simply because they cannot be undone).

[40]Scalia, *supra* note 4, at 861.

[41]F. Frankfurter, *The Commerce Clause* 80–81 (1937).

Without adherence to the original understanding, even the actual Bill of Rights could be pared or eliminated. It is asserted nonetheless, and sometimes on high authority, that the judicial philosophy of original understanding is fatally defective in any number of respects. If that were so, if the Constitution cannot be law that binds judges, there would remain only one democratically legitimate solution: judicial supremacy, the power of courts to invalidate statutes and executive actions in the name of the Constitution, would have to be abandoned. For the choice would then be either rule by judges according to their own desires or rule by the people according to theirs. Under our form of government, under the entire history of the American people, the choice between an authoritarian judicial oligarchy and a representative democracy can have only one outcome. But this is a false statement of alternatives, for judicial interpretation of the Constitution according to its original understanding is entirely possible. When that course is followed, judges are not a dictatorial oligarchy but the guardians of our liberties. I turn next to the objections that have been raised to this conclusion.

## QUESTIONS

1. Recall Bork's distinction between "public understanding" and "subjective intention" as to the meaning of the Constitution's words and his claim that it is the former, not the latter, that counts. The Fourteenth Amendment's Equal Protection Clause makes no mention at all of race, even though it is clear, as a matter of history, that racial equality and the elimination of slavery were very much on the minds of those who wrote, and those who then ratified, this amendment. Can you fully understand what the wording of this clause requires without appealing to principles of morality and justice *and* without appealing to the "subjective intention" of the amendment's framers and ratifiers?

2. Suppose that we grant for the sake of argument that *Griswold* v. *Connecticut*, as well as *Roe* v. *Wade*, were wrongly decided. The question now arises as to whether the Supreme Court ought to overrule its earlier mistaken decisions. How does the Court, by making appeal only to the plain meaning of the Constitution itself, and by making no appeal either to moral and political philosophy, or to the political considerations that properly belong to a legislature, decide whether to overrule?

3. Bork says, "The Court can act as a legal rather than a political institution only if it is neutral as well in the way it derives and defines the principles it applies." Would it satisfy Bork if the principles the Court uses now "fit" earlier cases, that is, could be used to derive the holdings in those earlier cases given their fact situations? Explain why or why not.

4. Bork says that a judge who is committed to the philosophy of original understanding is supposed to "find the meaning of a text . . . and to apply that text to a particular situation." Think of the various arguments in favor of, and those against, the idea that there is some single meaning of a written document like a statute or a constitutional provision that we are to count as "the meaning" of that text.

## Stephen Macedo
# MORALITY AND CONSTITUTIONAL LAW*

Before considering what, in substance, a principled constitutional jurisprudence should be, it is necessary to contend with the New Right's skeptical, derisive attitude toward the judicial invocation of moral principles. The New Right's moral skepticism is utterly implausible, ignoble, and deeply at odds with America's morally robust constitutional tradition.

Bork insists, uncontroversially, that judicial decisions must rest on "reasoned opinions," that is, a "legitimate" court must have "a valid theory, derived from the Constitution" to justify its actions.[58] Bork's view of what constitutes a constitutional principle is, however, extremely narrow: valid constitutional principles are drawn only from the text interpreted in light of specific historical intentions; the "framers' intentions with respect to freedoms are the sole legitimate premise from which constitutional analysis may proceed."[59] On Bork's reading, therefore, the equal protection clause of the Fourteenth Amendment has two requirements: "formal procedural equality," as the bare text clearly requires, and no government discrimination along racial lines, because a concern with race is revealed by the history of the Fourteenth Amendment.

Cut loose from plain text and historical intentions, there is, for Bork, "no principled way of saying which . . . inequalities are permissible."[60] Beyond text and historical intention are "matters of morality," which "belong . . . to the political community."[61] Political morality is of no help in deciding constitutional questions because, says Bork, any system of "moral and ethical values . . . has no objective or intrinsic validity of its own"; there is, in effect, no right and wrong because all that can be said about morality is that "men can and do differ."[62] As if to make moral skepticism or subjectivism official U.S. government policy, Attorney General Meese approvingly quotes Bork's aphorism: "The judge who looks outside the Constitution always looks inside himself and nowhere else."[63]

Bork's skepticism turns to cynicism when he reduces all moral claims to claims for "gratification": "Every clash between a minority claiming freedom and a majority claiming power to regulate involves a choice between the gratifications of two groups."[64] When examining *Griswold* v. *Connecticut*, a case in which married couples asserted, as a matter of constitutional and political morality, the right to use contraceptives in the privacy of their own home, Bork sees no serious moral problem but only a question of "sexual gratification." Since there is no principled way, according to Bork, to discriminate between kinds of "gratification," the majority should have its way.[65] Bork would extend First Amendment protections only to *political* speech that is within the bounds of

---

*From *The New Right v. The Constitution* (1987) by Stephen Macedo, Chap. 4. Reprinted by permission of the CATO Institute.

[58]Bork, "Neutral Principles," p. 3.

[59]Bork, *Tradition*, p. 10.

[60]Bork, "Neutral Principles," p. 11.

[61]Ibid., p. 12.

[62]Ibid., p. 10

[63]Meese, Federalist Society address, p. 11.

[64]Bork, "Neutral Principles," p. 20.

[65]Ibid., p. 11; and see *Griswold* v. *Connecticut*, 381 U.S. 479 (1965).

the established legal order; he would extend no judicial protection to academic, literary, or any other forms of expression.[66]

Chief Justice Rehnquist, generally considered an intellectual leader of the conservative bloc on the Supreme Court, shares Bork's moral skepticism: "Many of us necessarily feel strongly and deeply about our own moral judgments, but they remain only personal moral judgments until in some way given the sanction of law."[67] What Rehnquist, like Bork, gives us is moral skepticism in the service of majoritarianism, masquerading as an innocent respect for the constitutional text.

Judge Posner expresses a similar skepticism about "value judgments":

[It is] inevitable that many judicial decisions will be based on value judgments rather than technical determinations; and decisions so made are by definition not scientific, and therefore are not readily falsifiable and hence not readily verifiable either—and as a consequence are not always profitably discussable.[68]

Although Posner's skepticism has a scientific gloss, and his position is arguably more sophisticated than Bork's, he agrees with Bork in urging judges to confine themselves to principles that have "public approbation" and "values that are widely . . . held" in the community.[69]

The New Right's attitude to rights claims appears to have the advantage of a tough-minded, down-to-earth, realism. Bork makes much of preferring the "common sense of the people" to the "theorists of moral abstraction," to "intellectuals," and to "what-have-you philosophy."[70] But the appearance of realism is spurious, for Americans could not make sense of their traditions, practices, and habitual ways of thinking, acting, and judging, or of the Constitution, if they accepted the New Right's radical moral skepticism. Indeed, it is hard to see how one could reconcile the New Right's apparently principled preference for democracy with its moral skepticism. (After all, why should anyone, except on the basis of a principle of moral equality, prefer the gratifications of the majority to a minority? Why should we prefer democracy to totalitarianism?)

The apparent lesson of the New Right's derision of rights and moral reflection is that moral claims can be ignored because they are no more than the way that "intellectuals" dress up their preferences and gratifications. In reducing rights claims to demands for "gratification," the New Right theorists destroy the distinction between moral reasons and mere arbitrary preferences. And as Sotirios Barber points out, to insist that a community's enforced ethical values need express no more than the merely subjective preferences of the majority is to put forward "a sophisticated version of the maxim that might makes right."[71]

In telling the majority, those with the strength of numbers, that morality may be ignored (because moral reasons are mere preferences), the New Right calls upon what is worst, not what is best, in the public. The

---

[66]Bork, "Neutral Principles," p. 20.

[67]William H. Rehnquist, "The Notion of a Living Constitution," *Texas Law Review* 54 (1976): 704.

[68]Richard A. Posner, "The Meaning of Judicial Self-Restraint," *Indiana Law Journal* 59 (1983): 6.

[69]Ibid., pp. 10, 23.

[70]Bork, *Tradition*, pp. 7–11.

[71]Sotirios Barber, "Judge Bork's Constitution," in *Courts, Judges, and Politics,* 3d ed., ed. Walter F. Murphy and C. Herman Pritchett (New York: Random House, forthcoming), pp. 691–95. Barber also has pointed out to the present author that Bork's position is essentially the same as that of Thrasymachus, in Plato's *Republic,* who argued against Socrates that justice is no more than the interest of the stronger.

Framers recognized this stance; indeed, they feared it. They feared the untutored, unrefined "prejudices" of the people, and they regarded those who would flatter and enflame these prejudices as demagogues.

The Framers feared the "passions" of the people, and they argued that "the reason, alone, of the public . . . ought to control and regulate the government."[72] The Framers were not simple democrats, but republicans who rejected the idea that popular government was necessarily good government. They sought to ensure that political power would be in the hands of the wisest members of the community and not those most responsive to popular prejudices: "The republican principle demands that the deliberate sense of the community should govern."[73] And, unlike Bork and others in today's New Right, the Framers were neither morally skeptical nor derisive of abstract ideas. For what else but abstract ideas are the "self-evident" truths of the Declaration of Independence? What else but philosophical principles are "unalienable Rights" that belong naturally to all men? And how else, except as the assertion of an abstract moral claim, can one understand the Framers' assertion that "Justice is the end of government"?[74]

Fortunately, despite its apparent tough-mindedness, the New Right's conception of morality is so counterintuitive that hardly anyone would accept it and so implausible that no one should. Who really believes that moral claims express only desires for "gratification," as Bork asserts? To accept Bork's position, one would have to believe that there is no moral difference between the "gratification" of a murderer and the "gratification" of his potential victim who wishes to live. According to Bork, "Anything some

people want has, to that degree, social value."[75] But what of the desires of the rapist, the thief, and the arsonist? Do these desires have social value? And do they fail to win moral approval and become lawful only because they are the desires of minorities?

Contrary to Bork, the truth is that we can and do distinguish between mere gratifications and genuine moral claims all the time. We say with moral confidence that the gratifications of those who enjoy murdering, raping, stealing, burning other people's homes, or violating rights in other ways count for nothing. We believe in fundamental rights, to freedom of conscience and of speech, to life and to at least some forms of privacy, on the basis of moral reason and not on the basis of absurd calculations about net gratifications.

The New Right's moral theory is nothing if not audacious, but it would take more than audacity to seriously argue either that the Framers of the Constitution shared this deep skepticism or that the American people do so today. The Framers were suspicious of democracy and confident that certain standards of political morality transcend the will of any majority. And they sought, in the deliberations on the ratification of the Constitution, to direct the public's attention toward reflection on justice and away from arbitrary preferences and immediate "gratifications": the conduct of this country would decide, said Hamilton in the first paragraph of the first *Federalist*, "whether societies of men are capable or not of establishing good government from reflection and choice" rather than "accident and force." And Thomas Paine expressed the faith of his generation when he claimed, "The Independence of America was accompanied by a Revolution in the principles and practices of Governments. . . . Government founded on a

[72]*Federalist*, no. 49.
[73]*Federalist*, no. 71.
[74]*Federalist*, no. 51.
[75]Bork, "Neutral Principles," p. 29.

moral theory . . . on the indefeasible heredi-tary Rights of Man, is now revolving from West to East."[76]

Bork basks in his derision of moral ab-stractions and claims that his posture ex-presses reverence for the founders and our political tradition. But moral abstractions, such as rights and justice, did play a central role in the minds of the Founders and do form an essential part of America's constitu-tional tradition.

The main sources of the political ideas of the founding generation were the legal au-thorities Edward Coke and William Black-stone and the great classical liberal political theorist John Locke.[77] All three accepted the political centrality of "natural law" morality. Coke and Locke, in particular, con-tinually stressed that moral standards defin-ing individual rights were binding on all political actors, including popular majorities and legislatures.

Most importantly for the argument at hand, in the period of the revolution, the "higher law," or natural moral law, was held to embody judicially enforceable limits on legislatures and positive law. Coke, whose *Commentaries* Jefferson called "the universal lawbook of students," argued that "when an act of Parliament is against common right and reason, or repugnant, or impossible to be performed, the common law will control it and adjudge such act to be void."[78]

John Locke, the political thinker who ex-ercised the greatest influence on the repub-lic's founding generation, argued that men gave up none of their natural rights when entering political society; they gave to gov-ernment only the power to better "preserve" their natural rights to "liberty and prop-erty."[79] Thomas Jefferson echoed Lockean theory when, in 1816, he asserted,

> Our legislators are not sufficiently apprised of the rightful limits of their power; that their true office is to declare and enforce only our natural rights and duties, and to take none of them from us. . . . When the laws have declared and enforced all this, they have fulfilled their functions; and the idea is quite unfounded that on entering so-ciety we give up any natural right.[80]

Not all the Founders adhered strictly, even in theory, to Lockeanism, and none of them acted solely on the basis of morality. Prudence, together with forms of political wisdom beyond moral reflection, comes into play in any successful act of statecraft. These facts notwithstanding, it is safe to say that the Founders did not doubt the existence of moral rights that bind popular governments. The Constitution itself, moreover, does not confer rights, but only "secures" them. And the Ninth Amendment explicitly calls upon constitutional interpreters not to "deny or disparage" the existence of rights not stated explicitly in the Constitution. By implication, then, the Constitution calls upon all citizens and public officials to reflect upon the rights that people have even in the absence of ex-plicit political acknowledgment. The Ninth

---

[76]Thomas Paine, *The Rights of Man*, quoted in Thomas Pangle, "Patriotism American Style," *National Review*, November 29, 1985, pp. 30–34.

[77]On the influence of Locke, see Bernard Bailyn, *The Ideological Origins of the American Revolution* (Cambridge: Harvard University Press, 1982), especially pp. 27–28. On Locke and Coke, see Edward S. Corwin, *The "Higher Law" Background of American Constitutionalism* (Ithaca, N.Y.: Cornell University Press, 1979). On Blackstone's teaching on "natural law" and his influence on the Founders, see W. A. Mell, "James Wilson, Alexander Hamilton, and William Blackstone," doctoral dissertation, University of Oregon, 1976 (reprinted by University Microfilms, Ann Arbor, Mich., 1980).

[78]Corwin, p. 42.

[79]John Locke, *Two Treatises on Government*, Second Treatise, ed. Peter Laslett (New York: New American Library, 1965), par. 131, pp. 398–99.

[80]Thomas Jefferson, as quoted in Murphy, "Art," p. 140.

Amendment calls upon conscientious interpreters to reflect upon natural rights and so to engage in moral theory.

The New Right's moral skepticism, as well as its disparaging attitude toward rights not explicitly stated in the text of the Constitution, find little support in the ideas of the Founders or in the text of the Constitution. Not surprisingly, then, judicially enforceable moral principles, even those not explicitly stated in the Constitution, have played an important role throughout U. S. history. Early on, Justice Chase invoked, in *Calder* v. *Bull*, "the general principles of law and reason" that constrain legislators even in the absence of explicit constitutional provisions.[81]

Chief Justice Marshall, an ardent nationalist, could have struck down Georgia's revocation of a land grant in *Fletcher* v. *Peck* by invoking only the Constitution's contracts clause. Instead, he went beyond the text of the Constitution and engaged in a considerable discussion of "the great principles of justice, whose authority is universally acknowledged."[82] Seventeen years later, in *Ogden* v. *Saunders*, Marshall invoked the "abstract philosophy" of natural rights: "Individuals do not derive from government their right to contract, but bring that right with them into society. . . . [E]very man retains [the right] to acquire property, to dispose of that property according to his own judgment, and to pledge himself for a future act."[83]

When one thinks of the American political tradition at its best, Abraham Lincoln must rank alongside the greatest of the Founders. Lincoln's political morality, his central concern with human equality as a moral principle, stands sharply at odds with Bork's skepticism. In the Gettysburg Address, Lincoln described the central proposition of the Declaration of Independence, to which the nation was dedicated at its birth, as "an abstract truth applicable to all men and all times." Lincoln, unlike Bork, held that right and wrong depend on standards of judgment independent of mere opinion. What Lincoln would have thought of the assertion that the gratifications of slave traders and slaves, for instance, are not morally distinguishable, or are distinguishable only quantitatively, may easily be inferred from his Peoria speech of 1854:

> All these free blacks are the descendants of slaves, or have been slaves themselves, and they would be now, but for *something* which has operated on their white owners, inducing them, at vast pecuniary sacrifices, to liberate them. What is that *something*? Is there any mistaking it? In all these cases it is your sense of justice, and human sympathy, continually telling you, that the poor negro has some natural right to himself—that those who deny it, and make merchandise of him, deserve kicking, contempt, and death.[84]

After the Civil War, the development of the doctrine of "substantive due process" carried forward the "higher law" tradition in the form of judicially protected economic liberties. Accordingly, Bork's disparaging attitude toward moral rights neglects not only the ideas of the Framers but also important aspects of the American constitutional and political tradition.

Bork is on firmer ground when he charges that in recent times the Supreme Court, in defining values sufficiently "fundamental"

[81]3 Dall. 395 (1798).

[82]3 L.Ed. 162 (1810).

[83]2 Wheaton 213 (1827).

[84]Abraham Lincoln, speech delivered at Peoria, Ill., 1854, as quoted in Harry V. Jaffa, *Crisis of the House Divided* (Seattle: University of Washington Press, 1973), p. 312. For a discussion of Lincoln's view of the moral status of the Declaration of Independence, see Jaffa, chap. 14; and Gary J. Jacobsohn, "Abraham Lincoln 'On this Question of Judicial Authority': The Theory of Constitutional Aspiration," *Western Political Quarterly* 36, no. 1 (1983): 52–70.

to warrant judicial protection, has neglected some rights, especially economic ones, for no good reason. In this way, the Court has indeed been "political"; it has ignored the high standing of economic rights in the Constitution's text, in our political tradition, and in moral theory. The modern Court has erected a constitutional double standard by giving high place to "personal rights" while neglecting economic rights that are at least as well founded in the Constitution.

The Supreme Court can and should be criticized for the narrow way in which it has defined those "fundamental" values and "preferred" freedoms worthy of judicial protection. It should not be concluded, however, that the active judicial defense of liberty and rights should be abandoned, for this defense is supported by the Constitution's text, by the ideas of the Framers, and by our political tradition. The proper course, it seems, is for conscientious interpreters of the Constitution to correct, not abandon, judicial activism.

There is clearly a close fit between the three levels of the New Right's jurisprudence. The resort to historical intentions to construe rights narrowly is supported by the preference for majority power over individual liberty, and that in turn is supported by moral skepticism. And yet at each level, the New Right's position is diametrically opposed to the ideas of the Framers, to the text of the Constitution, and to morality itself, which limits and defines our ultimate political duties. . . .

# QUESTIONS

1. Macedo says, "Contrary to Bork, the truth is that we can and do distinguish between mere gratifications and genuine moral claims all the time. We say with moral confidence that the gratifications of those who enjoy murdering, raping, stealing, burning other people's homes, or violating rights in other ways count for nothing." Suppose we begin with a utilitarian view that pleasure is the one intrinsic good in the world, while suffering is the one thing that is intrinsically bad. What are some ways in which such utilitarian moral theory might plausibly make a distinction between the gratification of a murder and the gratification of his potential victim who wants to live?

2. The Ninth Amendment to the U. S. Constitution reads: "The enumeration in the Constitution, of certain rights, shall not be construed to deny or disparage others retained by the people." Read it first for its plain meaning. Then, if you wish to pursue it further, look into the history of the amendment. Why would the framers of a constitution want to include an amendment like this one? What was the purpose of including the amendment in *this* Constitution?

3. Macedo, like many others who maintain that reasoning about moral rights must be part of constitutional reasoning, mentions the Ninth Amendment's call not to "deny or disparage" rights not explicitly mentioned in the Constitution. What can a defender of the "original meaning" method of constitutional interpretation say about this reference to the Ninth Amendment?

4. In criticism of Macedo's argument and in defense of the Jurisprudence of Original Intention (*The New Right v. The Constitution* [p. 106; not reprinted here]), Gary L. McDowell says that "it does not matter what James Madison or Alexander Hamilton or

anyone else of that generation felt about, say, abortion as a moral matter. What does matter is whether such questions as abortion are properly handled by the federal judiciary or are appropriately left to the legislatures of the several states as a result of the Constitution's principle of federalism." Comment on whether this program of deciding what is properly decided by the federal judiciary or the state legislatures is itself a program which can be carried out without slipping back into what originalists such as Bork dislike and protest.

# Rights

## *John Stuart Mill*
# ON THE CONNECTION BETWEEN JUSTICE AND UTILITY*

In all ages of speculation one of the strongest obstacles to the reception of the doctrine that utility or happiness is the criterion of right and wrong has been drawn from the idea of justice. The powerful sentiment and apparently clear perception which that word recalls with a rapidity and certainty resembling an instinct have seemed to the majority of thinkers to point to an inherent quality in things; to show that the just must have an existence in nature as something absolute, generically distinct from every variety of the expedient and, in idea, opposed to it, though (as is commonly acknowledged) never, in the long run, disjoined from it in fact.

In the case of this, as of our other moral sentiments, there is no necessary connection between the question of its origin and that of its binding force. That a feeling is bestowed on us by nature does not necessarily legitimate all its promptings. The feeling of justice might be a peculiar instinct, and might yet require, like our other instincts, to be controlled and enlightened by a higher reason. If we have intellectual instincts leading us to judge in a particular way, as well as animal instincts that prompt us to act in a particular way, there is no necessity that the former should be more infallible in their sphere than the latter in theirs; it may as well happen that wrong judgments are occasionally suggested by those, as wrong actions by these. But though it is one thing to believe that we have natural feelings of justice, and another to acknowledge them as an ultimate criterion of conduct, these two opinions are very closely connected in point of fact. Mankind are always predisposed to believe that any subjective feeling, not otherwise accounted for, is a revelation of some objective reality. Our present object is to determine whether the reality to which the feeling of justice corresponds is one which needs any such special revelation, whether the justice or injustice of an action is a thing intrinsically peculiar and distinct from all its other qualities or only a combination of certain of those qualities presented under a peculiar aspect. For the purpose of this inquiry it is practically important to consider whether the feeling itself, of justice and injustice, is *sui generis* like our sensations of color and taste or a derivative feeling formed by a combination of others. And this it is the more essential to examine, as people are in general willing enough to allow that objectively the dictates of justice coincide with a part of the field of general expediency; but inasmuch as the subjective mental feeling of justice is different from that which commonly attaches to simple expediency, and, except in the extreme cases of the latter, is far move imperative in its demands, people find it difficult to see in justice only a particular kind or branch of general utility, and think that its superior binding force requires a totally different origin.

To throw light upon this question, it is necessary to attempt to ascertain what is the distinguishing character of justice, or of injustice; what is the quality, or whether there is any quality, attributed in common to all modes of conduct designated as unjust (for justice, like may other moral attributes, is best defined by its opposite), and distinguishing them from such modes of conduct as are disapproved, but without having that particular epithet of disapprobation applied to them. If in everything which men are accustomed to characterize as just or unjust some one common attribute or collection of attributes is always present, we may judge

*From *Utilitarianism*, Chap. 5. First published in 1863.

whether this particular attribute or combination of attributes would be capable of gathering round it a sentiment of that peculiar character and intensity by virtue of the general laws of our emotional constitution, or whether the sentiment is inexplicable and requires to be regarded as a special provision of nature. If we find the former to be the case, we shall, in resolving this question, have resolved also the main problem; if the latter, we shall have to seek for some other mode of investigating it.

To find the common attributes of a variety of objects, it is necessary to begin by surveying the objects themselves in the concrete. Let us therefore advert successively to the various modes of action and arrangements of human affairs which are classed, by universal or widely spread opinion, as just or as unjust. The things well known to excite the sentiments associated with those names are of a very multifarious character. I shall pass them rapidly in review, without studying any particular arrangement.

In the first place, it is mostly considered unjust to deprive anyone of his personal liberty, his property, or any other thing which belongs to him by law. Here, therefore, is one instance of the application of the terms "just" and "unjust" in a perfectly definite sense, namely, that it is just to respect, unjust to violate, the *legal rights* of anyone. But this judgment admits of several exceptions, arising from the other forms in which the notions of justice and injustice present themselves. For example, the person who suffers the deprivation may (as the phrase is) have *forfeited* the rights which he is so deprived of—a case to which we shall return presently. But also—

Secondly, the legal rights of which he is deprived may be rights which *ought* not to have belonged to him; in other words, the law which confers on him these rights may be a bad law. When it is so or when (which is the same thing for our purpose) it is supposed to be so, opinions will differ as to the justice or injustice of infringing it. Some maintain that no law, however bad, ought to be disobeyed by an individual citizen; that his opposition to it, if shown at all, should only be shown in endeavoring to get it altered by competent authority. This opinion (which condemns many of the most illustrious benefactors of mankind, and would often protect pernicious institutions against the only weapon which, in the state of things existing at the time, have any chance of succeeding against them) is defended by those who hold it on grounds of expediency, principally on that of the importance to the common interest of mankind, of maintaining inviolate the sentiment of submission to law. Other persons, again, hold the directly contrary opinion that any law, judged to be bad, may blamelessly be disobeyed, even though it be not judged to be unjust but only inexpedient, while others would confine the license of disobedience to the case of unjust laws; but, again, some say that all laws which are inexpedient are unjust, since every law imposes some restriction on the natural liberty of mankind, which restriction is an injustice unless legitimated by tending to their good. Among these diversities of opinion it seems to be universally admitted that there may be unjust laws, and that law, consequently, is not the ultimate criterion of justice, but may give to one person a benefit, or impose on another an evil, which justice condemns. When, however, a law is thought to be unjust, it seems always to be regarded as being so in the same way in which a breach of law is unjust, namely, by infringing somebody's right, which as it cannot in this case be a legal right, receives a different appellation and is called a moral right. We may say, therefore, that a second case of injustice consists in taking or withholding from any person that to which he has a *moral right*.

Thirdly, it is universally considered just that each person should obtain that (whether good or evil) which he *deserves*, and unjust that he should obtain a good or be made to undergo an evil which he does not deserve. This is, perhaps, the clearest and most emphatic form in which the idea of justice is conceived by the general mind. As it involves the notion of desert, the question arises what constitutes desert? Speaking in a general way, a person is understood to deserve good if he does right, evil if he does wrong; and in a more particular sense, to deserve good from those to whom he does or has done good, and evil from those to whom he does or has done evil. The precept of returning good for evil has never been regarded as a case of the fulfillment of justice, but as one in which the claims of justice are waived, in obedience to other considerations.

Fourthly, it is confessedly unjust to *break faith* with anyone: to violate an engagement, either express or implied, or disappoint expectations raised by our own conduct, at least if we have raised those expectations knowingly and voluntarily. Like the other obligations of justice already spoken of, this one is not regarded as absolute, but as capable of being overruled by a stronger obligation of justice on the other side, or by such conduct on the part of the person concerned as is deemed to absolve us from our obligation to him and to constitute a *forfeiture* of the benefit which he has been led to expect.

Fifthly, it is, by universal admission, inconsistent with justice to be *partial*—to show favor or preference to one person over another in matters to which favor and preference do not properly apply. Impartiality, however, does not seem to be regarded as a duty in itself, but rather as instrumental to some other duty; for it is admitted that favor and preference are not always censurable, and, indeed, the cases in which they are condemned are rather the exception than the rule. A person would be more likely to be blamed than applauded for giving his family or friends no superiority in good offices over strangers when he could do so without violating any other duty; and no one thinks it unjust to seek one person in preference to another as a friend, connection, or companion. Impartiality where rights are concerned is of course obligatory, but this is involved in the more general obligation of giving to everyone his right. A tribunal, for example,

must be impartial because it is bound to award, without regard to any consideration, a disputed object to the one of two parties who has the right to it. There are other cases in which impartiality means being solely influenced by desert, as with those who, in the capacity of judges, preceptors, or parents, administer reward and punishment as such. There are cases, again, in which it means being solely influenced by consideration for the public interest, as in making a selection among candidates for a government employment. Impartiality, in short, as an obligation of justice, may be said to mean being exclusively influenced by the considerations which it is supposed ought to influence the particular case in hand, and resisting solicitation of any motives which prompt to conduct different from what those considerations would dictate.

Nearly allied to the idea of impartiality is that of *equality*, which often enters as a component part both into the conception of justice and into the practice of it, and, in the eyes of many person, constitutes its essence. But in this, still more than in any other case, the notion of justice varies in different persons, and always conforms in its variations to their notion of utility. Each person maintains that equality is the dictate of justice, except where he thinks that expediency requires inequality. The justice of giving equal protection to the rights of all is maintained by those who support the most outrageous inequality in the rights themselves. Even in slave countries it is theoretically admitted that the rights of the slave, such as they are, ought to be as sacred as those of the master, and that a tribunal which fails to enforce them with equal strictness is wanting in justice; while, at the same time, institutions which leave to the slave scarcely any rights to enforce are not deemed unjust because they are not deemed inexpedient. Those who think that utility requires distinctions of rank do not consider it unjust that riches and social privileges should be unequally dispensed; but those who think this inequality inexpedient think it unjust also. Whoever thinks that government is necessary sees no injustice in as much inequality as is constituted by giving to the magistrate powers not granted to other people. Even among those who hold leveling doctrines, there are differences of opinion about expediency. Some communists consider it unjust that the produce of the labor of the community should be shared on any other principle than that of exact equality; others think it just that those should receive most whose wants are greatest; while others hold that those who work harder, or who produce more, or whose services are more valuable to the community, may justly claim a larger quota in the division of the produce. And the sense of natural justice may be plausibly appealed to in behalf of every one of these opinions.

Among so many diverse applications of the term "justice," which yet is not regarded as ambiguous, it is a matter of some difficulty to seize the mental link which holds them together, and on which the moral sentiment adhering to the term essentially depends. Perhaps, in this embarrassment, some help may be derived from the history of the word, as indicated by its etymology.

In most if not in all languages, the etymology of the word which corresponds to "just" points distinctly to an origin connected with the ordinance of law. *Justum* is a form of *jussum*, that which has been ordered. *Dikaion* comes directly from *dike*, a suit at law. *Recht*, from which came *right* and *righteous*, is synonymous with law. The courts of justice, the administration of justice, are the courts and the administration of law. *La justice*, in French, is the established term for judicature. I am not committing the fallacy, imputed with some show of truth to Horne Tooke, of assuming that a word must still continue to mean what it originally meant. Etymology is slight evidence of what the idea now signified is, but the very best evidence of how it sprang up. There can, I think, be no doubt that the *idée mère*, the primitive element, in the formation of the notion of justice was conformity to law. It constituted the entire idea among the Hebrews, up to the birth of Christianity; as might be expected in the case of a people whose laws attempted to embrace all subjects on which precepts were required, and who believed those laws to be a direct emanation from the Supreme Being. But other nations, and in particular the Greeks and Romans, who knew that their laws had been made originally, and still continued to be made, by men, were not afraid to admit that those men might make bad laws; might do by law, the same things, and from the same motive, which if done by individuals without the sanction of law would be called unjust. And hence the sentiment of injustice came to be attached, not to all violations of law, but only to violations of such laws as *ought* to exist, including such as ought to exist but do not, and to laws themselves if supposed to be contrary to what ought to be law. In this manner the idea of law and of its injunctions was still predominant in the notion of justice, even when the laws actually in force ceased to be accepted as the standard of it.

It is true that mankind consider the idea of justice and its obligations as applicable to many things which neither are, nor is it desired that they should be, regulated by law. Nobody desires that laws should interfere with the whole detail of private life; yet everyone allows that in all daily conduct a person may and does show himself to be either just or unjust. But even here, the idea of the breach of what ought to be law still lingers in a modified shape. It would always give us pleasure, and chime in with our feelings of fitness, that acts which we deem unjust should be punished, though we do not always think it expedient that this should be done by the tribunals. We forego that gratification on account of incidental inconveniences. We should be glad to see just conduct enforced and injustice repressed, even in the minutest details, if we were not, with reason, afraid of trusting the magistrate with so unlimited an amount of power over individuals. When we think that a person is bound in justice to do a thing, it is an ordinary form of language to say that he ought to be compelled to do it. We should be gratified to see the obligation enforced by anybody who had the power. If we see that its enforcement by law would be inexpedient, we lament the impossibility, we consider the impunity given to injustice as an evil, and strive to make amends for it by bringing a strong expression of our own and the public disapprobation to bear upon the offender. Thus the idea of legal constraint is still the generating idea of the notion of justice, though undergoing several transformations before that notion as it exists in an advanced state of society becomes complete.

The above is, I think, a true account, as far as it goes, of the origin and progressive growth of the idea of justice. But we must observe that it contains as yet nothing to distinguish that obligation from moral obligation in general. For the truth is that the idea of penal sanction, which is the essence of law, enters not only into the conception of injustice, but into that of any kind of wrong. We do not call anything wrong unless we mean to imply that a person ought to be punished in some way or other for doing it—if not by law, by the opinion of his fellow creatures; if not by opinion, by the reproaches of his own conscience. This seems the real turning point of the distinction between morality and simple expediency. It is a part of the notion of duty in every one of its forms that a person may rightfully be compelled to fulfill it. Duty is a thing which may be *exacted* from a person, as one exacts a debt. Unless we think that it may be exacted from him, we do not call it his duty. Reasons of prudence, or the interest of other people, may militate against actually exacting it, but the person himself, it is clearly understood, would not be entitled to complain. There are other things, on the contrary, which we wish that people should do, which we like or admire them for doing, perhaps dislike or despise them for not doing, but yet admit that they are not bound to do; it is not a case of moral obligation; we do not blame them, that is, we do not think that they are proper objects of punishment. How we come by these ideas of deserving and not deserving punishment will appear, perhaps, in the sequel; but I think there is no doubt that this distinction lies at the bottom of the notions of right and wrong; that we call any conduct wrong, or employ, instead, some other term of dislike or disparagement, according as we think that person ought, or ought not, to be punished for it; and we say it would be right to do so and so, or merely that it would be desirable or laudable, according as we would wish to see the person whom it concerns compelled, or only persuaded and exhorted, to act in that manner.*

This, therefore, being the characteristic difference which marks off, not justice, but morality in general from the remaining provinces of expediency and worthiness, the character is still to be sought which distinguishes justice from other branches of morality. Now it is known that ethical writers divide moral duties into two classes, denoted by the ill-chosen expressions, duties of perfect and of imperfect obligation; the latter being those in which, though the act is obligatory, the particular occasions of performing it are left to our choice, as in the case of charity or beneficence, which we are indeed bound to practice but not toward any definite person, nor at any prescribed time. In the more precise language of philosophic jurists, duties of perfect obligation are those duties in virtue of which a correlative *right* resides in some person or persons; duties of imperfect obligation are those moral obligations which

*See this point enforced and illustrated by Professor Bain, in an admirable chapter (entitled "The Ethical Emotions, or the Moral Sense"), of the second of the two treatises composing his elaborate and profound work on the Mind.

do not give birth to any right. I think it will be found that this distinction exactly coincides with that which exists between justice and the other obligations of morality. In our survey of the various popular acceptations of justice, the term appeared generally to involve the idea of a personal right—a claim on the part of one or more individuals, like that which the law gives when it confers a proprietary or other legal right. Whether the injustice consists in depriving a person of a possession, or in breaking faith with him, or in treating him worse than he deserves, or worse than other people who have no greater claims—in each case the supposition implies two things: a wrong done, and some assignable person who is wronged. Injustice may also be done by treating a person better than others; but the wrong in this case is to his competitors, who are also assignable persons. It seems to me that this feature in the case—a right in some person, correlative to the moral obligation—constitutes the specific difference between justice and generosity or beneficence. Justice implies something which it is not only right to do, and wrong not to do, but which some individual person can claim from us as his moral right. No one has a moral right to our generosity or beneficence because we are not morally bound to practice those virtues toward any given individual. And it will be found with respect to this as to every correct definition that the instances which seem to conflict with it are those which most confirm it. For if a moralist attempts, as some have done, to make out that mankind generally, though not any given individual, have a right to all the good we can do them, he at once, by that thesis, includes generosity and beneficence within the category of justice. He is obliged to say that our utmost exertions are *due* to our fellow creatures, thus assimilating them to a debt: or that nothing less can be a sufficient *return* for what society does for us, thus classing the case as one of gratitude; both of which are acknowledged cases of justice, and not of the virtue of beneficence; and whoever does not

place the distinction between justice and morality in general, where we have now placed it, will be found to make no distinction between them at all, but to merge all morality in justice.

Having thus endeavored to determine the distinctive elements which enter into the composition of the idea of justice, we are ready to enter on the inquiry whether the feeling which accompanies the idea is attached to it by a special dispensation of nature, or whether it could have grown up, by any known laws, out of the idea itself; and, in particular, whether it can have originated in considerations of general expediency.

I conceive that the sentiment itself does not arise from anything which would commonly or correctly be termed an idea of expediency, but that, though the sentiment does not, whatever is moral in it does.

We have seen that the two essential ingredients in the sentiment of justice are the desire to punish a person who has done harm and the knowledge or belief that there is some definite individual or individuals to whom harm has been done.

Now it appears to me that the desire to punish a person who has done harm to some individual is a spontaneous outgrowth from two sentiments, both in the highest degree natural and which either are or resemble instincts: the impulse of self-defense and the feeling of sympathy.

It is natural to resent and to repel or retaliate any harm done or attempted against ourselves or against those with whom we sympathize. The origin of this sentiment it is not necessary here to discuss. Whether it be an instinct or a result of intelligence, it is, we know, common to all animal nature; for every animal tries to hurt those who have hurt, or who it thinks are about to hurt, itself or its young. Human beings, on this point, only differ from other animals in two particulars. First, in being capable of sympathizing, not solely with their offspring, or, like some of the more noble animals, with some superior animal who is kind to them, but with all human, and even with all sentient, beings; secondly, in having a more developed intelligence, which gives a wider range to the whole of their sentiments, whether self-regarding or sympathetic. By virtue of his superior intelligence, even apart from his superior range of sympathy, a human being is capable of apprehending a community of interest between himself and the human society of which he forms a part, such that any conduct which threatens the security of the society generally is threatening to his own, and calls forth his instinct (if instinct it be) of self-defense. The same superiority of intelligence, joined to the power of sympathizing with human beings generally, enables him to attach himself to the collective idea of his tribe, his country, or mankind in such a manner that any act hurtful to them raises his instinct of sympathy and urges him to resistance.

The sentiment of justice, in that one of its elements which consists of the desire to punish, is thus, I conceive, the natural feeling of retaliation or vengeance, rendered by intellect and sympathy applicable to those injuries, that is, to those hurts, which wound us through, or in common with, society at large. This sentiment, in itself, has nothing moral in it; what is moral is the exclusive subordination of it to the social sympathies, so as to wait on and obey their call. For the natural feeling would make us resent indiscriminately whatever anyone does that is disagreeable to us; but, when moralized by the social feeling, it only acts in the directions conformable to the general good: just persons resenting a hurt to society, though not otherwise a hurt to themselves, and not resenting a hurt to themselves, however painful, unless it be of the kind which society has common interest with them in the repression of.

It is no objection against this doctrine to say that, when we feel our sentiment of justice outraged, we are not thinking of society at large or of any collective interest, but only of the individual case. It is common enough,

certainly, though the reverse of commendable, to feel resentment merely because we have suffered pain; but a person whose resentment is really a moral feeling, that is, who considers whether an act is blamable before he allows himself to resent it—such a person, though he may not say expressly to himself that he is standing up for the interest of society, certainly does feel that he is asserting a rule which is for the benefit of others as well as for his own. If he is not feeling this, if he is regarding the act solely as it affects him individually, he is not consciously just; he is not concerning himself about the justice of his actions. This is admitted even by anti-utilitarian moralists. When Kant (as before remarked) propounds as the fundamental principle of morals, "So act that thy rule of conduct might be adopted as a law by all rational beings," he virtually acknowledges that the interest of mankind collectively, or at least of mankind indiscriminately, must be in the mind of the agent when conscientiously deciding on the morality of the act. Otherwise he uses words without a meaning; for that a rule even of utter selfishness could not *possibly* be adopted by all rational beings—that there is any insuperable obstacle in the nature of things to its adoption—cannot be even plausibly maintained. To give any meaning to Kant's principle, the sense put upon it must be that we ought to shape our conduct by a rule which all rational beings might adopt *with benefit to their collective interest.*

To recapitulate: the idea of justice supposes two things—a rule of conduct and a sentiment which sanctions the rule. The first must be supposed common to all mankind and intended for their good. The other (the sentiment) is a desire that punishment may be suffered by those who infringe the rule. There is involved, in addition, the conception of some definite person who suffers by the infringement, whose rights (to use the expression appropriated to the case) are violated by it. And the sentiment of justice appears to me to be the animal desire to repel or retaliate a hurt or damage to oneself or to those with whom one sympathizes, widened so as to include all persons, by the human capacity of enlarged sympathy and the human conception of intelligent self-interest. From the latter elements the feeling derives its morality; from the former, its peculiar impressiveness and energy of self-assertion.

I have, throughout, treated the idea of a *right* residing in the injured person and violated by the injury, not as a separate element in the composition of the idea and sentiment, but as one of the forms in which the other two elements clothe themselves. These elements are a hurt to some assignable person or persons, on the one hand, and a demand for punishment, on the other. An examination of our own minds, I think, will show that these two things include all that we mean when we speak of violation of a right. When we call anything a person's right, we mean that he has a valid claim on society to protect him in the possession of it, either by the force of law or by that of education and opinion. If he has what we consider a sufficient claim, on whatever account, to have something guaranteed to him by society, we say that he has a right to it. If we desire to prove that anything does not belong to him by right, we think this done as soon as it is admitted that society ought not to take measures for securing it to him, but should leave him to chance or to his own exertions. Thus a person is said to have a right to what he can earn in fair professional competition, because society ought not to allow any other person to hinder him from endeavoring to earn in that manner as much as he can. But he has not a right to three hundred a year, though he may happen to be earning it; because society is not called onto provide that he shall earn that sum. On the contrary, if he owns ten thousand pounds three-per-cent stock, he *has* a right to three hundred a year because society has come under an obligation to provide him with an income of that amount.

To have a right, then, is, I conceive, to have something which society ought to defend me in the possession of. If the objector goes on to ask why it ought, I can give him no other reason than general utility. If that expression does not seem to convey a sufficient feeling of the strength of the obligation, nor to account for the peculiar energy of the feeling, it is because there goes to the composition of the sentiment, not a rational only but also an animal element—the thirst for retaliation; and this thirst derives its intensity, as well as its moral justification, from the extraordinarily important and impressive kind of utility which is concerned. The interest involved is that of security, to everyone's feeling the most vital of all interests. All other earthly benefits are needed by one person, not needed by another; and many of them can, if necessary, be cheerfully foregone or replaced by something else; but security no human being can possibly do without; on it we depend for all our immunity from evil and for the whole value of all and every good, beyond the passing moment, since nothing but the gratification of the instant could be of any worth to us if we could be deprived of everything the next instant by whoever was momentarily stronger than ourselves. Now this most indispensable of all necessaries, after physical nutriment, cannot be had unless the machinery for providing it is kept unintermittedly in active play. Our notion, therefore, of the claim we have on our fellow creatures to join in making safe for us the very groundwork of our existence gathers feelings around it so much more intense than those concerned in any of the more common cases of utility that the difference in degree (as is often the case in psychology) becomes a real difference in kind. The claim assumes that character of absoluteness, that apparent infinity and incommensurability with all other considerations which constitute the distinction between the feeling of right and wrong and that of ordinary expediency and inexpediency. The feelings concerned are so powerful, and we count so positively on finding a responsive feeling in others (all being alike interested) that *ought* and *should* grow into *must*, and recognized indispensability becomes a moral necessity, analogous to physical, and often not inferior to it in binding force.

If the preceding analysis, or something resembling it, be not the correct account of the notion of justice—if justice be totally independent of utility, and be a standard *per se*, which the mind can recognize by simple introspection of itself—it is hard to understand why that internal oracle is so ambiguous, and why so many things appear either just or unjust, according to the light in which they are regarded.

We are continually informed that utility is an uncertain standard, which every different person interprets differently, and that there is no safety but in the immutable, ineffaceable, and unmistakable dictates of justice, which carry their evidence in themselves and are independent of the fluctuations of opinion. One would suppose from this that on questions of justice there could be no controversy; that, if we take that for our rule, its application to any given case could leave us in as little doubt as a mathematical demonstration. So far is this from being the fact that there is as much difference of opinion, and as much discussion, about what is just as about what is useful to society. Not only have different nations and individuals different notions of justice, but in the mind of one and the same individual, justice is not some one rule, principle, or maxim, but many which do not always coincide in their dictates, and, in choosing between which, he is guided either by some extraneous standard or by his own personal predilections.

For instance, there are some who say that it is unjust to punish anyone for the sake of example to others, that punishment is just only when intended for the good of the sufferer himself. Others maintain the extreme reverse, contending that to punish persons who have attained years of discretion, for their own benefit, is despotism and injustice, since, if the matter at issue is solely their own good, no one has a right to control their own judgment of it; but that they may justly be punished to prevent evil to others, this being the exercise of the legitimate right of self-defense. Mr. Owen, again, affirms that it is unjust to punish at all, for the criminal did not make his own character; his education and the circumstances which surrounded him have made him a criminal, and for these he is not responsible. All these opinions are extremely plausible; and so long as the question is argued as one of justice simply, without going down to the principles which lie under justice and are the source of its authority, I am unable to see how any of these reasoners can be refuted. For in truth every one of the three builds upon rules of justice confessedly true. The first appeals to the acknowledged injustice of singling out an individual and making him a sacrifice, without his consent, for other people's benefit. The second relies on the acknowledged justice of self-defense and the admitted injustice of forcing one person to conform to another's notions of what constitutes his good. The Owenite invokes the admitted principle that it is unjust to punish anyone for what he cannot help. Each is triumphant so long as he is not compelled to take into consideration any other maxims of justice than the one he has selected; but as soon as their several maxims are brought face to face, each disputant seems to have exactly as much to say for himself as the others. No one of them can carry out his own notion of justice without trampling upon another equally binding. These are difficulties; they have always been felt to be such; and many devices have been invented to turn rather than to overcome them. As a refuge from the last of the three, men imagined what they called the freedom of the will—fancying that they could not justify punishing a man whose will is in a thoroughly hateful state unless it be supposed to have come into that state through no influence of anterior circumstances. To escape from the other difficulties, a favorite contrivance has been the fiction of a contract whereby at some unknown period all the members of society engaged to obey the laws and consented to be punished for any disobedience to them, thereby giving to their legislators the right, which it is assumed they would not otherwise have had, of punishing them, either for their own good or for that of society. This happy thought was considered to get rid of the whole difficulty and to legitimate the infliction of punishment, in virtue of another received maxim. of justice, *volenti non fit injuria*—that is not unjust which is done with the consent of the person who is supposed to be hurt by it. I need hardly remark that, even if the consent were not a mere fiction, this maxim is not superior in authority to the others which it is brought in to supersede. It is, on the contrary, an instructive specimen of the loose and irregular manner in which supposed principles of justice grow up. This particular one evidently came into use as a help to the coarse exigencies of courts of law, which are sometimes obliged to be content with very uncertain presumptions, on account of the greater evils which should often arise from any attempt on their part to cut finer. But even courts of law are not able to adhere consistently to the maxim, for they allow voluntary engagements to be set aside on the ground of fraud, and sometimes on that of mere mistake or misinformation.

Again, when the legitimacy of inflicting punishment is admitted, how many conflicting conceptions of justice come to light in discussing the proper apportionment of punishments to offenses. No rule on the subject recommends itself so strongly to the primitive and spontaneous sentiment of justice as the *lex talionis*, an eye for an eye and a tooth for a tooth. Though this principle of the Jewish and of the Mohammedan law has been generally abandoned in Europe as a practical maxim, there is, I suspect, in most minds, a secret hankering after it; and when retribution accidentally falls on an offender in that precise shape, the general feeling of satisfaction evinced bears witness how natural is the sentiment to which this repayment in kind is acceptable. With many, the test of justice in penal infliction is that the punishment should be proportioned to the offense, meaning that it should be exactly measured by the moral guilt of the culprit (whatever be their standard for measuring moral guilt), the consideration what amount of punishment is necessary to deter from the offense having nothing to do with the question of justice, in the estimation; while there are others to whom that consideration is all in all, who maintain that it is not just, at least for man, to inflict on a fellow creature, whatever may be his offenses, any amount of suffering beyond the least that will suffice to prevent him from repeating, and others from imitating, his misconduct.

To take another example from a subject already once referred to. In co-operative industrial association, is it just or not that talent or skill should give a title to superior remuneration? On the negative side of the question it is argued that whoever does the best he can deserves equally well, and ought not in justice to be put in a position of inferiority for no fault of his own; that superior abilities have already advantages more than enough, in the admiration they excite, the personal influence they command, and the internal sources of satisfaction attending them, without adding to these a superior share of the world's goods; and that society is bound in justice rather to make compensation to the less favored for this unmerited inequality of advantages than to aggravate it. On the contrary side it is contended that society receives more from the more efficient laborer; that, his services being more useful, society owes him a larger return for them; that a greater share of the joint result is actually his work, and not to allow his claim to it is a kind of robbery; that, if he is only to receive as much as others, he can only be justly required to produce as much, and to give a smaller amount of time and exertion, proportioned to his superior efficiency. Who shall decide between these appeals to conflicting principles of justice? Justice has in this case two sides to it, which it is impossible to bring into harmony, and the two disputants have chosen opposite sides; the one looks to what it is just that the individual should receive, the other to what it is just that the community should give. Each, from his own point of view, is unanswerable; and any choice between them, on grounds of justice, must be perfectly arbitrary. Social utility alone can decide the preference.

How many, again, and how irreconcilable are the standards of justice to which reference is made in discussing the repartition of taxation. One opinion is that payment to the state should be in numerical proportion to pecuniary means. Others think that justice dictates what they term graduated taxation—taking a higher percentage from those who have more to spare. In point of natural justice a strong case might be made for disregarding means altogether, and taking the same absolute sum (whenever it could be got) from everyone; as the subscribers to a mess or to a club all pay the same sum for the same privileges, whether they can all equally afford it or not. Since the protection (it might be said) of law and government is afforded to and is equally required by all, there is no injustice in making all buy it at the same price. It is reckoned justice, not injustice, that a dealer should charge to all customers the same price for the same article, not a price varying according to their means of payment. This doctrine, as applied to taxation, finds no advocates because it conflicts so strongly with man's feelings of humanity and of social expediency; but the principle of justice which it invokes is as true and as binding as those which can be appealed to against it. Accordingly it exerts a tacit influence on the line of defense employed for other modes of assessing taxation. People feel obliged to argue that the state does more for the rich man than for the poor, as a justification for its taking more from them, though this is in reality not true, for the rich would be far better able to protect themselves, in the absence of law or government,

than the poor, and indeed would probably be successful in converting the poor into their slaves. Others, again, so far defer to the same conception of justice as to maintain that all should pay an equal capitation tax for the protection of their persons (these being of equal value to all), and an unequal tax for the protection of their property, which is unequal. To this others reply that the all of one man is as valuable to him as the all of another. From these confusions there is no other mode of extrication than the utilitarian.

Is, then, the difference between the just and expedient a merely imaginary distinction? Have mankind been under a delusion in thinking that justice is a more sacred thing than policy, and that the latter ought only to be listened to after the former has been satisfied? By no means. The exposition we have given of the nature and origin of the sentiment recognizes a real distinction; and no one of those who profess the most sublime contempt for the consequences of actions as an element in their morality attaches more importance to the distinction than I do. While I dispute the pretensions of any theory which sets up an imaginary standard of justice not grounded on utility, I account the justice which is grounded on utility to be the chief part, and incomparably the most sacred and binding part, of all morality. Justice is a name for certain classes of moral rules which concern the essentials of human well-being more nearly, and are therefore of more absolute obligation, than any other rules for the guidance of life; and the notion which we have found to be of the essence of the idea of justice—that of a right residing in an individual—implies and testifies to this more binding obligation.

The moral rules which forbid mankind to hurt one another (in which we must never forget to include wrongful interference with each other's freedom) are more vital to human well-being than any maxims, however important, which only point out the best mode of managing some department of human affairs. They have also the peculiarity that they are the main element in determining the whole of the social feelings of mankind. It is their observance which alone preserves peace among human beings; if obedience to them were not the rule, and disobedience the exception, everyone would see in everyone else an enemy against whom he must be perpetually guarding himself. What is hardly less important, these are the precepts which mankind have the strongest and the most direct inducements for impressing upon one another. By merely giving to each other prudential instruction or exhortation, they may gain, or think they gain, nothing; in inculcating on each other the duty of positive beneficence, they have an unmistakable interest, but far less in degree; a person may possibly not need the benefits of others, but he always needs that they should not do him hurt. Thus the moralities which protect every individual from being harmed by others, either directly or by being hindered in his freedom of pursuing his own good, are at once those which he himself has most at heart and those which he has the strongest interest in publishing and enforcing by word and deed. It is by a person's observance of these that his fitness to exist as one of the fellowship of human beings is tested and decided; for on that depends his being a nuisance or not to those with whom he in contact. Now it is these moralities primarily which compose the obligations of justice. The most marked cases of injustice, and those which give the tone to the feeling of repugnance which characterizes the sentiment, are acts of wrongful aggression or wrongful exercise of power over someone; the next are those which consist in wrongfully withholding from him something which is his due—in both cases inflicting on him a positive hurt, either in the form of direct suffering or of the privation of some good which he had reasonable ground, either of a physical or of a social kind, for counting upon.

The same powerful motives which command the observance of these primary moralities enjoin the punishment of those who violate them, and as the impulses of self-defense, of defense of others, and of vengeance are all called forth against such persons, retribution, or evil for evil, becomes closely connected with the sentiment of justice, and is universally included in the idea. Good for good is also one of the dictates of justice; and this, though its social utility is evident, and though it carries with it a natural human feeling, has not at first sight that obvious connection with hurt or injury which, existing in the most elementary cases of just and unjust, is the source of the characteristic intensity of the sentiment. But the connection, though less obvious, is not less real. He who accepts benefits and denies a return of them when needed inflicts a real hurt by disappointing one of the most natural and reasonable of expectations, and one which he must at least tacitly have encouraged, otherwise the benefits would seldom have been conferred. The important rank, among human evils and wrongs, of the disappointment of expectation is shown, in the fact that it constitutes the principal criminality of two such highly immoral acts as a breach of friendship and a breach of promise. Few hurts which human beings can sustain are greater, and none wound more, than when that on which they habitually and with full assurance relied fails them in the hour of need; and few wrongs are greater than this mere withholding of good; none excite more resentment, either in the person suffering or in a sympathizing spectator. The principle, therefore, of giving to each what they deserve, that is, good for good as well as evil for evil, is not only included within the idea of justice as we have defined it, but is a proper object of that intensity of sentiment which places the just in human estimation above the simply expedient.

Most of the maxims of justice current in the world, and commonly appealed to in its transactions, are simply instrumental to carrying into effect the principles of justice which we have now spoken of. That a person is only responsible for what he has done voluntarily, or could voluntarily have avoided, that it is unjust to condemn any person unheard; that the punishment ought to be proportioned to the offense, and the like, are maxims intended to prevent the just principle of evil for evil from being perverted to the infliction of evil without that justification. The greater part of these common maxims have come into use from the practice of courts of justice, which have been naturally led to a more complete recognition and elaboration than was likely to suggest itself to others, of the rules necessary to enable them to fulfill their double function—of inflicting punishment when due, and of awarding to each person his right.

That first of judicial virtues, impartiality, is an obligation of justice, partly for the reason last mentioned, as being a necessary condition of the fulfillment of other obligations of justice. But this is not the only source of the exalted rank, among human obligations, of those maxims of equality and impartiality, which, both in popular estimation and in that of the most enlightened, are included among the precepts of justice. In one point of view, they may be considered as corollaries from the principles already laid down. If it is a duty to do to each according to his deserts, returning good for good, as well as repressing evil by evil, it necessarily follows that we should treat all equally well (when no higher duty forbids) who have deserved equally well of *us*, and

that society should treat all equally well who have deserved equally well of *it*, that is, who have deserved equally well absolutely. This is the highest abstract standard of social and distributive justice, toward which all institutions and the efforts of all virtuous citizens should be made in the utmost possible degree to converge. But this great moral duty rests upon a still deeper foundation, being a direct emanation from the first principle of morals, and not a mere logical corollary from secondary or derivative doctrines. It is involved in the very meaning of utility, or the greatest happiness principle. That principle is a mere form of words without rational signification unless one person's happiness, supposed equal in degree (with the proper allowance made for kind), is counted for exactly as much as another's. These conditions being supplied, Bentham's dictum, "everybody to count for one, nobody for more than one," might be written under the principle of utility as an explanatory commentary.* The equal claim of everybody to happiness, in the estimation of the moralist and of the legislator, involves an equal claim to all the means of happiness except in so far as the inevitable conditions of human life and the general interest in which that of every individual is included set limits to the maxim; and those limits ought to be strictly construed. As every other maxim of justice, so this is by no means applied or held applicable universally; on the contrary, as I have already

---

*This implication, in the first principle of the utilitarian scheme, of perfect impartiality between persons is regarded by Mr. Herbert Spencer (in his *Social Statics*) as a disproof of the pretensions of utility to be a sufficient guide to right; since (he says) the principle of utility presupposes the anterior principle that everybody has an equal right to happiness. It may be more correctly described as supposing that equal amounts of happiness are equally desirable, whether felt by the same or different persons. This, however, is not a *pre*supposition, not a premise needful to support the principle of utility, but the very principle itself; for what is the principle of utility if it be not that "happiness" and "desirable" are synonymous terms? If there is any anterior principle implied, it can be no other than this, that the truths of arithmetic are applicable to the valuation of happiness, as of all other measurable quantities.

(Mr. Herbert Spencer, in a private communication on the subject of the preceding note, objects to being considered an opponent of utilitarianism and states that he regards happiness as the ultimate end of morality; but deems the end only partially attainable by empirical generalizations from the observed results of conduct, and completely attainable only by deducing, from the laws of life and the conditions of existence, what kinds of action necessarily tend to produce happiness and what kinds to produce unhappiness. With the exception of the word "necessarily," I have no dissent to express from this doctrine; and (omitting that word) I am not aware that any modern advocate of utilitarianism is of a different opinion. Bentham, certainly, to whom in the *Social Statics*

remarked, it bends to every person's ideas of social expediency. But in whatever case it is deemed applicable at all, it is held to be the dictate of justice. All persons are deemed to have a *right* to equality of treatment, except when some recognized social expediency requires the reverse. And hence all social inequalities which have ceased to be considered expedient assume the character, not of simple inexpediency, but of injustice, and appear so tyrannical that people are apt to wonder how they ever could have been tolerated—forgetful that they themselves, perhaps, tolerate other inequalities under an equally mistaken notion of expediency, the correction of which would make that which they approve seem quite as monstrous as what they have at last learned to condemn. The entire history of social improvement has been a series of transitions by which one custom or institution after another, from being a supposed primary necessity of social existence, has passed into the rank of a universally stigmatized injustice and tyranny. So it has been with the distinctions of slaves and freemen, nobles and serfs, patricians and plebeians; and so it will be and in part already is, with the aristocracies of color, race, and sex.

It appears from what has been said that justice is a name for certain moral requirements which, regarded collectively, stand higher in the scale of social utility, and are therefore of more paramount obligation, than any others, though particular cases may occur in which some other social duty is so important as to overrule any one of the general maxims of justice. Thus, to save a life, it may not only be allowable, but a duty, to steal or take by force the necessary food or medicine, or to kidnap and compel to officiate the only qualified medical practitioner.

In such cases, as we do not call anything justice which is not a virtue, we usually say, not that justice must give way to some other moral principle, but that what is just in ordinary cases is, by reason of that other principle, not just in the particular case. By this useful accommodation of language, the character of indefeasibility attributed to justice is kept up, and we are saved from the necessity of maintaining that there can be laudable injustice.

The considerations which have now been adduced resolve, I conceive, the only real difficulty in the utilitarian theory of morals. It has always been evident that all cases of justice are also cases of expediency; the difference is in the peculiar sentiment which attaches to the former, as contradistinguished from the latter. If this characteristic sentiment has been sufficiently accounted for; if there is no necessity to assume for it any peculiarity of origin; if it is simply the natural feeling of resentment, moralized by being made coextensive with the demands of social good; and if this feeling not only does but ought to exist in all the classes of cases to which the idea of justice corresponds—that idea no longer presents itself as a stumbling block to the utilitarian ethics. Justice remains the appropriate name for certain social utilities which are vastly more important, and therefore more absolute and imperative, than any others are as a class (though not more so than others may be in particular cases); and which, therefore, ought to be, as well as naturally are, guarded by a sentiment, not only different in degree, but also in kind; distinguished from the milder feeling which attaches to the mere idea of promoting human pleasure or convenience at once by the more definite nature of its commands and by the sterner character of its sanctions.

Mr. Spencer particularly referred, is, least of all writers, chargeable with unwillingness to deduce the effect of actions on happiness from the laws of human nature and the universal conditions of human life. The common charge against him is of relying too exclusively upon such deductions and declining altogether to be bound by the generalizations from specific experience which Mr. Spencer thinks that utilitarians generally confine themselves to. My own opinion (and, as I collect, Mr. Spencer's) is that in ethics, as in all other branches of scientific study, the consilience of the results of both these processes, each corroborating and verifying the other, is requisite to give to any general proposition the kind and degree of evidence which constitutes scientific proof.)

## QUESTIONS

1. Mill says that "To have a right . . . is . . . to have something that society ought to defend me in the possession of." What factors would tend to support the claim that society ought to defend me in the possession of something, rather than leave me to my own defense of it? What factors would tend to support the claim that society ought not to get involved?

2. What sorts of considerations properly incline us to leave the "punishment" of some injustice to the pangs of conscience and informal social pressure?

3. Using Mill's account of duty, give definitions of (a) duty according to prevailing morality; (b) duty according to ideal morality; (c) legal duty.

4. Justice would require that property that had been stolen from a rich miser and then given to the poor be returned. Does returning such property to the owner, even where its theft was a secret in the first place, always do more good than letting the poor keep it? If not, what other utilitarian reasons would there be for returning the stolen property?

5. Using Mill's account of rights, how would one argue to support the claim that (a) a child has a right to parental support; (b) a homeless person that you encounter on the street has a right to a cash contribution from you?

## *Gerald J. Postema*
# THE CONCEPT OF RIGHTS[6]*

The semantic realm of rights is the realm of practical deliberation and normative argument—the realm of goals and aims, duties and obligations, justification and liability. To understand the language of rights we need to mark out its distinctive place in this complex of fundamental normative notions. Rights assertions are thickly textured normative assertions. Their structure is different and more complex than assertions of value, statements of goals or aims, and propositions ascribing duties to particular agents.[7] Assertions of rights typically take the form:

*J has a right to X relative to (or 'against') K.*

A right is a certain kind of normative relation (or set of such relations) between a *bearer* (J), *respecters* (K), and the *object* of the right (X). The nature of this relation itself is complex, and can vary considerably across the range of rights we claim

*From "In Defence of 'French Nonsense': Fundamental Rights in Constitutional Jurisprudence" in *Enlightenment, Rights, and Revolution* (1989), edited by Neil MacCormick and Zenon Bankowski. Reprinted by permission of the author.

[6]The discussion in this section depends heavily on recent work on the concept of rights, in particular D.N. MacCormick, 'Rights in Legislation', in P.M.S. Hacker and J. Raz, eds., *Law, Morality, and Society* (Oxford: Clarendon Press, 1977); J. Raz, *The Morality of Freedom* (Oxford: Clarendon Press, 1986), chs. 7, 8, and 10; and J. Coleman, 'Rethinking the Theory of Legal Rights', in Coleman, *Markets, Morals and the Law* (Cambridge: Cambridge University Press, 1988), 28–63.

[7]C.Wellman, *A Theory of Rights* (Totowa, NJ: Rowman & Alanheld, 1985), 10.

for ourselves and others. Over the next several pages I will explore this complex texture of rights assertions.

## Interests and the Focus of Rights

While the *concept* of rights imposes few limits on the range of objects of rights, it does assume that the objects are linked to certain interests, or components of the good, of bearers.[8] Rights assertions necessarily presuppose that securing the object to the bearer is good *because* or *insofar* as the object answers to the interest of the bearer, that is, insofar as it is component of, or means to, the good of the bearer.[9]

It is often said that rights are essentially concerned with securing interests of *individual* human beings.[10] As a claim about the logic of rights this is false, although it may be true on some substantive theories of rights. It is true, however, that rights are 'focused' in a way that distinguishes them from other kinds of moral or political aims and marks out the peculiar niche rights occupy in the logical environment of normative deliberation and argument. Relative to a class of moral subjects, rights focus on the good of 'each and every member severally' (MacCormick, 205), rather than the aggregate or collective good of that class. The logic of rights requires that we distinguish between goods of the class understood *collectively* or *in the aggregate* and goods of the class understood *distributively*, but it does not require that the members of the class be *individual* human beings. There is no logical barrier to speaking of rights of groups, classes, states, corporations, nations, or families, which rights are not reducible to rights of members considered apart from their membership in the group. (Of course, some group rights may *indirectly imply*, or give rise to, rights of their members.) It is conceivable, then, that some rights might secure collective goods or interests.

Again, it is often said that the essential 'normative function' of rights assertions is to express a compelling demand which ordinarily will defeat ('trump') considerations of aggregate or collective good.[11] But this seems to confuse a claim about the logic of rights with a substantive claim about their relative weight. From the fact that assertions of rights are logically distinct from statements of collective or aggregate goals, and that these two kinds of normative assertions can come into conflict, nothing *follows* about the weight of either kind of consideration.[12] If rights regularly 'trump' considerations of collective or aggregate good when they conflict, this is so in virtue of their place in a substantive moral or political theory—and in particular in virtue of the substantive importance of the interests secured by the rights—not in virtue of their logic alone.

---

[8] This thesis is neutral between the so-called 'will theory' of rights and its rival the 'benefit theory'. They are best understood not as theses about the *concept* of rights, but as *substantive* theories about the components of what I will call below the 'exercise–respect structure' of all rights. (See Coleman, 'Rethinking', 38.) The will theory, as I understand it, holds the substantive thesis that there is one interest the securing of which is common to all actual rights, viz., the interest of the bearer in autonomy, or control over some area of life (or public recognition of this autonomy).

[9] In some cases, the benefit to a particular bearer of a given right *is imputed* or *assumed* rather than *actual*. This is possible because rights are typically ascribed to members of a *class* of bearers and the ascription of a right will seem appropriate if the object answers to interests of the members of that class generally speaking. See MacCormick, 'Rights in Legislation', 202.

[10] MacCormick, 205; this also seems to be Dworkin's view in *Taking Rights Seriously* (Cambridge, Mass.: Harvard Univeristy Press, 1978), xi and *passim*.

[11] See J.S. Mill. *Utilitarianism*, G. Scher, ed. (Indianapolis: Hackett Publishing Co., 1979), 53; Dworkin, *Taking Rights Seriously*, xi, 92, 191–2; Dworkin, *A Matter of Principle* (Cambridge Mass.: Harvard University Press, 1985), 359; L. W. Sumner, *Moral Foundations of Rights* (Oxford: Clarendon Press, 1986), 15.

[12] Why, then, think this is a defining feature of rights? Because, Professor Dworkin suggests, '[w]e need rights, as a distinct element in political theory, only when some decision that injures some people nevertheless finds *prima*

## The Content of Rights

Rights, then, are normative relations focused around the interests of bearers. We can better appreciate the complex texture of rights if we inquire after the nature of these normative relations. Consider the content of rights. **Rights as grounds.** Let us begin with Bentham's positivist analysis of rights. One has a right, says Bentham, *just in case* one is the intended beneficiary of a (regularly enforced) obligation.[13] On this analysis, talk of rights is empty except where there are legally (or informal socially) enforced obligations already in place. Moreover, the language of rights becomes entirely dispensable, since everything we want to say about rights can be said equally well with the language of obligation (Hart, 'Legal Rights', 181–2). Because of his reductionist aims, Bentham was not much bothered by these implications.[14] But they troubled others, including John Stuart Mill.

Mill shifted the focus of Bentham's analysis of rights. To say a person has a right, says Mill, is to say

> that he has a valid claim upon society to protect him in the possession of it, either by force of law or by that of education and opinion. If he has what we consider a sufficient claim, on whatever account, to have something guaranteed him by society, we say he has a right to it. To have a right, then, is, I conceive, to have something that society ought to defend me in the possession of (*Utilitarianism*, 52)

Rights, on Mill's view, are not statements about protections actually provided by law or society for certain interests, but rather about *grounds* or reasons of a certain sort *for* these protections.

Joseph Raz recently proposed a slightly more refined version of this account. X has a right, Raz maintains, if and only if 'X can have rights and, other things being equal, an aspect of X's well-being (his interest) is a sufficient reason for holding some other person(s) to be under a duty.'[15] This proposal seems vulnerable to Bentham's retort that 'reasons for wishing there were such things as rights are not rights . . . want is not supply—hunger is not bread' (*Anarchical Fallacies, 501*). But the Mill–Raz thesis is not that rights are reasons for rights, which of course is nonsense, but that one has a right to X just in case one's interest in X is sufficient reason for (constitutes 'a valid claim upon') society to guarantee or protect one's enjoyment of X.

The nature of rights, I have said, is determined by their role in moral/political deliberation and argument. On the Mill–Raz proposal, the role of assertions of rights is to link certain interests of rights bearers to a network of what Neil MacCormick calls 'normative protections'. The link is provided, specifically, by the assertion that the interest is sufficiently important to *ground* or *justify* these normative protections. Rights, then, should be identified with neither the interests which ought to be protected, nor the protections that are or ought to be provided.

---

*facie* support in the claim that it will make the community as a whole better off . . .' (*Matter of Principle*, 371). But this seems false. We need rights as a distinct element in political theory whenever we find it important to recognize *distributively* certain claims of members of a class or group, regardless of the logical character of the competing moral or political considerations. Rights are distinctive normative assertions in virtue of their complex texture. They retain this distinctive character, and have a distinctive impact on practical deliberation in consequence, as long as they are capable of competing with other practical considerations, including other rights.

[13] J. Bentham, *Pannomial Fragments*, Bowring iii, 218. See Hart, 'Natural Rights: Bentham and John Stuart Mill', and 'Legal Rights' both in *Essays on Bentham* (Oxford: Clarendon Press, 1982).

[14] For a general discussion of the motivations behind Bentham's rational reconstruction of central moral and jurisprudential concepts see my *Bentham and the Common Law Tradition* (Oxford: Clarendon Press, 1986), 317–28 (hereafter 'BCLT').

[15] Raz, *Morality of Freedom*, 166. See also N. MacCormick, 'Rights in Legislation', 204.

Rather, rights assertions are normative bridges between certain interests and certain sets of normative protections.

I have put the Mill–Raz thesis in terms of *normative protections*, rather than just *duties* and *obligations* as Raz (and Mill implicitly) does. I have done this for two reasons. First, the structure and composition of the normative protections can be complex and varied; they can include elements other than duties. These protections consist of a set of normative relations which determine what the *bearer* may or is empowered to do or say relative to certain other parties, and what is *owed* to the bearer by those parties. I shall call this set of relations the 'exercise–respect structure' (the E–R structure) of a right[16], because it determines specifically how the right may be exercised by the bearer and is to be respected by others.[17] Second, the components of the E–R structure (the 'content') of rights—whether of some species of rights, or of rights in general—is a matter for substantive rights theory, not formal analysis, to determine.[18] The E–R structure is determined by the weight and importance of the background interest in the circumstances in which the right will be exercised and respected, and so will depend on the respect structure of other rights, as well as the importance of other competing moral or political considerations. Let me elaborate on each of these points.

THE E–R STRUCTURE OF RIGHTS. Hohfeld's conceptual scheme is best understood not as typology of *rights* (or discrete legal relationships, as he proposed), but as a typology of components of the E–R structure of rights. If we look around at the rights people tend to claim for themselves or others it will be clear that they involve more or less complex clusters of Hohfeldian elements,[19] that is, sets of Hohfeldian claims, duties and liberties, or sets of powers, immunities, and disabilities, or (more typically) a complex combination of both. For any given right, these relations may be quite different for different respecters.[20]

Much has been made recently of the 'directionality' of duties associated with rights.[21] This is not surprising, since such duties are prominent in the E–R structure of many rights. But note that the claims, liberties, powers, and disabilities *of bearers* are equally 'directed' *toward respecters*. It is not the relational character of the E–R structure of rights itself that explains the sense that rights are directed to the bearer, but rather the fact that the *normative ground* of that E–R structure is an important interest of the bearer.

Similarly, the E–R structure is thought to provide 'normative advantages' to the bearer. But this is not because the bearer enjoys liberties, powers and immunities ('advantages'), and only the respecters suffer constraints on their choices and actions in the form of duties, liabilities, and disabilities

[16]Coleman calls this the 'transaction structure' of the right ('Rethinking', 35). I follow Coleman here, although my notion is somewhat broader.

[17]This way of conceptualizing rights brings the modern notion back to its roots in pre-imperial Roman law. (See R. Tuck, *Natural Rights Theories* (Cambridge: Cambridge University Press, 1979), 9–10.) *Iura* were not *possessions* of an individual over which he had sovereign control, but rather established relations and responsibilities between parties arising from an agreement between them. The modern concept of rights differs from the Roman concept in this respect: whereas *iura* were grounded in agreements between the parties, modern rights are grounded in certain interests of one of the parties. In virtue of this fact, we designate that party the right-*bearer*, even though both bearers and respecters may have liberties, powers, disabilities, etc., relative to each other.

[18]This is effectively argued by Coleman, 'Rethinking'.

[19]See MacCormick, 'Rights in Legislation', 205-6; J. Waldron, 'Introduction' to his, *Theories of Rights* (Oxford: Oxford University Press, 1984), 10-11.

[20]These relations, *pace* Hohfeld, need not be diadic: they may well be one-many relations. See MacCormick, 206; and Wellman, *Theory of Rights*, 24, 43.

[21]See, e.g., Sumner, *Moral Foundations*, 42–3.

('disadvantages'). For bearers often 'suffer' such constraints as well. An 'inalienability rule', for example, imposes a disability on the bearer as well as conferring on him or her immunity. The 'normative advantages' enjoyed by the bearer can be explained only in terms of the anticipated effects of the cluster of normative protections defined by the E–R structure on social interactions.

PRIMARY VS SECONDARY E–R STRUCTURES. Mill's analysis of rights quoted above, however, is deficient in one important respect.[22] Mill mentions explicitly only one party to whom bearers are related, viz., society, but surely it is possible for one to have rights against individuals, too. Moreover, Mill says that as a right bearer one has a claim to society's protection of one's *rights*. But that seems to commit Mill either to a viciously circular analysis of rights, or to the confusion of rights with arguments for them which Bentham pointed out.

The problem is that Mill failed to recognize that the E–R structure of rights is layered.[23] The *primary* layer of a right's E–R structure consists of the cluster of Hohfeldian elements I described above. The *secondary* layer—which also may include a complex set of claims, duties, powers, immunities, and the like—is designed to *enforce* the normative relations at the primary level. These Hohfeldian normative elements come into play when the primary elements are violated or improperly invoked. Like the primary E–R structure, the secondary structure is determined by the weight and importance of the background interest of the bearer in the circumstances in which the right will be exercised and respected. Thus, it will depend on the nature of the primary structure, the need for enforcing it, available means for enforcing it, their costs, etc.[24]

While the primary E–R structure may define relations between individuals, the secondary structure typically (though not necessarily) involves claims against the community more generally (or government acting as its agent) to underwrite and vindicate the primary structure. Mill's mistake was to focus exclusively on the secondary E–R structure of some rights.

## Interests and the E–R Structure of Rights

It is likely that different rights will combine Hohfeldian elements into different E–R structures, some relatively simple, others very complex. The bearer's *focal interest* generates and unifies the bundle of Hohfeldian elements of any given right, and preserves the integrity of the right through changes in its E–R structure.[25] The exact nature of the E–R structure for any given right depends

---

[22]See Hart, 'Natural Rights', 92–3.

[23]The terminology is mine, but the basic distinction was introduced by Coleman, 'Rethinking', 34, 36.

[24]It is tempting to think of the distinction between the primary and secondary layers in terms of the distinction between moral and legal rights. But this would be a mistake. First, we can find this layering in *both* legal and moral rights. In the former, the distinction between layers parallels roughly the distinction between rights and remedies (if we include in the latter category also certain procedural rights). In the latter, there are informal analogues to the enforcement structure. For example, it would determine those who may and who *are authorized* to make or press the claims defined by the primary structure. Second, while some legal rights may rest on more fundamental and moral rights, other moral rights imply at most that there *ought to be* legal recognition of them, *not that there is* such recognition. Moreover, there may be some moral rights, with at least minimal secondary E–R structures, for which legal recognition would be undesirable. Fourth, some legal rights do not rest on moral rights at all, but still have both primary and secondary exercise–respect structures.

[25]Waldron, 'Introduction' in *Theories*, 11. Brandt points out that 'A manifesto of the Women's Movement might list innumerable duties of men, corporations, or government, in respect of women. But such a list would lack focus. After all there is a target here: that women have an equal opportunity for a good life. That is what all these duties are aimed at; the duties are what other people must do if women are to have an equally good life. In talking of a right to equal opportunity, we focus attention on the intended good.' R. Brandt. 'The Concept of a Moral Right', *Journal of Philosophy*, 80 (1983), 44.

on the nature and moral importance of the right's focal interest and how an interest of that kind and that degree of importance can best be protected in the circumstances in which the bearer and respecters interact.

Furthermore, a right can be said to *exist* only if the focal interest is of the appropriate kind and of sufficient moral weight in the circumstances to justify a specific E–R structure relative to certain bearers and respecters (Raz, *Morality of Freedom*, 181–3). It must be possible to justify this structure in light of the burdens or restrictions it places on people and the opportunity costs and other costs consequent upon respecting it. As Carl Wellman observes, 'any complete justification of the assertion that some specified right exists must have a complexity comparable to the complex structure of the rights justified . . . the grounds of rights can only be the sorts of reasons that would establish the existence of claims, liberties, powers and immunities' (*Theory of Rights*, 5).

Thus, the existence and *content* of an alleged right depend on the kind of interest it seeks to protect, its moral weight or importance, and the circumstances in which it will be exercised and respected. That is to say, they depend on matters for substantive moral/political argument. It has always been recognized that what rights *there are*— that is, *who* has rights to *what*—is a morally/ politically substantive matter. It is now clear that *what it is to have or enjoy* any given right is also in large part a morally/politically substantive matter.

Thus, if our view of an alleged right's focal interest changes, or its moral importance relative to other goals or principles changes, so too may our view of the right's content (the E–R structure), or even its existence, change. Even if we keep constant our view of a given right's focal interest, the right can generate new duties, disabilities, and the like, if the circumstances in which bearers and respecters interact change materially. As Raz has pointed out, rights have thus a 'dynamic aspect'. No closed list of du-

ties (or other components of the E–R structure) correspond to any given right (*Morality of Freedom*, 171). That which preserves continuity of the right through changes in its E–R structure is the right's focal interest.

Raz also correctly observes that it may be possible to recognize that an interest is morally important enough to justify *some* significant E–R structure, without yet identifying in detail all the components of that structure (*Morality of Freedom*, 184–5). Rights assertions often take this form especially in rhetoric of politics. We must keep in mind, however, that in this form they function as enthymemes in an extended moral/political argument, as invitations to more detailed inquiry and argument. Such inquiry and argument would have to extend both 'behind' the right to a more careful and detailed accounting of the importance of its focal interest and the place of that interest in a larger moral/political theory, and 'ahead' to a more detailed definition of its E–R structure and its place in the existing network of rights and other social relationships.

Given what we have learned here about the texture of rights assertions and their role in moral or political argument, we should not be surprised to find that rights assertions are highly contestable. Parties may agree that some right exists, but disagree about the components of the E–R structure that the right is supposed to ground and consequently disagree about the practical implications to be drawn from the existence of the right. This may be due to different general substantive theories of rights, or to disagreements localized to the species of right in question. Disagreement may turn on different characterisations of the focal interest of the right, or different assessments of its weight or importance, or different views of the context of social relationships (actual or ideal) in which the right takes on concrete life, or different views of the best way to protect or promote that interest.

Thus, rights assertions, especially when they ascribe to bearers relatively abstract rights the *existence* of which we may all grant, are likely to be invitations to extended argument and debate, rather than major premises in a very short practical syllogism. For this reason I am skeptical of Raz's intriguing view that the 'mediational' role of rights in moral/political argument makes possible 'a common culture . . . formed round shared intermediate conclusions in spite of a great degree of haziness and disagreement, concerning ultimate values' (*Morality of Freedom*, 181). The 'shared intermediate conclusions' regarding the existence of certain rights are important for shaping a common culture, but not because they make it possible for us to agree on concrete practical conclusions while disagreeing about fundamentals. Because rights assertions are *bridges between* fundamental ideals and social visions and concrete social life, the disagreements about fundamentals are very likely to emerge in the concrete implications drawn from the 'shared intermediate conclusions'. They are as likely to generate disagreement as consensus. Their contribution to a common political culture lies in their ability to focus and structure the debate in a distinctive constructive way, to pose common questions and problems, to bring our conflicting ideals and social visions into contact with common facts about our community's history and future. . . .

# QUESTIONS

1. Postema says that "one has a right to X just in case one's interest in X is sufficient reason for . . . society to guarantee or protect one's enjoyment of X." Is this true as it stands? Must it be the *bearer's* interest that is sufficient reason for this protection, or might the interest of others in some cases be sufficient? Consider the right to free speech. What if the justification for a right to free speech rests primarily on the benefits to others from being able to hear what people have to say? In that case, my interest in speaking freely might be viewed as relatively unimportant and an inadequate basis for a right, while society's interest in hearing various points of view would be a reason of sufficient importance to ground a right.

2. What implications does Postema's account of the existence and content of rights have for the debate over the Supreme Court's recognition, in *Griswold v. Connecticut,* of a right of privacy that is nowhere mentioned in the Constitution?

3. Remembering the brief discussion of Hohfeld in the introduction to Part 3, explain what Postema means by saying that "Hohfeld's conceptual scheme is best understood not as a typology of *rights* . . . , but as a typology of components of the E–R structure of rights."

# PART FOUR

# Law and Economics: Economic Efficiency as Goal and Explanation

The economic analysis of law is a new field of research that has gained considerable momentum in recent years. It is a program that is both ambitious and controversial: ambitious because it aims at providing a unifying account of many disparate areas of law such as contracts, property and nuisance law; controversial because its very attempt to unify so many segments of law has seemed to critics to be a gross oversimplification which, if also accepted as a goal of public policy, would lead to injustice.

The unifying principle of the law and economics movement is the principle of economic efficiency, or wealth maximization. (As we shall see, these are actually two closely related but slightly different principles.) The most ambitious version of the law and economics program includes both a descriptive component and a normative component. The descriptive component seeks to explain the development of the law as an outgrowth of the principle of efficiency. Whether in property law, contracts, torts, or even criminal law, judges and legislators have, according to this explanation, worked either consciously or unconsciously toward making the law more efficient. The normative component of the law and economics movement proposes the principle of efficiency as the proper goal of legislative and judicial strivings. Here the claim is that economic efficiency is what *ought* to guide the development of the law. Just as the great classical utilitarians Bentham and Mill proposed the maximization of utility as the proper goal of law, contemporary economic analysts advance ideas either to show how the law in some area already has developed on its own in a way that promotes economic efficiency or, if it has failed in this, these analysts attempt to show how the law ought to be reformed to make it more efficient.

## CONCEPTS AND APPLICATIONS

CONCEPTS OF EFFICIENCY: THE PARETO PRINCIPLE. The principle of efficiency, usually called the *Pareto principle,* is an economist's invention. While the principle may be new to those who have studied no economics, it is simple enough to state and apply. The principle enables us to compare distributions of things among people. The things whose distributions are compared can be almost anything, ranging from manufactured goods to land, to more abstract things like the rights and privileges of office. The Pareto principle has two parts. The first allows us to compare some distributions:

(Pareto superiority): Distribution $D_1$ is *superior* to distribution $D_2$ if and only if (a) $D_1$ makes at least one person better off than $D_2$, and (b) $D_1$ makes no one worse off than $D_2$.

As an illustration, think of any state of affairs in which two people would be better off if each traded something with the other: $A$ would be better off by trading with $B$ in return for something $B$ has, and vice versa. If no one else is adversely affected by the trade, then the resulting distribution after the trade will be Pareto-superior to the distribution before the trade. How do we determine what makes a person "better off"? Answering this can lead us deeply into controversies within political and moral philosophy. For our purposes here, we shall keep matters simple. We shall assume that, in most circumstances anyway, people are the best judges of what makes them better off, and hence that being made better off is to be equated with getting what one prefers. If randomly put together sack lunches are randomly distributed to a group of people, it will be highly likely that some distribution would be superior to the one that results from the random process. So the best mechanism for arriving at a superior distribution would be to allow the people in possession of the lunches to trade with one another: an apple for an orange, a chicken sandwich for a cheese sandwich, and so on. We should reflect here on what needs to be the case for this mechanism of "free trade" to result in improvements in the initial distribution. If $A$ and $B$ would both be better off if $A$'s chicken sandwich is traded for $B$'s cheese sandwich, the trade may still fail to occur if $A$ and $B$ do not have information about each other's possessions and willingness to trade. Getting the necessary information may be costly or impossible. The trade may also fail to occur if $A$ and $B$ are far from one another and the costs of negotiating a deal outweigh its value to one or both of the parties. These costs of getting information and bringing about the trade are usually called *transaction costs.*

Let us suppose that the mechanism works perfectly, and that the people in the imagined group carry out mutual trades of lunch portions until no further move toward greater Pareto superiority is possible. The second part of the Pareto principle then defines this situation as optimal:

(Pareto optimality): A distribution $D_x$ is *optimal* if and only if there is no distribution $D_y$ that is superior to $D_x$.

So defined, optimality gives us one important meaning of "efficiency." Notice that even at this point it is easy to see that the Pareto conceptions of superiority and optimality carry some internal limitations. Perhaps the most important of these limitations is that a distribution can be judged superior or optimal only relative to a given starting point. For example, consider the situation in which A has a sack containing a complete lunch while B has nothing. Since any redistribution would make A worse off, the existing distribution would be optimal. And yet the same would be true of the reverse situation in which B had everything and A had nothing. To some, this limitation constitutes one of the main reasons why the Pareto principle could not be satisfactory as a principle of justice. The principle would make the desirability of a distribution too heavily dependent on factors that are arbitrary from a moral point of view, like the accidental fact of how assets were initially distributed among persons.[1] For other thinkers, this is no objection. To them, the justice of a distribution is not called into question by the mere fact that it arose out of the accidental facts of some initial distribution.[2]

A BROADER CONCEPT: EFFICIENCY AS WEALTH MAXIMIZATION. The concept of economic efficiency as defined by the Pareto principle is rather narrow since it designates as superior only those redistributions that would not be objected to by anyone. Because of obstacles standing in the way of reaching an agreement, various people may object to activities which are economically beneficial on the whole, at least in the sense that they maximize wealth in the community. Suppose, for example, that S objects to the building of a skyscraper on nearby property because the skyscraper would block the sun coming through S's window. Due to various legal and other obstacles, it might be difficult or impossible for S to enter into an agreement with the developer that would result in S's putting these objections aside. Since S objects to the skyscraper, the building of the skyscraper would not result in a Pareto-superior situation. Yet the skyscraper's existence would surely add far more wealth to the community than it would take away by casting an afternoon shadow on S's house. So it is often useful to economists to define a broader concept of efficiency as wealth maximization. This is usually called the *Kaldor-Hicks principle* of efficiency:

(K-H efficiency): Distribution $D_1$ is *K-H superior* to $D_2$ if and only if the gains in $D_1$ could be redistributed so that at least one person would be better off and no one would be worse off.

It is important to notice that, for $D_1$ to be superior to $D_2$, it is not necessary that the gains *actually* be redistributed; only that they are sufficient so that they *could* be used to provide for actual Pareto superiority.[3] What is important to K-H superiority, therefore, is net improvement in the total production of wealth. On this criterion, the situation resulting from the building of the skyscraper would be K-H superior to that in which it is not built (at least if we may assume that the existence of the skyscraper will result in enough wealth to more than compensate S for the loss of sunlight). As Posner indicates in the reading in this section, we do not need to take into account here the costs of carrying out an actual compensation, because it is potential, not actual, compensation that is the issue.

---

[1]See the discussion of the Pareto principle in John Rawls, *A Theory of Justice* (Cambridge, Mass.: Harvard University Press, 1971).

[2]See Robert Nozick, *Anarchy, State, and Utopia* (New York: Basic Books, 1974), especially Chap. 7, for a contrary view.

[3]A useful discussion of the difference between the Pareto and Kaldor-Hicks principles is found in Jules Coleman, "The Economic Analysis of Law," in *Ethics, Economics, & the Law*, ed. J. Ronald Pennock and John W. Chapman (New York: New York University Press, 1982), Chap. 4.

Efficiency as measured by one of these standards, then, is the goal that is supposed to guide the law's development. Sometimes people will reach the most efficient solution when they are left on their own to buy, sell, or use property under the familiar institutions of private property. In other cases this will not be enough, and legal institutions will have to be structured somewhat differently if wealth is to be maximized. A simple example of the economic analysis of pollution and nuisance law will illustrate these points.

AN EXAMPLE: EFFICIENT RESPONSES TO POLLUTION. Imagine a restaurant that is directly adjacent to a small hotel. Smoke from the restaurant's kitchen drifts over to the hotel, making the hotel substantially less desirable as a place to stay. With the pollution from the restaurant's kitchen smoke, hotel owner (H) makes $10,000 less profit yearly than if there were no smoke. Restaurant owner (R) could eliminate the smoke by installing a filtering system, but that would cost R $3,000 yearly. Clearly, the situation is not efficient. It would be a more efficient situation if R were to install the filter. But whether this actually happens depends on more than its being abstractly desirable from the standpoint of efficiency. So the challenge for the law is to facilitate, or otherwise bring about, the efficient result. In this simple example, we can imagine two possibilities. One is that H has a property right, enforceable with the power of getting a court injunction, that R's restaurant not pollute the neighborhood. The other is that R has a property right, likewise enforceable with the power of getting a court injunction against H, that H not interfere with the ongoing (and polluting) operations of the restaurant. Relevant at this point is one of the most influential doctrines of economic analysis of law, the *Coase theorem*,[4] which states that, in an ideal situation in which the relevant parties have full information, transaction costs are zero, and the parties are prepared to act cooperatively, it will not matter to the achievement of efficiency which of these initial assignments of rights holds. In either case, the efficient outcome will result. If R initially has the right to pollute, H will buy that right from R for some price greater than $3,000 and less than $10,000. If H initially has the right to be free of the pollution, then H can get an injunction against R, and R will have to buy the filter. In either case, the filter is installed, and the hotel gets to operate without the pollution.

Of course, the neat demonstration of this outcome depended on several assumptions: The parties R and H were willing to cooperate, they had full information about one another's situation, and so on. But it is a notorious fact that these assumptions do not always hold. In addition, there may be another problem. What if there are many parties affected by this pollution such that, if they all got together to negotiate with the polluter, each could contribute enough so that together, and only together, they could buy the right to pollute from the polluter? It is not worthwhile for any of the affected parties to act individually, so success depends on collective action. The problem is that there are difficulties and costs involved in getting together, working out a plan of action among themselves, and then insuring that each affected party makes the assigned contribution needed to buy the rights from the polluter. We are no longer talking about a situation in which transaction costs are zero.

---

[4]The theorem is named for Ronald Coase, winner of the 1991 Nobel Prize in economics. Coase has over the years become famous for his identification of the problem of transaction costs in economic activity and for the implications these have for the institution of property and the free market. See especially his "The Problem of Social Cost," in *Journal of Law & Economics*, vol. 3 (1960), p. 1.

On the contrary, they may be sufficiently great to prevent the efficient outcome. The polluter will go on polluting, reducing in the process the creation of wealth in the community. It is the job of economic analysis of law to propose a solution guided by the idea that the law should work to advance that outcome which comes closest to economic efficiency, or the result that would have been produced had conditions been ideal.

Given obstacles such as the fact that many parties are affected and collective action is difficult, we can no longer rely on the buying and selling of property rights in a free market to solve the problem. How, then, should the law assign entitlements and then enforce them to bring about the efficient outcome? Economic analysts of law have made a helpful distinction between enforcing an entitlement using a *property* rule and enforcing an entitlement using a *liability* rule.[5] An entitlement is protected by a property rule if it can be removed from its possessor only by purchase in a voluntary transaction. The holder of an entitlement is protected from encroachments by the threat of punishment directed at would-be violators. Having an entitlement that is protected by a property rule is an all-or-nothing thing: If *H* is entitled to be free of pollution, then anyone who causes pollution for *H* can be punished. Their only recourse is to purchase the entitlement in advance in a voluntary transaction. On the other hand, if an entitlement is protected by a liability rule, the would-be polluter may violate the entitlement by dumping pollution on the entitlement holder, but can be made to pay compensation for the damages caused. The amount of compensation to be paid is an objective amount determined by the actual damages caused. It is not a punishment aimed at deterring would-be violators of the entitlement. Protection of entitlements by liability rule is therefore not an all-or-nothing matter. Now suppose that there are many hotels and other establishments similarly affected by the pollution. Each can act separately to obtain compensation from *R* for the pollution caused by *R*'s restaurant. In this way, the need for collective action, otherwise an obstacle to an efficient outcome, is obviated. The negative external effects, or costs, of *R*'s otherwise beneficial activity are internalized in this way in *R*'s calculations. The full social cost to the community from this form of activity is taken into account, and *R* can use this fact as a basis for deciding whether to purchase and install a filter.

AUTOMOBILE-PEDESTRIAN ACCIDENTS. The capacity of economic analysis of law to be extended in often surprising ways to new areas of law and behavior emerges in its analysis of the tradeoffs between walking and automobile driving. The classic problem for economic analysis that of a conflict between two kinds of activity, each of which is beneficial in its own way, but impinges on the other. In the pollution example, *R*'s restaurant produced something of value, though inflicting a cost on *H*'s hotel in the process. What we want from a social point of view is the most efficient tradeoff.[6] Walking versus automobile driving is also such a tradeoff. The presence of pedestrians creates obstacles for automobiles, slowing them down. And the presence of automobiles in the area where pedestrians are walking means that some pedestrians will be injured or killed. More generally, the driving of automobiles in

---

[5]The main statement of this distinction is in Guido Calabresi and A. Douglas Melamed, "Property Rules, Liability Rules, and Inalienability: One View of the Cathedral," in *Harvard Law Review*, vol. 85 (1972), p. 1089.

[6]A useful brief discussion in economic terms of automobile accidents is to be found in A. Mitchell Polinsky, *An Introduction to Law and Economics* (Boston: Little, Brown and Company, 1983), Chap. 6.

the neighborhood creates a risk of accidents. A risk of harm, of course, is not the same as actual harm, but it is a negative effect, much like pollution. As such, economic analysis suggests that the legal remedies be arranged so that the outcome will be efficient, with the external negative effects of automobile driving for pedestrians being taken into account. We can measure the risk of a particular kind of harm by multiplying the disvalue of that harm by the probability that it will occur. If the disvalue of a particular kind of accident can be measured as a cost of $1,000, and the probability of its occurrence as 0.01, then the expected cost of such an accident = $10.

We can again imagine two assignments of entitlement and two ways of protecting entitlements. As between automobile drivers and pedestrians, either automobile drivers could be given an entitlement to impose risks on pedestrians, or pedestrians could be given an entitlement to be free of risks imposed by automobile driving. And the entitlements themselves could be protected either by a property rule or a liability rule. Which combination would lead to the efficient result? Because there are so many potential drivers and pedestrians, this would seem to be a classic example of a case in which protection of an entitlement by use of property rule would be inefficient. For suppose that pedestrians are granted the entitlement to be free of automobile-imposed risk of accident. If transaction costs were zero and a fully cooperative attitude reigned, automobile drivers could negotiate with pedestrians for the right to drive. The amount paid for the right would no doubt be reasonable. But in reality, transaction costs would be far from zero; they would in fact be enormous. The number of parties to the negotiations would be staggering. So protection of the entitlement by use of a property rule would surely not lead to an efficient result. Protection of a pedestrian's entitlement via a liability rule is more promising. Under such a rule, a pedestrian who is injured would be able to obtain compensation from the automobile driver(s) involved in the accident.

There are further questions which might be answered within the conceptual framework of economic analysis. One concerns the fault system of liability. If automobile driver D causes harm to pedestrian P, should D's liability to pay P compensatory damages be made to depend on D's being at fault? Or should we have a system of strict liability in which the mere causing of harm is sufficient for liability? A strict liability system would force automobile drivers to bear the costs of injuries they cause. Since no inquiry would be made into the question of the driver's fault, whether the injury occurred as a result of driving too fast would be irrelevant to the awarding of compensatory damages. From the social point of view of economic efficiency and the maximization of wealth, we want automobiles to be used, for their use produces wealth. Moreover, we want them to be driven at an optimum speed, high enough to serve their purposes well, but not so high as to begin to produce a net loss due to the costs of accidents they cause. Will a strict liability system be efficient? Yes, according to the following argument. Being strictly liable for all the accidents to pedestrians they cause, rational drivers will choose their driving speed depending on what maximizes the social benefit for their driving, where social benefit = (benefit of the driving – cost imposed by the driving on others). Thus if we imagine that driving 10 mph faster will yield $100 worth of additional profits, it will not be worth the bargain if it can be expected to cause $110 worth of additional costs to the driver in the form of compensatory damages.

Economic analysis can also shed light on the fault system in which negligence is a necessary condition for a driver's liability. Judgments of negligence involve the application of standards of care, including care in not imposing undue risks on others. Limiting ourselves again to the issue of driver's speed, there will be some driving speed which constitutes the line of demarcation between negligence and non-negligence. Sometimes this line varies from one situation to another, and judgments must be individualized for the particular circumstances, usually by a court. More usually, and for reasons of simplicity of enforcement, this line is not individualized, but established by legislation. In either case, we need to know where this line should be set. Economic analysis proposes that the line be set at the level that is efficient. This solution, though theoretically neat, is difficult to apply in practice. Determining the economically efficient speed for automobiles requires that the governmental official making the determination have a great deal of information. Indeed, unlike enforcing entitlements using a property rule, the liability rule method of enforcing entitlements brings with it just such additional burdens on judges and legislatures. They must be sure to impose compensatory damages that equal the harm actually caused and, where a negligence system is used, they must use standards of negligence that truly reflect the requirements of economic efficiency.

## SOME PROBLEMS

In addition to its vigorous proponents, the program of law and economics has had many equally vigorous critics. Here as elsewhere, the critics have sometimes taken accurate aim, while in other cases their criticisms have been wide of the mark. Let us confine our attention in this introduction to a few of the objections that focus on the acceptability of the principle of efficiency as a normative principle.

Perhaps the easiest objection to level against the principle of efficiency in either of the versions mentioned above is what it designates as an efficient allocation depends heavily on the initial distribution, and this may be grossly unequal, unjust, or both. This is related to the fact that what people are willing to pay for depends on the resources they have available. Neither version of the efficiency principle takes any account of such matters as how wealth was initially distributed, or whether demand for goods and services is based on fundamental needs or a developed taste for frivolous luxuries.

This criticism, however, is valid only against those who propose the unrestricted use of the principle of efficiency in all areas of law and policy. But the proponent of efficiency need not always be understood in this way. For example, it is possible to propose a constrained pursuit of economic efficiency, that is, an operative standard only against a background in which wealth and resources are distributed approximately equally, or in some other way that one takes to be consistent with justice. And the proponent of efficiency may also be right in insisting that, whether or not we allow the law to be shaped by the principle of efficiency, we should at least use economic analysis to give us some idea of what things would be like if the principle were to operate without restriction. We may choose to restrict the free market in the interests of justice, fairness, or moral decency, but, reflecting on what a free market would be like in some area in which we are not used to seeing it operate, we may also decide that our rejection of it was based on irrational prejudice. For example, we may on reflection decide that Richard Posner's suggestion[7] for a market in babies ought to be rejected on moral grounds. But in thinking about how such a market would work, we will be able to confront directly our deepest reasons for thinking it unacceptable. Then again, we may decide that such a market is desirable and our moral objections to it were unfounded.

There is another way in which the unrestricted use of the principle of efficiency would indeed be objectionable. It is one thing to suggest that public, general, prospective laws enacted by a legislature ought to be framed with the goal of promoting economic efficiency, at least in a way consistent with the rule of law. It is quite another to suggest that courts ought to dispose of individual cases in accordance with the principle of maximizing wealth in the community. Recall that bringing about K-H efficiency does not require actual compensation of the losers in a wealth-producing redistribution; it requires only that they *could* be compensated. As one of Ronald Dworkin's[8] examples illustrates, actions done directly to maximize wealth can be both unjust and inconsistent with the integrity of law. Imagine a poor and sick man who is willing to sell a book of his for $5 to buy medicine. The grandson of the author would be willing to pay $10 for the book in order to autograph it and re-sell it for $11. It would be K-H wealth maximizing simply to take it from the owner and give it to the person willing to pay $10. The forced transfer would save the transaction costs of negotiation. This example suggests that an important ethical dimension is missing in a principle that would allow transfer without negotiation and actual consent.


## THE READINGS

In his article reprinted here, Richard Posner attempts to provide an ethical justification for the Kaldor-Hicks principle of efficiency. Though Posner recognizes the appeal of the Pareto principle, he clearly favors the Kaldor-Hicks wealth maximization version because of its broader applicability. But the adoption of any political and moral principle, especially a potentially controversial one like K-H wealth maximization, requires a justification. This Posner attempts to provide by relying broadly on the idea of consent, an idea that has long played an important role in political and moral philosophy. One who fully and freely consents to law has by that fact provided a good argument for being held to its requirements. However, instead of relying on the claim that the principle of wealth maximization is directly and actually consented to, Posner's claim is that the principle's consequences either are indirectly consented to in much the same sense that the outcome of a lottery is consented to by your playing it ("ex ante" compensation), or that the wealth maximization it approves would be consented to if conditions were ideal ("implied" or "hypothetical" consent).

Ronald Dworkin's comments on Posner greatly illuminate the scope and validity of consent arguments in political philosophy. He points out, for example, that consenting to playing a game in which you know you might lose does not entail consenting to losing.

[7]Richard A. Posner, *Economic Analysis of Law*, 2d ed. (Boston: Little, Brown and Company, 1977), pp. 111–116.
[8]This example is taken from Ronald Dworkin, *Law's Empire* (Cambridge, Mass.: Harvard University Press, 1986), pp. 286–87.

One's consent to the game may mean that being stuck with the loss after the game has been properly played is *fair*, but this is different from one's having consented to the loss. In addition, Dworkin points out that even if we make the questionable assumption that a principle like wealth maximization is in one's interest, it does not follow that one has consented to it or that one would consent to it.

*Richard A. Posner*
# THE ETHICAL AND POLITICAL BASIS OF THE EFFICIENCY NORM IN <u>COMMON</u> LAW ADJUDICATION*

In a recent article I argued that a society which aims at maximizing wealth, unlike a society which aims a maximizing utility (happiness), will produce an ethically attractive combination of happiness, of rights (to liberty and property), and of sharing with the less fortunate members of society.[1] Evidently, I did not explain adequately why this combination was ethically attractive.[2] The present Article began as an attempt to extend the argument of the last one by considering this question in greater depth. But as the paper took shape, it became both narrower and broader than the original conception. It narrowed as my interest shifted to showing that wealth maximization was an ethically attractive objective to guide common law adjudication, rather than social choice generally.[3] It broadened as I began to see that the same considerations which made wealth maximization an ethically attractive norm in common law adjudication might help to explain why it has played an important role in shaping the substantive rules and procedures of the common law.[4]

The main ethical argument of this Article, developed in the first section, is that wealth maximization, especially in the common law setting, derives support from the principle of consent that can also be regarded as underlying the otherwise quite different approach of Pareto ethics. The second section shifts the focus from normative to positive. I argue that the political counterpart of consent—consensus—explains the role of wealth maximization in shaping the common law. The principle of consent supports the wealth-maximization norm in the common law setting precisely because common law judges deal with problems, and by methods, in which redistributive considerations are not salient. This means that consent to efficient solutions can be presumed; but it also means that politically influential groups can do no better, in general, than to support efficient policies. Such policies maximize aggregate wealth in a setting where, by hypothesis, altering the shares (redistribution) is not a feasible means by which a group can increase its wealth. I also briefly discuss whether the common law is utilitarian or wealth maximizing.

## THE CONSENSUAL BASIS OF EFFICIENCY

### From Pareto to Kaldor-Hicks

Pareto superiority is the principle that one allocation of resources is superior to another if at least one person is better off under the first allocation than under the second and no one is worse off.[5] Pareto invented the principle as an answer to the traditional problem

---

*From *Hofstra Law Review*, vol. 8, no. 3 (Spring 1980), pp. 487–507. Reprinted by permission of the *Hofstra Law Review*. Some internal footnotes to this volume of the *Review* have been omitted.

[1]Posner, *Utilitarianism, Economics, and Legal Theory*, 8 J. LEGAL STUD. 103 (1979).

[2]*See* Dworkin, *Is Wealth a Value?*, 9 J. LEGAL STUD. 191 (1980); Kronman, *Wealth Maximization as a Normative Principle*, 9 J. LEGAL STUD. 227 (1980). I reply to these critics in Posner, *The Value of Wealth: A Reply to Dworkin and Kronman*, 9 J. LEGAL STUD. 243 (1980).

[3]I consider it an attractive objective to guide social choice generally, but do not pursue the argument for that position in this Article.

[4]For a recent statement of the "efficiency theory" of the common law, see Posner, *Some Uses and Abuses of Economics in Law*, 46 U. CHI. L. REV. 281, 288–95 (1979).

[5]For a lucid discussion of Pareto ethics by a philosopher, see Coleman, *Efficiency, Exchange, and Auction: Philosophic Aspects of the Economic Approach to Law*, 68 CAL. L. REV. 221 (1980). And for a good recent textbook treatment by an economist, see C. PRICE, WELFARE ECONOMICS IN THEORY AND PRACTICE (1977).

of practical utilitarianism, that of measuring happiness across persons for purposes of determining the effect of a policy on total utility.[6] The change to a Pareto-superior allocation must yield a net increase in utility, since no one is made worse off and at least one person is made better off by the change, even though the *amount* by which total utility has been increased may not be measurable.

But, as is well known,[7] the solution is apparent rather than real. Because of the impossibility of measuring utility directly, the only way to demonstrate that a change in the allocation of resources is Pareto superior is to show that everyone affected by the change consented to it. If A sells a tomato to B for $2 and no one else is affected by the transaction, we can be sure that the utility to A of $2 is greater than the utility of the tomato to A, and vice versa for B, even though we do not know how much A's and B's utility has been increased by the transaction. But because the crucial assumption in this example, the absence of third-party effects, is not satisfied with regard to *classes* of transactions, the Pareto-superiority criterion is useless for most policy questions. For example, if the question is not whether, given a free market in tomatoes, A's sale to B is a Pareto-superior change, but whether a free market in tomatoes is Pareto superior to a market in which there is a ceiling on the price of tomatoes, the concept of Pareto superiority is unhelpful. The price ceiling will result in a lower market price, a lower quantity produced, lower rents to land specialized to the growing of tomatoes, and other differences from the results of a free market in tomatoes. It would be impossible to identify, let alone negotiate for the consent of, everyone affected by a move from a price-regulated to a free tomato-market, so the criterion of Pareto superiority cannot be satisfied. Stating this conclusion differently, one cannot say that the movement to a free market would increase total utility or, conversely, that if we had a free market in tomatoes, imposing a price ceiling would reduce total utility.[8]

I have been speaking thus far of Pareto ethics and specifically of the concept of Pareto superiority as an answer, though not a practical one, to the utilitarian's problem of the interpersonal comparison of utilities. But it is also possible to locate Pareto ethics in a different philosophical tradition from the utilitarian, in the tradition, broadly Kantian, which attaches a value over and above the utilitarian to individual autonomy. One ethical criterion of change that is highly congenial to the Kantian emphasis on autonomy is consent. And consent is the operational basis of the concept of Pareto superiority. It is not the theoretical basis, at least if Pareto superiority is viewed as a tool of utilitarian ethics, because if the utilitarian could devise a practical utility-metric he could dispense with the consensual or transactional method of determining whether an allocation of resources was Pareto superior; indeed, he could dispense with the concept of Pareto superiority itself.

Suppose we consider consent an ethically attractive basis for permitting changes in the allocation of resources, on Kantian grounds

---

[6] *See* V. Tarascio, Pareto's Methodological Approach to Economics 79–84 (1968).

[7] *See, e.g.,* G. Calabresi & P. Bobbitt, Tragic Choices 83–85 (1978).

[8] The revealed-preference approach, *see generally* P. Samuelson, Foundations of Economic Analysis 146–56 (1947), offers a method, unfortunately not very practical either, of determining whether a change is Pareto superior that does not require express consent. Imagine that C is a third party affected by the transaction between A and B in the example in the text. Before the transaction, C's income is X and he uses it to purchase commodities a . . . n. The transaction may affect C's income, as well as the prices of a . . . n. If, however, after the transaction C's income, now Y, is large enough to enable him to purchase a . . . n at their current prices, then we may say (without having to consult C) that the transaction between A and B did not make him worse off. But the information necessary to apply this approach is rarely available, in part because some of the commodities that C buys may not be priced in any market (love, respect, etc.) and his ability to obtain them may be adversely affected by the transaction between A and B.

unrelated to the fact that a consensual trans-action is likely to increase the happiness at least of the immediate parties to it. We are then led, in the manner of Nozick and Epstein,[9] to an ethical defense of market transactions that is unrelated to their effect in promoting efficiency either in the Pareto sense or in the sense of wealth maximization.

In the setting of a market free from third-party effects, it is clear that forbidding trans-actions would reduce both the wealth of society and personal autonomy, so that the goals of maximizing wealth and of protect-ing autonomy coincide. But the setting is a special one. For example, suppose that a company decides to close a factory in town A and open a new one in B, and that in nei-ther location are there significant pollution, congestion, or other technological externali-ties from the plant. The move may still lower property values in A and raise them in B, making landowners in A worse off and those in B better off. The parties to the move will not take account of these effects and their failure to do so makes it impossible for the plant's move to satisfy the criterion of a Pareto-superior move.[10]

That the third-party effects are merely "pecuniary" externalities, meaning that they result simply from a change in demand rather than from the consumption of some scarce resource (e.g., clean air, in the case of pollution, which is a technological external-ity), or, stated otherwise, that they have no net effect on the wealth of the society, is ir-relevant from the standpoint of Pareto supe-riority. Not only is it impossible to say that no one will be made worse off by the plant move, but it is in fact certain that some peo-ple will be made worse off—the landowners

in A and others, such as workers in A who have skills specialized to the plant that is being closed and positive costs of relocating in B. By the same token—and here the rela-tionship of the Pareto-superiority criterion to utilitarian thought is clear—one cannot be sure that the move will increase total util-ity.[11] The disutility to the losers from the move may exceed the utility to the winners, even though, by the assumption that only pecuniary externalities are involved, the total wealth of the people affected by, but not party to, the transaction is unchanged, so that the transaction is wealth maximizing.

In a case such as the one I have put, the wealth-maximization criterion elaborated in my previous Article indicates that the trans-action should be allowed. So, equivalently, as Jules Coleman has pointed out, does the Kaldor-Hicks criterion (sometimes called "Potential Pareto Superiority"), which re-quires, not that no one be made worse off by the move, but only that the increase in value be sufficiently large that the losers could be fully compensated.[12] Since the decrease in land values in A is matched by the increase in B, in principle (i.e., ignoring transfer costs) the landowners in A could be compensated and then no one would be worse off. But neither the Pareto criterion itself nor the utilitarian imperative underlying the Pareto criterion—to maximize utility—would be satisfied, because there is no way of know-ing whether the utility to the winners of not having to pay compensation will exceed the disutility to the losers of not receiving com-pensation. Suppose the landowners in A in-curred a loss of 100 utiles (an arbitrary measure of utility) because of the $1 million decrease in property values in A resulting

[9]See R. Nozick, Anarchy, State, and Utopia (1974); Epstein, *Causation and Corrective Justice: A Reply to Two Critics*, 8 J. Legal Stud. 477, 487–88 (1979).

[10]I ignore for the moment the possibility of ex ante compensation of the affected landowners. . . .

[11]The externalities could be internalized by the cities' offering tax inducements to the plant's owner. But that would not make the plant's moving (or remaining) Pareto superior, since those people who paid the higher taxes necessary to finance these inducements would be worse off.

[12]See Coleman, *supra* note 5, at 239–42.

from the move of the plant, while the land-owners in *B* obtained only 80 utiles from the $1 million increase in their property values. The Kaldor-Hicks criterion would be satisfied but the Pareto-superiority criterion would not be.

## Wealth Maximization and the Principle of Consent

I want to defend the Kaldor-Hicks or wealth-maximization approach, not by reference to Pareto-superiority as such or its utilitarian premise, but by reference to the idea of consent that I have said provides an alternative basis to utilitarianism for the Pareto criterion. The notion of consent used here is what economists call ex ante compensation.[13] I contend, I hope uncontroversially, that if you buy a lottery ticket and lose the lottery, then, so long as there is no question of fraud or duress, you have consented to the loss. Many of the involuntary, uncompensated losses experienced in the market, or tolerated by the institutions that take the place of the market where the market cannot be made to work effectively, are fully compensated ex ante and hence are consented to. Suppose some entrepreneur loses money because a competitor develops a superior product. Since the return to entrepreneurial activity will include a premium to cover the risk of losses due to competition, the entrepreneur is compensated for those losses ex ante. Similarly, the landowners in *A*, in my previous example, were compensated when they bought the land. The probability that the plant would move was discounted in the purchase price they paid.[14]

The concept of ex ante compensation provides an answer to the argument that the wealth-maximization criterion, applied unflinchingly in market settings such as my plant-relocation example, would violate the principle of consent. A more difficult question is raised, however, by the similar attempt to ground nonmarket, but arguably wealth-maximizing institutions, such as the embattled negligence system of automobile accident liability, in the principle of consent. In what sense may the driver injured by another driver in an accident in which neither was at fault be said to have consented to the injury, so as not to be entitled, under a negligence system, to compensation?

To answer this question, we must consider the effect on the costs of driving of insisting on ex post compensation, as under a system of strict liability. By hypothesis they would be higher; otherwise the negligence system would not be the wealth-maximizing system and no issue of justifying wealth maximization by reference to the principle of consent would arise. Would drivers be willing to incur higher costs of driving in order to preserve the principle of ex post compensation? They would not. Any driver who wanted to be assured of compensation in the event of an accident regardless of whether he was at fault need only buy first-party, or accident, insurance, by hypothesis at lower cost than he could obtain compensation ex post through a system of strict liability.

This can be most easily visualized by imagining that everyone involved in a traffic accident is identical—everyone is the same age, drives the same amount, and so on. In these circumstances everyone will pay the

---

[13] The argument that follows is sketched in Posner, *Epstein's Tort Theory: A Critique*, 8 J. LEGAL STUD. 457, 460, 464 (1979). A similar argument is made independently in Michelman, *Constitutions, Statutes, and the Theory of Efficient Adjudication*, 9 J. LEGAL STUD. 431, 438–40 (1980). Both arguments resemble a position taken by many welfare economists: that the Kaldor-Hicks criterion for deciding whether to undertake a public project satisfies the Pareto-superiority criterion provided that there is a sufficient probability that an individual will benefit in the long run from such projects, though he may be a loser from a particular one. *See* Polinsky, *Probabilistic Compensation Criteria*, 86 Q. J. ECON. 407 (1972), and references cited therein.

[14] A parallel, but because of possible information costs more difficult, case is that of the worker who loses his job and incurs positive relocation costs when the demand for his services collapses as a result of the development of a superior substitute product.

same rate for both liability insurance and accident insurance. The difference between negligence and strict liability will be that under negligence, liability-insurance rates will be lower and accident insurance rates higher, because fewer accidents will give rise to liability, while under strict liability the reverse will be true. But if, as I am assuming, negligence is the more efficient system, the *sum* of the liability and accident insurance premiums will be lower under negligence,[15] and everyone will prefer this.

All this assumes, of course, that people are identical; the implications of relaxing that assumption will be considered later. It also depends on my initial assumption that negligence is a cheaper system of automobile accident liability than strict liability would be. But that assumption is immaterial to my basic point, which is that an institution predicated on wealth maximization may be justifiable by reference to the consent of those affected by it even though the institution authorizes certain takings, such as the taking of life, health, or property of an individual injured in an accident in which neither party is negligent, without requiring compensation ex post.

I have used the example of negligence versus strict liability because it has been used to argue that the wealth-maximization approach is inconsistent with an approach consistent with notions of personal autonomy or, in the terminology of this Article, consent.[16] Other examples could be offered, but it is not the purpose of this Article to deduce the institutional structure implied by wealth maximization; it is to show that social institutions that maximize wealth without requiring ex post compensation need not on that account be viewed as inconsistent

with an ethical system premised on the principle of consent.

Some may object to the above analysis on the ground that the consent on the basis of which I am prepared, in principle at least, to justify institutions such as the negligence system is fictitious because no one has given his *express* consent. It would indeed be naïve to regard the political survival of negligence in the automobile accident arena as evidence of such consent; the radical imperfections of the political system in registering preferences are the subject of a vast literature in social choice and in the economic theory of legislation. Nevertheless, the objection founders, in my opinion, precisely on the unavailability of a practical method of eliciting express consent, not so much to individual market transactions—though even there the consent of third parties affected by those transactions often cannot feasibly be elicited—as to *institutions*, such as the negligence system or indeed the market itself. If there is no reliable mechanism for eliciting express consent, it follows, not that we must abandon the principle of consent, but rather that we should look for implied consent, as by trying to answer the hypothetical question whether, if transaction costs were zero, the affected parties would have agreed to the institution. This procedure[19] resembles a judge's imputing the intent of parties to a contract that fails to provide expressly for some contingency. Although the task of imputation is easier in the contract case, that case is still significant in showing that implicit consent is a meaningful form of consent. The absence of an underlying contract is relevant to the confidence with which an inference of implicit consent can be drawn rather than to the propriety of drawing such inferences.

---

[15]This assumes that all accident costs are reflected in insurance rates. Most accident-prevention costs (*e.g.*, the value of time lost in driving more slowly) are not. Presumably, these costs would also be higher under strict liability if that is indeed the less efficient liability rule.

[16]*See* Epstein, *A Theory of Strict Liability*, 2 J. Legal Stud. 151 (1973).

[19]One, incidentally, that many economists use to make judgments of Pareto efficiency. For a recent example *see* S. Shavell, Accidents, Liability, and Insurance 5–7 (June 1979) (Harv. Inst. Econ. Research, Discussion Paper No. 685).

To be sure, "[a] proposal is not legislation simply because all the members of the legislature are in favor of it.[20] But this is because there is a mechanism by which legislators can express actual consent to a proposal. Sometimes the mechanism is inoperative, as when a question arises as to the scope or meaning of a past legislative enactment, and then we allow the courts to infer the legislative intent. This is an example of implicit but meaningful consent.

Another objection to using consent to justify institutions which maximize wealth is that the consent will rarely be unanimous. Contrary to my earlier assumption, people are not identical ex ante. Even if the costs of driving would be higher under a system of strict liability than under a negligence system, why should nondrivers prefer the negligence system? To the extent that groups of this sort could actually be identified, one might grant them the protection of a strict liability system if one placed a high value on autonomy.[21] But this may not be required by the principle of consent. Most people who do not drive do not stay at home either; they use other modes of transportation—taxi, buses, or subways, to name a few—whose costs would by assumption be higher under a system of strict liability. Those costs, or a large fraction of them at least, would be borne by the users. Even the nondrivers might therefore consent to a negligence system of liability for transport accidents if it were cheaper than a system of strict liability.[22] No institution, of course, will command the implicit consent of everyone. But only a fanatic would insist that absolute unanimity is required to legitimize a social institution such as the negligence system.

To summarize, the wealth-maximization or Kaldor-Hicks criterion can sometimes be applied without violating the principle of consent. While Kaldor-Hicks is not a Pareto criterion as such, it will sometimes function as a tolerable and, more to the point, administrable approximation of the Pareto-superiority criterion. To attempt to defend wealth-maximization on Pareto grounds, however, is to raise the following question: why should not the principle that guides society by the protection and enhancement of personal autonomy, the value that underlies the principle of consent, rather than the maximization of wealth? One objection to using autonomy directly as an ethical norm, an objection well illustrated by the choice between strict liability and negligence, is that it requires an arbitrary initial assignment of rights. I assumed that the victim of an accident had some kind of moral claim to compensation, ex post or ex ante, even though the injurer was not at fault. One could equally well assume that people have a right not to be hampered in their activities by being held liable for accidents that they could not have prevented at reasonable cost. No liability denies the autonomy of the victim, and strict liability the autonomy of the injurer. To differentiate the two *when neither is at fault* is no simple task.[23]

Another objection to building an ethical system directly on the idea of autonomy is that, just as literal adherence to the Pareto-superiority criterion could be paralyzing, so the ethics of personal autonomy, interpreted and applied without regard for the consequences for human welfare, would lead to a great deal of misery. This is conceded by the adherents to the ethics of personal autonomy in modern jurisprudential thought,

---

[20]Epstein, *supra* note 9, at 496.

[21]As suggested in Fletcher, *Fairness and Utility in Tort Theory*, 85 Harv. L. Rev. 537, 543–51 (1972). . . .

[22]This leaves open the possibility of further subdividing the transport industry for liability purposes and of having one rule for buses, another for autos, etc.

[23]For the divergent view of Kantian philosophers on this question, *see* Posner, *supra* note 1, at 115 n. 43.

such as Charles Fried and Richard Epstein.[24] Wealth maximization as an ethical norm has the property of giving weight both to preferences, though less heavily than utilitarianism does, and to consent, though less heavily than Kant himself would have done. Also, as explained in my previous article, it gives weight to the human impulse, apparently genetically based, to share wealth with people who are less effective in producing it.[25]

These characteristics of wealth maximization are not, as Professor Dworkin has suggested, accidental.[26] The perfectly free market, in which there are no third-party effects, is paradigmatic of how utility is promoted noncoercively, through the voluntary transactions of autonomous, utility-seeking individuals. The system of wealth maximization consists of institutions that facilitate, or where that is infeasible approximate, the operations of a free market and thus maximize autonomous, utility-seeking behavior. Because utility seeking in a market requires inducing others to enter into transactions advantageous to them, wealth is automatically transferred to those who have productive assets, whether goods or time. By the same token, those who have no productive assets have no ethical claim on the assets of others. This is not necessarily a result that maximizes utility; it is of course uncongenial to those who believe that the individual is separable from his endowments of skill, energy, and character. It is

consistent, however, with a desire, rooted in the principles of autonomy and consent, to minimize coercion.

The system of wealth maximization outlined in this and my previous Article could be viewed as one of constrained utilitarianism. The constraint, which is not ad hoc but is supplied by the principle of consent, is that people may seek to promote their utility only through the market or institutions modeled on the market. As I have been at pains to stress, transactions that are consensual between the immediate parties may be coercive as to third parties. But as the negligence example showed, the amount of coercion in a system of wealth maximization is easily exaggerated; where it is wealth maximizing to deny compensation ex post, ex ante the potentially affected parties may prefer that such compensation be denied.

## Comparison to Rawls' Approach

My discussion of the choice that the individual is assumed to make between negligence and strict liability systems before an accident occurs—a choice under uncertainty from which consent to a social institution is then inferred—may seem derivative of Rawls' analysis of justice.[27] In fact, both Rawls' analysis and the analysis in this Article have common roots. The "original position" approach was apparently first used by economists seeking to establish the consensual foundations of

---

[24]See C. Fried, Right and Wrong 9–10 (1978); Epstein, *Nuisance Law: Corrective Justice and Its Utilitarian Constraints*, 8 J. Legal Stud. 49, 74–75, 79 (1979).

[25]See Posner, *supra* note 1, at 123, 129 n. 80, arguing that the producer puts more into society than he takes out, because he cannot (barring perfect price discrimination) appropriate the entire consumer surplus generated by his production. It is true that the marginal producer creates no consumer surplus—he takes out exactly what he puts in—and so if each producer is the marginal producer none would reduce the wealth of other people by withdrawing from the market. However, not every producer is marginal; we may be reasonably confident that the American people would have been poorer if Henry Ford had decided to become a Trappist monk rather than an automobile manufacturer. More important, even in an industry where each producer is marginal and his withdrawal from the industry would not reduce consumer surplus, the withdrawal of a group of producers would. Each producer's contribution to consumer surplus is negligible but the sum of their contributions is not.

[26]See Dworkin, *supra* note 2.

[27]See J. Rawls, A Theory of Justice 17–22 (1971).

utility maximization in a somewhat similar fashion to what I have done here.[28] As Kenneth Arrow has explained, they

> start[ed] from the position . . . that choice under risky conditions can be described as the maximization of expected utility. In the original position, each individual may with equal probability be any member of the society. If there are $n$ members of the society and if the $i$th member will have utility $u_i$ under some given allocation decision, then the value of that allocation to any individual is $\Sigma u_i \ (1/n)$, since $1/n$ is the probability of being individual $i$. Thus, in choosing among alternative allocations of goods, each individual in the original position will want to maximize this expectation, or, what is the same thing for a given population, maximize the sum of utilities.[29]

The twist that Rawls gave to choice in the original position was to argue that people would choose to maximize, not expected utility, but the utility of the worst outcomes in the distribution.[30] Again in the words of Arrow:

> It has, however, long been remarked that the maximin theory has some implications that seem hardly acceptable. It implies that any benefit, no matter how small, to the worst-off member of society, will outweigh any loss to a better-off individual, provided it does not reduce the second below the level of the first. Thus, there can easily exist medical procedures which serve to keep people barely alive but with little satisfaction and which are yet so expensive as to reduce the rest of the population to poverty. A maximin principle would apparently imply that such procedures be adopted.[31]

If, with Arrow, one finds expected utility a more plausible maximand than maximin is, one will be driven to the startling conclusion that utilitarianism has a firmer basis in the principle of consent than Rawls' "justice as fairness." But any theory of consent that is based on choice in the original position is unsatisfactory, not only because of the well-known difficulties of describing the preference functions of people in that position, but also because the original position approach opens the door to the claims of the unproductive. In the original position, no one knows whether he has productive capabilities, so choices made in that position will presumably reflect some probability that the individual making the choice will turn out not to be endowed with any such capabilities. In effect, the choices of the unproductive are weighted equally with those of the productive. This result obscures the important moral distinction, between capacity to enjoy and capacity to produce for others, that distinguishes utility from wealth.[32] I prefer therefore to imagine actual people, deploying actual endowments of skill and energy and character, making choices under uncertainty. I prefer, that is, to imagine choice under conditions of natural ignorance to choice under the artificial ignorance of the original position.

---

[28] See Arrow, *Some Ordinalist-Utilitarian Notes on Rawls's Theory of Justice*, 70 J. PHILOSOPHY 245, 250 (1973).

[29] *Id.*

[30] J. RAWLS, *supra* note 27, at 150–61.

[31] Arrow, *supra* note 28, at 251.

[32] My concept of wealth includes, as noted in the previous article, Posner, *supra* note 1, at 105 n. 11, the dollar value (or cost) that people who are not risk-neutral attach to uncertain outcomes. Thus, my concept is similar to what most economists mean when they say expected utility. I avoid the latter word, however, because utilitarian philosophers (and perhaps implicitly therefore those economists who think of themselves as applied utilitarians) do not differentiate between preferences backed by willingness to pay and preferences backed simply by desire. In my analysis, only the former preferences enter into a determination as to which choices are wealth maximizing.

### Limitations of Wealth Maximization as an Ethical Norm Founded on Consent

The domain within which the principle of consent can supply an ethical justification for social institutions that maximize wealth is limited in at least two principal respects.

1. Where the distributive impact of a wealth-maximizing policy is substantial and nonrandom, broad consent will be difficult to elicit or impute without actual compensation. I mentioned this possibility in connection with the choice between negligence and strict liability to govern traffic accidents but it seemed unimportant there. Suppose, however, the issue was whether to substitute a proportionate income tax for the current progressive one. The substitution would increase the wealth of society if the increase in output (counting both work and leisure as output) by upper bracket taxpayers, whose marginal-tax rate would be lowered by the substitution, exceeded the reduction in output caused by raising the marginal tax rate of lower bracket taxpayers. However, unless the net increase in output was sufficiently great to result in an increase in the after-tax incomes even of those taxpayers who would be paying higher taxes under a proportionate than under a progressive income tax— and let us assume it was not—the lower bracket taxpayers could hardly be assumed to consent to the tax change, even though it would be wealth maximizing.

I was first stimulated to investigate the ethical foundations of wealth maximization by the suggestion that it was too unappealing a value to ascribe to common law judges.[33] Yet it is precisely in the context of common law adjudication, as contrasted with the redistributive statutory domain illustrated by my tax example, that a consensual basis for wealth maximization is most plausible. The rules that govern the acquisition and transfer of property rights, the making and enforcement of contracts, and liability for accidents and the kinds of naked aggression that were made crimes at common law are supported by a broad consensus and distribute their benefits very widely. For example, only a naïve analysis of the economic consequences of refusing to enforce the leases that poor people sign with presumably wealthier landlords would conclude that the poor would be better off under such a regime. Landlords would either charge higher rentals because of the greater risk of loss or shift their property into alternative uses, so that the low-income housing supply would be smaller and its price higher.[34] If we can generalize from this example that the choice between common law rules usually does not have systematic distributive consequences, then it is reasonable to suppose that there is—or would be, if it paid people to inform themselves in these matters—general consent to those common law rules that maximize wealth. If so, a common law judge guided by the wealth-maximization criterion will at the same time be promoting personal autonomy.

2. Another area in which the principle of consent and the principle of wealth maximization are potentially in conflict, aside from redistributive policies such as those embodied in the progressive income tax, is in the initial assignment of property rights, the starting point for a market system.

What if $A$'s labor is worth more to $B$ than to $A$? Then it would be efficient to make $A$ the slave of $B$ but this result would hardly comport with the principle of consent. Such cases must be very rare. Not only will $A$ probably have a better idea than anyone else where he could be most productively employed, but the costs of overcoming $A$'s

---

[33]For a recent statement of this argument, see Michelman, *A Comment on Some Uses and ABuses of Economics in Law*, 46 U. Chi. L. Rev. 307, 308 (1979).

[34]Komesar, *Return to Slumville: A Critique of the Ackerman Analysis of Housing Code Enforcement and the Poor*; 82 Yale L. J. 1175, 1187–91 (1973).

disincentive to work hard when the benefits of his hard work would enure exclusively to another are likely to make the net value of his labor less than if he owned it himself. If there are cases where the costs of physical coercion are so low relative to the costs of administering contracts as to make slavery a more efficient method of organizing production than any voluntary system, they either arise under such different social conditions from our own as to make ethical comparison difficult,[35] or involve highly unusual circumstances (*e.g.*, military discipline) to which the term slavery is not attached.

A related problem is that where large allocative questions are involved, as in the initial assignment of rights, the very concept of wealth maximization becomes problematic. Since the wealth of society is the output of all tangible and intangible commodities multiplied by their market values, it is difficult to compare the wealth of two states of society in which prices are different. The prices in a social order in which one person owned all the other members of society might be different from the prices in a social order where everyone was his own master. But even here guesses may be possible. For example, if we started with a society where one person owned all the others, soon most of the others would have bought their freedom from that person because their output would be greater as free individuals than as slaves, enabling them to pay more for the right to their labor than that right was worth to the slave owner.[36] It would be clear, then, that the slave society was inefficient, even though the prices in a slave and free society might be different for many commodities.

Consider the following example of how the initial assignment of rights might appear to have such an effect on prices that the wealth of society under alternative assignments could not be compared.[37] Imagine that A, if a free man, would derive a lifetime market income of 100 in present value from working and a nonmarket income of 50 from leisure, for a total income of 150, but that if A is B's slave, A will be forced to produce an output having a market value of 110 and will obtain zero nonpecuniary income. A's wealth is higher in the free than in the slave state (150 versus zero), so that if he has the right to his labor he will not sell that right to B. Freedom is therefore wealth maximizing if A is free to begin with. But if B owns the right to A's labor, then it may seem that A will not be able to buy it back from B. How can A pay more than 100 since that is the value of his output as a free man? A's output is worth 110 to B, and A cannot use his nonpecuniary income in the free state to buy his freedom because his leisure has no value to anyone else.[38] Therefore, it seems that slavery is wealth maximizing if the initial assignment of rights is to make A the slave of B.

But this analysis overlooks the possibility of converting nonpecuniary into pecuniary income. A's preferred mixture of work and leisure is such as to yield 100 in market income and 50 in nonpecuniary income from leisure, but A could work harder, as he does for B. Suppose by working harder (but not all the time), A could earn a market income of 120 and leisure income of 10. A could then buy his freedom from B. It is true that, having done so, A would be worse off than if he had the right to his labor in the first place. The point of the analysis, however, is that freedom is indeed more efficient than slavery, because by giving A his freedom in the first place we obviate the need for a transaction whereby A buys his freedom from B.

[35]One the costs of monitoring economic activity in primitive societies, see Posner, *A Theory of Primitive Society, with Special Reference to Law*; 23 J. L. & ECON. 1 (1980).

[36]The slave would borrow against his future earnings to finance the purchase of his freedom.

[37]A similar example is analyzed in Dworkin, *supra* note 2, at 208–10.

[38]A's leisure might have value to another, but let us assume that it does not.

Thus, while the theoretical possibility exists that efficiency might dictate slavery or some other monstrous rights assignment, it is difficult to give examples where this would actually happen. I conclude that it is possible to deduce a structure of rights congruent with our ethical intuitions from the wealth-maximization premise.

## SOME IMPLICATIONS FOR THE POSITIVE ECONOMIC ANALYSIS OF LAW

### Why the Common Law Is Efficient

Scholars like myself who have argued that the common law is best explained as an effort, however inarticulate, to promote efficiency have lacked a good reason why this should be so—making them seem, perhaps, the naïve adherents of the outmoded "public interest" theory of the state.[39] This is the theory that the state operates, albeit imperfectly, to promote widely shared social goals—of which wealth maximization is surely one, regardless of how important a goal it may be. The state promotes efficiency by arranging for the provision of "public goods," that is, goods that confer benefits not limited to those who pay for them and hence that are produced in suboptimal amounts by private markets. One of these public goods is a legal system that corrects sources of market failure such as externalities.

The public-interest theory of the state has been under severe attack from the proponents of the "interest group" or, more narrowly, the "producer protection" theory of the governmental process.[40] This theory assigns primary importance to redistribution as an object of public policy. The redistributive emphasis stems from treating governmental action as a commodity, much like other commodities, that is allocated in accordance with the forces of supply and demand. The focus of research has been on demand. The characteristics that enable an industry or other group to overcome free-rider problems and thereby outbid rival claimants for governmental protection and largesse have been studied, and the conclusion has been reached that compact groups will generally outbid diffuse ones for government favor.

The interest-group theory is an economic theory because it links governmental action to utility maximization by the people seeking such action. The public-interest theory is a description, rather than an economic theory, of the political process because it does not show how utility maximizing by individuals results in governmental action that promotes the interest of such diffuse groups as the "public," consumers, or taxpayers. The implication of the interest group theory that diffuse groups are likely to lose out in competition with more compact groups for government protection undermines the plausibility of the public-interest theory even as description.

However, common law doctrines that satisfy the Pareto-superiority criterion in the "principle of consent" form in which I have cast it in this Article (no common law doctrine would satisfy a literal interpretation of the Pareto criterion) are plausible candidates for survival even in a political system otherwise devoted to redistribution. The reason is that a rule or institution that satisfies the principle of consent cannot readily be altered, at least not by the remedies available to common law judges, in a way that will redistribute wealth toward some politically effective interest group. This is particularly clear in cases, such as the landlord-tenant case discussed earlier, where the parties to litigation have a preexisting voluntary relationship. In effect, the court would be changing

---

[38] For a review of the rival theories of government discussed in this part of the Article, see Posner, *Theories of Economic Regulation*, 5 BELL J. ECON. & MGT. SCI. 335 (1974).

[40] The semnal article in the economic theory of interest-group politics (as distinct from the earlier political-science theory) is Stigler, *The Theory of Economic Regulation*, 2 BELL J. ECON. & MGT. SCI. 3 (1971).

only one term of a contract, and the parties could alter the other contract terms in the future.[42] This is not an effective method of redistributing wealth. Even if the dispute does not arise from a contract, the parties may be interrelated in a way that totally or largely cancels any wealth effects from a change in the rule of liability. For example, since farmers were the major customers of railroads in the nineteenth century, it would not have made much sense to try to transfer wealth from railroads to farmers or vice versa simply by increasing or decreasing the liability of railroads for damage caused to crops growing along railroad rights of way.

The potential for using the common law to redistribute wealth is not great even in cases involving complete strangers. Consider again the negligence system of automobile-accident liability. It is hard to see how moving to a system of strict liability would increase the wealth of a compact, readily identifiable, and easily organizable group in the society. The principal effect would simply be to increase or decrease most people's wealth a small amount, depending upon whether strict liability is more or less efficient than negligence in the automobile setting.

There is a literature that contends that the common law has been biased in favor of the rich—has served, that is, systematic and perverse redistributive ends.[43] The above analysis makes this an implausible contention, though it would carry me too far afield to attempt to refute it in detail here.[44] If I am correct that the common law is not an effective method of redistributing wealth,[45] whether from rich or poor, farmers or railroads, tenants or landlords, or between any reasonably well defined, plausibly effective interest

groups, then there is no reason to expect the common law to be dominated by redistributive concerns even if legislatures are.

To say what the common law is not is not to say what it is, but that too can be derived from the preceding analysis. There are numerous politically effective groups in the society; the question is what their rational objectives are likely to be in areas regulated by common law methods. Probably their self-interest is promoted by supporting the efficiency norm in those areas. By doing so they increase the wealth of the society; they will get a share of that increased wealth; and there is no alternative norm that would yield a larger share. To be sure, none of them will devote substantial resources to promoting the efficiency norm in the common law, because the benefits that each group derives will be small and because each will be tempted to take a free ride on the others. But few resources have to be devoted to promoting the efficiency norm for it to survive: its distributive neutrality operates to reduce potential opposition as well as support.

This analysis implicitly treats judges simply as agents of the government and hence does not confront the difficulties that judicial independence from political control poses for any self-interest theory of judicial behavior. That is a problem in the economics of agency. The utility of the analysis is in relating the efficiency theory of the common law to the redistributive theory of the state, albeit some of the links in the chain are obscure. Notice that it is an implication of the theory that where legislatures legislate within the area of common law regulation— as with respect to rights and remedies in torts, contracts, property, and related fields—

---

[42] It is noteworthy that Professor Ackerman, a leading advocate of using tort law to force landlords to increase the quality of slum housing, couples this with a proposal for a public subsidy to prevent tort liability from leading to a reduction in the supply of housing for the poor. *See* Ackerman, *Regulating Slum Housing Markets on Behalf of the Poor: Of Housing Codes, Housing Subsidies, and Income Redistribution Policy*, 80 YALE L.J. 1093 (1971).

[43] *See, e.g.*, M. HORWITZ, THE TRANSFORMATION OF AMERICAN LAW, 1780–1860, ch. III (1977).

[44] For some criticism of the literature, see R. POSNER, ECONOMIC ANALYSIS OF LAW § 8.2 (2d. ed. 1977).

[45] As also argued on theoretical grounds in S. Shavell, A Note on Efficiency vs. Equity in Legal Rulemaking: Should Equity Matter, Given Optimal Income Taxation? (1979) (unpublished paper Harv. Univ. Dep't of Econ.).

they too will be trying to promote efficiency. For, in this view, it is not the nature of the regulating institution,[46] but the subjects and methods of regulation, that determine whether the government will promote efficiency or redistribute wealth.

The relationship of the above political analysis to the ethical discussion in the earlier parts of the Article should now be clear. The principle of consent that I extracted from the Pareto-superiority criterion was another name for an absence of systematic distributive effects. The probabilistic compensation discussed in connection with the negligence system of automobile accident liability made it possible to ignore ex post distributive effects in evaluating that system. By the same token, no group can hope to benefit ex ante from a change in the system, assuming the system is the most efficient one possible, and those few and scattered parties who lose out ex post are a diffuse and therefore ineffective interest group. If this example can be generalized to the common law as a whole, it provides a reason for believing that the political forces in the society will converge in seeking efficiency in common law adjudication. In this instance what is ethical is also politic.

### Is the Common Law Efficient or Utilitarian?

I want to consider finally and very briefly whether it is possible to distinguish empiri-cally between the efficiency theory of the common law and a theory that says that in the heyday of the common law the judges subscribed to the dominant utilitarian ideology of the nineteenth century. My previous article noted that some influential figures in legal scholarship described the common law as utilitarian.[47] Did they mean utilitarian in contradistinction to economic? I think not, for I can think of no instances in which utilitarian deviates from economic teaching where the common law followed the utilitarian approach. For example, income equality, protection of animals, and prohibition of begging are all policies that were advocated by Bentham,[48] the most thoroughgoing utilitarian, yet no traces of these policies can be found in the common law. Bentham also believed in imposing a legal duty to be a good Samaritan, but the common law, perhaps on economic grounds, rejected such a duty.[49] There is also no trace in the common law of sympathy for thieves, rapists, or other criminals who seek to defend their crimes on the ground that they derived more pleasure from the act than the pain suffered by their victims. Of course utilitarianism is a flexible enough philosophy to accommodate arguments as to why allowing a criminal such a defense would not really maximize happiness over the long term. But this is just to say that enlightened utilitarianism will incorporate the sorts of constraints that makes wealth maximization an appealing ethical norm.

---

[46] In this analysis, the features of the judicial process that I have argued elsewhere tend to suppress distributive considerations, *see, e.g.,* R. POSNER, *supra* note 44, § 19.2, are thus viewed as effects rather than as causes of the judicial emphasis on efficiency.

[47] *See* Posner, *supra* note 1, at 106.

[48] *See* Posner, *Blackstone and Bentham*, 19 J.L. & ECON. 569, 590–600 (1976).

[49] *Compare* J. BENTHAM, THEORY OF LEGISLATION 189–90 (R. Hildreth ed. 1864), *with* Landes & Posner, *Salvors, Finders, Good Samaritans, and Other Rescuers: An Economic Study of Law and Altruism*, 7 J. LEGAL STUD. 83, 119–27 (1978).

## QUESTIONS

1. Explain what Posner means by saying that the concept of Pareto superiority should be an answer to the "utilitarian's problem of the interpersonal comparison of utilities."

2. In Posner's example, when the factory closes in town *A* and opens in town *B*, landowners in *A* will be worse off. What reasons (following either Posner's or your own thinking) could be given to these landowners to explain why they ought to accept this change?

3. Would the principle of wealth maximization authorize slavery under certain conditions? Evaluate Posner's arguments that it would not.

4. It is sometimes said that economic analysis is of limited applicability because it is based on ideal assumptions that are almost never true in the real world. How deeply does this sort of criticism cut against Posner's idea of wealth maximization as a tool of analysis and recommendation?

5. Posner believes that, where express consent is not available, "we should look for implied consent, as by trying to answer the hypothetical question whether, if transaction costs are zero, the affected parties would have agreed to the institution." "This procedure," Posner says, "resembles a judge's imputing the intent of parties to a contract that fails to provide expressly for some contingency." Is Posner confusing the situation in which we try to *reconstruct* what someone has *actually* consented to with the situation in which we try to imagine what someone *would* consent to under certain conditions? [On the distinction between reconstructed consent and hypothetical consent, see Daniel Brudney, "Hypothetical Consent and Moral Force," *Law and Philosophy*, vol. 10, no. 3 (August 1991), pp. 235–70.]

## *Ronald Dworkin*
## POSNER'S WRONG START*

Professor Posner believes that agencies of government, and particularly courts, should make political decisions in such a way as to maximize social wealth.[11] In the present article he narrows his claim and offers a new argument. He wishes to show, not as before why society as a whole should seek wealth maximization in every political decision, but only why common law judges should decide cases so as to maximize wealth. He offers two arguments meant to be connected (or perhaps even to be only one argument). First, everyone (or at least almost everyone) may be deemed to have consented in advance to the principles or rules that judges who seek to maximize wealth will apply. Second, the enforcement of these principles and rules is in fact in the interest of everyone (or almost everyone) including those who thereby lose law suits. The first—the argument from consent—is supposed to introduce the idea of autonomy (and therefore a strain of Kant) to the case for wealth. The second—the argument from universal interest—insists in the

*Pp. 573–590 from Ronald Dworkin, "Why Efficiency?" in *Hofstra Law Review*, vol. 8, no. 3 (Spring 1980). Reprinted by permission of the *Hofstra Law Review*. Numerous footnotes have been omitted.
[11] Posner, *Utilitarianism, Economics, and Legal Theory*, 8.J. Legal Stud. 103 (1979).

continuing relevance of welfare to justice, and therefore is supposed to add a dose of utilitarianism. The combined arguments, Posner suggests, show that wealth maximization—at least by judges—provides the best of both these traditional theories of political morality and avoids their famous problems.

Posner illustrates the second claim by showing why, if negligence rules are superior from the standpoint of wealth maximization to rules of strict liability, it follows that all those who benefit from reduced driving costs—almost everyone—would be better off under a regime of negligence than a regime of strict liability. The first claim—about consent—is then supposed to follow directly: If it is in fact true that almost everyone would be better off under a regime of negligence than strict liability, then it is fair to assume that almost everyone would have chosen negligence if offered the choice between these two regimes at a suitably early time, and therefore fair to deem almost everyone to have consented to negligence even though, of course, no one has actually done so.

## The Argument from Consent

In fact both these arguments are more complex and I think more confused than first appears. (I discussed them both at length several years ago.) It is important to remember, first, that consent and self-interest are independent concepts that have independent roles in political justification. If I have consented in advance to governance by a certain rule, then this counts as some reason for enforcing against me the rule to which I have consented. Of course, in determining how much reason my actual consent provides we must look to the circumstances of my consent, in particular to see whether it was informed and uncoerced. In this latter investigation the question of whether it was in my self-interest to have consented may figure only as evidence: if it was plainly not in my self-interest, this might suggest, though it does not prove, that my consent was either uninformed or coerced. But the bare fact that my consent was against my own interest provides no argument in itself against enforcing my consent against my later wishes.

Conversely, the fact that it would have been in my self-interest to have consented to something is sometimes evidence that I did in fact consent, if the question of whether I did actually consent is for some reason in doubt. But only evidence: the fact of self-interest, of course, in no way constitutes an actual consent. In some circumstances, however, the fact of self-interest is good evidence for what we might call a counterfactual consent: that is, the proposition that I would have consented had I been asked. But a counterfactual consent provides no reason in itself for enforcing against me that to which I would have (but did not) consent. Perhaps the fact of my earlier self-interest does provide an argument for enforcing the principle against me now. I shall consider that later. But the counterfactual consent, of which the self-interest is evidence, can provide no further argument beyond whatever argument the self-interest itself provides. Since Posner's argument from consent depends entirely on counterfactual consent, and since counterfactual consent is in itself irrelevant to political justification, the argument from consent wholly fails. Posner's appeal to "autonomy"—and his associated claim to have captured what is most worthwhile in "Kantian" theories—is wholly spurious.

Autonomy is, I agree, a different concept from consent. It contemplates what is sometimes called—perhaps misleadingly—authentic consent, meaning the consent of the true or genuine person. That dark idea is often elaborated as a kind of hypothetical or counterfactual consent. But then the authenticity is provided by—and everything turns on—the way the conditions of the counterfactual consent are specified. Kant himself deployed a complex metaphysical psychology to identify the consent of the genuine person counterfactually. Rawls constructs an elaborate "original position" for an arguably similar purpose.

But Posner's argument lacks any comparable structure, and so provides no reason to think that the counterfactual consent he describes has more claim to authenticity—and hence to autonomy—than any other choice people might have, but did not, make.

Why has Posner confused self-interest and consent in this apparently elementary way? His present article provides a variety of clues. Consider the following extraordinary passage:

> The notion of consent used here is what economists call ex ante compensation. I contend, I hope uncontroversially, that if you buy a lottery ticket and lose the lottery . . . you have consented to the loss. Many of the involuntary, uncompensated losses experienced in the market, or tolerated by the institutions that take the place of the market where the market cannot be made to work effectively, are fully compensated ex ante and hence are consented to.

This passage confuses two questions: Is it fair that someone should bear some loss? Has he consented to bear that loss? If I buy a lottery ticket knowing the odds, and was uncoerced, it is perhaps fair that I bear the loss that follows, because I received a benefit ("compensation") for assuming the risk. But it hardly follows, nor is it true, that I have consented to that loss. What, indeed, would that mean? (Perhaps that I agreed that the game should be rigged so that I must lose.)

In some circumstances it may be said that I consented to the *risk* of loss, which is different, though even this stretches a point and in many cases is just false. Suppose (with no question of fraud or duress) I wildly overestimated my chance of winning—perhaps I thought it a sure thing. It may nevertheless be fair that I lose, if the ticket was in fact fairly priced, even though I would not have bet if I had accurately assessed my chances of winning. All this—the importance of distinguishing between fairness and consent—is even clearer in the case

of the "entrepreneurial risks" Posner discusses. He imagines a case in which someone buys land which then falls in value when the biggest plant in town unexpectedly moves. He says that the loss was compensated ex ante (and hence "consented to") because "[t]he probability that the plant would move was discounted in the purchase price that they paid." The latter suggestion is mysterious. Does it assume that the price was lower because both parties to the sale expected the move? But then the plant's move would not have been unexpected. Or does it mean simply that anyone buying or selling anything knows that the unexpected may happen? In either case the argument begs the question even as an argument that it is fair that the buyer bear the loss. For it assumes that it has already been established and understood by the parties that the buyer must bear the loss—otherwise the price would not have reflected just the risk that the plant would move, but also the risk that the buyer would be required to bear the loss if it did move.

But in any event it is just wrong to say, in either case, that the buyer consented to the loss. Perhaps, though the buyer knew that the plant would very likely move and that he was getting a bargain price because the seller expected that the buyer would bear the loss if the plant did move, the buyer hoped that he might be able to persuade some court to rescind the sale if the feared move did take place or to persuade some legislature to bail him out. It would be fair, in these circumstances, for the court to refuse rescission, but dead wrong to say that the buyer had consented to bear the loss. The argument of fairness must stand on its own, that is, and gains nothing from any supposition about consent. Autonomy is simply not a concept here in play.

So Posner may have conflated interest and consent because he has conflated consent more generally with the grounds of fairness. A second clue is provided by his remarks about what he calls "implied consent." He acknowledges that plaintiffs in negligence suits cannot be said to have consented expressly to rules of negligence rather than strict liability—even in the way he believes buyers of lottery tickets have consented to losing. But he says that courts can *impute* consent to such plaintiffs the way courts impute intentions to parties to a contract who have spelled out every term, or to legislatures whose statutes are dark with ambiguity. Once again, Posner's analogy betrays a confusion; in this case, it is a confusion between unexpressed and counterfactual consent.

Lawyers disagree about how best to describe contractual or statutory interpretation. According to one theory, the court takes what the parties or the legislators say expressly as evidence—as clues to the existence of some individual or group psychological state which is an actual intention, though one that is never expressed formally in the requisite document. According to the competing theory, the court does not purport to discover such a hidden psychological state, but rather uses the fiction of an unexpressed psychological state as a vehicle for some argument about what the parties or the legislature would have done (or, perhaps, should have done) if they had attended to the issue now in question. These are different and competing theories of constructive intention, precisely because they describe very different justifications for a judicial decision. If a judge really has discovered a hidden but actual psychological state—some common understanding of parties to a contract or of members of a legislative group—then the fact of that common understanding provides a direct argument for his decision. But if the putative psychological state is fiction only, then the fiction can of course provide no argument in itself. In that case it is the arguments the judge himself deploys, about what the parties or the legislature would or should have done, that do all the work, and the idea of consent plays no role whatsoever. When Posner says that the courts might impute consent to plaintiffs in automobile-accident cases, there can be no doubt which kind of description he means to suggest. He does not suppose that plaintiffs have really but secretly consented to negligence rules, taking a silent vow to that effect each morning before breakfast. He means that the imputed consent would be a fiction. He has in mind only counterfactual, not unexpressed, consent. But a counterfactual consent is not some pale form of consent. It is no consent at all.

The third clue Posner offers us is more interesting. He notices that Rawls (and Harsanyi and other economists) have built elaborate arguments for theories of justice that are based on counterfactual consent. He means to make the same sort of argument, though, as he makes plain, he has in mind a different basis for counterfactual consent and a different theory of justice. He asks himself, not what parties to some original position would consent to under conditions of radical uncertainty, but what actual people, each of whom knows his particular situation in full detail, would consent to in the fullness of that understanding. He answers that they would consent, not to principles seeking maximin over wealth or even average utility, but to just those rules that common law judges concerned about maximizing social wealth would employ.

But Posner ignores the fact that Rawls' (and Harsanyi's) arguments have whatever force they do have just because the questions they describe must be answered under conditions of radical uncertainty. Indeed (as I have tried to make plain elsewhere) Rawls' original position is a powerful mechanic for thinking about justice because the design of that position embodies and enforces the theory of deep equality described in the last part of this essay. It embodies that theory precisely through the stipulation that parties consent to principles of justice with no knowledge of any qualities or attributes that give them advantages over others, and with no knowledge of what conception of the good they hold as distinct from others.

Posner says that his own arguments improve on Rawls because Posner is concerned with actual people making choices under what he calls "natural" ignorance—he means, I suppose, ignorance about whether they will actually be unlucky—rather than under what he calls Rawls' "artificial" and more radical ignorance. But this "improvement" is fatal. Posner does not contemplate, as we saw, actual consent. If he did, then the degree of "natural" ignorance to attribute to the choosers (or, what comes to the same thing, the date at which to define that ignorance) would be given. It would be the date of the actual, historical choice. But since Posner has in mind a counterfactual rather than an actual choice, any selection of a degree or date of ignorance must be wholly arbitrary, and different selections would dictate very different rules as fair. It would plainly be arbitrary, for example, to construct "natural" ignorance so that no one knew whether he was one of the few inveterate pedestrians whose expected welfare would be improved by strict liability rather than negligence for automobile accidents. But if natural ignorance does not exclude such self-knowledge, then Posner cannot claim that even the counterfactual consent would be unanimous. If must be a matter of the counterfactual choice of most people and that provides, as we shall see, not an improved version of a Rawlsian argument, but a utilitarian argument only.

In fact, the situation is worse even than that. For if only "natural" ignorance is in play, then there is no nonarbitrary reason to exclude the knowledge of those who know that they have already been unlucky—that is, the plaintiffs of the particular law suits the judge is asked to decide by imposing a wealth-maximizing rule. After all, at any moment, some people are in that position, and their consent will not be forthcoming then, even counterfactually. Posner plainly wants to invite consent under what turns out to be, not natural ignorance, but a tailored ignorance that is even more artificial

than Rawls' original position. For any particular plaintiff, he wants to invite consent at some time after that person's driving habits are sufficiently well formed so that he is a gainer from reduced driving costs, but before the time he has suffered an uninsured nonnegligence accident. What time is that? Why is that time decisive? Rawls chose his original position, with its radical ignorance, for reasons of political morality: the original position, so defined, is a device for enforcing a theory of deep equality. Posner seems to be able to define his conditions of counterfactual choice only so as to reach the results he wants.

## The Argument from Interest

Posner's second main argument, as I said earlier, is an argument from the self-interest of most people. He offers to show that it is in the interest of almost everyone that judges decide common law cases by enforcing those rules that maximize social wealth. Even those people who do not drive, he notices, use motor vehicles—they take buses or are driven by others—and so gain from reduced driving costs. If a regime of negligence rules, rather than rules of strict liability, would reduce driving costs, and if nearly everyone would benefit overall from that reduction, then something very like a Pareto justification on the welfare space is available for negligence. Almost everyone is better off and almost no one is worse off. Of course not absolutely everyone will be better off—we can imagine someone who is always a pedestrian and never even a passenger—but "only a fanatic" would insist on complete unanimity when a Pareto justification is in play.

That is Posner's argument from nonfanatical Paretianism, shorn of its autonomy or consent claims. What are we to make of it? We must first of all try to become clearer about whom the "almost everyone" proviso leaves out. Suppose I am an automobile driver who benefits steadily over my whole life from the reduced driving costs made possible by the institution of negligence. One day I am run down (on one of my rare walks around the block) by a nonnegligent driver, and I suffer medical and other costs far in excess of the amount I formerly saved from reduced driving costs, and will save from reduced ambulance charges and motorized wheelchair costs in the future. In what sense do I benefit from a regime of negligence, which denies me recovery, over a regime of strict liability? Only in the sense of what might be called my antecedent self-interest. I was better off under the system of negligence before I was run down, at least on the reasonable assumption that I had no more chance of being run down than any one else. After all (by hypothesis) I could have bought insurance against being run down with part of what I saved, as a motorist, from the lower driving costs. But of course *after* the accident (if I have not in fact bought such insurance) I would be better off under a system of strict liability. The difference can also be expressed not temporally, but as a difference in expected welfare under different states of knowledge. When I do not know that it is I who will be run down, my expected welfare is higher under negligence. When I do know that, my expected welfare is higher under strict liability.

But what is the appropriate point (expressed either temporally or as a function of knowledge) at which to calculate my expected welfare? Suppose my case is a hard case at law because it has not yet been decided in my jurisdiction whether negligence or strict liability governs cases like mine. (It is, after all, just in such hard cases that we need a theory of adjudication like the one Posner proposes.) Now the fact that I would have been better off, before my accident, under a system of negligence seems irrelevant. I did not in fact have the benefits of a negligence rule. In such a case the question—under which rule will everyone be better off—must look to the future only. And I, for one, will not be better off under negligence. I will be better off under strict liability.

But suppose it is said that at least everyone else—or everyone else except the few who walk and never drive or are driven—will be better off. Only I and these inveterate pedestrians will be worse off. Is that true? It is true that (ignoring these inveterate pedestrians) everyone else's expected welfare, fixed at the time of my lawsuit, will be improved. But it is not true that everyone's actual welfare will be improved. For there will be some who will not, in fact, take out the appropriate insurance, and who will be unlucky. They will suffer so much uncompensated loss from nonnegligent accidents that they would have been better off, ex post, had the court laid down a regime of strict liability in my case, even when their reduced driving costs in the meantime, and their reduced ambulance costs thereafter, have been taken into account. Suppose you are one of these unlucky people. You sue. You cannot say that you have had no benefit from the system of negligence, but you nevertheless suggest that the system of negligence be abandoned now and strict liability instituted, starting with your case.

It cannot be said, as a reason for refusing your request, that you in fact gained more than you lost from the decision in my case. You did not—you lost more than you gained. But suppose it were true that you gained more than you lost. Let me change the facts once again so that is so. Suppose that your present accident arises near the end of your expected life and that you did arrange insurance after the decision in my case so that you will now suffer only a short-lived increase in your premium if you lose your case. You have gained more in reduced driving costs in the meantime than you will lose even if you lose your case. Nevertheless it is not true that you will gain more *in the future* if the judge in your case refuses your request and maintains the system of negligence. Even under the new set of facts you will gain more if strict liability is now instituted, starting with your case. Otherwise (being rational) you would not have made the request that you did.

I hope the point is now clear. If we set out to justify any particular common law decisions on Pareto grounds, then the class of exceptions—the class of those worse off through the decision—must include, at a minimum, those who lose the lawsuit and others in like cases. It does not improve the Pareto justification that the rule now imposed would have increased the expected welfare of the loser had it been imposed earlier. Nor that the rule was in fact imposed earlier so that his expected welfare was in fact increased at some earlier date. Nor that, because the rule was in fact imposed earlier, the loser in the present suit gained more from that past rule than he now loses. Each of these is irrelevant because a Pareto justification is a forward-looking, not a backward-looking, justification. It proposes that a decision is right because no one is worse off through *that* decision being taken. But then all those who are worse off from a forward-looking point of view must stand as counter examples to a proposed Pareto justification. Of course these different *backward*-looking considerations might well be relevant to a different kind of justification of judicial decision. They might, in particular, be relevant to a familiar sort of argument from fairness. (I shall, in fact, consider that argument later.) But they are not relevant to a Pareto justification, which justification Posner is at pains to supply.

Is Posner saved here by his caveat, that only a fanatic would insist on absolute unanimity? Perhaps it does sound fanatical to insist that every last person must benefit—or at least not lose—before any social decision is taken. If we accepted that constraint almost no social decision would be justified. Nevertheless that is exactly what the Pareto criterion requires. It insists that no one be worse off, and if any one is, then the Pareto justification is not simply weakened; it is destroyed. Pareto is all or nothing, like pregnancy and legal death.

Why? Because unless the Pareto criterion is treated as all or nothing, as fanatical in this way, it simply collapses into the utilitarian criterion. In particular, it assumes the burden of both the conceptual and the moral defects of utilitarian theories. Suppose we state the Pareto criterion in the following, nonfanatical way: "A political (including a judicial) decision is justified if it will make the vast bulk of people better off and only a relatively few people worse off." Surely we must interpret this test so as to take account of the quantity of welfare gained or lost as well as the numbers who gain or lose. Otherwise it might justify devastating losses to a few in exchange for such trivial gains to the many that the sum of the latter, on any reckoning, falls short of the sum of the former. But when we do introduce the dimension of quantity of welfare gained and lost we also introduce the familiar problems of inter-personal comparisons of utility. One important claim for the Pareto criterion is that it avoids such comparisons; if it turns out not to avoid them after all, then this claim must be withdrawn.

A second claim for the Pareto criterion is a claim of political morality. Utilitarianism faces the problem of explaining to someone who loses in a Benthamite calculation why it is fair to make him suffer simply so that others may prosper. Critics of utilitarianism hold that any Benthamite justification offered to him will commit what I have called the ambiguous sin of ignoring the difference between people. Now if a fanatical Pareto justification is available for a given political decision, than this problem—explaining why someone must be worse off in order that others be better off—is avoided. I do not mean that Pareto justifications are wholly unproblematical. Someone who holds a deep-egalitarian theory of absolute equality of welfare will object to a decision that makes some better off and no one worse off if that decision destroys a preexisting absolute equality of welfare. But fanatical Pareto justifications do avoid the obviously more serious problem of justifying losses to some so that others may gain.

It is important to see, moreover, that this is not a problem of the numbers of who lose. Suppose only one person loses in a Benthamite calculation. If the fact that the gain to others outweighs, in total, the loss to that one person provides a justification for the loss to him, then that same justification must obviously be available when the number of losers increases to any number, provided, of course, that the aggregate gain still exceeds the aggregate loss. The issue of principle is raised, decisively, in the individual case. That is the eye of the needle; if utility can pass through that eye it gains heaven. So our relaxed Pareto criterion can have no advantage of political morality over straightforward Benthamism. Nonfanatical Paretianism is utilitarianism merely.

It is time for a reckoning. Posner is pleased to claim that wealth maximization combines the most appealing features of both the Kantian concern with autonomy and the utilitarian concern with individual preferences, while avoiding the excesses of either of these traditional theories. His argument from counterfactual consent is meant to supply the Kantian features. But this is spurious: In fact the idea of consent does no work at all in the theory and the appeal to autonomy is therefore a facade. His argument from the common interest is meant to supply the utilitarian features. But it does this too well. He cannot claim a genuine Pareto justification for common law decisions, in either hard or easy cases. His relaxed version of Paretianism is simply utilitarianism with all the warts. The voyage of his present essay ends in the one traditional theory he was formerly most anxious to disown.

## Beyond Consent and Interest

Can we discover, in Posner's various discussions, some more attractive argument of fairness than those he makes explicitly? The following general principle (we may call it the antecedent-interest principle) seems some-

how in play. If a rule is in everyone's antecedent interest at the time it is enacted, then it is fair to enforce that rule even against those who turn out, in the event, to lose by its adoption, provided that they were, in advance, no more likely to lose by it than others were. That is not, as we have seen, the Pareto criterion, nor will everyone agree that it is, in fact, a fair principle. Indeed I shall provide reasons to doubt it. But it has enough initial appeal for us to ask whether it provides a base for Posner's arguments for wealth maximization in adjudication.

The antecedent-interest principle cannot, of course, be used directly in favor of any particular wealth-maximizing rule a judge might adopt, for the first time, in a hard case. For any particular rule will fail the test the principle provides: It will not be in the interest of the party against whom it is used at the time of its adoption, because the time of its adoption is just the time at which it is used against him. But the antecedent-interest principle does seem to support a *meta-rule* of adjudication (call it alpha) which provides that in a hard case judges should choose and apply that rule, if any, that is in the then antecedent interests of the vast bulk of people though not in the interests of the party who then loses. Once alpha has been in force in a community for some time, at least, alpha itself meets the antecedent-interest-principle test. For each individual, alpha may unhappily make it more likely that some rule will be adopted that will work against his interests. For inveterate pedestrians, for example, alpha may make it more likely that the negligence rule will be adopted. But since each individual will gain through the adoption of other rules in virtue of alpha—inveterate pedestrians will gain through all manner of common law rules that work in their benefit as well as the benefit of most others—it may plausibly be said that alpha *itself* is in the antecedent interest of absolutely everyone. But even if it turns out that this is wrong—that a certain economic or other minority exists such that that minority characteristically loses by a wide range of particular rules meeting the test of alpha—then alpha can be suitably amended. Let us therefore restate alpha this way: In a hard case, judges should choose that rule, if any, that is in the then antecedent interests of the vast bulk of people and not against the interests of the worst-off economic group or any other group that would be generally and antecedently disadvantaged, as a group, by the enforcement of this principle without this qualification.

Now Posner believes that alpha (taken hereafter to be amended in this way) would require judges to adopt a wealth-maximizing test for common law adjudication, at least in general. If this is so, then the combination of the antecedent-interest rule and alpha might seem to provide an argument of fairness in favor of (at least general) wealth-maximizing adjudication at common law. That would be an important conclusion and, in my opinion, a clear advance over previous attempts to justify wealth maximization as a standard for adjudication. It is more convincing to argue that, under the conditions of common law adjudication, wealth-maximizing rules are fair, than to say either that wealth is good in itself or that it is causally related to other, independently stated, goods in such a way as to justify instrumentally the doctrine that society should single-mindedly pursue wealth.

So we have good reason to ask whether the antecedent interest principle is fair. We should notice that if that principle could be sensibly applied by the parties to Rawls' original position, and if they chose to apply it, then they would select the principle of average utility as the fundamental principle of justice rather than the principles Rawls says they would select, (Harsanyi and others, as Posner reminds us, have argued for average utility in just this way.) We can immediately see one reason, however, why parties to the original position, under one description of their interests, would not accept the antecedent-interest principle. If they were con-

servative about risks and adopted a maximin strategy for that reason, they would avoid the principle, because it works against those who in one way or another have very bad luck.

We have already seen why this is so. Suppose alpha has been in force for generations. But the question of whether negligence or strict liability holds for automobile accidents has never been settled. Some person who is injured by a nonnegligent driver, and is uninsured, finds that a court, responding to alpha, chooses a negligence rule, and he is therefore ruined by medical expenses. He argues that this is unfair. It is not an appealing reply that the economic group to which he belongs gains along with everyone else under a regime of negligence. He loses. Nor is it necessarily true that as things turned out, he gained more than he lost from alpha being accepted in his community. It is hard to guess at how much he gained. We should have to ask what other arguments were in favor of the rules that were adopted earlier in virtue of alpha in order to decide whether the same rules would have been adopted even if alpha had been rejected from the outset. But if he is absolutely ruined by his uncompensated accident he might well be better off, ex post, had alpha never been recognized.

Suppose we say to him, in reply to his complaint, that he should have known that alpha would settle any case testing negligence against strict liability for accidents, should have calculated that alpha required negligence, and should have purchased appropriate insurance against nonnegligent injury. He will answer, with some force, that we have begged every important question. First it does not follow, from the fact that alpha in fact recommends negligence, that the argument that it does was, in the appropriate sense, publicly available. That argument might rest on reasonably recondite economic analysis developed and worked through for the first time in connection with this litigation. Second, our reply assumes that alpha is fair, so that he should have made provisions for insurance in its light, though that is just what he questions. He did not, of course, consent to alpha just because it was in his antecedent interest when established—that claim simply repeats Posner's initial mistake. Nor does he accept that it is fair to impose some standard on him just because he has had some benefit from it in the past, particularly if he had no choice whether to accept that benefit.[26] We must show that the principle of antecedent interest is fair, not just assume it.

We shall clarify these objections, I think, if we construct a different principle (call it beta). Beta is not, in its basic formulation, a principle for adjudication, as alpha is, but it furnishes one. Beta is basically a theory of social responsibility. We might formulate it in its most abstract form this way. People should take responsibility for such costs of accidents (defined, as elsewhere in this Article, broadly) if responsibility for such costs would be assigned to them by legislation in an ideal community in which everyone acted and voted with a sense of justice and with mutual and equal concern and respect, based on information that is also easily, publicly, and reliably available to the actor. Beta (stated at that level of abstraction) might well be said to be only a schema for a principle of responsibility not a principle itself. Reasonable people who accept it will nevertheless disagree about what it requires because they disagree about how just people would act and vote. (Beta, we might say, admits of different interpretations or conceptions.) But even put so abstractly beta if far from empty. On the contrary, it is very demanding—perhaps too demanding—because it proposes to enforce legislation that would be adopted in certain unlikely circumstances but in fact has not yet been. Beta is a strong theory of responsibility because it is a theory of natural responsibility tied to

counterfactual propositions about legislation. Someone might intelligibly believe that beta requires people to take responsibility themselves for the costs of nonnegligent accidents, and yet deny that they should do so until and unless the legislation described in beta is actually in force. He accepts, that is, that beta requires some particular assumption of responsibility, but rejects beta.

Though beta is a theory of natural responsibility, it furnishes a recommendation for adjudication, particularly against the background of a general theory of adjudication, which argues that, in principle, natural rights and duties should be enforced in court. Suppose someone now says, however, that beta is in fact nothing but alpha. Or (perhaps a bit more plausibly) that alpha is one interpretation or conception of beta. Either would be a mistake, and a serious confusion. For alpha will, under certain circumstances all too familiar, recommend judicial decisions that no plausible interpretation of beta could countenance. Suppose, as we just imagined, that a particular rule will in fact meet the requirements of alpha, but for reasons that are neither familiar nor generally available but are developed in adjudication in just the way in which recondite economic data or analysis might properly be developed looking towards legislation. Alpha will insist that that rule must be applied to someone who, even though aware of alpha, could not reliably have anticipated the rule. Beta, of course, will not eliminate all surprises: If people disagree radically about what it requires, because they disagree about the underlying moral issues, then someone may indeed be surprised by its application. But the grounds and incidents of this surprise differ greatly between the two principles.

A second difference seems to me more important. Consider the following familiar argument about the consequences of a principle

---

[26] See Simmons, *The Principle of Fair Play*, 8 PHILOSOPHY & PUB. AFF. 307 (1979).

like alpha. Suppose considerations of fairness recommend that members of some group—the poor, for example, or the uneducated—should have certain contractual privileges or immunities, either through special rules or through general rules that will have special importance for people in their situation. But if a court adopts such a rule members of that group will in fact suffer in the long run, because merchants or other contractors will be less likely to contract with them, or will insist on compensatory price increases or other conditions, or will in some other way thwart the purpose of the rule in question. Alpha now argues against the immediately protective rule. If alpha is followed, someone loses in the present case who is told that, although fairness would justify a decision for him if his case could be considered on its own merits, he must lose in order to protect others in his economic class in the future. Beta, on the other hand, argues the other way. It regards the fact that others would act so as to undermine the requirements of fairness as irrelevant to the question of natural responsibility, and so irrelevant to the question put for adjudication. The merchants who will ignore the claims of the disadvantaged group, claims we assume *arguendo* to be required by justice, are not behaving as they would in the counterfactual conditions stipulated for fixing natural responsibility.

Legislators would be wiser, no doubt, to consider the real world rather than these counterfactual conditions, and so to prefer alpha to beta as a guide for forward-looking legislation about contractual immunities, responsibility for accidents, and so forth. Some people might think that judges deciding hard cases at law should also prefer alpha to beta, though others, perhaps more sensitive to the differences between the questions put to the two institutions, will disagree. My present point is only that beta is different from alpha, both in what it requires and in its philosophical basis.

But beta will in fact require much of what alpha requires. If Posner is right about the fact and the distribution of the cost savings under a negligence rule, for example, both beta and alpha will recommend a regime of negligence rather than strict liability over a certain range of cases. Under even more plausible assumptions beta as well as alpha will recommend some version of the Hand test[27] as the basis for computing negligence. Perhaps beta as well as alpha would characteristically recommend wealth-maximizing rules for the sorts of disputes that come to adjudication under common law. (Perhaps beta would recommend the wealth-maximizing rule in more of such cases than alpha would.)

What conclusions should we draw? Beta seems to me inherently more attractive as a guide to adjudication than alpha does. Beta is itself a principle about natural responsibility, and so, as a guide for adjudication, unites adjudication and private morality and permits the claim that a decision in a hard case, assigning responsibility to some party, simply recognizes that party's moral responsibility. Alpha is not itself a principle of responsibility at all, but only a guide to wise forward-looking legislation. It must rely on the antecedent-interest principle to supply an argument of fairness in adjudication, and that principle (as we noticed in considering the complaints of someone who loses when alpha is applied) is seriously flawed.

In any case, however, there is a fatal objection to relying on the combination of alpha and the antecedent-interest principle to justify wealth-maximizing decisions in our own legal system. I skirted over this problem in explaining the argument for alpha, but must confront it now. The antecedent-interest principle could never justify introducing alpha itself in a hard case, for if some member of the then community loses who would not otherwise have lost—either the losing party in that case or someone else—then the antecedent-interest principle is violated. It is only after

<hr>

[27] *See* United States v. Carroll Towing Co., 159 F. 2d 169, 173 (2d Cir. 1947).

alpha has been in force for some time that it could be in the antecedent interest of every *then* member of the community to *have* introduced it. It can never be fair to introduce alpha for the first time (if the fairness of doing so depends on the antecedent-interest principle) though the unfairness of having introduced it may disappear over time.

Is this a boring technical point, calling attention only to some presumed unfairness in a past long dead, or something of practical importance? That depends on what is taken to be the adoption of alpha. Can we say that alpha has already been adopted as a principle of adjudication within a legal system when the decisions the courts have reached (or tended to reach) are the same as the decisions that alpha would have required had it been expressly adopted? Or only when alpha has in fact been expressly adopted and relied on in reaching those decisions? The antecedent-interest principle supports alpha only after alpha has been adopted in the second sense. That principle supposes a moment at which people's antecedent or expected welfare is improved by a social decision to adjudicate in a certain way, and that moment is not supplied simply by a set of decisions that would have been reached by an institution that had taken that decision. For no one's expected welfare would be improved in the way alpha promises simply by a course of decisions, however consistent with alpha, that did not carry a commitment to enforce alpha generally, and this is true even if that course of decisions worked to enforce alpha not by coincidence, but through some invisible hand, or even by the subconscious motivation of judges. What is essential is a commitment, and that can be achieved only by adoption in the second sense.

But since that is so, alpha has never been adopted in our own legal system in the pertinent sense, even if the positive claims of Posner and others about the explanatory power of wealth maximization are accepted

in full. So we cannot rely on alpha to show that wealth-maximizing decisions in the past were fair through some combination of alpha and the antecedent-interest principle. Nor can we rely on that combination to justify any wealth-maximizing decisions in the future. On a more careful look, that is, alpha drops away as a candidate for the basis of a normative theory of wealth maximization.

We might well be left with beta. Beta does not, of course, rely on the antecedent-interest principle in the way alpha did. Beta is itself a principle of fairness—it is, as I said, a principle of natural responsibility—and though it will seem to some too demanding, it requires no help from the antecedent-interest principle to count as an argument of fairness in adjudication. So it is irrelevant that beta has never been expressly recognized as a commitment of our legal system. It carries, as it were, its own claims to be a principle of fairness. If it can be shown that past decisions were those that beta would have justified, that does count as an argument that these decisions were fair. If the same can be shown for future decisions, that, without more, recommends these decisions as fair.

So it would be well to carry further than I have here the possibility that beta requires common law decisions that (at least over a certain range of cases) are just those decisions that maximize wealth. If beta does have that consequence, then a Kantian justification of wealth maximization may indeed be available. Posner's long search for a philosophical basis for his normative theory of adjudication may therefore end in what seemed, at the beginning, unlikely territory for him. For the roots of Kantian morality (as beta practically shouts) are deeply egalitarian. Incidentally, at the close of his letter Calabresi[a] seems to use "policy" as I use "principle." So it appears we do agree about the role of principle in adjudication though perhaps still disagree about what principle requires.

[a]Not reprinted here.

# QUESTIONS

1. Is it fair for a court to enforce against you today a liability rule that you undoubtedly would have consented to last year before your accident, but which you probably would not consent to now? Is it fair to enforce such a rule against you if you actually did consent to it last year?

2. Dworkin speaks of the "dark idea" of "authentic consent" of "the true or genuine person." Give examples of ways in which one's consent would not count as authentic, or that of the real person, and explain why such consent would not be genuine.

3. Suppose that a rule providing for liability only for negligently caused harm has long existed in A's society, and A has enjoyed being a net gainer over the years due to the rule's existence. Now A suffers injury from the non-negligent acts of another person. Is it fair now to enforce the rule, making A a net loser? Explain why or why not.

4. What does Dworkin mean by a "nonfanatical" Pareto criterion? Explain Dworkin's arguments against the nonfanatical version of the Pareto criterion, and why it amounts to "utilitarianism merely."

5. If total net wealth in a community is maximized, does that also maximize the community's total net *utility*? (Suppose that utility = satisfaction of desires.)

# PART FIVE

# Varieties of Skepticism About Legal Reasoning

In Part 5 we need to bring together a number of concepts that we encountered in earlier sections. This is necessary because skepticism about legal reasoning includes doubts about many of the most time-honored ideas that have been developed by legal philosophy. Let us begin by recalling the basic idea of a legal rule that is supposed to be binding on judges in their decisions of cases. In one view of legal reasoning, a deductivist conception that was quite popular in this country during the last century, judges are supposed to apply preexisting rules to the particular facts of a case they are trying to decide and then deduce the proper holding, whether for the plaintiff or the defendant. If there is a legal rule that any person $X$ who negligently injures another person $Y$ is liable to $Y$ for damages, and it is established in court that John negligently injured Mary, then, in the deductivist view, it follows that John may be held liable to pay damages to Mary. Of course, not all applications of an existing legal rule will be as simple as this one. Legal rules embodied in a tax code can be very complicated. In addition, not all legal rules exist because of legislative enactment. Many rules develop out of the precedent-setting decisions of other courts. But whether complicated or simple and whether it comes from legislation or precedent, the rule is to be applied by judges, not created by them. The correct answers to legal problems are already there to be derived by a more or less straightforward piece of deductive inference. As we shall see, this deductivist ideal and the rule of law are often connected.

## THE READINGS

AMERICAN LEGAL REALISM. The intellectual movement known as Legal Realism (LR) was in significant part a strong reaction against deductivism in legal reasoning. Legal realists maintained that judges do not in fact reason as deductivism claims they do. More importantly, they claimed that judges ought not to apply rules so mechanically to cases as the deductivist model suggests. Judges often rely on "hunch" or intuition to decide cases, using talk about rules as rhetorical window dressing in their opinions to make decisions appear acceptable after the fact. This is often made easier, LR contends, by the fact that there are typically many conflicting legal rules, any one of which a judge could refer to. Moreover, legal realists usually contend that it would involve rule worship and sometimes injustice if judges tried to do what the deductivist thinks they ought to do. We can see why by pursuing our simple example a bit further. In addition to the facts about John's negligently injuring Mary, suppose that Mary's injury is also partly the result of Mary's own negligence. Had Mary herself not been negligent at the time, John's negligent act would have caused her only a minor bruise. But because she too was acting negligently, her leg was broken. The general rule about $X$ negligently injuring $Y$ does not take $Y$'s contributory negligence into account, and so, when the deduction is carried out, Mary's contributory negligence will not be taken into account. Yet our intuitions about fairness suggest that Mary's contributory negligence ought at least to reduce the amount of damages she can rightly receive from John. It would be an abdication of both moral and legal responsibility for a judge to follow the rule for no reason other than the fact that it is a rule. After all, the thought runs, legal rules are only instruments to be used toward human ends; they are not ends in themselves. The notion that rules are only instruments to be dispensed with when they do not serve their purposes is characteristic of LR.

Now it becomes clear why the deductivist ideal is often associated with that of the rule of law. If it is understood that judges are to deduce their conclusions by applying the facts to fixed legal rules, those affected by their decisions can know in advance what to expect. The rules are public, one knows the facts of one's situation or some hypothetical situation, and anyone with an understanding of elementary logic can carry out the deduction. On the other hand, if judges feel free to depart from the rules whenever they feel that justice requires it, the certainty and fair notice provided by the rule of law are threatened. This, then, is one of the long-standing dilemmas of legal philosophy: either provide for legal certainty and fair notice, or provide for particular justice by taking into account all the compelling facts about individual cases. But one cannot do both. Sticking to rules in order to promote legal certainty at all costs means rigidity at the expense of justice to the individual. And trying to do justice solely on the merits of each case as it comes along means uncertainty and confusion and injustice to those who relied on known rules and their consistent enforcement. Of course, the dilemma may not be as sharp and inflexible as this suggests. When sufficiently complex legal rules have been developed to take account of a wide variety of situations that may be expected to arise, the need to depart from them in the interest of particular justice will be rare. And, if judges are bound in their decisions by principles in addition to rules, as Ronald Dworkin has argued, doing justice in particular cases will not be a mere matter of the judge's discretion. (See the Dworkin readings in Parts 1 and 3.)

Using this additional set of standards to guide legal reasoning and legal predictions, judicial decisions will no doubt be much more predictable and much more in accord with publicly known standards of legal reasoning than would be the case if rules alone governed legal decision. Ronald Dworkin's arguments about the existence of nonrule binding standards are relatively recent. In the continuing debate, it has been left to Critical Legal Studies (CLS) to develop a deeper skepticism about all standards that putatively "bind" judges.

The excerpt from Jerome Frank's book *Law and the Modern Mind* (1930) provides a sampling of some of LR's main ideas from one of its leading figures. Frank attacks deductivism in this excerpt primarily by attacking the doctrine of precedent. Recall now certain features of that doctrine. The doctrine of precedent holds that judges are bound by precedents established by judicial decisions in earlier cases. By examining the facts of earlier cases, along with the decisions reached in those cases, judges, by a process of logical induction or reasoning from particular cases to general rules, can arrive at the rules which bind them today. These rules are then to be applied by the deductive method. We might call this the *past-oriented* part of the doctrine of precedent, because it concerns what today's judge must do in order to find the law which is to be applied today. But there is also a *future-oriented* part of the doctrine of precedent. Today's judge must realize that her or his decision will set a precedent for future judges deciding future cases. And that in turn implies that ordinary people, seeing that today's decision will have the effect of setting a precedent, will adjust their behavior on that expectation. So the doctrine of precedent requires that today's judge look both to the past, to see how earlier decisions constrain those in the present, and to the future, so see how present decisions will change people's behavior for better or worse. All of this imposes a heavy responsibility on today's judge.

In "Illusory Precedents," Frank expresses doubts about both the past- and the future-oriented aspects of the doctrine of precedent. He suggests that rules of law derived from precedent cannot be relied on anyway, because today's judges do not know enough about the particular facts of those earlier cases, nor do they know enough about the processes of thinking that led earlier judges to decide the way they did. Frank also implies that, even if judges could always discover some clear and unequivocal rule in past decisions, that rule should not weigh heavily in the present case. Each case is unique and should be considered on its merits. The judicial process involves, as Frank puts it, "unceasing adjustment and individualization." To allow oneself to be governed by rules would be rule worship. And just as the attempt to follow rules makes judges too much slaves of the past, the future-oriented part of the doctrine of precedent also serves to take judges' attention away from the wise settlement of the particular dispute at hand, wrongly shifting attention to the unreachable goal of legal certainty. In short, it is an illusion to think that judges should be ruled by the past and equally an illusion to think that judges should attempt to rule the future. The judge's real job is to be the arbitrator of the particular dispute at hand. That job is necessarily focused on particulars and not on rules.

How, then, are individual cases to be decided? If they are not to be decided by following precedents already established in other cases, then what is the judge to use in determining whether plaintiff or defendant should win? LR has mostly been concerned with criticizing deductivism and the doctrine of precedent, remaining open to constructive suggestions about how judges ought to proceed. One possibility that has attracted some legal realists derives from the tradition of the great utilitarians, Jeremy Bentham and John Stuart Mill. The suggestion is that the judge ought to decide each case with a view to producing the greatest overall good, whether that be pleasure or happiness.

To illustrate this, let us consider the sort of example that utilitarians so often use in their debates. Think of an impoverished widow who, because of a mortgage payment she is unable to make, is the defendant in a lawsuit brought by her creditor, a rich, smug miser.[1] It might seem that the most overall good would be produced by preventing the rich plaintiff from foreclosing on the widow. She needs the house far more than he needs the money. But if the defendant's obligation is not enforced against her, that will have the bad effect of making it more difficult for people to borrow money, especially people in need.

So there is at least an indirect reason for the judge to enforce the rule which makes such obligations enforceable: To do so promotes trust, confidence, and legal certainty. Notice that such reasons can be taken into account by the utilitarian who is only interested in the merits of individual cases and has no respect for rules as such. But a utilitarian judge who thinks in these terms would only be concerned about the effect of this particular failure to enforce the terms of this widow's mortgage. If deciding in favor of this widow will not shake public confidence in the enforceability of such agreements, then effects on public confidence need be considered no further. Notice also that the legal realist who adopts such a utilitarian view, though a skeptic about rules, is not a skeptic about the underlying conception of the good that judicial decisions are supposed to promote. A deeper skepticism about the objectivity of any such concept of the good emerges in the Critical Legal Studies movement.

**CRITICAL LEGAL STUDIES.**  The decades of 1920 to 1950 were the heyday of American Legal Realism. In more recent years, what has come to be known as Critical Legal Studies (CLS), in many ways the intellectual descendant of LR, has gained influence. CLS has broadened the attack on some traditional ideas that were already the object of LR's criticism and has opened new attacks in other areas.

One major object of attack for CLS is the ideal of the rule of law. Recall that the rule of law is an ideal that makes certain demands of officials who exercise power. Laws are to be public, general, and relatively fixed. They are to offer a publicly known framework within which individuals may pursue their projects and by means of which the citizenry may hold officials accountable for their actions. The rule of law is supposed to insulate citizens from the arbitrary will and the subjective decisions of those who wield power. Legal realist critics of rules like Jerome Frank had by their criticisms already undercut the foundations of the rule of law. CLS, however, has developed a more frontal attack on the concept of the rule of law, and on the underlying ideal of liberal legalism. Among the leading ideas of liberal legalism are those providing for the maximum feasible individual liberty, as well as providing for the neutrality of the legal system toward various individual values, convictions, and lifestyles. The rule of law helps to secure the objectives of liberal legalism by providing a clear framework of reasonably fixed general public rules and a well-defined sphere of liberty for the individual. Since everyone can understand the value of peaceful

[1] For an extended discussion of utilitarian reasoning built around similar examples, see Richard Wasserstrom, *The Judicial Decision* (Stanford: Stanford University Press, 1961), esp. Chap. 7.

cooperation among diverse members of a pluralistic society, the impartial enforcement of the rules is supposed to be based on values to which everyone can subscribe, thus providing for neutrality on the part of the state and its officials.

The rule of law and its counterpart liberal legalism belong to the core of legal and political thinking in Western democracies. But CLS has raised serious questions about these ideas,[2] claiming that they do not reflect the actual workings of contemporary legal systems and that they are, for that matter, mostly unworkable in principle. This is so, CLS contends, because there are many ways in which controversial moral and political doctrines will creep into the interpretation of legal rules, whether they be the case-law rules that derive from many judicial decisions over the years, or from the rules enacted by legislatures. Legislated rules contain terms that are elastic. They are what philosophers like H.L.A. Hart call "open-textured."[3] The U.S. Constitution contains many such terms: "cruel and unusual punishments" (Amendment VIII); "unreasonable searches and seizures" (Amendment IV); and "due process of law" (Amendments V and XIV). In many areas of the law, both in legislation and in case law, use is made of the famous "reasonable man" standard to measure the conduct of one accused of a crime or a breach of contract. These terms invite, if not require, appeal to political and moral principles as aids to filling our their meaning. Indeed, many of the arguments we have encountered in this book, particularly those advanced by Ronald Dworkin claiming that the decision of hard cases requires use of moral principles, seem to play into the hands of CLS theorists.

If controversial ideology cannot be kept out of legal argument, then it is hard to see how the ideal of the legal system's neutrality can be secured. Whether a rule is to be interpreted as favoring the plaintiff or as favoring the defendant in some lawsuit, say, about property rights, then depends on matters of morality and ideology about which people, including judges, are likely to have deep differences. Whichever decision is reached by the court, the court will not have succeeded in remaining neutral.

So, the thought runs, the notion that the state can stand above the ideological battle, remaining neutral among conflicting moral convictions and lifestyles, a notion that is a centerpiece of liberal legalism, is an idle dream, a myth. That liberal legalism is based on this myth has been a dominant theme of much of the CLS literature. Indeed, according to this criticism of liberal legalism, the liberal state confronts another problem, the problem of community. The more the state is committed to a robust moral and political ideology, the less chance that its laws will be based on principles that everyone can accept or, to put it differently, on principles that are neutral among the various convictions and lifestyles represented in a pluralistic culture. But the more the ideology of the state is restricted to values with which everyone can agree, the less basis there is for a genuine sense of community. Such values may be acceptable and right, but what is needed is a sense of solidarity, of belonging to a joint enterprise that is inspiring, not merely acceptable. A thin ideology that stresses nothing more than such fundamental values as protecting everyone from injuries inflicted by others would no doubt be just that: acceptable but uninspiring.

[2]For more on these matters, see Andrew Altman, *Critical Legal Studies: A Liberal Critique* (Princeton, N.J.: Princeton University Press, 1990).

[3]H.L.A. Hart, *The Concept of Law* (Oxford: The Clarendon Press, 1961), Chap. VII.

Roberto Unger's *Knowledge and Politics* (1975), a small portion of which is excerpted here, has been a seminal work for the CLS movement. The excerpt here touches on several problems, one of which concerns the justification, or theoretical foundation, of rules of law. Rules of law are necessary in order to coordinate human action to provide a basis for resolving disputes among people who are in competition with one another. Left to the uncontrolled pursuit of their own ends, individuals would soon be in a mutually destructive war with one another. So there must be legal rules which stand above this clash. They are to be impartial and neutral. But the whole idea of governing human behavior by rules must be based on some notion of the ends, or good, that those rules are supposed to promote. And in constructing this concept of the good, Unger thinks, the political and legal theory of liberalism faces several serious dilemmas.

One of these dilemmas is the choice between positivism and natural right. The positivist route, exemplified well by John Austin, leads to a kind of "legislative agnosticism," according to Unger, for it holds merely that the law is what the sovereign commands it to be, and it refuses to apply any further standard to determine whether the sovereign's commands are really law or not. We can recall here that, in Austin's view of legislation, neither moral nor constitutional limits have any real bearing on the question of an enactment's legal validity. The sovereign's power cannot be legally limited. But the sovereign is just another person or human group, and in theory there is no assurance that the sovereign will not simply become another party to the conflict, betraying the hope of impartiality and neutrality. On the other hand, the other route, that taken by natural right, does attempt to recognize limits on the sovereign's authority to enact law. A prime example is St. Thomas Aquinas's natural law conception, on which nothing that human beings enact can be law if it is not derivable from the natural law. But Unger reminds us that such conceptions face the notorious difficulty of explaining how we can derive conclusions about the natural law, that is, how we can derive normative standards about how people ought to behave from facts about how they do behave. And if we think of the good as simply something that happens to be agreed upon, that leaves open the possibility that this agreement can be renegotiated, and that we may agree to deviate from it on particular occasions we happen to choose. In short, law would then turn out to be perilously close to politics, and our hope for an impartial, neutral standard set apart from the clash of individual pursuits would again have to be abandoned.

In this connection, Unger levels a charge against political liberalism that has by now become quite common. It is that liberalism is committed to the subjectivity of values and has no basis upon which to erect a conception of the community good except that of individuals' preferences. As he puts it, "Subjectivity emphasizes that an end is an end simply because someone holds it, whereas individuality means that there must always be a particular person whose end it is." If the very existence of values depends on human choice, and if all values ultimately reflect the choices that particular individuals happen to have made, that is yet another reason why the hope to anchor legal rules in some objective, independently demonstrable validity seems doomed to fail.

If correct, this charge would be troublesome to the liberal, because it calls into question the ultimate defensibility of the legal rules which define individual rights, including those of free speech and privacy. The problem arises in two ways. First, if the rules and the rights they define are called into question, and if they have no more secure basis than the fact that they reflect, or once reflected, the preferences of those who enacted them, they are open to the charge that those preferences are or were only those of a small and powerful elite. Second, the problem also arises when there are disagreements about how those rules are to be interpreted and applied, for the results of interpreting any rule in a hard case are bound to depend on the value that the rule is supposed to advance. If that value is controversial, the interpretation itself, being a mere act of will, must also become controversial as well as unstable.

Mark Tushnet's 1986 article on the origins of CLS provides helpful insights into the connection between CLS and its intellectual predecessor, LR. Tushnet distinguishes between LR's critical program, with which most in the CLS movement agree, and LR's constructive program, which itself now becomes the object of critical skepticism, this time under the sponsorship of CLS. A major part of this constructive program is to replace rules and deductivism with policy analysis. Now for our purposes, policy analysis, as Tushnet describes it, is essentially a form of utilitarian decision making. (It might also be a form of wealth maximization decision making as proposed by law and economics.) The decision maker, whether judge or legislator, is supposed to determine what "social interests" are at issue in a particular controversy. In doing this, the decision maker is to determine how people's established wants and preferences will be affected by deciding one way as opposed to another. Doing so requires decision makers to balance interests against one another, much as an old-fashioned classical utilitarian like Bentham would have us balance the pleasures and suffering that would be brought about by various available actions.

But this program requires a concept of what is good and valuable, and it also requires a concept of how values are to be balanced against one another in case of conflict. And on this matter, Tushnet points out, the CLS movement has generally been skeptical. In the absence of any satisfactory theory of the objectively valuable, we must ultimately rely on whatever consensus about the good that might exist. As Tushnet puts it, CLS here "makes a simple point"—the decision makers are not, as a matter of fact, truly representative of the populace. They represent a small elite who are likely to take their own preferences for those of the populace. Indeed, the preferences of the populace itself are shaped by existing legal rules, so the status of those preferences is suspect. This Tushnet calls the "social construction of values." The idea that values are socially constructed is sometimes made in tandem with the claim that those values are suspect because they arise from conditions in which people are unfree or unequal. Notice that this objection to policy analysis seems not to involve the claim that all preferences are inherently subjective and too shaky a foundation for utilitarian decision making. Instead, it seems to imply that, if preferences were taken *under suitable conditions* (of equality, freedom from pressures and influence, and so on), they would then be a true foundation for a concept of the good, and then for policy analysis with an objective basis. Such a suggestion as this, however, runs headlong into another feature the Tushnet attributes to CLS: its drive to shatter or undermine "settled understandings." If, as Tushnet suggests toward the end of his article, no such "congealed form of life" has any real system and integrity of its own, then neither could any such utilitarian proposal for taking people's preferences, whether under ideal conditions or not, escape the CLS attack. Utilitarian proposals belong to constructive system building. They are not part of deconstructionist criticism.

# American Legal Realism

## Jerome Frank
# ILLUSORY PRECEDENTS: THE FUTURE: JUDICIAL SOMNAMBULISM*

Lawyers and judges purport to make large use of precedents; that is, they purport to rely on the conduct of judges in past cases as a means of procuring analogies for action in new cases. But since what was actually decided in the earlier cases is seldom revealed, it is impossible, in a real sense, to rely on these precedents. What the courts in fact do is to manipulate the language of former decisions.[1] They could approximate a system of real precedents only if the judges, in rendering those former decisions, had reported with fidelity the precise steps by which they arrived at their decisions. The paradox of the situation is that, granting there is value in a system of precedents, our present use of illusory precedents makes the employment of real precedents impossible.

The decision of a judge after trying a case is the product of a unique experience. "Of the many things which have been said of the mystery of the judicial process," writes Yntema,[1] "the most salient is that *decision is reached after an emotive experience in which principles and logic play a secondary part.* The function of juristic logic and the principles which it employs seem to be like that of language, to describe the event which has already transpired. These considerations must reveal to us the impotence of general principles to control decision. Vague because of their generality, they mean nothing save what they suggest in the organized experience of one who thinks them, and, because of their vagueness, they only remotely compel the organization of that experience. The important problem . . . is not the formulation of the rule but the ascertainment of the cases to which, and the extent to which, it applies. And this, even if we are seeking uniformity in the administration of justice, will lead us again to the

---

*From *Law and the Modern Mind*, originally published by Brentano's, Inc., in 1930. The Anchor Books edition is published by arrangement with Barbara Frank Kristein. Reprinted by permission of the Estate of Barbara Frank Kristein.  Bracketed [] footnotes are from the Appendix of the original work. Unbracketed footnotes are from the main text of the original work.

[1]There are the two following effective methods employed by the courts for "distinguishing" (*i.e.* evading or sterilizing) a rule laid down in an earlier case:

(1) The rule is limited to the "precise question" involved in the earlier case. *"Minute differences in the circumstances of two cases,"* said a well-known English judge, *"will prevent any argument being deduced from one to the other."* The "decision consists in what is done, not in what is said by the court in doing it," writes Judge Cuthbert Pound. The United States Supreme Court has stated that every "opinion must be read as a whole in view of the facts on which it was based. The facts are the foundation of the entire structure, which cannot safely be used without reference to the facts." The generality of expressions used by a court must, according to Lord Halsbury, "be governed and qualified by the particular facts of the case in which such expressions are found. . . . I entirely deny that [a case] can be quoted for a proposition that may seem to follow logically from it."

(2) It is often asserted that the "authoritative" part of a decision is not what was decided or the rule on which the court based its decision but something (lying back of the decision and the rule) called the "ratio decidendi"—the "right principle upon which the case was decided." In determining whether an earlier decision is a precedent to be followed, a judge need pay scant heed to what the court in the earlier case decided, nor even to what that court stated or believed to be the "ratio decidendi" for its judgment. "It is," says Allen, a defender of the doctrine of "stare decisis" (*i.e.* standing by the precedents), "it is for the court, of whatever degree, which is called upon to consider the precedent, to determine what the *true* ratio decidendi was." The "authoritative" part of a former decision, on this theory, is not the rule announced by the judge in the former case, nor what that judge thought was the principle back of the rule he was applying. What "binds" the judge in any later case is what that judge determines was the "true" principle or "juridical motive" involved in the prior decision. *The*

circumstances of the concrete case. . . . The reason why the general principle cannot control is because it does not inform. . . . It should be obvious that when we have observed a recurrent phenomenon in the decisions of the courts, we may appropriately express the classification in a rule. But the rule will be only a mnemonic device, a useful but hollow diagram of what has been. It will be intelligible only if we *relive again the experience of the classifier.*"

The rules a judge announces when publishing his decision are, therefore, intelligible only if one can relive the judge's unique experience while he was trying the case—which, of course, cannot be done. One cannot even approximate that experience as long as opinions take the form of abstract rules applied to facts formally described. Even if it were desirable that, despite its uniqueness, the judge's decision should be followed, as an analogy, by other judges while trying other cases, this is impossible when the manner in which the judge reached his judgment in the earlier case is most inaccurately reported, as it now is. You are not really applying his decision as a precedent in another case unless you can say, in effect, that, having relived his experience in the earlier case, you believe that he would

have thought his decision applicable to the facts of the latter case.[2] And as opinions are now written, it is impossible to guess what the judge did experience in trying a case. The facts of all but the simplest controversies are complicated and unlike those of any other controversy; in the absence of a highly detailed account by the judge of how he reacted to the evidence, no other person is capable of reproducing his actual reactions. The rules announced in his opinions are therefore often insufficient to tell the reader why the judge reached his decision.

Dickinson admits that the "personal bent of the judge" to some extent affects his decisions. But this "personal bent," he insists, is a factor only in the selection of new rules for unprovided cases. However, *in a profound sense the unique circumstances of almost any case make it an "unprovided case" where no well-established rule "authoritatively" compels a given result.* The uniqueness of the facts and of the judge's reaction thereto is often concealed because the judge so states the facts that they appear to call for the application of a settled rule. But that concealment does not mean that the judge's personal bent has been inoperative or that his emotive experience is simple and reproducible.[3]

---

*earlier case means only what the judge in the later case says it means.* Any case is an "authoritative" precedent only for a judge who, as a result of his own reflection, decides that it is authoritative.

See Allen, "Law in the Making," for a discussion of these two more or less inconsistent theories of the use of precedents. Allen is as unaware of this inconsistency as of the casuistry involved in the process of "distinguishing" cases. He points out that in arriving at the true principles behind the precedents, the judge may and often does employ not only his own reasoning powers but the views of text-writers and scholars. This leads to the result (which Allen fails to perceive) that *anyone can make a legal rule or principle.* When a case comes before a judge, your rule or mine may be more acceptable to him than any theretofore announced from any bench. The authoritative (*i.e.* compulsory or dictatorial) character of legal rules, principles, precepts or other legal generalities, is therefore non-existent. . . .

[1]37 Yale Law Journal, 468, 480.

[2] "The plea that by admitting a principle in one case," says F .C. S Schiller, "we have admitted it in all, is an attempt to cheat us out of a recognition that circumstances alter cases and that cases must be considered on their merits."

"All of us," warned Anatole France, "judge everything by our own measure. How could we do otherwise, since to judge is to compare, and we have only one measure, which is ourselves; and this measure is constantly changing."

[3] . . . Of course there are cases where the facts are so simple and undisputed and stereotyped that the judge must either apply a settled rule or frankly over-rule the precedents. The indications are that there are fewer such cases than most persons assume. *When the judges develop their processes so as more adequately to individualize all cases to the extent they do now in many "socialized" courts, such type cases will become markedly fewer. Today the judicial conventions artificially simplify many cases, so that they appear to come within settled rules, with resulting injustice to one or the other of the parties.*

Oliphant has argued that the courts have been paying too much attention to the language of prior cases and that the proper use of the doctrine of following the precedents should lead the courts to pay more attention to what judges in earlier cases have *decided* as against what they have *said* in their opinions.[2] It may be true that in a limited number of simple cases we can guess what the judges believed to be the facts, and therefore can guess what facts, in any real sense, he was passing on. But usually there are so many and such diverse factors in the evidence which combine in impelling the judge's mind to a decision, that what he decided is unknown—except in the sense that he gave judgment for A, or sent B to prison for ten years, or enjoined C from interfering with D.

At any rate, that will be true while the present method of reporting and deciding cases is adhered to. If and when we have judges trained to observe their own mental processes and such judges with great particularity set forth in their opinions all the factors which they believe led to their conclusions, a judge in passing on a case may perhaps find it possible, to some considerable extent, intelligently to use as a control or guide, the opinion of another judge announced while passing on another case. But as matters stand, reliance on precedents is illusory because judges can seldom tell precisely what has been theretofore decided.

Every lawyer of experience comes to know (more or less unconsciously) that in the great majority of cases, the precedents are none too good as bases of prediction. Somehow or other, there are plenty of precedents to go around. A recent writer, a believer in the use of precedents, has said proudly that "it is very seldom indeed that a judge cannot find guidance of some kind, direct or indirect, in the mass of our reported decisions—by this time a huge accumulation of facts as well as rules." In plain English, as S. S. Gregory or Judge Hutcheson would have put it, a court can usually find earlier decisions which can be made to appear to justify almost any conclusion.[4]

What has just been said is not intended to mean that most courts arrive at their conclusions arbitrarily or apply a process of casuistical deception in writing their opinions. The process we have been describing involves no insincerity or duplicity. The average judge

---

[2]Oliphant is doubtless right as far as he goes. A given conclusion may be correct although the arguments by which it is justified may be inadequate. It is possible to work out a considerable number of syllogisms in which the same conclusion is derived from varying premises. When a judge attaches an opinion to his decision he may explain that his judgment was derived from a certain rule or principle as its major premise. The decision with respect to the facts of the particular case may be quite satisfactory. It is possible, however, to relate this judgment to a markedly different principle as the major premise.

There are many dark spots in legal history owing to the fact that judges, seduced by the wisdom of a *decision* rendered by a judge in an earlier case, have gone beyond the use of the earlier *decision* as an analogy and have used the "*principle*" to which the judge in his opinion in the earlier case purported to relate his conclusion. Thus seduced, they feel obliged to follow the "principle" announced in the earlier opinion and thence to reason syllogistically, using this "principle" as a major premise.

See Goodhart, 15 Cornell Law Quarterly, 173 at 185, to the effect that Oliphant's suggested return from *stare dictis* to real *stare decisis* resembles Rousseau's demand for a return to a law of nature which never existed. See also Dean Green, 28 Columbia Law Review, 1014 at 1038.

[4]Judge Cuthbert Pound quotes the doctrine that "when a court has once laid down a principle of law as applicable to a certain state of facts, it will adhere to that principle and apply it to all future cases where the facts are substantially the same, and this does for the stability and certainty of the law." Judge Pound adds, "The courts and judges state this doctrine of stability with repetitious and tedious emphasis. Yet it is not infrequently reasoned away to the vanishing point. One may wade through a morass of decisions only to sink into a quicksand of uncertainty. The decisions . . . are mere illustrations of the common law as applied to particular cases and unless the precedent cited is 'on all fours' with the case at bar the principle relied on does not necessarily apply, if some other principle is found to be more applicable. . . . The courts state general principles but the force of their observations lies in the application of them and this application cannot be predicted with accuracy."

sincerely believes that he is using his intellect as "a cold logic engine" in applying rules and principles derived from the earlier cases to the objective facts of the case before him.

A satirist might indeed suggest that it is regrettable that the practice of precedent-mongering does not involve *conscious* deception, for it would be comparatively easy for judges entirely aware of what they were doing, to abandon such conscious deception and to report accurately how they arrived at their decisions. Unfortunately, most judges have no such awareness. Worse than that, they are not even aware that they are not aware. Judges Holmes, Cardozo, Hand, Hutcheson, Lehman and a few others have attained the enlightened state of awareness of their unawareness. A handful of legal thinkers off the bench have likewise come to the point of noting the ignorance of all of us as to just how decisions, judicial and otherwise, are reached. Until many more lawyers and judges become willing to admit that ignorance which is the beginning of wisdom and from that beginning work forward painstakingly and consciously, we shall get little real enlightenment on that subject.[5]

Perhaps one of the worst aspects of rule-fetichism and veneration for what judges have done in the past is that the judges, in writing their opinions, are constrained to think of themselves altogether too much as if they were addressing posterity. Swayed by the belief that their opinions will serve as precedents and will therefore bind the thought processes of judges in cases which may thereafter arise, they feel obliged to consider excessively not only what has previously been said by other judges but also the future effect of those generalizations which they themselves set forth as explanations of their own decisions.[3] When publishing the rules which are supposed to be the core of their decisions, they thus feel obligated to look too far both backwards and forwards. Many a judge, when unable to find old word-patterns which will fit his conclusions, is overcautious about announcing a so-called new rule for fear that, although the new rule may lead to a just conclusion in the case before him, it may lead to undesirable results in the future—that is, in cases not then before the court.[a] Once trapped by the belief that the announced rules are the paramount thing in the law, and that uniformity and certainty are of major importance and are to be procured by uniformity and certainty in the phrasing of rules, a judge is likely to be affected, in determining what is fair to the parties in the unique situation before him, by consideration of the possible, yet scarcely imaginable, bad effect of a just opinion in the instant case on possible unlike cases which may later be brought into court. He then refuses to do justice in the case on trial because he fears that "hard cases make bad laws." And thus arises what may aptly be called "injustice according to the law."

Such injustice is particularly tragic because it is based on a hope doomed to futility, a hope of controlling the future. Of course, present problems will be clarified by reference to future ends; but ends, although they have a future bearing, must obtain their significance in present consequences, otherwise those ends lose their significance. For it is the nature of

---

[5]One wishes, for instance, that Judge Hutcheson would not stop with the mere statement that his decisions are the result of inspirational hunches, but would some day give a detailed statement of his reactions throughout the course of a trial and during the time when he was hunching and gathering together the materials for his "opinion," or as he has happily called it, the "apologia" for his decision.

[3]If all judges were completely sophisticated and casuistical, they could usually avoid this problem by deliberately insincere expressions of the reasoning which they employ in their opinions. In other words, in many cases they could mouth the old formulas, even when they knew they were actually reaching conclusions that were at variance with the established doctrines. But professional conscientiousness prevents the deliberate and conscious use of such disingenuous methods.

[a]Footnote deleted.

the future that it never arrives. If all decisions are to be determined with reference to a time to come, then the law is indeed chasing a will-o'-the-wisp. "Yesterday today was to-morrow." To give too much attention to the future is to ignore the problem which is demanding solution today. Any future, when it becomes the present, is sure to bring new complicating and individualized problems. "Future problems" can never be solved. There is much wisdom in Valéry's reference to the "anachronism of the future."

Indeed, alleged interest in the future may be a disguise for too much devotion to the past, and a means of avoiding the necessity for facing unpleasant risks in the present. If the decision of a particular case takes the form of the enunciation of a rule with emphasis on its future incidence, the tendency will be to connect the past by smooth continuities with the future, and the consequence will be an overlooking of the distinctive novelties of the present. There will be undue stress on the past, habitual ways of doing things.

What is more significant is that this regard for the future serves also to conceal that factor in judging which is most disturbing to the rule-minded—the personality of the judge. Thus in a recent book[4] the author finds an advantage in the technique of abstract logic which judges purport to employ in that it requires the judges to

"raise their minds above the facts of the immediate case before them and subordinate their feelings and impressions to a process of intricate abstract reasoning. *One danger in the administration of justice is that the necessities of the future and the interest of parties not before the court may be sacrificed in favor of present litigants . . . .* Nothing is so effective to prevent this outcome as that judges should approach the decision of a controversy with minds directed to considerations having no connection with the immediate situation or interest in the parties. Judges are human instruments, with prejudices, passions, and weaknesses. As it is, they often decide a new point or a doubtful point, ignore a principle, narrow a rule, or explain a concept under the influence of these human limitations. But this influence is enormously diminished by the necessity of centering their attention on a mass of considerations which lie outside the color of the case at bar; and by the habit of coming at every question from the angle of a dry and abstract logic."

It might be more accurately said that the influence of this point of view promotes judicial self-delusion and produces that ineffectual suppression of the judge's personality which leads to the indirect, unobserved and harmful effects of his personality on judicial decisions.

Present problems should be worked out with reference to present events. We cannot rule the future. We can only imagine it in terms of the present. And the only way to do that is as thoroughly as possible to know the present.[7]

---

[4]Dickinson, "Administrative Justice and the Supremacy of Law." Dickinson in this book was struggling away from an obsessive interest in rules, an interest which expresses itself in such of his language as the following: "It is the reason embodied in the purposes of the law and not the arbitrary discretion of the judge that must determine whether or not a particular legal concept controls a case which from some angles fits within it. A concept ought never to be held inapplicable to a case to which it seems to apply unless it ought also to be held inapplicable to all similar cases where its application would similarly defeat the purpose of the law. What is needed is not arbitrary discretion, but a rule for making exceptions,—a rule for breaking a rule—and of such rules the law is of course full." Can there, indeed, be a "rule"—*i.e.* a general abstract formula—for breaking a rule?

There are other passages in which Dickinson approaches the problem of judicial discretion more realistically; his realistic trend finds still more marked expression in his more recent articles in "The Law Behind Law," 29 Columbia Law Review, 114, 284. See comments on Dickinson in Appendix II.

[7]Many of our judges have become golfers; they would do well to take over into the law something of the golfing technique of keeping the eye on the ball. The golfer wants to know where the ball is to go: but to play well he must concentrate to a large extent on the ball itself. So the judge with regard to present facts and future consequences.

We come to this: The desire to regulate the future is in part a desire for impossible uniformity, security and certainty, for over-simplification, for a world regulated and controlled as a child would have it regulated and controlled.

In the interest of preserving the appearance of such a world, much effort is devoted to "keeping the record straight"; that is, to making it appear that decisions and opinions have more of the logical and less of the psychological than is possible. This desire manifests itself in many curious comments and suggestions.

Thus a writer, not long since, suggested that there was growing an unfortunate tendency of courts to decide cases on their merits, that this was making the law chaotic, but that a return to certainty and predictability could be procured, in spite of this tendency, if the courts would cease writing opinions. The suggestion was made naively and without cognizance of the fact that it meant merely that the failure of the courts to adhere to mechanical applications of rules would be less obvious, if the courts merely recorded their judgments without opinions and thus made it more difficult to scrutinize the means by which they arrived at their judgments.

And again, it has been urged that, in the interest of maintaining respect for the courts, dissenting opinions should never be rendered, the intent being that thereby the public will not be made aware that able judges, sitting side by side and passing on the same set of facts, can disagree about the law.

The point of all such proposals is that they tacitly concede the impossibility of obtaining legal conformity, but seek to cover up the more obvious manifestations of this lack. The healthier method would be not only to recognize the gross evidences of uncertainty but to make evident the actual but now concealed circumstances which make certainty an impossibility, to the end that by describing accurately the real nature of the judicial process we may learn to better it.

*The judge, at his best, is an arbitrator*, a "sound man" who strives to do justice to the parties by exercising a wise discretion with reference to the peculiar circumstances of the case. He does not merely "find" or invent some generalized rule which he "applies" to the facts presented to him. He does "equity" in the sense in which Aristotle—when thinking most clearly—described it. "It is equity," he wrote in his Rhetoric, "to pardon human failings, and to look to the law giver and not to the law; . . . to prefer arbitration to judgment, for the arbitrator sees what is equitable, but the judge only the law, and for this an arbitrator was first appointed, in order that equity might flourish."[8] The bench and bar usually try to conceal the arbitral function of the judge. (Dicey represents the typical view. A judge, he says, "when deciding any case must act, *not as arbitrator, but strictly as a judge; . . . it is a judge's business to determine not what may be fair as between A and X in a given case*, but what according to some principle of law, are the respective rights of A and X.") But although fear of legal uncertainty leads to this

---

[8] The reader will recall the discussion of Aristotle's unfortunate separation of "law" and "equity."

Is not the present-day growth of non-judicial arbitration largely due to an attempt to have that equity flourish which the courts have seemed to deny?

Interestingly enough, the tendency is to set up non-governmental arbitration tribunals which are required to follow their own precedents. The judges (who are really trained arbitrators) are to be superseded by seeming arbitrators who are instructed to act as judges (*i.e.*, as judges seem to act). Unfortunately, as the system develops, the precedents are sure to accumulate and the untrained arbitrators will be baffled by a lack of an effective technique for skillfully evading their own former decisions. *We shall, in effect, be exchanging moderately expert arbitrators for quite inefficient judges.*

concealment, the arbitral function is the central fact in the administration of justice. The concealment has merely made the labor of the judges less effective.[9]

We must stop playing ostrich, one is tempted to say. And then one remembers the amusing remarks of Stefansson on that cliché and its cognates: There is, he says, an African ostrich, a zoölogical bird. There is also the ostrich of literature, philosophy and morals. The latter buries his head when frightened. The former does not. The literary ostrich, however, has for two thousand years survived all attacks from careful first-hand observation of the zoölogical bird. He has survived because, like the literary wolf or the literary Eskimo, he is a part of "knowledge-by-definition" which is more stable than constantly changing empirical knowledge. The average human has a passion for order and symmetry[10] in the universe, a craving for absolute knowledge, an abhorrence of chaos. Let us, then, suggests Stefansson with nice sarcasm, find a new basis for all knowledge. Let us in all fields have knowledge that is incapable of being contradicted. Knowledge-by-definition (defined facts; truths that are standardized errors, but are not allowed to be contradicted) will eliminate the embarrassment of adaptation to the discovery of newly observed facts.

The plan of standardizing error, which Stefansson ridicules, has a purpose: the complete exclusion from attention of all facts which annoyingly interfere with our theories does create the appearance of a thoroughly controlled and ordered universe.[11] But the belief in such a disciplined universe is consistently acted upon only by primitive men, children and the insane.[5] To the extent that anyone relies on such a belief he becomes the victim of the very uncertainties which he ignores and which he therefore fails to allow for.

To be sure, whoever rejects the childish habit of standardizing error attains increasing knowledge of the ways of the objective world, and makes his world picture ever more complex. Life will then disclose itself to him as far more precarious and difficult to conciliate than it appeared to primitive man or than it appears to the idiot or to the child. But just in proportion as he learns more about what was previously unknown, he reduces his chances of being crushed by unobserved dangers. That is the paradox of wisdom: In so far as we become mindful that life is more dangerous than we had naïvely supposed in childhood, we help ourselves to approach nearer to actual security.[6] We should never have had steam-engines if

---

[9]Among the numerous resulting harms is the fact that the judges must think one way and talk another. This would be bad enough if they did so consciously and hypocritically. But it is far worse because they are unaware or only half aware of the difficulty. . . .

[10]Several writers note, as the explanation of the excessive desire for a legal certainty, the "aesthetic impulse" or "the sense of symmetry." But is not an excessive demand for symmetry perhaps the result of an undue prolongation of emotional infancy? The aesthetic impulse, when it takes that form, should be more accurately called "the anaesthetic impulse." It is related to that undue desire for rest which is regressive.

[11]Cf. Zane's statement that "the machinery of justice must provide some method of *decently veiling violations of the general rule in particular cases.*"

[5]Cf. the writings of Frazer, Leuba, Hart and Piaget.

[6]Cf. Clerk Maxwell's ideal of freedom of will, "whereby, instead of being consciously free and really in subjection to unknown law, it becomes consciously active law, and really free from interference of an unrecognized law." Quoted in Otto, "Natural Laws and Human Hopes," 60.

Compare the following from Wm. Stern (quoted in Gmelin, loc. cit., 106): "The great forward movements of science are not composed of the sudden emergence of new concepts and ideas out of nothingness, but rather consist in this, that familiar experiences, which hitherto were accepted as matters of course, are subjected to criticism, so that their problematic character is recognized and an endeavor to understand them is put in the place of an acquiescence in what is supposed to be self-evident."

See Appendix III

men had been content with dream-engines. Airplanes were not invented by believers in wishing rugs.[b]

And so in respect to the law: If we relinquish the assumption that law can be made mathematically certain, if we honestly recognize the judicial process as involving unceasing adjustment and individualization, we may be able to reduce the uncertainty which characterizes much of our present judicial output to the extent that such uncertainty is undesirable. By abandoning an infantile hope of absolute legal certainty we may augment markedly the amount of actual legal certainty.[13]

To the somnambulist, sleep-walking may seem more pleasant and less hazardous than wakeful walking, but the latter is the wiser mode of locomotion in the congested traffic of a modern community. It is about time to abandon judicial somnambulism.[14]

## QUESTIONS

1. Frank says, "as opinions are now written, it is impossible to guess what the judge did experience in trying a case." To what extent does following precedent require that we know "what the [earlier] judge did experience"?

2. Frank suggests that we should "relinquish the assumption that law can be made mathematically certain." Is this equally sound and desirable advice both for (a) determining what past decisions imply about how one must decide the present case, and (b) trying to lay down a rule for the future? Is one of the two, (a) or (b), the more important function for a judge?

3. Frank says, "Present problems should be worked out with reference to present events. We cannot rule the future." What does this mean? Is it possible to decide today's case in a way that will have no effects for the decisions of cases in the future?

4. Suppose that, within earshot of the rest of the class, a student asks his professor for special permission to take the final exam two weeks early, so that he can be best man at his friend's wedding. The professor quickly grants the permission, only to find out within the next several days that some nine other students also want permission to take the exam early. They have various reasons. Some want to get an early start at a summer job, some want to go on a vacation with parents, and one student wants very much to attend the wedding of her cousin, whom she hasn't seen in years. Does the first permission create a precedent for likewise granting the other requests? If the professor then realizes that giving the first student permission was a mistake, what should she do? Revoke that permission and grant no other requests? Or stick with it and grant the other requests too? Or should she treat it as an individual case with no implications for the later requests? When you consider these issues, reflect on whether this situation is really analogous to a judge deciding cases. If so, what general advice would Frank give the professor?

---

[b]Footnote deleted.

[13]The reader will recall that this is a *"partial* explanation."

[14]"In some cases," says Bentham, "jurisprudence may be defined the art of being methodically ignorant of what everybody knows."

# Critical Legal Studies

## Roberto Mangabeira Unger
# LAW AND LIBERAL POLITICAL THEORY*

### THE PRINCIPLE OF RULES AND VALUES

The distinction between rules and values, as the two basic elements of social order, is the first principle of liberal political thought. It may be called simply the principle of rules and values. It articulates the conception, embraced by the unreflective view of society, that the eternal hostility of men to one another requires that order and freedom be maintained by government under law.

To explain what is meant by the principle of rules and values and to work out its implications, I begin by defining the concepts of value and of rule. Then I discuss how the relationship between rules and values is conceived. Lastly, I suggest ways in which the idea of a society governed by law ties together several seemingly unrelated aspects of liberal thought.

### Value and Rule

Value is the social face of desire. It refers to an end of action or to a want when the emphasis is on relations among persons. In contrast, the term desire is used when the discussion concerns the relation within an individual between the setting of goals and the understanding of facts. End, objective, goal, and will are generic concepts that cover both usages.

The satisfaction of an individual's wants is his good. Assuredly, through lack of understanding, men may fail to appreciate that a single-minded insistence on the pursuit of a particular objective may prejudice the attainment of other goals. Moreover, they may

also distinguish between what they think is right or proper and what they want. In this sense, the concept of value is ambiguous as between want or interest and standard or ideal. Nevertheless, as the discussion of liberal psychology has already suggested and the study of liberal political thought will confirm, the second sense of value ultimately collapses into the first. The sole measure of good that remains is the wants of an individual or some combination of the wants of different individuals revealed by the choices they make. The good has no existence outside the will.[2]

The need for rules arises from the undying enmity and the demands of collaboration that mark social life. Because there are no conceptions of the good that stand above the conflict and impose limits on it, artificial limits must be created. Otherwise, the natural hostility men have for one another will run its course relentlessly to the prejudice of their interdependence.

Self-interest, the generalized search for comfort and glory, and any sharing of common values will all be insufficient to keep the peace. It is in the individual's self-interest to benefit from a system of laws established by others but not to obey or establish that system himself. As long as most persons are not robbers, robbery can be a profitable business.[3] Furthermore, though everyone has similar interests in comfort and glory, they are interests that, because of the scarcity of their objects, throw men against one another as much a they bring men together. Finally, every other sharing of values is bound to be

---

[2]See Hobbes, *Leviathan*, ch. 6, p. 41.

[3]For a modern development of this idea, see Mancur Olson, *The Logic of Collective Action* (Cambridge, Harvard, 1973), p. 11.

both precarious and morally indifferent. It is precarious because the individual will is the true and only seat of value, forever changing direction as the dangers and opportunities of the struggle for comfort and glory shift. The sharing of values is also without ethical significance. We are not entitled to pass from the fact that we happen to agree upon our ends to the claim that someone else ought to agree to them, or at least should do nothing to stop us from attaining them.

Peace must therefore be established by rules. By its significance to society, by its origin, and by its form, a rule differs from a value. A good way to develop the point is to make the concept of rule used in liberal political thought more precise. One can do this by distinguishing different kinds of rules with respect to their uses in social life and then by focusing on the type of rule with which liberal political doctrine is most directly concerned.

Rules are general and they bear on conduct. Beyond this, however, little can be said before we have distinguished three sorts of rules: constitutive, technical or instrumental, and prescriptive.[4]

Constitutive rules define a form of conduct in such a way that the distinction between the rule and the ruled activity disappears. It has been said that the rules of games and the rules of logic are of this sort. The moves of a game and thus the game as a whole are defined by its rules. The laws of identity and contradiction determine a particular mode of discourse.[5]

Technical or instrumental rules are guides for the choice of the most effective means to an end. They take the form, do $x$ if you want $y$.

They simply state a generalization about what means are most likely on the whole to produce the desired result. In any given situation, one may find a more efficient means than the one indicated by the rule.[6]

Prescriptive rules are imperatives that state what some category of persons may do, ought to do, or ought not to do. Accordingly, they are permissions, general commands, and prohibitions. Prescriptive rules differ from constitutive rules because they are clearly distinguishable from the conduct they govern and from instrumental rules because they are not hypothetical.

The rules to which the first principle of liberal political doctrine refers must be prescriptive. The war of men against one another lacks the voluntary or unthinking stability of conduct presupposed by constitutive rules. Moreover, the same antagonism precludes the constant and general agreement about ends that would be necessary for instrumental rules to serve effectively as a basis for the ordering of social relations.

The prescriptive rules established by government are usually called laws. Many laws, to be sure, lend themselves easily to being viewed as instrumental or constitutive rules.[7] Indeed, it is possible to see the whole legal order as either instrumental or constitutive; the implications of these alternative possibilities will be mentioned later. Nevertheless, for the moment it is enough to remember that for a powerful if not dominant strain in liberal political thought laws are above all prescriptive rules.

They place limits on the pursuit of private ends, thereby ensuring that natural egoism will not turn into a free-for-all in which everyone

[4]See Georg Henrik von Wright, *Norm and Action* (London, Routledge, 1963), pp. 6–16.

[5]The conception of constitutive rules is developed in Ludwig Wittgenstein, *Philosophical Investigations* (New York, Macmillan, 1969), §§80–91, 197–241, pp. 38–42, 80–88.

[6]On the conception of instrumental rules, see John Rawls, "Two Concepts of Rules," *Philosophical Review* (1956), vol. LXIV, pp. 18–29.

[7]The constitutive conception of rules, made into the basis of a social theory of law, may serve as the tool of a communitarian critique of liberal political and legal theory. (See ch. 6, note 7.) The instrumental view of rules is the handmaiden of utilitarian jurisprudence.

and everything is endangered. They also facilitate mutual collaboration. The two tasks are connected because a peaceful social order in which we know what to expect from others is a condition for the accomplishment of any of our goals. More specifically, it is the job of the laws to guarantee the supreme goods of social life, order, and freedom.

## Positivism and Natural Right

The two basic manners in which the political doctrine of liberalism defines the opposition of rules and values correspond to two ideas about the source of the laws and to two conceptions of how freedom and order may be established. To establish order and freedom the laws must be impersonal. They must embody more than the values of an individual or of a group. Rules whose source is the interest of a single person or class of persons destroy the good of freedom because, by definition, they constitute a dominion of some wills over the wills of others. Furthermore, they leave order without any support except the terror by which it is imposed, for the oppressed will not love the laws.

There are other ways to avoid the dictatorship of private interest. One way is to imagine that public rules are made by a will that stands above the contending private wills and somehow represents them. Hobbes' sovereign monarch and Hegel's bureaucratic class and king exemplify this notion of a political deity.[8] The political deity's circumstances supposedly allow it to understand and to promote the common interests men have in the control of hostility and in the furtherance of collaboration.

According to this view, which one might call in an ample sense positivism or absolutism, the problem of determining *in general* the best way to guarantee coordination and to limit antagonism is insoluble. This may be either because there are no solid standards for choosing the best solution or because the complexity of the task exceeds the powers of the mind. The right laws will therefore be whatever rules are chosen by the sovereign, whose condition allegedly places him beyond the contention of individual wants.

The absolutist view leads to a kind of legislative agnosticism that makes it impossible to define when the laws are impersonal other than by the standard of their origin. Moreover, the sovereign, the government, or the class in whose impartiality the positivist conception trusts are always in danger of sinking into the very battle of private interests from which they claim to escape. Indeed, given the impossibility of rising above individual choice as a measure of the good, this disaster seems unavoidable.

For these reasons, there arises within liberal thought a second family of attempts to define the relationship between rules and values. It consists in trying to formulate standards or procedures that will establish in a general fashion which laws are impersonal and therefore capable of securing order and freedom in society. The more familiar liberal theories of legislation fall into this category.

Among such views, there is one that calls for separate and immediate treatment because of its direct bearing on the relationship between rules and values. It starts from the premise that the circumstances of reciprocal hostility and need, and the universal interest in comfort and glory, carry implications of their own for how society ought to be arranged. Intelligence can spell out the implications and then take them as a basis for impersonal legislation. Thus, the solution to problems of order and freedom preexists the making of the laws and can be used as a standard with which to judge them. It is this preexisting solution that settles the entitlements of individuals; rights precede rules.

---

[8]See Hobbes, *Leviathan*, ch. 18, pp. 133–141; Hegel, *Grundlinien der Philosophie des Rechts*, §§205, 275–286, *Sämtliche Werke*, ed. H. Glockner (Stuttgart, Fromman, 1928), vol. VII, pp. 377–395.

Here you have the core of the modern theory of natural right, under whose star the liberal state was born.[9]

There is in most statements of the natural rights conception an ambiguity that obscures a fatal dilemma. If we treat the rights as somehow derived from the circumstances of social life, we are forced to explain how evaluative standards can be inferred from facts. If, on the contrary, we present the rights as simply prudent means to achieve agreed-upon ends, like peace and prosperity, we have to explain how we go about judging divergence from these ends and what happens when, in a particular case, the purpose seems to be better served by disrespecting the right.[10] These and other consequences of such an attempt to view the law as a system of instrumental rules are discussed at greater length later on.

Despite their divergence, the positivist and natural right interpretations of the principle of rules and values have in common the insistence that it is on the whole better for men to live under laws than to be without them. The two doctrines agree that the absence of coercively enforced public rules would deny us the blessings of collaboration and security in the search for comfort and glory. The point can be put in an altogether more inclusive form. Whenever we want something, we must also want not to have it kept away from us or taken away once it is already ours. When we want to carry out a course of action, we must also want not to be stopped by others from executing it.

To will intelligently and consequentially is to will that others respect our objectives. We wish to be entitled to the objects of our choices. Entitlements, however, are possible only when there is a system of general rules that limits the wants of each man in comparison to those of his fellows so that each may be safe in the enjoyment of what is his. In short, will implies the will to be entitled, which in turn implies the acceptance of a system of rules either to distribute or to confirm and enforce the entitlements. With similar arguments, some have even suggested that a legal order is entailed by the very concept of a society of men with conflicting values.[11]

At a still more basic level, positivism and natural rights theory may be viewed as expressions in political thought of opposing yet complementary views of the dualism of the universal and the particular. In Chapter One, I pointed out that this dualism is the common ground of the antinomies of theory and fact and of reason and desire. In this chapter, it will reappear as the basis of an antinomy of rules and values.

To the positivist, society has no inherent order of its own. He sees rules as the impositions of a will, even though of an enlightened one, on the chaos of social life. The universal laws are simply conventions which set the boundaries among particular interests so that these interests will not destroy each other.

The natural rights theorist, on the contrary, claims to discover an intrinsic order in social relations, an order it is his purpose to make explicit and to develop. For him the universals that describe this order—rights, rules, and institutional categories—have an existence and a worth quite independent of the particular interests that may take advantage of them. Thus, the natural rights thinker treats the system of private law concepts of contract and property or the doctrine of separation of powers in public law as if they had an autonomous logic that survived in all their transmutations.

---

[9]Hobbes develops both the natural rights and the positivist strand in liberal political thought. From this flow many of the paradoxes as well as much of the greatness of his thought. See *Leviathan*, chs. 14–15, pp. 99–123. See also Locke, *Two Treatises*, especially bk. 2, ch. 11, §§134–142, vol V, pp. 416–424.

[10]Hobbes recognizes the problem in *Leviathan*, ch. 15, pp. 111–112.

[11]Kant, *Metaphysische Anfangsgründe der Rechtslehre*, §44, *Kants Werke*, ed. Prussian Academy (Berlin, Gruyter, 1968), vol. VI, §44, pp. 312–313.

Though they differ in the priorities they assign to the universal and the particular, positivism and natural rights doctrine are at one in accepting a radical distinction between universals and particulars and in identifying the former with the abstract and the latter with the concrete. The significance of this assumption for the entire system of liberal thought will gradually become clear.

## The Legal Mentality

To explain the principle of rules and values, I have defined its constituent terms and suggested how the liberal doctrine conceives their relationship to each other. Now I shall complete my study of the principle by describing some of its links to a more general view of social life.

The society evoked and described by the first postulate of liberal political thought is a society governed by law. Only a system of prescriptive rules with the characteristics of law can resolve the problems of order and freedom. These characteristics are already implicit in the preceding discussion of what prescriptive rules have to be like to satisfy the requirement of impersonality. For liberal political thought, the laws must be general, uniform, public, and capable of coercive enforcement.

Because the laws are general, it is possible to state what sorts of acts are commanded, prohibited, or permitted to categories of persons before specific problems of choice under the laws arise. The generality of the laws makes it possible for them to be impersonal either because they may represent some ideal outcome of conflicting private interests or because they somehow abstract altogether from considerations of private interest.

To be meaningful, generality requires uniformity of application. Some decisions under the rules may be attacked as mistaken, and others defended as correct. Entitlements or rights are interests of individuals protected by uniformly applied laws.

If they are impersonal, the laws must also be public. They are the rules established by a particular institution, the government or the state. The state is viewed either as above the antagonism of private values or as the framework within which those interests are represented and reconciled. Only such an institution can hope to frame laws that do more than embody a factional interest.

Hence, a clear line is drawn between the state and other social groups, and between the laws of the former and the rules of the latter. But the distinction is always breaking down. The government takes on the characteristics of a private body because private interests are the only interests that exist in the situation of which it is a part. Thus, the state is like the gods on Olympus, who were banished from the earth and endowed with superhuman powers, but condemned to undergo the passions of mortals.

Lastly, the laws must on the whole be capable of coercive enforcement. Failure to achieve one's goals has an automatic sanction. In psychology, the sanction is described as discontentment; in political thought, as the loss of comfort and glory. If, however, the laws, by virtue of their very impersonality, fail to live up completely to the interests of any person, obedience to the public rules cannot be spontaneously protected by self-interest. A sufficiently stiff punishment, however, will make it in the interest of all to obey them by outweighing the advantages that might be gained from disobedience.

Generality, uniformity, publicity, and coercion are therefore the distinguishing attributes of impersonal laws. Each of them is connected with a deeper set of presuppositions about thought or society. The relationship of the attributes of law to their assumptions, and of the assumptions to one another, is neither logical nor causal, but is of a kind described later as a relationship of common meaning. These foundations of the idea of law are aspects of the peculiar legal mentality that animates liberal political thought.

Generality is associated with the political ideal of formal equality and with the moral ideal of universalism. Formal equality means that as citizens of the state and legal persons men are viewed and treated by the law as fundamentally equal. Social circumstances must therefore be clearly distinguished from legal-political status. By disregarding or accepting the inequality of the former in order to emphasize all the more intensely the equality of the latter, we commit ourselves to general laws. To equalize men's social circumstances with respect to even a few of the divergences among those circumstances, we would have to treat each man or each group differently and thus to move away from the attribute of generality. The language of formal equality is a language of rights as abstract opportunities to enjoy certain advantages rather than a language of the concrete and actual experience of social life.[12]

The ethical analogue to formal equality is universalism. It is the belief that moral judgment, like political order, is primarily a matter of rights and duties. The rights and duties are established by principles whose formulation becomes more general and therefore more perfect and less their applicability turns on who and where one is. The morality of reason is a classic form of the universalist ethic.

Formal equality and moral universalism both include the conception of universals and particulars encountered before. The legal person or the moral agent are constructed, as abstract and formal universals, out of individual lives, and then treated as if they were real and independent beings. Particular interests, experiences, or circumstances are viewed as a contingent substance of the forms, or as concrete examples of the abstract propositions. Thus, one can define a right independently of the interests an individual may use it to promote.

The basis of uniformity is the formal conception of reason. Reason cannot establish the ends of action, nor does it suffice to determine the concrete implications of general values on which we may happen to agree. That is why rules are so important in the first place. Nevertheless, if the laws are to be uniformly applied, we need a technique of rule application. This technique must rely on the powers that reason possesses because it is a machine for analysis and combination: the capacity to deduce conclusions from premises and the ability to choose efficient means to accepted ends. Consequently, the major liberal theories of adjudication view the task of applying law either as one of making deductions from the rules or as one of choosing the best means to advance the ends the rules themselves are designed to foster.

The public character of law has its immediate ground in the distinction between state and society and in the more inclusive dichotomy of public and private life. The state appears in a double light, as the providential alternative to the blindness of private cupidity and as the supreme weapon of some men in the self-interested struggle against others. The separation of the public and the private alternates with the destruction of the latter by the former. In either event, the conflict between the two is never resolved.

The assumption of the belief that the laws must be capable of coercive enforcement is the artificial view of society. According to this view, even though society may have an implicit order, as the natural rights theorist claims, it is not a self-regulating or self-enforcing one. Because individuals and individual interests are the primary elements of social life, and because they are locked in a perpetual struggle with one another, social order must be established by acts of will and protected against the ravages of self-interest.

---

[12]Franz Neumann, "Der Funktionswandel des Gesetzes im Recht der bürgerlichen Gesellschaft," *Zeitschrift für Sozialforschung* (1937), vol. VI, pp. 542–596.

The ideas that there is no natural community of common ends and that group life is a creature of will help explain the importance of rules and of their coercive enforcement. But the same factors may also account for the fascination of terror, the systematic use of violence unlimited by law, as a device of social organization. The less one's ability to rely on participation in common ends, the greater the importance of force as a bond among individuals. Punishment and fear take the place of community.

Moreover, when they view everything in the social world as a creation of the will, men come to believe there is nothing in society a will sufficiently violent cannot preserve or destroy. Thus, legalism and terrorism, the commitment to rules and the seduction of violence, are rival brothers, but brothers nonetheless.[13]

The legal mentality described in the preceding pages is no mere invention of philosophers. It is a way of thinking about social life, a mode of consciousness that is bound together with both a doctrine and an experience of social life. For the present, let me continue to focus on the doctrine. As the argument moves forward, I shall come back to the consciousness and examine the experience.

## THE PRINCIPLE OF SUBJECTIVE VALUE

There is an aspect of the principle of rules and values so important that it deserves to be distinguished and developed in its own right. It is the proposition that all values are individual and subjective, the principle of subjective value. My discussion of this principle will proceed in three steps. First, I shall explain what I mean by individuality and subjectivity and contrast the conception of individual and subjective value with an alternative view. Then, I shall examine the relation of the principle to other aspects of liberal political theory. The last step of the argument will show how the idea of subjective value serves as the connecting link between the repudiation of intelligible essences and the central political problems of lawmaking and law application.

Ends are viewed by liberal theory as individual in the sense that they are always the objectives of particular individuals. By contrast, values are called communal when they are understood as the aims of groups, and of individuals only to the extent that the individuals are members of those groups. The political doctrine of liberalism does not acknowledge communal values. To recognize

---

[13] The discovery of a connection between the appeal to terror and the artificial view of society has played an important part in the criticism of liberal thought. The decisive event in this respect was the French Revolution. Both the theme of an absence of community between the Republic and its enemies and that of the subordination of society to will are already implicit in the original justification of the "Reign of Terror." See Maximilien Robespierre, *Rapport sur les Principes du Gouvernement Revolutionnaire*, in *Discours et Rapports de Robespierre*, ed. C. Vellay (Paris, Charpentier, 1908), pp. 332–333. The idea that the disintegration of community makes fear the supreme social bond recurs in the history of the conservative attack on liberalism. See Edmund Burke, *Reflections on the Revolution in France, Works of Edmund Burke* (London, Rivington, 1801), vol. V, p. 202. The relationship of voluntarism to terror is in turn brought out by Hegel's remarks on "absolute freedom and terror." See *Phänomenologie des Geistes, Sämtliche Werke*, ed H. Glockner (Stuttgart, Fromman, 1927), vol. II, pp. 449–459. An analogous argument is developed by Marx and by some of his followers. See, for example, Marx's article in *Vorwärts* of August 7, 1844, *Marx-Engels Werke* (Berlin, Dietz, 1957), vol. I, p. 392; and Lenin, *The Proletarian Revolution and Kautsky the Renegade*, in *Collected Works* (Moscow, Progress, 1965), vol. XXVIII, pp. 227–325. Still another perspective on the matter is offered by the development in social theory of the view that in 'premodern' societies a clear line is drawn between what is immutable in the social order and what falls under the discretion of the rulers, whereas in modern states every aspect of social life becomes subject in principle to the political will. See Henry Maine, *Lectures on the Early History of Institutions* (London, Murray, 1897), pp. 373–386; and Max Weber, *Wirtschaft und Gesellschaft*, ed. J. Winckelmann (Tübingen, Mohr, 1972), ch. 3, §6, p. 130. In a very different context, the relationship of legalism to terrorism is highlighted by the doctrines of the Chinese 'Legalists.' See *The Complete Works of Han Fei Tzŭ*, 2 vols., trans. W. Liao (London, Probsthain, 1939); and *The Book of Lord Shang*, trans. J. Duyvendak (London, Probsthain, 1928).

their existence, it would be necessary to begin with a vision of the basic circumstances of social life that took groups rather than individuals as the intelligible and primary units of social life. The individuality of values is the very basis of personal identity in liberal thought, a basis the communal conception of value destroys.

Values are subjective in the sense that they are determined by choice. Subjectivity emphasizes that an end is an end simply because someone holds it, whereas individuality means that there must always be a particular person whose end it is. The opposing conception is the idea of objective value, a major theme of the philosophy of the ancients. Objective values are standards and goals of conduct that exist independently of human choice. Men may embrace or reject objective values, but they cannot establish or undo their authority.

From the start, liberal political thought has been in revolt against the conception of objective value.[14] If we were able to perceive such values, they would become the true foundation of the social order. Public rules would be relegated to a subsidiary role, as devices for the specification of the objective standards, when those standards were imprecise, or for their enforcement, when they were disobeyed. The problems of order and freedom would be cast in a different light if we could think of these norms of conduct as ends whose fulfillment would bring our worthiest capacities to their richest development rather than as constraints imposed by an external will. Even the premises of liberal psychology would be affected by an objective theory of value. Ends would be at least as intelligible as facts. They would be things that exist in the world, like triangles, if not like tables. The distinction between the objective understanding of facts and the arbitrary choice of goals would therefore collapse.

For all these reasons, the teachings of liberalism must be, and almost always have

been, uncompromisingly hostile to the classic idea of objective good. The theoretical antagonism is accompanied and in part inspired by a historical process, the progressive disintegration of the system of fixed social classes or estates in postfeudal European societies. It is only in the context of a well-defined hierarchy for the distribution of wealth and power that the objective values of the earlier philosophy seemed precise in their implications. As a result of the dissolution of that hierarchical order and of the expansion of the market economy, concepts like 'just price' in exchange and distribution according to 'virtue' lost their meaning.

Granted that the doctrine of objective value is incompatible with the premises of liberalism and that its political implications are unclear, might it nevertheless be true? For the present, I shall be content to suggest some preliminary reasons why I think it is false, but the main argument will have to wait. The criticism of the rival doctrine of subjective value will be developed in the course of this chapter.

First, the theory of objective value presupposes that the mind can grasp and establish moral essences or goods. But this has never been shown, and the conception of reason on which it rests has been discredited in nonmoral areas of thought.

Second, the doctrine denies any significance to choice other than the passive acceptance or rejection of independent truths. Our experience of moral judgment, however, seems to be one of at least contributing to shape the ends we pursue. A conception that puts this fact aside disregards the significance of choice as an expression of personality.

Third, the inability of the theory of objective value to determine how we should act in particular situations is no remediable mishap. To make the doctrine plausible in the absence of divinely revealed moral truth, its proponents rely on references to moral opinions shared by men of many different

---

[14] See Hobbes, *Leviathan*, ch. 6 ("good and evil apparent"), p. 48. See note 18 to my ch. 1.

ages and societies. The more concrete the allusions to this allegedly timeless moral agreement, the less convincing they become. Therefore, to make their case, the proponents of objective value must restrict themselves to a few abstract ideals whose vagueness allows almost any interpretation.

There is a conception of the place of values in society that does not at first seem to fit into the categories of the individual and the communal, the subjective and the objective, but that nevertheless plays an overpowering role in our everyday views, in the modern social sciences, and in classical liberal thought itself. It is the idea that the more or less stable sharing of values among persons is a fundamental fact about society. Theories like Hutcheson's doctrine of benevolence or Hume's doctrine of sympathy foreshadowed this idea by emphasizing the extent to which the unity of human nature allows men to enter into each other's sentiments. However, as long as the sharing of ends is conceived simply as a convergence of individual preferences, with no change of other postulates of liberal thought, it does not truly qualify the principle that values are individual and subjective.

On the other hand, each convergence of preferences remains a precarious alliance of interests. The source of value continues to be the individual will, given the derivative and artificial character of groups according to the principle of individualism I later describe. Hence, the individuality of values persists despite the possibility of varying degrees of consensus at different moments.

On the other hand, reliance on combinations of interests as a mechanism of social order is consistent with the premise that these interests are significant only because they happen to be agreed upon. Democracy may require that the shared ends of the majority be imposed on a minority that does not share them. The liberal theorist, however, will be careful to point out that the duty of a minority to obey laws that advance the goals of a majority must be founded on the minority's rationally self-interested con-

sent. The rules or the procedures for rule-making are in the minority's enlightened self-interest even when they operate prejudicially in particular cases (Locke). Or perhaps the will to obey the laws is implied in all the more concrete desires one has, when those desires are clearly understood (Kant). In no way, then, does the idea of sharing of values, as it appears in liberal thought, disrespect the subjectivity of values.

We have seen that the principle of subjective value is closely linked with the liberal conception of rules as the basis of order and freedom in society and with the psychological distinction of reason and desire, description and evaluation. But to understand the principle fully we must return to the problem of intelligible essences. The temporary retreat to a level of even greater generality and abstraction will enable us to see how the postulate of subjective value bears on much more concrete issues of political and legal theory.

The doctrine that there are no intelligible essences is the ultimate basis of the principle of subjective value. The theory of intelligible essences states that there are a limited number of classes of things in the world, that each thing has characteristics that determine the class to which it belongs, and that these characteristics can be known directly by the mind.

Were we to make any concessions to the doctrine of intelligible essences in our view of natural facts, there seems to be no way we could keep the doctrine from penetrating into the sphere of language, conduct, and values. This is an obvious conclusion in a philosophy that denies the separation of values from facts. For such a philosophy our notions of right and wrong, good and bad, have to be taken as interpretations of objective standards of value just as our capacity to distinguish tables from chairs is a consequence of our ability to perceive the respective essences of each.

But even a doctrine like the liberal one that contrasts facts and values cannot ultimately uphold the ontological distinction between them. Values may be experienced as subjective, and desires as arbitrary, but there is still an important sense in which they are facts like all other facts. The arbitrariness of desires and the subjectivity of values have to do with the significance of ends as bases for the criticism or justification of conduct. The fundamental point remains: precisely because ends are denied an objective existence, they must be conceived as psychic events going on in the heads of particular men. If events in general had intelligible essences, so would these psychic events. The battle against objective values would be lost. Thus, to maintain the principle of subjective value, we must reject the doctrine of intelligible essences completely. Not only did the classic liberal thinkers recognize the truth of this conclusion, but they devoted a large part of their efforts to dealing with its many troublesome implications.[15]

Now, however, a difficulty arises. If there are no intelligible essences, how do we go about classifying facts and situations, especially social facts and social situations? Because facts have no intrinsic identity, everything depends on the names we give them. The conventions of naming rather than any perceived quality of 'tableness' will determine whether an object is to count as a table. In the same way, convention rather than nature will dictate whether a particular bargain is to be treated as a contract.

It is not surprising, then, that language should become an obsession of the liberal thinker, for he worships it as the demiurge of the world. But the real sovereigns that stand behind the demiurge are the interests that lead men to classify things as they do. He who has the power to decide what a thing will be called has the power to decide what it

is. This is as true of persons as of things. There cannot be patricians and plebeians unless we are able to distinguish the two groups. To distinguish them is to name them because there is no essential quality that determines who is patrician; who plebeian.[16]

Properly understood, the system of public rules is itself a language. Every rule is addressed to a category of persons and acts, and marks its addressees off from others. To mark off is to name. To apply the rules to particular cases is to subsume individual persons and acts under the special branch of the general theory of naming.

At last, I can state the great political problem toward which I have been winding my way. The resort to a set of public rules as the foundation of order and freedom is a consequence of the subjective conception of value. The subjective conception of value in turn presupposes the abandonment of the doctrine of intelligible essences. In the absence of intelligible essences, however, there are no obvious criteria for defining general categories of acts and persons when we make the rules. (The making of rules is legislation.) Nor are there clear standards by which to classify the particular instances under rules when we come to the stage of applying the rules we have made. (The application of rules is adjudication.)

All the fundamental issues of modern political and legal theory have to do with the need to supply standards of legislation and adjudication when intelligible essences, and therefore objective values, are rejected. Each attempt to provide guides for the making and application of the laws seems to undermine the system of thought it was meant to support. . . .

---

[15]See Hobbes' fear that the doctrine of intelligible essences would imply a limitation on state power. *Leviathan* ch. 46, pp. 526–527.

[16]On the theory of naming and its political importance, see Hobbes, *Leviathan* ch. 4, pp. 23–32.

# QUESTIONS

1. What is Unger's reason for saying that "the doctrine of objective value is incompatible with the premises of liberalism"? Is this true? Is it possible to defend consistently a Millian or Rawlsian (say) political liberalism while also defending the view that there are objective values?

2. Subjectivity of values, Unger says, means that values are "determined by choice." Objective values, on the other hand, "are standards and goals of conduct that exist independently of human choice." It is a fact that people often need water even when, not feeling thirsty, they do not know it. Consequently, they do not ask for water or seek it out. Without enough water, weakness and malaise can result. Apply Unger's definitions. Is getting enough water in such conditions a subjective value, or an objective value?

3. "The less one's ability to rely on participation in common ends," Unger says, "the greater the importance of force as a bond among individuals." Suppose that someone demonstrated conclusively that there is a common end, which all have a moral obligation to promote, say, the equal opportunity of all to have a rewarding and satisfying life. Would demonstrating the validity of this end reduce the need for rules and force as a bond? Why or why not?

4. Unger says, "It [the principle of rules and values] articulates the conception, embraced by the unreflective view of society, that the eternal hostility of men to one another requires that order and freedom be maintained by government under law." Are legal rules necessary only to deal with situations arising out of mutual hostility? Imagine a society overflowing with mutual love. Would any rules be needed?

## *Mark Tushnet*
# CRITICAL LEGAL STUDIES: AN INTRODUCTION TO ITS ORIGINS AND UNDERPINNINGS[1]*

These comments take on the task of explaining why Critical Legal Studies (CLS) forms an appropriate part of a jurisprudence course. Additionally, it provides an overview of what might be included in that part of the course. Material from CLS is already infiltrating the materials used in the first-year curriculum, and at least one prominent British text on jurisprudence has included a brief discussion of CLS in its chapter on American Legal Realism.[2] As that discussion suggests, Legal Realism is one of the intellectual origins of CLS; the other is the progressive tradition in American historiography.

*From *Journal of Legal Education*, vol. 36 (1986), pp. 505–517. Reprinted by permission of the *Journal of Legal Education* and the author.

[1] The proximate source of this introduction was a talk given at the Workshop on Jurisprudence sponsored by the AALS on March 20–22, 1986.

[2] Lord Lloyd of Hampstead & M.D.A. Freeman, Lloyds's Introduction to Jurisprudence 709–16, 5th ed. (London, 1985).

In many ways CLS is a direct descendant of American Legal Realism, which flourished in the 1920s and 1930s and left an important legacy to all legal thought.[3] CLS interprets Legal Realism along the following lines. The Realists offered a critical analysis of law as they saw it. At the time the Realists wrote, many lawyers, judges, and scholars seemed to think that they could draw on a relatively small collection of fairly abstract concepts—CLS has focused on "liberty of contract" and "property rights"—as the basis for decisions in particular cases. Results could either be deduced from the necessary meanings of the concepts or intuited from the social understanding of their meanings. The critical dimension of Legal Realism established that these assumptions were unfounded.[4] The concepts were so abstract that they led to contradictory conclusions, and because of social divisions—between employers and organized labor, for example—there could be no broadly shared social understandings on which intuitions could properly be based.[5]

The second intellectual source of CLS is the progressive tradition in American historiography. Like Legal Realism, progressive historiography flourished in the 1920s and 1930s. The progressive historians, including Charles Beard and Vernon Parrington, argued that the best way to understand the course of American history was to pay atten-

tion to the play of interest groups in American society.[6] Much of their work was devoted to debunking the claims of filiopietistic writers that the best way to understand the course of American history was as the working out of the idea of progress within a generally liberal political framework. The progressive historians looked at American policies and politics and saw much more of economic interest at work; for that they were, rather like CLS people today, called Marxists.[7]

In CLS the most important voice for the progressive tradition has been that of Morton Horwitz.[8] Historians found Horwitz's work entirely congenial—so congenial that they awarded his book their most prestigious professional award, the Bancroft Prize—because he told a story with which historians were familiar. He looked at antebellum courts and found that they were making decisions that, as he interpreted them, promoted the advance of American corporate enterprise and industrialization. Historians had heard versions of this story before. In the late 1940s Louis Hartz and Oscar Handlin, for example, had written studies that made the same point.[9] But while Hartz and Handlin had examined legislative policies and found that they promoted industrialization, Horwitz reached the same conclusion after examining judicial decisions.

[3]It is a matter of some controversy whether CLS offers anything that the most thorough going Legal Realists did not. See e.g., Robert Gordon, Critical Legal Histories, 36 Stan. L. Rev. 57, 102 n. 102 (1984). Like Gordon, I doubt that much of interest turns on the resolution of that controversy. As I discuss below, I believe that CLS has in some ways deepened the basic insights of Legal Realism, but whether that counts as an innovation seems to me an uninteresting question.

[4]Here as elsewhere I use words such as "established" to indicate my view that the arguments offered by the Legal Realists were correct. Those interested in the discussion as an effort to retrieve the intellectual background of CLS may substitute words that do not express such evaluations.

[5]See, e.g., Oliver Wendell Holmes, Herbert Spencer: Legislation and Empiricism, 7 Am. L. Rev. 582 (1873).

[6]See Richard Hofstadter, The Progressive Historians: Turner, Beard Parrington (New York, 1968).

[7]It may be worth noting that "debunking" is just another word for "trashing" or "demystification."

[8]See Morton Horwitz. The Transformation of American Law. 1780–1860 (Cambridge, Mass., 1977).

[9]Louis Hartz, Economic Policy and Democratic Thought: Pennsylvania, 1776–1860 (Cambridge, Mass., 1948); Oscar & Mary Handlin, Commonwealth, A Study of the Role of Government in the American Economy: Massachusetts, 1774–1861 (New York, 1947).

Unlike the historians, lawyers felt threatened by Horwitz's story, and the reviews by lawyers were much more critical.[10] The reason is that, for lawyers if not for historians, there has to be a difference between judges and legislators;[11] otherwise the distinction between law and politics collapses. The role of the progressive tradition in CLS has been to support the general judgment that there is no tenable distinction between law and politics, just as the Realists' critique of rules had argued. The general point of both traditions was to emphasize the importance of relations of power in the employment and development of law—what CLS has come to refer to as the importance of illegitimate hierarchy as an ordering institution in our society.

The Realists made another important point, which was constructive rather than critical. They argued that deduction and intuition had to be replaced by explicit and fairly systematic policy analysis. This constructive program had three elements. First, decision-makers, whether judges, legislators, or lawyers advising clients, had to identify those social interests actually at issue in a particular controversy, and had to think about how those interests might be affected by the various courses of action that might be pursued. Understanding the consequences of legal decisions required studying the actual operation of the legal system, drawing on sociology and political science for organizing concepts.[12] This study came to be called policy analysis, and it is now so widely accepted a way of thinking about law that the forms for student evaluation of teaching routinely ask whether the teacher adequately explored policy issues in the course.

Second, according to the Realists, although lawyers should abandon abstract legal concepts as the basis for decision, they should still pay attention to some important but nonetheless abstract social interests, such as promoting human freedom and material well-being. For while people might disagree about *how* those interests should be advanced and *whether* other particular values ought to be promoted, no one would disagree *that* these most fundamental values are important. Thus policy analysis could be grounded on these newly identified and broadly shared social understandings.

The third element in the Realists' constructive program was a method of legal analysis, the method of balancing. Once the precise interests at stake have been identified and their relation to the broad social values understood, decision-makers should balance the interests to arrive at an appropriate decision.

The Realists' constructive program provides the framework for most legal thought today. One need only read a randomly selected law review article or—perhaps a better indicator of what we teach our students—a randomly selected student note of comment to find that the right answer to the question at issue can be found by balancing the interests identified in the appropriate three-part test.

CLS accepts the critical aspect of Legal Realism but challenges its constructive program. Because it does so by using the critical techniques developed by the Realists, CLS is in this sense a true descendant of Realism. The way in which CLS is concerned with the political dimensions of law and domination can be explored by examining the CLS attack

---

[10]See, e.g., John Reid, Book Review, 55 Tex. L. Rev. 1307 (1977); Peter Teachout, Book Review, 53 NYU L. Rev. 291 (1977); A.B. Simpson, The Horwitz Thesis and the History of Contracts, 46 U. Chi. L. Rev. 533 (1979). Citations to other reviews can be found in Wythe Holt, Morton Horwitz and the Transformation of American Legal History, 23 Wm. & Mary L. Rev. 633, 666 nn. 8–9 (1982).

[11]This is not to contend that Horwitz's analysis was unflawed. what is of interest here is the comparison between the lawyers' and the historians' responses, not the accuracy of their respective judgments.

[12]The usual citation for this point is Harold Lasswell & Myres McDougal, Legal Education and Public Policy: Professional Training in the Public Interest, 52 Yale L.J. 203 (1943).

on policy analysis, balancing, and shared social values—that is, on the constructive program of Legal Realism.

The CLS attack on policy analysis has focused on what is at present the most popular systematic form of policy analysis, law-and-economics. Law-and-economics attempts to identify what the most efficient solution to a legal problem is. That is, suppose we know how wealth is distributed in a particular society and the preferences of its members. Law-and-economics attempts to determine what rule will allow that society to achieve the most of what its members want, given the existing distribution of wealth. Everyone knows that many interesting questions are assumed away when law-and-economics takes the distribution of wealth as a given. But its proponents claim that answers to many questions are insensitive to the distribution of wealth—there could be large changes in that distribution and no changes in the efficient rules—and that, in any event, if you care about wealth distribution, it is pretty silly to worry about tort or contract law rather than, for example, the tax system.[13]

CLS has attacked law-and-economics in a number of ways. I am not competent to evaluate the technical attack, but I can describe it: The legal system, through its rules of property, contract, and tort, creates a set of entitlements. These entitlements constitute the pattern of wealth-holding in the society. If you are trying to figure out what the efficient rule of contract law is, you cannot take the distribution of wealth as given, because the rule you come up with defines the distribution of wealth. A second line of attack is that economic analysis—and by extension policy analysis more generally—necessarily proceeds by making simplifying assumptions about the world. Law-and-economics has increasingly relaxed those assumptions to make the economic models more realistic. But as the realism of the models increases the conclusions that we can draw become weaker and weaker.

The most sophisticated economic analyses and end up where the Legal Realists began, with a list of things we ought to think about. The third attack on policy analysis is still more general. Legal rules, and the distribution of wealth, do not merely *reflect* individual preferences. To some degree the rules shape those preferences. Decision-makers must therefore ask not only "What can we do to provide what people want" but, "How will what we do affect what people want?"

The Legal Realists' constructive program answered this question by offering its method of balancing. Sensible decision-makers, brought up in their society and sensitive to its present desires and its aspirations, would be able to take into account everything that policy analysis identified and could come up with the right answers. Here CLS makes a simple point. In our society the class of decision-makers is not representative enough to provide the assurance the Realists wanted. Decision-makers are an elite, demographically unrepresentative and socialized into a set of beliefs about society and technology that skew the balance that they reach. The CLS challenge to balancing, then, is the claim that balancing is a social process that needs to be examined sociologically. The concern for sociological analysis of the actual exercise of power is one part of the legacy of progressive historiography. Sociological analysis inevitably raises political questions. For example, CLS argues that the Realists did not go far enough in demanding a democratization of law and, notably, that neither the New Deal nor the present Democratic Party does so either.

Concern for the politics of legal thought is even more evident in the most fundamental part of the CLS challenge to the Legal Realists' constructive program. The Realists wanted lawyers to worry about how the legal system promoted broadly shared social values. Parts of the CLS argument here are simple applications of the Realists' critical arguments: The

---

[13]See e.g., A. Mitchell Polinsky, An Introduction to Law and Economics 105–13 (Boston, 1983).

social values are described so abstractly that they could justify any decision, and there is some disagreement even about these abstract values—consider the environmentalists' challenge to arguments for increasing a society's material wealth. But the more important part of the CLS argument goes deeper. CLS insists that the social values, on which there may well be agreement, are not valuable in some abstract and timeless sense. They are values because of our society is structured to produce in its members just that set of values. But if that is so, the entire constructive enterprise collapses on itself, because you cannot think about altering legal rules to conform to a society's values when those values are constructed partly on the basis of the legal rules themselves.

Taken together, the CLS arguments are bound to be unsettling. If the argument about the social construction of values is correct, people who talk about radical changes in social organization are likely to seem at least weird and off-the-wall.[14] CLS tries to put into question the deepest values of a society: Because there is nothing timeless about those values, we might simply decide to abandon them. CLS might not be able to make much headway with these arguments were is not aided by developments in other disciplines such as philosophy and sociology, whose important thinkers have also argued that social reality is itself socially constructed.

My reference to developments in other disciplines indicates where CLS goes beyond the progressive historians as well. Progressive historians tend to tell a story in which social and political developments were more or less strongly dependent upon or derived from economic developments; that is why they were sometimes called Marxists. In emphasizing economics they relied on the dominant methodological theories of historical knowledge available to them. These theories were quite strongly influenced by the model of the natural sciences and tended in the direction of a fairly strong determinism.

CLS has developed a critique of these versions of social theory which draws on the legacy of Legal Realism. One version of the critique is straightforward. Social theories attempt to provide systematic explanations of many aspects of the social order by drawing on a much smaller list of aspects that the theory identifies as fundamental. Virtually all social theories identify as fundamental some aspects whose definition requires recourse to legal concepts. For example, in its classical versions Marxism derives its conclusions from premises that involve statements about ownership of the means of production. Yet if, as Legal Realism showed, the concept of ownership, like all other legal concepts, is empty and meaningless—in the sense that it can have any content and implications whatever—nothing can be derived from it. To the extent that social theories rely on legal concepts, they cannot find the explanations that they seek.

The second version of the critique of social theory goes beyond the perhaps accidental fact that most social theories use legal terms. It applies Legal Realism to the effort of social theorists to provide "law"-like explanations. Stated most abstractly, Legal Realism established that particular conclusions—outcomes in cases—could not be derived from general concepts—rules of law. It did so by showing, in example after example, that however one defined the general concepts, a critic could derive contradictory conclusions by, for instance, exploiting ambiguities in the concepts or drawing on other concepts that could not be kept out of the discussion. These analytic techniques can be used to develop a general critique of the effort to link general concepts to particular results, and that critique undermines social

---

[14]And after all, if their argument is correct, where do *their* values come from? Well, CLS does not argue that contemporary society is hermetically sealed against values that might, for example, be remembered as attractive relics of the past, or might be imagined by appreciating what modern art tells us about ourselves.

theory. Taken as a whole, the CLS challenge to social theory suggests that the initial effort to provide a general theoretical account of how domination occurred was misguided. At present, CLS takes the position that no such general account is available. All that we can have are examples of how domination occurs in particular settings.

This critique of social theory has a number of consequences that I will discuss presently. For the moment, the point I would like to make is that, just as progressive historiography and Legal Realism fit into the available discourses in other disciplines in the 1930s, so CLS fits into the discourses current today. The critique of rules, and more particularly the critique of social theory, has strong affinities to discussions of method in the philosophy of the social and natural sciences, as well as in various disciplines in the humanities.[15]

I turn now to a description of the current state of CLS. First, however, I must interject a number of qualifications. CLS is a developing body of thought, and it would be unsound to attempt to freeze it with an absolutely precise description. Further, different participants in the effort to push CLS ahead have different opinions, and as one of the participants, I have my own views on matters in controversy.[16]

One issue should be mentioned, only to be put aside. It seems to be a standard line in statements by critics of CLS that CLS has no constructive program. As I will indicate at the conclusion of these remarks, there is a deep sense in which that is correct. But in the superficial sense that these critics appear to intend, their comments are simply wrong. CLS offers many proposals for alternative programs. These proposals run from the mundane, such as William Simon's suggestion that a random selection of welfare determinations be automatically subjected to review on appeal,[17] to the grandiose, such as Roberto Unger's description of various forms of public control over investment.[18] I suppose that the critics' point is that, though they can *read* these statements about what ought to be done, they cannot quite understand how those practical proposals are related to the critical or theoretical dimensions of CLS.

Here I will give the short answer to this criticism and will devote the rest of my paper to explaining that answer. The short answer is that the point of the proposals is to continue the critique of existing society, not to get these particular proposals adopted in the short run. This position is, as I will now try to argue, related to ongoing discussions within CLS.

To illustrate this relation, I will describe what is, or at least what was, probably the central debate within CLS.[19] The early position in CLS was that one could say something systematic about the relation between legal rules and power—for example, we can say, though with many qualifications, that the legal system is tilted in favor of capitalism. So long as it is not bound by too many qualifications, that statement or some variant has a fairly obvious intuitive appeal.

The dominant position responds by identifying—or perhaps more precisely by stressing more strongly than the early position —the difficulties inherent even in heavily qualified versions of the early formulations. Three of its arguments have been particularly

---

[15] A useful recent overview of these developments, which includes a helpful bibliography, is Quentin Skinner, ed., The Return of Grand Theory in the Human Sciences (New York, 1985).

[16] I should probably note my guess that I am in the minority these days on most of the issues I will mention.

[17] William Simon, Legality, Bureaucracy, and Class in the Welfare System, 92 Yale L. J. 1198, 1267–68 (1983).

[18] Roberto Unger, The Critical Legal Studies Movement, 96 Harv. L. Rev. 561, 596–97 (1983).

[19] The labels that have been attached to the polar positions in this debate are "rationalist" and "irrationalist." See, e.g., Clare Dalton, Book Review, 6 Harv. Women's L.J. 229, 231 (1983). I have concluded that these labels are more misleading than helpful in providing an initial orientation to the discussions, and I have decided simply to call one the early position and the other the dominant position.

effective. The first emphasizes the Legal Realists' skepticism about rules, which made it impossible to say that "the legal system" is tilted in any direction at all: If decision-makers can in principle reach any conclusion they wish within the legal system, "the system" cannot be tilted, though of course the decision-makers might be biased. The second argument is that no one has shown that any particular aspect of the legal system, or even the legal system as a whole, serves the interests of capitalism better than do obvious alternatives, including wholesale rejection of vast bodies of law. For any particular rule in the law of contracts in some state in the United States which might be thought to support capitalism, there is a precisely contrary rule, within an equally capitalist system, that is, in another state. International comparisons demonstrated that capitalist economic systems could be found in countries with widely divergent legal systems. The final argument against tilt is that the legal system in fact has little direct impact on the maintenance of capitalism. It provides a framework within which bargains can be struck, and its rules are a sort of disaster insurance against unforseen calamities. But it is difficult to see how an institution whose purposes are so limited could have much of systemic impact.

These arguments have forced a reformulation of the early position. Agreeing that tilt could not be found systematically in the rules of the legal system, the reformulation argued that it is located in the construction of the categories used to organize legal thought and in the construction of the operations used to relate those categories.[20] This seems to me the present state of the position: It claims an analytic program, but has not

yet made much progress in demonstrating the program's power.

The renunciation of the theoretical dimension of the initial project of CLS helps explain an otherwise curious characteristic of recent critical legal scholarship. Although it devotes a great deal of attention to phenomena that occurred in the past, much of the work is relentlessly ahistorical. It focuses synchronically on particular moments in the past[21] or offers a sort of comparative statics,[22] but never gives a diachronic account of transformation over time. I believe that this ahistoricism is linked to the critique of social theory, because diachronic accounts explicitly or implicitly rely on social theory to give them coherence. One tradition in the philosophy of history holds that narratives must draw on covering laws—the generalizations of social theory—of which sequences of particular events are specific instances based on identified initial conditions. Another tradition is less explicitly theoretical and claims only that historians provide narratives of past events. But the selection of the events that are placed in the narrative's sequence, out of all the possible events that could be used, seems to require some (usually implicit) theoretical account, if only the common sense theories held by well-socialized readers of historical narratives. Having renounced social theory, CLS is barred/precluded from using these standard traditions of historical writing—thus its characteristic ahistoricism.

Alternatively, one could provide a multitude of competing stories about how things changed, while insisting that none of the stories has the sort of epistemological priority that social theories gives to the narratives of the standard traditions. Or one could rely on

---

[20] See, e.g., Gordon, *supra* note 3, at 109–13.

[21] See, e.g., Duncan Kennedy, The Structure of Blackstone's Commentaries, 28 Buff. L. Rev. 205 (1979); Mark Tushnet, The American Law of Slavery, 1810–1860: Considerations of Humanity and Interest 9 (Princeton, N.J., 1981) (describing efforts to analyze a "general" law of slavery without regard to variation over time). As the latter example suggests, the "moment" can be extended for a rather long period—fifty years in my book on the law of slavery. But the ahistoricism remains because no change that the study seeks to explain occurs during the extended period.

[22] See, e.g., Gary Peller, The Metaphysics of American Law, 73 Cal. L. Rev. 1151 (1985).

the critique of social theory as a background against which only one account was offered, demanding that readers abjure the usual expectations they might hold about the epistemological claims implicit in such narratives. Either of these courses—the many stories or the one told with a raised eyebrow—could force readers to consider what might be the basis for the critical legal scholar's choice or stories to tell. And that would bring the politics of CLS directly into the discussion.

The view of historical analysis that I have just sketched is implicit in much recent critical legal scholarship, but I believe that the body of work would be strengthened by explicit discussions of these issues. More often the issues have been taken up in the use of structuralist and deconstructionist methods. These methods lie behind much of the currently dominant practice. As soon as an analyst offers a systematic explanation of something, the dominant strain in CLS decenters the explanation, rearranging the terms and categories used in the explanation to demonstrate that the reorganized explanation is just as good as the original one.[23] This decentering project has no termination.

The use of deconstruction has developed its insistence that general social-theoretical explanations are unavailable into the position that all one can do is provide minutely detailed maps or descriptions of phenomena. At this point the open question for the dominant view arises. In general, though it has abandoned the search for social theory, it has not abandoned the view that social power (illegitimate hierarchy) exists. Somehow the detailed descriptions are to reveal how power actually operates. They do so not by invoking social theory of covering laws, but by educing, in an essentially intuitive way, understanding out of the reader's immersion in details. But we need to ask, how is this understanding supposed to emerge?

One possible answer is that the dominant program does not really aim at understanding in the usual sense. Rather, this view maintains, proponents of the dominant program have made a strategic judgment that in the present circumstances their political goals are more likely to be reached by using deconstructive methods. This view breaks the connection between the analytic program and the politics of critical legal studies.

A second possibility is that understanding emerges because of the essentially literary techniques used by those presenting the detailed descriptions. It might be that these techniques operate in a sphere epistemologically distinct from that in which social theory is thought to operate. If so, the emptiness of social theory need not imply that we cannot gain knowledge via deconstruction.[24]

A third possibility, and the one that I believe many critical legal scholars would prefer to pursue, is that we can analyze the ways in which intuitive understanding emerges from detailed descriptions. The anthropologist Clifford Geertz has argued that all knowledge is this sort of "local knowledge."[25] But neither Geertz nor anyone who has appropriated his terminology has done much to explain the sense in which "local knowledge" is knowledge. The effort to do so seems sensible for two reasons. First, we know that people sometimes have different intuitions about a particular problem, and we ought to be curious about how and why intuitive understandings are sometimes shared and sometimes divergent. Second, the analytic effort may be required by the CLS emphasis on domination and illegitimate hierarchy. These terms have normative connotations that suggest that any accurate understanding of hierarchial situations would refer to domination. But that judgment plainly needs some sort of defense.

---

[23]See, e.g., David Kennedy, The Turn to Interpretation, 58 S. Cal. L. Rev. 251 (1985).

[24]Though I am not competent to evaluate this possibility, I gather that the French post-structuralists have been unable to sustain their similar epistemological claims.

[25]Clifford Geertz, Local Knowledge (New York, 1983).

One line of defense, which appears in some works, is to rely on an essentially romantic view of human nature. Joseph Singer, for example, counters hard-nosed views that "what people *really* like is doing horrible things to each other" with the sensible response that they "do not want just to be beastly to each other. . . . [T]hey also want not to harm others."[26] The difficulty is that as Singer pursues his analysis, he forgets the implication of the "not just" and "also"; in other words, he forgets that people do indeed sometimes want to be beastly. What to those on the bottom is an illegitimate hierarchy is to those on the top a perfectly sensible one.[27] The romantic view of human nature denies that anyone could hold the latter belief in good faith, but, in the absence of a fairly elaborate late Sartrean exposition of the concept of bad faith, the denial is unpersuasive.

A second line of defense for judgments about domination can be called strategic silence. Gary Peller's analysis of the reification of consent in the law of rape provides a useful example.[28] In a standard deconstructive analysis, Peller argues that the concept of consent can be applied in particular settings only by "construct[ing] the context which is supposed to provide the ground for representing the event," a course that "promises total circularity."[29] Peller's aim is to demonstrate that the use of consent as a defense in the law of rape projects "the ideological message . . . that consensual sexuality is consistent with male domination in society."[30] But it should be clear that the same analysis could be used to explain what might be called the Maileresque assessment that female domination requires men to engage in sexual behavior that society creates to be coercive. The technique of deconstruction, that is, cannot in itself support the political conclusions implicit in the use of the term "domination" as applied to particular arrangements. Because the political open-endedness of the deconstructive technique is so obvious, the silence about it in the CLS literature should be understood as strategic, designed to place on the table the political judgments implied by any use of language.

But strategic silence only raises the political issues; it does not explain why one ought to adopt the feminist interpretation of consent and reject the Maileresque interpretation of coercion. This fact suggests that the idea of strategic silence could be extended. The extension would hold that there is nothing beyond that silence, that the process of decentering our understandings is indeed interminable. One offers the feminist interpretation of rape because one has made a political judgment that in our society congealed forms of domination are more likely to be broken up by that interpretation than by the Maileresque alternative. But that is an ungrounded political judgment, open to discussion and alteration as times, circumstances, and understandings change.

The critique of social theory thus replaces one form of political analysis with another. Instead of having political positions flow from social theory, the dominant CLS project simply takes political positions. But not just any political positions. The politics of the dominant position is the politics of decentering, disrupting whatever understandings happen to be settled, criticizing the existing order whatever that order is. Some CLS proponents are attracted to small-scale decentralized socialism.[31] But that attraction must be understood as the embodiment of a critique of large-scale centralized capitalism. It cannot

---

[26] Joseph Singer, The Player and the Cards: Nihilism and Legal Theory, 94 Yale L.J. 1, 54 (1984).

[27] In one sense the topic of my book, *supra* note 21, was the examination of how people could come to have that belief.

[28] Peller, *supra* note 22, at 1187–91.

[29] *Id.* at 1189–90.

[30] *Id.* at 1191.

[31] See, e.g., Gerald Frug, The City as a Legal Concept, 93 Harv. L. Rev. 1057 (1980); Mark Tushnet, Federalism and the Traditions of American Political Theory, 19 Ga. L. Rev. 981 (1985).

set forth a permanent program, the realization of which would be the end of politics.[32] In fact, in a socialist society, the critical legal scholar would criticize socialism as denying the importance of individual achievement, and decentralization as an impediment to material and spiritual achievement. Roberto Unger captured this dimension of the irrationalist project in his description of destablization rights, "claims to the disruption of established institutions . . . that have . . . contributed to the very kind of crystallized plan of social hierarchy and division that the entire constitution wants to avoid."[33]

With all this in hand, we can in conclusion turn to the implications of the critique of social theory for the future of CLS. Of course the Legal Realist analysis of rules will continue to be used; the legal academy's commitment to the coherence of rules is strong enough to require repeated assaults. It might be useful as well to develop detailed analyses of how law and beliefs about law are implicated in practices of domination and liberation, but the institutional impediments to sustained empirical research by legal academics are so substantial that it is unlikely that critical legal scholars will produce much along these lines.

I should mention too that one part of the future of CLS is continued institutionalization as part of the pluralist intellectual world of the legal academy. It now seems to be a more or less standard practice in symposia and workshops to include someone from CLS, or at least to feel bad if you do not manage to round one up (or if you willfully ignore them.)[34]

But the most important implication of the dominant CLS analysis is that any critique of the existing order is consistent with the project of CLS. Statistical studies, casual empiricism, classical social theory, the most old-fashioned doctrinal analysis—all might be critical legal studies so long as three conditions are met. First, the work should not be defended on grounds that suggest that something more enduring than interminable critique might result from following it through. Second, it must be designed as a critique rather than as a defense of the existing order—or of a slightly modified version of the existing order that, once modified, would be the end of politics. Finally, the work should actually operate as a critique.[35]

Perhaps the program of interminable critique swallows itself. If it is widely accepted, people may at first resign themselves to their inability to transcend critique. But they may come to see that inability is itself transcendent, creating a new form of life in which the terms on which critique must proceed today have become unintelligible.

I would like to close by elaborating this point about interminable critique. I will do so by describing one of the more controversial CLS arguments, which has been called the critique of rights. According to this argument, it would seem that we could abandon such valued rights as the constitutional protections our society gives to free speech and to the antidiscrimination principle. The CLS argument has two parts. The first applies the critique of legal concepts to the concepts embodied in these ideas about rights. Here the

---

[32]The same point must be made in connection with the assertions that altruism and paternalism should play a more vital role in our law as compared with its present individuals [sic]. See, e.g., Duncan Kennedy, Form and Substance in Private Law Adjudication, 89 Harv. L. Rev. 1685 (1976); Duncan Kennedy, Distributive and Paternalist Motives in Contract and Tort Law, with Special Reference to Compulsory Terms and Unequal Bargaining Power, 41 Md. L. Rev. 563 (1982).

[33]Unger, *supra* note 18, at 600, 611–15

[34]I suspect that CLS is about to become one of the quotas that law schools feel they ought to fill: one trusts-and-estates teacher, one teacher of jurisprudence, one representative of law-and-economics sort, one of CLS. (As with all quotas, of course, the more categories any one person occupies the better—imagine finding someone who wanted to teach trusts and estates, jurisprudence, and law-and-economics.)

[35]This final pragmatic criterion may be controversial, for some critical legal scholars may claim that a statistical study or a doctrinal analysis or a social theory of the classical type cannot actually function as a critique in our society as it is presently constituted. I disagree, but will reserve my comments on this issue for another forum.

critique argues that the rights are defined on too abstract a level to be helpful in resolving the claims presented in particular cases. Nor will recourse to underlying values or to a balancing process help, for reasons I have already reviewed. This aspect of the argument is not unusual or, in itself, particularly bothersome, because it relies on positions for which the Realists were thought to have adequate answers.

One person to whom, the critique of rights was described reacted by calling the world that it depicted "Kafkaesque." According to the critique of rights, people cannot know what rights they have, and there are no political methods that guarantee those rights. The term "Kafkaesque" is perfectly appropriate and provides a clue to the justification for the constructive program—or for the program of interminable critique. For by invoking Kafka's vision, the term allows CLS to say that it, like Kafka, is describing the condition of the modern world. Those reared in, or attracted to, premodernist traditions may well find the world so described quite distasteful. But the point of modernism is precisely that that is just the way things are these days.

CLS is thus the form that modernism takes in legal thought. Like modernism in philosophy and sociology, it displaces settled understandings, insisting that whatever we have is something we create and recreate daily. As a form of modernism, CLS argues that our lives are structured by institutions that we create and sustain, and that our lives have no meaning outside those institutions and the processes by which we create them—and create ourselves. So, in part, the CLS program is justified in the way all modernist programs are: The program consists of shattering congealed forms of life by showing that they have no particular integrity. And whatever makes that demonstration effective—utopian yearnings, close analysis of legal texts, concrete proposals—is part of the program.

Perhaps this analysis could be continued indefinitely. But if the CLS critique is interminable, this article is not.

## QUESTIONS

1. It has been said that the politician looks to the next election, while those trying to apply principles look to the indefinite future. Can this insight be developed into an answer to CLS's claim (according to Tushnet) "that there is no tenable distinction between law and politics"?

2. Read either or both of the excerpts from Ronald Dworkin's writings reprinted in Parts 1 and 3. Develop your own criticisms of Dworkin's views, using Tushnet's account of CLS as your starting point.

3. Consider what John Rawls says about the nature and function of what he calls an "overlapping consensus." (See his "The Idea of an Overlapping Consensus" in Part 2.) Again taking Tushnet's account of CLS doctrines as your starting point, how would CLS view Rawls's suggestion that an overlapping consensus serves to take certain matters, including comprehensive philosophical and religious doctrines, off the political agenda? Does Rawls help us to answer CLS's claim that there is no real distinction between law and politics?

4. What, according to Tushnet, is "the argument about the social construction of values"? In what sense are values socially constructed? If it turns out that they are socially constructed, what implications would that have?

5. "CLS, as described by Tushnet, is not so much and alternative set of legal doctrines as a skeptical and critical attitude toward the foundations of any established legal doctrine." Comment.

# PART SIX

# Theories of Punishment

Questions about legal punishment are among the most serious and constant that arise in the philosophy of law. Punishment is a phenomenon that forces itself on our attention, raising questions that demand answers. The urgency of the philosophical questions it raises is no doubt due to the fact that punishment involves doing things to people that in other circumstances are wrong, even the greatest of wrongs: intentionally inflicting pain and suffering, sometimes even death. Without an adequate philosophical justification of punishment, those who have learned and internalized the flat moral prohibition against killing will have a hard time understanding why that prohibition does not apply to the state's intentional infliction of suffering or death.

To fix ideas, we begin with a definition. We may define legal punishment as:

1. the infliction of suffering, or what would normally be considered an evil;
2. by those who claim to act within their authority as legal officials, and
3. who claim to inflict this evil for an offense against legal rules.

This definition leaves open for discussion and argument two things that have been at the core of philosophical debate about punishment. So far as the definition is concerned, it does not specify that the person who is punished must be the one who committed the offense, nor does it rule out the possibility that the officials who administer the punishment do so with the knowledge that the punished person is in fact innocent. These are serious issues, and it is important that we not close off debate about them by definitional fiat.[1]

[1]See H.L.A. Hart, "Prolegomenon to the Principles of Punishment," in *Punishment and Responsibility: Essays in the Philosophy of Law* (New York: Oxford University Press, 1968).

Theories of punishment are supposed to answer such questions as the following: Is punishment justified, and if so, under what circumstances? Who ought to be punished? What governs the amount of punishment that ought to be meted out? A theory of punishment may seek to provide a single principle from which answers to all of these and some other questions can be derived, or it may provide different principles to answer different questions.

As in other areas of the philosophy of law, attempts to provide systematic answers to these questions about punishment have resulted in a classic conflict. Two families of theories have been in regular contention with one another: utilitarianism and retributivism. However, if one studies theories of punishment carefully, one soon discovers that it can be a real challenge to put a particular theory in one or the other of these categories. It can even be a challenge to get a precise idea of what makes one theory utilitarian and what makes another retributivist. Let us begin with an attempt to clarify the general differences between utilitarianism and retributivism.

Philosophers usually point out that the utilitarian justification for punishment is *future-oriented*, holding that what justifies punishing someone is the happiness or other kind of good that is likely to be produced as a result of the punishment. A retributivist justification is *past-oriented*, holding instead that we punish for a crime that has been committed, not for the good that it will do. Retributivists think that to inflict suffering on someone for the reason that it will bring about some future good would be a fundamental injustice. Oriented toward the other direction in time, utilitarians think that the crime cannot be undone and our sole concern must therefore be to affect the future, whether that be by reducing crime, reforming or morally improving the wrongdoer, or satisfying the desire for revenge.

Making the distinction between retributivism and utilitarianism in this way is helpful only as a rough, starting approximation. The main problem is that retributivism too can be described as being oriented toward the future. If (to use language retributivists tend to use) we punish in order to rectify injustice, to restore equality, or to vindicate rights that have been violated, then we are punishing in order to bring about a state of affairs in which injustice is rectified, equality is restored, or rights are vindicated. All of these purposes look to the future. So the difference between utilitarianism and retributivism needs to be made clearer.

The retributivist's main concern is that the justification for punishment should have this general form: We punish a person *for* (and only for) a crime committed by *that* person. Thus the reason for punishment begins with a particular agent's wrongdoing and directs the punishment back onto the individual whose willful action was the crime in question.

Utilitarian theory does not start with this tight connection between a punishment and a crime. The utilitarian's main concern is that punishing, like any other action, should produce the most good overall. It is then only a contingent fact if punishing a person for a crime that person has committed will produce the most good overall. In some cases, not punishing for a crime might do the most good; in others, punishing a person other than the wrongdoer might do the most good; and in others, punishing though there was no crime at all might be the utilitarian thing to do. If a utilitarian theory ultimately supports a tight connection between $X$'s punishment and $X$'s crime, it is not because it begins with the idea of a tight connection as retributivism does, but because it establishes the connection indirectly.

This tight connection between punishment and crime—that we punish a person for and only for a crime committed by that person—is the core idea of retributivism. Different versions of retributivism argue for this core idea in different ways. However, if a particular theory provides only a contingent or shaky basis for this connection, we must ask whether that theory is really retributivist after all.

As an illustration, suppose that a theory of punishment claims that punishment is justified because of the good that it does for the wrongdoer. What, we ask, is the nature of this good? If we can still obtain this same kind of good by inflicting punishment on someone who is innocent, then the theory fails to support the needed tight connection between punishment and crime. For example, if we punish in order to teach the wrongdoer a stern, character-building lesson, could we not also punish an innocent person in order to teach the same character-building lesson to the public, who may falsely believe this person to be guilty?

Let us now summarize the differences between retributivism and utilitarianism in the theory of punishment. To set up the clearest contrast between the two, first consider each theory in its most robust form, remembering that there are many ways in which the extreme form can be modified to answer criticisms. The most robust form of retributivism consists of three theses:

(R1)  Anyone who commits a legal offense must be punished by legal authorities for that offense.

(R2)  No one may be punished by legal authorities except for a legal offense.

(R3)  The punishment must fit, or be proportional to, the crime.

Thesis (R1) will be especially likely to attract criticism from utilitarians because punishment, involving as it does doing unpleasant things to people, seems hard to justify in a particular instance if it will do no good. So some retributivists might be inclined to soften (R1) a bit to something like the following:

(R1a)  Anyone who commits a legal offense may justifiably be punished by legal authorities for that offense.

(R1a) allows punishment, but does not mandate it. Those who make decisions about applying punishment would presumably need criteria to determine which persons, among those who may be punished, will be punished. These criteria might be utilitarian in nature, selecting for punishment only those individuals where punishment will produce net benefit. But if the criteria are utilitarian, two questions will arise, one practical, the other theoretical. The practical question has to do with discretion: Does it not grant too much discretion to officials to tell them to punish the guilty when and only when doing so will produce the most good overall? The theoretical question concerns the status of this new theory of punishment. Is it still a version of retributivism? Or is it now an uneasy and unstable compromise between retributivism and utilitarianism? If the latter, what objection is there to adopting a full-fledged utilitarian theory of punishment?

Thesis (R3) might also attract criticism from utilitarians, because it rules out less severe punishment of serious crimes, even though punishing up to the point of full proportionality may do no good, or even harm. In addition, (R3) would seem to be difficult to apply in practice, for it is not clear how to proceed in establishing equalities, or rank–orderings, between punishments and offenses. So (R1), and to some extent (R3), are the most vulnerable to attack, both from the standpoint of utilitarian theory, as well as from the standpoint of common convictions about penal justice.

Thesis (R2), on the other hand, is by far the most appealing thesis of retributivism. Not only does it deeply appeal to the convictions that ordinary people have about justice but (R2) has also usually been thought so important by philosophers that utilitarians themselves go to great lengths to show that their theory of punishment, despite appearances to the contrary, would in fact never require the punishment of an innocent person. The strongest point in favor of retributivism, then, is thesis (R2), and it is precisely the difficulty that utilitarianism has in establishing its own version of thesis (R2) that many think is its weakest point.

Extreme utilitarianism holds one simple thesis about the right thing for legislators, judges, and law enforcement officers to do, and from this thesis two corollaries can be derived. This basic thesis is that

(U) That action (of legislating, punishing, etc.) is right which produces the most good overall (where good=happiness).

Among the corollaries of (U) are the following:

(UC1)  If punishing an innocent person produces the most good overall, then that action is right.

(UC2)  If not punishing a guilty person produces the most good overall, then that action is right.

So from the standpoint of the ordinary person's convictions about justice, the strengths and weaknesses of utilitarianism and retributivism are mirror images of one another. The utilitarian corollary (UC2) reflects the common conviction that (R1) is too harsh: Punishment should not be pursued if it really does no good. But, on the other side, (UC1) is even further out of touch with the common convictions reflected in retributivism's (R2): Punishing the innocent is wrong no matter how much good it might do.

Although the main challenge for the utilitarian theory of punishment is to show that it would never in fact require punishing the innocent, there are related problems posed by cases that are intermediate between outright innocence and outright guilt. One such case is that in which the agent does a legally forbidden thing, like selling liquor to underage persons, but with the sincere belief that they are not underage. Not having purposely or knowingly sold liquor to minors, the agent did not have what lawyers sometimes call *mens rea* (i.e., "guilty mind," or "criminal intent"). Such a person is not really guilty in the ordinary sense. Nor is that person unequivocally innocent, for he or she did engage in an activity (selling liquor) which risks bringing about this kind of a result (selling liquor to a minor).

After all, anyone who gets into the retail liquor business knows that, no matter how careful someone in the business might be, one might still someday unknowingly sell liquor to an underage person.

*Strict liability* criminal laws make violators liable to criminal punishment (fines, perhaps even jail sentences) regardless of whether they acted purposely or knowingly, or even recklessly. Less common and more controversial, though a real possibility, are *vicarious liability* criminal laws which make one person liable to criminal punishment for certain illegal actions of another person, for example, a child or other member of one's family. Many people have fundamental moral objections to strict liability criminal laws, and especially to vicarious criminal liability.

Circumstances can easily be imagined in which utilitarian theory would recommend criminal punishment based either on strict liability, or vicarious liability, or some mixture of both. As a measure to reduce certain forms of undesirable behavior, strict criminal liability might be effective. Thus liquor retailers who know that liability for selling liquor to a minor is strict may as a result be far more cautious and even stay out of the business entirely if they cannot take the extra precautions. And in some societies, where family members can exercise close supervision of one another, the knowledge that one can punished for the offenses of a sister or son might well cause stricter intrafamilial control of behavior. This does not mean that either strict liability or vicarious liability is fair or having it is admirable; only that it might be effective as a means of controlling behavior. (This topic is raised again in Part 7 of this book.) In any case, an important dimension of a theory of punishment is its implications about the appropriateness of strict and vicarious forms of liability.

Some philosophers, unhappy both with extreme retributivism and extreme utilitarianism, have attempted to combine the important insights of both in a mixed theory that has the major defects of neither. For example, H.L.A. Hart once provided the basis for such a mixed view by making a distinction between the *general justifying aim* of a system of punishment and the *principles of distribution* of punishments to particular persons.[2] The general justifying aim provides us with an answer to the question, "Why should we punish people for legal offenses?" Principles of distribution provide an answer to the separate question, "Whom should we punish, and in what amount?" The innovation in such a mixed theory is that it allows a retributivist answer to one question without ruling out a utilitarian answer to the other question. Thus the general justifying aim of a system of punishment might properly be the utilitarian one of reducing harmful behavior, while punishment is distributed in accordance with a principle of fairness that makes the purposeful or knowing commission of an offense a necessary condition for punishablilty. The resulting justification of punishment thus embodies a mixture of two principles that limit and check one another: the utilitarian principle requiring that the overall system be justified by the good that it does and the retributivist principle of fairness requiring that individuals be punished only for those violations of law that involve mens rea.

Still other philosophers believe that an adequate theory of punishment is available if extreme utilitarianism is rejected in favor of a modified utilitarianism. The modification is

[2]Ibid.

*rule* utilitarianism, or the view that, in some departments of life at least, the right thing to do is to follow a public, rule-defined practice. It is then the practice itself, not the particular action falling under it, which is to be evaluated for the good that it does.

In the case of punishment, we can compare two practices: one which leaves it to the discretion of officials to decide whether punishing a person—any person, whether innocent or guilty—would do the most good overall, and a practice which permits punishment only of those who have been convicted in a public trial in which rigorous, public procedures have been followed in reaching a conviction. Which practice will do the most good? The latter, it seems likely. One needs only to think of the uncertainty and general insecurity that should result if officials were known to have broad discretion to punish on the basis of nothing more that their own belief that it will produce the most good. Such a modified utilitarianism counts as a mixed view in that it incorporates elements from standard retributivism. Even though the overall system of punishing a certain type of behavior is defined by rules is based squarely on the idea of bringing about good, the question whether an individual may be punished is a question that must focus on the crimes of the individual to be punished. But whether such a modified utilitarianism counts as a mixed view at its very foundation depends on whether the idea of punishing only the guilty for their crimes is itself explained by reference to the utilitarian principle of doing good, or is simply left as an idea that is supposed to stand on its own, serving as a limit to the utilitarian principle.

## THE READINGS

RETRIBUTIVISM. Immanuel Kant (1724–1804), one of the most influential figures in the history of philosophy generally, is also known for his philosophy of law and his retributivist philosophy of punishment. In Kant's view, it is characteristic of legal punishment that it involves the application of coercion. Indeed, it is the possibility of enforcement through coercion which is the distinguishing characteristic of the sphere of *juridical* legislation, such as the legal obligation not to injure another person, or the duty to pay one's bills. The performance of legal obligations can be brought about through external motivation in the form of the threat of punishment. Such external threats will be insufficient to bring about the performance of moral obligations. Moral obligations are supplied with an internal motivation: The idea of the duty itself is its own motivation. Since punishment involves the application of coercion, the main problem for a theory of punishment is to explain when the application of coercion is legitimate and why.

Crucial to an understanding of Kant's theory of justified punishment is that the function of law, in Kant's view, is to provide a system of equal liberty. Although there are of course some connections between liberty and happiness, it is not the function of law to provide for happiness, as a utilitarian might say; instead, the law establishes a system of equal liberty in which individuals can pursue their own ends, be those ends happiness, pleasure, knowledge, or something else.

When an individual commits a crime, whether theft, rape, or murder, that action involves the taking of liberty at the expense of another's liberty. Thus to punish a person in order to cancel this crime is a legitimate use of coercion, for in doing so we respect rational individual choice. First, a system of equal liberty is what rational persons, knowing only that they are persons with ends, would choose. And as part of this choice, rational persons would want the system of equal liberty to be upheld by punishing those, and only those, who violate its terms.

Second, the criminal's choice on the occasion of the crime is respected in that, knowing that the contemplated action would violate the law and make one subject to punishment, the criminal chose to violate it anyway. On the other hand, to punish a person simply in order to produce greater happiness in the community would be an illegitimate use of coercion, for it would involve taking one particular and by no means universal end, that of happiness, and using it as the reason for coercing another human being. This would involve using that person not as an end as such, but as a means to someone's particular end.

Kant's theory is thus clearly retributivist in that it implies (R1), (R2), and (R3). His theory agrees with utilitarian theories only in the minimal sense that criminal punishment is used in order to maintain a good. In Kant's case, however, this good is that of a system of equal liberty in which people are free to adopt and pursue their own ends and in which punishments are imposed on individuals because of their own choices.

**UTILITARIANISM.** Jeremy Bentham (1748–1832) is perhaps the preeminent example of a classical utilitarian. His concern to reform the legal system, ridding it of archaic laws and punishments that have no real purpose, was premised on the simple idea that all laws and actions of government ought to implement the principle of utility, that is, to promote the total happiness of the community.

Happiness, in Bentham's conception, is reducible to pleasure, which is the only thing that is good in and of itself. Moreover, the amount of an individual's pleasure is something that can in principle be quantified. It varies with, among other things, its intensity and duration: Other things being equal, the same pleasure experienced either with twice the intensity, or for twice the length of time, has twice the value. The total happiness of the community is the sum that can be obtained by adding up the pleasures of individuals and subtracting their suffering. This is so because a community can in Bentham's view be nothing more than a set of individuals and a community's happiness can be nothing more than the sum total of their pleasures.

Now if we are rationally to decide on a course of action that maximizes pleasure, we must first recognize that the consequences of our contemplated actions are typically a matter of probability rather than of certainty. So when deciding on the best course of action, we weigh its possible outcomes by multiplying the utilitarian value of an outcome by its probability. An action with an outcome of modest but highly probable utility is thus to be chosen over one whose consequences have a greater but highly improbable utility.

Bentham's discussion of punishment is an attempt to draw out the implications of the utilitarian principle for legislation and judicial action. Individuals, in his view, seek where they can to maximize their own pleasure. Sometimes in doing so they produce misery for the community as a whole. It is the job of law and government to insure that the private maximization of pleasure will be consistent with the overall happiness of the community. So Bentham's aim is to show where punishment is justified because of its value in reducing "mischief," and where it may be unjustified because it is either pointless or inefficacious.

When reading Bentham's advice on punishment, it is important to distinguish between two quite different ways in which his views might be open to criticism. One is to attack his views at their very foundation by rejecting the principle of utility itself. This is what both retributivists and defenders of mixed views have tended to do. The other is to question whether some of Bentham's particular conclusions about the efficacy or point of punishment really do follow from his utilitarian premise. Accordingly, some have questioned Bentham's view that punishment must always be inefficacious in cases where the wrong was done unintentionally.

Another classical utilitarian, John Stuart Mill (1806–1873), was a distinguished philosopher and economist and, for a time, member of Parliament. His prominent position enabled him to apply utilitarian ideas to some of the major political debates of his time. In his 1868 speech on capital punishment reprinted here, Mill uses utilitarian arguments to defend the death penalty, at least for the most "atrocious" crimes, against the familiar claim that it is inhumanly severe.

Mill's strategy is to argue, first, that the infliction of death is far less painful to the one who suffers it than the most likely punishment alternatives not involving death. Mill's use of utilitarian ideas is evident in this argument. As he puts it, "It is not human life only, not human life as such, that ought to be sacred to us, but human feelings."

The second main part of his strategy is to argue that, whether or not hardened criminals are deterred by the existence of the death penalty, ordinary innocent persons are. In short, it is in Mill's view a common mistake both to overestimate the painfulness of the death penalty for those who are put to death and to underestimate its deterrent effect on the innocent who know of it.

Mill's conclusions are remarkable, both because his tough-minded position favoring the death penalty may seem surprising to those used to thinking of death as the ultimate suffering and because Mill does not shrink from the consistent application of his utilitarian principle, even when doing so puts him at odds with what is ordinarily thought to be the side of humanitarian benevolence.

**MIXED VIEWS.** Recall the corollary (UC1) of extreme utilitarianism: If punishing an innocent person produces the most good overall, then that action is right. How does utilitarianism deal with the obvious objection to this, namely, that punishing an innocent person is wrong no matter how much good it does? The excerpt from John Rawls's (1955) essay on rules makes an important point that is meant to deal specifically with this objection.

There is a difference in kind, Rawls reminds us, between questions about the justification of a particular instance of an action, like that of keeping a promise or of punishing someone, and questions about the justification for the general practice of promise keeping or of punishing for lawbreaking. And this means that the kind of answer appropriate to questions about the justification of a practice will be different from the sort of answer to questions about justifying a particular application of the practice. Thus Rawls asks us to imagine the two different questions: (1) "Why was J put in jail yesterday?" and (2) "Why do people put other people in jail?" Extreme utilitarianism attempts to answer both questions by reference to utility and thus makes the rightness of punishing the innocent depend solely on whether it will do the most good.

Rawls's modified utilitarianism, on the other hand, pushes the role of utilitarian answers further back. Whether it is right to punish some particular person is a matter to be referred to a practice which must in turn be defined by a public rule. It is only when we ask questions about whether the publicly defined practice is itself justified that a utilitarian answer becomes appropriate. Rawls is confident that any public rule granting discretion to officials to punish someone simply for the good of it, regardless of whether that person committed any crime, could not be justified on utilitarian grounds. It would create too much insecurity and fear.

Rawls's account of the justification of punishment has raised some new questions. Two of these concern the rationale for adhering to a practice defined by a public rule: If it clearly would do the most good overall to trump up charges against, and punish, an innocent person, what is the utilitarian reason for adhering to the rule, or is there some nonutilitarian principle operating here—one that is in conflict with utilitarian ideas? And what philosophical justification can be given for the notion that the rules officials are to follow in imposing punishments must be *public* rules?[3] Finally, it has been suggested that a rule utilitarian theory like Rawls's might still authorize punishing, say, an uninvolved relative of a wrongdoer, purely on a basis of vicarious liability.[4]

Jean Hampton's (1984) article on the moral education theory of punishment represents yet another kind of attempt to combine utilitarian and retributivist insights into a single theory. Recall that one of the standing objections to the utilitarian theory is that it proposes, in effect, to use one person for the good of others, recommending that we inflict suffering in order to deter others from crime and thus to provide for the general safety. Not only does this involve using one for the good of others, but the punishment operates only as a simple threat, appealing to fear and self-interest rather than to one's moral capacities. It is the sort of thing one does when one raises a stick before a dog. Retributivism disallows the punishment of any person for the purpose of advancing a social goal.

But in its rejection of the idea that punishment has a goal, retributivism seems to go too far, making it hard to understand why we should be engaging in this activity at all. Hampton claims that punishment does have a goal, though it is a very specific and focused goal, having to do with the good of the person who is punished. The function of punishment, in her view, is to teach a moral lesson, to communicate something. As such, punishment presupposes, rather than denies, the moral capacities of those to whom the criminal law is addressed. Since punishment's aim is to communicate a moral lesson which if successful will improve the offender, it does not involve using the offender for the benefit of others.

Hampton's view raises a number of questions. If the decision to punish depends on whether it is likely to teach a moral lesson, what about criminals who are so hardened that they are beyond being taught a lesson? And is imprisonment, or any kind of infliction of suffering for that matter, really the best way to teach a moral lesson?

---

[3] For a discussion of this, see Conrad D. Johnson, *Moral Legislation* (New York: Cambridge University Press, 1991), Chaps 3–4.

[4] See David A.J. Richards, *The Moral Criticism of Law* (Encino and Belmont, Calif.: Dickenson Publishing Co., 1977), pp. 234–35.

**Cases.** The cases in this part show some of the interesting ways in which decisions about the existing law have touched on philosophical theories of punishment. The Supreme Court case of *Gregg v. Georgia* (1976) addresses the question of the constitutional permissibility of capital punishment in light of the Eighth Amendment's prohibition on "cruel and unusual punishments." In the interpretation of this rather vague phrase, *Gregg* takes seriously the opinions and standards of decency prevailing in American society about punishment, particularly as those standards are expressed in federal and state legislation. While the Supreme Court takes consistency with existing standards of decency as something close to a necessary condition for punishment's not being cruel and unusual, this is not a sufficient condition. In the two-level system, in which the trial has both a guilt phase and a sentencing phase, the legislature must have taken concrete steps to limit arbitrariness and discretion on the part of the jury. The majority opinion lists the sorts of questions which, the legislature deemed, must be answered by the jury in their deliberations about inflicting the death penalty.

The Supreme Court case of *Payne v. Tennessee* (1991) is philosophically interesting for several reasons. It could just as easily have been included in any of two or three other parts of this book. The primary issue in *Payne* was the kind of consideration that can properly go into a jury's thinking in their decision whether to impose the death penalty. Is it allowable to let the jury hear about the good moral character of the victim and the impact of the crime on the victim's family? Or should the presentation of such evidence be disallowed on grounds that it is irrelevant and is likely only to inflame the emotions of the jury?

Each side in this issue can trace connections to a deeper philosophical debate in moral philosophy. On the one side there are those who hold that punishment and blame are properly directed at the wrongdoer and the wrongdoer's culpability. This, they say, is a question that focuses exclusively on the wrongdoer's *internal will*, that is, the wrongdoer's intentions and knowledge. If we compare two equally evil wrongdoers *A* and *B* who have equally evil intentions, perhaps *A*'s crime had worse consequences for the victim's family and friends than *B*'s crime did. But that is an accidental fact that has no bearing on the comparative culpability of *A* and *B*.

On the other side there are those who say that culpability and blameworthiness are partly a matter of *moral luck*.[5] If *A*'s crime had worse consequences for its victims than *B*'s crime did, then *A* is indeed more culpable and deserving of more severe punishment, and that is just the way it turned out. If you do wrong, you assume a risk that things will go especially badly, and your culpability will be greater than that of a wrongdoer who has better moral luck.

The majority in *Payne v. Tennessee* weigh in on the side of "moral luck" rather than on the side of the "internal will" school of thought about culpability. But it was exactly the other way around in the earlier case of *Booth v. Maryland* (1987). In that case Justice Scalia was in the dissenting minority when he wrote that "the amount of harm one causes does bear upon the extent of his 'personal responsibility.'"

The dramatic departure from *Booth* gives rise to a second heatedly debated issue in *Payne*: that concerning the role of *stare decisis*, the doctrine that the decisions in earlier cases set a precedent that must be followed. May earlier decisions like that of *Booth v.*

---

[5]On moral luck, see Thomas Nagel, "Moral Luck" in *Mortal Questions* (New York: Cambridge University Press, 1979), Chap. 3; and Bernard Williams, *Moral Luck* (New York: Cambridge University Press, 1981), Chap. 2.

*Maryland* be overruled? Do consistency and continuity require a court to adhere to an earlier decision even if it is assumed that the decision was mistaken? Or is it both desirable as well as just to undo a mistaken decision once the mistake is recognized? The opinions in *Payne* thus recall and further illuminate some issues about legal reasoning that were explored in Parts 3 and 5 of this book.

# Retributivism

## Immanuel Kant

# PENAL LAW AND THE UNIVERSAL PRINCIPLE OF JUSTICE*

### OF THE SUBDIVISION OF A METAPHYSICS OF MORALS

All legislation (whether it prescribes internal or external actions, and these either a priori through mere reason or through another person's will) consists of two elements: first, a law that objectively represents the action that is to be done as necessary, that is, that makes the action a duty; second, an incentive that subjectively links the ground determining will to this action with the representation of the law. So this second element amounts to this, that the law makes duty the incentive. Through the former element, the action is represented as a duty; as such, it is mere theoretical knowledge of the possible determination of will, that is, a knowledge of practical rules. Through the latter element, the obligation so to act is combined in the subject with a determining ground of will in general.

Therefore (even though one legislation may agree with another with regard to actions that are required as duties; for example, the actions might in all cases be external ones) all legislation can nevertheless be differentiated with regard to the incentives. If legislation makes an action a duty and at the same time makes this duty the incentive, it is *ethical*. If it does not include the latter condition in the law and therefore admits an incentive other than the Idea of duty itself, it is *juridical*. As regards juridical legislation, it is easily seen that the incentive here, being different from the Idea of duty, must be derived from pathological grounds determining will, that is, from inclinations and disinclinations and, among these, specifically from disinclinations, since it is supposed to be the kind of legislation that constrains, not an allurement that invites.

The mere agreement or disagreement of an action with the law, without regard to the incentive of the action , is called *legality*; but, when the Idea of duty arising from the law is at the same time the incentive of the action, then the agreement is called the *morality* of the action.

Duties in accordance with juridical legislation can be only external duties because such legislation does not require that the Idea of this duty, which is internal, be of itself the ground determining the will of the agent. Because such legislation still requires a suitable incentive for the law, it can combine only external incentives with the law. On the other hand, ethical legislation also makes internal actions duties, but does not, however, exclude external actions; rather, it applies generally to everything that is a duty. But, for the very reason that ethical legislation includes in its law the internal incentive of the action (the Idea of duty), which is a determination that must by no means be mixed with external legislation, ethical legislation cannot be external (not even the external legislation of a divine Will), although it may adopt duties that rest on external legislation and take them, insofar as they are duties, as incentives in its own legislation.

From this it can be seen that all duties, simply because they are duties, belong to Ethics.[12] But their legislation is not therefore always included under Ethics; in the case of many duties, it is quite outside Ethics. Thus, Ethics commands me to fulfill my pledge

---

*Reprinted by permission of Macmillan Publishing Company from *The Metaphysical Elements of Justice* translated by John Ladd. Copyright © 1985 by Macmillan Publishing Company. Copyright © 1965. Some footnotes have been deleted.

[12][*Ethik* is translated "Ethics," with a capital E; "ethics" is the translation of *Tugendlehre*. For the most part, Kant uses these terms interchangeably.]

given in a contract, even though the other party could not compel me to do so; but the law (*pacta sunt servanda*[13]) and the duty corresponding to it are taken by Ethics from jurisprudence. Accordingly, the legislation that promises must be kept is contained in *jus*,[14] and not in Ethics. Ethics teaches only that, if the incentive that juridical legislation combines with that duty, namely, external coercion, were absent, the Idea of duty alone would still be sufficient as an incentive. If this were not so and if the legislation itself were not juridical and the duty arising from it thus not properly a duty of justice (in contradistinction to a duty of virtue), then keeping faith (in accordance with one's promise in a contract) would be put in the same class with actions of benevolence and the manner in which we are bound to perform them as a duty, and this certainly must not happen. It is not a duty of virtue to keep one's promise, but a duty of justice, one that we can be coerced to perform. Nevertheless, it is a virtuous action (proof of virtue) to do so where no coercion is to be feared. Jurisprudence and ethics [*Rechtslehre* and *Tugendlehre*] are distinguished, therefore, not so much by their differing duties as by the difference in the legislation that combines one or the other incentive with the law.

Ethical legislation is that which cannot be external (though the duties may be external); juridical legislation is that which can also be external. Thus, to keep one's promise in a contract is an external duty; but the command to do so merely because it is a duty, without regard to any other incentive, belongs only to internal legislation. Accordingly, this obligation is reckoned as belonging to Ethics, not as being a special kind of duty (a special kind of action to which one is bound)—for it is an external

duty in Ethics as well as in justice[15]—but because the legislation in this case is internal and cannot have an external legislator. For the same reason, duties of benevolence, though they are external duties (obligations to external actions), are reckoned as belonging to Ethics because their legislation can only be internal.

To be sure, Ethics also has duties peculiar to itself (for example, duties to oneself); but it also has duties in common with justice, though the manner of being bound to such duties differs. The peculiarity of ethical legislation is that it requires actions to be performed simply because they are duties and makes the basic principles of duty itself, no matter whence the duty arises, into the sufficient incentive of will. Hence, though there are many directly ethical duties, internal legislation also makes all the rest indirectly ethical. . . .

## § C. UNIVERSAL PRINCIPLE OF JUSTICE

"Every action is just [right] that in itself or in its maxim is such that the freedom of the will of each can coexist together with the freedom of everyone in accordance with a universal law."

If, therefore, my action or my condition in general can coexist with the freedom of everyone in accordance with a universal law, then anyone who hinders me in performing the action or in maintaining the condition does me an injustice, inasmuch as this hindrance (this opposition) cannot coexist with freedom in accordance with universal laws.

It also follows that I cannot be required to adopt as one of my maxims this principle of all maxims, that is, to make this principle a

---

[13]["Agreements ought to be kept."]

[14]["Right," "Law", "justice." This is the word that Kant translates *Rechtslehre* ("jurisprudence"). He uses *jus* here and *Recht* ("justice") later in the paragraph instead of *Rechtslehre* because these two nouns are of neuter gender, and, in his typical style, Kant wants to draw the distinction grammatically as well.]

[15][See note 14.]

maxim of my action. For anyone can still be free, even though I am quite indifferent to his freedom or even though I might in my heart wish to infringe on his freedom, as long as I do not through an external action violate his freedom. That I adopt as a maxim the maxim of acting justly is a requirement that Ethics [rather than jurisprudence] imposes on me.

Hence the universal law of justice is: act externally in such a way that the free use of your will is compatible with the freedom of everyone according to a universal law. Admittedly, this law imposes an obligation on me, but I am not at all expected, much less required, to restrict my freedom to these conditions for the sake of this obligation itself. Rather, reason says only that, in its very Idea, freedom is restricted in this way and may be so restricted by others in practice. Moreover, it states this as a postulate not susceptible of further proof. Given that we do not intend to teach virtue, but only to give an account of what is just, we may not and ought not to represent this law of justice as being itself an incentive.

## §D. JUSTICE IS UNITED WITH THE AUTHORIZATION TO USE COERCION

Any opposition that counteracts the hindrance of an effect promotes that effect and is consistent with it. Now, everything that is unjust is a hindrance to freedom according to universal laws. Coercion, however, is a hindrance or opposition to freedom. Consequently, if a certain use of freedom is itself a hindrance to freedom according to universal laws (that is, is unjust), then the use of coercion to counteract it, inasmuch as it is the prevention of a hindrance to freedom, is consistent with freedom according to universal laws; in other words, this use of coercion is just. It follows by the law of contradiction that justice [a right] is united with the autho-

rization to use coercion against anyone who violates justice [or a right]. . . .

## E. The Penal Law and the Law of Pardon

I [THE RIGHT TO PUNISH] The right to punish contained in the penal law [*das Strafrecht*] is the right that the magistrate has to inflict pain on a subject in consequence of his having committed a crime. It follows that the suzerain of the state cannot himself be punished; we can only remove ourselves from his jurisdiction. A transgression of the public law that makes him who commits it unfit to be a citizen is called either simply a crime (*crimen*) or a public crime (*crimen publicum*). [If, however, we call it a public crime, then we can use the term "crime" generically to include both private and public crimes.][11] The first (a private crime) is brought before a civil court, and the second (a public crime), before a criminal, court. Embezzlement, that is, misappropriation of money or wares entrusted in commerce, and fraud in buying and selling, if perpetrated before the eyes of the party who suffers, are private crimes. On the other hand, counterfeiting money or bills of exchange, theft, robbery, and similar acts are public crimes, because through them the commonwealth and not just a single individual is exposed to danger. These crimes may be divided into those of a base character (*indolis abjectae*) and those of a violent character (*indolis violentae*).

Judicial punishment (*poena forensis*) is entirely distinct from natural punishment (*poena naturalis*). In natural punishment, vice punishes itself, and this fact is not taken into consideration by the legislator. Judicial punishment can never be used merely as a means to promote some other good for the criminal himself or for civil society but instead it must in all cases be imposed on him only on the ground that he has committed a crime; for a human being can never be manipulated merely as a

---

[11] [Natorp and Cassirer agree that there is something wrong with the sentence following this one. Either a sentence has been omitted or the sentence in question has been misplaced. Kant's meaning is, however, perfectly clear, and I have inserted a sentence to provide the transition.]

means to the purposes of someone else and can never be confused with the objects of the Law of things [*Sachenrecht*]. His innate personality [that is, his right as a person] protects him against such treatment, even though he may indeed be condemned to lose his civil personality. He must first be found to be deserving of punishment before any consideration is given to the utility of this punishment for himself or for his fellow citizens. The law concerning punishment is a categorical imperative, and woe to him who rummages around in the winding paths of a theory of happiness looking for some advantage to be gained by releasing the criminal from punishment or by reducing the amount of it—in keeping with the Pharisaic motto: "It is better that one man should die than that the whole people should perish." If legal justice perishes, then it is no longer worth while for men to remain alive on this earth. If this is so, what should one think of the proposal to permit a criminal who has been condemned to death to remain alive, if, after consenting to allow dangerous experiments to be made on him, he happily survives such experiments and if doctors thereby obtain new information that benefits the community? Any court of justice would repudiate such a proposal with scorn if it were suggested by a medical college, for [legal] justice ceases to be justice if it can be bought for a price.

What kind and what degree of punishment does public legal justice adopt as its principle and standard? None other than the principle of equality (illustrated by the pointer on the scales of justice), that is, the principle of not treating one side more favorably than the other. Accordingly, any undeserved evil that you inflict on someone else among the people is one that you do to yourself. If you vilify him, you vilify yourself; if you steal from him, you steal from yourself; if you kill him, you kill yourself. Only the Law of retribution (*jus talionis*) can determine exactly the kind and degree of punishment; it must be well understood, however, that this determination [must be made] in the chambers of a court of justice (and not in your private judgment). All other standards fluctuate back and forth and, because extraneous considerations are mixed with them, they cannot be compatible with the principle of pure and strict legal justice.

Now it might seem that the existence of class distinctions would not allow for the [application of the] retributive principle of returning like for like. Nevertheless, even though these class distinctions may not make it possible to apply this principle to the letter, it can still always remain applicable in its effects if regard is had to the special sensibilities of the higher classes. Thus, for example, the imposition of a fine for a verbal injury has no proportionality to the original injury, for someone who has a good deal of money can easily afford to make insults whenever he wishes. On the other hand, the humiliation of the pride of such an offender comes much closer to equaling an injury done to the honor of the person offended; thus the judgment and Law might require the offender, not only to make a public apology to the offended person, but also at the same time to kiss his hand, even though he be socially inferior. Similarly, if a man of a higher class has violently attacked an innocent citizen who is socially inferior to him, he may be condemned, not only to apologize but to undergo solitary and painful confinement, because by this means, in addition to the discomfort suffered, the pride of the offender will be painfully affected, and thus his humiliation will compensate for the offense as like for like.

But what is meant by the statement: "If you steal from him, you steal from yourself"? Inasmuch as someone steals, he makes the ownership of everyone else insecure, and hence he robs himself (in accordance with the Law of retribution) of the security of any possible ownership. He has nothing and can also acquire nothing, but he still wants to live, and this is not possible unless others provide him with nourishment. But, because the state will not support him gratis, he must let the state have his labor at any kind of work it may wish to use him for (convict labor), and so he becomes a slave, either for a certain period of time or indefinitely, as the case may be.

If, however, he has committed a murder, he must die. In this case, there is no substitute that will satisfy the requirements of legal justice. There is no sameness of kind between death and remaining alive even under the most miserable conditions, and consequently there is also no equality between the crime and the retribution unless the criminal is judicially condemned and put to death. But the death of the criminal must be kept entirely free of any maltreatment that would make an abomination of the humanity residing in the person suffering it. Even if a civil society were to dissolve itself by common agreement of all its members (for example, if the people inhabiting an island decided to separate and disperse themselves around the world), the last murderer remaining in prison must first be executed, so that everyone will duly receive what his actions are worth and so that the bloodguilt thereof will not be fixed on the people because they failed to insist on carrying out the punishment; for if they fail to do so, they may be regarded as accomplices in this public violation of legal justice.

Furthermore, it is possible for punishment to be equal in accordance with the strict Law of retribution only if the judge pronounces the death sentence. This is clear because only in this way will the death sentence be pronounced on all criminals in proportion to their inner viciousness (even if the crime involved is not murder, but some other crime against the state that can be expiated only by death). To illustrate this point, let us consider a situation, like the last Scottish rebellion, in

which the participants are motivated by varying purposes, just as in that rebellion some believed that they were only fulfilling their obligations to the house of Stuart (like Balmerino and others),[12] and others, in contrast, were pursuing their own private interests. Suppose that the highest court were to pronounce as follows: Each person shall have the freedom to choose between death and penal servitude. I say that a man of honor would choose death and that the knave would choose servitude. This is implied by the nature of human character, because the first recognizes something that he prizes more highly than life itself, namely, honor whereas the second thinks that a life covered with disgrace is still better than not being alive at all (*animam praeferre pudori*).[13] The first is without doubt less deserving of punishment than the other, and so, if they are both condemned to die, they will be punished exactly in proportion [to their inner viciousness]; the first will be punished mildly in terms of his kind of sensibility, and the second will be punished severely in terms of his kind of sensibility. On the other hand, if both were condemned to penal servitude, the first would be punished too severely and the second too mildly for their baseness. Thus, even in sentences imposed on a number of criminals united in a plot, the best equalizer before the bar of public legal justice is death.

It may also be pointed out that no one has ever heard of anyone condemned to death on account of murder who complained that he was getting too much [punishment] and therefore was being treated unjustly; everyone would laugh in his face if he were to make such a statement. Indeed, otherwise we would have to

---

[12][Arthur Elphinstone, Sixth Baron Balmerino (1688–1746), participated in the Jacobite rebellion that attempted to put Prince Charles Edward Stuart on the British throne. He was captured, tried, found guilty, and beheaded. He is said to have acted throughout with great constancy and courage.]

[13]["To prefer life to honor"—Juvenal, *Satire* 8. 83. The complete text, lines 79–84, is quoted by Kant in the *Critique of Practical Reason*, Part II: "Be a stout soldier, a faithful guardian, and an incorruptible judge; if summoned to bear witness in some dubious and uncertain cause, though Phalaris himself should command you to tell lies and bring up his bull and dictate to you a perjury, count it the greatest of all sins to prefer life to honour, and to lose, for the sake of living, all that makes life worth having." Trans. G. G. Ramsey, "Loeb classical Library." (Phalaris, tyrant of Agrigentum, had criminals burned to death in a brass ox.)]

assume that, although the treatment accorded the criminal is not unjust according to the law, the legislative authority still is not authorized to decree this kind of punishment and that, if it does so, it comes into contradiction with itself.

Anyone who is a murderer—that is, has committed a murder, commanded one, or taken part in one—must suffer death. This is what [legal] justice as the Idea of the judicial authority wills in accordance with universal laws that are grounded a priori. The number of accomplices (*correi*) in such a deed might, however, be so large that the state would soon approach the condition of having no more subjects if it were to rid itself of these criminals, and this would lead to its dissolution and a return to the state of nature, which is much worse, because it would be a state of affairs without any external legal justice whatsoever. Since a sovereign will want to avoid such consequences and above all, will want to avoid adversely affecting the feelings of the people by the spectacle of such butchery, he must have it within his power in case of necessity (*casus necessitatis*) to assume the role of judge and to pronounce a judgment that, instead of imposing the death penalty on the criminals, assigns some other punishment that will make the preservation of the mass of the people possible, such as, for example, deportation. Such a course of action would not come under a public law, but would be an executive decree [*Machtspruch*], that is, an act based on the right of majesty, which, as an act of reprieve, can be exercised only in individual cases.

In opposition to this view, the Marquis of Beccaria,[14] moved by sympathetic sentimentality and an affectation of humanitarianism, has asserted that all capital punishment is illegitimate. He argues that it could not be contained in the original civil contract, inasmuch as this would imply that every one of the people has agreed to forfeit his life if he murders another (of the people); but such an agreement would be impossible, for no one can dispose of his own life.

No one suffers punishment because he has willed the punishment, but because he has willed a punishable action. If what happens to someone is also willed by him, it cannot be a punishment. Accordingly, it is impossible to will to be punished. To say, "I will to be punished if I murder someone," can mean nothing more than, "I submit myself along with everyone else to those laws which, if there are any criminals among the people, will naturally include penal laws." In my role as colegislator making the penal law, I cannot be the same person who, as subject, is punished by the law; for, as a subject who is also a criminal, I cannot have a voice in legislation. (The legislator is holy.) When, therefore, I enact a penal law against myself as a criminal it is the pure juridical legislative reason (*homo noumenon*) in me that submits myself to the penal law as a person capable of committing a crime, that is, as another person (*homo phaenomenon*) along with all the others in the civil union who submit themselves to this law. In other words, it is not the people (considered as individuals) who dictate the death penalty, but the court (public legal justice); that is, someone other than the criminal. The social contract does not include the promise to permit oneself to be punished and thus to dispose of oneself and of one's life, because, if the only ground that authorizes the punishment of an evildoer were a promise that expresses his willingness to be punished, then it would have to be left up to him to find himself liable to punishment, and the criminal would be his own judge. The chief error contained in this sophistry (πρωτον ψευδος) consists in the confusion of the criminal's own judgment (which one must necessarily attribute to his reason) that he must forfeit

14[Cesare Bonesana, Marquis di Beccaria (1738–1794), Italian publicist. His *Dei delitti e delle pene* (1764) (*On Crimes and Punishments*, trans. Henry Paolucci, "The Library of Liberal Arts," No. 107 [New York:"The Liberal Arts press, 1963]) was widely read and had great influence on the reform of the penal codes of various European states.]

his life with a resolution of the Will to take his own life. The result is that the execution of the Law and the adjudication thereof are represented as united in the same person.

There remain, however, two crimes deserving of death with regard to which it still remains doubtful whether legislation is authorized to impose the death penalty. In both cases, the crimes are due to the sense of honor. One involves the honor of womanhood; the other, military honor. Both kinds of honor are genuine, and duty requires that they be sought after by every individual in each of these two classes. The first crime is infanticide at the hands of the mother (*infanticidium maternale*); the other is the murder of a fellow soldier (*commilitonicidium*) in a duel.

Now, legislation cannot take away the disgrace of an illegitimate child, nor can it wipe away the stain of suspicion of cowardice from a junior officer who fails to react to a humiliating affront with action that would show that he has the strength to overcome the fear of death. Accordingly, it seems that, in such circumstances, the individuals concerned find themselves in a state of nature, in which killing another (*homicidium*) can never be called murder (*homicidium dolosum*); in both cases, they are indeed deserving of punishment, but they cannot be punished with death by the supreme power. A child born into the world outside marriage is outside the law (for this is [implied by the concept of] marriage), and consequently it is also outside the protection of the law. The child has crept surreptitiously into the commonwealth (much like prohibited wares), so that its existence as well as its destruction can be ignored (because by right it ought not to have come into existence in this way); and the mother's disgrace if the illegitimate birth becomes known cannot be wiped out by any official decree.

Similarly, a military man who has been commissioned a junior officer may suffer an insult and as a result feel obliged by the opinions of his comrades in arms to seek satisfaction and to punish the person who insulted him, not by appealing to the law and taking him to court, but instead, as would be done in a state of nature, by challenging him to a duel; for even though in doing so he will be risking his life, he will thereby be able to demonstrate his military valor, on which the honor of his profession rests. If, under such circumstances his opponent should be killed, this cannot properly be called a murder (*homicidium dolosum*), inasmuch as it takes place in a combat openly fought with the consent of both parties, even though they may have participated in it only reluctantly.

What then, is the actual Law of the land with regard to these two cases (which come under criminal justice)? This question presents penal justice with a dilemma: either it must declare that the concept of honor (which is no delusion in these cases) is null and void in the eyes of the law and that these acts should be punished by death or it must abstain from imposing the death penalty for these crimes, which merit it; thus it must be either too cruel or too lenient. The solution to this dilemma is as follows: the categorical imperative involved in the legal justice of punishment remains valid (that is, the unlawful killing of another person must be punished by death), but legislation itself (including also the civil constitution), as long as it remains barbaric and undeveloped, is responsible for the fact that incentives of honor among the people do not accord (subjectively) with the standards that are (objectively) appropriate to their purpose, with the result that public legal justice as administered by the state is injustice from the point of view of the people.[15]

---

[15][See Appendix, §5. In the *Critique of Pure Reason*, trans. Kemp Smith, B 373, Kant writes: "The more legislation and government are brought into harmony with the . . . idea . . . (of a constitution allowing the *greatest possible human freedom* in accordance with laws by which the *freedom of each is made to be consistent with that of all others*) . . . the rarer would punishments become, and it is therefore quite rational to maintain, as Plato does, that in a perfect state no punishments whatsoever would be required." The order of the sentence has been changed.]

II [The Right to Pardon] The right to pardon a criminal (*jus aggratiandi*), either by mitigating or by entirely remitting the punishment, is certainly the most slippery of all the rights of the sovereign. By exercising it he can demonstrate the splendor of his majesty and yet thereby wreak injustice (*unrecht*) to a high degree. With respect to a crime of one subject against another, he absolutely cannot exercise this right, for in such cases exemption from punishment (*impunitas criminis*) constitutes the greatest injustice toward his subjects. Consequently, he can make use of this right of pardon only in connection with an injury committed against himself (*crimen laesae majestatis*). But, even in these cases, he cannot allow a crime to go unpunished if the safety of the people might be endangered thereby. The right to pardon is the only one that deserves the name of a "right of majesty.". . .

## QUESTIONS

1. In explaining the claim that, in stealing from someone, you steal from yourself, Kant says that someone who steals "makes the ownership of everyone else insecure. . . ." Does Kant mean that any single instance of theft, no matter how small or done in secret, threatens the security of ownership? Explain.

2. Kant says: "If what happens to someone is also willed by him, it cannot be a punishment." In what sense or senses, then, does Kant believe that punishment respects the will of the person being punished, and how is his view consistent with the quotation?

3. It is sometimes said that "You can't legislate morality." Explain, using Kant's distinction between the morality and the legality of an action, at least one thing that might be meant by this statement.

4. When addressing the question of the kind and amount of punishment required for a crime, Kant says that it is "None other than the principle of equality. . . , that is, the principle of not treating one side more favorable than the other". Using the various comments Kant makes on this subject, construct, as best you can, some helpful practical criteria to guide legislators and judges in assigning punishments according to the Kantian principle.

5. Kant says, "a human being can never be manipulated merely as a means to the purposes of someone else and can never be confused with the objects of the Law of things." Would a utilitarian theory of punishment like Bentham's satisfy this demand? Explain why or why not.

# Utilitarianism

# Jeremy Bentham
# PRINCIPLES OF MORALS AND LEGISLATION*

## CASES UNMEET FOR PUNISHMENT

### § I. General View of Cases Unmeet for Punishment.

I. The general object which all laws have, or ought to have, in common, is to augment the total happiness of the community; and therefore, in the first place, to exclude, as far as may be, everything that tends to subtract from that happiness: in other words, to exclude mischief.

II. But all punishment is mischief: all punishment in itself is evil. Upon the principle of utility, if it ought at all to be admitted, it ought only to be admitted in as far as it promises to exclude some greater evil[1].

III. It is plain, therefore, that in the following cases punishment ought not to be inflicted.

1. Where it is *groundless:* where there is no mischief for it to prevent; the act not being mischievous upon the whole.

2. Where it must be *inefficacious:* where it cannot act so as to prevent the mischief.

3. Where it is *unprofitable*, or too *expensive:* where the mischief it would produce would be greater than what it prevented.

4. Where it is *needless:* where the mischief may be prevented, or cease of itself, without it: that is, at a cheaper rate.

### § 2. Cases in Which Punishment Is Groundless.

These are,

IV. I. Where there has never been any mischief: where no mischief has been produced to any body by the act in question. Of this number are those in which the act was such as might, on some occasions, be mischievous or disagreeable, but the person whose interest it concerns gave his *consent* to the performance of it. This consent, provided it be free, and fairly obtained, is the best proof that can be produced, that, to the person who gives it, no mischief, at least no immediate mischief, upon the whole, is done. For no man can be so good a judge as the man himself, what it is gives him pleasure or displeasure.

*From *The Principles of Morals and Legislation* (1823), Chaps. 13–14. First published in 1789. Annotations, all footnotes to footnotes, and some footnotes have been deleted.

[1]What follows, relative to the subject of punishment, ought regularly to be preceded by a distinct chapter on the ends of punishment. But having little to say on that particular branch of the subject, which has not been said before, it seemed better, in a work, which will at any rate be but too voluminous, to omit this title, reserving it for another, hereafter to be published, intituled *The Theory of Punishment*. To the same work I must refer the analysis of the several possible modes of punishment, a particular and minute examination of the nature of each, and of its advantages and disadvantages, and various other disquisitions, which did not seem absolutely necessary to be inserted here. A very few words, however, concerning the *ends* of punishment, can scarcely be dispensed with.

The immediate principal end of punishment is to control action. This action is either that of the offender, or of others: that of the offender it controls by its influence, either on his will, in which case it is said to operate in the way of *reformation*; or on his physical power in which case it is said to operate by *disablement*: that of others it can influence no otherwise than by its influence over their wills; in which case it is said to operate in the way of *example*. A kind of collateral end, which it has a natural tendency to answer, is that of affording a pleasure or satisfaction to the party injured, where there is one, and, in general, to parties whose ill-will, whether on a self-regarding account, or on the account of sympathy or antipathy, has been excited by the offence. This purpose, as far as it can be answered *gratis*, is a beneficial one. But no punishment ought to be allotted merely to this purpose, because (setting aside its effects in the way of control) no such pleasure is ever produced by punishment as can be equivalent to the pain. The punishment, however, which is allotted to the other purpose, ought, as far as it can be done without expense, to be accommodated to this. Satisfaction thus administered to a party injured, in the shape of a dissocial pleasure, may be styled a vindictive satisfaction or compensation: as a compensation, administered in the shape of a self-regarding profit, or stock of pleasure, may be styled a lucrative one. See B. L. tit. vi [Compensation]. Example is the most important end of all, in proportion as the *number* of the persons under temptation to offend is to *one*.

V. 2. Where the mischief was *outweighed*: although a mischief was produced by that act, yet the same act was necessary to the production of a benefit which was of greater value[1] than the mischief. This may be the case with any thing that is done in the way of precaution against instant calamity, as also with any thing that is done in the exercise of the several sorts of powers necessary to be established in every community, to wit, domestic, judicial, military, and supreme[2].

VI. 3. Where there is a certainty of an adequate compensation: and that in all cases where the offence can be committed. This supposes two things: 1. That the offence is such as admits of an adequate compensation: 2. That such a compensation is sure to be forthcoming. Of these suppositions, the latter will be found to be a merely ideal one: a supposition that cannot, in the universality here given to it, be verified by fact. It cannot, therefore, in practice, be numbered amongst the grounds of absolute impunity. It may, however, be admitted as a ground for an abatement of that punishment, which other considerations, standing by themselves, would seem to dictate[3].

§ 3. Cases in Which Punishment Must Be Inefficacious.

These are,

VII. I. Where the penal provision is *not established* until after the act is done. Such are the cases, 1. Of an *ex-post facto* law; where the legislator himself appoints not a punishment till after the act is done. 2. Of a sentence beyond the law; where the judge, of his own authority, appoints a punishment which the legislator had not appointed.

VIII. 2. Where the penal provision, though established, is *not conveyed* to the notice of the person on whom it seems intended that it should operate. Such is the case where the law has omitted to employ any of the expedients which are necessary, to make sure that every person whatsoever, who is within the reach of the law, be apprized of all the cases whatsoever, in which (being in the station of life he is in) he can be subjected to the penalties of the law[1].

IX. 3. Where the penal provision, though it were conveyed to a man's notice, *could produce no effect* on him, with respect to the preventing him from engaging in any act of the *sort* in question. Such is the case, 1. In extreme *infancy*; where a man has not yet attained that state or disposition of mind in which the prospect of evils so distant as those which are held forth by the law, has the effect of influencing his conduct. 2. In *insanity*, where the person, if he has attained to that disposition, has since been deprived of it through the influence of some permanent though unseen cause. 3. In *intoxication*; where he has been deprived of it by the transient influence of a visible cause: such as the use of wine, or opium, or other drugs, that act in this manner on the nervous system: which condition is indeed neither more nor less than a temporary insanity produced by an assignable cause[2].

[1]See supra, ch. iv. [Value].

[2]See Book I. tit. [Justifications].

[3]This, for example, seems to have been one ground, at least, of the favour shown by perhaps all systems of laws, to such offenders as stand upon a footing of responsibility: shown, not directly indeed to the persons themselves; but to such offences as none but responsible persons are likely to have the opportunity of engaging in. In particular, this seems to be the reason why embezzlement, in certain cases, has not commonly been punished upon the footing of theft: nor mercantile frauds upon that of common sharping.

[1]See B. II. Appendix, tit. iii. [Promulgation].

[2]Notwithstanding what is here said, the cases of infancy and intoxication (as we shall see hereafter) cannot be looked upon in practice as affording sufficient grounds for absolute impunity. But this exception in point of practice is no objection to the propriety of the rule in point of theory. The ground of the exception is neither more nor less than the difficulty there is of ascertaining the matterr of fact: viz. whether at the requisite point of time the party was actually in the state of question; that is, whether a given case comes really under the rule. Suppose the matter of fact capable of being perfectly asertained, without danger or mistake, the impropriety of punishment would be as indubitable in these cases as in any other.

X. 4. Where the penal provision (although, being conveyed to the party's notice, it might very well prevent his engaging in those acts of the sort in question, provided he knew that it related to those acts) could not have this effect, with regard to the *individual* act he is about to engage in: to wit, because he knows not that it is of the number of those to which the penal provision relates. This may happen, 1. In the case of *unintentionality*; where he intends not to engage, and thereby knows not that he is about to engage, in the *act* in which eventually he is about to engage[1]. 2. In the case of *unconsciousness*; where, although he may know that he is about to engage in the act itself, yet, from not knowing all the material *circumstances* attending it, he knows not of the *tendency* it has to produce that mischief, in contemplation of which it has been made penal in most instances. 3. In the case of *missupposal*; where, although he may know of the tendency the act has to produce that degree of mischief, he supposes it, though mistakenly, to be attended with some circumstance, or set of circumstances, which if it had been attended with, it would either not have been productive of that mischief, or have been productive of such a greater degree of good, as has determined the legislator in such a case not to make it penal[2].

XI. 5. Where, though the penal clause might exercise a full and prevailing influence, were it to act alone, yet by the *predomi-* *nant* influence of some opposite cause upon the will, it must necessarily be ineffectual; because the evil which he sets himself about to undergo, in the case of his *not* engaging in the act, is so great, that the evil denounced by the penal clause, in case of his engaging in it, cannot appear greater. This may happen, 1. In the case of *physical danger*; where the evil is such as appears likely to be brought about by the unassisted powers of *nature*. 2. In the case of a *threatened mischief*; where it is such as appears likely to be brought about through the intentional and conscious agency of *man*[1].

XII. 6. Where (though the penal clause may exert a full and prevailing influence over the *will* of the party) yet his *physical faculties* (owing to the predominant influence of some physical cause) are not in a condition to follow the determination of the will: insomuch that the act is absolutely *involuntary*. Such is the case of physical *compulsion* or *restraint*, by whatever means brought about; where the man's hand, for instance, is pushed against some object which his will disposes him *not* to touch; or tied down from touching some object which his will disposes him to touch.

## § 4. Cases Where Punishment Is Unprofitable.

These are,

XIII. 1. Where, on the one hand, the nature of the offence, on the other hand, that of the

---

The reason that is commonly assigned for the establishing an exemption from punishment in favour of infants, insane persons, and persons under intoxication, is either false in fact, or confusedly expressed. The phrase is, that the will of these persons concurs not with the act; that they have no vicious will; or, that they have not the free use of their will. But suppose all this to be true? What is it to the purpose? Nothing: except in as far as it implies the reason given in the text.

[1]See ch. viii. [Intentionality].

[2]See ch. ix. [Consciousness].

[1]The influences of the *moral* and *religious* sanctions, or, in other words, of the motives of *love of reputation* and *religion*, are other causes, the force of which may, upon particular occasions, come to be greater than that of any punishment which the legislator is *able*, or at least which he will *think proper*, to apply. These, therefore, it will be proper for him to have his eye upon. But the force of these influences is variable and different in different times and places: the force of the foregoing influences is constant and the same, at all times and every where. These, therefore, it can never be proper to look upon as safe grounds for establishing absolute impunity: owing (as in the above-mentioned cases of infancy and intoxication) to the impracticability of ascertaining the matter of fact.

punishment, are, *in the ordinary state of things*, such, that when compared together, the evil of the latter will turn out to be greater than that of the former.

XIV. Now the evil of the punishment divides itself into four branches, by which so many different sets of persons are affected. 1. The evil of *coercion* or *restraint*: or the pain which it gives a man not to be able to do the act, whatever it be, which by the apprehension of the punishment he is deterred from doing. This is felt by those by whom the law is *observed*. 2. The evil of *apprehension*: or the pain which a man, who has exposed himself to punishment, feels at the thoughts of undergoing it. This is felt by those by whom the law has been *broken*, and who feel themselves in *danger* of its being executed upon them. 3. The evil of *sufferance*[1]: or the pain which a man feels, in virtue of the punishment itself, from the time when he begins to undergo it. This is felt by those by whom the law is broken, and upon whom it comes actually to be executed. 4. The pain of sympathy, and the other *derivative* evils resulting to the persons who are in *connection* with the several classes of original sufferers just mentioned.[2] Now of these four lots of evil, the first will be greater or less, according to the nature of the act from which the party is restrained; the second and third according to the nature of the punishment which stands annexed to that offence.

XV. On the other hand, as to the evil of the offence, this will also, of course, be greater or less, according to the nature of each offence. The proportion between the one evil and the other will therefore be different in the case of each particular offence. The cases, therefore, where punishment is unprofitable on this ground, can by no other means be discovered, than by an examination of each particular offence;which is what will be the business of the body at work.

XVI. 2. Where, although in the *ordinary state* of things, the evil resulting from the punishment is not greater than the benefit which is likely to result from the force with which it operates, during the same space of time, towards the excluding the evil of the offences, yet it may have been rendered so by the influence of some *occasional circumstances*. In the number of these circumstances may be, 1. The multitude of delinquents at a particular juncture; being such as would increase, beyond the ordinary measure, the *quantum* of the second and third lots, and thereby also of a part of the fourth lot, in the evil of the punishment. 2. The extraordinary value of the services of some one delinquent; in the case where the effect of the punishment would be to deprive the community of the benefit of those services. 3. The displeasure of the *people*; that is, of an indefinite number of the members of the *same* community, in cases where (owing to the influence of some occasional incident) they happen to conceive, that the offence or the offender ought not to be punished at all, or at least ought not to be punished in the way in question. 4. The displeasure of *foreign powers*; that is, of some governing body, or a considerable number of the members of some *foreign* community or communities, with which the community in question is connected.

### § 5. Cases Where Punishment Is Needless.

These are,

XVII. I. Where the purpose of putting an end to the practice may be attained as effectually at a cheaper rate; by instruction, for instance, as well as by terror; by informing the understanding, as well as by exercising an immediate influence on the will. This seems to be the case with respect to all those offences which consist in the disseminating pernicious principles in matters of duty; of whatever kind the duty be; whether political, or

---

[1]See ch. v. [Pleasures and Pains].
[2]See ch. xii. [Consequences] iv.

moral, or religious. And this, whether such principles be disseminated *under*, or even *without*, a sincere persuasion of their being beneficial. I say, even *without*: for though in such a case it is not instruction that can prevent the writer from endeavouring to inculcate his principles, yet it may the readers from adopting them: without which, his endeavouring to inculcate them will do no harm. In such a case, the sovereign will commonly have little need to take an active part: if it be the interest of *one* individual to inculcate principles that are pernicious, it will as surely be the interest of *other* individuals to expose them. But if the sovereign must needs take a part in the controversy, the pen is the proper weapon to combat error with, not the sword.

## OF THE PROPORTION BETWEEN PUNISHMENTS AND OFFENSES

I. We have seen that the general object of all laws is to prevent mischief; that is to say, when it is worth while; but that, where there are no other means of doing this than punishment, there are four cases in which it is *not* worth while.

II. When it *is* worth while, there are four subordinate designs or objects, which, in the course of his endeavours to compass, as far as may be, that one general object, a legislator, whose views are governed by the principle of utility, comes naturally to propose to himself.

III. 1. His first, most extensive, and most eligible object is to prevent, in as far as it is possible, and worth while, all sorts of offences whatsoever[1]: in other words, so to manage, that no offence whatsoever may be committed.

IV. 2. But if a man must needs commit an offence of some kind or other, the next object is to induce him to commit an offence *less* mischievous, *rather* than one *more* mischievous: in other words, to choose always the *least* mischievous, of two offenses that will either of them suit his purpose.

V. 3. When a man has resolved upon a particular offence, the next object is to dispose him to do *no more* mischief than is *necessary* to his purpose: in other words, to do as little mischief as is consistent with the benefit he has in view.

VI. 4. The last object is, whatever the mischief be, which it is proposed to prevent, to prevent it at as *cheap* a rate as possible.

VII. Subservient to these four objects, or purposes, must be the rules or canons by which the proportion of punishments[1] to offences is to be governed.

VIII. Rule. I. I. The first object, it has been seen, is to prevent, in as far as it is worth while, all sorts of offenses; therefore

*The value of the punishment must not be less in any case than what is sufficient to outweigh that of the profit[2] of the offence[3].*

---

[1]By *offences* I mean, at present, acts which appear to him to have a tendency to produce mischief

[1]The same rules (it is to be observed) may be applied, with little variation, to rewards as well as punishment: in short, to motives in general, which, according as they are of the pleasurable or painful kind, are of the nature of *reward* or *punishment*: and, according as the act they are applied to produce is of the positive or negative kind, are styled impelling or restraining.

[2]By the profit of an offence, is to be understood, not merely the pecuniary profit, but the pleasure or advantage, of whatever kind it be, which a man reaps, or expects to reap, from the gratification of the desire which prompted him to engage in the offence.

It is the profit (that is, the expectation of the profit) of the offence that constitutes the *impelling* motive, or, where there are several, the sum of the impelling motives, by which a man is prompted to engage in the offence. It is the punishment, that is, the expectation of the punishment, that constitutes the *restraining* motive, which, either by itself, or in conjunction with others, is to act upon him in a *contrary* direction, so as to induce him to abstain from engaging in the offence. Accidental circumstances apart, the strength of the temptation is as the force of the seducing, that is, of the impelling motive or motives. To say then, as authors of great merit and great name have said, that the punishment ought not to increase with the strength of the temptation, is as much as to say in

If it be, the offence (unless some other considerations, independent of the punishment, should intervene and operate efficaciously in the character of tutelary motives[4]) will be sure to be committed notwithstanding[5]: the whole lot of punishment will be thrown away: it will be altogether *inefficacious*[1].

IX. The above rule has been often objected to, on account of its seeming harshness: but this can only have happened for want of its being properly understood. The strength of the temptation, *coeteris paribus*, is as the profit of the offence: the quantum of the punishment must rise with the profit of the offence: *coeteris paribus*, it must therefore rise with the strength of the temptation. This there is no disputing. True it is, that the stronger the temptation, the less conclusive is the indication which the act of delinquency affords of the depravity of the offender's disposition[2]. So far then as the absence of any aggravation arising from extraordinary depravity of disposition, may operate, or at the utmost, so far as the presence of a ground of extenuation, resulting from the innocence or beneficence of the offender's disposition, can operate, the strength of the temptation may operate in

abatement of the demand for punishment. But it can never operate so far as to indicate the propriety of making the punishment ineffectual, which it is sure to be when brought below the level of the apparent profit of the offence.

The partial benevolence which should prevail for the reduction of it below this level, would counteract as well those purposes which such a motive would actually have in view, as those more extensive purposes which benevolence ought to have in view: it would be cruelty not only to the public, but to the very persons in whose behalf it pleads: in its effects, I mean, however opposite in its intention. Cruelty to the public, that is cruelty to the innocent, by suffering them, for want of an adequate protection, to lie exposed to the mischief of the offence: cruelty even to the offender himself, by punishing him to no purpose, and without the chance of compassing that beneficial end, by which alone the introduction of the evil of punishment is to be justified.

X. Rule 2. But whether a given offence shall be prevented in a given degree by a given quantity of punishment, is never any thing better than a chance; for the purchasing

---

mechanics, that the moving force or *momentum* of the *power* need not increase in proportion to the momentum of the *burthen*.

[3]Beccaria, dei diletti, § 6. id. trad. par. Morellet, § 23.

[4]See ch. xi. [Dispositions] xxix.

[5]It is a well-known adage, though it is to be hoped not a true one, that every man has his price. It is commonly meant of a man's virtue. This saying, though in a very different sense, was strictly verified by some of the Anglo-Saxon laws: by which a fixed price was set, not upon a man's virtue indeed, but upon his life: that of the sovereign himself among the rest. For 200 shillings you might have killed a peasant: for six times as much, a nobleman: for six-and-thirty times as much you might have killed the king. A king in those days was worth exactly 7,200 shillings. If then the heir to the throne, for example, grew weary of waiting for it, he had a secure and legal way of gratifying his impatience: he had but to kill the king with one hand, and pay himself with the other, and all was right. An earl Godwin, or a duke Streon, could have bought the lives of a whole dynasty. It is plain, that if ever a king in those days died in his bed, he must have had something else, besides this law, to thank for it. This being the production of a remote and barbarous age, the absurdity of it is presently recognised: but, upon examination, it would be found, that the freshest laws of the most civilised nations are continually falling into the same error. This, in short, is the case wheresoever the punishment is fixed while the profit of delinquency is indefinite: or, to speak more precisely, where the punishment is limited to such a mark, that the profit of delinquency may reach beyond it.

[1]See ch. xiii. [Cases unmeet], § I.

[2]See ch. xi. [Dispositions], xlii.

of which, whatever punishment is employed, is so much expended in advance. However, for the sake of giving it the better chance of outweighing the profit of the offence.

*The greater the mischief of the offence, the greater is the expense, which it may be worth while to be at, in the way of punishment*[1].

XI. Rule 3. The next object is, to induce a man to choose always the least mischievous of two offenses; therefore

*Where two offenses come in competition, the punishment for the greater offence must be sufficient to induce a man to prefer the less*[2].

XII. Rule 4. When a man has resolved upon a particular offence, the next object is, to induce him to do no more mischief than what is necessary for his purpose: therefore

*The punishment should be adjusted in such manner to each particular offence, that for every part of the mischief there may be a motive to restrain the offender from giving birth to it*[3].

XIII. Rule 5. The last object is, whatever mischief is guarded against, to guard against it at as cheap a rate as possible: therefore

*The punishment ought in no case to be more than what is necessary to bring it into conformity with the rules here given*

XIV. Rule 6. It is further to be observed, that owing to the different manners and degrees in which persons under different circumstances are affected by the same exciting cause, a punishment which is the same in name will not always either really produce, or even so much as appear to others to produce, in two different persons the same degree of pain: therefore

*That the quantity actually inflicted on each individual offender may correspond to the quantity intended for similar offenders in general, the several circumstances influencing sensibility ought always to be taken into account*[1].

XV. Of the above rules of proportion, the four first, we may perceive, serve to mark out the limits on the side of diminution; the limits *below* which a punishment ought not to be *diminished*: the fifth, the limits on the side of increase; the limits *above* which it ought not to be *increased*. The five first are calculated to serve as guides to the legislator: the sixth is calculated, in some measure, indeed, for the same purpose; but principally for guiding the judge in his endeavours to conform, on both sides, to the intentions of the legislator.

XVI. Let us look back a little. The first rule, in order to render it more conveniently applicable to practice, may need perhaps to be a little particularly unfolded. It is to be observed, then, that for the sake of accuracy, it was necessary, instead of the word *quantity* to make use of the less perspicuous term *value*. For the word *quantity* will not properly include the circumstances either of certainty or proximity: circumstances which, in estimating the value of a lot of pain or pleasure,

---

[1] For example, if it can ever be worth while to be at the expense of so horrible a punishment as that of burning alive, it will be more so in the view of preventing such a crime as that of murder or incendiarism, than in the view of preventing the uttering of a piece of bad money.

[2] Espr. des Loix, L. vi. c. 16.

[3] If any one have any doubt of this, let him conceive the offence to be divided into as many separate offences as there are distinguishable parcels of mischief that result from it. Let it consist, for example, in a man's giving you ten blows, or stealing from you ten shillings. If then, for giving you ten blows , he is punished no more than for giving you five, the giving you five of these ten blows is an offence for which there is no punishment at all: which being understood, as often as a man gives you five blows, he will be sure to give you five more, since he may have the pleasure of giving you these five for nothing. In like manner, if for stealing from you ten shillings, he is punished no more than for stealing five, the stealing of the remaining five of those ten shillings is an offence for which there is no punishment at all. This rule is violated in almost every page of every body of laws I have ever seen.

The profit, it is to be observed, though frequently, is not constantly, proportioned to the mischief: for example, where a thief, along with the things he covets, steals others which are of no use to him. This may happen through wantonness, indolence, precipitation, &c. &c.

[1] See ch. vi. [Sensibility].

must always be taken into the account[1]. Now, on the one hand, a lot of punishment is a lot of pain; on the other hand, the profit of an offence is a lot of pleasure, or what is equivalent to it. But the profit of the offence *is* commonly more *certain* than the punishment, or, what comes to the same thing, *appears* so at least to the offender. It is at any rate commonly more *immediate*. It follows, therefore, that, in order to maintain its superiority over the profit of the offence, the punishment must have its value made up in some other way, in proportion to that whereby it falls short in the two points of *certainty* and *proximity*. Now there is no other way in which it can receive any addition to its *value*, but by receiving an addition in point of *magnitude*. Wherever then the value of the punishment falls short, either in point of *certainty*, or of *proximity*, of that of the profit of the offence, it must receive a proportionable addition in point of *magnitude*[2].

XVII. Yet farther. To make sure of giving the value of the punishment the superiority over that of the offence, it may be necessary, in some cases, to take into the account the profit not only of the *individual* offence to which the punishment is to be annexed, but also of such *other* offences of the *same sort* as the offender is likely to have already committed without detection. This random mode of calculation, severe as it is, it will be impossible to avoid having recourse to, in certain cases: in such, to wit, in which the profit is pecuniary, the chance of detection very small, and the obnoxious act of such a nature as indicates a habit: for example, in the case of frauds against the coin. If it be *not* recurred to, the practice of committing the offence will be sure to be, upon the balance of the account, a gainful practice. That being the case, the legislator will be absolutely sure of *not*

being able to suppress it, and the whole punishment that is bestowed upon it will be thrown away. In a word (to keep to the same expressions we set out with) that whole quantity of punishment will be *inefficacious*.

XVIII. Rule 7. These things being considered, the three following rules may be laid down by way of supplement and explanation to Rule 1.

*To enable the value of the punishment to outweigh that of the profit of the offence, it must be increased, in point of magnitude, in proportion as it falls short in point of certainty.*

XIX. Rule 8. *Punishment must be further increased in point of magnitude, in proportion as it falls short in point of proximity.*

XX. Rule 9. *Where the act is conclusively indicative of a habit, such an increase must be given to the punishment as may enable it to outweigh the profit not only of the individual offence, but of such other like offences as are likely to have been committed with impunity by the same offender.*

XXI. There may be a few other circumstances or considerations which may influence, in some small degree, the demand for punishment: but as the propriety of these is either not so demonstrable, or not so constant, or the application of them not so determinate, as that of the foregoing, it may be doubted whether they be worth putting on a level with the others.

XXII. Rule 10. *When a punishment which in point of quality is particularly well calculated to answer its intention, cannot exist in less than a certain quantity, it may sometimes be of use, for the sake of employing it, to stretch a little beyond that quantity which, on other accounts, would be strictly necessary.*

XXIII. Rule 11. *In particular, this may sometimes be the case, where the punishment proposed is of such a nature as to be particularly well calculated to answer the purpose of a moral lesson*[1].

[1] See ch. iv. [Value].

[2] It is for this reason, for example, that simple compensation is never looked upon as sufficient punishment for theft or robbery.

[1] A punishment may be said to be calculated to answer the purpose of a moral lesson, when, by reason of the ignominy it stamps upon the offence, it is calculated to inspire the public with sentiments of aversion towards those pernicious habits and dispositions with which the offence appears to be connected; and thereby to inculcate the opposite beneficial habits and dispositions.

XXIV. Rule 12. The tendency of the above considerations is to dictate an augmentation in the punishment: the following rule operates in the way of diminution. There are certain cases (it has been seen[1]) in which, by the influence of accidental circumstances, punishment may be rendered unprofitable in the whole: in the same cases it may chance to be rendered unprofitable as to a part only. Accordingly,

*In adjusting the quantum of punishment, the circumstances, by which all punishment may be rendered unprofitable, ought to be attended to.*

XXV. Rule 13. It is to be observed, that the more various and minute any set of provisions are, the greater the chance is that any given article in them will not be borne in mind: without which, no benefit can ensue from it. Distinctions, which are more complex than what the conceptions of those whose conduct it is designed to influence can take in, will even be worse than useless. The whole system will present a confused appearance: and thus the effect, not only of the proportions established by the articles in question, but of whatever is connected with them, will be destroyed[2]. To draw a precise line of direction in such case seems impossible. However, by way of memento, it may be of some use to subjoin the following rule.

*Among provisions designed to perfect the proportion between punishments and offences, if any occur, which, by their own particular good effects, would not make up for the harm they* would do by adding to the intricacy of the Code, they should be omitted[3].

XXVI. It may be remembered, that the political sanction, being that to which the sort of punishment belongs, which in this chapter is all along in view, is but one of four sanctions, which may all of them contribute their share towards producing the same effects. It may be expected, therefore, that in adjusting the quantity of political punishment, allowance should be made for the assistance it may meet with from those other controlling powers. True it is, that from each of these several sources a very powerful assistance may sometimes be derived. But the case is, that (setting aside the moral sanction, in the case where the force of it is expressly adopted into and modified by the political) the force of those other powers is never determinate enough to be depended upon. It can never be reduced, like political punishment, into exact lots, nor meted out in number, quantity, and value. The legislator is therefore obliged to provide the full complement of punishment, as if he were sure of not receiving any assistance whatever from any of those quarters. If he does, so much the better: but lest he should not, it is necessary he should, at all events, make that provision which depends upon himself.

XXVII. It may be of use, in this place, to recapitulate the several circumstances, which, in establishing the proportion betwixt punishments and offences, are to be attended to. These seem to be as follows:

---

It is this, for example, if any thing, that must justify the application of so severe a punishment as the infamy of a public exhibition, hereinafter proposed, for him who lifts up his hand against a woman, or against his father.

It is partly on this principle, I suppose, that military legislators have justified to themselves the inflicting death on the soldier who lifts up his hand against his superior officer.

[1] See ch. xiii. [Cases unmeet], § 4.

[2] See B II. tit. [Purposes], Append. tit. [Composition].

[3] Notwithstanding this rule, my fear is, that in the ensuing model, I may be thought to have carried my endeavours at proportionality too far. Hitherto scarce any attention has been paid to it. Montesquieu seems to have been almost the first who has had the least idea of any such thing. In such a matter, therefore, excess seemed more eligible than defect. The difficulty is to invent: that done, if any thing seems superfluous, it is easy to retrench.

I. *On the part of the offence*:

1. The profit of the offence;
2. The mischief of the offence;
3. The profit and mischief of other greater or lesser offences, of different sorts, which the offender may have to choose out of;
4. The profit and mischief of other offences, of the same sort, which the same offender may probably have been guilty of already.

II. *On the part of the punishment*:

5. The magnitude of the punishment: composed of its intensity and duration;
6. The deficiency of the punishment in point of certainty;
7. The deficiency of the punishment in point of proximity;
8. The quality of the punishment;
9. The accidental advantage in point of quality of a punishment, not strictly needed in point of quantity;
10. The use of a punishment of a particular quality, in the character of a moral lesson.

III. *On the part of the offender*:

11. The responsibility of the class of persons in a way to offend;
12. The sensibility of each particular offender;
13. The particular merits or useful qualities of any particular offender, in case of a punishment which might deprive the community of the benefit of them;
14. The multitude of offenders on any particular occasion.

IV. *On the part of the public, at any particular conjuncture*:

15. The inclinations of the people, for or against any quantity or mode of punishment;
16. The inclinations of foreign powers.

V. *On the part of the law*: that is, of the public for a continuance:

17. The necessity of making small sacrifices, in point of proportionality, for the sake of simplicity.

XXVIII. There are some, perhaps, who, at first sight, may look upon the nicety employed in the adjustment of such rules, as so much labour lost: for gross ignorance, they will say, never troubles itself about laws, and passion does not calculate. But the evil of ignorance admits of cure: and as to the proposition that passion does not calculate, this, like most of these very general and oracular propositions, is not true. When matters of such importance as pain and pleasure are at stake, and these in the highest degree (the only matters, in short, that can be of importance) who is there that does not calculate? Men calculate, some with less exactness, indeed, some with more: but all men calculate. I would not say, that even a madman does not calculate[1]. Passion calculates, more or less, in every man: in different men, according to the warmth or coolness of their dispositions: according to the firmness or irritability of their minds: according to the nature of the motives by which they are acted upon. Happily, of all passions, that is the most given to calculation, from the excesses of which, by reason of its strength, constancy, and universality, society has most to apprehend[2]: I mean that which corresponds to the motive of pecuniary interest: so that these niceties, if such they are to be called, have the best chance of being efficacious, where efficacy is of the most importance.

[1] There are few madmen but what are observed to be afraid of the strait waistcoat.
[2] See ch. xii. [Consequences]. xxxiii.

## QUESTIONS

1. Bentham says that punishment must be inefficacious where the agent's action was unintentional. Does Bentham mean by this that laws making punishment a matter of strict liability, making wrongdoers punishable regardless of whether the wrong was done intentionally or not, must be inefficacious? If so, is this correct?

2. Bentham remarks that, while a certain kind of crime ought in the ordinary case to be punished, punishment may be unprofitable in certain special cases due to "the influence of some *occasional circumstances*." Do you accept his account of what these special circumstances are? Comment on whether a public practice of recognizing such special circumstances would likely be as beneficial as Bentham thinks.

3. If it is true, as Bentham believes it is, that a penal provision could produce no effect on one who is intoxicated from "the use of wine, or opium, or other drugs" that produce "a temporary insanity," then under what circumstances, if any, is punishment for acts done while intoxicated ever effective?

4. Bentham thinks (XXV, Rule 13) that there are utilitarian reasons for making the criminal code simple: "Distinctions, which are more complex than what the conceptions of those whose conduct it is designed to influence can take in, will even be worse than useless." To what extent does utilitarian reasoning call for the whole criminal code, including tax laws and laws governing such things as the purchase and sale of stock, to be simple enough to be understandable to everyone?

## *John Stuart Mill*
# SPEECH BEFORE THE HOUSE OF COMMONS, 1868*

Mr. J. STUART MILL: It would be a great satisfaction to me if I were able to support this Motion. It is always a matter of regret to me to find myself, on a public question, opposed to those who are called—sometimes in the way of honour and sometimes in what is intended for ridicule—the philanthropists. Of all persons who take part in public affairs, they are those for whom, on the whole, I feel the greatest amount of respect; for their characteristic is, that they devote their time, their labour, and much of their money to objects purely public, with a less admixture of either personal or class selfishness, than any other class of politicians whatever. On almost all the great questions, scarcely any politicians are so steadily and almost uniformly to be found on the side of right; and they seldom err, but by an exaggerated application of some just and highly important principle. On the very subject that is now occupying us we all know what signal service they have rendered. It is through their efforts that our criminal laws—which within my memory hanged people for stealing in a dwelling house to the value of 40s.—laws by virtue of which rows of human beings might be seen suspended in front of Newgate by those who ascended or descended Ludgate Hill—have so greatly relaxed their most revolting and most impolitic ferocity, that aggravated murder is now practically the only crime which is punished with death by any of our lawful tribunals; and we are even now

*From *Hansard's Parliamentary Debates,* 3rd series (London: Cornelius Buck, 1868).

deliberating whether the extreme penalty should be retained in that solitary case. This vast gain, not only to humanity, but to the ends of penal justice, we owe to the philanthropists; and if they are mistaken, as I cannot but think they are, in the present instance, it is only in not perceiving the right time and place for stopping in a career hitherto so eminently beneficial. Sir, there is a point at which, I conceive, that career ought to stop. When there has been brought home to any one, by conclusive evidence, the greatest crime known to the law; and when the attendant circumstances suggest no palliation of the guilt, no hope that the culprit may even yet not be unworthy to live among mankind, nothing to make it probable that the crime was an exception to his general character rather than a consequence of it, then I confess it appears to me that to deprive the criminal of the life of which he has proved himself to be unworthy—solemnly to blot him out from the fellowship of mankind and from the catalogue of the living—is the most appropriate, as it is certainly the most impressive, mode in which society can attach to so great a crime the penal consequences which for the security of life it is indispensable to annex to it. I defend this penalty, when confined to atrocious cases, on the very ground on which it is commonly attacked—on that of humanity to the criminal; as beyond comparison the least cruel mode in which it is possible adequately to deter from the crime. If, in our horror of inflicting death, we endeavour to devise some punishment for the living criminal which shall act on the human mind with a deterrent force at all comparable to that of death, we are driven to inflictions less severe indeed in appearance, and therefore less efficacious, but far more cruel in reality. Few, I think, would venture to propose, as a punishment for aggravated murder, less than imprisonment with hard labour for life; that is the fate to which a murderer would be consigned by the mercy which shrinks from putting him to death. But has it been suffi-

ciently considered what sort of a mercy this is, and what kind of life it leaves to him? If, indeed, the punishment is not really inflicted—if it becomes the sham which a few years ago such punishments were rapidly becoming—then, indeed, its adoption would be almost tantamount to giving up the attempt to repress murder altogether. But if it really is what it professes to be, and if it is realized in all its rigour by the popular imagination, as it very probably would not be, but as it must be if it is to be efficacious, it will be so shocking that when the memory of the crime is no longer fresh, there will be almost insuperable difficulty in executing it. What comparison can there really be, in point of severity, between consigning a man to the short pang of a rapid death, and immuring him in a living tomb, there to linger out what may be a long life in the hardest and most monotonous toil, without any of its alleviations or rewards—debarred from all pleasant sights and sounds, and cut off from all earthly hope, except a slight mitigation of bodily restraint, or a small improvement of diet? Yet even such a lot as this, because there is no one moment at which the suffering is of terrifying intensity, and, above all, because it does not contain the element, so imposing to the imagination, of the unknown, is universally reputed a milder punishment than death—stands in all codes as a mitigation of the capital penalty, and is thankfully accepted as such. For it is characteristic of all punishments which depend on duration for their efficacy—all, therefore, which are not corporal or pecuniary—that they are more rigorous than they seem; while it is, on the contrary, one of the strongest recommendations a punishment can have, that it should seem more rigorous than it is; for its practical power depends far less on what it is than on what it seems. There is not, I should think, any human infliction which makes an impression on the imagination so entirely out of proportion to its real severity as the punishment of death. The punishment must be mild indeed which does not add more to the sum of human misery than is necessarily or directly added by the execution of a criminal. As my hon. Friend the Member for Northampton (Mr. Gilpin) has himself remarked, the most that human laws can do to anyone in the matter of death is to hasten it; the man would have died at any rate; not so very much later, and on the average, I fear, with a considerably greater amount of bodily suffering. Society is asked, then, to denude itself of an instrument of punishment which, in the grave cases to which alone it is suitable, effects its purpose at a less cost of human suffering than any other; which, while it inspires more terror, is less cruel in actual fact than any punishment that we should think of substituting for it. My hon. Friend says that it does not inspire terror, and that experience proves it to be a failure. But the influence of a punishment is not to be estimated by its effect on hardened criminals. Those whose habitual way of life keeps them, so to speak, at all times within sight of the gallows, do grow to care less about it; as, to compare good things with bad, an old soldier is not much affected by the chance of dying in battle. I can afford to admit all that is often said about the indifference of professional criminals to the gallows. Though of that indifference one-third is probably bravado and another third confidence that they shall have the luck to escape, it is quite probable that the remaining third is real. But the efficacy of a punishment which acts principally through the imagination, is chiefly to be measured by the impression it makes on those who are still innocent: by the horror with which it surrounds the first prompting of guilt; the restraining influence it exercises over the beginning of the thought which, if indulged, would become a temptation; the check which it exerts over the gradual descension towards the state—never suddenly attained—in which crime no longer revolts, and punishment no longer terrifies. As for what is called the failure of death punishment, who is able to judge of that? We partly know who those are whom it has not deterred; but who is there who knows whom it has deterred, or how many human beings it has saved who would have lived to be murderers if that awful association had not been thrown round the idea of murder from their earliest infancy? Let us not forget that the most imposing fact loses its power over the imagination if it is made too cheap. When a punishment fit only for the most atrocious crimes is lavished on small offences until human feeling recoils from it, then, indeed, it ceases to intimidate, because it ceases to be believed in. The failure of capital punishment in cases of theft is easily accounted for: the thief did not believe that it would be inflicted. He had learnt by experience that jurors would perjure themselves rather than find him guilty; that Judges would seize any excuse for not sentencing him to death, or for recommending him to mercy; and that if neither jurors nor Judges were merciful, there were still hopes from an authority above both. When things had come to this pass it was high time to give up the vain attempt. When it is impossible to inflict a punishment, or when its infliction becomes a public scandal, the idle threat cannot too soon disappear from the statute book. And in the case of the host of offences which were formerly capital, I heartily rejoice that it did become impracticable to execute the law. If the same state of public feeling comes to exist in the case of murder; if the time comes when jurors refuse to find a murderer guilty; when Judges will not sentence him to death, or will recommend him to mercy; or when, if juries and Judges do not flinch from their duty, Home Secretaries, under pressure of deputations and memorials, shrink from theirs, and the threat becomes, as it became in the other cases, a mere *brutum fulmen*; then, indeed, it may become necessary to do in this case what has been done in those—to abrogate the penalty. That time may come— my hon. Friend thinks that it has nearly come. I hardly know whether he lamented it or boasted of it; but he and his Friends are entitled to the boast: for if it comes it will be their doing, and they will have gained what I cannot but call a fatal victory, for they will have achieved it by bringing about, if they will forgive me for saying so, an enervation, an effeminacy, in the general mind of the country. For what else than effeminacy is it to be so much more shocked by taking a man's life than by depriving him of all that makes life desirable or valuable? Is death, then, the greatest of all earthly ills? *Usque adeone mori miserum est*? Is it indeed, so dreadful a thing to die? Has it not been from of old one chief part of a manly education to make us despise death—teaching us to account it, if an evil at all, by no means high in the list of evils; at all events, as an inevitable one, and to hold, as it were, our lives in our hands, ready to be given or risked at any moment, for a sufficiently worthy object? I am sure that my hon. Friends know all this as well, and have as much of all these feelings as any of the rest of us; possibly more. But I cannot think that this is likely to be the effect of their teaching on the general mind. I cannot think that the cultivating of a peculiar sensitiveness of conscience on this one point, over and above what results from the general cultivation of the moral sentiments, is permanently consistent with assigning in our own minds to the fact of death no more than the degree of relative importance which belongs to it among the other incidents of our humanity. The men of old cared too little about death, and gave their own lives or took those of others with equal recklessness. Our danger is of the opposite kind, lest we should be so much shocked by death, in general and in the abstract, as to care too much about it in individual cases, both those of other people and our own, which call for its being risked. And I am not putting things at the worst, for it is proved by the experience of other countries that horror of the executioner by no means necessarily implies horror of the assassin. The stronghold, as we all know, of hired assassination in the 18th century was Italy; yet it is said that in some of

the Italian populations the infliction of death by sentence of law was in the highest degree offensive and revolting to popular feeling. Much has been said of the sanctity of human life, and the absurdity of supposing that we can teach respect for life by ourselves destroying it. But I am surprised at the employment of this argument, for it is one which might be brought against any punishment whatever. It is not human life only, not human life as such, that ought to be sacred to us, but human feelings. The human capacity of suffering is what we should cause to be respected, not the mere capacity of existing. And we may imagine somebody asking how we can teach people not to inflict suffering by ourselves inflicting it? But to this I should answer—all of us would answer—that to deter by suffering from inflicting suffering is not only possible, but the very purpose of penal justice. Does fining a criminal show want of respect for property, or imprisoning him, for personal freedom? Just as unreasonable is it to think that to take the life of a man who has taken that of another is to show want of regard for human life. We show, on the contrary, most emphatically our regard for it, by the adoption of a rule that he who violates that right in another forfeits it for himself, and that while no other crime that he can commit deprives him of his right to live, this shall. There is one argument against capital punishment, even in extreme cases, which I cannot deny to have weight—on which my hon. Friend justly laid great stress, and which never can be entirely got rid of. It is this—that if by an error of justice an innocent person is put to death, the mistake can never be corrected; all compensation, all reparation for the wrong is impossible. This would be indeed a serious objection if these miserable mistakes—among the most tragical occurrences in the whole round of human affairs—could not be made extremely rare. The argument is invincible where the mode of criminal procedure is dangerous to the innocent, or where the Courts of Justice are not trusted. And this probably is the reason why the objection to an irreparable punishment began (as I believe it did) earlier, and is more intense and more widely diffused, in some parts of the Continent of Europe than it is here. There are on the Continent great and enlightened countries, in which the criminal procedure is not so favourable to innocence, does not afford the same security against erroneous conviction, as it does among us; countries where the Courts of Justice seem to think they fail in their duty unless they find somebody guilty; and in their really laudable desire to hunt guilt from its hiding-places, expose themselves to a serious danger of condemning the innocent. If our own procedure and Courts of Justice afforded ground for similar apprehension, I should be the first to join in withdrawing the power of inflicting irreparable punishment from such tribunals. But we all know that the defects of our procedure are the very opposite. Our rules of evidence are even too favourable to the prisoner: and juries and Judges carry out the maxim, "It is better that ten guilty should escape than that one innocent person should suffer," not only to the letter, but beyond the letter. Judges are most anxious to point out, and juries to allow for, the barest possibility of the prisoner's innocence. No human judgment is infallible: such sad cases as my hon. Friend cited will sometimes occur; but in so grave a case as that of murder, the accused, in our system, has always the benefit of the merest shadow of a doubt. And this suggests another consideration very germane to the question. The very fact that death punishment is more shocking than any other to the imagination, necessarily renders the Courts of Justice more scrupulous in requiring the fullest evidence of guilt. Even that which is the greatest objection to capital punishment, the impossibility of correcting an error once committed, must make, and does make, juries and Judges more careful in forming their opinion, and more jealous in their scrutiny of the evidence. If the substitution of penal servi-

tude for death in cases of murder should cause any relaxation in this conscientious scrupulosity, there would be a great evil to set against the real, but I hope rare, advantage of being able to make reparation to a condemned person who was afterwards discovered to be innocent. In order that the possibility of correction may be kept open wherever the chance of this sad contingency is more than infinitesimal, it is quite right that the Judge should recommend to the Crown a commutation of the sentence, not solely when the proof of guilt is open to the smallest suspicion, but whenever there remains anything unexplained and mysterious in the case, raising a desire for more light, or making it likely that further information may at some future time be obtained. I would also suggest that whenever the sentence is commuted the grounds of the commutation should, in some authentic form, be made known to the public. Thus much I willingly concede to my hon. Friend; but on the question of total abolition I am inclined to hope that the feeling of the country is not with him, and that the limitation of death punishment to the cases referred to in the Bill of last year will be generally considered sufficient. The mania which existed a short time ago for paring down all our punishments seems to have reached its limits, and not before it was time. We were in danger of being left without any effectual punishment, except for small offences. What was formerly our chief secondary punishment—transportation—before it was abolished, had become almost a reward. Penal servitude, the substitute for it, was becoming, to the classes who were principally subject to it, almost nominal, so comfortable did we make our prisons, and so easy had it become to get quickly out of them. Flogging—a most objectionable punishment in ordinary cases, but a particularly appropriate one for crimes of brutality, especially crimes against women—we would not hear of, except, to be sure, in the case of garroters, for whose peculiar benefit we re-established it in a hurry, immediately after a Member of Parliament had been garotted. With this exception, offences, even of an atrocious kind, against the person, as my hon. and learned Friend the Member for Oxford (Mr. Neate) well remarked, not only were, but still are, visited with penalties so ludicrously inadequate, as to be almost an encouragement to the crime. I think, Sir, that in the case of most offences, except those against property, there is more need of strengthening our punishments than of weakening them: and that severer sentences, with an apportionment of them to the different kinds of offences which shall approve itself better then at present to the moral sentiments of the community, are the kind of reform of which our penal system now stands in need. I shall therefore vote against the Amendment.

## QUESTIONS

1. Some people claim that the death penalty should be eliminated because its use by the state expresses, and causes, disrespect for human life. Mill argues against this view by using an analogical argument. Is his analogy a good one? Explain.

2. Speaking of the human history of torture and cruelty, Friedrich Nietzsche remarked (in *The Genealogy of Morals*) that perhaps "pain did not hurt so much as it does nowadays . . . . ." Mill himself suggests that "men of old cared too little about death." If there is an element of truth in these claims, what might be the explanation for it?

3. Judging from everything Mill says here on the death penalty, would he be in favor of televising executions? Explain your answer.

4. The death penalty is commonly thought to be the severest of punishments currently in use. Mill disagrees. What are the best reasons for thinking that the death penalty is uniquely severe? Is it (a) its finality? (b) its presumed painfulness? (c) the indignity it inflicts on the one being killed? (d) the hard attitude toward human beings and human life that it expresses? (e) or something else?

# Mixed Views

## *John Rawls*
# RULES AND PUNISHMENT*

IN THIS paper I want to show the importance of the distinction between justifying a practice[1] and justifying a particular action falling under it, and I want to explain the logical basis of this distinction and how it is possible to miss its significance. While the distinction has frequently been made,[2] and is now becoming commonplace, there remains the task of explaining the tendency either to overlook it altogether, or to fail to appreciate its importance.

To show the importance of the distinction I am going to defend utilitarianism against those objections which have traditionally been made against it in connection with punishment and the obligation to keep promises. I hope to show that if one uses the distinction in question then one can state utilitarianism in a way which makes it a much better explication of our considered moral judgments than these traditional objections would seem to admit.[3] Thus the importance of the distinction is shown by the

way it strengthens the utilitarian view regardless of whether that view is completely defensible or not.

To explain how the significance of the distinction may be overlooked, I am going to discuss two conceptions of rules. One of these conceptions conceals the importance of distinguishing between the justification of a rule or practice and the justification of a particular action falling under it. The other conception makes it clear why this distinction must be made and what is its logical basis.

## I

The subject of punishment, in the sense of attaching legal penalties to the violation of legal rules, has always been a troubling moral question.[4] The trouble about it has not been that people disagree as to whether or not punishment is justifiable. Most people have held that, freed from certain abuses, it

---

*From *The Philosophical Review*, vol. 64 (1955), pp. 3–13, 18–29 Reprinted by permission of *The Philosophical Review* and the author.

[1] I use the word "practice" throughout as a sort of technical term meaning any form of activity specified by a system of rules which defines offices, roles, moves, penalties, defenses, and so on, and which gives the activity its structure. As examples one may think of games and rituals, trials and parliaments.

[2] The distinction is central to Hume's discussion of justice in *A Treatise of Human Nature*, bk. III, pt. II, esp. secs. 2–4. It is clearly stated by John Austin in the second lecture of *Lectures on Jurisprudence* (4th ed.; London, 1873), I, 116ff. (1st ed., 1832). Also it may be argued that J. S. Mill took it for granted in *Utilitarianism*; on this point cf. J. O. Urmson, "The Interpretation of the Moral Philosophy of J. S. Mill," *Philosophical Quarterly*, vol. III (1953). In addition to the arguments given by Urmson there are several clear statements of the distinction in *A System of Logic* (8th ed.; London, 1872), bk. VI, ch. xii pars. 2, 3, 7. The distinction is fundamental to J. D. Mabbott's important papers, "Punishment," *Mind*, n.s., vol. XLVIII (April, 1939). More recently the distinction has been stated with particular emphasis by S. E. Toulmin in *The Place of Reason in Ethics* (Cambridge, 1950), see esp. ch. xi, where it plays a major part in his account of moral reasoning. Toulmin doesn't explain the basis of the distinction, nor how one might overlook its importance, as I try to in this paper, and in my review of his book ((*Philosophical Review*, vol. LX [October, 1951]), as some of my criticisms show, I failed to understand the force of it. See also H. D. Aiken, "The Levels of Moral Discourse," *Ethics*, vol. LXII (1952), A. M. Quinton, "Punishment," *Analysis*, vol. XIV (June, 1954), and P. H. Nowell-Smith, *Ethics* (London 1954), pp. 236–239, 271–273.

[3] On the concept of explication see the author's paper *Philosophical Review*, vol. LX (April, 1951).

[4] While this paper was being revised, Quinton's appeared; footnote 2 supra. There are several respects in which my remarks are similar to his. Yet as I consider some further questions and rely on somewhat different arguments, I have retained the discussion of punishment and promises together as two test cases for utilitarianism.

is an acceptable institution. Only a few have rejected punishment entirely, which is rather surprising when one considers all that can be said against it. The difficulty is with the justification of punishment: various arguments for it have been given by moral philosophers, but so far none of them has won any sort of general acceptance; no justification is without those who detest it. I hope to show that the use of the aforementioned distinction enables one to state the utilitarian view in a way which allows for the sound points of its critics.

For our purposes we may say that there are two justifications of punishment. What we may call the retributive view is that punishment is justified on the grounds that wrongdoing merits punishment. It is morally fitting that a person who does wrong should suffer in proportion to his wrongdoing. That a criminal should be punished follows from his guilt, and the severity of the appropriate punishment depends on the depravity of his act. The state of affairs where a wrongdoer suffers punishment is morally better than the state of affairs where he does not; and it is better irrespective of any of the consequences of punishing him.

What we may call the utilitarian view holds that on the principle that bygones are bygones and that only future consequences are material to present decisions, punishment is justifiable only by reference to the probable consequences of maintaining it as one of the devices of the social order. Wrongs committed in the past are, as such, not relevant considerations for deciding what to do. If punishment can be shown to promote effectively the interest of society it is justifiable, otherwise it is not.

I have stated these two competing views very roughly to make one feel the conflict between them: one feels the force of *both* arguments and one wonders how they can be reconciled. From my introductory remarks it is obvious that the resolution which I am going to propose is that in this case one must distinguish between justifying a practice as a system of rules to be applied and enforced, and justifying a particular action which falls under these rules; utilitarian arguments are appropriate with regard to questions about practices, while retributive arguments fit the application of particular rules to particular cases.

We might try to get clear about this distinction by imagining how a father might answer the question of his son. Suppose the son asks, "Why was $J$ put in jail yesterday?" The father answers, "Because he robbed the bank at $B$. He was duly tried and found guilty. That's why he was put in jail yesterday." But suppose the son had asked a different question, namely, "Why do people put other people in jail?" Then the father might answer, "To protect good people from bad people" or "To stop people from doing things that would make it uneasy for all of us; for otherwise we wouldn't be able to go to bed at night and sleep in peace." There are two very different questions here. One question emphasizes the proper name: it asks why $J$ was punished rather than someone else, or it asks what he was punished for. The other question asks why we have the institution of punishment: why do people punish one another rather than, say, always forgiving one another?

Thus the father says in effect that a particular man is punished rather than some other man, because he is guilty, and he is guilty because he broke the law (past tense). In his case the law looks back, the judge looks back, the jury looks back, and a penalty is visited upon him for something he did. That a man is to be punished, and what his punishment is to be, is settled by its being shown that he broke the law and that the law assigns that penalty for the violation of it.

On the other hand we have the institution of punishment itself, and recommend and accept various changes in it, because it is thought by the (ideal) legislator and by those to whom the law applies that, as a part of a system of law impartially applied from case to case arising under it, it will have the consequence, in the long run, of furthering the interests of society.

One can say, then, that the judge and the legislator stand in different positions and look in different directions: one to the past, the other to the future. The justification of what the judge does, *qua* judge, sounds like the retributive view; the justification of what the (ideal) legislator does, *qua* legislator, sounds like the utilitarian view. Thus both views have a point (this is as it should be since intelligent and sensitive persons have been on both sides of the argument); and one's initial confusion disappears once one sees that these views apply to persons holding different offices with different duties, and situated differently with respect to the system of rules that make up the criminal law.[5]

One might say, however, that the utilitarian view is more fundamental since it applies to a more fundamental office, for the judge carries out the legislator's will so far as he can determine it. Once the legislator decides to have laws and to assign penalties for their violation (as things are there must be both the law and the penalty) an institution is set up which involves a retributive conception of particular cases. It is part of the concept of the criminal law as a system of rules that the application and enforcement of these rules in particular cases should be justifiable by arguments of a retributive character. The decision whether or not to use law rather than some other mechanism of social control, and the decision as to what laws to have and what penalties to assign, may be settled by utilitarian arguments; but if one decides to have laws then one has decided on something

whose working in particular cases is retributive in form.[6]

The answer, then, to the confusion engendered by the two views of punishment is quite simple: one distinguishes two offices, that of the judge and that of the legislator, and one distinguishes their different stations with respect to the system of rules which make up the law; and then one notes that the different sorts of considerations which would usually be offered as reasons for what is done under the cover of these offices can be paired off with the competing justifications of punishment. One reconciles the two views by the time-honored device of making them apply to different situations.

But can it really be this simple? Well, this answer allows for the apparent intent of each side. Does a person who advocates the retributive view necessarily advocate, as an *institution*, legal machinery whose essential purpose is to set up and preserve a correspondence between moral turpitude and suffering? Surely not.[7] What retributionists have rightly insisted upon is that no man can be punished unless he is guilty, that is, unless he has broken the law. Their fundamental criticism of the utilitarian account is that, as they interpret it, it sanctions an innocent person's being punished (if one may call it that) for the benefit of society.

On the other hand, utilitarians agree that punishment is to be inflicted only for the violation of law. They regard this much as understood from the concept of punishment itself.[8] The point of the utilitarian account concerns the institution as a system of rules: utilitarianism seeks to limit its use by declar-

[5]Note the fact that different sorts of arguments are suited to different offices. One way of taking the differences between ethical theories is to regard them as accounts of the reasons expected in different offices.

[6]In this connection see Mabbott, *op. cit*, pp. 163–164.

[7]On this point see Sir David Ross, *The Right and the Good* (Oxford, 1930), pp. 57–60.

[8]See Hobbes's definition of punishment in *Leviathan*, ch. xxviii; and Bentham's definition in *The Principle of Morals and Legislation*, ch. xii, par. 36, ch. xv, par. 28, and in *The Rationale of Punishment*, (London, 1830), bk. I, ch. i. They could agree with Bradley that: "Punishment is punishment only when it is deserved. We pay the penalty, because we owe it, and for no other reason; and if punishment is inflicted for any other reason whatever than because it is merited by wrong, it is a gross immorality, a crying injustice, an abominable crime, and not what it pretends to be." *Ethical Studies* (2nd ed.; Oxford, 1927), pp. 26–27. Certainly by definition it isn't what it pretends to be. The innocent can only be punished by mistake; deliberate "punishment" of the innocent necessarily involves fraud.

ing it justifiable only if it can be shown to foster effectively the good of society. Historically it is a protest against the indiscriminate and ineffective use of the criminal law.[9] It seeks to dissuade us from assigning to penal institutions the improper, if not sacrilegious, task of matching suffering with moral turpitude. Like others, utilitarians want penal institutions designed so that, as far as humanly possible, only those who break the law run afoul of it. They hold that no official should have discretionary power to inflict penalties whenever he thinks it for the benefit of society; for on utilitarian grounds an institution granting such power could not be justified.[10]

The suggested way of reconciling the retributive and the utilitarian justifications of punishment seems to account for what both sides have wanted to say. There are, however, two further questions which arise, and I shall devote the remainder of this section to them.

First, will not a difference of opinion as to the proper criterion of just law make the proposed reconciliation unacceptable to retributionists? Will they not question whether, if the utilitarian principle is used as the criterion, it follows that those who have broken the law are guilty in a way which satisfies their demand that those punished deserve to be punished? To answer this difficulty, suppose that the rules of the criminal law are justified on utilitarian grounds (it is only for laws that meet his criterion that the utilitarian can be held responsible). Then it follows that the actions which the criminal law specifies as offenses are such that, if they were tolerated, terror and alarm would spread in society. Consequently, retributionists can only

deny that those who are punished deserve to be punished if they deny that such actions are wrong. This they will not want to do.

The second question is whether utilitarianism doesn't justify too much. One pictures it as an engine of justification which, if consistently adopted, could be used to justify cruel and arbitrary institutions. Retributionists may be supposed to concede that utilitarians *intend* to reform the law and to make it more humane; that utilitarians do not *wish* to justify any such thing as punishment of the innocent; and that utilitarians may appeal to the fact that punishment presupposes guilt in the sense that by punishment one understands an institution attaching penalties to the infraction of legal rules, and therefore that it is logically absurd to suppose that utilitarians in justifying *punishment* might also have justified punishment (if we may call it that) of the innocent. The real question, however, is whether the utilitarian, in justifying punishment, hasn't used arguments which commit him to accepting the infliction of suffering on innocent persons if it is for the good of society (whether or not one calls this punishment). More generally, isn't the utilitarian committed in principle to accepting many practices which he, as a morally sensitive person, wouldn't want to accept? Retributionists are inclined to hold that there is no way to stop the utilitarian principle from justifying too much except by adding to it a principle which distributes certain rights to individuals. Then the amended criterion is not the greatest benefit of society *simpliciter,* but the greatest benefit of society subject to the constraint that no one's rights may be violated. Now while I think that the classical utilitari-

[9]Cf. Leon Radzinowicz, *A History of English Criminal Law: The Movement for Reform 1750–1833* (London, 1948), esp. ch. xi on Bentham.

[10]Bentham discusses how corresponding to a punitory provision of a criminal law there is another provision which stands to it as an antagonist and which needs a name as much as the punitory. He calls it, as one might expect, the *anaetiosostic,* and of it he says: "The punishment of guilt is the object of the former one: the preservation of innocence that of the latter." In the same connection he asserts that it is never thought fit to give the judge the option of deciding whether a thief (that is, a person whom he believes to be a thief, for the judge's belief is what the question must always turn upon) should hang or not, and so the law writes the provision: "The judge shall not cause a thief to be hanged unless he has been duly convicted and sentenced in course of law." (*The Limits of Jurisprudence Defined*, ed. C. W. Everett [New York, 1945] pp. 238–239).

ans proposed a criterion of this more complicated sort, I do not want to argue that point here.[11] What I want to show is that there is *another* way of preventing the utilitarian principle from justifying too much, or at least of making it much less likely to do: namely, by stating utilitarianism in a way which accounts for the distinction between the justification of an institution and the justification of a particular action falling under it.

I begin by defining the institution of punishment as follows: a person is said to suffer punishment whenever he is legally deprived of some of the normal rights of a citizen on the ground that he has violated a rule of law, the violation having been established by trial according to the due process of law, provided that the deprivation is carried out by the recognized legal authorities of the state, that the rule of law clearly specifies both the offense and the attached penalty, that the courts construe statutes strictly, and that the statute was on the books prior to the time of the offense.[12] This definition specifies what I shall understand by punishment. The question is whether utilitarian arguments may be found to justify institutions widely different from this and such as one would find cruel and arbitrary.

This question is best answered, I think, by taking up a particular accusation. Consider the following from Carritt:

> . . . the utilitarian must hold that we are justified in inflicting pain always and only to prevent worse pain or bring about greater happiness. This, then, is all we need to consider in so-called punishment, which must be purely preventive. But if some kind of very cruel crime becomes common, and none of the criminals can be caught, it might be highly expedient, as an example, to hang an innocent man, if a charge against him could be so framed that he were universally thought guilty; indeed this would only fail

to be an ideal instance of utilitarian 'punishment' because the victim himself would not have been so likely as a real felon to commit such a crime in the future; in all other respects it would be perfectly deterrent and therefore felicific.[13]

Carritt is trying to show that there are occasions when a utilitarian argument would justify taking an action which would be generally condemned; and thus that utilitarianism justifies too much. But the failure of Carritt's argument lies in the fact that he makes no distinction between the justification of the general system of rules which constitutes penal institutions and the justification of particular applications of these rules to particular cases by the various officials whose job it is to administer them. This becomes perfectly clear when one asks who the "we" are of whom Carritt speaks. Who is this who has a sort of absolute authority on particular occasions to decide that an innocent man shall be "punished" if everyone can be convinced that he is guilty? Is this person the legislator, or the judge, or the body of private citizens, or what? It is utterly crucial to know who is to decide such matters, and by what authority, for all of this must be written into the rules of the institution. Until one knows these things one doesn't know what the institution is whose justification is being challenged; and as the utilitarian principle applies to the institution one doesn't know whether it is justifiable on utilitarian grounds or not.

Once this is understood it is clear what the countermove to Carritt's argument is. One must describe more carefully what the *institution* is which his example suggests, and then ask oneself whether or not it is likely that having this institution would be for the benefit of society in the long run. One must not content oneself with the vague thought that,

[11]By the classical utilitarians I understand Hobbes, Hume, Bentham, J. S. Mill, and Sidgwick.
[12]All these features of punishment are mentioned by Hobbes; cf. *Leviathan*, ch. xxviii.
[13]*Ethical and Political Thinking* (Oxford, 1947), p. 65

when it's a question of *this* case, it would be a good thing if *somebody* did something even if an innocent person were to suffer.

Try to imagine, then, an institution (which we may call "telishment") which is such that the officials set up by it have authority to arrange a trial for the condemnation of an innocent man whenever they are of the opinion that doing so would be in the best interests of society. The discretion of officials is limited, however, by the rule that they may not condemn an innocent man to undergo such an ordeal unless there is, at the time, a wave of offenses similar to that with which they charge him and telish him for. We may imagine that the officials having the discretionary authority are the judges of the higher courts in consultation with the chief of police, the minister of justice, and a committee of the legislature.

Once one realizes that one is involved in setting up an *institution*, one sees that the hazards are very great. For example, what check is there on the officials? How is one to tell whether or not their actions are authorized? How is one to limit the risks involved in allowing such systematic deception? How is one to avoid giving anything short of complete discretion to the authorities to telish anyone they like? In addition to these considerations, it is obvious that people will come to have a very different attitude towards their penal system when telishment is adjoined to it. They will be uncertain as to whether a convicted man has been punished or telished. They will wonder whether or not they should feel sorry for him. They will wonder whether the same fate won't at any time fall on them. If one pictures how such an institution would actually work, and the enormous risks involved in it, it seems clear that it would serve no useful purpose. A utilitarian justification for this institution is most unlikely.

It happens in general that as one drops off the defining features of punishment one ends up with an institution whose utilitarian justification is highly doubtful. One reason for this is that punishment works like a kind of price system: by altering the prices one has to pay for the performance of actions it supplies a motive for avoiding some actions and doing others. The defining features are essential if punishment is to work in this way; so that an institution which lacks these features, e.g., an institution which is set up to "punish" the innocent, is likely to have about as much point as a price system (if one may call it that) where the prices of things change at random from day to day and one learns the price of something after one has agreed to buy it.[14]

If one is careful to apply the utilitarian principle to the institution which is to authorize particular actions, then there is *less* danger of its justifying too much. Carritt's example gains plausibility by its indefiniteness and by its concentration on the particular case. His argument will only hold if it can be shown that there are utilitarian arguments which justify an institution whose publicly ascertainable offices and powers are such as to permit officials to exercise that kind of discretion in particular cases. But the requirement of having to build the ar-

---

[14]The analogy with the price system suggests an answer to the question how utilitarian considerations insure that punishment is proportional to the offense. It is interesting to note that Sir David Ross, after making the distinction between justifying a penal law and justifying a particular application of it, and after stating that utilitarian considerations have a large place in determining the former, still holds back from accepting the utilitarian justification of punishment on the grounds that justice requires that punishment be proportional to the offense, and that utilitarianism is unable to account for this. Cf. *The Right and the Good*, pp. 61–62. I do not claim that utilitarianism can account for this requirement as Sir David might wish, but it happens, nevertheless, that if utilitarian considerations are followed, penalties will be proportional to offenses in this sense: the order of offenses according to seriousness can be paired off with the order of penalties according to severity. Also the absolute level of penalties will be as low as possible. This follows from the assumption that people are rational (i.e., that they are able to take into account the "prices" the state puts on actions), the utilitarian rule that a penal system should provide a motive for preferring the less serious offense, and the principle that punishment as such is an evil. All this was carefully worked out by Bentham in *The Principles of Morals and Legislation*, chs. xiii-xv.

bitrary features of the particular decision into the institutional practice makes the justification much less likely to go through. . . .

## III

So far I have tried to show the importance of the distinction between the justification of a practice and the justification of a particular action falling under it by indicating how this distinction might be used to defend utilitarianism against two longstanding objections. One might be tempted to close the discussion at this point by saying that utilitarian considerations should be understood as applying to practices in the first instance and not to particular actions falling under them except insofar as the practices admit of it. One might say that in this modified form it is a better account of our considered moral opinions and let it go at that. But to stop here would be to neglect the interesting question as to how one can fail to appreciate the significance of this rather obvious distinction and can take it for granted that utilitarianism has the consequence that particular cases may always be decided on general utilitarian grounds.[21] I want to argue that this mistake may be connected with misconceiving the logical status of the rules of practices; and to show this I am going to examine two conceptions of rules, two ways of placing them within the utilitarian theory.

The conception which conceals from us the significance of the distinction I am going to call the summary view. It regards rules in the following way: one supposes that each person decides what he shall do in particular cases by applying the utilitarian principle; one supposes further that different people will decide the same particular case in the same way and that there will be recurrences of cases similar to those previously decided. Thus it will happen that in cases of certain kinds the same decision will be made either by the same person at different times or by different persons at the same time. If a case occurs frequently enough one supposes that a rule is formulated to cover that sort of case. I have called this conception the summary view because rules are pictured as summaries of past decisions arrived at by the *direct* application of the utilitarian principle to particular cases. Rules are regarded as reports that cases of a certain sort have been found on *other* grounds to be properly decided in a certain way (although, of course, they do not *say* this).

There are several things to notice about this way of placing rules within the utilitarian theory.[22]

1. The point of having rules derives from the fact that similar cases tend to recur and that one can decide cases more quickly if one records past decisions in the form of rules. If similar cases didn't recur, one would be required to apply the utilitarian principles directly, case by case, and rules reporting past decisions would be of no use.

2. The decisions made on particular cases are logically prior to rules. Since rules gain their point from the need to apply the utilitarian principle to many similar cases, it follows

---

[21]So far as I can see it is not until Moore that the doctine is expressly stated in this way. See, for example, *Principia Ethica*, p. 147, where it is said that the statement "I am morally bound to perform this action" is identical with the statement "*This* action will produce the greatest possible amount of good in the Universe" (my italics). It is important to remember that those whom I have called the classical utilitarians were largely interested in social institutions. They were among the leading economists and political theorists of their day, and they were not infrequently reformers interested in practical affairs. Utilitarianism historically goes together with a coherent view of society, and is not simply an ethical theory, much less an attempt at philosophical analysis in the modern sense. The utilitarian principle was quite naturally thought of, and used, as a criterion for judging social institutions (practices) and as a basis for urging reforms. It is not clear, therefore, how far it is necessary to amend utilitarianism in its classical form. For a discussion of utilitarianism as an integral part of a theory of society, see L. Robbins, *The Theory of Economic Policy in English Classical Political Economy* (London, 1952).

[22]This footnote should read after sec. 3 and presupposes what I have said there. It provides a few references to statements by leading utilitarians of the summary conception. In general it appears that when they discussed the logical features of rules the summary conception prevailed and that it was typical of the way they talked about moral rules. I cite a rather lengthy group of passages from Austin as a full illustration.

that a particular case (or several cases similar to it) may exist whether or not there is a rule covering that case We are pictured as recognizing particular cases prior to there being a rule which covers them, for it is only if we meet with a number of cases of a certain sort that we formulate a rule. Thus we are able to describe a particular case as a particular case of the requisite sort whether there is a rule regarding *that* sort of case or not. Put another way: what the *A*'s and the *B*'s refer to in rules of the form 'Whenever *A* do *B*' may be described as *A*'s and *B*'s whether or not there is the rule 'Whenever *A* do *B*', or whether or not there is any body of rules which make up a practice of which that rule is a part.

To illustrate this consider a rule, or maxim, which could arise in this way: suppose that a person is trying to decide whether to tell someone who is fatally ill what his illness is when he has been asked to do so. Suppose the person to reflect and then decide, on utilitarian grounds, that he should not answer truthfully; and suppose that on the basis of this and other like occasions he formulates a rule to the effect that when asked by someone fatally ill what his illness is, one should not tell him. The point to notice is that someone's being fatally ill and asking what his illness is, and someone's telling him, are things that can be described as such whether or not there is this rule. The performance of the action to

John Austin in his *Lectures on Jurisprudence* meets the objection that deciding in accordance with the utilitarian principle case by case is impractical by saying that this is a misinterpretation of utilitarianism. According to the utilitarian view " . . . our conduct would conform to *rules* inferred from the tendencies of actions, but would not be determined by a direct resort to the principle of general utility. Utility would be the test of our conduct, ultimately, but not immediately: the immediate test of the rules to which our conduct would conform, but not the immediate test of specific or individual actions. Our rules would be fashioned on utility; our conduct, on our rules" (vol. I, p. 116). As to how one decides on the tendency of an action he says: "If we would try the tendency of a specific or individual act, we must not contemplate the act as if it were single and insulated, but must look at the class of acts to which it belongs. We must suppose that acts of the class were generally done or omitted, and consider the probable effect upon the general happiness or good. We must gress the consequences which would follow, if the class of acts were general; and also the consequences which would follow, if they were generally omitted. We must then compare the consequences on the positive and negative sides, and determine on which of the two the *balance* of advantage lies . . . . If we truly try the tendency of a specific or individual act, we try the tendency of the class to which that act belongs. The *particular* conclusion which we draw, with regard to the single act, implies a *general* conclusion embracing all similar acts. . . . To the rules thus inferred, and lodged in the memory, our conduct would conform *immediately* if it were truly adjusted to utility" (*ibid.*, p. 117). One might think that Austin meets the objection by stating the practice conception of rules; and perhaps he did intend to. But it is not clear that he has stated this conception. Is the generality he refers to of the statistical sort? This is suggested by the notion of tendency. Or does he refer to the utility of setting up a practice? I don't know; but what suggests the summary view is his subsequent remarks. He says: "To consider the specific consequences of single or individual acts, would *seldom* [my italics] consist with that ultimate principle" (*ibid.*, p. 117). But would one ever do this? He continues:" . . . this being admitted, the necessity of pausing and calculating, which the objection in question supposes, is an imagined necessity. To preface each act or forbearance by a conjecture and comparison of consequences, were clearly *superfluous* [my italics] and mischievous. It were clearly superfluous, inasmuch as the *result of that process* (my italics) would be embodied in a known *rule*. It were clearly mischievous, inasmuch as the *true* result would be expressed by that rule, whilst the process would probably be faulty, if it were done on the spur of the occasion" (*ibid.*, pp. 117–118). He goes on: "If our experience and observation of particulars were not *generalized*, our experience and observation of particulars would seldom avail us in *practice*. . . .The inferences suggested to our mind by repeated experience and observation are, therefore, drawn into *principles*, or compressed into *maxims*. These we carry about us ready for use, and apply to individual cases promptly . . . without reverting to the process by which they were obtained; or without recalling, and arraying before our minds, the numerous and intricate considerations of which they are *handy abridgments* [my italics] . . . True theory is a *compendium* of particular truths. . . . Speaking then, generally, human conduct is inevitably *guided* (my italics) by *rules*, or by *principle* or *maxims* (*ibid.*, pp. 117–118). I need not trouble to show how all these remarks incline to the summary view. Further, when Austin comes to deal with cases "of comparatively rare occurrence" he holds that specific considerations may outweigh the general. "Looking at the reasons from which we had inferred the rule, it were absurd to think it inflexible. We should therefore dismiss the *rule*; resort directly to the *principle* upon which our rules were fashioned; and calculate *specific* consequences to the best of our knowledge and ability" (*ibid.*, pp. 120–121). Austin's view is interesting because it shows how one may come close to the practice conception and then slide away from it.

which the rule refers doesn't require the stage-setting of a practice of which this rule is a part. This is what is meant by saying that on the summary view particular cases are logically prior to rules.

3. Each person is in principle always entitled to reconsider the correctness of a rule and to question whether or not it is proper to follow it in a particular case. As rules are guides and aids, one may ask whether in past decisions there might not have been a mistake in applying the utilitarian principle to get the rule in question, and wonder whether or not it is best in this case. The reason for rules is that people are not able to apply the utilitarian principle effortlessly and flawlessly; there is need to save time and to post a guide. On this view a society of rational utilitarians would be a society without rules in which each person applied the utilitarian principle directly and smoothly,

and without error, case by case. On the other hand, ours is a society in which rules are formulated to serve as aids in reaching these ideally rational decisions on particular cases, guides which have been built up and tested by the experience of generations, If one applies this view to rules, one is interpreting them as maxims, as "rules of thumb"; and it is doubtful that anything to which the summary conception did apply would be called a *rule*. Arguing as if one regarded rules in this way is a mistake one makes while doing philosophy.

4. The concept of a *general* rule takes the following form. One is pictured as estimating on what percentage of the cases likely to arise a given rule may be relied upon to express the correct decision, that is, the decision that would be arrived at if one were to correctly apply the utilitarian principle case by case. If one estimates that by and large the

In *A System of Logic*, bk. VI, ch. xii, par. 2, Mill distinguishes clearly between the position of judge and legislator and in doing so suggests the distinction between the two concepts of rules. However, he distinguishes the two positions to illustrate the difference between cases where one is to apply a rule already established and cases where one must formulate a rule to govern subsequent conduct. It's the latter case that interests him and he takes the "maxim of policy" of a legislator as typical of rules. In par. 3 the summary conception is very clearly stated. For example, he says of rules of conduct that they should be taken provisionally, as they are made for the most numerous cases. He says that they "point out" the manner in which it is least perilous to act; they serve as an "admonition" that a certain mode of conduct has been found suited to the most common occurrences. In *Utilitarianism*, ch. ii, par. 24, the summary conception appears in Mill's answer to the same objection Austin considered. Here he speaks of rules as "corollaries" from the principle of utility; these "secondary" rules are compared to "landmarks" and "direction-posts." They are based on long experience and so make it unnecessary to apply the utilitarian principle to each case. In par. 25 Mill refers to the task of the utilitarian principle in adjudicating between competing moral rules. He talks here as if one then applies the utilitarian principle directly to the particular case. On the practice view one would rather use the principle to decide which of the ways that make the practice consistent is the best. It should be noted that while in par. 10 Mill's definition of utilitarianism makes the utilitarian principle apply to morality, i.e., to the rules and precepts of human conduct, the definition in par. 2 uses the phrase "actions are right in *proportion* as they *tend* to promote happiness" [my italics] and this inclines towards the summary view. In the last paragraph of the essay "On the Definition of Political Economy," *Westminster Review* (October 1836), Mill says that it is only in art, as distinguished from science, that one can properly speak of exceptions. In a question of practice, if something is fit to be done "in the majority of cases" then it is made the rule. "We may . . . in talking of art *unobjectionably* speak of the *rule* and the *exception*, meaning by the rule the cases in which there exists a preponderance . . . of inducemnts for acting in a particular way; and by the exception, the cases in which the preponderance is on the contrary side." These remarks, too, suggest the summary view.

In Moore's *Principia Ethica*, ch. v, there is a complicated and difficult discussion of moral rules. I will not examine it here except to express my suspicion that the summary conception prevails. To be sure, Moore speaks frequently of the utility of rules as generally followed, and of actions as generally practiced. But it is possible that these passages fit the statistical notion of generality which the summary conception allows. This conception is suggested by Moore's taking the utilitarian principle as applying directly to particular actions (pp. 147–148) and by his notion of a rule as something indicating which of the few alternatives likely to occur to anyone will generally produce greater total good in the immediate future (p. 154). He talks of an "ethical law" as a prediction, and as a generalization (pp. 146, 155). The summary conception is also suggested by his discussion of exceptions (pp. 162–163) and of the force of examples of breaching a rule (pp. 163–164).

rule will give the correct decision, or if one estimates that the likelihood of making a mistake by applying the utilitarian principle directly on one's own is greater than the likelihood of making a mistake by following the rule, and if these considerations held of persons generally, then one would be justified in urging its adoption as a general rule. In this way *general* rules might be accounted for on the summary view. It will still make sense, however, to speak of applying the utilitarian principle case by case, for it was by trying to foresee the results of doing this that one got the initial estimates upon which acceptance of the rule depends. That one is taking a rule in accordance with the summary conception will show itself in the naturalness with which one speaks of the rule as a guide, or as a maxim, or as a generalization from experience, and as something to be laid aside in extraordinary cases where there is no assurance that the generalization will hold and the case must therefore be treated on its merits. Thus there goes with this conception the notion of a particular exception which renders a rule suspect on a particular occasion.

The other conception of rules I will call the practice conception. On this view rules are pictured as defining a practice. Practices are set up for various reasons, but one of them is that in many areas of conduct each person's deciding what to do on utilitarian grounds case by case leads to confusion, and that the attempt to coordinate behavior by trying to foresee how others will act is bound to fail. As an alternative one realizes that what is required is the establishment of a practice, the specification of a new form of activity; and from this one sees that a practice necessarily involves the abdication of full liberty to act on utilitarian and prudential grounds. It is the mark of a practice that being taught how to engage in it involves being instructed in the rules which define it, and that appeal is made to those rules to correct the behavior of those engaged in it. Those engaged in a practice recognize the rules as defining it. The rules cannot be taken as simply describing how those en-

gaged in the practice in fact behave: it is not simply that they act as if they were obeying the rules. Thus it is essential to the notion of a practice that the rules are publicly known and understood as definitive; and it is essential also that the rules of a practice can be taught and can be acted upon to yield a coherent practice. On this conception then, rules are not generalizations from the decisions of individuals applying the utilitarian principle directly and independently to recurrent particular cases. On the contrary, rules define practice and are themselves the subject of the utilitarian principle.

To show the important differences between this way of fitting rules into the utilitarian theory and the previous way, I shall consider the differences between the two conceptions on the points previously discussed.

1. In contrast with the summary view, the rules of practices are logically prior to particular cases. This is so because there cannot be a particular case of an action falling under a rule of a practice unless there is the practice. This can be made clearer as follows: in a practice there are rules setting up offices, specifying certain forms of action appropriate to various offices, establishing penalties for the breach of rules, and so on. We may think of the rules of a practice as defining offices, moves, and offenses. Now what is meant by saying that the practice is logically prior to particular cases is this: given any rule which specifies a form of action (a move), a particular action which would be taken as falling under this rule given that there is the practice would not be *described* as that sort of action unless there was the practice. In the case of actions specified by practices it is logically impossible to perform them outside the stage-setting provided by those practices, for unless there is the practice, and unless the requisite proprieties are fulfilled, whatever one does, whatever movements one makes, will fail to count as a form of action which the practice specifies. What one does will be described in some *other* way.

One may illustrate this point from the game of baseball. Many of the actions one performs in a game of baseball one can do by oneself or with others whether there is the game or not. For example, one can throw a ball, run, or swing a peculiarly shaped piece of wood. But one cannot steal base, or strike out, or draw a walk, or make an error, or balk; although one can do certain things which appear to resemble these actions such as sliding into a bag, missing a grounder and so on. Striking out, stealing a base, balking, etc., are all actions which can only happen in a game. No matter what a person did, what he did would not be described as stealing a base or striking out or drawing a walk unless he could also be described as playing baseball, and for him to be doing this presupposes the rule-like practice which constitutes the game. The practice is logically prior to particular cases: unless there is the practice the terms referring to actions specified by it lack a sense.[23]

2. The practice view leads to an entirely different conception of the authority which each person has to decide on the propriety of following a rule in particular cases. To engage in a practice, to perform those actions specified by a practice, means to follow the appropriate rules. If one wants to do an action which a certain practice specifies then there is no way to do it except to follow the rules which define it. Therefore, it doesn't make sense for a person to raise the question whether or not a rule of a practice correctly applies to *his* case where the action he contemplates is a form of action defined by a practice. If someone were to raise such a question, he would simply show that he didn't understand the situation in which he was acting. If one wants to perform an action specified by a practice, the only legitimate

question concerns the nature of the practice itself ("How do I go about making a will?")

This point is illustrated by the behavior expected of a player in games. If one wants to play a game, one doesn't treat the rules of the game as guides as to what is best in particular cases. In a game of baseball if a batter were to ask "Can I have four strikes?" it would be assumed that he was asking what the rule was; and if, when told what the rule was, he were to say that he meant that on this occasion he thought it would be best on the whole for him to have four strikes rather than three, this would be most kindly taken as a joke. One might contend that baseball would be a better game if four strikes were allowed instead of three; but one cannot picture the rules as guides to what is best on the whole in particular cases, and question their applicability to particular cases as particular cases.

3 and 4. To complete the four points of comparison with the summary conception, it is clear from what has been said that rules of practices are not guides to help one decide particular cases correctly as judged by some higher ethical principle. And neither the quasi-statistical notion of generality, nor the notion of a particular exception, can apply to the rules of practices. A more or less general rule of a practice must be a rule which according to the structure of the practice applies to more or fewer of the kinds of cases arising under it; or it must be a rule which is more or less basic to the understanding of the practice. Again, a particular case cannot be an exception to a rule of a practice. An exception is rather a qualification or a further specification of the rule.

It follows from what we have said about the practice conception of rules that if a per-

---

[23]One might feel that it is a mistake to say that a practice is logically prior to the forms of action it specifies on the grounds that if there were never any instances of actions falling under a practice then we should be strongly inclined to say that there wasn't the practice either. Blue-prints for a practice do not make a practice. That there is a practice entails that there are instances of people having been engaged and now being engaged in it (with suitable qualifications). This is correct, but it doesn't hurt the claim that any given particular instance of a form of action specified by a practice presupposes the practice. This isn't so on the summary picture, as each instance must be "there" prior to the rules, so to speak, as something from which one gets the rule by applying the utilitarian principle to it directly.

son is engaged in a practice, and if he is asked why *he* does what *he* does, or if he is asked to defend what he does, then his explanation, or defense, lies in referring the questioner to the practice. He cannot say of *his* action, if it is an action specified by a practice, that he does it rather than some other because he thinks it is best on the whole.[24] When a man engaged in a practice is queried about his action he must assume that the questioner either doesn't know that he is engaged in it ("Why are you in a hurry to pay him?" "I promised to pay him today") or doesn't know what the practice is. One doesn't so much justify one's particular action as explain, or show, that it is in accordance with the practice. The reason for this is that it is only against the stage-setting of the practice that one's particular action is described as it is. Only by reference to the practice can one *say* what one is doing. To explain or to defend one's action, as a particular action, one fits it into the practice which defines it. If this is not accepted it's a sign that a different question is being raised as to whether one is justified in accepting the practice, or in tolerating it. When the challenge is to the practice, citing the rules (saying what the practice is) is naturally to no avail. But when the challenge is to the particular action defined by the practice, there is nothing one can do but refer to the rules. Concerning particular actions there is only a question for one who isn't clear as to what the practice is, or who doesn't know that it is being engaged in. This is to be contrasted with the case of a maxim which may be taken as pointing to the correct decision on the case as decided on *other* grounds, and so giving a challenge on

the case a sense by having it question whether these other grounds really support the decision on this case.

If one compares the two conceptions of rules I have discussed one can see how the summary conception misses the significance of the distinction between justifying a practice and justifying actions falling under it. On this view rules are regarded as guides whose purpose it is to indicate the ideally rational decision on the given particular case which the flawless application of the utilitarian principle would yield. One has, in principle, full option to use the guides or to discard them as the situation warrants without one's moral office being altered in any way: whether one discards the rules or not, one always holds the office of a rational person seeking case by case to realize the best on the whole. But on the practice conception, if one holds an office defined by a practice then questions regarding one's actions in this office are settled by reference to the rules which define the practice. If one seeks to question these rules, then one's office undergoes a fundamental change: one then assumes the office of one empowered to change and criticize the rules, or the office of a reformer, and so on. The summary conception does away with the distinction of offices and the various forms of argument appropriate to each. On that conception there is one office and so no offices at all. It therefore obscures the fact that the utilitarian principle must, in the case of actions and offices defined by a practice, apply to the practice, so that general utilitarian arguments are not available to those who act in offices so defined.[25]

[24] A philosophical joke (in the mouth of Jeremy Bentham): "When I run to the other wicket after my partner has struck a good ball I do so because it is best on the whole."

[25] How do these remarks apply to the case of the promise known only to father and son? Well, at first sight the son certainly holds the office of promisor, and so he isn't allowed by the practice to weigh the particular case on general utilitarian grounds. Suppose instead that he wishes to consider himself in the office of one empowered to criticize and change the practice, leaving aside the question as to his right to move from his previously assumed office to another. Then he may consider utilitarian arguments as applied to the practice; but once he does this he will see that there are such arguments for not allowing a general utilitarian defense in the practice for this sort of case. For to do so would make it impossible to ask for and to give a kind of promise which one often wants to be able to ask for and to give. Therefore he will not want to change the practice, and so as a promisor he has no option but to keep his promise.

Some qualifications are necessary in what I have said. First, I may have talked of the summary and the practice conceptions of rules as if only one of them could be true of rules, and if true of any rules, then necessarily true of *all* rules. I do not, of course, mean this. (It is the critics of utilitarianism who make this mistake insofar as their arguments against utilitarianism presuppose a summary conception of the rules of practices.) Some rules will fit one conception, some rules the other; and so there are rules of practices (rules in the strict sense), and maxims and "rules of thumb."

Secondly, there are further distinctions that can be made in classifying rules, distinctions which should be made if one were considering other questions. The distinctions which I have drawn are those most relevant for the rather special matter I have discussed, and are not intended to be exhaustive.

Finally, there will be many border-line cases about which it will be difficult, if not impossible, to decide which conception of rules is applicable. One expects border-line cases with any concept, and they are especially likely in connection with such involved concepts as those of a practice, institution, game, rule, and so on. Wittgenstein has shown how fluid these notions are.[26] What I have done is to emphasize and sharpen two conceptions for the limited purpose of this paper. . . .

# QUESTIONS

1. Suppose that someone says: "Ultimately, the only thing that is relevant to the rightness of any action, whether it is keeping a promise, taking from the rich to give to the poor, or punishing an innocent person on trumped up charges, is whether it will do the most good overall. The only reason we have for thinking that breaking a promise or punishing an innocent person is wrong is that, *most* of the time, these things don't do the most good, everything considered." Using Rawls's argument as a source of ideas and starting point, construct a rule-utilitarian answer to this claim.

2. Think of the following as the statement of a rule: "It is wrong to break a promise." Explain what it would mean if understood as (a) a summary rule, and then as (b) a practice rule.

3. What, in Rawls's conception of justifying punishment, would one have to establish in order to show that one was justified in sending a parent to jail for her child's conviction on a charge of selling marijuana at summer camp?

4. Rawls gives the following analogy from baseball: "[I]f, when told what the rule was, he were to say that he meant that on this occasion he thought it would be best on the whole for him to have four strikes rather than three, this would be most kindly taken as a joke." Analyze Rawls's analogy. Why would this question be taken as a joke? Is it also out of the question to make an exception to a rule about applying punishment? If one must stick to the rule in both cases, are the reasons for doing so the same for the two cases? Is the practice of applying punishment sufficiently like playing a game to make the analogy compelling?

5. Explain, and then either defend or criticize, the following assertion: "Utilitarianism is a philosophy most appropriate for legislatures; retributivism, a philosophy most appropriate for judges. "

[26]*Philosophical Investigations* (Oxford, 1953), I, pars. 65–71, for example.

## *Jean Hampton*
# THE MORAL EDUCATION THEORY OF PUNISHMENT*

We ought not to repay injustice with injustice or to do harm to any man, no matter what we may have suffered from him.

Plato, *Crito*, X, 49

There are few social practices more time-honored or more widely accepted throughout the world than the practice of punishing wrongdoers. Yet if one were to listen to philosophers discussing this practice, one would think punishment impossible to justify and difficult even to understand. However, I do not believe that one should conclude that punishment as a practice is morally unjustifiable or fundamentally irrational. Instead I want to explore the promise of another theory of punishment which incorporates certain elements of the deterrence, retributivist, and rehabilitation views, but whose justification for punishment and whose formula for determining what punishment a wrongdoer deserves are distinctive and importantly different from the reasons and formulas characterizing the traditional theories.

This view, which I call the moral education theory of punishment, is not new. There is good reason to believe Plato and Hegel accepted something like it,[1] and more recently, Herbert Morris and Robert Nozick have maintained that the moral education which punishment effects is at least part of punishment's justification.[2] I want to go farther, however, and suggest that by reflecting on the educative character of punishment we can provide a full and complete justification for it. Hence my discussion of the moral education theory in this paper is meant to develop it as a complete justification of punishment and to distinguish it from its traditional rivals. Most of my discussion will focus on the theory's application to the state's punishment of criminal offenders, but I will also be looking at the theory's implications for punishment within other societal institutions, most notably the family.

I will not, however, be able to give an adequate development of the theory in this paper. It is too complex, and too closely connected to many difficult issues, including the nature of law, the foundation of ethical reasoning, and the way human beings develop ethical concepts. Hence what I shall do is simply to *introduce* the theory, sketching its outlines in the first half, and suggesting what seem to be certain advantages and

*Reprinted by permission of Princeton University Press. Jean Hampton, "The Moral Education Theory of Punishment," *Philosophy & Public Affairs*, vol. 13, no. 3 (Summer 1984), copyright © 1984 by Princeton University Press. pp. 208–38 reprinted by permission.

[1] See Hegel, *Philosophy of Right*, tran. T. Knox (Oxford: Clarendon Press, 1952), sections 90–104 (pp. 66–74); and see Plato, in particular the dialogues: *The Laws* (bks. 5 and 9), *Gorgias* (esp. pp. 474ff.), *Protagoras* (esp. pp. 323ff.) and Socrates's discussion of his own punishment in the *Apology* and the *Crito*. I am not convinced that this characterization of either Hegel's or Plato's views is correct, but I do not have time to pursue those issues here. J. E. McTaggart has analyzed Hegel's position in a way that suggests it is a moral education view. See his "Hegel's Theory of Punishment," *International Journal of Ethics* 6 (1896), pp. 482–99; portions reprinted in *Philosophical Perspectives On Punishment*, ed. Gertrude Ezorsky (Albany, NY: State University of New York Press, 1972). In her *Plato on Punishment*, M. M. Mackenzie's presentation of Plato's position suggests it is not a strict moral education view.

[2] Recently Morris has been explicitly advocating this view in "A Paternalistic Theory of Punishment," *American Philosophical Quarterly* 18, no. 4 (October 1981), but only as *one aspect* of the justification of punishment. Morris argues that punishment is sufficiently complicated to require a justification incorporating all of the justificatory reasons offered by the traditional theories of punishment as well as by the moral education view. I do not think this sort of patchwork approach to punishment will work and, in this article, I explore the idea that the moral education view can, by itself, give an adequate justification of punishment.

See also Nozick's recent book *Philosophical Explanations* (Cambridge: Harvard University Press, 1981), pp. 363–97.

drawbacks of the view in the second half. Much more work needs to be done before anyone is in a position to embrace the view wholeheartedly, hence I won't even attempt to argue in any detailed way here that it is superior to the three traditional views. But I hope my discussion will show that this theory is promising, and merits considerably more discussion and study by the larger intellectual community.

## I. THE JUSTIFICATION

Philosophers who write about punishment spend most of their time worrying about whether the state's punishment of criminals is justifiable, so let us begin with that particular issue.

When does punishment by the state take place? The answer to this question seems simple: the state carries out punishment upon a person when he or she has broken a *law*. Yet the fact that the state's punishment always follows the transgression of a law is surely neither coincidental nor irrelevant to the understanding and justification of this practice. What is the nature of law? This is a thorny problem which has vexed philosophers for hundreds of years. For the purposes of this article, however, let us agree with Hart that there are (at least) two kinds of law, those which are power-conferring rules, for example, rules which specify how to make a contract or a will, and those which are "rules of obligation."[3] We are concerned with the latter kind of rule, and philosophers and legal theorists have generally analyzed the structure of this sort of law as "orders backed by threats" made by the state.

What is the subject matter of these orders? I will contend (consistent with a positivist account of law) that the subject matter *ought* to be (although it might not always be) drawn either from ethical imperatives, of the form "don't steal," or "don't murder," or else from imperatives made necessary for moral reasons, for example, "drive on the right"— so that the safety of others on the road is insured, or "advertise your university job in the professional journals"—so that blacks and women will not be denied an opportunity to secure the job.[4] The state makes these two kinds of commands not only to define a minimal set of duties which a human being in that community must follow in his or her dealings with others, but also to designate actions which, when followed by all members of the society, will solve various problems of conflict and coordination.[5]

And the threat? What role does it play? In the end, this is the central question for which we must have an adequate answer if we are to construct a viable theory of punishment.

The threat, which specifies the infliction of pain if the imperative is not obeyed, gives people a nonmoral incentive, that is, the avoidance of pain, to refrain from the prohibited action. The state hopes this incentive will block a person's performance of the immoral action whenever the ethical incentive fails to do so. But insofar as the threat given in the law is designed to play this kind of "deterring" role, carrying out the threat, that is, punishing someone when he or she has broken the law, is, at least in part, a way of "making good" on the threat. The threat will only deter the disobedience of the state's orders if people believe there is a good chance the pain will be inflicted upon them after they commit the crime. But if the state punishes

---

[3]See Hart, *The Concept of Law* (Oxford: Clarendon Press, 1961), chaps. 5 and 6.

[4]As stated, this is a positivist definition of law. However, with John Chipman Gray I am maintaining that morality, although not the same as law, should be the source of law. (See Gray's *The Nature and Source of Law* [New York: Macmillan, 1921], p, 84.)

[5]See Edna Ullman-Margalit, *The Emergence of Norms* (Oxford: Clarendon Press, 1977) for a discussion of how law can solve coordination and conflict problems.

in order to make good on its threats, then the deterrence of future crime cannot be wholly irrelevant to the justification of punishment. And anyone, including Kant, who analyzes laws as orders backed by threats must recognize that fact.[6]

Moreover, I believe we must accept the deterrence theorist's contention that the justification of punishment is connected with the fact that it is a necessary tool for preventing future crime and promoting the public's well-being. Consider standard justifications of the state: philosophers from Plato to Kant to Hart have argued that because a community of people cannot tolerate violent and destructive behavior in its midst, it is justified in establishing a state which will coercively interfere in people's lives for publicly announced and agreed-upon reasons so that an unacceptable level of violence and harm can be prevented. Whereas we normally think the state has to respect its citizens' choices about how to live, certain choices, for example, choices to rape, to murder, or to steal, cannot be respected by a community which is committed to preserving and pursuing the well-being of its members. So when the state annexes punishment to these damaging activities, it says that such activities are not a viable option for anyone in that community.

But to say that the state's punishment is needed to prevent crime is not to commit oneself to the deterrence justification of punishment—it all depends on what one takes prevention to entail. And, as Hegel says, if we aimed to prevent wrongdoing only by deterring its commission, we would be treating human beings in the same way that we treat dogs.[7] Consider the kind of lesson an animal learns when, in an effort to leave a pasture, it runs up against an electrified fence. It experiences pain and is conditioned, after a series of encounters with the fence, to stay away from it and thus remain in the pasture. A human being in the same pasture will get the same message and learn the same lesson—"if you want to avoid pain, don't try to transgress the boundary marked by this fence." But, unlike the animal in the pasture, a human being will also be able to reflect on the reasons for that fence's being there, to theorize about *why* there is this barrier to his freedom.

Punishments are like electrified fences. At the very least they teach a person, via pain, that there is "barrier" to the action she wants to do, and so, at the very least, they aim to deter. But because punishment "fences" are marking *moral* boundaries, the pain which these "fences" administer (or threaten) conveys a larger message to beings who are able to reflect on the reasons for these barriers' existence: they convey that there is a barrier to these actions *because* they are morally wrong. Thus, according to the moral education theory, punishment is not intended as a way of conditioning a human being to do what society wants her to do (in the way that an animal is conditioned by an electrified fence to stay within a pasture); rather, the theory maintains that punishment is intended as a way of teaching the wrongdoer that the action she did (or wants to do) is forbidden because it is morally wrong and should not be done for that reason. The theory also regards that lesson as public, and thus as directed to the rest of society. When the state makes its criminal law and its en-

---

[6]Although Kant's position on punishment is officially retributive (see his *Metaphysical Elements of Justice*, trans, J. Ladd [Indianapolis: Bobbs-Merrill, 1965], p. 100, Academy edition, p. 331), his definition of law conflicts with his retributivist position. Note, for example, the deterrent flavor of his justification of law:

> if a certain use of freedom is itself a hindrance to freedom according to universal laws (that is, unjust), then the use of coercion to counteract it, inasmuch as it is the prevention of a hindrance to freedom according to universal laws, is consistent with freedom according to universal laws; in other words, this use of coercion is just (p. 36, Academy edition, p. 231; see also *Metaphysical Elements of Justice* pp. 18–19, 33–45; Academy edition, pp. 218–21, 229–39).

[7]Hegel, *Philosophy of Right*, addition to par. 99, p. 246.

forcement practices known, it conveys an educative message not only to the convicted criminal but also to anyone else in the society who might be tempted to do what she did.

Comparing punishments to electrical fences helps to make clear how a certain kind of deterrent message is built into the larger moral point which punishment aims to convey. If one wants someone to understand that an offense is immoral, at the very least, one has to convey to him or her that it is prohibited—that it ought not to occur. Pain is the way to convey that message. The pain says "Don't!" and gives the wrongdoer a reason for not performing the action again; an animal shocked by a fence gets the same kind of message and the same kind of incentive. But the state also wants to use the pain of punishment to get the human wrongdoer to reflect on the moral reasons for that barrier's existence, so that he will make the decision to reject the prohibited action for *moral* reasons, rather than for the self-interested reason of avoiding pain.

If those who are punished (or who watch the punishment take place) reject the moral message implicit in the punishment, at least they will learn from it that there is a barrier to the actions they committed (or are tempted to commit). Insofar as they choose to respond to their punishment (or the punishment of others) merely as a threat, it can keep them within moral boundaries in the same way that fences keep animals in a pasture. This deterrent effect of punishment is certainly welcome by the state whose role is to protect its citizens, and which has erected a "punishment barrier" to certain kinds of actions precisely because those actions will seriously harm its citizens. But on the moral education view, it is incorrect to regard simple deterrence as the aim of punishment; rather, to state it succinctly, the view maintains that punishment is justified as a way to prevent wrongdoing insofar as it can teach both wrongdoers and the public at large the moral reasons for *choosing* not to perform an offense.

I said at the outset that one of the reasons any punishment theory is complicated is that it involves one in taking stands on many difficult ethical and legal issues. And it should be quite clear already that particular positions on the nature of morality and human freedom are presupposed by the moral education view which distinguish the theory from its traditional rivals. Given that the goal of punishment, whether carried out by the state on criminals or by parents on children, is the offender's (as well as other potential offenders') realization of an action's wrongness, the moral education view naturally assumes that there is a fact of the matter about what is right and what is wrong. That is, it naturally rests on ethical objectivism. Perhaps certain sophisticated subjectivists could adapt the theory to accommodate their ontological commitments (punishment, they might say, teaches what society defines as right and wrong). But such an accommodation, in my view, does real damage to the theory, which purports to explain punishment as a way of conveying when an action *is* wrong. Given that the theory holds that punishment is a way of teaching ethical *knowledge*, if there is no such thing, the practice seems highly suspect.

The theory also takes a strong stand on human freedom. It rests on the idea that we can act freely in a way that animals cannot. If we were only like animals, attempts at punishment would affect us in the way that electrical fences affect animals—they would deter us, nothing more. But this theory assumes that we are autonomous, that we can choose and be held accountable for our actions. Thus it holds that punishments must attempt to do more than simply deter us from performing certain offenses; they must also, on this view, attempt to provide us with moral reasons for our *choosing* not to perform these actions. Only creatures who are free to determine their lives according to their moral values can choose not to do an action because it is wrong. Insofar as the moral education view justifies punishment as a way of promoting that moral choice, it assumes that punishment is (and ought only to be) inflicted on beings who are free in this sense.[8] It might be that human beings who have lost their autonomy and who have broken a law can be justifiably treated in a painful way so as to deter them (even as we would deter dangerous animals) from behaving similarly in the future, but this theory would not call such treatment punishment.

Thus one distinction between the moral education view and the deterrence justification of punishment is that on the moral education view, the state is not concerned to use pain coercively so as to progressively eliminate certain types of behavior; rather, it is concerned to educate its citizens morally so that they choose to engage in this behavior. Moreover, there is another important difference between the two views. On the deterrence view, the infliction of pain on certain individuals is justified as a way of promoting a larger social end. But critics of the deterrence view have pointed out that this is just to say that it is all right to *use* certain individuals to achieve a desirable social goal. The moral education theory, however, does not sanction the use of a criminal for social purposes; on the contrary, it attempts to justify punishment as a way to benefit the person who will experience it, a way of helping him to gain moral knowledge if he chooses to listen. Of course other desirable social goals will be achieved through his punishment, goals which include the education of the larger community about the immorality of the offense, but none of these ends is to be achieved at the expense of the criminal. Instead the moral good which punishment attempts to accomplish within the wrongdoer makes it something which is done *for* him, not *to* him.

There are also sharp differences between the moral education view and various rehabilitative theories of criminal "treatment." An advocate of the moral education view does not perceive punishment as a way of treating a "sick" person for a mental disease, but rather as a way of sending a moral message to a person who has acted immorally and who is to be held responsible for her actions.[9] And whereas both theorists are concerned with the good which punishment can do for the wrongdoer, they disagree about what that good is, one defining it as moral growth, the other as the wrongdoer's acceptance of society's mores and her successful operation in the community. In addition, as we shall discuss in Section II, they disagree about what methods to use to achieve these different ends.

Some readers might wonder how close the moral education view is to the old retribution theory. Indeed references in the literature to a view of this type frequently characterize it as a variant of retribution.[10] Nonetheless, there are sharp and important differences between the two views, which we will explore in more detail in Section II. Suffice to say now that whereas retributivism understands punishment as performing the rather metaphysical task of "negating the wrong" and "reasserting the right," the moral education theorist argues that there is a concrete moral goal which punishment should be designed to accomplish, and that goal includes the benefiting of the criminal himself. The state, as it punishes the lawbreaker, is trying to

[8]Kantians who see a close connection between autonomy and moral knowledge will note that this connection is suggested in these remarks.

[9]Rehabilitationists disagree about exactly what disease criminals suffer from. See for example the various psychiatric diagnoses of Benjamin Karpman in "Criminal Psychodynamics: A Platform," reprinted in *Punishment and Rehabilitation,* ed. J. Murphy (Belmont, CA: Wadsworth, 1973) as opposed to the behaviorist analysis of criminal behavior offered by B. F. Skinner in *Science and Human Behavior* (New York: Macmillan, 1953), pp. 182–93 and 446–49.

[10]See for example Nozick's characterization of the view as "teleological retributivism," pp. 370–74 and Gertrude Ezorsky's use of that term in *Philosophical Perspectives on Punishment.*

promote his moral personality; it realizes that "(h)is soul is in jeopardy as his victim's is not."[11] Thus, it punishes him as a way of communicating a moral message to him, which he can accept or not, as he chooses.

Certain retributivists have also been very attracted to the idea that punishment is a kind of speech act. For example, Robert Nozick in his book *Philosophical Explanations* has provided a nice nine-point analysis of punishment which presents it as a kind of communication and which fits the account of meaning put forward by H. P. Grice.[12] Yet if punishment is a way of (morally) speaking with a wrongdoer, then why doesn't this show that it is fundamentally justified as a *communication*, in virtue of what it is trying to communicate, rather than, in Nozick's view, as some kind of symbolic "linkage" of the criminal with "correct values"?[13]

Indeed, I would maintain that regarding punishment as a kind of moral communication is intuitively very natural and attractive. Consider, for example, what we say when we punish others: a father who punishes his child explains that he does so in order that the child "learn his lesson"; someone who has been physically harmed by another demands punishment "so that she will understand what she did to me"; a judge recently told a well-known user of cocaine that he was receiving a stiff sentence because his "matter-of-fact dabbling in cocaine . . . tells the whole world it is all right to use it."[14] These kinds of remarks accompanying our punishment efforts suggest that our principal concern as we punish is to get the wrongdoer to stop doing the immoral action by communicating to her that her offense was immoral. And the last remark by the judge to the cocaine user shows that when the state punishes it is important that these communications be public, so that other members of society will hear the same moral message. Even people who seem to be seeking revenge on wrongdoers behave in ways which show that they too want to make a moral point not only to the wrongdoer, but to anyone else who will listen. The hero seeking revenge in a Western movie, for example, never simply shoots the bad guy in the back when he finds him—he always confronts the bad guy first (usually in the presence of other people) and tells him *why* he is about to die. Indeed, the movie would be unsatisfying if he didn't make that communication. And surely, the hero's desire to explain his actions is linked with his desire to convey to the bad guy and to others in society that the bad guy had "done him wrong."[15]

Moreover, if one understands punishment as a moral message aimed at educating both the wrongdoer and the rest of society about the immorality of the offense, one has a powerful explanation (at least as powerful as the one offered by retributivism) of why victims so badly want their assailants punished. If the point of punishment is to convey to the criminal (and others) that the criminal *wronged* the victim, then punishment is implicitly recognizing the victim's plight, and honoring the moral claims of that individual. Punishment affirms as a *fact* that the victim has been wronged, and as a *fact* that he is owed a certain kind of treatment from others. Hence, on this view, it is natural for

---

[11]Morris, "The Paternalistic Theory of Punishment," p. 268.

[12]Nozick, pp. 369–80.

[13]Ibid, pp. 374ff. The point is that if one is going to accept the idea that punishment is a communication, one is connecting it with human purposive activity, and hence the *purpose* of speaking to the criminal (as well as to the rest of society) becomes central to the justification of the communication itself. To deny this is simply to regard punishment as something fundamentally different from a species of communication (for example, to regard it as some kind of "value-linkage device") which Nozick seems reluctant to do.

[14]*Los Angeles Times*, 30 July 1981, part 4, p. I.

[15]Nozick has also found the "communication" element in comic book stories about revenge; see *Philosophical Explanations*, pp. 368–69.

the victim to demand punishment because it is a way for the community to restore his moral status after it has been damaged by his assailant.

Thus far, I have concentrated on how the state's punishment of criminals can be justified as an attempt at moral education. But I want to contend that punishment efforts by *any* institution or individual should be perceived as efforts at moral education, although the nature and extensiveness of the legitimate educative roles of these institutions and individuals might differ sharply. For example, I believe it is quite clear that parents want to make such a moral communication through their punishments.[16] Suppose for example, that a mother sees her daughter hitting another child. After stepping in to stop this violent behavior, the mother will reflect on what she can do to prevent its reoccurrence. If the mother chooses to try to do this by punishing her daughter, one of the things she "says" through the punishment is, "if you do this again, you will experience the same unpleasantness," and this message is directed at any other children in the family, as well as at this daughter. Hence, one of the things the mother is doing is introducing the incentive of avoiding pain into the children's "calculations" about how to act if and when they are tempted in the future to hurt each other. If a genuine concern for each other's well-being is absent from the children's minds, at least this incentive (as well as fear of losing her approval) might be strong enough to prevent them from hurting each other in the future.[17] But

clearly the mother is also trying to get her children to appreciate that there is a *moral* reason for prohibiting this action. The punishment is supposed to convey the message, "don't do this action again because it is *wrong*; love and not hatred or unwarranted violence is what one should display towards one another." The ultimate goal of the punishment is not merely to deter the child from performing the bad action in the future, but to deter her *by convincing her* (as well as the other children) to renounce the action because it is wrong. And the older and more ethically mature the child becomes, the less the parent will need to resort to punishment to make her moral point, and the more other techniques like moral suasion, discussion, or debate, will be appropriate.

However, although both state and parental punishment should, according to this theory, be understood as efforts at moral communication and education, the theory does not regard the two kinds of punishment as exactly the same. While punishment should always be regarded as moral education, the "character" of that education can vary enormously, depending in particular on the nature of the institution or individual charged with inflicting the punishment. For example, a parent who is responsible for the full maturation and moral development of her child is naturally thought to be entitled to punish her children for many more offenses and in very different ways, than the children's schoolteacher, or the neighbor down the street. We also think of a university as having punishment rights over its students,

[16]Parental punishment can take many forms; although spanking and various kinds of corporal punishment are usually what spring to mind when one thinks of parental punishment, many parents punish through the expression of anger or disapproval, which can be interpreted by the child as a withdrawal of love or as the (at least temporary) loss of the parent's friendship. Such deprivations are in many ways far more serious than the momentary experience of bodily pain or the temporary loss of certain privileges, and hence, although they seem to be mild forms of punishment, they can in actuality be very severe. I am indeed indebted to Herbert Morris for suggesting this point.

[17]Because children are not completely responsible, rational beings, punishing them can also be justified as a way of encouraging in them certain kinds of morally desirable habits, insofar as it has "conditioning like" effects. Aristotle seems to regard punishment of children as, at least in part, playing this role. See for example *Nicomachean Ethics*, bk. I. chap. 4. I would not want to deny that aspect of parental punishment.

but we certainly reject the idea that this sort of institution acts *in loco parentis* towards its students generally. Hence, the theory would not have us understand the punishment role of all institutions and particularly governments, as the *same* as punishment by parents.[18] None of us, I believe, thinks that the state's role is to teach its citizens the entire contents of morality—a role we might characterize as "moral paternalism." A variety of considerations are important in limiting the mode and extent of the state's punishment.

Nonetheless, some readers still might think the moral education theory implies a paternalistic theory of the state—after all, doesn't it maintain that the state can interfere in people's lives for their own good? But when such philosophers as John Stuart Mill have rejected paternalism, what they have rejected is a certain position on what should be law; specifically, they have rejected the state's passing any law which would restrict what an individual can do to *himself* (as opposed to what he can do to another). They have not objected to the idea that when the state justifiably interferes in someone's life *after* he has broken a law (which prohibited harm to another), it should intend good rather than evil towards the criminal. Now it is possible they might call this theory paternalistic anyway, not because it takes any stand on what should be law, but because it views the state's punishment as interference in his life plans without his consent for his own good. But why should paternalism in this sense be offensive? It would be strange indeed if philosophers insisted that the state should only try to prevent further harm to the community by actively intending to harm, or at least be indifferent to, the people it punishes!

But, Mill might complain, if you are willing to allow the state to morally educate those who harm others, why not allow it to morally educate those who harm themselves? This is a good question, but one the moral education theory cannot answer. Indeed, answering it is the same as answering the question: What ought to be made law? Or, alternatively, what is the appropriate area for legislation? Though central to political theory, these questions are ones to which the moral education theory can give no answer, for while the theory maintains that punishment of a certain sort should follow the transgression of a law, it is no part of the theory to say *what* ethical reasons warrant the imposition of a law. Indeed, one of the advantages of the theory is that one can adopt it no matter what position one occupies on the political spectrum.

But, critics might insist, isn't this theory arguing that the state should be in the business of deciding and enforcing morality, overriding the autonomous moral decisions of its citizens? Yes, that is exactly the theory's point, the state *is* in that business in a very limited way. Imagine a murderer saying: "You, the state, have no right to tell me that my murder of this man is wrong," or a rapist protesting: "Who is the state to tell me that my rape of this woman is immoral?" These statements sound absurd, because we believe not merely that such actions are wrong, but that they are also heinous and morally appalling. The state is justified in punishing rapists and murderers because their choices about what to do betray a serious inability to make decisions about immoral and moral actions, which has resulted in substantial harm to some members of that community. And while some readers might find it offensive to contemplate the state presuming to morally educate anyone but serious felons, is this not exactly the kind of sentiment behind the libertarians' call for extensive constraints on the state's role and power?

---

[18]It is because I believe there are sharp and important differences between parental and state punishment that I eschew Herbert Morris's title for this type of punishment theory (that is, his title, "the paternalistic theory of punishment").

Moreover, I wonder whether, by calling this theory paternalistic, one might not be irritated more by the thought of being governed than by the thought of what this particular theory says being governed involves. Yet, unless one is prepared to be an anarchist, one must admit that being governed is necessary as long as we, as human beings, are prone to immoral acts. We do not outgrow cruelty, or meanness, or the egoistic disregard for others when we reach the age of majority. On this view, the state exists because even adults need to be governed, although not in the way that children require governing by their parents. (Indeed, these ideas suggested by the theory form a germ of an argument against anarchism, which I can only pursue in another place.)

But, critics might insist, it is this theory's view of what governing involves that is objectionable. Who and what is the state, that it can presume to teach us a moral lesson? Yet I regard this question not as posing a challenge to the moral education view itself, but rather as posing a challenge *by* that theory to any existing state. Not only does the theory offer a partial explanation of the state's role, but it also proposes a view of what the state *ought* to be like if its punishment activities have any legitimacy. For example, insofar as the state should be morally educating when it punishes, this theory implies that the state's laws should be arrived at by reflection on what is right or wrong, and not on what is in the best interest of a particular class, or race, or sex. That this is not always true of the laws of our society is an indictment of our state, and punishments inflicted as a way of enforcing these biased laws cannot be justified. Moreover, if we accept the idea that the state is supposed to morally educate its citizens, it is natural to argue that all of its citizens should participate either directly or through representatives in the legislative branch of that institution in order to control and supervise its moral enforcement so that the resulting laws reflect the moral consensus of the community rather than the views of one class. Hence the moral education view can underlie an argument for the democratic structure of a state.

Finally, I would contend that the moral education theory illuminates better than any of its theoretical rivals the strategy of those who are civilly disobedient. Martin Luther King, Jr. wrote that it is critical for anyone who wants to be civilly disobedient to accept the penalty for his or her lawbreaking, not only to express "the very highest respect for law" but also "to arouse the conscience of the community over its injustice."[19] The moral education theory explains how both these objectives are achieved. The civilly disobedient person, when she accepts the penalty for lawbreaking, is respecting the state's right to punish transgressors of its laws, but she is also forcing the state to commit itself, in full view of the rest of society, to the idea that her actions show she needs moral education. And when that person is protesting, as Gandhi or King did, offensive and unjust laws, she knows the state's punishment will appear morally outrageous and will arouse the conscience of anyone sensitive to the claims of justice. Therefore, the civilly disobedient person is, on this view, using the idea of what the state and its laws ought to be like if its punishment activities have legitimacy in order to effect moral improvement in the legal system.

## II. QUESTIONS AND CRITICISMS

Although I will not fully develop and defend the moral education view in this article, I now want to put some flesh on the skeletal presentation of the view just given by considering some questions which spring naturally to mind as one reflects on the theory.

[19]Martin Luther King, Jr., "Letter from a Birmingham Jail," from *Civil Disobedience*, ed. H. A. Bedau (New York: Pegasus, 1969), pp. 78–9.

1. *What is this theory's punishment formula?* Punishment formulas always follow directly from punishment justifications. If punishment is justified as a deterrent, then it follows from that justification that particular punishments should be structured so as to deter. But if punishment is justified as a way of morally educating the wrongdoer and the rest of society about the immorality of the act, then it follows that one should punish in ways that promote this two-part goal. But how do we go about structuring punishments that morally educate? And would this way of determining punishments yield intuitively more just punishments than those yielded by the formulas of the traditional theories?

One reason these formulas of all the traditional theories have been attacked as unjust is that all of them fail to incorporate an acceptable upper bound on what punishments can be legitimately inflicted on an offender. Consider that, once the deterrence theorist has defined his deterrence goal, any punishment that will achieve this goal is justified, including the most brutalizing. Similarly, the retributivist's *lex talionis* punishment formula (dictating that punishments are to be somehow equal to the crime) would seem to recommend, for example, torturing the torturer, murdering *all* murderers, and such recommendations cast serious doubt on the formula's moral adequacy.[20] Even the rehabilitation theory does not place strict limits on the kinds of "treatments" which can legitimately be given to offenders. If the psychiatric "experts" decide that powerful drugs, shock treatments, lobotomies or other similar medical procedures are legitimate and

necessary treatments of certain criminals, why shouldn't they be used? The only upper bound on the treatments inherent in this theory derives from the consciences of psychiatrists and the consensus about what constitutes "reasonable" treatment, and many contend that history has shown such an upper bound to be far too high.[21]

The moral education theory, however, does seem to have the resources to generate a reasonable upper limit on how much punishment the state can legitimately administer. Because part of the goal of punishment is to educate the criminal, this theory insists that as he is educated, his autonomy must be respected. The moral education theorist does not want "education" confused with "conditioning." Shock treatments or lobotomies that would damage or destroy the criminal's freedom to choose are not appropriate educative techniques. On this view the goal of punishment is not to destroy the criminal's freedom of choice, but to persuade him to use his freedom in a way consistent with the freedom of others. Thus, any punishment that would damage the autonomy of the criminal is ruled out by this theory.

In addition, it is important to remember that, on this view, punishments should be designed to convey to the criminal and to the rest of society the idea that the criminal's act was wrong. And it seems difficult if not impossible for the state to convey this message if it is carrying out cruel and disfiguring punishments such as torture or maiming. When the state climbs into the moral gutter with the criminal in this way it cannot credibly convey either to the criminal or to the public

---

[20]Some retributivists have tried to argue that the *lex talionis* needn't be regarded as a formula whose upper bound *must* be respected; see, for example, K. C. Armstrong, "The Retributivist Hits Back," *Philosophy of Punishment*, ed. H. B. Acton (London: Macmillan, 1969). However, critics can object that Armstrong's weaker retributivist position still does not *rule out* barbaric punishments (like torture) as permissible, nor does it explain why and when punishments which are less in severity than the criminal act can be legitimately inflicted.

[21]Consider the START program used in a Connecticut prison to "rehabilitate" child molesters: electrodes were connected to the prisoner's skin, and then pictures of naked boys and girls were flashed on a screen while electric shocks were applied. The Federal Bureau of Prisons canceled this program just before they were about to lose a court challenge to the program's constitutionality (see David J. Rothman's discussion of this in "Behavior Modification in Total Institutions," *Hastings Center Report* 5, no. I [1975]: 22].

its moral message that human life must always be respected and preserved, and such actions can even undercut its justification for existing. Note that both of these considerations indicate this theory rules out execution as punishment.[22] (Of course, the moral education theory says nothing about whether the execution of criminals might be justified not as punishment but as a method of "legitimate elimination" of criminals who are judged to have lost all of their essential humanity, making them wild beasts of prey on a community that must, to survive, destroy them. Whether such a justification of criminal execution can be morally tolerable is something I do not want to explore here.)

But, the reader might wonder, how can inflicting *any* pain upon a criminal be morally educational? And why isn't the infliction of mild sorts of pains and deprivations also climbing into the moral gutter with the criminal? The moral education theorist must provide an explanation of why certain sorts of painful experiences (whose infliction on others we would normally condemn) may legitimately be inflicted in order to facilitate moral growth. But is such an explanation possible? And even if it is, would the infliction of pain always be the right way to send a moral message? If a criminal's psychological makeup is such that pain would not reform him, whereas "inflicting" a pleasurable experience would produce this reform, are we therefore justified only in giving him that pleasurable experience? Retributivists like Robert Nozick think the answer to this last question is yes, and thus reject the view as an adequate justification of punishment by itself.[23]

All three of these worries would be allayed if the moral education theorist could show that only the infliction of pain of a certain sort following a wrongdoing is *necessarily* connected with the promotion of the goal of moral education. In order to establish this necessary connection between certain sorts of painful experiences and moral growth, the moral education theorist needs an account of what moral concepts are, and an account of how human beings come to acquire them (that is, what moral education is). I cannot even attempt to propose, much less develop, answers to these central ethical issues here. But I will try to offer reasons for thinking that painful experiences of a particular sort would seem to be necessary for the communication of a certain kind of moral message.

It is useful to start our discussion by getting a good understanding of what actions count as punishment. First, if we see punishment from the offender's standpoint, we appreciate that it involves the loss of her freedom. This is obviously true when one is locked up in a penitentiary, but it is also true when, for example, parents stop their child's allowance (money that has previously been defined as hers is withheld—whether she likes it or not) or when they force her to experience a spanking or a lecture. I would argue that this loss of freedom is why (autonomous) human beings so dislike punishment. Second, whereas it is very natural to characterize punishment as involving pain or other unpleasant consequences, the infliction of what we intuitively want to call punishment might involve the wrongdoer in performing actions which one would not normally describe as painful or unpleasant. For example, a doctor who cheated the Medicare system and is sentenced to compulsory weekend service in a state-supported clinic would not be undergoing what one would normally describe as a painful or

---

[22]Apart from the fact that killing someone is hardly an appropriate technique for educating him, it is likely that this action sends a poor message to the rest of society about the value of human life. Indeed, in one of their national meetings, the Catholic bishops of the United States argued that repeal of capital punishment would send "a message that we can break the cycle of violence, that we need not take life for life, that we can envisage more human and more hopeful and effective responses to the growth of violent crime." ("Statement on Capital Punishment," *Origins* 10, no. 24 [27 November 1980]: 374.)

[23]Nozick, pp. 373–74.

unpleasant experience (he isn't being incarcerated, whipped, fined). Nonetheless, insofar as some of his free time is being taken away from him, the state is depriving him of his freedom to carry out his own plans and to pursue the satisfaction of his own interests. In this case, the state is clearly punishing an offender, but it sounds distorted to say that it is inflicting pain on him. Thus we need a phrase to describe punishment which will capture better than "infliction of pain" all of the treatments which we intuitively want to call punishment. For this purpose I propose the phrase "disruption of the freedom to pursue the satisfaction of one's desires," a phrase which is suitably general and which fits a wide variety of experiences that we want to call experiences of *punishment*. (It may well be *too* general, but I do not want to pursue that issue here.)[24]

Thus I understand punishment as an experience which a wrongdoer is forced by an authority to undergo in virtue of the fact that he has transgressed (what ought to be) a morally derived rule laid down by that authority, and which disrupts (in either a major or a minor way) the wrongdoer's freedom to pursue the satisfaction of his desires. Given that punishment is understood in this way, how do coercion and disruption of one's self-interested pursuits convey a *moral* message?

Before answering this question, it is important to make clear that punishment is only *one* method of moral education. Upon reflection, it is clear, I think, that we choose to employ this method only when we're trying to teach someone that an action is *wrong*, rather than when we are trying to teach someone what (imperfect) moral duties he or she ought to recognize. (We punish a child when he kicks his brother: we don't

punish him in order to get him to give Dad a present on Father's Day.)

What is one trying to get across when one wants to communicate an action's wrongness? The first thing one wants to convey is that the action is forbidden, prohibited, "fenced off." Consider a mother who sees her child cheating at solitaire. She might say to the child, "You mustn't do that." Or if she saw her child putting his left shoe on his right foot, she would likely say, "No, you mustn't dress that way." In both cases it would be highly inappropriate for her to follow these words with punishment. She is communicating to her child that what he is doing in these circumstances is inadvisable, imprudent, not playing by the rules, but she is not communicating (and not trying to communicate) the idea that such actions violate one's moral duty to others (or, for that matter, one's moral duty to oneself). Now consider this mother seeing her son kick the neighbor's young daughter. Once again she might say, "You mustn't do that," to the child, but the "mustn't" in the mother's words here is unique. It is more than "you shouldn't" or "it isn't advisable" or "it's against the rules of the game." Rather, it attempts to convey the idea that the action is forbidden, prohibited, intolerable.

But merely telling the child that he "mustn't do that" will not effectively convey to the child that there is this profound moral boundary. Without punishment why shouldn't the child regard the "mustn't" in the parent's statement just as he did the "mustn't" in "You mustn't cheat at solitaire"? The mother needs to get across to the child the very special nature of the prohibition against this immoral act. How can she do this? Consider the fact that someone who (for no moral reason) violates a positive duty to others is not acting

---

[24]George Fletcher, in *Rethinking Criminal Law* (Boston: Little, Brown, 1978), p. 410, worries about defining punishment so that it doesn't include too much (for example, it should not include the impeachment of President Nixon, despite the fact that it would be a case of unpleasant consequences inflicted on Nixon by an authority in virtue of a wrongdoing). I do not have time here to consider how to hone my definition such that it will not encompass impeachments, deportation, tort damages, and so forth. Indeed, perhaps the only way one can do this is to bring into the definition of punishment its justification as moral education.

out of any interest in the other's well-being. A teenager who steals from a passer-by because she needs the money, a man who rapes a woman so that he can experience a sense of power and mastery—such people are performing immoral acts in order to satisfy their own needs and interests, insensitive to the needs and interests of the people they hurt. The way to communicate to such people that there is a barrier of a very special sort against these kinds of actions would seem to be to link performance of the actions with what such people care about most—the pursuit of their own pleasure. Only when disruption of that pursuit takes place will a wrongdoer appreciate the special force of the "mustn't" in the punisher's communication. So the only effective way to "talk to" such people is through the disruption of their own interests, that is, through punishment (which has been defined as just such a disruption.)

What conclusions will a person draw from this disruption of his pleasure? At the very least he will conclude that his society (in the guise of the family, the state, the university, etc.) has erected a barrier to that kind of action, and that if he wants to pursue the satisfaction of his own desires, he won't perform that action again. So at the very least, he will understand his punishment as society's attempt to deter him from committing the action in the future. Such a conclusion does not have moral content. The person views his punishment only as a sign of society's condemnation of the act, not as a sign of the act's *wrongness*. But it is a start, and a *necessary first start*. If a wrongdoer has little or no conception of an action's wrongness, then the first thing one must do is to communicate to him that the action is prohibited. We must put up the electrical fence in an attempt to keep him out of a forbidden realm.

But given that we want the offender to understand the moral reasons for the action's condemnation, how can punishment communicate those reasons? The punisher wants the wrongdoer to move from the first stage of the educative process initiated by punishment—the realization that society prohibits the action—to a second stage, where the moral reasons for the condemnation of the action are understood and accepted. Can punishment, involving the disruption of a person's self-interested pursuits, help an offender to arrive at this final moral conclusion, to understand, in other words, why this fence has been erected?

What is it that one wants the wrongdoer to see? As we noted before, someone who (for no moral reason) violates her (perfect) moral duty to others is not thinking about the others' needs and interests, and most likely has little conception of, or is indifferent to, the pain her actions caused another to suffer. Hence, what the punisher needs to do is to communicate to the wrongdoer *that* her victims suffered and how much they suffered, so that the wrongdoer can appreciate the harmfulness of her action. How does one get this message across to a person insensitive to others? Should not such a person be made to endure an unpleasant experience designed, in some sense, to "represent" the pain suffered by her victim(s)? This is surely the institution behind the *lex talionis* but it best supports the concept of punishment as moral education. As Nozick admits,[25] it is very natural to regard the pain or unpleasantness inflicted by the wrongdoer as the punisher's way of saying: "This is what you did to another. You hate it; so consider how your victim felt." By giving a wrongdoer something like what she gave to others, you are trying to drive home to her just how painful and damaging her action was for her victims, and this experience will, one hopes, help the wrongdoer to understand the immorality of her action.

Of course, the moral education formula does not recommend that punishments be specifically *equal* to the crime—in many instances this doesn't even make sense. But

---

[25]Compare Nozick's discussion of the content of the Gricean message of punishment. pp. 370–74.

what does the "representation" of the wrongful act involve, if not actual equality? This is a terribly difficult question, and I find I can only offer tentative, hesitant answers. One way the moral education theorist can set punishments for crimes is to think about "fit." Irrespective of how severe a particular crime is, there will sometimes be a punishment that seems naturally suited to it; for example, giving a certain youth charged with burglarizing and stealing money from a neighbor's house the punishment of supervised compulsory service to this neighbor for a period of time, or giving a doctor charged with cheating a government medical insurance program the punishment of compulsory unremunerated service in a state medical institution. And probably such punishments seem to fit these crimes because they force the offender to compensate the victim, and thus help to heal more effectively the "moral wound" which the offense has caused. Another way the moral education theorist can make specific punishment recommendations is to construct an ordinal scale of crimes, going from most offensive to least offensive, and then to link determinate sentences to each crime, respecting this ordinal comparison, and insuring proportionality between crime and punishment. But it is not easy to use either method to fashion a tidy punishment table because it is not easy to determine which painful experiences will be educative but not cruel, both proportional to the offense committed and somehow relevant to that offense. Indeed, our society has been notoriously unsuccessful in coming up with punishments that are in any way morally educative. And I would argue that it speaks in favor of this theory that it rejects many forms of incarceration used today as legitimate punishments, insofar as they tend to make criminals morally worse rather than better.

But even if this theory can tell us how to represent wrongdoing in a punishment, it must still handle other questions which I do not have time to pursue properly in this article. For example, how does that representation help the wrongdoer to understand and *accept* the fact that she did wrong and should do otherwise in the future? And if we want to send the most effective message possible in order to bring about this acceptance, should we try to tailor punishments to the particular psychological and moral deficiencies of the wrongdoer, or must considerations of equal treatment and fairness override this? Finally, does the view justify the state's punishing people who are innocent of any illegal act but who seem to need moral education?

The theory has a very interesting and complicated response to this last question. We have said that punishment is not the appropriate method to teach every sort of moral lesson, but only the lesson that a certain action is wrong. But on whom is the state justified in imposing such a lesson?—clearly, a person who has shown she needs the lesson by committing a wrong which the state had declared illegal, and clearly *not* a person who has shown she already understands this lesson (at least in some sense) by conscientiously obeying that law. We also believe that the state is justified in imposing this lesson on a person who has not broken that law but who has *tried* to do so. She might, for example, be punished for "attempted murder" or "attempted kidnapping." (And do we make the punishments for such attempts at wrongdoing less than for successful wrongdoings because we're not sure the attempts provide conclusive evidence that such people would have carried through?) But what about a person who has not broken a law or even attempted to do so but who has, say, talked about doing so publicly? Is that enough evidence that she needs a moral education? Probably—by *some* person or institution, but not by the state. The point is that we believe the state should refrain from punishing immoral people who have nonetheless committed no illegal act, not because they don't need moral education but because the state is not the appropriate institution to effect that education. Indeed, one of the reasons we insist that the state operate by enacting laws is that doing so defines when it may coercively interfere in the lives of its citizens and when it may not; its legislation, in other words, defines the extent of its educative role (and there might exist constitutional rules guiding this legislation). So if the state were to interfere with its citizens' lives when they had not broken its laws, it would exceed its own legitimate role. In the end, the state may not punish immoral people who are innocent of any crime not because they don't need moral education, but because the state is not justified in giving it to them.

However, there is another question relevant to the issue of punishing the innocent. Given that I have represented the moral education theory as having a two-part goal—the moral education of the criminal and the moral education of the rest of society—it might be that a punishment which would achieve one part of this goal would not be an effective way of realizing the other part. Must we choose between these two objectives, or is it possible to show that they are inextricably linked? And if they are not, could it be that in order to pursue the goal of morally educating *society*, it would be necessary to punish an innocent person? More generally, could it be justifiable on this view to punish a wrongdoer much more (or much less) severely than her offense (if any) would seem to warrant if doing so would further society's moral education? If this were true, the theory would not preserve proportionality between crime and punishments. However, there are reasons for thinking that educating the criminal and educating the community are inextricably linked. For example, if the state aims to convey a moral lesson to the community about how other human beings should be treated, it will completely fail to do so if it inflicts pain on someone innocent of any wrongdoing—indeed, it would send a message exactly contrary to the one it had intended. But even if we suppose, for the sake of argument, that

these educational objectives could become disengaged, we can preserve proportionality between a person's crime and her punishment by making the moral education of the criminal lexically prior to the moral education of the community (after all we *know* she needs the lesson, we're less sure about the community.)[26]

However, giving adequate arguments for solutions to any of the problems I have posed in this section requires a much more fully developed account of what moral education is and of how punishment would help to effect it. Some readers might think that developing such an account is simply an empirical rather than a philosophical task. But before we can know how to morally educate, we need a better theoretical understanding of what moral knowledge is, and why human beings do wrong. (Is it because, as Kant insists, we choose to defy the power of the moral law or because, as Socrates argues, we are morally ignorant?) Moreover, we need a better appreciation of the source and extent of the state's authority if we are to understand its legitimate role as moral educator. Further work on this theory has to come to grips with these issues in moral and political philosophy before we can know whether to embrace it. But I have tried to suggest in my remarks in this section that certain kinds of approaches to these issues are at least promising.

2. *Is the moral education of most criminals just a pipe dream?* How can we really expect hard-core criminals convicted of serious offenses to be able to change and morally improve? In answer to this last question, the moral education theorist will admit that the state can predict that many of the criminals it punishes will refuse to accept the moral message it delivers. As I have stressed, the moral education theory rests on the assumption of individual autonomy, and thus an advocate of this theory must not only admit but insist that the choice of whether to listen

[26]I have profited from discussions with Katherine Shamey on this point.

to the moral message contained in the punishment belongs to the criminal. Thus it is very unlikely that society will be 100 percent successful in its moral education efforts, no matter how well it uses the theory to structure punishments.

But at least the punishment the state delivers can have a deterrent effect; even if the criminal refuses to understand the state's communication about why there is a barrier to his action, at least he will understand *that* the barrier exists. Hegel once wrote that if a criminal is coerced by a punishment, it is because he *chooses* to be so coerced; such a person rejects the moral message and accepts instead the avoidance of pain as his sole reason for avoiding the action.[27] In the end, punishments might only have deterrent effects because that is all wrongdoers will let them have.

However, neither the state nor anyone else can determine who the "losers" are. None of us can read another's mind, none of us knows the pressures, beliefs, and concerns motivating another's actions and decisions. The state cannot, even with the help of a thousand psychiatrists, *know for sure* who is a hopeless case and who isn't. Nor is this just a simple epistemological problem. Insofar as the state, on this view, should regard each person it punishes as autonomous, it is committed to the view that the choice of whether to reform or not is a free one, and hence one the state cannot hope to predict. Finally, the state's assumption that the people it is entitled to punish are free means it must never regard any one it punishes as hopeless, insofar as it is assuming that each of these persons still has the ability to choose to be moral. Thus, as Hegel puts it,[28] punishment is the criminal's "right" as a free person—to refuse to punish him on the grounds that he has been diagnosed as hopeless is to regard him as something other than a rational human being.

But even if it seems likely that punishing some criminals will not effect their moral growth, and may not even deter them, the moral education of the community about the nature of their crimes can still be promoted by their punishment. Indeed any victim of crime is going to be very sensitive to this fact, insofar as he has been the one against whom the wrong has been committed, and is the one who is most interested in having the community acknowledge that what happened to him *shouldn't* have happened. And as long as the person whom we punish is admitted to be an autonomous human being, we cannot be convicted of using her as we educate the community about the wrongness of her offense, because we are doing something to her which is *for* her, which can achieve a great deal of good for her, if she will but let it.

3. *Shouldn't the moral education theory imply an indeterminate sentencing policy?* Throughout your discussion, rehabilitationists might complain, you have been assuming that punishment by the state should proceed from determinate sentences for specific crimes. But isn't indeterminate sentencing fairer? Why keep a criminal who has learned his moral lesson in jail just because his sentence has not run out, and why release a criminal who is unrepentant and who will probably harm the public again, just because his sentence has run out?

However, the moral education theorist has very good reasons, provided by the foundations of the theory itself, for rejecting the concepts of indeterminate sentences and parole boards. First, this theorist would strongly disagree with the idea that a criminal should continue to receive "treatment" until his reform has been effected. Recall that it is an important tenet of the view that the criminals we punish are free beings, responsible for their actions. And you can't *make*

[27]See Hegel, *Philosophy of Right*, sec. 91.
[28]Ibid, sec. 100, p. 70.

a free human being believe something. In particular, you can't coerce people to be just for justice's sake. Punishment is the state's attempt to teach a moral lesson, but whether or not the criminal will listen and accept it is up to the criminal himself.

The moral education theorist takes this stand not simply because she believes one ought to respect the criminal's autonomy, but also because she believes one has no choice but to respect it. The fact that parole boards in this country have tried to coerce repentance is, from the standpoint of this theorist, a grave and lamentable mistake. (Consider James McConnell's claim, in an article in *Psychology Today*, that "Somehow we've got to *force* people to love one another, to force them to want to behave properly.")[29] Indeed, critics of present parole systems in the United States maintain that these systems only open the way for manipulation.[30] The parole board uses the threat of the refusal of parole to get the kind of behavior it wants from the criminal, and the criminal manipulates back—playing the game, acting reformed, just to get out. In the process, no moral message is conveyed to the criminal, and probably no real reformation takes place. The high recidivism rate in the United States tells the tale of how successful parole boards have been in evaluating the rehabilitation of prisoners. As one prisoner put it: "If they ask if this yellow wall is blue, I'll say, of course it's blue. I'll say anything they want me to say if they're getting ready to let me go."[31]

The moral education theorist doesn't want the state to play this game. A sentence for a crime is set, and when the criminal breaks a law, the sentence is inflicted on him as a way of teaching him that what he did was wrong. When the sentence is up, the criminal is released. The state hopes its message was effective, but whether it was or not is largely up to the criminal himself.

There is another important reason why the moral education theorist does not want to insist on repentance before release. Even a good state can make mistakes when it enacts law. It is not just possible but probable that the state at one time or another will declare a certain action immoral which some of its citizens will regard as highly moral. These citizens will often decide to disobey this "immoral" law, and while being punished, will steadfastly refuse to repent for an action they believe was right. Martin Luther King, Jr. never repented for breaking various segregation laws in the South while he was in jail; few draft resisters repented for refusing to go to Vietnam when they were in prison. By not insisting on the repentance of its criminals, the state is, once again, respecting the freedom of its citizens—particularly each citizen's freedom of conscience, and their right, as free beings, to disagree with its rulings. Hence, the moral education theorist doesn't want the state to insist on repentance because it doesn't want Solzhenitsyns rotting in jail until they have "reformed."[32]

How can the moral education theorist justify the punishment of a criminal who is already repentant prior to his sentencing, or who repents before his sentence is completely served? The theorist's response to this question is complicated. Because it is difficult to be sure that a seemingly repentant

[29]From "Criminals Can be Brainwashed—Now," *Psychology Today*, April 1970, p. 14: also quoted in Rick Carlson's *The Dilemma of Corrections* (Lexington, MA: Lexington Books, 1976), p. 35.

[30]See "The Crime of Treatment," American Friends Service Committee from *The Struggle for Justice*, chap. 6 (New York: Hill and Wang, 1971) reprinted in *Punishment: Selected Readings*, eds., Feinberg and Gross.

[31]Quoted by Carlson, p. 161; from David Fogel, *We Are the Living Proof* (Cincinnati: W. H. Anderson, n.d.).

[32]Jeffrie Murphy has argued that instituting a rehabilitationist penal system would deny prisoners many of their present due process rights. See "Criminal Punishment and Psychiatric Fallacies," especially pp. 207–209, in *Punishment and Rehabilitation*, ed. J. Murphy. The American Friends Service Committee has also charged that the California penal system, which was heavily influenced by the rehabilitation theory, has in fact done this. See "The Crime of Treatment," pp. 91–93, in Feinberg et al.

criminal is *truly* repentant, and thus because a policy of suspending or shortening sentences for those who seem repentant to the authorities could easily lead the criminal to fake repentance before a court or a parole board, the moral education theorist would be very reluctant to endorse such a policy.

Moreover, it might well be the case that, prior to or during sentencing, a criminal's experience of repentance is produced in large part by the expectation of receiving the full punishment, so that the state's subsequent failure to inflict it could lead to a weakening of the criminal's renunciation of the action. Like a bad but repentant child who will conclude, if he is not punished by his parents, that his action must not have been so bad, the repentant criminal might well need to experience his complete sentence in order to "learn his lesson" effectively.

Finally, the lesson learning effected by punishment can also involve a purification process for a wrongdoer, a process of healing. As Herbert Morris has written, experiencing the pain of punishment can be a kind of catharsis for the criminal, a way of "burning out" the evil in his soul.[33] Novelists like Dostoyevsky have explored the criminal's need, born of guilt and shame, to experience pain at the hands of the society he has wronged in order to be reconciled with them. Thus the rehabilitationist who would deny the criminal the experience of pain at the hands of the state would deny him what he may want and need to be forgiven—both by society and by himself. And punishment understood as moral education would explain how it could be perceived as a purification process. For how is it that one overcomes shame? Is it not by becoming a person different from the one who did the immoral action? The subsiding of shame in us seems to go along with the idea. "Given who I was, I did the action then, but I'm different now—I'm *better* now—and I wouldn't

do the same act again." But how do we become different, how do we change, improve? Insofar as punishment is seen as a way of educating oneself about the offense, undergoing that experience is a way of changing for the better. It might well be the yearning for that change which drives a person like Raskolnikov towards his punishment.

Nonetheless, if there were clear evidence that a criminal was very remorseful for his action and had already experienced great pain because of his crime (had "suffered enough"), this theory would endorse a suspension of his sentence or else a pardon (*not* just a parole). His moral education would have already been accomplished, and the example of his repentance would be lesson enough for the general public. (Indeed, punishment under these circumstances would make the state appear vindictive.) In addition, because the state conceives itself to be punishing a wrong, it is appropriate for it to allow certain sorts of excuses and mitigating circumstances to lessen the penalty normally inflicted for the crime in question.

4. *Does the moral education theory actually presuppose the truth of retribution?* Retributivists have a very interesting criticism of the moral education theory available to them. Granted, they might maintain, that punishment is connected with moral education, still this only provides an additional reason for punishing someone—it does not provide the fundamental justification of punishment. That fundamental justification, they would argue, is retributive: wrongdoers simply deserve to experience pain for the sake of the wrong they have committed. As Kant has argued, however much good one intends one's punishment to effect,

> yet it must first be justified in itself as punishment i.e. as mere harm, so that if it stopped there, and the person punished

---

[33]See Morris's discussion of certain wrongdoers' need to experience punishment in "The Paternalistic Theory of Punishment," p. 267.

could get no glimpse of kindness hidden behind this harshness, he must yet admit that justice was done him, and that his reward was perfectly suitable to his conduct.[34]

Moreover, such modern retributivists as Walter Moberly have argued that it is only when the wrongdoer can assent to his punishment as already justified in virtue of his offense that the punishment can do him any good.[35]

In a certain sense, Moberly's point is simply that a criminal will perceive his punishment as vindictive and vengeful unless he understands or accepts the fact that it is justified. But should the justification of punishment be cashed out in terms of the retributive concept of desert, given that it has been difficult for retributivists to say what they mean by the criminal's "deserving" punishment simply in virtue of his offense? Robert Nozick tries to cash out the retributive link between crime and "deserved" punishment by saying that the punishment represents a kind of "linkage" between the criminal and "right values."[36] But why is inflicting pain on someone a way of effecting this linkage? Why isn't the infliction of a pleasurable experience for the sake of the crime just as good a way of linking the wrongdoer with these right values? And if Nozick explains the linkage of pain with crime by saying that the pain is necessary in order to communicate to the criminal that his action was wrong, he has answered the question but lost his retributive theory.

Other philosophers, like Hegel,[37] speak of punishment as a way of "annulling" or "canceling" the crime and hence "deserved" for that reason. But although Hegel's words have a nice metaphorical ring to them, it is hard to see how they can be given a literal force that will explain the retributivist concept of desert. As J. L. Mackie has written, insofar as punishment occurs after the crime, it certainly cannot cancel it—past events are not eliminated by later ones.[38]

It is partly because retributivists have been at a loss to explain the notion of desert implicit in their theory of punishment that I have sought to propose and explore a completely nonretributivist justification of punishment. But my reasons for rejecting retributivism are deeper. The retributive position is that it is somehow morally appropriate to inflict pain for pain, to take an eye for an eye, a tooth for a tooth. But how is it ever morally appropriate to inflict one evil for the sake of another? How is the society that inflicts the second evil any different from the wrongdoer who has inflicted the first? He strikes first, they strike back; why is the second strike acceptable but the first not? Plato, in a passage quoted at the start of this article, insists that both harms are wrong; and Jesus attacks retributivism[39] for similar reasons:

You have learned that they were told, 'Eye for eye, tooth for tooth'. But what I tell you is this: Do not set yourself against the man who wrongs you. . . . You have heard that

---

[34]Kant, *Critique of Practical Reason*, "The Analytic of Pure Practical Reason," Remark II. (Abbott trans. in *Kant's Theory of Ethics* [London: Longman, 1959], p. 127; Academy edition, p.38.)

[35]Walter Moberly, *The Ethics of Punishment*, (London: Faber & Faber, 1968), p. 141.

[36]Nozick. pp. 374ff.

[37]For example, see Hegel, *The Philosophy of Right*, sec. 101–103.

[38]J. L. Mackie, "Morality and the Retributive Emotions, " in *Criminal Justice Ethics* I, no. I (Winter/Spring 1982): 3–10. In the face of the retributivists' failure to explain why punishment is deserved, Mackie wants to argue that our retributive intuitions spring from fundamental retributive emotions, which are part of a human being's fundamental moral make-up (and he gives a sketch of how our evolution as a species could have generated such emotions). But many retributivists, particularly the Kantian sort, would eschew such an explanation which, in any case, is hardly *justification* of the retributive impulse itself.

[39]Jesus rejected not only "negative retributivism," that is, the idea that we deserve bad for doing bad, but also "positive retributivism," that is, the idea that we deserve good for doing good, but I cannot go into that here.

they were told 'Love your neighbor, hate your enemy'. But what I tell you is this: Love your enemy and pray for your persecutors; only so can you be children of your heavenly father, who makes the sun rise on good and bad alike, and sends the rain on the honest and dishonest. [Matt. 5:38-9, 43-6]

In other words, both reject retributivism because they insist that the only thing human beings "deserve" in this life is *good*, that no matter what evil a person has committed, no one is justified in doing further evil to her.

But if one accepts the idea that no one can ever deserve ill, can we hope to justify punishment? Yes, if punishment can be shown to be a good for the wrongdoer. The moral education theory makes just such an attempt to explain punishment as a good for those who experience it, as something done *for* them, not to them, something designed to achieve a goal that includes their own moral well-being. This is the justification of punishment the criminal needs to hear so that he can accept it as legitimate rather than dismiss it as vindictive. Therefore, my interest in the moral education theory is connected with my desire to justify punishment *as a good* for those who experience it, and to avoid any theoretical justification of punishment that would regard it as a deserved evil.[40] Reflection on the punishment activities of those who truly love the people they punish, for example, the infliction of pain by a parent on a beloved but naughty child, suggests to me that punishment should not be justified as a deserved evil, but rather as an attempt, by someone who cares, to improve a wayward person.

Still, the moral education theory can incorporate a particular notion of desert which might be attractive to retributivists. Anyone who is punished according to this theory would know that his punishment is "deserved," that is, morally required, insofar as the community cannot morally tolerate the immoral lesson that his act conveys to others (for example, the message that raping a woman is all right if it gives one a feeling of self-mastery) and cannot morally allow that he receive no education about the evil of his act.

So the theory's point is this: Wrong occasions punishment not because pain deserves pain, but because evil deserves correction.

## QUESTIONS

1. Do all laws reflect moral distinctions or moral principles? In particular, does punishing a person for failing to file an income tax return by April 15 teach a moral lesson in the same sense that punishing the violator of a law against assaulting another person is supposed to teach a moral lesson?

2. Hampton says that punishment is an unpleasant experience serving to "communicate to the wrongdoer *that* her victims suffered . . . , so that the wrongdoer can appreciate the harmfulness of her action." Suppose that the wrongdoer is an intelligent sadist who was able most effectively to torture others precisely because she knew exactly what would harm them, and how much. Does punishment of such a person then teach her any lesson she does not already know? How would Hampton's view be defended in light of this kind of example?

3. Hampton says, "as long as the person whom we punish is admitted to be an autonomous human being, we cannot be convicted of using her as we educate the community about

[40]Indeed, I believe that it is because retribution would justify punishment as a deserved evil that it strikes many as much too close to revenge.

the wrongness of her offense, because we are doing something to her which is *for* her, which can achieve a great deal of good for her, if she will but let it." Does it make sense to say that we are punishing someone *for* her moral education when we know with certainty that the punishment will not produce the desired result?

4. If judges had a rough idea of the extent to which various convicted wrongdoers would learn a moral lesson from punishment, would it be required, in Hampton's theory, to punish or not depending on whether the wrongdoer would learn from the experience? Why or why not?

5. Suppose that S would have no compunction about committing burglary or assault, and that this is part of the reason he is confused about a very vivid dream he had: He mistakenly believes that he actually is guilty. Would officials be justified, according to Hampton's theory, in punishing him for the imagined crime if they could do so without revealing his real innocence? Why or why not?

# Cases on Punishment

# United States Supreme Court*
## GREGG v. GEORGIA

. . . Judgment of the Court, and opinion of MR. JUSTICE STEWART, MR. JUSTICE POWELL, and MR. JUSTICE STEVENS, announced by MR. JUSTICE STEWART.

The issue in this case is whether the imposition of the sentence of death for the crime of murder under the law of Georgia violates the Eighth and Fourteenth Amendments.

## I

The petitioner, Troy Gregg, was charged with committing armed robbery and murder. In accordance with Georgia procedure in capital cases, the trial was in two stages, a guilt stage and a sentencing stage. The evidence at the guilt trial established that on November 21, 1973, the petitioner and a traveling companion, Floyd Allen, while hitchhiking north in Florida were picked up by Fred Simmons and Bob Moore. Their car broke down, but they continued north after Simmons purchased another vehicle with some of the cash he was carrying. While still in Florida, they picked up another hitchhiker, Dennis Weaver, who rode with them to Atlanta, where he was let out about 11 p.m. A short time later the four men interrupted their journey for a rest stop along the highway. The next morning the bodies of Simmons and Moore were discovered in a ditch nearby.

On November 23, after reading about the shootings in an Atlanta newspaper, Weaver communicated with the Gwinnett County police and related information concerning the journey with the victims, including a description of the car. The next afternoon, the petitioner and Allen, while in Simmons' car, were arrested in Asheville, N. C. In the search incident to the arrest a .25-caliber pistol, later shown to be that used to kill

Simmons and Moore, was found in the petitioner's pocket. After receiving the warnings required by *Miranda* v. *Arizona*, 384 U. S. 436 (1966), and signing a written waiver of his rights, the petitioner signed a statement in which he admitted shooting, then robbing Simmons and Moore. He justified the slayings on grounds of self-defense. The next day, while being transferred to Lawrenceville, Ga., the petitioner and Allen were taken to the scene of the shootings. Upon arriving there, Allen recounted the events leading to the slayings. His version of these events was as follows: After Simmons and Moore left the car, the petitioner stated that he intended to rob them. The petitioner then took his pistol in hand and positioned himself on the car to improve his aim. As Simmons and Moore came up an embankment toward the car, the petitioner fired three shots and the two men fell near a ditch. The petitioner, at close range, then fired a shot into the head of each. He robbed them of valuables and drove away with Allen.

A medical examiner testified that Simmons died from a bullet wound in the eye and that Moore died from bullet wounds in the cheek and in the back of the head. He further testified that both men had several bruises and abrasions about the face and head which probably were sustained either from the fall into the ditch or from being dragged or pushed along the embankment. Although Allen did not testify, a police detective recounted the substance of Allen's statements about the slayings and indicated that directly after Allen had made these statements the petitioner had admitted that Allen's account was accurate. The petitioner testified in his own defense. He confirmed that Allen had made the statements described by the

*428 U.S. 153 (1976). Numerous citations omitted without so specifying.

detective, but denied their truth or ever having admitted to their accuracy. He indicated that he had shot Simmons and Moore because of fear and in self-defense, testifying they had attacked Allen and him, one wielding a pipe and the other a knife.

The trial judge submitted the murder charges to the jury on both felony-murder and nonfelony-murder theories. He also instructed on the issue of self-defense but declined to instruct on manslaughter. He submitted the robbery case to the jury on both an armed-robbery theory and on the lesser included offense of robbery by intimidation. The jury found the petitioner guilty of two counts of armed robbery and two counts of murder.

At the penalty stage, which took place before the same jury, neither the prosecutor nor the petitioner's lawyer offered any additional evidence. Both counsel, however, made lengthy arguments dealing generally with the propriety of capital punishment under the circumstances and with the weight of the evidence of guilt. The trial judge instructed the jury that it could recommend either a death sentence or a life prison sentence on each count. The judge further charged the jury that in determining what sentence was appropriate the jury was free to consider the facts and circumstances, if any, presented by the parties in mitigation or aggravation.

Finally, the judge instructed the jury that it "would not be authorized to consider [imposing] the penalty of death" unless it first found beyond a reasonable doubt one of these aggravating circumstances:

"One—That the offense of murder was committed while the offender was engaged in the commission of two other capital felonies, to-wit the armed robbery of [Simmons and Moore].

"Two—That the offender committed the offense of murder for the purpose of receiving money and the automobile described in the indictment.

"Three—The offense of murder was outrageously and wantonly vile, horrible and inhuman, in that they [sic] involved the depravity of [the] mind of the defendant."

Finding the first and second of these circumstances, the jury returned verdicts of death on each count.

The Supreme Court of Georgia affirmed the convictions and the imposition of the death sentences for murder. After reviewing the trial transcript and the record, including the evidence, and comparing the evidence and sentence in similar cases in accordance with the requirements of Georgia law, the court concluded that, considering the nature of the crime and the defendant, the sentences of death had not resulted from prejudice or any other arbitrary factor and were not excessive or disproportionate to the penalty applied in similar cases. The death sentences imposed for armed robbery, however, were vacated on the grounds that the death penalty had rarely been imposed in Georgia for that offense and that the jury improperly considered the murders as aggravating circumstances for the robberies after having considered the armed robberies as aggravating circumstances for the murders.

We granted the petitioner's application for a writ of certiorari limited to his challenge to the imposition of the death sentences in this case as "cruel and unusual" punishment in violation of the Eighth and the Fourteenth Amendments. . . .

We address initially the basic contention that the punishment of death for the crime of murder is, under all circumstances, "cruel and unusual" in violation of the Eighth and Fourteenth Amendments of the Constitution. In Part IV of this opinion, we will consider the sentence of death imposed under the Georgia statutes at issue in this case.

The Court on a number of occasions has both assumed and asserted the constitutionality of capital punishment. In several cases that assumption provided a necessary foundation for the decision, as the Court was asked to decide whether a particular method of carrying out a capital sentence would be allowed to stand under the Eighth Amendment. But until *Furman* v. *Georgia*, 408 U. S. 238 (1972), the Court never confronted squarely the fundamental claim that the punishment of death always, regardless of the enormity of the offense or the procedure followed in imposing the sentence, is cruel and unusual punishment in violation of the Constitution. Although this issue was presented and addressed in *Furman*, it was not resolved by the Court. Four Justices would have held that capital punishment is not unconstitutional *per se*; two Justices would have reached the opposite conclusion; and three Justices, while agreeing that the statutes before the Court were invalid as applied, left open the question whether such punishment may ever be imposed. We now hold that the punishment of death does not invariably violate the Constitution.

## A

The history of the prohibition of "cruel and unusual" punishment already has been reviewed at length. The phrase first appeared in the English Bill of Rights of 1689, which was drafted by Parliament at the accession of William and Mary. See Granucci, "Nor Cruel and Unusual Punishments Inflicted:" The Original Meaning, 57 Calif. L. Rev. 839, 852–853 (1969). The English version appears to have been directed against punishments

unauthorized by statute and beyond the jurisdiction of the sentencing court, as well as those disproportionate to the offense involved. *Id.*, at 860. The American draftsmen, who adopted the English phrasing in drafting the Eighth Amendment, were primarily concerned, however, with proscribing "tortures" and other "barbarous" methods of punishment." *Id.*, at 842.[17]

In the earliest cases raising Eighth Amendment claims, the Court focused on particular methods of execution to determine whether they were too cruel to pass constitutional muster. The constitutionality of the sentence of death itself was not at issue, and the criterion used to evaluate the mode of execution was its similarity to "torture" and other "barbarous" methods. See *Wilkerson* v. *Utah*, 99 U. S. 130, 136 (1879) ("[I]t is safe to affirm that punishments of torture . . . and all others in the same line of unnecessary cruelty, are forbidden by that amendment . . . "): *In re Kemmler*, 136 U. S. 436, 447 (1890) ("Punishments are cruel when they involve torture or a lingering death . . . "). See also *Louisiana ex rel. Francis* v. *Resweber*, 329 U. S. 459, 464 (1947) (second attempt at electrocution found not to violate Eighth Amendment, since failure of initial execution attempt was "an unforeseeable accident" and "[t]here [was] no purpose to inflict unnecessary pain nor any unnecessary pain involved in the proposed execution").

But the Court has not confined the prohibition embodied in the Eighth Amendment to "barbarous" methods that were generally outlawed in the 18th century. Instead, the Amendment has been interpreted in a flexible

---

[17]This conclusion derives primarily from statements made during the debates in the various state conventions called to ratify the Federal Constitution. For example, Virginia delegate Patrick Henry objected vehemently to the lack of a provision banning "cruel and unusual punishments":

"What has distinguished our ancestors?—That they would not admit of tortures, or cruel and barbarous punishment. But Congress may introduce the practice of the civil law, in preference to that of the common law. They may introduce the practice of France, Spain, and German—of torturing, to extort a confession of the crime." 3 J. Elliot, Debates 447–448 (1863).

A similar objection was made in the Massachusetts convention: "They are nowhere restrained from inventing the most cruel and unheard-of punishments and annexing them to crimes; and there is no constitutional check on them, but that *racks* and *gibbets* may be amongst the most mild instruments of their discipline." 2 Elliot, *supra*, at 111.

and dynamic manner. The Court early recognized that "a principle to be vital must be capable of wider application than the mischief which gave it birth." *Weems* v. *United States*, 217 U. S. 349, 373 (1910). Thus the Clause forbidding "cruel and unusual" punishments "is not fastened to the obsolete but may acquire meaning as public opinion becomes enlightened by a humane justice." *Id.*, at 378.

In *Weems* the Court addressed the constitutionality of the Philippine punishment of *cadena temporal* for the crime of falsifying an official document. That punishment included imprisonment for at least 12 years and one day, in chains, at hard and painful labor; the loss of many basic civil rights; and subjection to lifetime surveillance. Although the Court acknowledged the possibility that "the cruelty of pain" may be present in the challenged punishment, 217 U. S., at 366, it did not rely on that factor, for it rejected the proposition that the Eighth Amendment reaches only punishments that are "inhuman and barbarous, torture and the like." *Id.*, at 368. Rather, the Court focused on the lack of proportion between the crime and the offense:

> "Such penalties for such offenses amaze those who have formed their conception of the relation of a state to even its offending citizens from the practice of the American commonwealths, and believe that it is a precept of justice that punishment for crime should be graduated and proportioned to offense." *Id.*, at 366–367.

Later, in *Trop* v. *Dulles, supra*, the Court reviewed the constitutionality of the punishment of denationalization imposed upon a soldier who escaped from an Army stockade and became a deserter for one day. Although the concept of proportionality was not the basis of the holding, the plurality observed in dicta that "[f]ines, imprisonment and even execution may be imposed depending upon the enormity of the crime." 356 U. S., at 100.

The substantive limits imposed by the Eighth Amendment on what can be made criminal and punished were discussed in *Robinson* v. *California*, 370 U. S. 660 (1962). The Court found unconstitutional a state statute that made the status of being addicted to a narcotic drug a criminal offense. It held, in effect, that it is "cruel and unusual" to impose any punishment at all for the mere status of addiction. The cruelty in the abstract of the actual sentence imposed was irrelevant: "Even one day in prison would be a cruel and unusual punishment for the 'crime' of having a common cold." Most recently, in *Furman* v. *Georgia, supra*, three Justices in separate concurring opinions found the Eighth Amendment applicable to procedures employed to select convicted defendants for the sentence of death.

It is clear from the foregoing precedents that the Eighth Amendment has not been regarded as a static concept. As Mr. Chief Justice Warren said, in an oft-quoted phrase, "[t]he Amendment must draw its meaning from the evolving standards of decency that mark the progress of a maturing society." *Trop* v. *Dulles, supra*, at 101. Thus, an assessment of contemporary values concerning the infliction of a challenged sanction is relevant to the application of the Eighth Amendment. As we develop below more fully, this assessment does not call for a subjective judgment. It requires, rather, that we look to objective indicia that reflect the public attitude toward a given sanction.

But our cases also make clear that public perceptions of standards of decency with respect to criminal sanctions are not conclusive. A penalty also must accord with "the dignity of man," which is the "basic concept underlying the Eighth Amendment." *Trop* v. *Dulles, supra*, at 100 (plurality opinion). This means, at least, that the punishment not be "excessive." When a form of punishment in the abstract (in this case, whether capital punishment may ever be imposed as a sanction for murder) rather than in the particular (the propriety of death as a penalty to be applied to a specific defendant for a specific crime) is under consideration, the inquiry into "excessiveness" has two aspects. First, the punishment must not involve the unnecessary and wanton infliction of pain. Second, the punishment must not be grossly out of proportion to the severity of the crime. . . .

Four years ago, the petitioners in *Furman* and its companion cases predicated their argument primarily upon the asserted proposition that standards of decency had evolved to the point where capital punishment no longer could be tolerated. The petitioners in those cases said, in effect, that the evolutionary process had come to an end, and that standards of decency required that the Eighth Amendment be construed finally as prohibiting capital punishment for any crime regardless of its depravity and impact on society. This view was accepted by two Justices. Three other Justices were unwilling to go so far; focusing on the procedures by which convicted defendants were selected for the death penalty rather than on the actual punishment inflicted, they joined in the conclusion that the statutes before the Court were constitutionally invalid.

The petitioners in the capital cases before the Court today renew the "standards of decency" argument, but developments during the four years since *Furman* have undercut substantially the assumptions upon which their argument rested. Despite the continuing debate, dating back to the 19th century, over the morality and utility of capital punishment, it is now evident that a large proportion of American society continues to regard it as an appropriate and necessary criminal sanction.

The most marked indication of society's endorsement of the death penalty for murder is the legislative response to *Furman*. The legislatures of at least 35 States have enacted new statutes that provide for the death penalty for at least some crimes that result in the death of another person. And the Congress of the United States, in 1974, enacted a statute providing the death penalty for aircraft piracy that results in death. These recently adopted statutes have attempted to address the concerns expressed by the Court in *Furman* primarily (i) by specifying the factors to be weighed and the procedures to be followed in deciding when to impose a capital sentence, or (ii) by making the death penalty mandatory for specified crimes. But all of the post-*Furman* statutes make clear that capital punishment itself has not been rejected by the elected representatives of the people.

In the only statewide referendum occurring since *Furman* and brought to our attention, the people of California adopted a constitutional amendment that authorized capital punishment, in effect negating a prior ruling by the Supreme Court of California in *People* v. *Anderson*, 6 Cal. 3d 628, 493 P. 2d 880, cert. denied, 406 U. S. 958 (1972), that the death penalty violated the California Constitution.

The jury also is a significant and reliable objective index of contemporary values because it is so directly involved. See *Furman* v. *Georgia*, 408 U. S., at 439–440 (POWELL, J., dissenting). See generally Powell, Jury Trial of Crimes, 23 Wash. & Lee L. Rev. 1 (1966). The Court has said that "one of the most important functions any jury can perform in making . . . a selection [between life imprisonment and death for a defendant convicted in a capital case] is to maintain a link between contemporary community values and the penal system." *Witherspoon* v. *Illinois*, 391 U. S. 510, 519 n. 15 (1968). It may be true that evolving standards have influenced juries in recent decades to be more discriminating in imposing the sentence of death. But the relative infrequency of jury verdicts imposing the death sentence does not indicate rejection of capital punishment *per se*. Rather, the reluctance of juries in many cases to impose the sentence may well reflect the human feeling that this most irrevocable of sanctions should be reserved for a small number of extreme cases. See *Furman* v. *Georgia, supra*, at 388 (BURGER, C. J., dissenting). Indeed, the actions of juries in many States since *Furman* are fully compatible with the legislative judgments, reflected in the new statutes, as to the continued utility and necessity of capital punishment in appropriate cases. At the close of 1974 at least 254 persons had been sentenced to death since *Furman*, and by the end of March 1976, more than 460 persons were subject to death sentences.

As we have seen, however, the Eighth Amendment demands more than that a challenged punishment be acceptable to contemporary society. The Court also must ask whether it comports with the basic concept of human dignity at the core of the Amendment. *Trop* v. *Dulles*, 356 U. S., at 100 (plurality opinion). Although we cannot "invalidate a category of penalties because we deem less severe penalties adequate to serve the ends of penology," *Furman* v. *Georgia, supra*, at 451 (POWELL, J., dissenting), the sanction imposed cannot be so totally without penological justification that it results in the gratuitous infliction of suffering. Cf. *Wilkerson* v. *Utah*, 99 U. S., at 135–136; *In re Kemmler*, 136 U. S., at 447.

The death penalty is said to serve two principal social purposes: retribution and deterrence of capital crimes by prospective offenders.[28]

In part, capital punishment is an expression of society's moral outrage at particularly offensive conduct.[29] This function may be unappealing to many, but it is essential in an ordered society that asks its citizens to rely on legal processes rather than self-help to vindicate their wrongs.

> "The instinct for retribution is part of the nature of man, and channeling that instinct in the administration of criminal justice serves an important purpose in promoting the stability of a society governed by law. When people begin to believe that organized society is unwilling or unable to impose upon criminal offenders the punishment they 'deserve,' then there are sown the seeds of anarchy—of self-help, vigilante justice, and lynch law." *Furman* v. *Georgia, supra*, at 308 (STEWART, J., concurring).

"Retribution is no longer the dominant objective of the criminal law," *Williams* v. *New York*, 337 U. S. 241, 248 (1949), but neither is it a forbidden objective nor one inconsistent with our respect for the dignity of men. Indeed, the decision that capital punishment may be the appropriate sanction in extreme cases is an expression of the community's belief that certain crimes are themselves so grievous an affront to humanity that the only adequate response may be the penalty of death.

Statistical attempts to evaluate the worth of the death penalty as a deterrent to crimes by potential offenders have occasioned a great deal of debate. The results simply have been inconclusive. As one opponent of capital punishment has said:

> "[A]fter all possible inquiry, including the probing of all possible methods of inquiry, we do not know, and for systematic and easily visible reasons cannot know, what the truth about this 'deterrent' effect may be. . . .
>
> "The inescapable flaw is . . . that social conditions in any state are not constant through time, and that social conditions are not the same in any two states. If an effect were observed (and the observed effects, one way or another, are not large) then one could not at all tell whether any of this effect is attributable to the presence or absence of capital punishment. A 'scientific'—that is to say, a soundly based—conclusion is simply impossible, and no methodological path out of this tangle suggests itself." C. Black, Capital Punishment: The Inevitability of Caprice and Mistake 25–26 (1974).

Although some of the studies suggest that the death penalty may not function as a significantly greater deterrent than lesser penalties, there is no convincing empirical evidence either supporting or refuting this view. We may nevertheless assume safely that there are murderers, such as

---

[28]Another purpose that has been discussed is the incapacitation of dangerous criminals and the consequent prevention of crimes that they may otherwise commit in the future. See *People* v. *Anderson*, 6 Cal. 3d 628, 651, 493 P. 2d 880, 896, cert. denied, 406 U. S. 958 (1972): *Commonwealth* v. *O'Neal, supra*, at —, 339 N. E. 2d, at 685–686.

[29]See H. Packer, Limits of the Criminal Sanction 43–44 (1968).

those who act in passion, for whom the threat of death has little or no deterrent effect. But for many others, the death penalty undoubtedly is a significant deterrent. There are carefully contemplated murders, such as murder for hire, where the possible penalty of death may well enter into the cold calculus that precedes the decision to act. And there are some categories of murder, such as murder by a life prisoner, where other sanctions may not be adequate.

The value of capital punishment as a deterrent of crime is a complex factual issue the resolution of which properly rests with the legislatures, which can evaluate the results of statistical studies in terms of their own local conditions and with a flexibility of approach that is not available to the courts. *Furman* v. *Georgia, supra,* at 403–405 (BURGER, C. J., dissenting). Indeed, many of the post-*Furman* statutes reflect just such a responsible effort to define those crimes and those criminals for which capital punishment is most probably an effective deterrent.

In sum, we cannot say that the judgment of the Georgia Legislature that capital punishment may be necessary in some cases is clearly wrong. Considerations of federalism, as well as respect for the ability of a legislature to evaluate, in terms of its particular State, the moral consensus concerning the death penalty and its social utility as a sanction, require us to conclude, in the absence of more convincing evidence, that the infliction of death as a punishment for murder is not without justification and thus is not unconstitutionally severe.

Finally, we must consider whether the punishment of death is disproportionate in relation to the crime for which it is imposed. There is no question that death as a punishment is unique in its severity and irrevocability. When a defendant's life is at stake, the Court has been particularly sensitive to insure that every safeguard is observed. But we are concerned here only with the imposition of capital punishment for the crime of murder, and when a life has been taken deliberately by the offender, we cannot say

that the punishment is invariably disproportionate to the crime. It is an extreme sanction, suitable to the most extreme of crimes.

We hold that the death penalty is not a form of punishment that may never be imposed, regardless of the circumstances of the offense, regardless of the character of the offender, and regardless of the procedure followed in reaching the decision to impose it. . . .

We now turn to consideration of the constitutionality of Georgia's capital-sentencing procedures. In the wake of *Furman,* Georgia amended its capital punishment statute, but chose not to narrow the scope of its murder provisions. Thus, now as before *Furman,* in Georgia "[a] person commits murder when he unlawfully and with malice aforethought, either express or implied, causes the death of another human being." Ga. Code Ann., § 26–1101 (a) (1972). All persons convicted of murder "shall be punished by death or by imprisonment for life." § 26–1101 (c) (1972).

Georgia did act, however, to narrow the class of murderers subject to capital punishment by specifying 10 statutory aggravating circumstances, one of which must be found by the jury to exist beyond a reasonable doubt before a death sentence can ever be imposed. In addition, the jury is authorized to consider any other appropriate aggravating or mitigating circumstances. § 27–2534.1 (b) (Supp. 1975). The jury is not required to find any mitigating circumstance in order to make a recommendation of mercy that is binding on the trial court, see § 27–2302 (Supp. 1975), but it must find a *statutory* aggravating circumstance before recommending a sentence of death.

These procedures require the jury to consider the circumstances of the crime and the criminal before it recommends sentence. No longer can a Georgia jury do as Furman's jury did: reach a finding of the defendant's guilt and then, without guidance or direction, decide whether he should live or die. Instead, the jury's attention is directed to the specific circumstances of the crime: Was it committed in the course of another capital felony? Was it committed for money? Was it committed upon a peace officer or judicial officer? Was it committed in a particularly heinous way or in a manner that endangered the lives of many persons? In addition, the jury's attention is focused on the characteristics of the person who committed the crime: Does he have a record of prior convictions for capital offenses? Are there any special facts about this defendant that mitigate against imposing capital punishment (*e.g.*, his youth, the extent of his cooperation with the police, his emotional state at the time of the crime). As a result, while some jury discretion still exists, "the discretion to be exercised is controlled by clear and objective standards so as to produce non-discriminatory application." *Coley* v. *State*, 231 Ga. 829, 834, 204 S. E. 2d 612, 615 (1974).

As an important additional safeguard against arbitrariness and caprice, the Georgia statutory scheme provides for automatic appeal of all death sentences to the State's Supreme Court. That court is required by statute to review each sentence of death and determine whether it was imposed under the influence of passion or prejudice, whether the evidence supports the jury's finding of a statutory aggravating circumstance, and whether the sentence is disproportionate compared to those sentences imposed in similar cases. § 27–2537 (c) (Supp. 1975).

In short, Georgia's new sentencing procedures require as a prerequisite to the imposition of the death penalty, specific jury findings as to the circumstances of the crime or the character of the defendant. Moreover, to guard further against a situation comparable to that presented in *Furman*, the Supreme Court of Georgia compares each death sentence with the sentences imposed on similarly situated defendants to ensure that the sentence of death in a particular case is not disproportionate. On their face these procedures seem to satisfy the concerns of *Furman*. No longer should there be "no meaningful basis for distinguishing the few cases in which [the death penalty] is imposed from the many cases in which it is not." 408 U. S., at 313 (WHITE, J., concurring).

The petitioner contends, however, that the changes in the Georgia sentencing procedures are only cosmetic, that the arbitrariness and capriciousness condemned by *Furman* continue to exist in Georgia—both in traditional practices that still remain and in the new sentencing procedures adopted in response to *Furman*.

## 1

First, the petitioner focuses on the opportunities for discretionary action that are inherent in the processing of any murder case under Georgia law. He notes that the state prosecutor has unfettered authority to select those persons whom he wishes to prosecute for a capital offense and to plea bargain with them. Further, at the trial the jury may choose to convict a defendant of a lesser included offense rather than find him guilty of a crime punishable by death, even if the evidence would support a capital verdict. And finally, a defendant who is convicted and sentenced to die may have his sentence commuted by the Governor of the State and the Georgia Board of Pardons and Paroles.

The existence of these discretionary stages is not determinative of the issues before us. At each of these stages an actor in the criminal justice system makes a decision which may remove a defendant from consideration as a candidate for the death penalty. *Furman*, in contrast, dealt with the decision to impose the death sentence on a specific individual who had been convicted of a capital offense. Nothing in any of our cases suggests that the decision to afford an individual defendant mercy violates the Constitution. *Furman* held only that, in order to minimize the risk that the death penalty would be imposed on a capriciously selected group of offenders, the decision to impose it had to be guided by standards so that the sentencing authority would focus on the particularized circumstances of the crime and the defendant.

**2**

The petitioner further contends that the capital-sentencing procedures adopted by Georgia in response to *Furman* do not eliminate the dangers of arbitrariness and caprice in jury sentencing that were held in *Furman* to be violative of the Eighth and Fourteenth Amendments. He claims that the statute is so broad and vague as to leave juries free to act as arbitrarily and capriciously as they wish in deciding whether to impose the death penalty. While there is no claim that the jury in this case relied upon a vague or overbroad provision to establish the existence of a statutory aggravating circumstance, the petitioner looks to the sentencing system as a whole (as the Court did in *Furman* and we do today) and argues that it fails to reduce sufficiently the risk of arbitrary infliction of death sentences. Specifically, Gregg urges that the statutory aggravating circumstances are too broad and too vague, that the sentencing procedure allows for arbitrary grants of mercy, and that the scope of the evidence and argument that can be considered at the presentence hearing is too wide.

The petitioner attacks the seventh statutory aggravating circumstance, which authorizes imposition of the death penalty if the murder was "outrageously or wantonly vile, horrible or inhuman in that it involved torture, depravity of mind, or an aggravated battery to the victim," contending that it is so broad that capital punishment could be imposed in any murder case. It is, of course, arguable that any murder involves depravity of mind or an aggravated battery. But this language need not be construed in this way, and there is no reason to assume that the Supreme Court of Georgia will adopt such an open-ended construction. In only one case has it upheld a jury's decision to sentence a defendant to death when the only statutory aggravating circumstance found was that of the seventh, see *McCorquodale* v. *State*, 233 Ga. 369, 211 S. E. 2d 577 (1974), and that homicide was a horrifying torture-murder.

The petitioner also argues that two of the statutory aggravating circumstances are vague and therefore susceptible of widely differing interpretations, thus creating a substantial risk that the death penalty will be arbitrarily inflicted by Georgia juries. In light of the decisions of the Supreme Court of Georgia we must disagree. First, the petitioner attacks that part of § 27–2534.1 (b) (1) that authorizes a jury to consider whether a defendant has a "substantial history of serious assaultive criminal convictions." The Supreme Court of Georgia, however, has demonstrated a concern that the new sentencing procedures provide guidance to juries. It held this provision to be impermissibly vague in *Arnold* v. *State*, 236 Ga. 534, 540, 224 S. E. 2d 386, 391 (1976), because it did not provide the jury with "sufficiently 'clear and objective standards.'" Second, the petitioner points to § 27–2534.1 (b) (3) which speaks of creating a "great risk of death to more than one person." While such a phrase might be susceptible of an overly broad interpretation, the Supreme Court of Georgia has not so construed it. The only case in which the court upheld a conviction in reliance on this aggravating circumstance involved a man who stood up in a church and fired a gun indiscriminately into the audience. On the other hand, the court expressly reversed a finding of great risk when the victim was simply kidnapped in a parking lot.

The petitioner next argues that the requirements of *Furman* are not met here because the jury has the power to decline to impose the death penalty even if it finds that one or more statutory aggravating circumstances are present in the case. This contention misinterprets *Furman*. Moreover, it ignores the role of the Supreme Court of Georgia which reviews each death sentence to determine whether it is proportional to other sentences imposed for similar crimes. Since the proportionality requirement on review is intended to prevent caprice in the decision to inflict the penalty, the isolated decision of a jury to afford mercy does not render unconstitutional death sentences imposed on defendants who were sentenced under a system that does not create a substantial risk of arbitrariness or caprice.

The petitioner objects, finally, to the wide scope of evidence and argument allowed at presentence hearings. We think that the Georgia court wisely has chosen not to impose unnecessary restrictions on the evidence that can be offered at such a hearing and to approve open and far-ranging argument. So long as the evidence introduced and the arguments made at the presentence hearing do not prejudice a defendant, it is preferable not to impose restrictions. We think it desirable for the jury to have as much information before it as possible when it makes the sentencing decision.

**3**

Finally, the Georgia statute has an additional provision designed to assure that the death penalty will not be imposed on a capriciously selected group of convicted defendants. The new sentencing procedures require that the State Supreme Court review each death sentence to determine whether it was imposed under the influence of passion, prejudice, or any other arbitrary factor, whether the evidence supports the findings of a statutory aggravating circumstance, and "[w]hether the sentence of death is excessive or disproportionate to the penalty imposed in similar cases, considering both the crime and the defendant." In performing its sentence-review function, the Georgia court has held that "if the death penalty is only rarely imposed for an act or it is substantially out of line with sentences imposed for other acts it will be set aside as excessive." *Coley* v. *State*, 231 Ga., at 834, 204 S. E. 2d, at 616. The court on another occasion stated that "we view it to be our duty under the similarity standard to assure that no death sentence is affirmed unless in similar cases throughout the state the death penalty has been imposed generally. . . . " *Moore* v. *State*, 233 Ga. 861, 864, 213 S. E. 2d 829, 832 (1975).

It is apparent that the Supreme Court of Georgia has taken its review responsibilities seriously. In *Coley*, it held that "[t]he prior cases indicate that the past practice among juries faced with similar factual situations and like aggravating circumstances has been to impose only the sentence of life imprisonment for the offense of rape, rather than death." 231 Ga., at 835, 204 S. E. 2d, at 617. It thereupon reduced Coley's sentence from death to life imprisonment. Similarly, although armed robbery is a capital offense under Georgia law, the Georgia court concluded that the death sentences imposed in this case for that crime were "unusual in that they are rarely imposed for [armed robbery]. Thus, under the test provided by statute, . . . they must be considered to be excessive or disproportionate to the penalties imposed in similar cases." 233 Ga., at 127, 210 S. E. 2d, at 667. The court therefore vacated Gregg's death sentences for armed robbery and has followed a similar course in every other armed robbery death penalty case to come before it.

The provision for appellate review in the Georgia capital-sentencing system serves as a check against the random or arbitrary imposition of the death penalty. In particular, the proportionality review substantially eliminates the possibility that a person will be sentenced to die by the action of an aberrant jury. If a time comes when juries generally do not impose the death sentence in a certain kind of murder case, the appellate review procedures assure that no defendant convicted under such circumstances will suffer a sentence of death.

**V**

The basic concern of *Furman* centered on those defendants who were being condemned to death capriciously and arbitrarily. Under the procedures before the Court in that case, sentencing authorities were not directed to give attention to the nature or circumstances of the crime committed or to the character or record of the defendant. Left unguided, juries imposed the death sentence in a way that could only be called freakish. The new Georgia sentencing procedures, by contrast, focus the jury's attention on the particularized nature of the crime and the particularized characteristics of the individual defendant. While the jury is permitted to consider any aggravating or mitigating circumstances, it must find and identify at least one statutory aggravating factor before it may impose a penalty of death. In this way the jury's discretion is channeled. No longer can a jury wantonly and freakishly impose the death sentence; it is always circumscribed by the legislative guidelines. In addition, the review function of the Supreme Court of Georgia affords additional assurance that the concerns that prompted our decision in *Furman* are not present to any significant degree in the Georgia procedure applied here.

For the reasons expressed in this opinion, we hold that the statutory system under which Gregg was sentenced to death does not violate the Constitution. Accordingly, the judgment of the Georgia Supreme Court is affirmed.

*It is so ordered. . . .*

MR. JUSTICE BRENNAN, dissenting.

The Cruel and Unusual Punishments Clause "must draw its meaning from the evolving standards of decency that mark the progress of a maturing society." The opinions of MR. JUSTICE STEWART, MR. JUSTICE POWELL, and MR. JUSTICE STEVENS today hold that "evolving standards of decency" require focus not on the essence of the death penalty itself but primarily upon the procedures employed by the State to single out persons to suffer the penalty of death. Those opinions hold further that, so viewed, the Clause invalidates the mandatory infliction of the death penalty but not its infliction under sentencing procedures that MR. JUSTICE STEWART, MR. JUSTICE POWELL, and MR. JUSTICE STEVENS conclude adequately

safeguard against the risk that the death penalty was imposed in an arbitrary and capricious manner.

In *Furman* v. *Georgia*, I read "evolving standards of decency" as requiring focus upon the essence of the death penalty itself and not primarily or solely upon the procedures under which the determination to inflict the penalty upon a particular person was made. I there said:

"From the beginning of our Nation, the punishment of death has stirred acute public controversy. Although pragmatic arguments for and against the punishment have been frequently advanced, this longstanding and heated controversy cannot be explained solely as the result of differences over the practical wisdom of a particular government policy. At bottom, the battle has been waged on moral grounds. The country has debated whether a society for which the dignity of the individual is the supreme value can, without a fundamental inconsistency, follow the practice of deliberately putting some of its members to death. In the United States, as in other nations of the western world, 'the struggle about this punishment has been one between ancient and deeply rooted beliefs in retribution, atonement or vengeance on the one hand, and, on the other, beliefs in the personal value and dignity of the common man that were born of the democratic movement of the eighteenth century, as well as beliefs in the scientific approach to an understanding of the motive forces of human conduct, which are the result of the growth of the sciences of behavior during the nineteenth and twentieth centuries.' It is this essentially moral conflict that forms the backdrop for the past changes in and the present operation of our system of imposing death as a punishment for crime."

That continues to be my view. For the Clause forbidding cruel and unusual punishments under our constitutional system of government embodies in unique degree moral principles restraining the punishments that our civilized society may impose on those persons who transgress its laws. Thus, I too say: "For myself, I do not hesitate to assert the proposition that the only way the law has progressed from the days of the rack, the screw and the wheel is the development of moral concepts, or, as stated by the Supreme Court . . . the application of 'evolving standards of decency'. . . . "

This Court inescapably has the duty, as the ultimate arbiter of the meaning of our Constitution, to say whether, when individuals condemned to death stand before our Bar, "moral concepts" require us to hold that the law has progressed to the point where we should declare that the punishment of death, like punishments on the rack, the screw, and the wheel, is no longer morally tolerable in our civilized society. My opinion in *Furman* v. *Georgia* concluded that our civilization and the law had progressed to this point and that therefore the punishment of death, for whatever crime and under all circumstances, is "cruel and unusual" in violation of the Eighth and Fourteenth Amendments of the Constitution. I shall not again canvass the reasons that led to that conclusion. I emphasize only that foremost among the "moral concepts" recognized in our cases and inherent in the Clause is the primary moral principle that the State, even as it punishes, must treat its citizens in a manner consistent with their intrinsic worth as human beings—a punishment must not be so severe as to be degrading to human dignity. A judicial determination whether the punishment of death comports with human dignity is therefore not only permitted but compelled by the Clause.

I do not understand that the Court disagrees that "[i]n comparison to all other punishments today . . . the deliberate extinguishment of human life by the State is uniquely degrading to human dignity." For three of my Brethren hold today that mandatory infliction of the death penalty constitutes the penalty cruel and unusual punishment. I perceive no principled basis for this limitation. Death for whatever crime and under all circumstances "is truly an awesome punishment. The calculated killing of a human being by the State involves, by its very nature, a denial of the executed person's humanity. . . . An executed person has indeed 'lost the right to have rights.'" Death is not only an unusually severe punishment, unusual in its pain, in its finality, and in its enormity, but it serves no penal purpose more effectively than a less severe punishment; therefore the principle inherent in the Clause that prohibits pointless infliction of excessive punishment when less severe punishment can adequately achieve the same purpose invalidates the punishment.

The fatal constitutional infirmity in the punishment of death is that it treats "members of the human race as nonhumans, as objects to be toyed with and discarded. [It is] thus inconsistent with the fundamental premise of the Clause that even the vilest criminal remains a human being possessed of common human dignity." As such it is a penalty that "subjects the individual to a fate forbidden by the principle of civilized treatment guaranteed by the [Clause]." I therefore would hold on that ground alone, that death is today a cruel and unusual punishment prohibited by the Clause. "Justice of this kind is obviously no less shocking than the crime itself, and the new 'official' murder, far from offering redress for the offense committed against society, adds instead a second defilement to the first."

I dissent from the judgments in No. 74-6257, *Gregg* v. *Georgia*, No. 75–5706, *Proffitt* v. *Florida*, and No. 75–5394, *Jurek* v. *Texas*, insofar as each upholds the death sentences challenged in those cases. I would set aside the death sentences imposed in those cases as violative of the Eighth and Fourteenth Amendments.

MR. JUSTICE MARSHALL, dissenting.

In *Furman* v. *Georgia*, I set forth at some length my views on the basic issue presented to the Court in these cases. The death penalty, I concluded, is a cruel and unusual punishment prohibited by the Eighth and Fourteenth Amendments. That continues to be my view.

I have no intention of retracing the "long and tedious journey," that led to my conclusion in *Furman*. My sole purposes here are to consider the suggestion that my conclusion in *Furman* has been undercut by developments since then, and briefly to evaluate the basis for my Brethren's holding that the extinction of life is a permissible form of punishment under the Cruel and Unusual Punishments Clause.

In *Furman* I concluded that the death penalty is constitutionally invalid for two reasons. First, the death penalty is excessive. And second, the American people, fully informed as to the purposes of the death penalty and its liabilities, would in my view reject it as morally unacceptable.

Since the decision in *Furman*, the legislatures of 35 States have enacted new statutes authorizing the imposition of the death sentence for certain crimes, and Congress has enacted a law providing the death penalty for air piracy resulting in death. I would be less than candid if I did not acknowledge that these developments have a significant bearing on a realistic assessment of the moral acceptability of the death penalty to the American people. But if the constitutionality of the death penalty turns, as I have urged, on the opinion of an *informed* citizenry, then even the enactment of new death statutes cannot be viewed as conclusive. In *Furman*, I observed that the American people are largely unaware of the information critical to a judgment on the morality of the death penalty, and concluded that it they were better informed they would consider it shocking, unjust, and unacceptable. A recent study, conducted after the enactment of the post-*Furman* statutes, has confirmed that the American people know little about the death penalty, and that the opinions of an informed public would differ significantly from those of a public unaware of the consequences and effects of the death penalty.

Even assuming, however, that the post-*Furman* enactment of statutes authorizing the death penalty renders the prediction of the views of an informed citizenry an uncertain basis for a constitutional decision, the enactment of those statutes has no bearing whatsoever on the conclusion that the death penalty is unconstitutional because it is excessive. An excessive penalty is invalid under the Cruel and Unusual Punishments Clause "even though popular sentiment may favor" it. The inquiry here, then, is simply whether the death penalty is necessary to accomplish the legitimate legislative purposes in punishment, or whether a less severe penalty—life imprisonment—would do as well.

The two purposes that sustain the death penalty as nonexcessive in the Court's view are general deterrence and retribution. In *Furman*, I canvassed the relevant data on the deterrent effect of capital punishment. 408 U. S., at 347–354. The state of knowledge at that point, after literally centuries of debate, was summarized as follows by a United Nations Committee:

> "It is generally agreed between the retentionists and abolitionists, whatever their opinions about the validity of comparative studies of deterrence, that the data which now exist show no correlation between the existence of capital punishment and lower rates of capital crime."

The available evidence, I concluded in *Furman*, was convincing that "capital punishment is not necessary as a deterrent to crime in our society." . . .

The other principal purpose said to be served by the death penalty is retribution. The notion that retribution can serve as a moral justification for the sanction of death finds credence in the opinion of my Brothers STEWART, POWELL, and STEVENS, and that of my Brother WHITE in *Roberts* v. *Louisiana, post,* p. 337. See also *Furman* v. *Georgia,* 408 U. S., at 394–395 (BURGER, C. J., dissenting). It is this notion that I find to be the most disturbing aspect of today's unfortunate decisions.

The concept of retribution is a multifaceted one, and any discussion of its role in the criminal law must be undertaken with caution. On one level, it can be said that the notion of retribution or reprobation is the basis of our insistence that only those who have broken the law be punished, and in this sense the notion is quite obviously central to a just system of criminal sanctions. But our recognition that retribution plays a crucial role in determining who may be punished by no means requires approval of retribution as a general justification for punishment.[15] It is the question whether retribution can provide a moral justification for punishment—in particular, capital punishment—that we must consider.

My Brothers STEWART, POWELL, and STEVENS offer the following explanation of the retributive justification for capital punishment:

> "'The instinct for retribution is part of the nature of man, and channeling that instinct in the administration of criminal justice serves an important purpose in promoting the stability of a society governed by law. When people begin to believe that organized society is unwilling or unable to impose upon criminal offenders the punishment they 'deserve,' then there are sown the seeds of anarchy—of self-help, vigilante justice, and lynch law.'"
> *Ante,* at 183, quoting from *Furman* v. *Georgia, supra,* at 308 (STEWART, J., concurring).

This statement is wholly inadequate to justify the death penalty. As my Brother BRENNAN stated in *Furman,* "[t]here is no evidence whatever that utilization of imprisonment rather than death encourages private blood feuds and other disorders." It simply defies belief to suggest that the death penalty is necessary to prevent the American people from taking the law into their own hands.

In a related vein, it may be suggested that the expression of moral outrage through the imposition of the death penalty serves to reinforce basic moral values—that it marks some crimes as particularly offensive and therefore to be avoided. The argument is akin to a deterrence argument, but differs in that it contemplates the individual's shrinking from antisocial conduct, not because he fears punishment, but because he has been told in the strongest possible way that the conduct is wrong. This contention, like the previous one, provides no support for the death penalty. It is inconceivable that any individual concerned about conforming his conduct to what society says is "right" would fail to realize that murder is "wrong" if the penalty were simply life imprisonment.

The foregoing contentions—that society's expression of moral outrage through the imposition of the death penalty pre-empts the citizenry from taking the law into its own hands and reinforces moral values—are not retributive in the purest sense. They are essentially utilitarian in that they portray the death penalty as valuable because of its beneficial results. These justifications for the death penalty are inadequate because the penalty is, quite clearly I think, not necessary to the accomplishment of those results.

There remains for consideration, however, what might be termed the purely retributive justification for the death penalty—that the death penalty is appropriate, not because of its beneficial effect on society, but because the taking of the murderer's life is itself morally good.[17] Some of the language of the

[15]See, *e. g.,* H. Hart, Punishment and Responsibility 8–10, 71–83 (1968): H. Packer, Limits of the Criminal Sanction 38–39, 66 (1968).

[17]See Hart, *supra,* n. 15, at 72, 74–75, 234–235; Packer, *supra,* n. 15, at 37–39.

opinion of my Brothers STEWART, POWELL, and STEVENS in No. 74–6257 appears positively to embrace this notion of retribution for its own sake as a justification for capital punishment.[18] They state:

> "[T]he decision that capital punishment may be the appropriate sanction in extreme cases is an expression of the community's belief that certain crimes are themselves so grievous an affront to humanity that the only adequate response may be the penalty of death." *Ante,* at 184 (footnote omitted).

They then quote with approval from Lord Justice Denning's remarks before the British Royal Commission on Capital Punishment:

> "'The truth is that some crimes are so outrageous that society insists on adequate punishment, because the wrong-doer deserves it, irrespective of whether it is a deterrent or not.'"

Of course, it may be that these statements are intended as no more than observations as to the popular demands that it is thought must be responded to in order to prevent anarchy. But the implication of the statements appears to me to be quite different—namely, that society's judgment that the murderer "deserves"

death must be respected not simply because the preservation of order requires it, but because it is appropriate that society make the judgment and carry it out. It is this latter notion, in particular, that I consider to be fundamentally at odds with the Eighth Amendment. The mere fact that the community demands the murderer's life in return for the evil he has done cannot sustain the death penalty, for as JUSTICES STEWART, POWELL, and STEVENS remind us, "the Eighth Amendment demands more than that a challenged punishment be acceptable to contemporary society." To be sustained under the Eighth Amendment, the death penalty must "compor[t] with the basic concept of human dignity at the core of the Amendment," *ibid.;* the objective in imposing it must be "[consistent] with our respect for the dignity of [other] men." Under these standards, the taking of life "because the wrong-doer deserves it" surely must fall, for such a punishment has as its very basis the total denial of the wrongdoer's dignity and worth.

The death penalty, unnecessary to promote the goal of deterrence or to further any legitimate notion of retribution, is an excessive penalty forbidden by the Eighth and Fourteenth Amendments. I respectfully dissent from the Court's judgment upholding the sentences of death imposed upon the petitioners in these cases.

## QUESTIONS

1. In his dissenting opinion, Justice Brennan claims that the punishment of death is uniquely degrading to human dignity. Compare this conclusion, and his reasons for it, with the views of one or more of the following: Kant, Bentham, or Mill.

2. Is it a good idea to make our understanding of what punishments are "cruel and unusual" depend on prevailing community standards and attitudes? Why or why not?

[18]MR. JUSTICE WHITE'S view of retribution as a justification for the death penalty is not altogther clear. "The widespread reenactment of the death penalty," he states at one point, "answers any claims that life imprisonment is adequate punishment to satisfy the need for reprobation or retribution." *Roberts* v. *Louisiana, post,* at 354. (WHITE, J., dissenting). But MR. JUSTICE WHITE later states: "It will not do to denigrate these legislative judgments as some form of vestigial savagery or as purely retributive in motivation; for they are solemn judgements, reasonably based, that imposition of the death penalty will save the lives of innocent persons." *Post,* at 355.

3. The plurality opinion in *Gregg* suggests that we should presume the validity of a statute, rather than placing the burden of proof on those who claim it serves some legitimate end, such as deterrence. Is a statute providing for a death penalty of sufficient seriousness that the burden of proof ought to be placed on those who claim it serves a legitimate purpose? Why or why not?

4. Assume for the sake of argument that the death penalty is deserved for certain crimes. Now assume also that (a) due to inevitable imperfections in the criminal justice system, not all who deserve the death penalty will receive that punishment. Would the death penalty still be justified in practice, or would its administration be too unfair for it to be justified? If you believe that it would be justified even on assumption (a), does your answer change if you make the additional assumption that (b) in the administration of the death penalty, those deserving of death but who escape it are disproportionately rich rather than poor, or white rather than black? Why or why not?

5. Justice Marshall says that the American people would reject the death penalty as morally unacceptable if they were "better informed" about it. What, in your view, would be required for the public to be better informed? Would it require that executions be televised in detail? Or would it be enough to have observers' descriptions, along with a few still photographs, available in the newspapers?

## *United States Supreme Court**
## PAYNE v. TENNESSEE

CHIEF JUSTICE REHNQUIST delivered the opinion of the court.

In this case we reconsider our holdings in *Booth* v. *Maryland*, 482 U. S. 496 (1987), and *South Carolina* v. *Gathers*, 490 U. S. 805 (1989), that the Eighth Amendment bars the admission of victim impact evidence during the penalty phase of a capital trial.

The petitioner, Pervis Tyrone Payne, was convicted by a jury on two counts of first-degree murder and one count of assault with intent to commit murder in the first degree. He was sentenced to death for each of the murders, and to 30 years in prison for the assault.

The victims of Payne's offenses were 28-year-old Charisse Christopher, her 2-year-old daughter Lacie, and her 3-year-old son Nicholas. The three lived together in an apartment in Millington, Tennessee, across the hall from Payne's girlfriend, Bobbie Thomas. . . .

In *Booth*, the defendant robbed and murdered an elderly couple. As required by a state statute, a victim impact statement was prepared based on interviews with the victims' son, daughter, son-in-law, and granddaughter. The statement, which described the personal characteristics of the victims, the emotional impact of the crimes on the family, and set forth the family members' opinions and characterizations of the crimes and the defendant, was submitted to the jury at sentencing. The jury imposed the death penalty. The conviction and sentence were affirmed on appeal by the State's highest court.

*112 S. Ct. 28 (1991). Numerous citations omitted without so specifying.

This Court held by a 5-to-4 vote that the Eighth Amendment prohibits a jury from considering a victim impact statement at the sentencing phase of a capital trial. The Court made clear that the admissibility of victim impact evidence was not to be determined on a case-by-case basis, but that such evidence was *per se* inadmissible in the sentencing phase of a capital case except to the extent that it "relate[d] directly to the circumstances of the crime." In *Gathers*, decided two years later, the Court extended the rule announced in *Booth* to statements made by a prosecutor to the sentencing jury regarding the personal qualities of the victim.

The *Booth* Court began its analysis with the observation that the capital defendant must be treated as a "'uniquely individual human bein[g],'" and therefore the Constitution requires the jury to make an individualized determination as to whether the defendant should be executed based on the "'character of the individual and the circumstances of the crime.'" The Court concluded that while no prior decision of this Court had mandated that only the defendant's character and immediate characteristics of the crime may constitutionally be considered, other factors are irrelevant to the capital sentencing decision unless they have "some bearing on the defendant's 'personal responsibility and moral guilt.'" To the extent that victim impact evidence presents "factors about which the defendant was unaware, and that were irrelevant to the decision to kill," the Court concluded, it has nothing to do with the "blameworthiness of a particular defendant." Evidence of the victim's character, the Court observed, "could well distract the sentencing jury from its constitutionally required task [of] determining whether the death penalty is appropriate in light of the background and record of the accused and the particular circumstances of the crime." The Court concluded that, except to the extent that victim impact evidence relates "directly to the circumstances of the crime," the prosecution may not introduce

such evidence at a capital sentencing hearing because "it creates an impermissible risk that the capital sentencing decision will be made in an arbitrary manner."

*Booth* and *Gathers* were based on two premises: that evidence relating to a particular victim or to the harm that a capital defendant causes a victim's family do not in general reflect on the defendant's "blameworthiness," and that only evidence relating to "blameworthiness" is relevant to the capital sentencing decision. However, the assessment of harm caused by the defendant as a result of the crime charged has understandably been an important concern of the criminal law, both in determining the elements of the offense and in determining the appropriate punishment. Thus, two equally blameworthy criminal defendants may be guilty of different offenses solely because their acts cause differing amounts of harm. "If a bank robber aims his gun at a guard, pulls the trigger, and kills his target, he may be put to death. If the gun unexpectedly misfires, he may not. His moral guilt in both cases is identical, but his responsibility in the former is greater." *Booth*, 482 U. S., at 519 (SCALIA, J., dissenting). The same is true with respect to two defendants, each of whom participates in a robbery, and each of whom acts with reckless disregard for human life; if the robbery in which the first defendant participated results in the death of a victim, he may be subjected to the death penalty, but if the robbery in which the second defendant participates does not result in the death of a victim, the death penalty may not be imposed.

The principles which have guided criminal sentencing—as opposed to criminal liability—have varied with the times. The book of Exodus prescribes the *Lex talionis*, "An eye for an eye, a tooth for a tooth." Exodus 21:22-23. In England and on the continent of Europe, as recently as the 18th century crimes which would be regarded as quite minor today were capital offenses. Writing in the 18th century, the Italian criminologist Cesare Beccaria advocated the idea that "the punishment should fit the crime." He said that "[w]e have seen that the true measure of crimes is the injury done to society." J. Farrer, Crimes and Punishments, 199 (London, 1880).

Gradually the list of crimes punishable by death diminished, and legislatures began grading the severity of crimes in accordance with the harm done by the criminal. The sentence for a given offense, rather than being precisely fixed by the legislature, was prescribed in terms of a minimum and a maximum, with the actual sentence to be decided by the judge. With the increasing importance of probation, as opposed to imprisonment, as a part of the penological process, some States such as California developed the "indeterminate sentence," where the time of incarceration was left almost entirely to the penological authorities rather than to the courts. But more recently the pendulum has swung back. The Federal Sentencing Guidelines, which went into effect in 1987, provided for very precise calibration of sentences, depending upon a number of factors. These factors relate both to the subjective guilt of the defendant and to the harm caused by his acts.

Wherever judges in recent years have had discretion to impose sentence, the consideration of the harm caused by the crime has been an important factor in the exercise of that discretion:

"The first significance of harm in Anglo-American jurisprudence is, then, as a prerequisite to the criminal sanction. The second significance of harm—one no less important to judges—is as a measure of the seriousness of the offense and therefore as a standard for determining the severity of the sentence that will be meted out." S. Wheeler, K. Mann, and A. Sarat, Sitting in judgment: The Sentencing of White-Collar Criminals 56 (1988).

Whatever the prevailing sentencing philosophy, the sentencing authority has always been free to consider a wide range of relevant material. In the federal system, we observed that "a judge may appropriately conduct an inquiry broad in scope, largely unlimited as to the kind of information he may consider, or the source from which it may come." Even in the context of capital sentencing, prior to *Booth* the joint opinion of Justices STEWART, POWELL, and STEVENS in *Gregg* v. *Georgia*, 428 U. S. 153, 203–204 (1976), had rejected petitioner's attack on the Georgia statute because of the "wide scope of evidence and argument allowed at presentence hearings." The joint opinion stated:

"We think that the Georgia court wisely has chosen not to impose unnecessary restrictions on the evidence that can be offered at such a hearing and to approve open and far-ranging argument. . . . So long as the evidence introduced and the arguments made at the presentence hearing do not prejudice a defendant, it is preferable not to impose restrictions. We think it desirable for the jury to have as much information before it as possible when it makes the sentencing decision."

The Maryland statute involved in *Booth* required that the presentence report in all felony cases include a "victim impact statement" which would describe the effect of the crime on the victim and his family. Congress and most of the States have, in recent years, enacted similar legislation to enable the sentencing authority to consider information about the harm caused by the crime committed by the defendant. The evidence involved in the present case was not admitted pursuant to any such enactment, but its purpose and effect was much the same as if it had been. While the admission of this particular kind of evidence—designed to portray for the sentencing authority the actual harm caused by a particular crime—is of recent origin, this fact hardly renders it unconstitutional. . . .

"We have held that a State cannot preclude the sentencer from considering 'any relevant mitigating evidence' that the defendant proffers in support of a sentence less than death." *Eddings* v. *Oklahoma*, 455 U. S. 104, 114 (1982). Thus we have, as the Court observed in *Booth*, required that the capital defendant be treated as a "'uniquely individual human bein[g]'" But it was never held or even suggested in any of our cases preceding *Booth* that the defendant, entitled as he was to individualized consideration, was to receive that consideration wholly apart from the crime which he had committed. The language quoted from *Woodson* in the *Booth* opinion was not intended to describe a class of evidence that *could not* be received, but a class of evidence which *must* be received. Any doubt on the matter is dispelled by comparing the language in *Woodson* with the language from *Gregg* v. *Georgia*, quoted above, which was handed down the same day as *Woodson*. This misreading of precedent in *Booth* has, we think, unfairly weighted the scales in a capital trial; while virtually no limits are placed on the relevant mitigating evidence a capital defendant may introduce concerning his own circumstances, the State is barred from either offering "a glimpse of the life" which a defendant "chose to extinguish," Mills, 486 U. S. at 397, (REHNQUIST, C. J., dissenting), or demonstrating the loss to the victim's family and to society which have resulted from the defendant's homicide.

*Booth* reasoned that victim impact evidence must be excluded because it would be difficult, if not impossible, for the defendant to rebut such evidence without shifting the focus of the sentencing hearing away from the defendant, thus creating a "'mini-trial' on the victim's character." *Booth, supra,* at 506-507. In many cases the evidence relating to the victim is already before the jury at least in part because of its relevance at the guilt phase of the trial. But even as to additional evidence admitted at the sentencing phase, the mere fact that for tactical reasons it might not be prudent for the defense to rebut victim impact evidence makes the case no different than others in which a party is faced with this sort of a dilemma. As we explained in rejecting the contention that expert testimony on future dangerousness should be excluded from capital trials, "the rules of evidence generally extant at the federal and state levels anticipate that relevant, unprivileged evidence should be admitted and its weight left to the fact-finder, who would have the benefit of cross examination and contrary evidence by the opposing party." *Barefoot* v. *Estelle,* 463 U. S. 880, 898 (1983).

Payne echoes the concern voiced in *Booth*'s case that the admission of victim impact evidence permits a jury to find that defendants whose victims were assets to their community are more deserving of punishment than those whose victims are perceived to be less worthy. As a general matter, however, victim impact evidence is not offered to encourage comparative judgments of this kind—for instance, that the killer of a hardworking, devoted parent deserves the death penalty, but that the murderer of a reprobate does not. It is designed to show instead *each* victim's "uniqueness as an individual human being," whatever the jury might think the loss to the community resulting from his death might be. The facts of *Gathers* are an excellent illustration of this: the evidence showed that the victim was an out of work, mentally handicapped individual, perhaps not, in the eyes of most, a significant contributor to society, but nonetheless a murdered human being.

Under our constitutional system, the primary responsibility for defining crimes against state law, fixing punishments for the commission of these crimes, and establishing procedures for criminal trials rests with the States. The state laws respecting crimes, punishments, and criminal procedure are of course subject to the overriding provisions of the United States Constitution. Where the State imposes the death penalty for a particular crime, we have held that the Eighth

Amendment imposes special limitations upon that process.

"First, there is a required threshold below which the death penalty cannot be imposed. In this context, the State must establish rational criteria that narrow the decisionmaker's judgment as to whether the circumstances of a particular defendant's case meet the threshold. Moreover, a societal consensus that the death penalty is disproportionate to a particular offense prevents a State from imposing the death penalty for that offense. Second, States cannot limit the sentencer's consideration of any relevant circumstance that could cause it to decline to impose the penalty. In this respect, the State cannot challenge the sentencer's discretion, but must allow it to consider any relevant information offered by the defendant." *McCleskey* v. *Kemp*, 481 U. S. 279, 305-306 (1987).

But, as we noted in *California* v. *Ramos*, 463 U. S. 992, 1001 (1983), "[b]eyond these limitations . . . the Court has deferred to the State's choice of substantive factors relevant to the penalty determination."

"Within the constitutional limitations defined by our cases, the States enjoy their traditional latitude to prescribe the method by which those who commit murder should be punished." *Blystone* v. *Pennsylvania*, 494 U. S. 299, 309 (1990). The States remain free, in capital cases, as well as others, to devise new procedures and new remedies to meet felt needs. Victim impact evidence is simply another form or method of informing the sentencing authority about the specific harm caused by the crime in question, evidence of a general type long considered by sentencing authorities. We think the *Booth* Court was wrong in stating that this kind of evidence leads to the arbitrary imposition of the death penalty. In the majority of cases, and in this case, victim impact evidence serves entirely legitimate purposes. In the event that evidence is introduced that is so unduly prejudicial that it renders the trial fundamentally unfair, the Due Process Clause of the Fourteenth Amendment provides a mechanism for relief. Courts have always taken into consideration the harm done by the defendant in imposing sentence, and the evidence adduced in this case was illustrative of the harm caused by Payne's double murder.

We are now of the view that a State may properly conclude that for the jury to assess meaningfully the defendant's moral culpability and blameworthiness, it should have before it at the sentencing phase evidence of the specific harm caused by the defendant. "[T]he State has a legitimate interest in counteracting the mitigating evidence which the defendant is entitled to put in, by reminding the sentencer that just as the murderer should be considered as an individual, so too the victim is an individual whose death represents a unique loss to society and in particular to his family." By turning the victim into a "faceless stranger at the penalty phase of a capital trial," *Booth* deprives the State of the full moral force of its evidence and may prevent the jury from having before it all the information necessary to determine the proper punishment for a first-degree murder.

The present case is an example of the potential for such unfairness. The capital sentencing jury heard testimony from Payne's girlfriend that they met at church, that he was affectionate, caring, kind to her children, that he was not an abuser of drugs or alcohol, and that it was inconsistent with his character to have committed the murders. Payne's parents testified that he was a good son, and a clinical psychologist testified that Payne was an extremely polite prisoner and suffered from a low IQ. None of this testimony was related to the circumstances of Payne's brutal crimes. In contrast, the only evidence of the impact of Payne's offenses during the sentencing phase was Nicholas' grandmother's description—in response to a single question—that the child misses his mother and baby sister. Payne argues that the Eighth Amendment commands that the jury's death sentence must be set aside because the jury heard this testimony. But the testimony illustrated quite poignantly some of the harm that Payne's killing had caused; there is nothing unfair about allowing the jury to bear in mind that harm at the same time as it considers the mitigating evidence introduced by the defendant. The Supreme Court of Tennessee in this case obviously felt the unfairness of the rule pronounced by *Booth* when it said "[i]t is an affront to the civilized members of the human race to say that at sentencing in a capital case, a parade of witnesses may praise the background, character and good deeds of Defendant (as was done in this case), without limitation as to relevancy, but nothing may be said that bears upon the character of, or the harm imposed, upon the victims."

In *Gathers*, as indicated above, we extended the holding of *Booth* barring victim impact evidence to the prosecutor's argument to the jury. Human nature being what it is, capable lawyers trying cases to juries try to convey to the jurors that the people involved in the underlying events are, or were, living human beings, with something to be gained or lost from the jury's verdict. Under the aegis of the Eighth Amendment, we have given the broadest latitude to the defendant to introduce relevant mitigating evidence reflecting on his individual personality, and the defendant's attorney may argue that evidence to the jury. Petitioner's attorney in this case did just that. For the reasons discussed above, we now reject the view—expressed in *Gathers*—that a State may not permit the prosecutor to similarly argue to the jury the human cost of the crime of which the defendant stands convicted. We affirm the view expressed by Justice Cardozo in *Snyder* v. *Massachusetts*, 291 U. S. 97, 122 (1934): "justice, though due to the accused, is due to the accuser also. The concept of fairness must not be strained till it is narrowed to a filament. We are to keep the balance true."

We thus hold that if the State chooses to permit the admission of victim impact evidence and prosecutorial argument on that subject, the Eighth Amendment erects no *per se* bar. A State may legitimately conclude that evidence about the victim and about the impact of the murder on the victim's family is relevant to the jury's decision as to whether or not the death penalty should be imposed. There is no reason to treat such evidence differently than other relevant evidence is treated.

Payne and his *amicus* argue that despite these numerous infirmities in the rule created by *Booth* and *Gathers*, we should adhere to the doctrine of *stare decisis* and stop short of overruling those cases. *Stare decisis* is the preferred course because it promotes the evenhanded, predictable, and consistent development of legal principles, fosters reliance on judicial decisions, and contributes to the actual and perceived integrity of the judicial process. See *Vasquez* v. *Hillery*, 474 U. S. 254, 265-266 (1986). Adhering to precedent "is usually the wise policy, because in most matters it is more important that the applicable rule of law be settled than it be settled right." *Burnet* v. *Coronado Oil & Gas Co.*, 285 U. S. 393, 406 (1932) (Brandeis, J., dissenting). Nevertheless, when governing decisions are unworkable or are badly reasoned, "this Court has never felt constrained to follow precedent." *Smith* v. *Allwright*, 321 U. S. 649, 665 (1944). *Stare decisis* is not an inexorable command; rather, it "is a principle of policy and not a mechanical formula of adherence to the latest decision." *Helvering* v. *Hallock*, 309 U. S. 106, 119 (1940). This is particularly true in constitutional cases, because in such cases "correction through legislative action is practically impossible." *Burnet* v. *Coronado Oil & Gas Co., supra*, at 407 (Brandeis, J., dissenting). Considerations in favor of *stare decisis* are at their acme in cases involving property and contract rights, where reliance interests are involved, the opposite is true in cases such as the present one involving procedural and evidentiary rules.

Applying these general principles, the Court has during the past 20 Terms overruled in whole or in part 33 of its previous constitutional decisions. *Booth* and *Gathers* were decided by the narrowest of margins, over spirited dissents challenging the basic underpinnings of those decisions. They have been questioned by members of the Court in later decisions, and have defied consistent application by the lower courts. . . . Reconsidering these decisions now, we conclude for the reasons heretofore stated, that they were wrongly decided and should be, and now are, overruled.[2] We accordingly affirm the judgment of the Supreme Court of Tennessee.

*Affirmed.*

JUSTICE SCALIA, with whom JUSTICE O'CONNOR and JUSTICE KENNEDY join as to Part II, concurring. . . .

The response to JUSTICE MARSHALL'S strenuous defense of the virtues of *stare decisis* can be found in the writings of JUSTICE MARSHALL himself. That doctrine, he has reminded us, "is not 'an imprisonment of reason.'" If there was ever a case that defied reason, it was *Booth* v. *Maryland*, imposing a constitutional rule that had absolutely no basis in constitutional text, in historical practice, or in logic. JUSTICE MARSHALL has also explained that "'[t]he jurist concerned with public confidence in, and acceptance of the judicial system might well consider that, however admirable its resolute adherence to the law as it was, a decision contrary to the public sense of justice as it is, operates, so far as it is known, to diminish respect for the courts and for law itself.'" *Booth*'s stunning *ipse dixit*, that a crime's unanticipated consequences must be deemed "irrelevant" to the sentence, conflicts with a public sense of justice keen enough that it has found voice in a nationwide "victim's rights" movement.

Today, however, JUSTICE MARSHALL demands of us some "special justification"—*beyond* the mere conviction that the rule of *Booth* significantly harms our criminal justice system and is egregiously wrong—before we can be absolved of exercising "[p]ower, not reason." I do not think that is fair. In fact, quite to the contrary, what would enshrine power as the governing principle of this Court is the notion that an important constitutional decision with plainly inadequate rational support *must* be left in place for the sole reason that it once attracted five votes.

It seems to me difficult for those who were in the majority in *Booth* to hold themselves forth as ardent apostles of *stare decisis*. That doctrine, to the extent it rests upon anything more than administrative convenience, is merely the application to judicial precedents of a more general principle that the settled practices and expectations of a democratic society should generally not be disturbed by the courts. It is hard to have a genuine regard for *stare decisis* without honoring that more general principle as well. A decision of this Court which, while not overruling a prior holding, nonetheless announces a novel rule, contrary to long and unchallenged practice, and pronounces it to be the Law of the Land—such a decision, no less than an explicit ruling, should be approached with great caution. It was, I suggest, *Booth*, and not today's decision, that compromised the fundamental values underlying the doctrine of *stare decisis*.

JUSTICE SOUTER, with whom JUSTICE KENNEDY joins, concurring. . . .

I so view the relevance of the two categories of victim impact evidence at issue here, and I fully agree with the majority's conclusion, and the opinions expressed by the dissenters in *Booth* and *Gathers*, that nothing in the Eighth Amendment's condemnation of cruel and unusual punishment would require that evidence to be excluded. . . .

---

[2]Our holding today is limited to the holdings of *Booth* v. *Maryland*, 482 U. S. 496 (1987), and *South Carolina* v. *Gathers*, 490 U. S. 805 (1989), that evidence and argument relating to the victim and the impact of the victim's death on the victim's family are inadmissible at a capital sentencing hearing. *Booth* also held that the admission of a victim's family members' characterizations and opinions about the crime, the defendant, and the appropriate sentence violates the Eighth Amendment. No evidence of the latter sort was presented at the trial in this case.

I do not, however, rest my decision to overrule wholly on the constitutional error that I see in the cases in question. I must rely as well on my further view that *Booth* sets an unworkable standard of constitutional relevance that threatens, on its own terms, to produce such arbitrary consequences and uncertainty of application as virtually to guarantee a result far diminished from the case's promise of appropriately individualized sentencing for capital defendants. These conclusions will be seen to result from the interaction of three facts. First, although *Booth* was prompted by the introduction of a systematically prepared "victim impact statement" at the sentencing phase of the trial, *Booth*'s restriction of relevant facts to what the defendant knew and considered in deciding to kill applies to any evidence, however derived or presented. Second, details of which the defendant was unaware, about the victim and survivors, will customarily be disclosed by the evidence introduced at the guilt phase of the trial. Third, the jury that determines guilt will usually determine, or make recommendations about, the imposition of capital punishment.

A hypothetical case will illustrate these facts and raise what I view as the serious practical problems with application of the *Booth* standard. Assume that a minister, unidentified as such and wearing no clerical collar, walks down a street to his church office on a brief errand, while his wife and adolescent daughter wait for him in a parked car. He is robbed and killed by a stranger, and his survivors witness his death. What are the circumstances of the crime that can be considered at the sentencing phase under *Booth*? The defendant did not know his victim was a minister, or that he had a wife and child, let alone that they were watching. Under *Booth*, these facts were irrelevant to his decision to kill, and they should be barred from consideration at sentencing. Yet evidence of them will surely be admitted at the guilt phase of the trial. The widow will testify to what she saw, and in so doing she will not be asked to pretend that she was a mere bystander. She could not succeed at that if she tried. The daughter may well testify too. The jury will not be kept from knowing that the victim was a minister, with a wife and child, on an errand to his church. This is so not only because the widow will not try to deceive the jury about her relationship, but also because the usual standards of trial relevance afford factfinders enough information about surrounding circumstances to let them make sense of the narrowly material facts of the crime itself. No one claims that jurors in a capital case should be deprived of such common contextual evidence, even though the defendant knew nothing about the errand, the victim's occupation or his family. And yet, if these facts are not kept from the jury at the guilt stage, they will be in the jurors' minds at the sentencing stage.

*Booth* thus raises a dilemma with very practical consequences. If we were to require the rules of guilt-phase evidence to be changed to guarantee the full effect of *Booth*'s promise to exclude consideration of specific facts unknown to the defendant and thus supposedly without significance in morally evaluating his decision to kill, we would seriously reduce the comprehensibility of most trials by depriving jurors of those details of context that allow them to understand what is being described. If, on the other hand, we are to leave the rules of trial evidence alone, *Booth*'s objective will not be attained without requiring a separate sentencing jury to be empaneled. This would be a major imposition on the States, however, and I suppose that no one would seriously consider adding such a further requirement.

But, even if *Booth* were extended one way or the other to exclude completely from the sentencing proceeding all facts about the crime's victims not known by the defendant, the case would be vulnerable to the further charge that it would lead to arbitrary sentencing results. In the preceding hypothetical, *Booth* would require that all evidence about the victim's family, including its very existence, be excluded from sentencing consideration because the defendant did not know of it when he killed the victim. Yet, if the victim's daughter had screamed "Daddy, look out," as the defendant approached the victim with drawn gun, then the evidence of at least the daughter's survivorship would be admissible even under a strict reading of *Booth*, because the defendant, prior to killing, had been made aware of the daughter's existence, which therefore became relevant in evaluating the defendant's decision to kill. Resting a decision about the admission of impact evidence on such a fortuity is arbitrary.

Thus, the status quo is unsatisfactory and the question is whether the case that has produced it should be overruled. In this instance, as in any other, overruling a precedent of this Court is a matter of no small import, for "the doctrine of *stare decisis* is of fundamental importance to the rule of law." . . . But, even in constitutional cases, the doctrine carries such persuasive force that we have always required a departure from precedent to be supported by some "special justification."

The Court has a special justification in this case. *Booth* promises more than it can deliver, given the unresolved tension between common evidentiary standards at the guilt phase and *Booth*'s promise of a sentencing determination free from the consideration of facts unknown to the defendant and irrelevant to his decision to kill. An extension of the case to guarantee a sentencing authority free from the influence of information extraneous under *Booth* would be either an unworkable or a costly extension of an erroneous principle and would itself create a risk of arbitrary results. There is only one other course open to us. We can recede from the erroneous holding that created the tension and extended the false promise, and there is precedent in our *stare decisis* jurisprudence for doing just this. In prior cases, when this Court has confronted a wrongly decided, unworkable precedent calling for some further action by the Court, we have chosen not to compound the original error, but to overrule the precedent. Following this course here not only has itself the support of precedent but of practical sense as well. Therefore, I join the Court in its partial overruling of *Booth* and *Gathers*.

JUSTICE MARSHALL, with whom JUSTICE BLACKMUN joins, dissenting.

Power, not reason, is the new currency of this Court's decisionmaking. Four Terms ago, a five-Justice majority of this Court held that "victim impact" evidence of the type at issue in this case could not constitutionally be introduced during the penalty phase of a capital trial. By another 5–4 vote, a majority of this court rebuffed an attack upon this ruling just two Terms ago. Nevertheless, having expressly invited respondent to renew the attack, today's majority overrules *Booth* and *Gathers* and credits the dissenting views expressed in those cases. Neither the law nor the facts supporting *Booth* and *Gathers* underwent any change in the last four years. Only the personnel of this Court did.

In dispatching *Booth* and *Gathers* to their graves, today's majority ominously suggests that an even more extensive upheaval of this Court's precedents may be in store. Renouncing this Court's historical commitment to a conception of "the judiciary as a source of impersonal and reasoned judgments," the majority declares itself free to discard any principle of constitutional liberty which was recognized or reaffirmed over the dissenting votes of four Justices and with which five or more Justices *now* disagree. The implications of this radical new exception to the doctrine of *stare decisis* are staggering. The majority today sends a clear signal that scores of established constitutional liberties are now ripe for reconsideration, thereby inviting the very type of open defiance of our precedents that the majority rewards in this case. Because I believe that this Court owes more to its constitutional precedents in general and to *Booth* and *Gathers* in particular, I dissent. . . .

The overruling of one of this Court's precedents ought to be a matter of great moment and consequence. Although the doctrine of *stare decisis* is not an "inexorable command," this Court has repeatedly stressed that fidelity to precedent is fundamental to "a society governed by the rule of law." ("[I]t is indisputable that *stare decisis* is a basic self-governing principle within the Judicial Branch, which is entrusted with the sensitive and difficult task of fashioning and preserving a jurisprudential system that is not based upon 'an arbitrary discretion.'" . . .

Consequently, this Court has never departed from precedent without "special justification." Such justifications include the advent of "subsequent changes or development in the law" that undermine a decision's rationale; the need "to bring [a decision] into agreement with experience and with facts newly ascertained"; and a showing that a particular precedent has become a "detriment to coherence and consistency in the law."

The majority cannot seriously claim that *any* of these traditional bases for overruling a precedent applies to *Booth* or *Gathers*. The majority does not suggest that the legal rationale of these decisions has been undercut by changes or developments in doctrine during the last two years. Nor does the majority claim that experience over that period of time has discredited the principle that "any decision to impose the death sentence be, and appear to be, based on reason rather than caprice or emotion," . . .

It takes little real detective work to discern just what *has* changed since this Court decided *Booth* and *Gathers*: this Court's own personnel. Indeed, the majority candidly explains why this particular contingency, which until now has been almost universally understood *not* to be sufficient to warrant overruling a precedent, *is* sufficient to justify overruling *Booth* and *Gathers*. "Considerations in favor of *stare decisis* are at their acme," the majority explains, "in cases involving property and contract rights, where reliance interests are involved[;] the opposite is true in cases such as the present one involving procedural and evidentiary rules." In addition, the majority points out, "*Booth* and *Gathers* were decided by the narrowest of margins, over spirited dissents" and thereafter were "questioned by members of the Court." Taken together, these considerations make it legitimate, in the majority's view, to elevate the position of the *Booth* and *Gathers* dissenters into the law of the land.

This truncation of the Court's duty to stand by its own precedents is astonishing. By limiting full protection of the doctrine of *stare decisis* to "cases involving property and contract rights," the majority sends a clear signal that essentially *all* decisions implementing the personal liberties protected by the Bill of Rights and the Fourteenth Amendment are open to reexamination. Taking into account the majority's additional criterion for overruling—that a case either was decided or reaffirmed by a 5-4 margin "over spirited dissen[t]," the continued vitality of literally scores of decisions must be understood to depend on nothing more than the proclivities of the individuals who *now* comprise a majority of this Court. . . .

In my view, this impoverished conception of *stare decisis* cannot possibly be reconciled with the values that inform the proper judicial function. Contrary to what the majority suggests, *stare decisis* is important not merely because individuals rely on precedent to structure their commercial activity but because fidelity to precedent is part and parcel of a conception of "the judiciary as a source of impersonal and reasoned judgments." Indeed, this function of *stare decisis* is in many respects even *more* critical in adjudication involving constitutional liberties than in adjudication involving commercial entitlements. Because enforcement of the Bill of Rights and the Fourteenth Amendment frequently requires this Court to rein in the forces of democratic politics, this Court can legitimately lay claim to compliance with its directives only if the public understands the Court to be implementing "principles . . .

founded in the law rather than in the pro-clivities of individuals.". . .

Carried to its logical conclusion, the majority's debilitated conception of *stare decisis* would destroy the Court's very capacity to resolve authoritatively the abiding conflicts between those with power and those without. If this Court shows so little respect for its own precedents, it can hardly expect them to be treated more respectfully by the state actors whom these decisions are supposed to bind. By signaling its willingness to give fresh consideration to any constitutional liberty recognized by a 5-4 vote "over spirited dissen[t]," the majority invites state actors to renew the very policies deemed unconstitutional in the hope that this Court may now reverse course, even if it has only recently reaffirmed the constitutional liberty in question.

Indeed, the majority's disposition of this case nicely illustrates the rewards of such a strategy of defiance. The Tennessee Supreme Court did nothing in this case to disguise its contempt for this Court's decisions in *Booth* and *Gathers*. Summing up its reaction to those cases, it concluded:

> "It is an affront to the civilized members of the human race to say that at sentencing in a capital case, a parade of witnesses may praise the background, character and good deeds of Defendant (as was done in this case), without limitation as to relevancy, but nothing may be said that bears upon the character of, or harm imposed, upon the victims."

Offering no explanation for how this case could possibly be distinguished from *Booth* and *Gathers*—for obviously, there is none to offer—the court perfunctorily declared that the victim-impact evidence and the prosecutor's argument based on this evidence "did not violate either[of those decisions]." It cannot be clearer that the court simply declined to be bound by this Court's precedents.

Far from condemning this blatant disregard for the rule of law, the majority applauds it. In the Tennessee Supreme Court's denigration of *Booth* and *Gathers* as "an affront to the civilized members of the human race," the majority finds only confirmation of "the unfairness of the rule pronounced by" the majorities in those cases. It is hard to imagine a more complete abdication of this Court's historic commitment to defending the supremacy of its own pronouncements on issues of constitutional liberty. . . . In light of the cost that such abdication exacts on the authoritativeness of *all* of this Court's pronouncements, it is also hard to imagine a more short-sighted strategy for effecting change in our constitutional order.

Today's decision charts an unmistakable course. If the majority's radical reconstruction of the rules for overturning this Court's decisions is to be taken at face value—and the majority offers us no reason why it should not—then the overruling of *Booth* and *Gathers* is but a preview of an even broader and more far-reaching assault upon this Court's precedents. Cast aside today are those condemned to face society's ultimate penalty. Tomorrow's victims may be minorities, women, or the indigent. Inevitably, this campaign to resurrect yesterday's "spirited dissents" will squander the authority and the legitimacy of this Court as a protector of the powerless.

I dissent.

## QUESTIONS

1. The majority opinion says, "But it was never held or even suggested in any of our cases preceding *Booth* that the defendant, entitled as he was to individualized consideration, was to receive that consideration wholly apart from the crime which he committed."

Does "the crime" for which one is to be punished include the various consequences that one did not know or intend at the time of the crime? Or does "the crime" include only that which formed part of one's intentions or, at least, knowledge?

2. Suppose that A and B, with equally wicked intentions, take aim at their targets. A pulls the trigger and succeeds in the murderous plan, but B does not, being distracted at the last second by a bird that gets in the way. Are A and B equally blameworthy? Should they be punished equally severely by the law? Should attempts to commit crime X be punished as severely as the actual crime X? Explain your answers.

3. Assuming that the earlier case of *Booth v. Maryland* was wrongly decided, are there nevertheless sufficient reasons for adhering to the precedent set in that case? (See the sorts of reasons that Justice Marshall lists as sufficient to justify overruling an earlier decision.) Is the admissibility of victim impact statements the sort of issue that gives stare decisis especially great weight, or not?

4. Do you agree with the view that it is unfair to allow details about the defendant's character to be presented to the jury while details about a victim's character are kept from the jury? Or do you agree with the view that the use of victim impact statements is unfair because they have a tendency to inflame a jury into making judgments that are, or appear to be, based on emotion rather than reason?

# PART 7

# Responsibility

## SOME BASIC CONCEPTS

Suppose that *S* enters the classroom as usual, two minutes before class is to begin. As is *S*'s habit, *S* flips on the light switch. But unknown to *S*, a terrorist has connected the light switch to a bomb, and *S*'s action of flipping the switch kills ten people in another room. Notice how many different questions having to do with responsibility it seems natural to ask: Was *S* responsible for their deaths? Was *S*'s *action* responsible for the deaths? Was *S* responsible for checking to see how the light switch was hooked up before turning it on? Is *S* now or was *S* then a responsible person? This matter obviously requires some sorting out, for it seems evident that these questions point inquiries in quite different directions. To lay the groundwork, we need to clarify the concept of responsibility and its role in judgments that lead to blaming and punishment. That is the topic of Part 7.

To begin, we need a framework of basic concepts. The commission of a punishable crime involves an *actus reus*, or an action that is legally prohibited. Doing something that brings about another's death, setting fire to another's property, or unlawfully taking another's property are all examples of such actions. They are prohibited by law, typically because they are the kinds of actions that are either individually or collectively harmful. Notice that one can engage in such an action unknowingly and unintentionally. When flipping the light switch in the example above, *S* neither knew nor intended the awful result that ten people would be killed. So it is certainly possible to do something that is legally prohibited, but to do it without the knowledge, intention, or other state of mind normally requisite to its being a punishable crime. Thus most legal systems would not provide for punishment of an action

635

like $S$'s. Notice also that not just any mere behavior counts as an act. Twitching in your sleep is not even an act, and the reason for this would seem to be that one's twitching is not (leaving out the case of dreaming) the result of any belief, plan, or intention. It simply occurs. But $S$ was performing an act that was intentional at least under one description: $S$ intended to flip the switch to turn on the light.

Since doing a legally forbidden thing is typically only a necessary, and not a sufficient, condition for punishability, a central concern of the law is the agent's mental stance toward that action at the time it occurred. The law makes a useful conceptual distinction between prohibited actions that are *justified*, and those that are *excused*. A justified action is one that the agent had good reason to do—good reason, that is, from an impersonal, social perspective. Suppose, that in order to prevent the further spread of a destructive fire, the agent sets fire to a piece of property. Although this action may fit the legal definition of arson, the agent was justified in doing it because it was necessary to prevent even greater destruction. Far from being the appropriate object of punishment, a justified action may actually be a reason for praising the agent, and we may hope that other similarly situated agents will do the same in the future. The agent's claim to be acting for the greater social good has a basis in objective fact.

By contrast, an unlawful though excusable action may still be regrettable from an impersonal, social perspective. It is not the kind of action that we would hope for or encourage more of. A typical example of an excusable action is one that is done because of some reasonable though mistaken belief about the facts of one's situation or of what one is doing: killing another with the mistaken belief that you must do so to defend yourself, when in fact you are only being "threatened" with a toy gun; shooting what you believe to be a deer when it is in fact a man wearing antlers during hunting season, and so on. Another clear example of an excuse recognized by the law is that of duress, where the agent is threatened with harm to life or limb if he or she does not do some wrongful action, such as stealing merchandise or committing perjury. If the agent, in response to the situation, does do the wrongful action, it is not justified, though it can be excused. As such, it is either not punished at all or it is punished less than it otherwise would be. Although it might have been best from an impersonal, social point of view if the threats had been resisted, the law does not punish people merely for failing to do the heroic thing.

So far, we have three of the conditions, each of which can be viewed as necessary for an agent to be punishable: (1) The agent did a legally prohibited act, and did it (2) without a justification, and (3) without excuse. In addition, a fourth issue can bear on the punishability of the agent, and this brings us to one of the standard uses of the terms "responsible" and "responsibility": (4) To be punishable, the agent must have been responsible for his or her actions in the sense that the agent had normal capacities of understanding, perception, and control. Infancy and insanity are the paradigm cases in which this condition is not satisfied. Infancy is different from insanity, of course, as it is a kind of standing background condition of incapacity, whereas insanity can be a short-term lapse at the time of the act.

When a person's action is determined to be not punishable because of infancy or insanity, it is natural to speak of that person as "not responsible," or of "diminished responsibility." Such judgments point to the agent's lack of certain capacities, such as the ability to understand the difference between right and wrong, to know within normal limits the probable consequences of one's actions, and the ability to control one's behavior to keep it in conformity with the requirements of law and morality. This notion is termed "*capacity* responsibility" in H.L.A. Hart's useful categorization of ideas.[1]

Hart's distinctions among various notions of responsibility are helpful in clarifying different kinds of judgments made in law and morality. In addition to that of capacity responsibility, another is that of *causal* responsibility, as when we say such things as, "The recent hurricane was responsible for all the damage you see around here." In this case, our use of "responsible for" marks nothing more or less than a singular causal connection between two events or states of affairs. There need be no implication whatever that anything or anyone is blamable, punishable, or had even a potential capacity to understand anything. Of course, we also make judgments of causal responsibility in law, as well as in morality, when we link an agent's action to some outcome: "*S*'s flipping the light switch was responsible for the bomb going off at 1:59 P.M." "Linda's swerving her car out of the way of the truck was responsible for the three-car accident." Statements like these can be used to make singular causal judgments which leave open the question of whether any person was responsible in any further sense, such as being blameworthy or legally liable for harm caused.

A third category of assertions about responsibility mark what Hart calls "*role* responsibility": "Mary is responsible for feeding the animals, and Johnny's responsibility is to keep their pens clean." Or, "One of the responsibilities of a commanding officer is to see that the troops are properly fed and provided for." In these cases, the term "responsibility" is virtually interchangeable with "duty." More specifically, the duties in such cases exist over an extended period of time and typically arise from one's occupying a position or role, though in some cases the duty may be occasional and brief. (Perhaps Mary and Johnny agreed to divide their responsibilities for one occasion only.)

The fourth main category of judgments are those of *liability* responsibility. A judgment about someone's liability responsibility is in the most general sense a judgment about what can be exacted from that person or what that person can be made to pay for his or her misdeeds. The specific nature of this exactment depends on whether the judgment is a moral judgment, one of civil law, or one of criminal law. To determine that a person is responsible for certain behavior is to judge that that person is the appropriate object of blame and censure and feelings of guilt (where there is moral liability at issue), or can be made to pay damages (in civil cases), or can be punished (in the criminal law). Judgments of liability responsibility can depend on conclusions about each of the other kinds of responsibility. Whether one is liable for damages arising from one's negligent actions, for example, depends on whether those actions played a causal role in bringing about the harm in question. And whether one's actions were even negligent in the first place, or whether one's failure to act amounted to a criminal omission, can both depend on what one's role responsibilities were. If you have a special duty to look after someone or something, your failure to carry out your duty can lead to civil liability, criminal liability, or both. Finally, we have already seen that one's lack of capacity responsibility can, via the insanity defense, negate criminal liability for one's actions.

---

[1]H.L.A. Hart, "Postscript: Responsibility and Retribution," in *Punishment and Responsibility: Essays in the Philosophy of Law* (New York: Oxford University Press, 1968), pp. 210–37.

## ANALYSES OF THE "GUILTY MIND"

When *S* flipped the light switch, *S* had no idea that it would cause the result it did. If we were making a moral judgment about this action, we would say that *S* was not guilty of anything and should not be blamed. Analogously, the law usually makes liability—especially criminal liability—depend on fault. Using the legal Latin phrase, one would say that *S* acted without *mens rea* (or "guilty mind"). However, this phrase is vague, and it can be quite misleading. The idea of an action taking place with mens rea is the sort of idea that has fortunately received considerable philosophical analysis. Most importantly, philosophers and legal theorists have repeatedly asked: What is the root idea underlying this notion of mens rea? One possibility, that to act with mens rea is simply to act with a *morally* guilty mind, can be rejected from the start. This is so because mens rea is something more like a *relation* between agent and prohibited action. Thus even a terribly unjust and evil law, such as a law requiring citizens to cooperate in torturing members of a minority group, could be violated with mens rea. Were a citizen intentionally to defy such a law, he or she would certainly not be exhibiting a morally evil mind. Quite the contrary.

One way of understanding the legal concept of mens rea focuses on the system of excuses recognized in the law. This approach gives us, in effect, a list of conditions, such as duress, mistake of fact, acting in self-defense, and so on, each of which would negate the inference that a defendant who violated the law acted with mens rea. A second approach to understanding the concept makes distinctions among grades or degrees of the agent's culpability. This approach has been set forth in the American Law Institute's Model Penal Code (MPC). Since this approach proceeds by giving analytical definitions of four concepts that have frequent use in the law and analogous use in moral thinking, it will help us to examine them briefly here.

The MPC defines four grades of agent culpability corresponding to four kinds of mental stance that the agent might have with respect to the various "material elements" of an offense, such as the agent's physical conduct or the result of that conduct. (Think here of the earlier example of *S*'s physical conduct and its results.) The four kinds of culpability are as follows[2]:

1. *Purposely.* "A person acts purposely with respect to a material element of an offense when . . . it is his conscious object to engage in conduct of that nature or to cause such a result. . . . "

2. *Knowingly.* "A person acts knowingly with respect to a material element of an offense when . . . he is aware that his conduct is of that nature or . . . he is aware that it is practically certain that his conduct will cause such a result."

3. *Recklessly.* "A person acts recklessly with respect to a material element of an offense when he consciously disregards a substantial and unjustifiable risk that the material element exists or will result from his conduct. The risk must be of such a nature and degree that, considering the nature and purpose of the actor's conduct and the circumstances known to him, its disregard involves a gross deviation from the standard of conduct that a law-abiding person would observe in the actor's situation."

[2]Model Penal Code, Proposed Official Draft, 1962, Sec. 2.02.

4. *Negligently.* "A person acts negligently with respect to a material element of an offense when he should be aware of a substantial and unjustifiable risk. . . . " [remainder the same except that standard of care is that of the "reasonable man"]

Notice that each of these, with the sole exception of negligence, involves a defective or undesirable state of mind toward the law's requirements. But unlike the others, the culpability in negligently doing wrong does not consist even in an awareness of any risk of doing wrong. The negligent person causes harm through a kind of stumbling inadvertence, not through anything we would ordinarily recognize as evil motivation. For this reason, some would refuse to recognize negligence as a true form of culpability.

The MPC analysis of culpability gives us some insight into the idea of mens rea. But we can still ask for a deeper, unifying theory that, in addition to explaining what the MPC's kinds of culpability have in common, will explain why we ought to recognize some actions as excused and others as justified.

Richard Brandt, a philosopher whose article on the insanity defense is reprinted here, proposes one such unifying theory that he calls the "motivation theory."[3] The main idea is that the law expects individuals to have a certain level of motivation to obey the law and to avoid harming people. He summarizes the theory this way: "[L]egally wrongful acts ought to be subject to legal punishment only if they are at least partially caused by a defective state of the agent's (long-term) motivation."[4] Depending on the circumstances surrounding a law-breaking act, we may or may not be able to infer some defect in the agent's motivation to avoid harming others or breaking the law.

If the circumstances of the act do warrant the inference that the agent's motivation is faulty, we attribute mens rea to the agent and think of punishment as warranted, otherwise not. For example, think of a mistake of fact. The agent mistakenly believes that the property he takes has been abandoned, when in fact this is not the case. Can we infer from this that the agent had an insufficient aversion to theft? Not at all. His mistaken belief, not any defect of motivation, explains his action. In consequence, we think of the action as excused. The same is true of one who steals expensive jewelry under threat of physical mutilation. The law does not expect one to respect the law so much as to be willing to undergo physical mutilation to avoid disobeying it. On the other hand, one who has a normal aversion to killing will not yield to the threat, "Kill your wife or our relationship is finished." Notice that the theory also allows us to explain why neither excused nor justified acts should be punished, and also why we still look at excused lawbreakings differently from justified ones. In typical cases of either an excused or a justified action, circumstances do not warrant the inference that the agent had a motivational defect. And in the case of a justified action, such as setting fire to a building in order to prevent larger destruction, the agent's motivation not only does not show a defect but it also shows itself to be positively desirable.

---

[3]See Richard B. Brandt, "A Motivational Theory of Excuses in the Criminal Law," in *Criminal Justice* (*Nomos* XXVII), edited by J. Roland Pennock and John W. Chapman (New York: New York University Press, 1985), pp. 165–98.

[4]Ibid., p. 169.

## STRICT LIABILITY AND THE RATIONALE OF MENS REA

For several reasons, the law's recognition of excuses requires a philosophical rationale. One relatively minor reason for this is the challenge posed by causal determinism. Causal determinism is the view that all of our actions are caused, and since this is the case, we cannot properly be held responsible for any of them. Those who defend the compatibility of responsibility with causal determinism generally do so by attempting to show that there is still a point in distinguishing between those wrongdoers who had mens rea and those who did not, even if all of our actions are caused.

Brandt, as well as a number of other thinkers who have offered theories of mens rea, believe their theories to be compatible with causal determinism. Brandt's motivation theory attempts to show that this point is partly to distinguish between those who have sufficient motivation to obey the law and those whose defective motivation could be improved through the application of punishment. These purposes are clearly consistent with causal determinism.

Other theories have explained the point of mens rea and the system of excuses somewhat differently, but again to be consistent with causal determinism. H.L.A. Hart, for example, has relied on the idea of unfairness: We have reason not to punish or blame someone whose action was excusable on account of duress, self-defense, or reasonable mistake of fact, because it is unfair to punish someone unless the agent had a fair opportunity to avoid doing the thing for which he or she is to be punished.[5]

That some philosophical rationale for recognizing excuses is needed is also clear from the significant and even increased reliance on strict liability in the criminal law. Strict liability is liability imposed merely for violation of the law without reference to whether the actor could prove the absence of mens rea, say, by showing that there was an accident or mistake. A prominent example of strict liability laws are those prohibiting the sale of impure or harmful foods, such as contaminated meat or milk. Another example is the offense of statutory rape, where a defendant is not allowed the defense of having made an honest and reasonable mistake as to the age of the alleged victim. Is there an acceptable justification for strict liability offenses in the criminal law? One candidate is a utilitarian rationale, which might weigh in on the side of strict liability, arguing that to exclude defenses of mistake or accident could well serve the purpose of deterring others even in those cases where it had no beneficial effect on the punished. In the case of laws prohibiting the sale of contaminated foodstuffs, strict liability can cause operators of such businesses to be even more cautious than they would otherwise be. Where the punishment involved is nothing more than a stiff fine, such laws can serve to keep all but the most careful operators out of an enterprise, the proper operation of which is so important to the public welfare.

When considering the advantages and disadvantages of strict liability, it is also important to keep in mind that excuses must be viewed in the practical legal context of presumptions and burdens of proof within which they operate. A defendant's claim of an ordinary excuse like mistake of fact or self-defense must be rebutted beyond a reasonable doubt by the prosecution. The result is that the law's recognition of these excuses makes it significantly more difficult to get convictions. On the other hand, for purposes of the insanity defense, a criminal defendant is presumed to be sane, and the burden of proving otherwise rests with the defendant. The law's use of presumptions and its placement of

---

[5]H.L.A. Hart, "Changing Conceptions of Responsibility," in *Punishment and Responsibility,* pp. 186–209.

burdens of proof can make a great deal of difference to the outcomes of criminal cases where criteria of responsibility are applied. The recognition of an excusing condition can place a new burden of proof on the prosecution, and this in turn raises the possibility that the excuse can be successfully faked and that some wrongdoers will go unpunished.

Strict liability in such cases may be effective, but is it fair? Greater utilitarian effectiveness, it seems, does require some compromise in pursuing the ideal of fairness to individuals, but not its total sacrifice. It would indeed be extremely unfair if liability were so strict that individuals had no way of knowing in advance how to avoid liability or at least reduce the risk of it. Suddenly finding yourself in the position of having to go to jail or pay a stiff penalty without having had the slightest clue that you were even running the risk of liability would be unacceptable no matter how otherwise effective it might be as a device for controlling the behavior of others.

But purveyors of foodstuffs, having had advance warning of the costs and risks of their business, are not in this position. Nor, according to one line of thought, is anyone whose background behavior is clearly wrongful in the first place. One who commits an arson that has someone's death as an unintended result is subject to the felony-murder rule, a rule which imposes liability as though the agent setting the fire did so with murderous intent. Although the arsonist may have had no intention to murder, the agent knew that arson is wrong and punishable. According to this line of thought, people can avoid criminal liability by staying out of the whole sphere of wrongful behavior from the start.

## SELF-DEFENSE

A successful claim of self-defense exculpates an agent for an act that otherwise would be punishable. And both in the law and in our moral thinking, there are conflicting and changing attitudes about how self-defense ought to be regarded. This makes the theory of self-defense one of the most fertile areas for philosophical reflection and analysis.

The conflicting attitudes that people have about self-defense are evident in their reactions to highly publicized and controversial cases like that of Bernhard Goetz (see George Fletcher's discussion of the case in this section). One attitude toward self-defense sees an aggressor's aggression, whether toward one's family, property, or person, as a justification for one to take whatever steps against the aggressor one deems appropriate, the onus being on the aggressor for having violated your rights in the first place. Viewed in this way, one who acts from self-defense is seen as having a justification, as doing something that can even be admirable. George Fletcher has called this the "individualist" conception of self-defense.

What Fletcher calls the "social" conception is quite a different attitude. It sees self-defense as an unfortunately necessary though understandable step that you might have to take against an aggressor who, in spite of having committed an act of aggression, is still a human being who has rights and whose life has value. Viewed from this perspective, self-defense amounts to an excuse, though the action may still be seen as unfortunate or regrettable.[6] These opposing conceptions of self-defense have very different implications about what the victim of aggression may do in reply to the aggression.

[6]Further explanation of these two models of self-defense can be found in George Fletcher, *Rethinking Criminal Law* (Boston: Little, Brown and Company, 1978), pp. 855–75, and his "Punishment and Self-Defense," in *Law and Philosophy*, vol. 8, no. 2 (August 1989), pp. 201–15.

The individualist conception gives victims of aggression wide latitude in deciding what is necessary to repel the aggression. The victim need do little to proportion the extent of the response to the nature of the aggressor's threat. Shooting to kill a petty thief running away with a stolen purse comes within the range of permissible response. The social conception, however, imposes more of an impersonal, utilitarian perspective on judgments about self-defense, requiring the victim to take account of the aggressor's interests as well. Weighing the value of the aggressor's life in the balance, you will not be justified in shooting someone in order to prevent him from running off with your property. But shooting to kill would be excusable if it is an "either-or" situation: the aggressor's life or yours.

Philosophical reflection on these two models of self-defense brings us very quickly to background moral and political philosophy. Does utilitarianism support the individualist or the social conception? At first, it might seem that a utilitarian theory would support the social conception, and that the individualist conception would be supported by only a non-utilitarian theory like Kant's—one that takes as fundamental the idea that individuals have an equal right to liberty. (See the discussion of Kant's theory of punishment in the introduction to Part 6.) But it might turn out, in some societies at least, that the individualist conception would have a utilitarian advantage that would favor it: that of turning over to individuals part of the task of "enforcing" the law. Whether this advantage would outweigh the obvious disadvantage of giving individuals too much discretion to respond in the emotion and heat of the moment remains to be debated.

## THE INSANITY DEFENSE

Many of the issues about mens rea and the rationale for recognizing excuses come together when we consider the problem of formulating the insanity defense. The central problem for courts and legal scholars has been to come up with a legal definition of insanity, a formulation of the insanity defense that both derives from a defensible conception of what insanity is and is usable in practice. Filling this bill has not been easy, as the materials reprinted in this part show.

An acceptable formulation of the insanity defense must satisfy several criteria:

(1) It must make a morally defensible, nonarbitrary distinction between wrongdoing which is blamable because it springs from evil motives and wrongdoing which is not blamable because of insanity. The formula must therefore reflect the recognition that evil motives are not automatically to be categorized as insane.

(2) The formula must be usable in the sense that it can be understood and applied by lawyers, judges, and juries without causing too much confusion or error. For example, a vague unstructured formula excusing all who "cannot justly be held responsible" would not satisfy this criterion.

(3) The formula must be consistent with medical and scientific knowledge, taking account of the full range of ways in which insanity can manifest itself, but without placing too much weight on the testimony of medical expert witnesses. Thus a definition of insanity like the *M'Naghten* test, focusing narrowly on cognitive defects such as the inability

to know what one is doing or to know the difference between right and wrong, would be too narrow. It would not take account of those kinds of insanity that result mostly in an individual's inability to control behavior. At the same time, to solve the problem of narrowness by using the all-inclusive formula of *Durham v. United States* (1954), "that an accused is not criminally responsible if his unlawful act was the product of mental disease or mental defect," is to turn over too much unstructured discretion to the judgments of medical experts, people whose views are often in conflict with one another and whose reasons can easily appear arbitrary and obscure to laypersons.

Partly because of the difficulties in arriving at an adequate definition of insanity, some have come to the conclusion that the effort is a misguided one from the start. One well-known radical proposal would eliminate the insanity defense, replacing the defense's focus on mens rea with a system of strict liability. The "Wootton proposal" (after its author, Barbara Wootton[7]) would authorize legal measures to be taken against anyone whose action fit the definition of a crime, whether that action was done with mens rea or not. Those legal measures might include some form of incarceration, medical treatment, or might involve doing nothing at all. The particular measure to be taken would depend on the results of an investigation looking into the individual's medical condition, personality traits, and behavioral history. Whether the defendant acted with what would traditionally be regarded as mens rea then becomes just one of many factors to be considered, and would no longer be a necessary condition for compulsory measures to be taken.

One of Wootton's main ideas is that the criminal law's concern about mens rea is outdated and based on the mistaken notion that there is such a thing as evil which inheres in minds and actions and must be punished as such. She believes that we should replace this mistaken retributivist idea with a forward-looking utilitarian conception. Our sole concern should then be the utilitarian one of reducing crime and promoting security. Accordingly, our main question concerning an individual wrongdoer ought to be whether these purposes are best served by compulsory treatment, incarceration, or release.

Reflection on the Wootton proposal helps highlight the real reasons for incorporating in the criminal law something closer to the traditional system of excuses. Wootton's suggestion makes violation of the law, but not mens rea, a necessary condition for compulsory measures. However, if we begin with the simple utilitarian premise of crime prevention, limiting compulsory measures to those who have violated a law has no rationale. For if a person shows a dangerous personality or dangerous tendencies, it would not seem to matter for preventive purposes whether that individual had actually done something forbidden by law. A system of truly strict liability would allow intervention without observing niceties about the commission of any criminal acts.

But we do make the violation of law a necessary condition for compulsory measures, and we do this for much the same kind of reason that we refuse to punish someone whose act was due to mistake, because, out of fairness and respect for individual liberty, we seek to mark out in advance a sphere of behavior that will be free of legal sanction. Individuals will then know that their choices will be respected and that they will have a fair opportunity to plan their lives avoiding the law's sanctions.

[7]Barbara Wootton, *Crime and the Criminal Law* (London: Sweet & Maxwell, 1963).

## RESPONSIBILITY IN TORTS

Suppose that N inattentively and carelessly turns on an electric saw while T, standing near the saw, is adjusting the blade. The blade cuts T's hand and causes serious injury. In addition to experiencing pain and suffering, T has large medical bills and is out of work for several weeks. What recourse does T have? No doubt N has committed no crime. N's act was only an instance of ordinary negligence, and that is typically not enough to lead to criminal liability. But T can probably sue for damages on the grounds that N's act was a tort.

Notice first the main differences between a tort and a crime. It is the state that prosecutes wrongdoers for criminal behavior, but it is individual wronged parties who take tort cases to court. Had N committed a crime, it would be the job of the government to make the case against N in court, and the subsequent case would have some such title as "*Nevada v. N,*" "*Tennessee v. N,*" or "*U.S. v. N.*" Given that N's action constitutes a tort and not a crime, T (no doubt through T's lawyer) will be the party who takes the case to court, and the case's title will reflect the fact that the dispute is between two private parties: "*T v. N.*"

For the most part, therefore, the function of tort law is not retributive punishment for its own sake, but to shift losses from one private party to another. Rather than leaving the losses on T where they fell, the law shifts them to N, who caused them in the first place and who happens also to have been the one who was negligent.

A further difference between torts and crimes arises from the fact that the main function of tort law is to shift losses while that of the criminal law is to punish wrongs. Criminal liability attaches only to actions that have been explicitly defined as wrongs by the legislature. In this way, people are given fair notice of what is required of them. This is a constitutional requirement in many countries, including the United States, where it is an element of due process. In the case of torts, however, standards of conduct can be much more vague and general, and there is no obstacle to a court's recognizing a new tort on the spot without benefit of clear legislative definition of the conduct in question.

To summarize, the main elements of standard tort liability are: (1) an action or omission on A's part; (2) that caused B's harm or loss; and such that (3) A was at fault. Unlike crimes, torts (a) typically do not involve violation of a legislated prohibition that defines a wrong; (b) do not require the degree of culpability on the part of the actor that is typically required for criminal liability; (c) employ a "preponderance of the evidence" standard of proof rather than the criminal law's "beyond a reasonable doubt"; and (d) are conceived as issues, not between the state and a private party, but between one private party and another. As in the case of crimes, however, torts are sometimes made a matter of strict liability. In that case, (3) then drops out as an element of a tort.

## THE READINGS

**SELF-DEFENSE.** The case of Bernhard Goetz was one of the most notorious and controversial of the 1980s. On December 22, 1984, in New York City, Goetz, 37 years old and a slightly built white man, walked from his apartment to a subway station, entered a car on the IRT express going downtown. Sitting down next to four boisterous black youths, Goetz was approached by one of them. When Goetz asked him what he wants, he said, "Give me five dollars." Then there were four gunshots, one aimed at each of the youths. These events subsequently led to a great outpouring of public support for Goetz as a kind of avenger in the style of the Charles Bronson movie *Death Wish*. The incident also provoked outrage on the part of some that there should be so much public support for a white man who so unhesitatingly "took the law into his own hands" and shot and injured four young blacks. Professor George Fletcher had written on the theory of self-defense[8] some years before Goetz's trial took place. In the public mind, two conceptions of self-defense, both of which had been outlined in Fletcher's writings, were in conflict. (See the discussion above.) Thus the Goetz case, and the trial which Fletcher attended in its entirety, provide us with an important testing ground for our intuitions about self-defense.

**RESPONSIBILITY AND INSANITY.** The rules in the *M'Naghten* case (1843) belong to the classic legal literature on the insanity defense. The defendant, Daniel M'Naghten, had shot Edward Drummond, the secretary to the prime minister. In M'Naghten's trial for the eventual death of Drummond, evidence was presented that he had morbid and insane delusions and had really wanted to kill the prime minister. The rules in this case have long carried authority in courts of law, though their exclusive focus on cognitive failures has long since come to be regarded as too narrow. Mental disease can manifest itself in many ways other than morbid delusion, and some of these manifestations can as surely lead to murder as did M'Naghten's delusions. Conforming to the requirements of law and morality is not merely a matter of knowing what is wrong, but also of being able to resist doing what one knows is wrong. If inability to avoid wrongdoing in the circumstances was itself due to insanity, then that is the kind of act that ought to be covered by the insanity defense. Yet it would not be covered by the M'Naghten rules.

Recognizing the ways in which determinations of insanity had a scientific dimension, courts increasingly came to formulate their opinions and proposed criteria for insanity in scientific terms, leaving it to experts to account for the sources of insanity and insane actions. *Durham v. United States* (1954) represents the high-water mark in this development. As the opinion in *Durham* shows, after *M'Naghten* there had already been legal recognition of the fact that insane acts could be the outcome of inability to control behavior. This recognition came in the use of the "irresistible impulse" test as a supplement to the *M'Naghten* criteria. But, as Judge Bazelon's opinion shows, even these two tests taken together are too narrow, for they still take no account of "mental illness characterized by brooding and reflection." Thus the court in *Durham* arrives at its own test for insanity, surely the broadest and most sweeping of all.

Dissatisfaction with *Durham's* overly broad, unstructured insanity test has led to widespread adoption of the kind of test proposed in the Model Penal Code (MPC). The MPC employs a disjunctive test, one prong of which refers to cognitive incapacity and the other prong of which refers to inability to control one's conduct: "lacks substantial capacity either to appreciate the criminality [wrongfulness] of his conduct or to conform his conduct to the requirements of law."[9]

[8]See his *Rethinking Criminal Law.*
[9]4.01 (1).

Richard Brandt's article is an attempt to apply his motivation theory of excuses (see above) to the MPC's insanity defense formula. Recall that the motivation theory of excuses would have us ask whether the circumstances of the agent's action allow the inference that the agent had an insufficient aversion to breaking the law, injuring others, and so on. Breaking the law as the result of mistake of fact is the sort of thing that blocks this inference. Brandt's suggestion is that insanity ought to be viewed in much the same way. What should interest us is whether the action would have occurred in the presence of a sufficient level of the appropriate standing aversions. However, what Brandt calls a "mental/brain state" sometimes gets in the way, and even a fully adequate level of standing motivation will not prevent the wrongful behavior. In these circumstances, the fact of the mental/brain state intervenes: It blocks the inference to motivation defect, and the behavior is nonculpable.

RESPONSIBILITY IN TORTS. A typical philosophical question to ask about torts, as about other areas of the law, concerns its justification, or rationale. Why should we shift the losses to the one who negligently caused the loss in the first place? Indeed, is it even germane to ask whether the one who caused the loss was at fault? Why not replace the fault system with one of strict liability? At the opposite extreme, one might ask why inquiring into causal connection between negligent act and harm should be so important. If two people are equally at fault, doing equally risky and dangerous things, and one's behavior just happens to cause a lot of harm while the other's though sheer luck does not, why should we treat them differently? Why make one pay for all the damage while the other pays nothing?

Questions like these emerge in the two pieces reprinted here: Judith Jarvis Thomson's "Remarks on Causation and Liability," and the case, *Summers v. Tice* (1948). The *Summers* case is one that forces us to confront the questions why the accidental facts of actual causal connection should make so much difference, for there were two parties whose behavior with respect to the plaintiff's injury was indistinguishable in every respect. Indeed, it could not be determined which party's gun and bullet actually caused the injury, so the court determined that the plaintiff could collect damages from either defendant.

But suppose that evidence had come to light indicating which of the two equally negligent parties actually caused the injury. Why would this matter? Thomson argues that the concept of individual freedom of action can do much to provide a rationale for tort liability and for the role that causal connection plays in particular judgments of tort liability. Each individual is recognized by the law to have freedom of action. Making a claim on A's assets would wrongly impinge on A's freedom of action unless A had caused losses to B. A's impinging on B's freedom of action in this way does not necessarily involve any fault, blameworthiness, or punishability. Quite apart from anyone's fault, we still need to know who is to bear the loss. The legal system's refusal to act would itself be an answer to this question.

# Self-Defense

## George P. Fletcher
# PASSION AND REASON IN SELF-DEFENSE*

SELF-DEFENSE was always the central issue in the Goetz case—from the decision of the first grand jury not to indict on the shooting charges to the final verdict in June 1987. A legal system is possible only if the state enjoys a monopoly of force. When private individuals appeal to force and decide who shall enjoy the right to "life, liberty and the pursuit of happiness," there can be no pretense of the rule of law. Yet the state's monopoly also entails an obligation to secure its citizens against violence. When individuals are threatened with immediate aggression, when the police cannot protect them, the monopoly of the state gives way. The individual right of survival reasserts itself. No inquiry could be more important than probing this boundary between the state's obligation to protect us and the individual's right to use force, even deadly force, to repel and disarm an aggressor. There is no simple rule that traces this boundary between the authority of the state and the right of individuals to protect themselves. The inquiry itself generates an ongoing debate about the values that lie at the foundation of the legal system.

As the Goetz case wound its way through the courts, the lawyers and judges proceeded on a general set of assumptions about the contours of self-defense. Merely examining these general points of law, however, will not be sufficient to understand the fierce, continuing debate about the legitimacy of Goetz's shooting Troy Canty, Barry Allen, James Ramseur, and Darrell Cabey. Behind the general principles of self-defense swirl conflicting moral and ideological theories about when and why self-defense is legitimate. Some of these theories appeal to our passions; others, to our reason. Our passions pull us in the direction of seeing the act of defense as punitive, as the vengeful response of a private citizen against those who deserve to suffer. The passionate response is captured in the refrain heard throughout the Goetz trial: "These kids got what they deserved." Our reason pulls toward understanding self-defense not as an act of punitive justice, but as a necessary means for vindicating a stable social order. By examining these conflicting theories, we can begin to understand why, from the outset, blacks and whites, liberals and conservatives, have disagreed so vehemently about the Goetz case.

The New York Penal Law (NYPL), under which Goetz was tried, identifies self-defense as one of several justifications for crimes of violence.[1] Other examples of justification are the provisions on necessity (choosing the lesser evil under the circumstances),[2] and the use of force in law enforcement.[3] Consent is also a justification for physical intrusions and taking the property of another, even though the New York statute does not discuss consent as a distinct defense. The point of a justification is that it renders a nominal violation lawful—in conformity with the jus, or higher, unwritten law of legitimate conduct.

Claims of justification are distinguishable from other claims that bar conviction for crime, such as the claims of duress ("Someone forced me to do it") and insanity ("My disease forced me to do it.").[4] These claims do not render conduct lawful and proper. No one would say that an insane man has a right to kill, or that

---

*Reprinted with permission of The Free Press, a Division of Macmillan, Inc., from *A Crime of Self-Defense* by George P. Fletcher. Copyright © 1988 by George P. Fletcher.

[1]See NYPL § 35.15.

[2]See NYPL § 35.05.

[3]See NYPL § 35.30.

[4]See NYPL § § 40.00; 30.05.

his killing conforms with higher principles of rightful conduct. These other claims of defense, often called excuses, merely negate the actor's personal responsibility for the violation. It is unquestionably wrong for an insane man to kill, but his mental condition undercuts his responsibility for his wicked deed.

The struggle between passion and reason in the law of self-defense is played out against a background of shared, albeit vague, assumptions about the contours of defense. First, in order to be properly resisted, an attack must be *imminent*. Further, the defender's response must be both *necessary* and *proportional* to the feared attack. And finally, the defender must act with the *intention* not of hurting the victim per se, but of thwarting the attack. There is no statute or authoritative legal source that expresses this consensus, but lawyers all over the world would readily concur that these are the basic, structural elements of a valid claim of self-defense.

The requirement of *imminence* means that the time for defense is now! The defender cannot wait any longer. This requirement distinguishes self-defense from the illegal use of force in two temporally related ways. A preemptive strike against a feared aggressor is illegal force used too soon; and retaliation against a successful aggressor is illegal force used too late. Legitimate self-defense must be neither too soon nor too late.

In the case of a preemptive strike, the defender calculates that the enemy is planning an attack or surely is likely to attack in the future, and therefore it is wiser to strike first than wait until the actual aggression. Preemptive strikes are illegal in international law as they are illegal internally in every legal system of the world. They are illegal because they are not based on a visible manifestation of aggression; they are grounded in a prediction of how the feared enemy is likely to behave in the future.

The line between lawful self-defense and an unlawful preemptive strike is not so easily staked out, but there are some clear instances of both categories. Because the general principles of international law are the same as those of domestic legal systems, we can ponder some dramatic examples among current international events.

Think about the various military moves that Israel has made against Arab forces in the last 20 years. The strike against the Iraqi nuclear reactor in 1981 was clearly preemptive, for the supposition that the Iraqis would use the reactor for military purposes was based on an inference from private Israeli military intelligence. Even if it is true that the Iraqis intended to manufacture a nuclear bomb, that activity hardly constitutes an attack against Israel. Israel has its own nuclear weapons, and its government would hotly contest the inference that this fact alone establishes its intention to bomb Arab territory.

Preemptive strikes are always based on assumptions, more or less rational, that the enemy is likely to engage in hostile behavior. Israel could well argue that it did not wish to take the chance that Iraq would use nuclear weapons against the Jewish state as well as against Iran and other opponents of the Baghdad regime. Be that as it may, there is no doubt that the air attacks on the reactor constituted a preemptive strike. The possible attack by Iraq was not sufficiently imminent to justify a response in self-defense.

More controversial is Israel's attack against Egypt in June 1967, initiating the spectacular Israeli victory in the Six-Day War. Egypt closed the Straits of Tiran to Israeli shipping, amassed its troops on Israel's borders, and secured command control over the armies of Jordan and Iraq. In the two weeks preceding the Israeli response on June 5, Nasser had repeatedly made bellicose threats, including the total destruction of Israel. The question is whether Egypt's threat was sufficiently imminent to justify Israel's response under international law. Perhaps Egypt was merely bluffing; perhaps its leaders did not know whether they intended to attack or not. There is no doubt, however, that Egypt was attempting to intimidate Israel by behaving as though it were about to attack (unlike Iraq in the reactor incident). Israel took the Egyptians at face value; it responded to what appeared to be an attack in the offing. Could Israel have waited longer? Of course it could have. But the requirement of imminence does not require that guns actually fire, that bombs be in the air. And if anything short of letting the missiles fly constitutes an imminent attack, then that requirement was fulfilled in the June 1967 conflict between Egypt and Israel.

The distinction between a preemptive strike and a response to an imminent attack haunts our analysis of the Goetz case. We know that Canty asked Goetz for five dollars. But we don't know his tone of voice and his body language. The request for five dollars could be understood as panhandling, as harassment, as intimidation (hand it over or else!), or as a prelude to a violent assault whatever Goetz did. If Canty was merely begging, with no threat implicit in his request, there was no imminent attack. If the request was a veiled threat of violence, the circumstances are much closer to an imminent attack.

In cases of interpersonal as well as international violence, the outbreak might be neither defensive nor preemptive. It could be simply a passionate retaliation for past wrongs suffered by the person resorting to violence. Retaliatory acts seek to even the score—to inflict harm because harm has been suffered in the past.

Retaliation, as opposed to defense, is a common problem in cases arising from wife battering and domestic violence. The injured wife waits for the first possibility of striking against a distracted or unarmed husband.[5] The man may even be asleep when the wife finally reacts. Goetz's response to the four young blacks was retaliatory so far as he perceived them as "four young muggers" rather than as individuals; he was striking back for having been mugged by the "same type of guys" in 1981 and suffering lasting injuries to his knee and chest.

Retaliation is the standard case of "taking the law into one's own hands." There is no way, under the law, to justify killing a wife batterer or a rapist as retaliation or revenge, however much sympathy there may be for the wife wreaking retaliation. Private citizens cannot function as judge and jury toward each other. They have no authority to pass judgment and to punish each other for past wrongs.

Those who defend the use of violence rarely admit that their purpose is retaliation for a past wrong. The argument typically is that the actor feared a recurrence of the past violence, thus the focus shifts from past to future violence, from retaliation to an argument of defending against an imminent attack. This is the standard maneuver in battered-wife cases. In view of her prior abuse, the wife arguably has reason to fear renewed violence. Killing the husband while he is asleep then comes into focus as an arguably legitimate defensive response rather than an illegitimate act of vengeance for past wrongs.

The New York statute on self-defense recognizes two distinct forms of imminent attack on which Goetz could and did ground his claim of self-defense. The first is that one is subject to the "imminent use of deadly physical force"; the second, making New York more favorable than many states to claims of self-defense, is that a robbery is about to be committed.* In both cases, provided that other conditions of self-defense are satisfied, Goetz would be entitled to respond with deadly force.

In the latter case of robbery, the requirement of an imminent attack finds expression in the question whether the aggressor is about to commit or attempting to commit a robbery. How do we know and how should Goetz know whether Canty's behavior amounted to an attempted robbery? In a case of self-defense, there is obviously no time to confer with a lawyer.

---

[5]See, e.g., People v. Torres, 128 Misc. 2d 129 (1985), recognizing the admissibility of expert testimony on the "battered wife" syndrome.

*The requirement of "imminence" is expressed in the statutory reference to a robbery's being "about" to be committed.

Whether Canty was in fact engaged in an attempted robbery is far from obvious, both as a matter of fact and a matter of law. Of course, if his intention was merely to beg for five dollars, there was no attempt to rob. But let us assume that Canty was bent on mischief. If Goetz had not given him the five dollars, he might have demanded the whole wallet. If Goetz had refused, Canty and his three companions might have begun to abuse him, with the risk that the abuse would lead to a brawl and a beating on the floor of the subway car. Does the implicit threat of physical violence render Canty's demand for money an attempted robbery?

Robbery is defined at common law and in the New York statute as "forcible stealing."[6] Simple stealing, such as picking pockets, is not robbery and therefore there would certainly be no right to use deadly force to prevent a thief from getting away with a pilfered wallet. The additional element for robbery is that the thief must threaten to use force "upon a person" in order either to overcome resistance or to compel the owner "to deliver up" the property. The threatened force must be both immediate and to a person. If Canty had said, "Give me five dollars or I'll beat you up the next time I see you," that act would have supported a conviction for larceny by extortion[7] but not for robbery.

In order to think of Canty's act as an incipient robbery, therefore, one has to read into his demand an implicit threat to use force against Goetz and to use it immediately if Goetz should refuse to cooperate. This is precisely the picture of the subway encounter that the defense sought to portray.

If we assume that the requirement of an imminent attack is satisfied, the question remains whether the other elements of justifi- able self-defense are present in his subway shooting. Goetz's firing each of the five shots must have been *necessary* under the circumstances.[8] Was there an effective response less drastic than firing the gun at the four feared assailants? Was it necessary to shoot? Would it not have been enough merely to show the gun in its holster? Or to draw and point the weapon without firing? Goetz had twice scared off muggers on the street merely by drawing the gun.

But the uneven grind of the accelerating train made Goetz's footing uncertain. During his initial exchange with Canty he rose to his feet and was standing in close quarters with his feared assailants. Showing the gun in the holster or drawing it would have risked one of the four young men's taking the gun away and shooting him. Gauging necessity under the circumstances turns, in the end, on an elusive prediction of what would have happened if Goetz had tried this or that maneuver short of shooting. There is no objective way of knowing for sure what indeed was necessary under the circumstances.*

The requirement of *proportionality* adds a problem beyond the necessity of the defensive response. To understand the distinction between proportionality and necessity, think about the ratio between the means of resistance and the gravity of the attack. Necessity speaks to the question whether some less costly means of defense, such as merely showing the gun or firing a warning shot into the air, might be sufficient to ward off the attack. The requirement of proportionality addresses the ratio of harms emanating from both the attack and the defense. The harm done in disabling the aggressor must not be excessive or disproportionate relative to the harm threatened and likely to result from the attack.

---

[6]NYPL § 160.00.

[7]NYPL § 155.05(2)(e)(i).

[8]Note that I am treating the question of actual necessity separately from the question of Goetz's mistaken belief in the necessity of using deadly physical force in response.

*On the problem of whether Goetz "reasonably perceived" that it was necessary to shoot, see the discussion [below].

Some examples will illuminate the distinction. Suppose that a liquor store owner has no means of preventing a thief from escaping with a few bottles of scotch except to shoot him. Most people would recoil from the notion that protecting property justifies shooting and risking the death of escaping thieves. It is better from a social point of view to suffer the theft of a few bottles of liquor than to inflict serious physical harm on a fellow human being.

It is not simply that property rights must sometimes give way to our concern for the lives and well-being even of aggressors. Suppose that the only way for a woman to avoid being touched by a man harassing her is to respond with deadly force—by, say, cutting him with a razor blade. May she engage in this act necessary for her defense rather than suffer the personal indignity of being touched? It is not so clear. Of course, if she were threatened with rape, she could use every necessary means at her disposal to protect herself. No legal system in the Western world would expect a woman to endure rape if her only means of defense required that she risk the death of her aggressor.

Proportionality in self-defense requires a balancing of competing interests, the interests of the defender and those of the aggressor. As the innocent party in the fray, a woman defending against rape has interests that weigh more than those of the aggressor. She may kill to ward off a threat to her sexual autonomy, but she has no license to take life in order to avoid every petty interference with her autonomy. If the only way she can avoid being touched is to kill, that response seems clearly excessive relative to the interests at stake. Even if our thumb is on the scale in favor of the defender, there comes a point at which the

aggressor's basic human interests will outweigh those of an innocent victim, thumb and all. There is obviously no way to determine the breaking point, even theoretically. At a certain point our sensibilities are triggered, our compassion for the human being behind the mask of the evil aggressor is engaged, and we have to say, "Stop! That's enough."

The New York Penal Law has a rough principle of proportionality built into it. The provision on self-defense distinguishes between two levels of defensive response: The former is permissible to prevent the "imminent use of physical force" against oneself or against a third person;[9] the more serious response, the use of deadly force, is permissible in specified cases where the threatened force is more serious. Of the cases enumerated in the provision on self-defense, the threats relevant to the justification of Goetz's conduct are (1) the threat to "use deadly physical force," and (2) the attempt to commit a robbery.[10]

Admittedly, the provision on attempted robbery is a peculiarity of New York law. It seems paradoxical for the statute to demand in its first part that the defender face the imminent use of "deadly physical force" and then in its second part to lower the threshold of deadly defensive force to protecting against a robbery that might entail a minimal threat of assault. Even more curiously, deadly force is permissible against an imminent attack of deadly physical force only if the defender first retreats whenever he knows that he can do so safely,[11] but he may use deadly force against an imminent robbery without first retreating. But paradoxical or not,[12] this is the New York statute and Justice Crane and the Goetz jury had to apply it as is.[13]

The preceding three characteristics of self-defense—imminence, necessity, and propor-

---

[9]NYPL § 35.15 on self-defense does not distinguish between the defense of self and the defense of third parties.

[10]NYPL § 35.15(2)(b) (robbery is among four enumerated crimes sufficiently serious to warrant a defense with deadly force; the others are kidnapping, forcible rape, and forcible sodomy).

[11]NYPL § 35.15 ("if he knows he can [retreat] with complete safety as to himself and others").

[12]The best explanation for this apparent contradiction (duty to retreat from the more, not the less serious attack) is that the statute combines two distinct traditions in the theory of using deadly force. One theory, generating a

tionality—speak to the objective characteristics of the attack and the defense in response. In order to establish that these requirements are satisfied, we need not ask any questions about what Goetz himself knew and thought as he shot the four youths. But suppose that while being attacked without knowing it, he started shooting with the aim of inflicting harm on the four black youths. In this hypothetical situation, could he invoke self-defense on the ground that his act in fact frustrated the attack? It would be a de facto act of self-defense, even though Goetz had his own reasons for shooting.

The consensus among Western legal systems is that in order to invoke a sound claim of self-defense, the defender must know about the attack and act with the *intention* of repelling it. Why should Goetz receive the benefit of a justification if he acted maliciously, without fear of attack? Surprisingly, some leading scholars think that in a case of criminal homicide, the accused should be able to invoke self-defense even if he does not know about the attack.[14] Their argument is that if you cannot be guilty of homicide by killing someone who is already dead (no matter what your intent), you should not be guilty of homicide by killing an aggressor (no matter what your intent). No harm, no crime. And there is arguably no harm in killing an aggressor.

Yet there is an important moral difference between pumping lead into a dead body and killing an aggressor in self-defense. We can comfortably say that there is no harm in the former case (except perhaps interference with a dead body), but injuring or killing a human being remains a harm, even if the harm is inflicted in self-defense. Troy Canty, Barry Allen, James Ramseur, and Darrell Cabey are victims even if it turns out that Goetz's shooting them is justified under the law. If they are victims of self-defense (unlike dead bodies that are not harmed), the least the law can demand is that the defender inflict harm only when he has good reason to act. If he does not know that he is being attacked, he cannot have a good reason for claiming four human beings as his victims.

Think about the screwdrivers that Ramseur and Cabey were carrying when they were shot. In the first few weeks after the shooting, some circles in the press reported, in blatant disregard of the available facts, that the screwdrivers were sharpened. The screwdrivers, sharpened or not, confirmed what most people wanted to believe: that these four kids were about to mug Goetz and that therefore his response was justified as self-defense. Yet there was no evidence that Goetz knew of the three screwdrivers. Not one of the four victims pulled a screwdriver from his pocket, either before or during the shooting. If Goetz did not know of the screwdrivers, however, they could not contribute to his justification. They had no more relevance than a secret, undisclosed plan to kill Goetz because he was white.

These four elements, then—imminence, necessity, proportionality, and intention— provide the general framework for the law of

---

duty to retreat, is based on personal defense. The other, not requiring retreat, is based on the authority of every citizen to prevent the occurrence of a serious felony. See supra note 10.

[13]Many of the academic commentators who have spoken or written about the Goetz case seem to lack expertise in New York law. They rely upon the general principles of law taught in our law schools and repeated in basic texts on criminal law. For example, Harvard professor Arthur Miller opined in the "20/20" show on the Goetz case, March 21, 1985, that legitimate self-defense presupposes a threat of deadly physical force. His colleague Alan Dershowitz wrote after the verdict, "Any person who is in immediate danger of death or serious bodily harm may use any means necessary to prevent the assault." *Los Angeles Times*, Op-Ed page, June 17, 1987. Both ignore the distinct ground in the New York statute that speaks directly to the prevention of a robbery.

[14]See G. Williams, *Textbook of Criminal Law* 504 (2d ed., 1983) ("The law would be oppressive if it said: it is true that you took this action because you felt it in your bones that you were in peril, and it is true that you were right, but you cannot now assign reasonable grounds for your belief, so you were only right by a fluke and will be convicted"); 2 P. Robinson, *Defenses to Crime* 12–29 (1984).

self-defense. The first three elements bear on the objective reality of the circumstances of using force; the fourth element of intention speaks to what the actor knows and his reasons for acting. The actor's subjective perceptions of reality introduce an additional element in the analysis that goes beyond his intention to repel the attack. If Goetz was mistaken about whether an attack was imminent and whether his defensive response was necessary and proportional, he might well be excused for acting under circumstances that do not meet the objective requirements of self-defense. In most legal systems of the world, the case of mistaken or putative self-defense is clearly distinguished, in terminology and legal consequences, from real self-defense based upon the criteria of imminence, necessity, and proportionality. The essential difference is that real self-defense justifies the use of force, while putative self-defense merely excuses it.[15]

Under American law, and in particular New York law, there is no distinction between mistaken self-defense and real self-defense. Indeed the law is geared to the case of mistaken self-defense, the assumption being that whatever is true about the case of a subjective but mistaken perception of reality would be true about a correct perception of imminence, necessity, and proportionality. The New York statute applies, therefore, whenever the defendant "reasonably believes" that the conditions of self-defense are present. Of this phrase and its problematic meaning, there will be more to say later.[16]

The requirements of imminence, necessity, and proportionality, expressed in different terms in different languages, are found in virtually every legal system in the world. Yet these basic structural elements account only for the surface language of the law.

Beneath the surface there surge conflicting moral and ideological forces that drive the interpretation of the law in particular directions. We may all be united in the terms in which we discuss self-defense, but we are divided in our loyalties to unarticulated theories that account for our willingness now to stretch the law broadly, now to interpret it narrowly. These deeper forces shaping our interpretation reflect the confrontation between passion and reason in the law.

On the surface, the doctrine of self-defense purports to be a unified whole. New York has a single statutory provision on the subject, and Justice Crane tried to give a single explanation of self-defense to the jury.[17] Beneath the surface, however, there are at least four theories, four models of the defense, that run through New York law and that interweave in the debate about Goetz's shooting, pulling our sentiments in at least four different directions. Terms like imminence, necessity, and proportionality take on differing connotations, depending on the theory in which they are anchored. In presenting evidence, cross-examining witnesses, and making arguments to the jury, Waples and Slotnick sought to tap the jury's underlying and unexamined sentiments about self-defense. By articulating these conflicting value systems, we come to understand the larger issues at stake in the rhetoric of the Goetz case.

Our passion for justice and for the symbolic expiation of evil pulls us in the direction of thinking of self-defense as a form of just punishment. The individual acts in place of the state in inflicting on wrongdoers their just deserts. If Troy Canty, Barry Allen, James Ramseur, and Darrell Cabey were in fact muggers, then this rough principle of justice holds that "they got what they deserved." These are the exact words of a black witness,

---

[15]For further elaboration of this distinction, see my article "The Right and the Reasonable," 98 *Harvard Law Review* 949 (1985), cited by the Court of Appeals in People v. Goetz, 68 NY2d 98, 112 (1987).

[16]See Chapter Three [not reprinted here].

[17]In fact, he changed his instruction several times, but on relatively minor points. See Chapter Nine [not reprinted here].

Andrea Reid. Present with her baby in the subway car at the time of the shooting, she was also afraid of the four "punks who were bothering the white man." Barry Slotnick referred to her words "they got what they deserved" dozens of times in the course of the trial. Sometimes he paraphrased the comment in a more respectable legal idiom: "They got what the law allowed."

Goetz became a folk hero because, as the folk saw it, his shooting brought these arrogant predators to their knees. Yet even under a punitive theory of giving criminals what they deserve, there remain questions of fact. Did these kids have records long enough to support the judgment that they were criminals and predators? Or is the public perception of Canty, Cabey, Ramseur, and Allen as criminal types largely a function of their race and youth? When our passions seek gratification, when our lust to avenge gains the upper hand, we don't always ponder the facts and weigh the gradations of evil and its fitting punishment.

That people should be rewarded and punished on the basis of their character and their lifelong behavior expresses a principle of justice, but it is a principle better suited for infallible divine punishment than the imperfect institutions of the law. In fairy tales, the witch may receive her comeuppance at the end. But surely it is not the business of human institutions—not to mention a loner riding the subway—to determine who is a witch, or a wicked person or a habitual criminal.

The law wisely limits itself to the question whether a particular act constitutes a crime and merits punishment or whether, in the context of self-defense, a particular aggressive act properly triggers a defensive response. The general character of suspects is important neither for human punishment nor for the assessment whether defensive force was permissible in a particular situation. Some people who passionately sided with Goetz's victims may think that when Goetz's lawyer Slotnick

was jumped and assaulted a few weeks after the trial was over, he too got what he deserved. They are entitled to their opinion. But their passion for justice on the streets should not be heard in court. Nor should Slotnick's repeated reiteration of Andrea Reid's words "they got what they deserved" have been heard as a persuasive argument about the proper scope of self-defense.

But a persuasive argument it may have been. And therefore we have to ask the question, If a juror thinks about self-defense as a form of punishment, how would he or she be inclined to interpret the requirements of imminence, necessity, and proportionality? First, he would probably loosen up on the requirements both of imminence and necessity; further, he would blur the line between legitimate defense and a preemptive attack. He would probably see Canty's demand for five dollars as sufficiently close to a real attack to warrant a defensive response. An actual, unavoidable attack is simply not important to someone whose thinking is geared to the punitive theory. What counts is the justice of the response, given the generally evil character of the aggressor.

Thinking about the proportionality of Goetz's punitive response requires that we distinguish between punishing the four kids for what they were and punishing them for their specific acts on December 22, 1984. Perhaps if they were being punished for what they were and one believed they were the embodiment of our urban ills, one might—in the irrationality of hatred—think they received what they deserved. But there is no way that one could think of Goetz's shooting them as fair punishment for their specific acts in the subway car.

Proportionality in punishment—making the punishment fit the crime—is more rigorous than proportionality in self-defense. Using the death penalty for rape, for example, violates the principles of proportional punishment as expressed in the Eighth Amendment, which prohibits cruel and unusual punishment.[18] Yet

[18]See Coker v. Georgia, 433 U.S. 584 (1977).

if a woman is threatened by rape, she may legally resist by killing the aggressor. Even legal systems that have abolished the death penalty permit the use of deadly force in the defense of vital interests. While proportionality in punishment requires that the sentence fit the crime, clearly more is permitted in self-defense.

Thinking of self-defense as a form of punishment, then, should strengthen the requirement of proportionality. The defensive response would have to fit the "crime" committed by Goetz's four adversaries. So far as their crime on that day is at issue, we can only wonder what people might mean when they say that those "punks"—Troy Canty, Barry Allen, James Ramseur and Darrell Cabey—got what they deserved. What, after all, was their crime? Even if they were about to subject Goetz to a fierce beating, they would hardly deserve a punishment of being shot, paralyzed, being brought to the edge of death. No modern legal system would countenance a penalty of maiming or death for the crime of mugging.

Another significant approach to self-defense shifts our focus away from our anger toward the aggressor and our passion to punish and directs our attention instead to the personal plight of the defender. In the closing portions of his summation to the jury, Barry Slotnick played on this theme. He stressed Goetz's fear, his back to the steel wall of the subway car, with no choice but to strike back.

The theme of fear invokes the primordial form of self-defense in English law. From roughly the 13th to the 16th century, the plea of self-defense, called *se defendendo*, came into consideration whenever a fight broke out and one party retreated as far as he could go before resorting to defensive force. His back had to be literally against the wall.

If he then killed the aggressor, *se defendendo* had the effect of saving the defendant from execution, but it left intact the other stigmatizing effects of the criminal law. The defendant forfeited his goods as expiation of his having taken human life. The murder weapon was also forfeited to the crown as a deodand, a tainted object. Killing *se defendendo* was called excusable homicide, for though the wrong of homicide had occurred, the circumstances generated a personal excuse that saved the manslayer from execution. The defense of *se defendendo* springs more from compassion for the predicament of the trapped defender than from a passion for justice or the dictates of reason. If we would all act the same way if caught in the same circumstances, we can hardly condemn and execute the manslayer who had no choice.

Conceiving of self-defense as an excuse, based on the defender's uncontrollable reaction to the specter of death, leads, it would seem, to tightening the screws on the issues of imminence and necessity, but loosening them on proportionality. The former two must be strictly applied in order to assure that the defense is indeed an involuntary response to the terror of the situation. Yet if the reaction is indeed voluntary, greater tolerance should be allowed for the defender's overreacting and inflicting disproportionate harm.

The punitive theory of self-defense loosens the imminence and necessity requirements and should lead to a stricter application of proportionality as a value. Conceiving of self-defense as an excuse based on fear has the opposite effect in all three dimensions. Ingeniously, the defense brought both of these theories into play on behalf of Goetz's shooting the four youths.

Most legal systems today think of self-defense neither as a form of punishment nor as an excuse based on the defender's involuntary response to an overwhelming threat. We have come to think of acting to ward off aggression as the exercise of a basic right—an act, grounded in the dictates of reason, that justifies inflicting injuries and even killing the aggressor. To understand this emergence of self-defense as a justification, we must first consider the shortcoming in the law left by the defense of *se defendendo*. The only way for the defendant to avoid the harsh consequence of forfeiting his property on a successful plea of *se defendendo* was to argue that the death of the victim was not his act at all. If the killing was not his act, there was no blot on his escutcheon, nothing for him to expiate. The jury would acquit him outright and he would retain his goods.

The line between killing and passively being the instrument of death is, of course, a fine one. Sir Mathew Hale distinguishes between a defender's stabbing a victim (*se defendendo*) and a victim's impaling himself on the defender's motionless sword.[19] Like many other poets in history, Shakespeare had little patience for this kind of legal hair-splitting. His satire in *Hamlet* is worth recalling.

If Ophelia killed herself by her own hand, she was not entitled to a Christian burial. She appears to have done just that. When the Clown's partner tells him that Ophelia is entitled to a Christian burial, he is dumbfounded:[20]

CLOWN: How can that be, unless she drowned herself in her own defense?

OTHER: Why, 'tis found so.

CLOWN: It must be *se offendendo*; it cannot be else. For here lies the point: If I drown myself wittingly, it argues an act, and an act hath three branches; it is to act, to do, to perform: argal, she drowned herself wittingly.

OTHER: Nay, but hear you, goodman deliver.

CLOWN: Give me leave. Here lies the water; good: here stands the man; good: if the man go to the water and drowns himself, it is, will he, nill he, he goes; mark you that? But if the water comes to him and drown him, he drowns not himself; argal he that is not guilty of his own death shortens not his own life.

The Clown's mockery of lawyers and their reasoning is so effective precisely because he understands the legal relevance of action and the rationale for *se defendendo*. It all depends, as he says, on whether Ophelia comes to the water or the water comes to Ophelia. Of course, if she throws herself into the river, there would seem to be little doubt about who comes to what. But the view that she "shortens not [her] own life" turns on the whimsical view that the stream comes to her. The Clown's colleague sees through the play on the logical distinction with the kind of comment that today would be regarded as an insight into the class struggle: he claims that if she were not of aristocratic birth, "she should have been buried out of Christian burial."

The common law was obviously incomplete. Could it be the case that killing to save one's life always left a taint on the defender? At early stages of the common law, as in Roman law, there was no offense in killing a thief caught in the act—a *fur manifestus*. Why should not the defense against an apparent murderer be treated in the same way? Lawyers of 15th and 16th centuries paid close attention to the jurisprudence of the Bible; in Exodus 22 we read that there is no bloodguilt, no taint, in killing a thief who seeks at night to break into one's home. Why should the common law suppose, in opposition to Exodus, that there is a taint requiring forfeiture of goods? Why should the only escape from this conclusion be the whimsical argument that the thief came to the knife, rather than the knife to the thief?

Even before Shakespeare's wit conceived of "se offendendo," Parliament came center stage and filled the role left vacant in the common law. Significantly, Parliament's statute enacted in 1532 licenses the killing, without any taint whatsoever, of robbers and other assailants on the public highway. The modern analogue to these highwaymen feared in the 16th century is muggers on our underground public highways—subways. This statutory defense came to be called justifiable as opposed to excusable homicide. The defense is not based on compassion for someone with his back to the wall, but

[19]1 Mathew Hale, *History of the Pleas of the Crown* 413 (1736).

[20]W. Shakespeare, *Hamlet*, act V, scene 1 ("Universal" ed., 1893).

rather it expresses a right to hold one's ground against wrongful aggressors. The claim is not "I could not do otherwise," but rather "Don't tread on me!" As the leading scholar of the 17th century Sir Edward Coke said of this defense, "no man shall ever give way to a thief, etc. neither shall he forfeit anything."[21] The consequence of justifiable homicide, as the 1532 statute prescribes, is total acquittal. There was no forfeiture of goods, no need to ponder whether the killer was really acting.

This version of self-defense is appropriately called "individualist," for it takes the vindication of individual autonomy as its fundamental imperative. Its philosophical champions were John Locke and Immanuel Kant. Locke insisted that yielding even an inch to an aggressor would put one on the path to submission and slavery.[22] Kant conceived of an unqualified right of self-defense as the foundation of a liberal legal system in which each citizen recognized and willed maximum freedom for himself as well as for his fellow citizens. That the legal system should be organized on the basis of maximum freedom was, for Kant, the implication of pure reason in human affairs.

Relying implicitly on this tradition, Slotnick invoked the individualist theory in his opening statement:[23]

> [N]o one can ever take away your inalienable right to protect your property or your life or your family. No one can walk up to me and say, "give me that watch," "give me your ring," "give me five dollars." And if they do, heaven help them if I'm armed, because I know what the law allows.

The "individualist" stands in contrast to the "social" variation of justifiable self-defense. The difference between the two is expressed in a very loose as opposed to a very strict approach to proportionality. The extreme version of the individualist defense rejects proportionality altogether. Any encroachment on an individual's rights represents an intolerable violation of personal autonomy. The affected individual can do everything in his power, deploy all necessary means to end the encroachment and vindicate his autonomy. The expansive attitude toward self-defense in the individualist theory leads, as well, to more generous interpretations of imminence and necessity.

The individualist theory has always expressed itself more strongly in the protection of one's home. Any intrusion against one's castle, against one's refuge from the heartless world, seems intolerable. The individualist theory would vindicate the use of all necessary means to defend one's home against an attempted intrusion. Perhaps, as Kant would say, our moral concern for the welfare of others would lead us not to exercise our right of defense,[24] but liberal writings leave no doubt that freedom entails the option to resist all forms of encroachment.

The social variation of the same defense rejects absolutes like the imperative to secure one's rights, one's autonomy, or one's private physical space. The individualist treats every person as an island, entitled to full sovereignty in his own domain. This theory, which treats human beings as though they were nation-states, ignores our interdependence, both in shaping our sense of self and in cooperating in society for mutual advantage. The aggressor is another member of the same society of interdependent selves. He has interests that we cannot ignore even if he acts wrongfully in aggressing against someone else. These interests are expressed in the obligation of the defender to consider the aggressor not merely as an intrusive force, but as a human being.

---

[21]3 E. Coke, *Third Institute* 55 (1644).

[22]J. Locke, *Treatise of Civil Government* 14 (Sherman ed., 1937).

[23]Record at 4888.

[24]See I. Kant, *Metaphysical Elements of Justice* 41 (1797) (J. Ladd translation) ("for even in such a situation [i.e., "an unjust assailant on my own life"] the recommendation of moderation is not of [law], but belongs only to ethics").

Recognizing the humanity of the aggressor implies that in some situations the defender must absorb an encroachment on his autonomy rather than inflict an excessive cost on the aggressor. If the only way to prevent an intrusion and nonviolent theft in one's home is to kill the aggressor, the defender may voluntarily have to forgo the defense and risk losing his property. He must suffer a minor invasion and hope that the police will recover his goods; the alternative of killing the aggressor is too costly and too callous a disregard of the human interests of the aggressor.

Blackstone's influential argument for the social interpretation of justifiable self-defense harks back to the punitive theory that we considered at the beginning of this discussion. As he puts it, if the courts do not execute a petty thief for his crime, neither the police nor a private citizen should be able to kill him to prevent his theft.[25] The analogy is powerful. If punishment is limited by the principle of proportionality, it makes sense to limit self-defense by a version of the same principle.

Yet self-defense is not punishment. The purpose of a defensive act is not to inflict harm according to the desert of the aggressor. Its purpose is to repel the attack. And if there is a principle of proportionality that restricts self-defense, it cannot be the same principle of justice that governs sentencing after trial and conviction.[26] As the example of repelling rape by deadly force demonstrates, the right to subject an aggressor to a risk of death attaches even when capital punishment would be unacceptable.

In the 1950s and the 1960s a strong defense of the social theory emerged from the general and seemingly uncontroversial view that the purpose of criminal law was to further the public good. After all, who could be against the public good? The consequence of this view in the thinking of criminal law reformers was that the purpose of punishment was primarily to encourage people to act in a socially desirable way, and the determination of socially desirable conduct turned largely on the assessment of the costs and benefits of acting in particular ways.

The consequence of thinking about self-defense as a measure furthering the public welfare led courts and legislatures, for a time, to eschew all absolutist thinking about the right of people to defend their autonomy against aggressive attacks. In cases of burglary, for example, the lawmakers demanded that for a homeowner to use deadly force against an intruder, he must fear violence to himself or the other occupants; the fear of theft would not be sufficient to justify fighting off the burglar with force endangering his life.

An illustrative case is the decision of the California Supreme Court in *People v. Ceballos*,[27] which held that injuring a burglar with a spring gun could not be justified. Since no one was at home at the time of the intrusion, the burglary did not subject an occupant to the risk of violence, and therefore the only interest at stake on the side of the homeowner was his property. Defending property alone did not justify the use of deadly force against the burglar.

The social theory of self-defense says, in short, that burglars and muggers also have rights, and the rights of the victims must therefore be restricted when their exercise inflicts an excessive cost on those who attack them. It would be fair to say that if the public at large supported this philosophy a generation ago, their feelings about crime and the rights of criminals have shifted dramatically since then.

---

[25]4 W. Blackstone, *Commentaries on the Laws of England* 181 (1765–69).

[26]If there were any relationship between self-defense and punishment, you would think that less force would be tolerable in self-defense before trial than in punishing the convicted offender after trial; the trial reduces the risk of mistake in treating an ambiguous intrusion—like that of Tony Canty—as a punishable crime.

[27]116 Cal. Rptr. 233, 526 P2d 241, 12 C.3d 470 (1974).

There is little sympathy today for the welfare of those who aggress against others. We are witnessing a return to absolutist thinking about self-defense, a return to the individualist philosophy that ignores the costs of a necessary defense to the aggressor. This is evident in legislative changes. When Illinois adopted its criminal code in 1962, it restricted the use of deadly force in burglary cases "to prevent the commission of forcible felonies in the dwelling."[28] In 1967 the legislature dropped the word "forcible," making it clear that deadly force would also be permissible merely to prevent larceny—a felony that does not require the use of force. The same pattern is evident in New York. In 1968, the New York legislature amended the new Penal Law, just three years old, to make the commission of a burglary a sufficient ground, in itself, for resistance with deadly force.[29]

Some changes in the last few years have been even more dramatic. Colorado enacted a statute in 1985 that begins with the bold declaration that "the citizens of Colorado have a right to expect absolute safety in their homes." The statute goes on to postulate that self-defense should be applicable if an intruder in one's home is "committing or intends to commit a crime . . . [even] against property" and "the occupant reasonably believes that [the intruder] might use any physical force, no matter how slight, against any occupant."[30]

The problem faced by Bernhard Goetz is not exactly the same as that faced by a homeowner confronted by an unlawful intruder, but there is an important analogy. Goetz also felt that his rightful space was being intruded upon by a stranger confronting him and demanding money. As a homeowner does not know for sure that an intruder will injure him or his family, Goetz did not know for sure that had he said, "No, I have no money," Canty and his friends would have assaulted him. The social theory of self-defense requires the victim to suffer a loss of property rather than fight back with deadly force.

There is no doubt that from a social point of view, life and limb are more important than property rights. What the social theory of self-defense ignores, however, is the ever-present risk that a burglar or intruder into your space on the subway will do much more than merely take your money or your watch. The individualist theory acknowledges that risk as real and holds that it is wrong to force innocent, law-abiding individuals to suffer a risk of personal violence. As the Colorado statute endorses deadly force whenever there is a risk that an intruder "might use physical force, no matter how slight," many who sympathize with Goetz would argue that he too should have been able to use deadly force to counteract the risk of "physical force, no matter how slight."

What, then, is the balance that we can draw from all these conflicting theories of self-defense? Several of these perspectives support an expansive interpretation of Goetz's right to use deadly force. The theory of self-defense as an excuse generates an acquittal for virtually any degree of force that Goetz, in his state of fear, with his back against the wall, felt compelled to use. The individualist theory of self-defense as a justification also vindicates the use of deadly force, when necessary, to uphold the defender's rights to his personal security, his autonomy, and his liberty of movement.

[28]Ill. Rev. Stat. § 38, § 7–1.

[29]NYPL § 35.15(2) (c).

[30]Colo. Rev. Stat. § 18–1–704.5 Cf. Cal. Penal Code § 198.5 (if an unlawful and forcible entry has occurred, an occupant who uses deadly force against the intruder "shall be presumed to have held a reasonable fear of imminent peril of death or great bodily harm"). Both statutes appear to be limited to cases in which the owner is on the premises, and therefore neither justifies the use of spring guns against burglars.

Strains of all but the social theory of self-defense interweave in the defense's appeals to the jury in the Goetz trial. When the focus fell on Goetz's fear, the argument implicitly invoked the theory of self-defense as an excuse. When the emphasis was directed to a subway passenger's right not to surrender his money or his watch, the argument rested on the individualist theory of self-defense as a justification.

The defense also relied heavily on the punitive theory, although a careful analysis of "what those punks deserved" could hardly support a finding that they were rightly subject to a potentially fatal shooting. If they were convicted for what they did, both that day and in the past, their legal punishment would not even approach the suffering of Darrell Cabey.

The only perspective that unequivocally stood for a narrow interpretation of Goetz's right of self-defense was the social variation of self-defense as a justification. It is only by thinking of the alleged aggressors as people with interests to be balanced against those of the defender Goetz that a jury could be led to think of Goetz's response as excessive and illegitimate. The more Troy Canty, Barry Allen, James Ramseur, and Darrell Cabey come into focus as human beings worthy of our compassion, the more we might expect Goetz to have taken some risks that he could exit from the confrontation on the train without inflicting the human costs that he did.

From the perspective of our efforts to understand the rhetoric of the Goetz case, the four theories of self-defense provide an invaluable matrix of interpretation. Rhetorical gambits like "they got what they deserved" make sense as an appeal to a particular conception of self-defense. Emphasizing Goetz's fears draws

on a different strain in the accretions of the legal tradition, and appealing to Goetz's right to be free of harassment invokes yet another perspective. Understanding the rhetoric of the Goetz case requires, above all, that we grasp the theoretical forces driving the debate.

Passion and reason interact in the law of self-defense, then, by generating conflicting theories that nag at our loyalties when we seek to interpret the vague contours of the defense. Passions impel us to think of defensive force as punitive and vengeful, inflicting deserved harm on wrongdoers. Reason invites us to think of self-defense as a means of maintaining order and harmony among independent, autonomous persons. The historic struggle of the law has been from passion to reason, from inflicting just deserts to the vindication of the defense's autonomy. Other theories, such as self-defense as an excuse based on an involuntary response and the social theory of justifiable self-defense, complicate the task of reason.

Could it be the case that reason requires a single theory of self-defense? Or is reason tolerant of diverse theories within the same legal system? The question whether reason tolerates diversity invites us to think about diverse perceptions of an ambiguous situation like Troy Canty's approaching Bernhard Goetz and asking for five dollars. As there are many approaches to self-defense, there are potentially many plausible interpretations of what might have happened in that subway encounter. In the end, the inquiry must turn to Goetz's subjective perception of what was about to happen to him. His claim of self-defense resolved into an inquiry whether his perception of the events was consistent with reason. Reason in the law drives us toward the truth, but it can also be tolerant of sensible error.

# QUESTIONS

1. Fletcher says, "When individuals are threatened with immediate aggression, when the police cannot protect them, the monopoly of the state gives way." In which circumstances would the individualist version of self-defense be most appealing: in a society in which the state's enforcement of law is weak and uncertain, or one in which the state's protection of individuals from crime is reliable and strong?

2. In what ways is self-defense different from punishment? In what ways is self-defense like punishment?

3. Fletcher says, "The passionate response is captured in the refrain heard throughout the Goetz trial: 'These kids got what they deserved.'" If we believe that retributivism, with its idea that punishment must fit the crime, is the proper measure of deserved punishment, then did Goetz mete out deserved punishment?

4. Fletcher says, "Proportionality in punishment—making the punishment fit the crime—is more rigorous than proportionality in self-defense. Using the death penalty for rape, for example, violates the principles of proportional punishment as expressed in the Eighth Amendment, which prohibits cruel and unusual punishment." Provide a rationale for this difference between proportionality in punishment and proportionality in self-defense.

5. Which model, Fletcher's social version or his individualist version, agrees most with your initial feelings about self-defense? Apart from these feelings, for which of these models can you give the most plausible rationale?

6. One writer suggests that, since we regard killing in self-defense as morally permissible, it follows that we cannot regard killing per se as wrong. [Jeffrey H. Reiman,, "Justice, Civilization, and the Death Penalty," *Philosophy & Public Affairs*, vol. 14, no. 2 (Spring 1985), p. 116.] Reflect on what you have learned about different conceptions of self-defense, and then consider this question: Are there some relevant differences between killing in self-defense and administering the death penalty that weaken this argument?

# Responsibility and Insanity

## House of Lords
# THE RULES IN M'NAGHTEN'S CASE*

(Q.I.) "What is the law respecting alleged crimes committed by persons afflicted with insane delusion in respect of one or more particular subjects or persons: as for instance, where at the time of the commission of the alleged crime, the accused knew he was acting contrary to law, but did the act complained of with a view, under the influence of insane delusion, of redressing or revenging some supposed grievance or injury, or of producing some supposed public benefit?

(A.I.) "Assuming that your lordships" inquiries are confined to those persons who labor under such partial delusions only, and are not in other respects insane, we are of opinion that notwithstanding the accused did the act complained of with a view, under the influence of insane delusion, or redressing or avenging some supposed grievance or injury, or of producing some public benefit, he is nevertheless punishable, according to the nature of the crime committed, if he knew at the time of committing such crime that he was acting contrary to law, by which expression we understand your lordships to mean the law of the land."

(Q.II.) "What are the proper questions to be submitted to the jury where a person alleged to be afflicted with insane delusion respecting one or more particular subjects or persons is charged with the commission of a crime (murder, for example), and insanity is set up as a defence?"

(Q.III.) "In what terms ought the question to be left to the jury as to the prisoner's state of mind at the time when the act was committed?"

(A.II and A.III.) "As these two questions appear to us to be more conveniently answered together, we submit our opinion to be that the jury ought to be told in all cases

that every man is presumed to be sane, and to possess a sufficient degree of reason to be responsible for his crimes, until the contrary be proved to their satisfaction; and that to establish a defence on the ground of insanity it must be clearly proved that, at the time of committing the act, the accused was labouring under such a defect of reason, from disease of the mind, as not to know the nature and quality of the act he was doing, or, if he did know it, that he did not know he was doing what was wrong. The mode of putting the latter part of the question to the jury on these occasions has generally been whether the accused at the time of doing the act knew the difference between right and wrong: which mode, though rarely, if ever, leading to any mistake with the jury, is not, as we conceive, so accurate when put generally and in the abstract as when put with reference to the party's knowledge of right and wrong, in respect to the very act with which he is charged. If the question were to be put as to the knowledge of the accused solely and exclusively with reference to the law of the land, it might tend to confound the jury, by inducing them to believe that an actual knowledge of the law of the land was essential in order to lead to conviction: whereas, the law is administered upon the principle that everyone must be taken conclusively to know it, without proof that he does know it. If the accused was conscious that the act was one that he ought not do, and if that act was at the same time contrary to the law of the land, he is punishable; and the usual course, therefore, has been to leave the question to the jury, whether the accused had a sufficient degree of reason to know that he was doing an act that was wrong;

*(1843) 10 Cl. & F. 200, 8 Eng. Rep. 718.

and this course we think is correct, accompanied with such observations and explanations as the circumstances of each particular case may require."

(Q.IV.) "If a person under an insane delusion as to existing facts commits an offence in consequence thereof, is he thereby excused?"

(A.IV.) "The answer must, of course, depend on the nature of the delusion; but making the same assumption as we did before, namely, that he labors under such partial delusion only, and is not in other respects insane, we think he must be considered in the same situation as to responsibility as if the facts with respect to which the delusion exists were real. For example, if under the influence of his delusion he supposes another man to be in the act of attempting to take away his life, and he kills that man, as he supposes in self-defence, he would be exempt from punishment. If his delusion was that the deceased had inflicted a serious injury to his character and fortune, and he killed him in revenge for such supposed injury, he would be liable to punishment."

## U.S. Court of Appeals, District of Columbia*
## DURHAM v. UNITED STATES

BAZELON, Circuit Judge.

Monte Durham was convicted of housebreaking,[1] by the District Court sitting without a jury. The only defense asserted at the trial was that Durham was of unsound mind at the time of the offense. We are now urged to reverse the conviction (1) because the trial court did not correctly apply existing rules governing the burden of proof on the defense of insanity, and (2) because existing tests of criminal responsibility are obsolete and should be superseded.[2]

### I.

Durham has a long history of imprisonment and hospitalization. In 1945, at the age of 17, he was discharged from the Navy after a psychiatric examination had shown that he suffered "from a profound personality disorder which renders him unfit for Naval service." In 1947 he pleaded guilty to violating the National Motor Theft Act[3] and was placed on probation for one to three years. He attempted suicide, was taken to Gallinger Hospital for observation, and was transferred to St. Elizabeths Hospital, from which he was discharged after two months. In January of 1948, as a result of a conviction in the District of Columbia Municipal Court for passing bad checks, the District Court revoked his probation and he commenced service of his Motor Theft sentence. His conduct within the first few days in jail led to a lunacy inquiry in the Municipal Court where a jury found him to be of unsound mind. Upon commitment to St. Elizabeths, he was diagnosed as suffering from "psychosis with psychopathic personality." After 15 months of treatment, he was discharged in July 1949

*214 F. 2d 862 (1954).

[1] D.C. Code §§ 22–1801, 22–2201 and 22–2202 (1951).

[2] Because the questions raised are of general and crucial importance, we called upon the Government and counsel whom we appointed for the indigent appellant to brief and argue this case a second time. Their able presentations have been of great assistance to us. On the question of the adequacy of prevailing tests of criminal responsibility, we received further assistance from the able brief and argument of Abram Chayes, *amicus curiae* by appointment of this Court, in Stewart v. United States, 94 U.S. App. D.C.—, 214 F.2d 879.

[3] 18 U.S.C. § 408 (1946). 1948 Revision, 18 U.S.C. §§ 10, 2311–2313.

as "recovered" and was returned to jail to serve the balance of his sentence. In June 1950 he was conditionally released. He violated the conditions by leaving the District. When he learned of a warrant for his arrest as a parole violator, he fled to the "South and Midwest obtaining money by passing a number of bad checks." After he was found and returned to the District, the Parole Board referred him to the District Court for a lunacy inquisition, wherein a jury again found him to be of unsound mind. He was readmitted to St. Elizabeths in February 1951. This time the diagnosis was "without mental disorder, psychopathic personality." He was discharged for the third time in May 1951. The housebreaking which is the subject of the present appeal took place two months later, on July 13, 1951.

According to his mother and the psychiatrist who examined him in September 1951, he suffered from hallucinations immediately after his May 1951 discharge from St. Elizabeths. Following the present indictment, in October 1951, he was adjudged of unsound mind in proceedings under § 4244 of Title 18 U.S.C., upon the affidavits of two psychiatrists that he suffered from "psychosis with psychopathic personality." He was committed to St. Elizabeths for the fourth time and given subshock insulin therapy. This commitment lasted 16 months— until February 1953—when he was released to the custody of the District Jail on the certificate of Dr. Silk, Acting Superintendent of St. Elizabeths, that he was "mentally competent to stand trial and * * * able to consult with counsel to properly assist in his own defense."

He was thereupon brought before the court on the charge involved here. The prosecutor told the court:

"So I take this attitude, in view of the fact that he has been over there [St. Elizabeths] a couple of times and these cases that were charged against him were dropped. I don't think I should take the responsibility of dropping these cases against him; then Saint Elizabeths would let him out on the street, and if that man committed a murder next week then it is my responsibility. So we decided to go to trial on one case, that is the case where we found him right in the house, and let him bring in the defense, if he wants to, of unsound mind at the time the crime was committed, and then Your Honor will find him on that, and in your decision send him back to Saint Elizabeths Hospital, and then if they let him out on the street it is their responsibility."

Shortly thereafter, when the question arose whether Durham could be considered competent to stand trial merely on the basis of Dr. Silk's ex parte statement, the court said to defense counsel:

"I am going to ask you this, Mr. Ahern: I have taken the position that if once a person has been found of unsound mind after a lunacy hearing, an ex parte certificate of the Superintendent of Saint Elizabeths is not sufficient to set aside that finding and I have held another lunacy hearing. That has been my custom. However, if you want to waive that you may do it, if you admit that he is now of sound mind."

[1] The court accepted counsel's waiver on behalf of Durham, although it had been informed by the prosecutor that a letter from Durham claimed need of further hospitalization, and by defense counsel that "* * * the defendant does say that even today he thinks he does need hospitalization; he told me that this morning."[4] Upon being so informed, the court said, "Of course, if I hold he is not mentally incompetent to stand trial I send him back to

---

[4]Durham showed confusion when he testified. These are but two examples:

"Q. Do you remember writing it? A. No. Don't you forget? People get all mixed up in machines.

Saint Elizabeths Hospital and they will send him back again in two or three months."[5] In this atmosphere Durham's trial commenced.

[2-4] His conviction followed the trial court's rejection of the defense of insanity in these words:

"I don't think it has been established that the defendant was of unsound mind as of July, 13, 1951, in the sense that he didn't know the difference between right and wrong or that even if he did, he was subject to an irresistible impulse by reason of the derangement of mind.

"While, of course, the burden of proof on the issue of mental capacity to commit a crime is upon the Government, just as it is on every other issue, nevertheless, the Court finds that there is not sufficient to contradict the usual presumption of [sic] the usual inference of sanity.

"*There is no testimony concerning the mental state of the defendant as of July, 13, 1951, and therefore the usual presumption of sanity governs.*

"*While if there was some testimony as to his mental state as of that date to the effect that he was incompetent on that date, the burden of proof would be on the Government to overcome it. There has been no such testimony, and the usual presumption of sanity prevails.*

\*      \*      \*      \*      \*

"Mr. Ahern, I think you have done very well by your client and defended him very ably, but I think under the circumstances there is nothing that anybody could have done." [Emphasis supplied.]

We think this reflects error requiring reversal.

In Tatum v. United States we said, "When lack of mental capacity is raised as a defense to a charge of crime, the law accepts the general experience of mankind and presumes that all people, including those accused of crime, are sane."[6] So long as this presumption prevails, the prosecution is not required to prove the defendant's sanity. But "as soon as 'some evidence of mental disorder is introduced, \* \* \* sanity, like any other fact, must be proved as a part of the prosecution's case beyond a reasonable doubt.'"[7] Here it appears that the trial judge recognized this rule but failed to find "some evidence." We hold that the court erred and that the requirement of "some evidence" was satisfied.[8]

---

"Q. What kind of a machine? A. I don't know, they just get mixed up.

"Q. Are you cured now? A. No, sir.

"Q. In your opinion? A. No, sir.

"Q. What is the matter with you? A. You hear people bother you.

"Q. What? You say you hear people bothering you? A. Yes.

"Q. What kind of people? What do they bother you about? A. (No response.)"

Although we think the court erred in accepting counsel's admission that Durham was of sound mind, the matter does not require discussion since we reverse on other grounds and the principles governing this issue are fully discussed in our decision today in Gunther v. United States, 94 U.S.App.D.C.—, 215 F.2d 493.

[5]The court also accepted a waiver of trial by jury when Durham indicated, in response to the court's question, that he preferred to be tried without a jury and that he waived his right to a trial by jury.

[6]1951, 88 U.S.App.D.C. 386, 389, 190 F. 2d 612, 615.

[7]88 U.S.App.D.C. at page 389, 190 F.2d at page 615, quoting Glueck, Mental Disorder and the Criminal Law 41–42 (1925).

[8]In its brief, the prosecution confounds the "some evidence" test with the "evidence sufficient to create a reasonable doubt" test, despite our explanation in Tatum that the "'evidence sufficient to create a reasonable doubt' test" applies only after the issue has been raised by "some evidence" and the burden is already upon the Government to prove the defendant's sanity beyond a reasonable doubt. 88 U.S.App.D.C. at page 390, 190 F.2d at page 616.

In Tatum we held that requirement satisfied by considerably less than is present here. Tatum claimed lack of memory concerning the critical events and three lay witnesses testified that he appeared to be in "more or less of a trance," or "abnormal," but two psychiatrists testified that he was of "sound mind" both at the time of examination and at the time of the crime. Here, the psychiatric testimony was unequivocal that Durham was of unsound mind at the time of the crime. Dr. Gilbert, the only expert witness heard,[9] so stated at least four times. This crucial testimony is set out in the margin.[10] Intensive questioning by the court failed to produce any retraction of Dr. Gilbert's testimony that the "period of insanity would have embraced the date July 13, 1951." And though the prosecution sought unsuccessfully in its cross- and recross-examination of Dr. Gilbert to establish that Durham was a malingerer who feigned insanity whenever he was trapped for his misdeeds, it failed to present any expert testimony to support this theory. In addition to Dr. Gilbert's testimony, there was testimony by Durham's mother to the effect that in the interval between his discharge from St. Elizabeths in May 1951, and

[9]Dr. Amino Perretti, who also examined Durham in connection with those proceedings and furnished an affidavit that Durham was of unsound mind, was unable to testify due to illness.

[10](1) "Q. [Mr. Ahern]. As a result of those examinations did you reach a conclusion as to the sanity or insanity of the defendant? A. Yes, I did arrive at an opinion as to his mental condition.

"Q. And what is that opinion? A. That he at that time was of unsound mind.

"Q. Can you tell us what disorder he was suffering from, Doctor? A. The report of his case at the time, as of October 9, 1951, I used the diagnosis of undifferentiated psychosis, but according to the record the diagnosis was at the time of commitment psychosis with psychopathic personality.

\*     \*     \*     \*     \*     \*     \*     \*     \*

"Q. At that time were you able to make a determination as to how long this condition had existed? A. According to the record I felt at the time that he had been in that attitude or mental disorder for a period of some few to several months."

(2) "Q. [Mr. Ahern]. Directing your attention specifically to July 13, 1951, will you give us your opinion as to the mental condition of the defendant at that time? A. From my previous testimony and previous opinion, to repeat, it was my opinion that he had been of unsound mind from sometime not long after a previous release from Saint Elizabeths Hospital [i.e., May 14, 1951]."

(3) "Q. [Mr. Ahern]. In any event, Doctor, is it your opinion that that period of insanity would have embraced the date July 13, 1951? A. Yes. My examination would antedate that; that is, the symptoms obtained, according to my examinations, included that—the symptoms of the mental disorder.

"Q. Can you tell us what symptoms you found, Doctor? A. Well, he was trying to work for a while, he stated, and while he was working at one of these People's Drug Stores he began to hear false voices and suffer from hallucinations and believed that the other employees and others in the store talked about him, watched him, and the neighbors did the same, watching him from their windows, talking about him, and those symptoms continued and were present through the time that I examined him in September and October.

\*     \*     \*     \*     \*     \*     \*     \*     \*

"Q. [Mr. McLaughlin]. You were asked the specific question, Doctor, whether or not in your opinion on July 13, 1951, this defendant was of unsound mind and didn't know the difference between right and wrong. Can you express an opinion as to that? A. Yes. It is my opinion he was of unsound mind."

(4) "Q. [Mr. McLaughlin]. Can you tell us—this is for my own information, I would like to know this—you say that this defendant, at the time you examined him in 1951 was of unsound mind and had been of unsound mind sometime prior to that; is that your statement? A. Yes, sir.

"Q. Can you tell us how long prior to that time he was of unsound mind? A. Well, while he was working in People's Drug Store the symptoms were present, and how long before that, I didn't get the date of that.

"Q. When was he working in People's Drug Store?

\*     \*     \*     \*     \*     \*     \*     \*     \*

"A. Sometime after his discharge from Saint Elizabeths Hospital.

"Q. In 1947? A. Oh, no; 1951."

the crime "he seemed afraid of people" and had urged her to put steel bars on his bedroom windows.

Apparently the trial judge regarded this psychiatric testimony as "no testimony" on two grounds: (1) it did not adequately cover Durham's condition on July 13, 1951, the date of the offense; and (2) it was not directed to Durham's capacity to distinguish between right and wrong. We are unable to agree that for either of these reasons the psychiatric testimony could properly be considered "no testimony."

(1) Following Dr. Gilbert's testimony that the condition in which he found Durham on September 3, 1951 was progressive and did not "arrive overnight," Dr. Gilbert responded to a series of questions by the court:

> "Q. [Court]. Then it is reasonable to assume that it is not possible to determine *how far* this state of unsound mind had progressed by July 13th? Isn't that so? A. [Dr. Gilbert]. As to the seriousness of the symptoms as compared with them and the time I observed him, that's true, except that his travels were based, according to his statements to me, on certain of the symptoms and his leaving Washington, his giving up his job and work and leaving the work that he had tried to do.
>
> "Q. But you can't tell, can you, *how far* those symptoms had progressed and become worse by the 13th of July? A. No, not *how far* they were, that is correct." [Emphasis supplied.]

Thereafter, when the prosecutor on re-cross asked Dr. Gilbert whether he would change his opinion concerning Durham's mental condition on July 13, 1951, if he knew that Durham had been released from St. Elizabeths just two months before as being of sound mind, the court interrupted to say: "Just a minute. The Doctor testified in answer to my question that he doesn't know and he can't express a definite opinion as to his mental condition on the 13th of July." This, we think, overlooks the witness' unequivocal testimony on direct and cross-examination,[11] and misconceives what he had said in response to questioning by the court, namely, that certain symptoms of mental disorder antedated the crime, although it was impossible to say how far they had progressed.

Moreover, any conclusion that there was "no testimony" regarding Durham's mental condition at the time of the crime disregards the testimony of his mother. Her account of his behavior after his discharge from St. Elizabeths in May 1951 was directly pertinent to the issue of his sanity at the time of the crime.

(2) On re-direct examination, Dr. Gilbert was asked whether he would say that Durham "knew the difference between right and wrong on July 13, 1951; that is, his ability to distinguish between what was right and what was wrong." He replied: "As I have stated before, if the question of the right and wrong were propounded to him he could give you the right answer." Then the court interrupted to ask:

> "The Court. No, I don't think that is the question, Doctor—not whether he could give a right answer to a question, but whether he, himself, knew the difference between right and wrong in connection with governing his own actions. * * * If you are unable to answer, why, you can say so; I mean if you are unable to form an opinion.
>
> "The Witness. I can only answer this way: That I can't tell how much the abnormal thinking and the abnormal experiences in the form of hallucinations and delusions—delusions of persecutions—had to do with his anti-social behavior.

---

[11] See note 10, supra.

"I don't know how anyone can answer that question categorically, except as one's experience leads him to know that most mental cases can give you a categorical answer of right and wrong, but what influence these symptoms have on abnormal behavior or anti-social behavior—

"The Court. Well, your answer is that you are unable to form an opinion, is that it?

"The Witness. I would say that is essentially true, for the reasons that I have given."

Later, when defense counsel sought elaboration from Dr. Gilbert on his answers relating to the "right and wrong" test, the court cut off the questioning with the admonition that "you have answered the question, Doctor."

The inability of the expert to give categorical assurance that Durham was unable to distinguish between right and wrong did not destroy the effect of his previous testimony that the period of Durham's "insanity" embraced July 13, 1951. It is plain from our decision in Tatum that this previous testimony was adequate to prevent the presumption of sanity from becoming conclusive and to place the burden of proving sanity upon the Government. None of the testimony before the court in Tatum was couched in terms of "right and wrong."

[5] Finally, even assuming *arguendo* that the court, contrary to the plain meaning of its words, recognized that the prosecution had the burden of proving Durham's sanity, there would still be a fatal error. For once the issue of insanity is raised by the introduction of "some evidence," so that the presumption of sanity is no longer absolute, it is incumbent upon the trier of fact to weigh and consider "the whole evidence, including that supplied by the presumption of sanity * * *" on the issue of "the capacity in law of the accused to commit" the crime.[12] Here, manifestly, the court as the trier of fact did not and could not weigh "the whole evidence," for it found there was "no testimony concerning the mental state" of Durham.

For the foregoing reasons, the judgment is reversed and the case is remanded for a new trial.

## II.

It has been ably argued by counsel for Durham that the existing tests in the District of Columbia for determining criminal responsibility, *i.e.*, the so-called right-wrong test supplemented by the irresistible impulse test, are not satisfactory criteria for determining criminal responsibility. We are urged to adopt a different test to be applied on the retrial of this case. This contention has behind it nearly a century of agitation for reform.

A. The right-wrong test, approved in this jurisdiction in 1882,[13] was the exclusive test of criminal responsibility in the District of Columbia until 1929 when we approved the irresistible impulse test as a supplementary test in Smith v. United States.[14] The right-wrong test has its roots in England. There, by the first quarter of the eighteenth century, an accused escaped punishment if he could not distinguish "good and evil," *i.e.*, if he "doth not know what he is doing, no more than * * * a wild beast."[15] Later in the same century, the "wild beast" test was abandoned and "right and wrong" was substituted for "good and evil."[16] And toward

[12]Davis v. United States, 1895, 160 U.S. 469, 488, 16 S.Ct. 353, 358, 40 L.Ed. 499.

[13]1882, 12 D.C. 498, 550, 1 Mackey 498, 550. The right-wrong test was reaffirmed in United States v. Lee, 1886, 15 D.C. 489, 496, 4 Mackey 489, 496.

[14]1920, 59 App.D.C. 144, 36 F.2d 548, 70 A.L.R. 654.

[15]Glueck, Mental Disorder and the Criminal Law 138–39 (1925), citing Rex v. Arnold, 16 How.St.Tr. 695, 764 (1724).

[16]Id. at 142–52, citing Earl Ferrer's case, 19 How.St.Tr. 886 (1760). One writer has stated that these tests originated in England in the 13th or 14th century, when the law began to define insanity in terms of intellect for purposes of determining capacity to manage feudal estates. Comment, *Lunacy and Idiocy—The Old Law and Its Incubus*, 18 U. of Chi.L.Rev. 361 (1951).

the middle of the nineteenth century, the House of Lords in the famous M'Naghten case[17] restated what had become the accepted "right-wrong" test[18] in a form which has since been followed, not only in England[19] but in most American jurisdictions[20] as an exclusive test of criminal responsibility:

"* * * the jurors ought to be told in all cases that every man is to be presumed to be sane, and to possess a sufficient degree of reason to be responsible for his crimes, until the contrary be proved to their satisfaction; and that, to establish a defense on the ground of insanity, it must be clearly proved that, at the time of the committing of the act, the party accused was labouring under such a defect of reason, from disease of the mind, as not to know the nature and quality of the act he was doing, or, if

he did know it, that he did not know he was doing what was wrong."[21]

As early as 1838, Isaac Ray, one of the founders of the American Psychiatric Association, in his now classic Medical Jurisprudence of Insanity, called knowledge of right and wrong a "fallacious" test of criminal responsibility.[22] This view has long since been substantiated by enormous developments in knowledge of mental life.[23] In 1928 Mr. Justice Cardozo said to the New York Academy of Medicine: "Everyone concedes that the present [legal] definition of insanity has little relation to the truths of mental life."[24]

Medico-legal writers in large number,[25] The Report of the Royal Commission on Capital Punishment 1949–1953,[26] and The Preliminary Report by the Committee on Forensic

[17]8 Eng.Rep. 718 (1843).

[18]Hall, Principles of Criminal Law 480, n. 6 (1947).

[19]Royal Commission on Capital Punishment 1949–1953 Report (Cmd. 8932) 79 (1953) (hereinafter cited as Royal Commission Report).

[20]Weihofen, *The M'Naghten Rule in Its Present Day Setting*, Federal Probation 8 (Sept. 1953); Weihofen, Insanity as a Defense in Criminal Law 15, 64–68, 109–47 (1933); Leland v. State of Oregon, 1952, 343 U.S. 790, 800, 72 S.Ct. 1002, 96 L.Ed. 1302.
"In five States the M'Naghten Rules have been in substance re-enacted by statute." Royal Commission Report 409; see. e.g., "Sec. 1120 of the [New York State] Penal Law [McK.Consol. Laws, c. 40] [which] provides that a person is not excused from liability on the grounds of insanity, idiocy or imbecility, except upon proof that at the time of the commission of the criminal act he was laboring under such a defect of reason as (1) not to know the nature and quality of the act he was doing or (2) not to know that the act was wrong." Ploscowe, *Suggested Changes in the New York Laws and Procedures Relating to the Criminally Insane and Mentally Defective Offenders*, 43 J. Crim.L., Criminology & Police Sci. 312, 314 (1952).

[21]8 Eng.Rep. 718, 722 (1843). "Today, Oregon is the only state that requires the accused, on a plea of insanity, to establish that defense beyond a reasonable doubt. Some twenty states, however, place the burden on the accused to establish his insanity by a preponderance of the evidence or some similar measure of persuasion." Leland v. State of Oregon, supra, note 20, 343 U.S. at page 798, 72 S.Ct. 1002. Since Davis v. United States, 1895, 160 U.S. 469, 484, 16 S.Ct. 353, 40 L.Ed. 499, a contrary rule of procedure has been followed in the Federal courts. For example, in compliance with Davis, we held in Tatum v. United States, supra, note 8, 88 U.S.App.D.C. 386, 389, 190 F.2d 612, 615, and text, "as soon as 'some evidence of mental disorder is introduced, * * * sanity, like any other fact, must be proved as part of the prosecution's case beyond a reasonable doubt.'"

[22]Ray, Medical Jurisprudence of Insanity 47 and 34 et seq. (1st ed. 1838). "That the insane mind is not entirely deprived of this power of moral discernment, but in many subjects is perfectly rational, and displays the exercise of a sound and well balanced mind is one of those facts now so well established, that to question it would only betray the height of ignorance and presumption." Id. at 32.

[23]See Zilboorg, *Legal Aspects of Psychiatry* in One Hundred Years of American Psychiatry 1844–1944, 507, 552 (1944).

[24]Cardozo, What Medicine Can Do For the Law 32 (1930).

[25]For a detailed bibliography on Insanity as a Defense to Crime, see 7 The Record of the Association of the Bar of the City of New York 158–62 (1952). And see, *e.g.*, Alexander, the Criminal, the Judge and the Public 70 et

Psychiatry of the Group for the Advancement of Psychiatry[27] present convincing evidence that the right and wrong test is "based on an entirely obsolete and misleading conception of the nature of insanity."[28] The science of psychiatry now recognizes that a man is an integrated personality and that reason, which is only one element in that personality, is not the sole determinant of his conduct. The right-wrong test, which considers knowledge of reason alone, is therefore an inadequate guide to mental responsibility for criminal behavior. As Professor Sheldon Glueck of the Harvard Law School points out in discussing the right-wrong tests, which he calls the knowledge tests:

"It is evident that the knowledge tests unscientifically abstract out of the mental make-up but one phase or element of mental life, the cognitive, which, in this era of dynamic psychology, is beginning to be regarded as not the most important factor in conduct and its disorders. In brief, these tests proceed upon the following question-

able assumptions of an outworn era in psychiatry: (1) that lack of knowledge of the 'nature or quality' of an act (assuming the meaning of such terms to be clear) or incapacity to know right from wrong, is the sole or even the most important symptom of mental disorder; (2) that such knowledge is the sole instigator and guide of conduct, or at least the most important element therein, and consequently should be the sole criterion of responsibility when insanity is involved; and (3) that the capacity of knowing right from wrong can be completely intact and functioning perfectly even though a defendant is otherwise demonstrably of disordered mind."[29]

Nine years ago we said:

"The modern science of psychology * * * does not conceive that there is a separate little man in the top of one's head called reason whose function is to guide another unruly little man called instinct, emotion, or impulse in the way he should go."[30]

seq. (1931); Cardozo, What Medicine Can Do For the Law 28 et seq. (1930); Cleckley, the Mask of Sanity 491 et seq. (2d ed.1950); Deutsch, The Mentally Ill In America 389–417 (2d ed.1949); Glueck, Mental Disorder and the Criminal Law (1925), Crime and Justice 96 et seq. (1936); Guttmacher & Weihofen, Psychiatry and the Law 218, 403–23 (1952); Hall, Principles of Criminal Law 477–538 (1947); Menninger, The Human Mind 450 (1937); Hall & Menninger, *Psychiatry and the Law*—A Dual Review, 38 Iowa L.Rev. 687 (1953); Overholser, The Psychiatrist and the Law 41–43 (1953); Overholser & Richmond, Handbook of Psychiatry 208–15 (1947); Ploscowe, *Suggested Changes in the New York Laws and Procedures Relating to the Criminally Insane and Mentally Defective Offenders*, 43 J.Crim.L., Criminology & Police Sci. 312, 314 (1952); Ray, Medical Jurisprudence of Insanity (1st ed.1838) (4th ed.1860); Reik, *The Doe-Ray Correspondence: A Pioneer Collaboration in the Jurisprudence of Mental Disease*, 63 Yale L.J. 183 (1953); Weihofen, Insanity as a Defense in Criminal Law (1933), *The M'Naghten Rule in Its Present Day Setting*, Federal Probation 8 (Sept. 1953); Zilboorg, Mind, Medicine and Man 246–97 (1943), *Legal Aspects of Psychiatry*, American Psychiatry 1844–1944, 507 (1944).

[26]Royal Commission Report 73–129.

[27]The Committee on Forensic Psychiatry (whose report is hereinafter cited as Gap Report) was composed of Drs. Philip Q. Roche, Frank S. Curran, Lawrence Z. Freedman and Manfred S. Guttmacher. They were assisted in their deliberations by leading psychiatrists, jurists, law professors, and legal practitioners.

[28]Royal Commission Report 80.

[29]Glueck, *Psychiatry and the Criminal Law*, 12 Mental Hygiene 575, 580 (1928), as quoted in Deutsch, The Mentally Ill in America 396 (2d ed. 1949); and see, *e.g.*, Menninger, The Human Mind 450 (1937); Guttmacher & Weihofen, Psychiatry and the Law 403–08 (1952).

[30]Holloway v. United States, 1945, 80 U.S.App.D.C. 3, 5, 148 F.2d 665, 667, certiorari denied, 1948, 334 U.S. 852, 68 S.Ct. 1507, 92 L.Ed. 1774.

More recently, the Royal Commission, after an exhaustive survey of legal, medical and lay opinion in many Western countries, including England and the United States made a similar finding. It reported:
"The gravamen of the charge against the M'Naghten Rules is that they are not in harmony with modern medical science, which, as we have seen, is reluctant to divide the mind into separate compartments—the intellect, the emotions and the will—but looks at it as a whole and considers that insanity distorts and impairs the action of the mind as a whole." Royal Commission Report 113. The Commission lends vivid support to this conclusion by

By its misleading emphasis on the cognitive, the right-wrong test requires court and jury to rely upon what is, scientifically speaking, inadequate, and most often, invalid[31] and irrelevant testimony in determining criminal responsibility.[32]

The fundamental objection to the right-wrong test, however, is not that criminal responsibility is made to rest upon an inadequate, invalid or indeterminable symptom or manifestation, but that it is made to rest upon *any* particular symptom.[33] In attempting to define insanity in terms of a symptom, the courts have assumed an impossible role,[34] not merely one for which they have no

special competence.[35] As the Royal Commission emphasizes, it is dangerous "to abstract particular mental faculties, and to lay it down that unless these particular faculties are destroyed or gravely impaired, an accused person, whatever the nature of his mental disease, must be held to be criminally responsible * * *."[36] In this field of law as in others, the fact finder should be free to consider all information advanced by relevant scientific disciplines.[37]

Despite demands in the name of scientific advances, this court refused to alter the right-wrong test at the turn of the century.[38]

---

pointing out that "It would be impossible to apply modern methods of care and treatment in mental hospitals, and at the same time to maintain order and discipline, if the great majority of the patients, even among the grossly insane, did not know what is forbidden by the rules and that, if they break them, they are liable to forfeit some privilege. Examination of a number of individual cases in which a verdict of guilty but insane [the nearest English equivalent of our acquittal by reason of insanity] was returned, and rightly returned, has convinced us that there are few indeed where the accused can truly be said not to have known that his act was wrong." Id. at 103.

[31]See Guttmacher & Weihofen, Psychiatry and the Law 421, 422 (1952). The M'Naghten rules "constitute not only an arbitrary restriction on vital medical data, but also impose an improper onus of decision upon the expert witness. The Rules are unanswerable in that they have no consensus with established psychiatric criteria of symptomatic description save for the case of disturbed consciousness or of idiocy, * * *." From statement by Dr. Philip Q. Roche, quoted id. at 407. See also United States ex rel. Smith v. Baldi, 3 Cir., 1951, 192 F.2d 540, 567 (dissenting opinion).

[32]In a very recent case, the Supreme Court of New Mexico recognized the inadequacy of the right-wrong test, and adopted what it called an "extension of the M'Naghten Rules." Under this extension, lack of knowledge of right and wrong is not essential for acquittal "if, by reason of disease of the mind, defendant has been deprived of or lost the power of his will * * *." State v. White, N.M. 270 P.2d 727, 730.

[33]Deutsch, The Mentally Ill in America 400 (2d ed.1949); Keedy, *Irresistible Impulse as a Defense in Criminal Law*, 100 U. of Pa.L.Rev. 956, 992 (1952).

[34]Professor John Whitehorn of the Johns Hopkins Medical School, who recently prepared an informal memorandum on this subject for a Commission on Legal Psychiatry appointed by the Governor of Maryland, has said: "Psychiatrists are challenged to set forth a crystal-clear statement of what constitutes insanity. It is impossible to express this adequately in words, alone, since such diagnostic judgments involve clinical skill and experience which cannot wholly be verbalized. * * * The medical profession would be baffled if asked to write into the legal code universally valid criteria for the diagnosis of the many types of psychotic illness which may seriously disturb a person's responsibility, and even if this were attempted, the diagnostic criteria would have to be rewritten from time to time, with the progress of psychiatric knowledge." Quoted in Guttmacher & Wiehofen, Psychiatry and the Law 419–20 (1952).

[35]"* * * the legal profession were invading the province of medicine, and attempting to install old exploded medical theories in the place of facts established in the progress of scientific knowledge." State v. Pike, 1870, 49 N.H. 399, 438.

[36]Royal Commission Report 114. And see State v. Jones, 1871, 50 N.H. 369, 392–393.

[37]Keedy, *Irresistible Impulse as a Defense in Criminal Law*, 100 U. of Pa.L. Rev. 956, 992–93 (1952).

[38]See, *e.g.*, Taylor v. United States, 1895, 7 App.D.C. 27, 41–44, where we rejected "emotional insanity" as a defense, citing with approval the following from the trial court's instruction to the jury: "Whatever may be the cry of scientific experts, the law does not recognize, but condemns the doctrine of emotional insanity—that a man may be sane up until a moment before he commits a crime, insane while he does it, and sane again soon afterwards. Such a doctrine would be dangerous in the extreme. The law does not recognize it; and a jury cannot without violating their oaths." This position was emphatically reaffirmed in Snell v. United States, 1900, 16 App.D.C. 501, 524.

But in 1929, we reconsidered in response to "the cry of scientific experts" and added the irresistible impulse test as a supplementary test for determining criminal responsibility. Without "hesitation" we declared, in Smith v. United States, "it to be the law of this District that, in cases where insanity is interposed as a defense, and the facts are sufficient to call for the application of the rule of irresistible impulse, the jury should be so charged."[39] We said:

"* * * The modern doctrine is that the degree of insanity which will relieve the accused of the consequences of a criminal act must be such as to create in his mind an uncontrollable impulse to commit the offense charged. This impulse must be such as to override the reason and judgment and obliterate the sense of right and wrong to the extent that the accused is deprived of the power to choose between right and wrong. The mere ability to distinguish right from wrong is no longer the correct test either in civil or criminal cases, where the defense of insanity is interposed. The accepted rule in this day and age, with the great advancement in medical science as an enlightening influence on this subject, is that the accused must be capable, not only of distinguishing between right and wrong, but that he was not impelled to do the act by an irresistible impulse, which means before it will justify a verdict of acquittal that his reasoning powers were so far dethroned by his diseased mental condition as to deprive him of the will power to resist the

insane impulse to perpetrate the deed, though knowing it to be wrong."[40]

As we have already indicated, this has been the test in the District.

Although the Smith case did not abandon the right-wrong test, it did liberate the fact finder from exclusive reliance upon that discredited criterion by allowing the jury to inquire also whether the accused suffered from an undefined "diseased mental condition [which] deprive[d] him of the will power to resist the insane impulse * * *."[41] The term "irresistible impulse," however, carries the misleading implication that "diseased mental condition[s]" produce only sudden, momentary or spontaneous inclinations to commit unlawful acts.[42]

As the Royal Commission found:

"* * * In many cases * * * this is not true at all. The sufferer from [melancholia, for example] experiences a change of mood which alters the whole of his existence. He may believe, for instance, that a future of such degradation and misery awaits both him and his family that death for all is a less dreadful alternative. Even the thought that the acts he contemplates are murder and suicide pales into insignificance in contrast with what he otherwise expects. The criminal act, in such circumstances, may be the reverse of impulsive. It may be coolly and carefully prepared; yet it is still the act of a madman. This is merely an illustration; similar states of mind are likely

---

[39]1929, 59 App.D.C. 144, 146, 36 F.2d 548, 550, 70 A.L.R. 654.

[40]59 App.D.C. at page 145, 36 F.2d at page 549.

[41]59 App.D.C. at page 145, 36 F2d at page 549.

[42]Impulse, as defined by Webster's New International Dictionary (2d ed.1950), is:

"1. Act of impelling, or driving onward with *sudden* force; impulsion, esp., force so communicated as to produce motion *suddenly*, or *immediately* * *.

"2. An incitement of the mind or spirit, esp. in the form of an *abrupt* and vivid suggestion, prompting some *unpremeditated* action or leading to unforeseen knowledge or insight; a *spontaneous* inclination * * *.

"3. * * * motion produced by a *sudden* or *momentary* force * * *." [Emphasis supplied.]

to lie behind the criminal act when murders are committed by persons suffering from schizophrenia or paranoid psychoses due to disease of the brain."[43]

[6] We find that as an exclusive criterion the right-wrong test is inadequate in that (a) it does not take sufficient account of psychic realities and scientific knowledge, and (b) it is based upon one symptom and so cannot validly be applied in all circumstances. We find that the "irresistible impulse" test is also inadequate in that it gives no recognition to mental illness characterized by brooding and reflection and so relegates acts caused by such illness to the application of the inadequate right-wrong test. We conclude that a broader test should be adopted.[44]

[7, 8] B. In the District of Columbia, the formulation of tests of criminal responsibility is entrusted to the courts[45] and, in adopting a new test, we invoke our inherent power to make the change prospectively.[46]

[9] The rule we now hold must be applied on the retrial of this case and in future cases is not unlike that followed by the New Hampshire court since 1870.[47] It is simply that an accused is not criminally responsible if his unlawful act was the product of mental disease or mental defect.[48]

[10] We use "disease" in the sense of a condition which is considered capable of either improving or deteriorating. We use "defect" in the sense of a condition which is not considered capable of either improving or deteriorating and which may be either congenital, or the result of an injury, or the residual effect of a physical or mental disease.

[43]Royal Commission Report 110; for additional comment on the irresistible impulse test, see Glueck, Crime and Justice 101–03 (1936); Guttmacher & Weihofen, Psychiatry and the Law 410–12 (1952); Hall, General Principles of Criminal Law 505–26 (1947); Keedy, *Irresistible Impulse as a Defense in Criminal Law*, 100 U. of Pa.L.Rev. 956 (1952); Wertham, The Show of Violence 14 (1949).

The New Mexico Supreme Court in recently adopting a broader criminal insanity rule, note 32, supra, observed: "* * * insanity takes the form of the personality of the individual and, if his tendency is toward depression, his wrongful act may come at the conclusion of a period of complete lethargy, thoroughly devoid of excitement."

[44]As we recently said, "* * * former common law should not be followed where changes in conditions have made it obsolete. We have never hesitated to exercise the usual judicial function of revising and enlarging the common law." Linkins v. Protestant Episcopal Cathedral Foundation, 1950, 87 U.S.App.D.C. 351, 355, 187 F.2d 357, 361, 28 A.L.R.2d 521. Cf. Funk v. United States, 1933, 290 U.S. 371, 381–382, 54 S.Ct. 212, 78 L.Ed. 369.

[45]Congress, like most State legislatures, has never undertaken to define insanity in this connection, although it recognizes the fact that an accused may be acquitted by reason of insanity. See D.C.Code § 24–301 (1951). And as this court made clear in Hill v. United States, Congress has left no doubt that "common-law procedure, in all matters relating to crime * * * still continues in force here in all cases except where special provision is made by statute to the exclusion of the common-law procedure." 22 App. D.C. 395, 401 (1903), and statutes cited therein; Linkins v. Protestant Episcopal Cathedral Foundation, 87 U.S.App.D.C. at pages 354–55, 187 F.2d at pages 360–361; and see Fisher v. United States, 1946, 328 U.S. 463, 66 S.Ct. 1318, 90 L. Ed. 1382.

[46]See Great Northern R. v. Sunburst Oil & Refining Co., 1932, 287 U.S. 358, 53 S. Ct. 145, 77 L.Ed. 360; National Labor Relations Board v. Guy F. Atkinson Co., 9 Cir., 1952, 195 F.2d 141, 148; Concurring opinion of Judge Frank in Aero Spark Plug Co. v. B. G. Corporation, 2 Cir., 1942, 130 F.2d 290, 298, and note 24; Warring v. Colpoys, 1941, 74 App. D.C. 303, 122 F.2d 642, 645, 136 A.L.R. 1025; Moore & Oglebay, *The Supreme Court, Stare Decisis and Law of the Case*, 21 Texas L.Rev. 514, 535 (1943); Carpenter, *Court Decisions and the Common Law*, 17 Col.L.Rev. 593, 606–07 (1917). But see von Moschzisker, *Stare Decisis in Courts of Last Resort*, 37 Harv.L.Rev. 409, 426 (1924). Our approach is similar to that of the Supreme Court of California in People v. Maughs, 1906, 149 Cal. 253, 86 P. 187, 191, where the court prospectively invalidated a previously accepted instruction, saying:

"* * * we think the time has come to say that in all future cases which shall arise, and where, after this warning, this instruction shall be given, this court will hold the giving of it to be so prejudicial to the rights of a defendant, secured to him by our Constitution and laws, as to call for the reversal of any judgment which may be rendered against him."

[47]State v. Pike, 1870, 49 N.H. 399.

[48]Cf. State v. Jones, 1871, 50 N.H. 369, 398.

[11,12] Whenever there is "some evidence" that the accused suffered from a diseased or defective mental condition at the time the unlawful act was committed, the trial court must provide the jury with guides for determining whether the accused can be held criminally responsible. We do not, and indeed could not, formulate an instruction which would be either appropriate or binding in all cases. But under the rule now announced, any instruction should in some way convey to the jury the sense and substance of the following: If you the jury believe beyond a reasonable doubt that the accused was not suffering from a diseased or defective mental condition at the time he committed the criminal act charged, you may find him guilty. If you believe he was suffering from a diseased or defective mental condition when he committed the act, but believe beyond a reasonable doubt that the act was not the product of such mental abnormality, you may find him guilty. Unless you believe beyond a reasonable doubt either that he was not suffering from a diseased or defective mental condition, or that the act was not a product of such abnormality, you must find the accused not guilty by reason of insanity. Thus your task would not be completed upon finding, if you did find, that the accused suffered from a mental disease or defect. He would still be responsible for his unlawful act if there was no causal connection between such mental abnormality and the act.[49] These questions must be determined by you from the facts which you find to be fairly deducible from the testimony and the evidence in this case.[50]

[13] The questions of fact under the test we now lay down are as capable of determination by the jury as, for example, the questions juries must determine upon a claim of total disability under a policy of insurance where the state of medical knowledge concerning the disease involved, and its effects, is obscure or in conflict. In such cases, the jury is not required to depend on arbitrarily selected "symptoms, phases or manifestations"[51] of the disease as criteria for determining the ultimate questions of fact upon which the claim depends. Similarly, upon a claim of criminal irresponsibility, the jury will not be required to rely on such symptoms as criteria for determining the ultimate question of fact upon which such claim depends. Testimony as to such "symptoms, phases or manifestations," along with other relevant evidence, will go to the jury upon the ultimate questions of fact which it alone can finally determine. Whatever the state of psychiatry, the psychiatrist will be permitted to carry out his principal court function which, as we noted in Holloway v. U.S., "is to inform the jury of the character of [the accused's] mental disease [or defect]."[52] The jury's range of inquiry will not be limited to, but may include, for example, whether an

---

[49] "There is no *a priori* reason why every person suffering from any form of mental abnormality or disease, or from any particular kind of mental disease, should be treated by the law as not answerable for any criminal offence which he may commit, and be exempted from conviction and punishment. Mental abnormalities vary infinitely in their nature and intensity and in their effects on the character and conduct of those who suffer from them. Where a person suffering from a mental abnormality commits a crime, there must always be some likelihood that the abnormality has played some part in the causation of the crime; and, generally speaking, the graver the abnormality, * * * the more probable it must be that there is a casual connection between them. But the closeness of this connection will be shown by the facts brought in evidence in individual cases and cannot be decided on the basis of any general medical principle." Royal Commission Report 99.

[50] The court may always, of course, if it deems it advisable for the assistance of the jury, point out particular areas of agreement and conflict in the expert testimony in each case, just as it ordinarily does in summing up any other testimony.

[51] State v. Jones, 1871, 50 N.H. 369, 398.

[52] 1945, 80 U.S.App.D.C. 3, 5, 148 F.2d 665, 667.

accused, who suffered from a mental disease or defect did not know the difference between right and wrong, acted under the compulsion of an irresistible impulse, we had "been deprived of or lost the power of his will * * *."[53]

Finally, in leaving the determination of the ultimate question of fact to the jury, we permit it to perform its traditional function which, as we said in Holloway, is to apply "our inherited ideas of moral responsibility to individuals prosecuted for crime * * *."[54] Juries will continue to make moral judgments, still operating under the fundamental precept that "Our collective conscience does not allow punishment where it cannot impose blame."[55] But in making such judgments, they will be guided by wider horizons of knowledge concerning mental life. The question will be simply whether the accused acted because of a mental disorder, and not whether he displayed particular symptoms which medical science has long recognized do not necessarily, or even typically, accompany even the most serious mental disorder.[56]

[14,15] The legal and moral traditions of the western world require that those who, of their own free will and with evil intent (sometimes called *mens rea*), commit acts which violate the law, shall be criminally responsible for those acts. Our traditions also require that where such acts stem from and are the product of a mental disease or defect as those terms are used herein, moral blame shall not attach, and hence there will not be criminal responsibility.[57] The rule we state in this opinion is designed to meet these requirements.

Reversed and remanded for a new trial. . . .

## QUESTIONS

1. Would the broad phrase "mental disease or defect" allow one to argue that, since defendant's crime was so horrible, that fact in itself is evidence of "mental disease or defect"? Should such an argument be acceptable in a court of law? Would it be acceptable to allow an expert witness to offer such judgments to the jury? Why or why not?

2. Why did the witness Dr. Gilbert have such a hard time applying the *M'Naghten* right-wrong test?

[53]State V. White, see n. 32, supra.
[54]80 U.S.App.D.C. at page 5, 148 F.2d at page 667.
[55]80 U.S.App.D.C. at pages 4–5, 148 F.2d at pages 666–667.
[56]See text, supra, 214 F.2d 870–872.
[57]An accused person who is acquitted by reason of insanity is presumed to be insane, Orencia v. Overholser, 1947, 82 U.S.App.D.C. 285, 163 F.2d 768; Barry v. White, 1933, 62 App.D.C. 69, 64 F.2d 707, and may be committed for an indefinite period to a "hospital for the insane." D.C.Code § 24–301 (1951).

We think that even where there has been a specific finding that the accused was competent to stand trial and to assist in his own defense, the court would be well advised to invoke this Code provision so that the accused may be confined as long as "the public safety and * * * [his] welfare" require. Barry v. White, 62 App.D.C. at page 71, 64 F.2d at page 709.

3. One writer analogizes the idea of mental disease to inadequate vision, claiming that, while each concept may at first appear to be a medical concept, neither concept is in fact a medical concept. [Herbert Fingarette, *The Meaning of Criminal Insanity* (1972), Chap. 1.] Reflect on this claim, listing various analogies and disanalogies between defective vision and mental disease.

4. Some have claimed that the *M'Naghten* test, while overly narrow, will in fact be stretched and applied sufficiently broadly by medical expert witnesses, so that any genuine case of insanity can be successfully made out in court. If so, would that be a reason for leaving an overly narrow test like *M'Naghten* in place and unamended?

## R. B. Brandt
# THE INSANITY DEFENSE
# AND THE THEORY OF MOTIVATION*

The rule which makes insanity a defense against criminal culpability obviously needs some justification beyond just the intuitive belief that insane persons are to be excused, or that it is pointless and unjust to punish them in view of the (supposed) fact that they are unable to obey the law. The rule needs to be consistent with and supported by what we know of psychology, and with a general philosophical theory of the system of criminal justice. What follows is an attempt in this direction.

What might a philosophical justification of the system of criminal law be like? There have been recent claims that a convicted criminal should be punished, as payment of a debt to society, or to make up for the unfair advantage he has taken others who are lawabiding. But a widely accepted view is that the criminal law—and indeed every human institution—is justified if it can function so that it optimizes the general good. This view could be questioned, and if it is we could go on to defend it by examining the story on a deeper level, arguing that rational and informed persons would support, or want, for a society in which they expect to live a lifetime, only institutions which are benefit-maximizing.[1] (This view is not very different from that of Rawls[2] if we make some additions to his concept of rationality and drop his proposed strategy of maximum reasoning, along lines suggested by John Harsanyi.)[3]

If we take the benefit-maximizing line, we can go along with a thesis described by Plato:

In punishing wrongdoers, no one concentrates on the fact that a man has done wrong in the past, or punishing him on that account,

*From *Law and Philosophy*, vol. 7, no. 2 (August 1988), pp. 123–46. © 1988 by *Kluwer Academic Publishers*. Reprinted by permission of Kluwer Academic Publishers.

[1]See R.B. Brandt, *A Theory of the Good and the Right* (Oxford: Clarendon Press, 1979) chs. 10 and 11. What is there said about a social moral system can be transposed to hold of a legal institution.

[2]John Rawls, *A Theory of Justice* (Cambridge: Harvard University Press, 1971) chs. 1–3.

[3]John Harsanyi has argued that Rawls' basic conception leads to the idea that institutions including morality should be devised so as to maximize average utility. 'Can the Maximin Principle Serve as a Basis for Morality? A Critique of John Rawls' Theory', *American Political Science Review* **69**, 37–63; 'Morality and the Theory of Rational Behavior,' *Social Research* **44**, 631–6; and 'Basic Moral Decisions and Alternative Concepts of Rationality', *Social Theory and Practice* **9**, 231–44.

unless taking vengeance like a beast. No, punishment is not inflicted by a rational man for the sake of the crime that has been committed—after all one cannot undo the past—but for the sake of the future, to prevent either the same man or, by the spectacle of his punishment, someone else, from doing wrong again. . . . Punishment is inflicted as a deterrent.[4]

If we are receptive to this general view about when institutions are acceptable, we hold that the aim of the legal system should be to maximize the general well-being, taking all the costs into account. More specifically, what the *criminal* law should aim to do is to maximize the general well-being, and to minimize the damage of crime and anxiety about the possibility of crime, at least human cost—that is, in part, without the infliction of pointless injury or suffering on anyone. It is widely, and rightly, supposed that this objective is best achieved by the public enunciation of general prohibitions (primarily against injury to others or their property), accompanied by threats of punishment for those who fail to conform, threats that are mostly made good. But since the liberty and welfare of the nonconformers are themselves goods which have an equal claim to respect, the system must be devised so that their rights to liberty and welfare are overridden only to the extent necessary for the general welfare. It is partly in order to protect these rights of the nonconformers that the system of criminal justice recognizes a set of justifications and excuses which protect the nonconformers when punishing them would serve no important social purpose. So much for general philosophical background.

The general idea, then, is that an optimal system of criminal justice will provide protection of the general welfare by a system of threats aimed at deterring the convicted from repeating, and deterring others from emulating them. But what is deterrence? Presumably, it is the impact on the motivation of possible offenders so that they are more inclined to obey the law than they otherwise would have been.

## 1. THE THEORY OF MOTIVATION

I now turn to the theory of human motivation. If this theory is accepted, the psychological assumptions on which the insanity defense is based must be substantially revised, but not necessarily the main thrust of the insanity rule itself, although I think that it too may be improved in certain details.

But, first let me note a general assumption of psychological work on the theory of motivation (and all other branches of psychology): that human behavior is an instance of causal laws.[5] As the Statement of the American Psychiatric Association on the Insanity Defense says: "Psychiatry is a deterministic discipline that views all human behavior as, to a good extent, 'caused'".[6] Various legal writers would reject this assumption, regarding it as inconsistent with any defensible theory of criminal justice, some writers saying that if everything a person does is caused then illness and badness are merged and the law should excuse everything. But there is, as we shall see, no reason to think that the law must excuse everything if causal determinism is accepted. And, suppose we adopted the alternative view that human behavior is not caused; then must we not regard it as random? Would this view make possible a defensible view of responsibility? Indeed, the system of criminal justice, in holding

[4]Put in the mouth of Protagoras, in *Protagoras* 324. But see *Republic* 614 ff. and *Laws* 862 ff.

[5]Anyone who is doubtful whether anything is really known about "laws" of motivation or the brain-state background should consult a very recent review, Douglas C. Mook, *Motivation: The Organization of Action* (New York: W.W. Norton and Company, 1987) chs. 3,9, and 10.

[6]December 1982, p.14.

that legal sanctions may improve the criminal and deter him and others, seems to suppose that human behavior is caused. A few philosophers[7] think there is a viable middle position, but I propose to ignore them.

Some writers who reject the view that human behavior is caused seem to take this view because they think a person can be justly punished only if and to the degree that his action was *morally blameworthy*. How, they ask, can a person be morally blameworthy for an action if its occurrence was written in the stars? But what does the term "morally blameworthy" mean? Need we think that the applicability of this term presupposes that behavior is uncaused? I suggest that a useful interpretation of "the act was morally blameworthy" is "the agent would not have committed that act but for an unacceptable level of character or moral/legal motivation".[8] (This is like saying that dropping a fly ball is an "error" only if so doing shows a substandard level of skill.) This proposal does not tell us how we are to define "unacceptable level of character or moral/legal motivation", and I shall come to that. But it is clear that, given this explanation, an act can be morally blameworthy independent of its having been caused—and irrespective of how an agent got his character and motivation. An act can be morally

blameworthy on this conception if it manifests an unacceptably substandard motivation *now*, even if its agent is as he is because of his genes, faulty upbringing, etc. One might ask: why define "morally blameworthy" in this way? One answer is that such a definition has implications acceptable to our intuitions. Another is that the definition makes it sensible for the agents of blameworthy acts to be negatively reinforced by punishment of social disapproval, thereby profitably improving the level of their motivation, which "blameworthy" implies is defective and needs improvement.[9]

With these background remarks behind us, let us consider what the theory of motivation affirms about human behavior.

In the first place, motivation theory, like the law, is concerned only with *acts*, bodily movements which are *voluntary* in a sense which excludes movements which are reflex, i.e., that occur during unconsciousness or sleep and during hypnosis. This agrees with the view of the Model Penal Code (hereafter MPC), which says that a culpable action must be a "product of the effort or determination of the actor, either conscious or habitual."[10]

About acts of this type the theory of motivation puts forward some "laws". These laws could stand more evidence, but I think they are the best we have at the present time.[11]

---

[7]R.M. Chisholm, 'Freedom of Action', in K. Lehrer (ed.), *Freedom and Determinism* (New York: Random House, 1966), 28–44; and 'The Agent as Cause', in *Action Theory*, eds. M. Brand and D. Walton (Dordrecht: Reidel, 1976), 199–211. Also Richard Taylor, *Action and Purpose* (Englewood Cliffs, N.J.: Prentice-Hall, 1966). These theorists can argue that the criminal law does not *cause* any modification for behavior, but simply makes clear to the prospective criminal that his *options* for choice are narrower or more unpleasant, than he might otherwise have thought.

[8]Cf. R.B. Brandt 'Blameworthiness and Obligation' in *Essays in Moral Philosophy* ed. A.I. Melden (Seattle: University of Washington Press, 1958); and R.B. Brandt, *Ethical Theory* (Englewood Cliffs, N.J.: Prentice-Hall, 1959) chap. 18; and 'Traits of Character: A Conceptual Analysis', *American Philosophical Quarterly* 7, 23–37.

[9]It is worth noting that the frequent affirmation of the importance of "free will" in the literature on punishment in general and the insanity defense in particular may have been misunderstood by some; it may well be that at least many writers have no intention of using "free will" to imply lack of causal law. They may think that all free will really requires is that people make choices in the normal "rational" way: noting their options for action, their likely consequences, the desirability of these, and choosing accordingly. This conception does not imply lack of causation.

[10]1.13 (2) and 2.01 (2).

[11]Persons who have put forward these laws often, I think, do not assume that they are basic laws, but speculate that they are ultimately explainable by the physiology of the brain, in other words by principles of physics and chemistry, given the way the brain is structured. We can leave this open.

The empirical evidence for the laws comes from such work as that on achievement motivation, experiments in industrial psychology, etc.[12] But the laws are also just an empirically supported elaboration of the common-sense view that, when making a decision, we line up the pros and cons for each action (the outcomes), estimate the probability of each, and ask ourselves how much we want each. Then we try to sum.

What, as I think, the currently best-attested psychological (non-neurological) theory asserts is that every voluntary action is a function of the following variables: (1) what the agent manages to think of (at the time of decision) as options for choice; (2) the agent's beliefs, at the time of choice, about the possible consequences of these various options (counting the kind of act as itself a consequence), as well as how likely they are, given a particular act; (3) how *strongly* the agent wants (possibly unconsciously), or is averse to, the act and its expected consequences, at the time of choice; and (4) *how vividly* the agent represents these outcomes and their relationship to the act—what a person in some sense believes but is not salient in his thought may not influence his choice.

We might put this in other words as follows: the *strength* of an agent's *tendency* to choose one of the options open to him is a sum, of the intensity of his desire/aversion toward *each* anticipated *consequence* of that option, reduced by the believed improbability of the consequence occurring if that option is taken, and reduced again by any lack of salience of that consequence and its relation to taking that option in the awareness of the agent—summing over all the anticipated consequences of taking that option. The theory affirms that the choice the agent actually makes is for the option he has the strongest *tendency* to take—for which this sum is greatest. (One may wonder how in the world numbers are to be assigned to these, so that it is sensible to talk of the largest "sum". I am going to assume that there is an intuitive understanding or at least an ordering of how much we want certain outcomes, how probable we think they are, and more dimly how nearly the representation of each approaches the vividness, say, of sensory perception). This "law" is only approximate and needs to be filled out in many details. For obviously the ordinary person has only vague notions of probability, has little idea of what it is to want something more or less strongly or how to form a product of this strength of want and probability, much less how to go about summing these products. There is a large literature about the contortions people go through when they are trying to decide which car to buy, or even which sandwich to purchase—within the framework of the sketched conception of laws applicable to human behavior.[13]

A good many philosophers who do not question the above psychological causal account want this causal account filled out with a good many more details. What these details are is controversial. But something like the following is probably as near as we can get to an agreed view. First, a person's thought of a possible course of action being most strongly wanted, along the lines I have sketched, will result in the *formation of an*

---

[12]For a review of some of the evidence with citations of data see R.B. Brandt, *A Theory of the Good and the Right* (Oxford: Clarendon Press, 1979) chap. 3. For a much fuller account, see Mook, *op cit,.*, chs. 9 and 10.

[13]Experimental data show that individuals do not very reliably estimate the probabilities of outcomes, given their evidence. Moreover, we are not equipped with any summing device which enables us to know which sum of products comes out highest. There are all sorts of strategies individuals use to solve this problem, and all sorts of proposals as to what these strategies are. See Mook, *op. cit.*, and various review articles in the *Annual Review of Psychology*: J.R. Bettman, 'Consumer Psychology', 37, 257–89; G.F. Pitz and N.J. Sachs, 'Judgment and Decision' 35, 139–63; H.J. Einhorn and R.M. Hogarth, 'Behavioral Decision Theory: Processes of Judgment and Choice' 32, 53–88, especially 69–77; and P. Slovik, B. Fischhoff, and S. Lichtenstein, 'Behavior Decision Theory' 28, 1–39. Also see D. Kahneman and A. Tversky, 'Prospect Theory: An Analysis of Decision under Risk' *Econometrica* **47**, 263–91.

*intention* or disposition to follow a staged *plan* of action. (Some philosophers debate what an "intention" is, some holding it is just an everything-considered preference for or pro-attitude toward an action plan,[14] others insisting that it is more than this, partly because intentions persist and mould future plans.[15]) This intended plan of action will presumably fix when it should be executed, and when that time is (believed to be) *now* the agent will (supported by the intention but also by the underlying desire for the outcome) begin to execute the plan by trying, or willing, to bring about the first stage of the plan, usually a certain bodily action—a "willing" the nature of which is itself debated (sometimes thought of as the focusing of attention on the projected bodily action, sometimes as involving an image of the sensation characteristic of the intended movement). This action will result in the setting of an appropriate next stage of the plan, or even in the wanted outcome. (If one wants more light in the room, the act of pulling the drapes aside will be enough.) The intention will, unless there is a change of mind, remain through the period necessary for reaching the desired outcome, monitoring the sequence of actions in view of the feedback resulting from earlier members of the sequence, and other information.[16]

We should note that all of this is consistent with holding that, directly or indirectly, acts are caused by a complex of the agent's beliefs and desires/aversions.

Among the desires/aversions which control behavior are some of especial interest to the law: (1) empathic/sympathetic concern for others, including an aversion to injuring others and to disasters like a nuclear explosion, and a desire to give assistance to others in distress; (2) aversions to theft, lies, rape, etc., learned in various ways, but probably mostly because of its having been made clear to an agent that they are normally harmful to others;[17] (3) a desire to pay attention to laws, because they are intended for the welfare of all and enacted by a democratically elected body; (4) an aversion to doing what is considered morally wrong; (5) finally, motivation not to perform actions for which the law provides sanctions—to do so is risking unpleasant consequences. I shall call these "moral/legal motivations".

Now, if the above model of motivation theory is correct, these motives have to compete with various other desires: for food, water, sex, human company, compliments,

[14]Donald Davidson, *Essays on Action and Events* (Oxford: Clarendon Press, 1980) pp. 98–100. For more clarification of this view see the following footnote on his reply to Bratman and pp. 220 ff.

[15]See Michael Bratman, 'Davidson's Theory of Intention', in *Essays on Davidson: Actions and Events*, eds. B. Vermazen and M. Hintikka (Oxford: Clarendon Press, 1985). Also his forthcoming (Harvard) *Intentions, Plans and Practical Reasons*; and his 'Taking Plans Seriously', *Social Theory and Practice* **9**, 271–87. Davidson replies lucidly in eds. B. Vermazen and M. Hintikka, ibid.

[16]See , for example, Bruce Aune, Reason and Action (Dordrecht: Reidel, 1977) chaps. 1 and 2, pp. 137–142; A.I. Goldman, *loc. cit.*, and 'The Volitional Theory Revisited' in *Action Theory*, eds. M. Brand and D. Walton, (Dordrecht: Reidel, 1976); Hugh McCann, 'Volition and Basic Action', *Philosophical Review* **83**, 451–73; L.H. Davis, *Theory of Action* (Englewood Cliffs, N.J.: Prentice-Hall, 1979), 38 ff., 59–93; John Searle, *Intentionality* (Cambridge: Cambridge University Press, 1983) pp. 83–135; Wayne Davis, 'A Causal Theory of Intending', *American Philosophical Quarterly* **21**, 43–54; G.A. Miller, E. Galanter and K.H. Pribram, *Plans and the Structure of Behavior* (New York: Holt, Rinehart and Winston, 1960), especially Ch. 4; William James, *The Principles of Psychology* (New York: Henry Holt and Company, 1913), II, 487–92; A.G. Greenwald, 'Sensory Feedback Mechanisms in Performance Control: With Special Reference to the Ideo-Motor Mechanism', *Psychological Review* 77, 73–101.

[17]See Martin Hoffman, 'Developmental Synthesis of Affect and Cognition and Its Implications for Altruistic Motivations', *Developmental Psychology* 11, 607–22, 'Moral Development' in *Carmichael's Manual of Child Psychology*, ed. P. Mussen (New York: John Wiley and Sons, 1970), II pp. 261–359, part on "the inductive method"; and 'The Contribution of Empathy to Justice and Moral Development', in *Empathy: A Developmental Perspective*, eds. N. Eisenberg and J. Strayer (New York: Cambridge University Press, 1987).

financial security. Moreover, there are emotion-based desires. People desire to act aggressively when angry, to escape when fearful, to restore a relationship when grieving. When emotions occur they markedly change the structure of motivations in the person at the time.

There is one feature of what I am calling "moral/legal motivations" which distinguishes them from many of the desires/aversions with which they compete for control of conduct. This is that they may be called "standing"; they are relatively fixed and permanent unlike desires for food or sex. (They are not the only desires with this status; a person's motivation to achieve is also relatively unchanging.) An empathic person does not suddenly cease to be so on the following day. The same for aversion to injury of others, theft, lies, rape, etc. And the same for the aversion to being the target of the law's criminal sanctions. Of course, these standing motives may not always control conduct; each has a certain level of strength, and in many situations this will not be enough to control behavior in the face of desires stronger at that time.

## II. WHAT CAN THE SYSTEM OF CRIMINAL JUSTICE DO?

Let us now address ourselves to the question: What can the system of criminal justice do to insure that people conform to the law?

First, I have listed five kinds of desires/aversions which are forces inclining a person to conform his conduct to the law. Can the system of legal penalties strengthen any of these? Of course it can strengthen the fifth (motivation to avoid the penalties of the law) by making the penalty heavier or more certain; and it can add to the strength of the first and second (aversions to injuring and to specific offenses like theft), by conditioning, by negative reinforcement of the agent or vicariously by his observation of what happens to others. The law can also bring about, by conditioning, that we *notice* more options for action, and attain a more *vivid awareness* of the consequences. (A hefty fine for running a red light tends to make one think that one had better begin to slow down when the yellow light appears. Lengthy incarceration may not have this effect.)

A different thing that might be done is to reduce the strength of desires/aversions which lead to a breach of law: whether to get money, satisfy sexual desires, obtain a position of status in the community, and so on. Since such motives are formed mostly by the example of parents or other prestige figures, by the educational system or by fare provided by the mass media such as television, there is not much the law can do about them. What the legal system can mostly do is increase competing aversions, to theft, etc., in the way already suggested.

Now if the purpose of the system of criminal justice is to enhance general well-being by control of crime at least cost, we can see why it should and mostly does refrain from punishing various types of infringement of the statutes. For sometimes it is *better* that people *do* infringe the *statutes*, e.g., by actions to promote public goods, such as burning down a house when necessary in order to prevent a general conflagration. We *want* behavior of this sort. We call this sort of infringement of the statutes "justified" infringement of the statutes—"lawful" in the broad sense. Violators of this sort are not held guilty of unlawful action. But there is a wider group of cases in which the law should not and generally does not punish (what we may call "excused" unlawful behavior), e.g., when the act would have been lawful if the situation had been what the agent thought or at least reasonably thought it was; when there was ignorance of the law (perhaps ignorance from which a reasonable man would suffer); action under "duress"; actions done as a result of involuntary intoxication by alcohol or drugs (perhaps because of addiction); "entrapment"; and (as mitigating) provocation. (Some of these "excuses" can be accommodated in the *definitions* of various offenses, requiring that be done willfully, purposefully, recklessly, or negligently.)[18]

Why not punish in these cases? In the case of justifications, the answer is obvious: we *want* people generally to do what the agents did, in their circumstances. The answer in the case of excused behavior is different. We must recall that the primary effect of punishment on the convicted is to affect motivations (and vividness of representations). But in the case of "excused" behavior punishment may not optimize the good, for change of motivations is not needed since as far as we know the agent's motivations are already at an acceptable level. A person who acts illegally because of an honest mistake is not shown thereby to have a defect of motivation. There is no point in trying to improve the agent's motivation, if he is, as far as we know, already where he ought to be. And as for the effects on others, there is not evidence that failure to punish in "excused" cases decreases deterrence, that is, the motivation of others not to commit crime because of their knowledge of punishment in the nonexcused cases. Much less would punishment, or the threat of it, affect the motivation of those to whose behavior such excuses would apply, since the threat of punishment can hardly operate to deter a person who commits an offense because he is ignorant of facts which make his act illegal. The system of excuses avoids inflicting pointless harm on persons who have not conformed with the law.

Some may be disturbed by the implication that a main aim of the criminal system should be to affect *motivations* in one way or another. It is true that the effect of the law may be somewhat educational cognitively: by emphasizing the standards of conduct as

well as the probable consequences of a certain kind of action. But the main impact of the criminal system must surely be to affect motivation. This may seem to conflict with the idea that the criminal law does not concern itself with motivation. But this conception that the law is not concerned with motivation seems to ignore the fact that there are *two* kinds of motivation, the motives which *lead one* to break the law, and also motives (mostly *aversions*) about breaking the law, stealing, killing, etc. These latter motives surely *are* of interest to the law. Suppose we say Jane is guilty of a crime because she tampered with the brakes of her husband's car, knowing it would bring about his death. The legal scholar may say Jane has *mens rea* because she *knowingly* acted to bring about his death. But when we take motivation theory (and common sense) into account, it is clear that what is responsible for Jane's tampering with the brakes and thereby producing the death of her husband was not merely her wanting the money etc., and knowing that tampering with the brakes would bring about the things she wanted; what is also responsible is her relative *indifference* to bringing about her husband's death. So, but for that difference, her action would not have occurred. Thus, while the MPC makes the normal condition of criminality that the agent do something forbidden, either having the act or its consequences as his "conscious object", or knowingly (=willfully)[19] performing the act with its anticipated consequences, or recklessly (with awareness of the risk) doing a forbidden thing, it could as well say that a condition for conviction of a crime is *failure to be motivated to avoid* a foreseen forbidden consequence, or to be indifferent to a substantial risk that it occur. Thus talk about intention or foresight (which some have thought identical with *mens rea*) is misleading; it is true that an

---

[18]The MPC appears to compound confusion by putting these mental conditions into the *definition* of the crime. As Glanville Williams has pointed out, this move makes for difficulties in deciding the criminality of accessories. See his 'The Theory of Excuses', *Criminal Law Review* 1982, 734 ff.

[19]MPC 2.028.

intentional act is in part a cognitive occurrence—there must be a plan, a cognitive map for future action, however simple—but it is an essential part of an intentional action that there should be *motivation* to get the end envisaged by the plan (or to avoid it), and what a person foresees but ignores is evidence about what he is indifferent to.[20]

In view of the foregoing, it seems the law *could* say that a prohibited action, unjustified, is *culpable* only if it manifests (has as a *necessary* condition, in the circumstances) a defective level of *moral/legal motivation*. (The defective motivation is a "necessary condition" of an action if and only if the action would not have occurred but for the motivation.)[21] This is a conclusion of considerable importance.

It might be objected that this proposal cannot be right, for it supposes a person can be convicted of a crime only when there is known to be a defect of character/motivation, when in many cases all we know about a person's mental state is this single action—and how then could we be justified in saying that the condition of defective motivation is met? (One might equally well ask whether the action was purposeful or done knowingly.) But this objection overlooks how we can justifiably make judgments about motivation on the strength of a single action. If a person is playing a friendly game of tennis, and if in the middle of it a child has a bad spill from his bicycle in the next court, and is screaming and covered with blood, and the person calmly continues with his tennis, we *do* draw an inference about his motivation, and it is a well-founded inference if we do,

at least absent some explanation.[22] Not that this inference comes out of the blue: we know how sympathetic or empathic people normally behave in comparable circumstances. This man can hardly be either.

So the commission of an illegal unjustified act can be viewed as prima facie evidence (which is rebuttable by further explanation) that there is a defective level of character or moral/legal motivation. *What a legal "excuse" does* is *not* provide evidence that the agent's character/motivations are *perfect*, but merely shows that in the circumstances it is *unwarranted to infer* defective motivation from the particular unlawful act. And if defective motivation is a condition of culpability then an excuse is a shield against culpability.

This is as it should be since, as remarked above, one of the purposes of the criminal law is to improve in the agent (and others) any defective level of motivation relevant to lawabidingness, and if there is no ground in the agent's actions for thinking his motivation defective, the punishment is uncalled for, serves no purpose—even that of deterrence of others.

## III. THE INSANITY DEFENSE

The thesis I suggest about the insanity defense is that it is essentially the claim that the state of mind of the agent at the time of his unlawful act prevents conclusive inference from his act to a defective level of moral/legal motivation (as being its necessary condition), hence it provides a release from culpability. Some of the concepts in this proposal need

---

[20]There are parts of the MPC which take motivation in my broad sense (both desires and aversions) into account: in its statement about the excuse of duress., about the effect of renunciation of criminal purpose when there has been an attempt, about "extreme indifference to the value of human life" (210.2 (1b)), or about the aggravating effect of the purpose of a murder being "pecuniary gain", or the act's "manifesting exceptional depravity" (210.6 (3) g, h)).

[21]What I mean by saying that a certain motivational defect is a necessary condition of an event (illegal act) in the circumstances, is that there is a general natural law to the effect that whenever an act of the type in question occurs in circumstances like the present, there is always a defect of legal/moral motivation of some sort. This is to say that when the act occurs, the defect must have been present, or the act would not have occurred but for the defect.

[22]See R.B. Brandt, 'Traits of Character: a Conceptual Analysis', *American Philosophical Quarterly 7*, 26.

explanation, which I propose to offer. This proposal differs from the widespread view that the justification for excusing acts done in an insane frame of mind is basically that insanity involves an *incapacity* to obey the law, either cognitive (can't know what the law requires) or volitional (knows what the law requires, but unable to conform conduct to it). And it is thought to be senseless and unjust to punish in face of this incapacity: senseless because penal sanctions could not reach him (or others in his situation by the threat of them), and about the kind of incapacity there is to obey the law. Hence we shall see that there is reason to be unhappy with the legal rule about have a "fair chance" to obey the law.) We shall see, however, that there is obscurity about both the sense in which there is a cognitive defect, and about the kind of incapacity there is to obey the law. Hence we shall see that there is reason to be unhappy with the legal rule about the insanity defense as it now stands, and with this standard rationale.

Let us look both into this obscurity and at the same time into problems of the law about insanity as it now stands.

Let us look at the statement in MPC, the most widely accepted rule at present. It says[23] that a person "is not responsible for unlawful conduct if at the time . . . as a *result* of mental *disease* or *defect* he lacks *substantial capacity* either to *appreciate* the *criminality* [wrongfulness] of his conduct or to conform his conduct to the requirements of law" [my italics]. Further, "mental disease or defect" does not include any abnormality manifested only by repeated criminal or otherwise anti-social conduct.[24] The statement of law does not say anything about a rationale,

There are some things about the MPC rule which are not satisfactory. First, a minor point. We might ask what is a "disease" or "defect".[25] Is this to include a mild neurosis, or any one of the problems listed in the Diagnostic and Statistical Manual (of the Psychiatric Association) edition III, or an I.Q. below 80? The implication of the MPC is that *any* level passes if it is serious enough to cause a "substantial inability" to identify illegal conduct or to avoid conduct which is illegal.[26] Very well. "Substantial inability" is rather vague, but this is probably not a defect since the concept probably could not be spelled out in detail, and there are some things which can be left to the good sense of the jury and judge.

But, and more serious in its vagueness, what is to "appreciate" the immorality/criminality of one's act? Evidently something more than just readiness to *say* that an act is wrong. What else more? Some writers talk about the "emotional meaning" of the act (or of "immorality" or "illegality"). Does this mean ability to represent the whole situation (and the wrongness of the act?) to one's self *vividly* (a factor which we saw above is one of those of which action is a function), with corresponding emotional repercussions? Or is it awareness of generally accepted social standards for behavior of the kind in question? Or is it to have at least *some reasonably strong aversion* to performing acts of that kind for reasons other than self-interest—a state which many contemporary philosophers would say is a part of what it is for a person to think a certain action is morally wrong? Moreover, the MPC does not make up its mind whether responsibility is contingent on a person's believing that his act is "criminal" or "(morally) wrongful". If the accused's belief that his action was immoral is relevant for responsibility, then someone needs to straighten out just

[23]4.01 (1).

[24]4.01 (2).

[25]Thomas Maeder offers a definition in *Crime and Madness* (New York: Harper and Row, 1985), p. 85.

[26]The American Psychiatric Association, in its 1982 report on 'The Insanity Defense', proposed that exculpating mental disorders "must be *serious*. Such disorders should usually be of the severity—if not always of the quality—of conditions that psychiatrists diagnose as psychoses". This view conflicts with the MPC and is too restrictive, as will become clear below.

what "thinks the action was immoral" actually means. Such an important concept in the statement of the law ought to be reasonably precise in meaning. Just what is the cognitive condition for culpability supposed to be?[27]

Finally, and most important, the vagueness in the concept of lack of "substantial capacity . . . to . . . conform his conduct to the requirements of the law". There are, of course, some things a person physically cannot do—for instance, move his car in a no-stopping zone when there is a traffic jam. The law does not require him to do these things. From the determinist's point of view a person in a sense cannot do anything other than what he in fact does, being the kind of person he has become. So presumably "lack of capacity" must refer to something else. Usually there is no question but that the accused was physically able to refrain from doing what he did, e.g., fire a revolver. Is it an inability to *control* behavior?[28] But if our account of motivational psychology is correct, this concept hardly belongs in a scientific psychology and what is called "self-control" boils down to some fact about the relative strength of *aversions* to a certain sort of behavior. ("Self-control" is the fact that the act/consequences are so aversive that they stand out in the agent's thinking and he is motivated to avoid them.)

I suggest, then, that, in line with our psychological knowledge, we might explain this "lack of capacity" as follows: to say that a person *lacks capacity* to conform is to say that, even if his legal/moral motivations were at an acceptable level, he might still not

obey the law on account of some (other) mental/brain state he is in.[29] (In the case of such a person a defective state of motivations is *not* a necessary condition of his failure to obey.) This proposal would seem to allow us to excuse the effect of the sudden impulses of the kleptomaniac, or of deep brooding, or of the inability to represent the relation of consequences to action, or of some breakdown of the whole system of motivational control, perhaps as a result of brain-damage—the concept of "other mental/brain state" is open-ended.

I suggest then that what the law expects of a person, if he is to be held nonculpable for some offense, is that the strength of the agent's standing motivations mentioned as support for obedience to law—empathy/sympathy, aversion to the act-type in question, respect for law, fear of the penal sanctions of the law—be in sum not less than an acceptable (not necessarily average) level. And the function of argument for nonculpability in the law, and of the insanity defense, is to make it reasonable to believe that what the agent did is causally (not merely logically) compatible with his (moral, etc.) desires/aversions not being below that acceptable level, although prima facie unlawful behavior indicates a defect of moral/legal motivation.

The basic idea of the insanity defense, then, I suggest, should be that *some* actual mental/brain state of the agent (not necessarily a "mental disease or defect" in some specified sense, like those identified as of a type listed in DSM III) other than the "standard" grounds for excuse could have prevented him

---

[27]See the opinion by Judge Cardozo in People v. Schmidt, 216 N.Y. 324, 110 N.E. 945 (1915).

[28]Wechsler seemed to explain "will" and "self-control" in terms of "amenability to influence by the law". Correspondence between M.S. Guttmacher and Herbert Wechsler in *Model Penal Code, Tentative Draft #4*, (Philadelphia: American Law Institute, 1955), printed in American Law Institute, *Model Penal Code*, Tentative Drafts Nos. 1, 2, 3 and 4, American Law Institute, 1956, p. 192.

Sir James Stephen remarked in 1883 that the "power of self-control must mean a power to attend to distant motives and general principles of conduct, and to connect them rationally with the particular act under consideration, and a disease of the brain which so weakens the sufferer's powers as to prevent him from attending, or referring to such considerations, or from connecting the general theory with the particular fact, deprives him of the power of self-control". *A History of the Criminal Law of England*, II (1883), p. 170.

[29]Guttmacher speaks of the "overwhelming force of the unconscious in many seriously disordered patients". *Loc cit.*, p. 172.

from abiding by the law despite the presence of an acceptable level of moral/legal motivation. We might put this more formally as follows: "A person is culpable (responsible) only if his act—an act within the meaning of the law (as explained earlier)—would not have occurred *in the presence of a sum-total acceptable level of standing aversion to breach of law, and to immorality, and to injury to others, and to the specific type of action in question, and to the sanctions of the law*". Alternatively, we can say that an unlawful act is *nonculpable* when an agent's mental/brain condition is such that his act (might have) occurred even if he otherwise possessed an acceptable level of moral/legal motivations.[30] (Of course, we need some explanation of "an acceptable level" of moral/legal motivations.) My suggestion is that the statement of the MPC should be interpreted in this way.

This proposal is not really different from the MPC in its implications for the obvious cases. It is the conceptual framework that is different, and there could be difference on border-line cases, depending on how the MPC is interpreted. (I say nothing about the final clause relating to sociopathic cases since a defense of insanity would hardly be mounted on the basis merely of a criminal record.) The MPC *could* be construed to say, if it takes motivational theory into account, that no defect of motivation is proven on account of mental disease or defect; whereas my proposal is that no defect of motivation is proven on account of the presence of *some* other state of mind, including ones not identified as some recognized form of insanity. On either view, there is no point for law to aim at improving the legal/moral motivations of the accused for they may not need improvement. Nor can punishment be justified on the ground of deterring others (not merely those mentally like the accused) in view of the infrequency of the insanity defense and the even smaller frequency of its success. My proposal enables the insanity defense to be a part of a general theory of excuses. My proposal is also compatible with essentially a "product" theory of the insanity defense: the excused offense might not have occurred but for some mental/brain state of the agent different from his moral/legal motivations.

My proposal, then, is that an agent should be held culpable or nonculpable in the circumstances cited. But it is a different question under what conditions we can properly *infer* (or the court or jury can infer) that one of these conclusions fits the evidence, that it is defective motivations or possibly "some other" mental/brain state. The answer to this can seemingly only be that the truth of one assessment or the other can properly be inferred from its being the best and simplest explanation of the unlawful act when the *total evidence* is taken into account.

It is reasonable to expect that it is the job of the *defense* to bring forward and support arguments in favor of such a claim of nonculpability, and to expect to succeed by a preponderance of the evidence, not beyond a reasonable doubt.

It is in presenting and interpreting the "total evidence" that the psychiatrist (or a character witness) will enter the picture. If he is testifying for the defense presumably he will explain the evidence for thinking that the accused's motivation, emotional state, defect of cognitive processing, or total breakdown of the machinery (e.g., extreme schizophrenia) was of a certain sort as well as why his evidence calls for a certain sort of interpretation. It is for the jury to decide whether such an explanation offered by the defense psychiatrist, or a defective level of moral/legal motivation as asserted presumably by the psychiatrist for the prosecution, is the best and simplest explanation of all the facts.

---

[30]The U.S. Court of Appeals, D.C. District Circuit (312 F. 2d at 851) held that a "mental disease or defect includes *any abnormal* condition of the mind which substantially affects mental or emotional processes and substantially impairs behavior controls" [my italics]. This leaves open the question of how to determine that a state of mind is "abnormal".

What sort of evidence might support a conclusion that the accused should be excused as "not guilty by reason of insanity" (as distinct from being excused on some such ground as mistake of fact or duress)? One would be a record of emotional instability in the past, e.g., if the accused had been under treatment by a psychiatrist for that reason. Another would be the record of a recent head injury of a kind often followed by bizarre behavior. Another would be just reports of recent strange behavior or the reports of examination by a psychiatrist. In contrast to this would be "character"-witnesses: evidently the past manifestation of a high level of moral/legal motivation (say when there was strong self-interested motivation to do something incompatible with this) is pertinent—and we think that such motivation is relatively permanent. What the jury has to do is to make a common-sense reconstruction of the accused's motivation. The very absence of a motive for the crime is itself a relevant fact. The jury must try to identify the motive (if any) which led to the crime and whether this motive should have been weaker than acceptable contrary moral/legal motivation. Or it may find that the accused's motives had no rational connection with what he did, thereby pointing to an infirmity of the reasoning process rather than to defective motivation as the source of the offense.

This proposal may at first seem less precise and convincing than the formulation in the MPC. But provided we can make a couple of conceptions clearer, it seems more simple. Moreover, it has the virtue of placing in center stage the concept of adequate moral/legal motivations thus making clear why an insanity defense is sensible. The law excuses when all that its sanctions can affect is, as far as we know, already in good condition, when punishment would inflict pointless harm.

I have suggested that the proposal contains some terms which call for explanation. These are: "the best or simplest explanation", and "an acceptable level of moral/legal motivation". We must say something about them.

The first does not present any real difficulty. Philosophers have argued at length about the proper meaning to be assigned to "best and simplest explanation". But the general idea is familiar enough for a jury to work with. They are presumably familiar with discussions of what is "the best explanation" of the Challenger disaster, or the collapse of a bridge, or the failure of a car to start. No more than such examples, I think, is needed for understanding the concept involved.

The second notion, that of an "acceptable level of moral/legal motivation" is another story and calls for a fuller account.

The first thing to note is that apparently the ordinary person's conception—hence the community standard—of an "acceptable level of moral/legal motivation" is roughly close to the law, as indicated by the relative severity of authorized sentences. People regard a willingness to kill another adult human being except in defense of self and others as wholly unacceptable, although there are circumstances in which a person's killing is less than normally objectionable, i.e., when there is provocation, or extreme need. Of course, a man's foresight into consequences and the representation of them may be dimmed by angry desire which makes his behavior less objectionable (and is a mitigating factor) but still not acceptable—his anger would not have controlled his behavior if his aversion to killing had been up to par. What a person does recklessly, indifferent to a risk, say of killing someone, is also unacceptable but *less* objectionable than killing someone either as an end in itself, or as a means to the agent's ends, or as an expected consequence of an act. All this conforms with legal conceptions of merited punishment. How about assault or battery? It is clear that a person is falling short of community standards if he strikes (except in games, etc.) or even touches another in an unwelcome way. But, as in the law, this is viewed as far less objectionable than a willingness to kill. And so on down the line. For the most part, community standards agree that a man's lack of aversion to an act-type can be *ordered in degree* of acceptability, in roughly the same order as is indicated by the range of sentences authorized by the law. But only in general. Laws which impose a penalty on behavior which does not injure anyone in person or property conform less well with community standards. The same applies for the felony-murder rule. Moreover, there is so much disagreement on some matters that one can hardly claim there is a "community" standard at all, e.g., euthanasia and various kinds of sexual behavior. But despite these reservations the extension of the concept "an acceptable level of legal/moral motivation" seems not objectionably unclear. Of course, the jury will have to draw the line about when motivation is "acceptable". Members of a jury may disagree among themselves, but the hope is that their conclusion about what motivation is acceptable, after discussion, will be representative of "community standards". Presumably members of the jury will be reasonably familiar with community standards on such points, and indeed are themselves, we hope, representative of those standards, so that mostly they need only look within.

Some courts have not overlooked the importance of community standards as something which a jury should bear in mind in its decision whether an act shows defective motivation (= morally blameworthy). The Supreme Court of Rhode Island[31] said that the jury is to "evaluate the defendant's blameworthiness in light of prevailing community standards".

There is, of course, no black or white line here which makes it easy for the jury to decide which is the "best explanation". One can feel some sympathy with George Will's remark,[32] cited by Joseph E. diGenova and Victoria Toensing,[33] "The most morally indefensible crimes are becoming the most legally defend-able . . . the more odious the crime—premeditated or spontaneous—the more reasonable doubt there is about the person's sanity at the time". This objection, however, will hardly be convincing to readers who reflect on a recent case of Henriette Cornier, a woman who asked to be allowed to take a neighbor's 19-month-old child for a walk, took the child up to her room, severed its head, threw the head out of the window, and calmly waited for the police.[34] Is this a "morally indefensible crime?" The act was morally wrong all right, but this is not to say it was morally blameworthy. Was there possibly something very wrong with the accused's mind/brain state, different from her standing moral/legal aversions, which produced such a hideous action? The decision by the jury in some such cases may not be easy. Mr. Will is right that when something horrible is done which seems wholly unmotivated, which members of a jury cannot imagine a normal person doing in those circumstances, there *is* some presumption of "some other" mental problem, unrelated to standing moral/legal motivations. This is where the record of previous behavior (and while in detention) is relevant. The jury may make mistakes where there is no sharp line but the job of the jury to do the best it can.[35] (It is not clear that the decision is any harder than that required by MPC: whether the accused was suffering from such mental defect or illness that he was substantially unable to conform to, or appreciate the legality [morality] of his action.) The severity of the problem is somewhat mitigated, as we shall see in a moment, in that the disposition of convicted criminals and those judged not guilty by reason of insanity will not be very different in a rational system of penal and mental institutions. Incidentally, the proposal comes out exactly where the MPC does on

---

[31]State v. Johnson 399 A. 2d 469, 1979, Cited by D.H.J. Hermann, *The Insanity Defense* (1983: Charles Thomas, Springfield, Il.), p. 55 f.

[32]*Baltimore Sun*, June 24, 1982, A19.

[33]The Federal Insanity Defense: a Time for Change in the Post-Hinckley Era', *South Texas Law Journal*, 1984, 728.

[34]Cited by Maeder, *op. cit.*, p. 42.

[35]The British Royal Commission on Capital Punishment proposed (1953) an equally indeterminate job for the jury, affirming that a person is not responsible for his unlawful act if "at the time of the act the accused was suf-

the matter of sociopathic individuals who seem precisely to lack adequate moral/legal motivation and are therefore guilty.

## V. THE DISPOSITION OF THE NOT GUILTY BY REASON OF INSANITY

What should happen to persons who are judged not guilty by reason of insanity or "guilty but insane"? Obviously they should be committed to an institution for observation and treatment. Release could come fairly rapidly (the court having decided they were "insane" at the time of the offense but possibly not now). The use of drugs may remove the symptoms (say, of schizophrenia) quite rapidly and they may remain suppressed for some length of time, perhaps permanently. Psychological therapy can have the same effect. If the crime was a crime of violence, of course, procedures should be more strict for it is already known that the person is somewhat dangerous to society. In such cases gradual discharge, probation, frequent reports to the therapist for a time, and general monitoring of progress are in order and should be mandatory.[36] Some of these may be beyond treatment, and hence their free circulation in society would be a dangerous thing. The prospect of early release will not encourage average persons with standard legal/moral motivations to break the law. Deterrence will be maximized for the average person by the mere prospect of a criminal trial. The stigma of being judged mentally defective will itself be a substantial discouragement to crime.

How will this differ from treatment of persons who are convicted, in view of their unlawful action, having manifested a defective level of their moral/legal motivations? A defect of moral/legal motivation is itself a kind of mind/brain defect. One hopes that many cases of this can be treated successfully by therapy, probation with regular reports to a probation officer, placement in a job and so on. In the case of "sociopaths" or "hardened criminals" this may not be possible. It may be that their defect was a result of experiences during the early years of life and cannot be remedied by anything done later. Then they should be kept out of circulation for the sake of protection of society, except in so far as determinate sentences are required by the values of a liberal democratic society.

There is another point to be remembered: if one is a determinist, one will think that defect of legal/moral motivation resulting in crime is no less a matter of genes, upbringing, etc., than is the case with the mind/brain problem of those adjudged insane. Some persons have had the advantage of good genes (intelligence, health, energy) and family upbringing and location in society which not only produce good moral/legal motivation, but also assure that they will not be put in a position where they are strongly motivated to disobey the law. With others the opposite is the case. There is an unjustified inequality in the lottery of life, which bestows good things on some and bad things on others. We all have a moral obligation to work toward the amelioration or removal of these inequalities. But that is not the job of the criminal law. The system of criminal justice is an uneasy compromise, attempting to accommodate both the need to protect society from harm and to avoid imposing pointless suffering on those who have broken the law.

---

fering from disease of the mind (or mental deficiency) to such a degree that he ought not to be held responsible". Cited by S.H. Kadish, S.J. Schulhofer, and M.G. Paulsen, *Criminal Law and its Processes* (Boston: Little, Brown and Company, 1983), p. 834.

[36] As proposed by the court in Benham v. Edwards, U.S. District Court ND Georgia 501 Suppl 1050, 1980.

# QUESTIONS

1. Brandt says, "An act can be morally blameworthy independent of its having been caused—and irrespective of how an agent got his character and motivation." Explain what the point could be in blaming someone for behavior that was causally determined.

2. In Brandt's account, the main point of punishment is to affect the motivations of the convicted, or other people. Could conviction and punishment of one who acted with an excuse serve to improve the motivations of *other* people, even if not of the one who is punished?

3. Assuming that Brandt's definition of culpability is correct, would you recommend its adoption for use by courts and juries? Why or why not?

4. If our concern in punishing is exclusively one of getting the convicted and others to conform to the law, should we be as concerned as we are about the mental state, aversions, and so forth, of the actor *at the time of the criminal act?*

# Responsibility in Torts

# California Supreme Court, 1948*
## SUMMERS V. TICE ET AL.

Appeal from Superior Court, Los Angeles County; John A. Holland, Judge pro tem.

Actions by Charles A. Summers against Harold W. Tice and against Ernest Simonson for negligently shooting plaintiff while hunting. From judgments for plaintiff, defendants appeal, and the appeals were consolidated pursuant to stipulation.

Affirmed. . . .

CARTER, Justice.

Each of the two defendants appeals from a judgment against them in an action for personal injuries. Pursuant to stipulation the appeals have been consolidated.

Plaintiff's action was against both defendants for an injury to his right eye and face as the result of being struck by bird shot discharged from a shotgun. The case was tried by the court without a jury and the court found that on November 20, 1945, plaintiff and the two defendants were hunting quail on the open range. Each of the defendants was armed with a 12 gauge shotgun loaded with shells containing 7½ size shot. Prior to going hunting plaintiff discussed the hunting procedure with defendants, indicating that they were to exercise care when shooting and to "keep in line." In the course of hunting plaintiff proceeded up a hill, thus placing the hunters at the points of a triangle. The view of defendants with reference to plaintiff was unobstructed and they knew his location. Defendant Tice flushed a quail which rose in flight to a ten foot elevation and flew between plaintiff and defendants. Both defendants shot at the quail, shooting in plaintiff's direction. At that time defendants were 75 yards from plaintiff. One shot struck plaintiff in his eye and another in his upper lip. Finally it was found by the court that as a direct result of the shooting by the defendants the shots struck plaintiff as above

mentioned and that defendants were negligent in so shooting and plaintiff was not contributorily negligent.

[1] First, on the subject of negligence, defendant Simonson contends that the evidence is insufficient to sustain the finding on that score, but he does not point out wherein it is lacking. There is evidence that both defendants, at about the same time or one immediately after the other, shot at a quail and in so doing shot toward plaintiff who was uphill from them, and that they knew his location. That is sufficient from which the trial court could conclude that they acted with respect to plaintiff other than as persons of ordinary prudence. The issue was one of fact for the trial court.

Defendant Tice states in his opening brief, "we have decided not to argue the insufficiency of negligence on the part of defendant Tice." It is true he states in his answer to plaintiff's petition for a hearing in this court that he did not concede this point but he does not argue it. Nothing more need be said on the subject.

[2,3] Defendant Simonson urges that plaintiff was guilty of contributory negligence and assumed the risk as a matter of law. He cites no authority for the proposition that by going on a hunting party the various hunters assume the risk of negligence on the part of their companions. Such a tenet is not reasonable. It is true that plaintiff suggested that they all "stay in line," presumably abreast, while hunting, and he went uphill at somewhat of a right angle to the hunting line, but he also cautioned that they use care, and defendants knew plaintiff's position. We hold, therefore, that the trial court was justified in

*33 Cal. 2d 80, 199 P. 2d 1 (1948). Some citations deleted without so specifying.

finding that he did not assume the risk or act other than as a person of ordinary prudence under the circumstances. None of the cases cited by Simonson are in point.

The problem presented in this case is whether the judgment against both defendants may stand. It is argued by defendants that they are not joint tort feasors, and thus jointly and severally liable, as they were not acting in concert, and that there is not sufficient evidence to show which defendant was guilty of the negligence which caused the injuries—the shooting by Tice or that by Simonson. Tice argues that there is evidence to show that the shot which struck plaintiff came from Simonson's gun because of admissions allegedly made by him to third persons and no evidence that they came from his gun. Further in connection with the latter contention, the court failed to find on plaintiff's allegation in his complaint that he did not know which one was at fault—did not find which defendant was guilty of the negligence which caused the injuries to plaintiff.

[4] Considering the last argument first, we believe it is clear that the court sufficiently found on the issue that defendants were jointly liable and that thus the negligence of both was the cause of the injury or to that legal effect. It found that both defendants were negligent and "That as a direct and proximate result of the shots fired by *defendants, and each of them,* a birdshot pellet was caused to and did lodge in plaintiff's right eye and that another birdshot pellet was caused to and did lodge in plaintiff's upper lip." In so doing the court evidently did not give credence to the admissions of Simonson to third persons that he fired the shots, which it was justified in doing. It thus determined that the negligence of both defendants was the legal cause of the injury— or that both were responsible. Implicit in such finding is the assumption that the court was unable to ascertain whether the shots were from the gun of one defendant or the other or one shot from each of them. The one shot that entered plaintiff's eye was the major factor in assessing damages and that shot could not have come from the gun of both defendants. It was from one or the other only.

It has been held that where a group of persons are on a hunting party, or otherwise engaged in the use of firearms, and two of them are negligent in firing in the direction of a third person who is injured thereby, both of those so firing are liable for the injury suffered by the third person, although the negligence of only one of them could have caused the injury. Moore v. Foster, Miss., 180 So. 73; Oliver v. Miles, Miss., 110 So. 666, 50 A.L.R. 357; Reyher v. Mayne, 90 Colo. 856, 10 P.2d 1109; Benson v. Ross, 143 Mich. 452, 106 N.W, 1120, 114 Am.St. Rep. 675. The same rule has been applied in criminal cases (State v. Newburg, 129 Or. 564, 278 P. 568, 63 A.L.R. 1225), and both drivers have been held liable for the negligence of one where they engaged in a racing contest causing an injury to a third person. Saisa v. Lilja, 1 Cir., 76 F.2d 380. These cases speak of the action of defendants as being in concert as the ground of decision, yet it would seem they are straining that concept and the more reasonable basis appears in Oliver v. Miles, supra. There two persons were hunting together. Both shot at some partridges and in so doing shot across the highway injuring plaintiff who was travelling on it. The court stated they were acting in concert and thus both were liable. The court then stated [110 So. 668]: "We think that * * * each is liable for the resulting injury to the boy, although no one can say definitely who actually shot him. *To hold otherwise would be to exonerate both from liability, although each was negligent, and the injury resulted from such negligence.*" [Emphasis added.] 110 So. p. 668. It is said in the Restatement: "For harm resulting to a third person from the tortious conduct of another, a person is liable if he * * * (b) knows that the other's conduct constitutes a breach of duty and gives substantial assistance or encouragement to the other so to conduct himself, or (c) gives substantial assistance to the other in accomplishing a tortious result and his own conduct, separately considered, constitutes a breach of duty to the third person." (Rest., Torts, sec. 876(b) (c).) Under subsection (b) the example is given: "A and B are members of a hunting party. Each of them in the presence of the other shoots across a public road at an animal, this being negligent as to persons on the road. A hits the animal. B's bullet strikes C, a traveler on the road. A is liable to C." (Rest., Torts, Sec. 876 (b), Com., Illus. 3.) An illustration given under subsection (c) is the same as above except the factor of both defendants shooting is missing and joint liability is not imposed. It is further said that: "If two forces are actively operating, one because of the actor's negligence, the other not because of any misconduct on his part, and each of itself is sufficient to bring about harm to another, the actor's negligence may be held by the jury to be a substantial factor in bringing it about." (Rest., Torts, sec. 432.) Dean Wigmore has this to say: "When two or more persons by their acts are possibly the sole cause of a harm, or when two or more acts of the same person are possibly the sole cause, and the plaintiff has introduced evidence that the one of the two persons, or the one of the same person's two acts, is culpable, then the defendant has the burden of proving that the other person, or his other act, was the sole cause of the harm. (b) * * * The real reason for the rule that each joint tortfeasor is responsible for the whole damage is the practical unfairness of denying the injured person redress simply because he cannot prove how much damage each did, when it is certain that between them they did all; let them be the ones to apportion it among themselves. Since, then, the difficulty of proof is the reason, the rule should apply whenever the harm has plural causes, and not merely when they acted in conscious concert. * * *" (Wigmore, Select Cases on the Law of Torts, sec. 153.) Similarly Professor Carpenter has said: "[Suppose] the case where A and B independently shoot at C and but one bullet touches C's body. In such case, such proof as is ordinarily required that either A or B shot C, of course fails. It is suggested that there should be a relaxation of the proof required of the plaintiff * * * where the injury occurs as a result of one where more than one independent force is operating, and it is impossible to determine that the force set in operation by defendant did not in fact constitute a cause of the damage, and where it may have caused the damage, but the plaintiff is unable to establish that it was a cause." (20 Cal. L. Rev. 406.)

[5] When we consider the relative position of the parties and the results that would flow if plaintiff was required to pin the injury on one of the defendants only, a requirement that the burden of proof on that subject be shifted to defendants become manifest. They are both wrongdoers—both negligent toward plaintiff. They brought about a situation where the negligence of one of them injured the plaintiff, hence it should rest with them each to absolve himself if he can. The injured party has been placed by defendants in the unfair position of pointing to which defendant caused the harm. If one can escape the other may also and plaintiff is remediless. Ordinarily defendants are in a far better position to offer evidence to determine which one caused the injury. This reasoning has recently found favor in this Court. In a quite analogous situation this Court held that a patient injured while unconscious on an operating table in a hospital could hold all or any of the persons who had any connection with the operation even though he could not select the particular acts by the particular person which led to his disability. Ybarra v. Spangard, 25 Cal. 2d 486, 154 P.2d 687, 162 A.L.R. 1258. There the Court was considering whether the patient could avail himself of res ipsa loquitur, rather than where the burden of the proof lay, yet the effect of the decision is that plaintiff has made out a case when he

has produced evidence which gives rise to an inference of negligence which was the proximate cause of the injury. It is up to defendants to explain the cause of the injury. It was there said: "If the doctrine is to continue to serve a useful purpose, we should not forget that 'the particular force and justice of the rule, regarded as a presumption throwing upon the party charged the duty of producing evidence, consists in the circumstances that the chief evidence of the true cause, whether culpable or innocent, is practically accessible to him but inaccessible to the injured person.'" 25 Cal. 2d at page 490, 154 P.2d at page 689, 162 A.L.R. 1258. Similarly in the instant case plaintiff is not able to establish which of defendants caused his injury.

The foregoing discussion disposes of the authorities cited by defendants such as Kraft v. Smith, 24 Cal.2d 124, 148 P.2d 23, and Hernandez v. Southern California Gas Co., 213 Cal. 384, 2 P.2d 360, stating the general rule that one defendant is not liable for the independent tort of the other defendant, or that ordinarily the plaintiff must show a causal connection between the negligence and the injury. There was an entire lack of such connection in the Hernandez case and there were not several negligent defendants, one of whom must have caused the injury.

Defendants rely upon Christensen v. Los Angeles Electrical Supply Co., 112 Cal.App. 629, 297 P. 614, holding that a defendant is not liable where he negligently knocked down with his car a pedestrian and a third person then ran over the prostrate person. That involves the question of intervening cause which we do not have here. Moreover it is out of harmony with the current rule on that subject and was properly questioned in Hill v. Peres, 136 Cal.App. 132, 28 P.2d 946 (hearing in this Court denied), and must be deemed disapproved. See, Mosley v. Arden Farms Co., 26 Cal.2d 213, 157 P.2d 372, 158 A.L.R. 872; Sawyer v. Southern California Gas Co., 206 Cal. 366, 274 P. 544; 6 Cal.Jur. Ten

Yr.Supp., Automobiles, sec. 349; 19 Cal.Jur. 570–572.

Cases are cited for the opposition that where two or more tort feasors acting independently of each other cause an injury to plaintiff, they are not tort feasors and plaintiff must establish the portion of the damage caused by each, even though it is impossible to prove the portion of the injury caused by each. See, Slater v. Pacific American Oil Co., 212 Cal. 648, 300 P. 31; Miller v. Highland Ditch Co., 87 Cal. 430, 25 P. 550, 22 Am.St.Rep. 254; People v. Gold Run D. & M. Co., 66 Cal. 138, 4 P. 1152, 56 Am.Rep. 80; Wade v. Thorsen, 5 Cal.App.2d 706, 43 P.2d 592; California Orange Co., v. Riverside P.C. Co., 50 Cal. App. 522, 195 P. 694; City of Oakland v. Pacific Gas & E. Co., 47 Cal.App.2d 444, 118 P.2d 328. In view of the foregoing discussion it is apparent that defendants in cases like the present one may be treated as liable on the same basis as joint tort feasors, and hence the last cited cases are distinguishable inasmuch as they involve independent tort feasors.

[6] In addition to that, however, it should be pointed out that the same reasons of policy and justice shift the burden to each of the defendants to absolve himself if he can—relieving the wronged person of the duty of apportioning the injury to a particular defendant, apply here where we are concerned with whether plaintiff is required to supply evidence for the apportionment of damages. If defendants are independent tort feasors and thus each liable for the damage caused by him alone, and, at least, where the matter of apportionment is incapable of proof, the innocent wronged party should not be deprived of his right to redress. The wrongdoers should be left to work out between themselves any apportionment. See, Colonial Ins. Co., v. Industrial Acc. Com., 29 Cal.2d 79, 172 P.2d 884. Some of the cited cases refer to the difficulty of apportioning the burden of damages between the independent tort feasors, and say that where factually a correct division cannot be made, the trier of fact

may make it the best it can, which would be more or less a guess, stressing the factor that the wrongdoers are not in a position to complain of uncertainty. California Orange Co., v. Riverside P. C. Co., supra.

[7] It is urged that plaintiff now has changed the theory of his case in claiming a concert of action; that he did not plead or prove such concert. From what has been said it is clear that there has been no change in theory. The joint liability, as well as the lack of knowledge as to which defendant was liable, was pleaded and the proof developed the case under either theory. We have seen that for the reasons of policy discussed herein, the case is based upon the legal proposition that, under the circumstances here presented, each defendant is liable for the whole damage whether they are deemed to be acting in concert or independently.

The judgment is affirmed.

## QUESTIONS

1. Suppose that all the other facts about this case remain unchanged except that it is discovered that it was birdshot from Tice's gun only that caused injury to Summers. If Simonson's behavior was equally negligent and could just as easily have been the one that caused the harm but for his luck, why should he not also be made to pay? Why reward Simonson for mere luck, for something so arbitrary from a moral point of view?

2. Suppose that we can determine the rough extent of lung disease and other harm caused to nonsmokers from their passive inhalation of smoke from smokers. Would it be fair to require smokers equally to bear the costs, even though no one knows exactly whose smoke caused what harm? What are the analogies and disanalogies between this and the facts of Summers v. Tice? If we were to use the reasoning in Summers, how would we proceed to apportion liability where there are literally thousands of people whose negligence could have contributed to the harm?

3. Tice and Simonson were acting "independently" and not "in concert." Think about the differences between acting in concert and acting independently. Would it be more justifiable to hold both Tice and Simonson liable if they had been acting in concert? Why or why not?

## Judith Jarvis Thomson
## REMARKS ON CAUSATION AND LIABILITY*

**I**

Under traditional tort law, a plaintiff had to show three things in order to win a case: that he suffered harm or loss, that an act or omission of the defendant's caused that harm or loss, and that the defendant was at fault in so acting or refraining from acting. It is widely known by non-lawyers that liability may nowadays be imposed in many kinds of cases in which there is no showing that the third requirement is met. Strict product liability is

*Reprinted by permission of Princeton University Press. Judith Jarvis Thomson, "Remarks on Causation and Liability," *Philosophy & Public Affairs*, vol. 13, no. 2 (Spring 1984), copyright © 1984 by Princeton University Press. Pp. 101–16 reprinted by permission.

one example. Thus if you buy a lawn mower, and are harmed when you use it, then (other things being equal) you win your suit against the manufacturer if you show that you suffered a harm when you used it, and that the harm you suffered was caused by a defect in the lawn mower—as it might be, a missing bolt. You do not need also to show the manufacturer was at fault for the defect; it is enough that the lawn mower was defective when it left his hands, and that the defect caused your harm.

What may be less widely known by nonlawyers is that there have been some recent cases which were won without plaintiff's having shown that the second requirement was met, namely, that of causation. Perhaps the most often discussed nowadays is *Sindell v. Abbott Laboratories*,[1] which was decided by the California Supreme Court in 1980. Plaintiff Sindell had brought an action against eleven drug companies that had manufactured, promoted, and marketed diethylstilbesterol (DES) between 1941 and 1971. The plaintiff's mother took DES to prevent miscarriage. The plaintiff alleged that the defendants knew or should have known that DES was ineffective as a miscarriage-preventitive, and that it would cause cancer in the daughters of the mothers who took it, and that they nevertheless continued to market the drug as a miscarriage-preventitive. The plaintiff also alleged that she developed cancer as a result of the drug taken by her mother. Due to the passage of time and to the fact that the drug was often sold under its generic name, the plaintiff was unable to identify the particular company which had manufactured the DES taken by her mother; and the trial court therefore dismissed the case. The California Supreme Court reversed. It held that if the plaintiff "joins in the action the manufacturers of a substantial share of the DES which her mother might have taken," then she need not carry the burden of showing which manufactured the quantity of DES that her mother took; rather the burden shifts to them to show they could not have manufactured it.[2] And it held also that if damages are awarded her, they should be apportioned among the defendants who cannot make such a showing in accordance with their percentage of "the appropriate market" in DES.

In short, then, the plaintiff need not show about any defendant company that it caused the harm in order to win her suit.

Was the Court's decision in *Sindell* fair? I think most people will be inclined to think it was. On the other hand, it is not easy to give principled reasons why it should be thought fair, for some strong moral intuitions get in the way of quick generalization. What I want to do is to bring out some of the sources of worry.

But the case is in fact extremely complicated, so I suggest we begin with a simpler case, *Summers v. Tice*,[3] which the same court had decided in 1948, and which the plaintiff in Sindell offered as a precedent.

## II

Plaintiff Summers had gone quail hunting with the two defendants, Tice and Simonson. A quail was flushed, and the defendants fired negligently in the plaintiff's direction; one shot struck the plaintiff in the eye. The defendants were equally distant from the plaintiff, and both had an unobstructed view of him. Both were using the same kind of gun and the same kind of birdshot; and it was not possible to determine which gun the pellet in the plaintiff's eye had come from. The trial court found in the plaintiff's favor, and held both defendants "jointly and severally liable." That is, it declared the plaintiff entitled to collect damages from whichever defendant he chose.

[1]26 Cal. 3d 588, 163 Cal. Rptr. 132, 607 P. 2d 924 (1980).
[2]One defendant had already been dismissed from the action on the ground that it had not manufactured DES until after the plaintiff was born.
[3]33 Cal. 2d 80, 199 P. 2d 1 (1948).

The defendants appealed, and their appeals were consolidated. The California Supreme Court affirmed the judgement.

Was the Court's decision in *Summers* fair? There are two questions to be addressed. First, why should either defendant be held liable for any of the costs? And second, why should each defendant be held liable for all of the costs— that is, why should the plaintiff be entitled to collect all of the costs from either?

Why should either defendant be held liable for any of the costs? The facts suggest that in the case of each defendant, it was only .5 probable that he caused the injury; normally, however, a plaintiff must show that it is more likely than not, and thus more than .5 probable, that the defendant caused the harm complained of if he is to win his case.

The Court's reply is this:

When we consider the relative positions of the parties and the results that would flow if plaintiff was required to pin the injury on one of the defendants only, a requirement that the burden of proof on that subject be shifted to defendants becomes manifest. They are both wrongdoers—both negligent toward plaintiff. They brought about a situation where the negligence of one of them injured the plaintiff, hence it should rest with them each to absolve himself if he can. The injured party has been placed by defendants in the unfair position of pointing to which defendant caused the harm. If one can escape the other may also and plaintiff is remediless.

The Court's argument seems to me to go as follows. The plaintiff cannot determine which defendant caused the harm. If the plaintiff has the burden of determining which defendant caused the harm, he will therefore be without remedy. But both defendants acted negligently "toward plaintiff," and the negligence of one of them caused the harm. Therefore the plaintiff should not be without remedy. Therefore it is manifest that the burden should shift to each defendant to show that he did not cause the injury; and, if neither can carry that burden, then both should be held liable.

The argument does not say merely that both defendants are wrongdoers, or that both defendants acted negligently: it says that both defendants acted negligently "toward plaintiff"—that is; both were in breach of a duty of care that they owed to the plaintiff. Suppose, for example, that the plaintiff had brought suit, not against the two hunters who were out quail hunting with him, but against three people: the two hunters and Jones, who was driving negligently in New York that afternoon. All three members of the class of defendants were wrongdoers, all three acted negligently, and indeed one of the three caused the harm, though it is not possible to tell which. But it could hardly be thought fair for all of them, and so a fortiori, for Jones to have to carry the burden of showing that *his* negligence did not cause the harm. Perhaps he could carry that burden easily; but it would not be fair to require that he do so on pain of liability for the harm. The argument excludes Jones, however, for although he was negligent, he was not negligent toward the plaintiff.

And even that qualification is not enough— we must suppose a further qualification to lie in the background of the argument. Consider Smith, who was driving negligently in California that day, and who in fact nearly ran the plaintiff down as the plaintiff was on his way to go quail hunting. And suppose that the plaintiff had brought his suit against the following three people: the two hunters and Smith. All three were wrongdoers, all three acted negligently, and indeed negligently toward the plaintiff, and one of the three caused the harm, though it is not possible to tell which. But it could hardly be thought fair for all of them, and so a fortiori for Smith to have to carry the burden of showing that *his* negligence did not cause the harm. As it stands, the argument does not exclude Smith, for he *was* negligent toward the plaintiff. So we must suppose that the Court had in mind not merely that all the defendants were negligent toward the plaintiff, but also that their negligent acts were in a measure likely to have caused the harm for which the plaintiff sought compensation.

There lurks behind these considerations what I take to be a deep and difficult question, namely: Why does it matter to us whose negligent act caused the harm in deciding who is to compensate the victim?

## III

It will help to focus on a hypothetical variant of the case, which I shall call *Summers II*. Same plaintiff, same defendants, same negligence, same injury as in *Summers*; but *Summers II* differs in that during the course of the trial, evidence suddenly becomes available which makes it as certain as empirical matters ever get to be, that the pellet lodged in plaintiff Summers' eye came from defendant Tice's gun. Tort law being what it is, defendant Simonson is straightaway dismissed from the case. And isn't that the right outcome? Don't we feel that Tice alone should be held liable in *Summers II*? We do not feel that Simonson should be dismissed with a blessing: he acted very badly indeed. So did Tice act badly. But Tice also caused the harm, and (other things being equal) fairness requires that he pay for it.[4] But why? After all, both defendants acted equally negligently toward Summers in shooting as they did; and it simple good luck for Simonson that, as things turned out, he did not cause the harm to Summers.

It is arguable that there is no principled stopping place other than Tice.[5] Consider, for example, a rule which says: Liability is to be shared among the actual harm-causer and anyone else (if there is anyone else) who acted as negligently toward the victim, and who nearly caused him a harm of the same kind as the actual harm-causer did. Under this rule, liability should presumably be shared between Tice and Simonson in *Summers II*. But only presumably, since what, after all, counts for these purposes as a "harm of the same kind"? (Compare Smith of the preceding section.) And by what principle should liability be shared only among those who acted negligently toward the victim? (Compare Jones of the preceding section.)

Moreover, even if there is no principled stopping place *other than* Tice, it would remain to be answered what is the principle behind a rule which stops liability *at* Tice:

It pays to begin by asking: What if Tice has an insurance policy that covers him for the costs of harms he causes? We would not feel it unfair for the insurance company to pay Summers off for Tice.

Nor do we feel there would be any unfairness if a friendly philanthropist paid Summers off for Tice.

But the insurance company could simply be living up to its contract with Tice to pay what Tice would have had to pay if he had had no such contract; and the philanthropist would simply be making a gift to Tice—paying a debt for Tice which Tice would otherwise have had to pay himself.

Nevertheless these considerations do bring out that paying Summers' costs is not something we wish to impose on Tice by way of retribution or punishment for his act. If imposing this were a punishment, we would not regard it as acceptable that a third party (insurance company, friendly philanthropist) suffer it as a surrogate for Tice.[6]

What we are concerned with here is not blame, but only who is to be out of pocket for the costs. More precisely, why it is Tice

---

[4]Some people feel that Summers himself should share in the costs, in the thought that Summers assumed a risk in going out quail hunting with Tice and Simonson. I do not myself share that intuition. Anyone who does is invited to imagine, instead, that Summers is a farmer, who was passing by, on his way to market.

[5]See Wex S. Malone, "Ruminations Cause-In-Fact," *Stanford Law Review* 9 (December 1956): 66.

[6]A number of people have drawn attention to the general point at work here. See, for example, Jules Coleman, "On the Moral Argument for the Fault System," *The Journal of Philosophy* 71, no. 14 (15 August 1974).

who is to be out of pocket for the costs. It pays to take note of what lies on the other side of this coin. You and your neighbor work equally hard, and equally imaginatively, on a cure for the common cold. Nature then smiles on you: a sudden gust of wind blows your test tubes together, and rattles your chemicals, and lo, there you have it. Both of you acted well; but who is to be in pocket for the profits? You are. Why? That is as deep and difficult a question as the one we are attending to. I think that the considerations I shall appeal to for an answer to our question could also be helpfully appealed to for an answer to this one, but I shall not try to show how.

There is something quite general at work here. "B is responsible for the damage to A's fence; so B should repair it." "The mess on A's floor is B's fault; so B should clean it up." Or anyway, B should have the fence repaired, the mess cleaned up. The step is common, familiar, entirely natural. But what warrants taking it?

It is a plausible first idea that the answer lies in the concept 'enrichment.' Suppose I steal your coffee mug. I am thereby enriched, and at your expense. Fairness calls for return for the good: I must return the coffee mug.

That model is oversimple, of course: it cannot be brought to bear directly. For only I can return the coffee mug, whereas by contrast, anyone can pay the costs of having the fence repaired or the mess cleaned up, either in his own time and effort, or in whatever it takes to get someone else to do these things.

Well, fairness needn't call for the return of the very coffee mug I took, and surely can't call for this if I have now smashed it. Replacement costs might do just as well. Or perhaps something more than replacement costs, to cover your misery while thinking you'd lost your mug. In any case, anyone can pay those costs. But I must pay them to you because I was the person enriched by the theft of the mug, and at your expense. So similarly, perhaps we can say that B must pay the costs of having the fence repaired because B was the person who enriched himself, and at A's expense, by the doing of whatever it was he did by the doing of which he damaged the fence.

Enrichment? Perhaps so: B might literally have made a profit by doing whatever it was he did by the doing of which he made a mess on A's floor. (E.g., mudpie-making for profit.) Or anyway, he might have greatly enjoyed himself. (E.g., mud-pie-making for fun.) Perhaps he made the mess out of negligence? Then he at least made a saving: he saved the expense in time or effort or whatever he would have had to expend to take due care. And he made that saving at A's expense.

But this cannot really be the answer—it certainly cannot be the whole answer. For consider Tice and Simonson again. They fired their guns negligently in Summers' direction, and Tice's bullet hit Summers. Why should Tice pay Summers' costs? Are we to say that that is because Tice enriched himself at Summers' expense? Or anyway, that Tice made a saving at Summers' expense—a saving in time and effort or whatever he would have had to expend to take due care? Well, Simonson saved the same as Tice did, for they acted equally negligently.[7] It would have to be said "Ah, but Tice's saving was a saving *at Summers' expense*—and Simonson's was not." But what made Tice's saving *be* a saving at Summers' expense? Plainly not the fact that his negligence was negligence 'toward' Summers, for as the Court said, Tice and Simonson were both "negligent toward plaintiff." If it is said that what made Tice's saving be a saving at Summers' expense is the fact that it was Tice's negligence that caused Summers' injury, then we are back where we were: for what we began with was why that fact should make the difference.

[7]The general point I illustrate here was made by Jules Coleman, in "Corrective Justice and Wrongful Gain," *The Journal of Legal Studies* II, no. 2 (June 1982).

Drawing attention to cases in which two are equally enriched also brings out more clearly a problem which is already present when only one is. Why is it B who must pay the costs of having the mess on A's floor cleaned up, when it is B who caused it to be there? Because in doing what he did which caused it to be there he enriched himself ( or made a saving) at A's expense. But if what made the enrichment be *at A's expense* is the fact that his act caused the mess to be there, then the question has not been answered; we have merely been offered new language in which to ask it.

Perhaps it pays to set aside the concept 'enrichment' and attend, instead, to what we have in mind when we characterize a person as "responsible." Consider again: "B is responsible for the damages to A's fence; so B should repair it." Doesn't the responsible *person* pay the costs of damage he or she is responsible *for*? And don't we place a high value on being a responsible person?

Similarly, the responsible person pays the costs of damage which is his or her fault.

This is surely right; but what lies behind it? *Why* do we think it a good trait in a man that he pays the costs of a damage he is responsible for? Why do we expect him to?

I hazard a guess that the, or anyway an, answer may be found in the value we place on freedom of action, by which I mean to include freedom to plan on action in the future, for such ends as one chooses for oneself. We take it that people are entitled to a certain 'moral space' in which to assess possible ends, make choices, and then work for the means to reach those ends. Freedom of action is obviously not the only thing we value; but let us attend only to considerations of freedom of action, and bring out how they bear on the question in hand.

If A is injured, his planning is disrupted: he will have to take assets he meant to devote to such and such chosen purpose, and use them to pay the costs of his injury. Or that is so unless he is entitled to call on the assets of another, or others, to pay the costs

for him. His moral space would be considerably larger if he were entitled to have such costs paid for him.

But who is to pay A's costs? On whose assets is it to be thought he is entitled call? Whose plans may *he* disrupt?

A might say to the rest of us, "Look, you share my costs with me now, and I'll share with you when you are injured later." And we might then agree to adopt a cost-spreading arrangement under which the costs of all (or some) of our injuries are shared; indeed, we might the better secure freedom of action for all of us if we did agree to such an arrangement. The question which needs answering, however, is whether A may call on this or that person's assets in the absence of an agreement.

One thing A is not entitled to do is choose a person X at random, and call on X's assets to pay his costs. That seems right; but I think it is not easy to say exactly why. That is, it will not suffice to say that if all we know about X is that X is a person chosen at random, then we know of no reason to think that a world in which X pays A's costs is better than a world in which A pays A's costs. That is surely true. But by the same token, if all we know about X is that X is a person chosen at random, then we know of no reason to think that a world in which A pays A's costs is better than a world in which X pays A's costs. So far, it looks as if flipping a coin would be in order.

What I think we should do is to look at A's situation *before* any costs have been incurred. A has been injured. Now he wants to be 'made whole': he wants the world changed in such a way as to make him be as nearly as possible what he would have been had he not been injured. That is what he needs money for. But the freedom of action of other people lends weight to the following: If A wants the world changed in that (or any other) way, then—other things being equal—A has to pay the costs, in money, time, energy, whatever is needed, unless he can get the voluntary agreement of those others to contribute to those costs. Again, *A*'s wanting the world changed in that (or any other) way is not by itself a reason to think he may call on another person to supply him with what he needs to change it. It follows that *A* is not entitled to call on a person unless that person has a feature other than just that of being a person, which marks *his* pockets as open to *A*. *A* cannot, then, choose a person *X* at random, and call on *X* to pay the costs—on pain of infringing *X*'s freedom of action.

And it could hardly be thought that while *A* is not entitled to call on *X*'s assets before *A* has spent anything, *A* becomes entitled to call on *X*'s assets the moment he has.

So *A* is not entitled to choose a person *X* at random, and call on *X*'s assets to pay his costs.

Well, here is *B*, who is considerably richer than *A*. Perhaps some people will feel that that does entitle *A* to call on *B*. I want to set this aside. As I said, freedom of action is not the only thing we value, but I want to bring out *its* bearing on the question in hand; so I shall sidestep this issue by inviting you to imagine that no one is any richer than anyone else.

*A* is injured. Let us supply his injury with a certain history. Suppose, first, that *A* himself caused it—freely and wittingly, for purposes of his own. And suppose, second, that it is not also true of any other person *X* that *X* caused it, or even that *X* in any way causally contributed to it. Thus:

(1)   *A* caused *A*'s injury, freely, wittingly, for purposes of his own; and no one other than *A* caused it, or even causally contributed to it.

We can easily construct examples of injuries which consist in loss or damage to property which have histories of this kind—for example, *A* might have broken up one of his chairs, to use as kindling to light a fire to get the pleasure of looking at a fire. It is harder to construct examples of injuries which consist in physical harm which have histories of this kind. But it is possible—for example, *A* might have cut off a gangrenous toe to save his life. *A* might have cut off his nose to spite his face.

Suppose now that having caused himself the injury, *A* wants for one or another reason to be made whole again. That will cost him something. Here is *B*. Since (I) is true of *A*'s injury, *B*'s freedom of action protects him against *A*: *A* is not entitled to call on *B*'s assets for the purpose—*A* is not entitled to disrupt *B*'s planning to reverse an outcome wholly of his own planning which he now finds unsatisfactory.

That seems right. And it seems right whatever we imagine true of *B*. *B* may be vicious or virtuous, fat or thin, tall or short; none of this gives *A* a right to call on *B*'s assets. Again, *B* might have been acting very badly indeed contemporaneously with *A*'s taking the steps he took to cause his own injury: *B* might even have been imposing risks of very serious injuries on *A* concurrently with *A*'s act—for example, *B* might have been playing Russian roulette on *A*, or throwing bricks at him. No matter: if *A*'s injury has the history I described in (I), then *B*'s freedom of action protects him against the costs of it.

If that is right, then the answer to our question falls out easily enough. Let us suppose that *A* is injured, and that *B* did not cause the injury, indeed, that he in no way causally contributed to *A*'s injury. Then whatever did in fact cause *A*'s injury—whether it was *A* himself who caused his injury, or whether his injury was due entirely to natural causes, or whether *C* or *D* caused it—there is nothing true of *B* which rules out that *A*'s injury had the history described in (I), and therefore nothing true of *B* which rules out that *A* should bear his own costs. Everything true of *B* is compatible with its being the case that *A*'s costs should lie where they fell. So there is no feature of *B* which marks his pockets as open to *A*—*A* is no more entitled to call on *B* than he is entitled to call any person *X* chosen at random.

Causality matters to us, then, because if *B* did not cause (or even causally contribute to) *A*'s injury, then *B*'s freedom of action protects him against liability for *A*'s costs. And in particular, it is Simonson's freedom of action which protects him against liability for Summers' costs in *Summers II*, for in that case it was discovered that Tice had caused the injury.

I have been saying that freedom of action is not the only thing we value, and that is certainly true. But if I am right that it is freedom of action which lies behind our inclination to think causality matters—and in particular, our inclination to think it right that Simonson be dismissed once it has been discovered that he did not cause Summers' injury—then these considerations by themselves show we place a very high value on it, for those inclinations are very strong.

Since the question we began with was the question why causality matters to us, we could acceptably stop here. But I think it pays to press on, to see how far attention to freedom of action will carry us.

For as we know, however much causality matters to us in assessing liability, it is on no plausible view sufficient for liability. The fact that Tice caused Summers' injury does not by itself yield the conclusion that he is properly to be held liable for it; what yields this conclusion is the conjunction of the fact that Tice caused the injury *and* the relevant facts about Tice's fault—that he was negligent, that the injury was of a kind such that Tice's act was negligent in that he did not exercise the care which is called for precisely in order to avoid causing an injury of that kind, and so on. Suppose *A*'s injury was caused by *B* as in

(2) *B* caused *A*'s injury by some freak accident—by doing something which he took all due care in the doing of, and which he could not have been expected to foresee would lead to harm.

Then alas for *A*, it seems right that *A*'s costs lie where they fell: the fact that *B* caused the injury does not suffice for imposing liability on him. When fault is added to causality, however, things look very different to us. If *A*'s injury was caused by *B* as in

(3) *B* caused *A*'s injury wrongfully—by intention, or out of negligence

then *B* must plainly pay.

Why this difference between (2) and (3)? It might be thought we could say this. In (3), *B* caused *A*'s injury by doing what it was a wrong in him to do, and freedom of action has its limits: one is not free to act wrongly. By contrast, in (2), there was nothing *B* did which it was a wrong in him to do, no constraint of morality that he violated; so it is his freedom of action that protects him against liability for *A*'s costs in (2).

But I think this account of (2) and (3) is oversimple. In the first place, I think we *are* free to act wrongly—so long, that is, as we cause no harm to others (more generally, infringe no right of theirs) in doing so. It is not the fact that *B* acted wrongly in (3) that makes him liable for *A*'s costs in (3): *B* can have been acting as wrongfully as you like concurrently with the coming about of *A*'s injury and is all the same not liable for *A*'s costs if *A* caused his own injury—as in (I). What makes *B* liable for *A*'s costs in (3) is rather that in (3) he wrongfully caused *A*'s injury. It is *that* which fixes that his freedom of action does not protect him against liability for *A*'s costs in (3).

Second, it is not the fact that *B* did not act wrongfully in (2) that protects him against liability for *A*'s costs in (2). For what if *A*'s injury had a history of the following kind:

(4) *B* caused *A*'s injury, and did so freely and wittingly, but did so to save himself from a very much greater injury, and was justified in so acting.

*B* did not act wrongly in (4), and is all the same properly held liable for *A*'s costs in (4). A case of the kind I have in mind, which comes from the legal literature, is *Vincent v. Lake Erie Transportation Co.*,[8] in which a ship's captain tied his ship to a dock to protect it from the risk of being sunk in a storm. The dock-owner's dock was damaged by the ship's banging against it in the storm, and he sued the ship-owner. The declared that the ship's captain had acted properly and well; but it (surely right) awarded damages to the plaintiff. A second case of the kind I have in mind, which comes from the literature of moral theory, is Joel Feinberg's story of a hiker, lost in a sudden mountain storm, who broke into an empty cabin and burned the furniture to keep warm; the hiker was plainly justified in so acting, but he owes the cabin-owner compensation for the damage he did.[9]

Why is *B* protected against liability for *A*'s costs in (2) but not in (4)? *B* acted wrongly in neither case, and it is not at all easy to see the source of the difference.

Richard A. Epstein offers the following justification for the imposition of liability on the defendant in Vincent:

Had the Lake Erie Transportation Company owned both the dock and the ship, there could have been no lawsuit as a result of the incident. The Transportation Company, now the sole party involved, would, when faced with the storm, apply some form of cost-benefit analysis in order to decide whether to sacrifice its ship or its dock to the elements. Regardless of the choice made, it would bear the consequences and would have no recourse against anyone else. There is no reason why the company as a defendant in a lawsuit should be able to shift the loss in question because the dock belonged to someone else. The action in tort in effect enables the injured party to require the defendant to

treat the loss he has inflicted on another as though it were his own. If the Transportation Company must bear all the costs in those cases in which it damages its own property, then it should bear those costs when it damages the property of another.[10]

These seem to me to be very helpful remarks. Suppose the name of the man who actually owns the dock is Jones. What Epstein points to is this: If the dock had belonged, not to Jones, but to the Lake Erie Transportation Company, then the Company would not have been entitled to call on Jones's assets for funds to repair it. Why not? Consider again

(I)  *A* caused *A*'s injury, freely, wittingly, for purposes of his own; and no one other than *A* caused it, or even causally contributed to it.

If the dock had belonged to the Lake Erie Transportation Company, then the Company would have caused itself an injury (by causing an injury to its own dock); so the history of its injury would have been as described in (I), and the Company would not have been entitled to call on Jones's assets for the costs.

So far so good. But all of that is counterfactual. The dock in fact belongs to Jones, not to the Lake Erie Transportation Company, and how do we get from the counterfactual remarks about what would have been the case if the Company had owned the dock to that Jones is entitled to, given Jones does own the dock? Perhaps Epstein's thought is that the step is warranted by what is said in the final sentence of the passage I quoted above: "If the Transportation Company must bear all the costs in those cases in which it damages its own property, then it should

[8]10 Minn. 456, 124 NW 221 (1910).

[9]Joel Feinberg, "Voluntary Euthanasia and the Inalienable Right to Life," *Philosophy & Public Affairs* 7, no. 2 (Winter 1978), reprinted in Joel Feinberg, *Rights, Justice, and the Bounds of Liberty: Essays in Social Philosophy* (Princeton: Princeton University Press, 1980).

[10]Richard A. Epstein, "A theory of Strict Liability," *The Journal of Legal Studies* 2, no. 1 (January 1973): 158.

bear those costs when it damages the property of another." Thus: since (or: just as?) the Company has to bear the costs of repair when it damages its own property, the Company has to bear the costs of repair when it damages the property of another.

But that is unfortunately overstrong. If $B$ has to pay the costs of any injury of $A$'s which $B$ causes (as $B$ has to pay the costs of any injury of his own which he causes), then $B$ may properly be held liable, not merely in

(4) $B$ caused $A$'s injury, and did so freely and wittingly, but did so to save himself from a very much greater injury, and was justified in so acting.

but also in

(2) $B$ caused $A$'s injury by some freak accident—by doing something which he took all due care in the doing of, and which he could not have expected to foresee would lead to harm.

Doesn't $B$ have to pay the costs of any injury of his own which he causes himself by accident? But it really does seem wrong to hold $B$ liable in (2).

I suppose it is arguable that what makes it seem wrong to hold $B$ liable in (2) is not any consideration of fairness to $B$, and in particular, that it is not $B$'s own freedom of action that protects him against liability in (2). For it is arguable that what blocks shifting $A$'s costs to $B$ in (2) is a rule-utilitarian argument issuing from our concern for freedom of action for all of us—that is, from our desire to be able to count on being free of costs for harms which we cause others, but which we could not, or anyway, morally speaking need not have foreseen and planned for.[11] (Such an argument would have to make out, more strongly, that we prefer being free of costs for harms which we cause others in this way to being free of costs for harms which we are caused by others in this way.) If that is the ground for leaving $A$'s costs to lie where they fell in (2), then Epstein's point could be restated as follows: *in general B must pay the costs of any injury of A's which B causes—but that is not so where utility is maximized by the adoption of a rule which relieves B of liability, and utility is maximized by the adoption of a rule which relieves B of liability in (2), but not so in (4).*

But I fancy that there is more to be said about (4) than Epstein says. Let us look, not at what $B$'s actions caused, but at the content of $B$'s planning before he acts. In a case that will later be describable by (4), $B$ has an end in view that he wants to reach, and he figures he will be able to reach it if he does something which he is aware will cause $A$ a harm, and thereby impose costs on $A$. I stress: $B$ is aware of the fact that his acting will cause $A$ a harm. In a case that will later be describable by (2), $B$ is not aware of the fact that his acting will cause $A$ a harm, and has no moral duty to find out whether it will. Considerations of freedom of action (namely, $A$'s), however, suggest that if $B$ is

---

[11]Compare Hart's rule-utilitarian argument for restricting punishment to voluntary acts:

[Restricting punishment in that way] increases the power of individuals to identify beforehand periods when the law's punishments will not interfere with them and to plan their lives accordingly. . . . Where punishment is not so restricted individuals will be liable to have their plans frustrated by punishments for what they do unintentionally, in ignorance, by accident or mistake. . . . [Failing to restrict punishment in that way] would diminish the individual's power to identify beforehand particular periods during which he will be free from them. This is so because we can have very little ground for confidence that during a particular period we will not do something unintentionally, accidently, etc.; whereas from their own knowledge of themselves many can say with justified confidence that for some period ahead they are not likely to engage intentionally in crime and can plan their lives from point to point in confidence that they will be left free during that period.

H.L.A. Hart, "Prolegomenon to the Principles of Punishment," in *Punishment and Responsibility: Essays in the Philosophy of Law* (Oxford: Oxford University Press, 1968), pp. 23–24.

aware that his acting will cause *A* a harm, then—other things being equal—*B* must buy from *A* the right to cause *A* that harm, and must do this before acting. In *Vincent,* the dock-owner was not there to be bargained with. (So also was the cabin-owner not there to be bargained with in Feinberg's story of the hiker.) So other things were not equal in *Vincent.* But surely the fact that a right-holder is not there to be bargained with for possession of the right cannot be thought to entitle the one who wants it to have it free.

These remarks are far too brief: the differences between (2) and (4) call for far closer attention than they can be given here. But I have in any case wanted only to suggest that considerations of freedom of action will take us a long way—not merely into the question why causality matters, but also into the question when and where it does. . . .

## QUESTIONS

1. Suppose that *A,* negligently firing his shotgun, hits and causes harm to *B*. *B*'s harm does not enrich *A*. Is there any sense in which *A* took or otherwise gained something? If so, was the gain wrongful or unfair?

2. Thomson says, "Causality matters to us, then, because if *B* did not cause (or even causally contribute to) *A*'s injury, then *B*'s freedom of action protects him against liability for *A*'s costs." Try to apply this idea to answer the following questions:

   a. From a legal point of view, one is free to be negligent, so long as one's negligent behavior does not cause harm or losses. Did Simonson, in *Summers II,* have the moral freedom to act negligently? Does anyone?

   b. If we have the freedom to act negligently so long as we do not cause losses to others, is it only because imposing legal liability on us would be worse (i.e., more costly and dangerous) than doing nothing?

   c. Would Thomson's idea here make sense if applied to criminal attempts, that is, could we say that, if *B* did not cause or contribute to *A*'s injury even though *B* tried to kill *A,* that *B*'s freedom of action protects him against criminal liability? Why or why not?

3. Compare the desirability of (a) a system that would make negligent behavior (like Simonson's in *Summers II*) punishable as a crime whether or not it in fact caused anyone losses with (b) a system that imposes only civil liability after the fact for losses actually caused.